America's
Top-Rated Cities:
A Statistical Handbook

Volume 2

2023
Thirtieth Edition

America's
Top-Rated Cities:
A Statistical Handbook

Volume 2: Western Region

Grey House
Publishing

Cover image: Albuquerque, New Mexico

PUBLISHER: Leslie Mackenzie
EDITORIAL DIRECTOR: Stuart Paterson
SENIOR EDITOR: David Garoogian

RESEARCHER & WRITER: Jael Bridgemahon; Laura Mars
MARKETING DIRECTOR: Jessica Moody

Grey House Publishing, Inc.
4919 Route 22
Amenia, NY 12501
518.789.8700 • Fax 845.373.6390
www.greyhouse.com
books@greyhouse.com

Publisher's Cataloging-in-Publication Data
(Prepared by The Donohue Group, Inc.)

America's top-rated cities. Vol. 2, Western region : a statistical handbook. — 1992-

   v. : ill. ; cm.
   Annual, 1995-
   Irregular, 1992-1993
   ISSN: 1082-7102

1. Cities and towns—Ratings—Western States—Statistics—Periodicals. 2. Cities and towns—Western States—Statistics— Periodicals. 3. Social indicators—Western States—Periodicals. 4. Quality of life—Western States—Statistics—Periodicals. 5. Western States—Social conditions—Statistics—Periodicals. I. Title: America's top rated cities. II. Title: Western region

HT123.5.S6 A44
307.76/0973/05   95644648

4-Volume Set   ISBN: 978-1-63700-534-7
Volume 1   ISBN: 978-1-63700-536-1
Volume 2   **ISBN: 978-1-63700-537-8**
Volume 3   ISBN: 978-1-63700-538-5
Volume 4   ISBN: 978-1-63700-539-2

Albuquerque, New Mexico

Anchorage, Alaska

Boise City, Idaho

Boulder, Colorado

Colorado Springs, Colorado

Denver, Colorado

Fort Collins, Colorado

Greeley, Colorado

Honolulu, Hawaii

Las Cruces, New Mexico

Las Vegas, Nevada

Los Angeles, California

Phoenix, Arizona

Portland, Oregon

Provo, Utah

Reno, Nevada

Sacramento, California

Salem, Oregon

Salt Lake City, Utah

San Diego, California

Tucson, Arizona

Appendixes

Introduction

This thirtieth edition of *America's Top-Rated Cities* is a concise, statistical, 4-volume work identifying America's top-rated cities with estimated populations of approximately 100,000 or more. It profiles 100 cities that have received high marks for business and living from prominent sources such as *Forbes, Fortune, U.S. News & World Report, The Brookings Institution, U.S. Conference of Mayors, The Wall Street Journal,* and *CNNMoney*.

Each volume covers a different region of the country—Southern, Western, Central, Eastern—and includes a detailed Table of Contents, City Chapters, Appendices, and Maps. Each city chapter incorporates information from hundreds of resources to create the following major sections:

- **Background**—lively narrative of significant, up-to-date news for both businesses and residents. These combine historical facts with current developments, "known-for" annual events, and climate data.
- **Rankings**—fun-to-read, bulleted survey results from over 221 books, magazines, and online articles, ranging from general (Great Places to Live), to specific (Friendliest Cities), and everything in between.
- **Statistical Tables**—88 tables and detailed topics that offer an unparalleled view of each city's Business and Living Environments. They are carefully organized with data that is easy to read and understand.
- **Appendices**—five in all, appearing at the end of each volume. These range from listings of Metropolitan Statistical Areas to Comparative Statistics for all 100 cities.

This new edition of *America's Top-Rated Cities* includes cities that not only surveyed well, but ranked highest using our unique weighting system. We looked at violent crime, property crime, population growth, median household income, housing affordability, poverty, educational attainment, and unemployment. You'll find that we have included several American cities despite less-than-stellar numbers. New York, Los Angeles, and Miami remain world-class cities despite challenges faced by many large urban centers. Part of the criteria, in most cases, is that it be the "primary" city in a given metropolitan area. For example, if the metro area is Raleigh-Cary, NC, we would consider Raleigh, not Cary. This allows for a more equitable core city comparison. In general, the core city of a metro area is defined as having substantial influence on neighboring cities. A final consideration is location—we strive to include as many states in the country as possible.

New to this edition are:
Volume 1 - Brownsville, TX
Volume 2 - Greeley, CO; Salem, OR
Volume 4 - Greensboro, NC; Worcester, MA

Praise for previous editions:

> *"...[ATRC] has...proven its worth to a wide audience...from businesspeople and corporations planning to launch, relocate, or expand their operations to market researchers, real estate professionals, urban planners, job-seekers, students...interested in...reliable, attractively presented statistical information about larger U.S. cities."*
> —ARBA

> *"...For individuals or businesses looking to relocate, this resource conveniently reports rankings from more than 300 sources for the top 100 US cities. Recommended..."*
> —Choice

> *"...While patrons are becoming increasingly comfortable locating statistical data online, there is still something to be said for the ease associated with such a compendium of otherwise scattered data. A well-organized and appropriate update...*
> —Library Journal

BACKGROUND

Each city begins with an informative Background that combines history with current events. These narratives often reflect changes that have occurred during the past year, and touch on the city's environment, politics, employment, cultural offerings, and climate, and include interesting trivia. For example: Peregrine Falcons were rehabilitated and released into the wild from Boise City's World Center for Birds of Prey; Grand Rapids was the first city to introduce fluoride into its drinking water in 1945; and Thomas Alva Edison discovered the phonograph and the light bulb in the city whose name was changed in 1954 from Raritan Township to Edison in his honor.

RANKINGS

This section has rankings from a possible 221 books, articles, and reports. For easy reference, these Rankings are categorized into 16 topics including Business/Finance, Dating/Romance, and Health/Fitness.

The Rankings are presented in an easy-to-read, bulleted format and include results from both annual surveys and one-shot studies. **Fastest-Growing Economies** . . . **Best Drivers** . . . **Most Well-Read** . . . **Most Wired** . . . **Healthiest for Women** . . . **Best for Minority Entrepreneurs** . . . **Safest** . . . **Best to Retire** . . . **Most Polite** . . . **Best for Moviemakers** . . . **Most Frugal** . . . **Best for Bikes** . . . **Most Cultured** . . . **Least Stressful** . . . **Best for Families** . . . **Most Romantic** . . . **Most Charitable** . . . **Best for Telecommuters** . . . **Best for Singles** . . . **Nerdiest** . . . **Fittest** . . . **Best for Dogs** . . . **Most Tattooed** . . . **Best for Wheelchair Users**, and more.

Sources for these Rankings include both well-known magazines and other media, including *Forbes, Fortune, USA Today, Condé Nast Traveler, Gallup, Kiplinger's Personal Finance, Men's Journal,* and *Travel + Leisure,* as well as *Asthma & Allergy Foundation of America, American Lung Association, League of American Bicyclists, The Advocate, National Civic League, National Alliance to End Homelessness, MovieMaker Magazine, National Insurance Crime Bureau, Center for Digital Government, National Association of Home Builders,* and *Milken Institute.*

Rankings cover a variety of geographic areas; see Appendix B for full geographic definitions.

STATISTICAL TABLES

Each city chapter includes 88 tables and detailed topics—45 in Business and 43 in Living. Over 90% of statistical data has been updated. This edition also includes newly released data from the 2020 Census. A new table on household relationships has also be added, which includes information on same-sex spouses and unmarried partners.

Business Environment includes hard facts and figures on 8 major categories, including Demographics, Income, Economy, Employment, and Taxes. *Living Environment* includes 11 major categories, such as Cost of Living, Housing, Health, Education, Safety, and Climate.

To compile the Statistical Tables, editors have again turned to a wide range of sources, some well known, such as the *U.S. Census Bureau, U.S. Environmental Protection Agency, Bureau of Labor Statistics, Centers for Disease Control and Prevention,* and the *Federal Bureau of Investigation*, plus others like *The Council for Community and Economic Research, Texas A&M Transportation Institute,* and *Federation of Tax Administrators.*

APPENDIXES: Data for all cities appear in all volumes.
- **Appendix A**—*Comparative Statistics*
- **Appendix B**—*Metropolitan Area Definitions*
- **Appendix C**—*Government Type and County*
- **Appendix D**—*Chambers of Commerce and Economic Development Organizations*
- **Appendix E**—*State Departments of Labor and Employment*

Material provided by public and private agencies and organizations was supplemented by original research, numerous library sources and Internet sites. *America's Top-Rated Cities, 2023,* is designed for a wide range of readers: private individuals considering relocating a residence or business; professionals considering expanding their businesses or changing careers; corporations considering relocating, opening up additional offices or creating new divisions; government agencies; general and market researchers; real estate consultants; human resource personnel; urban planners; investors; and urban government students.

Customers who purchase the four-volume set receive free online access to *America's Top-Rated Cities* allowing them to download city reports and sort and rank by 50-plus data points.

©Larry Mandelin 2023

AMERICA'S TOP-RATED CITIES

	CBSA: Core Based Statistical Area
	STATE
○	Top Rated City
	South Region - VOLUME 1
	West Region - VOLUME 2
	Central Region - VOLUME 3
	East Region - VOLUME 4

Cities (labels)

Maine, Manchester, Boston, Providence, New Haven, New York, Worcester, NH, MA, CT, RI, VT, Edison, Allentown, New Jersey, Philadelphia, Baltimore, Washington, DE, MD, Richmond, Virginia Beach, Pittsburgh, Pennsylvania, New York, Cleveland, Columbus, Ohio, Durham, Raleigh, NC, Wilmington, Charleston, Columbia, SC, Greensboro, Winston-Salem, Charlotte, Miami, Orlando, Jacksonville, Savannah, Cape Coral, Tampa, Florida, Georgia, Athens, Atlanta, Alabama, Huntsville, Tuscaloosa, Nashville, Knoxville, Lexington, Louisville, Cincinnati, Clarksville, Kentucky, Tennessee, Indianapolis, Fort Wayne, Indiana, Ann Arbor, MI, Grand Rapids, Green Bay, Milwaukee, Chicago, Wisconsin, Madison, Rochester, Minneapolis, Minnesota, Fargo, North Dakota, Sioux Falls, South Dakota, Cedar Rapids, Davenport, Des Moines, Iowa, Omaha, Lincoln, Nebraska, Springfield, St. Louis, Columbia, Kansas City, Missouri, Wichita, Kansas, Oklahoma City, Tulsa, Oklahoma, Little Rock, Arkansas, New Orleans, Louisiana, Lafayette, Mississippi, College Station, Houston, Brownsville, TX, Dallas, Fort Worth, Austin, San Antonio, Texas, Midland, El Paso, Las Cruces, New Mexico, Albuquerque, Colorado Springs, Colorado, Greeley, CO, Denver, Boulder, Fort Collins, Wyoming, Montana, Idaho, Boise City, Salt Lake City, Provo, Utah, Arizona, Phoenix, Tucson, Las Vegas, Nevada, Reno, Sacramento, San Francisco, San Jose, Santa Rosa, California, Los Angeles, San Diego, Seattle, Portland, Salem, Washington, Oregon, Honolulu, HI, Anchorage, Alaska

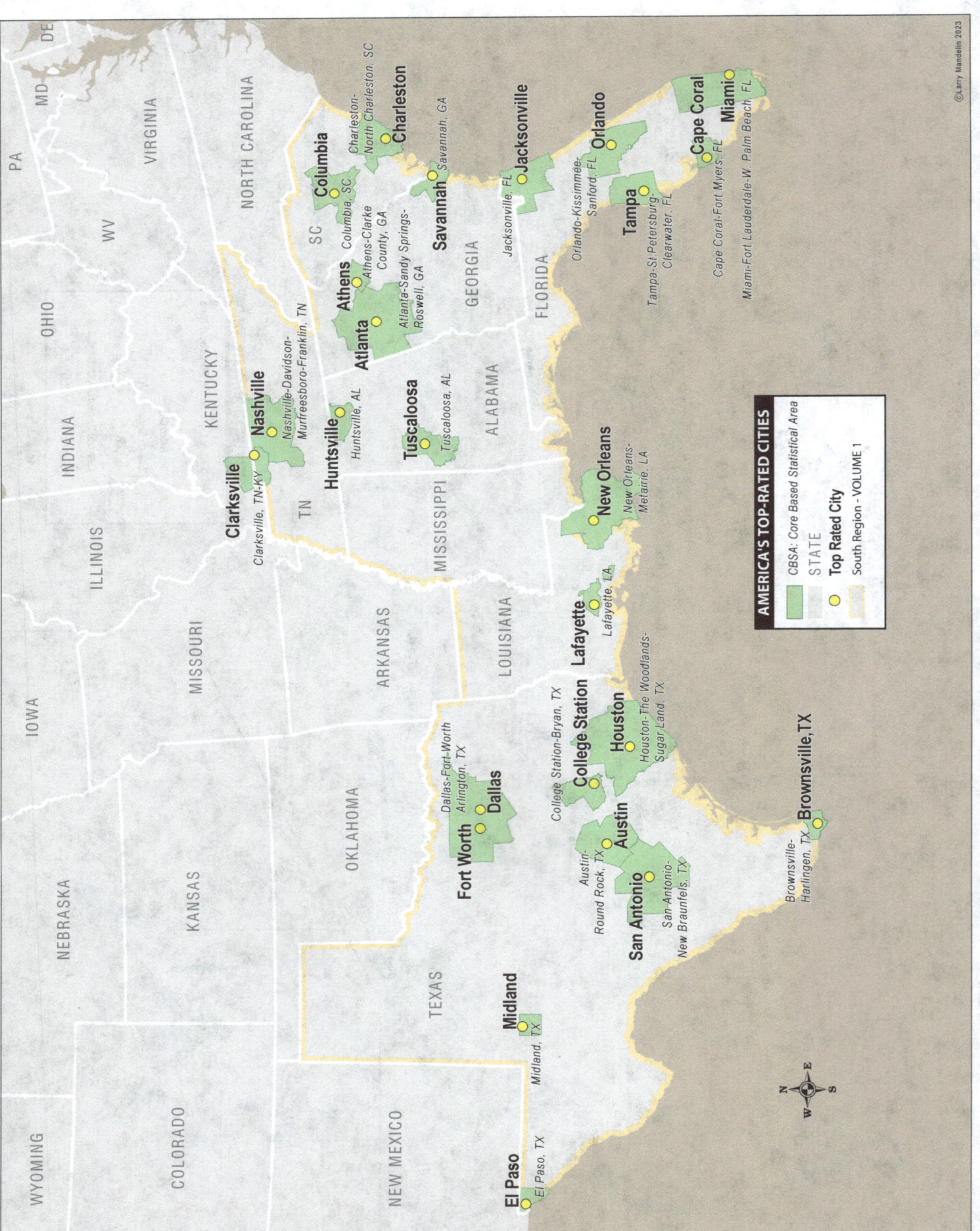

AMERICA'S TOP-RATED CITIES

CBSA: Core Based Statistical Area
STATE
Top Rated City
South Region - VOLUME 1

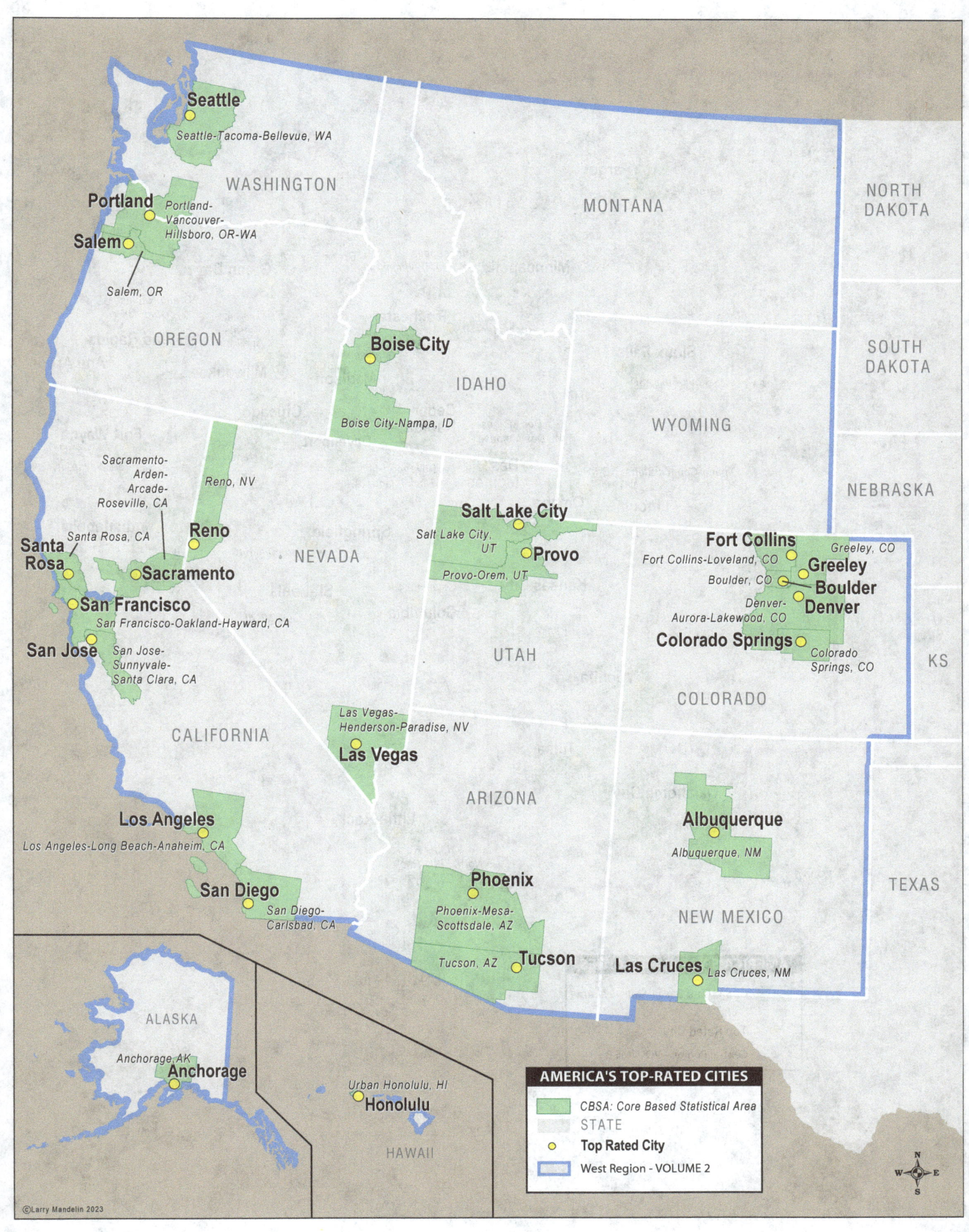

Seattle
Seattle-Tacoma-Bellevue, WA

WASHINGTON

Portland
Portland-Vancouver-Hillsboro, OR-WA

Salem
Salem, OR

OREGON

Boise City
Boise City-Nampa, ID

IDAHO

MONTANA

NORTH DAKOTA

SOUTH DAKOTA

WYOMING

NEBRASKA

Sacramento-Arden-Arcade-Roseville, CA

Reno, NV

Santa Rosa, CA

Santa Rosa

Reno

Sacramento

San Francisco
San Francisco-Oakland-Hayward, CA

San Jose
San Jose-Sunnyvale-Santa Clara, CA

NEVADA

Salt Lake City
Salt Lake City, UT

Provo
Provo-Orem, UT

UTAH

Fort Collins
Fort Collins-Loveland, CO

Greeley, CO

Boulder, CO

Greeley

Boulder

Denver

Denver-Aurora-Lakewood, CO

Colorado Springs
Colorado Springs, CO

COLORADO

KS

CALIFORNIA

Las Vegas-Henderson-Paradise, NV

Las Vegas

ARIZONA

Albuquerque
Albuquerque, NM

Los Angeles
Los Angeles-Long Beach-Anaheim, CA

San Diego
San Diego-Carlsbad, CA

Phoenix
Phoenix-Mesa-Scottsdale, AZ

Tucson, AZ
Tucson

NEW MEXICO

TEXAS

Las Cruces
Las Cruces, NM

ALASKA

Anchorage, AK
Anchorage

Urban Honolulu, HI
Honolulu

HAWAII

AMERICA'S TOP-RATED CITIES

CBSA: Core Based Statistical Area
STATE
○ Top Rated City
West Region - VOLUME 2

©Larry Mandelin 2023

N
W   E
S

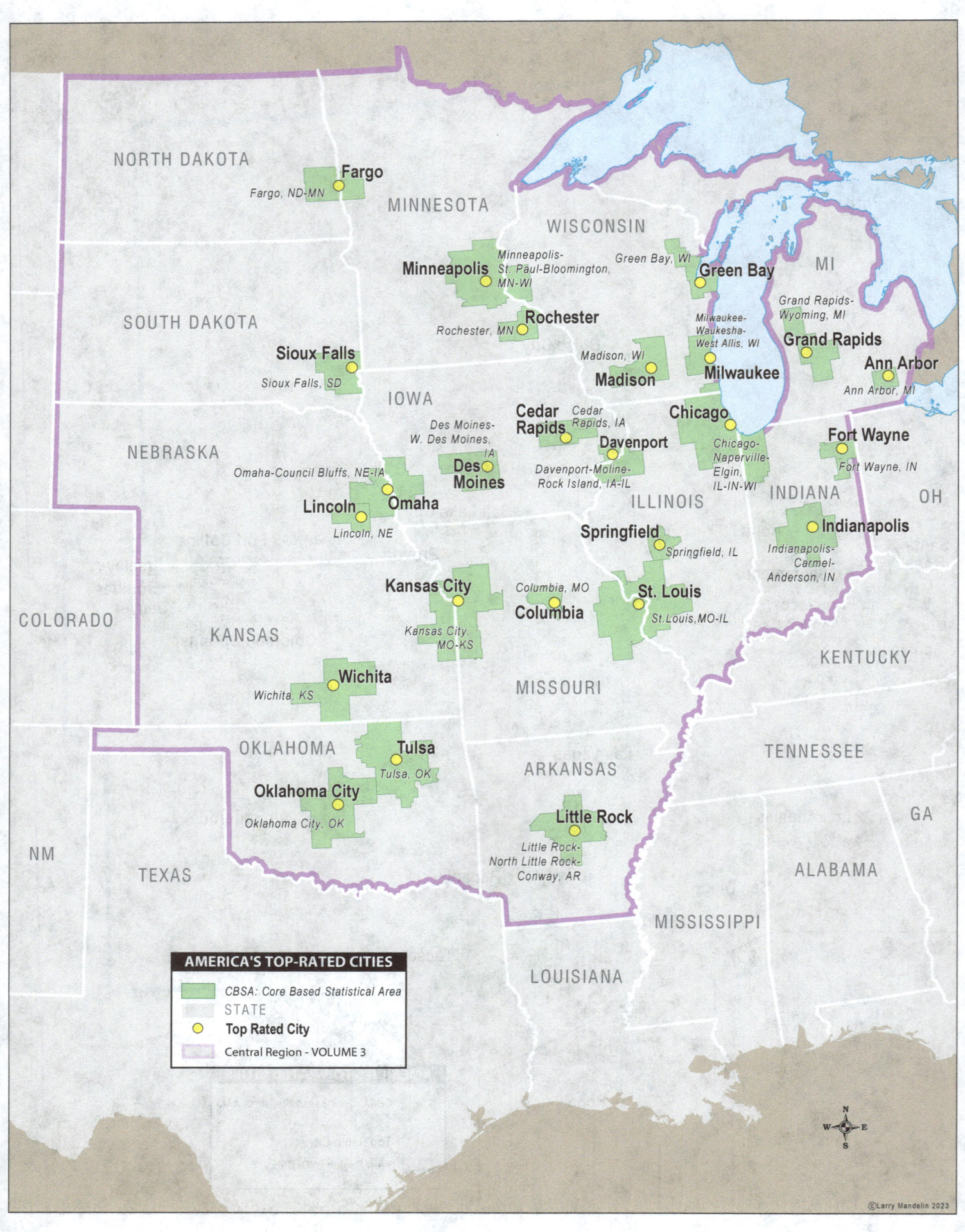

AMERICA'S TOP-RATED CITIES

CBSA: Core Based Statistical Area
STATE
Top Rated City
East Region - VOLUME 4

MAINE

VT   NH
NEW YORK   **Manchester**
Manchester-Nashua, NH   Boston-Cambridge-Newton, MA-NH
Worcester   **Boston**
Worcester, MA-CT   **Providence**
MA   CT   Providence-Warwick, RI-MA
RI
New Haven
Allentown-Bethlehem-Easton,   New Haven-Milford, CT
PA-NJ
Allentown   **New York**
PENNSYLVANIA   **Edison**   New York-Newark-Jersey City,
Cleveland   NY-NJ-PA
Cleveland-Elyria, OH   **Pittsburgh**   **Philadelphia**
OHIO   Pittsburgh, PA   Baltimore-Columbia-   NJ   Philadelphia-Camden-Wilmington,
Towson, MD   PA-NJ-DE-MD
Columbus   **Baltimore**
INDIANA   Columbus, OH   DE   **Washington**   MD
Cincinnati, OH-KY-IN   WV   Washington-Arlington-Alexandria, DC-VA-MD-WV
IL   **Cincinnati**   **Richmond**
Louisville/Jefferson   VA   Virginia Beach-Norfolk-Newport News, VA-NC
County, KY-IN   **Lexington**
Richmond, VA
Louisville   Lexington-Fayette, KY   **Virginia Beach**
KENTUCKY   **Durham**   Durham-Chapel Hill, NC
Greensboro   **Raleigh**
Winston-Salem   Raleigh, NC
Winston-Salem, NC
Greensboro-High Point, NC
NC
TENNESSEE   Wilmington, NC
Charlotte
Charlotte-   **Wilmington**
Concord-
Gastonia, NC-SC
S.CAROLINA   N
W   E
S
MS   ALABAMA   GEORGIA

MICHIGAN

©Larry Mandelin 2023

Albuquerque, New Mexico

Background

Pueblo Indians originally inhabited what is now the Albuquerque metropolitan area. In the sixteenth century, Spaniards began arriving from Mexico in search of riches, but it was not until 1706 that they founded the settlement, naming it after the viceroy of New Spain, San Francisco de Alburquerque, a duke whose permission was needed to set up the town. Eventually, the city's name would lose a consonant and become Albuquerque. The city earned the sobriquet "Duke City" because of its namesake.

In the early nineteenth century, Mexico secured her independence from Spanish rule and allowed Americans to enter the province of New Mexico to trade. During the Mexican War of the 1840s, Americans under the command of General Stephen Kearny captured the town, and New Mexico became part of the United States in the Treaty of Guadalupe Hidalgo, ending the war.

During the Civil War, Confederates held the town briefly before surrendering it to a besieging Union army. After the war, the railroad arrived in 1880, bringing with it people and business. In 1891 the town received a city charter. Albuquerque became an important site for tuberculosis sanatoriums during the next few decades because of the healing nature of the dry desert air.

World War II had a great impact on Albuquerque, as Kirtland Air Force Base became an important site for the manufacture of the atomic bomb. Sandia National Laboratories was founded in the city after the war and was important in defense-related research during the Cold War.

The defense industry is of prime significance to Albuquerque. Institutions in the city that were once dedicated to defense research are now involved in applying such technology to the private sector, making the city a perfect place for high-tech concerns. In addition to Sandia, the city hosts a branch of the Air Force Research Laboratories and the Los Alamos National Laboratory. Biotech and semiconductor industries also have had a positive impact on the city's economy.

Albuquerque and New Mexico have many programs to assist business. The state has property taxes that are among the lowest in the nation. The city consistently ranks high in business and engineering careers, and generally among best places to live. Additionally, traditional jobs, such as ranching, still have a large presence in the city.

Albuquerque is also a critical transportation center for the American Southwest, with two major interstates that intersect there. Its airport, Albuquerque International Sunport, is served by both major commercial and commuter carriers. The city is home to state-of-the-art manufacturing and shipping facilities and Mesa del Sol, a mixed-used development site connected to the airport by light-rail and a commuter rail line that also serves the region. The New Mexico Rail Runner Express system as well as the Rapid Ride bus service serves Albuquerque's residents. The city also gets high points for its walkability. According to 2022 figures, the city's Park Management Division maintains and manages more than 288 park sites.

There are various venues for higher education located in Albuquerque, the most significant of which is the University of New Mexico.

There are popular festive events scheduled throughout the year, including the annual International Albuquerque International Balloon Fiesta and the annual Gathering of Nations Powwow, an international event that is North America's biggest powwow. featuring over 3,000 indigenous Native American dancers and singers representing more than 500 tribes. The city is also the setting for television shows *Breaking Bad*, *Get Shorty*, and *Succession*. In 2018, the United Soccer League expanded into New Mexico with its headquarters in Albuquerque.

Albuquerque enjoys a dry, arid climate, with plenty of sunshine, low humidity, and scant rainfall. More than three-fourths of the daylight hours have sunshine, summer and winter. As in all desert climates, temperatures can fluctuate widely between day and night, all year round. Precipitation is meager during the winter, more abundant in summer with afternoon and evening thunderstorms.

Rankings

General Rankings

- For its "Best for Vets: Places to Live 2019" rankings, *Military Times* evaluated 599 cities (83 large, 234 medium, 282 small) and compared the locations across three broad categories: veteran and military culture/services; economic indicators; and livability factors such as health, crime, traffic, and school quality. Albuquerque ranked #14 out of the top 25, in the large city category (population of more than 250,000). Data points more specific to veterans and the military weighed more heavily than others. *rebootcamp.militarytimes.com, "Military Times Best Places to Live 2019," September 10, 2018*

- Albuquerque was selected as one of the best places to live in America by *Outside Magazine*. Criteria centered on diversity; sustainability; outdoor equity; and affordability. Local experts shared highlights from hands-on experience in each location. *Outside Magazine, "The 20 Most Livable Towns and Cities in America," October 15, 2021*

Business/Finance Rankings

- Albuquerque was the #13-ranked city for savers, according to a study by the finance site GOBankingRates, which considered the prospects for people trying to save money. Criteria: average monthly cost of grocery items; median home listing price; median rent; median income; transportation costs; gas prices; and the cost of eating out for an inexpensive and mid-range meal in 100 U.S. cities. *www.gobankingrates.com, "The 20 Best (and Worst) Places to Live If You're Trying to Save Money," August 27, 2019*

- Albuquerque was ranked #13 among 100 U.S. cities for most difficult conditions for savers, according to a study by the finance site GOBankingRates. Criteria: average monthly cost of grocery items; median home listing price; median rent; median income; transportation costs; gas prices; and the cost of eating out for an inexpensive and mid-range meal. *www.gobankingrates.com, "The 20 Best (and Worst) Places to Live If You're Trying to Save Money," August 27, 2019*

- The Brookings Institution ranked the nation's largest cities based on income inequality. Albuquerque was ranked #52 (#1 = greatest inequality). Criteria: the "95/20 ratio," a figure representing the income at which a household earns more than 95 percent of all other households, divided by the income at which a household earns more than only 20 percent of all other households. *Brookings Institution, "Household Income Inequality, Largest Cities of 97 Large U.S. Metro Areas, 2014-2016," February 5, 2018*

- The Brookings Institution ranked the 100 largest metro areas in the U.S. based on income inequality. Albuquerque was ranked #21 (#1 = greatest inequality). Criteria: the "95/20 ratio," a figure representing the income at which a household earns more than 95 percent of all other households, divided by the income at which a household earns more than only 20 percent of all other households. *Brookings Institution, "Household Income Inequality, 100 Largest U.S. Metro Areas, 2014-2016," February 5, 2018*

- The Albuquerque metro area appeared on the Milken Institute "2022 Best Performing Cities" list. Rank: #75 out of 200 large metro areas (population over 250,000). Criteria: job growth; wage and salary growth; high-tech output growth; housing affordability; household broadband access. *Milken Institute, "Best-Performing Cities 2022," March 28, 2022*

- *Forbes* ranked the 200 most populous metro areas to determine the nation's "Best Places for Business and Careers." The Albuquerque metro area was ranked #126. Criteria: costs (business and living); job growth (past and projected); income growth; quality of life; educational attainment (college and high school); projected economic growth; cultural and leisure opportunities; workplace tolerance laws; net migration patterns. *Forbes, "The Best Places for Business and Careers 2019: Seattle Still On Top," October 30, 2019*

Culture/Performing Arts Rankings

- Albuquerque was selected as one of the 25 best cities for moviemakers in North America. Great film cities are places where filmmaking dreams can come true, that offer more creative space, lower costs, and great outdoor locations. NYC & LA were intentionally excluded. Criteria: longstanding reputations as film-friendly communities; film community and culture; affordability; and quality of life. The city was ranked #5. *MovieMaker Magazine, "Best Places to Live and Work as a Moviemaker, 2023," January 18, 2023*

Education Rankings

■ Personal finance website *WalletHub* analyzed the 150 largest U.S. metropolitan statistical areas to determine where the most educated Americans are putting their degrees to work. Criteria: education levels; percentage of workers with degrees; education quality and attainment gap; public school quality rankings; quality and enrollment of each metro area's universities. Albuquerque was ranked #47 (#1 = most educated city). *www.WalletHub.com, "Most & Least Educated Cities in America," July 18, 2022*

■ Albuquerque was selected as one of America's most literate cities. The city ranked #33 out of the 84 largest U.S. cities. Criteria: number of booksellers; library resources; Internet resources; educational attainment; periodical publishing resources; newspaper circulation. *Central Connecticut State University, "America's Most Literate Cities, 2018," February 2019*

Environmental Rankings

■ Albuquerque was highlighted as one of the 25 most ozone-polluted metro areas in the U.S. during 2019 through 2021. The area ranked #24. *American Lung Association, "State of the Air 2023," April 19, 2023*

Health/Fitness Rankings

■ For each of the 100 largest cities in the United States, the American Fitness Index®, compiled in partnership between the American College of Sports Medicine and the Elevance Health Foundation, evaluated community infrastructure and 34 health behaviors including preventive health, levels of chronic disease conditions, food insecurity, sleep quality, pedestrian safety, air quality, and community/environment resources that support physical activity. Albuquerque ranked #33 for "community fitness." *americanfitnessindex.org, "2022 ACSM American Fitness Index Summary Report," July 12, 2022*

■ Albuquerque was identified as a "2022 Spring Allergy Capital." The area ranked #79 out of 100. Three groups of factors were used to identify the most challenging cities for people with allergies during the spring season: annual spring pollen scores; over the counter allergy medicine use; number of board-certified allergy specialists. *Asthma and Allergy Foundation of America, "Spring Allergy Capitals 2022," March 2, 2022*

■ Albuquerque was identified as a "2022 Fall Allergy Capital." The area ranked #80 out of 100. Three groups of factors were used to identify the most challenging cities for people with allergies during the fall season: annual fall pollen scores; over the counter allergy medicine use; number of board-certified allergy specialists. *Asthma and Allergy Foundation of America, "Fall Allergy Capitals 2022," March 2, 2022*

■ Albuquerque was identified as a "2022 Asthma Capital." The area ranked #81 out of the nation's 100 largest metropolitan areas. Criteria: estimated asthma prevalence; asthma-related mortality; and ER visits due to asthma. Risk factors analyzed but not factored in the rankings: annual pollen score; annual air quality; public smoking laws; access to board-certified asthma specialists; rescue and controller medication use; uninsured rate; poverty rate. *Asthma and Allergy Foundation of America, "Asthma Capitals 2022: The Most Challenging Places to Live With Asthma," September 14, 2022*

Real Estate Rankings

■ *WalletHub* compared the most populated U.S. cities to determine which had the best markets for real estate agents. Albuquerque ranked #135 where demand was high and pay was the best. Criteria: sales per agent; annual median wage for real-estate agents; monthly average starting salary for real estate agents; real estate job density and competition; unemployment rate; home turnover rate; housing-market health index; and other relevant metrics. *www.WalletHub.com, "2021 Best Places to Be a Real Estate Agent," May 12, 2021*

■ Albuquerque was ranked #18 in the top 20 out of the 100 largest metro areas in terms of house price appreciation in 2022 (#1 = highest rate). *Federal Housing Finance Agency, House Price Index, 4th Quarter 2022*

■ Albuquerque was ranked #126 out of 235 metro areas in terms of housing affordability in 2022 by the National Association of Home Builders (#1 = most affordable). Criteria: the share of homes sold in that area affordable to a family earning the local median income, based on standard mortgage underwriting criteria. *National Association of Home Builders®, NAHB-Wells Fargo Housing Opportunity Index, 4th Quarter 2022*

Safety Rankings

- To identify the most dangerous cities in America, *24/7 Wall St.* focused on violent crime categories—murder, non-negligent manslaughter, rape, robbery, and aggravated assault—as reported for every 100,000 residents using data from the FBI's 2020 annual Uniform Crime Report. For cities with populations over 25,000, Albuquerque was ranked #28. *247wallst.com, "America's Most Dangerous Cities" November 12, 2021*

- Allstate ranked the 200 largest cities in America in terms of driver safety. Albuquerque ranked #58. Criteria: internal property damage claims over a two-year period from January 2016 to December 2017. The report helps increase the importance of safety and awareness behind the wheel. *Allstate, "Allstate America's Best Drivers Report, 2019" June 24, 2019*

- Albuquerque was identified as one of the most dangerous cities in America by NeighborhoodScout. The city ranked #30 out of 100 (#1 = most dangerous). Criteria: number of violent crimes per 1,000 residents. The editors evaluated cities with 25,000 or more residents. *NeighborhoodScout.com, "2023 Top 100 Most Dangerous Cities in the U.S.," January 12, 2023*

- The National Insurance Crime Bureau ranked 390 metro areas in the U.S. in terms of per capita rates of vehicle theft. The Albuquerque metro area ranked #4 (#1 = highest rate). Criteria: number of vehicle theft offenses per 100,000 inhabitants in 2021. *National Insurance Crime Bureau, "Hot Spots 2021," September 1, 2022*

Seniors/Retirement Rankings

- From its Best Cities for Successful Aging indexes, the Milken Institute generated rankings for metropolitan areas, weighing data in nine categories—health care, wellness, living arrangements, transportation and convenience, financial characteristics, education, employment, community engagement, and overall livability. The Albuquerque metro area was ranked #87 overall in the large metro area category. *Milken Institute, "Best Cities for Successful Aging, 2017" March 14, 2017*

- Albuquerque was identified as #13 of 20 most popular places to retire in the Southwest region by *Topretirements.com*. The site separated its annual "Best Places to Retire" list by major U.S. regions for 2019. The list reflects the 20 cities that visitors to the website are most interested in for retirement, based on the number of times a city's review was viewed on the website. *Topretirements.com, "20 Most Popular Places to Retire in the Southwest for 2019," October 2, 2019*

Sports/Recreation Rankings

- Albuquerque was chosen as one of America's best cities for bicycling. The city ranked #47 out of 50. Criteria: cycling infrastructure that is safe and friendly for all ages; energy and bike culture. The editors evaluated cities with populations of 100,000 or more. *Bicycling, "The 50 Best Bike Cities in America," October 10, 2018*

Women/Minorities Rankings

- *Women's Health*, together with the site Yelp, identified the 15 "Wellthiest" spots in the U.S. Albuquerque appeared among the top for happiest, healthiest, outdoorsiest and Zen-iest. *Women's Health, "The 15 Wellthiest Cities in the U.S." July 5, 2017*

- Personal finance website *WalletHub* compared more than 180 U.S. cities across two key dimensions, "Hispanic Business-Friendliness" and "Hispanic Purchasing Power," to arrive at the most favorable conditions for Hispanic entrepreneurs. Albuquerque was ranked #39 out of 182. Criteria includes: share of Hispanic-Owned Businesses; Hispanic entrepreneurship rate to median annual income of Hispanics; Small Business-Friendliness score; cost of living; and number of Hispanics with at least a bachelor's degree. *WalletHub.com, "2019's Best Cities for Hispanic Entrepreneurs," May 1, 2019*

Miscellaneous Rankings

- Albuquerque was selected as a 2022 Digital Cities Survey winner. The city ranked #8 in the large city (500,000 or more population) category. The survey examined and assessed how city governments are utilizing technology to continue innovation, engage with residents, and persevere through the challenges of the pandemic. Survey questions focused on ten initiatives: cybersecurity; citizen experience; disaster recovery; business intelligence; IT personnel; data governance; business automation; IT governance; infrastructure modernization; and broadband connectivity. *Center for Digital Government, "2022 Digital Cities Survey," November 10, 2022*

- *WalletHub* compared the 150 most populated U.S. cities to determine their operating efficiency. A "Quality of Services" score was constructed for each city and then divided by the total budget per capita to reveal which were managed the best. Albuquerque ranked #23. Criteria: financial stability; economy; education; safety; health; infrastructure and pollution. *www.WalletHub.com, "2022's Best- & Worst-Run Cities in America," June 21, 2022*

Business Environment

DEMOGRAPHICS

Population Growth

Area	1990 Census	2000 Census	2010 Census	2020 Census	Population Growth (%) 1990-2020	Population Growth (%) 2010-2020
City	388,375	448,607	545,852	564,559	45.4	3.4
MSA[1]	599,416	729,649	887,077	916,528	52.9	3.3
U.S.	248,709,873	281,421,906	308,745,538	331,449,281	33.3	7.4

Note: (1) Figures cover the Albuquerque, NM Metropolitan Statistical Area
Source: U.S. Census Bureau, 1990 Census, 2000 Census, 2010 Census, 2020 Census

Race

Area	White Alone[2] (%)	Black Alone[2] (%)	Asian Alone[2] (%)	AIAN[3] Alone[2] (%)	NHOPI[4] Alone[2] (%)	Other Race Alone[2] (%)	Two or More Races (%)
City	52.2	3.5	3.4	5.6	0.1	14.2	21.0
MSA[1]	52.8	2.8	2.5	6.6	0.1	14.5	20.6
U.S.	61.6	12.4	6.0	1.1	0.2	8.4	10.2

Note: (1) Figures cover the Albuquerque, NM Metropolitan Statistical Area; (2) Alone is defined as not being in combination with one or more other races; (3) American Indian and Alaska Native; (4) Native Hawaiian and Other Pacific Islander
Source: U.S. Census Bureau, 2020 Census

Hispanic or Latino Origin

Area	Total (%)	Mexican (%)	Puerto Rican (%)	Cuban (%)	Other (%)
City	49.8	29.7	0.7	0.4	19.0
MSA[1]	49.7	29.0	0.7	0.4	19.7
U.S.	18.4	11.2	1.8	0.7	4.7

Note: Persons of Hispanic or Latino origin can be of any race; (1) Figures cover the Albuquerque, NM Metropolitan Statistical Area
Source: U.S. Census Bureau, 2017-2021 American Community Survey 5-Year Estimates

Age

Area	Under Age 5	Age 5–19	Age 20–34	Age 35–44	Age 45–54	Age 55–64	Age 65–74	Age 75–84	Age 85+	Median Age
City	5.1	18.6	21.8	13.2	11.7	12.7	10.2	4.9	1.9	38.2
MSA[1]	5.1	19.2	19.8	12.6	11.7	13.4	11.0	5.2	1.8	39.4
U.S.	5.6	19.2	20.2	12.7	12.4	13.1	10.0	4.9	1.9	38.8

Note: (1) Figures cover the Albuquerque, NM Metropolitan Statistical Area
Source: U.S. Census Bureau, 2020 Census

Disability by Age

Area	All Ages	Under 18 Years Old	18 to 64 Years Old	65 Years and Over
City	14.2	4.3	12.3	35.3
MSA[1]	15.1	4.2	13.2	36.3
U.S.	12.6	4.4	10.3	33.4

Note: Figures show percent of the civilian noninstitutionalized population that reported having a disability. Disability status is determined from six types of difficulty: vision, hearing, cognitive, ambulatory, self-care, and independent living. For children under 5 years old, hearing and vision difficulty are used to determine disability status. For children between the ages of 5 and 14, disability status is determined from hearing, vision, cognitive, ambulatory, and self-care difficulties. For people aged 15 years and older, they are considered to have a disability if they have difficulty with any one of the six difficulty types; Note: (1) Figures cover the Albuquerque, NM Metropolitan Statistical Area
Source: U.S. Census Bureau, 2017-2021 American Community Survey 5-Year Estimates

Ancestry

Area	German	Irish	English	American	Italian	Polish	French[2]	Scottish	Dutch
City	9.2	7.6	7.8	3.3	3.2	1.4	1.8	1.4	0.9
MSA[1]	9.2	7.2	7.7	3.9	3.1	1.3	1.7	1.5	0.7
U.S.	12.8	9.6	8.1	5.7	5.0	2.7	2.2	1.6	1.1

Note: Figures are the percentage of the total population reporting a particular ancestry. The nine most commonly reported ancestries in the U.S. are shown. Figures include multiple ancestries (e.g. if a person reported being Irish and Italian, they were included in both columns); (1) Figures cover the Albuquerque, NM Metropolitan Statistical Area; (2) Excludes Basque
Source: U.S. Census Bureau, 2017-2021 American Community Survey 5-Year Estimates

Foreign-born Population

Area	Any Foreign Country	Percent of Population Born in							
		Asia	Mexico	Europe	Caribbean	Central America[2]	South America	Africa	Canada
City	10.2	2.5	5.1	0.9	0.4	0.1	0.4	0.5	0.1
MSA[1]	8.9	1.9	4.9	0.8	0.3	0.2	0.3	0.4	0.1
U.S.	13.6	4.2	3.3	1.5	1.4	1.1	1.1	0.8	0.2

Note: (1) Figures cover the Albuquerque, NM Metropolitan Statistical Area; (2) Excludes Mexico.
Source: U.S. Census Bureau, 2017-2021 American Community Survey 5-Year Estimates

Household Size

Area	Persons in Household (%)							Average Household Size
	One	Two	Three	Four	Five	Six	Seven or More	
City	36.4	33.0	13.7	10.2	4.7	1.3	0.7	2.40
MSA[1]	32.3	34.7	14.3	10.7	5.1	1.7	1.1	2.50
U.S.	28.1	33.8	15.5	12.9	6.0	2.3	1.4	2.60

Note: (1) Figures cover the Albuquerque, NM Metropolitan Statistical Area
Source: U.S. Census Bureau, 2017-2021 American Community Survey 5-Year Estimates

Household Relationships

Area	House-holder	Opposite-sex Spouse	Same-sex Spouse	Opposite-sex Unmarried Partner	Same-sex Unmarried Partner	Child[2]	Grand-child	Other Relatives	Non-relatives
City	42.1	15.1	0.3	3.4	0.3	27.0	2.5	4.6	3.2
MSA[1]	40.1	16.3	0.3	3.1	0.3	27.7	3.1	4.6	2.9
U.S.	38.3	17.5	0.2	2.5	0.2	28.3	2.4	4.8	3.4

Note: Figures are percent of the total population; (1) Figures cover the Albuquerque, NM Metropolitan Statistical Area; (2) Includes biological, adopted, and stepchildren of the householder
Source: U.S. Census Bureau, 2020 Census

Gender

Area	Males	Females	Males per 100 Females
City	274,173	290,386	94.4
MSA[1]	449,092	467,436	96.1
U.S.	162,685,811	168,763,470	96.4

Note: (1) Figures cover the Albuquerque, NM Metropolitan Statistical Area
Source: U.S. Census Bureau, 2020 Census

Marital Status

Area	Never Married	Now Married[2]	Separated	Widowed	Divorced
City	38.2	40.1	1.4	5.5	14.8
MSA[1]	35.6	43.5	1.4	5.5	14.1
U.S.	33.8	48.0	1.8	5.6	10.8

Note: Figures are percentages and cover the population 15 years of age and older; (1) Figures cover the Albuquerque, NM Metropolitan Statistical Area; (2) Excludes separated
Source: U.S. Census Bureau, 2017-2021 American Community Survey 5-Year Estimates

Religious Groups by Family

Area	Catholic	Baptist	Methodist	LDS[2]	Pentecostal	Lutheran	Islam	Adventist	Other
MSA[1]	32.6	3.2	0.9	2.7	1.7	0.4	0.7	1.5	10.8
U.S.	18.7	7.3	3.0	2.0	1.8	1.7	1.3	1.3	11.6

Note: Figures are the number of adherents as a percentage of the total population and cover the eight largest religious groups in the U.S; (1) Figures cover the Albuquerque, NM Metropolitan Statistical Area; (2) Church of Jesus Christ of Latter-day Saints
Sources: 2020 U.S. Religion Census, Association of Statisticians of American Religious Bodies; The Association of Religion Data Archives (ARDA)

Religious Groups by Tradition

Area	Catholic	Evangelical Protestant	Mainline Protestant	Black Protestant	Islam	Judaism	Hinduism	Orthodox	Buddhism
MSA[1]	32.6	13.4	2.2	0.5	0.7	0.2	0.2	0.1	0.6
U.S.	18.7	16.5	5.2	2.3	1.3	0.6	0.4	0.4	0.3

Note: Figures are the number of adherents as a percentage of the total population; (1) Figures cover the Albuquerque, NM Metropolitan Statistical Area
Sources: 2020 U.S. Religion Census, Association of Statisticians of American Religious Bodies; The Association of Religion Data Archives (ARDA)

ECONOMY

Gross Metropolitan Product

Area	2020	2021	2022	2023	Rank[2]
MSA[1]	45.1	50.3	56.1	58.2	70

Note: Figures are in billions of dollars; (1) Figures cover the Albuquerque, NM Metropolitan Statistical Area;
(2) Rank is based on 2021 data and ranges from 1 to 381
Source: U.S. Conference of Mayors, U.S. Metro Economies: U.S. Metros Compared to Global and State
Economies, June 2022

Economic Growth

Area	2018-20 (%)	2021 (%)	2022 (%)	2023 (%)	Rank[2]
MSA[1]	-0.4	5.6	4.6	3.6	167
U.S.	-0.6	5.7	3.1	2.9	–

Note: Figures are real gross metropolitan product (GMP) growth rates and represent average annual percent
change; (1) Figures cover the Albuquerque, NM Metropolitan Statistical Area; (2) Rank is based on 2020
2-year average annual percent change and ranges from 1 to 381
Source: U.S. Conference of Mayors, U.S. Metro Economies: U.S. Metros Compared to Global and State
Economies, June 2022

Metropolitan Area Exports

Area	2016	2017	2018	2019	2020	2021	Rank[2]
MSA[1]	999.7	624.2	771.5	1,629.7	1,265.3	2,215.0	101

Note: Figures are in millions of dollars; (1) Figures cover the Albuquerque, NM Metropolitan Statistical Area;
(2) Rank is based on 2021 data and ranges from 1 to 388
Source: U.S. Department of Commerce, International Trade Administration, Office of Trade and Economic
Analysis, Industry and Analysis, Exports by Metropolitan Area, data extracted March 16, 2023

Building Permits

Area	Single-Family			Multi-Family			Total		
	2021	2022	Pct. Chg.	2021	2022	Pct. Chg.	2021	2022	Pct. Chg.
City	773	707	-8.5	894	902	0.9	1,667	1,609	-3.5
MSA[1]	2,535	2,002	-21.0	1,486	1,055	-29.0	4,021	3,057	-24.0
U.S.	1,115,400	975,600	-12.5	621,600	689,500	10.9	1,737,000	1,665,100	-4.1

Note: (1) Figures cover the Albuquerque, NM Metropolitan Statistical Area; Figures represent new,
privately-owned housing units authorized (unadjusted data); All permit data are based on estimates with
imputation
Source: U.S. Census Bureau, Manufacturing, Mining, and Construction Statistics, Building Permits, 2021,
2022

Bankruptcy Filings

Area	Business Filings			Nonbusiness Filings		
	2021	2022	% Chg.	2021	2022	% Chg.
Bernalillo County	21	15	-28.6	560	383	-31.6
U.S.	14,347	13,481	-6.0	399,269	374,240	-6.3

Note: Business filings include Chapter 7, Chapter 9, Chapter 11, Chapter 12, Chapter 13, Chapter 15, and
Section 304; Nonbusiness filings include Chapter 7, Chapter 11, and Chapter 13
Source: Administrative Office of the U.S. Courts, Business and Nonbusiness Bankruptcy, County Cases
Commenced by Chapter of the Bankruptcy Code, During the 12-Month Period Ending December 31, 2021 and
Business and Nonbusiness Bankruptcy, County Cases Commenced by Chapter of the Bankruptcy Code, During
the 12-Month Period Ending December 31, 2022

Housing Vacancy Rates

Area	Gross Vacancy Rate[2] (%)			Year-Round Vacancy Rate[3] (%)			Rental Vacancy Rate[4] (%)			Homeowner Vacancy Rate[5] (%)		
	2020	2021	2022	2020	2021	2022	2020	2021	2022	2020	2021	2022
MSA[1]	5.1	5.3	5.3	4.9	5.1	5.1	5.4	6.4	5.5	1.4	0.5	1.0
U.S.	10.6	10.8	10.5	8.2	8.4	8.2	6.3	6.1	5.8	1.0	0.9	0.8

Note: (1) Figures cover the Albuquerque, NM Metropolitan Statistical Area; (2) The percentage of the total
housing inventory that is vacant; (3) The percentage of the housing inventory (excluding seasonal units) that is
year-round vacant; (4) The percentage of rental inventory that is vacant for rent; (5) The percentage of
homeowner inventory that is vacant for sale
Source: U.S. Census Bureau, Housing Vacancies and Homeownership Annual Statistics: 2020, 2021, 2022

INCOME

Income

Area	Per Capita ($)	Median Household ($)	Average Household ($)
City	33,494	56,366	76,833
MSA[1]	32,622	58,335	78,771
U.S.	37,638	69,021	97,196

Note: (1) Figures cover the Albuquerque, NM Metropolitan Statistical Area
Source: U.S. Census Bureau, 2017-2021 American Community Survey 5-Year Estimates

Household Income Distribution

Area	Percent of Households Earning							
	Under $15,000	$15,000 -$24,999	$25,000 -$34,999	$35,000 -$49,999	$50,000 -$74,999	$75,000 -$99,999	$100,000 -$149,999	$150,000 and up
City	13.1	8.9	9.8	12.9	18.0	11.6	14.8	10.9
MSA[1]	12.0	8.9	9.3	13.0	18.0	12.3	15.0	11.5
U.S.	9.4	7.8	8.2	11.4	16.8	12.8	16.3	17.3

Note: (1) Figures cover the Albuquerque, NM Metropolitan Statistical Area
Source: U.S. Census Bureau, 2017-2021 American Community Survey 5-Year Estimates

Poverty Rate

Area	All Ages	Under 18 Years Old	18 to 64 Years Old	65 Years and Over
City	16.2	21.0	15.7	11.7
MSA[1]	15.3	19.5	14.9	11.3
U.S.	12.6	17.0	11.8	9.6

Note: Figures are percentage of people whose income during the past 12 months was below the poverty level;
(1) Figures cover the Albuquerque, NM Metropolitan Statistical Area
Source: U.S. Census Bureau, 2017-2021 American Community Survey 5-Year Estimates

EMPLOYMENT

Labor Force and Employment

Area	Civilian Labor Force			Workers Employed		
	Dec. 2021	Dec. 2022	% Chg.	Dec. 2021	Dec. 2022	% Chg.
City	286,208	278,969	-2.5	272,867	270,719	-0.8
MSA[1]	445,726	434,352	-2.6	424,396	421,074	-0.8
U.S.	161,696,000	164,224,000	1.6	155,732,000	158,872,000	2.0

Note: Data is not seasonally adjusted and covers workers 16 years of age and older; (1) Figures cover the Albuquerque, NM Metropolitan Statistical Area
Source: Bureau of Labor Statistics, Local Area Unemployment Statistics

Unemployment Rate

Area	2022											
	Jan.	Feb.	Mar.	Apr.	May	Jun.	Jul.	Aug.	Sep.	Oct.	Nov.	Dec.
City	4.9	4.3	4.0	3.9	3.7	4.4	4.1	4.0	4.0	3.6	3.2	3.0
MSA[1]	5.1	4.4	4.1	4.0	3.8	4.6	4.3	4.1	4.2	3.7	3.3	3.1
U.S.	4.4	4.1	3.8	3.3	3.4	3.8	3.8	3.8	3.3	3.4	3.4	3.3

Note: Data is not seasonally adjusted and covers workers 16 years of age and older; (1) Figures cover the Albuquerque, NM Metropolitan Statistical Area
Source: Bureau of Labor Statistics, Local Area Unemployment Statistics

Average Wages

Occupation	$/Hr.	Occupation	$/Hr.
Accountants and Auditors	35.62	Maintenance and Repair Workers	20.91
Automotive Mechanics	21.48	Marketing Managers	61.49
Bookkeepers	20.91	Network and Computer Systems Admin.	44.73
Carpenters	23.25	Nurses, Licensed Practical	28.50
Cashiers	13.53	Nurses, Registered	41.94
Computer Programmers	39.45	Nursing Assistants	16.74
Computer Systems Analysts	44.30	Office Clerks, General	16.26
Computer User Support Specialists	25.04	Physical Therapists	44.66
Construction Laborers	17.98	Physicians	129.51
Cooks, Restaurant	15.25	Plumbers, Pipefitters and Steamfitters	25.36
Customer Service Representatives	17.46	Police and Sheriff's Patrol Officers	27.99
Dentists	92.90	Postal Service Mail Carriers	26.30
Electricians	27.76	Real Estate Sales Agents	22.73
Engineers, Electrical	63.45	Retail Salespersons	15.08
Fast Food and Counter Workers	12.75	Sales Representatives, Technical/Scientific	37.39
Financial Managers	59.44	Secretaries, Exc. Legal/Medical/Executive	20.16
First-Line Supervisors of Office Workers	27.81	Security Guards	15.37
General and Operations Managers	58.98	Surgeons	n/a
Hairdressers/Cosmetologists	13.60	Teacher Assistants, Exc. Postsecondary*	14.88
Home Health and Personal Care Aides	13.30	Teachers, Secondary School, Exc. Sp. Ed.*	28.99
Janitors and Cleaners	14.36	Telemarketers	20.16
Landscaping/Groundskeeping Workers	16.24	Truck Drivers, Heavy/Tractor-Trailer	22.67
Lawyers	54.41	Truck Drivers, Light/Delivery Services	20.43
Maids and Housekeeping Cleaners	13.69	Waiters and Waitresses	16.14

Note: Wage data covers the Albuquerque, NM Metropolitan Statistical Area; (*) Hourly wages were calculated from annual wage data based on a 40 hour work week; n/a not available.
Source: Bureau of Labor Statistics, Metro Area Occupational Employment & Wage Estimates, May 2022

Employment by Industry

Sector	MSA[1]		U.S.
	Number of Employees	Percent of Total	Percent of Total
Construction, Mining, and Logging	25,100	6.2	5.4
Private Education and Health Services	67,600	16.6	16.1
Financial Activities	20,500	5.0	5.9
Government	79,100	19.4	14.5
Information	5,800	1.4	2.0
Leisure and Hospitality	43,100	10.6	10.3
Manufacturing	17,200	4.2	8.4
Other Services	11,800	2.9	3.7
Professional and Business Services	67,500	16.6	14.7
Retail Trade	42,800	10.5	10.2
Transportation, Warehousing, and Utilities	14,900	3.7	4.9
Wholesale Trade	11,500	2.8	3.9

Note: Figures are non-farm employment as of December 2022. Figures are not seasonally adjusted and include workers 16 years of age and older; (1) Figures cover the Albuquerque, NM Metropolitan Statistical Area
Source: Bureau of Labor Statistics, Current Employment Statistics, Employment, Hours, and Earnings

Employment by Occupation

Occupation Classification	City (%)	MSA[1] (%)	U.S. (%)
Management, Business, Science, and Arts	44.9	42.6	40.3
Natural Resources, Construction, and Maintenance	7.2	8.6	8.7
Production, Transportation, and Material Moving	7.9	8.8	13.1
Sales and Office	21.6	21.6	20.9
Service	18.4	18.4	17.0

Note: Figures cover employed civilians 16 years of age and older; (1) Figures cover the Albuquerque, NM Metropolitan Statistical Area
Source: U.S. Census Bureau, 2017-2021 American Community Survey 5-Year Estimates

Occupations with Greatest Projected Employment Growth: 2022 – 2024

Occupation[1]	2022 Employment	2024 Projected Employment	Numeric Employment Change	Percent Employment Change
Home Health and Personal Care Aides	35,710	37,830	2,120	5.9
Construction Laborers	14,780	15,630	850	5.8
Cooks, Restaurant	8,140	8,950	810	10.0
Fast Food and Counter Workers	21,760	22,500	740	3.4
Heavy and Tractor-Trailer Truck Drivers	12,510	13,190	680	5.4
Stockers and Order Fillers	14,010	14,680	670	4.8
Waiters and Waitresses	11,520	12,090	570	4.9
Maids and Housekeeping Cleaners	6,690	7,240	550	8.2
Registered Nurses	18,320	18,850	530	2.9
Laborers and Freight, Stock, and Material Movers, Hand	8,870	9,400	530	6.0

Note: Projections cover New Mexico; (1) Sorted by numeric employment change
Source: www.projectionscentral.com, State Occupational Projections, 2022–2024 Short-Term Projections

Fastest-Growing Occupations: 2022 – 2024

Occupation[1]	2022 Employment	2024 Projected Employment	Numeric Employment Change	Percent Employment Change
Fitness Trainers and Aerobics Instructors	1,690	2,000	310	18.3
Amusement and Recreation Attendants	840	990	150	17.9
Gaming Change Persons and Booth Cashiers	440	500	60	13.6
Lodging Managers	460	520	60	13.0
Hotel, Motel, and Resort Desk Clerks	3,620	4,030	410	11.3
Nurse Practitioners	1,370	1,520	150	10.9
Roustabouts, Oil and Gas	2,780	3,070	290	10.4
Industrial Truck and Tractor Operators	1,770	1,950	180	10.2
Cooks, Restaurant	8,140	8,950	810	10.0
Insurance Sales Agents	1,890	2,060	170	9.0

Note: Projections cover New Mexico; (1) Sorted by percent employment change and excludes occupations with numeric employment change less than 50
Source: www.projectionscentral.com, State Occupational Projections, 2022–2024 Short-Term Projections

CITY FINANCES

City Government Finances

Component	2020 ($000)	2020 ($ per capita)
Total Revenues	1,503,206	2,682
Total Expenditures	1,130,403	2,017
Debt Outstanding	1,475,292	2,632
Cash and Securities[1]	1,098,446	1,960

Note: (1) Cash and security holdings of a government at the close of its fiscal year, including those of its dependent agencies, utilities, and liquor stores.
Source: U.S. Census Bureau, State & Local Government Finances 2020

City Government Revenue by Source

Source	2020 ($000)	2020 ($ per capita)	2020 (%)
General Revenue			
From Federal Government	70,085	125	4.7
From State Government	257,343	459	17.1
From Local Governments	229,304	409	15.3
Taxes			
Property	159,990	285	10.6
Sales and Gross Receipts	299,316	534	19.9
Personal Income	0	0	0.0
Corporate Income	0	0	0.0
Motor Vehicle License	0	0	0.0
Other Taxes	14,776	26	1.0
Current Charges	243,895	435	16.2
Liquor Store	0	0	0.0
Utility	157,549	281	10.5

Source: U.S. Census Bureau, State & Local Government Finances 2020

City Government Expenditures by Function

Function	2020 ($000)	2020 ($ per capita)	2020 (%)
General Direct Expenditures			
Air Transportation	49,215	87	4.4
Corrections	0	0	0.0
Education	0	0	0.0
Employment Security Administration	0	0	0.0
Financial Administration	8,870	15	0.8
Fire Protection	79,027	141	7.0
General Public Buildings	11,338	20	1.0
Governmental Administration, Other	20,867	37	1.8
Health	41,960	74	3.7
Highways	60,296	107	5.3
Hospitals	0	0	0.0
Housing and Community Development	52,526	93	4.6
Interest on General Debt	41,357	73	3.7
Judicial and Legal	5,712	10	0.5
Libraries	12,074	21	1.1
Parking	5,012	8	0.4
Parks and Recreation	99,471	177	8.8
Police Protection	196,952	351	17.4
Public Welfare	20,944	37	1.9
Sewerage	112,248	200	9.9
Solid Waste Management	52,198	93	4.6
Veterans' Services	0	0	0.0
Liquor Store	0	0	0.0
Utility	209,398	373	18.5

Source: U.S. Census Bureau, State & Local Government Finances 2020

TAXES

State Corporate Income Tax Rates

State	Tax Rate (%)	Income Brackets ($)	Num. of Brackets	Financial Institution Tax Rate (%)[a]	Federal Income Tax Ded.
New Mexico	4.8 - 5.9	500,000	2	4.8 - 5.9	No

Note: Tax rates as of January 1, 2023; (a) Rates listed are the corporate income tax rate applied to financial institutions or excise taxes based on income. Some states have other taxes based upon the value of deposits or shares.
Source: Federation of Tax Administrators, State Corporate Income Tax Rates, January 1, 2023

State Individual Income Tax Rates

State	Tax Rate (%)	Income Brackets ($)	Personal Exemptions ($)			Standard Ded. ($)	
			Single	Married	Depend.	Single	Married
New Mexico	1.7 - 5.9	5,500 - 210,000 (r)	(d)	(d)	(d)	13,850	27,700 (d)

Note: Tax rates as of January 1, 2023; Local- and county-level taxes are not included; Federal income tax is not deductible on state income tax returns; (d) These states use the personal exemption/standard deduction amounts provided in the federal Internal Revenue Code; (r) The income brackets reported for New Mexico are for single individuals. For married couples filing jointly, the same tax rates apply to income brackets ranging from $8,000 to $315,000.
Source: Federation of Tax Administrators, State Individual Income Tax Rates, January 1, 2023

Various State Sales and Excise Tax Rates

State	State Sales Tax (%)	Gasoline[1] ($/gal.)	Cigarette[2] ($/pack)	Spirits[3] ($/gal.)	Wine[4] ($/gal.)	Beer[5] ($/gal.)	Recreational Marijuana (%)
New Mexico	5	0.19	2.00	6.06	1.70	0.41	(n)

Note: All tax rates as of January 1, 2023; (1) The American Petroleum Institute has developed a methodology for determining the average tax rate on a gallon of fuel. Rates may include any of the following: excise taxes, environmental fees, storage tank fees, other fees or taxes, general sales tax, and local taxes; (2) The federal excise tax of $1.0066 per pack and local taxes are not included; (3) Rates are those applicable to off-premise sales of 40% alcohol by volume (a.b.v.) distilled spirits in 750ml containers. Local excise taxes are excluded; (4) Rates are those applicable to off-premise sales of 11% a.b.v. non-carbonated wine in 750ml containers; (5) Rates are those applicable to off-premise sales of 4.7% a.b.v. beer in 12 ounce containers; (n) 12% excise tax (retail price)
Source: Tax Foundation, 2023 Facts & Figures: How Does Your State Compare?

State Business Tax Climate Index Rankings

State	Overall Rank	Corporate Tax Rank	Individual Income Tax Rank	Sales Tax Rank	Property Tax Rank	Unemployment Insurance Tax Rank
New Mexico	22	12	36	35	1	9

Note: The index is a measure of how each state's tax laws affect economic performance. The lower the rank, the more favorable a state's tax system is for business. States without a given tax are given a ranking of 1. The scores/rankings for the District of Columbia do not affect other states. The 2023 index represents the tax climate as of July 1, 2022.
Source: Tax Foundation, State Business Tax Climate Index 2023

TRANSPORTATION

Means of Transportation to Work

Area	Car/Truck/Van		Public Transportation			Bicycle	Walked	Other Means	Worked at Home
	Drove Alone	Car-pooled	Bus	Subway	Railroad				
City	76.6	8.9	1.3	0.0	0.1	0.8	1.9	1.1	9.4
MSA[1]	76.8	9.4	1.0	0.0	0.1	0.6	1.7	1.1	9.4
U.S.	73.2	8.6	2.0	1.6	0.5	0.5	2.5	1.5	9.7

Note: Figures are percentages and cover workers 16 years of age and older; (1) Figures cover the Albuquerque, NM Metropolitan Statistical Area
Source: U.S. Census Bureau, 2017-2021 American Community Survey 5-Year Estimates

Travel Time to Work

Area	Less Than 10 Minutes	10 to 19 Minutes	20 to 29 Minutes	30 to 44 Minutes	45 to 59 Minutes	60 to 89 Minutes	90 Minutes or More
City	11.0	35.9	27.8	18.1	3.1	2.5	1.6
MSA[1]	10.7	31.5	26.0	20.7	5.7	3.5	1.8
U.S.	12.4	28.5	21.0	20.9	8.2	6.2	2.9

Note: Note: Figures are percentages and include workers 16 years old and over; (1) Figures cover the Albuquerque, NM Metropolitan Statistical Area
Source: U.S. Census Bureau, 2017-2021 American Community Survey 5-Year Estimates

Key Congestion Measures

Measure	1990	2000	2010	2015	2020
Annual Hours of Delay, Total (000)	6,255	15,165	16,874	19,390	10,229
Annual Hours of Delay, Per Auto Commuter	21	39	37	43	22
Annual Congestion Cost, Per Auto Commuter ($)	406	620	877	944	516

Note: Covers the Albuquerque NM urban area
Source: Texas A&M Transportation Institute, 2021 Urban Mobility Report

Freeway Travel Time Index

Measure	1985	1990	1995	2000	2005	2010	2015	2020
Urban Area Index[1]	1.07	1.07	1.11	1.14	1.14	1.15	1.16	1.06
Urban Area Rank[1,2]	48	74	66	62	73	65	57	75

Note: Freeway Travel Time Index—the ratio of travel time in the peak period to the travel time at free-flow conditions. For example, a value of 1.30 indicates a 20-minute free-flow trip takes 26 minutes in the peak (20 minutes x 1.30 = 26 minutes); (1) Covers the Albuquerque NM urban area; (2) Rank is based on 101 larger urban areas (#1 = highest travel time index)
Source: Texas A&M Transportation Institute, 2021 Urban Mobility Report

Public Transportation

Agency Name / Mode of Transportation	Vehicles Operated in Maximum Service[1]	Annual Unlinked Passenger Trips[2] (in thous.)	Annual Passenger Miles[3] (in thous.)
ABQ Ride			
Bus (directly operated)	87	2,865.5	10,199.7
Bus Rapid Transit (directly operated)	14	1,111.1	4,378.0
Demand Response (directly operated)	62	90.3	671.2

Note: (1) Number of revenue vehicles operated by the given mode and type of service to meet the annual maximum service requirement. This is the revenue vehicle count during the peak season of the year; on the week and day that maximum service is provided. Vehicles operated in maximum service (VOMS) exclude atypical days and one-time special events; (2) Number of passengers who boarded public transportation vehicles. Passengers are counted each time they board a vehicle no matter how many vehicles they use to travel from their origin to their destination. (3) Sum of the distances ridden by all passengers during the entire fiscal year.
Source: Federal Transit Administration, National Transit Database, 2021

Air Transportation

Airport Name and Code / Type of Service	Passenger Airlines[1]	Passenger Enplanements	Freight Carriers[2]	Freight (lbs)
Albuquerque International (ABQ)				
Domestic service (U.S. carriers - 2022)	28	2,317,709	15	59,072,354
International service (U.S. carriers - 2021)	0	0	0	0

Note: (1) Includes all U.S.-based major, minor and commuter airlines that carried at least one passenger during the year; (2) Includes all U.S.-based airlines and freight carriers that transported at least one pound of freight during the year.
Source: Bureau of Transportation Statistics, The Intermodal Transportation Database, Air Carriers: T-100 Domestic Market (U.S. Carriers), 2022; Bureau of Transportation Statistics, The Intermodal Transportation Database, Air Carriers: T-100 International Market (U.S. Carriers), 2021

BUSINESSES

Major Business Headquarters

Company Name	Industry	Rankings	
		Fortune[1]	Forbes[2]
No companies listed	-	-	-

Note: (1) Companies that produce a 10-K are ranked 1 to 500 based on 2021 revenue; (2) All private companies with at least $2 billion in annual revenue through the end of their most current fiscal year are ranked 1 to 246; companies listed are headquartered in the city; dashes indicate no ranking
Source: Fortune, "Fortune 500," 2022; Forbes, "America's Largest Private Companies," 2022

Living Environment

COST OF LIVING

Cost of Living Index

Composite Index	Groceries	Housing	Utilities	Trans-portation	Health Care	Misc. Goods/ Services
92.9	98.4	87.6	91.7	92.5	90.9	95.4

Note: The Cost of Living Index measures regional differences in the cost of consumer goods and services, excluding taxes and non-consumer expenditures, for professional and managerial households in the top income quintile. It is based on more than 50,000 prices covering almost 60 different items for which prices are collected three times a year by chambers of commerce, economic development organizations or university applied economic centers in each participating urban area. The numbers shown should be read as a percentage above or below the national average of 100. For example, a value of 115.4 in the groceries column indicates that grocery prices are 15.4% higher than the national average. Small differences in the index numbers should not be interpreted as significant; Figures cover the Albuquerque NM urban area.
Source: The Council for Community and Economic Research, Cost of Living Index, 2022

Grocery Prices

Area[1]	T-Bone Steak ($/pound)	Frying Chicken ($/pound)	Whole Milk ($/half gal.)	Eggs ($/dozen)	Orange Juice ($/64 oz.)	Coffee ($/11.5 oz.)
City[2]	11.88	1.01	2.29	2.30	3.89	5.52
Avg.	13.81	1.59	2.43	2.25	3.85	4.95
Min.	10.17	0.90	1.51	1.30	2.90	3.46
Max.	19.35	3.30	4.32	4.32	5.31	8.59

*Note: (1) Values for the local area are compared with the average, minimum and maximum values for all 286 areas in the Cost of Living Index; (2) Figures cover the Albuquerque NM urban area; **T-Bone Steak** (price per pound); **Frying Chicken** (price per pound, whole fryer); **Whole Milk** (half gallon carton); **Eggs** (price per dozen, Grade A, large); **Orange Juice** (64 oz. Tropicana or Florida Natural); **Coffee** (11.5 oz. can, vacuum-packed, Maxwell House, Hills Bros, or Folgers).*
Source: The Council for Community and Economic Research, Cost of Living Index, 2022

Housing and Utility Costs

Area[1]	New Home Price ($)	Apartment Rent ($/month)	All Electric ($/month)	Part Electric ($/month)	Other Energy ($/month)	Telephone ($/month)
City[2]	383,227	1,215	-	107.21	43.71	191.37
Avg.	450,913	1,371	176.41	99.93	76.96	190.22
Min.	229,283	546	100.84	31.56	27.15	174.27
Max.	2,434,977	4,569	356.86	249.59	272.24	208.31

*Note: (1) Values for the local area are compared with the average, minimum and maximum values for all 286 areas in the Cost of Living Index; (2) Figures cover the Albuquerque NM urban area; **New Home Price** (2,400 sf living area, 8,000 sf lot, in urban area with full utilities); **Apartment Rent** (950 sf 2 bedroom/1.5 or 2 bath, unfurnished, excluding all utilities except water); **All Electric** (average monthly cost for an all-electric home); **Part Electric** (average monthly cost for a part-electric home); **Other Energy** (average monthly cost for natural gas, fuel oil, coal, wood, and any other forms of energy except electricity); **Telephone** (price includes the base monthly rate plus taxes and fees for three lines of mobile phone service).*
Source: The Council for Community and Economic Research, Cost of Living Index, 2022

Health Care, Transportation, and Other Costs

Area[1]	Doctor ($/visit)	Dentist ($/visit)	Optometrist ($/visit)	Gasoline ($/gallon)	Beauty Salon ($/visit)	Men's Shirt ($)
City[2]	114.36	105.38	123.65	3.81	45.00	29.72
Avg.	124.91	107.77	117.66	3.86	43.31	34.21
Min.	36.61	58.25	51.79	2.90	22.18	13.05
Max.	250.21	162.58	371.96	5.54	85.61	63.54

*Note: (1) Values for the local area are compared with the average, minimum and maximum values for all 286 areas in the Cost of Living Index; (2) Figures cover the Albuquerque NM urban area; **Doctor** (general practitioners routine exam of an established patient); **Dentist** (adult teeth cleaning and periodic oral examination); **Optometrist** (full vision eye exam for established adult patient); **Gasoline** (one gallon regular unleaded, national brand, including all taxes, cash price at self-service pump if available); **Beauty Salon** (woman's shampoo, trim, and blow-dry); **Men's Shirt** (cotton/polyester dress shirt, pinpoint weave, long sleeves).*
Source: The Council for Community and Economic Research, Cost of Living Index, 2022

HOUSING

Homeownership Rate

Area	2015 (%)	2016 (%)	2017 (%)	2018 (%)	2019 (%)	2020 (%)	2021 (%)	2022 (%)
MSA[1]	64.3	66.9	67.0	67.9	70.0	69.5	66.5	67.3
U.S.	63.7	63.4	63.9	64.4	64.6	66.6	65.5	65.8

Note: (1) Figures cover the Albuquerque, NM Metropolitan Statistical Area
Source: U.S. Census Bureau, Housing Vacancies and Homeownership Annual Statistics: 2015-2022

House Price Index (HPI)

Area	National Ranking[2]	Quarterly Change (%)	One-Year Change (%)	Five-Year Change (%)	Since 1991Q1 (%)
MSA[1]	67	0.95	14.03	58.76	256.02
U.S.[3]	–	0.34	8.41	58.44	289.08

Note: The HPI is a weighted repeat sales index. It measures average price changes in repeat sales or refinancings on the same properties. This information is obtained by reviewing repeat mortgage transactions on single-family properties whose mortgages have been purchased or securitized by Fannie Mae or Freddie Mac since January 1975; (1) Figures cover the Albuquerque, NM Metropolitan Statistical Area; (2) Rankings are based on annual percentage change for all metro areas containing at least 15,000 transactions over the last 10 years and ranges from 1 to 257; (3) figures based on a weighted average of Census Division estimates using a seasonally adjusted, purchase-only index; all figures are for the period ending December 31, 2022
Source: Federal Housing Finance Agency, Change in FHFA Metropolitan Area House Price Indexes, 2022Q4

Median Single-Family Home Prices

Area	2020	2021	2022[p]	Percent Change 2021 to 2022
MSA[1]	248.1	292.5	336.6	15.1
U.S. Average	300.2	357.1	392.6	9.9

Note: Figures are median sales prices of existing single-family homes in thousands of dollars; (p) preliminary; (1) Figures cover the Albuquerque, NM Metropolitan Statistical Area
Source: National Association of Realtors, Median Sales Price of Existing Single-Family Homes for Metropolitan Areas, 4th Quarter 2022

Qualifying Income Based on Median Sales Price of Existing Single-Family Homes

Area	With 5% Down ($)	With 10% Down ($)	With 20% Down ($)
MSA[1]	100,675	95,377	84,779
U.S. Average	112,234	106,237	94,513

Note: Figures are preliminary; Qualifying income is based on a mortgage rate of 6.77%. Monthly principal and interest payment is limited to 25% of income; (1) Figures cover the Albuquerque, NM Metropolitan Statistical Area
Source: National Association of Realtors, Qualifying Income Based on Median Sales Price of Existing Single-Family Homes for Metropolitan Areas, 4th Quarter 2022

Home Value

Area	Under $100,000	$100,000 -$199,999	$200,000 -$299,999	$300,000 -$399,999	$400,000 -$499,999	$500,000 -$999,999	$1,000,000 or more	Median ($)
City	8.2	36.2	31.9	13.0	5.9	4.2	0.6	214,600
MSA[1]	11.7	34.6	28.4	12.3	5.9	5.9	1.1	210,700
U.S.	16.2	24.2	20.1	13.6	8.3	13.6	4.1	244,900

Note: Figures are percentages except for median and cover owner-occupied housing units; (1) Figures cover the Albuquerque, NM Metropolitan Statistical Area
Source: U.S. Census Bureau, 2017-2021 American Community Survey 5-Year Estimates

Year Housing Structure Built

Area	2020 or Later	2010 -2019	2000 -2009	1990 -1999	1980 -1989	1970 -1979	1960 -1969	1950 -1959	1940 -1949	Before 1940	Median Year
City	0.2	5.7	16.1	14.9	15.1	19.1	9.8	11.8	4.3	3.1	1981
MSA[1]	0.2	5.9	17.2	17.3	16.8	17.8	8.7	9.3	3.6	3.2	1984
U.S.	0.2	7.3	13.6	13.6	13.2	14.8	10.3	10.0	4.7	12.2	1979

Note: Figures are percentages except for Median Year; Note: (1) Figures cover the Albuquerque, NM Metropolitan Statistical Area
Source: U.S. Census Bureau, 2017-2021 American Community Survey 5-Year Estimates

Gross Monthly Rent

Area	Under $500	$500 -$999	$1,000 -$1,499	$1,500 -$1,999	$2,000 -$2,499	$2,500 -$2,999	$3,000 and up	Median ($)
City	7.3	49.4	31.5	9.8	1.1	0.5	0.5	932
MSA[1]	7.2	47.4	32.9	10.2	1.3	0.4	0.5	952
U.S.	8.1	30.5	30.8	16.8	7.3	3.1	3.5	1,163

Note: Figures are percentages except for median; Gross rent is the contract rent plus the estimated average monthly cost of utilities (electricity, gas, and water and sewer) and fuels (oil, coal, kerosene, wood, etc.) if these are paid by the renter (or paid for the renter by someone else); (1) Figures cover the Albuquerque, NM Metropolitan Statistical Area
Source: U.S. Census Bureau, 2017-2021 American Community Survey 5-Year Estimates

HEALTH

Health Risk Factors

Category	MSA[1] (%)	U.S. (%)
Adults aged 18–64 who have any kind of health care coverage	90.7	90.9
Adults who reported being in good or better health	81.7	85.2
Adults who have been told they have high blood cholesterol	37.7	35.7
Adults who have been told they have high blood pressure	32.2	32.4
Adults who are current smokers	11.5	14.4
Adults who currently use e-cigarettes	7.5	6.7
Adults who currently use chewing tobacco, snuff, or snus	2.9	3.5
Adults who are heavy drinkers[2]	4.9	6.3
Adults who are binge drinkers[3]	13.1	15.4
Adults who are overweight (BMI 25.0 - 29.9)	37.1	34.4
Adults who are obese (BMI 30.0 - 99.8)	32.8	33.9
Adults who participated in any physical activities in the past month	78.9	76.3

Note: (1) Figures cover the Albuquerque, NM Metropolitan Statistical Area; (2) Heavy drinkers are classified as adult men having more than 14 drinks per week and adult women having more than 7 drinks per week; (3) Binge drinkers are classified as males having five or more drinks on one occasion or females having four or more drinks on one occasion
Source: Centers for Disease Control and Prevention, Behaviorial Risk Factor Surveillance System, SMART: Selected Metropolitan Area Risk Trends, 2021

Acute and Chronic Health Conditions

Category	MSA[1] (%)	U.S. (%)
Adults who have ever been told they had a heart attack	3.3	4.0
Adults who have ever been told they have angina or coronary heart disease	1.9	3.8
Adults who have ever been told they had a stroke	2.5	3.0
Adults who have ever been told they have asthma	14.5	14.9
Adults who have ever been told they have arthritis	25.2	25.8
Adults who have ever been told they have diabetes[2]	13.6	10.9
Adults who have ever been told they had skin cancer	6.2	6.6
Adults who have ever been told they had any other types of cancer	6.5	7.5
Adults who have ever been told they have COPD	5.7	6.1
Adults who have ever been told they have kidney disease	4.5	3.0
Adults who have ever been told they have a form of depression	22.1	20.5

Note: (1) Figures cover the Albuquerque, NM Metropolitan Statistical Area; (2) Figures do not include pregnancy-related, borderline, or pre-diabetes
Source: Centers for Disease Control and Prevention, Behaviorial Risk Factor Surveillance System, SMART: Selected Metropolitan Area Risk Trends, 2021

Health Screening and Vaccination Rates

Category	MSA[1] (%)	U.S. (%)
Adults who have ever been tested for HIV	35.5	34.9
Adults who have had their blood cholesterol checked within the last five years	80.3	85.2
Adults aged 65+ who have had flu shot within the past year	71.3	68.6
Adults aged 65+ who have ever had a pneumonia vaccination	77.5	71.0

Note: (1) Figures cover the Albuquerque, NM Metropolitan Statistical Area.
Source: Centers for Disease Control and Prevention, Behaviorial Risk Factor Surveillance System, SMART: Selected Metropolitan Area Risk Trends, 2021

Disability Status

Category	MSA[1] (%)	U.S. (%)
Adults who reported being deaf	8.4	7.2
Are you blind or have serious difficulty seeing, even when wearing glasses?	4.8	4.8
Are you limited in any way in any of your usual activities due to arthritis?	11.8	11.1
Do you have difficulty doing errands alone?	7.9	7.0
Do you have difficulty dressing or bathing?	4.5	3.6
Do you have serious difficulty concentrating/remembering/making decisions?	14.8	12.1
Do you have serious difficulty walking or climbing stairs?	15.4	12.8

Note: (1) Figures cover the Albuquerque, NM Metropolitan Statistical Area.
Source: Centers for Disease Control and Prevention, Behaviorial Risk Factor Surveillance System, SMART: Selected Metropolitan Area Risk Trends, 2021

Mortality Rates for the Top 10 Causes of Death in the U.S.

ICD-10[a] Sub-Chapter	ICD-10[a] Code	Crude Mortality Rate[1] per 100,000 population	
		County[2]	U.S.
Malignant neoplasms	C00-C97	163.6	182.6
Ischaemic heart diseases	I20-I25	133.4	113.1
Other forms of heart disease	I30-I51	42.1	64.4
Other degenerative diseases of the nervous system	G30-G31	43.4	51.0
Cerebrovascular diseases	I60-I69	48.0	47.8
Other external causes of accidental injury	W00-X59	81.5	46.4
Chronic lower respiratory diseases	J40-J47	48.8	45.7
Organic, including symptomatic, mental disorders	F01-F09	32.4	35.9
Hypertensive diseases	I10-I15	16.9	35.0
Diabetes mellitus	E10-E14	27.0	29.6

Note: (a) ICD-10 = International Classification of Diseases 10th Revision; (1) Crude mortality rates are a three-year average covering 2019-2021; (2) Figures cover Bernalillo County.
Source: Centers for Disease Control and Prevention, National Center for Health Statistics. National Vital Statistics System, Mortality 2018-2021 on CDC WONDER Online Database

Mortality Rates for Selected Causes of Death

ICD-10[a] Sub-Chapter	ICD-10[a] Code	Crude Mortality Rate[1] per 100,000 population	
		County[2]	U.S.
Assault	X85-Y09	14.2	7.0
Diseases of the liver	K70-K76	37.4	19.8
Human immunodeficiency virus (HIV) disease	B20-B24	1.4	1.5
Influenza and pneumonia	J09-J18	13.3	14.7
Intentional self-harm	X60-X84	24.1	14.3
Malnutrition	E40-E46	15.7	4.3
Obesity and other hyperalimentation	E65-E68	4.4	3.0
Renal failure	N17-N19	11.1	15.7
Transport accidents	V01-V99	19.0	13.6
Viral hepatitis	B15-B19	2.5	1.2

Note: (a) ICD-10 = International Classification of Diseases 10th Revision; (1) Crude mortality rates are a three-year average covering 2019-2021; (2) Figures cover Bernalillo County; Data are suppressed when the data meet the criteria for confidentiality constraints; Crude mortality rates are flagged as unreliable when the rate would be calculated with a numerator of 20 or less.
Source: Centers for Disease Control and Prevention, National Center for Health Statistics. National Vital Statistics System, Mortality 2018-2021 on CDC WONDER Online Database

Health Insurance Coverage

Area	With Health Insurance	With Private Health Insurance	With Public Health Insurance	Without Health Insurance	Population Under Age 19 Without Health Insurance
City	92.1	60.6	44.2	7.9	4.3
MSA[1]	92.0	60.1	45.5	8.0	4.7
U.S.	91.2	67.8	35.4	8.8	5.3

Note: Figures are percentages that cover the civilian noninstitutionalized population; (1) Figures cover the Albuquerque, NM Metropolitan Statistical Area
Source: U.S. Census Bureau, 2017-2021 American Community Survey 5-Year Estimates

Number of Medical Professionals

Area	MDs[3]	DOs[3,4]	Dentists	Podiatrists	Chiropractors	Optometrists
County[1] (number)	3,195	149	591	60	169	110
County[1] (rate[2])	472.2	22.0	87.6	8.9	25.1	16.3
U.S. (rate[2])	289.3	23.5	72.5	6.2	28.7	17.4

Note: Data as of 2021 unless noted; (1) Data covers Bernalillo County; (2) Rate per 100,000 population; (3) Data as of 2020 and includes all active, non-federal physicians; (4) Doctor of Osteopathic Medicine
Source: U.S. Department of Health and Human Services, Health Resources and Services Administration, Bureau of Health Professions, Area Resource File (ARF) 2021-2022

EDUCATION

Public School District Statistics

District Name	Schls	Pupils	Pupil/ Teacher Ratio	Minority Pupils[1] (%)	LEP/ELL[2] (%)	IEP[3] (%)
Albuquerque Public Schools	176	81,762	13.6	80.2	17.0	18.5

Note: Table includes school districts with 2,000 or more students; (1) Percentage of students that are not non-Hispanic white; (2) Percentage of students that are Limited English Proficient or English Language Learners (2018-19); (3) Percentage of students that have an Individualized Education Program (2019-20).
Source: U.S. Department of Education, National Center for Education Statistics, Common Core of Data, Local Education Agency (School District) Universe Survey: School Year 2021-2022

Best High Schools

According to *U.S. News,* Albuquerque is home to two of the top 500 high schools in the U.S.: **Albuquerque Institute of Math and Science** (#53); **Cottonwood Classical Prep** (#190). Nearly 18,000 public, magnet and charter schools were ranked based on their performance on state assessments and how well they prepare students for college. *U.S. News & World Report, "Best High Schools 2022"*

Highest Level of Education

Area	Less than H.S.	H.S. Diploma	Some College, No Deg.	Associate Degree	Bachelor's Degree	Master's Degree	Prof. School Degree	Doctorate Degree
City	9.1	21.8	22.7	9.1	20.4	11.5	2.9	2.6
MSA[1]	10.0	23.8	23.2	9.2	18.6	10.5	2.4	2.2
U.S.	11.1	26.5	20.0	8.7	20.6	9.3	2.2	1.5

Note: Figures cover persons age 25 and over; (1) Figures cover the Albuquerque, NM Metropolitan Statistical Area
Source: U.S. Census Bureau, 2017-2021 American Community Survey 5-Year Estimates

Educational Attainment by Race

Area	High School Graduate or Higher (%)					Bachelor's Degree or Higher (%)				
	Total	White	Black	Asian	Hisp.[2]	Total	White	Black	Asian	Hisp.[2]
City	90.9	93.0	94.3	87.7	84.8	37.4	41.1	36.2	54.1	24.3
MSA[1]	90.0	92.1	92.0	89.6	83.8	33.7	37.5	34.4	54.4	21.7
U.S.	88.9	91.4	87.2	87.6	71.2	33.7	35.5	23.3	55.6	18.4

Note: Figures shown cover persons 25 years old and over; (1) Figures cover the Albuquerque, NM Metropolitan Statistical Area; (2) People of Hispanic origin can be of any race
Source: U.S. Census Bureau, 2017-2021 American Community Survey 5-Year Estimates

School Enrollment by Grade and Control

Area	Preschool (%)		Kindergarten (%)		Grades 1 - 4 (%)		Grades 5 - 8 (%)		Grades 9 - 12 (%)	
	Public	Private	Public	Private	Public	Private	Public	Private	Public	Private
City	57.2	42.8	86.7	13.3	86.7	13.3	90.7	9.3	91.7	8.3
MSA[1]	57.8	42.2	84.8	15.2	86.4	13.6	89.8	10.2	90.8	9.2
U.S.	58.8	41.2	86.3	13.7	88.3	11.7	88.6	11.4	89.4	10.6

Note: Figures shown cover persons 3 years old and over; (1) Figures cover the Albuquerque, NM Metropolitan Statistical Area
Source: U.S. Census Bureau, 2017-2021 American Community Survey 5-Year Estimates

Higher Education

Four-Year Colleges			Two-Year Colleges			Medical Schools[1]	Law Schools[2]	Voc/ Tech[3]
Public	Private Non-profit	Private For-profit	Public	Private Non-profit	Private For-profit			
1	0	1	3	0	2	1	1	6

Note: Figures cover institutions located within the Albuquerque, NM Metropolitan Statistical Area and include main campuses only; (1) includes schools accredited by the Liaison Committee on Medical Education and the American Osteopathic Association's Commission on Osteopathic College Accreditation; (2) includes ABA-accredited schools, schools with provisional ABA accreditation, and state accredited schools; (3) includes all schools with programs that are less than 2 years.
Source: National Center for Education Statistics, Integrated Postsecondary Education System (IPEDS), 2021-22; Wikipedia, List of Medical Schools in the United States, accessed April 10, 2023; Wikipedia, List of Law Schools in the United States, accessed April 10, 2023

According to *U.S. News & World Report,* the Albuquerque, NM metro area is home to one of the top 100 law schools in the U.S.: **University of New Mexico** (#91 tie). The rankings are based on a weighted average of 12 measures of quality: peer assessment score; assessment score by lawyers/judges; median LSAT scores; median undergrad GPA; acceptance rate; employment rates for graduates; placement success; bar passage rate; faculty resources; expenditures per student; student/faculty ratio; and library resources. *U.S. News & World Report, "America's Best Graduate Schools, Law, 2023"*

EMPLOYERS

Major Employers

Company Name	Industry
Central New Mexico Community College	Vocational schools
City of Albuquerque	Municipal government
City of Albuquerque Police Department	Municipal police
Jack Henry & Associates	Computers
Laguna Development Corporation	Grocery stores, independent
Mediplex of Massachusetts	Nursing home, exc skilled & intermediate care facility
Sandia Corporation	Noncommercial research organizations
The Boeing Company	Aircraft
U.S. Fish and Wildlife Service	Fish & wildlife conservation agency, government
United States Department of Energy	Energy development & conservation agency, government
United States Department of the Air Force	Testing laboratories
University of New Mexico	University
University of New Mexico Hospital	General medical & surgical hospitals
USAF	U.S. military
Veterans Health Administration	Administration of veterans' affiars
Veterans Hospital	General medical & surgical hospitals

Note: Companies shown are located within the Albuquerque, NM Metropolitan Statistical Area.
Source: Hoovers.com; Wikipedia

PUBLIC SAFETY

Crime Rate

Area	Total Crime	Violent Crime Rate				Property Crime Rate		
		Murder	Rape[3]	Robbery	Aggrav. Assault	Burglary	Larceny -Theft	Motor Vehicle Theft
City	6,355.7	14.2	78.5	256.0	994.9	902.9	3,225.8	883.3
Suburbs[1]	2,025.9	1.9	34.6	40.4	405.3	354.2	870.1	319.4
Metro[2]	4,660.5	9.4	61.3	171.6	764.1	688.1	2,303.5	662.5
U.S.	2,356.7	6.5	38.4	73.9	279.7	314.2	1,398.0	246.0

Note: Figures are crimes per 100,000 population; (1) All areas within the metro area that are located outside the city limits; (2) Figures cover the Albuquerque, NM Metropolitan Statistical Area; (3) All figures shown were reported using the revised Uniform Crime Reporting (UCR) definition of rape; Due to the transition to the National Incident-Based Reporting System (NIBRS), limited city and metro area data was released for 2021.
Source: FBI Uniform Crime Reports, 2020

Hate Crimes

Area	Number of Quarters Reported	Number of Incidents per Bias Motivation					
		Race/Ethnicity/ Ancestry	Religion	Sexual Orientation	Disability	Gender	Gender Identity
City[1]	4	26	3	9	1	2	2
U.S.	4	5,227	1,244	1,110	130	75	266

Note: (1) Figures include one incident reported with more than one bias motivation; Due to the transition to the National Incident-Based Reporting System (NIBRS), limited crime data was released for 2021.
Source: Federal Bureau of Investigation, Hate Crime Statistics 2020

Identity Theft Consumer Reports

Area	Reports	Reports per 100,000 Population	Rank[2]
MSA[1]	1,590	174	201
U.S.	1,108,609	339	-

Note: (1) Figures cover the Albuquerque, NM Metropolitan Statistical Area; (2) Rank ranges from 1 to 391 where 1 indicates greatest number of identity theft reports per 100,000 population
Source: Federal Trade Commission, Consumer Sentinel Network Data Book 2022

Fraud and Other Consumer Reports

Area	Reports	Reports per 100,000 Population	Rank[2]
MSA[1]	8,589	938	131
U.S.	4,064,520	1,245	-

Note: (1) Figures cover the Albuquerque, NM Metropolitan Statistical Area; (2) Rank ranges from 1 to 391 where 1 indicates greatest number of fraud and other consumer reports per 100,000 population
Source: Federal Trade Commission, Consumer Sentinel Network Data Book 2022

POLITICS

2020 Presidential Election Results

Area	Biden	Trump	Jorgensen	Hawkins	Other
Bernalillo County	61.0	36.6	1.5	0.5	0.4
U.S.	51.3	46.8	1.2	0.3	0.5

Note: Results are percentages and may not add to 100% due to rounding
Source: Dave Leip's Atlas of U.S. Presidential Elections

SPORTS

Professional Sports Teams

Team Name	League	Year Established
No teams are located in the metro area		

Source: Wikipedia, Major Professional Sports Teams of the United States and Canada, April 12, 2023

CLIMATE

Average and Extreme Temperatures

Temperature	Jan	Feb	Mar	Apr	May	Jun	Jul	Aug	Sep	Oct	Nov	Dec	Yr.
Extreme High (°F)	69	76	85	89	98	105	105	101	100	91	77	72	105
Average High (°F)	47	53	61	71	80	90	92	89	83	72	57	48	70
Average Temp. (°F)	35	40	47	56	65	75	79	76	70	58	45	36	57
Average Low (°F)	23	27	33	41	50	59	65	63	56	44	31	24	43
Extreme Low (°F)	-17	-5	8	19	28	40	52	50	37	21	-7	-7	-17

Note: Figures cover the years 1948-1992
Source: National Climatic Data Center, International Station Meteorological Climate Summary, 9/96

Average Precipitation/Snowfall/Humidity

Precip./Humidity	Jan	Feb	Mar	Apr	May	Jun	Jul	Aug	Sep	Oct	Nov	Dec	Yr.
Avg. Precip. (in.)	0.4	0.4	0.5	0.4	0.5	0.5	1.4	1.5	0.9	0.9	0.4	0.5	8.5
Avg. Snowfall (in.)	3	2	2	1	Tr	0	0	0	Tr	Tr	1	3	11
Avg. Rel. Hum. 5am (%)	68	64	55	48	48	45	60	65	61	60	63	68	59
Avg. Rel. Hum. 5pm (%)	41	33	25	20	19	18	27	30	29	29	35	43	29

Note: Figures cover the years 1948-1992; Tr = Trace amounts (<0.05 in. of rain; <0.5 in. of snow)
Source: National Climatic Data Center, International Station Meteorological Climate Summary, 9/96

Weather Conditions

Temperature			Daytime Sky			Precipitation		
10°F & below	32°F & below	90°F & above	Clear	Partly cloudy	Cloudy	0.01 inch or more precip.	0.1 inch or more snow/ice	Thunder-storms
4	114	65	140	160	65	60	9	38

Note: Figures are average number of days per year and cover the years 1948-1992
Source: National Climatic Data Center, International Station Meteorological Climate Summary, 9/96

HAZARDOUS WASTE

Superfund Sites

The Albuquerque, NM metro area is home to three sites on the EPA's Superfund National Priorities List: **AT&SF (Albuquerque)** (final); **Fruit Avenue Plume** (final); **South Valley** (final). There are a total of 1,165 Superfund sites with a status of proposed or final on the list in the U.S. *U.S. Environmental Protection Agency, National Priorities List, April 12, 2023*

AIR QUALITY

Air Quality Trends: Ozone

	1990	1995	2000	2005	2010	2015	2018	2019	2020	2021
MSA[1]	0.072	0.070	0.072	0.073	0.066	0.066	0.074	0.067	0.071	0.071
U.S.	0.087	0.089	0.081	0.080	0.072	0.067	0.069	0.065	0.065	0.067

Note: (1) Data covers the Albuquerque, NM Metropolitan Statistical Area. The values shown are the composite ozone concentration averages among trend sites based on the highest fourth daily maximum 8-hour concentration in parts per million. These trends are based on sites having an adequate record of monitoring data during the trend period. Data from exceptional events are included.
Source: U.S. Environmental Protection Agency, Air Quality Monitoring Information, "Air Quality Trends by City, 1990-2021"

Air Quality Index

Area	Percent of Days when Air Quality was...[2]					AQI Statistics[2]	
	Good	Moderate	Unhealthy for Sensitive Groups	Unhealthy	Very Unhealthy	Maximum	Median
MSA[1]	23.6	70.7	5.2	0.5	0.0	166	62

Note: (1) Data covers the Albuquerque, NM Metropolitan Statistical Area; (2) Based on 365 days with AQI data in 2021. Air Quality Index (AQI) is an index for reporting daily air quality. EPA calculates the AQI for five major air pollutants regulated by the Clean Air Act: ground-level ozone, particle pollution (aka particulate matter), carbon monoxide, sulfur dioxide, and nitrogen dioxide. The AQI runs from 0 to 500. The higher the AQI value, the greater the level of air pollution and the greater the health concern. There are six AQI categories: "Good" AQI is between 0 and 50. Air quality is considered satisfactory; "Moderate" AQI is between 51 and 100. Air quality is acceptable; "Unhealthy for Sensitive Groups" When AQI values are between 101 and 150, members of sensitive groups may experience health effects; "Unhealthy" When AQI values are between 151 and 200 everyone may begin to experience health effects; "Very Unhealthy" AQI values between 201 and 300 trigger a health alert; "Hazardous" AQI values over 300 trigger warnings of emergency conditions (not shown).
Source: U.S. Environmental Protection Agency, Air Quality Index Report, 2021

Air Quality Index Pollutants

Area	Percent of Days when AQI Pollutant was...[2]					
	Carbon Monoxide	Nitrogen Dioxide	Ozone	Sulfur Dioxide	Particulate Matter 2.5	Particulate Matter 10
MSA[1]	0.0	0.0	49.6	(3)	16.7	33.7

Note: (1) Data covers the Albuquerque, NM Metropolitan Statistical Area; (2) Based on 365 days with AQI data in 2021. The Air Quality Index (AQI) is an index for reporting daily air quality. EPA calculates the AQI for five major air pollutants regulated by the Clean Air Act: ground-level ozone, particle pollution (also known as particulate matter), carbon monoxide, sulfur dioxide, and nitrogen dioxide. The AQI runs from 0 to 500. The higher the AQI value, the greater the level of air pollution and the greater the health concern; (3) Sulfur dioxide is no longer included in this table (as of December 8, 2021) because SO_2 concentrations tend to be very localized and not necessarily representative of broad geographical areas like counties and CBSAs.
Source: U.S. Environmental Protection Agency, Air Quality Index Report, 2021

Maximum Air Pollutant Concentrations: Particulate Matter, Ozone, CO and Lead

	Particulate Matter 10 (ug/m^3)	Particulate Matter 2.5 Wtd AM (ug/m^3)	Particulate Matter 2.5 24-Hr (ug/m^3)	Ozone (ppm)	Carbon Monoxide (ppm)	Lead (ug/m^3)
MSA[1] Level	221	11.3	28	0.076	1	n/a
NAAQS[2]	150	15	35	0.075	9	0.15
Met NAAQS[2]	No	Yes	Yes	No	Yes	n/a

Note: (1) Data covers the Albuquerque, NM Metropolitan Statistical Area; Data from exceptional events are included; (2) National Ambient Air Quality Standards; ppm = parts per million; ug/m^3 = micrograms per cubic meter; n/a not available.
Concentrations: Particulate Matter 10 (coarse particulate)—highest second maximum 24-hour concentration; Particulate Matter 2.5 Wtd AM (fine particulate)—highest weighted annual mean concentration; Particulate Matter 2.5 24-Hour (fine particulate)—highest 98th percentile 24-hour concentration; Ozone—highest fourth daily maximum 8-hour concentration; Carbon Monoxide—highest second maximum non-overlapping 8-hour concentration; Lead—maximum running 3-month average
Source: U.S. Environmental Protection Agency, Air Quality Monitoring Information, "Air Quality Statistics by City, 2021"

Maximum Air Pollutant Concentrations: Nitrogen Dioxide and Sulfur Dioxide

	Nitrogen Dioxide AM (ppb)	Nitrogen Dioxide 1-Hr (ppb)	Sulfur Dioxide AM (ppb)	Sulfur Dioxide 1-Hr (ppb)	Sulfur Dioxide 24-Hr (ppb)
MSA[1] Level	8	44	n/a	3	n/a
NAAQS[2]	53	100	30	75	140
Met NAAQS[2]	Yes	Yes	n/a	Yes	n/a

Note: (1) Data covers the Albuquerque, NM Metropolitan Statistical Area; Data from exceptional events are included; (2) National Ambient Air Quality Standards; ppm = parts per million; ug/m^3 = micrograms per cubic meter; n/a not available.
Concentrations: Nitrogen Dioxide AM—highest arithmetic mean concentration; Nitrogen Dioxide 1-Hr—highest 98th percentile 1-hour daily maximum concentration; Sulfur Dioxide AM—highest annual mean concentration; Sulfur Dioxide 1-Hr—highest 99th percentile 1-hour daily maximum concentration; Sulfur Dioxide 24-Hr—highest second maximum 24-hour concentration
Source: U.S. Environmental Protection Agency, Air Quality Monitoring Information, "Air Quality Statistics by City, 2021"

Anchorage, Alaska

Background

Anchorage, in south central Alaska, is the state's largest city and a center for the state's communication, transportation, health care, and finance industries. Originally powered by the railroads and the fishing industry, Anchorage's economy has in more recent times been closely tied to petroleum production, which accounts for more than 20 percent of the nation's oil reserves.

This modern city lies in a spectacular natural setting, with the Chugach Mountain Range across its eastern skyline and the waters of the Cook Inlet to the west. The city boasts all the advantages of a dynamic urban center, while its residents enjoy a natural environment that teems with bear, moose, caribou, fox, eagles, wolves, Dall sheep, orcas, and beluga whales.

The city was incorporated in 1920 and grew slowly for several decades. During World War II, when airfields and roads were constructed to aid in the war effort, the population expanded dramatically; by 1946, Anchorage was home to more than 40,000 people.

In 1964, the region was hit by the strongest earthquake ever to strike North America. There was extensive damage and some loss of life, but the city was quickly rebuilt; in fact, reconstruction was so prompt, efficient, and successful that many look back on the period with considerable civic pride. Earthquakes are not uncommon to the region, and a moderate 5.7 event occurred in Anchorage in January 2009.

In 1951, Anchorage International Airport, now Ted Stevens International Airport (ANC), was completed, and the city became vital to the emerging air transport industry as new routes were created. Ted Stevens International Airport flies nearly 600 transcontinental cargo flights each week and is the busiest cargo airport in the country. Elmendorf Air Force Base at the northeast end of town, and Anchorage's pioneering development of bush aviation, which serves the entire interior of Alaska, further testify to the importance of air travel to the city's development. Also located at the airport are Fort Richardson Army Post and Kulis Air National Guard Base that together employ 8,500.

Oil in Alaska was first discovered in 1957, and 17 oil companies subsequently set up headquarters in Anchorage, giving the city a tremendous economic boost. In 1968, when the large North Slope field was discovered, Anchorage was again a major beneficiary. With the completion of the Trans-Alaskan Pipeline System in 1977, Anchorage entered its contemporary period of sustained population growth and dynamic economic development.

Tourism accounts for 1 in 9 jobs in Anchorage. More than $30 million is collected in local hotel and car rental taxes alone, and visitors spend hundreds of millions in Anchorage annually. Anchorage is also known as a tax-friendly city, with no sales or personal income tax.

The city's cultural amenities include the Anchorage Museum at Rasmuson Center and the Alaska Aviation Heritage Museum, which chronicles the story of Alaska's early and pioneering air transport system. Near the city is the Potter Section House Railway Museum, which pays homage to the state's vital rail industry. The city also boasts the Alaska Center for the Performing Arts and the Alaska Botanical Garden. Delaney Park, also known as the Park Strip, is a venerable and valued recreational resource in the city's business district, and its ongoing improvement looks toward a year-round "Central Park" for Anchorage. The Alaska State Fair has been recognized as one of the Top 100 Events in North America.

The city is an educational center with two universities and many technical, vocational, and private schools. A campus of the University of Alaska has been in Anchorage since 1954, and the city is also home to Alaska Pacific University.

The natural environment of Anchorage is spectacular, and at nearby Portage Glacier, one can watch the glacier "calving," as huge blocks of ice crash into the lake below. Anchorage is also located at one end of the famous annual Iditarod Trail Sled Dog Race.

Because of its long summer days and relatively mild temperatures, Anchorage is called "The City of Lights and Flowers," and open grassy expanses are adorned throughout the summer season with lights and flowers. Summer also brings out a friendly competition among the city's residents, who plant colorful flowers along streets, in parks, private gardens, window boxes, and lobbies.

The weather in Anchorage, contrary to what many believe, is not savagely cold. It is tempered by the city's location on the coast and by the Alaska Mountain Range, which acts as a barrier to very cold air from the north. Snow season lasts from October to May. Summers can bring fog and rain.

Rankings

General Rankings

- For its "Best for Vets: Places to Live 2019" rankings, *Military Times* evaluated 599 cities (83 large, 234 medium, 282 small) and compared the locations across three broad categories: veteran and military culture/services; economic indicators; and livability factors such as health, crime, traffic, and school quality. Anchorage ranked #15 out of the top 25, in the large city category (population of more than 250,000). Data points more specific to veterans and the military weighed more heavily than others. *rebootcamp.militarytimes.com, "Military Times Best Places to Live 2019," September 10, 2018*

- *Insider* listed 23 places in the U.S. that travel industry trends reveal would be popular destinations in 2023. This year the list trends towards cultural and historical happenings, sports events, wellness experiences and invigorating outdoor escapes. According to the website insider.com Anchorage is a place to visit in 2023. *Insider, "23 of the Best Places You Should Travel to in the U.S. in 2023," December 17, 2022*

- In their ninth annual survey, Livability.com looked at data for more than 2,300 mid-sized U.S. cities to determine the rankings for Livability's "Top 100 Best Places to Live" in 2022. Anchorage ranked #23. Criteria: housing and economy; social and civic engagement; education; demographics; health care options; transportation & infrastructure; and community amenities. *Livability.com, "Top 100 Best Places to Live 2022" July 19, 2022*

Business/Finance Rankings

- The Anchorage metro area appeared on the Milken Institute "2022 Best Performing Cities" list. Rank: #196 out of 200 large metro areas (population over 250,000). Criteria: job growth; wage and salary growth; high-tech output growth; housing affordability; household broadband access. *Milken Institute, "Best-Performing Cities 2022," March 28, 2022*

- *Forbes* ranked the 200 most populous metro areas to determine the nation's "Best Places for Business and Careers." The Anchorage metro area was ranked #185. Criteria: costs (business and living); job growth (past and projected); income growth; quality of life; educational attainment (college and high school); projected economic growth; cultural and leisure opportunities; workplace tolerance laws; net migration patterns. *Forbes, "The Best Places for Business and Careers 2019: Seattle Still On Top," October 30, 2019*

Education Rankings

- Personal finance website *WalletHub* analyzed the 150 largest U.S. metropolitan statistical areas to determine where the most educated Americans are putting their degrees to work. Criteria: education levels; percentage of workers with degrees; education quality and attainment gap; public school quality rankings; quality and enrollment of each metro area's universities. Anchorage was ranked #57 (#1 = most educated city). *www.WalletHub.com, "Most & Least Educated Cities in America," July 18, 2022*

- Anchorage was selected as one of America's most literate cities. The city ranked #52 out of the 84 largest U.S. cities. Criteria: number of booksellers; library resources; Internet resources; educational attainment; periodical publishing resources; newspaper circulation. *Central Connecticut State University, "America's Most Literate Cities, 2018," February 2019*

Health/Fitness Rankings

- For each of the 100 largest cities in the United States, the American Fitness Index®, compiled in partnership between the American College of Sports Medicine and the Elevance Health Foundation, evaluated community infrastructure and 34 health behaviors including preventive health, levels of chronic disease conditions, food insecurity, sleep quality, pedestrian safety, air quality, and community/environment resources that support physical activity. Anchorage ranked #56 for "community fitness." *americanfitnessindex.org, "2022 ACSM American Fitness Index Summary Report," July 12, 2022*

Real Estate Rankings

- *WalletHub* compared the most populated U.S. cities to determine which had the best markets for real estate agents. Anchorage ranked #140 where demand was high and pay was the best. Criteria: sales per agent; annual median wage for real-estate agents; monthly average starting salary for real estate agents; real estate job density and competition; unemployment rate; home turnover rate; housing-market health index; and other relevant metrics. *www.WalletHub.com, "2021 Best Places to Be a Real Estate Agent," May 12, 2021*

- Anchorage was ranked #65 out of 235 metro areas in terms of housing affordability in 2022 by the National Association of Home Builders (#1 = most affordable). Criteria: the share of homes sold in that area affordable to a family earning the local median income, based on standard mortgage underwriting criteria. *National Association of Home Builders®, NAHB-Wells Fargo Housing Opportunity Index, 4th Quarter 2022*

Safety Rankings

- To identify the most dangerous cities in America, *24/7 Wall St.* focused on violent crime categories—murder, non-negligent manslaughter, rape, robbery, and aggravated assault—as reported for every 100,000 residents using data from the FBI's 2020 annual Uniform Crime Report. For cities with populations over 25,000, Anchorage was ranked #38. *247wallst.com, "America's Most Dangerous Cities" November 12, 2021*

- Allstate ranked the 200 largest cities in America in terms of driver safety. Anchorage ranked #27. Criteria: internal property damage claims over a two-year period from January 2016 to December 2017. The report helps increase the importance of safety and awareness behind the wheel. *Allstate, "Allstate America's Best Drivers Report, 2019" June 24, 2019*

- Anchorage was identified as one of the most dangerous cities in America by NeighborhoodScout. The city ranked #59 out of 100 (#1 = most dangerous). Criteria: number of violent crimes per 1,000 residents. The editors evaluated cities with 25,000 or more residents. *NeighborhoodScout.com, "2023 Top 100 Most Dangerous Cities in the U.S.," January 12, 2023*

- The National Insurance Crime Bureau ranked 390 metro areas in the U.S. in terms of per capita rates of vehicle theft. The Anchorage metro area ranked #79 (#1 = highest rate). Criteria: number of vehicle theft offenses per 100,000 inhabitants in 2021. *National Insurance Crime Bureau, "Hot Spots 2021," September 1, 2022*

Seniors/Retirement Rankings

- From its Best Cities for Successful Aging indexes, the Milken Institute generated rankings for metropolitan areas, weighing data in nine categories—health care, wellness, living arrangements, transportation and convenience, financial characteristics, education, employment, community engagement, and overall livability. The Anchorage metro area was ranked #52 overall in the small metro area category. *Milken Institute, "Best Cities for Successful Aging, 2017" March 14, 2017*

Women/Minorities Rankings

- *Women's Health*, together with the site Yelp, identified the 15 "Wellthiest" spots in the U.S. Anchorage appeared among the top for happiest, healthiest, outdoorsiest and Zen-iest. *Women's Health, "The 15 Wellthiest Cities in the U.S." July 5, 2017*

- Anchorage was selected as one of the queerest cities in America by *The Advocate*. The city ranked #20 out of 25. Criteria, among many: Trans Pride parades/festivals; gay rugby teams; lesbian bars; LGBTQ centers; theater screenings of "Moonlight"; LGBTQ-inclusive nondiscrimination ordinances; and gay bowling teams. *The Advocate, "Queerest Cities in America 2017" January 12, 2017*

- Personal finance website *WalletHub* compared more than 180 U.S. cities across two key dimensions, "Hispanic Business-Friendliness" and "Hispanic Purchasing Power," to arrive at the most favorable conditions for Hispanic entrepreneurs. Anchorage was ranked #49 out of 182. Criteria includes: share of Hispanic-Owned Businesses; Hispanic entrepreneurship rate to median annual income of Hispanics; Small Business-Friendliness score; cost of living; and number of Hispanics with at least a bachelor's degree. *WalletHub.com, "2019's Best Cities for Hispanic Entrepreneurs," May 1, 2019*

Miscellaneous Rankings

- *WalletHub* compared the 150 most populated U.S. cities to determine their operating efficiency. A "Quality of Services" score was constructed for each city and then divided by the total budget per capita to reveal which were managed the best. Anchorage ranked #90. Criteria: financial stability; economy; education; safety; health; infrastructure and pollution. *www.WalletHub.com, "2022's Best- & Worst-Run Cities in America," June 21, 2022*

Business Environment

DEMOGRAPHICS

Population Growth

Area	1990 Census	2000 Census	2010 Census	2020 Census	Population Growth (%) 1990-2020	Population Growth (%) 2010-2020
City	226,338	260,283	291,826	291,247	28.7	-0.2
MSA[1]	266,021	319,605	380,821	398,328	49.7	4.6
U.S.	248,709,873	281,421,906	308,745,538	331,449,281	33.3	7.4

Note: (1) Figures cover the Anchorage, AK Metropolitan Statistical Area
Source: U.S. Census Bureau, 1990 Census, 2000 Census, 2010 Census, 2020 Census

Race

Area	White Alone[2] (%)	Black Alone[2] (%)	Asian Alone[2] (%)	AIAN[3] Alone[2] (%)	NHOPI[4] Alone[2] (%)	Other Race Alone[2] (%)	Two or More Races (%)
City	56.5	5.0	9.5	8.1	3.4	3.5	14.0
MSA[1]	62.1	3.9	7.3	7.7	2.6	3.0	13.3
U.S.	61.6	12.4	6.0	1.1	0.2	8.4	10.2

Note: (1) Figures cover the Anchorage, AK Metropolitan Statistical Area; (2) Alone is defined as not being in combination with one or more other races; (3) American Indian and Alaska Native; (4) Native Hawaiian and Other Pacific Islander
Source: U.S. Census Bureau, 2020 Census

Hispanic or Latino Origin

Area	Total (%)	Mexican (%)	Puerto Rican (%)	Cuban (%)	Other (%)
City	9.5	4.6	1.5	0.4	3.0
MSA[1]	8.4	4.1	1.3	0.4	2.6
U.S.	18.4	11.2	1.8	0.7	4.7

Note: Persons of Hispanic or Latino origin can be of any race; (1) Figures cover the Anchorage, AK Metropolitan Statistical Area
Source: U.S. Census Bureau, 2017-2021 American Community Survey 5-Year Estimates

Age

Area	Percent of Population Under Age 5	Age 5–19	Age 20–34	Age 35–44	Age 45–54	Age 55–64	Age 65–74	Age 75–84	Age 85+	Median Age
City	6.4	19.6	23.4	13.7	11.7	12.6	8.3	3.1	0.9	35.2
MSA[1]	6.5	20.4	22.2	13.7	11.8	12.7	8.6	3.1	0.9	35.5
U.S.	5.6	19.2	20.2	12.7	12.4	13.1	10.0	4.9	1.9	38.8

Note: (1) Figures cover the Anchorage, AK Metropolitan Statistical Area
Source: U.S. Census Bureau, 2020 Census

Disability by Age

Area	All Ages	Under 18 Years Old	18 to 64 Years Old	65 Years and Over
City	11.1	3.8	10.0	33.3
MSA[1]	11.7	3.8	10.7	33.9
U.S.	12.6	4.4	10.3	33.4

Note: Figures show percent of the civilian noninstitutionalized population that reported having a disability. Disability status is determined from six types of difficulty: vision, hearing, cognitive, ambulatory, self-care, and independent living. For children under 5 years old, hearing and vision difficulty are used to determine disability status. For children between the ages of 5 and 14, disability status is determined from hearing, vision, cognitive, ambulatory, and self-care difficulties. For people aged 15 years and older, they are considered to have a disability if they have difficulty with any one of the six difficulty types; Note: (1) Figures cover the Anchorage, AK Metropolitan Statistical Area
Source: U.S. Census Bureau, 2017-2021 American Community Survey 5-Year Estimates

Ancestry

Area	German	Irish	English	American	Italian	Polish	French[2]	Scottish	Dutch
City	13.8	9.4	8.5	3.6	3.2	2.0	2.3	1.9	1.3
MSA[1]	14.7	9.9	8.8	4.0	3.0	2.0	2.4	2.0	1.4
U.S.	12.8	9.6	8.1	5.7	5.0	2.7	2.2	1.6	1.1

Note: Figures are the percentage of the total population reporting a particular ancestry. The nine most commonly reported ancestries in the U.S. are shown. Figures include multiple ancestries (e.g. if a person reported being Irish and Italian, they were included in both columns); (1) Figures cover the Anchorage, AK Metropolitan Statistical Area; (2) Excludes Basque
Source: U.S. Census Bureau, 2017-2021 American Community Survey 5-Year Estimates

Foreign-born Population

Area	Any Foreign Country	Percent of Population Born in							
		Asia	Mexico	Europe	Caribbean	Central America[2]	South America	Africa	Canada
City	11.0	6.1	0.7	1.0	0.6	0.2	0.5	0.6	0.4
MSA[1]	9.0	4.8	0.6	1.1	0.4	0.2	0.4	0.4	0.4
U.S.	13.6	4.2	3.3	1.5	1.4	1.1	1.1	0.8	0.2

Note: (1) Figures cover the Anchorage, AK Metropolitan Statistical Area; (2) Excludes Mexico.
Source: U.S. Census Bureau, 2017-2021 American Community Survey 5-Year Estimates

Household Size

Area	Persons in Household (%)							Average Household Size
	One	Two	Three	Four	Five	Six	Seven or More	
City	26.9	32.9	15.6	13.6	6.2	2.6	2.2	2.70
MSA[1]	25.7	33.4	15.5	13.5	6.8	2.8	2.3	2.70
U.S.	28.1	33.8	15.5	12.9	6.0	2.3	1.4	2.60

Note: (1) Figures cover the Anchorage, AK Metropolitan Statistical Area
Source: U.S. Census Bureau, 2017-2021 American Community Survey 5-Year Estimates

Household Relationships

Area	House-holder	Opposite-sex Spouse	Same-sex Spouse	Opposite-sex Unmarried Partner	Same-sex Unmarried Partner	Child[2]	Grand-child	Other Relatives	Non-relatives
City	37.5	17.0	0.2	3.0	0.2	28.3	1.9	4.6	4.2
MSA[1]	37.1	17.6	0.2	2.9	0.1	29.1	1.9	4.2	4.0
U.S.	38.3	17.5	0.2	2.5	0.2	28.3	2.4	4.8	3.4

Note: Figures are percent of the total population; (1) Figures cover the Anchorage, AK Metropolitan Statistical Area; (2) Includes biological, adopted, and stepchildren of the householder
Source: U.S. Census Bureau, 2020 Census

Gender

Area	Males	Females	Males per 100 Females
City	147,894	143,353	103.2
MSA[1]	203,277	195,051	104.2
U.S.	162,685,811	168,763,470	96.4

Note: (1) Figures cover the Anchorage, AK Metropolitan Statistical Area
Source: U.S. Census Bureau, 2020 Census

Marital Status

Area	Never Married	Now Married[2]	Separated	Widowed	Divorced
City	33.6	48.9	1.9	3.6	12.0
MSA[1]	32.2	50.5	1.8	3.8	11.8
U.S.	33.8	48.0	1.8	5.6	10.8

Note: Figures are percentages and cover the population 15 years of age and older; (1) Figures cover the Anchorage, AK Metropolitan Statistical Area; (2) Excludes separated
Source: U.S. Census Bureau, 2017-2021 American Community Survey 5-Year Estimates

Religious Groups by Family

Area	Catholic	Baptist	Methodist	LDS[2]	Pentecostal	Lutheran	Islam	Adventist	Other
MSA[1]	4.9	3.4	1.0	5.1	1.7	1.5	0.1	1.7	16.3
U.S.	18.7	7.3	3.0	2.0	1.8	1.7	1.3	1.3	11.6

Note: Figures are the number of adherents as a percentage of the total population and cover the eight largest religious groups in the U.S; (1) Figures cover the Anchorage, AK Metropolitan Statistical Area; (2) Church of Jesus Christ of Latter-day Saints
Sources: 2020 U.S. Religion Census, Association of Statisticians of American Religious Bodies; The Association of Religion Data Archives (ARDA)

Religious Groups by Tradition

Area	Catholic	Evangelical Protestant	Mainline Protestant	Black Protestant	Islam	Judaism	Hinduism	Orthodox	Buddhism
MSA[1]	4.9	19.2	2.4	0.9	0.1	0.1	0.1	0.5	1.3
U.S.	18.7	16.5	5.2	2.3	1.3	0.6	0.4	0.4	0.3

Note: Figures are the number of adherents as a percentage of the total population; (1) Figures cover the Anchorage, AK Metropolitan Statistical Area
Sources: 2020 U.S. Religion Census, Association of Statisticians of American Religious Bodies; The Association of Religion Data Archives (ARDA)

ECONOMY

Gross Metropolitan Product

Area	2020	2021	2022	2023	Rank[2]
MSA[1]	25.8	28.3	31.3	32.6	112

Note: Figures are in billions of dollars; (1) Figures cover the Anchorage, AK Metropolitan Statistical Area; (2) Rank is based on 2021 data and ranges from 1 to 381
Source: U.S. Conference of Mayors, U.S. Metro Economies: U.S. Metros Compared to Global and State Economies, June 2022

Economic Growth

Area	2018-20 (%)	2021 (%)	2022 (%)	2023 (%)	Rank[2]
MSA[1]	-2.4	0.4	2.3	2.9	323
U.S.	-0.6	5.7	3.1	2.9	—

Note: Figures are real gross metropolitan product (GMP) growth rates and represent average annual percent change; (1) Figures cover the Anchorage, AK Metropolitan Statistical Area; (2) Rank is based on 2020 2-year average annual percent change and ranges from 1 to 381
Source: U.S. Conference of Mayors, U.S. Metro Economies: U.S. Metros Compared to Global and State Economies, June 2022

Metropolitan Area Exports

Area	2016	2017	2018	2019	2020	2021	Rank[2]
MSA[1]	1,215.4	1,675.9	1,510.8	1,348.0	990.9	n/a	n/a

Note: Figures are in millions of dollars; (1) Figures cover the Anchorage, AK Metropolitan Statistical Area; (2) Rank is based on 2021 data and ranges from 1 to 388
Source: U.S. Department of Commerce, International Trade Administration, Office of Trade and Economic Analysis, Industry and Analysis, Exports by Metropolitan Area, data extracted March 16, 2023

Building Permits

Area	Single-Family			Multi-Family			Total		
	2021	2022	Pct. Chg.	2021	2022	Pct. Chg.	2021	2022	Pct. Chg.
City	840	124	-85.2	293	31	-89.4	1,133	155	-86.3
MSA[1]	877	166	-81.1	306	47	-84.6	1,183	213	-82.0
U.S.	1,115,400	975,600	-12.5	621,600	689,500	10.9	1,737,000	1,665,100	-4.1

Note: (1) Figures cover the Anchorage, AK Metropolitan Statistical Area; Figures represent new, privately-owned housing units authorized (unadjusted data); All permit data are based on estimates with imputation
Source: U.S. Census Bureau, Manufacturing, Mining, and Construction Statistics, Building Permits, 2021, 2022

Bankruptcy Filings

Area	Business Filings			Nonbusiness Filings		
	2021	2022	% Chg.	2021	2022	% Chg.
Anchorage Borough	12	4	-66.7	116	77	-33.6
U.S.	14,347	13,481	-6.0	399,269	374,240	-6.3

Note: Business filings include Chapter 7, Chapter 9, Chapter 11, Chapter 12, Chapter 13, Chapter 15, and Section 304; Nonbusiness filings include Chapter 7, Chapter 11, and Chapter 13
Source: Administrative Office of the U.S. Courts, Business and Nonbusiness Bankruptcy, County Cases Commenced by Chapter of the Bankruptcy Code, During the 12-Month Period Ending December 31, 2021 and Business and Nonbusiness Bankruptcy, County Cases Commenced by Chapter of the Bankruptcy Code, During the 12-Month Period Ending December 31, 2022

Housing Vacancy Rates

Area	Gross Vacancy Rate[2] (%)			Year-Round Vacancy Rate[3] (%)			Rental Vacancy Rate[4] (%)			Homeowner Vacancy Rate[5] (%)		
	2020	2021	2022	2020	2021	2022	2020	2021	2022	2020	2021	2022
MSA[1]	n/a	n/a	n/a	n/a	n/a	n/a	n/a	n/a	n/a	n/a	n/a	n/a
U.S.	10.6	10.8	10.5	8.2	8.4	8.2	6.3	6.1	5.8	1.0	0.9	0.8

Note: (1) Figures cover the Anchorage, AK Metropolitan Statistical Area; (2) The percentage of the total housing inventory that is vacant; (3) The percentage of the housing inventory (excluding seasonal units) that is year-round vacant; (4) The percentage of rental inventory that is vacant for rent; (5) The percentage of homeowner inventory that is vacant for sale; n/a not available
Source: U.S. Census Bureau, Housing Vacancies and Homeownership Annual Statistics: 2020, 2021, 2022

INCOME

Income

Area	Per Capita ($)	Median Household ($)	Average Household ($)
City	43,125	88,871	113,873
MSA[1]	41,201	86,252	109,817
U.S.	37,638	69,021	97,196

Note: (1) Figures cover the Anchorage, AK Metropolitan Statistical Area
Source: U.S. Census Bureau, 2017-2021 American Community Survey 5-Year Estimates

Household Income Distribution

Area	Percent of Households Earning							
	Under $15,000	$15,000 -$24,999	$25,000 -$34,999	$35,000 -$49,999	$50,000 -$74,999	$75,000 -$99,999	$100,000 -$149,999	$150,000 and up
City	5.5	5.1	5.5	9.0	17.1	14.1	20.2	23.6
MSA[1]	6.1	5.5	5.7	9.0	17.1	14.1	20.1	22.4
U.S.	9.4	7.8	8.2	11.4	16.8	12.8	16.3	17.3

Note: (1) Figures cover the Anchorage, AK Metropolitan Statistical Area
Source: U.S. Census Bureau, 2017-2021 American Community Survey 5-Year Estimates

Poverty Rate

Area	All Ages	Under 18 Years Old	18 to 64 Years Old	65 Years and Over
City	9.1	11.1	8.8	6.8
MSA[1]	9.6	11.5	9.2	7.4
U.S.	12.6	17.0	11.8	9.6

Note: Figures are percentage of people whose income during the past 12 months was below the poverty level;
(1) Figures cover the Anchorage, AK Metropolitan Statistical Area
Source: U.S. Census Bureau, 2017-2021 American Community Survey 5-Year Estimates

EMPLOYMENT

Labor Force and Employment

Area	Civilian Labor Force			Workers Employed		
	Dec. 2021	Dec. 2022	% Chg.	Dec. 2021	Dec. 2022	% Chg.
City	154,601	155,471	0.6	148,017	150,605	1.7
MSA[1]	205,827	206,845	0.5	196,305	199,569	1.7
U.S.	161,696,000	164,224,000	1.6	155,732,000	158,872,000	2.0

Note: Data is not seasonally adjusted and covers workers 16 years of age and older; (1) Figures cover the Anchorage, AK Metropolitan Statistical Area
Source: Bureau of Labor Statistics, Local Area Unemployment Statistics

Unemployment Rate

Area	2022											
	Jan.	Feb.	Mar.	Apr.	May	Jun.	Jul.	Aug.	Sep.	Oct.	Nov.	Dec.
City	4.8	4.4	4.0	3.9	3.7	3.8	3.6	2.9	2.9	3.1	3.3	3.1
MSA[1]	5.3	4.9	4.5	4.3	4.0	4.2	3.9	3.2	3.2	3.3	3.6	3.5
U.S.	4.4	4.1	3.8	3.3	3.4	3.8	3.8	3.8	3.3	3.4	3.4	3.3

Note: Data is not seasonally adjusted and covers workers 16 years of age and older; (1) Figures cover the Anchorage, AK Metropolitan Statistical Area
Source: Bureau of Labor Statistics, Local Area Unemployment Statistics

Average Wages

Occupation	$/Hr.	Occupation	$/Hr.
Accountants and Auditors	38.08	Maintenance and Repair Workers	24.49
Automotive Mechanics	28.88	Marketing Managers	52.64
Bookkeepers	25.34	Network and Computer Systems Admin.	42.70
Carpenters	35.06	Nurses, Licensed Practical	31.62
Cashiers	16.27	Nurses, Registered	49.59
Computer Programmers	47.28	Nursing Assistants	20.50
Computer Systems Analysts	47.93	Office Clerks, General	22.26
Computer User Support Specialists	31.03	Physical Therapists	49.64
Construction Laborers	26.21	Physicians	112.03
Cooks, Restaurant	18.32	Plumbers, Pipefitters and Steamfitters	43.11
Customer Service Representatives	20.61	Police and Sheriff's Patrol Officers	47.16
Dentists	86.58	Postal Service Mail Carriers	25.73
Electricians	38.38	Real Estate Sales Agents	34.80
Engineers, Electrical	51.77	Retail Salespersons	18.27
Fast Food and Counter Workers	14.73	Sales Representatives, Technical/Scientific	36.27
Financial Managers	72.72	Secretaries, Exc. Legal/Medical/Executive	20.62
First-Line Supervisors of Office Workers	32.44	Security Guards	20.74
General and Operations Managers	54.98	Surgeons	n/a
Hairdressers/Cosmetologists	15.13	Teacher Assistants, Exc. Postsecondary*	17.44
Home Health and Personal Care Aides	17.28	Teachers, Secondary School, Exc. Sp. Ed.*	36.14
Janitors and Cleaners	16.95	Telemarketers	n/a
Landscaping/Groundskeeping Workers	21.00	Truck Drivers, Heavy/Tractor-Trailer	27.93
Lawyers	58.26	Truck Drivers, Light/Delivery Services	26.04
Maids and Housekeeping Cleaners	15.86	Waiters and Waitresses	13.47

Note: Wage data covers the Anchorage, AK Metropolitan Statistical Area; (*) Hourly wages were calculated from annual wage data based on a 40 hour work week; n/a not available.
Source: Bureau of Labor Statistics, Metro Area Occupational Employment & Wage Estimates, May 2022

Employment by Industry

Sector	MSA[1]		U.S.
	Number of Employees	Percent of Total	Percent of Total
Construction	8,900	5.1	5.0
Private Education and Health Services	32,100	18.4	16.1
Financial Activities	7,900	4.5	5.9
Government	33,500	19.2	14.5
Information	3,400	1.9	2.0
Leisure and Hospitality	18,800	10.8	10.3
Manufacturing	2,300	1.3	8.4
Mining and Logging	1,900	1.1	0.4
Other Services	6,300	3.6	3.7
Professional and Business Services	19,700	11.3	14.7
Retail Trade	20,000	11.5	10.2
Transportation, Warehousing, and Utilities	14,800	8.5	4.9
Wholesale Trade	4,800	2.8	3.9

Note: Figures are non-farm employment as of December 2022. Figures are not seasonally adjusted and include workers 16 years of age and older; (1) Figures cover the Anchorage, AK Metropolitan Statistical Area
Source: Bureau of Labor Statistics, Current Employment Statistics, Employment, Hours, and Earnings

Employment by Occupation

Occupation Classification	City (%)	MSA[1] (%)	U.S. (%)
Management, Business, Science, and Arts	41.6	39.9	40.3
Natural Resources, Construction, and Maintenance	8.3	10.4	8.7
Production, Transportation, and Material Moving	11.1	11.1	13.1
Sales and Office	21.0	20.8	20.9
Service	18.0	17.9	17.0

Note: Figures cover employed civilians 16 years of age and older; (1) Figures cover the Anchorage, AK Metropolitan Statistical Area
Source: U.S. Census Bureau, 2017-2021 American Community Survey 5-Year Estimates

Occupations with Greatest Projected Employment Growth: 2022 – 2024

Occupation[1]	2022 Employment	2024 Projected Employment	Numeric Employment Change	Percent Employment Change
Fast Food and Counter Workers	6,510	6,800	290	4.5
Waiters and Waitresses	4,520	4,750	230	5.1
Operating Engineers and Other Construction Equipment Operators	2,610	2,810	200	7.7
Home Health and Personal Care Aides	6,150	6,340	190	3.1
Maids and Housekeeping Cleaners	3,330	3,520	190	5.7
Construction Laborers	3,730	3,910	180	4.8
Food Preparation Workers	3,750	3,910	160	4.3
Office Clerks, General	6,200	6,340	140	2.3
Service Unit Operators, Oil, Gas, and Mining	720	860	140	19.4
Airline Pilots, Copilots, and Flight Engineers	2,210	2,350	140	6.3

Note: Projections cover Alaska; (1) Sorted by numeric employment change
Source: www.projectionscentral.com, State Occupational Projections, 2022–2024 Short-Term Projections

Fastest-Growing Occupations: 2022 – 2024

Occupation[1]	2022 Employment	2024 Projected Employment	Numeric Employment Change	Percent Employment Change
Roustabouts, Oil and Gas	350	430	80	22.9
Service Unit Operators, Oil, Gas, and Mining	720	860	140	19.4
Flight Attendants	410	460	50	12.2
Commercial Pilots	1,000	1,100	100	10.0
Transportation Attendants, Except Flight Attendants	620	680	60	9.7
Reservation and Transportation Ticket Agents and Travel Clerks	1,000	1,090	90	9.0
Welders, Cutters, Solderers, and Brazers	560	610	50	8.9
Cargo and Freight Agents	680	740	60	8.8
Hotel, Motel, and Resort Desk Clerks	930	1,010	80	8.6
First-Line Supervisors of Construction Trades and Extraction Workers	700	760	60	8.6

Note: Projections cover Alaska; (1) Sorted by percent employment change and excludes occupations with numeric employment change less than 50
Source: www.projectionscentral.com, State Occupational Projections, 2022–2024 Short-Term Projections

CITY FINANCES

City Government Finances

Component	2020 ($000)	2020 ($ per capita)
Total Revenues	1,715,835	5,958
Total Expenditures	1,667,328	5,789
Debt Outstanding	1,639,532	5,693
Cash and Securities[1]	769,726	2,673

Note: (1) Cash and security holdings of a government at the close of its fiscal year, including those of its dependent agencies, utilities, and liquor stores.
Source: U.S. Census Bureau, State & Local Government Finances 2020

City Government Revenue by Source

Source	2020 ($000)	2020 ($ per capita)	2020 (%)
General Revenue			
From Federal Government	44,054	153	2.6
From State Government	531,829	1,847	31.0
From Local Governments	0	0	0.0
Taxes			
Property	558,102	1,938	32.5
Sales and Gross Receipts	75,911	264	4.4
Personal Income	0	0	0.0
Corporate Income	0	0	0.0
Motor Vehicle License	17,638	61	1.0
Other Taxes	9,694	34	0.6
Current Charges	148,111	514	8.6
Liquor Store	0	0	0.0
Utility	236,454	821	13.8

Source: U.S. Census Bureau, State & Local Government Finances 2020

City Government Expenditures by Function

Function	2020 ($000)	2020 ($ per capita)	2020 (%)
General Direct Expenditures			
Air Transportation	4,932	17	0.3
Corrections	0	0	0.0
Education	676,860	2,350	40.6
Employment Security Administration	0	0	0.0
Financial Administration	23,107	80	1.4
Fire Protection	115,630	401	6.9
General Public Buildings	0	0	0.0
Governmental Administration, Other	16,487	57	1.0
Health	23,616	82	1.4
Highways	93,947	326	5.6
Hospitals	0	0	0.0
Housing and Community Development	70	< 1	< 0.1
Interest on General Debt	36,988	128	2.2
Judicial and Legal	7,388	25	0.4
Libraries	9,051	31	0.5
Parking	7,597	26	0.5
Parks and Recreation	42,273	146	2.5
Police Protection	147,957	513	8.9
Public Welfare	4,035	14	0.2
Sewerage	54,256	188	3.3
Solid Waste Management	46,686	162	2.8
Veterans' Services	0	0	0.0
Liquor Store	0	0	0.0
Utility	240,490	835	14.4

Source: U.S. Census Bureau, State & Local Government Finances 2020

TAXES

State Corporate Income Tax Rates

State	Tax Rate (%)	Income Brackets ($)	Num. of Brackets	Financial Institution Tax Rate (%)[a]	Federal Income Tax Ded.
Alaska	0 - 9.4	25,000 - 222,000	10	0 - 9.4	No

Note: Tax rates as of January 1, 2023; (a) Rates listed are the corporate income tax rate applied to financial institutions or excise taxes based on income. Some states have other taxes based upon the value of deposits or shares.
Source: Federation of Tax Administrators, State Corporate Income Tax Rates, January 1, 2023

State Individual Income Tax Rates

State	Tax Rate (%)	Income Brackets ($)	Personal Exemptions ($) Single	Married	Depend.	Standard Ded. ($) Single	Married
Alaska			– No state income tax –				

Note: Tax rates as of January 1, 2023; Local- and county-level taxes are not included
Source: Federation of Tax Administrators, State Individual Income Tax Rates, January 1, 2023

Various State Sales and Excise Tax Rates

State	State Sales Tax (%)	Gasoline[1] ($/gal.)	Cigarette[2] ($/pack)	Spirits[3] ($/gal.)	Wine[4] ($/gal.)	Beer[5] ($/gal.)	Recreational Marijuana (%)
Alaska	None	0.1513	2.00	12.80	2.50	1.07	(a)

Note: All tax rates as of January 1, 2023; (1) The American Petroleum Institute has developed a methodology for determining the average tax rate on a gallon of fuel. Rates may include any of the following: excise taxes, environmental fees, storage tank fees, other fees or taxes, general sales tax, and local taxes; (2) The federal excise tax of $1.0066 per pack and local taxes are not included; (3) Rates are those applicable to off-premise sales of 40% alcohol by volume (a.b.v.) distilled spirits in 750ml containers. Local excise taxes are excluded; (4) Rates are those applicable to off-premise sales of 11% a.b.v. non-carbonated wine in 750ml containers; (5) Rates are those applicable to off-premise sales of 4.7% a.b.v. beer in 12 ounce containers; (a) $50/oz. mature flowers; $25/oz. immature flowers; $15/oz. trim, $1 per clone
Source: Tax Foundation, 2023 Facts & Figures: How Does Your State Compare?

State Business Tax Climate Index Rankings

State	Overall Rank	Corporate Tax Rank	Individual Income Tax Rank	Sales Tax Rank	Property Tax Rank	Unemployment Insurance Tax Rank
Alaska	3	28	1	5	26	44

Note: The index is a measure of how each state's tax laws affect economic performance. The lower the rank, the more favorable a state's tax system is for business. States without a given tax are given a ranking of 1. The scores/rankings for the District of Columbia do not affect other states. The 2023 index represents the tax climate as of July 1, 2022.
Source: Tax Foundation, State Business Tax Climate Index 2023

TRANSPORTATION

Means of Transportation to Work

Area	Car/Truck/Van		Public Transportation			Bicycle	Walked	Other Means	Worked at Home
	Drove Alone	Car-pooled	Bus	Subway	Railroad				
City	73.7	12.1	1.4	0.0	0.0	0.9	2.6	2.1	7.1
MSA[1]	73.7	11.5	1.2	0.0	0.0	0.8	2.4	3.0	7.4
U.S.	73.2	8.6	2.0	1.6	0.5	0.5	2.5	1.5	9.7

Note: Figures are percentages and cover workers 16 years of age and older; (1) Figures cover the Anchorage, AK Metropolitan Statistical Area
Source: U.S. Census Bureau, 2017-2021 American Community Survey 5-Year Estimates

Travel Time to Work

Area	Less Than 10 Minutes	10 to 19 Minutes	20 to 29 Minutes	30 to 44 Minutes	45 to 59 Minutes	60 to 89 Minutes	90 Minutes or More
City	16.1	44.4	23.4	11.2	2.1	1.2	1.6
MSA[1]	15.0	40.4	21.8	11.4	4.5	4.1	2.7
U.S.	12.4	28.5	21.0	20.9	8.2	6.2	2.9

Note: Note: Figures are percentages and include workers 16 years old and over; (1) Figures cover the Anchorage, AK Metropolitan Statistical Area
Source: U.S. Census Bureau, 2017-2021 American Community Survey 5-Year Estimates

Key Congestion Measures

Measure	1990	2000	2010	2015	2020
Annual Hours of Delay, Total (000)	1,848	3,973	5,279	6,397	3,080
Annual Hours of Delay, Per Auto Commuter	19	32	37	41	18
Annual Congestion Cost, Per Auto Commuter ($)	566	917	974	1,088	563

Note: Covers the Anchorage AK urban area
Source: Texas A&M Transportation Institute, 2021 Urban Mobility Report

Freeway Travel Time Index

Measure	1985	1990	1995	2000	2005	2010	2015	2020
Urban Area Index[1]	1.03	1.07	1.10	1.14	1.16	1.16	1.18	1.07
Urban Area Rank[1,2]	89	74	72	62	57	54	41	57

Note: Freeway Travel Time Index—the ratio of travel time in the peak period to the travel time at free-flow conditions. For example, a value of 1.30 indicates a 20-minute free-flow trip takes 26 minutes in the peak (20 minutes x 1.30 = 26 minutes); (1) Covers the Anchorage AK urban area; (2) Rank is based on 101 larger urban areas (#1 = highest travel time index)
Source: Texas A&M Transportation Institute, 2021 Urban Mobility Report

Public Transportation

Agency Name / Mode of Transportation	Vehicles Operated in Maximum Service[1]	Annual Unlinked Passenger Trips[2] (in thous.)	Annual Passenger Miles[3] (in thous.)
Municipality of Anchorage, dba Public Transportation			
Bus (directly operated)	47	1,953.1	8,780.5
Demand Response (purchased transportation)	26	89.8	525.4
Vanpool (purchased transportation)	70	151.0	6,278.4

Note: (1) Number of revenue vehicles operated by the given mode and type of service to meet the annual maximum service requirement. This is the revenue vehicle count during the peak season of the year; on the week and day that maximum service is provided. Vehicles operated in maximum service (VOMS) exclude atypical days and one-time special events; (2) Number of passengers who boarded public transportation vehicles. Passengers are counted each time they board a vehicle no matter how many vehicles they use to travel from their origin to their destination. (3) Sum of the distances ridden by all passengers during the entire fiscal year.
Source: Federal Transit Administration, National Transit Database, 2021

Air Transportation

Airport Name and Code / Type of Service	Passenger Airlines[1]	Passenger Enplanements	Freight Carriers[2]	Freight (lbs)
Anchorage International (ANC)				
Domestic service (U.S. carriers - 2022)	22	2,530,255	28	2,747,019,423
International service (U.S. carriers - 2021)	3	188	10	505,219,014

Note: (1) Includes all U.S.-based major, minor and commuter airlines that carried at least one passenger during the year; (2) Includes all U.S.-based airlines and freight carriers that transported at least one pound of freight during the year.
Source: Bureau of Transportation Statistics, The Intermodal Transportation Database, Air Carriers: T-100 Domestic Market (U.S. Carriers), 2022; Bureau of Transportation Statistics, The Intermodal Transportation Database, Air Carriers: T-100 International Market (U.S. Carriers), 2021

BUSINESSES

Major Business Headquarters

Company Name	Industry	Rankings	
		Fortune[1]	Forbes[2]
No companies listed	-	-	-

Note: (1) Companies that produce a 10-K are ranked 1 to 500 based on 2021 revenue; (2) All private companies with at least $2 billion in annual revenue through the end of their most current fiscal year are ranked 1 to 246; companies listed are headquartered in the city; dashes indicate no ranking
Source: Fortune, "Fortune 500," 2022; Forbes, "America's Largest Private Companies," 2022

Living Environment

COST OF LIVING

Cost of Living Index

Composite Index	Groceries	Housing	Utilities	Trans-portation	Health Care	Misc. Goods/ Services
126.7	124.6	136.7	118.0	114.3	150.5	121.4

Note: The Cost of Living Index measures regional differences in the cost of consumer goods and services, excluding taxes and non-consumer expenditures, for professional and managerial households in the top income quintile. It is based on more than 50,000 prices covering almost 60 different items for which prices are collected three times a year by chambers of commerce, economic development organizations or university applied economic centers in each participating urban area. The numbers shown should be read as a percentage above or below the national average of 100. For example, a value of 115.4 in the groceries column indicates that grocery prices are 15.4% higher than the national average. Small differences in the index numbers should not be interpreted as significant; Figures cover the Anchorage AK urban area.
Source: The Council for Community and Economic Research, Cost of Living Index, 2022

Grocery Prices

Area[1]	T-Bone Steak ($/pound)	Frying Chicken ($/pound)	Whole Milk ($/half gal.)	Eggs ($/dozen)	Orange Juice ($/64 oz.)	Coffee ($/11.5 oz.)
City[2]	16.43	2.25	2.85	2.16	4.61	6.29
Avg.	13.81	1.59	2.43	2.25	3.85	4.95
Min.	10.17	0.90	1.51	1.30	2.90	3.46
Max.	19.35	3.30	4.32	4.32	5.31	8.59

Note: (1) Values for the local area are compared with the average, minimum and maximum values for all 286 areas in the Cost of Living Index; (2) Figures cover the Anchorage AK urban area; T-Bone Steak (price per pound); Frying Chicken (price per pound, whole fryer); Whole Milk (half gallon carton); Eggs (price per dozen, Grade A, large); Orange Juice (64 oz. Tropicana or Florida Natural); Coffee (11.5 oz. can, vacuum-packed, Maxwell House, Hills Bros, or Folgers).
Source: The Council for Community and Economic Research, Cost of Living Index, 2022

Housing and Utility Costs

Area[1]	New Home Price ($)	Apartment Rent ($/month)	All Electric ($/month)	Part Electric ($/month)	Other Energy ($/month)	Telephone ($/month)
City[2]	656,122	1,516	-	102.07	130.31	188.62
Avg.	450,913	1,371	176.41	99.93	76.96	190.22
Min.	229,283	546	100.84	31.56	27.15	174.27
Max.	2,434,977	4,569	356.86	249.59	272.24	208.31

Note: (1) Values for the local area are compared with the average, minimum and maximum values for all 286 areas in the Cost of Living Index; (2) Figures cover the Anchorage AK urban area; New Home Price (2,400 sf living area, 8,000 sf lot, in urban area with full utilities); Apartment Rent (950 sf 2 bedroom/1.5 or 2 bath, unfurnished, excluding all utilities except water); All Electric (average monthly cost for an all-electric home); Part Electric (average monthly cost for a part-electric home); Other Energy (average monthly cost for natural gas, fuel oil, coal, wood, and any other forms of energy except electricity); Telephone (price includes the base monthly rate plus taxes and fees for three lines of mobile phone service).
Source: The Council for Community and Economic Research, Cost of Living Index, 2022

Health Care, Transportation, and Other Costs

Area[1]	Doctor ($/visit)	Dentist ($/visit)	Optometrist ($/visit)	Gasoline ($/gallon)	Beauty Salon ($/visit)	Men's Shirt ($)
City[2]	228.37	152.08	252.89	4.49	55.00	34.08
Avg.	124.91	107.77	117.66	3.86	43.31	34.21
Min.	36.61	58.25	51.79	2.90	22.18	13.05
Max.	250.21	162.58	371.96	5.54	85.61	63.54

Note: (1) Values for the local area are compared with the average, minimum and maximum values for all 286 areas in the Cost of Living Index; (2) Figures cover the Anchorage AK urban area; Doctor (general practitioners routine exam of an established patient); Dentist (adult teeth cleaning and periodic oral examination); Optometrist (full vision eye exam for established adult patient); Gasoline (one gallon regular unleaded, national brand, including all taxes, cash price at self-service pump if available); Beauty Salon (woman's shampoo, trim, and blow-dry); Men's Shirt (cotton/polyester dress shirt, pinpoint weave, long sleeves).
Source: The Council for Community and Economic Research, Cost of Living Index, 2022

HOUSING

Homeownership Rate

Area	2015 (%)	2016 (%)	2017 (%)	2018 (%)	2019 (%)	2020 (%)	2021 (%)	2022 (%)
MSA[1]	n/a	n/a	n/a	n/a	n/a	n/a	n/a	n/a
U.S.	63.7	63.4	63.9	64.4	64.6	66.6	65.5	65.8

Note: (1) Figures cover the Anchorage, AK Metropolitan Statistical Area; n/a not available
Source: U.S. Census Bureau, Housing Vacancies and Homeownership Annual Statistics: 2015-2022

House Price Index (HPI)

Area	National Ranking[2]	Quarterly Change (%)	One-Year Change (%)	Five-Year Change (%)	Since 1991Q1 (%)
MSA[1]	215	-0.36	8.00	27.30	235.38
U.S.[3]	–	0.34	8.41	58.44	289.08

Note: The HPI is a weighted repeat sales index. It measures average price changes in repeat sales or refinancings on the same properties. This information is obtained by reviewing repeat mortgage transactions on single-family properties whose mortgages have been purchased or securitized by Fannie Mae or Freddie Mac since January 1975; (1) Figures cover the Anchorage, AK Metropolitan Statistical Area; (2) Rankings are based on annual percentage change for all metro areas containing at least 15,000 transactions over the last 10 years and ranges from 1 to 257; (3) figures based on a weighted average of Census Division estimates using a seasonally adjusted, purchase-only index; all figures are for the period ending December 31, 2022
Source: Federal Housing Finance Agency, Change in FHFA Metropolitan Area House Price Indexes, 2022Q4

Median Single-Family Home Prices

Area	2020	2021	2022p	Percent Change 2021 to 2022
MSA[1]	n/a	n/a	n/a	n/a
U.S. Average	300.2	357.1	392.6	9.9

Note: Figures are median sales prices of existing single-family homes in thousands of dollars; (p) preliminary; n/a not available; (1) Figures cover the Anchorage, AK Metropolitan Statistical Area
Source: National Association of Realtors, Median Sales Price of Existing Single-Family Homes for Metropolitan Areas, 4th Quarter 2022

Qualifying Income Based on Median Sales Price of Existing Single-Family Homes

Area	With 5% Down ($)	With 10% Down ($)	With 20% Down ($)
MSA[1]	n/a	n/a	n/a
U.S. Average	112,234	106,237	94,513

Note: Figures are preliminary; Qualifying income is based on a mortgage rate of 6.77%. Monthly principal and interest payment is limited to 25% of income; n/a not available; (1) Figures cover the Anchorage, AK Metropolitan Statistical Area
Source: National Association of Realtors, Qualifying Income Based on Median Sales Price of Existing Single-Family Homes for Metropolitan Areas, 4th Quarter 2022

Home Value

Area	Under $100,000	$100,000 -$199,999	$200,000 -$299,999	$300,000 -$399,999	$400,000 -$499,999	$500,000 -$999,999	$1,000,000 or more	Median ($)
City	6.7	10.2	25.3	28.2	13.9	14.3	1.4	327,500
MSA[1]	6.7	12.7	28.8	26.2	12.5	12.0	1.1	306,700
U.S.	16.2	24.2	20.1	13.6	8.3	13.6	4.1	244,900

Note: Figures are percentages except for median and cover owner-occupied housing units; (1) Figures cover the Anchorage, AK Metropolitan Statistical Area
Source: U.S. Census Bureau, 2017-2021 American Community Survey 5-Year Estimates

Year Housing Structure Built

Area	2020 or Later	2010 -2019	2000 -2009	1990 -1999	1980 -1989	1970 -1979	1960 -1969	1950 -1959	1940 -1949	Before 1940	Median Year
City	<0.1	4.7	11.9	11.9	25.8	28.0	10.2	5.8	1.2	0.5	1982
MSA[1]	0.1	6.4	17.2	13.3	25.0	23.5	8.3	4.7	1.0	0.5	1985
U.S.	0.2	7.3	13.6	13.6	13.2	14.8	10.3	10.0	4.7	12.2	1979

Note: Figures are percentages except for Median Year; Note: (1) Figures cover the Anchorage, AK Metropolitan Statistical Area
Source: U.S. Census Bureau, 2017-2021 American Community Survey 5-Year Estimates

Gross Monthly Rent

Area	Under $500	$500 -$999	$1,000 -$1,499	$1,500 -$1,999	$2,000 -$2,499	$2,500 -$2,999	$3,000 and up	Median ($)
City	4.8	20.1	34.7	23.1	11.6	4.0	1.8	1,350
MSA[1]	5.1	21.7	34.9	22.4	10.8	3.5	1.5	1,314
U.S.	8.1	30.5	30.8	16.8	7.3	3.1	3.5	1,163

Note: Figures are percentages except for median; Gross rent is the contract rent plus the estimated average monthly cost of utilities (electricity, gas, and water and sewer) and fuels (oil, coal, kerosene, wood, etc.) if these are paid by the renter (or paid for the renter by someone else); (1) Figures cover the Anchorage, AK Metropolitan Statistical Area
Source: U.S. Census Bureau, 2017-2021 American Community Survey 5-Year Estimates

HEALTH

Health Risk Factors

Category	MSA[1] (%)	U.S. (%)
Adults aged 18–64 who have any kind of health care coverage	88.8	90.9
Adults who reported being in good or better health	85.7	85.2
Adults who have been told they have high blood cholesterol	31.4	35.7
Adults who have been told they have high blood pressure	29.6	32.4
Adults who are current smokers	15.3	14.4
Adults who currently use e-cigarettes	6.7	6.7
Adults who currently use chewing tobacco, snuff, or snus	4.8	3.5
Adults who are heavy drinkers[2]	8.5	6.3
Adults who are binge drinkers[3]	17.4	15.4
Adults who are overweight (BMI 25.0 - 29.9)	34.6	34.4
Adults who are obese (BMI 30.0 - 99.8)	33.5	33.9
Adults who participated in any physical activities in the past month	80.9	76.3

Note: (1) Figures cover the Anchorage, AK Metropolitan Statistical Area; (2) Heavy drinkers are classified as adult men having more than 14 drinks per week and adult women having more than 7 drinks per week; (3) Binge drinkers are classified as males having five or more drinks on one occasion or females having four or more drinks on one occasion
Source: Centers for Disease Control and Prevention, Behaviorial Risk Factor Surveillance System, SMART: Selected Metropolitan Area Risk Trends, 2021

Acute and Chronic Health Conditions

Category	MSA[1] (%)	U.S. (%)
Adults who have ever been told they had a heart attack	3.0	4.0
Adults who have ever been told they have angina or coronary heart disease	3.3	3.8
Adults who have ever been told they had a stroke	3.2	3.0
Adults who have ever been told they have asthma	15.2	14.9
Adults who have ever been told they have arthritis	23.4	25.8
Adults who have ever been told they have diabetes[2]	7.9	10.9
Adults who have ever been told they had skin cancer	4.4	6.6
Adults who have ever been told they had any other types of cancer	6.5	7.5
Adults who have ever been told they have COPD	5.4	6.1
Adults who have ever been told they have kidney disease	2.4	3.0
Adults who have ever been told they have a form of depression	20.4	20.5

Note: (1) Figures cover the Anchorage, AK Metropolitan Statistical Area; (2) Figures do not include pregnancy-related, borderline, or pre-diabetes
Source: Centers for Disease Control and Prevention, Behaviorial Risk Factor Surveillance System, SMART: Selected Metropolitan Area Risk Trends, 2021

Health Screening and Vaccination Rates

Category	MSA[1] (%)	U.S. (%)
Adults who have ever been tested for HIV	45.6	34.9
Adults who have had their blood cholesterol checked within the last five years	79.3	85.2
Adults aged 65+ who have had flu shot within the past year	57.8	68.6
Adults aged 65+ who have ever had a pneumonia vaccination	65.2	71.0

Note: (1) Figures cover the Anchorage, AK Metropolitan Statistical Area.
Source: Centers for Disease Control and Prevention, Behaviorial Risk Factor Surveillance System, SMART: Selected Metropolitan Area Risk Trends, 2021

Disability Status

Category	MSA[1] (%)	U.S. (%)
Adults who reported being deaf	6.4	7.2
Are you blind or have serious difficulty seeing, even when wearing glasses?	4.7	4.8
Are you limited in any way in any of your usual activities due to arthritis?	10.8	11.1
Do you have difficulty doing errands alone?	6.6	7.0
Do you have difficulty dressing or bathing?	3.0	3.6
Do you have serious difficulty concentrating/remembering/making decisions?	12.1	12.1
Do you have serious difficulty walking or climbing stairs?	10.7	12.8

Note: (1) Figures cover the Anchorage, AK Metropolitan Statistical Area.
Source: Centers for Disease Control and Prevention, Behaviorial Risk Factor Surveillance System, SMART: Selected Metropolitan Area Risk Trends, 2021

Mortality Rates for the Top 10 Causes of Death in the U.S.

ICD-10[a] Sub-Chapter	ICD-10[a] Code	Crude Mortality Rate[1] per 100,000 population	
		County[2]	U.S.
Malignant neoplasms	C00-C97	140.2	182.6
Ischaemic heart diseases	I20-I25	63.4	113.1
Other forms of heart disease	I30-I51	46.3	64.4
Other degenerative diseases of the nervous system	G30-G31	29.1	51.0
Cerebrovascular diseases	I60-I69	28.0	47.8
Other external causes of accidental injury	W00-X59	51.1	46.4
Chronic lower respiratory diseases	J40-J47	25.0	45.7
Organic, including symptomatic, mental disorders	F01-F09	29.2	35.9
Hypertensive diseases	I10-I15	21.2	35.0
Diabetes mellitus	E10-E14	20.5	29.6

Note: (a) ICD-10 = International Classification of Diseases 10th Revision; (1) Crude mortality rates are a three-year average covering 2019-2021; (2) Figures cover Anchorage Borough.
Source: Centers for Disease Control and Prevention, National Center for Health Statistics. National Vital Statistics System, Mortality 2018-2021 on CDC WONDER Online Database

Mortality Rates for Selected Causes of Death

ICD-10[a] Sub-Chapter	ICD-10[a] Code	Crude Mortality Rate[1] per 100,000 population	
		County[2]	U.S.
Assault	X85-Y09	8.0	7.0
Diseases of the liver	K70-K76	27.1	19.8
Human immunodeficiency virus (HIV) disease	B20-B24	Suppressed	1.5
Influenza and pneumonia	J09-J18	5.2	14.7
Intentional self-harm	X60-X84	22.8	14.3
Malnutrition	E40-E46	2.9	4.3
Obesity and other hyperalimentation	E65-E68	2.4	3.0
Renal failure	N17-N19	11.6	15.7
Transport accidents	V01-V99	10.9	13.6
Viral hepatitis	B15-B19	Unreliable	1.2

Note: (a) ICD-10 = International Classification of Diseases 10th Revision; (1) Crude mortality rates are a three-year average covering 2019-2021; (2) Figures cover Anchorage Borough; Data are suppressed when the data meet the criteria for confidentiality constraints; Crude mortality rates are flagged as unreliable when the rate would be calculated with a numerator of 20 or less.
Source: Centers for Disease Control and Prevention, National Center for Health Statistics. National Vital Statistics System, Mortality 2018-2021 on CDC WONDER Online Database

Health Insurance Coverage

Area	With Health Insurance	With Private Health Insurance	With Public Health Insurance	Without Health Insurance	Population Under Age 19 Without Health Insurance
City	89.5	69.7	32.7	10.5	7.6
MSA[1]	88.6	68.1	33.5	11.4	9.0
U.S.	91.2	67.8	35.4	8.8	5.3

Note: Figures are percentages that cover the civilian noninstitutionalized population; (1) Figures cover the Anchorage, AK Metropolitan Statistical Area
Source: U.S. Census Bureau, 2017-2021 American Community Survey 5-Year Estimates

Number of Medical Professionals

Area	MDs[3]	DOs[3,4]	Dentists	Podiatrists	Chiropractors	Optometrists
Borough[1] (number)	1,113	131	376	16	185	90
Borough[1] (rate[2])	383.0	45.1	130.5	5.6	64.2	31.2
U.S. (rate[2])	289.3	23.5	72.5	6.2	28.7	17.4

Note: Data as of 2021 unless noted; (1) Data covers Anchorage Borough; (2) Rate per 100,000 population; (3) Data as of 2020 and includes all active, non-federal physicians; (4) Doctor of Osteopathic Medicine
Source: U.S. Department of Health and Human Services, Health Resources and Services Administration, Bureau of Health Professions, Area Resource File (ARF) 2021-2022

EDUCATION

Public School District Statistics

District Name	Schls	Pupils	Pupil/ Teacher Ratio	Minority Pupils[1] (%)	LEP/ELL[2] (%)	IEP[3] (%)
Anchorage School District	97	43,054	17.2	59.6	15.8	15.4

Note: Table includes school districts with 2,000 or more students; (1) Percentage of students that are not non-Hispanic white; (2) Percentage of students that are Limited English Proficient or English Language Learners (2018-19); (3) Percentage of students that have an Individualized Education Program (2019-20).
Source: U.S. Department of Education, National Center for Education Statistics, Common Core of Data, Local Education Agency (School District) Universe Survey: School Year 2021-2022

Highest Level of Education

Area	Less than H.S.	H.S. Diploma	Some College, No Deg.	Associate Degree	Bachelor's Degree	Master's Degree	Prof. School Degree	Doctorate Degree
City	5.8	23.7	25.0	8.6	22.8	9.8	2.8	1.3
MSA[1]	6.0	26.2	25.5	9.1	20.9	8.8	2.4	1.2
U.S.	11.1	26.5	20.0	8.7	20.6	9.3	2.2	1.5

Note: Figures cover persons age 25 and over; (1) Figures cover the Anchorage, AK Metropolitan Statistical Area
Source: U.S. Census Bureau, 2017-2021 American Community Survey 5-Year Estimates

Educational Attainment by Race

Area	High School Graduate or Higher (%)					Bachelor's Degree or Higher (%)				
	Total	White	Black	Asian	Hisp.[2]	Total	White	Black	Asian	Hisp.[2]
City	94.2	96.4	93.2	88.4	85.6	36.8	44.0	21.6	26.4	24.5
MSA[1]	94.0	95.8	92.9	88.2	86.4	33.3	38.1	21.8	26.1	24.3
U.S.	88.9	91.4	87.2	87.6	71.2	33.7	35.5	23.3	55.6	18.4

Note: Figures shown cover persons 25 years old and over; (1) Figures cover the Anchorage, AK Metropolitan Statistical Area; (2) People of Hispanic origin can be of any race
Source: U.S. Census Bureau, 2017-2021 American Community Survey 5-Year Estimates

School Enrollment by Grade and Control

Area	Preschool (%)		Kindergarten (%)		Grades 1 - 4 (%)		Grades 5 - 8 (%)		Grades 9 - 12 (%)	
	Public	Private	Public	Private	Public	Private	Public	Private	Public	Private
City	50.1	49.9	91.5	8.5	87.5	12.5	89.0	11.0	92.0	8.0
MSA[1]	51.6	48.4	90.9	9.1	87.2	12.8	88.1	11.9	90.9	9.1
U.S.	58.8	41.2	86.3	13.7	88.3	11.7	88.6	11.4	89.4	10.6

Note: Figures shown cover persons 3 years old and over; (1) Figures cover the Anchorage, AK Metropolitan Statistical Area
Source: U.S. Census Bureau, 2017-2021 American Community Survey 5-Year Estimates

Higher Education

Four-Year Colleges			Two-Year Colleges			Medical Schools[1]	Law Schools[2]	Voc/ Tech[3]
Public	Private Non-profit	Private For-profit	Public	Private Non-profit	Private For-profit			
1	2	0	0	0	1	0	0	0

Note: Figures cover institutions located within the Anchorage, AK Metropolitan Statistical Area and include main campuses only; (1) includes schools accredited by the Liaison Committee on Medical Education and the American Osteopathic Association's Commission on Osteopathic College Accreditation; (2) includes ABA-accredited schools, schools with provisional ABA accreditation, and state accredited schools; (3) includes all schools with programs that are less than 2 years.
Source: National Center for Education Statistics, Integrated Postsecondary Education System (IPEDS), 2021-22; Wikipedia, List of Medical Schools in the United States, accessed April 10, 2023; Wikipedia, List of Law Schools in the United States, accessed April 10, 2023

EMPLOYERS

Major Employers

Company Name	Industry
ASRC Energy Services	Oil & gas field services
AT&T	Telephone communication, except radio
BP Transportation (Alaska)	Crude petroleum production
Bureau of Land Management	Information bureau
Carrs/Safeway	Grocery stores
Federal Aviation Administration	Aircraft regulating agencies
Federal Express Corporation	Air cargo carrier, scheduled
Fred Meyer	Retail
Galen Hospital Alaska	General medical & surgical hospitals
Indian Health Service	General medical & surgical hospitals
Municipality of Anchorage	Mayors' office
Nabors Alaska Drilling	Drilling oil & gas wells
Providence Health Services	Healthcare
U.S. Fish and Wildlife Service	Fish & wildlife conservation agency, government
United States Department of the Air Force	U.S. military
USPHS AK Native Medical Center	General medical & surgical hospitals
Wal-Mart Stores	Retail

Note: Companies shown are located within the Anchorage, AK Metropolitan Statistical Area.
Source: Hoovers.com; Wikipedia

PUBLIC SAFETY

Crime Rate

Area	Total Crime	Violent Crime Rate				Property Crime Rate		
		Murder	Rape[3]	Robbery	Aggrav. Assault	Burglary	Larceny -Theft	Motor Vehicle Theft
City	4,659.4	6.3	194.8	194.8	816.4	504.2	2,541.7	401.2
Suburbs[1]	3,312.3	0.0	63.6	42.4	445.2	233.2	2,247.1	280.9
Metro[2]	4,576.1	5.9	186.7	185.4	793.4	487.5	2,523.4	393.8
U.S.	2,356.7	6.5	38.4	73.9	279.7	314.2	1,398.0	246.0

Note: Figures are crimes per 100,000 population; (1) All areas within the metro area that are located outside the city limits; (2) Figures cover the Anchorage, AK Metropolitan Statistical Area; (3) All figures shown were reported using the revised Uniform Crime Reporting (UCR) definition of rape; Due to the transition to the National Incident-Based Reporting System (NIBRS), limited city and metro area data was released for 2021.
Source: FBI Uniform Crime Reports, 2020

Hate Crimes

Area	Number of Quarters Reported	Number of Incidents per Bias Motivation					
		Race/Ethnicity/ Ancestry	Religion	Sexual Orientation	Disability	Gender	Gender Identity
City	4	3	0	1	0	1	0
U.S.	4	5,227	1,244	1,110	130	75	266

Note: Due to the transition to the National Incident-Based Reporting System (NIBRS), limited crime data was released for 2021.
Source: Federal Bureau of Investigation, Hate Crime Statistics 2020

Identity Theft Consumer Reports

Area	Reports	Reports per 100,000 Population	Rank[2]
MSA[1]	479	120	324
U.S.	1,108,609	339	-

Note: (1) Figures cover the Anchorage, AK Metropolitan Statistical Area; (2) Rank ranges from 1 to 391 where 1 indicates greatest number of identity theft reports per 100,000 population
Source: Federal Trade Commission, Consumer Sentinel Network Data Book 2022

Fraud and Other Consumer Reports

Area	Reports	Reports per 100,000 Population	Rank[2]
MSA[1]	3,811	954	120
U.S.	4,064,520	1,245	-

Note: (1) Figures cover the Anchorage, AK Metropolitan Statistical Area; (2) Rank ranges from 1 to 391 where 1 indicates greatest number of fraud and other consumer reports per 100,000 population
Source: Federal Trade Commission, Consumer Sentinel Network Data Book 2022

POLITICS

2020 Presidential Election Results

Area	Biden	Trump	Jorgensen	Hawkins	Other
Alaska	42.8	52.8	2.5	0.0	1.9
U.S.	51.3	46.8	1.2	0.3	0.5

Note: Results are percentages and may not add to 100% due to rounding
Source: Dave Leip's Atlas of U.S. Presidential Elections

SPORTS

Professional Sports Teams

Team Name	League	Year Established

No teams are located in the metro area
Source: Wikipedia, Major Professional Sports Teams of the United States and Canada, April 12, 2023

CLIMATE

Average and Extreme Temperatures

Temperature	Jan	Feb	Mar	Apr	May	Jun	Jul	Aug	Sep	Oct	Nov	Dec	Yr.
Extreme High (°F)	50	48	51	65	77	85	82	82	73	61	53	48	85
Average High (°F)	22	25	33	43	55	62	65	63	55	41	28	22	43
Average Temp. (°F)	15	18	25	36	47	55	59	57	48	35	22	16	36
Average Low (°F)	8	11	17	28	39	47	51	49	41	28	15	10	29
Extreme Low (°F)	-34	-26	-24	-4	17	33	36	31	19	-5	-21	-30	-34

Note: Figures cover the years 1953-1995
Source: National Climatic Data Center, International Station Meteorological Climate Summary, 9/96

Average Precipitation/Snowfall/Humidity

Precip./Humidity	Jan	Feb	Mar	Apr	May	Jun	Jul	Aug	Sep	Oct	Nov	Dec	Yr.
Avg. Precip. (in.)	0.8	0.8	0.7	0.6	0.7	1.0	1.9	2.4	2.7	1.9	1.1	1.1	15.7
Avg. Snowfall (in.)	10	12	10	5	Tr	0	0	0	Tr	8	12	15	71
Avg. Rel. Hum. 6am (%)	74	74	72	75	73	74	80	84	84	78	78	78	77
Avg. Rel. Hum. 3pm (%)	73	67	57	54	50	55	62	64	64	64	67	74	64

Note: Figures cover the years 1953-1995; Tr = Trace amounts (<0.05 in. of rain; <0.5 in. of snow)
Source: National Climatic Data Center, International Station Meteorological Climate Summary, 9/96

Weather Conditions

Temperature			Daytime Sky			Precipitation		
0°F & below	32°F & below	65°F & above	Clear	Partly cloudy	Cloudy	0.01 inch or more precip.	0.1 inch or more snow/ice	Thunder-storms
32	194	41	50	115	200	113	49	2

Note: Figures are average number of days per year and cover the years 1953-1995
Source: National Climatic Data Center, International Station Meteorological Climate Summary, 9/96

HAZARDOUS WASTE

Superfund Sites

The Anchorage, AK metro area is home to two sites on the EPA's Superfund National Priorities List: **Elmendorf Air Force Base** (final); **Fort Richardson (USARMY)** (final). There are a total of 1,165 Superfund sites with a status of proposed or final on the list in the U.S. *U.S. Environmental Protection Agency, National Priorities List, April 12, 2023*

AIR QUALITY

Air Quality Trends: Ozone

	1990	1995	2000	2005	2010	2015	2018	2019	2020	2021
MSA[1]	n/a	n/a	n/a	n/a	n/a	n/a	n/a	n/a	n/a	n/a
U.S.	0.087	0.089	0.081	0.080	0.072	0.067	0.069	0.065	0.065	0.067

Note: (1) Data covers the Anchorage, AK Metropolitan Statistical Area; n/a not available. The values shown are the composite ozone concentration averages among trend sites based on the highest fourth daily maximum 8-hour concentration in parts per million. These trends are based on sites having an adequate record of monitoring data during the trend period. Data from exceptional events are included.
Source: U.S. Environmental Protection Agency, Air Quality Monitoring Information, "Air Quality Trends by City, 1990-2021"

Air Quality Index

Area	Percent of Days when Air Quality was...[2]					AQI Statistics[2]	
	Good	Moderate	Unhealthy for Sensitive Groups	Unhealthy	Very Unhealthy	Maximum	Median
MSA[1]	80.3	18.6	0.8	0.3	0.0	160	25

Note: (1) Data covers the Anchorage, AK Metropolitan Statistical Area; (2) Based on 365 days with AQI data in 2021. Air Quality Index (AQI) is an index for reporting daily air quality. EPA calculates the AQI for five major air pollutants regulated by the Clean Air Act: ground-level ozone, particle pollution (aka particulate matter), carbon monoxide, sulfur dioxide, and nitrogen dioxide. The AQI runs from 0 to 500. The higher the AQI value, the greater the level of air pollution and the greater the health concern. There are six AQI categories: "Good" AQI is between 0 and 50. Air quality is considered satisfactory; "Moderate" AQI is between 51 and 100. Air quality is acceptable; "Unhealthy for Sensitive Groups" When AQI values are between 101 and 150, members of sensitive groups may experience health effects; "Unhealthy" When AQI values are between 151 and 200 everyone may begin to experience health effects; "Very Unhealthy" AQI values between 201 and 300 trigger a health alert; "Hazardous" AQI values over 300 trigger warnings of emergency conditions (not shown).
Source: U.S. Environmental Protection Agency, Air Quality Index Report, 2021

Air Quality Index Pollutants

Area	Percent of Days when AQI Pollutant was...[2]					
	Carbon Monoxide	Nitrogen Dioxide	Ozone	Sulfur Dioxide	Particulate Matter 2.5	Particulate Matter 10
MSA[1]	0.0	0.0	0.0	(3)	68.5	31.5

Note: (1) Data covers the Anchorage, AK Metropolitan Statistical Area; (2) Based on 365 days with AQI data in 2021. The Air Quality Index (AQI) is an index for reporting daily air quality. EPA calculates the AQI for five major air pollutants regulated by the Clean Air Act: ground-level ozone, particle pollution (also known as particulate matter), carbon monoxide, sulfur dioxide, and nitrogen dioxide. The AQI runs from 0 to 500. The higher the AQI value, the greater the level of air pollution and the greater the health concern; (3) Sulfur dioxide is no longer included in this table (as of December 8, 2021) because SO_2 concentrations tend to be very localized and not necessarily representative of broad geographical areas like counties and CBSAs.
Source: U.S. Environmental Protection Agency, Air Quality Index Report, 2021

Maximum Air Pollutant Concentrations: Particulate Matter, Ozone, CO and Lead

	Particulate Matter 10 (ug/m³)	Particulate Matter 2.5 Wtd AM (ug/m³)	Particulate Matter 2.5 24-Hr (ug/m³)	Ozone (ppm)	Carbon Monoxide (ppm)	Lead (ug/m³)
MSA[1] Level	97	6	21	n/a	2	n/a
NAAQS[2]	150	15	35	0.075	9	0.15
Met NAAQS[2]	Yes	Yes	Yes	n/a	Yes	n/a

Note: (1) Data covers the Anchorage, AK Metropolitan Statistical Area; Data from exceptional events are included; (2) National Ambient Air Quality Standards; ppm = parts per million; ug/m³ = micrograms per cubic meter; n/a not available.
Concentrations: Particulate Matter 10 (coarse particulate)—highest second maximum 24-hour concentration; Particulate Matter 2.5 Wtd AM (fine particulate)—highest weighted annual mean concentration; Particulate Matter 2.5 24-Hour (fine particulate)—highest 98th percentile 24-hour concentration; Ozone—highest fourth daily maximum 8-hour concentration; Carbon Monoxide—highest second maximum non-overlapping 8-hour concentration; Lead—maximum running 3-month average
Source: U.S. Environmental Protection Agency, Air Quality Monitoring Information, "Air Quality Statistics by City, 2021"

Maximum Air Pollutant Concentrations: Nitrogen Dioxide and Sulfur Dioxide

	Nitrogen Dioxide AM (ppb)	Nitrogen Dioxide 1-Hr (ppb)	Sulfur Dioxide AM (ppb)	Sulfur Dioxide 1-Hr (ppb)	Sulfur Dioxide 24-Hr (ppb)
MSA[1] Level	n/a	n/a	n/a	n/a	n/a
NAAQS[2]	53	100	30	75	140
Met NAAQS[2]	n/a	n/a	n/a	n/a	n/a

Note: (1) Data covers the Anchorage, AK Metropolitan Statistical Area; Data from exceptional events are included; (2) National Ambient Air Quality Standards; ppm = parts per million; ug/m³ = micrograms per cubic meter; n/a not available.
Concentrations: Nitrogen Dioxide AM—highest arithmetic mean concentration; Nitrogen Dioxide 1-Hr—highest 98th percentile 1-hour daily maximum concentration; Sulfur Dioxide AM—highest annual mean concentration; Sulfur Dioxide 1-Hr—highest 99th percentile 1-hour daily maximum concentration; Sulfur Dioxide 24-Hr—highest second maximum 24-hour concentration
Source: U.S. Environmental Protection Agency, Air Quality Monitoring Information, "Air Quality Statistics by City, 2021"

Boise City, Idaho

Background

Boise (boy-see) is the capital and largest city in Idaho, lying along the Boise River adjacent to the foothills of the Rocky Mountains. The city is located southwest of the western slopes of the Rockies and is the site of a great system of natural warm water springs.

Boise's spectacular natural location is its most popular, and obvious, attraction, and this, coupled with its dynamic economic growth in recent decades, makes Boise an altogether remarkable city. The splendor of its surroundings, together with an average 18-minute drive to work, has allowed the city to combine pleasure and production in an enviable mix.

French-Canadian trappers were familiar with Boise and its environs by 1811, and the name of the city is an Anglicization of the French Les Bois—the trees. The first substantial European settlement dates to 1863 when, in the spring of that year, I.M. Coston built from pegged driftwood a great house that served as a hub for the activities of prospectors, traders, and Native Americans. In the same year, the U.S. Army built Fort Boise, and considerable deposits of gold and silver were discovered in the area. The U.S. Assay Office in Boise, in 1870-71 alone, is said to have valuated more than $75 million in precious metals.

The area is rich in gold rush lore, and there is still talk of buried treasure from that era: The eastbound stagecoach from Boise was said to have been waylaid by a robber, six miles above the city on the south side of the river, who, though wounded in the attack, managed to drag off a strongbox filled with $50,000 in gold. The robber died of his wounds and was discovered the next day, but the loot was never found.

The Boise area was subsequently developed for farming, as crops of grains, vegetables, and fruits, replaced the mines as its source of wealth. It became the territorial capital of Idaho in 1864 and the state capital in 1890. Education was served with the opening of a university in 1932, which became Boise State University in 1974 and now enrolls about 20,000 students.

The city's natural setting offers a great range of outdoor activities that are pursued energetically by its citizens. Its rivers, mountains, deserts, and lakes offer world-class skiing, hiking, camping, kayaking, river rafting, hunting, and fishing. Bike paths run throughout the city and into Boise's large outdoor trail network, the Boise River Greenbelt. Recreational wilderness exists extensively just outside the city's limits. The Word Center for Birds of Prey is located on the city's southern frontier and is the site of the Peregrine Falcon's rehabilitation and release into the wild.

Many large regional, national, and international companies are headquartered in Boise, including major call centers for DIRECTV and T-Mobile.

The city produces high- and low-tech products and everything in between: software, computer components, steel and sheet metal products, mobile homes, lumber products, farm machinery, packed meats, and processed foods. Increasingly an advanced technological center, it continues to serve as a trading center for the greater agricultural region.

By virtue of its history and geographical character, the city can be considered a presence on the Pacific Rim. In a more tangible vein, Boise, with nine airlines operating at its airport, is conveniently tied to the wider world.

Boise's Basque community is the largest in the United States and the third largest in the world outside Argentina and the Basque Country in Spain and France. A large Basque festival known as Jaialdi is held once every five years, with the next scheduled for 2025. Boise (along with Valley and Boise Counties) hosted the 2009 Special Olympics World Winter Games. More than 2,500 athletes from over 100 countries participated.

The city is protected by the mountains to the north in such a way that it is largely unbothered by the extreme blizzards that affect eastern Idaho and parts of neighboring states. Boise, and this section of western Idaho generally, is affected by climatic influences from the Pacific Ocean and exhibits an unusually mild climate for this latitude. Summers can be hot, but nights are almost always cool, and sunshine generally prevails.

Rankings

General Rankings

- For its "Best for Vets: Places to Live 2019" rankings, *Military Times* evaluated 599 cities (83 large, 234 medium, 282 small) and compared the locations across three broad categories: veteran and military culture/services; economic indicators; and livability factors such as health, crime, traffic, and school quality. Boise City ranked #13 out of the top 50, in the medium-sized city category (population of 100,000-249,999). Data points more specific to veterans and the military weighed more heavily than others. *rebootcamp.militarytimes.com, "Military Times Best Places to Live 2019," September 10, 2018*

- *US News & World Report* conducted a survey of more than 3,600 people and analyzed the 150 largest metropolitan areas to determine what matters most when selecting where to settle down. Boise City ranked #15 out of the top 25 as having the best combination of desirable factors. Criteria: cost of living; quality of life and education; net migration; job market; desirability; and other factors. *money.usnews.com, "The 25 Best Places to Live in the U.S. in 2022-2023," May 17, 2022*

- The Boise City metro area was identified as one of America's fastest-growing areas in terms of population and business growth by *MagnifyMoney.* The area ranked #8 out of 35. The 100 most populous metro areas in the U.S. were evaluated on their change from 2011 to 2016 in the following categories: people and housing; workforce and employment opportunities; growing industry. *www.businessinsider.com, "The 35 Cities in the US with the Biggest Influx of People, the Most Work Opportunities, and the Hottest Business Growth," August 12, 2018*

- The Boise City metro area was identified as one of America's fastest-growing areas in terms of population and economy by *Forbes.* The area ranked #1 out of 25. The 100 most populous metro areas in the U.S. were evaluated on the following criteria: estimated population growth; employment; economic output; wages; home values. *Forbes, "America's Fastest-Growing Cities 2018," February 28, 2018*

- Boise City was selected as one of the best places to live in the United States by *Money* magazine. The city ranked #11 out of 50. This year's list focused on cities that would be welcoming to a broader group of people and with populations of at least 20,000. Beginning with a pool of 1,370 candidates, editors looked at 350 data points, organized into the these nine categories: income and personal finance, cost of living, economic opportunity, housing market, fun and amenities, health and safety, education, diversity, and quality of life. *Money, "The 50 Best Places to Live in the U.S. in 2022-2023" September 29, 2022*

- In their ninth annual survey, Livability.com looked at data for more than 2,300 mid-sized U.S. cities to determine the rankings for Livability's "Top 100 Best Places to Live" in 2022. Boise City ranked #35. Criteria: housing and economy; social and civic engagement; education; demographics; health care options; transportation & infrastructure; and community amenities. *Livability.com, "Top 100 Best Places to Live 2022" July 19, 2022*

Business/Finance Rankings

- The Brookings Institution ranked the nation's largest cities based on income inequality. Boise City was ranked #60 (#1 = greatest inequality). Criteria: the "95/20 ratio," a figure representing the income at which a household earns more than 95 percent of all other households, divided by the income at which a household earns more than only 20 percent of all other households. *Brookings Institution, "Household Income Inequality, Largest Cities of 97 Large U.S. Metro Areas, 2014-2016," February 5, 2018*

- The Brookings Institution ranked the 100 largest metro areas in the U.S. based on income inequality. Boise City was ranked #89 (#1 = greatest inequality). Criteria: the "95/20 ratio," a figure representing the income at which a household earns more than 95 percent of all other households, divided by the income at which a household earns more than only 20 percent of all other households. *Brookings Institution, "Household Income Inequality, 100 Largest U.S. Metro Areas, 2014-2016," February 5, 2018*

- The Boise City metro area appeared on the Milken Institute "2022 Best Performing Cities" list. Rank: #15 out of 200 large metro areas (population over 250,000). Criteria: job growth; wage and salary growth; high-tech output growth; housing affordability; household broadband access. *Milken Institute, "Best-Performing Cities 2022," March 28, 2022*

- *Forbes* ranked the 200 most populous metro areas to determine the nation's "Best Places for Business and Careers." The Boise City metro area was ranked #29. Criteria: costs (business and living); job growth (past and projected); income growth; quality of life; educational attainment (college and high school); projected economic growth; cultural and leisure opportunities; workplace tolerance laws; net migration patterns. *Forbes, "The Best Places for Business and Careers 2019: Seattle Still On Top," October 30, 2019*

Dating/Romance Rankings

- Boise City was ranked #3 out of 25 cities that stood out for inspiring romance and attracting diners on the website OpenTable.com. Criteria: percentage of people who dined out on Valentine's Day in 2018; percentage of romantic restaurants as rated by OpenTable diner reviews; and percentage of tables seated for two. *OpenTable, "25 Most Romantic Cities in America for 2019," February 7, 2019*

Education Rankings

- Personal finance website *WalletHub* analyzed the 150 largest U.S. metropolitan statistical areas to determine where the most educated Americans are putting their degrees to work. Criteria: education levels; percentage of workers with degrees; education quality and attainment gap; public school quality rankings; quality and enrollment of each metro area's universities. Boise City was ranked #50 (#1 = most educated city). *www.WalletHub.com, "Most & Least Educated Cities in America," July 18, 2022*

Environmental Rankings

- Boise City was highlighted as one of the 25 metro areas most polluted by short-term particle pollution (24-hour PM 2.5) in the U.S. during 2019 through 2021. The area ranked #21. *American Lung Association, "State of the Air 2023," April 19, 2023*

Food/Drink Rankings

- Boise City was selected as one of America's 10 most vegan-friendly areas. The city was ranked #5. Criteria now includes smaller urban areas, following the migration to smaller cities due to the pandemic. *People for the Ethical Treatment of Animals, "Top 10 Vegan-Friendly Towns and Small Cities of 2020," December 14, 2020*

Health/Fitness Rankings

- For each of the 100 largest cities in the United States, the American Fitness Index®, compiled in partnership between the American College of Sports Medicine and the Elevance Health Foundation, evaluated community infrastructure and 34 health behaviors including preventive health, levels of chronic disease conditions, food insecurity, sleep quality, pedestrian safety, air quality, and community/environment resources that support physical activity. Boise City ranked #12 for "community fitness." *americanfitnessindex.org, "2022 ACSM American Fitness Index Summary Report," July 12, 2022*

- Boise City was identified as a "2022 Spring Allergy Capital." The area ranked #82 out of 100. Three groups of factors were used to identify the most challenging cities for people with allergies during the spring season: annual spring pollen scores; over the counter allergy medicine use; number of board-certified allergy specialists. *Asthma and Allergy Foundation of America, "Spring Allergy Capitals 2022," March 2, 2022*

- Boise City was identified as a "2022 Fall Allergy Capital." The area ranked #85 out of 100. Three groups of factors were used to identify the most challenging cities for people with allergies during the fall season: annual fall pollen scores; over the counter allergy medicine use; number of board-certified allergy specialists. *Asthma and Allergy Foundation of America, "Fall Allergy Capitals 2022," March 2, 2022*

- Boise City was identified as a "2022 Asthma Capital." The area ranked #80 out of the nation's 100 largest metropolitan areas. Criteria: estimated asthma prevalence; asthma-related mortality; and ER visits due to asthma. Risk factors analyzed but not factored in the rankings: annual pollen score; annual air quality; public smoking laws; access to board-certified asthma specialists; rescue and controller medication use; uninsured rate; poverty rate. *Asthma and Allergy Foundation of America, "Asthma Capitals 2022: The Most Challenging Places to Live With Asthma," September 14, 2022*

Real Estate Rankings

- *WalletHub* compared the most populated U.S. cities to determine which had the best markets for real estate agents. Boise City ranked #107 where demand was high and pay was the best. Criteria: sales per agent; annual median wage for real-estate agents; monthly average starting salary for real estate agents; real estate job density and competition; unemployment rate; home turnover rate; housing-market health index; and other relevant metrics. *www.WalletHub.com, "2021 Best Places to Be a Real Estate Agent," May 12, 2021*

- The Boise City metro area was identified as one of the 20 worst housing markets in the U.S. in 2022. The area ranked #184 out of 187 markets. Criteria: year-over-year change of median sales price of existing single-family homes between the 4th quarter of 2021 and the 4th quarter of 2022. *National Association of Realtors®, Median Sales Price of Existing Single-Family Homes for Metropolitan Areas, 4th Quarter 2022*

- Boise City was ranked #213 out of 235 metro areas in terms of housing affordability in 2022 by the National Association of Home Builders (#1 = most affordable). Criteria: the share of homes sold in that area affordable to a family earning the local median income, based on standard mortgage underwriting criteria. *National Association of Home Builders®, NAHB-Wells Fargo Housing Opportunity Index, 4th Quarter 2022*

Safety Rankings

- Allstate ranked the 200 largest cities in America in terms of driver safety. Boise City ranked #2. Criteria: internal property damage claims over a two-year period from January 2016 to December 2017. The report helps increase the importance of safety and awareness behind the wheel. *Allstate, "Allstate America's Best Drivers Report, 2019" June 24, 2019*

- The National Insurance Crime Bureau ranked 390 metro areas in the U.S. in terms of per capita rates of vehicle theft. The Boise City metro area ranked #325 (#1 = highest rate). Criteria: number of vehicle theft offenses per 100,000 inhabitants in 2021. *National Insurance Crime Bureau, "Hot Spots 2021," September 1, 2022*

Seniors/Retirement Rankings

- From its Best Cities for Successful Aging indexes, the Milken Institute generated rankings for metropolitan areas, weighing data in nine categories—health care, wellness, living arrangements, transportation and convenience, financial characteristics, education, employment, community engagement, and overall livability. The Boise City metro area was ranked #34 overall in the large metro area category. *Milken Institute, "Best Cities for Successful Aging, 2017" March 14, 2017*

- Boise City was identified as #13 of 20 most popular places to retire in the Western region by *Topretirements.com*. The site separated its annual "Best Places to Retire" list by major U.S. regions for 2019. The list reflects the 20 cities that visitors to the website are most interested in for retirement, based on the number of times a city's review was viewed on the website. *Topretirements.com, "20 Best Places to Retire in the West-2019," November 11, 2019*

Sports/Recreation Rankings

- Boise City was chosen as one of America's best cities for bicycling. The city ranked #21 out of 50. Criteria: cycling infrastructure that is safe and friendly for all ages; energy and bike culture. The editors evaluated cities with populations of 100,000 or more. *Bicycling, "The 50 Best Bike Cities in America," October 10, 2018*

Women/Minorities Rankings

- Personal finance website *WalletHub* compared more than 180 U.S. cities across two key dimensions, "Hispanic Business-Friendliness" and "Hispanic Purchasing Power," to arrive at the most favorable conditions for Hispanic entrepreneurs. Boise City was ranked #35 out of 182. Criteria includes: share of Hispanic-Owned Businesses; Hispanic entrepreneurship rate to median annual income of Hispanics; Small Business-Friendliness score; cost of living; and number of Hispanics with at least a bachelor's degree. *WalletHub.com, "2019's Best Cities for Hispanic Entrepreneurs," May 1, 2019*

Miscellaneous Rankings

- *WalletHub* compared the 150 most populated U.S. cities to determine their operating efficiency. A "Quality of Services" score was constructed for each city and then divided by the total budget per capita to reveal which were managed the best. Boise City ranked #2. Criteria: financial stability; economy; education; safety; health; infrastructure and pollution. *www.WalletHub.com, "2022's Best-& Worst-Run Cities in America," June 21, 2022*

Business Environment

DEMOGRAPHICS

Population Growth

Area	1990 Census	2000 Census	2010 Census	2020 Census	Population Growth (%)	
					1990-2020	2010-2020
City	144,317	185,787	205,671	235,684	63.3	14.6
MSA[1]	319,596	464,840	616,561	764,718	139.3	24.0
U.S.	248,709,873	281,421,906	308,745,538	331,449,281	33.3	7.4

Note: (1) Figures cover the Boise City, ID Metropolitan Statistical Area
Source: U.S. Census Bureau, 1990 Census, 2000 Census, 2010 Census, 2020 Census

Race

Area	White Alone[2] (%)	Black Alone[2] (%)	Asian Alone[2] (%)	AIAN[3] Alone[2] (%)	NHOPI[4] Alone[2] (%)	Other Race Alone[2] (%)	Two or More Races (%)
City	81.2	2.3	3.6	0.7	0.3	3.5	8.5
MSA[1]	80.0	1.3	2.1	0.9	0.3	5.9	9.6
U.S.	61.6	12.4	6.0	1.1	0.2	8.4	10.2

Note: (1) Figures cover the Boise City, ID Metropolitan Statistical Area; (2) Alone is defined as not being in combination with one or more other races; (3) American Indian and Alaska Native; (4) Native Hawaiian and Other Pacific Islander
Source: U.S. Census Bureau, 2020 Census

Hispanic or Latino Origin

Area	Total (%)	Mexican (%)	Puerto Rican (%)	Cuban (%)	Other (%)
City	8.8	6.4	0.5	0.1	1.9
MSA[1]	14.1	11.5	0.5	0.1	2.0
U.S.	18.4	11.2	1.8	0.7	4.7

Note: Persons of Hispanic or Latino origin can be of any race; (1) Figures cover the Boise City, ID Metropolitan Statistical Area
Source: U.S. Census Bureau, 2017-2021 American Community Survey 5-Year Estimates

Age

Area	Percent of Population									Median Age
	Under Age 5	Age 5–19	Age 20–34	Age 35–44	Age 45–54	Age 55–64	Age 65–74	Age 75–84	Age 85+	
City	5.1	18.4	23.4	13.6	11.7	12.0	9.5	4.5	1.8	37.1
MSA[1]	5.9	21.8	19.7	13.4	11.9	11.7	9.5	4.6	1.6	36.9
U.S.	5.6	19.2	20.2	12.7	12.4	13.1	10.0	4.9	1.9	38.8

Note: (1) Figures cover the Boise City, ID Metropolitan Statistical Area
Source: U.S. Census Bureau, 2020 Census

Disability by Age

Area	All Ages	Under 18 Years Old	18 to 64 Years Old	65 Years and Over
City	11.3	4.2	9.4	29.7
MSA[1]	12.1	4.4	10.6	31.6
U.S.	12.6	4.4	10.3	33.4

Note: Figures show percent of the civilian noninstitutionalized population that reported having a disability. Disability status is determined from six types of difficulty: vision, hearing, cognitive, ambulatory, self-care, and independent living. For children under 5 years old, hearing and vision difficulty are used to determine disability status. For children between the ages of 5 and 14, disability status is determined from hearing, vision, cognitive, ambulatory, and self-care difficulties. For people aged 15 years and older, they are considered to have a disability if they have difficulty with any one of the six difficulty types; Note: (1) Figures cover the Boise City, ID Metropolitan Statistical Area
Source: U.S. Census Bureau, 2017-2021 American Community Survey 5-Year Estimates

Ancestry

Area	German	Irish	English	American	Italian	Polish	French[2]	Scottish	Dutch
City	16.9	12.1	18.1	4.4	4.2	1.9	2.2	3.2	1.7
MSA[1]	16.4	10.2	17.6	4.9	3.5	1.4	2.4	2.9	1.9
U.S.	12.8	9.6	8.1	5.7	5.0	2.7	2.2	1.6	1.1

Note: Figures are the percentage of the total population reporting a particular ancestry. The nine most commonly reported ancestries in the U.S. are shown. Figures include multiple ancestries (e.g. if a person reported being Irish and Italian, they were included in both columns); (1) Figures cover the Boise City, ID Metropolitan Statistical Area; (2) Excludes Basque
Source: U.S. Census Bureau, 2017-2021 American Community Survey 5-Year Estimates

Foreign-born Population

Area	Percent of Population Born in								
	Any Foreign Country	Asia	Mexico	Europe	Caribbean	Central America[2]	South America	Africa	Canada
City	6.5	2.8	1.1	1.2	0.1	0.0	0.3	0.5	0.5
MSA[1]	6.5	1.5	2.7	1.0	0.0	0.2	0.4	0.3	0.3
U.S.	13.6	4.2	3.3	1.5	1.4	1.1	1.1	0.8	0.2

Note: (1) Figures cover the Boise City, ID Metropolitan Statistical Area; (2) Excludes Mexico.
Source: U.S. Census Bureau, 2017-2021 American Community Survey 5-Year Estimates

Household Size

Area	Persons in Household (%)							Average Household Size
	One	Two	Three	Four	Five	Six	Seven or More	
City	31.7	36.6	14.9	9.9	4.9	1.4	0.6	2.40
MSA[1]	24.7	36.1	15.3	12.5	6.5	3.1	1.7	2.70
U.S.	28.1	33.8	15.5	12.9	6.0	2.3	1.4	2.60

Note: (1) Figures cover the Boise City, ID Metropolitan Statistical Area
Source: U.S. Census Bureau, 2017-2021 American Community Survey 5-Year Estimates

Household Relationships

Area	Householder	Opposite-sex Spouse	Same-sex Spouse	Opposite-sex Unmarried Partner	Same-sex Unmarried Partner	Child[2]	Grandchild	Other Relatives	Non-relatives
City	41.4	17.8	0.2	3.2	0.2	24.7	1.3	2.9	5.4
MSA[1]	36.6	19.5	0.2	2.5	0.1	29.7	1.9	3.5	3.8
U.S.	38.3	17.5	0.2	2.5	0.2	28.3	2.4	4.8	3.4

Note: Figures are percent of the total population; (1) Figures cover the Boise City, ID Metropolitan Statistical Area; (2) Includes biological, adopted, and stepchildren of the householder
Source: U.S. Census Bureau, 2020 Census

Gender

Area	Males	Females	Males per 100 Females
City	116,758	118,926	98.2
MSA[1]	380,892	383,826	99.2
U.S.	162,685,811	168,763,470	96.4

Note: (1) Figures cover the Boise City, ID Metropolitan Statistical Area
Source: U.S. Census Bureau, 2020 Census

Marital Status

Area	Never Married	Now Married[2]	Separated	Widowed	Divorced
City	34.8	47.0	1.0	4.4	12.9
MSA[1]	29.1	53.3	1.1	4.3	12.2
U.S.	33.8	48.0	1.8	5.6	10.8

Note: Figures are percentages and cover the population 15 years of age and older; (1) Figures cover the Boise City, ID Metropolitan Statistical Area; (2) Excludes separated
Source: U.S. Census Bureau, 2017-2021 American Community Survey 5-Year Estimates

Religious Groups by Family

Area	Catholic	Baptist	Methodist	LDS[2]	Pentecostal	Lutheran	Islam	Adventist	Other
MSA[1]	13.0	0.8	2.5	15.0	1.6	0.8	0.3	1.7	10.0
U.S.	18.7	7.3	3.0	2.0	1.8	1.7	1.3	1.3	11.6

Note: Figures are the number of adherents as a percentage of the total population and cover the eight largest religious groups in the U.S; (1) Figures cover the Boise City, ID Metropolitan Statistical Area; (2) Church of Jesus Christ of Latter-day Saints
Sources: 2020 U.S. Religion Census, Association of Statisticians of American Religious Bodies; The Association of Religion Data Archives (ARDA)

Religious Groups by Tradition

Area	Catholic	Evangelical Protestant	Mainline Protestant	Black Protestant	Islam	Judaism	Hinduism	Orthodox	Buddhism
MSA[1]	13.0	11.9	3.9	<0.1	0.3	0.1	0.2	0.1	0.1
U.S.	18.7	16.5	5.2	2.3	1.3	0.6	0.4	0.4	0.3

Note: Figures are the number of adherents as a percentage of the total population; (1) Figures cover the Boise City, ID Metropolitan Statistical Area
Sources: 2020 U.S. Religion Census, Association of Statisticians of American Religious Bodies; The Association of Religion Data Archives (ARDA)

ECONOMY

Gross Metropolitan Product

Area	2020	2021	2022	2023	Rank[2]
MSA[1]	37.9	42.9	46.9	50.4	80

Note: Figures are in billions of dollars; (1) Figures cover the Boise City, ID Metropolitan Statistical Area; (2) Rank is based on 2021 data and ranges from 1 to 381
Source: U.S. Conference of Mayors, U.S. Metro Economies: U.S. Metros Compared to Global and State Economies, June 2022

Economic Growth

Area	2018-20 (%)	2021 (%)	2022 (%)	2023 (%)	Rank[2]
MSA[1]	2.0	7.4	3.2	4.2	35
U.S.	-0.6	5.7	3.1	2.9	–

Note: Figures are real gross metropolitan product (GMP) growth rates and represent average annual percent change; (1) Figures cover the Boise City, ID Metropolitan Statistical Area; (2) Rank is based on 2020 2-year average annual percent change and ranges from 1 to 381
Source: U.S. Conference of Mayors, U.S. Metro Economies: U.S. Metros Compared to Global and State Economies, June 2022

Metropolitan Area Exports

Area	2016	2017	2018	2019	2020	2021	Rank[2]
MSA[1]	3,021.7	2,483.3	2,771.7	2,062.8	1,632.9	1,937.1	110

Note: Figures are in millions of dollars; (1) Figures cover the Boise City, ID Metropolitan Statistical Area; (2) Rank is based on 2021 data and ranges from 1 to 388
Source: U.S. Department of Commerce, International Trade Administration, Office of Trade and Economic Analysis, Industry and Analysis, Exports by Metropolitan Area, data extracted March 16, 2023

Building Permits

Area	Single-Family			Multi-Family			Total		
	2021	2022	Pct. Chg.	2021	2022	Pct. Chg.	2021	2022	Pct. Chg.
City	856	392	-54.2	1,165	1,210	3.9	2,021	1,602	-20.7
MSA[1]	8,342	5,925	-29.0	3,854	4,550	18.1	12,196	10,475	-14.1
U.S.	1,115,400	975,600	-12.5	621,600	689,500	10.9	1,737,000	1,665,100	-4.1

Note: (1) Figures cover the Boise City, ID Metropolitan Statistical Area; Figures represent new, privately-owned housing units authorized (unadjusted data); All permit data are based on estimates with imputation
Source: U.S. Census Bureau, Manufacturing, Mining, and Construction Statistics, Building Permits, 2021, 2022

Bankruptcy Filings

Area	Business Filings			Nonbusiness Filings		
	2021	2022	% Chg.	2021	2022	% Chg.
Ada County	13	16	23.1	393	326	-17.0
U.S.	14,347	13,481	-6.0	399,269	374,240	-6.3

Note: Business filings include Chapter 7, Chapter 9, Chapter 11, Chapter 12, Chapter 13, Chapter 15, and Section 304; Nonbusiness filings include Chapter 7, Chapter 11, and Chapter 13
Source: Administrative Office of the U.S. Courts, Business and Nonbusiness Bankruptcy, County Cases Commenced by Chapter of the Bankruptcy Code, During the 12-Month Period Ending December 31, 2021 and Business and Nonbusiness Bankruptcy, County Cases Commenced by Chapter of the Bankruptcy Code, During the 12-Month Period Ending December 31, 2022

Housing Vacancy Rates

Area	Gross Vacancy Rate[2] (%)			Year-Round Vacancy Rate[3] (%)			Rental Vacancy Rate[4] (%)			Homeowner Vacancy Rate[5] (%)		
	2020	2021	2022	2020	2021	2022	2020	2021	2022	2020	2021	2022
MSA[1]	n/a	n/a	n/a	n/a	n/a	n/a	n/a	n/a	n/a	n/a	n/a	n/a
U.S.	10.6	10.8	10.5	8.2	8.4	8.2	6.3	6.1	5.8	1.0	0.9	0.8

Note: (1) Figures cover the Boise City, ID Metropolitan Statistical Area; (2) The percentage of the total housing inventory that is vacant; (3) The percentage of the housing inventory (excluding seasonal units) that is year-round vacant; (4) The percentage of rental inventory that is vacant for rent; (5) The percentage of homeowner inventory that is vacant for sale; n/a not available
Source: U.S. Census Bureau, Housing Vacancies and Homeownership Annual Statistics: 2020, 2021, 2022

INCOME

Income

Area	Per Capita ($)	Median Household ($)	Average Household ($)
City	40,056	68,373	93,693
MSA[1]	35,114	69,801	92,742
U.S.	37,638	69,021	97,196

Note: (1) Figures cover the Boise City, ID Metropolitan Statistical Area
Source: U.S. Census Bureau, 2017-2021 American Community Survey 5-Year Estimates

Household Income Distribution

Area	Under $15,000	$15,000 -$24,999	$25,000 -$34,999	$35,000 -$49,999	$50,000 -$74,999	$75,000 -$99,999	$100,000 -$149,999	$150,000 and up
				Percent of Households Earning				
City	7.6	7.6	8.6	12.4	18.5	13.9	15.7	15.7
MSA[1]	7.0	7.1	7.6	12.0	20.4	14.6	17.3	14.2
U.S.	9.4	7.8	8.2	11.4	16.8	12.8	16.3	17.3

Note: (1) Figures cover the Boise City, ID Metropolitan Statistical Area
Source: U.S. Census Bureau, 2017-2021 American Community Survey 5-Year Estimates

Poverty Rate

Area	All Ages	Under 18 Years Old	18 to 64 Years Old	65 Years and Over
City	11.6	13.8	11.6	8.6
MSA[1]	9.9	11.2	9.9	7.6
U.S.	12.6	17.0	11.8	9.6

Note: Figures are percentage of people whose income during the past 12 months was below the poverty level;
(1) Figures cover the Boise City, ID Metropolitan Statistical Area
Source: U.S. Census Bureau, 2017-2021 American Community Survey 5-Year Estimates

EMPLOYMENT

Labor Force and Employment

Area	Civilian Labor Force			Workers Employed		
	Dec. 2021	Dec. 2022	% Chg.	Dec. 2021	Dec. 2022	% Chg.
City	135,152	140,433	3.9	132,075	137,857	4.4
MSA[1]	400,832	416,686	4.0	390,861	407,819	4.3
U.S.	161,696,000	164,224,000	1.6	155,732,000	158,872,000	2.0

Note: Data is not seasonally adjusted and covers workers 16 years of age and older; (1) Figures cover the Boise City, ID Metropolitan Statistical Area
Source: Bureau of Labor Statistics, Local Area Unemployment Statistics

Unemployment Rate

Area	2022											
	Jan.	Feb.	Mar.	Apr.	May	Jun.	Jul.	Aug.	Sep.	Oct.	Nov.	Dec.
City	2.8	2.7	2.5	2.0	2.0	2.4	2.2	2.3	2.3	2.4	2.3	1.8
MSA[1]	3.1	3.0	2.8	2.4	2.2	2.7	2.6	2.7	2.5	2.6	2.5	2.1
U.S.	4.4	4.1	3.8	3.3	3.4	3.8	3.8	3.8	3.3	3.4	3.4	3.3

Note: Data is not seasonally adjusted and covers workers 16 years of age and older; (1) Figures cover the Boise City, ID Metropolitan Statistical Area
Source: Bureau of Labor Statistics, Local Area Unemployment Statistics

Average Wages

Occupation	$/Hr.	Occupation	$/Hr.
Accountants and Auditors	34.92	Maintenance and Repair Workers	20.73
Automotive Mechanics	22.86	Marketing Managers	51.10
Bookkeepers	21.24	Network and Computer Systems Admin.	39.68
Carpenters	21.41	Nurses, Licensed Practical	27.38
Cashiers	13.64	Nurses, Registered	39.06
Computer Programmers	37.89	Nursing Assistants	17.88
Computer Systems Analysts	44.85	Office Clerks, General	17.66
Computer User Support Specialists	26.11	Physical Therapists	43.44
Construction Laborers	19.73	Physicians	148.73
Cooks, Restaurant	15.37	Plumbers, Pipefitters and Steamfitters	28.88
Customer Service Representatives	18.74	Police and Sheriff's Patrol Officers	30.67
Dentists	71.88	Postal Service Mail Carriers	27.00
Electricians	26.06	Real Estate Sales Agents	21.80
Engineers, Electrical	55.65	Retail Salespersons	16.72
Fast Food and Counter Workers	11.97	Sales Representatives, Technical/Scientific	41.57
Financial Managers	56.23	Secretaries, Exc. Legal/Medical/Executive	18.67
First-Line Supervisors of Office Workers	27.15	Security Guards	16.67
General and Operations Managers	38.95	Surgeons	n/a
Hairdressers/Cosmetologists	15.45	Teacher Assistants, Exc. Postsecondary*	14.04
Home Health and Personal Care Aides	13.80	Teachers, Secondary School, Exc. Sp. Ed.*	27.88
Janitors and Cleaners	14.80	Telemarketers	17.64
Landscaping/Groundskeeping Workers	17.90	Truck Drivers, Heavy/Tractor-Trailer	25.05
Lawyers	48.56	Truck Drivers, Light/Delivery Services	24.37
Maids and Housekeeping Cleaners	15.14	Waiters and Waitresses	14.76

Note: Wage data covers the Boise City, ID Metropolitan Statistical Area; (*) Hourly wages were calculated from annual wage data based on a 40 hour work week; n/a not available.
Source: Bureau of Labor Statistics, Metro Area Occupational Employment & Wage Estimates, May 2022

Employment by Industry

Sector	MSA[1]		U.S.
	Number of Employees	Percent of Total	Percent of Total
Construction, Mining, and Logging	32,600	8.4	5.4
Private Education and Health Services	57,500	14.8	16.1
Financial Activities	22,700	5.8	5.9
Government	51,400	13.2	14.5
Information	4,700	1.2	2.0
Leisure and Hospitality	39,400	10.1	10.3
Manufacturing	29,600	7.6	8.4
Other Services	13,100	3.4	3.7
Professional and Business Services	59,900	15.4	14.7
Retail Trade	41,400	10.6	10.2
Transportation, Warehousing, and Utilities	17,300	4.4	4.9
Wholesale Trade	19,300	5.0	3.9

Note: Figures are non-farm employment as of December 2022. Figures are not seasonally adjusted and include workers 16 years of age and older; (1) Figures cover the Boise City, ID Metropolitan Statistical Area
Source: Bureau of Labor Statistics, Current Employment Statistics, Employment, Hours, and Earnings

Employment by Occupation

Occupation Classification	City (%)	MSA[1] (%)	U.S. (%)
Management, Business, Science, and Arts	47.2	40.3	40.3
Natural Resources, Construction, and Maintenance	7.5	10.8	8.7
Production, Transportation, and Material Moving	8.9	11.3	13.1
Sales and Office	20.4	22.1	20.9
Service	16.0	15.5	17.0

Note: Figures cover employed civilians 16 years of age and older; (1) Figures cover the Boise City, ID Metropolitan Statistical Area
Source: U.S. Census Bureau, 2017-2021 American Community Survey 5-Year Estimates

Occupations with Greatest Projected Employment Growth: 2022 – 2024

Occupation[1]	2022 Employment	2024 Projected Employment	Numeric Employment Change	Percent Employment Change
Home Health and Personal Care Aides	17,940	18,580	640	3.6
Office Clerks, General	18,710	19,290	580	3.1
Registered Nurses	15,340	15,880	540	3.5
Customer Service Representatives	19,630	20,160	530	2.7
Heavy and Tractor-Trailer Truck Drivers	12,780	13,260	480	3.8
Carpenters	9,750	10,180	430	4.4
Retail Salespersons	27,960	28,380	420	1.5
General and Operations Managers	13,910	14,320	410	2.9
Construction Laborers	8,570	8,920	350	4.1
Laborers and Freight, Stock, and Material Movers, Hand	9,230	9,560	330	3.6

Note: Projections cover Idaho; (1) Sorted by numeric employment change
Source: www.projectionscentral.com, State Occupational Projections, 2022–2024 Short-Term Projections

Fastest-Growing Occupations: 2022 – 2024

Occupation[1]	2022 Employment	2024 Projected Employment	Numeric Employment Change	Percent Employment Change
Semiconductor Processors	870	930	60	6.9
Electronics Engineers, Except Computer	1,900	2,010	110	5.8
Telecommunications Equipment Installers and Repairers, Except Line Installers	910	960	50	5.5
Postal Service Mail Carriers	2,430	2,560	130	5.3
Drywall and Ceiling Tile Installers	1,520	1,600	80	5.3
Heating, Air Conditioning, and Refrigeration Mechanics and Installers	3,190	3,360	170	5.3
Electrical and Electronics Engineering Technicians	970	1,020	50	5.2
Cement Masons and Concrete Finishers	2,950	3,100	150	5.1
Plumbers, Pipefitters, and Steamfitters	2,040	2,140	100	4.9
Electrical, Electronic, and Electromechanical Assemblers, Except Coil Winders, Tapers, and Fini	1,220	1,280	60	4.9

Note: Projections cover Idaho; (1) Sorted by percent employment change and excludes occupations with numeric employment change less than 50
Source: www.projectionscentral.com, State Occupational Projections, 2022–2024 Short-Term Projections

CITY FINANCES

City Government Finances

Component	2020 ($000)	2020 ($ per capita)
Total Revenues	443,538	1,937
Total Expenditures	442,074	1,931
Debt Outstanding	89,133	389
Cash and Securities[1]	347,315	1,517

Note: (1) Cash and security holdings of a government at the close of its fiscal year, including those of its dependent agencies, utilities, and liquor stores.
Source: U.S. Census Bureau, State & Local Government Finances 2020

City Government Revenue by Source

Source	2020 ($000)	2020 ($ per capita)	2020 (%)
General Revenue			
From Federal Government	10,321	45	2.3
From State Government	35,548	155	8.0
From Local Governments	0	0	0.0
Taxes			
Property	174,063	760	39.2
Sales and Gross Receipts	8,302	36	1.9
Personal Income	0	0	0.0
Corporate Income	0	0	0.0
Motor Vehicle License	0	0	0.0
Other Taxes	9,794	43	2.2
Current Charges	181,150	791	40.8
Liquor Store	0	0	0.0
Utility	0	0	0.0

Source: U.S. Census Bureau, State & Local Government Finances 2020

City Government Expenditures by Function

Function	2020 ($000)	2020 ($ per capita)	2020 (%)
General Direct Expenditures			
Air Transportation	31,755	138	7.2
Corrections	0	0	0.0
Education	0	0	0.0
Employment Security Administration	0	0	0.0
Financial Administration	7,859	34	1.8
Fire Protection	60,763	265	13.7
General Public Buildings	2,967	13	0.7
Governmental Administration, Other	15,154	66	3.4
Health	1,245	5	0.3
Highways	0	0	0.0
Hospitals	0	0	0.0
Housing and Community Development	29,265	127	6.6
Interest on General Debt	3,554	15	0.8
Judicial and Legal	5,773	25	1.3
Libraries	12,766	55	2.9
Parking	0	0	0.0
Parks and Recreation	57,152	249	12.9
Police Protection	68,477	299	15.5
Public Welfare	0	0	0.0
Sewerage	55,820	243	12.6
Solid Waste Management	36,500	159	8.3
Veterans' Services	0	0	0.0
Liquor Store	0	0	0.0
Utility	0	0	0.0

Source: U.S. Census Bureau, State & Local Government Finances 2020

TAXES

State Corporate Income Tax Rates

State	Tax Rate (%)	Income Brackets ($)	Num. of Brackets	Financial Institution Tax Rate (%)[a]	Federal Income Tax Ded.
Idaho	5.8 (f)	Flat rate	1	5.8 (f)	No

Note: Tax rates as of January 1, 2023; (a) Rates listed are the corporate income tax rate applied to financial institutions or excise taxes based on income. Some states have other taxes based upon the value of deposits or shares; (f) Idaho's minimum tax on a corporation is $20. The $10 Permanent Building Fund Tax must be paid by each corporation in a unitary group filing a combined return. Taxpayers with gross sales in Idaho under $100,000, and with no property or payroll in Idaho, may elect to pay 1% on such sales (instead of the tax on net income).
Source: Federation of Tax Administrators, State Corporate Income Tax Rates, January 1, 2023

State Individual Income Tax Rates

State	Tax Rate (%)	Income Brackets ($)	Personal Exemptions ($) Single	Married	Depend.	Standard Ded. ($) Single	Married
Idaho	5.8	Flat rate	(d)	(d)	(d)	13,850	27,700 (d)

Note: Tax rates as of January 1, 2023; Local- and county-level taxes are not included; Federal income tax is not deductible on state income tax returns; (d) These states use the personal exemption/standard deduction amounts provided in the federal Internal Revenue Code.
Source: Federation of Tax Administrators, State Individual Income Tax Rates, January 1, 2023

Various State Sales and Excise Tax Rates

State	State Sales Tax (%)	Gasoline[1] ($/gal.)	Cigarette[2] ($/pack)	Spirits[3] ($/gal.)	Wine[4] ($/gal.)	Beer[5] ($/gal.)	Recreational Marijuana (%)
Idaho	6	0.33	0.57	12.15	0.45	0.15	Not legal

Note: All tax rates as of January 1, 2023; (1) The American Petroleum Institute has developed a methodology for determining the average tax rate on a gallon of fuel. Rates may include any of the following: excise taxes, environmental fees, storage tank fees, other fees or taxes, general sales tax, and local taxes; (2) The federal excise tax of $1.0066 per pack and local taxes are not included; (3) Rates are those applicable to off-premise sales of 40% alcohol by volume (a.b.v.) distilled spirits in 750ml containers. Local excise taxes are excluded; (4) Rates are those applicable to off-premise sales of 11% a.b.v. non-carbonated wine in 750ml containers; (5) Rates are those applicable to off-premise sales of 4.7% a.b.v. beer in 12 ounce containers.
Source: Tax Foundation, 2023 Facts & Figures: How Does Your State Compare?

State Business Tax Climate Index Rankings

State	Overall Rank	Corporate Tax Rank	Individual Income Tax Rank	Sales Tax Rank	Property Tax Rank	Unemployment Insurance Tax Rank
Idaho	15	26	19	10	3	47

Note: The index is a measure of how each state's tax laws affect economic performance. The lower the rank, the more favorable a state's tax system is for business. States without a given tax are given a ranking of 1. The scores/rankings for the District of Columbia do not affect other states. The 2023 index represents the tax climate as of July 1, 2022.
Source: Tax Foundation, State Business Tax Climate Index 2023

TRANSPORTATION

Means of Transportation to Work

Area	Car/Truck/Van Drove Alone	Car-pooled	Public Transportation Bus	Subway	Railroad	Bicycle	Walked	Other Means	Worked at Home
City	73.8	6.9	0.5	0.0	0.0	2.5	2.9	1.6	11.7
MSA[1]	76.4	7.9	0.2	0.0	0.0	1.1	1.9	1.3	11.0
U.S.	73.2	8.6	2.0	1.6	0.5	0.5	2.5	1.5	9.7

Note: Figures are percentages and cover workers 16 years of age and older; (1) Figures cover the Boise City, ID Metropolitan Statistical Area
Source: U.S. Census Bureau, 2017-2021 American Community Survey 5-Year Estimates

Travel Time to Work

Area	Less Than 10 Minutes	10 to 19 Minutes	20 to 29 Minutes	30 to 44 Minutes	45 to 59 Minutes	60 to 89 Minutes	90 Minutes or More
City	13.6	44.5	26.2	11.4	1.6	1.5	1.2
MSA[1]	12.8	33.4	25.0	19.7	5.5	2.2	1.4
U.S.	12.4	28.5	21.0	20.9	8.2	6.2	2.9

Note: Note: Figures are percentages and include workers 16 years old and over; (1) Figures cover the Boise City, ID Metropolitan Statistical Area
Source: U.S. Census Bureau, 2017-2021 American Community Survey 5-Year Estimates

Key Congestion Measures

Measure	1990	2000	2010	2015	2020
Annual Hours of Delay, Total (000)	1,913	5,019	9,599	10,855	5,102
Annual Hours of Delay, Per Auto Commuter	16	28	35	43	18
Annual Congestion Cost, Per Auto Commuter ($)	229	451	692	720	341

Note: Covers the Boise ID urban area
Source: Texas A&M Transportation Institute, 2021 Urban Mobility Report

Freeway Travel Time Index

Measure	1985	1990	1995	2000	2005	2010	2015	2020
Urban Area Index[1]	1.01	1.04	1.06	1.11	1.15	1.15	1.15	1.05
Urban Area Rank[1,2]	100	94	93	79	68	65	67	85

Note: Freeway Travel Time Index—the ratio of travel time in the peak period to the travel time at free-flow conditions. For example, a value of 1.30 indicates a 20-minute free-flow trip takes 26 minutes in the peak (20 minutes x 1.30 = 26 minutes); (1) Covers the Boise ID urban area; (2) Rank is based on 101 larger urban areas (#1 = highest travel time index)
Source: Texas A&M Transportation Institute, 2021 Urban Mobility Report

Public Transportation

Agency Name / Mode of Transportation	Vehicles Operated in Maximum Service[1]	Annual Unlinked Passenger Trips[2] (in thous.)	Annual Passenger Miles[3] (in thous.)
Ada County Highway District, dba ACHD Commuteride			
Vanpool (directly operated)	82	104.0	4,198.7
Boise State University			
Bus (directly operated)	9	42.0	n/a

Note: (1) Number of revenue vehicles operated by the given mode and type of service to meet the annual maximum service requirement. This is the revenue vehicle count during the peak season of the year; on the week and day that maximum service is provided. Vehicles operated in maximum service (VOMS) exclude atypical days and one-time special events; (2) Number of passengers who boarded public transportation vehicles. Passengers are counted each time they board a vehicle no matter how many vehicles they use to travel from their origin to their destination. (3) Sum of the distances ridden by all passengers during the entire fiscal year.
Source: Federal Transit Administration, National Transit Database, 2021

Air Transportation

Airport Name and Code / Type of Service	Passenger Airlines[1]	Passenger Enplanements	Freight Carriers[2]	Freight (lbs)
Boise Air Terminal-Gowen Field (BOI)				
Domestic service (U.S. carriers - 2022)	20	2,230,165	10	48,367,630
International service (U.S. carriers - 2021)	0	0	0	0

Note: (1) Includes all U.S.-based major, minor and commuter airlines that carried at least one passenger during the year; (2) Includes all U.S.-based airlines and freight carriers that transported at least one pound of freight during the year.
Source: Bureau of Transportation Statistics, The Intermodal Transportation Database, Air Carriers: T-100 Domestic Market (U.S. Carriers), 2022; Bureau of Transportation Statistics, The Intermodal Transportation Database, Air Carriers: T-100 International Market (U.S. Carriers), 2021

BUSINESSES

Major Business Headquarters

Company Name	Industry	Rankings	
		Fortune[1]	Forbes[2]
Albertsons	Food and drug stores	52	-
Boise Cascade	Wholesalers, diversified	432	-
JR Simplot	Food, drink & tobacco	-	49
Micron Technology	Semiconductors and other electronic components	127	-
WinCo Foods	Food markets	-	60

Note: (1) Companies that produce a 10-K are ranked 1 to 500 based on 2021 revenue; (2) All private companies with at least $2 billion in annual revenue through the end of their most current fiscal year are ranked 1 to 246; companies listed are headquartered in the city; dashes indicate no ranking
Source: Fortune, "Fortune 500," 2022; Forbes, "America's Largest Private Companies," 2022

Fastest-Growing Businesses

According to *Inc.*, Boise City is home to three of America's 500 fastest-growing private companies: **Proud Source Water** (#223); **Lovevery** (#263); **Gymreapers** (#291). Criteria: must be an independent, privately-held, for-profit, U.S. corporation, proprietorship or partnership as of December 31, 2021; revenues must be at least $100,000 in 2018 and $2 million in 2021; must have four-year operating/sales history. *Inc., "America's 500 Fastest-Growing Private Companies," 2022*

According to Deloitte, Boise City is home to one of North America's 500 fastest-growing high-technology companies: **Tackle** (#17). Companies are ranked by percentage growth in revenue over a four-year period. Criteria for inclusion: company must be headquartered within North America; must own proprietary intellectual property or technology that is sold to customers in products that contributes to a significant portion of the company's operating revenue; must have been in business for a minumum of four years with 2018 operating revenues of at least $50,000 USD/CD and 2021 operating revenues of at least $5 million USD/CD. *Deloitte, 2022 Technology Fast 500™*

Living Environment

COST OF LIVING

Cost of Living Index

Composite Index	Groceries	Housing	Utilities	Trans-portation	Health Care	Misc. Goods/ Services
107.7	96.0	125.6	80.1	114.1	99.6	105.2

Note: The Cost of Living Index measures regional differences in the cost of consumer goods and services, excluding taxes and non-consumer expenditures, for professional and managerial households in the top income quintile. It is based on more than 50,000 prices covering almost 60 different items for which prices are collected three times a year by chambers of commerce, economic development organizations or university applied economic centers in each participating urban area. The numbers shown should be read as a percentage above or below the national average of 100. For example, a value of 115.4 in the groceries column indicates that grocery prices are 15.4% higher than the national average. Small differences in the index numbers should not be interpreted as significant; Figures cover the Boise ID urban area.
Source: The Council for Community and Economic Research, Cost of Living Index, 2022

Grocery Prices

Area[1]	T-Bone Steak ($/pound)	Frying Chicken ($/pound)	Whole Milk ($/half gal.)	Eggs ($/dozen)	Orange Juice ($/64 oz.)	Coffee ($/11.5 oz.)
City[2]	13.59	1.60	2.21	1.69	3.58	5.27
Avg.	13.81	1.59	2.43	2.25	3.85	4.95
Min.	10.17	0.90	1.51	1.30	2.90	3.46
Max.	19.35	3.30	4.32	4.32	5.31	8.59

Note: (1) Values for the local area are compared with the average, minimum and maximum values for all 286 areas in the Cost of Living Index; (2) Figures cover the Boise ID urban area; T-Bone Steak (price per pound); Frying Chicken (price per pound, whole fryer); Whole Milk (half gallon carton); Eggs (price per dozen, Grade A, large); Orange Juice (64 oz. Tropicana or Florida Natural); Coffee (11.5 oz. can, vacuum-packed, Maxwell House, Hills Bros, or Folgers).
Source: The Council for Community and Economic Research, Cost of Living Index, 2022

Housing and Utility Costs

Area[1]	New Home Price ($)	Apartment Rent ($/month)	All Electric ($/month)	Part Electric ($/month)	Other Energy ($/month)	Telephone ($/month)
City[2]	576,971	1,640	-	63.81	63.35	174.27
Avg.	450,913	1,371	176.41	99.93	76.96	190.22
Min.	229,283	546	100.84	31.56	27.15	174.27
Max.	2,434,977	4,569	356.86	249.59	272.24	208.31

Note: (1) Values for the local area are compared with the average, minimum and maximum values for all 286 areas in the Cost of Living Index; (2) Figures cover the Boise ID urban area; New Home Price (2,400 sf living area, 8,000 sf lot, in urban area with full utilities); Apartment Rent (950 sf 2 bedroom/1.5 or 2 bath, unfurnished, excluding all utilities except water); All Electric (average monthly cost for an all-electric home); Part Electric (average monthly cost for a part-electric home); Other Energy (average monthly cost for natural gas, fuel oil, coal, wood, and any other forms of energy except electricity); Telephone (price includes the base monthly rate plus taxes and fees for three lines of mobile phone service).
Source: The Council for Community and Economic Research, Cost of Living Index, 2022

Health Care, Transportation, and Other Costs

Area[1]	Doctor ($/visit)	Dentist ($/visit)	Optometrist ($/visit)	Gasoline ($/gallon)	Beauty Salon ($/visit)	Men's Shirt ($)
City[2]	140.88	86.46	138.00	4.43	39.00	43.44
Avg.	124.91	107.77	117.66	3.86	43.31	34.21
Min.	36.61	58.25	51.79	2.90	22.18	13.05
Max.	250.21	162.58	371.96	5.54	85.61	63.54

Note: (1) Values for the local area are compared with the average, minimum and maximum values for all 286 areas in the Cost of Living Index; (2) Figures cover the Boise ID urban area; Doctor (general practitioners routine exam of an established patient); Dentist (adult teeth cleaning and periodic oral examination); Optometrist (full vision eye exam for established adult patient); Gasoline (one gallon regular unleaded, national brand, including all taxes, cash price at self-service pump if available); Beauty Salon (woman's shampoo, trim, and blow-dry); Men's Shirt (cotton/polyester dress shirt, pinpoint weave, long sleeves).
Source: The Council for Community and Economic Research, Cost of Living Index, 2022

HOUSING

Homeownership Rate

Area	2015 (%)	2016 (%)	2017 (%)	2018 (%)	2019 (%)	2020 (%)	2021 (%)	2022 (%)
MSA[1]	n/a	n/a	n/a	n/a	n/a	n/a	n/a	n/a
U.S.	63.7	63.4	63.9	64.4	64.6	66.6	65.5	65.8

Note: (1) Figures cover the Boise City, ID Metropolitan Statistical Area; n/a not available
Source: U.S. Census Bureau, Housing Vacancies and Homeownership Annual Statistics: 2015-2022

House Price Index (HPI)

Area	National Ranking[2]	Quarterly Change (%)	One-Year Change (%)	Five-Year Change (%)	Since 1991Q1 (%)
MSA[1]	256	-6.44	1.06	96.45	501.63
U.S.[3]	–	0.34	8.41	58.44	289.08

Note: The HPI is a weighted repeat sales index. It measures average price changes in repeat sales or refinancings on the same properties. This information is obtained by reviewing repeat mortgage transactions on single-family properties whose mortgages have been purchased or securitized by Fannie Mae or Freddie Mac since January 1975; (1) Figures cover the Boise City, ID Metropolitan Statistical Area; (2) Rankings are based on annual percentage change for all metro areas containing at least 15,000 transactions over the last 10 years and ranges from 1 to 257; (3) figures based on a weighted average of Census Division estimates using a seasonally adjusted, purchase-only index; all figures are for the period ending December 31, 2022
Source: Federal Housing Finance Agency, Change in FHFA Metropolitan Area House Price Indexes, 2022Q4

Median Single-Family Home Prices

Area	2020	2021	2022[p]	Percent Change 2021 to 2022
MSA[1]	353.9	468.6	491.6	4.9
U.S. Average	300.2	357.1	392.6	9.9

Note: Figures are median sales prices of existing single-family homes in thousands of dollars; (p) preliminary; (1) Figures cover the Boise City, ID Metropolitan Statistical Area
Source: National Association of Realtors, Median Sales Price of Existing Single-Family Homes for Metropolitan Areas, 4th Quarter 2022

Qualifying Income Based on Median Sales Price of Existing Single-Family Homes

Area	With 5% Down ($)	With 10% Down ($)	With 20% Down ($)
MSA[1]	136,966	129,758	115,340
U.S. Average	112,234	106,237	94,513

Note: Figures are preliminary; Qualifying income is based on a mortgage rate of 6.77%. Monthly principal and interest payment is limited to 25% of income; (1) Figures cover the Boise City, ID Metropolitan Statistical Area
Source: National Association of Realtors, Qualifying Income Based on Median Sales Price of Existing Single-Family Homes for Metropolitan Areas, 4th Quarter 2022

Home Value

Area	Under $100,000	$100,000 -$199,999	$200,000 -$299,999	$300,000 -$399,999	$400,000 -$499,999	$500,000 -$999,999	$1,000,000 or more	Median ($)
City	5.2	12.8	27.2	22.0	13.5	17.2	2.3	322,300
MSA[1]	6.9	15.9	25.8	21.3	13.1	14.9	2.1	306,300
U.S.	16.2	24.2	20.1	13.6	8.3	13.6	4.1	244,900

Note: Figures are percentages except for median and cover owner-occupied housing units; (1) Figures cover the Boise City, ID Metropolitan Statistical Area
Source: U.S. Census Bureau, 2017-2021 American Community Survey 5-Year Estimates

Year Housing Structure Built

Area	2020 or Later	2010 -2019	2000 -2009	1990 -1999	1980 -1989	1970 -1979	1960 -1969	1950 -1959	1940 -1949	Before 1940	Median Year
City	0.1	9.0	11.0	22.5	15.8	17.1	7.8	6.8	3.9	6.2	1985
MSA[1]	0.5	14.3	23.2	20.7	9.8	14.1	5.2	4.3	2.8	5.2	1994
U.S.	0.2	7.3	13.6	13.6	13.2	14.8	10.3	10.0	4.7	12.2	1979

Note: Figures are percentages except for Median Year; Note: (1) Figures cover the Boise City, ID Metropolitan Statistical Area
Source: U.S. Census Bureau, 2017-2021 American Community Survey 5-Year Estimates

Gross Monthly Rent

Area	Under $500	$500 -$999	$1,000 -$1,499	$1,500 -$1,999	$2,000 -$2,499	$2,500 -$2,999	$3,000 and up	Median ($)
City	4.2	34.8	42.3	15.3	1.9	0.7	0.8	1,103
MSA[1]	6.5	32.7	40.5	16.2	2.6	0.8	0.7	1,107
U.S.	8.1	30.5	30.8	16.8	7.3	3.1	3.5	1,163

Note: Figures are percentages except for median; Gross rent is the contract rent plus the estimated average monthly cost of utilities (electricity, gas, and water and sewer) and fuels (oil, coal, kerosene, wood, etc.) if these are paid by the renter (or paid for the renter by someone else); (1) Figures cover the Boise City, ID Metropolitan Statistical Area
Source: U.S. Census Bureau, 2017-2021 American Community Survey 5-Year Estimates

HEALTH

Health Risk Factors

Category	MSA[1] (%)	U.S. (%)
Adults aged 18–64 who have any kind of health care coverage	89.5	90.9
Adults who reported being in good or better health	88.5	85.2
Adults who have been told they have high blood cholesterol	32.7	35.7
Adults who have been told they have high blood pressure	28.6	32.4
Adults who are current smokers	12.5	14.4
Adults who currently use e-cigarettes	8.1	6.7
Adults who currently use chewing tobacco, snuff, or snus	4.3	3.5
Adults who are heavy drinkers[2]	7.8	6.3
Adults who are binge drinkers[3]	14.8	15.4
Adults who are overweight (BMI 25.0 - 29.9)	36.0	34.4
Adults who are obese (BMI 30.0 - 99.8)	30.2	33.9
Adults who participated in any physical activities in the past month	80.9	76.3

Note: (1) Figures cover the Boise City, ID Metropolitan Statistical Area; (2) Heavy drinkers are classified as adult men having more than 14 drinks per week and adult women having more than 7 drinks per week; (3) Binge drinkers are classified as males having five or more drinks on one occasion or females having four or more drinks on one occasion
Source: Centers for Disease Control and Prevention, Behaviorial Risk Factor Surveillance System, SMART: Selected Metropolitan Area Risk Trends, 2021

Acute and Chronic Health Conditions

Category	MSA[1] (%)	U.S. (%)
Adults who have ever been told they had a heart attack	4.3	4.0
Adults who have ever been told they have angina or coronary heart disease	3.4	3.8
Adults who have ever been told they had a stroke	3.1	3.0
Adults who have ever been told they have asthma	13.9	14.9
Adults who have ever been told they have arthritis	22.9	25.8
Adults who have ever been told they have diabetes[2]	10.2	10.9
Adults who have ever been told they had skin cancer	8.2	6.6
Adults who have ever been told they had any other types of cancer	7.5	7.5
Adults who have ever been told they have COPD	4.9	6.1
Adults who have ever been told they have kidney disease	2.7	3.0
Adults who have ever been told they have a form of depression	24.7	20.5

Note: (1) Figures cover the Boise City, ID Metropolitan Statistical Area; (2) Figures do not include pregnancy-related, borderline, or pre-diabetes
Source: Centers for Disease Control and Prevention, Behaviorial Risk Factor Surveillance System, SMART: Selected Metropolitan Area Risk Trends, 2021

Health Screening and Vaccination Rates

Category	MSA[1] (%)	U.S. (%)
Adults who have ever been tested for HIV	33.8	34.9
Adults who have had their blood cholesterol checked within the last five years	82.8	85.2
Adults aged 65+ who have had flu shot within the past year	66.2	68.6
Adults aged 65+ who have ever had a pneumonia vaccination	71.8	71.0

Note: (1) Figures cover the Boise City, ID Metropolitan Statistical Area.
Source: Centers for Disease Control and Prevention, Behaviorial Risk Factor Surveillance System, SMART: Selected Metropolitan Area Risk Trends, 2021

Disability Status

Category	MSA[1] (%)	U.S. (%)
Adults who reported being deaf	7.2	7.2
Are you blind or have serious difficulty seeing, even when wearing glasses?	5.2	4.8
Are you limited in any way in any of your usual activities due to arthritis?	8.6	11.1
Do you have difficulty doing errands alone?	6.5	7.0
Do you have difficulty dressing or bathing?	2.8	3.6
Do you have serious difficulty concentrating/remembering/making decisions?	13.3	12.1
Do you have serious difficulty walking or climbing stairs?	10.8	12.8

Note: (1) Figures cover the Boise City, ID Metropolitan Statistical Area.
Source: Centers for Disease Control and Prevention, Behaviorial Risk Factor Surveillance System, SMART: Selected Metropolitan Area Risk Trends, 2021

Mortality Rates for the Top 10 Causes of Death in the U.S.

ICD-10[a] Sub-Chapter	ICD-10[a] Code	Crude Mortality Rate[1] per 100,000 population County[2]	U.S.
Malignant neoplasms	C00-C97	151.4	182.6
Ischaemic heart diseases	I20-I25	68.8	113.1
Other forms of heart disease	I30-I51	52.0	64.4
Other degenerative diseases of the nervous system	G30-G31	55.1	51.0
Cerebrovascular diseases	I60-I69	37.6	47.8
Other external causes of accidental injury	W00-X59	33.2	46.4
Chronic lower respiratory diseases	J40-J47	37.2	45.7
Organic, including symptomatic, mental disorders	F01-F09	26.8	35.9
Hypertensive diseases	I10-I15	22.2	35.0
Diabetes mellitus	E10-E14	18.8	29.6

Note: (a) ICD-10 = International Classification of Diseases 10th Revision; (1) Crude mortality rates are a three-year average covering 2019-2021; (2) Figures cover Ada County.
Source: Centers for Disease Control and Prevention, National Center for Health Statistics. National Vital Statistics System, Mortality 2018-2021 on CDC WONDER Online Database

Mortality Rates for Selected Causes of Death

ICD-10[a] Sub-Chapter	ICD-10[a] Code	Crude Mortality Rate[1] per 100,000 population County[2]	U.S.
Assault	X85-Y09	Unreliable	7.0
Diseases of the liver	K70-K76	17.8	19.8
Human immunodeficiency virus (HIV) disease	B20-B24	Suppressed	1.5
Influenza and pneumonia	J09-J18	6.3	14.7
Intentional self-harm	X60-X84	17.6	14.3
Malnutrition	E40-E46	6.0	4.3
Obesity and other hyperalimentation	E65-E68	1.6	3.0
Renal failure	N17-N19	6.0	15.7
Transport accidents	V01-V99	8.3	13.6
Viral hepatitis	B15-B19	Unreliable	1.2

Note: (a) ICD-10 = International Classification of Diseases 10th Revision; (1) Crude mortality rates are a three-year average covering 2019-2021; (2) Figures cover Ada County; Data are suppressed when the data meet the criteria for confidentiality constraints; Crude mortality rates are flagged as unreliable when the rate would be calculated with a numerator of 20 or less.
Source: Centers for Disease Control and Prevention, National Center for Health Statistics. National Vital Statistics System, Mortality 2018-2021 on CDC WONDER Online Database

Health Insurance Coverage

Area	With Health Insurance	With Private Health Insurance	With Public Health Insurance	Without Health Insurance	Population Under Age 19 Without Health Insurance
City	92.1	75.5	28.2	7.9	4.2
MSA[1]	90.5	72.3	30.7	9.5	5.4
U.S.	91.2	67.8	35.4	8.8	5.3

Note: Figures are percentages that cover the civilian noninstitutionalized population; (1) Figures cover the Boise City, ID Metropolitan Statistical Area
Source: U.S. Census Bureau, 2017-2021 American Community Survey 5-Year Estimates

Number of Medical Professionals

Area	MDs[3]	DOs[3,4]	Dentists	Podiatrists	Chiropractors	Optometrists
County[1] (number)	1,413	168	415	20	273	106
County[1] (rate[2])	283.7	33.7	81.1	3.9	53.3	20.7
U.S. (rate[2])	289.3	23.5	72.5	6.2	28.7	17.4

Note: Data as of 2021 unless noted; (1) Data covers Ada County; (2) Rate per 100,000 population; (3) Data as of 2020 and includes all active, non-federal physicians; (4) Doctor of Osteopathic Medicine
Source: U.S. Department of Health and Human Services, Health Resources and Services Administration, Bureau of Health Professions, Area Resource File (ARF) 2021-2022

EDUCATION

Public School District Statistics

District Name	Schls	Pupils	Pupil/ Teacher Ratio	Minority Pupils[1] (%)	LEP/ELL[2] (%)	IEP[3] (%)
Boise Independent District	51	23,270	15.4	27.7	9.2	12.6

Note: Table includes school districts with 2,000 or more students; (1) Percentage of students that are not non-Hispanic white; (2) Percentage of students that are Limited English Proficient or English Language Learners (2018-19); (3) Percentage of students that have an Individualized Education Program (2019-20).
Source: U.S. Department of Education, National Center for Education Statistics, Common Core of Data, Local Education Agency (School District) Universe Survey: School Year 2021-2022

Best High Schools

According to *U.S. News,* Boise City is home to one of the top 500 high schools in the U.S.: **Sage International School of Boise** (#405). Nearly 18,000 public, magnet and charter schools were ranked based on their performance on state assessments and how well they prepare students for college. *U.S. News & World Report, "Best High Schools 2022"*

Highest Level of Education

Area	Less than H.S.	H.S. Diploma	Some College, No Deg.	Associate Degree	Bachelor's Degree	Master's Degree	Prof. School Degree	Doctorate Degree
City	4.8	20.4	22.8	8.3	28.0	10.8	2.8	2.0
MSA[1]	7.9	24.1	24.9	9.2	22.6	8.1	1.9	1.3
U.S.	11.1	26.5	20.0	8.7	20.6	9.3	2.2	1.5

Note: Figures cover persons age 25 and over; (1) Figures cover the Boise City, ID Metropolitan Statistical Area
Source: U.S. Census Bureau, 2017-2021 American Community Survey 5-Year Estimates

Educational Attainment by Race

Area	High School Graduate or Higher (%)					Bachelor's Degree or Higher (%)				
	Total	White	Black	Asian	Hisp.[2]	Total	White	Black	Asian	Hisp.[2]
City	95.2	96.2	78.5	90.0	82.7	43.7	43.9	31.0	57.7	26.7
MSA[1]	92.1	94.1	80.8	88.2	70.7	33.9	35.1	25.3	52.0	16.6
U.S.	88.9	91.4	87.2	87.6	71.2	33.7	35.5	23.3	55.6	18.4

Note: Figures shown cover persons 25 years old and over; (1) Figures cover the Boise City, ID Metropolitan Statistical Area; (2) People of Hispanic origin can be of any race
Source: U.S. Census Bureau, 2017-2021 American Community Survey 5-Year Estimates

School Enrollment by Grade and Control

Area	Preschool (%)		Kindergarten (%)		Grades 1 - 4 (%)		Grades 5 - 8 (%)		Grades 9 - 12 (%)	
	Public	Private	Public	Private	Public	Private	Public	Private	Public	Private
City	32.0	68.0	77.1	22.9	89.8	10.2	91.7	8.3	88.4	11.6
MSA[1]	35.5	64.5	84.5	15.5	87.8	12.2	90.3	9.7	89.0	11.0
U.S.	58.8	41.2	86.3	13.7	88.3	11.7	88.6	11.4	89.4	10.6

Note: Figures shown cover persons 3 years old and over; (1) Figures cover the Boise City, ID Metropolitan Statistical Area
Source: U.S. Census Bureau, 2017-2021 American Community Survey 5-Year Estimates

Higher Education

Four-Year Colleges			Two-Year Colleges			Medical Schools[1]	Law Schools[2]	Voc/ Tech[3]
Public	Private Non-profit	Private For-profit	Public	Private Non-profit	Private For-profit			
1	3	2	1	0	1	1	1	7

Note: Figures cover institutions located within the Boise City, ID Metropolitan Statistical Area and include main campuses only; (1) includes schools accredited by the Liaison Committee on Medical Education and the American Osteopathic Association's Commission on Osteopathic College Accreditation; (2) includes ABA-accredited schools, schools with provisional ABA accreditation, and state accredited schools; (3) includes all schools with programs that are less than 2 years.
Source: National Center for Education Statistics, Integrated Postsecondary Education System (IPEDS), 2021-22; Wikipedia, List of Medical Schools in the United States, accessed April 10, 2023; Wikipedia, List of Law Schools in the United States, accessed April 10, 2023

EMPLOYERS

Major Employers

Company Name	Industry
Ada County	Administration - local government
Albertsons Companies	Retail grocery
Boise City ISD #1	Education - local government
Boise State University	Education - state government
City of Boise	Municipal government
DirectTV Customer Service	Administrative & waste service
Hewlett-Packard Co.	Manufacturing
Idaho Power Co	Utilities
J R Simplot Co	Manufacturing
McDonalds	Accommodation & food services
Meridian JSD #2	Education - local government
Micron Technology	Manufacturing
Nampa School District #13	Education - local government
St. Alphonsus Regional Medical Center	Health care
St. Lukes Health Systems	Health care
State of Idaho Department of Health	State government
State of Idaho Dept of Corrections	State government
U.S. Postal Service	Transportation & warehousing
U.S. Veterans Administration	Federal government, health care
Wal-Mart Stores	Retail trade
WDS Global	Administrative & waste service
Wells Fargo	Finance & insurance

Note: Companies shown are located within the Boise City, ID Metropolitan Statistical Area.
Source: Hoovers.com; Wikipedia

PUBLIC SAFETY

Crime Rate

Area	Total Crime	Violent Crime Rate				Property Crime Rate		
		Murder	Rape[3]	Robbery	Aggrav. Assault	Burglary	Larceny -Theft	Motor Vehicle Theft
City	1,933.2	1.7	73.5	23.8	193.8	207.2	1,312.6	120.7
Suburbs[1]	1,206.5	1.9	52.0	6.9	189.1	178.4	674.0	104.3
Metro[2]	1,424.4	1.8	58.5	11.9	190.5	187.0	865.5	109.2
U.S.	2,356.7	6.5	38.4	73.9	279.7	314.2	1,398.0	246.0

Note: Figures are crimes per 100,000 population; (1) All areas within the metro area that are located outside the city limits; (2) Figures cover the Boise City, ID Metropolitan Statistical Area; (3) All figures shown were reported using the revised Uniform Crime Reporting (UCR) definition of rape; Due to the transition to the National Incident-Based Reporting System (NIBRS), limited city and metro area data was released for 2021.
Source: FBI Uniform Crime Reports, 2020

Hate Crimes

Area	Number of Quarters Reported	Number of Incidents per Bias Motivation					
		Race/Ethnicity/ Ancestry	Religion	Sexual Orientation	Disability	Gender	Gender Identity
City	4	10	5	2	0	1	1
U.S.	4	5,227	1,244	1,110	130	75	266

Note: Due to the transition to the National Incident-Based Reporting System (NIBRS), limited crime data was released for 2021.
Source: Federal Bureau of Investigation, Hate Crime Statistics 2020

Identity Theft Consumer Reports

Area	Reports	Reports per 100,000 Population	Rank[2]
MSA[1]	1,154	158	236
U.S.	1,108,609	339	-

Note: (1) Figures cover the Boise City, ID Metropolitan Statistical Area; (2) Rank ranges from 1 to 391 where 1 indicates greatest number of identity theft reports per 100,000 population
Source: Federal Trade Commission, Consumer Sentinel Network Data Book 2022

Fraud and Other Consumer Reports

Area	Reports	Reports per 100,000 Population	Rank[2]
MSA[1]	6,044	827	198
U.S.	4,064,520	1,245	-

Note: (1) Figures cover the Boise City, ID Metropolitan Statistical Area; (2) Rank ranges from 1 to 391 where 1 indicates greatest number of fraud and other consumer reports per 100,000 population
Source: Federal Trade Commission, Consumer Sentinel Network Data Book 2022

POLITICS

2020 Presidential Election Results

Area	Biden	Trump	Jorgensen	Hawkins	Other
Ada County	46.1	50.0	2.0	0.1	1.8
U.S.	51.3	46.8	1.2	0.3	0.5

Note: Results are percentages and may not add to 100% due to rounding
Source: Dave Leip's Atlas of U.S. Presidential Elections

SPORTS

Professional Sports Teams

Team Name	League	Year Established

No teams are located in the metro area
Source: Wikipedia, Major Professional Sports Teams of the United States and Canada, April 12, 2023

CLIMATE

Average and Extreme Temperatures

Temperature	Jan	Feb	Mar	Apr	May	Jun	Jul	Aug	Sep	Oct	Nov	Dec	Yr.
Extreme High (°F)	63	70	81	92	98	105	111	110	101	94	74	65	111
Average High (°F)	36	44	53	62	71	80	90	88	78	65	48	38	63
Average Temp. (°F)	29	36	42	49	58	66	74	73	63	52	40	31	51
Average Low (°F)	22	27	31	37	44	52	58	57	48	39	30	23	39
Extreme Low (°F)	-17	-15	6	19	22	31	35	34	23	11	-3	-25	-25

Note: Figures cover the years 1948-1995
Source: National Climatic Data Center, International Station Meteorological Climate Summary, 9/96

Average Precipitation/Snowfall/Humidity

Precip./Humidity	Jan	Feb	Mar	Apr	May	Jun	Jul	Aug	Sep	Oct	Nov	Dec	Yr.
Avg. Precip. (in.)	1.4	1.1	1.2	1.2	1.2	0.9	0.3	0.3	0.6	0.7	1.4	1.4	11.8
Avg. Snowfall (in.)	7	4	2	1	Tr	Tr	0	0	0	Tr	2	6	22
Avg. Rel. Hum. 7am (%)	81	80	75	69	65	59	48	50	58	67	77	81	68
Avg. Rel. Hum. 4pm (%)	68	58	45	35	34	29	22	23	28	36	55	67	42

Note: Figures cover the years 1948-1995; Tr = Trace amounts (<0.05 in. of rain; <0.5 in. of snow)
Source: National Climatic Data Center, International Station Meteorological Climate Summary, 9/96

Weather Conditions

Temperature			Daytime Sky			Precipitation		
5°F & below	32°F & below	90°F & above	Clear	Partly cloudy	Cloudy	0.01 inch or more precip.	0.1 inch or more snow/ice	Thunder-storms
6	124	45	106	133	126	91	22	14

Note: Figures are average number of days per year and cover the years 1948-1995
Source: National Climatic Data Center, International Station Meteorological Climate Summary, 9/96

HAZARDOUS WASTE

Superfund Sites

The Boise City, ID metro area has no sites on the EPA's Superfund Final National Priorities List.
There are a total of 1,165 Superfund sites with a status of proposed or final on the list in the U.S. *U.S. Environmental Protection Agency, National Priorities List, April 12, 2023*

AIR QUALITY

Air Quality Trends: Ozone

	1990	1995	2000	2005	2010	2015	2018	2019	2020	2021
MSA[1]	n/a	n/a	n/a	n/a	n/a	n/a	n/a	n/a	n/a	n/a
U.S.	0.087	0.089	0.081	0.080	0.072	0.067	0.069	0.065	0.065	0.067

Note: (1) Data covers the Boise City, ID Metropolitan Statistical Area; n/a not available. The values shown are the composite ozone concentration averages among trend sites based on the highest fourth daily maximum 8-hour concentration in parts per million. These trends are based on sites having an adequate record of monitoring data during the trend period. Data from exceptional events are included.
Source: U.S. Environmental Protection Agency, Air Quality Monitoring Information, "Air Quality Trends by City, 1990-2021"

Air Quality Index

Area	Percent of Days when Air Quality was...[2]					AQI Statistics[2]	
	Good	Moderate	Unhealthy for Sensitive Groups	Unhealthy	Very Unhealthy	Maximum	Median
MSA[1]	55.1	39.5	4.4	1.1	0.0	168	49

Note: (1) Data covers the Boise City, ID Metropolitan Statistical Area; (2) Based on 365 days with AQI data in 2021. Air Quality Index (AQI) is an index for reporting daily air quality. EPA calculates the AQI for five major air pollutants regulated by the Clean Air Act: ground-level ozone, particle pollution (aka particulate matter), carbon monoxide, sulfur dioxide, and nitrogen dioxide. The AQI runs from 0 to 500. The higher the AQI value, the greater the level of air pollution and the greater the health concern. There are six AQI categories: "Good" AQI is between 0 and 50. Air quality is considered satisfactory; "Moderate" AQI is between 51 and 100. Air quality is acceptable; "Unhealthy for Sensitive Groups" When AQI values are between 101 and 150, members of sensitive groups may experience health effects; "Unhealthy" When AQI values are between 151 and 200 everyone may begin to experience health effects; "Very Unhealthy" AQI values between 201 and 300 trigger a health alert; "Hazardous" AQI values over 300 trigger warnings of emergency conditions (not shown).
Source: U.S. Environmental Protection Agency, Air Quality Index Report, 2021

Air Quality Index Pollutants

Area	Percent of Days when AQI Pollutant was...[2]					
	Carbon Monoxide	Nitrogen Dioxide	Ozone	Sulfur Dioxide	Particulate Matter 2.5	Particulate Matter 10
MSA[1]	0.0	0.8	44.9	(3)	51.2	3.0

Note: (1) Data covers the Boise City, ID Metropolitan Statistical Area; (2) Based on 365 days with AQI data in 2021. The Air Quality Index (AQI) is an index for reporting daily air quality. EPA calculates the AQI for five major air pollutants regulated by the Clean Air Act: ground-level ozone, particle pollution (also known as particulate matter), carbon monoxide, sulfur dioxide, and nitrogen dioxide. The AQI runs from 0 to 500. The higher the AQI value, the greater the level of air pollution and the greater the health concern; (3) Sulfur dioxide is no longer included in this table (as of December 8, 2021) because SO_2 concentrations tend to be very localized and not necessarily representative of broad geographical areas like counties and CBSAs.
Source: U.S. Environmental Protection Agency, Air Quality Index Report, 2021

Maximum Air Pollutant Concentrations: Particulate Matter, Ozone, CO and Lead

	Particulate Matter 10 (ug/m³)	Particulate Matter 2.5 Wtd AM (ug/m³)	Particulate Matter 2.5 24-Hr (ug/m³)	Ozone (ppm)	Carbon Monoxide (ppm)	Lead (ug/m³)
MSA[1] Level	113	9.2	37	0.075	1	n/a
NAAQS[2]	150	15	35	0.075	9	0.15
Met NAAQS[2]	Yes	Yes	No	Yes	Yes	n/a

Note: (1) Data covers the Boise City, ID Metropolitan Statistical Area; Data from exceptional events are included; (2) National Ambient Air Quality Standards; ppm = parts per million; ug/m³ = micrograms per cubic meter; n/a not available.
Concentrations: Particulate Matter 10 (coarse particulate)—highest second maximum 24-hour concentration; Particulate Matter 2.5 Wtd AM (fine particulate)—highest weighted annual mean concentration; Particulate Matter 2.5 24-Hour (fine particulate)—highest 98th percentile 24-hour concentration; Ozone—highest fourth daily maximum 8-hour concentration; Carbon Monoxide—highest second maximum non-overlapping 8-hour concentration; Lead—maximum running 3-month average
Source: U.S. Environmental Protection Agency, Air Quality Monitoring Information, "Air Quality Statistics by City, 2021"

Maximum Air Pollutant Concentrations: Nitrogen Dioxide and Sulfur Dioxide

	Nitrogen Dioxide AM (ppb)	Nitrogen Dioxide 1-Hr (ppb)	Sulfur Dioxide AM (ppb)	Sulfur Dioxide 1-Hr (ppb)	Sulfur Dioxide 24-Hr (ppb)
MSA[1] Level	10	45	n/a	2	n/a
NAAQS[2]	53	100	30	75	140
Met NAAQS[2]	Yes	Yes	n/a	Yes	n/a

Note: (1) Data covers the Boise City, ID Metropolitan Statistical Area; Data from exceptional events are included; (2) National Ambient Air Quality Standards; ppm = parts per million; ug/m³ = micrograms per cubic meter; n/a not available.
Concentrations: Nitrogen Dioxide AM—highest arithmetic mean concentration; Nitrogen Dioxide 1-Hr—highest 98th percentile 1-hour daily maximum concentration; Sulfur Dioxide AM—highest annual mean concentration; Sulfur Dioxide 1-Hr—highest 99th percentile 1-hour daily maximum concentration; Sulfur Dioxide 24-Hr—highest second maximum 24-hour concentration
Source: U.S. Environmental Protection Agency, Air Quality Monitoring Information, "Air Quality Statistics by City, 2021"

Boulder, Colorado

Background

Boulder lies at the foot of the Rocky Mountains in Boulder County. It is the eighth largest city in Colorado. Tourism is a major industry in Boulder, which offers spectacular views from its elevation of 5,430 feet and many outdoor recreation opportunities in over 31,000 acres of open space.

Boulder Valley originally was home to the Southern Arapahoe tribe. The first white settlement was established by gold miners in 1858 near the entrance to Boulder Canyon at Red Rocks. In 1859, the Boulder City Town Company was formed. The town's first schoolhouse was built in 1860, and in 1874 the University of Colorado opened.

Boulder was incorporated as a town in 1871 and as a city in 1882. By 1890, the railroad provided service from Boulder to Golden, Denver, and the western mining camps. In 1905, amidst a weakening economy, Boulder began promoting tourism to boost its finances. The city raised money to construct a first-class hotel, which was completed in 1908 and named Hotel Boulderado.

Although tourism remained strong until the late 1930s, it had begun to decline by World War II. The U.S. Navy's Japanese language school, housed at the city's University of Colorado, proved to be an impressive introduction to the area and students, professionals, and veterans attending the university on the GI Bill, returned to Boulder. Consequently, Boulder's population grew from 12,958 in 1940 to 20,000 in 1950. To accommodate this huge increase, new public buildings, highways, residential areas, and shopping centers developed, spurring further economic expansion.

Many major tech companies have operations in Boulder, as does NOAA, the National Oceanic and Atmospheric Administration.

Boulder is home to the University of Colorado, which houses a robust research park. Cultural venues in the city include the Boulder Dushanbe Teahouse, a gift to the city from its sister city of Dushanbe in Tajikistan, and the Pearl Street Mall, an open-air walkway that was the city's original downtown and is rich with restaurants, cafes, bookstores, and street entertainers. Boulder offers many scenic opportunities for outdoor activities, with parks, recreation areas, and hiking trails. The city boasts hundreds of miles of bike trails, lanes, and paths as a part of their renowned network of citywide bikeways. Boulder has been recognized by the League of American Bicyclists as a leading bicyclist-friendly city.

Keeping with Boulder's tradition of outdoor recreation, BOLDERBoulder, a popular race for over 50,000 runners, joggers, walkers, and wheelers, happens on May 29, 2023, with over 100,000 spectators.

Annual attractions include the Creek Festival in May, Art Fair in July, Fall Festival, and Lights of December Parade. The annual Boulder International Film Festival (BIFF) is held in February and has created a name for itself in the international film community.

Like the rest of Colorado, Boulder enjoys a cool, dry highland continental climate. In winter, the mountains to the west shield the city from the coldest temperatures. Humidity is generally low. Winter storms moving east from the Pacific drop most of their moisture on the mountains to the west, while summer precipitation comes from scattered thunderstorms.

Rankings

General Rankings

- *US News & World Report* conducted a survey of more than 3,600 people and analyzed the 150 largest metropolitan areas to determine what matters most when selecting where to settle down. Boulder ranked #4 out of the top 25 as having the best combination of desirable factors. Criteria: cost of living; quality of life and education; net migration; job market; desirability; and other factors. *money.usnews.com, "The 25 Best Places to Live in the U.S. in 2022-2023," May 17, 2022*

Business/Finance Rankings

- According to *Business Insider*, the Boulder metro area is a prime place to run a startup or move an existing business to. The area ranked #4. More than 300 metro areas were analyzed for factors that were of top concern to new business owners. Data was based on the 2019 U.S. Census Bureau American Community Survey, statistics from the CDC, Bureau of Labor Statistics employment report, and University of Chicago analysis. Criteria: business formations; percentage of vaccinated population; percentage of households with internet subscriptions; median household income; and share of work that can be done from home. *www.businessinsider.com, "The 20 Best Cities for Starting a Business in 2022 Include Baltimore, Boulder, and Boston," January 5, 2022*

- *24/7 Wall St.* used metro data from the Bureau of Labor Statistics' Occupational Employment database to identify the cities with the highest percentage of those employed in jobs requiring knowledge in the science, technology, engineering, and math (STEM) fields as well as average wages for STEM jobs. The Boulder metro area was #4. *247wallst.com, "15 Cities with the Most High-Tech Jobs," January 11, 2020*

- The Boulder metro area appeared on the Milken Institute "2022 Best Performing Cities" list. Rank: #41 out of 200 large metro areas (population over 250,000). Criteria: job growth; wage and salary growth; high-tech output growth; housing affordability; household broadband access. *Milken Institute, "Best-Performing Cities 2022," March 28, 2022*

- *Forbes* ranked the 200 most populous metro areas to determine the nation's "Best Places for Business and Careers." The Boulder metro area was ranked #25. Criteria: costs (business and living); job growth (past and projected); income growth; quality of life; educational attainment (college and high school); projected economic growth; cultural and leisure opportunities; workplace tolerance laws; net migration patterns. *Forbes, "The Best Places for Business and Careers 2019: Seattle Still On Top," October 30, 2019*

Environmental Rankings

- Niche compiled a list of the nation's snowiest cities, based on the National Oceanic and Atmospheric Administration's 30-year average snowfall data. Among cities with a population of at least 50,000, Boulder ranked #6. *Niche.com, Top 25 Snowiest Cities in America, December 10, 2018*

- The U.S. Environmental Protection Agency (EPA) released its list of mid-size U.S. metropolitan areas with the most ENERGY STAR certified buildings in 2022. The Boulder metro was ranked #8 out of 10. *U.S. Environmental Protection Agency, "2023 Energy Star Top Cities," April 26, 2023*

Health/Fitness Rankings

- The Sharecare Community Well-Being Index evaluates 10 individual and social health factors in order to measure what matters to Americans in the communities in which they live. The Boulder metro area ranked #10 in the top 10 across all 10 domains. Criteria: access to healthcare, food, and community resources; housng and transportation; economic security; feeling of purpose; physical, financial, social, and community well-being. *www.sharecare.com, "Community Well-Being Index: 2020 Metro Area & County Rankings Report," August 30, 2021*

Real Estate Rankings

- The Boulder metro area was identified as one of the 20 worst housing markets in the U.S. in 2022. The area ranked #177 out of 187 markets. Criteria: year-over-year change of median sales price of existing single-family homes between the 4th quarter of 2021 and the 4th quarter of 2022. *National Association of Realtors®, Median Sales Price of Existing Single-Family Homes for Metropolitan Areas, 4th Quarter 2022*

- The Boulder metro area was identified as one of the 20 least affordable housing markets in the U.S. in 2022. The area ranked #179 out of 186 markets. Criteria: qualification for a mortgage loan with a 10 percent down payment on a typical home. *National Association of Realtors®, Qualifying Income Based on Sales Price of Existing Single-Family Homes for Metropolitan Areas, 2022*

- Boulder was ranked #185 out of 235 metro areas in terms of housing affordability in 2022 by the National Association of Home Builders (#1 = most affordable). Criteria: the share of homes sold in that area affordable to a family earning the local median income, based on standard mortgage underwriting criteria. *National Association of Home Builders®, NAHB-Wells Fargo Housing Opportunity Index, 4th Quarter 2022*

Safety Rankings

- The National Insurance Crime Bureau ranked 390 metro areas in the U.S. in terms of per capita rates of vehicle theft. The Boulder metro area ranked #82 (#1 = highest rate). Criteria: number of vehicle theft offenses per 100,000 inhabitants in 2021. *National Insurance Crime Bureau, "Hot Spots 2021," September 1, 2022*

Seniors/Retirement Rankings

- From its Best Cities for Successful Aging indexes, the Milken Institute generated rankings for metropolitan areas, weighing data in nine categories—health care, wellness, living arrangements, transportation and convenience, financial characteristics, education, employment, community engagement, and overall livability. The Boulder metro area was ranked #11 overall in the small metro area category. *Milken Institute, "Best Cities for Successful Aging, 2017" March 14, 2017*

- Boulder was identified as #11 of 20 most popular places to retire in the Western region by *Topretirements.com*. The site separated its annual "Best Places to Retire" list by major U.S. regions for 2019. The list reflects the 20 cities that visitors to the website are most interested in for retirement, based on the number of times a city's review was viewed on the website. *Topretirements.com, "20 Best Places to Retire in the West-2019," November 11, 2019*

Sports/Recreation Rankings

- Boulder was chosen as one of America's best cities for bicycling. The city ranked #12 out of 50. Criteria: cycling infrastructure that is safe and friendly for all ages; energy and bike culture. The editors evaluated cities with populations of 100,000 or more. *Bicycling, "The 50 Best Bike Cities in America," October 10, 2018*

Women/Minorities Rankings

- *Travel + Leisure* listed the best cities in and around the U.S. for a memorable and fun girls' trip, even on a budget. Whether it is for a special occasion, to make new memories or just to get away, Boulder is sure to have something for all the ladies in your tribe. *Travel + Leisure, "25 Affordable Girls Weekend Getaways That Won't Break the Bank," November 25, 2022*

- *Women's Health*, together with the site Yelp, identified the 15 "Wellthiest" spots in the U.S. Boulder appeared among the top for happiest, healthiest, outdoorsiest and Zen-iest. *Women's Health, "The 15 Wellthiest Cities in the U.S." July 5, 2017*

Business Environment

DEMOGRAPHICS

Population Growth

Area	1990 Census	2000 Census	2010 Census	2020 Census	Population Growth (%) 1990-2020	Population Growth (%) 2010-2020
City	87,737	94,673	97,385	108,250	23.4	11.2
MSA[1]	208,898	269,758	294,567	330,758	58.3	12.3
U.S.	248,709,873	281,421,906	308,745,538	331,449,281	33.3	7.4

Note: (1) Figures cover the Boulder, CO Metropolitan Statistical Area
Source: U.S. Census Bureau, 1990 Census, 2000 Census, 2010 Census, 2020 Census

Race

Area	White Alone[2] (%)	Black Alone[2] (%)	Asian Alone[2] (%)	AIAN[3] Alone[2] (%)	NHOPI[4] Alone[2] (%)	Other Race Alone[2] (%)	Two or More Races (%)
City	78.8	1.3	6.4	0.6	0.1	4.7	8.1
MSA[1]	77.4	1.0	5.0	0.8	0.1	5.8	10.0
U.S.	61.6	12.4	6.0	1.1	0.2	8.4	10.2

Note: (1) Figures cover the Boulder, CO Metropolitan Statistical Area; (2) Alone is defined as not being in combination with one or more other races; (3) American Indian and Alaska Native; (4) Native Hawaiian and Other Pacific Islander
Source: U.S. Census Bureau, 2020 Census

Hispanic or Latino Origin

Area	Total (%)	Mexican (%)	Puerto Rican (%)	Cuban (%)	Other (%)
City	10.6	6.3	0.4	0.4	3.6
MSA[1]	14.0	9.9	0.5	0.3	3.3
U.S.	18.4	11.2	1.8	0.7	4.7

Note: Persons of Hispanic or Latino origin can be of any race; (1) Figures cover the Boulder, CO Metropolitan Statistical Area
Source: U.S. Census Bureau, 2017-2021 American Community Survey 5-Year Estimates

Age

Area	Under Age 5	Age 5–19	Age 20–34	Age 35–44	Age 45–54	Age 55–64	Age 65–74	Age 75–84	Age 85+	Median Age
City	3.0	19.4	34.9	10.4	10.3	9.1	7.7	3.6	1.6	30.0
MSA[1]	4.2	19.0	23.5	12.7	12.7	12.5	9.7	4.2	1.6	37.6
U.S.	5.6	19.2	20.2	12.7	12.4	13.1	10.0	4.9	1.9	38.8

Note: (1) Figures cover the Boulder, CO Metropolitan Statistical Area
Source: U.S. Census Bureau, 2020 Census

Disability by Age

Area	All Ages	Under 18 Years Old	18 to 64 Years Old	65 Years and Over
City	6.6	2.9	4.7	23.1
MSA[1]	8.4	3.3	6.1	25.5
U.S.	12.6	4.4	10.3	33.4

Note: Figures show percent of the civilian noninstitutionalized population that reported having a disability. Disability status is determined from six types of difficulty: vision, hearing, cognitive, ambulatory, self-care, and independent living. For children under 5 years old, hearing and vision difficulty are used to determine disability status. For children between the ages of 5 and 14, disability status is determined from hearing, vision, cognitive, ambulatory, and self-care difficulties. For people aged 15 years and older, they are considered to have a disability if they have difficulty with any one of the six difficulty types; Note: (1) Figures cover the Boulder, CO Metropolitan Statistical Area
Source: U.S. Census Bureau, 2017-2021 American Community Survey 5-Year Estimates

Ancestry

Area	German	Irish	English	American	Italian	Polish	French[2]	Scottish	Dutch
City	16.2	11.5	11.4	2.4	6.0	3.6	2.4	3.3	1.3
MSA[1]	18.4	11.9	13.4	3.0	5.4	3.2	2.7	3.0	1.7
U.S.	12.8	9.6	8.1	5.7	5.0	2.7	2.2	1.6	1.1

Note: Figures are the percentage of the total population reporting a particular ancestry. The nine most commonly reported ancestries in the U.S. are shown. Figures include multiple ancestries (e.g. if a person reported being Irish and Italian, they were included in both columns); (1) Figures cover the Boulder, CO Metropolitan Statistical Area; (2) Excludes Basque
Source: U.S. Census Bureau, 2017-2021 American Community Survey 5-Year Estimates

Foreign-born Population

Area	Any Foreign Country	Asia	Mexico	Europe	Caribbean	Central America[2]	South America	Africa	Canada
City	10.6	4.4	0.9	3.0	0.2	0.5	0.7	0.3	0.5
MSA[1]	9.9	3.4	2.3	2.3	0.1	0.3	0.6	0.3	0.5
U.S.	13.6	4.2	3.3	1.5	1.4	1.1	1.1	0.8	0.2

Note: (1) Figures cover the Boulder, CO Metropolitan Statistical Area; (2) Excludes Mexico.
Source: U.S. Census Bureau, 2017-2021 American Community Survey 5-Year Estimates

Household Size

Area	One	Two	Three	Four	Five	Six	Seven or More	Average Household Size
City	35.8	35.9	14.0	10.6	2.7	0.5	0.5	2.20
MSA[1]	29.5	36.4	14.8	13.1	4.3	1.5	0.4	2.40
U.S.	28.1	33.8	15.5	12.9	6.0	2.3	1.4	2.60

Note: (1) Figures cover the Boulder, CO Metropolitan Statistical Area
Source: U.S. Census Bureau, 2017-2021 American Community Survey 5-Year Estimates

Household Relationships

Area	Householder	Opposite-sex Spouse	Same-sex Spouse	Opposite-sex Unmarried Partner	Same-sex Unmarried Partner	Child[2]	Grandchild	Other Relatives	Non-relatives
City	40.2	13.0	0.3	3.1	0.2	16.4	0.3	1.6	12.3
MSA[1]	40.1	18.0	0.3	2.8	0.2	23.8	1.0	2.6	6.8
U.S.	38.3	17.5	0.2	2.5	0.2	28.3	2.4	4.8	3.4

Note: Figures are percent of the total population; (1) Figures cover the Boulder, CO Metropolitan Statistical Area; (2) Includes biological, adopted, and stepchildren of the householder
Source: U.S. Census Bureau, 2020 Census

Gender

Area	Males	Females	Males per 100 Females
City	55,982	52,268	107.1
MSA[1]	166,794	163,964	101.7
U.S.	162,685,811	168,763,470	96.4

Note: (1) Figures cover the Boulder, CO Metropolitan Statistical Area
Source: U.S. Census Bureau, 2020 Census

Marital Status

Area	Never Married	Now Married[2]	Separated	Widowed	Divorced
City	56.1	31.2	0.7	2.5	9.5
MSA[1]	38.5	45.5	0.9	3.7	11.4
U.S.	33.8	48.0	1.8	5.6	10.8

Note: Figures are percentages and cover the population 15 years of age and older; (1) Figures cover the Boulder, CO Metropolitan Statistical Area; (2) Excludes separated
Source: U.S. Census Bureau, 2017-2021 American Community Survey 5-Year Estimates

Religious Groups by Family

Area	Catholic	Baptist	Methodist	LDS[2]	Pentecostal	Lutheran	Islam	Adventist	Other
MSA[1]	16.0	0.3	0.7	0.7	0.5	1.7	0.4	0.9	15.2
U.S.	18.7	7.3	3.0	2.0	1.8	1.7	1.3	1.3	11.6

Note: Figures are the number of adherents as a percentage of the total population and cover the eight largest religious groups in the U.S; (1) Figures cover the Boulder, CO Metropolitan Statistical Area; (2) Church of Jesus Christ of Latter-day Saints
Sources: 2020 U.S. Religion Census, Association of Statisticians of American Religious Bodies; The Association of Religion Data Archives (ARDA)

Religious Groups by Tradition

Area	Catholic	Evangelical Protestant	Mainline Protestant	Black Protestant	Islam	Judaism	Hinduism	Orthodox	Buddhism
MSA[1]	16.0	12.7	3.4	n/a	0.4	0.7	0.5	0.2	1.0
U.S.	18.7	16.5	5.2	2.3	1.3	0.6	0.4	0.4	0.3

Note: Figures are the number of adherents as a percentage of the total population; (1) Figures cover the Boulder, CO Metropolitan Statistical Area
Sources: 2020 U.S. Religion Census, Association of Statisticians of American Religious Bodies; The Association of Religion Data Archives (ARDA)

ECONOMY

Gross Metropolitan Product

Area	2020	2021	2022	2023	Rank[2]
MSA[1]	29.7	32.7	35.9	38.1	101

Note: Figures are in billions of dollars; (1) Figures cover the Boulder, CO Metropolitan Statistical Area; (2) Rank is based on 2021 data and ranges from 1 to 381
Source: U.S. Conference of Mayors, U.S. Metro Economies: U.S. Metros Compared to Global and State Economies, June 2022

Economic Growth

Area	2018-20 (%)	2021 (%)	2022 (%)	2023 (%)	Rank[2]
MSA[1]	1.5	5.6	3.5	3.8	49
U.S.	-0.6	5.7	3.1	2.9	–

Note: Figures are real gross metropolitan product (GMP) growth rates and represent average annual percent change; (1) Figures cover the Boulder, CO Metropolitan Statistical Area; (2) Rank is based on 2020 2-year average annual percent change and ranges from 1 to 381
Source: U.S. Conference of Mayors, U.S. Metro Economies: U.S. Metros Compared to Global and State Economies, June 2022

Metropolitan Area Exports

Area	2016	2017	2018	2019	2020	2021	Rank[2]
MSA[1]	956.3	1,012.0	1,044.1	1,014.9	1,110.4	1,078.0	152

Note: Figures are in millions of dollars; (1) Figures cover the Boulder, CO Metropolitan Statistical Area; (2) Rank is based on 2021 data and ranges from 1 to 388
Source: U.S. Department of Commerce, International Trade Administration, Office of Trade and Economic Analysis, Industry and Analysis, Exports by Metropolitan Area, data extracted March 16, 2023

Building Permits

Area	Single-Family			Multi-Family			Total		
	2021	2022	Pct. Chg.	2021	2022	Pct. Chg.	2021	2022	Pct. Chg.
City	41	35	-14.6	253	269	6.3	294	304	3.4
MSA[1]	343	661	92.7	894	981	9.7	1,237	1,642	32.7
U.S.	1,115,400	975,600	-12.5	621,600	689,500	10.9	1,737,000	1,665,100	-4.1

Note: (1) Figures cover the Boulder, CO Metropolitan Statistical Area; Figures represent new, privately-owned housing units authorized (unadjusted data); All permit data are based on estimates with imputation
Source: U.S. Census Bureau, Manufacturing, Mining, and Construction Statistics, Building Permits, 2021, 2022

Bankruptcy Filings

Area	Business Filings			Nonbusiness Filings		
	2021	2022	% Chg.	2021	2022	% Chg.
Boulder County	13	27	107.7	216	160	-25.9
U.S.	14,347	13,481	-6.0	399,269	374,240	-6.3

Note: Business filings include Chapter 7, Chapter 9, Chapter 11, Chapter 12, Chapter 13, Chapter 15, and Section 304; Nonbusiness filings include Chapter 7, Chapter 11, and Chapter 13
Source: Administrative Office of the U.S. Courts, Business and Nonbusiness Bankruptcy, County Cases Commenced by Chapter of the Bankruptcy Code, During the 12-Month Period Ending December 31, 2021 and Business and Nonbusiness Bankruptcy, County Cases Commenced by Chapter of the Bankruptcy Code, During the 12-Month Period Ending December 31, 2022

Housing Vacancy Rates

Area	Gross Vacancy Rate[2] (%)			Year-Round Vacancy Rate[3] (%)			Rental Vacancy Rate[4] (%)			Homeowner Vacancy Rate[5] (%)		
	2020	2021	2022	2020	2021	2022	2020	2021	2022	2020	2021	2022
MSA[1]	n/a	n/a	n/a	n/a	n/a	n/a	n/a	n/a	n/a	n/a	n/a	n/a
U.S.	10.6	10.8	10.5	8.2	8.4	8.2	6.3	6.1	5.8	1.0	0.9	0.8

Note: (1) Figures cover the Boulder, CO Metropolitan Statistical Area; (2) The percentage of the total housing inventory that is vacant; (3) The percentage of the housing inventory (excluding seasonal units) that is year-round vacant; (4) The percentage of rental inventory that is vacant for rent; (5) The percentage of homeowner inventory that is vacant for sale; n/a not available
Source: U.S. Census Bureau, Housing Vacancies and Homeownership Annual Statistics: 2020, 2021, 2022

INCOME

Income

Area	Per Capita ($)	Median Household ($)	Average Household ($)
City	52,057	74,902	123,606
MSA[1]	52,401	92,466	128,190
U.S.	37,638	69,021	97,196

Note: (1) Figures cover the Boulder, CO Metropolitan Statistical Area
Source: U.S. Census Bureau, 2017-2021 American Community Survey 5-Year Estimates

Household Income Distribution

Area	Percent of Households Earning							
	Under $15,000	$15,000 -$24,999	$25,000 -$34,999	$35,000 -$49,999	$50,000 -$74,999	$75,000 -$99,999	$100,000 -$149,999	$150,000 and up
City	13.1	7.8	6.7	8.9	13.6	9.5	13.8	26.6
MSA[1]	7.9	5.7	5.5	8.3	13.7	12.1	18.2	28.5
U.S.	9.4	7.8	8.2	11.4	16.8	12.8	16.3	17.3

Note: (1) Figures cover the Boulder, CO Metropolitan Statistical Area
Source: U.S. Census Bureau, 2017-2021 American Community Survey 5-Year Estimates

Poverty Rate

Area	All Ages	Under 18 Years Old	18 to 64 Years Old	65 Years and Over
City	20.9	8.6	25.6	6.4
MSA[1]	11.0	7.1	13.2	6.4
U.S.	12.6	17.0	11.8	9.6

Note: Figures are percentage of people whose income during the past 12 months was below the poverty level;
(1) Figures cover the Boulder, CO Metropolitan Statistical Area
Source: U.S. Census Bureau, 2017-2021 American Community Survey 5-Year Estimates

EMPLOYMENT

Labor Force and Employment

Area	Civilian Labor Force			Workers Employed		
	Dec. 2021	Dec. 2022	% Chg.	Dec. 2021	Dec. 2022	% Chg.
City	66,246	67,538	2.0	64,727	66,197	2.3
MSA[1]	198,590	201,887	1.7	193,073	197,458	2.3
U.S.	161,696,000	164,224,000	1.6	155,732,000	158,872,000	2.0

Note: Data is not seasonally adjusted and covers workers 16 years of age and older; (1) Figures cover the
Boulder, CO Metropolitan Statistical Area
Source: Bureau of Labor Statistics, Local Area Unemployment Statistics

Unemployment Rate

Area	2022											
	Jan.	Feb.	Mar.	Apr.	May	Jun.	Jul.	Aug.	Sep.	Oct.	Nov.	Dec.
City	2.6	2.7	2.3	2.1	2.2	2.8	3.0	2.4	2.3	2.6	2.7	2.0
MSA[1]	3.1	3.2	2.8	2.4	2.4	2.8	2.9	2.6	2.5	2.8	2.6	2.2
U.S.	4.4	4.1	3.8	3.3	3.4	3.8	3.8	3.8	3.3	3.4	3.4	3.3

Note: Data is not seasonally adjusted and covers workers 16 years of age and older; (1) Figures cover the
Boulder, CO Metropolitan Statistical Area
Source: Bureau of Labor Statistics, Local Area Unemployment Statistics

Average Wages

Occupation	$/Hr.	Occupation	$/Hr.
Accountants and Auditors	46.88	Maintenance and Repair Workers	27.19
Automotive Mechanics	27.50	Marketing Managers	85.56
Bookkeepers	24.94	Network and Computer Systems Admin.	48.32
Carpenters	27.55	Nurses, Licensed Practical	29.85
Cashiers	16.30	Nurses, Registered	44.57
Computer Programmers	71.67	Nursing Assistants	19.72
Computer Systems Analysts	61.71	Office Clerks, General	25.81
Computer User Support Specialists	37.04	Physical Therapists	48.20
Construction Laborers	20.81	Physicians	142.09
Cooks, Restaurant	18.99	Plumbers, Pipefitters and Steamfitters	32.34
Customer Service Representatives	21.92	Police and Sheriff's Patrol Officers	40.88
Dentists	77.69	Postal Service Mail Carriers	28.10
Electricians	28.91	Real Estate Sales Agents	49.41
Engineers, Electrical	61.37	Retail Salespersons	18.86
Fast Food and Counter Workers	16.24	Sales Representatives, Technical/Scientific	n/a
Financial Managers	90.26	Secretaries, Exc. Legal/Medical/Executive	22.19
First-Line Supervisors of Office Workers	34.38	Security Guards	21.46
General and Operations Managers	77.36	Surgeons	n/a
Hairdressers/Cosmetologists	23.64	Teacher Assistants, Exc. Postsecondary*	18.12
Home Health and Personal Care Aides	17.40	Teachers, Secondary School, Exc. Sp. Ed.*	35.67
Janitors and Cleaners	18.80	Telemarketers	17.68
Landscaping/Groundskeeping Workers	21.69	Truck Drivers, Heavy/Tractor-Trailer	26.67
Lawyers	n/a	Truck Drivers, Light/Delivery Services	24.66
Maids and Housekeeping Cleaners	17.31	Waiters and Waitresses	20.98

Note: Wage data covers the Boulder, CO Metropolitan Statistical Area; (*) Hourly wages were calculated from
annual wage data based on a 40 hour work week; n/a not available.
Source: Bureau of Labor Statistics, Metro Area Occupational Employment & Wage Estimates, May 2022

Employment by Industry

Sector	MSA[1]		U.S.
	Number of Employees	Percent of Total	Percent of Total
Construction, Mining, and Logging	5,900	2.9	5.4
Private Education and Health Services	26,300	12.7	16.1
Financial Activities	7,200	3.5	5.9
Government	40,100	19.4	14.5
Information	8,200	4.0	2.0
Leisure and Hospitality	19,600	9.5	10.3
Manufacturing	22,200	10.8	8.4
Other Services	8,300	4.0	3.7
Professional and Business Services	42,400	20.6	14.7
Retail Trade	16,500	8.0	10.2
Transportation, Warehousing, and Utilities	2,200	1.1	4.9
Wholesale Trade	7,400	3.6	3.9

Note: Figures are non-farm employment as of December 2022. Figures are not seasonally adjusted and include workers 16 years of age and older; (1) Figures cover the Boulder, CO Metropolitan Statistical Area
Source: Bureau of Labor Statistics, Current Employment Statistics, Employment, Hours, and Earnings

Employment by Occupation

Occupation Classification	City (%)	MSA[1] (%)	U.S. (%)
Management, Business, Science, and Arts	57.9	54.7	40.3
Natural Resources, Construction, and Maintenance	2.5	5.4	8.7
Production, Transportation, and Material Moving	6.0	7.8	13.1
Sales and Office	17.5	18.2	20.9
Service	16.0	13.9	17.0

Note: Figures cover employed civilians 16 years of age and older; (1) Figures cover the Boulder, CO Metropolitan Statistical Area
Source: U.S. Census Bureau, 2017-2021 American Community Survey 5-Year Estimates

Occupations with Greatest Projected Employment Growth: 2022 – 2024

Occupation[1]	2022 Employment	2024 Projected Employment	Numeric Employment Change	Percent Employment Change
Software Developers	43,570	47,290	3,720	8.5
Stockers and Order Fillers	45,230	48,030	2,800	6.2
Cooks, Restaurant	31,870	34,550	2,680	8.4
Fast Food and Counter Workers	79,850	82,410	2,560	3.2
Accountants and Auditors	42,150	43,910	1,760	4.2
Market Research Analysts and Marketing Specialists	28,150	29,830	1,680	6.0
Home Health and Personal Care Aides	43,200	44,870	1,670	3.9
Registered Nurses	53,590	55,060	1,470	2.7
General and Operations Managers	47,360	48,780	1,420	3.0
Sales Representatives of Services, Except Advertising, Insurance, Financial Services, and Travel	37,310	38,730	1,420	3.8

Note: Projections cover Colorado; (1) Sorted by numeric employment change
Source: www.projectionscentral.com, State Occupational Projections, 2022–2024 Short-Term Projections

Fastest-Growing Occupations: 2022 – 2024

Occupation[1]	2022 Employment	2024 Projected Employment	Numeric Employment Change	Percent Employment Change
Derrick Operators, Oil and Gas	550	640	90	16.4
Roustabouts, Oil and Gas	1,550	1,790	240	15.5
Service Unit Operators, Oil, Gas, and Mining	2,430	2,760	330	13.6
Flight Attendants	4,890	5,490	600	12.3
Epidemiologists	530	590	60	11.3
Information Security Analysts (SOC 2018)	6,100	6,760	660	10.8
Statisticians	1,410	1,550	140	9.9
Veterinary Assistants and Laboratory Animal Caretakers	2,360	2,590	230	9.7
Data Scientists	3,520	3,850	330	9.4
Solar Photovoltaic Installers	530	580	50	9.4

Note: Projections cover Colorado; (1) Sorted by percent employment change and excludes occupations with numeric employment change less than 50
Source: www.projectionscentral.com, State Occupational Projections, 2022–2024 Short-Term Projections

CITY FINANCES

City Government Finances

Component	2020 ($000)	2020 ($ per capita)
Total Revenues	385,049	3,644
Total Expenditures	287,982	2,725
Debt Outstanding	256,751	2,430
Cash and Securities[1]	520,739	4,928

Note: (1) Cash and security holdings of a government at the close of its fiscal year, including those of its dependent agencies, utilities, and liquor stores.
Source: U.S. Census Bureau, State & Local Government Finances 2020

City Government Revenue by Source

Source	2020 ($000)	2020 ($ per capita)	2020 (%)
General Revenue			
From Federal Government	1,542	15	0.4
From State Government	10,175	96	2.6
From Local Governments	788	7	0.2
Taxes			
Property	44,758	424	11.6
Sales and Gross Receipts	166,012	1,571	43.1
Personal Income	0	0	0.0
Corporate Income	0	0	0.0
Motor Vehicle License	0	0	0.0
Other Taxes	30,662	290	8.0
Current Charges	59,184	560	15.4
Liquor Store	0	0	0.0
Utility	30,323	287	7.9

Source: U.S. Census Bureau, State & Local Government Finances 2020

City Government Expenditures by Function

Function	2020 ($000)	2020 ($ per capita)	2020 (%)
General Direct Expenditures			
Air Transportation	1,013	9	0.4
Corrections	0	0	0.0
Education	0	0	0.0
Employment Security Administration	0	0	0.0
Financial Administration	4,740	44	1.6
Fire Protection	22,343	211	7.8
General Public Buildings	6,640	62	2.3
Governmental Administration, Other	6,320	59	2.2
Health	0	0	0.0
Highways	31,012	293	10.8
Hospitals	0	0	0.0
Housing and Community Development	36,671	347	12.7
Interest on General Debt	3,480	32	1.2
Judicial and Legal	5,820	55	2.0
Libraries	9,254	87	3.2
Parking	6,086	57	2.1
Parks and Recreation	69,803	660	24.2
Police Protection	37,307	353	13.0
Public Welfare	0	0	0.0
Sewerage	18,153	171	6.3
Solid Waste Management	0	0	0.0
Veterans' Services	0	0	0.0
Liquor Store	0	0	0.0
Utility	19,586	185	6.8

Source: U.S. Census Bureau, State & Local Government Finances 2020

TAXES

State Corporate Income Tax Rates

State	Tax Rate (%)	Income Brackets ($)	Num. of Brackets	Financial Institution Tax Rate (%)[a]	Federal Income Tax Ded.
Colorado	4.4	Flat rate	1	4.4	No

Note: Tax rates as of January 1, 2023; (a) Rates listed are the corporate income tax rate applied to financial institutions or excise taxes based on income. Some states have other taxes based upon the value of deposits or shares.
Source: Federation of Tax Administrators, State Corporate Income Tax Rates, January 1, 2023

State Individual Income Tax Rates

State	Tax Rate (%)	Income Brackets ($)	Personal Exemptions ($)			Standard Ded. ($)	
			Single	Married	Depend.	Single	Married
Colorado	4.4	Flat rate	(d)	(d)	(d)	13,850	27,700 (d)

Note: Tax rates as of January 1, 2023; Local- and county-level taxes are not included; Federal income tax is not deductible on state income tax returns; (d) These states use the personal exemption/standard deduction amounts provided in the federal Internal Revenue Code.
Source: Federation of Tax Administrators, State Individual Income Tax Rates, January 1, 2023

Various State Sales and Excise Tax Rates

State	State Sales Tax (%)	Gasoline[1] ($/gal.)	Cigarette[2] ($/pack)	Spirits[3] ($/gal.)	Wine[4] ($/gal.)	Beer[5] ($/gal.)	Recreational Marijuana (%)
Colorado	2.9	0.22	1.94	2.28	0.32	0.08	(d)

Note: All tax rates as of January 1, 2023; (1) The American Petroleum Institute has developed a methodology for determining the average tax rate on a gallon of fuel. Rates may include any of the following: excise taxes, environmental fees, storage tank fees, other fees or taxes, general sales tax, and local taxes; (2) The federal excise tax of $1.0066 per pack and local taxes are not included; (3) Rates are those applicable to off-premise sales of 40% alcohol by volume (a.b.v.) distilled spirits in 750ml containers. Local excise taxes are excluded; (4) Rates are those applicable to off-premise sales of 11% a.b.v. non-carbonated wine in 750ml containers; (5) Rates are those applicable to off-premise sales of 4.7% a.b.v. beer in 12 ounce containers; (d) 15% excise tax (levied on wholesale at average market rate); 15% excise tax (retail price)
Source: Tax Foundation, 2023 Facts & Figures: How Does Your State Compare?

State Business Tax Climate Index Rankings

State	Overall Rank	Corporate Tax Rank	Individual Income Tax Rank	Sales Tax Rank	Property Tax Rank	Unemployment Insurance Tax Rank
Colorado	21	7	14	40	36	42

Note: The index is a measure of how each state's tax laws affect economic performance. The lower the rank, the more favorable a state's tax system is for business. States without a given tax are given a ranking of 1. The scores/rankings for the District of Columbia do not affect other states. The 2023 index represents the tax climate as of July 1, 2022.
Source: Tax Foundation, State Business Tax Climate Index 2023

TRANSPORTATION

Means of Transportation to Work

Area	Car/Truck/Van		Public Transportation			Bicycle	Walked	Other Means	Worked at Home
	Drove Alone	Car-pooled	Bus	Subway	Railroad				
City	45.8	4.3	6.5	0.0	0.0	8.8	9.1	1.3	24.3
MSA[1]	60.1	6.6	3.9	0.0	0.0	3.6	4.0	1.1	20.8
U.S.	73.2	8.6	2.0	1.6	0.5	0.5	2.5	1.5	9.7

Note: Figures are percentages and cover workers 16 years of age and older; (1) Figures cover the Boulder, CO Metropolitan Statistical Area
Source: U.S. Census Bureau, 2017-2021 American Community Survey 5-Year Estimates

Travel Time to Work

Area	Less Than 10 Minutes	10 to 19 Minutes	20 to 29 Minutes	30 to 44 Minutes	45 to 59 Minutes	60 to 89 Minutes	90 Minutes or More
City	19.7	44.5	16.1	9.5	5.8	3.2	1.2
MSA[1]	14.5	33.4	20.5	17.6	7.6	4.8	1.6
U.S.	12.4	28.5	21.0	20.9	8.2	6.2	2.9

Note: Note: Figures are percentages and include workers 16 years old and over; (1) Figures cover the Boulder, CO Metropolitan Statistical Area
Source: U.S. Census Bureau, 2017-2021 American Community Survey 5-Year Estimates

Key Congestion Measures

Measure	1990	2000	2010	2015	2020
Annual Hours of Delay, Total (000)	997	2,194	3,362	4,092	2,312
Annual Hours of Delay, Per Auto Commuter	17	30	37	43	23
Annual Congestion Cost, Per Auto Commuter ($)	326	539	660	744	436

Note: Covers the Boulder CO urban area
Source: Texas A&M Transportation Institute, 2021 Urban Mobility Report

Freeway Travel Time Index

Measure	1985	1990	1995	2000	2005	2010	2015	2020
Urban Area Index[1]	1.04	1.08	1.13	1.17	1.20	1.21	1.21	1.08
Urban Area Rank[1,2]	81	62	47	36	36	33	36	44

Note: Freeway Travel Time Index—the ratio of travel time in the peak period to the travel time at free-flow conditions. For example, a value of 1.30 indicates a 20-minute free-flow trip takes 26 minutes in the peak (20 minutes x 1.30 = 26 minutes); (1) Covers the Boulder CO urban area; (2) Rank is based on 101 larger urban areas (#1 = highest travel time index)
Source: Texas A&M Transportation Institute, 2021 Urban Mobility Report

Public Transportation

Agency Name / Mode of Transportation	Vehicles Operated in Maximum Service[1]	Annual Unlinked Passenger Trips[2] (in thous.)	Annual Passenger Miles[3] (in thous.)
Community Transit Network			
Bus (directly operated)	286	20,803.7	93,150.4
Bus (purchased transportation)	194	10,766.8	42,419.1
Commuter Rail (directly operated)	8	763.1	6,809.5
Commuter Rail (purchased transportation)	36	5,822.3	75,820.0
Demand Response (purchased transportation)	278	605.0	5,696.8
Light Rail (directly operated)	111	10,016.2	67,364.6

Note: (1) Number of revenue vehicles operated by the given mode and type of service to meet the annual maximum service requirement. This is the revenue vehicle count during the peak season of the year; on the week and day that maximum service is provided. Vehicles operated in maximum service (VOMS) exclude atypical days and one-time special events; (2) Number of passengers who boarded public transportation vehicles. Passengers are counted each time they board a vehicle no matter how many vehicles they use to travel from their origin to their destination. (3) Sum of the distances ridden by all passengers during the entire fiscal year.
Source: Federal Transit Administration, National Transit Database, 2021

Air Transportation

Airport Name and Code / Type of Service	Passenger Airlines[1]	Passenger Enplanements	Freight Carriers[2]	Freight (lbs)
Denver International (40 miles) (DEN)				
Domestic service (U.S. carriers - 2022)	26	32,145,313	15	277,972,263
International service (U.S. carriers - 2021)	8	661,977	3	3,625,333

Note: (1) Includes all U.S.-based major, minor and commuter airlines that carried at least one passenger during the year; (2) Includes all U.S.-based airlines and freight carriers that transported at least one pound of freight during the year.
Source: Bureau of Transportation Statistics, The Intermodal Transportation Database, Air Carriers: T-100 Domestic Market (U.S. Carriers), 2022; Bureau of Transportation Statistics, The Intermodal Transportation Database, Air Carriers: T-100 International Market (U.S. Carriers), 2021

BUSINESSES

Major Business Headquarters

Company Name	Industry	Rankings	
		Fortune[1]	Forbes[2]
No companies listed	-	-	-

Note: (1) Companies that produce a 10-K are ranked 1 to 500 based on 2021 revenue; (2) All private companies with at least $2 billion in annual revenue through the end of their most current fiscal year are ranked 1 to 246; companies listed are headquartered in the city; dashes indicate no ranking
Source: Fortune, "Fortune 500," 2022; Forbes, "America's Largest Private Companies," 2022

Fastest-Growing Businesses

According to *Inc.*, Boulder is home to two of America's 500 fastest-growing private companies: **Ned** (#364); **RASA** (#369). Criteria: must be an independent, privately-held, for-profit, U.S. corporation, proprietorship or partnership as of December 31, 2021; revenues must be at least $100,000 in 2018 and $2 million in 2021; must have four-year operating/sales history. *Inc., "America's 500 Fastest-Growing Private Companies," 2022*

Living Environment

COST OF LIVING

Cost of Living Index

Composite Index	Groceries	Housing	Utilities	Trans-portation	Health Care	Misc. Goods/ Services
n/a	n/a	n/a	n/a	n/a	n/a	n/a

Note: The Cost of Living Index measures regional differences in the cost of consumer goods and services, excluding taxes and non-consumer expenditures, for professional and managerial households in the top income quintile. It is based on more than 50,000 prices covering almost 60 different items for which prices are collected three times a year by chambers of commerce, economic development organizations or university applied economic centers in each participating urban area. The numbers shown should be read as a percentage above or below the national average of 100. For example, a value of 115.4 in the groceries column indicates that grocery prices are 15.4% higher than the national average. Small differences in the index numbers should not be interpreted as significant; n/a not available.
Source: The Council for Community and Economic Research, Cost of Living Index, 2022

Grocery Prices

Area[1]	T-Bone Steak ($/pound)	Frying Chicken ($/pound)	Whole Milk ($/half gal.)	Eggs ($/dozen)	Orange Juice ($/64 oz.)	Coffee ($/11.5 oz.)
City[2]	n/a	n/a	n/a	n/a	n/a	n/a
Avg.	13.81	1.59	2.43	2.25	3.85	4.95
Min.	10.17	0.90	1.51	1.30	2.90	3.46
Max.	19.35	3.30	4.32	4.32	5.31	8.59

*Note: (1) Values for the local area are compared with the average, minimum and maximum values for all 286 areas in the Cost of Living Index; (2) Figures cover the Boulder CO urban area; n/a not available; **T-Bone Steak** (price per pound); **Frying Chicken** (price per pound, whole fryer); **Whole Milk** (half gallon carton); **Eggs** (price per dozen, Grade A, large); **Orange Juice** (64 oz. Tropicana or Florida Natural); **Coffee** (11.5 oz. can, vacuum-packed, Maxwell House, Hills Bros, or Folgers).*
Source: The Council for Community and Economic Research, Cost of Living Index, 2022

Housing and Utility Costs

Area[1]	New Home Price ($)	Apartment Rent ($/month)	All Electric ($/month)	Part Electric ($/month)	Other Energy ($/month)	Telephone ($/month)
City[2]	n/a	n/a	n/a	n/a	n/a	n/a
Avg.	450,913	1,371	176.41	99.93	76.96	190.22
Min.	229,283	546	100.84	31.56	27.15	174.27
Max.	2,434,977	4,569	356.86	249.59	272.24	208.31

*Note: (1) Values for the local area are compared with the average, minimum and maximum values for all 286 areas in the Cost of Living Index; (2) Figures cover the Boulder CO urban area; n/a not available; **New Home Price** (2,400 sf living area, 8,000 sf lot, in urban area with full utilities); **Apartment Rent** (950 sf 2 bedroom/1.5 or 2 bath, unfurnished, excluding all utilities except water); **All Electric** (average monthly cost for an all-electric home); **Part Electric** (average monthly cost for a part-electric home); **Other Energy** (average monthly cost for natural gas, fuel oil, coal, wood, and any other forms of energy except electricity); **Telephone** (price includes the base monthly rate plus taxes and fees for three lines of mobile phone service).*
Source: The Council for Community and Economic Research, Cost of Living Index, 2022

Health Care, Transportation, and Other Costs

Area[1]	Doctor ($/visit)	Dentist ($/visit)	Optometrist ($/visit)	Gasoline ($/gallon)	Beauty Salon ($/visit)	Men's Shirt ($)
City[2]	n/a	n/a	n/a	n/a	n/a	n/a
Avg.	124.91	107.77	117.66	3.86	43.31	34.21
Min.	36.61	58.25	51.79	2.90	22.18	13.05
Max.	250.21	162.58	371.96	5.54	85.61	63.54

*Note: (1) Values for the local area are compared with the average, minimum and maximum values for all 286 areas in the Cost of Living Index; (2) Figures cover the Boulder CO urban area; n/a not available; **Doctor** (general practitioners routine exam of an established patient); **Dentist** (adult teeth cleaning and periodic oral examination); **Optometrist** (full vision eye exam for established adult patient); **Gasoline** (one gallon regular unleaded, national brand, including all taxes, cash price at self-service pump if available); **Beauty Salon** (woman's shampoo, trim, and blow-dry); **Men's Shirt** (cotton/polyester dress shirt, pinpoint weave, long sleeves).*
Source: The Council for Community and Economic Research, Cost of Living Index, 2022

HOUSING

Homeownership Rate

Area	2015 (%)	2016 (%)	2017 (%)	2018 (%)	2019 (%)	2020 (%)	2021 (%)	2022 (%)
MSA[1]	n/a	n/a	n/a	n/a	n/a	n/a	n/a	n/a
U.S.	63.7	63.4	63.9	64.4	64.6	66.6	65.5	65.8

Note: (1) Figures cover the Boulder, CO Metropolitan Statistical Area; n/a not available
Source: U.S. Census Bureau, Housing Vacancies and Homeownership Annual Statistics: 2015-2022

House Price Index (HPI)

Area	National Ranking[2]	Quarterly Change (%)	One-Year Change (%)	Five-Year Change (%)	Since 1991Q1 (%)
MSA[1]	150	-1.96	10.66	47.80	588.29
U.S.[3]	–	0.34	8.41	58.44	289.08

Note: The HPI is a weighted repeat sales index. It measures average price changes in repeat sales or refinancings on the same properties. This information is obtained by reviewing repeat mortgage transactions on single-family properties whose mortgages have been purchased or securitized by Fannie Mae or Freddie Mac since January 1975; (1) Figures cover the Boulder, CO Metropolitan Statistical Area; (2) Rankings are based on annual percentage change for all metro areas containing at least 15,000 transactions over the last 10 years and ranges from 1 to 257; (3) figures based on a weighted average of Census Division estimates using a seasonally adjusted, purchase-only index; all figures are for the period ending December 31, 2022
Source: Federal Housing Finance Agency, Change in FHFA Metropolitan Area House Price Indexes, 2022Q4

Median Single-Family Home Prices

Area	2020	2021	2022[p]	Percent Change 2021 to 2022
MSA[1]	645.9	782.7	857.8	9.6
U.S. Average	300.2	357.1	392.6	9.9

Note: Figures are median sales prices of existing single-family homes in thousands of dollars; (p) preliminary; (1) Figures cover the Boulder, CO Metropolitan Statistical Area
Source: National Association of Realtors, Median Sales Price of Existing Single-Family Homes for Metropolitan Areas, 4th Quarter 2022

Qualifying Income Based on Median Sales Price of Existing Single-Family Homes

Area	With 5% Down ($)	With 10% Down ($)	With 20% Down ($)
MSA[1]	227,230	215,271	191,352
U.S. Average	112,234	106,237	94,513

Note: Figures are preliminary; Qualifying income is based on a mortgage rate of 6.77%. Monthly principal and interest payment is limited to 25% of income; (1) Figures cover the Boulder, CO Metropolitan Statistical Area
Source: National Association of Realtors, Qualifying Income Based on Median Sales Price of Existing Single-Family Homes for Metropolitan Areas, 4th Quarter 2022

Home Value

Area	Under $100,000	$100,000 -$199,999	$200,000 -$299,999	$300,000 -$399,999	$400,000 -$499,999	$500,000 -$999,999	$1,000,000 or more	Median ($)
City	5.2	3.5	3.6	5.3	6.9	44.1	31.4	790,100
MSA[1]	4.1	2.1	5.7	13.1	16.3	44.3	14.5	575,700
U.S.	16.2	24.2	20.1	13.6	8.3	13.6	4.1	244,900

Note: Figures are percentages except for median and cover owner-occupied housing units; (1) Figures cover the Boulder, CO Metropolitan Statistical Area
Source: U.S. Census Bureau, 2017-2021 American Community Survey 5-Year Estimates

Year Housing Structure Built

Area	2020 or Later	2010 -2019	2000 -2009	1990 -1999	1980 -1989	1970 -1979	1960 -1969	1950 -1959	1940 -1949	Before 1940	Median Year
City	0.1	7.9	7.7	12.0	16.7	19.6	17.7	9.0	1.7	7.7	1977
MSA[1]	0.2	9.4	11.7	19.4	16.4	19.7	10.6	4.8	1.3	6.3	1984
U.S.	0.2	7.3	13.6	13.6	13.2	14.8	10.3	10.0	4.7	12.2	1979

Note: Figures are percentages except for Median Year; Note: (1) Figures cover the Boulder, CO Metropolitan Statistical Area
Source: U.S. Census Bureau, 2017-2021 American Community Survey 5-Year Estimates

Gross Monthly Rent

Area	Under $500	$500 -$999	$1,000 -$1,499	$1,500 -$1,999	$2,000 -$2,499	$2,500 -$2,999	$3,000 and up	Median ($)
City	3.1	6.2	29.1	27.4	16.5	6.4	11.3	1,711
MSA[1]	3.5	7.0	27.3	31.3	15.9	6.9	8.0	1,694
U.S.	8.1	30.5	30.8	16.8	7.3	3.1	3.5	1,163

Note: Figures are percentages except for median; Gross rent is the contract rent plus the estimated average monthly cost of utilities (electricity, gas, and water and sewer) and fuels (oil, coal, kerosene, wood, etc.) if these are paid by the renter (or paid for the renter by someone else); (1) Figures cover the Boulder, CO Metropolitan Statistical Area
Source: U.S. Census Bureau, 2017-2021 American Community Survey 5-Year Estimates

HEALTH

Health Risk Factors

Category	MSA[1] (%)	U.S. (%)
Adults aged 18–64 who have any kind of health care coverage	n/a	90.9
Adults who reported being in good or better health	n/a	85.2
Adults who have been told they have high blood cholesterol	n/a	35.7
Adults who have been told they have high blood pressure	n/a	32.4
Adults who are current smokers	n/a	14.4
Adults who currently use e-cigarettes	n/a	6.7
Adults who currently use chewing tobacco, snuff, or snus	n/a	3.5
Adults who are heavy drinkers[2]	n/a	6.3
Adults who are binge drinkers[3]	n/a	15.4
Adults who are overweight (BMI 25.0 - 29.9)	n/a	34.4
Adults who are obese (BMI 30.0 - 99.8)	n/a	33.9
Adults who participated in any physical activities in the past month	n/a	76.3

Note: (1) Figures for the Boulder, CO Metropolitan Statistical Area were not available.
(2) Heavy drinkers are classified as adult men having more than 14 drinks per week and adult women having more than 7 drinks per week; (3) Binge drinkers are classified as males having five or more drinks on one occasion or females having four or more drinks on one occasion
Source: Centers for Disease Control and Prevention, Behaviorial Risk Factor Surveillance System, SMART: Selected Metropolitan Area Risk Trends, 2021

Acute and Chronic Health Conditions

Category	MSA[1] (%)	U.S. (%)
Adults who have ever been told they had a heart attack	n/a	4.0
Adults who have ever been told they have angina or coronary heart disease	n/a	3.8
Adults who have ever been told they had a stroke	n/a	3.0
Adults who have ever been told they have asthma	n/a	14.9
Adults who have ever been told they have arthritis	n/a	25.8
Adults who have ever been told they have diabetes[2]	n/a	10.9
Adults who have ever been told they had skin cancer	n/a	6.6
Adults who have ever been told they had any other types of cancer	n/a	7.5
Adults who have ever been told they have COPD	n/a	6.1
Adults who have ever been told they have kidney disease	n/a	3.0
Adults who have ever been told they have a form of depression	n/a	20.5

Note: (1) Figures for the Boulder, CO Metropolitan Statistical Area were not available.
(2) Figures do not include pregnancy-related, borderline, or pre-diabetes
Source: Centers for Disease Control and Prevention, Behaviorial Risk Factor Surveillance System, SMART: Selected Metropolitan Area Risk Trends, 2021

Health Screening and Vaccination Rates

Category	MSA[1] (%)	U.S. (%)
Adults who have ever been tested for HIV	n/a	34.9
Adults who have had their blood cholesterol checked within the last five years	n/a	85.2
Adults aged 65+ who have had flu shot within the past year	n/a	68.6
Adults aged 65+ who have ever had a pneumonia vaccination	n/a	71.0

Note: (1) Figures for the Boulder, CO Metropolitan Statistical Area were not available.
Source: Centers for Disease Control and Prevention, Behaviorial Risk Factor Surveillance System, SMART: Selected Metropolitan Area Risk Trends, 2021

Disability Status

Category	MSA[1] (%)	U.S. (%)
Adults who reported being deaf	n/a	7.2
Are you blind or have serious difficulty seeing, even when wearing glasses?	n/a	4.8
Are you limited in any way in any of your usual activities due to arthritis?	n/a	11.1
Do you have difficulty doing errands alone?	n/a	7.0
Do you have difficulty dressing or bathing?	n/a	3.6
Do you have serious difficulty concentrating/remembering/making decisions?	n/a	12.1
Do you have serious difficulty walking or climbing stairs?	n/a	12.8

Note: (1) Figures for the Boulder, CO Metropolitan Statistical Area were not available.
Source: Centers for Disease Control and Prevention, Behaviorial Risk Factor Surveillance System, SMART: Selected Metropolitan Area Risk Trends, 2021

Mortality Rates for the Top 10 Causes of Death in the U.S.

ICD-10[a] Sub-Chapter	ICD-10[a] Code	Crude Mortality Rate[1] per 100,000 population	
		County[2]	U.S.
Malignant neoplasms	C00-C97	126.6	182.6
Ischaemic heart diseases	I20-I25	57.1	113.1
Other forms of heart disease	I30-I51	40.8	64.4
Other degenerative diseases of the nervous system	G30-G31	45.3	51.0
Cerebrovascular diseases	I60-I69	39.2	47.8
Other external causes of accidental injury	W00-X59	34.6	46.4
Chronic lower respiratory diseases	J40-J47	26.9	45.7
Organic, including symptomatic, mental disorders	F01-F09	28.2	35.9
Hypertensive diseases	I10-I15	22.8	35.0
Diabetes mellitus	E10-E14	11.3	29.6

Note: (a) ICD-10 = International Classification of Diseases 10th Revision; (1) Crude mortality rates are a three-year average covering 2019-2021; (2) Figures cover Boulder County.
Source: Centers for Disease Control and Prevention, National Center for Health Statistics. National Vital Statistics System, Mortality 2018-2021 on CDC WONDER Online Database

Mortality Rates for Selected Causes of Death

ICD-10[a] Sub-Chapter	ICD-10[a] Code	Crude Mortality Rate[1] per 100,000 population	
		County[2]	U.S.
Assault	X85-Y09	2.8	7.0
Diseases of the liver	K70-K76	15.6	19.8
Human immunodeficiency virus (HIV) disease	B20-B24	Suppressed	1.5
Influenza and pneumonia	J09-J18	6.9	14.7
Intentional self-harm	X60-X84	20.0	14.3
Malnutrition	E40-E46	5.9	4.3
Obesity and other hyperalimentation	E65-E68	Unreliable	3.0
Renal failure	N17-N19	6.3	15.7
Transport accidents	V01-V99	10.1	13.6
Viral hepatitis	B15-B19	Suppressed	1.2

Note: (a) ICD-10 = International Classification of Diseases 10th Revision; (1) Crude mortality rates are a three-year average covering 2019-2021; (2) Figures cover Boulder County; Data are suppressed when the data meet the criteria for confidentiality constraints; Crude mortality rates are flagged as unreliable when the rate would be calculated with a numerator of 20 or less.
Source: Centers for Disease Control and Prevention, National Center for Health Statistics. National Vital Statistics System, Mortality 2018-2021 on CDC WONDER Online Database

Health Insurance Coverage

Area	With Health Insurance	With Private Health Insurance	With Public Health Insurance	Without Health Insurance	Population Under Age 19 Without Health Insurance
City	96.0	83.6	21.0	4.0	1.1
MSA[1]	95.4	79.9	26.0	4.6	2.3
U.S.	91.2	67.8	35.4	8.8	5.3

Note: Figures are percentages that cover the civilian noninstitutionalized population; (1) Figures cover the Boulder, CO Metropolitan Statistical Area
Source: U.S. Census Bureau, 2017-2021 American Community Survey 5-Year Estimates

Number of Medical Professionals

Area	MDs[3]	DOs[3,4]	Dentists	Podiatrists	Chiropractors	Optometrists
County[1] (number)	1,195	105	355	20	273	92
County[1] (rate[2])	361.2	31.7	107.7	6.1	82.8	27.9
U.S. (rate[2])	289.3	23.5	72.5	6.2	28.7	17.4

Note: Data as of 2021 unless noted; (1) Data covers Boulder County; (2) Rate per 100,000 population; (3) Data as of 2020 and includes all active, non-federal physicians; (4) Doctor of Osteopathic Medicine
Source: U.S. Department of Health and Human Services, Health Resources and Services Administration, Bureau of Health Professions, Area Resource File (ARF) 2021-2022

EDUCATION

Public School District Statistics

District Name	Schls	Pupils	Pupil/ Teacher Ratio	Minority Pupils[1] (%)	LEP/ELL[2] (%)	IEP[3] (%)
Boulder Valley SD No. Re2	56	29,008	16.9	32.9	6.3	n/a

Note: Table includes school districts with 2,000 or more students; (1) Percentage of students that are not non-Hispanic white; (2) Percentage of students that are Limited English Proficient or English Language Learners (2018-19); (3) Percentage of students that have an Individualized Education Program (2019-20).
Source: U.S. Department of Education, National Center for Education Statistics, Common Core of Data, Local Education Agency (School District) Universe Survey: School Year 2021-2022

Best High Schools

According to *U.S. News,* Boulder is home to one of the top 500 high schools in the U.S.: **Fairview High School** (#450). Nearly 18,000 public, magnet and charter schools were ranked based on their performance on state assessments and how well they prepare students for college. *U.S. News & World Report, "Best High Schools 2022"*

Highest Level of Education

Area	Less than H.S.	H.S. Diploma	Some College, No Deg.	Associate Degree	Bachelor's Degree	Master's Degree	Prof. School Degree	Doctorate Degree
City	3.1	5.9	10.6	3.6	37.1	25.0	5.7	9.0
MSA[1]	4.5	11.1	15.0	6.6	34.5	19.1	3.9	5.3
U.S.	11.1	26.5	20.0	8.7	20.6	9.3	2.2	1.5

Note: Figures cover persons age 25 and over; (1) Figures cover the Boulder, CO Metropolitan Statistical Area
Source: U.S. Census Bureau, 2017-2021 American Community Survey 5-Year Estimates

Educational Attainment by Race

Area	High School Graduate or Higher (%)					Bachelor's Degree or Higher (%)				
	Total	White	Black	Asian	Hisp.[2]	Total	White	Black	Asian	Hisp.[2]
City	96.9	98.2	89.2	95.5	81.4	76.8	78.0	34.2	84.3	51.2
MSA[1]	95.5	97.0	86.9	92.5	75.8	62.9	64.6	30.4	70.8	31.3
U.S.	88.9	91.4	87.2	87.6	71.2	33.7	35.5	23.3	55.6	18.4

Note: Figures shown cover persons 25 years old and over; (1) Figures cover the Boulder, CO Metropolitan Statistical Area; (2) People of Hispanic origin can be of any race
Source: U.S. Census Bureau, 2017-2021 American Community Survey 5-Year Estimates

School Enrollment by Grade and Control

Area	Preschool (%)		Kindergarten (%)		Grades 1 - 4 (%)		Grades 5 - 8 (%)		Grades 9 - 12 (%)	
	Public	Private	Public	Private	Public	Private	Public	Private	Public	Private
City	50.4	49.6	88.4	11.6	88.7	11.3	90.1	9.9	89.7	10.3
MSA[1]	50.1	49.9	84.8	15.2	90.1	9.9	90.4	9.6	94.6	5.4
U.S.	58.8	41.2	86.3	13.7	88.3	11.7	88.6	11.4	89.4	10.6

Note: Figures shown cover persons 3 years old and over; (1) Figures cover the Boulder, CO Metropolitan Statistical Area
Source: U.S. Census Bureau, 2017-2021 American Community Survey 5-Year Estimates

Higher Education

Four-Year Colleges			Two-Year Colleges			Medical Schools[1]	Law Schools[2]	Voc/ Tech[3]
Public	Private Non-profit	Private For-profit	Public	Private Non-profit	Private For-profit			
1	2	1	0	0	1	0	1	1

Note: Figures cover institutions located within the Boulder, CO Metropolitan Statistical Area and include main campuses only; (1) includes schools accredited by the Liaison Committee on Medical Education and the American Osteopathic Association's Commission on Osteopathic College Accreditation; (2) includes ABA-accredited schools, schools with provisional ABA accreditation, and state accredited schools; (3) includes all schools with programs that are less than 2 years.
Source: National Center for Education Statistics, Integrated Postsecondary Education System (IPEDS), 2021-22; Wikipedia, List of Medical Schools in the United States, accessed April 10, 2023; Wikipedia, List of Law Schools in the United States, accessed April 10, 2023

According to *U.S. News & World Report,* the Boulder, CO metro area is home to one of the top 200 national universities in the U.S.: **University of Colorado Boulder** (#97 tie). The indicators used to capture academic quality fall into a number of categories: assessment by administrators at peer institutions; retention of students; faculty resources; student selectivity; financial resources; alumni giving; high school counselor ratings of colleges; and graduation rate. *U.S. News & World Report, "America's Best Colleges 2023"*

According to *U.S. News & World Report,* the Boulder, CO metro area is home to one of the top 100 law schools in the U.S.: **University of Colorado—Boulder** (#49 tie). The rankings are based on a weighted average of 12 measures of quality: peer assessment score; assessment score by lawyers/judges; median LSAT scores; median undergrad GPA; acceptance rate; employment rates for graduates; placement success; bar passage rate; faculty resources; expenditures per student; student/faculty ratio; and library resources. *U.S. News & World Report, "America's Best Graduate Schools, Law, 2023"*

According to *U.S. News & World Report,* the Boulder, CO metro area is home to one of the top 75 business schools in the U.S.: **University of Colorado—Boulder (Leeds)** (#67 tie). The rankings are based on a weighted average of the following nine measures: quality assessment; peer assessment; recruiter assessment; placement success; mean starting salary and bonus; student selectivity; mean

GMAT and GRE scores; mean undergraduate GPA; and acceptance rate. *U.S. News & World Report, "America's Best Graduate Schools, Business, 2023"*

EMPLOYERS

Major Employers

Company Name	Industry
Agilent Technologies	Instruments to measure electricity
America's Note Network	Mortgage bankers & loan correspondents
Ball Aerospace & Technologies Corp.	Search & navigation equipment
Ball Corporation	Space research & technology
Corden Pharma Colorado	Pharmaceutical preparations
County of Boulder	County government
Crispin Porter Bogusky	Business services at non-commercial site
Health Carechain	Medical field-related associations
IBM	Magnetic storage devices, computer
Lockheed Martin Corporation	Search & navigation equipment
Micro Motion	Liquid meters
National Oceanic and Atmospheric Admin	Environmental protection agency, government
Natl Inst of Standards & Technology	Commercial physical research
Qualcomm Incorporated	Integrated circuits, semiconductor networks
Staffing Solutions Southwest	Temporary help services
The Regents of the University of Colorado	Noncommercial research organizations
Tyco Healthcare Group	Medical instruments & equipment, blood & bone work
University Corp for Atmospheric Research	Noncommercial research organizations
University of Colorado	Colleges & universities
Wall Street On Demand	Financial services
Whole Foods Market	Grocery stores

Note: Companies shown are located within the Boulder, CO Metropolitan Statistical Area.
Source: Hoovers.com; Wikipedia

PUBLIC SAFETY

Crime Rate

Area	Total Crime	Violent Crime Rate				Property Crime Rate		
		Murder	Rape[3]	Robbery	Aggrav. Assault	Burglary	Larceny -Theft	Motor Vehicle Theft
City	4,092.0	1.9	29.1	67.5	223.3	613.5	2,808.7	348.0
Suburbs[1]	2,552.6	0.9	66.0	30.7	181.8	304.8	1,686.2	282.2
Metro[2]	3,053.3	1.2	54.0	42.7	195.3	405.2	2,051.3	303.6
U.S.	2,356.7	6.5	38.4	73.9	279.7	314.2	1,398.0	246.0

Note: Figures are crimes per 100,000 population; (1) All areas within the metro area that are located outside the city limits; (2) Figures cover the Boulder, CO Metropolitan Statistical Area; (3) All figures shown were reported using the revised Uniform Crime Reporting (UCR) definition of rape; Due to the transition to the National Incident-Based Reporting System (NIBRS), limited city and metro area data was released for 2021.
Source: FBI Uniform Crime Reports, 2020

Hate Crimes

Area	Number of Quarters Reported	Number of Incidents per Bias Motivation					
		Race/Ethnicity/ Ancestry	Religion	Sexual Orientation	Disability	Gender	Gender Identity
City	4	8	1	1	0	0	0
U.S.	4	5,227	1,244	1,110	130	75	266

Note: Due to the transition to the National Incident-Based Reporting System (NIBRS), limited crime data was released for 2021.
Source: Federal Bureau of Investigation, Hate Crime Statistics 2020

Identity Theft Consumer Reports

Area	Reports	Reports per 100,000 Population	Rank[2]
MSA[1]	598	184	191
U.S.	1,108,609	339	-

Note: (1) Figures cover the Boulder, CO Metropolitan Statistical Area; (2) Rank ranges from 1 to 391 where 1 indicates greatest number of identity theft reports per 100,000 population
Source: Federal Trade Commission, Consumer Sentinel Network Data Book 2022

Fraud and Other Consumer Reports

Area	Reports	Reports per 100,000 Population	Rank[2]
MSA[1]	3,367	1,037	82
U.S.	4,064,520	1,245	-

Note: (1) Figures cover the Boulder, CO Metropolitan Statistical Area; (2) Rank ranges from 1 to 391 where 1 indicates greatest number of fraud and other consumer reports per 100,000 population
Source: Federal Trade Commission, Consumer Sentinel Network Data Book 2022

POLITICS

2020 Presidential Election Results

Area	Biden	Trump	Jorgensen	Hawkins	Other
Boulder County	77.2	20.6	1.2	0.3	0.6
U.S.	51.3	46.8	1.2	0.3	0.5

Note: Results are percentages and may not add to 100% due to rounding
Source: Dave Leip's Atlas of U.S. Presidential Elections

SPORTS

Professional Sports Teams

Team Name	League	Year Established

No teams are located in the metro area
Source: Wikipedia, Major Professional Sports Teams of the United States and Canada, April 12, 2023

CLIMATE

Average and Extreme Temperatures

Temperature	Jan	Feb	Mar	Apr	May	Jun	Jul	Aug	Sep	Oct	Nov	Dec	Yr.
Extreme High (°F)	73	76	84	90	93	102	103	100	97	89	79	75	103
Average High (°F)	43	47	52	62	71	81	88	86	77	67	52	45	64
Average Temp. (°F)	30	34	39	48	58	67	73	72	63	52	39	32	51
Average Low (°F)	16	20	25	34	44	53	59	57	48	37	25	18	37
Extreme Low (°F)	-25	-25	-10	-2	22	30	43	41	17	3	-8	-25	-25

Note: Figures cover the years 1948-1992
Source: National Climatic Data Center, International Station Meteorological Climate Summary, 9/96

Average Precipitation/Snowfall/Humidity

Precip./Humidity	Jan	Feb	Mar	Apr	May	Jun	Jul	Aug	Sep	Oct	Nov	Dec	Yr.
Avg. Precip. (in.)	0.6	0.6	1.3	1.7	2.5	1.7	1.9	1.5	1.1	1.0	0.9	0.6	15.5
Avg. Snowfall (in.)	9	7	14	9	2	Tr	0	0	2	4	9	8	63
Avg. Rel. Hum. 5am (%)	62	65	67	66	70	68	67	68	66	63	66	63	66
Avg. Rel. Hum. 5pm (%)	49	44	40	35	38	34	34	34	32	34	47	50	39

Note: Figures cover the years 1948-1992; Tr = Trace amounts (<0.05 in. of rain; <0.5 in. of snow)
Source: National Climatic Data Center, International Station Meteorological Climate Summary, 9/96

Weather Conditions

Temperature			Daytime Sky			Precipitation		
10°F & below	32°F & below	90°F & above	Clear	Partly cloudy	Cloudy	0.01 inch or more precip.	0.1 inch or more snow/ice	Thunder-storms
24	155	33	99	177	89	90	38	39

Note: Figures are average number of days per year and cover the years 1948-1992
Source: National Climatic Data Center, International Station Meteorological Climate Summary, 9/96

HAZARDOUS WASTE

Superfund Sites

The Boulder, CO metro area is home to two sites on the EPA's Superfund National Priorities List: **Captain Jack Mill** (final); **Marshall Landfill** (final). There are a total of 1,165 Superfund sites with a status of proposed or final on the list in the U.S. *U.S. Environmental Protection Agency, National Priorities List, April 12, 2023*

AIR QUALITY

Air Quality Trends: Ozone

	1990	1995	2000	2005	2010	2015	2018	2019	2020	2021
MSA[1]	n/a	n/a	n/a	n/a	n/a	n/a	n/a	n/a	n/a	n/a
U.S.	0.087	0.089	0.081	0.080	0.072	0.067	0.069	0.065	0.065	0.067

Note: (1) Data covers the Boulder, CO Metropolitan Statistical Area; n/a not available. The values shown are the composite ozone concentration averages among trend sites based on the highest fourth daily maximum 8-hour concentration in parts per million. These trends are based on sites having an adequate record of monitoring data during the trend period. Data from exceptional events are included.
Source: U.S. Environmental Protection Agency, Air Quality Monitoring Information, "Air Quality Trends by City, 1990-2021"

Air Quality Index

Area	Percent of Days when Air Quality was...[2]					AQI Statistics[2]	
	Good	Moderate	Unhealthy for Sensitive Groups	Unhealthy	Very Unhealthy	Maximum	Median
MSA[1]	55.9	34.5	8.8	0.8	0.0	159	48

Note: (1) Data covers the Boulder, CO Metropolitan Statistical Area; (2) Based on 365 days with AQI data in 2021. Air Quality Index (AQI) is an index for reporting daily air quality. EPA calculates the AQI for five major air pollutants regulated by the Clean Air Act: ground-level ozone, particle pollution (aka particulate matter), carbon monoxide, sulfur dioxide, and nitrogen dioxide. The AQI runs from 0 to 500. The higher the AQI value, the greater the level of air pollution and the greater the health concern. There are six AQI categories: "Good" AQI is between 0 and 50. Air quality is considered satisfactory; "Moderate" AQI is between 51 and 100. Air quality is acceptable; "Unhealthy for Sensitive Groups" When AQI values are between 101 and 150, members of sensitive groups may experience health effects; "Unhealthy" When AQI values are between 151 and 200 everyone may begin to experience health effects; "Very Unhealthy" AQI values between 201 and 300 trigger a health alert; "Hazardous" AQI values over 300 trigger warnings of emergency conditions (not shown).
Source: U.S. Environmental Protection Agency, Air Quality Index Report, 2021

Air Quality Index Pollutants

Area	Percent of Days when AQI Pollutant was...[2]					
	Carbon Monoxide	Nitrogen Dioxide	Ozone	Sulfur Dioxide	Particulate Matter 2.5	Particulate Matter 10
MSA[1]	0.0	0.0	74.8	(3)	24.7	0.5

Note: (1) Data covers the Boulder, CO Metropolitan Statistical Area; (2) Based on 365 days with AQI data in 2021. The Air Quality Index (AQI) is an index for reporting daily air quality. EPA calculates the AQI for five major air pollutants regulated by the Clean Air Act: ground-level ozone, particle pollution (also known as particulate matter), carbon monoxide, sulfur dioxide, and nitrogen dioxide. The AQI runs from 0 to 500. The higher the AQI value, the greater the level of air pollution and the greater the health concern; (3) Sulfur dioxide is no longer included in this table (as of December 8, 2021) because SO_2 concentrations tend to be very localized and not necessarily representative of broad geographical areas like counties and CBSAs.
Source: U.S. Environmental Protection Agency, Air Quality Index Report, 2021

Maximum Air Pollutant Concentrations: Particulate Matter, Ozone, CO and Lead

	Particulate Matter 10 (ug/m³)	Particulate Matter 2.5 Wtd AM (ug/m³)	Particulate Matter 2.5 24-Hr (ug/m³)	Ozone (ppm)	Carbon Monoxide (ppm)	Lead (ug/m³)
MSA[1] Level	51	10	54	0.082	n/a	n/a
NAAQS[2]	150	15	35	0.075	9	0.15
Met NAAQS[2]	Yes	Yes	No	No	n/a	n/a

Note: (1) Data covers the Boulder, CO Metropolitan Statistical Area; Data from exceptional events are included; (2) National Ambient Air Quality Standards; ppm = parts per million; ug/m³ = micrograms per cubic meter; n/a not available.
Concentrations: Particulate Matter 10 (coarse particulate)—highest second maximum 24-hour concentration; Particulate Matter 2.5 Wtd AM (fine particulate)—highest weighted annual mean concentration; Particulate Matter 2.5 24-Hour (fine particulate)—highest 98th percentile 24-hour concentration; Ozone—highest fourth daily maximum 8-hour concentration; Carbon Monoxide—highest second maximum non-overlapping 8-hour concentration; Lead—maximum running 3-month average
Source: U.S. Environmental Protection Agency, Air Quality Monitoring Information, "Air Quality Statistics by City, 2021"

Maximum Air Pollutant Concentrations: Nitrogen Dioxide and Sulfur Dioxide

	Nitrogen Dioxide AM (ppb)	Nitrogen Dioxide 1-Hr (ppb)	Sulfur Dioxide AM (ppb)	Sulfur Dioxide 1-Hr (ppb)	Sulfur Dioxide 24-Hr (ppb)
MSA[1] Level	n/a	n/a	n/a	n/a	n/a
NAAQS[2]	53	100	30	75	140
Met NAAQS[2]	n/a	n/a	n/a	n/a	n/a

Note: (1) Data covers the Boulder, CO Metropolitan Statistical Area; Data from exceptional events are included; (2) National Ambient Air Quality Standards; ppm = parts per million; ug/m³ = micrograms per cubic meter; n/a not available.
Concentrations: Nitrogen Dioxide AM—highest arithmetic mean concentration; Nitrogen Dioxide 1-Hr—highest 98th percentile 1-hour daily maximum concentration; Sulfur Dioxide AM—highest annual mean concentration; Sulfur Dioxide 1-Hr—highest 99th percentile 1-hour daily maximum concentration; Sulfur Dioxide 24-Hr—highest second maximum 24-hour concentration
Source: U.S. Environmental Protection Agency, Air Quality Monitoring Information, "Air Quality Statistics by City, 2021"

Colorado Springs, Colorado

Background

Colorado Springs is the seat of El Paso County in central Colorado and sits at the foot of Pike's Peak, the highest summit of the Southern Front Range of the Rock Mountains in North America. A dynamic and growing city, its economy is based on health care, high-tech manufacturing, tourism, and sports, with strong employment links to nearby military installations. With its economy and gorgeous surroundings, it is no wonder that Colorado Springs ranks as one of the fastest-growing cities in the country.

In 1806, Lieutenant Zebulon Pike visited the site and the mountain that now bears his name, but settlement did not begin in earnest until gold was discovered in 1859 and miners flooded into the area.

In 1871, General William Jackson Palmer, a railroad tycoon, purchased the site for $10,000 and began promoting the area as a health and recreation resort. Pike's Peak was already well known as a scenic landmark, and very soon the Garden of the Gods, Seven Falls, Cheyenne Mountain, and Manitou Springs were widely known for their spectacular natural beauty. Perhaps the highest testimonial came from Katherine Lee Bates, who, after a trip to Pike's Peak in 1893, wrote "America the Beautiful."

The planned community of Colorado Springs was incorporated in 1876. As a resort, it was wildly successful, hosting the likes of Oscar Wilde and John D. Rockefeller. It became a special favorite of English visitors, one of whom made the claim that there were two "civilized" places between the Atlantic and the Pacific—Chicago and Colorado Springs.

The English were so enamored of the place, in fact, that it came to be called "Little London," as English visitors settled in the area, introducing golf, cricket, polo, and fox hunting. Since there were no local foxes, an artificial scent was spread out for the hounds, or sometimes a coyote was substituted. Several sumptuous hotels were built during this period, as was an elegantly appointed opera house.

In 1891, gold was again discovered, and the city's population tripled to 35,000 in the following decade. Sufficient gold deposits allowed a lucky few to amass considerable fortunes and build huge houses north of the city. However, not all the newly minted millionaires were inclined toward conspicuous display; Winfield Scott Stratton, "Midas of the Rockies," bruised emerging aesthetic sensibilities by constructing a crude wooden frame house near the business district.

After the 1890s rush ended, Colorado Springs resumed a more measured pace of growth. World War II caused considerable development as Fort Carson and the Peterson Air Force Base were established, followed by the North American Aerospace Defense Command (NORAD) and the U.S. Air Force Academy in the 1950s. Today NORAD is primarily concerned with the tracking of Intercontinental Ballistic Missiles (ICBM) and celebrated its 64th anniversary in 2022. The city's military connection has contributed in large part to the economic base of the area, and its highly educated and technically skilled workforce. In late 2008, Fort Carson became the home station of the 4th Infantry Division, nearly doubling the population of the base.

Colorado Springs is the site of the headquarters of the United States Olympics Committee, which maintains an important Olympic training center there. The U.S. Olympic and Paralympic Museum opened in 2020.

The city is also home to the World Figure Skating Museum and Hall of Fame, the Pro Rodeo Hall of Fame, and Museum of the American Cowboy. The state-of-the-art Pikes Peak Summit Center opened in 2021, and includes a visitor center, utilities facility, and high-altitude research laboratory.

The city hosts several institutions of higher learning, including Colorado College (1874), the U.S. Air Force Academy (1954), a campus of the University of Colorado (1965), and Nazarene Bible College (1967). Cultural amenities include the Fine Arts Center and Theatreworks at the University of Colorado.

Although recreational marijuana is legal in Colorado, the Colorado Springs city council has yet to approve retail shops in the city. In 2022, while hundreds of medical marijuana dispensaries operate in the city, there are no recreational cannabis shops.

The region enjoys four seasons, with plenty of sunshine—300 days each year. Rainfall is relatively minimal, but snow can pile up.

Rankings

General Rankings

- For its "Best for Vets: Places to Live 2019" rankings, *Military Times* evaluated 599 cities (83 large, 234 medium, 282 small) and compared the locations across three broad categories: veteran and military culture/services; economic indicators; and livability factors such as health, crime, traffic, and school quality. Colorado Springs ranked #1 out of the top 25, in the large city category (population of more than 250,000). Data points more specific to veterans and the military weighed more heavily than others. *rebootcamp.militarytimes.com, "Military Times Best Places to Live 2019," September 10, 2018*

- *US News & World Report* conducted a survey of more than 3,600 people and analyzed the 150 largest metropolitan areas to determine what matters most when selecting where to settle down. Colorado Springs ranked #2 out of the top 25 as having the best combination of desirable factors. Criteria: cost of living; quality of life and education; net migration; job market; desirability; and other factors. *money.usnews.com, "The 25 Best Places to Live in the U.S. in 2022-2023," May 17, 2022*

- The Colorado Springs metro area was identified as one of America's fastest-growing areas in terms of population and business growth by *MagnifyMoney*. The area ranked #23 out of 35. The 100 most populous metro areas in the U.S. were evaluated on their change from 2011 to 2016 in the following categories: people and housing; workforce and employment opportunities; growing industry. *www.businessinsider.com, "The 35 Cities in the US with the Biggest Influx of People, the Most Work Opportunities, and the Hottest Business Growth," August 12, 2018*

- The Colorado Springs metro area was identified as one of America's fastest-growing areas in terms of population and economy by *Forbes*. The area ranked #18 out of 25. The 100 most populous metro areas in the U.S. were evaluated on the following criteria: estimated population growth; employment; economic output; wages; home values. *Forbes, "America's Fastest-Growing Cities 2018," February 28, 2018*

- In their ninth annual survey, Livability.com looked at data for more than 2,300 mid-sized U.S. cities to determine the rankings for Livability's "Top 100 Best Places to Live" in 2022. Colorado Springs ranked #16. Criteria: housing and economy; social and civic engagement; education; demographics; health care options; transportation & infrastructure; and community amenities. *Livability.com, "Top 100 Best Places to Live 2022" July 19, 2022*

Business/Finance Rankings

- The Brookings Institution ranked the nation's largest cities based on income inequality. Colorado Springs was ranked #87 (#1 = greatest inequality). Criteria: the "95/20 ratio," a figure representing the income at which a household earns more than 95 percent of all other households, divided by the income at which a household earns more than only 20 percent of all other households. *Brookings Institution, "Household Income Inequality, Largest Cities of 97 Large U.S. Metro Areas, 2014-2016," February 5, 2018*

- The Brookings Institution ranked the 100 largest metro areas in the U.S. based on income inequality. Colorado Springs was ranked #94 (#1 = greatest inequality). Criteria: the "95/20 ratio," a figure representing the income at which a household earns more than 95 percent of all other households, divided by the income at which a household earns more than only 20 percent of all other households. *Brookings Institution, "Household Income Inequality, 100 Largest U.S. Metro Areas, 2014-2016," February 5, 2018*

- The Colorado Springs metro area appeared on the Milken Institute "2022 Best Performing Cities" list. Rank: #9 out of 200 large metro areas (population over 250,000). Criteria: job growth; wage and salary growth; high-tech output growth; housing affordability; household broadband access. *Milken Institute, "Best-Performing Cities 2022," March 28, 2022*

- *Forbes* ranked the 200 most populous metro areas to determine the nation's "Best Places for Business and Careers." The Colorado Springs metro area was ranked #19. Criteria: costs (business and living); job growth (past and projected); income growth; quality of life; educational attainment (college and high school); projected economic growth; cultural and leisure opportunities; workplace tolerance laws; net migration patterns. *Forbes, "The Best Places for Business and Careers 2019: Seattle Still On Top," October 30, 2019*

Education Rankings

- Personal finance website *WalletHub* analyzed the 150 largest U.S. metropolitan statistical areas to determine where the most educated Americans are putting their degrees to work. Criteria: education levels; percentage of workers with degrees; education quality and attainment gap; public school quality rankings; quality and enrollment of each metro area's universities. Colorado Springs was ranked #13 (#1 = most educated city). *www.WalletHub.com, "Most & Least Educated Cities in America," July 18, 2022*

- Colorado Springs was selected as one of America's most literate cities. The city ranked #21 out of the 84 largest U.S. cities. Criteria: number of booksellers; library resources; Internet resources; educational attainment; periodical publishing resources; newspaper circulation. *Central Connecticut State University, "America's Most Literate Cities, 2018," February 2019*

Environmental Rankings

- Colorado Springs was highlighted as one of the 25 most ozone-polluted metro areas in the U.S. during 2019 through 2021. The area ranked #20. *American Lung Association, "State of the Air 2023," April 19, 2023*

- Colorado Springs was highlighted as one of the top 25 cleanest metro areas for year-round particle pollution (Annual PM 2.5) in the U.S. during 2019 through 2021. The area ranked #9. *American Lung Association, "State of the Air 2023," April 19, 2023*

Health/Fitness Rankings

- For each of the 100 largest cities in the United States, the American Fitness Index®, compiled in partnership between the American College of Sports Medicine and the Elevance Health Foundation, evaluated community infrastructure and 34 health behaviors including preventive health, levels of chronic disease conditions, food insecurity, sleep quality, pedestrian safety, air quality, and community/environment resources that support physical activity. Colorado Springs ranked #49 for "community fitness." *americanfitnessindex.org, "2022 ACSM American Fitness Index Summary Report," July 12, 2022*

- Colorado Springs was identified as a "2022 Spring Allergy Capital." The area ranked #78 out of 100. Three groups of factors were used to identify the most challenging cities for people with allergies during the spring season: annual spring pollen scores; over the counter allergy medicine use; number of board-certified allergy specialists. *Asthma and Allergy Foundation of America, "Spring Allergy Capitals 2022," March 2, 2022*

- Colorado Springs was identified as a "2022 Fall Allergy Capital." The area ranked #70 out of 100. Three groups of factors were used to identify the most challenging cities for people with allergies during the fall season: annual fall pollen scores; over the counter allergy medicine use; number of board-certified allergy specialists. *Asthma and Allergy Foundation of America, "Fall Allergy Capitals 2022," March 2, 2022*

- Colorado Springs was identified as a "2022 Asthma Capital." The area ranked #98 out of the nation's 100 largest metropolitan areas. Criteria: estimated asthma prevalence; asthma-related mortality; and ER visits due to asthma. Risk factors analyzed but not factored in the rankings: annual pollen score; annual air quality; public smoking laws; access to board-certified asthma specialists; rescue and controller medication use; uninsured rate; poverty rate. *Asthma and Allergy Foundation of America, "Asthma Capitals 2022: The Most Challenging Places to Live With Asthma," September 14, 2022*

Real Estate Rankings

- *WalletHub* compared the most populated U.S. cities to determine which had the best markets for real estate agents. Colorado Springs ranked #38 where demand was high and pay was the best. Criteria: sales per agent; annual median wage for real-estate agents; monthly average starting salary for real estate agents; real estate job density and competition; unemployment rate; home turnover rate; housing-market health index; and other relevant metrics. *www.WalletHub.com, "2021 Best Places to Be a Real Estate Agent," May 12, 2021*

- Colorado Springs was ranked #193 out of 235 metro areas in terms of housing affordability in 2022 by the National Association of Home Builders (#1 = most affordable). Criteria: the share of homes sold in that area affordable to a family earning the local median income, based on standard mortgage underwriting criteria. *National Association of Home Builders®, NAHB-Wells Fargo Housing Opportunity Index, 4th Quarter 2022*

Safety Rankings

- Allstate ranked the 200 largest cities in America in terms of driver safety. Colorado Springs ranked #13. Criteria: internal property damage claims over a two-year period from January 2016 to December 2017. The report helps increase the importance of safety and awareness behind the wheel. *Allstate, "Allstate America's Best Drivers Report, 2019" June 24, 2019*

- The National Insurance Crime Bureau ranked 390 metro areas in the U.S. in terms of per capita rates of vehicle theft. The Colorado Springs metro area ranked #39 (#1 = highest rate). Criteria: number of vehicle theft offenses per 100,000 inhabitants in 2021. *National Insurance Crime Bureau, "Hot Spots 2021," September 1, 2022*

Seniors/Retirement Rankings

- From its Best Cities for Successful Aging indexes, the Milken Institute generated rankings for metropolitan areas, weighing data in nine categories—health care, wellness, living arrangements, transportation and convenience, financial characteristics, education, employment, community engagement, and overall livability. The Colorado Springs metro area was ranked #46 overall in the large metro area category. *Milken Institute, "Best Cities for Successful Aging, 2017" March 14, 2017*

- Colorado Springs was identified as #16 of 20 most popular places to retire in the Western region by *Topretirements.com*. The site separated its annual "Best Places to Retire" list by major U.S. regions for 2019. The list reflects the 20 cities that visitors to the website are most interested in for retirement, based on the number of times a city's review was viewed on the website. *Topretirements.com, "20 Best Places to Retire in the West-2019," November 11, 2019*

Sports/Recreation Rankings

- Colorado Springs was chosen as one of America's best cities for bicycling. The city ranked #28 out of 50. Criteria: cycling infrastructure that is safe and friendly for all ages; energy and bike culture. The editors evaluated cities with populations of 100,000 or more. *Bicycling, "The 50 Best Bike Cities in America," October 10, 2018*

Women/Minorities Rankings

- Personal finance website *WalletHub* compared more than 180 U.S. cities across two key dimensions, "Hispanic Business-Friendliness" and "Hispanic Purchasing Power," to arrive at the most favorable conditions for Hispanic entrepreneurs. Colorado Springs was ranked #93 out of 182. Criteria includes: share of Hispanic-Owned Businesses; Hispanic entrepreneurship rate to median annual income of Hispanics; Small Business-Friendliness score; cost of living; and number of Hispanics with at least a bachelor's degree. *WalletHub.com, "2019's Best Cities for Hispanic Entrepreneurs," May 1, 2019*

Miscellaneous Rankings

- The watchdog site, Charity Navigator, conducted a study of charities in major markets both to analyze statistical differences in their financial, accountability, and transparency practices and to track year-to-year variations in individual philanthropic communities. The Colorado Springs metro area was ranked #28 among the 30 metro markets in the rating category of Overall Score. *www.charitynavigator.org, "2017 Metro Market Study," May 1, 2017*

- *WalletHub* compared the 150 most populated U.S. cities to determine their operating efficiency. A "Quality of Services" score was constructed for each city and then divided by the total budget per capita to reveal which were managed the best. Colorado Springs ranked #45. Criteria: financial stability; economy; education; safety; health; infrastructure and pollution. *www.WalletHub.com, "2022's Best- & Worst-Run Cities in America," June 21, 2022*

Business Environment

DEMOGRAPHICS

Population Growth

Area	1990 Census	2000 Census	2010 Census	2020 Census	Population Growth (%) 1990-2020	Population Growth (%) 2010-2020
City	283,798	360,890	416,427	478,961	68.8	15.0
MSA[1]	409,482	537,484	645,613	755,105	84.4	17.0
U.S.	248,709,873	281,421,906	308,745,538	331,449,281	33.3	7.4

Note: (1) Figures cover the Colorado Springs, CO Metropolitan Statistical Area
Source: U.S. Census Bureau, 1990 Census, 2000 Census, 2010 Census, 2020 Census

Race

Area	White Alone[2] (%)	Black Alone[2] (%)	Asian Alone[2] (%)	AIAN[3] Alone[2] (%)	NHOPI[4] Alone[2] (%)	Other Race Alone[2] (%)	Two or More Races (%)
City	70.3	5.9	3.4	1.1	0.3	6.2	12.8
MSA[1]	71.3	5.8	3.0	1.0	0.4	5.8	12.7
U.S.	61.6	12.4	6.0	1.1	0.2	8.4	10.2

Note: (1) Figures cover the Colorado Springs, CO Metropolitan Statistical Area; (2) Alone is defined as not being in combination with one or more other races; (3) American Indian and Alaska Native; (4) Native Hawaiian and Other Pacific Islander
Source: U.S. Census Bureau, 2020 Census

Hispanic or Latino Origin

Area	Total (%)	Mexican (%)	Puerto Rican (%)	Cuban (%)	Other (%)
City	18.4	12.1	1.2	0.3	4.9
MSA[1]	17.5	10.9	1.4	0.4	4.9
U.S.	18.4	11.2	1.8	0.7	4.7

Note: Persons of Hispanic or Latino origin can be of any race; (1) Figures cover the Colorado Springs, CO Metropolitan Statistical Area
Source: U.S. Census Bureau, 2017-2021 American Community Survey 5-Year Estimates

Age

Area	Under Age 5	Age 5–19	Age 20–34	Age 35–44	Age 45–54	Age 55–64	Age 65–74	Age 75–84	Age 85+	Median Age
City	5.9	19.0	23.7	13.2	11.3	12.2	8.9	4.1	1.6	35.9
MSA[1]	6.0	20.0	23.1	12.9	11.4	12.4	8.8	3.9	1.4	35.6
U.S.	5.6	19.2	20.2	12.7	12.4	13.1	10.0	4.9	1.9	38.8

Note: (1) Figures cover the Colorado Springs, CO Metropolitan Statistical Area
Source: U.S. Census Bureau, 2020 Census

Disability by Age

Area	All Ages	Under 18 Years Old	18 to 64 Years Old	65 Years and Over
City	13.1	5.2	12.1	30.9
MSA[1]	12.5	5.1	11.5	30.8
U.S.	12.6	4.4	10.3	33.4

Note: Figures show percent of the civilian noninstitutionalized population that reported having a disability. Disability status is determined from six types of difficulty: vision, hearing, cognitive, ambulatory, self-care, and independent living. For children under 5 years old, hearing and vision difficulty are used to determine disability status. For children between the ages of 5 and 14, disability status is determined from hearing, vision, cognitive, ambulatory, and self-care difficulties. For people aged 15 years and older, they are considered to have a disability if they have difficulty with any one of the six difficulty types; Note: (1) Figures cover the Colorado Springs, CO Metropolitan Statistical Area
Source: U.S. Census Bureau, 2017-2021 American Community Survey 5-Year Estimates

Ancestry

Area	German	Irish	English	American	Italian	Polish	French[2]	Scottish	Dutch
City	17.7	10.6	11.4	4.2	4.7	2.2	2.7	2.7	1.4
MSA[1]	17.8	10.6	10.9	4.4	4.5	2.3	2.6	2.6	1.4
U.S.	12.8	9.6	8.1	5.7	5.0	2.7	2.2	1.6	1.1

Note: Figures are the percentage of the total population reporting a particular ancestry. The nine most commonly reported ancestries in the U.S. are shown. Figures include multiple ancestries (e.g. if a person reported being Irish and Italian, they were included in both columns); (1) Figures cover the Colorado Springs, CO Metropolitan Statistical Area; (2) Excludes Basque
Source: U.S. Census Bureau, 2017-2021 American Community Survey 5-Year Estimates

Foreign-born Population

Area	Percent of Population Born in								
	Any Foreign Country	Asia	Mexico	Europe	Caribbean	Central America[2]	South America	Africa	Canada
City	7.5	2.2	2.0	1.5	0.3	0.4	0.4	0.4	0.4
MSA[1]	6.7	1.9	1.6	1.5	0.4	0.3	0.4	0.3	0.3
U.S.	13.6	4.2	3.3	1.5	1.4	1.1	1.1	0.8	0.2

Note: (1) Figures cover the Colorado Springs, CO Metropolitan Statistical Area; (2) Excludes Mexico.
Source: U.S. Census Bureau, 2017-2021 American Community Survey 5-Year Estimates

Household Size

Area	Persons in Household (%)							Average Household Size
	One	Two	Three	Four	Five	Six	Seven or More	
City	27.5	36.0	15.0	12.5	5.5	2.3	1.1	2.50
MSA[1]	24.6	35.7	15.9	13.3	6.6	2.3	1.5	2.60
U.S.	28.1	33.8	15.5	12.9	6.0	2.3	1.4	2.60

Note: (1) Figures cover the Colorado Springs, CO Metropolitan Statistical Area
Source: U.S. Census Bureau, 2017-2021 American Community Survey 5-Year Estimates

Household Relationships

Area	House-holder	Opposite-sex Spouse	Same-sex Spouse	Opposite-sex Unmarried Partner	Same-sex Unmarried Partner	Child[2]	Grand-child	Other Relatives	Non-relatives
City	39.7	18.3	0.3	2.6	0.2	27.5	1.9	3.6	4.3
MSA[1]	37.5	19.3	0.2	2.2	0.1	28.5	2.0	3.6	3.8
U.S.	38.3	17.5	0.2	2.5	0.2	28.3	2.4	4.8	3.4

Note: Figures are percent of the total population; (1) Figures cover the Colorado Springs, CO Metropolitan Statistical Area; (2) Includes biological, adopted, and stepchildren of the householder
Source: U.S. Census Bureau, 2020 Census

Gender

Area	Males	Females	Males per 100 Females
City	236,731	242,230	97.7
MSA[1]	379,052	376,053	100.8
U.S.	162,685,811	168,763,470	96.4

Note: (1) Figures cover the Colorado Springs, CO Metropolitan Statistical Area
Source: U.S. Census Bureau, 2020 Census

Marital Status

Area	Never Married	Now Married[2]	Separated	Widowed	Divorced
City	30.9	50.2	1.6	4.5	12.9
MSA[1]	29.5	53.3	1.4	4.0	11.7
U.S.	33.8	48.0	1.8	5.6	10.8

Note: Figures are percentages and cover the population 15 years of age and older; (1) Figures cover the Colorado Springs, CO Metropolitan Statistical Area; (2) Excludes separated
Source: U.S. Census Bureau, 2017-2021 American Community Survey 5-Year Estimates

Religious Groups by Family

Area	Catholic	Baptist	Methodist	LDS[2]	Pentecostal	Lutheran	Islam	Adventist	Other
MSA[1]	16.4	2.6	1.3	3.0	1.0	1.2	0.1	1.0	16.2
U.S.	18.7	7.3	3.0	2.0	1.8	1.7	1.3	1.3	11.6

Note: Figures are the number of adherents as a percentage of the total population and cover the eight largest religious groups in the U.S; (1) Figures cover the Colorado Springs, CO Metropolitan Statistical Area; (2) Church of Jesus Christ of Latter-day Saints
Sources: 2020 U.S. Religion Census, Association of Statisticians of American Religious Bodies; The Association of Religion Data Archives (ARDA)

Religious Groups by Tradition

Area	Catholic	Evangelical Protestant	Mainline Protestant	Black Protestant	Islam	Judaism	Hinduism	Orthodox	Buddhism
MSA[1]	16.4	18.3	2.9	0.9	0.1	<0.1	<0.1	0.1	0.3
U.S.	18.7	16.5	5.2	2.3	1.3	0.6	0.4	0.4	0.3

Note: Figures are the number of adherents as a percentage of the total population; (1) Figures cover the Colorado Springs, CO Metropolitan Statistical Area
Sources: 2020 U.S. Religion Census, Association of Statisticians of American Religious Bodies; The Association of Religion Data Archives (ARDA)

ECONOMY

Gross Metropolitan Product

Area	2020	2021	2022	2023	Rank[2]
MSA[1]	39.5	43.7	47.3	49.9	78

Note: Figures are in billions of dollars; (1) Figures cover the Colorado Springs, CO Metropolitan Statistical Area; (2) Rank is based on 2021 data and ranges from 1 to 381
Source: U.S. Conference of Mayors, U.S. Metro Economies: U.S. Metros Compared to Global and State Economies, June 2022

Economic Growth

Area	2018-20 (%)	2021 (%)	2022 (%)	2023 (%)	Rank[2]
MSA[1]	1.6	6.0	2.1	3.0	47
U.S.	-0.6	5.7	3.1	2.9	–

Note: Figures are real gross metropolitan product (GMP) growth rates and represent average annual percent change; (1) Figures cover the Colorado Springs, CO Metropolitan Statistical Area; (2) Rank is based on 2020 2-year average annual percent change and ranges from 1 to 381
Source: U.S. Conference of Mayors, U.S. Metro Economies: U.S. Metros Compared to Global and State Economies, June 2022

Metropolitan Area Exports

Area	2016	2017	2018	2019	2020	2021	Rank[2]
MSA[1]	786.9	819.7	850.6	864.2	979.2	866.9	175

Note: Figures are in millions of dollars; (1) Figures cover the Colorado Springs, CO Metropolitan Statistical Area; (2) Rank is based on 2021 data and ranges from 1 to 388
Source: U.S. Department of Commerce, International Trade Administration, Office of Trade and Economic Analysis, Industry and Analysis, Exports by Metropolitan Area, data extracted March 16, 2023

Building Permits

Area	Single-Family			Multi-Family			Total		
	2021	2022	Pct. Chg.	2021	2022	Pct. Chg.	2021	2022	Pct. Chg.
City	n/a	n/a	n/a	n/a	n/a	n/a	n/a	n/a	n/a
MSA[1]	5,074	3,646	-28.1	4,261	5,198	22.0	9,335	8,844	-5.3
U.S.	1,115,400	975,600	-12.5	621,600	689,500	10.9	1,737,000	1,665,100	-4.1

Note: (1) Figures cover the Colorado Springs, CO Metropolitan Statistical Area; Figures represent new, privately-owned housing units authorized (unadjusted data); All permit data are based on estimates with imputation
Source: U.S. Census Bureau, Manufacturing, Mining, and Construction Statistics, Building Permits, 2021, 2022

Bankruptcy Filings

Area	Business Filings			Nonbusiness Filings		
	2021	2022	% Chg.	2021	2022	% Chg.
El Paso County	22	19	-13.6	728	609	-16.3
U.S.	14,347	13,481	-6.0	399,269	374,240	-6.3

Note: Business filings include Chapter 7, Chapter 9, Chapter 11, Chapter 12, Chapter 13, Chapter 15, and Section 304; Nonbusiness filings include Chapter 7, Chapter 11, and Chapter 13
Source: Administrative Office of the U.S. Courts, Business and Nonbusiness Bankruptcy, County Cases Commenced by Chapter of the Bankruptcy Code, During the 12-Month Period Ending December 31, 2021 and Business and Nonbusiness Bankruptcy, County Cases Commenced by Chapter of the Bankruptcy Code, During the 12-Month Period Ending December 31, 2022

Housing Vacancy Rates

Area	Gross Vacancy Rate[2] (%)			Year-Round Vacancy Rate[3] (%)			Rental Vacancy Rate[4] (%)			Homeowner Vacancy Rate[5] (%)		
	2020	2021	2022	2020	2021	2022	2020	2021	2022	2020	2021	2022
MSA[1]	n/a	n/a	n/a	n/a	n/a	n/a	n/a	n/a	n/a	n/a	n/a	n/a
U.S.	10.6	10.8	10.5	8.2	8.4	8.2	6.3	6.1	5.8	1.0	0.9	0.8

Note: (1) Figures cover the Colorado Springs, CO Metropolitan Statistical Area; (2) The percentage of the total housing inventory that is vacant; (3) The percentage of the housing inventory (excluding seasonal units) that is year-round vacant; (4) The percentage of rental inventory that is vacant for rent; (5) The percentage of homeowner inventory that is vacant for sale; n/a not available
Source: U.S. Census Bureau, Housing Vacancies and Homeownership Annual Statistics: 2020, 2021, 2022

INCOME

Income

Area	Per Capita ($)	Median Household ($)	Average Household ($)
City	37,979	71,957	93,740
MSA[1]	37,650	75,641	97,647
U.S.	37,638	69,021	97,196

Note: (1) Figures cover the Colorado Springs, CO Metropolitan Statistical Area
Source: U.S. Census Bureau, 2017-2021 American Community Survey 5-Year Estimates

Household Income Distribution

Area	Percent of Households Earning							
	Under $15,000	$15,000 -$24,999	$25,000 -$34,999	$35,000 -$49,999	$50,000 -$74,999	$75,000 -$99,999	$100,000 -$149,999	$150,000 and up
City	7.8	6.6	7.6	12.0	18.0	14.2	17.3	16.4
MSA[1]	6.9	6.2	6.9	11.5	18.1	14.1	18.4	17.9
U.S.	9.4	7.8	8.2	11.4	16.8	12.8	16.3	17.3

Note: (1) Figures cover the Colorado Springs, CO Metropolitan Statistical Area
Source: U.S. Census Bureau, 2017-2021 American Community Survey 5-Year Estimates

Poverty Rate

Area	All Ages	Under 18 Years Old	18 to 64 Years Old	65 Years and Over
City	10.9	13.7	10.7	7.5
MSA[1]	9.5	12.0	9.2	6.6
U.S.	12.6	17.0	11.8	9.6

Note: Figures are percentage of people whose income during the past 12 months was below the poverty level;
(1) Figures cover the Colorado Springs, CO Metropolitan Statistical Area
Source: U.S. Census Bureau, 2017-2021 American Community Survey 5-Year Estimates

EMPLOYMENT

Labor Force and Employment

Area	Civilian Labor Force			Workers Employed		
	Dec. 2021	Dec. 2022	% Chg.	Dec. 2021	Dec. 2022	% Chg.
City	243,995	246,112	0.9	234,766	238,820	1.7
MSA[1]	364,630	367,853	0.9	350,819	356,889	1.7
U.S.	161,696,000	164,224,000	1.6	155,732,000	158,872,000	2.0

Note: Data is not seasonally adjusted and covers workers 16 years of age and older; (1) Figures cover the Colorado Springs, CO Metropolitan Statistical Area
Source: Bureau of Labor Statistics, Local Area Unemployment Statistics

Unemployment Rate

Area	2022											
	Jan.	Feb.	Mar.	Apr.	May	Jun.	Jul.	Aug.	Sep.	Oct.	Nov.	Dec.
City	4.1	4.2	3.6	3.2	3.1	3.4	3.8	3.6	3.5	3.7	3.5	3.0
MSA[1]	4.1	4.2	3.8	3.3	3.5	3.5	3.9	3.6	3.5	3.8	3.6	3.0
U.S.	4.4	4.1	3.8	3.3	3.4	3.8	3.8	3.8	3.3	3.4	3.4	3.3

Note: Data is not seasonally adjusted and covers workers 16 years of age and older; (1) Figures cover the Colorado Springs, CO Metropolitan Statistical Area
Source: Bureau of Labor Statistics, Local Area Unemployment Statistics

Average Wages

Occupation	$/Hr.	Occupation	$/Hr.
Accountants and Auditors	36.34	Maintenance and Repair Workers	22.51
Automotive Mechanics	25.04	Marketing Managers	79.04
Bookkeepers	21.56	Network and Computer Systems Admin.	47.29
Carpenters	25.51	Nurses, Licensed Practical	27.54
Cashiers	14.94	Nurses, Registered	39.78
Computer Programmers	56.28	Nursing Assistants	18.31
Computer Systems Analysts	53.00	Office Clerks, General	23.24
Computer User Support Specialists	31.65	Physical Therapists	45.18
Construction Laborers	20.22	Physicians	n/a
Cooks, Restaurant	17.67	Plumbers, Pipefitters and Steamfitters	28.01
Customer Service Representatives	19.52	Police and Sheriff's Patrol Officers	37.67
Dentists	88.61	Postal Service Mail Carriers	26.35
Electricians	27.65	Real Estate Sales Agents	34.84
Engineers, Electrical	54.86	Retail Salespersons	17.44
Fast Food and Counter Workers	14.73	Sales Representatives, Technical/Scientific	46.25
Financial Managers	83.92	Secretaries, Exc. Legal/Medical/Executive	19.90
First-Line Supervisors of Office Workers	31.26	Security Guards	17.50
General and Operations Managers	65.50	Surgeons	n/a
Hairdressers/Cosmetologists	23.17	Teacher Assistants, Exc. Postsecondary*	15.06
Home Health and Personal Care Aides	16.66	Teachers, Secondary School, Exc. Sp. Ed.*	26.75
Janitors and Cleaners	16.75	Telemarketers	19.45
Landscaping/Groundskeeping Workers	n/a	Truck Drivers, Heavy/Tractor-Trailer	24.71
Lawyers	53.62	Truck Drivers, Light/Delivery Services	22.21
Maids and Housekeeping Cleaners	16.06	Waiters and Waitresses	19.75

Note: Wage data covers the Colorado Springs, CO Metropolitan Statistical Area; (*) Hourly wages were calculated from annual wage data based on a 40 hour work week; n/a not available.
Source: Bureau of Labor Statistics, Metro Area Occupational Employment & Wage Estimates, May 2022

Employment by Industry

Sector	MSA[1]		U.S.
	Number of Employees	Percent of Total	Percent of Total
Construction, Mining, and Logging	18,800	5.9	5.4
Private Education and Health Services	43,900	13.8	16.1
Financial Activities	18,300	5.8	5.9
Government	56,400	17.7	14.5
Information	5,200	1.6	2.0
Leisure and Hospitality	38,500	12.1	10.3
Manufacturing	11,900	3.7	8.4
Other Services	21,500	6.8	3.7
Professional and Business Services	54,000	17.0	14.7
Retail Trade	32,800	10.3	10.2
Transportation, Warehousing, and Utilities	10,400	3.3	4.9
Wholesale Trade	6,400	2.0	3.9

Note: Figures are non-farm employment as of December 2022. Figures are not seasonally adjusted and include workers 16 years of age and older; (1) Figures cover the Colorado Springs, CO Metropolitan Statistical Area
Source: Bureau of Labor Statistics, Current Employment Statistics, Employment, Hours, and Earnings

Employment by Occupation

Occupation Classification	City (%)	MSA[1] (%)	U.S. (%)
Management, Business, Science, and Arts	44.2	43.8	40.3
Natural Resources, Construction, and Maintenance	7.8	8.5	8.7
Production, Transportation, and Material Moving	9.4	9.7	13.1
Sales and Office	20.7	20.7	20.9
Service	17.8	17.3	17.0

Note: Figures cover employed civilians 16 years of age and older; (1) Figures cover the Colorado Springs, CO Metropolitan Statistical Area
Source: U.S. Census Bureau, 2017-2021 American Community Survey 5-Year Estimates

Occupations with Greatest Projected Employment Growth: 2022 – 2024

Occupation[1]	2022 Employment	2024 Projected Employment	Numeric Employment Change	Percent Employment Change
Software Developers	43,570	47,290	3,720	8.5
Stockers and Order Fillers	45,230	48,030	2,800	6.2
Cooks, Restaurant	31,870	34,550	2,680	8.4
Fast Food and Counter Workers	79,850	82,410	2,560	3.2
Accountants and Auditors	42,150	43,910	1,760	4.2
Market Research Analysts and Marketing Specialists	28,150	29,830	1,680	6.0
Home Health and Personal Care Aides	43,200	44,870	1,670	3.9
Registered Nurses	53,590	55,060	1,470	2.7
General and Operations Managers	47,360	48,780	1,420	3.0
Sales Representatives of Services, Except Advertising, Insurance, Financial Services, and Travel	37,310	38,730	1,420	3.8

Note: Projections cover Colorado; (1) Sorted by numeric employment change
Source: www.projectionscentral.com, State Occupational Projections, 2022–2024 Short-Term Projections

Fastest-Growing Occupations: 2022 – 2024

Occupation[1]	2022 Employment	2024 Projected Employment	Numeric Employment Change	Percent Employment Change
Derrick Operators, Oil and Gas	550	640	90	16.4
Roustabouts, Oil and Gas	1,550	1,790	240	15.5
Service Unit Operators, Oil, Gas, and Mining	2,430	2,760	330	13.6
Flight Attendants	4,890	5,490	600	12.3
Epidemiologists	530	590	60	11.3
Information Security Analysts (SOC 2018)	6,100	6,760	660	10.8
Statisticians	1,410	1,550	140	9.9
Veterinary Assistants and Laboratory Animal Caretakers	2,360	2,590	230	9.7
Data Scientists	3,520	3,850	330	9.4
Solar Photovoltaic Installers	530	580	50	9.4

Note: Projections cover Colorado; (1) Sorted by percent employment change and excludes occupations with numeric employment change less than 50
Source: www.projectionscentral.com, State Occupational Projections, 2022–2024 Short-Term Projections

CITY FINANCES

City Government Finances

Component	2020 ($000)	2020 ($ per capita)
Total Revenues	1,588,071	3,321
Total Expenditures	1,318,935	2,758
Debt Outstanding	2,518,296	5,266
Cash and Securities[1]	664,026	1,389

Note: (1) Cash and security holdings of a government at the close of its fiscal year, including those of its dependent agencies, utilities, and liquor stores.
Source: U.S. Census Bureau, State & Local Government Finances 2020

City Government Revenue by Source

Source	2020 ($000)	2020 ($ per capita)	2020 (%)
General Revenue			
From Federal Government	73,530	154	4.6
From State Government	6,660	14	0.4
From Local Governments	1,282	3	0.1
Taxes			
Property	54,111	113	3.4
Sales and Gross Receipts	326,732	683	20.6
Personal Income	0	0	0.0
Corporate Income	0	0	0.0
Motor Vehicle License	0	0	0.0
Other Taxes	3,440	7	0.2
Current Charges	126,660	265	8.0
Liquor Store	0	0	0.0
Utility	822,380	1,720	51.8

Source: U.S. Census Bureau, State & Local Government Finances 2020

City Government Expenditures by Function

Function	2020 ($000)	2020 ($ per capita)	2020 (%)
General Direct Expenditures			
Air Transportation	15,400	32	1.2
Corrections	0	0	0.0
Education	0	0	0.0
Employment Security Administration	0	0	0.0
Financial Administration	38,520	80	2.9
Fire Protection	57,764	120	4.4
General Public Buildings	0	0	0.0
Governmental Administration, Other	29,604	61	2.2
Health	0	0	0.0
Highways	95,502	199	7.2
Hospitals	0	0	0.0
Housing and Community Development	58,397	122	4.4
Interest on General Debt	24,826	51	1.9
Judicial and Legal	10,487	21	0.8
Libraries	0	0	0.0
Parking	2,530	5	0.2
Parks and Recreation	28,218	59	2.1
Police Protection	121,202	253	9.2
Public Welfare	0	0	0.0
Sewerage	35,182	73	2.7
Solid Waste Management	0	0	0.0
Veterans' Services	0	0	0.0
Liquor Store	0	0	0.0
Utility	703,727	1,471	53.4

Source: U.S. Census Bureau, State & Local Government Finances 2020

TAXES

State Corporate Income Tax Rates

State	Tax Rate (%)	Income Brackets ($)	Num. of Brackets	Financial Institution Tax Rate (%)[a]	Federal Income Tax Ded.
Colorado	4.4	Flat rate	1	4.4	No

Note: Tax rates as of January 1, 2023; (a) Rates listed are the corporate income tax rate applied to financial institutions or excise taxes based on income. Some states have other taxes based upon the value of deposits or shares.
Source: Federation of Tax Administrators, State Corporate Income Tax Rates, January 1, 2023

State Individual Income Tax Rates

State	Tax Rate (%)	Income Brackets ($)	Personal Exemptions ($)			Standard Ded. ($)	
			Single	Married	Depend.	Single	Married
Colorado	4.4	Flat rate	(d)	(d)	(d)	13,850	27,700 (d)

Note: Tax rates as of January 1, 2023; Local- and county-level taxes are not included; Federal income tax is not deductible on state income tax returns; (d) These states use the personal exemption/standard deduction amounts provided in the federal Internal Revenue Code.
Source: Federation of Tax Administrators, State Individual Income Tax Rates, January 1, 2023

Various State Sales and Excise Tax Rates

State	State Sales Tax (%)	Gasoline[1] ($/gal.)	Cigarette[2] ($/pack)	Spirits[3] ($/gal.)	Wine[4] ($/gal.)	Beer[5] ($/gal.)	Recreational Marijuana (%)
Colorado	2.9	0.22	1.94	2.28	0.32	0.08	(d)

Note: All tax rates as of January 1, 2023; (1) The American Petroleum Institute has developed a methodology for determining the average tax rate on a gallon of fuel. Rates may include any of the following: excise taxes, environmental fees, storage tank fees, other fees or taxes, general sales tax, and local taxes; (2) The federal excise tax of $1.0066 per pack and local taxes are not included; (3) Rates are those applicable to off-premise sales of 40% alcohol by volume (a.b.v.) distilled spirits in 750ml containers. Local excise taxes are excluded; (4) Rates are those applicable to off-premise sales of 11% a.b.v. non-carbonated wine in 750ml containers; (5) Rates are those applicable to off-premise sales of 4.7% a.b.v. beer in 12 ounce containers; (d) 15% excise tax (levied on wholesale at average market rate); 15% excise tax (retail price)
Source: Tax Foundation, 2023 Facts & Figures: How Does Your State Compare?

State Business Tax Climate Index Rankings

State	Overall Rank	Corporate Tax Rank	Individual Income Tax Rank	Sales Tax Rank	Property Tax Rank	Unemployment Insurance Tax Rank
Colorado	21	7	14	40	36	42

Note: The index is a measure of how each state's tax laws affect economic performance. The lower the rank, the more favorable a state's tax system is for business. States without a given tax are given a ranking of 1. The scores/rankings for the District of Columbia do not affect other states. The 2023 index represents the tax climate as of July 1, 2022.
Source: Tax Foundation, State Business Tax Climate Index 2023

TRANSPORTATION

Means of Transportation to Work

Area	Car/Truck/Van		Public Transportation			Bicycle	Walked	Other Means	Worked at Home
	Drove Alone	Car-pooled	Bus	Subway	Railroad				
City	74.7	9.8	0.7	0.0	0.0	0.5	1.7	1.1	11.4
MSA[1]	73.8	9.6	0.5	0.0	0.0	0.3	3.2	1.0	11.4
U.S.	73.2	8.6	2.0	1.6	0.5	0.5	2.5	1.5	9.7

Note: Figures are percentages and cover workers 16 years of age and older; (1) Figures cover the Colorado Springs, CO Metropolitan Statistical Area
Source: U.S. Census Bureau, 2017-2021 American Community Survey 5-Year Estimates

Travel Time to Work

Area	Less Than 10 Minutes	10 to 19 Minutes	20 to 29 Minutes	30 to 44 Minutes	45 to 59 Minutes	60 to 89 Minutes	90 Minutes or More
City	11.5	35.9	28.0	15.9	3.3	2.9	2.5
MSA[1]	11.5	32.8	26.9	18.0	4.7	3.6	2.5
U.S.	12.4	28.5	21.0	20.9	8.2	6.2	2.9

Note: Note: Figures are percentages and include workers 16 years old and over; (1) Figures cover the Colorado Springs, CO Metropolitan Statistical Area
Source: U.S. Census Bureau, 2017-2021 American Community Survey 5-Year Estimates

Key Congestion Measures

Measure	1990	2000	2010	2015	2020
Annual Hours of Delay, Total (000)	4,139	11,169	15,234	17,103	12,116
Annual Hours of Delay, Per Auto Commuter	20	34	36	40	29
Annual Congestion Cost, Per Auto Commuter ($)	346	704	763	793	582

Note: Covers the Colorado Springs CO urban area
Source: Texas A&M Transportation Institute, 2021 Urban Mobility Report

Freeway Travel Time Index

Measure	1985	1990	1995	2000	2005	2010	2015	2020
Urban Area Index[1]	1.04	1.09	1.12	1.15	1.16	1.15	1.15	1.08
Urban Area Rank[1,2]	81	56	57	53	57	65	67	44

Note: Freeway Travel Time Index—the ratio of travel time in the peak period to the travel time at free-flow conditions. For example, a value of 1.30 indicates a 20-minute free-flow trip takes 26 minutes in the peak (20 minutes x 1.30 = 26 minutes); (1) Covers the Colorado Springs CO urban area; (2) Rank is based on 101 larger urban areas (#1 = highest travel time index)
Source: Texas A&M Transportation Institute, 2021 Urban Mobility Report

Public Transportation

Agency Name / Mode of Transportation	Vehicles Operated in Maximum Service[1]	Annual Unlinked Passenger Trips[2] (in thous.)	Annual Passenger Miles[3] (in thous.)
Colorado Springs Transit System			
Bus (purchased transportation)	48	1,827.2	7,404.5
Demand Response (purchased transportation)	32	92.9	828.8
Demand Response - Taxi	3	0.5	1.4
Vanpool (directly operated)	8	9.5	620.3

Note: (1) Number of revenue vehicles operated by the given mode and type of service to meet the annual maximum service requirement. This is the revenue vehicle count during the peak season of the year; on the week and day that maximum service is provided. Vehicles operated in maximum service (VOMS) exclude atypical days and one-time special events; (2) Number of passengers who boarded public transportation vehicles. Passengers are counted each time they board a vehicle no matter how many vehicles they use to travel from their origin to their destination. (3) Sum of the distances ridden by all passengers during the entire fiscal year.
Source: Federal Transit Administration, National Transit Database, 2021

Air Transportation

Airport Name and Code / Type of Service	Passenger Airlines[1]	Passenger Enplanements	Freight Carriers[2]	Freight (lbs)
City of Colorado Springs Municipal (COS)				
Domestic service (U.S. carriers - 2022)	21	1,073,752	6	7,990,300
International service (U.S. carriers - 2021)	0	0	0	0

Note: (1) Includes all U.S.-based major, minor and commuter airlines that carried at least one passenger during the year; (2) Includes all U.S.-based airlines and freight carriers that transported at least one pound of freight during the year.
Source: Bureau of Transportation Statistics, The Intermodal Transportation Database, Air Carriers: T-100 Domestic Market (U.S. Carriers), 2022; Bureau of Transportation Statistics, The Intermodal Transportation Database, Air Carriers: T-100 International Market (U.S. Carriers), 2021

BUSINESSES

Major Business Headquarters

Company Name	Industry	Rankings Fortune[1]	Forbes[2]
No companies listed	-	-	-

Note: (1) Companies that produce a 10-K are ranked 1 to 500 based on 2021 revenue; (2) All private companies with at least $2 billion in annual revenue through the end of their most current fiscal year are ranked 1 to 246; companies listed are headquartered in the city; dashes indicate no ranking
Source: Fortune, "Fortune 500," 2022; Forbes, "America's Largest Private Companies," 2022

Fastest-Growing Businesses

According to *Inc.*, Colorado Springs is home to two of America's 500 fastest-growing private companies: **Zap Mortgage** (#335); **SOLKOA** (#376). Criteria: must be an independent, privately-held, for-profit, U.S. corporation, proprietorship or partnership as of December 31, 2021; revenues must be at least $100,000 in 2018 and $2 million in 2021; must have four-year operating/sales history. *Inc., "America's 500 Fastest-Growing Private Companies," 2022*

According to Deloitte, Colorado Springs is home to one of North America's 500 fastest-growing high-technology companies: **Quantum Metric** (#244). Companies are ranked by percentage growth in revenue over a four-year period. Criteria for inclusion: company must be headquartered within North America; must own proprietary intellectual property or technology that is sold to customers in products that contributes to a significant portion of the company's operating revenue; must have been in business for a minumum of four years with 2018 operating revenues of at least $50,000 USD/CD and 2021 operating revenues of at least $5 million USD/CD. *Deloitte, 2022 Technology Fast 500™*

Living Environment

COST OF LIVING

Cost of Living Index

Composite Index	Groceries	Housing	Utilities	Trans-portation	Health Care	Misc. Goods/ Services
105.0	99.0	110.4	103.6	100.6	103.4	105.0

Note: The Cost of Living Index measures regional differences in the cost of consumer goods and services, excluding taxes and non-consumer expenditures, for professional and managerial households in the top income quintile. It is based on more than 50,000 prices covering almost 60 different items for which prices are collected three times a year by chambers of commerce, economic development organizations or university applied economic centers in each participating urban area. The numbers shown should be read as a percentage above or below the national average of 100. For example, a value of 115.4 in the groceries column indicates that grocery prices are 15.4% higher than the national average. Small differences in the index numbers should not be interpreted as significant; Figures cover the Colorado Springs CO urban area.
Source: The Council for Community and Economic Research, Cost of Living Index, 2022

Grocery Prices

Area[1]	T-Bone Steak ($/pound)	Frying Chicken ($/pound)	Whole Milk ($/half gal.)	Eggs ($/dozen)	Orange Juice ($/64 oz.)	Coffee ($/11.5 oz.)
City[2]	14.09	1.35	2.17	2.04	3.53	5.14
Avg.	13.81	1.59	2.43	2.25	3.85	4.95
Min.	10.17	0.90	1.51	1.30	2.90	3.46
Max.	19.35	3.30	4.32	4.32	5.31	8.59

*Note: (1) Values for the local area are compared with the average, minimum and maximum values for all 286 areas in the Cost of Living Index; (2) Figures cover the Colorado Springs CO urban area; **T-Bone Steak** (price per pound); **Frying Chicken** (price per pound, whole fryer); **Whole Milk** (half gallon carton); **Eggs** (price per dozen, Grade A, large); **Orange Juice** (64 oz. Tropicana or Florida Natural); **Coffee** (11.5 oz. can, vacuum-packed, Maxwell House, Hills Bros, or Folgers).*
Source: The Council for Community and Economic Research, Cost of Living Index, 2022

Housing and Utility Costs

Area[1]	New Home Price ($)	Apartment Rent ($/month)	All Electric ($/month)	Part Electric ($/month)	Other Energy ($/month)	Telephone ($/month)
City[2]	497,622	1,512	-	104.56	85.71	186.39
Avg.	450,913	1,371	176.41	99.93	76.96	190.22
Min.	229,283	546	100.84	31.56	27.15	174.27
Max.	2,434,977	4,569	356.86	249.59	272.24	208.31

*Note: (1) Values for the local area are compared with the average, minimum and maximum values for all 286 areas in the Cost of Living Index; (2) Figures cover the Colorado Springs CO urban area; **New Home Price** (2,400 sf living area, 8,000 sf lot, in urban area with full utilities); **Apartment Rent** (950 sf 2 bedroom/1.5 or 2 bath, unfurnished, excluding all utilities except water); **All Electric** (average monthly cost for an all-electric home); **Part Electric** (average monthly cost for a part-electric home); **Other Energy** (average monthly cost for natural gas, fuel oil, coal, wood, and any other forms of energy except electricity); **Telephone** (price includes the base monthly rate plus taxes and fees for three lines of mobile phone service).*
Source: The Council for Community and Economic Research, Cost of Living Index, 2022

Health Care, Transportation, and Other Costs

Area[1]	Doctor ($/visit)	Dentist ($/visit)	Optometrist ($/visit)	Gasoline ($/gallon)	Beauty Salon ($/visit)	Men's Shirt ($)
City[2]	134.96	108.29	123.36	3.96	47.60	44.38
Avg.	124.91	107.77	117.66	3.86	43.31	34.21
Min.	36.61	58.25	51.79	2.90	22.18	13.05
Max.	250.21	162.58	371.96	5.54	85.61	63.54

*Note: (1) Values for the local area are compared with the average, minimum and maximum values for all 286 areas in the Cost of Living Index; (2) Figures cover the Colorado Springs CO urban area; **Doctor** (general practitioners routine exam of an established patient); **Dentist** (adult teeth cleaning and periodic oral examination); **Optometrist** (full vision eye exam for established adult patient); **Gasoline** (one gallon regular unleaded, national brand, including all taxes, cash price at self-service pump if available); **Beauty Salon** (woman's shampoo, trim, and blow-dry); **Men's Shirt** (cotton/polyester dress shirt, pinpoint weave, long sleeves).*
Source: The Council for Community and Economic Research, Cost of Living Index, 2022

HOUSING

Homeownership Rate

Area	2015 (%)	2016 (%)	2017 (%)	2018 (%)	2019 (%)	2020 (%)	2021 (%)	2022 (%)
MSA[1]	n/a	n/a	n/a	n/a	n/a	n/a	n/a	n/a
U.S.	63.7	63.4	63.9	64.4	64.6	66.6	65.5	65.8

Note: (1) Figures cover the Colorado Springs, CO Metropolitan Statistical Area; n/a not available
Source: U.S. Census Bureau, Housing Vacancies and Homeownership Annual Statistics: 2015-2022

House Price Index (HPI)

Area	National Ranking[2]	Quarterly Change (%)	One-Year Change (%)	Five-Year Change (%)	Since 1991Q1 (%)
MSA[1]	231	-3.83	6.63	67.59	425.90
U.S.[3]	–	0.34	8.41	58.44	289.08

Note: The HPI is a weighted repeat sales index. It measures average price changes in repeat sales or refinancings on the same properties. This information is obtained by reviewing repeat mortgage transactions on single-family properties whose mortgages have been purchased or securitized by Fannie Mae or Freddie Mac since January 1975; (1) Figures cover the Colorado Springs, CO Metropolitan Statistical Area; (2) Rankings are based on annual percentage change for all metro areas containing at least 15,000 transactions over the last 10 years and ranges from 1 to 257; (3) figures based on a weighted average of Census Division estimates using a seasonally adjusted, purchase-only index; all figures are for the period ending December 31, 2022
Source: Federal Housing Finance Agency, Change in FHFA Metropolitan Area House Price Indexes, 2022Q4

Median Single-Family Home Prices

Area	2020	2021	2022[p]	Percent Change 2021 to 2022
MSA[1]	361.7	432.9	463.4	7.0
U.S. Average	300.2	357.1	392.6	9.9

Note: Figures are median sales prices of existing single-family homes in thousands of dollars; (p) preliminary; (1) Figures cover the Colorado Springs, CO Metropolitan Statistical Area
Source: National Association of Realtors, Median Sales Price of Existing Single-Family Homes for Metropolitan Areas, 4th Quarter 2022

Qualifying Income Based on Median Sales Price of Existing Single-Family Homes

Area	With 5% Down ($)	With 10% Down ($)	With 20% Down ($)
MSA[1]	132,658	125,676	111,712
U.S. Average	112,234	106,237	94,513

Note: Figures are preliminary; Qualifying income is based on a mortgage rate of 6.77%. Monthly principal and interest payment is limited to 25% of income; (1) Figures cover the Colorado Springs, CO Metropolitan Statistical Area
Source: National Association of Realtors, Qualifying Income Based on Median Sales Price of Existing Single-Family Homes for Metropolitan Areas, 4th Quarter 2022

Home Value

Area	Under $100,000	$100,000 -$199,999	$200,000 -$299,999	$300,000 -$399,999	$400,000 -$499,999	$500,000 -$999,999	$1,000,000 or more	Median ($)
City	4.6	11.0	28.1	26.0	14.7	14.1	1.4	324,100
MSA[1]	4.6	10.9	26.6	25.1	14.8	16.3	1.6	331,300
U.S.	16.2	24.2	20.1	13.6	8.3	13.6	4.1	244,900

Note: Figures are percentages except for median and cover owner-occupied housing units; (1) Figures cover the Colorado Springs, CO Metropolitan Statistical Area
Source: U.S. Census Bureau, 2017-2021 American Community Survey 5-Year Estimates

Year Housing Structure Built

Area	2020 or Later	2010 -2019	2000 -2009	1990 -1999	1980 -1989	1970 -1979	1960 -1969	1950 -1959	1940 -1949	Before 1940	Median Year
City	0.3	9.5	14.7	15.4	18.9	17.2	9.4	7.0	2.0	5.5	1985
MSA[1]	0.3	10.7	17.8	16.4	17.6	16.2	8.1	6.2	1.6	5.1	1987
U.S.	0.2	7.3	13.6	13.6	13.2	14.8	10.3	10.0	4.7	12.2	1979

Note: Figures are percentages except for Median Year; Note: (1) Figures cover the Colorado Springs, CO Metropolitan Statistical Area
Source: U.S. Census Bureau, 2017-2021 American Community Survey 5-Year Estimates

Gross Monthly Rent

Area	Under $500	$500 -$999	$1,000 -$1,499	$1,500 -$1,999	$2,000 -$2,499	$2,500 -$2,999	$3,000 and up	Median ($)
City	3.3	21.7	39.4	25.1	6.5	2.8	1.2	1,300
MSA[1]	3.3	20.8	36.2	28.6	7.6	2.6	1.1	1,349
U.S.	8.1	30.5	30.8	16.8	7.3	3.1	3.5	1,163

Note: Figures are percentages except for median; Gross rent is the contract rent plus the estimated average monthly cost of utilities (electricity, gas, and water and sewer) and fuels (oil, coal, kerosene, wood, etc.) if these are paid by the renter (or paid for the renter by someone else); (1) Figures cover the Colorado Springs, CO Metropolitan Statistical Area
Source: U.S. Census Bureau, 2017-2021 American Community Survey 5-Year Estimates

HEALTH

Health Risk Factors

Category	MSA[1] (%)	U.S. (%)
Adults aged 18–64 who have any kind of health care coverage	92.5	90.9
Adults who reported being in good or better health	85.3	85.2
Adults who have been told they have high blood cholesterol	33.6	35.7
Adults who have been told they have high blood pressure	25.3	32.4
Adults who are current smokers	12.9	14.4
Adults who currently use e-cigarettes	9.0	6.7
Adults who currently use chewing tobacco, snuff, or snus	3.6	3.5
Adults who are heavy drinkers[2]	5.2	6.3
Adults who are binge drinkers[3]	13.8	15.4
Adults who are overweight (BMI 25.0 - 29.9)	34.0	34.4
Adults who are obese (BMI 30.0 - 99.8)	28.5	33.9
Adults who participated in any physical activities in the past month	83.0	76.3

Note: (1) Figures cover the Colorado Springs, CO Metropolitan Statistical Area; (2) Heavy drinkers are classified as adult men having more than 14 drinks per week and adult women having more than 7 drinks per week; (3) Binge drinkers are classified as males having five or more drinks on one occasion or females having four or more drinks on one occasion
Source: Centers for Disease Control and Prevention, Behaviorial Risk Factor Surveillance System, SMART: Selected Metropolitan Area Risk Trends, 2021

Acute and Chronic Health Conditions

Category	MSA[1] (%)	U.S. (%)
Adults who have ever been told they had a heart attack	3.0	4.0
Adults who have ever been told they have angina or coronary heart disease	1.7	3.8
Adults who have ever been told they had a stroke	2.1	3.0
Adults who have ever been told they have asthma	16.4	14.9
Adults who have ever been told they have arthritis	27.7	25.8
Adults who have ever been told they have diabetes[2]	7.4	10.9
Adults who have ever been told they had skin cancer	6.8	6.6
Adults who have ever been told they had any other types of cancer	6.2	7.5
Adults who have ever been told they have COPD	5.7	6.1
Adults who have ever been told they have kidney disease	2.6	3.0
Adults who have ever been told they have a form of depression	25.4	20.5

Note: (1) Figures cover the Colorado Springs, CO Metropolitan Statistical Area; (2) Figures do not include pregnancy-related, borderline, or pre-diabetes
Source: Centers for Disease Control and Prevention, Behaviorial Risk Factor Surveillance System, SMART: Selected Metropolitan Area Risk Trends, 2021

Health Screening and Vaccination Rates

Category	MSA[1] (%)	U.S. (%)
Adults who have ever been tested for HIV	46.0	34.9
Adults who have had their blood cholesterol checked within the last five years	83.2	85.2
Adults aged 65+ who have had flu shot within the past year	73.5	68.6
Adults aged 65+ who have ever had a pneumonia vaccination	78.2	71.0

Note: (1) Figures cover the Colorado Springs, CO Metropolitan Statistical Area.
Source: Centers for Disease Control and Prevention, Behaviorial Risk Factor Surveillance System, SMART: Selected Metropolitan Area Risk Trends, 2021

Disability Status

Category	MSA[1] (%)	U.S. (%)
Adults who reported being deaf	5.6	7.2
Are you blind or have serious difficulty seeing, even when wearing glasses?	3.8	4.8
Are you limited in any way in any of your usual activities due to arthritis?	12.6	11.1
Do you have difficulty doing errands alone?	8.2	7.0
Do you have difficulty dressing or bathing?	3.8	3.6
Do you have serious difficulty concentrating/remembering/making decisions?	14.8	12.1
Do you have serious difficulty walking or climbing stairs?	11.5	12.8

Note: (1) Figures cover the Colorado Springs, CO Metropolitan Statistical Area.
Source: Centers for Disease Control and Prevention, Behaviorial Risk Factor Surveillance System, SMART: Selected Metropolitan Area Risk Trends, 2021

Mortality Rates for the Top 10 Causes of Death in the U.S.

ICD-10[a] Sub-Chapter	ICD-10[a] Code	Crude Mortality Rate[1] per 100,000 population	
		County[2]	U.S.
Malignant neoplasms	C00-C97	137.3	182.6
Ischaemic heart diseases	I20-I25	65.5	113.1
Other forms of heart disease	I30-I51	37.6	64.4
Other degenerative diseases of the nervous system	G30-G31	44.7	51.0
Cerebrovascular diseases	I60-I69	38.7	47.8
Other external causes of accidental injury	W00-X59	56.4	46.4
Chronic lower respiratory diseases	J40-J47	43.9	45.7
Organic, including symptomatic, mental disorders	F01-F09	24.7	35.9
Hypertensive diseases	I10-I15	37.3	35.0
Diabetes mellitus	E10-E14	22.5	29.6

Note: (a) ICD-10 = International Classification of Diseases 10th Revision; (1) Crude mortality rates are a three-year average covering 2019-2021; (2) Figures cover El Paso County.
Source: Centers for Disease Control and Prevention, National Center for Health Statistics. National Vital Statistics System, Mortality 2018-2021 on CDC WONDER Online Database

Mortality Rates for Selected Causes of Death

ICD-10[a] Sub-Chapter	ICD-10[a] Code	Crude Mortality Rate[1] per 100,000 population	
		County[2]	U.S.
Assault	X85-Y09	8.0	7.0
Diseases of the liver	K70-K76	23.3	19.8
Human immunodeficiency virus (HIV) disease	B20-B24	Unreliable	1.5
Influenza and pneumonia	J09-J18	6.7	14.7
Intentional self-harm	X60-X84	28.9	14.3
Malnutrition	E40-E46	4.7	4.3
Obesity and other hyperalimentation	E65-E68	3.3	3.0
Renal failure	N17-N19	8.1	15.7
Transport accidents	V01-V99	15.7	13.6
Viral hepatitis	B15-B19	1.3	1.2

Note: (a) ICD-10 = International Classification of Diseases 10th Revision; (1) Crude mortality rates are a three-year average covering 2019-2021; (2) Figures cover El Paso County; Data are suppressed when the data meet the criteria for confidentiality constraints; Crude mortality rates are flagged as unreliable when the rate would be calculated with a numerator of 20 or less.
Source: Centers for Disease Control and Prevention, National Center for Health Statistics. National Vital Statistics System, Mortality 2018-2021 on CDC WONDER Online Database

Health Insurance Coverage

Area	With Health Insurance	With Private Health Insurance	With Public Health Insurance	Without Health Insurance	Population Under Age 19 Without Health Insurance
City	92.1	69.2	36.4	7.9	4.6
MSA[1]	92.7	71.3	35.4	7.3	4.7
U.S.	91.2	67.8	35.4	8.8	5.3

Note: Figures are percentages that cover the civilian noninstitutionalized population; (1) Figures cover the Colorado Springs, CO Metropolitan Statistical Area
Source: U.S. Census Bureau, 2017-2021 American Community Survey 5-Year Estimates

Number of Medical Professionals

Area	MDs[3]	DOs[3,4]	Dentists	Podiatrists	Chiropractors	Optometrists
County[1] (number)	1,516	231	769	39	335	185
County[1] (rate[2])	207.1	31.6	104.2	5.3	45.4	25.1
U.S. (rate[2])	289.3	23.5	72.5	6.2	28.7	17.4

Note: Data as of 2021 unless noted; (1) Data covers El Paso County; (2) Rate per 100,000 population; (3) Data as of 2020 and includes all active, non-federal physicians; (4) Doctor of Osteopathic Medicine
Source: U.S. Department of Health and Human Services, Health Resources and Services Administration, Bureau of Health Professions, Area Resource File (ARF) 2021-2022

EDUCATION

Public School District Statistics

District Name	Schls	Pupils	Pupil/ Teacher Ratio	Minority Pupils[1] (%)	LEP/ELL[2] (%)	IEP[3] (%)
Academy School District No. 20	41	26,050	16.3	31.4	1.9	n/a
Cheyenne Mountain SD No. 12	9	3,663	14.5	27.7	2.1	n/a
Colorado Springs SD No. 11	57	23,359	16.0	51.7	6.2	n/a
Harrison School District No. 2	31	13,002	15.5	73.9	11.8	n/a
School District No. 3	18	9,369	16.0	54.3	1.4	n/a

Note: Table includes school districts with 2,000 or more students; (1) Percentage of students that are not non-Hispanic white; (2) Percentage of students that are Limited English Proficient or English Language Learners (2018-19); (3) Percentage of students that have an Individualized Education Program (2019-20).
Source: U.S. Department of Education, National Center for Education Statistics, Common Core of Data, Local Education Agency (School District) Universe Survey: School Year 2021-2022

Best High Schools

According to *U.S. News,* Colorado Springs is home to one of the top 500 high schools in the U.S.: **The Vanguard School** (#251). Nearly 18,000 public, magnet and charter schools were ranked based on their performance on state assessments and how well they prepare students for college. *U.S. News & World Report, "Best High Schools 2022"*

Highest Level of Education

Area	Less than H.S.	H.S. Diploma	Some College, No Deg.	Associate Degree	Bachelor's Degree	Master's Degree	Prof. School Degree	Doctorate Degree
City	6.1	19.1	24.0	10.7	24.3	12.0	2.3	1.7
MSA[1]	5.4	19.8	24.4	10.9	23.9	12.0	1.9	1.6
U.S.	11.1	26.5	20.0	8.7	20.6	9.3	2.2	1.5

Note: Figures cover persons age 25 and over; (1) Figures cover the Colorado Springs, CO Metropolitan Statistical Area
Source: U.S. Census Bureau, 2017-2021 American Community Survey 5-Year Estimates

Educational Attainment by Race

Area	High School Graduate or Higher (%)					Bachelor's Degree or Higher (%)				
	Total	White	Black	Asian	Hisp.[2]	Total	White	Black	Asian	Hisp.[2]
City	93.9	95.5	93.8	85.8	82.6	40.2	43.4	28.1	42.7	20.4
MSA[1]	94.6	95.8	95.1	87.2	84.7	39.4	41.9	29.6	42.2	21.4
U.S.	88.9	91.4	87.2	87.6	71.2	33.7	35.5	23.3	55.6	18.4

Note: Figures shown cover persons 25 years old and over; (1) Figures cover the Colorado Springs, CO Metropolitan Statistical Area; (2) People of Hispanic origin can be of any race
Source: U.S. Census Bureau, 2017-2021 American Community Survey 5-Year Estimates

School Enrollment by Grade and Control

Area	Preschool (%)		Kindergarten (%)		Grades 1 - 4 (%)		Grades 5 - 8 (%)		Grades 9 - 12 (%)	
	Public	Private	Public	Private	Public	Private	Public	Private	Public	Private
City	56.0	44.0	89.3	10.7	88.6	11.4	89.0	11.0	91.0	9.0
MSA[1]	58.9	41.1	87.2	12.8	88.7	11.3	90.1	9.9	90.8	9.2
U.S.	58.8	41.2	86.3	13.7	88.3	11.7	88.6	11.4	89.4	10.6

Note: Figures shown cover persons 3 years old and over; (1) Figures cover the Colorado Springs, CO Metropolitan Statistical Area
Source: U.S. Census Bureau, 2017-2021 American Community Survey 5-Year Estimates

Higher Education

Four-Year Colleges			Two-Year Colleges			Medical Schools[1]	Law Schools[2]	Voc/ Tech[3]
Public	Private Non-profit	Private For-profit	Public	Private Non-profit	Private For-profit			
3	2	1	0	0	4	0	0	4

Note: Figures cover institutions located within the Colorado Springs, CO Metropolitan Statistical Area and include main campuses only; (1) includes schools accredited by the Liaison Committee on Medical Education and the American Osteopathic Association's Commission on Osteopathic College Accreditation; (2) includes ABA-accredited schools, schools with provisional ABA accreditation, and state accredited schools; (3) includes all schools with programs that are less than 2 years.
Source: National Center for Education Statistics, Integrated Postsecondary Education System (IPEDS), 2021-22; Wikipedia, List of Medical Schools in the United States, accessed April 10, 2023; Wikipedia, List of Law Schools in the United States, accessed April 10, 2023

According to *U.S. News & World Report,* the Colorado Springs, CO metro area is home to two of the top 100 liberal arts colleges in the U.S.: **United States Air Force Academy** (#18 tie); **Colorado College** (#27 tie). The indicators used to capture academic quality fall into a number of categories: assessment by administrators at peer institutions; retention of students; faculty resources; student selectivity; financial resources; alumni giving; high school counselor ratings of colleges; and graduation rate. *U.S. News & World Report, "America's Best Colleges 2023"*

EMPLOYERS

Major Employers

Company Name	Industry
Children's Hospital Colorado	Healthcare
Colorado State University	Education
Community Hospital Assn	Healthcare
Denver International Airport	Airports
Exempla St Joseph Hospital	Healthcare
Great-West Funds Inc	Financial services
Great-West Life & Annuity Ins	Insurance
Keystone Resort	Recreation association
Level 3 Communications Inc	Communications
Lockheed Martin Corp	Technology
Lockheed Martin Space Systems	Defense systems & equipment
Memorial Hospital North	Healthcare
Penrose Hospital	Healthcare
Peterson AFB	U.S. military
Poudre Valley Hospital	Healthcare
Schriever Air Force Base	U.S. military
Terumo	Healthcare
University of Boulder	Education
University of Colorado Health	Healthcare
University of Colorado-Boulder	Education
University of Northern Colorado	Education
Verizon Wireless	Wireless communcations
Western Union Co	Payment services

Note: Companies shown are located within the Colorado Springs, CO Metropolitan Statistical Area.
Source: Hoovers.com; Wikipedia

PUBLIC SAFETY

Crime Rate

Area	Total Crime	Violent Crime Rate				Property Crime Rate		
		Murder	Rape[3]	Robbery	Aggrav. Assault	Burglary	Larceny-Theft	Motor Vehicle Theft
City	3,976.6	7.4	82.5	77.5	429.6	533.5	2,344.8	501.4
Suburbs[1]	1,620.4	4.1	66.6	24.3	191.2	193.8	966.8	173.6
Metro[2]	3,139.6	6.2	76.8	58.6	344.9	412.8	1,855.2	384.9
U.S.	2,356.7	6.5	38.4	73.9	279.7	314.2	1,398.0	246.0

Note: Figures are crimes per 100,000 population; (1) All areas within the metro area that are located outside the city limits; (2) Figures cover the Colorado Springs, CO Metropolitan Statistical Area; (3) All figures shown were reported using the revised Uniform Crime Reporting (UCR) definition of rape; Due to the transition to the National Incident-Based Reporting System (NIBRS), limited city and metro area data was released for 2021.
Source: FBI Uniform Crime Reports, 2020

Hate Crimes

Area	Number of Quarters Reported	Number of Incidents per Bias Motivation					
		Race/Ethnicity/Ancestry	Religion	Sexual Orientation	Disability	Gender	Gender Identity
City	4	15	2	3	0	0	0
U.S.	4	5,227	1,244	1,110	130	75	266

Note: Due to the transition to the National Incident-Based Reporting System (NIBRS), limited crime data was released for 2021.
Source: Federal Bureau of Investigation, Hate Crime Statistics 2020

Identity Theft Consumer Reports

Area	Reports	Reports per 100,000 Population	Rank[2]
MSA[1]	1,554	211	153
U.S.	1,108,609	339	-

Note: (1) Figures cover the Colorado Springs, CO Metropolitan Statistical Area; (2) Rank ranges from 1 to 391 where 1 indicates greatest number of identity theft reports per 100,000 population
Source: Federal Trade Commission, Consumer Sentinel Network Data Book 2022

Fraud and Other Consumer Reports

Area	Reports	Reports per 100,000 Population	Rank[2]
MSA[1]	8,314	1,130	56
U.S.	4,064,520	1,245	-

Note: (1) Figures cover the Colorado Springs, CO Metropolitan Statistical Area; (2) Rank ranges from 1 to 391 where 1 indicates greatest number of fraud and other consumer reports per 100,000 population
Source: Federal Trade Commission, Consumer Sentinel Network Data Book 2022

POLITICS

2020 Presidential Election Results

Area	Biden	Trump	Jorgensen	Hawkins	Other
El Paso County	42.7	53.5	2.4	0.3	1.0
U.S.	51.3	46.8	1.2	0.3	0.5

Note: Results are percentages and may not add to 100% due to rounding
Source: Dave Leip's Atlas of U.S. Presidential Elections

SPORTS

Professional Sports Teams

Team Name	League	Year Established

No teams are located in the metro area
Source: Wikipedia, Major Professional Sports Teams of the United States and Canada, April 12, 2023

CLIMATE

Average and Extreme Temperatures

Temperature	Jan	Feb	Mar	Apr	May	Jun	Jul	Aug	Sep	Oct	Nov	Dec	Yr.
Extreme High (°F)	71	72	78	87	93	99	98	97	94	86	78	75	99
Average High (°F)	41	44	51	61	68	79	85	81	75	63	49	41	62
Average Temp. (°F)	29	32	39	48	55	66	71	69	61	50	37	30	49
Average Low (°F)	17	20	26	34	42	52	57	55	48	36	24	17	36
Extreme Low (°F)	-20	-19	-3	8	22	36	48	39	22	7	-5	-24	-24

Note: Figures cover the years 1948-1993
Source: National Climatic Data Center, International Station Meteorological Climate Summary, 9/96

Average Precipitation/Snowfall/Humidity

Precip./Humidity	Jan	Feb	Mar	Apr	May	Jun	Jul	Aug	Sep	Oct	Nov	Dec	Yr.
Avg. Precip. (in.)	0.3	0.4	1.3	1.3	2.6	2.1	2.6	3.4	1.0	0.9	0.6	0.5	17.0
Avg. Snowfall (in.)	6	6	10	5	2	0	0	0	Tr	3	7	8	48
Avg. Rel. Hum. 5am (%)	57	60	62	62	69	67	66	71	66	59	60	59	63
Avg. Rel. Hum. 5pm (%)	48	43	39	34	39	36	36	43	36	36	45	52	41

Note: Figures cover the years 1948-1993; Tr = Trace amounts (<0.05 in. of rain; <0.5 in. of snow)
Source: National Climatic Data Center, International Station Meteorological Climate Summary, 9/96

Weather Conditions

Temperature			Daytime Sky			Precipitation		
10°F & below	32°F & below	90°F & above	Clear	Partly cloudy	Cloudy	0.01 inch or more precip.	0.1 inch or more snow/ice	Thunderstorms
21	161	18	108	157	100	98	33	49

Note: Figures are average number of days per year and cover the years 1948-1993
Source: National Climatic Data Center, International Station Meteorological Climate Summary, 9/96

HAZARDOUS WASTE

Superfund Sites

The Colorado Springs, CO metro area has no sites on the EPA's Superfund Final National Priorities List. There are a total of 1,165 Superfund sites with a status of proposed or final on the list in the U.S.
U.S. Environmental Protection Agency, National Priorities List, April 12, 2023

AIR QUALITY

Air Quality Trends: Ozone

	1990	1995	2000	2005	2010	2015	2018	2019	2020	2021
MSA[1]	n/a	n/a	n/a	n/a	n/a	n/a	n/a	n/a	n/a	n/a
U.S.	0.087	0.089	0.081	0.080	0.072	0.067	0.069	0.065	0.065	0.067

Note: (1) Data covers the Colorado Springs, CO Metropolitan Statistical Area; n/a not available. The values shown are the composite ozone concentration averages among trend sites based on the highest fourth daily maximum 8-hour concentration in parts per million. These trends are based on sites having an adequate record of monitoring data during the trend period. Data from exceptional events are included.
Source: U.S. Environmental Protection Agency, Air Quality Monitoring Information, "Air Quality Trends by City, 1990-2021"

Air Quality Index

Area	Percent of Days when Air Quality was...[2]					AQI Statistics[2]	
	Good	Moderate	Unhealthy for Sensitive Groups	Unhealthy	Very Unhealthy	Maximum	Median
MSA[1]	64.7	27.7	7.7	0.0	0.0	140	47

Note: (1) Data covers the Colorado Springs, CO Metropolitan Statistical Area; (2) Based on 365 days with AQI data in 2021. Air Quality Index (AQI) is an index for reporting daily air quality. EPA calculates the AQI for five major air pollutants regulated by the Clean Air Act: ground-level ozone, particle pollution (aka particulate matter), carbon monoxide, sulfur dioxide, and nitrogen dioxide. The AQI runs from 0 to 500. The higher the AQI value, the greater the level of air pollution and the greater the health concern. There are six AQI categories: "Good" AQI is between 0 and 50. Air quality is considered satisfactory; "Moderate" AQI is between 51 and 100. Air quality is acceptable; "Unhealthy for Sensitive Groups" When AQI values are between 101 and 150, members of sensitive groups may experience health effects; "Unhealthy" When AQI values are between 151 and 200 everyone may begin to experience health effects; "Very Unhealthy" AQI values between 201 and 300 trigger a health alert; "Hazardous" AQI values over 300 trigger warnings of emergency conditions (not shown).
Source: U.S. Environmental Protection Agency, Air Quality Index Report, 2021

Air Quality Index Pollutants

Area	Percent of Days when AQI Pollutant was...[2]					
	Carbon Monoxide	Nitrogen Dioxide	Ozone	Sulfur Dioxide	Particulate Matter 2.5	Particulate Matter 10
MSA[1]	0.0	0.0	95.1	(3)	4.9	0.0

Note: (1) Data covers the Colorado Springs, CO Metropolitan Statistical Area; (2) Based on 365 days with AQI data in 2021. The Air Quality Index (AQI) is an index for reporting daily air quality. EPA calculates the AQI for five major air pollutants regulated by the Clean Air Act: ground-level ozone, particle pollution (also known as particulate matter), carbon monoxide, sulfur dioxide, and nitrogen dioxide. The AQI runs from 0 to 500. The higher the AQI value, the greater the level of air pollution and the greater the health concern; (3) Sulfur dioxide is no longer included in this table (as of December 8, 2021) because SO_2 concentrations tend to be very localized and not necessarily representative of broad geographical areas like counties and CBSAs.
Source: U.S. Environmental Protection Agency, Air Quality Index Report, 2021

Maximum Air Pollutant Concentrations: Particulate Matter, Ozone, CO and Lead

	Particulate Matter 10 (ug/m³)	Particulate Matter 2.5 Wtd AM (ug/m³)	Particulate Matter 2.5 24-Hr (ug/m³)	Ozone (ppm)	Carbon Monoxide (ppm)	Lead (ug/m³)
MSA[1] Level	39	6	21	0.078	1	n/a
NAAQS[2]	150	15	35	0.075	9	0.15
Met NAAQS[2]	Yes	Yes	Yes	No	Yes	n/a

Note: (1) Data covers the Colorado Springs, CO Metropolitan Statistical Area; Data from exceptional events are included; (2) National Ambient Air Quality Standards; ppm = parts per million; ug/m³ = micrograms per cubic meter; n/a not available.
Concentrations: Particulate Matter 10 (coarse particulate)—highest second maximum 24-hour concentration; Particulate Matter 2.5 Wtd AM (fine particulate)—highest weighted annual mean concentration; Particulate Matter 2.5 24-Hour (fine particulate)—highest 98th percentile 24-hour concentration; Ozone—highest fourth daily maximum 8-hour concentration; Carbon Monoxide—highest second maximum non-overlapping 8-hour concentration; Lead—maximum running 3-month average
Source: U.S. Environmental Protection Agency, Air Quality Monitoring Information, "Air Quality Statistics by City, 2021"

Maximum Air Pollutant Concentrations: Nitrogen Dioxide and Sulfur Dioxide

	Nitrogen Dioxide AM (ppb)	Nitrogen Dioxide 1-Hr (ppb)	Sulfur Dioxide AM (ppb)	Sulfur Dioxide 1-Hr (ppb)	Sulfur Dioxide 24-Hr (ppb)
MSA[1] Level	n/a	n/a	n/a	10	n/a
NAAQS[2]	53	100	30	75	140
Met NAAQS[2]	n/a	n/a	n/a	Yes	n/a

Note: (1) Data covers the Colorado Springs, CO Metropolitan Statistical Area; Data from exceptional events are included; (2) National Ambient Air Quality Standards; ppm = parts per million; ug/m³ = micrograms per cubic meter; n/a not available.
Concentrations: Nitrogen Dioxide AM—highest arithmetic mean concentration; Nitrogen Dioxide 1-Hr—highest 98th percentile 1-hour daily maximum concentration; Sulfur Dioxide AM—highest annual mean concentration; Sulfur Dioxide 1-Hr—highest 99th percentile 1-hour daily maximum concentration; Sulfur Dioxide 24-Hr—highest second maximum 24-hour concentration
Source: U.S. Environmental Protection Agency, Air Quality Monitoring Information, "Air Quality Statistics by City, 2021"

Denver, Colorado

Background

From almost anywhere in Denver, you can command a breathtaking view of the 14,000-foot Rocky Mountains. The early settlers of Denver, however, were not attracted to the city because of its vistas, but because of its gold.

In 1858, there were rumors that gold had been discovered in Denver's Cherry Creek. It wasn't until 1867, however, that its gold and silver can be said to have established Denver on its way to the sparkling, dramatic skyline, and steel towers of the modern city.

Today's Denver bears little resemblance to the dusty frontier village of the nineteenth century. The "Mile High City" has become a manufacturing, distribution, and transportation center that serves not only the western regions of the United States, but the entire nation. Denver is also home to many companies that are engaged in alternative fuel research and development.

Denver has been the host city of the Democratic National Convention twice, first in 1908 and again in 2008. The city also hosted the international G7 (now G8) summit in 1997. These events bolstered Denver's international reputation both on a political and socioeconomic level.

The massively renovated Colorado Convention Center—now 584,000 square feet—is a magnet for regional and national conferences and shows and is enhanced by the 5,000-seat Wells Fargo Theatre and new Light Rail Train Station. The renovated historic Denver Union Station operates as a mixed-use retail and multi-modal transportation hub. Another architecturally interesting building is the Jeppesen Terminal at Denver's airport, the largest international hub in the United States. The unique roof is made of heat- and light-reflecting tension fabric. The airport is huge, with 53 square miles and 6 million square feet of public space and 93 gates.

The city is also home to a lively cultural, recreational, and educational scene, including concerts at the Boettcher Concert Hall and seasonal drives through the Denver Mountain Park Circle Drive. Awesome skiing and hiking the Rockies is just 90 minutes away. Other area attractions include the Denver Museum of Nature and Science, Colorado History Museum, Denver Art Museum, and the recently built condominiums, Museum Residences. In 2020 one of the city's many neighborhoods changed its name from Stapleton (a KKK member) to Central Park.

The city's multibillion-dollar public transportation expansion plan, FasTracks, is under construction in metropolitan Denver. New bus service, and several light rail and commuter rail lines have been completed, as has a $200 million renovation to Denver Union Station. Completion of all phases of the project is anticipated in 2050.

The city also has its share of offbeat, distinctive places, including the hip Capitol Hill district, which offers small music venues and dank bars that appeal to University of Denver students. Sports fans have the Colorado Avalanche hockey team, the Denver Nuggets basketball team, the Colorado Rockies baseball team, and the Denver Broncos football team. In 2019, the Denver Bandits became part of the Women's National Football League and the first professional women's football team in the state.

In 2005, Denver became the first major city in the U.S. to legalize the private possession of marijuana. In 2012, Colorado Amendment 64 was signed into law by Governor John Hickenlooper, in 2014 Colorado became the first state to allow the sale of marijuana for recreational use, and in 2019, Denver became the first U.S. city to decriminalize psilocybin mushrooms.

The Denver Zoo is open year-round and houses nearly 4,000 animals representing 700 species, including the okapi, red-bellied lemur, Amur leopard, black rhino, and Siberian tiger. The zoo continues to implement its master modernization plan of habitats, having recently completed Predator Ridge, home to 14 African species of mammals, birds and reptiles, and an indoor tropical rain forest.

The University of Denver, Community College of Denver, Metropolitan State College, and the University of Colorado at Denver are only a few of the many excellent educational opportunities available in the city.

Denver's invigorating climate matches much of the central Rocky Mountain region, without the frigidly cold mornings of the higher elevations during winter, or the hot afternoons of summer at lower altitudes. Extreme cold and heat are generally short-lived. Low relative humidity, light precipitation, and abundant sunshine characterize Denver's weather. Spring is the cloudiest, wettest, and windiest season, while autumn is the most pleasant. Air pollution remains challenging.

Rankings

General Rankings

- The Denver metro area was identified as one of America's fastest-growing areas in terms of population and business growth by *MagnifyMoney*. The area ranked #6 out of 35. The 100 most populous metro areas in the U.S. were evaluated on their change from 2011 to 2016 in the following categories: people and housing; workforce and employment opportunities; growing industry. *www.businessinsider.com, "The 35 Cities in the US with the Biggest Influx of People, the Most Work Opportunities, and the Hottest Business Growth," August 12, 2018*

- Denver was selected as one of the best places to live in the United States by *Money* magazine. The city ranked #28 out of 50. This year's list focused on cities that would be welcoming to a broader group of people and with populations of at least 20,000. Beginning with a pool of 1,370 candidates, editors looked at 350 data points, organized into the these nine categories: income and personal finance, cost of living, economic opportunity, housing market, fun and amenities, health and safety, education, diversity, and quality of life. *Money, "The 50 Best Places to Live in the U.S. in 2022-2023" September 29, 2022*

Business/Finance Rankings

- According to *Business Insider*, the Denver metro area is a prime place to run a startup or move an existing business to. The area ranked #11. More than 300 metro areas were analyzed for factors that were of top concern to new business owners. Data was based on the 2019 U.S. Census Bureau American Community Survey, statistics from the CDC, Bureau of Labor Statistics employment report, and University of Chicago analysis. Criteria: business formations; percentage of vaccinated population; percentage of households with internet subscriptions; median household income; and share of work that can be done from home. *www.businessinsider.com, "The 20 Best Cities for Starting a Business in 2022 Include Baltimore, Boulder, and Boston," January 5, 2022*

- *24/7 Wall St.* used metro data from the Bureau of Labor Statistics' Occupational Employment database to identify the cities with the highest percentage of those employed in jobs requiring knowledge in the science, technology, engineering, and math (STEM) fields as well as average wages for STEM jobs. The Denver metro area was #15. *247wallst.com, "15 Cities with the Most High-Tech Jobs," January 11, 2020*

- The Brookings Institution ranked the nation's largest cities based on income inequality. Denver was ranked #29 (#1 = greatest inequality). Criteria: the "95/20 ratio," a figure representing the income at which a household earns more than 95 percent of all other households, divided by the income at which a household earns more than only 20 percent of all other households. *Brookings Institution, "Household Income Inequality, Largest Cities of 97 Large U.S. Metro Areas, 2014-2016," February 5, 2018*

- The Brookings Institution ranked the 100 largest metro areas in the U.S. based on income inequality. Denver was ranked #59 (#1 = greatest inequality). Criteria: the "95/20 ratio," a figure representing the income at which a household earns more than 95 percent of all other households, divided by the income at which a household earns more than only 20 percent of all other households. *Brookings Institution, "Household Income Inequality, 100 Largest U.S. Metro Areas, 2014-2016," February 5, 2018*

- Payscale.com ranked the 32 largest metro areas in terms of wage growth. The Denver metro area ranked #20. Criteria: quarterly changes in private industry employee and education professional wage growth from the previous year. *PayScale, "Wage Trends by Metro Area-1st Quarter," April 20, 2023*

- The Denver metro area was identified as one of the most debt-ridden places in America by the finance site Credit.com. The metro area was ranked #10. Criteria: residents' average credit card debt as well as median income. *Credit.com, "25 Cities With the Most Credit Card Debt," February 28, 2018*

- Denver was identified as one of the unhappiest cities to work in by CareerBliss.com, an online community for career advancement. The city ranked #1 out of 5. Criteria: an employee's relationship with his or her boss and co-workers; general work environment; compensation; opportunities for advancement; company culture and job reputation; and resources. *Businesswire.com, "CareerBliss Unhappiest Cities to Work 2019," February 12, 2019*

- The Denver metro area appeared on the Milken Institute "2022 Best Performing Cities" list. Rank: #14 out of 200 large metro areas (population over 250,000). Criteria: job growth; wage and salary growth; high-tech output growth; housing affordability; household broadband access. *Milken Institute, "Best-Performing Cities 2022," March 28, 2022*

- *Forbes* ranked the 200 most populous metro areas to determine the nation's "Best Places for Business and Careers." The Denver metro area was ranked #4. Criteria: costs (business and living); job growth (past and projected); income growth; quality of life; educational attainment (college and high school); projected economic growth; cultural and leisure opportunities; workplace tolerance laws; net migration patterns. *Forbes, "The Best Places for Business and Careers 2019: Seattle Still On Top," October 30, 2019*

Dating/Romance Rankings

- Denver was selected as one of America's best cities for singles by the readers of *Travel + Leisure* in their annual "America's Favorite Cities" survey. Criteria included good-looking locals, cool shopping, an active bar scene and hipster-magnet coffee bars. *Travel + Leisure, "Best Cities in America for Singles," July 21, 2017*

Education Rankings

- Personal finance website *WalletHub* analyzed the 150 largest U.S. metropolitan statistical areas to determine where the most educated Americans are putting their degrees to work. Criteria: education levels; percentage of workers with degrees; education quality and attainment gap; public school quality rankings; quality and enrollment of each metro area's universities. Denver was ranked #14 (#1 = most educated city). *www.WalletHub.com, "Most & Least Educated Cities in America," July 18, 2022*

- Denver was selected as one of America's most literate cities. The city ranked #8 out of the 84 largest U.S. cities. Criteria: number of booksellers; library resources; Internet resources; educational attainment; periodical publishing resources; newspaper circulation. *Central Connecticut State University, "America's Most Literate Cities, 2018," February 2019*

Environmental Rankings

- Niche compiled a list of the nation's snowiest cities, based on the National Oceanic and Atmospheric Administration's 30-year average snowfall data. Among cities with a population of at least 50,000, Denver ranked #25. *Niche.com, Top 25 Snowiest Cities in America, December 10, 2018*

- The U.S. Environmental Protection Agency (EPA) released its list of U.S. metropolitan areas with the most ENERGY STAR certified buildings in 2022. The Denver metro area was ranked #6 out of 25. *U.S. Environmental Protection Agency, "2023 Energy Star Top Cities," April 26, 2023*

- The U.S. Conference of Mayors and Walmart Stores sponsor the Mayors' Climate Protection Awards Program which recognize mayors for outstanding and innovative practices that address the climate crisis: increase energy efficiency in their cities, reduce carbon emissions and expand renewable energy. Denver received an Honorable Mention in the large city category. *U.S. Conference of Mayors, "2022 Mayors' Climate Protection Awards," June 3, 2022*

- Denver was highlighted as one of the 25 most ozone-polluted metro areas in the U.S. during 2019 through 2021. The area ranked #6. *American Lung Association, "State of the Air 2023," April 19, 2023*

- Denver was highlighted as one of the 25 metro areas most polluted by short-term particle pollution (24-hour PM 2.5) in the U.S. during 2019 through 2021. The area ranked #18. *American Lung Association, "State of the Air 2023," April 19, 2023*

Food/Drink Rankings

- The U.S. Chamber of Commerce Foundation conducted an in-depth study on local food truck regulations, surveyed 288 food truck owners, and ranked 20 major American cities based on how friendly they are for operating a food truck. The compiled index assessed the following: procedures for obtaining permits and licenses; complying with restrictions; and financial obligations associated with operating a food truck. Denver ranked #2 overall (1 being the best). *www.foodtrucknation.us, "Food Truck Nation," March 20, 2018*

Health/Fitness Rankings

- For each of the 100 largest cities in the United States, the American Fitness Index®, compiled in partnership between the American College of Sports Medicine and the Elevance Health Foundation, evaluated community infrastructure and 34 health behaviors including preventive health, levels of chronic disease conditions, food insecurity, sleep quality, pedestrian safety, air quality, and community/environment resources that support physical activity. Denver ranked #9 for "community fitness." *americanfitnessindex.org, "2022 ACSM American Fitness Index Summary Report," July 12, 2022*

- The Denver metro area was identified as one of the worst cities for bed bugs in America by pest control company Orkin. The area ranked #15 out of 50 based on the number of bed bug treatments Orkin performed from December 2021 to November 2022. *Orkin, "The Windy City Can't Blow Bed Bugs Away: Chicago Ranks #1 For Third Consecutive Year On Orkin's Bed Bug Cities List," January 9, 2023*

- Denver was identified as a "2022 Spring Allergy Capital." The area ranked #98 out of 100. Three groups of factors were used to identify the most challenging cities for people with allergies during the spring season: annual spring pollen scores; over the counter allergy medicine use; number of board-certified allergy specialists. *Asthma and Allergy Foundation of America, "Spring Allergy Capitals 2022," March 2, 2022*

- Denver was identified as a "2022 Fall Allergy Capital." The area ranked #91 out of 100. Three groups of factors were used to identify the most challenging cities for people with allergies during the fall season: annual fall pollen scores; over the counter allergy medicine use; number of board-certified allergy specialists. *Asthma and Allergy Foundation of America, "Fall Allergy Capitals 2022," March 2, 2022*

- Denver was identified as a "2022 Asthma Capital." The area ranked #78 out of the nation's 100 largest metropolitan areas. Criteria: estimated asthma prevalence; asthma-related mortality; and ER visits due to asthma. Risk factors analyzed but not factored in the rankings: annual pollen score; annual air quality; public smoking laws; access to board-certified asthma specialists; rescue and controller medication use; uninsured rate; poverty rate. *Asthma and Allergy Foundation of America, "Asthma Capitals 2022: The Most Challenging Places to Live With Asthma," September 14, 2022*

Pet Rankings

- Denver appeared on *The Dogington Post* site as one of the top cities for dog lovers, ranking #1 out of 15. The real estate marketplace, Zillow®, and Rover, the largest pet sitter and dog walker network, introduced a new list of "Top Emerging Dog-Friendly Cities" for 2021. Criteria: number of new dog accounts on the Rover platform; and rentals and listings that mention features that attract dog owners (fenced-in yards, dog houses, dog door or proximity to a dog park). *www.dogingtonpost.com, "15 Cities Emerging as Dog-Friendliest in 2021," May 11, 2021*

Real Estate Rankings

- *WalletHub* compared the most populated U.S. cities to determine which had the best markets for real estate agents. Denver ranked #5 where demand was high and pay was the best. Criteria: sales per agent; annual median wage for real-estate agents; monthly average starting salary for real estate agents; real estate job density and competition; unemployment rate; home turnover rate; housing-market health index; and other relevant metrics. *www.WalletHub.com, "2021 Best Places to Be a Real Estate Agent," May 12, 2021*

- The Denver metro area was identified as one of the 20 least affordable housing markets in the U.S. in 2022. The area ranked #174 out of 186 markets. Criteria: qualification for a mortgage loan with a 10 percent down payment on a typical home. *National Association of Realtors®, Qualifying Income Based on Sales Price of Existing Single-Family Homes for Metropolitan Areas, 2022*

- Denver was ranked #165 out of 235 metro areas in terms of housing affordability in 2022 by the National Association of Home Builders (#1 = most affordable). Criteria: the share of homes sold in that area affordable to a family earning the local median income, based on standard mortgage underwriting criteria. *National Association of Home Builders®, NAHB-Wells Fargo Housing Opportunity Index, 4th Quarter 2022*

Safety Rankings

- Allstate ranked the 200 largest cities in America in terms of driver safety. Denver ranked #83. Criteria: internal property damage claims over a two-year period from January 2016 to December 2017. The report helps increase the importance of safety and awareness behind the wheel. *Allstate, "Allstate America's Best Drivers Report, 2019" June 24, 2019*

- Denver was identified as one of the most dangerous cities in America by NeighborhoodScout. The city ranked #85 out of 100 (#1 = most dangerous). Criteria: number of violent crimes per 1,000 residents. The editors evaluated cities with 25,000 or more residents. *NeighborhoodScout.com, "2023 Top 100 Most Dangerous Cities in the U.S.," January 12, 2023*

- The National Insurance Crime Bureau ranked 390 metro areas in the U.S. in terms of per capita rates of vehicle theft. The Denver metro area ranked #2 (#1 = highest rate). Criteria: number of vehicle theft offenses per 100,000 inhabitants in 2021. *National Insurance Crime Bureau, "Hot Spots 2021," September 1, 2022*

Seniors/Retirement Rankings

- From its Best Cities for Successful Aging indexes, the Milken Institute generated rankings for metropolitan areas, weighing data in nine categories—health care, wellness, living arrangements, transportation and convenience, financial characteristics, education, employment, community engagement, and overall livability. The Denver metro area was ranked #12 overall in the large metro area category. *Milken Institute, "Best Cities for Successful Aging, 2017" March 14, 2017*

Sports/Recreation Rankings

- Denver was chosen as one of America's best cities for bicycling. The city ranked #14 out of 50. Criteria: cycling infrastructure that is safe and friendly for all ages; energy and bike culture. The editors evaluated cities with populations of 100,000 or more. *Bicycling, "The 50 Best Bike Cities in America," October 10, 2018*

Transportation Rankings

- According to the INRIX "2022 Global Traffic Scorecard," Denver was identified as one of the most congested metro areas in the U.S. The area ranked #17 out of 25. Criteria: average annual time spent in traffic and average cost of congestion per motorist. *Inrix.com, "Return to Work, Higher Gas Prices & Inflation Drove Americans to Spend Hundreds More in Time and Money Commuting," January 10, 2023*

Women/Minorities Rankings

- The *Houston Chronicle* listed the Denver metro area as #3 in top places for young Latinos to live in the U.S. Research was largely based on housing and occupational data from the largest metropolitan areas performed by *Forbes* and NBC Universo. Criteria: percentage of 18-34 year-olds; Latino college grad rates; and diversity. *blog.chron.com, "The 15 Best Big Cities for Latino Millenials," January 26, 2016*

- Personal finance website *WalletHub* compared more than 180 U.S. cities across two key dimensions, "Hispanic Business-Friendliness" and "Hispanic Purchasing Power," to arrive at the most favorable conditions for Hispanic entrepreneurs. Denver was ranked #41 out of 182. Criteria includes: share of Hispanic-Owned Businesses; Hispanic entrepreneurship rate to median annual income of Hispanics; Small Business-Friendliness score; cost of living; and number of Hispanics with at least a bachelor's degree. *WalletHub.com, "2019's Best Cities for Hispanic Entrepreneurs," May 1, 2019*

Miscellaneous Rankings

- The watchdog site, Charity Navigator, conducted a study of charities in major markets both to analyze statistical differences in their financial, accountability, and transparency practices and to track year-to-year variations in individual philanthropic communities. The Denver metro area was ranked #22 among the 30 metro markets in the rating category of Overall Score. *www.charitynavigator.org, "2017 Metro Market Study," May 1, 2017*

- *WalletHub* compared the 150 most populated U.S. cities to determine their operating efficiency. A "Quality of Services" score was constructed for each city and then divided by the total budget per capita to reveal which were managed the best. Denver ranked #132. Criteria: financial stability; economy; education; safety; health; infrastructure and pollution. *www.WalletHub.com, "2022's Best- & Worst-Run Cities in America," June 21, 2022*

- Denver was selected as one of "America's Friendliest Cities." The city ranked #20 in the "Friendliest" category. Respondents to an online survey were asked to rate 38 top urban destinations in the United States as to general friendliness, as well as manners, politeness and warm disposition. *Travel + Leisure, "America's Friendliest Cities," October 20, 2017*

- The National Alliance to End Homelessness listed the 25 most populous metro areas with the highest rate of homelessness. The Denver metro area had a high rate of homelessness. Criteria: number of homeless people per 10,000 population in 2016. *National Alliance to End Homelessness, "Homelessness in the 25 Most Populous U.S. Metro Areas," September 1, 2017*

Business Environment

DEMOGRAPHICS

Population Growth

Area	1990 Census	2000 Census	2010 Census	2020 Census	Population Growth (%) 1990-2020	Population Growth (%) 2010-2020
City	467,153	554,636	600,158	715,522	53.2	19.2
MSA[1]	1,666,935	2,179,296	2,543,482	2,963,821	77.8	16.5
U.S.	248,709,873	281,421,906	308,745,538	331,449,281	33.3	7.4

Note: (1) Figures cover the Denver-Aurora-Lakewood, CO Metropolitan Statistical Area
Source: U.S. Census Bureau, 1990 Census, 2000 Census, 2010 Census, 2020 Census

Race

Area	White Alone[2] (%)	Black Alone[2] (%)	Asian Alone[2] (%)	AIAN[3] Alone[2] (%)	NHOPI[4] Alone[2] (%)	Other Race Alone[2] (%)	Two or More Races (%)
City	60.6	8.9	3.9	1.5	0.2	11.3	13.5
MSA[1]	66.7	5.6	4.6	1.2	0.2	8.8	12.8
U.S.	61.6	12.4	6.0	1.1	0.2	8.4	10.2

Note: (1) Figures cover the Denver-Aurora-Lakewood, CO Metropolitan Statistical Area; (2) Alone is defined as not being in combination with one or more other races; (3) American Indian and Alaska Native; (4) Native Hawaiian and Other Pacific Islander
Source: U.S. Census Bureau, 2020 Census

Hispanic or Latino Origin

Area	Total (%)	Mexican (%)	Puerto Rican (%)	Cuban (%)	Other (%)
City	29.4	22.6	0.7	0.3	5.9
MSA[1]	23.4	17.5	0.6	0.2	5.0
U.S.	18.4	11.2	1.8	0.7	4.7

Note: Persons of Hispanic or Latino origin can be of any race; (1) Figures cover the Denver-Aurora-Lakewood, CO Metropolitan Statistical Area
Source: U.S. Census Bureau, 2017-2021 American Community Survey 5-Year Estimates

Age

Area	Under Age 5	Age 5–19	Age 20–34	Age 35–44	Age 45–54	Age 55–64	Age 65–74	Age 75–84	Age 85+	Median Age
City	5.4	15.5	31.0	15.8	11.1	9.4	7.4	3.2	1.3	34.1
MSA[1]	5.5	18.8	23.0	14.7	12.6	11.7	8.5	3.7	1.4	36.6
U.S.	5.6	19.2	20.2	12.7	12.4	13.1	10.0	4.9	1.9	38.8

Note: (1) Figures cover the Denver-Aurora-Lakewood, CO Metropolitan Statistical Area
Source: U.S. Census Bureau, 2020 Census

Disability by Age

Area	All Ages	Under 18 Years Old	18 to 64 Years Old	65 Years and Over
City	9.7	3.5	7.6	32.3
MSA[1]	9.7	3.5	7.8	29.8
U.S.	12.6	4.4	10.3	33.4

Note: Figures show percent of the civilian noninstitutionalized population that reported having a disability. Disability status is determined from six types of difficulty: vision, hearing, cognitive, ambulatory, self-care, and independent living. For children under 5 years old, hearing and vision difficulty are used to determine disability status. For children between the ages of 5 and 14, disability status is determined from hearing, vision, cognitive, ambulatory, and self-care difficulties. For people aged 15 years and older, they are considered to have a disability if they have difficulty with any one of the six difficulty types; Note: (1) Figures cover the Denver-Aurora-Lakewood, CO Metropolitan Statistical Area
Source: U.S. Census Bureau, 2017-2021 American Community Survey 5-Year Estimates

Ancestry

Area	German	Irish	English	American	Italian	Polish	French[2]	Scottish	Dutch
City	13.9	10.1	9.0	2.6	5.0	2.7	2.1	2.1	1.1
MSA[1]	17.1	10.7	10.5	3.3	5.0	2.4	2.4	2.2	1.4
U.S.	12.8	9.6	8.1	5.7	5.0	2.7	2.2	1.6	1.1

Note: Figures are the percentage of the total population reporting a particular ancestry. The nine most commonly reported ancestries in the U.S. are shown. Figures include multiple ancestries (e.g. if a person reported being Irish and Italian, they were included in both columns); (1) Figures cover the Denver-Aurora-Lakewood, CO Metropolitan Statistical Area; (2) Excludes Basque
Source: U.S. Census Bureau, 2017-2021 American Community Survey 5-Year Estimates

Foreign-born Population

| Area | Percent of Population Born in | | | | | | | | |
	Any Foreign Country	Asia	Mexico	Europe	Caribbean	Central America[2]	South America	Africa	Canada
City	14.2	2.8	6.6	1.4	0.3	0.6	0.7	1.4	0.3
MSA[1]	12.0	3.3	4.6	1.4	0.2	0.5	0.6	1.1	0.3
U.S.	13.6	4.2	3.3	1.5	1.4	1.1	1.1	0.8	0.2

Note: (1) Figures cover the Denver-Aurora-Lakewood, CO Metropolitan Statistical Area; (2) Excludes Mexico.
Source: U.S. Census Bureau, 2017-2021 American Community Survey 5-Year Estimates

Household Size

| Area | Persons in Household (%) | | | | | | | Average Household Size |
	One	Two	Three	Four	Five	Six	Seven or More	
City	38.6	33.5	11.7	9.4	3.9	1.6	1.3	2.20
MSA[1]	28.4	34.5	15.1	13.1	5.3	2.2	1.3	2.50
U.S.	28.1	33.8	15.5	12.9	6.0	2.3	1.4	2.60

Note: (1) Figures cover the Denver-Aurora-Lakewood, CO Metropolitan Statistical Area
Source: U.S. Census Bureau, 2017-2021 American Community Survey 5-Year Estimates

Household Relationships

Area	House-holder	Opposite-sex Spouse	Same-sex Spouse	Opposite-sex Unmarried Partner	Same-sex Unmarried Partner	Child[2]	Grand-child	Other Relatives	Non-relatives
City	44.4	14.0	0.5	4.1	0.4	22.3	1.9	4.4	5.9
MSA[1]	39.4	17.9	0.3	2.9	0.2	27.4	1.9	4.4	4.3
U.S.	38.3	17.5	0.2	2.5	0.2	28.3	2.4	4.8	3.4

Note: Figures are percent of the total population; (1) Figures cover the Denver-Aurora-Lakewood, CO Metropolitan Statistical Area; (2) Includes biological, adopted, and stepchildren of the householder
Source: U.S. Census Bureau, 2020 Census

Gender

Area	Males	Females	Males per 100 Females
City	358,405	357,117	100.4
MSA[1]	1,481,349	1,482,472	99.9
U.S.	162,685,811	168,763,470	96.4

Note: (1) Figures cover the Denver-Aurora-Lakewood, CO Metropolitan Statistical Area
Source: U.S. Census Bureau, 2020 Census

Marital Status

Area	Never Married	Now Married[2]	Separated	Widowed	Divorced
City	43.4	39.6	1.6	3.5	11.8
MSA[1]	33.6	49.8	1.4	3.8	11.5
U.S.	33.8	48.0	1.8	5.6	10.8

Note: Figures are percentages and cover the population 15 years of age and older; (1) Figures cover the Denver-Aurora-Lakewood, CO Metropolitan Statistical Area; (2) Excludes separated
Source: U.S. Census Bureau, 2017-2021 American Community Survey 5-Year Estimates

Religious Groups by Family

Area	Catholic	Baptist	Methodist	LDS[2]	Pentecostal	Lutheran	Islam	Adventist	Other
MSA[1]	16.1	1.5	1.0	2.1	0.6	1.4	0.3	1.1	10.4
U.S.	18.7	7.3	3.0	2.0	1.8	1.7	1.3	1.3	11.6

Note: Figures are the number of adherents as a percentage of the total population and cover the eight largest religious groups in the U.S; (1) Figures cover the Denver-Aurora-Lakewood, CO Metropolitan Statistical Area; (2) Church of Jesus Christ of Latter-day Saints
Sources: 2020 U.S. Religion Census, Association of Statisticians of American Religious Bodies; The Association of Religion Data Archives (ARDA)

Religious Groups by Tradition

Area	Catholic	Evangelical Protestant	Mainline Protestant	Black Protestant	Islam	Judaism	Hinduism	Orthodox	Buddhism
MSA[1]	16.1	9.6	2.8	0.6	0.3	0.4	0.5	0.4	0.5
U.S.	18.7	16.5	5.2	2.3	1.3	0.6	0.4	0.4	0.3

Note: Figures are the number of adherents as a percentage of the total population; (1) Figures cover the Denver-Aurora-Lakewood, CO Metropolitan Statistical Area
Sources: 2020 U.S. Religion Census, Association of Statisticians of American Religious Bodies; The Association of Religion Data Archives (ARDA)

ECONOMY

Gross Metropolitan Product

Area[1]	2020	2021	2022	2023	Rank[2]
MSA[1]	223.1	246.9	271.0	286.2	18

Note: Figures are in billions of dollars; (1) Figures cover the Denver-Aurora-Lakewood, CO Metropolitan Statistical Area; (2) Rank is based on 2021 data and ranges from 1 to 381
Source: U.S. Conference of Mayors, U.S. Metro Economies: U.S. Metros Compared to Global and State Economies, June 2022

Economic Growth

Area	2018-20 (%)	2021 (%)	2022 (%)	2023 (%)	Rank[2]
MSA[1]	0.8	6.2	3.5	3.1	82
U.S.	-0.6	5.7	3.1	2.9	–

Note: Figures are real gross metropolitan product (GMP) growth rates and represent average annual percent change; (1) Figures cover the Denver-Aurora-Lakewood, CO Metropolitan Statistical Area; (2) Rank is based on 2020 2-year average annual percent change and ranges from 1 to 381
Source: U.S. Conference of Mayors, U.S. Metro Economies: U.S. Metros Compared to Global and State Economies, June 2022

Metropolitan Area Exports

Area	2016	2017	2018	2019	2020	2021	Rank[2]
MSA[1]	3,649.3	3,954.7	4,544.3	4,555.6	4,604.4	4,670.8	62

Note: Figures are in millions of dollars; (1) Figures cover the Denver-Aurora-Lakewood, CO Metropolitan Statistical Area; (2) Rank is based on 2021 data and ranges from 1 to 388
Source: U.S. Department of Commerce, International Trade Administration, Office of Trade and Economic Analysis, Industry and Analysis, Exports by Metropolitan Area, data extracted March 16, 2023

Building Permits

Area	Single-Family			Multi-Family			Total		
	2021	2022	Pct. Chg.	2021	2022	Pct. Chg.	2021	2022	Pct. Chg.
City	1,550	1,323	-14.6	8,450	6,973	-17.5	10,000	8,296	-17.0
MSA[1]	13,113	10,108	-22.9	16,893	13,368	-20.9	30,006	23,476	-21.8
U.S.	1,115,400	975,600	-12.5	621,600	689,500	10.9	1,737,000	1,665,100	-4.1

Note: (1) Figures cover the Denver-Aurora-Lakewood, CO Metropolitan Statistical Area; Figures represent new, privately-owned housing units authorized (unadjusted data); All permit data are based on estimates with imputation
Source: U.S. Census Bureau, Manufacturing, Mining, and Construction Statistics, Building Permits, 2021, 2022

Bankruptcy Filings

Area	Business Filings			Nonbusiness Filings		
	2021	2022	% Chg.	2021	2022	% Chg.
Denver County	72	37	-48.6	764	590	-22.8
U.S.	14,347	13,481	-6.0	399,269	374,240	-6.3

Note: Business filings include Chapter 7, Chapter 9, Chapter 11, Chapter 12, Chapter 13, Chapter 15, and Section 304; Nonbusiness filings include Chapter 7, Chapter 11, and Chapter 13
Source: Administrative Office of the U.S. Courts, Business and Nonbusiness Bankruptcy, County Cases Commenced by Chapter of the Bankruptcy Code, During the 12-Month Period Ending December 31, 2021 and Business and Nonbusiness Bankruptcy, County Cases Commenced by Chapter of the Bankruptcy Code, During the 12-Month Period Ending December 31, 2022

Housing Vacancy Rates

Area	Gross Vacancy Rate[2] (%)			Year-Round Vacancy Rate[3] (%)			Rental Vacancy Rate[4] (%)			Homeowner Vacancy Rate[5] (%)		
	2020	2021	2022	2020	2021	2022	2020	2021	2022	2020	2021	2022
MSA[1]	5.8	6.5	5.8	5.1	5.3	5.2	4.8	4.6	5.1	0.5	1.0	0.3
U.S.	10.6	10.8	10.5	8.2	8.4	8.2	6.3	6.1	5.8	1.0	0.9	0.8

Note: (1) Figures cover the Denver-Aurora-Lakewood, CO Metropolitan Statistical Area; (2) The percentage of the total housing inventory that is vacant; (3) The percentage of the housing inventory (excluding seasonal units) that is year-round vacant; (4) The percentage of rental inventory that is vacant for rent; (5) The percentage of homeowner inventory that is vacant for sale
Source: U.S. Census Bureau, Housing Vacancies and Homeownership Annual Statistics: 2020, 2021, 2022

INCOME

Income

Area	Per Capita ($)	Median Household ($)	Average Household ($)
City	50,642	78,177	111,981
MSA[1]	47,026	88,512	117,250
U.S.	37,638	69,021	97,196

Note: (1) Figures cover the Denver-Aurora-Lakewood, CO Metropolitan Statistical Area
Source: U.S. Census Bureau, 2017-2021 American Community Survey 5-Year Estimates

Household Income Distribution

Area	Percent of Households Earning							
	Under $15,000	$15,000 -$24,999	$25,000 -$34,999	$35,000 -$49,999	$50,000 -$74,999	$75,000 -$99,999	$100,000 -$149,999	$150,000 and up
City	8.6	6.1	6.4	10.3	16.9	12.4	17.0	22.2
MSA[1]	6.2	4.8	5.7	9.5	16.3	13.2	19.9	24.5
U.S.	9.4	7.8	8.2	11.4	16.8	12.8	16.3	17.3

Note: (1) Figures cover the Denver-Aurora-Lakewood, CO Metropolitan Statistical Area
Source: U.S. Census Bureau, 2017-2021 American Community Survey 5-Year Estimates

Poverty Rate

Area	All Ages	Under 18 Years Old	18 to 64 Years Old	65 Years and Over
City	11.6	16.0	10.4	11.3
MSA[1]	8.1	10.2	7.6	7.1
U.S.	12.6	17.0	11.8	9.6

Note: Figures are percentage of people whose income during the past 12 months was below the poverty level;
(1) Figures cover the Denver-Aurora-Lakewood, CO Metropolitan Statistical Area
Source: U.S. Census Bureau, 2017-2021 American Community Survey 5-Year Estimates

EMPLOYMENT

Labor Force and Employment

Area	Civilian Labor Force			Workers Employed		
	Dec. 2021	Dec. 2022	% Chg.	Dec. 2021	Dec. 2022	% Chg.
City	428,646	439,359	2.5	411,447	426,400	3.6
MSA[1]	1,691,446	1,735,541	2.6	1,629,015	1,687,640	3.6
U.S.	161,696,000	164,224,000	1.6	155,732,000	158,872,000	2.0

Note: Data is not seasonally adjusted and covers workers 16 years of age and older; (1) Figures cover the
Denver-Aurora-Lakewood, CO Metropolitan Statistical Area
Source: Bureau of Labor Statistics, Local Area Unemployment Statistics

Unemployment Rate

Area	2022											
	Jan.	Feb.	Mar.	Apr.	May	Jun.	Jul.	Aug.	Sep.	Oct.	Nov.	Dec.
City	4.3	4.3	3.9	3.4	3.3	3.4	3.6	3.6	3.5	3.7	3.4	2.9
MSA[1]	4.0	4.0	3.6	3.2	3.1	3.3	3.5	3.3	3.2	3.5	3.3	2.8
U.S.	4.4	4.1	3.8	3.3	3.4	3.8	3.8	3.8	3.3	3.4	3.4	3.3

Note: Data is not seasonally adjusted and covers workers 16 years of age and older; (1) Figures cover the
Denver-Aurora-Lakewood, CO Metropolitan Statistical Area
Source: Bureau of Labor Statistics, Local Area Unemployment Statistics

Average Wages

Occupation	$/Hr.	Occupation	$/Hr.
Accountants and Auditors	43.21	Maintenance and Repair Workers	25.27
Automotive Mechanics	26.75	Marketing Managers	86.32
Bookkeepers	24.91	Network and Computer Systems Admin.	50.59
Carpenters	26.47	Nurses, Licensed Practical	30.30
Cashiers	16.03	Nurses, Registered	42.21
Computer Programmers	59.06	Nursing Assistants	19.35
Computer Systems Analysts	58.10	Office Clerks, General	24.74
Computer User Support Specialists	33.31	Physical Therapists	47.13
Construction Laborers	20.88	Physicians	156.83
Cooks, Restaurant	18.61	Plumbers, Pipefitters and Steamfitters	31.18
Customer Service Representatives	21.35	Police and Sheriff's Patrol Officers	41.85
Dentists	73.17	Postal Service Mail Carriers	28.16
Electricians	29.06	Real Estate Sales Agents	40.40
Engineers, Electrical	53.05	Retail Salespersons	19.03
Fast Food and Counter Workers	15.81	Sales Representatives, Technical/Scientific	54.91
Financial Managers	94.94	Secretaries, Exc. Legal/Medical/Executive	22.11
First-Line Supervisors of Office Workers	34.80	Security Guards	19.02
General and Operations Managers	75.18	Surgeons	146.05
Hairdressers/Cosmetologists	21.59	Teacher Assistants, Exc. Postsecondary*	17.40
Home Health and Personal Care Aides	16.85	Teachers, Secondary School, Exc. Sp. Ed.*	32.50
Janitors and Cleaners	17.70	Telemarketers	20.16
Landscaping/Groundskeeping Workers	20.25	Truck Drivers, Heavy/Tractor-Trailer	27.32
Lawyers	84.07	Truck Drivers, Light/Delivery Services	23.68
Maids and Housekeeping Cleaners	16.80	Waiters and Waitresses	18.48

Note: Wage data covers the Denver-Aurora-Lakewood, CO Metropolitan Statistical Area; (*) Hourly wages
were calculated from annual wage data based on a 40 hour work week; n/a not available.
Source: Bureau of Labor Statistics, Metro Area Occupational Employment & Wage Estimates, May 2022

Employment by Industry

Sector	MSA[1]		U.S.
	Number of Employees	Percent of Total	Percent of Total
Construction, Mining, and Logging	110,500	6.9	5.4
Private Education and Health Services	194,800	12.2	16.1
Financial Activities	116,800	7.3	5.9
Government	202,900	12.7	14.5
Information	52,900	3.3	2.0
Leisure and Hospitality	168,800	10.6	10.3
Manufacturing	71,300	4.5	8.4
Other Services	66,200	4.1	3.7
Professional and Business Services	312,800	19.6	14.7
Retail Trade	141,500	8.9	10.2
Transportation, Warehousing, and Utilities	80,400	5.0	4.9
Wholesale Trade	78,900	4.9	3.9

Note: Figures are non-farm employment as of December 2022. Figures are not seasonally adjusted and include workers 16 years of age and older; (1) Figures cover the Denver-Aurora-Lakewood, CO Metropolitan Statistical Area
Source: Bureau of Labor Statistics, Current Employment Statistics, Employment, Hours, and Earnings

Employment by Occupation

Occupation Classification	City (%)	MSA[1] (%)	U.S. (%)
Management, Business, Science, and Arts	51.7	47.1	40.3
Natural Resources, Construction, and Maintenance	7.0	7.9	8.7
Production, Transportation, and Material Moving	7.9	9.5	13.1
Sales and Office	19.0	20.8	20.9
Service	14.5	14.7	17.0

Note: Figures cover employed civilians 16 years of age and older; (1) Figures cover the Denver-Aurora-Lakewood, CO Metropolitan Statistical Area
Source: U.S. Census Bureau, 2017-2021 American Community Survey 5-Year Estimates

Occupations with Greatest Projected Employment Growth: 2022 – 2024

Occupation[1]	2022 Employment	2024 Projected Employment	Numeric Employment Change	Percent Employment Change
Software Developers	43,570	47,290	3,720	8.5
Stockers and Order Fillers	45,230	48,030	2,800	6.2
Cooks, Restaurant	31,870	34,550	2,680	8.4
Fast Food and Counter Workers	79,850	82,410	2,560	3.2
Accountants and Auditors	42,150	43,910	1,760	4.2
Market Research Analysts and Marketing Specialists	28,150	29,830	1,680	6.0
Home Health and Personal Care Aides	43,200	44,870	1,670	3.9
Registered Nurses	53,590	55,060	1,470	2.7
General and Operations Managers	47,360	48,780	1,420	3.0
Sales Representatives of Services, Except Advertising, Insurance, Financial Services, and Travel	37,310	38,730	1,420	3.8

Note: Projections cover Colorado; (1) Sorted by numeric employment change
Source: www.projectionscentral.com, State Occupational Projections, 2022–2024 Short-Term Projections

Fastest-Growing Occupations: 2022 – 2024

Occupation[1]	2022 Employment	2024 Projected Employment	Numeric Employment Change	Percent Employment Change
Derrick Operators, Oil and Gas	550	640	90	16.4
Roustabouts, Oil and Gas	1,550	1,790	240	15.5
Service Unit Operators, Oil, Gas, and Mining	2,430	2,760	330	13.6
Flight Attendants	4,890	5,490	600	12.3
Epidemiologists	530	590	60	11.3
Information Security Analysts (SOC 2018)	6,100	6,760	660	10.8
Statisticians	1,410	1,550	140	9.9
Veterinary Assistants and Laboratory Animal Caretakers	2,360	2,590	230	9.7
Data Scientists	3,520	3,850	330	9.4
Solar Photovoltaic Installers	530	580	50	9.4

Note: Projections cover Colorado; (1) Sorted by percent employment change and excludes occupations with numeric employment change less than 50
Source: www.projectionscentral.com, State Occupational Projections, 2022–2024 Short-Term Projections

CITY FINANCES

City Government Finances

Component	2020 ($000)	2020 ($ per capita)
Total Revenues	3,943,201	5,422
Total Expenditures	4,326,488	5,949
Debt Outstanding	8,399,283	11,550
Cash and Securities[1]	6,260,391	8,609

Note: (1) Cash and security holdings of a government at the close of its fiscal year, including those of its dependent agencies, utilities, and liquor stores.
Source: U.S. Census Bureau, State & Local Government Finances 2020

City Government Revenue by Source

Source	2020 ($000)	2020 ($ per capita)	2020 (%)
General Revenue			
From Federal Government	16,059	22	0.4
From State Government	186,334	256	4.7
From Local Governments	59,392	82	1.5
Taxes			
Property	304,969	419	7.7
Sales and Gross Receipts	1,023,897	1,408	26.0
Personal Income	0	0	0.0
Corporate Income	0	0	0.0
Motor Vehicle License	32,020	44	0.8
Other Taxes	124,262	171	3.2
Current Charges	1,542,559	2,121	39.1
Liquor Store	0	0	0.0
Utility	317,155	436	8.0

Source: U.S. Census Bureau, State & Local Government Finances 2020

City Government Expenditures by Function

Function	2020 ($000)	2020 ($ per capita)	2020 (%)
General Direct Expenditures			
Air Transportation	1,182,840	1,626	27.3
Corrections	146,438	201	3.4
Education	0	0	0.0
Employment Security Administration	0	0	0.0
Financial Administration	113,390	155	2.6
Fire Protection	147,524	202	3.4
General Public Buildings	18,733	25	0.4
Governmental Administration, Other	89,407	122	2.1
Health	109,272	150	2.5
Highways	81,195	111	1.9
Hospitals	0	0	0.0
Housing and Community Development	166,037	228	3.8
Interest on General Debt	370,991	510	8.6
Judicial and Legal	96,040	132	2.2
Libraries	51,579	70	1.2
Parking	16,100	22	0.4
Parks and Recreation	358,517	493	8.3
Police Protection	280,689	386	6.5
Public Welfare	164,191	225	3.8
Sewerage	194,218	267	4.5
Solid Waste Management	12,976	17	0.3
Veterans' Services	0	0	0.0
Liquor Store	0	0	0.0
Utility	250,410	344	5.8

Source: U.S. Census Bureau, State & Local Government Finances 2020

TAXES

State Corporate Income Tax Rates

State	Tax Rate (%)	Income Brackets ($)	Num. of Brackets	Financial Institution Tax Rate (%)[a]	Federal Income Tax Ded.
Colorado	4.4	Flat rate	1	4.4	No

Note: Tax rates as of January 1, 2023; (a) Rates listed are the corporate income tax rate applied to financial institutions or excise taxes based on income. Some states have other taxes based upon the value of deposits or shares.
Source: Federation of Tax Administrators, State Corporate Income Tax Rates, January 1, 2023

State Individual Income Tax Rates

State	Tax Rate (%)	Income Brackets ($)	Personal Exemptions ($)			Standard Ded. ($)	
			Single	Married	Depend.	Single	Married
Colorado	4.4	Flat rate	(d)	(d)	(d)	13,850	27,700 (d)

Note: Tax rates as of January 1, 2023; Local- and county-level taxes are not included; Federal income tax is not deductible on state income tax returns; (d) These states use the personal exemption/standard deduction amounts provided in the federal Internal Revenue Code.
Source: Federation of Tax Administrators, State Individual Income Tax Rates, January 1, 2023

Various State Sales and Excise Tax Rates

State	State Sales Tax (%)	Gasoline[1] ($/gal.)	Cigarette[2] ($/pack)	Spirits[3] ($/gal.)	Wine[4] ($/gal.)	Beer[5] ($/gal.)	Recreational Marijuana (%)
Colorado	2.9	0.22	1.94	2.28	0.32	0.08	(d)

Note: All tax rates as of January 1, 2023; (1) The American Petroleum Institute has developed a methodology for determining the average tax rate on a gallon of fuel. Rates may include any of the following: excise taxes, environmental fees, storage tank fees, other fees or taxes, general sales tax, and local taxes; (2) The federal excise tax of $1.0066 per pack and local taxes are not included; (3) Rates are those applicable to off-premise sales of 40% alcohol by volume (a.b.v.) distilled spirits in 750ml containers. Local excise taxes are excluded; (4) Rates are those applicable to off-premise sales of 11% a.b.v. non-carbonated wine in 750ml containers; (5) Rates are those applicable to off-premise sales of 4.7% a.b.v. beer in 12 ounce containers; (d) 15% excise tax (levied on wholesale at average market rate); 15% excise tax (retail price)
Source: Tax Foundation, 2023 Facts & Figures: How Does Your State Compare?

State Business Tax Climate Index Rankings

State	Overall Rank	Corporate Tax Rank	Individual Income Tax Rank	Sales Tax Rank	Property Tax Rank	Unemployment Insurance Tax Rank
Colorado	21	7	14	40	36	42

Note: The index is a measure of how each state's tax laws affect economic performance. The lower the rank, the more favorable a state's tax system is for business. States without a given tax are given a ranking of 1. The scores/rankings for the District of Columbia do not affect other states. The 2023 index represents the tax climate as of July 1, 2022.
Source: Tax Foundation, State Business Tax Climate Index 2023

TRANSPORTATION

Means of Transportation to Work

Area	Car/Truck/Van		Public Transportation			Bicycle	Walked	Other Means	Worked at Home
	Drove Alone	Car-pooled	Bus	Subway	Railroad				
City	62.7	6.8	3.5	0.6	0.4	2.0	4.4	2.3	17.2
MSA[1]	69.8	7.5	2.2	0.3	0.2	0.8	2.1	1.7	15.4
U.S.	73.2	8.6	2.0	1.6	0.5	0.5	2.5	1.5	9.7

Note: Figures are percentages and cover workers 16 years of age and older; (1) Figures cover the Denver-Aurora-Lakewood, CO Metropolitan Statistical Area
Source: U.S. Census Bureau, 2017-2021 American Community Survey 5-Year Estimates

Travel Time to Work

Area	Less Than 10 Minutes	10 to 19 Minutes	20 to 29 Minutes	30 to 44 Minutes	45 to 59 Minutes	60 to 89 Minutes	90 Minutes or More
City	7.9	29.0	24.7	26.0	7.2	3.7	1.4
MSA[1]	8.4	25.1	23.0	26.5	9.6	5.5	1.9
U.S.	12.4	28.5	21.0	20.9	8.2	6.2	2.9

Note: Note: Figures are percentages and include workers 16 years old and over; (1) Figures cover the Denver-Aurora-Lakewood, CO Metropolitan Statistical Area
Source: U.S. Census Bureau, 2017-2021 American Community Survey 5-Year Estimates

Key Congestion Measures

Measure	1990	2000	2010	2015	2020
Annual Hours of Delay, Total (000)	21,111	58,062	87,604	103,318	46,181
Annual Hours of Delay, Per Auto Commuter	23	44	50	58	26
Annual Congestion Cost, Per Auto Commuter ($)	437	903	1,083	1,180	545

Note: Covers the Denver-Aurora CO urban area
Source: Texas A&M Transportation Institute, 2021 Urban Mobility Report

Freeway Travel Time Index

Measure	1985	1990	1995	2000	2005	2010	2015	2020
Urban Area Index[1]	1.13	1.14	1.19	1.27	1.32	1.29	1.31	1.09
Urban Area Rank[1,2]	19	26	23	10	8	13	15	40

Note: Freeway Travel Time Index—the ratio of travel time in the peak period to the travel time at free-flow conditions. For example, a value of 1.30 indicates a 20-minute free-flow trip takes 26 minutes in the peak (20 minutes x 1.30 = 26 minutes); (1) Covers the Denver-Aurora CO urban area; (2) Rank is based on 101 larger urban areas (#1 = highest travel time index)
Source: Texas A&M Transportation Institute, 2021 Urban Mobility Report

Public Transportation

Agency Name / Mode of Transportation	Vehicles Operated in Maximum Service[1]	Annual Unlinked Passenger Trips[2] (in thous.)	Annual Passenger Miles[3] (in thous.)
Denver Regional Transportation District (RTD)			
Bus (directly operated)	286	20,803.7	93,150.4
Bus (purchased transportation)	194	10,766.8	42,419.1
Commuter Rail (directly operated)	8	763.1	6,809.5
Commuter Rail (purchased transportation)	36	5,822.3	75,820.0
Demand Response (purchased transportation)	278	605.0	5,696.8
Light Rail (directly operated)	111	10,016.2	67,364.6

Note: (1) Number of revenue vehicles operated by the given mode and type of service to meet the annual maximum service requirement. This is the revenue vehicle count during the peak season of the year; on the week and day that maximum service is provided. Vehicles operated in maximum service (VOMS) exclude atypical days and one-time special events; (2) Number of passengers who boarded public transportation vehicles. Passengers are counted each time they board a vehicle no matter how many vehicles they use to travel from their origin to their destination. (3) Sum of the distances ridden by all passengers during the entire fiscal year. Source: Federal Transit Administration, National Transit Database, 2021

Air Transportation

Airport Name and Code / Type of Service	Passenger Airlines[1]	Passenger Enplanements	Freight Carriers[2]	Freight (lbs)
Denver International (DEN)				
Domestic service (U.S. carriers - 2022)	26	32,145,313	15	277,972,263
International service (U.S. carriers - 2021)	8	661,977	3	3,625,333

Note: (1) Includes all U.S.-based major, minor and commuter airlines that carried at least one passenger during the year; (2) Includes all U.S.-based airlines and freight carriers that transported at least one pound of freight during the year. Source: Bureau of Transportation Statistics, The Intermodal Transportation Database, Air Carriers: T-100 Domestic Market (U.S. Carriers), 2022; Bureau of Transportation Statistics, The Intermodal Transportation Database, Air Carriers: T-100 International Market (U.S. Carriers), 2021

BUSINESSES

Major Business Headquarters

Company Name	Industry	Rankings	
		Fortune[1]	Forbes[2]
DCP Midstream	Pipelines	344	-
DaVita	Health care, medical facilities	323	-
Leprino Foods	Food, drink & tobacco	-	155
Molson Coors Beverage	Beverages	352	-
Ovintiv	Mining, crude-oil production	400	-

Note: (1) Companies that produce a 10-K are ranked 1 to 500 based on 2021 revenue; (2) All private companies with at least $2 billion in annual revenue through the end of their most current fiscal year are ranked 1 to 246; companies listed are headquartered in the city; dashes indicate no ranking Source: Fortune, "Fortune 500," 2022; Forbes, "America's Largest Private Companies," 2022

Fastest-Growing Businesses

According to *Inc.*, Denver is home to eight of America's 500 fastest-growing private companies: **Matter Made** (#81); **Fluid Truck** (#101); **Maxwell** (#164); **Arrive Health** (#181); **Sugarwish** (#262); **Sheets & Giggles** (#309); **The Dingman Group** (#404); **LEVO Oil Infusion** (#449). Criteria: must be an independent, privately-held, for-profit, U.S. corporation, proprietorship or partnership as of December 31, 2021; revenues must be at least $100,000 in 2018 and $2 million in 2021; must have four-year operating/sales history. *Inc., "America's 500 Fastest-Growing Private Companies," 2022*

According to Deloitte, Denver is home to nine of North America's 500 fastest-growing high-technology companies: **Fluid Truck** (#9); **Pie Insurance** (#45); **Arrive Health** (#61); **Maxwell** (#62); **CyberGRX** (#220); **Edison Interactive** (#254); **Veritone** (#400); **EverCommerce** (#450); **Skupos** (#490). Companies are ranked by percentage growth in revenue over a four-year period. Criteria for inclusion: company must be headquartered within North America; must own proprietary intellectual property or technology that is sold to customers in products that contributes to a significant portion of the company's operating revenue; must have been in business for a minumum of four years with 2018 operating revenues of at least $50,000 USD/CD and 2021 operating revenues of at least $5 million USD/CD. *Deloitte, 2022 Technology Fast 500™*

Living Environment

COST OF LIVING

Cost of Living Index

Composite Index	Groceries	Housing	Utilities	Trans-portation	Health Care	Misc. Goods/ Services
110.5	94.3	135.9	86.8	100.1	99.2	107.6

Note: The Cost of Living Index measures regional differences in the cost of consumer goods and services, excluding taxes and non-consumer expenditures, for professional and managerial households in the top income quintile. It is based on more than 50,000 prices covering almost 60 different items for which prices are collected three times a year by chambers of commerce, economic development organizations or university applied economic centers in each participating urban area. The numbers shown should be read as a percentage above or below the national average of 100. For example, a value of 115.4 in the groceries column indicates that grocery prices are 15.4% higher than the national average. Small differences in the index numbers should not be interpreted as significant; Figures cover the Denver CO urban area.
Source: The Council for Community and Economic Research, Cost of Living Index, 2022

Grocery Prices

Area[1]	T-Bone Steak ($/pound)	Frying Chicken ($/pound)	Whole Milk ($/half gal.)	Eggs ($/dozen)	Orange Juice ($/64 oz.)	Coffee ($/11.5 oz.)
City[2]	13.30	1.65	2.07	2.07	3.66	4.97
Avg.	13.81	1.59	2.43	2.25	3.85	4.95
Min.	10.17	0.90	1.51	1.30	2.90	3.46
Max.	19.35	3.30	4.32	4.32	5.31	8.59

*Note: (1) Values for the local area are compared with the average, minimum and maximum values for all 286 areas in the Cost of Living Index; (2) Figures cover the Denver CO urban area; **T-Bone Steak** (price per pound); **Frying Chicken** (price per pound, whole fryer); **Whole Milk** (half gallon carton); **Eggs** (price per dozen, Grade A, large); **Orange Juice** (64 oz. Tropicana or Florida Natural); **Coffee** (11.5 oz. can, vacuum-packed, Maxwell House, Hills Bros, or Folgers).*
Source: The Council for Community and Economic Research, Cost of Living Index, 2022

Housing and Utility Costs

Area[1]	New Home Price ($)	Apartment Rent ($/month)	All Electric ($/month)	Part Electric ($/month)	Other Energy ($/month)	Telephone ($/month)
City[2]	639,886	1,841	-	58.60	78.48	190.08
Avg.	450,913	1,371	176.41	99.93	76.96	190.22
Min.	229,283	546	100.84	31.56	27.15	174.27
Max.	2,434,977	4,569	356.86	249.59	272.24	208.31

*Note: (1) Values for the local area are compared with the average, minimum and maximum values for all 286 areas in the Cost of Living Index; (2) Figures cover the Denver CO urban area; **New Home Price** (2,400 sf living area, 8,000 sf lot, in urban area with full utilities); **Apartment Rent** (950 sf 2 bedroom/1.5 or 2 bath, unfurnished, excluding all utilities except water); **All Electric** (average monthly cost for an all-electric home); **Part Electric** (average monthly cost for a part-electric home); **Other Energy** (average monthly cost for natural gas, fuel oil, coal, wood, and any other forms of energy except electricity); **Telephone** (price includes the base monthly rate plus taxes and fees for three lines of mobile phone service).*
Source: The Council for Community and Economic Research, Cost of Living Index, 2022

Health Care, Transportation, and Other Costs

Area[1]	Doctor ($/visit)	Dentist ($/visit)	Optometrist ($/visit)	Gasoline ($/gallon)	Beauty Salon ($/visit)	Men's Shirt ($)
City[2]	106.00	118.21	115.00	3.72	47.09	35.52
Avg.	124.91	107.77	117.66	3.86	43.31	34.21
Min.	36.61	58.25	51.79	2.90	22.18	13.05
Max.	250.21	162.58	371.96	5.54	85.61	63.54

*Note: (1) Values for the local area are compared with the average, minimum and maximum values for all 286 areas in the Cost of Living Index; (2) Figures cover the Denver CO urban area; **Doctor** (general practitioners routine exam of an established patient); **Dentist** (adult teeth cleaning and periodic oral examination); **Optometrist** (full vision eye exam for established adult patient); **Gasoline** (one gallon regular unleaded, national brand, including all taxes, cash price at self-service pump if available); **Beauty Salon** (woman's shampoo, trim, and blow-dry); **Men's Shirt** (cotton/polyester dress shirt, pinpoint weave, long sleeves).*
Source: The Council for Community and Economic Research, Cost of Living Index, 2022

HOUSING

Homeownership Rate

Area	2015 (%)	2016 (%)	2017 (%)	2018 (%)	2019 (%)	2020 (%)	2021 (%)	2022 (%)
MSA[1]	61.6	61.6	59.3	60.1	63.5	62.9	62.8	64.6
U.S.	63.7	63.4	63.9	64.4	64.6	66.6	65.5	65.8

Note: (1) Figures cover the Denver-Aurora-Lakewood, CO Metropolitan Statistical Area
Source: U.S. Census Bureau, Housing Vacancies and Homeownership Annual Statistics: 2015-2022

House Price Index (HPI)

Area	National Ranking[2]	Quarterly Change (%)	One-Year Change (%)	Five-Year Change (%)	Since 1991Q1 (%)
MSA[1]	216	-2.41	7.96	52.15	548.72
U.S.[3]	–	0.34	8.41	58.44	289.08

Note: The HPI is a weighted repeat sales index. It measures average price changes in repeat sales or refinancings on the same properties. This information is obtained by reviewing repeat mortgage transactions on single-family properties whose mortgages have been purchased or securitized by Fannie Mae or Freddie Mac since January 1975; (1) Figures cover the Denver-Aurora-Lakewood, CO Metropolitan Statistical Area; (2) Rankings are based on annual percentage change for all metro areas containing at least 15,000 transactions over the last 10 years and ranges from 1 to 257; (3) figures based on a weighted average of Census Division estimates using a seasonally adjusted, purchase-only index; all figures are for the period ending December 31, 2022
Source: Federal Housing Finance Agency, Change in FHFA Metropolitan Area House Price Indexes, 2022Q4

Median Single-Family Home Prices

Area	2020	2021	2022[p]	Percent Change 2021 to 2022
MSA[1]	492.7	607.1	670.1	10.4
U.S. Average	300.2	357.1	392.6	9.9

Note: Figures are median sales prices of existing single-family homes in thousands of dollars; (p) preliminary; (1) Figures cover the Denver-Aurora-Lakewood, CO Metropolitan Statistical Area
Source: National Association of Realtors, Median Sales Price of Existing Single-Family Homes for Metropolitan Areas, 4th Quarter 2022

Qualifying Income Based on Median Sales Price of Existing Single-Family Homes

Area	With 5% Down ($)	With 10% Down ($)	With 20% Down ($)
MSA[1]	191,478	181,400	161,244
U.S. Average	112,234	106,237	94,513

Note: Figures are preliminary; Qualifying income is based on a mortgage rate of 6.77%. Monthly principal and interest payment is limited to 25% of income; (1) Figures cover the Denver-Aurora-Lakewood, CO Metropolitan Statistical Area
Source: National Association of Realtors, Qualifying Income Based on Median Sales Price of Existing Single-Family Homes for Metropolitan Areas, 4th Quarter 2022

Home Value

Area	Under $100,000	$100,000 -$199,999	$200,000 -$299,999	$300,000 -$399,999	$400,000 -$499,999	$500,000 -$999,999	$1,000,000 or more	Median ($)
City	2.3	4.6	12.8	20.0	17.5	34.9	7.9	459,100
MSA[1]	3.2	3.4	11.5	22.5	21.7	32.8	4.9	443,400
U.S.	16.2	24.2	20.1	13.6	8.3	13.6	4.1	244,900

Note: Figures are percentages except for median and cover owner-occupied housing units; (1) Figures cover the Denver-Aurora-Lakewood, CO Metropolitan Statistical Area
Source: U.S. Census Bureau, 2017-2021 American Community Survey 5-Year Estimates

Year Housing Structure Built

Area	2020 or Later	2010 -2019	2000 -2009	1990 -1999	1980 -1989	1970 -1979	1960 -1969	1950 -1959	1940 -1949	Before 1940	Median Year
City	0.3	12.8	11.1	6.7	7.6	12.7	10.6	14.2	5.8	18.2	1971
MSA[1]	0.3	10.7	16.0	14.8	13.8	17.2	9.0	9.0	2.6	6.5	1984
U.S.	0.2	7.3	13.6	13.6	13.2	14.8	10.3	10.0	4.7	12.2	1979

Note: Figures are percentages except for Median Year; Note: (1) Figures cover the Denver-Aurora-Lakewood, CO Metropolitan Statistical Area
Source: U.S. Census Bureau, 2017-2021 American Community Survey 5-Year Estimates

Gross Monthly Rent

Area	Under $500	$500 -$999	$1,000 -$1,499	$1,500 -$1,999	$2,000 -$2,499	$2,500 -$2,999	$3,000 and up	Median ($)
City	7.1	10.5	32.7	27.6	14.0	5.1	3.0	1,495
MSA[1]	4.5	9.6	32.5	31.5	14.2	5.0	2.7	1,554
U.S.	8.1	30.5	30.8	16.8	7.3	3.1	3.5	1,163

Note: Figures are percentages except for median; Gross rent is the contract rent plus the estimated average monthly cost of utilities (electricity, gas, and water and sewer) and fuels (oil, coal, kerosene, wood, etc.) if these are paid by the renter (or paid for the renter by someone else); (1) Figures cover the Denver-Aurora-Lakewood, CO Metropolitan Statistical Area
Source: U.S. Census Bureau, 2017-2021 American Community Survey 5-Year Estimates

HEALTH

Health Risk Factors

Category	MSA[1] (%)	U.S. (%)
Adults aged 18–64 who have any kind of health care coverage	87.9	90.9
Adults who reported being in good or better health	87.6	85.2
Adults who have been told they have high blood cholesterol	30.7	35.7
Adults who have been told they have high blood pressure	25.5	32.4
Adults who are current smokers	11.2	14.4
Adults who currently use e-cigarettes	6.4	6.7
Adults who currently use chewing tobacco, snuff, or snus	2.8	3.5
Adults who are heavy drinkers[2]	7.6	6.3
Adults who are binge drinkers[3]	19.7	15.4
Adults who are overweight (BMI 25.0 - 29.9)	35.2	34.4
Adults who are obese (BMI 30.0 - 99.8)	24.8	33.9
Adults who participated in any physical activities in the past month	83.6	76.3

Note: (1) Figures cover the Denver-Aurora-Lakewood, CO Metropolitan Statistical Area; (2) Heavy drinkers are classified as adult men having more than 14 drinks per week and adult women having more than 7 drinks per week; (3) Binge drinkers are classified as males having five or more drinks on one occasion or females having four or more drinks on one occasion
Source: Centers for Disease Control and Prevention, Behaviorial Risk Factor Surveillance System, SMART: Selected Metropolitan Area Risk Trends, 2021

Acute and Chronic Health Conditions

Category	MSA[1] (%)	U.S. (%)
Adults who have ever been told they had a heart attack	2.3	4.0
Adults who have ever been told they have angina or coronary heart disease	2.3	3.8
Adults who have ever been told they had a stroke	1.7	3.0
Adults who have ever been told they have asthma	15.0	14.9
Adults who have ever been told they have arthritis	21.7	25.8
Adults who have ever been told they have diabetes[2]	6.8	10.9
Adults who have ever been told they had skin cancer	6.2	6.6
Adults who have ever been told they had any other types of cancer	6.5	7.5
Adults who have ever been told they have COPD	4.5	6.1
Adults who have ever been told they have kidney disease	2.7	3.0
Adults who have ever been told they have a form of depression	18.8	20.5

Note: (1) Figures cover the Denver-Aurora-Lakewood, CO Metropolitan Statistical Area; (2) Figures do not include pregnancy-related, borderline, or pre-diabetes
Source: Centers for Disease Control and Prevention, Behaviorial Risk Factor Surveillance System, SMART: Selected Metropolitan Area Risk Trends, 2021

Health Screening and Vaccination Rates

Category	MSA[1] (%)	U.S. (%)
Adults who have ever been tested for HIV	40.6	34.9
Adults who have had their blood cholesterol checked within the last five years	86.3	85.2
Adults aged 65+ who have had flu shot within the past year	74.2	68.6
Adults aged 65+ who have ever had a pneumonia vaccination	77.4	71.0

Note: (1) Figures cover the Denver-Aurora-Lakewood, CO Metropolitan Statistical Area.
Source: Centers for Disease Control and Prevention, Behaviorial Risk Factor Surveillance System, SMART: Selected Metropolitan Area Risk Trends, 2021

Disability Status

Category	MSA[1] (%)	U.S. (%)
Adults who reported being deaf	4.8	7.2
Are you blind or have serious difficulty seeing, even when wearing glasses?	3.8	4.8
Are you limited in any way in any of your usual activities due to arthritis?	7.9	11.1
Do you have difficulty doing errands alone?	4.8	7.0
Do you have difficulty dressing or bathing?	1.8	3.6
Do you have serious difficulty concentrating/remembering/making decisions?	9.3	12.1
Do you have serious difficulty walking or climbing stairs?	7.9	12.8

Note: (1) Figures cover the Denver-Aurora-Lakewood, CO Metropolitan Statistical Area.
Source: Centers for Disease Control and Prevention, Behaviorial Risk Factor Surveillance System, SMART: Selected Metropolitan Area Risk Trends, 2021

Mortality Rates for the Top 10 Causes of Death in the U.S.

ICD-10[a] Sub-Chapter	ICD-10[a] Code	Crude Mortality Rate[1] per 100,000 population	
		County[2]	U.S.
Malignant neoplasms	C00-C97	122.2	182.6
Ischaemic heart diseases	I20-I25	59.8	113.1
Other forms of heart disease	I30-I51	32.9	64.4
Other degenerative diseases of the nervous system	G30-G31	32.9	51.0
Cerebrovascular diseases	I60-I69	31.5	47.8
Other external causes of accidental injury	W00-X59	59.1	46.4
Chronic lower respiratory diseases	J40-J47	35.6	45.7
Organic, including symptomatic, mental disorders	F01-F09	24.5	35.9
Hypertensive diseases	I10-I15	25.8	35.0
Diabetes mellitus	E10-E14	20.7	29.6

Note: (a) ICD-10 = International Classification of Diseases 10th Revision; (1) Crude mortality rates are a three-year average covering 2019-2021; (2) Figures cover Denver County.
Source: Centers for Disease Control and Prevention, National Center for Health Statistics. National Vital Statistics System, Mortality 2018-2021 on CDC WONDER Online Database

Mortality Rates for Selected Causes of Death

ICD-10[a] Sub-Chapter	ICD-10[a] Code	Crude Mortality Rate[1] per 100,000 population	
		County[2]	U.S.
Assault	X85-Y09	9.0	7.0
Diseases of the liver	K70-K76	26.3	19.8
Human immunodeficiency virus (HIV) disease	B20-B24	1.6	1.5
Influenza and pneumonia	J09-J18	6.0	14.7
Intentional self-harm	X60-X84	21.1	14.3
Malnutrition	E40-E46	6.8	4.3
Obesity and other hyperalimentation	E65-E68	3.2	3.0
Renal failure	N17-N19	8.3	15.7
Transport accidents	V01-V99	12.1	13.6
Viral hepatitis	B15-B19	1.9	1.2

Note: (a) ICD-10 = International Classification of Diseases 10th Revision; (1) Crude mortality rates are a three-year average covering 2019-2021; (2) Figures cover Denver County; Data are suppressed when the data meet the criteria for confidentiality constraints; Crude mortality rates are flagged as unreliable when the rate would be calculated with a numerator of 20 or less.
Source: Centers for Disease Control and Prevention, National Center for Health Statistics. National Vital Statistics System, Mortality 2018-2021 on CDC WONDER Online Database

Health Insurance Coverage

Area	With Health Insurance	With Private Health Insurance	With Public Health Insurance	Without Health Insurance	Population Under Age 19 Without Health Insurance
City	90.4	66.9	31.3	9.6	5.5
MSA[1]	92.2	72.6	29.1	7.8	4.7
U.S.	91.2	67.8	35.4	8.8	5.3

Note: Figures are percentages that cover the civilian noninstitutionalized population; (1) Figures cover the Denver-Aurora-Lakewood, CO Metropolitan Statistical Area
Source: U.S. Census Bureau, 2017-2021 American Community Survey 5-Year Estimates

Number of Medical Professionals

Area	MDs[3]	DOs[3,4]	Dentists	Podiatrists	Chiropractors	Optometrists
County[1] (number)	4,386	228	576	46	280	120
County[1] (rate[2])	611.2	31.8	81.0	6.5	39.4	16.9
U.S. (rate[2])	289.3	23.5	72.5	6.2	28.7	17.4

Note: Data as of 2021 unless noted; (1) Data covers Denver County; (2) Rate per 100,000 population; (3) Data as of 2020 and includes all active, non-federal physicians; (4) Doctor of Osteopathic Medicine
Source: U.S. Department of Health and Human Services, Health Resources and Services Administration, Bureau of Health Professions, Area Resource File (ARF) 2021-2022

Best Hospitals

According to *U.S. News,* the Denver-Aurora-Lakewood, CO metro area is home to three of the best hospitals in the U.S.: **Craig Hospital** (1 adult specialty); **National Jewish Health at Denver-University of Colorado Hospital** (1 adult specialty); **UCHealth University of Colorado Hospital** (5 adult specialties). The hospitals listed were nationally ranked in at least one of 15 adult or 10 pediatric specialties. The number of specialties shown cover the parent hospital. Only 164 U.S. hospitals performed well enough to be nationally ranked in one or more specialties. Twenty hospitals in the U.S. made the Honor Roll. The Best Hospitals Honor Roll takes both the national rankings and the procedure and condition ratings into account. Hospitals received points if they were nationally ranked in one of the 15 adult specialties—the higher they ranked, the more points they got—and how many ratings of "high performing" they earned in the 17 procedures and conditions. *U.S. News Online, "America's Best Hospitals 2022-23"*

According to *U.S. News,* the Denver-Aurora-Lakewood, CO metro area is home to one of the best children's hospitals in the U.S.: **Children's Hospital Colorado** (Honor Roll/10 pediatric specialties). The hospital listed was highly ranked in at least one of 10 pediatric specialties. Eighty-six children's hospitals in the U.S. were nationally ranked in at least one specialty. Hospitals received points for being ranked in a specialty, and the 10 hospitals with the most points across the 10 specialties make up the Honor Roll. *U.S. News Online, "America's Best Children's Hospitals 2022-23"*

EDUCATION

Public School District Statistics

District Name	Schls	Pupils	Pupil/ Teacher Ratio	Minority Pupils[1] (%)	LEP/ELL[2] (%)	IEP[3] (%)
Mapleton School District No. 1	19	9,002	19.8	75.2	23.4	n/a
School District No. 1	206	88,911	14.5	74.5	27.4	n/a
State Charter School Institute	43	19,614	16.8	49.2	13.1	n/a

Note: Table includes school districts with 2,000 or more students; (1) Percentage of students that are not non-Hispanic white; (2) Percentage of students that are Limited English Proficient or English Language Learners (2018-19); (3) Percentage of students that have an Individualized Education Program (2019-20). Source: U.S. Department of Education, National Center for Education Statistics, Common Core of Data, Local Education Agency (School District) Universe Survey: School Year 2021-2022

Best High Schools

According to *U.S. News,* Denver is home to four of the top 500 high schools in the U.S.: **D'Evelyn Junior/Senior High School** (#85); **Denver School of the Arts** (#161); **DSST: Stapleton High School** (#192); **KIPP Denver Collegiate High School** (#372). Nearly 18,000 public, magnet and charter schools were ranked based on their performance on state assessments and how well they prepare students for college. *U.S. News & World Report, "Best High Schools 2022"*

Highest Level of Education

Area	Less than H.S.	H.S. Diploma	Some College, No Deg.	Associate Degree	Bachelor's Degree	Master's Degree	Prof. School Degree	Doctorate Degree
City	10.0	16.0	16.0	5.6	32.0	13.9	4.5	2.1
MSA[1]	8.1	19.2	18.9	7.6	29.1	12.5	2.8	1.8
U.S.	11.1	26.5	20.0	8.7	20.6	9.3	2.2	1.5

Note: Figures cover persons age 25 and over; (1) Figures cover the Denver-Aurora-Lakewood, CO Metropolitan Statistical Area Source: U.S. Census Bureau, 2017-2021 American Community Survey 5-Year Estimates

Educational Attainment by Race

Area	High School Graduate or Higher (%)					Bachelor's Degree or Higher (%)				
	Total	White	Black	Asian	Hisp.[2]	Total	White	Black	Asian	Hisp.[2]
City	90.0	93.6	89.8	85.6	69.6	52.5	60.7	27.7	56.5	19.4
MSA[1]	91.9	94.5	90.4	84.9	74.1	46.2	50.1	29.2	53.1	19.6
U.S.	88.9	91.4	87.2	87.6	71.2	33.7	35.5	23.3	55.6	18.4

Note: Figures shown cover persons 25 years old and over; (1) Figures cover the Denver-Aurora-Lakewood, CO Metropolitan Statistical Area; (2) People of Hispanic origin can be of any race Source: U.S. Census Bureau, 2017-2021 American Community Survey 5-Year Estimates

School Enrollment by Grade and Control

Area	Preschool (%)		Kindergarten (%)		Grades 1 - 4 (%)		Grades 5 - 8 (%)		Grades 9 - 12 (%)	
	Public	Private	Public	Private	Public	Private	Public	Private	Public	Private
City	57.4	42.6	85.2	14.8	90.6	9.4	89.6	10.4	91.8	8.2
MSA[1]	58.0	42.0	88.1	11.9	90.8	9.2	90.9	9.1	91.5	8.5
U.S.	58.8	41.2	86.3	13.7	88.3	11.7	88.6	11.4	89.4	10.6

Note: Figures shown cover persons 3 years old and over; (1) Figures cover the Denver-Aurora-Lakewood, CO Metropolitan Statistical Area Source: U.S. Census Bureau, 2017-2021 American Community Survey 5-Year Estimates

Higher Education

Four-Year Colleges			Two-Year Colleges			Medical Schools[1]	Law Schools[2]	Voc/ Tech[3]
Public	Private Non-profit	Private For-profit	Public	Private Non-profit	Private For-profit			
8	6	8	2	0	7	2	1	16

Note: Figures cover institutions located within the Denver-Aurora-Lakewood, CO Metropolitan Statistical Area and include main campuses only; (1) includes schools accredited by the Liaison Committee on Medical Education and the American Osteopathic Association's Commission on Osteopathic College Accreditation; (2) includes ABA-accredited schools, schools with provisional ABA accreditation, and state accredited schools; (3) includes all schools with programs that are less than 2 years.
Source: National Center for Education Statistics, Integrated Postsecondary Education System (IPEDS), 2021-22; Wikipedia, List of Medical Schools in the United States, accessed April 10, 2023; Wikipedia, List of Law Schools in the United States, accessed April 10, 2023

According to *U.S. News & World Report*, the Denver-Aurora-Lakewood, CO metro area is home to two of the top 200 national universities in the U.S.: **Colorado School of Mines** (#89 tie); **University of Denver** (#105 tie). The indicators used to capture academic quality fall into a number of categories: assessment by administrators at peer institutions; retention of students; faculty resources; student selectivity; financial resources; alumni giving; high school counselor ratings of colleges; and graduation rate. *U.S. News & World Report, "America's Best Colleges 2023"*

According to *U.S. News & World Report*, the Denver-Aurora-Lakewood, CO metro area is home to one of the top 100 law schools in the U.S.: **University of Denver (Sturm)** (#78 tie). The rankings are based on a weighted average of 12 measures of quality: peer assessment score; assessment score by lawyers/judges; median LSAT scores; median undergrad GPA; acceptance rate; employment rates for graduates; placement success; bar passage rate; faculty resources; expenditures per student; student/faculty ratio; and library resources. *U.S. News & World Report, "America's Best Graduate Schools, Law, 2023"*

According to *U.S. News & World Report*, the Denver-Aurora-Lakewood, CO metro area is home to one of the top 75 medical schools for research in the U.S.: **University of Colorado** (#27). The rankings are based on a weighted average of 11 measures of quality: quality assessment; peer assessment score; assessment score by residency directors; research activity; total research activity; average research activity per faculty member; student selectivity; median MCAT total score; median undergraduate GPA; acceptance rate; and faculty resources. *U.S. News & World Report, "America's Best Graduate Schools, Medical, 2023"*

According to *U.S. News & World Report*, the Denver-Aurora-Lakewood, CO metro area is home to one of the top 75 business schools in the U.S.: **University of Denver (Daniels)** (#71). The rankings are based on a weighted average of the following nine measures: quality assessment; peer assessment; recruiter assessment; placement success; mean starting salary and bonus; student selectivity; mean GMAT and GRE scores; mean undergraduate GPA; and acceptance rate. *U.S. News & World Report, "America's Best Graduate Schools, Business, 2023"*

EMPLOYERS

Major Employers

Company Name	Industry
Arvada House Preservation	Apartment building operators
Centura Health Corporation	General medical & surgical hospitals
Colorado Department of Transportation	Regulation, administration of transportation
County of Jefferson	County government
DISH Network Corporation	Cable & other pay television services
Gart Bros Sporting Goods Company	Sporting goods & bicycle shops
HCA Healthone	General medical & surgical hospitals
IBM	Printers, computer
Level 3 Communications	Telephone communication, except radio
Lockheed Martin Corporation	Aircraft & space vehicles
Mormon Church	Mormon church
MWH/Fni Joint Venture	Engineering services
Newmont Gold Company	Gold ores mining
Noodles and Company	Eating places
Strasburg Telephone Company	Telephone communication, except radio
Synergy Services	Payroll accounting service
TW Telecom Holdings	Telephone communication, except radio
Western Union Financial Services	Electronic funds transfer network, including switching

Note: Companies shown are located within the Denver-Aurora-Lakewood, CO Metropolitan Statistical Area.
Source: Hoovers.com; Wikipedia

Best Companies to Work For

PCL Construction Enterprises, headquartered in Denver, is among "The 100 Best Companies to Work For." To pick the best companies, *Fortune* partnered with the Great Place to Work Institute. Two-thirds of a company's score is based on the results of the Institute's Trust Index survey, which is sent to a random sample of employees from each company. The questions related to attitudes about management's credibility, job satisfaction, and camaraderie. The other third of the scoring is based on the company's responses to the Institute's Culture Audit, which includes detailed questions about pay and benefit programs, and a series of open-ended questions about hiring practices, internal communication, training, recognition programs, and diversity efforts. Any company that is at least five years old with more than 1,000 U.S. employees is eligible. *Fortune, "The 100 Best Companies to Work For," 2023*

CIENCE, headquartered in Denver, is among "Fortune's Best Workplaces for Women." To pick the best companies, *Fortune* partnered with the Great Place to Work Institute. To be considered for the list, companies must be Great Place To Work-Certified. Companies must also employ at least 50 women, at least 20% of their non-executive managers must be female, and at least one executive must be female. To determine the Best Workplaces for Women, Great Place To Work measured the differences in women's survey responses to those of their peers and assesses the impact of demographics and roles on the quality and consistency of women's experiences. Great Place To Work also analyzed the gender balance of each workplace, how it compared to each company's industry, and patterns in representation as women rise from front-line positions to the board of directors. *Fortune, "Best Workplaces for Women," 2022*

PUBLIC SAFETY

Crime Rate

Area	Total Crime	Violent Crime Rate				Property Crime Rate		
		Murder	Rape[3]	Robbery	Aggrav. Assault	Burglary	Larceny -Theft	Motor Vehicle Theft
City	5,506.6	13.1	90.8	165.1	588.9	708.0	2,800.8	1,139.9
Suburbs[1]	3,233.8	3.8	57.7	70.7	238.2	357.6	1,904.0	601.8
Metro[2]	3,793.1	6.1	65.8	93.9	324.5	443.9	2,124.7	734.2
U.S.	2,356.7	6.5	38.4	73.9	279.7	314.2	1,398.0	246.0

Note: Figures are crimes per 100,000 population; (1) All areas within the metro area that are located outside the city limits; (2) Figures cover the Denver-Aurora-Lakewood, CO Metropolitan Statistical Area; (3) All figures shown were reported using the revised Uniform Crime Reporting (UCR) definition of rape; Due to the transition to the National Incident-Based Reporting System (NIBRS), limited city and metro area data was released for 2021.
Source: FBI Uniform Crime Reports, 2020

Hate Crimes

Area	Number of Quarters Reported	Number of Incidents per Bias Motivation					
		Race/Ethnicity/ Ancestry	Religion	Sexual Orientation	Disability	Gender	Gender Identity
City	4	47	7	21	1	0	4
U.S.	4	5,227	1,244	1,110	130	75	266

Note: Due to the transition to the National Incident-Based Reporting System (NIBRS), limited crime data was released for 2021.
Source: Federal Bureau of Investigation, Hate Crime Statistics 2020

Identity Theft Consumer Reports

Area	Reports	Reports per 100,000 Population	Rank[2]
MSA[1]	6,156	210	154
U.S.	1,108,609	339	-

Note: (1) Figures cover the Denver-Aurora-Lakewood, CO Metropolitan Statistical Area; (2) Rank ranges from 1 to 391 where 1 indicates greatest number of identity theft reports per 100,000 population
Source: Federal Trade Commission, Consumer Sentinel Network Data Book 2022

Fraud and Other Consumer Reports

Area	Reports	Reports per 100,000 Population	Rank[2]
MSA[1]	33,778	1,153	48
U.S.	4,064,520	1,245	-

Note: (1) Figures cover the Denver-Aurora-Lakewood, CO Metropolitan Statistical Area; (2) Rank ranges from 1 to 391 where 1 indicates greatest number of fraud and other consumer reports per 100,000 population
Source: Federal Trade Commission, Consumer Sentinel Network Data Book 2022

POLITICS

2020 Presidential Election Results

Area	Biden	Trump	Jorgensen	Hawkins	Other
Denver County	79.6	18.2	1.2	0.3	0.7
U.S.	51.3	46.8	1.2	0.3	0.5

Note: Results are percentages and may not add to 100% due to rounding
Source: Dave Leip's Atlas of U.S. Presidential Elections

SPORTS

Professional Sports Teams

Team Name	League	Year Established
Colorado Avalanche	National Hockey League (NHL)	1995
Colorado Rapids	Major League Soccer (MLS)	1996
Colorado Rockies	Major League Baseball (MLB)	1993
Denver Broncos	National Football League (NFL)	1960
Denver Nuggets	National Basketball Association (NBA)	1967

Note: Includes teams located in the Denver-Aurora-Lakewood, CO Metropolitan Statistical Area.
Source: Wikipedia, Major Professional Sports Teams of the United States and Canada, April 12, 2023

CLIMATE

Average and Extreme Temperatures

Temperature	Jan	Feb	Mar	Apr	May	Jun	Jul	Aug	Sep	Oct	Nov	Dec	Yr.
Extreme High (°F)	73	76	84	90	93	102	103	100	97	89	79	75	103
Average High (°F)	43	47	52	62	71	81	88	86	77	67	52	45	64
Average Temp. (°F)	30	34	39	48	58	67	73	72	63	52	39	32	51
Average Low (°F)	16	20	25	34	44	53	59	57	48	37	25	18	37
Extreme Low (°F)	-25	-25	-10	-2	22	30	43	41	17	3	-8	-25	-25

Note: Figures cover the years 1948-1992
Source: National Climatic Data Center, International Station Meteorological Climate Summary, 9/96

Average Precipitation/Snowfall/Humidity

Precip./Humidity	Jan	Feb	Mar	Apr	May	Jun	Jul	Aug	Sep	Oct	Nov	Dec	Yr.
Avg. Precip. (in.)	0.6	0.6	1.3	1.7	2.5	1.7	1.9	1.5	1.1	1.0	0.9	0.6	15.5
Avg. Snowfall (in.)	9	7	14	9	2	Tr	0	0	2	4	9	8	63
Avg. Rel. Hum. 5am (%)	62	65	67	66	70	68	67	68	66	63	66	63	66
Avg. Rel. Hum. 5pm (%)	49	44	40	35	38	34	34	34	32	34	47	50	39

Note: Figures cover the years 1948-1992; Tr = Trace amounts (<0.05 in. of rain; <0.5 in. of snow)
Source: National Climatic Data Center, International Station Meteorological Climate Summary, 9/96

Weather Conditions

Temperature			Daytime Sky			Precipitation		
10°F & below	32°F & below	90°F & above	Clear	Partly cloudy	Cloudy	0.01 inch or more precip.	0.1 inch or more snow/ice	Thunder-storms
24	155	33	99	177	89	90	38	39

Note: Figures are average number of days per year and cover the years 1948-1992
Source: National Climatic Data Center, International Station Meteorological Climate Summary, 9/96

HAZARDOUS WASTE

Superfund Sites

The Denver-Aurora-Lakewood, CO metro area is home to eight sites on the EPA's Superfund National Priorities List: **Air Force Plant PJKS** (final); **Broderick Wood Products** (final); **Central City, Clear Creek** (final); **Chemical Sales Co.** (final); **Denver Radium Site** (final); **Lowry Landfill** (final); **Rocky Flats Plant (USDOE)** (final); **Rocky Mountain Arsenal (USARMY)** (final). There are a total of 1,165 Superfund sites with a status of proposed or final on the list in the U.S. *U.S. Environmental Protection Agency, National Priorities List, April 12, 2023*

AIR QUALITY

Air Quality Trends: Ozone

	1990	1995	2000	2005	2010	2015	2018	2019	2020	2021
MSA[1]	0.077	0.070	0.069	0.072	0.070	0.073	0.071	0.068	0.079	0.080
U.S.	0.087	0.089	0.081	0.080	0.072	0.067	0.069	0.065	0.065	0.067

Note: (1) Data covers the Denver-Aurora-Lakewood, CO Metropolitan Statistical Area. The values shown are the composite ozone concentration averages among trend sites based on the highest fourth daily maximum 8-hour concentration in parts per million. These trends are based on sites having an adequate record of monitoring data during the trend period. Data from exceptional events are included.
Source: U.S. Environmental Protection Agency, Air Quality Monitoring Information, "Air Quality Trends by City, 1990-2021"

Air Quality Index

Area	Percent of Days when Air Quality was...[2]					AQI Statistics[2]	
	Good	Moderate	Unhealthy for Sensitive Groups	Unhealthy	Very Unhealthy	Maximum	Median
MSA[1]	30.1	51.5	13.7	4.7	0.0	177	61

Note: (1) Data covers the Denver-Aurora-Lakewood, CO Metropolitan Statistical Area; (2) Based on 365 days with AQI data in 2021. Air Quality Index (AQI) is an index for reporting daily air quality. EPA calculates the AQI for five major air pollutants regulated by the Clean Air Act: ground-level ozone, particle pollution (aka particulate matter), carbon monoxide, sulfur dioxide, and nitrogen dioxide. The AQI runs from 0 to 500. The higher the AQI value, the greater the level of air pollution and the greater the health concern. There are six AQI categories: "Good" AQI is between 0 and 50. Air quality is considered satisfactory; "Moderate" AQI is between 51 and 100. Air quality is acceptable; "Unhealthy for Sensitive Groups" When AQI values are between 101 and 150, members of sensitive groups may experience health effects; "Unhealthy" When AQI values are between 151 and 200 everyone may begin to experience health effects; "Very Unhealthy" AQI values between 201 and 300 trigger a health alert; "Hazardous" AQI values over 300 trigger warnings of emergency conditions (not shown).
Source: U.S. Environmental Protection Agency, Air Quality Index Report, 2021

Air Quality Index Pollutants

Area	Percent of Days when AQI Pollutant was...[2]					
	Carbon Monoxide	Nitrogen Dioxide	Ozone	Sulfur Dioxide	Particulate Matter 2.5	Particulate Matter 10
MSA[1]	0.0	18.6	63.6	(3)	11.2	6.6

Note: (1) Data covers the Denver-Aurora-Lakewood, CO Metropolitan Statistical Area; (2) Based on 365 days with AQI data in 2021. The Air Quality Index (AQI) is an index for reporting daily air quality. EPA calculates the AQI for five major air pollutants regulated by the Clean Air Act: ground-level ozone, particle pollution (also known as particulate matter), carbon monoxide, sulfur dioxide, and nitrogen dioxide. The AQI runs from 0 to 500. The higher the AQI value, the greater the level of air pollution and the greater the health concern; (3) Sulfur dioxide is no longer included in this table (as of December 8, 2021) because SO_2 concentrations tend to be very localized and not necessarily representative of broad geographical areas like counties and CBSAs.
Source: U.S. Environmental Protection Agency, Air Quality Index Report, 2021

Maximum Air Pollutant Concentrations: Particulate Matter, Ozone, CO and Lead

	Particulate Matter 10 (ug/m³)	Particulate Matter 2.5 Wtd AM (ug/m³)	Particulate Matter 2.5 24-Hr (ug/m³)	Ozone (ppm)	Carbon Monoxide (ppm)	Lead (ug/m³)
MSA[1] Level	96	10.3	41	0.089	2	n/a
NAAQS[2]	150	15	35	0.075	9	0.15
Met NAAQS[2]	Yes	Yes	No	No	Yes	n/a

Note: (1) Data covers the Denver-Aurora-Lakewood, CO Metropolitan Statistical Area; Data from exceptional events are included; (2) National Ambient Air Quality Standards; ppm = parts per million; ug/m³ = micrograms per cubic meter; n/a not available.
Concentrations: Particulate Matter 10 (coarse particulate)—highest second maximum 24-hour concentration; Particulate Matter 2.5 Wtd AM (fine particulate)—highest weighted annual mean concentration; Particulate Matter 2.5 24-Hour (fine particulate)—highest 98th percentile 24-hour concentration; Ozone—highest fourth daily maximum 8-hour concentration; Carbon Monoxide—highest second maximum non-overlapping 8-hour concentration; Lead—maximum running 3-month average
Source: U.S. Environmental Protection Agency, Air Quality Monitoring Information, "Air Quality Statistics by City, 2021"

Maximum Air Pollutant Concentrations: Nitrogen Dioxide and Sulfur Dioxide

	Nitrogen Dioxide AM (ppb)	Nitrogen Dioxide 1-Hr (ppb)	Sulfur Dioxide AM (ppb)	Sulfur Dioxide 1-Hr (ppb)	Sulfur Dioxide 24-Hr (ppb)
MSA[1] Level	26	71	n/a	7	n/a
NAAQS[2]	53	100	30	75	140
Met NAAQS[2]	Yes	Yes	n/a	Yes	n/a

Note: (1) Data covers the Denver-Aurora-Lakewood, CO Metropolitan Statistical Area; Data from exceptional events are included; (2) National Ambient Air Quality Standards; ppm = parts per million; ug/m³ = micrograms per cubic meter; n/a not available.
Concentrations: Nitrogen Dioxide AM—highest arithmetic mean concentration; Nitrogen Dioxide 1-Hr—highest 98th percentile 1-hour daily maximum concentration; Sulfur Dioxide AM—highest annual mean concentration; Sulfur Dioxide 1-Hr—highest 99th percentile 1-hour daily maximum concentration; Sulfur Dioxide 24-Hr—highest second maximum 24-hour concentration
Source: U.S. Environmental Protection Agency, Air Quality Monitoring Information, "Air Quality Statistics by City, 2021"

Fort Collins, Colorado

Background

At 4,985 feet, Fort Collins lies high in the eastern base of the Rocky Mountains' front range along the Cache la Poudre River about one hour from Denver. Although not quite as large as Denver, Fort Collins, home to Colorado State University and its own symphony orchestra, offers virtually everything its citizens need with a spectacular landscape, strong economy, and world-class outdoor adventure opportunities.

Fort Collins owes its name to Colonel William Collins of the Civil War era, who was sent with a regiment of Union soldiers to guard farmers and ranchers scattered throughout the valley, and to provide security for the Overland Stage trail. Originally called Camp Collins, the place remained a military reservation until 1866 and was incorporated in 1879.

The early economy of the town depended first on lumber, and then on the raising of livestock and produce, with alfalfa, grain, and sugar beets as the chief crops. Sugar refineries, dairies, and meatpacking plants bolstered the wealth of the town, as did the products of mining and quarrying. Fort Collins is still the commercial center for a rich agricultural region that produces hay, barley, and sugar beets.

Colorado State University, the land-grant University of Colorado, was established in Fort Collins in 1879, and offers innumerable cultural, economic, and educational benefits to residents. More than 32,000 students are enrolled at CSU, which is the largest employer in the city. CSU offers a world-class range of undergraduate and graduate programs, and is an internationally recognized center for forestry, agricultural science, veterinary medicine, and civil engineering.

Fort Collins' businesses produce motion-picture film, combustion engines, prefabricated metal buildings, arc welders and rods, cement products, dental hygiene appliances, and miscellaneous plastics.

The Fort Collins public school system, within the Poudre School District, is one of the area's largest employers. The latest addition was the city's 32nd elementary school. The city's public library system, Poudre River Public Libraries, operates three branches.

Gateway Natural Area, 15 miles from Fort Collins, offers several recreation opportunities, including a quarter-mile nature trail and a designated boat launch. Lakes are easily accessible for all water sports, and the Cache La Poudre River offers some of the best trout fishing in Colorado. For hunters, the area is a paradise, with ample supplies of antelope, black bear, deer, elk, mountain lion, and small game.

Fort Collins also offers a great range of cultural amenities. The city's Lincoln Center presents year-round performances by a variety of artists. Old Town, a historic downtown shopping district, hosts several large festivals each year. Fort Collins Symphony, the Larimer Chorale, Open Stage Theatre, and the Canyon Concert Ballet call Fort Collins their home. The city also cultivates the visual arts, with "Art in Public Places" sponsored by the city, and provides exhibits at the Lincoln Center, Fort Collins Museum, and private galleries.

Transportation in and around the city is convenient. The municipality operates its own bus service, and interstate bus service is available. Residents are served by three nearby airports—Fort Collins/Loveland Airport, Cheyenne Municipal Airport, and Denver International Airport, one of the nation's busiest airports.

Fort Collins features four distinct seasons and, though high in the foothills, is buffered from both summer and winter temperature extremes. A typical day in Fort Collins is warm and dry with mild nights. The town enjoys on average more than 300 sunny days per year, and an annual snowfall of 51 inches, with far less rainfall. Summers are comfortable, while winters are cold.

Rankings

General Rankings

- In their ninth annual survey, Livability.com looked at data for more than 2,300 mid-sized U.S. cities to determine the rankings for Livability's "Top 100 Best Places to Live" in 2022. Fort Collins ranked #11. Criteria: housing and economy; social and civic engagement; education; demographics; health care options; transportation & infrastructure; and community amenities. *Livability.com, "Top 100 Best Places to Live 2022" July 19, 2022*

Business/Finance Rankings

- The Fort Collins metro area appeared on the Milken Institute "2022 Best Performing Cities" list. Rank: #43 out of 200 large metro areas (population over 250,000). Criteria: job growth; wage and salary growth; high-tech output growth; housing affordability; household broadband access. *Milken Institute, "Best-Performing Cities 2022," March 28, 2022*

- *Forbes* ranked the 200 most populous metro areas to determine the nation's "Best Places for Business and Careers." The Fort Collins metro area was ranked #27. Criteria: costs (business and living); job growth (past and projected); income growth; quality of life; educational attainment (college and high school); projected economic growth; cultural and leisure opportunities; workplace tolerance laws; net migration patterns. *Forbes, "The Best Places for Business and Careers 2019: Seattle Still On Top," October 30, 2019*

Children/Family Rankings

- Fort Collins was selected as one of the most playful cities in the U.S. by KaBOOM! The organization's Playful City USA initiative honors cities and towns across the nation that have made their communities more playable. Criteria: pledging to integrate play as a solution to challenges in their communities; making it easy for children to get active and balanced play; creating more family-friendly and innovative communities as a result. *KaBOOM! National Campaign for Play, "2017 Playful City USA Communities"*

- Fort Collins was selected as one of the best cities for newlyweds by *Rent.com*. The city ranked #13 of 15. Criteria: cost of living; availability of affordable rental inventory; annual household income; activities and restaurant options; percentage of married couples; concentration of millennials; safety. *Rent.com, "The 15 Best Cities for Newlyweds," December 11, 2018*

Environmental Rankings

- Fort Collins was highlighted as one of the 25 most ozone-polluted metro areas in the U.S. during 2019 through 2021. The area ranked #15. *American Lung Association, "State of the Air 2023," April 19, 2023*

Real Estate Rankings

- The Fort Collins metro area was identified as one of the 20 least affordable housing markets in the U.S. in 2022. The area ranked #171 out of 186 markets. Criteria: qualification for a mortgage loan with a 10 percent down payment on a typical home. *National Association of Realtors®, Qualifying Income Based on Sales Price of Existing Single-Family Homes for Metropolitan Areas, 2022*

- Fort Collins was ranked #190 out of 235 metro areas in terms of housing affordability in 2022 by the National Association of Home Builders (#1 = most affordable). Criteria: the share of homes sold in that area affordable to a family earning the local median income, based on standard mortgage underwriting criteria. *National Association of Home Builders®, NAHB-Wells Fargo Housing Opportunity Index, 4th Quarter 2022*

Safety Rankings

- Allstate ranked the 200 largest cities in America in terms of driver safety. Fort Collins ranked #7. Criteria: internal property damage claims over a two-year period from January 2016 to December 2017. The report helps increase the importance of safety and awareness behind the wheel. *Allstate, "Allstate America's Best Drivers Report, 2019" June 24, 2019*

- The National Insurance Crime Bureau ranked 390 metro areas in the U.S. in terms of per capita rates of vehicle theft. The Fort Collins metro area ranked #164 (#1 = highest rate). Criteria: number of vehicle theft offenses per 100,000 inhabitants in 2021. *National Insurance Crime Bureau, "Hot Spots 2021," September 1, 2022*

Seniors/Retirement Rankings

- From its Best Cities for Successful Aging indexes, the Milken Institute generated rankings for metropolitan areas, weighing data in nine categories—health care, wellness, living arrangements, transportation and convenience, financial characteristics, education, employment, community engagement, and overall livability. The Fort Collins metro area was ranked #88 overall in the small metro area category. *Milken Institute, "Best Cities for Successful Aging, 2017" March 14, 2017*

- Fort Collins was identified as #9 of 20 most popular places to retire in the Western region by *Topretirements.com*. The site separated its annual "Best Places to Retire" list by major U.S. regions for 2019. The list reflects the 20 cities that visitors to the website are most interested in for retirement, based on the number of times a city's review was viewed on the website. *Topretirements.com, "20 Best Places to Retire in the West-2019," November 11, 2019*

Sports/Recreation Rankings

- Fort Collins was chosen as one of America's best cities for bicycling. The city ranked #3 out of 50. Criteria: cycling infrastructure that is safe and friendly for all ages; energy and bike culture. The editors evaluated cities with populations of 100,000 or more. *Bicycling, "The 50 Best Bike Cities in America," October 10, 2018*

Miscellaneous Rankings

- *MoveHub* ranked 446 hipster cities across 20 countries, using its new and improved *alternative* Hipster Index and Fort Collins came out as #48 among the top 50. Criteria: population over 150,000; number of vintage boutiques; density of tattoo parlors; vegan places to eat; coffee shops; and density of vinyl record stores. *www.movehub.com, "The Hipster Index: Brighton Pips Portland to Global Top Spot," July 28, 2021*

- Fort Collins was selected as a 2022 Digital Cities Survey winner. The city ranked #5 in the mid-sized city (125,000 to 249,999 population) category. The survey examined and assessed how city governments are utilizing technology to continue innovation, engage with residents, and persevere through the challenges of the pandemic. Survey questions focused on ten initiatives: cybersecurity; citizen experience; disaster recovery; business intelligence; IT personnel; data governance; business automation; IT governance; infrastructure modernization; and broadband connectivity. *Center for Digital Government, "2022 Digital Cities Survey," November 10, 2022*

Business Environment

DEMOGRAPHICS

Population Growth

Area	1990 Census	2000 Census	2010 Census	2020 Census	Population Growth (%) 1990-2020	Population Growth (%) 2010-2020
City	89,555	118,652	143,986	169,810	89.6	17.9
MSA[1]	186,136	251,494	299,630	359,066	92.9	19.8
U.S.	248,709,873	281,421,906	308,745,538	331,449,281	33.3	7.4

Note: (1) Figures cover the Fort Collins, CO Metropolitan Statistical Area
Source: U.S. Census Bureau, 1990 Census, 2000 Census, 2010 Census, 2020 Census

Race

Area	White Alone[2] (%)	Black Alone[2] (%)	Asian Alone[2] (%)	AIAN[3] Alone[2] (%)	NHOPI[4] Alone[2] (%)	Other Race Alone[2] (%)	Two or More Races (%)
City	80.8	1.5	3.6	0.8	0.1	3.6	9.6
MSA[1]	82.4	1.1	2.4	0.8	0.1	3.8	9.4
U.S.	61.6	12.4	6.0	1.1	0.2	8.4	10.2

Note: (1) Figures cover the Fort Collins, CO Metropolitan Statistical Area; (2) Alone is defined as not being in combination with one or more other races; (3) American Indian and Alaska Native; (4) Native Hawaiian and Other Pacific Islander
Source: U.S. Census Bureau, 2020 Census

Hispanic or Latino Origin

Area	Total (%)	Mexican (%)	Puerto Rican (%)	Cuban (%)	Other (%)
City	12.6	9.0	0.5	0.1	3.0
MSA[1]	12.0	8.8	0.4	0.2	2.6
U.S.	18.4	11.2	1.8	0.7	4.7

Note: Persons of Hispanic or Latino origin can be of any race; (1) Figures cover the Fort Collins, CO Metropolitan Statistical Area
Source: U.S. Census Bureau, 2017-2021 American Community Survey 5-Year Estimates

Age

Area	Under Age 5	Age 5–19	Age 20–34	Age 35–44	Age 45–54	Age 55–64	Age 65–74	Age 75–84	Age 85+	Median Age
City	4.4	19.4	31.1	12.7	10.2	9.5	7.7	3.4	1.6	31.7
MSA[1]	4.6	18.5	23.6	12.9	11.0	12.4	10.5	4.8	1.8	37.4
U.S.	5.6	19.2	20.2	12.7	12.4	13.1	10.0	4.9	1.9	38.8

Note: (1) Figures cover the Fort Collins, CO Metropolitan Statistical Area
Source: U.S. Census Bureau, 2020 Census

Disability by Age

Area	All Ages	Under 18 Years Old	18 to 64 Years Old	65 Years and Over
City	8.4	2.7	6.8	28.0
MSA[1]	10.0	2.7	7.7	28.8
U.S.	12.6	4.4	10.3	33.4

Note: Figures show percent of the civilian noninstitutionalized population that reported having a disability. Disability status is determined from six types of difficulty: vision, hearing, cognitive, ambulatory, self-care, and independent living. For children under 5 years old, hearing and vision difficulty are used to determine disability status. For children between the ages of 5 and 14, disability status is determined from hearing, vision, cognitive, ambulatory, and self-care difficulties. For people aged 15 years and older, they are considered to have a disability if they have difficulty with any one of the six difficulty types; Note: (1) Figures cover the Fort Collins, CO Metropolitan Statistical Area
Source: U.S. Census Bureau, 2017-2021 American Community Survey 5-Year Estimates

Ancestry

Area	German	Irish	English	American	Italian	Polish	French[2]	Scottish	Dutch
City	23.4	12.9	13.0	3.6	5.8	3.0	3.2	3.3	1.8
MSA[1]	25.2	13.1	14.1	4.1	5.2	2.8	3.2	3.4	2.1
U.S.	12.8	9.6	8.1	5.7	5.0	2.7	2.2	1.6	1.1

Note: Figures are the percentage of the total population reporting a particular ancestry. The nine most commonly reported ancestries in the U.S. are shown. Figures include multiple ancestries (e.g. if a person reported being Irish and Italian, they were included in both columns); (1) Figures cover the Fort Collins, CO Metropolitan Statistical Area; (2) Excludes Basque
Source: U.S. Census Bureau, 2017-2021 American Community Survey 5-Year Estimates

Foreign-born Population

Area	Any Foreign Country	Asia	Mexico	Europe	Caribbean	Central America[2]	South America	Africa	Canada
City	7.3	2.9	1.4	1.4	0.1	0.3	0.6	0.3	0.2
MSA[1]	5.8	1.8	1.4	1.2	0.1	0.2	0.5	0.3	0.2
U.S.	13.6	4.2	3.3	1.5	1.4	1.1	1.1	0.8	0.2

Note: (1) Figures cover the Fort Collins, CO Metropolitan Statistical Area; (2) Excludes Mexico.
Source: U.S. Census Bureau, 2017-2021 American Community Survey 5-Year Estimates

Household Size

Area	One	Two	Three	Four	Five	Six	Seven or More	Average Household Size
City	25.2	37.4	17.7	14.0	4.0	1.1	0.5	2.40
MSA[1]	24.9	39.9	15.8	12.2	5.0	1.5	0.8	2.40
U.S.	28.1	33.8	15.5	12.9	6.0	2.3	1.4	2.60

Note: (1) Figures cover the Fort Collins, CO Metropolitan Statistical Area
Source: U.S. Census Bureau, 2017-2021 American Community Survey 5-Year Estimates

Household Relationships

Area	House-holder	Opposite-sex Spouse	Same-sex Spouse	Opposite-sex Unmarried Partner	Same-sex Unmarried Partner	Child[2]	Grand-child	Other Relatives	Non-relatives
City	39.9	16.0	0.2	3.3	0.2	22.1	0.9	2.4	9.0
MSA[1]	40.2	19.4	0.2	2.8	0.2	24.0	1.2	2.7	6.0
U.S.	38.3	17.5	0.2	2.5	0.2	28.3	2.4	4.8	3.4

Note: Figures are percent of the total population; (1) Figures cover the Fort Collins, CO Metropolitan Statistical Area; (2) Includes biological, adopted, and stepchildren of the householder
Source: U.S. Census Bureau, 2020 Census

Gender

Area	Males	Females	Males per 100 Females
City	84,217	85,593	98.4
MSA[1]	177,804	181,262	98.1
U.S.	162,685,811	168,763,470	96.4

Note: (1) Figures cover the Fort Collins, CO Metropolitan Statistical Area
Source: U.S. Census Bureau, 2020 Census

Marital Status

Area	Never Married	Now Married[2]	Separated	Widowed	Divorced
City	46.6	40.9	0.7	3.3	8.5
MSA[1]	34.5	51.3	0.8	4.0	9.4
U.S.	33.8	48.0	1.8	5.6	10.8

Note: Figures are percentages and cover the population 15 years of age and older; (1) Figures cover the Fort Collins, CO Metropolitan Statistical Area; (2) Excludes separated
Source: U.S. Census Bureau, 2017-2021 American Community Survey 5-Year Estimates

Religious Groups by Family

Area	Catholic	Baptist	Methodist	LDS[2]	Pentecostal	Lutheran	Islam	Adventist	Other
MSA[1]	9.9	1.2	1.3	4.0	2.7	2.5	<0.1	1.2	12.1
U.S.	18.7	7.3	3.0	2.0	1.8	1.7	1.3	1.3	11.6

Note: Figures are the number of adherents as a percentage of the total population and cover the eight largest religious groups in the U.S; (1) Figures cover the Fort Collins, CO Metropolitan Statistical Area; (2) Church of Jesus Christ of Latter-day Saints
Sources: 2020 U.S. Religion Census, Association of Statisticians of American Religious Bodies; The Association of Religion Data Archives (ARDA)

Religious Groups by Tradition

Area	Catholic	Evangelical Protestant	Mainline Protestant	Black Protestant	Islam	Judaism	Hinduism	Orthodox	Buddhism
MSA[1]	9.9	15.6	3.3	0.4	<0.1	n/a	0.1	0.1	0.1
U.S.	18.7	16.5	5.2	2.3	1.3	0.6	0.4	0.4	0.3

Note: Figures are the number of adherents as a percentage of the total population; (1) Figures cover the Fort Collins, CO Metropolitan Statistical Area
Sources: 2020 U.S. Religion Census, Association of Statisticians of American Religious Bodies; The Association of Religion Data Archives (ARDA)

ECONOMY

Gross Metropolitan Product

Area	2020	2021	2022	2023	Rank[2]
MSA[1]	21.6	23.7	25.7	27.3	130

Note: Figures are in billions of dollars; (1) Figures cover the Fort Collins, CO Metropolitan Statistical Area; (2) Rank is based on 2021 data and ranges from 1 to 381
Source: U.S. Conference of Mayors, U.S. Metro Economies: U.S. Metros Compared to Global and State Economies, June 2022

Economic Growth

Area	2018-20 (%)	2021 (%)	2022 (%)	2023 (%)	Rank[2]
MSA[1]	2.2	5.3	2.6	4.0	27
U.S.	-0.6	5.7	3.1	2.9	–

Note: Figures are real gross metropolitan product (GMP) growth rates and represent average annual percent change; (1) Figures cover the Fort Collins, CO Metropolitan Statistical Area; (2) Rank is based on 2020 2-year average annual percent change and ranges from 1 to 381
Source: U.S. Conference of Mayors, U.S. Metro Economies: U.S. Metros Compared to Global and State Economies, June 2022

Metropolitan Area Exports

Area	2016	2017	2018	2019	2020	2021	Rank[2]
MSA[1]	993.8	1,034.1	1,021.8	1,060.0	1,092.5	1,132.5	146

Note: Figures are in millions of dollars; (1) Figures cover the Fort Collins, CO Metropolitan Statistical Area; (2) Rank is based on 2021 data and ranges from 1 to 388
Source: U.S. Department of Commerce, International Trade Administration, Office of Trade and Economic Analysis, Industry and Analysis, Exports by Metropolitan Area, data extracted March 16, 2023

Building Permits

Area	Single-Family			Multi-Family			Total		
	2021	2022	Pct. Chg.	2021	2022	Pct. Chg.	2021	2022	Pct. Chg.
City	381	287	-24.7	458	515	12.4	839	802	-4.4
MSA[1]	2,149	1,385	-35.6	1,072	1,187	10.7	3,221	2,572	-20.1
U.S.	1,115,400	975,600	-12.5	621,600	689,500	10.9	1,737,000	1,665,100	-4.1

Note: (1) Figures cover the Fort Collins, CO Metropolitan Statistical Area; Figures represent new, privately-owned housing units authorized (unadjusted data); All permit data are based on estimates with imputation
Source: U.S. Census Bureau, Manufacturing, Mining, and Construction Statistics, Building Permits, 2021, 2022

Bankruptcy Filings

Area	Business Filings			Nonbusiness Filings		
	2021	2022	% Chg.	2021	2022	% Chg.
Larimer County	14	14	0.0	306	283	-7.5
U.S.	14,347	13,481	-6.0	399,269	374,240	-6.3

Note: Business filings include Chapter 7, Chapter 9, Chapter 11, Chapter 12, Chapter 13, Chapter 15, and Section 304; Nonbusiness filings include Chapter 7, Chapter 11, and Chapter 13
Source: Administrative Office of the U.S. Courts, Business and Nonbusiness Bankruptcy, County Cases Commenced by Chapter of the Bankruptcy Code, During the 12-Month Period Ending December 31, 2021 and Business and Nonbusiness Bankruptcy, County Cases Commenced by Chapter of the Bankruptcy Code, During the 12-Month Period Ending December 31, 2022

Housing Vacancy Rates

Area	Gross Vacancy Rate[2] (%)			Year-Round Vacancy Rate[3] (%)			Rental Vacancy Rate[4] (%)			Homeowner Vacancy Rate[5] (%)		
	2020	2021	2022	2020	2021	2022	2020	2021	2022	2020	2021	2022
MSA[1]	n/a	n/a	n/a	n/a	n/a	n/a	n/a	n/a	n/a	n/a	n/a	n/a
U.S.	10.6	10.8	10.5	8.2	8.4	8.2	6.3	6.1	5.8	1.0	0.9	0.8

Note: (1) Figures cover the Fort Collins, CO Metropolitan Statistical Area; (2) The percentage of the total housing inventory that is vacant; (3) The percentage of the housing inventory (excluding seasonal units) that is year-round vacant; (4) The percentage of rental inventory that is vacant for rent; (5) The percentage of homeowner inventory that is vacant for sale; n/a not available
Source: U.S. Census Bureau, Housing Vacancies and Homeownership Annual Statistics: 2020, 2021, 2022

INCOME

Income

Area	Per Capita ($)	Median Household ($)	Average Household ($)
City	38,949	72,932	96,301
MSA[1]	42,596	80,664	104,442
U.S.	37,638	69,021	97,196

Note: (1) Figures cover the Fort Collins, CO Metropolitan Statistical Area
Source: U.S. Census Bureau, 2017-2021 American Community Survey 5-Year Estimates

Household Income Distribution

Area	Percent of Households Earning							
	Under $15,000	$15,000 -$24,999	$25,000 -$34,999	$35,000 -$49,999	$50,000 -$74,999	$75,000 -$99,999	$100,000 -$149,999	$150,000 and up
City	9.6	6.7	7.5	11.0	16.5	13.0	17.2	18.5
MSA[1]	7.9	6.2	6.6	10.0	16.0	14.2	18.8	20.3
U.S.	9.4	7.8	8.2	11.4	16.8	12.8	16.3	17.3

Note: (1) Figures cover the Fort Collins, CO Metropolitan Statistical Area
Source: U.S. Census Bureau, 2017-2021 American Community Survey 5-Year Estimates

Poverty Rate

Area	All Ages	Under 18 Years Old	18 to 64 Years Old	65 Years and Over
City	15.7	8.9	18.7	7.3
MSA[1]	11.1	8.8	13.0	6.6
U.S.	12.6	17.0	11.8	9.6

Note: Figures are percentage of people whose income during the past 12 months was below the poverty level;
(1) Figures cover the Fort Collins, CO Metropolitan Statistical Area
Source: U.S. Census Bureau, 2017-2021 American Community Survey 5-Year Estimates

EMPLOYMENT

Labor Force and Employment

Area	Civilian Labor Force			Workers Employed		
	Dec. 2021	Dec. 2022	% Chg.	Dec. 2021	Dec. 2022	% Chg.
City	100,891	102,741	1.8	98,235	100,394	2.2
MSA[1]	208,863	212,087	1.5	202,604	207,057	2.2
U.S.	161,696,000	164,224,000	1.6	155,732,000	158,872,000	2.0

Note: Data is not seasonally adjusted and covers workers 16 years of age and older; (1) Figures cover the Fort Collins, CO Metropolitan Statistical Area
Source: Bureau of Labor Statistics, Local Area Unemployment Statistics

Unemployment Rate

Area	2022											
	Jan.	Feb.	Mar.	Apr.	May	Jun.	Jul.	Aug.	Sep.	Oct.	Nov.	Dec.
City	3.0	3.2	2.7	2.4	2.4	2.8	2.9	2.7	2.6	2.8	2.8	2.3
MSA[1]	3.4	3.5	3.1	2.7	2.6	2.9	3.0	2.8	2.7	2.9	2.8	2.4
U.S.	4.4	4.1	3.8	3.3	3.4	3.8	3.8	3.8	3.3	3.4	3.4	3.3

Note: Data is not seasonally adjusted and covers workers 16 years of age and older; (1) Figures cover the Fort Collins, CO Metropolitan Statistical Area
Source: Bureau of Labor Statistics, Local Area Unemployment Statistics

Average Wages

Occupation	$/Hr.	Occupation	$/Hr.
Accountants and Auditors	40.07	Maintenance and Repair Workers	22.69
Automotive Mechanics	25.91	Marketing Managers	87.40
Bookkeepers	23.02	Network and Computer Systems Admin.	43.41
Carpenters	25.81	Nurses, Licensed Practical	28.74
Cashiers	15.48	Nurses, Registered	40.85
Computer Programmers	47.61	Nursing Assistants	18.30
Computer Systems Analysts	50.60	Office Clerks, General	23.55
Computer User Support Specialists	30.99	Physical Therapists	42.61
Construction Laborers	20.70	Physicians	n/a
Cooks, Restaurant	17.57	Plumbers, Pipefitters and Steamfitters	29.30
Customer Service Representatives	19.06	Police and Sheriff's Patrol Officers	43.64
Dentists	n/a	Postal Service Mail Carriers	27.22
Electricians	28.15	Real Estate Sales Agents	33.68
Engineers, Electrical	54.42	Retail Salespersons	17.51
Fast Food and Counter Workers	14.91	Sales Representatives, Technical/Scientific	46.18
Financial Managers	86.90	Secretaries, Exc. Legal/Medical/Executive	21.02
First-Line Supervisors of Office Workers	31.88	Security Guards	16.93
General and Operations Managers	63.72	Surgeons	n/a
Hairdressers/Cosmetologists	26.75	Teacher Assistants, Exc. Postsecondary*	16.36
Home Health and Personal Care Aides	16.84	Teachers, Secondary School, Exc. Sp. Ed.*	28.98
Janitors and Cleaners	17.15	Telemarketers	18.28
Landscaping/Groundskeeping Workers	19.43	Truck Drivers, Heavy/Tractor-Trailer	25.19
Lawyers	88.05	Truck Drivers, Light/Delivery Services	22.91
Maids and Housekeeping Cleaners	16.17	Waiters and Waitresses	19.93

Note: Wage data covers the Fort Collins, CO Metropolitan Statistical Area; (*) Hourly wages were calculated from annual wage data based on a 40 hour work week; n/a not available.
Source: Bureau of Labor Statistics, Metro Area Occupational Employment & Wage Estimates, May 2022

Employment by Industry

| Sector | MSA[1] | | U.S. |
	Number of Employees	Percent of Total	Percent of Total
Construction, Mining, and Logging	12,100	6.8	5.4
Private Education and Health Services	19,500	10.9	16.1
Financial Activities	7,100	4.0	5.9
Government	42,900	24.0	14.5
Information	2,600	1.5	2.0
Leisure and Hospitality	21,300	11.9	10.3
Manufacturing	14,900	8.3	8.4
Other Services	6,500	3.6	3.7
Professional and Business Services	21,200	11.9	14.7
Retail Trade	20,400	11.4	10.2
Transportation, Warehousing, and Utilities	4,200	2.4	4.9
Wholesale Trade	5,800	3.2	3.9

Note: Figures are non-farm employment as of December 2022. Figures are not seasonally adjusted and include workers 16 years of age and older; (1) Figures cover the Fort Collins, CO Metropolitan Statistical Area
Source: Bureau of Labor Statistics, Current Employment Statistics, Employment, Hours, and Earnings

Employment by Occupation

Occupation Classification	City (%)	MSA[1] (%)	U.S. (%)
Management, Business, Science, and Arts	49.3	46.5	40.3
Natural Resources, Construction, and Maintenance	6.2	8.2	8.7
Production, Transportation, and Material Moving	7.8	9.5	13.1
Sales and Office	20.0	20.6	20.9
Service	16.7	15.3	17.0

Note: Figures cover employed civilians 16 years of age and older; (1) Figures cover the Fort Collins, CO Metropolitan Statistical Area
Source: U.S. Census Bureau, 2017-2021 American Community Survey 5-Year Estimates

Occupations with Greatest Projected Employment Growth: 2022 – 2024

Occupation[1]	2022 Employment	2024 Projected Employment	Numeric Employment Change	Percent Employment Change
Software Developers	43,570	47,290	3,720	8.5
Stockers and Order Fillers	45,230	48,030	2,800	6.2
Cooks, Restaurant	31,870	34,550	2,680	8.4
Fast Food and Counter Workers	79,850	82,410	2,560	3.2
Accountants and Auditors	42,150	43,910	1,760	4.2
Market Research Analysts and Marketing Specialists	28,150	29,830	1,680	6.0
Home Health and Personal Care Aides	43,200	44,870	1,670	3.9
Registered Nurses	53,590	55,060	1,470	2.7
General and Operations Managers	47,360	48,780	1,420	3.0
Sales Representatives of Services, Except Advertising, Insurance, Financial Services, and Travel	37,310	38,730	1,420	3.8

Note: Projections cover Colorado; (1) Sorted by numeric employment change
Source: www.projectionscentral.com, State Occupational Projections, 2022–2024 Short-Term Projections

Fastest-Growing Occupations: 2022 – 2024

Occupation[1]	2022 Employment	2024 Projected Employment	Numeric Employment Change	Percent Employment Change
Derrick Operators, Oil and Gas	550	640	90	16.4
Roustabouts, Oil and Gas	1,550	1,790	240	15.5
Service Unit Operators, Oil, Gas, and Mining	2,430	2,760	330	13.6
Flight Attendants	4,890	5,490	600	12.3
Epidemiologists	530	590	60	11.3
Information Security Analysts (SOC 2018)	6,100	6,760	660	10.8
Statisticians	1,410	1,550	140	9.9
Veterinary Assistants and Laboratory Animal Caretakers	2,360	2,590	230	9.7
Data Scientists	3,520	3,850	330	9.4
Solar Photovoltaic Installers	530	580	50	9.4

Note: Projections cover Colorado; (1) Sorted by percent employment change and excludes occupations with numeric employment change less than 50
Source: www.projectionscentral.com, State Occupational Projections, 2022–2024 Short-Term Projections

CITY FINANCES

City Government Finances

Component	2020 ($000)	2020 ($ per capita)
Total Revenues	691,477	4,062
Total Expenditures	804,694	4,727
Debt Outstanding	234,040	1,375
Cash and Securities[1]	673,580	3,957

Note: (1) Cash and security holdings of a government at the close of its fiscal year, including those of its dependent agencies, utilities, and liquor stores.
Source: U.S. Census Bureau, State & Local Government Finances 2020

City Government Revenue by Source

Source	2020 ($000)	2020 ($ per capita)	2020 (%)
General Revenue			
From Federal Government	102,908	604	14.9
From State Government	58,094	341	8.4
From Local Governments	376	2	0.1
Taxes			
Property	36,367	214	5.3
Sales and Gross Receipts	143,623	844	20.8
Personal Income	0	0	0.0
Corporate Income	0	0	0.0
Motor Vehicle License	0	0	0.0
Other Taxes	4,661	27	0.7
Current Charges	104,422	613	15.1
Liquor Store	0	0	0.0
Utility	181,386	1,065	26.2

Source: U.S. Census Bureau, State & Local Government Finances 2020

City Government Expenditures by Function

Function	2020 ($000)	2020 ($ per capita)	2020 (%)
General Direct Expenditures			
Air Transportation	0	0	0.0
Corrections	0	0	0.0
Education	0	0	0.0
Employment Security Administration	0	0	0.0
Financial Administration	4,931	29	0.6
Fire Protection	30,645	180	3.8
General Public Buildings	0	0	0.0
Governmental Administration, Other	8,164	48	1.0
Health	0	0	0.0
Highways	73,688	432	9.2
Hospitals	0	0	0.0
Housing and Community Development	49,175	288	6.1
Interest on General Debt	4,802	28	0.6
Judicial and Legal	0	0	0.0
Libraries	0	0	0.0
Parking	3,985	23	0.5
Parks and Recreation	51,756	304	6.4
Police Protection	51,381	301	6.4
Public Welfare	0	0	0.0
Sewerage	24,061	141	3.0
Solid Waste Management	0	0	0.0
Veterans' Services	0	0	0.0
Liquor Store	0	0	0.0
Utility	356,525	2,094	44.3

Source: U.S. Census Bureau, State & Local Government Finances 2020

TAXES

State Corporate Income Tax Rates

State	Tax Rate (%)	Income Brackets ($)	Num. of Brackets	Financial Institution Tax Rate (%)[a]	Federal Income Tax Ded.
Colorado	4.4	Flat rate	1	4.4	No

Note: Tax rates as of January 1, 2023; (a) Rates listed are the corporate income tax rate applied to financial institutions or excise taxes based on income. Some states have other taxes based upon the value of deposits or shares.
Source: Federation of Tax Administrators, State Corporate Income Tax Rates, January 1, 2023

State Individual Income Tax Rates

State	Tax Rate (%)	Income Brackets ($)	Personal Exemptions ($)			Standard Ded. ($)	
			Single	Married	Depend.	Single	Married
Colorado	4.4	Flat rate	(d)	(d)	(d)	13,850	27,700 (d)

Note: Tax rates as of January 1, 2023; Local- and county-level taxes are not included; Federal income tax is not deductible on state income tax returns; (d) These states use the personal exemption/standard deduction amounts provided in the federal Internal Revenue Code.
Source: Federation of Tax Administrators, State Individual Income Tax Rates, January 1, 2023

Various State Sales and Excise Tax Rates

State	State Sales Tax (%)	Gasoline[1] ($/gal.)	Cigarette[2] ($/pack)	Spirits[3] ($/gal.)	Wine[4] ($/gal.)	Beer[5] ($/gal.)	Recreational Marijuana (%)
Colorado	2.9	0.22	1.94	2.28	0.32	0.08	(d)

Note: All tax rates as of January 1, 2023; (1) The American Petroleum Institute has developed a methodology for determining the average tax rate on a gallon of fuel. Rates may include any of the following: excise taxes, environmental fees, storage tank fees, other fees or taxes, general sales tax, and local taxes; (2) The federal excise tax of $1.0066 per pack and local taxes are not included; (3) Rates are those applicable to off-premise sales of 40% alcohol by volume (a.b.v.) distilled spirits in 750ml containers. Local excise taxes are excluded; (4) Rates are those applicable to off-premise sales of 11% a.b.v. non-carbonated wine in 750ml containers; (5) Rates are those applicable to off-premise sales of 4.7% a.b.v. beer in 12 ounce containers; (d) 15% excise tax (levied on wholesale at average market rate); 15% excise tax (retail price)
Source: Tax Foundation, 2023 Facts & Figures: How Does Your State Compare?

State Business Tax Climate Index Rankings

State	Overall Rank	Corporate Tax Rank	Individual Income Tax Rank	Sales Tax Rank	Property Tax Rank	Unemployment Insurance Tax Rank
Colorado	21	7	14	40	36	42

Note: The index is a measure of how each state's tax laws affect economic performance. The lower the rank, the more favorable a state's tax system is for business. States without a given tax are given a ranking of 1. The scores/rankings for the District of Columbia do not affect other states. The 2023 index represents the tax climate as of July 1, 2022.
Source: Tax Foundation, State Business Tax Climate Index 2023

TRANSPORTATION

Means of Transportation to Work

Area	Car/Truck/Van		Public Transportation			Bicycle	Walked	Other Means	Worked at Home
	Drove Alone	Car-pooled	Bus	Subway	Railroad				
City	66.7	6.3	1.8	0.0	0.0	4.4	4.3	1.1	15.5
MSA[1]	70.7	6.4	1.1	0.1	0.0	2.4	2.8	1.1	15.4
U.S.	73.2	8.6	2.0	1.6	0.5	0.5	2.5	1.5	9.7

Note: Figures are percentages and cover workers 16 years of age and older; (1) Figures cover the Fort Collins, CO Metropolitan Statistical Area
Source: U.S. Census Bureau, 2017-2021 American Community Survey 5-Year Estimates

Travel Time to Work

Area	Less Than 10 Minutes	10 to 19 Minutes	20 to 29 Minutes	30 to 44 Minutes	45 to 59 Minutes	60 to 89 Minutes	90 Minutes or More
City	15.4	43.8	20.6	10.0	5.4	3.3	1.5
MSA[1]	13.5	35.4	21.8	15.9	6.3	4.9	2.2
U.S.	12.4	28.5	21.0	20.9	8.2	6.2	2.9

Note: Note: Figures are percentages and include workers 16 years old and over; (1) Figures cover the Fort Collins, CO Metropolitan Statistical Area
Source: U.S. Census Bureau, 2017-2021 American Community Survey 5-Year Estimates

Key Congestion Measures

Measure	1990	2000	2010	2015	2020
Annual Hours of Delay, Total (000)	n/a	n/a	n/a	5,902	3,465
Annual Hours of Delay, Per Auto Commuter	n/a	n/a	n/a	21	12
Annual Congestion Cost, Per Auto Commuter ($)	n/a	n/a	n/a	421	256

Note: n/a not available
Source: Texas A&M Transportation Institute, 2021 Urban Mobility Report

Freeway Travel Time Index

Measure	1985	1990	1995	2000	2005	2010	2015	2020
Urban Area Index[1]	n/a	n/a	n/a	n/a	n/a	n/a	1.10	1.07
Urban Area Rank[1,2]	n/a	n/a	n/a	n/a	n/a	n/a	n/a	n/a

Note: Freeway Travel Time Index—the ratio of travel time in the peak period to the travel time at free-flow conditions. For example, a value of 1.30 indicates a 20-minute free-flow trip takes 26 minutes in the peak (20 minutes x 1.30 = 26 minutes); (1) Covers the Fort Collins CO urban area; (2) Rank is based on 101 larger urban areas (#1 = highest travel time index); n/a not available
Source: Texas A&M Transportation Institute, 2021 Urban Mobility Report

Public Transportation

Agency Name / Mode of Transportation	Vehicles Operated in Maximum Service[1]	Annual Unlinked Passenger Trips[2] (in thous.)	Annual Passenger Miles[3] (in thous.)
Transfort			
Bus (directly operated)	28	994.0	4,256.1
Bus (purchased transportation)	2	6.9	22.3
Bus Rapid Transit (directly operated)	6	437.0	1,414.9
Demand Response (purchased transportation)	3	5.0	45.8
Demand Response - Taxi	10	23.9	121.0

Note: (1) Number of revenue vehicles operated by the given mode and type of service to meet the annual maximum service requirement. This is the revenue vehicle count during the peak season of the year; on the week and day that maximum service is provided. Vehicles operated in maximum service (VOMS) exclude atypical days and one-time special events; (2) Number of passengers who boarded public transportation vehicles. Passengers are counted each time they board a vehicle no matter how many vehicles they use to travel from their origin to their destination. (3) Sum of the distances ridden by all passengers during the entire fiscal year.
Source: Federal Transit Administration, National Transit Database, 2021

Air Transportation

Airport Name and Code / Type of Service	Passenger Airlines[1]	Passenger Enplanements	Freight Carriers[2]	Freight (lbs)
Denver International (60 miles) (DEN)				
Domestic service (U.S. carriers - 2022)	26	32,145,313	15	277,972,263
International service (U.S. carriers - 2021)	8	661,977	3	3,625,333

Note: (1) Includes all U.S.-based major, minor and commuter airlines that carried at least one passenger during the year; (2) Includes all U.S.-based airlines and freight carriers that transported at least one pound of freight during the year.
Source: Bureau of Transportation Statistics, The Intermodal Transportation Database, Air Carriers: T-100 Domestic Market (U.S. Carriers), 2022; Bureau of Transportation Statistics, The Intermodal Transportation Database, Air Carriers: T-100 International Market (U.S. Carriers), 2021

BUSINESSES

Major Business Headquarters

Company Name	Industry	Rankings	
		Fortune[1]	Forbes[2]
No companies listed	-	-	-

Note: (1) Companies that produce a 10-K are ranked 1 to 500 based on 2021 revenue; (2) All private companies with at least $2 billion in annual revenue through the end of their most current fiscal year are ranked 1 to 246; companies listed are headquartered in the city; dashes indicate no ranking
Source: Fortune, "Fortune 500," 2022; Forbes, "America's Largest Private Companies," 2022

Living Environment

COST OF LIVING

Cost of Living Index

Composite Index	Groceries	Housing	Utilities	Trans-portation	Health Care	Misc. Goods/ Services
n/a	n/a	n/a	n/a	n/a	n/a	n/a

Note: The Cost of Living Index measures regional differences in the cost of consumer goods and services, excluding taxes and non-consumer expenditures, for professional and managerial households in the top income quintile. It is based on more than 50,000 prices covering almost 60 different items for which prices are collected three times a year by chambers of commerce, economic development organizations or university applied economic centers in each participating urban area. The numbers shown should be read as a percentage above or below the national average of 100. For example, a value of 115.4 in the groceries column indicates that grocery prices are 15.4% higher than the national average. Small differences in the index numbers should not be interpreted as significant; n/a not available.
Source: The Council for Community and Economic Research, Cost of Living Index, 2022

Grocery Prices

Area[1]	T-Bone Steak ($/pound)	Frying Chicken ($/pound)	Whole Milk ($/half gal.)	Eggs ($/dozen)	Orange Juice ($/64 oz.)	Coffee ($/11.5 oz.)
City[2]	n/a	n/a	n/a	n/a	n/a	n/a
Avg.	13.81	1.59	2.43	2.25	3.85	4.95
Min.	10.17	0.90	1.51	1.30	2.90	3.46
Max.	19.35	3.30	4.32	4.32	5.31	8.59

*Note: (1) Values for the local area are compared with the average, minimum and maximum values for all 286 areas in the Cost of Living Index; (2) Figures cover the Fort Collins CO urban area; n/a not available; **T-Bone Steak** (price per pound); **Frying Chicken** (price per pound, whole fryer); **Whole Milk** (half gallon carton); **Eggs** (price per dozen, Grade A, large); **Orange Juice** (64 oz. Tropicana or Florida Natural); **Coffee** (11.5 oz. can, vacuum-packed, Maxwell House, Hills Bros, or Folgers).*
Source: The Council for Community and Economic Research, Cost of Living Index, 2022

Housing and Utility Costs

Area[1]	New Home Price ($)	Apartment Rent ($/month)	All Electric ($/month)	Part Electric ($/month)	Other Energy ($/month)	Telephone ($/month)
City[2]	n/a	n/a	n/a	n/a	n/a	n/a
Avg.	450,913	1,371	176.41	99.93	76.96	190.22
Min.	229,283	546	100.84	31.56	27.15	174.27
Max.	2,434,977	4,569	356.86	249.59	272.24	208.31

*Note: (1) Values for the local area are compared with the average, minimum and maximum values for all 286 areas in the Cost of Living Index; (2) Figures cover the Fort Collins CO urban area; n/a not available; **New Home Price** (2,400 sf living area, 8,000 sf lot, in urban area with full utilities); **Apartment Rent** (950 sf 2 bedroom/1.5 or 2 bath, unfurnished, excluding all utilities except water); **All Electric** (average monthly cost for an all-electric home); **Part Electric** (average monthly cost for a part-electric home); **Other Energy** (average monthly cost for natural gas, fuel oil, coal, wood, and any other forms of energy except electricity); **Telephone** (price includes the base monthly rate plus taxes and fees for three lines of mobile phone service).*
Source: The Council for Community and Economic Research, Cost of Living Index, 2022

Health Care, Transportation, and Other Costs

Area[1]	Doctor ($/visit)	Dentist ($/visit)	Optometrist ($/visit)	Gasoline ($/gallon)	Beauty Salon ($/visit)	Men's Shirt ($)
City[2]	n/a	n/a	n/a	n/a	n/a	n/a
Avg.	124.91	107.77	117.66	3.86	43.31	34.21
Min.	36.61	58.25	51.79	2.90	22.18	13.05
Max.	250.21	162.58	371.96	5.54	85.61	63.54

*Note: (1) Values for the local area are compared with the average, minimum and maximum values for all 286 areas in the Cost of Living Index; (2) Figures cover the Fort Collins CO urban area; n/a not available; **Doctor** (general practitioners routine exam of an established patient); **Dentist** (adult teeth cleaning and periodic oral examination); **Optometrist** (full vision eye exam for established adult patient); **Gasoline** (one gallon regular unleaded, national brand, including all taxes, cash price at self-service pump if available); **Beauty Salon** (woman's shampoo, trim, and blow-dry); **Men's Shirt** (cotton/polyester dress shirt, pinpoint weave, long sleeves).*
Source: The Council for Community and Economic Research, Cost of Living Index, 2022

HOUSING

Homeownership Rate

Area	2015 (%)	2016 (%)	2017 (%)	2018 (%)	2019 (%)	2020 (%)	2021 (%)	2022 (%)
MSA[1]	n/a	n/a	n/a	n/a	n/a	n/a	n/a	n/a
U.S.	63.7	63.4	63.9	64.4	64.6	66.6	65.5	65.8

Note: (1) Figures cover the Fort Collins, CO Metropolitan Statistical Area; n/a not available
Source: U.S. Census Bureau, Housing Vacancies and Homeownership Annual Statistics: 2015-2022

House Price Index (HPI)

Area	National Ranking[2]	Quarterly Change (%)	One-Year Change (%)	Five-Year Change (%)	Since 1991Q1 (%)
MSA[1]	141	-2.34	10.88	51.04	508.13
U.S.[3]	–	0.34	8.41	58.44	289.08

Note: The HPI is a weighted repeat sales index. It measures average price changes in repeat sales or refinancings on the same properties. This information is obtained by reviewing repeat mortgage transactions on single-family properties whose mortgages have been purchased or securitized by Fannie Mae or Freddie Mac since January 1975; (1) Figures cover the Fort Collins, CO Metropolitan Statistical Area; (2) Rankings are based on annual percentage change for all metro areas containing at least 15,000 transactions over the last 10 years and ranges from 1 to 257; (3) figures based on a weighted average of Census Division estimates using a seasonally adjusted, purchase-only index; all figures are for the period ending December 31, 2022
Source: Federal Housing Finance Agency, Change in FHFA Metropolitan Area House Price Indexes, 2022Q4

Median Single-Family Home Prices

Area	2020	2021	2022p	Percent Change 2021 to 2022
MSA[1]	446.0	514.3	610.0	18.6
U.S. Average	300.2	357.1	392.6	9.9

Note: Figures are median sales prices of existing single-family homes in thousands of dollars; (p) preliminary; (1) Figures cover the Fort Collins, CO Metropolitan Statistical Area
Source: National Association of Realtors, Median Sales Price of Existing Single-Family Homes for Metropolitan Areas, 4th Quarter 2022

Qualifying Income Based on Median Sales Price of Existing Single-Family Homes

Area	With 5% Down ($)	With 10% Down ($)	With 20% Down ($)
MSA[1]	175,112	165,896	147,463
U.S. Average	112,234	106,237	94,513

Note: Figures are preliminary; Qualifying income is based on a mortgage rate of 6.77%. Monthly principal and interest payment is limited to 25% of income; (1) Figures cover the Fort Collins, CO Metropolitan Statistical Area
Source: National Association of Realtors, Qualifying Income Based on Median Sales Price of Existing Single-Family Homes for Metropolitan Areas, 4th Quarter 2022

Home Value

Area	Under $100,000	$100,000 -$199,999	$200,000 -$299,999	$300,000 -$399,999	$400,000 -$499,999	$500,000 -$999,999	$1,000,000 or more	Median ($)
City	4.0	2.8	10.0	24.0	29.5	27.3	2.4	431,300
MSA[1]	4.9	3.0	11.4	25.9	23.2	28.1	3.4	420,200
U.S.	16.2	24.2	20.1	13.6	8.3	13.6	4.1	244,900

Note: Figures are percentages except for median and cover owner-occupied housing units; (1) Figures cover the Fort Collins, CO Metropolitan Statistical Area
Source: U.S. Census Bureau, 2017-2021 American Community Survey 5-Year Estimates

Year Housing Structure Built

Area	2020 or Later	2010 -2019	2000 -2009	1990 -1999	1980 -1989	1970 -1979	1960 -1969	1950 -1959	1940 -1949	Before 1940	Median Year
City	0.3	13.1	18.0	21.0	15.0	16.8	6.7	3.0	1.5	4.6	1991
MSA[1]	0.4	14.9	18.1	19.1	12.4	17.9	6.6	3.3	1.8	5.6	1991
U.S.	0.2	7.3	13.6	13.6	13.2	14.8	10.3	10.0	4.7	12.2	1979

Note: Figures are percentages except for Median Year; Note: (1) Figures cover the Fort Collins, CO Metropolitan Statistical Area
Source: U.S. Census Bureau, 2017-2021 American Community Survey 5-Year Estimates

Gross Monthly Rent

Area	Under $500	$500 -$999	$1,000 -$1,499	$1,500 -$1,999	$2,000 -$2,499	$2,500 -$2,999	$3,000 and up	Median ($)
City	2.0	17.4	34.7	28.6	13.4	2.2	1.7	1,443
MSA[1]	2.8	17.7	34.1	28.7	12.2	2.9	1.7	1,433
U.S.	8.1	30.5	30.8	16.8	7.3	3.1	3.5	1,163

Note: Figures are percentages except for median; Gross rent is the contract rent plus the estimated average monthly cost of utilities (electricity, gas, and water and sewer) and fuels (oil, coal, kerosene, wood, etc.) if these are paid by the renter (or paid for the renter by someone else); (1) Figures cover the Fort Collins, CO Metropolitan Statistical Area
Source: U.S. Census Bureau, 2017-2021 American Community Survey 5-Year Estimates

HEALTH

Health Risk Factors

Category	MSA[1] (%)	U.S. (%)
Adults aged 18–64 who have any kind of health care coverage	n/a	90.9
Adults who reported being in good or better health	n/a	85.2
Adults who have been told they have high blood cholesterol	n/a	35.7
Adults who have been told they have high blood pressure	n/a	32.4
Adults who are current smokers	n/a	14.4
Adults who currently use e-cigarettes	n/a	6.7
Adults who currently use chewing tobacco, snuff, or snus	n/a	3.5
Adults who are heavy drinkers[2]	n/a	6.3
Adults who are binge drinkers[3]	n/a	15.4
Adults who are overweight (BMI 25.0 - 29.9)	n/a	34.4
Adults who are obese (BMI 30.0 - 99.8)	n/a	33.9
Adults who participated in any physical activities in the past month	n/a	76.3

Note: (1) Figures for the Fort Collins, CO Metropolitan Statistical Area were not available.
(2) Heavy drinkers are classified as adult men having more than 14 drinks per week and adult women having more than 7 drinks per week; (3) Binge drinkers are classified as males having five or more drinks on one occasion or females having four or more drinks on one occasion
Source: Centers for Disease Control and Prevention, Behaviorial Risk Factor Surveillance System, SMART: Selected Metropolitan Area Risk Trends, 2021

Acute and Chronic Health Conditions

Category	MSA[1] (%)	U.S. (%)
Adults who have ever been told they had a heart attack	n/a	4.0
Adults who have ever been told they have angina or coronary heart disease	n/a	3.8
Adults who have ever been told they had a stroke	n/a	3.0
Adults who have ever been told they have asthma	n/a	14.9
Adults who have ever been told they have arthritis	n/a	25.8
Adults who have ever been told they have diabetes[2]	n/a	10.9
Adults who have ever been told they had skin cancer	n/a	6.6
Adults who have ever been told they had any other types of cancer	n/a	7.5
Adults who have ever been told they have COPD	n/a	6.1
Adults who have ever been told they have kidney disease	n/a	3.0
Adults who have ever been told they have a form of depression	n/a	20.5

Note: (1) Figures for the Fort Collins, CO Metropolitan Statistical Area were not available.
(2) Figures do not include pregnancy-related, borderline, or pre-diabetes
Source: Centers for Disease Control and Prevention, Behaviorial Risk Factor Surveillance System, SMART: Selected Metropolitan Area Risk Trends, 2021

Health Screening and Vaccination Rates

Category	MSA[1] (%)	U.S. (%)
Adults who have ever been tested for HIV	n/a	34.9
Adults who have had their blood cholesterol checked within the last five years	n/a	85.2
Adults aged 65+ who have had flu shot within the past year	n/a	68.6
Adults aged 65+ who have ever had a pneumonia vaccination	n/a	71.0

Note: (1) Figures for the Fort Collins, CO Metropolitan Statistical Area were not available.
Source: Centers for Disease Control and Prevention, Behaviorial Risk Factor Surveillance System, SMART: Selected Metropolitan Area Risk Trends, 2021

Disability Status

Category	MSA[1] (%)	U.S. (%)
Adults who reported being deaf	n/a	7.2
Are you blind or have serious difficulty seeing, even when wearing glasses?	n/a	4.8
Are you limited in any way in any of your usual activities due to arthritis?	n/a	11.1
Do you have difficulty doing errands alone?	n/a	7.0
Do you have difficulty dressing or bathing?	n/a	3.6
Do you have serious difficulty concentrating/remembering/making decisions?	n/a	12.1
Do you have serious difficulty walking or climbing stairs?	n/a	12.8

Note: (1) Figures for the Fort Collins, CO Metropolitan Statistical Area were not available.
Source: Centers for Disease Control and Prevention, Behaviorial Risk Factor Surveillance System, SMART: Selected Metropolitan Area Risk Trends, 2021

Mortality Rates for the Top 10 Causes of Death in the U.S.

ICD-10[a] Sub-Chapter	ICD-10[a] Code	Crude Mortality Rate[1] per 100,000 population	
		County[2]	U.S.
Malignant neoplasms	C00-C97	138.2	182.6
Ischaemic heart diseases	I20-I25	52.9	113.1
Other forms of heart disease	I30-I51	47.8	64.4
Other degenerative diseases of the nervous system	G30-G31	54.9	51.0
Cerebrovascular diseases	I60-I69	44.8	47.8
Other external causes of accidental injury	W00-X59	36.3	46.4
Chronic lower respiratory diseases	J40-J47	30.2	45.7
Organic, including symptomatic, mental disorders	F01-F09	35.7	35.9
Hypertensive diseases	I10-I15	29.0	35.0
Diabetes mellitus	E10-E14	17.2	29.6

Note: (a) ICD-10 = International Classification of Diseases 10th Revision; (1) Crude mortality rates are a three-year average covering 2019-2021; (2) Figures cover Larimer County.
Source: Centers for Disease Control and Prevention, National Center for Health Statistics. National Vital Statistics System, Mortality 2018-2021 on CDC WONDER Online Database

Mortality Rates for Selected Causes of Death

ICD-10[a] Sub-Chapter	ICD-10[a] Code	Crude Mortality Rate[1] per 100,000 population	
		County[2]	U.S.
Assault	X85-Y09	Unreliable	7.0
Diseases of the liver	K70-K76	18.1	19.8
Human immunodeficiency virus (HIV) disease	B20-B24	Suppressed	1.5
Influenza and pneumonia	J09-J18	6.2	14.7
Intentional self-harm	X60-X84	22.1	14.3
Malnutrition	E40-E46	2.0	4.3
Obesity and other hyperalimentation	E65-E68	Unreliable	3.0
Renal failure	N17-N19	8.0	15.7
Transport accidents	V01-V99	9.7	13.6
Viral hepatitis	B15-B19	Suppressed	1.2

Note: (a) ICD-10 = International Classification of Diseases 10th Revision; (1) Crude mortality rates are a three-year average covering 2019-2021; (2) Figures cover Larimer County; Data are suppressed when the data meet the criteria for confidentiality constraints; Crude mortality rates are flagged as unreliable when the rate would be calculated with a numerator of 20 or less.
Source: Centers for Disease Control and Prevention, National Center for Health Statistics. National Vital Statistics System, Mortality 2018-2021 on CDC WONDER Online Database

Health Insurance Coverage

Area	With Health Insurance	With Private Health Insurance	With Public Health Insurance	Without Health Insurance	Population Under Age 19 Without Health Insurance
City	93.9	78.5	23.9	6.1	5.1
MSA[1]	94.0	76.6	28.9	6.0	4.4
U.S.	91.2	67.8	35.4	8.8	5.3

Note: Figures are percentages that cover the civilian noninstitutionalized population; (1) Figures cover the Fort Collins, CO Metropolitan Statistical Area
Source: U.S. Census Bureau, 2017-2021 American Community Survey 5-Year Estimates

Number of Medical Professionals

Area	MDs[3]	DOs[3,4]	Dentists	Podiatrists	Chiropractors	Optometrists
County[1] (number)	904	113	303	22	206	77
County[1] (rate[2])	251.3	31.4	83.6	6.1	56.8	21.2
U.S. (rate[2])	289.3	23.5	72.5	6.2	28.7	17.4

Note: Data as of 2021 unless noted; (1) Data covers Larimer County; (2) Rate per 100,000 population; (3) Data as of 2020 and includes all active, non-federal physicians; (4) Doctor of Osteopathic Medicine
Source: U.S. Department of Health and Human Services, Health Resources and Services Administration, Bureau of Health Professions, Area Resource File (ARF) 2021-2022

Best Hospitals

According to *U.S. News,* the Fort Collins, CO metro area is home to one of the best hospitals in the U.S.: **UCHealth Medical Center of the Rockies** (1 adult specialty). The hospital listed was nationally ranked in at least one of 15 adult or 10 pediatric specialties. The number of specialties shown cover the parent hospital. Only 164 U.S. hospitals performed well enough to be nationally ranked in one or more specialties. Twenty hospitals in the U.S. made the Honor Roll. The Best Hospitals Honor Roll takes both the national rankings and the procedure and condition ratings into account. Hospitals received points if they were nationally ranked in one of the 15 adult specialties—the higher they ranked, the more points they got—and how many ratings of "high performing" they earned in the 17 procedures and conditions. *U.S. News Online, "America's Best Hospitals 2022-23"*

EDUCATION

Public School District Statistics

District Name	Schls	Pupils	Pupil/ Teacher Ratio	Minority Pupils[1] (%)	LEP/ELL[2] (%)	IEP[3] (%)
Poudre School District R-1	52	29,907	16.6	28.2	4.3	n/a

Note: Table includes school districts with 2,000 or more students; (1) Percentage of students that are not non-Hispanic white; (2) Percentage of students that are Limited English Proficient or English Language Learners (2018-19); (3) Percentage of students that have an Individualized Education Program (2019-20).
Source: U.S. Department of Education, National Center for Education Statistics, Common Core of Data, Local Education Agency (School District) Universe Survey: School Year 2021-2022

Best High Schools

According to *U.S. News,* Fort Collins is home to one of the top 500 high schools in the U.S.: **Liberty Common Charter School** (#125). Nearly 18,000 public, magnet and charter schools were ranked based on their performance on state assessments and how well they prepare students for college. *U.S. News & World Report, "Best High Schools 2022"*

Highest Level of Education

Area	Less than H.S.	H.S. Diploma	Some College, No Deg.	Associate Degree	Bachelor's Degree	Master's Degree	Prof. School Degree	Doctorate Degree
City	3.0	14.4	17.3	8.6	32.8	17.5	2.5	3.8
MSA[1]	3.7	17.4	20.4	9.1	29.5	14.4	2.4	3.1
U.S.	11.1	26.5	20.0	8.7	20.6	9.3	2.2	1.5

Note: Figures cover persons age 25 and over; (1) Figures cover the Fort Collins, CO Metropolitan Statistical Area
Source: U.S. Census Bureau, 2017-2021 American Community Survey 5-Year Estimates

Educational Attainment by Race

Area	High School Graduate or Higher (%)					Bachelor's Degree or Higher (%)				
	Total	White	Black	Asian	Hisp.[2]	Total	White	Black	Asian	Hisp.[2]
City	97.0	97.6	91.7	93.4	87.4	56.6	58.0	36.7	73.4	33.1
MSA[1]	96.3	96.9	94.2	93.2	84.3	49.4	50.0	33.0	66.7	28.5
U.S.	88.9	91.4	87.2	87.6	71.2	33.7	35.5	23.3	55.6	18.4

Note: Figures shown cover persons 25 years old and over; (1) Figures cover the Fort Collins, CO Metropolitan Statistical Area; (2) People of Hispanic origin can be of any race
Source: U.S. Census Bureau, 2017-2021 American Community Survey 5-Year Estimates

School Enrollment by Grade and Control

Area	Preschool (%)		Kindergarten (%)		Grades 1 - 4 (%)		Grades 5 - 8 (%)		Grades 9 - 12 (%)	
	Public	Private	Public	Private	Public	Private	Public	Private	Public	Private
City	44.8	55.2	89.3	10.7	93.6	6.4	93.0	7.0	93.8	6.2
MSA[1]	45.2	54.8	88.9	11.1	88.9	11.1	86.8	13.2	88.3	11.7
U.S.	58.8	41.2	86.3	13.7	88.3	11.7	88.6	11.4	89.4	10.6

Note: Figures shown cover persons 3 years old and over; (1) Figures cover the Fort Collins, CO Metropolitan Statistical Area
Source: U.S. Census Bureau, 2017-2021 American Community Survey 5-Year Estimates

Higher Education

Four-Year Colleges			Two-Year Colleges			Medical Schools[1]	Law Schools[2]	Voc/ Tech[3]
Public	Private Non-profit	Private For-profit	Public	Private Non-profit	Private For-profit			
1	0	0	0	0	1	0	0	2

Note: Figures cover institutions located within the Fort Collins, CO Metropolitan Statistical Area and include main campuses only; (1) includes schools accredited by the Liaison Committee on Medical Education and the American Osteopathic Association's Commission on Osteopathic College Accreditation; (2) includes ABA-accredited schools, schools with provisional ABA accreditation, and state accredited schools; (3) includes all schools with programs that are less than 2 years.
Source: National Center for Education Statistics, Integrated Postsecondary Education System (IPEDS), 2021-22; Wikipedia, List of Medical Schools in the United States, accessed April 10, 2023; Wikipedia, List of Law Schools in the United States, accessed April 10, 2023

According to *U.S. News & World Report,* the Fort Collins, CO metro area is home to one of the top 200 national universities in the U.S.: **Colorado State University** (#151 tie). The indicators used to capture academic quality fall into a number of categories: assessment by administrators at peer institutions; retention of students; faculty resources; student selectivity; financial resources; alumni giving; high school counselor ratings of colleges; and graduation rate. *U.S. News & World Report, "America's Best Colleges 2023"*

EMPLOYERS

Major Employers

Company Name	Industry
Advanced Energy Industrials	Special industry machinery
Anheuser Busch	Malt beverages
Animal and Plant Health Inspection	Management services
Aramark Corporation	Food/bars
Center Partners	Business services
City of Loveland	Municipal government
Colorado State University	Colleges & universities
Contibeef	Beef cattle feedlots
Deere and Company	Farm machinery/equipment
Hach Company	Analytical instruments
Hewlett-Packard Co.	Electronic computers
Medical Center of the Rockies	General medical & surgical hospitals
Poudre School District	Building cleaning service
Poudre Valley Health Systems	General medical & surgical hospitals
Woodward	Aircraft engines & engine parts

Note: Companies shown are located within the Fort Collins, CO Metropolitan Statistical Area.
Source: Hoovers.com; Wikipedia

PUBLIC SAFETY

Crime Rate

Area	Total Crime	Violent Crime Rate				Property Crime Rate		
		Murder	Rape[3]	Robbery	Aggrav. Assault	Burglary	Larceny -Theft	Motor Vehicle Theft
City	2,389.9	0.6	24.0	21.1	171.5	204.8	1,834.5	133.4
Suburbs[1]	1,855.9	1.1	44.9	14.6	189.3	184.4	1,296.7	124.9
Metro[2]	2,112.3	0.8	34.8	17.7	180.7	194.2	1,555.0	129.0
U.S.	2,510.4	5.1	42.6	81.8	250.4	340.5	1,569.2	220.8

Note: Figures are crimes per 100,000 population; (1) All areas within the metro area that are located outside the city limits; (2) Figures cover the Fort Collins, CO Metropolitan Statistical Area; (3) All figures shown were reported using the revised Uniform Crime Reporting (UCR) definition of rape; Due to the transition to the National Incident-Based Reporting System (NIBRS), limited city and metro area data was released for 2021.
Source: FBI Uniform Crime Reports, 2019 (data for 2020 was not available)

Hate Crimes

Area	Number of Quarters Reported	Number of Incidents per Bias Motivation					
		Race/Ethnicity/ Ancestry	Religion	Sexual Orientation	Disability	Gender	Gender Identity
City	4	2	1	0	0	0	0
U.S.	4	5,227	1,244	1,110	130	75	266

Note: Due to the transition to the National Incident-Based Reporting System (NIBRS), limited crime data was released for 2021.
Source: Federal Bureau of Investigation, Hate Crime Statistics 2020

Identity Theft Consumer Reports

Area	Reports	Reports per 100,000 Population	Rank[2]
MSA[1]	584	167	215
U.S.	1,108,609	339	-

Note: (1) Figures cover the Fort Collins, CO Metropolitan Statistical Area; (2) Rank ranges from 1 to 391 where 1 indicates greatest number of identity theft reports per 100,000 population
Source: Federal Trade Commission, Consumer Sentinel Network Data Book 2022

Fraud and Other Consumer Reports

Area	Reports	Reports per 100,000 Population	Rank[2]
MSA[1]	3,780	1,078	69
U.S.	4,064,520	1,245	-

Note: (1) Figures cover the Fort Collins, CO Metropolitan Statistical Area; (2) Rank ranges from 1 to 391 where 1 indicates greatest number of fraud and other consumer reports per 100,000 population
Source: Federal Trade Commission, Consumer Sentinel Network Data Book 2022

POLITICS

2020 Presidential Election Results

Area	Biden	Trump	Jorgensen	Hawkins	Other
Larimer County	56.2	40.8	1.8	0.3	0.9
U.S.	51.3	46.8	1.2	0.3	0.5

Note: Results are percentages and may not add to 100% due to rounding
Source: Dave Leip's Atlas of U.S. Presidential Elections

SPORTS

Professional Sports Teams

Team Name	League	Year Established
No teams are located in the metro area		

Source: Wikipedia, Major Professional Sports Teams of the United States and Canada, April 12, 2023

CLIMATE

Average and Extreme Temperatures

Temperature	Jan	Feb	Mar	Apr	May	Jun	Jul	Aug	Sep	Oct	Nov	Dec	Yr.
Extreme High (°F)	73	76	84	90	93	102	103	100	97	89	79	75	103
Average High (°F)	43	47	52	62	71	81	88	86	77	67	52	45	64
Average Temp. (°F)	30	34	39	48	58	67	73	72	63	52	39	32	51
Average Low (°F)	16	20	25	34	44	53	59	57	48	37	25	18	37
Extreme Low (°F)	-25	-25	-10	-2	22	30	43	41	17	3	-8	-25	-25

Note: Figures cover the years 1948-1992
Source: National Climatic Data Center, International Station Meteorological Climate Summary, 9/96

Average Precipitation/Snowfall/Humidity

Precip./Humidity	Jan	Feb	Mar	Apr	May	Jun	Jul	Aug	Sep	Oct	Nov	Dec	Yr.
Avg. Precip. (in.)	0.6	0.6	1.3	1.7	2.5	1.7	1.9	1.5	1.1	1.0	0.9	0.6	15.5
Avg. Snowfall (in.)	9	7	14	9	2	Tr	0	0	2	4	9	8	63
Avg. Rel. Hum. 5am (%)	62	65	67	66	70	68	67	68	66	63	66	63	66
Avg. Rel. Hum. 5pm (%)	49	44	40	35	38	34	34	34	32	34	47	50	39

Note: Figures cover the years 1948-1992; Tr = Trace amounts (<0.05 in. of rain; <0.5 in. of snow)
Source: National Climatic Data Center, International Station Meteorological Climate Summary, 9/96

Weather Conditions

Temperature			Daytime Sky			Precipitation		
10°F & below	32°F & below	90°F & above	Clear	Partly cloudy	Cloudy	0.01 inch or more precip.	0.1 inch or more snow/ice	Thunder-storms
24	155	33	99	177	89	90	38	39

Note: Figures are average number of days per year and cover the years 1948-1992
Source: National Climatic Data Center, International Station Meteorological Climate Summary, 9/96

HAZARDOUS WASTE

Superfund Sites

The Fort Collins, CO metro area has no sites on the EPA's Superfund Final National Priorities List. There are a total of 1,165 Superfund sites with a status of proposed or final on the list in the U.S. *U.S. Environmental Protection Agency, National Priorities List, April 12, 2023*

AIR QUALITY

Air Quality Trends: Ozone

	1990	1995	2000	2005	2010	2015	2018	2019	2020	2021
MSA[1]	0.066	0.072	0.074	0.075	0.072	0.070	0.073	0.065	0.070	0.077
U.S.	0.087	0.089	0.081	0.080	0.072	0.067	0.069	0.065	0.065	0.067

Note: (1) Data covers the Fort Collins, CO Metropolitan Statistical Area. The values shown are the composite ozone concentration averages among trend sites based on the highest fourth daily maximum 8-hour concentration in parts per million. These trends are based on sites having an adequate record of monitoring data during the trend period. Data from exceptional events are included.
Source: U.S. Environmental Protection Agency, Air Quality Monitoring Information, "Air Quality Trends by City, 1990-2021"

Air Quality Index

Area	Percent of Days when Air Quality was...[2]					AQI Statistics[2]	
	Good	Moderate	Unhealthy for Sensitive Groups	Unhealthy	Very Unhealthy	Maximum	Median
MSA[1]	54.0	36.4	8.8	0.8	0.0	156	50

Note: (1) Data covers the Fort Collins, CO Metropolitan Statistical Area; (2) Based on 365 days with AQI data in 2021. Air Quality Index (AQI) is an index for reporting daily air quality. EPA calculates the AQI for five major air pollutants regulated by the Clean Air Act: ground-level ozone, particle pollution (aka particulate matter), carbon monoxide, sulfur dioxide, and nitrogen dioxide. The AQI runs from 0 to 500. The higher the AQI value, the greater the level of air pollution and the greater the health concern. There are six AQI categories: "Good" AQI is between 0 and 50. Air quality is considered satisfactory; "Moderate" AQI is between 51 and 100. Air quality is acceptable; "Unhealthy for Sensitive Groups" When AQI values are between 101 and 150, members of sensitive groups may experience health effects; "Unhealthy" When AQI values are between 151 and 200 everyone may begin to experience health effects; "Very Unhealthy" AQI values between 201 and 300 trigger a health alert; "Hazardous" AQI values over 300 trigger warnings of emergency conditions (not shown).
Source: U.S. Environmental Protection Agency, Air Quality Index Report, 2021

Air Quality Index Pollutants

Area	Percent of Days when AQI Pollutant was...[2]					
	Carbon Monoxide	Nitrogen Dioxide	Ozone	Sulfur Dioxide	Particulate Matter 2.5	Particulate Matter 10
MSA[1]	0.0	0.0	91.0	(3)	9.0	0.0

Note: (1) Data covers the Fort Collins, CO Metropolitan Statistical Area; (2) Based on 365 days with AQI data in 2021. The Air Quality Index (AQI) is an index for reporting daily air quality. EPA calculates the AQI for five major air pollutants regulated by the Clean Air Act: ground-level ozone, particle pollution (also known as particulate matter), carbon monoxide, sulfur dioxide, and nitrogen dioxide. The AQI runs from 0 to 500. The higher the AQI value, the greater the level of air pollution and the greater the health concern; (3) Sulfur dioxide is no longer included in this table (as of December 8, 2021) because SO_2 concentrations tend to be very localized and not necessarily representative of broad geographical areas like counties and CBSAs.
Source: U.S. Environmental Protection Agency, Air Quality Index Report, 2021

Maximum Air Pollutant Concentrations: Particulate Matter, Ozone, CO and Lead

	Particulate Matter 10 (ug/m^3)	Particulate Matter 2.5 Wtd AM (ug/m^3)	Particulate Matter 2.5 24-Hr (ug/m^3)	Ozone (ppm)	Carbon Monoxide (ppm)	Lead (ug/m^3)
MSA[1] Level	n/a	8.5	29	0.085	1	n/a
NAAQS[2]	150	15	35	0.075	9	0.15
Met NAAQS[2]	n/a	Yes	Yes	No	Yes	n/a

Note: (1) Data covers the Fort Collins, CO Metropolitan Statistical Area; Data from exceptional events are included; (2) National Ambient Air Quality Standards; ppm = parts per million; ug/m^3 = micrograms per cubic meter; n/a not available.
Concentrations: Particulate Matter 10 (coarse particulate)—highest second maximum 24-hour concentration; Particulate Matter 2.5 Wtd AM (fine particulate)—highest weighted annual mean concentration; Particulate Matter 2.5 24-Hour (fine particulate)—highest 98th percentile 24-hour concentration; Ozone—highest fourth daily maximum 8-hour concentration; Carbon Monoxide—highest second maximum non-overlapping 8-hour concentration; Lead—maximum running 3-month average
Source: U.S. Environmental Protection Agency, Air Quality Monitoring Information, "Air Quality Statistics by City, 2021"

Maximum Air Pollutant Concentrations: Nitrogen Dioxide and Sulfur Dioxide

	Nitrogen Dioxide AM (ppb)	Nitrogen Dioxide 1-Hr (ppb)	Sulfur Dioxide AM (ppb)	Sulfur Dioxide 1-Hr (ppb)	Sulfur Dioxide 24-Hr (ppb)
MSA[1] Level	n/a	n/a	n/a	n/a	n/a
NAAQS[2]	53	100	30	75	140
Met NAAQS[2]	n/a	n/a	n/a	n/a	n/a

Note: (1) Data covers the Fort Collins, CO Metropolitan Statistical Area; Data from exceptional events are included; (2) National Ambient Air Quality Standards; ppm = parts per million; ug/m^3 = micrograms per cubic meter; n/a not available.
Concentrations: Nitrogen Dioxide AM—highest arithmetic mean concentration; Nitrogen Dioxide 1-Hr—highest 98th percentile 1-hour daily maximum concentration; Sulfur Dioxide AM—highest annual mean concentration; Sulfur Dioxide 1-Hr—highest 99th percentile 1-hour daily maximum concentration; Sulfur Dioxide 24-Hr—highest second maximum 24-hour concentration
Source: U.S. Environmental Protection Agency, Air Quality Monitoring Information, "Air Quality Statistics by City, 2021"

Greeley, Colorado

Background

Greeley is a city built on farming and agriculture that does its best to follow modern technologies and trends, making it both stable and friendly, yet bustling and active. It is the most populous municipality in Weld County, Colorado, and is growing in popularity each year.

Greeley is situated in northern Colorado, 49 miles from Denver. To the south of the Greeley/Evans area is the South Platte River; to the north is the Cache la Poudre River.

The city's namesake, Horace Greeley, visited the area in 1859, and was the founder and editor of the *New York Tribune*. The city was first founded as the Union Colony in 1869, the city changed its name in honor of Greeley and incorporated in 1886. The city's population has more than doubled since 1970, and is now over 100,000.

The original incarnation of Greeley was an experimental utopian community built on "temperance, religion, agriculture, education and family values"; Greeley stills treasures many of these aspects today. Greeley's economy relies heavily on farming, energy, and agriculture; its largest employers include meatpacker Swift & Company, a subsidary of JBS, Hensel Phelps Construction, natural gas utility Atmos Energy, wind turbine manufacturer Vestas, and Halliburton Energy Services. A new hospital was opened in Greeley in 2019. Construction continues on a new factory by Leprino Foods.

Despite its small town appeal, Greeley is an innovative city for both technology and culture. In 1958 Greeley was the first city to establish a Department of Culture, and the Greeley Creative District is officially state certified. Greeley is home to the Union Colony Civic Center, one of the largest performing arts venues in Colorado. Helsen Phelps Theatre hosts The Stampede Troupe, and a variety of lectures and small performances. The Tointon Gallery features local and national artists. As a sister city to Moriya, Japan, it hosts a number of Japanese students every year for a week-long stay.

Greeley is also a media center for Colorado, recognized as the state's principal city for newspapers, television, and radio. Due to media's influence, Greely's famous sons and daughters include voice actor Dee Bradley Baker, UFC fighter Shane Carwin, and composer Miriam Gideon. Author James A. Michener conceived the idea for his acclaimed 1974 novel *Centennial* during his stay in Greeley at the University of Northern Colorado in 1936-37, which is just one of the multiple colleges and universities in the city.

In 2020, the city expanded its regional bus service and launched Poudre Express, connecting Greeley to Fort Collins and Windsor.

Its climate is semi-arid, with major variation in temperature due to mountains and lower elevation, especially between day and night. Air quality in Greeley is extremely dry, with the city experiencing less precipitation and fewer thunderstorms than adjacent areas. Extra-tropical cyclones which disrupt the Eastern two-thirds of the United States often originate in Colorado, which means that Greeley does not frequently experience fully developed storm systems.

Rankings

Business/Finance Rankings

- The Greeley metro area appeared on the Milken Institute "2022 Best Performing Cities" list. Rank: #101 out of 200 large metro areas (population over 250,000). Criteria: job growth; wage and salary growth; high-tech output growth; housing affordability; household broadband access. *Milken Institute, "Best-Performing Cities 2022," March 28, 2022*

- *Forbes* ranked the 200 most populous metro areas to determine the nation's "Best Places for Business and Careers." The Greeley metro area was ranked #52. Criteria: costs (business and living); job growth (past and projected); income growth; quality of life; educational attainment (college and high school); projected economic growth; cultural and leisure opportunities; workplace tolerance laws; net migration patterns. *Forbes, "The Best Places for Business and Careers 2019: Seattle Still On Top," October 30, 2019*

Children/Family Rankings

- Greeley was selected as one of the best cities for newlyweds by *Rent.com*. The city ranked #5 of 15. Criteria: cost of living; availability of affordable rental inventory; annual household income; activities and restaurant options; percentage of married couples; concentration of millennials; safety. *Rent.com, "The 15 Best Cities for Newlyweds," December 11, 2018*

Safety Rankings

- The National Insurance Crime Bureau ranked 390 metro areas in the U.S. in terms of per capita rates of vehicle theft. The Greeley metro area ranked #58 (#1 = highest rate). Criteria: number of vehicle theft offenses per 100,000 inhabitants in 2021. *National Insurance Crime Bureau, "Hot Spots 2021," September 1, 2022*

Seniors/Retirement Rankings

- From its Best Cities for Successful Aging indexes, the Milken Institute generated rankings for metropolitan areas, weighing data in nine categories—health care, wellness, living arrangements, transportation and convenience, financial characteristics, education, employment, community engagement, and overall livability. The Greeley metro area was ranked #170 overall in the small metro area category. *Milken Institute, "Best Cities for Successful Aging, 2017" March 14, 2017*

Business Environment

DEMOGRAPHICS

Population Growth

Area	1990 Census	2000 Census	2010 Census	2020 Census	Population Growth (%) 1990-2020	Population Growth (%) 2010-2020
City	60,887	76,930	92,889	108,795	78.7	17.1
MSA[1]	131,816	180,926	252,825	328,981	149.6	30.1
U.S.	248,709,873	281,421,906	308,745,538	331,449,281	33.3	7.4

Note: (1) Figures cover the Greeley, CO Metropolitan Statistical Area
Source: U.S. Census Bureau, 1990 Census, 2000 Census, 2010 Census, 2020 Census

Race

Area	White Alone[2] (%)	Black Alone[2] (%)	Asian Alone[2] (%)	AIAN[3] Alone[2] (%)	NHOPI[4] Alone[2] (%)	Other Race Alone[2] (%)	Two or More Races (%)
City	62.0	2.7	2.0	1.8	0.1	14.8	16.6
MSA[1]	70.5	1.4	1.8	1.3	0.1	11.2	13.8
U.S.	61.6	12.4	6.0	1.1	0.2	8.4	10.2

Note: (1) Figures cover the Greeley, CO Metropolitan Statistical Area; (2) Alone is defined as not being in combination with one or more other races; (3) American Indian and Alaska Native; (4) Native Hawaiian and Other Pacific Islander
Source: U.S. Census Bureau, 2020 Census

Hispanic or Latino Origin

Area	Total (%)	Mexican (%)	Puerto Rican (%)	Cuban (%)	Other (%)
City	40.3	33.0	0.9	0.1	6.3
MSA[1]	30.0	24.5	0.5	0.2	4.8
U.S.	18.4	11.2	1.8	0.7	4.7

Note: Persons of Hispanic or Latino origin can be of any race; (1) Figures cover the Greeley, CO Metropolitan Statistical Area
Source: U.S. Census Bureau, 2017-2021 American Community Survey 5-Year Estimates

Age

Area	Percent of Population Under Age 5	Age 5–19	Age 20–34	Age 35–44	Age 45–54	Age 55–64	Age 65–74	Age 75–84	Age 85+	Median Age
City	6.9	22.5	25.0	12.3	10.2	9.8	7.9	3.9	1.6	31.9
MSA[1]	6.9	22.6	21.3	13.9	11.6	11.1	8.0	3.4	1.2	34.5
U.S.	5.6	19.2	20.2	12.7	12.4	13.1	10.0	4.9	1.9	38.8

Note: (1) Figures cover the Greeley, CO Metropolitan Statistical Area
Source: U.S. Census Bureau, 2020 Census

Disability by Age

Area	All Ages	Under 18 Years Old	18 to 64 Years Old	65 Years and Over
City	11.9	3.4	11.1	33.5
MSA[1]	10.7	3.6	9.1	34.7
U.S.	12.6	4.4	10.3	33.4

Note: Figures show percent of the civilian noninstitutionalized population that reported having a disability. Disability status is determined from six types of difficulty: vision, hearing, cognitive, ambulatory, self-care, and independent living. For children under 5 years old, hearing and vision difficulty are used to determine disability status. For children between the ages of 5 and 14, disability status is determined from hearing, vision, cognitive, ambulatory, and self-care difficulties. For people aged 15 years and older, they are considered to have a disability if they have difficulty with any one of the six difficulty types; Note: (1) Figures cover the Greeley, CO Metropolitan Statistical Area
Source: U.S. Census Bureau, 2017-2021 American Community Survey 5-Year Estimates

Ancestry

Area	German	Irish	English	American	Italian	Polish	French[2]	Scottish	Dutch
City	16.6	8.4	7.5	3.1	2.7	1.6	1.6	1.9	1.0
MSA[1]	20.5	10.1	9.7	4.1	3.7	1.9	1.9	1.8	1.4
U.S.	12.8	9.6	8.1	5.7	5.0	2.7	2.2	1.6	1.1

Note: Figures are the percentage of the total population reporting a particular ancestry. The nine most commonly reported ancestries in the U.S. are shown. Figures include multiple ancestries (e.g. if a person reported being Irish and Italian, they were included in both columns); (1) Figures cover the Greeley, CO Metropolitan Statistical Area; (2) Excludes Basque
Source: U.S. Census Bureau, 2017-2021 American Community Survey 5-Year Estimates

Foreign-born Population

Area	Percent of Population Born in								
	Any Foreign Country	Asia	Mexico	Europe	Caribbean	Central America[2]	South America	Africa	Canada
City	12.2	0.8	8.3	0.5	0.1	1.1	0.2	1.2	0.1
MSA[1]	8.9	0.8	6.0	0.5	0.1	0.7	0.2	0.5	0.1
U.S.	13.6	4.2	3.3	1.5	1.4	1.1	1.1	0.8	0.2

Note: (1) Figures cover the Greeley, CO Metropolitan Statistical Area; (2) Excludes Mexico.
Source: U.S. Census Bureau, 2017-2021 American Community Survey 5-Year Estimates

Household Size

Area	Persons in Household (%)							Average Household Size
	One	Two	Three	Four	Five	Six	Seven or More	
City	25.4	32.8	16.2	13.5	7.4	3.0	1.7	2.70
MSA[1]	20.2	34.4	16.4	15.9	8.1	3.3	1.7	2.80
U.S.	28.1	33.8	15.5	12.9	6.0	2.3	1.4	2.60

Note: (1) Figures cover the Greeley, CO Metropolitan Statistical Area
Source: U.S. Census Bureau, 2017-2021 American Community Survey 5-Year Estimates

Household Relationships

Area	House-holder	Opposite-sex Spouse	Same-sex Spouse	Opposite-sex Unmarried Partner	Same-sex Unmarried Partner	Child[2]	Grand-child	Other Relatives	Non-relatives
City	34.9	15.8	0.2	2.5	0.1	29.4	2.6	5.0	5.1
MSA[1]	34.6	19.3	0.1	2.2	0.1	31.5	2.4	4.6	3.6
U.S.	38.3	17.5	0.2	2.5	0.2	28.3	2.4	4.8	3.4

Note: Figures are percent of the total population; (1) Figures cover the Greeley, CO Metropolitan Statistical Area; (2) Includes biological, adopted, and stepchildren of the householder
Source: U.S. Census Bureau, 2020 Census

Gender

Area	Males	Females	Males per 100 Females
City	53,848	54,947	98.0
MSA[1]	164,843	164,138	100.4
U.S.	162,685,811	168,763,470	96.4

Note: (1) Figures cover the Greeley, CO Metropolitan Statistical Area
Source: U.S. Census Bureau, 2020 Census

Marital Status

Area	Never Married	Now Married[2]	Separated	Widowed	Divorced
City	35.4	46.5	1.9	4.8	11.4
MSA[1]	28.7	55.2	1.4	4.0	10.7
U.S.	33.8	48.0	1.8	5.6	10.8

Note: Figures are percentages and cover the population 15 years of age and older; (1) Figures cover the Greeley, CO Metropolitan Statistical Area; (2) Excludes separated
Source: U.S. Census Bureau, 2017-2021 American Community Survey 5-Year Estimates

Religious Groups by Family

Area	Catholic	Baptist	Methodist	LDS[2]	Pentecostal	Lutheran	Islam	Adventist	Other
MSA[1]	14.1	0.5	0.9	2.9	1.1	1.2	<0.1	1.1	6.1
U.S.	18.7	7.3	3.0	2.0	1.8	1.7	1.3	1.3	11.6

Note: Figures are the number of adherents as a percentage of the total population and cover the eight largest religious groups in the U.S; (1) Figures cover the Greeley, CO Metropolitan Statistical Area; (2) Church of Jesus Christ of Latter-day Saints
Sources: 2020 U.S. Religion Census, Association of Statisticians of American Religious Bodies; The Association of Religion Data Archives (ARDA)

Religious Groups by Tradition

Area	Catholic	Evangelical Protestant	Mainline Protestant	Black Protestant	Islam	Judaism	Hinduism	Orthodox	Buddhism
MSA[1]	14.1	7.8	2.1	<0.1	<0.1	n/a	n/a	<0.1	0.2
U.S.	18.7	16.5	5.2	2.3	1.3	0.6	0.4	0.4	0.3

Note: Figures are the number of adherents as a percentage of the total population; (1) Figures cover the Greeley, CO Metropolitan Statistical Area
Sources: 2020 U.S. Religion Census, Association of Statisticians of American Religious Bodies; The Association of Religion Data Archives (ARDA)

ECONOMY

Gross Metropolitan Product

Area	2020	2021	2022	2023	Rank[2]
MSA[1]	16.7	17.9	20.0	22.3	162

Note: Figures are in billions of dollars; (1) Figures cover the Greeley, CO Metropolitan Statistical Area; (2) Rank is based on 2021 data and ranges from 1 to 381
Source: U.S. Conference of Mayors, U.S. Metro Economies: U.S. Metros Compared to Global and State Economies, June 2022

Economic Growth

Area	2018-20 (%)	2021 (%)	2022 (%)	2023 (%)	Rank[2]
MSA[1]	-4.3	3.2	5.5	9.1	366
U.S.	-0.6	5.7	3.1	2.9	–

Note: Figures are real gross metropolitan product (GMP) growth rates and represent average annual percent change; (1) Figures cover the Greeley, CO Metropolitan Statistical Area; (2) Rank is based on 2020 2-year average annual percent change and ranges from 1 to 381
Source: U.S. Conference of Mayors, U.S. Metro Economies: U.S. Metros Compared to Global and State Economies, June 2022

Metropolitan Area Exports

Area	2016	2017	2018	2019	2020	2021	Rank[2]
MSA[1]	1,539.6	1,492.8	1,366.5	1,439.2	1,480.4	2,022.6	109

Note: Figures are in millions of dollars; (1) Figures cover the Greeley, CO Metropolitan Statistical Area; (2) Rank is based on 2021 data and ranges from 1 to 388
Source: U.S. Department of Commerce, International Trade Administration, Office of Trade and Economic Analysis, Industry and Analysis, Exports by Metropolitan Area, data extracted March 16, 2023

Building Permits

Area	Single-Family			Multi-Family			Total		
	2021	2022	Pct. Chg.	2021	2022	Pct. Chg.	2021	2022	Pct. Chg.
City	315	345	9.5	600	1,725	187.5	915	2,070	126.2
MSA[1]	3,814	3,203	-16.0	1,454	2,940	102.2	5,268	6,143	16.6
U.S.	1,115,400	975,600	-12.5	621,600	689,500	10.9	1,737,000	1,665,100	-4.1

Note: (1) Figures cover the Greeley, CO Metropolitan Statistical Area; Figures represent new, privately-owned housing units authorized (unadjusted data); All permit data are based on estimates with imputation
Source: U.S. Census Bureau, Manufacturing, Mining, and Construction Statistics, Building Permits, 2021, 2022

Bankruptcy Filings

Area	Business Filings			Nonbusiness Filings		
	2021	2022	% Chg.	2021	2022	% Chg.
Weld County	9	16	77.8	447	400	-10.5
U.S.	14,347	13,481	-6.0	399,269	374,240	-6.3

Note: Business filings include Chapter 7, Chapter 9, Chapter 11, Chapter 12, Chapter 13, Chapter 15, and Section 304; Nonbusiness filings include Chapter 7, Chapter 11, and Chapter 13
Source: Administrative Office of the U.S. Courts, Business and Nonbusiness Bankruptcy, County Cases Commenced by Chapter of the Bankruptcy Code, During the 12-Month Period Ending December 31, 2021 and Business and Nonbusiness Bankruptcy, County Cases Commenced by Chapter of the Bankruptcy Code, During the 12-Month Period Ending December 31, 2022

Housing Vacancy Rates

Area	Gross Vacancy Rate[2] (%)			Year-Round Vacancy Rate[3] (%)			Rental Vacancy Rate[4] (%)			Homeowner Vacancy Rate[5] (%)		
	2020	2021	2022	2020	2021	2022	2020	2021	2022	2020	2021	2022
MSA[1]	n/a	n/a	n/a	n/a	n/a	n/a	n/a	n/a	n/a	n/a	n/a	n/a
U.S.	10.6	10.8	10.5	8.2	8.4	8.2	6.3	6.1	5.8	1.0	0.9	0.8

Note: (1) Figures cover the Greeley, CO Metropolitan Statistical Area; (2) The percentage of the total housing inventory that is vacant; (3) The percentage of the housing inventory (excluding seasonal units) that is year-round vacant; (4) The percentage of rental inventory that is vacant for rent; (5) The percentage of homeowner inventory that is vacant for sale; n/a not available
Source: U.S. Census Bureau, Housing Vacancies and Homeownership Annual Statistics: 2020, 2021, 2022

INCOME

Income

Area	Per Capita ($)	Median Household ($)	Average Household ($)
City	28,480	60,601	78,033
MSA[1]	35,707	80,843	99,568
U.S.	37,638	69,021	97,196

Note: (1) Figures cover the Greeley, CO Metropolitan Statistical Area
Source: U.S. Census Bureau, 2017-2021 American Community Survey 5-Year Estimates

Household Income Distribution

Area	Percent of Households Earning							
	Under $15,000	$15,000 -$24,999	$25,000 -$34,999	$35,000 -$49,999	$50,000 -$74,999	$75,000 -$99,999	$100,000 -$149,999	$150,000 and up
City	10.3	8.2	9.7	13.9	16.1	13.7	17.9	10.3
MSA[1]	6.6	5.7	7.3	10.2	16.7	14.3	22.2	16.9
U.S.	9.4	7.8	8.2	11.4	16.8	12.8	16.3	17.3

Note: (1) Figures cover the Greeley, CO Metropolitan Statistical Area
Source: U.S. Census Bureau, 2017-2021 American Community Survey 5-Year Estimates

Poverty Rate

Area	All Ages	Under 18 Years Old	18 to 64 Years Old	65 Years and Over
City	15.3	20.5	14.5	9.1
MSA[1]	9.7	12.1	9.0	7.7
U.S.	12.6	17.0	11.8	9.6

Note: Figures are percentage of people whose income during the past 12 months was below the poverty level;
(1) Figures cover the Greeley, CO Metropolitan Statistical Area
Source: U.S. Census Bureau, 2017-2021 American Community Survey 5-Year Estimates

EMPLOYMENT

Labor Force and Employment

Area	Civilian Labor Force			Workers Employed		
	Dec. 2021	Dec. 2022	% Chg.	Dec. 2021	Dec. 2022	% Chg.
City	51,681	51,829	0.3	49,366	50,105	1.5
MSA[1]	167,574	168,716	0.7	161,228	163,640	1.5
U.S.	161,696,000	164,224,000	1.6	155,732,000	158,872,000	2.0

Note: Data is not seasonally adjusted and covers workers 16 years of age and older; (1) Figures cover the Greeley, CO Metropolitan Statistical Area
Source: Bureau of Labor Statistics, Local Area Unemployment Statistics

Unemployment Rate

Area	2022											
	Jan.	Feb.	Mar.	Apr.	May	Jun.	Jul.	Aug.	Sep.	Oct.	Nov.	Dec.
City	4.9	5.0	4.4	3.7	3.5	3.9	4.5	3.9	3.8	3.9	3.7	3.3
MSA[1]	4.2	4.3	3.9	3.4	3.3	3.6	3.8	3.6	3.4	3.7	3.5	3.0
U.S.	4.4	4.1	3.8	3.3	3.4	3.8	3.8	3.8	3.3	3.4	3.4	3.3

Note: Data is not seasonally adjusted and covers workers 16 years of age and older; (1) Figures cover the Greeley, CO Metropolitan Statistical Area
Source: Bureau of Labor Statistics, Local Area Unemployment Statistics

Average Wages

Occupation	$/Hr.	Occupation	$/Hr.
Accountants and Auditors	40.39	Maintenance and Repair Workers	25.25
Automotive Mechanics	26.16	Marketing Managers	80.70
Bookkeepers	22.81	Network and Computer Systems Admin.	41.55
Carpenters	25.71	Nurses, Licensed Practical	29.06
Cashiers	14.89	Nurses, Registered	41.14
Computer Programmers	42.19	Nursing Assistants	17.60
Computer Systems Analysts	47.48	Office Clerks, General	23.36
Computer User Support Specialists	33.01	Physical Therapists	47.67
Construction Laborers	20.70	Physicians	n/a
Cooks, Restaurant	17.40	Plumbers, Pipefitters and Steamfitters	26.96
Customer Service Representatives	18.44	Police and Sheriff's Patrol Officers	36.95
Dentists	65.47	Postal Service Mail Carriers	26.49
Electricians	27.92	Real Estate Sales Agents	52.77
Engineers, Electrical	50.58	Retail Salespersons	18.12
Fast Food and Counter Workers	14.57	Sales Representatives, Technical/Scientific	47.78
Financial Managers	83.73	Secretaries, Exc. Legal/Medical/Executive	20.32
First-Line Supervisors of Office Workers	32.68	Security Guards	16.95
General and Operations Managers	64.82	Surgeons	n/a
Hairdressers/Cosmetologists	19.24	Teacher Assistants, Exc. Postsecondary*	16.03
Home Health and Personal Care Aides	16.62	Teachers, Secondary School, Exc. Sp. Ed.*	27.26
Janitors and Cleaners	17.37	Telemarketers	n/a
Landscaping/Groundskeeping Workers	20.33	Truck Drivers, Heavy/Tractor-Trailer	26.14
Lawyers	67.70	Truck Drivers, Light/Delivery Services	23.11
Maids and Housekeeping Cleaners	16.09	Waiters and Waitresses	18.76

Note: Wage data covers the Greeley, CO Metropolitan Statistical Area; (*) Hourly wages were calculated from annual wage data based on a 40 hour work week; n/a not available.
Source: Bureau of Labor Statistics, Metro Area Occupational Employment & Wage Estimates, May 2022

Employment by Industry

Sector	MSA[1]		U.S.
	Number of Employees	Percent of Total	Percent of Total
Construction, Mining, and Logging	16,800	15.1	5.4
Private Education and Health Services	11,000	9.9	16.1
Financial Activities	4,500	4.1	5.9
Government	18,300	16.5	14.5
Information	500	0.5	2.0
Leisure and Hospitality	10,300	9.3	10.3
Manufacturing	13,600	12.3	8.4
Other Services	3,500	3.2	3.7
Professional and Business Services	11,600	10.5	14.7
Retail Trade	11,800	10.6	10.2
Transportation, Warehousing, and Utilities	4,700	4.2	4.9
Wholesale Trade	4,400	4.0	3.9

Note: Figures are non-farm employment as of December 2022. Figures are not seasonally adjusted and include workers 16 years of age and older; (1) Figures cover the Greeley, CO Metropolitan Statistical Area
Source: Bureau of Labor Statistics, Current Employment Statistics, Employment, Hours, and Earnings

Employment by Occupation

Occupation Classification	City (%)	MSA[1] (%)	U.S. (%)
Management, Business, Science, and Arts	31.2	36.1	40.3
Natural Resources, Construction, and Maintenance	13.5	12.8	8.7
Production, Transportation, and Material Moving	17.6	15.1	13.1
Sales and Office	20.2	20.4	20.9
Service	17.5	15.6	17.0

Note: Figures cover employed civilians 16 years of age and older; (1) Figures cover the Greeley, CO Metropolitan Statistical Area
Source: U.S. Census Bureau, 2017-2021 American Community Survey 5-Year Estimates

Occupations with Greatest Projected Employment Growth: 2022 – 2024

Occupation[1]	2022 Employment	2024 Projected Employment	Numeric Employment Change	Percent Employment Change
Software Developers	43,570	47,290	3,720	8.5
Stockers and Order Fillers	45,230	48,030	2,800	6.2
Cooks, Restaurant	31,870	34,550	2,680	8.4
Fast Food and Counter Workers	79,850	82,410	2,560	3.2
Accountants and Auditors	42,150	43,910	1,760	4.2
Market Research Analysts and Marketing Specialists	28,150	29,830	1,680	6.0
Home Health and Personal Care Aides	43,200	44,870	1,670	3.9
Registered Nurses	53,590	55,060	1,470	2.7
General and Operations Managers	47,360	48,780	1,420	3.0
Sales Representatives of Services, Except Advertising, Insurance, Financial Services, and Travel	37,310	38,730	1,420	3.8

Note: Projections cover Colorado; (1) Sorted by numeric employment change
Source: www.projectionscentral.com, State Occupational Projections, 2022–2024 Short-Term Projections

Fastest-Growing Occupations: 2022 – 2024

Occupation[1]	2022 Employment	2024 Projected Employment	Numeric Employment Change	Percent Employment Change
Derrick Operators, Oil and Gas	550	640	90	16.4
Roustabouts, Oil and Gas	1,550	1,790	240	15.5
Service Unit Operators, Oil, Gas, and Mining	2,430	2,760	330	13.6
Flight Attendants	4,890	5,490	600	12.3
Epidemiologists	530	590	60	11.3
Information Security Analysts (SOC 2018)	6,100	6,760	660	10.8
Statisticians	1,410	1,550	140	9.9
Veterinary Assistants and Laboratory Animal Caretakers	2,360	2,590	230	9.7
Data Scientists	3,520	3,850	330	9.4
Solar Photovoltaic Installers	530	580	50	9.4

Note: Projections cover Colorado; (1) Sorted by percent employment change and excludes occupations with numeric employment change less than 50
Source: www.projectionscentral.com, State Occupational Projections, 2022–2024 Short-Term Projections

CITY FINANCES

City Government Finances

Component	2020 ($000)	2020 ($ per capita)
Total Revenues	244,612	2,251
Total Expenditures	232,303	2,138
Debt Outstanding	177,477	1,633
Cash and Securities[1]	303,369	2,792

Note: (1) Cash and security holdings of a government at the close of its fiscal year, including those of its dependent agencies, utilities, and liquor stores.
Source: U.S. Census Bureau, State & Local Government Finances 2020

City Government Revenue by Source

Source	2020 ($000)	2020 ($ per capita)	2020 (%)
General Revenue			
From Federal Government	5,777	53	2.4
From State Government	11,611	107	4.7
From Local Governments	3,401	31	1.4
Taxes			
Property	21,964	202	9.0
Sales and Gross Receipts	95,527	879	39.1
Personal Income	0	0	0.0
Corporate Income	0	0	0.0
Motor Vehicle License	352	3	0.1
Other Taxes	9,242	85	3.8
Current Charges	37,012	341	15.1
Liquor Store	0	0	0.0
Utility	42,938	395	17.6

Source: U.S. Census Bureau, State & Local Government Finances 2020

City Government Expenditures by Function

Function	2020 ($000)	2020 ($ per capita)	2020 (%)
General Direct Expenditures			
Air Transportation	0	0	0.0
Corrections	0	0	0.0
Education	0	0	0.0
Employment Security Administration	0	0	0.0
Financial Administration	5,153	47	2.2
Fire Protection	16,483	151	7.1
General Public Buildings	16,217	149	7.0
Governmental Administration, Other	11,083	102	4.8
Health	50	< 1	< 0.1
Highways	27,936	257	12.0
Hospitals	0	0	0.0
Housing and Community Development	8,574	78	3.7
Interest on General Debt	2,681	24	1.2
Judicial and Legal	2,871	26	1.2
Libraries	0	0	0.0
Parking	37	< 1	< 0.1
Parks and Recreation	24,792	228	10.7
Police Protection	26,446	243	11.4
Public Welfare	186	1	0.1
Sewerage	26,980	248	11.6
Solid Waste Management	255	2	0.1
Veterans' Services	0	0	0.0
Liquor Store	0	0	0.0
Utility	57,289	527	24.7

Source: U.S. Census Bureau, State & Local Government Finances 2020

TAXES

State Corporate Income Tax Rates

State	Tax Rate (%)	Income Brackets ($)	Num. of Brackets	Financial Institution Tax Rate (%)[a]	Federal Income Tax Ded.
Colorado	4.4	Flat rate	1	4.4	No

Note: Tax rates as of January 1, 2023; (a) Rates listed are the corporate income tax rate applied to financial institutions or excise taxes based on income. Some states have other taxes based upon the value of deposits or shares.
Source: Federation of Tax Administrators, State Corporate Income Tax Rates, January 1, 2023

State Individual Income Tax Rates

State	Tax Rate (%)	Income Brackets ($)	Personal Exemptions ($)			Standard Ded. ($)	
			Single	Married	Depend.	Single	Married
Colorado	4.4	Flat rate	(d)	(d)	(d)	13,850	27,700 (d)

Note: Tax rates as of January 1, 2023; Local- and county-level taxes are not included; Federal income tax is not deductible on state income tax returns; (d) These states use the personal exemption/standard deduction amounts provided in the federal Internal Revenue Code.
Source: Federation of Tax Administrators, State Individual Income Tax Rates, January 1, 2023

Various State Sales and Excise Tax Rates

State	State Sales Tax (%)	Gasoline[1] ($/gal.)	Cigarette[2] ($/pack)	Spirits[3] ($/gal.)	Wine[4] ($/gal.)	Beer[5] ($/gal.)	Recreational Marijuana (%)
Colorado	2.9	0.22	1.94	2.28	0.32	0.08	(d)

Note: All tax rates as of January 1, 2023; (1) The American Petroleum Institute has developed a methodology for determining the average tax rate on a gallon of fuel. Rates may include any of the following: excise taxes, environmental fees, storage tank fees, other fees or taxes, general sales tax, and local taxes; (2) The federal excise tax of $1.0066 per pack and local taxes are not included; (3) Rates are those applicable to off-premise sales of 40% alcohol by volume (a.b.v.) distilled spirits in 750ml containers. Local excise taxes are excluded; (4) Rates are those applicable to off-premise sales of 11% a.b.v. non-carbonated wine in 750ml containers; (5) Rates are those applicable to off-premise sales of 4.7% a.b.v. beer in 12 ounce containers; (d) 15% excise tax (levied on wholesale at average market rate); 15% excise tax (retail price)
Source: Tax Foundation, 2023 Facts & Figures: How Does Your State Compare?

State Business Tax Climate Index Rankings

State	Overall Rank	Corporate Tax Rank	Individual Income Tax Rank	Sales Tax Rank	Property Tax Rank	Unemployment Insurance Tax Rank
Colorado	21	7	14	40	36	42

Note: The index is a measure of how each state's tax laws affect economic performance. The lower the rank, the more favorable a state's tax system is for business. States without a given tax are given a ranking of 1. The scores/rankings for the District of Columbia do not affect other states. The 2023 index represents the tax climate as of July 1, 2022.
Source: Tax Foundation, State Business Tax Climate Index 2023

TRANSPORTATION

Means of Transportation to Work

Area	Car/Truck/Van		Public Transportation			Bicycle	Walked	Other Means	Worked at Home
	Drove Alone	Car-pooled	Bus	Subway	Railroad				
City	76.0	12.4	0.5	0.0	0.0	0.5	3.1	0.7	6.8
MSA[1]	76.7	10.4	0.4	0.0	0.0	0.2	1.9	0.8	9.5
U.S.	73.2	8.6	2.0	1.6	0.5	0.5	2.5	1.5	9.7

Note: Figures are percentages and cover workers 16 years of age and older; (1) Figures cover the Greeley, CO Metropolitan Statistical Area
Source: U.S. Census Bureau, 2017-2021 American Community Survey 5-Year Estimates

Travel Time to Work

Area	Less Than 10 Minutes	10 to 19 Minutes	20 to 29 Minutes	30 to 44 Minutes	45 to 59 Minutes	60 to 89 Minutes	90 Minutes or More
City	15.9	37.3	15.3	14.4	5.9	9.2	1.9
MSA[1]	11.6	26.7	18.8	22.8	9.8	8.1	2.3
U.S.	12.4	28.5	21.0	20.9	8.2	6.2	2.9

Note: Note: Figures are percentages and include workers 16 years old and over; (1) Figures cover the Greeley, CO Metropolitan Statistical Area
Source: U.S. Census Bureau, 2017-2021 American Community Survey 5-Year Estimates

Key Congestion Measures

Measure	1990	2000	2010	2015	2020
Annual Hours of Delay, Total (000)	n/a	n/a	n/a	2,725	1,412
Annual Hours of Delay, Per Auto Commuter	n/a	n/a	n/a	22	11
Annual Congestion Cost, Per Auto Commuter ($)	n/a	n/a	n/a	454	250

Note: n/a not available
Source: Texas A&M Transportation Institute, 2021 Urban Mobility Report

Freeway Travel Time Index

Measure	1985	1990	1995	2000	2005	2010	2015	2020
Urban Area Index[1]	n/a	n/a	n/a	n/a	n/a	n/a	1.14	1.08
Urban Area Rank[1,2]	n/a	n/a	n/a	n/a	n/a	n/a	n/a	n/a

Note: Freeway Travel Time Index—the ratio of travel time in the peak period to the travel time at free-flow conditions. For example, a value of 1.30 indicates a 20-minute free-flow trip takes 26 minutes in the peak (20 minutes x 1.30 = 26 minutes); (1) Covers the Greeley CO urban area; (2) Rank is based on 101 larger urban areas (#1 = highest travel time index); n/a not available
Source: Texas A&M Transportation Institute, 2021 Urban Mobility Report

Public Transportation

Agency Name / Mode of Transportation	Vehicles Operated in Maximum Service[1]	Annual Unlinked Passenger Trips[2] (in thous.)	Annual Passenger Miles[3] (in thous.)
City of Greeley - Transit Services			
Bus (directly operated)	17	398.7	n/a
Demand Response (directly operated)	7	17.3	n/a

Note: (1) Number of revenue vehicles operated by the given mode and type of service to meet the annual maximum service requirement. This is the revenue vehicle count during the peak season of the year; on the week and day that maximum service is provided. Vehicles operated in maximum service (VOMS) exclude atypical days and one-time special events; (2) Number of passengers who boarded public transportation vehicles. Passengers are counted each time they board a vehicle no matter how many vehicles they use to travel from their origin to their destination. (3) Sum of the distances ridden by all passengers during the entire fiscal year.
Source: Federal Transit Administration, National Transit Database, 2021

Air Transportation

Airport Name and Code / Type of Service	Passenger Airlines[1]	Passenger Enplanements	Freight Carriers[2]	Freight (lbs)
Denver International (55 miles) (DEN)				
Domestic service (U.S. carriers - 2022)	26	32,145,313	15	277,972,263
International service (U.S. carriers - 2021)	8	661,977	3	3,625,333

Note: (1) Includes all U.S.-based major, minor and commuter airlines that carried at least one passenger during the year; (2) Includes all U.S.-based airlines and freight carriers that transported at least one pound of freight during the year.
Source: Bureau of Transportation Statistics, The Intermodal Transportation Database, Air Carriers: T-100 Domestic Market (U.S. Carriers), 2022; Bureau of Transportation Statistics, The Intermodal Transportation Database, Air Carriers: T-100 International Market (U.S. Carriers), 2021

BUSINESSES

Major Business Headquarters

Company Name	Industry	Rankings	
		Fortune[1]	Forbes[2]
Hensel Phelps Construction	Construction	-	91

Note: (1) Companies that produce a 10-K are ranked 1 to 500 based on 2021 revenue; (2) All private companies with at least $2 billion in annual revenue through the end of their most current fiscal year are ranked 1 to 246; companies listed are headquartered in the city; dashes indicate no ranking
Source: Fortune, "Fortune 500," 2022; Forbes, "America's Largest Private Companies," 2022

Living Environment

COST OF LIVING

Cost of Living Index

Composite Index	Groceries	Housing	Utilities	Trans- portation	Health Care	Misc. Goods/ Services
n/a	n/a	n/a	n/a	n/a	n/a	n/a

Note: The Cost of Living Index measures regional differences in the cost of consumer goods and services, excluding taxes and non-consumer expenditures, for professional and managerial households in the top income quintile. It is based on more than 50,000 prices covering almost 60 different items for which prices are collected three times a year by chambers of commerce, economic development organizations or university applied economic centers in each participating urban area. The numbers shown should be read as a percentage above or below the national average of 100. For example, a value of 115.4 in the groceries column indicates that grocery prices are 15.4% higher than the national average. Small differences in the index numbers should not be interpreted as significant; n/a not available.
Source: The Council for Community and Economic Research, Cost of Living Index, 2022

Grocery Prices

Area[1]	T-Bone Steak ($/pound)	Frying Chicken ($/pound)	Whole Milk ($/half gal.)	Eggs ($/dozen)	Orange Juice ($/64 oz.)	Coffee ($/11.5 oz.)
City[2]	n/a	n/a	n/a	n/a	n/a	n/a
Avg.	13.81	1.59	2.43	2.25	3.85	4.95
Min.	10.17	0.90	1.51	1.30	2.90	3.46
Max.	19.35	3.30	4.32	4.32	5.31	8.59

*Note: (1) Values for the local area are compared with the average, minimum and maximum values for all 286 areas in the Cost of Living Index; (2) Figures cover the Greeley CO urban area; n/a not available; **T-Bone Steak** (price per pound); **Frying Chicken** (price per pound, whole fryer); **Whole Milk** (half gallon carton); **Eggs** (price per dozen, Grade A, large); **Orange Juice** (64 oz. Tropicana or Florida Natural); **Coffee** (11.5 oz. can, vacuum-packed, Maxwell House, Hills Bros, or Folgers).*
Source: The Council for Community and Economic Research, Cost of Living Index, 2022

Housing and Utility Costs

Area[1]	New Home Price ($)	Apartment Rent ($/month)	All Electric ($/month)	Part Electric ($/month)	Other Energy ($/month)	Telephone ($/month)
City[2]	n/a	n/a	n/a	n/a	n/a	n/a
Avg.	450,913	1,371	176.41	99.93	76.96	190.22
Min.	229,283	546	100.84	31.56	27.15	174.27
Max.	2,434,977	4,569	356.86	249.59	272.24	208.31

*Note: (1) Values for the local area are compared with the average, minimum and maximum values for all 286 areas in the Cost of Living Index; (2) Figures cover the Greeley CO urban area; n/a not available; **New Home Price** (2,400 sf living area, 8,000 sf lot, in urban area with full utilities); **Apartment Rent** (950 sf 2 bedroom/1.5 or 2 bath, unfurnished, excluding all utilities except water); **All Electric** (average monthly cost for an all-electric home); **Part Electric** (average monthly cost for a part-electric home); **Other Energy** (average monthly cost for natural gas, fuel oil, coal, wood, and any other forms of energy except electricity); **Telephone** (price includes the base monthly rate plus taxes and fees for three lines of mobile phone service).*
Source: The Council for Community and Economic Research, Cost of Living Index, 2022

Health Care, Transportation, and Other Costs

Area[1]	Doctor ($/visit)	Dentist ($/visit)	Optometrist ($/visit)	Gasoline ($/gallon)	Beauty Salon ($/visit)	Men's Shirt ($)
City[2]	n/a	n/a	n/a	n/a	n/a	n/a
Avg.	124.91	107.77	117.66	3.86	43.31	34.21
Min.	36.61	58.25	51.79	2.90	22.18	13.05
Max.	250.21	162.58	371.96	5.54	85.61	63.54

*Note: (1) Values for the local area are compared with the average, minimum and maximum values for all 286 areas in the Cost of Living Index; (2) Figures cover the Greeley CO urban area; n/a not available; **Doctor** (general practitioners routine exam of an established patient); **Dentist** (adult teeth cleaning and periodic oral examination); **Optometrist** (full vision eye exam for established adult patient); **Gasoline** (one gallon regular unleaded, national brand, including all taxes, cash price at self-service pump if available); **Beauty Salon** (woman's shampoo, trim, and blow-dry); **Men's Shirt** (cotton/polyester dress shirt, pinpoint weave, long sleeves).*
Source: The Council for Community and Economic Research, Cost of Living Index, 2022

HOUSING

Homeownership Rate

Area	2015 (%)	2016 (%)	2017 (%)	2018 (%)	2019 (%)	2020 (%)	2021 (%)	2022 (%)
MSA[1]	n/a	n/a	n/a	n/a	n/a	n/a	n/a	n/a
U.S.	63.7	63.4	63.9	64.4	64.6	66.6	65.5	65.8

Note: (1) Figures cover the Greeley, CO Metropolitan Statistical Area; n/a not available
Source: U.S. Census Bureau, Housing Vacancies and Homeownership Annual Statistics: 2015-2022

House Price Index (HPI)

Area	National Ranking[2]	Quarterly Change (%)	One-Year Change (%)	Five-Year Change (%)	Since 1991Q1 (%)
MSA[1]	207	-3.14	8.35	53.74	462.73
U.S.[3]	—	0.34	8.41	58.44	289.08

Note: The HPI is a weighted repeat sales index. It measures average price changes in repeat sales or refinancings on the same properties. This information is obtained by reviewing repeat mortgage transactions on single-family properties whose mortgages have been purchased or securitized by Fannie Mae or Freddie Mac since January 1975; (1) Figures cover the Greeley, CO Metropolitan Statistical Area; (2) Rankings are based on annual percentage change for all metro areas containing at least 15,000 transactions over the last 10 years and ranges from 1 to 257; (3) figures based on a weighted average of Census Division estimates using a seasonally adjusted, purchase-only index; all figures are for the period ending December 31, 2022
Source: Federal Housing Finance Agency, Change in FHFA Metropolitan Area House Price Indexes, 2022Q4

Median Single-Family Home Prices

Area	2020	2021	2022p	Percent Change 2021 to 2022
MSA[1]	n/a	n/a	n/a	n/a
U.S. Average	300.2	357.1	392.6	9.9

Note: Figures are median sales prices of existing single-family homes in thousands of dollars; (p) preliminary; n/a not available; (1) Figures cover the Greeley, CO Metropolitan Statistical Area
Source: National Association of Realtors, Median Sales Price of Existing Single-Family Homes for Metropolitan Areas, 4th Quarter 2022

Qualifying Income Based on Median Sales Price of Existing Single-Family Homes

Area	With 5% Down ($)	With 10% Down ($)	With 20% Down ($)
MSA[1]	n/a	n/a	n/a
U.S. Average	112,234	106,237	94,513

Note: Figures are preliminary; Qualifying income is based on a mortgage rate of 6.77%. Monthly principal and interest payment is limited to 25% of income; n/a not available; (1) Figures cover the Greeley, CO Metropolitan Statistical Area
Source: National Association of Realtors, Qualifying Income Based on Median Sales Price of Existing Single-Family Homes for Metropolitan Areas, 4th Quarter 2022

Home Value

Area	Under $100,000	$100,000 -$199,999	$200,000 -$299,999	$300,000 -$399,999	$400,000 -$499,999	$500,000 -$999,999	$1,000,000 or more	Median ($)
City	9.3	8.9	33.0	31.0	10.6	6.8	0.3	296,300
MSA[1]	7.1	7.0	21.1	28.5	17.5	17.3	1.5	352,000
U.S.	16.2	24.2	20.1	13.6	8.3	13.6	4.1	244,900

Note: Figures are percentages except for median and cover owner-occupied housing units; (1) Figures cover the Greeley, CO Metropolitan Statistical Area
Source: U.S. Census Bureau, 2017-2021 American Community Survey 5-Year Estimates

Year Housing Structure Built

Area	2020 or Later	2010 -2019	2000 -2009	1990 -1999	1980 -1989	1970 -1979	1960 -1969	1950 -1959	1940 -1949	Before 1940	Median Year
City	0.1	9.4	17.2	16.7	10.2	21.2	9.4	6.4	2.2	7.2	1984
MSA[1]	0.7	16.2	26.7	15.4	7.2	14.6	5.6	3.9	1.9	7.7	1996
U.S.	0.2	7.3	13.6	13.6	13.2	14.8	10.3	10.0	4.7	12.2	1979

Note: Figures are percentages except for Median Year; Note: (1) Figures cover the Greeley, CO Metropolitan Statistical Area
Source: U.S. Census Bureau, 2017-2021 American Community Survey 5-Year Estimates

Gross Monthly Rent

Area	Under $500	$500 -$999	$1,000 -$1,499	$1,500 -$1,999	$2,000 -$2,499	$2,500 -$2,999	$3,000 and up	Median ($)
City	9.1	29.7	37.4	16.2	6.0	1.1	0.5	1,134
MSA[1]	7.1	26.4	33.6	21.2	7.5	2.6	1.6	1,234
U.S.	8.1	30.5	30.8	16.8	7.3	3.1	3.5	1,163

Note: Figures are percentages except for median; Gross rent is the contract rent plus the estimated average monthly cost of utilities (electricity, gas, and water and sewer) and fuels (oil, coal, kerosene, wood, etc.) if these are paid by the renter (or paid for the renter by someone else); (1) Figures cover the Greeley, CO Metropolitan Statistical Area
Source: U.S. Census Bureau, 2017-2021 American Community Survey 5-Year Estimates

HEALTH

Health Risk Factors

Category	MSA[1] (%)	U.S. (%)
Adults aged 18–64 who have any kind of health care coverage	n/a	90.9
Adults who reported being in good or better health	n/a	85.2
Adults who have been told they have high blood cholesterol	n/a	35.7
Adults who have been told they have high blood pressure	n/a	32.4
Adults who are current smokers	n/a	14.4
Adults who currently use e-cigarettes	n/a	6.7
Adults who currently use chewing tobacco, snuff, or snus	n/a	3.5
Adults who are heavy drinkers[2]	n/a	6.3
Adults who are binge drinkers[3]	n/a	15.4
Adults who are overweight (BMI 25.0 - 29.9)	n/a	34.4
Adults who are obese (BMI 30.0 - 99.8)	n/a	33.9
Adults who participated in any physical activities in the past month	n/a	76.3

Note: (1) Figures for the Greeley, CO Metropolitan Statistical Area were not available.
(2) Heavy drinkers are classified as adult men having more than 14 drinks per week and adult women having more than 7 drinks per week; (3) Binge drinkers are classified as males having five or more drinks on one occasion or females having four or more drinks on one occasion
Source: Centers for Disease Control and Prevention, Behaviorial Risk Factor Surveillance System, SMART: Selected Metropolitan Area Risk Trends, 2021

Acute and Chronic Health Conditions

Category	MSA[1] (%)	U.S. (%)
Adults who have ever been told they had a heart attack	n/a	4.0
Adults who have ever been told they have angina or coronary heart disease	n/a	3.8
Adults who have ever been told they had a stroke	n/a	3.0
Adults who have ever been told they have asthma	n/a	14.9
Adults who have ever been told they have arthritis	n/a	25.8
Adults who have ever been told they have diabetes[2]	n/a	10.9
Adults who have ever been told they had skin cancer	n/a	6.6
Adults who have ever been told they had any other types of cancer	n/a	7.5
Adults who have ever been told they have COPD	n/a	6.1
Adults who have ever been told they have kidney disease	n/a	3.0
Adults who have ever been told they have a form of depression	n/a	20.5

Note: (1) Figures for the Greeley, CO Metropolitan Statistical Area were not available.
(2) Figures do not include pregnancy-related, borderline, or pre-diabetes
Source: Centers for Disease Control and Prevention, Behaviorial Risk Factor Surveillance System, SMART: Selected Metropolitan Area Risk Trends, 2021

Health Screening and Vaccination Rates

Category	MSA[1] (%)	U.S. (%)
Adults who have ever been tested for HIV	n/a	34.9
Adults who have had their blood cholesterol checked within the last five years	n/a	85.2
Adults aged 65+ who have had flu shot within the past year	n/a	68.6
Adults aged 65+ who have ever had a pneumonia vaccination	n/a	71.0

Note: (1) Figures for the Greeley, CO Metropolitan Statistical Area were not available.
Source: Centers for Disease Control and Prevention, Behaviorial Risk Factor Surveillance System, SMART: Selected Metropolitan Area Risk Trends, 2021

Disability Status

Category	MSA[1] (%)	U.S. (%)
Adults who reported being deaf	n/a	7.2
Are you blind or have serious difficulty seeing, even when wearing glasses?	n/a	4.8
Are you limited in any way in any of your usual activities due to arthritis?	n/a	11.1
Do you have difficulty doing errands alone?	n/a	7.0
Do you have difficulty dressing or bathing?	n/a	3.6
Do you have serious difficulty concentrating/remembering/making decisions?	n/a	12.1
Do you have serious difficulty walking or climbing stairs?	n/a	12.8

Note: (1) Figures for the Greeley, CO Metropolitan Statistical Area were not available.
Source: Centers for Disease Control and Prevention, Behaviorial Risk Factor Surveillance System, SMART: Selected Metropolitan Area Risk Trends, 2021

Mortality Rates for the Top 10 Causes of Death in the U.S.

ICD-10[a] Sub-Chapter	ICD-10[a] Code	Crude Mortality Rate[1] per 100,000 population	
		County[2]	U.S.
Malignant neoplasms	C00-C97	126.3	182.6
Ischaemic heart diseases	I20-I25	54.4	113.1
Other forms of heart disease	I30-I51	36.4	64.4
Other degenerative diseases of the nervous system	G30-G31	36.1	51.0
Cerebrovascular diseases	I60-I69	24.9	47.8
Other external causes of accidental injury	W00-X59	40.3	46.4
Chronic lower respiratory diseases	J40-J47	33.3	45.7
Organic, including symptomatic, mental disorders	F01-F09	15.9	35.9
Hypertensive diseases	I10-I15	23.3	35.0
Diabetes mellitus	E10-E14	21.0	29.6

Note: (a) ICD-10 = International Classification of Diseases 10th Revision; (1) Crude mortality rates are a three-year average covering 2019-2021; (2) Figures cover Weld County.
Source: Centers for Disease Control and Prevention, National Center for Health Statistics. National Vital Statistics System, Mortality 2018-2021 on CDC WONDER Online Database

Mortality Rates for Selected Causes of Death

ICD-10[a] Sub-Chapter	ICD-10[a] Code	Crude Mortality Rate[1] per 100,000 population	
		County[2]	U.S.
Assault	X85-Y09	4.1	7.0
Diseases of the liver	K70-K76	22.9	19.8
Human immunodeficiency virus (HIV) disease	B20-B24	Suppressed	1.5
Influenza and pneumonia	J09-J18	6.0	14.7
Intentional self-harm	X60-X84	17.3	14.3
Malnutrition	E40-E46	Unreliable	4.3
Obesity and other hyperalimentation	E65-E68	Unreliable	3.0
Renal failure	N17-N19	8.8	15.7
Transport accidents	V01-V99	15.0	13.6
Viral hepatitis	B15-B19	Suppressed	1.2

Note: (a) ICD-10 = International Classification of Diseases 10th Revision; (1) Crude mortality rates are a three-year average covering 2019-2021; (2) Figures cover Weld County; Data are suppressed when the data meet the criteria for confidentiality constraints; Crude mortality rates are flagged as unreliable when the rate would be calculated with a numerator of 20 or less.
Source: Centers for Disease Control and Prevention, National Center for Health Statistics. National Vital Statistics System, Mortality 2018-2021 on CDC WONDER Online Database

Health Insurance Coverage

Area	With Health Insurance	With Private Health Insurance	With Public Health Insurance	Without Health Insurance	Population Under Age 19 Without Health Insurance
City	90.2	60.8	40.2	9.8	5.1
MSA[1]	91.2	68.7	32.3	8.8	4.7
U.S.	91.2	67.8	35.4	8.8	5.3

Note: Figures are percentages that cover the civilian noninstitutionalized population; (1) Figures cover the Greeley, CO Metropolitan Statistical Area
Source: U.S. Census Bureau, 2017-2021 American Community Survey 5-Year Estimates

Number of Medical Professionals

Area	MDs[3]	DOs[3,4]	Dentists	Podiatrists	Chiropractors	Optometrists
County[1] (number)	419	60	157	7	79	44
County[1] (rate[2])	126.4	18.1	46.2	2.1	23.2	12.9
U.S. (rate[2])	289.3	23.5	72.5	6.2	28.7	17.4

Note: Data as of 2021 unless noted; (1) Data covers Weld County; (2) Rate per 100,000 population; (3) Data as of 2020 and includes all active, non-federal physicians; (4) Doctor of Osteopathic Medicine
Source: U.S. Department of Health and Human Services, Health Resources and Services Administration, Bureau of Health Professions, Area Resource File (ARF) 2021-2022

EDUCATION

Public School District Statistics

District Name	Schls	Pupils	Pupil/ Teacher Ratio	Minority Pupils[1] (%)	LEP/ELL[2] (%)	IEP[3] (%)
Greeleyschool District No. 6	34	21,997	17.6	70.9	18.0	n/a

Note: Table includes school districts with 2,000 or more students; (1) Percentage of students that are not non-Hispanic white; (2) Percentage of students that are Limited English Proficient or English Language Learners (2018-19); (3) Percentage of students that have an Individualized Education Program (2019-20).
Source: U.S. Department of Education, National Center for Education Statistics, Common Core of Data, Local Education Agency (School District) Universe Survey: School Year 2021-2022

Highest Level of Education

Area	Less than H.S.	H.S. Diploma	Some College, No Deg.	Associate Degree	Bachelor's Degree	Master's Degree	Prof. School Degree	Doctorate Degree
City	16.4	26.0	22.8	8.8	15.9	7.7	1.4	1.2
MSA[1]	11.9	25.4	23.8	9.5	19.3	7.8	1.3	1.1
U.S.	11.1	26.5	20.0	8.7	20.6	9.3	2.2	1.5

Note: Figures cover persons age 25 and over; (1) Figures cover the Greeley, CO Metropolitan Statistical Area
Source: U.S. Census Bureau, 2017-2021 American Community Survey 5-Year Estimates

Educational Attainment by Race

Area	High School Graduate or Higher (%)					Bachelor's Degree or Higher (%)				
	Total	White	Black	Asian	Hisp.[2]	Total	White	Black	Asian	Hisp.[2]
City	83.6	86.1	69.8	81.6	64.7	26.1	28.3	21.9	50.3	9.1
MSA[1]	88.1	90.1	79.6	89.1	67.8	29.5	31.3	31.0	41.1	10.1
U.S.	88.9	91.4	87.2	87.6	71.2	33.7	35.5	23.3	55.6	18.4

Note: Figures shown cover persons 25 years old and over; (1) Figures cover the Greeley, CO Metropolitan Statistical Area; (2) People of Hispanic origin can be of any race
Source: U.S. Census Bureau, 2017-2021 American Community Survey 5-Year Estimates

School Enrollment by Grade and Control

Area	Preschool (%)		Kindergarten (%)		Grades 1 - 4 (%)		Grades 5 - 8 (%)		Grades 9 - 12 (%)	
	Public	Private	Public	Private	Public	Private	Public	Private	Public	Private
City	72.4	27.6	92.8	7.2	94.1	5.9	92.8	7.2	94.4	5.6
MSA[1]	71.5	28.5	91.2	8.8	92.1	7.9	91.7	8.3	94.2	5.8
U.S.	58.8	41.2	86.3	13.7	88.3	11.7	88.6	11.4	89.4	10.6

Note: Figures shown cover persons 3 years old and over; (1) Figures cover the Greeley, CO Metropolitan Statistical Area
Source: U.S. Census Bureau, 2017-2021 American Community Survey 5-Year Estimates

Higher Education

Four-Year Colleges			Two-Year Colleges			Medical Schools[1]	Law Schools[2]	Voc/ Tech[3]
Public	Private Non-profit	Private For-profit	Public	Private Non-profit	Private For-profit			
1	0	0	1	0	0	0	0	1

Note: Figures cover institutions located within the Greeley, CO Metropolitan Statistical Area and include main campuses only; (1) includes schools accredited by the Liaison Committee on Medical Education and the American Osteopathic Association's Commission on Osteopathic College Accreditation; (2) includes ABA-accredited schools, schools with provisional ABA accreditation, and state accredited schools; (3) includes all schools with programs that are less than 2 years.
Source: National Center for Education Statistics, Integrated Postsecondary Education System (IPEDS), 2021-22; Wikipedia, List of Medical Schools in the United States, accessed April 10, 2023; Wikipedia, List of Law Schools in the United States, accessed April 10, 2023

EMPLOYERS

Major Employers

Company Name	Industry
A&W Water Services	Energy services
Anadarko Petroleum	Petroleum and natural gas exploration and production
Halliburton Energy Services	Oil field service
JB Swift & Company	Food processing
Noble Energy	Petroleum and natural gas exploration and production
North Colorado Medical Center	Medical center
Select Energy Services	Energy services
State Farm	Insurance
TeleTech	Business process outsourcing
Vestas	Wind turbines

Note: Companies shown are located within the Greeley, CO Metropolitan Statistical Area.
Source: Hoovers.com; Wikipedia

PUBLIC SAFETY

Crime Rate

Area	Total Crime	Murder	Rape[3]	Robbery	Aggrav. Assault	Burglary	Larceny -Theft	Motor Vehicle Theft
		Violent Crime Rate				Property Crime Rate		
City	2,888.6	8.1	48.0	70.6	298.6	333.9	1,774.6	354.7
Suburbs[1]	2,286.0	3.2	56.2	25.4	188.9	212.4	1,410.9	389.1
Metro[2]	2,487.0	4.8	53.4	40.4	225.5	253.0	1,532.2	377.6
U.S.	2,356.7	6.5	38.4	73.9	279.7	314.2	1,398.0	246.0

Note: Figures are crimes per 100,000 population; (1) All areas within the metro area that are located outside the city limits; (2) Figures cover the Greeley, CO Metropolitan Statistical Area; (3) All figures shown were reported using the revised Uniform Crime Reporting (UCR) definition of rape; Due to the transition to the National Incident-Based Reporting System (NIBRS), limited city and metro area data was released for 2021.
Source: FBI Uniform Crime Reports, 2020

Hate Crimes

Area	Number of Quarters Reported	Race/Ethnicity/ Ancestry	Religion	Sexual Orientation	Disability	Gender	Gender Identity
		Number of Incidents per Bias Motivation					
City	4	0	0	1	0	0	0
U.S.	4	5,227	1,244	1,110	130	75	266

Note: Due to the transition to the National Incident-Based Reporting System (NIBRS), limited crime data was released for 2021.
Source: Federal Bureau of Investigation, Hate Crime Statistics 2020

Identity Theft Consumer Reports

Area	Reports	Reports per 100,000 Population	Rank[2]
MSA[1]	484	153	251
U.S.	1,108,609	339	-

Note: (1) Figures cover the Greeley, CO Metropolitan Statistical Area; (2) Rank ranges from 1 to 391 where 1 indicates greatest number of identity theft reports per 100,000 population
Source: Federal Trade Commission, Consumer Sentinel Network Data Book 2022

Fraud and Other Consumer Reports

Area	Reports	Reports per 100,000 Population	Rank[2]
MSA[1]	2,342	743	263
U.S.	4,064,520	1,245	-

Note: (1) Figures cover the Greeley, CO Metropolitan Statistical Area; (2) Rank ranges from 1 to 391 where 1 indicates greatest number of fraud and other consumer reports per 100,000 population
Source: Federal Trade Commission, Consumer Sentinel Network Data Book 2022

POLITICS

2020 Presidential Election Results

Area	Biden	Trump	Jorgensen	Hawkins	Other
Weld County	39.6	57.6	1.7	0.2	0.9
U.S.	51.3	46.8	1.2	0.3	0.5

Note: Results are percentages and may not add to 100% due to rounding
Source: Dave Leip's Atlas of U.S. Presidential Elections

SPORTS

Professional Sports Teams

Team Name	League	Year Established

No teams are located in the metro area
Source: Wikipedia, Major Professional Sports Teams of the United States and Canada, April 12, 2023

CLIMATE

Average and Extreme Temperatures

Temperature	Jan	Feb	Mar	Apr	May	Jun	Jul	Aug	Sep	Oct	Nov	Dec	Yr.
Extreme High (°F)	73	76	84	90	93	102	103	100	97	89	79	75	103
Average High (°F)	43	47	52	62	71	81	88	86	77	67	52	45	64
Average Temp. (°F)	30	34	39	48	58	67	73	72	63	52	39	32	51
Average Low (°F)	16	20	25	34	44	53	59	57	48	37	25	18	37
Extreme Low (°F)	-25	-25	-10	-2	22	30	43	41	17	3	-8	-25	-25

Note: Figures cover the years 1948-1992
Source: National Climatic Data Center, International Station Meteorological Climate Summary, 9/96

Average Precipitation/Snowfall/Humidity

Precip./Humidity	Jan	Feb	Mar	Apr	May	Jun	Jul	Aug	Sep	Oct	Nov	Dec	Yr.
Avg. Precip. (in.)	0.6	0.6	1.3	1.7	2.5	1.7	1.9	1.5	1.1	1.0	0.9	0.6	15.5
Avg. Snowfall (in.)	9	7	14	9	2	Tr	0	0	2	4	9	8	63
Avg. Rel. Hum. 5am (%)	62	65	67	66	70	68	67	68	66	63	66	63	66
Avg. Rel. Hum. 5pm (%)	49	44	40	35	38	34	34	34	32	34	47	50	39

Note: Figures cover the years 1948-1992; Tr = Trace amounts (<0.05 in. of rain; <0.5 in. of snow)
Source: National Climatic Data Center, International Station Meteorological Climate Summary, 9/96

Weather Conditions

Temperature			Daytime Sky			Precipitation		
10°F & below	32°F & below	90°F & above	Clear	Partly cloudy	Cloudy	0.01 inch or more precip.	0.1 inch or more snow/ice	Thunder-storms
24	155	33	99	177	89	90	38	39

Note: Figures are average number of days per year and cover the years 1948-1992
Source: National Climatic Data Center, International Station Meteorological Climate Summary, 9/96

HAZARDOUS WASTE

Superfund Sites

The Greeley, CO metro area has no sites on the EPA's Superfund Final National Priorities List. There are a total of 1,165 Superfund sites with a status of proposed or final on the list in the U.S. *U.S. Environmental Protection Agency, National Priorities List, April 12, 2023*

AIR QUALITY

Air Quality Trends: Ozone

	1990	1995	2000	2005	2010	2015	2018	2019	2020	2021
MSA[1]	0.076	0.072	0.069	0.078	0.073	0.073	0.073	0.065	0.072	0.076
U.S.	0.087	0.089	0.081	0.080	0.072	0.067	0.069	0.065	0.065	0.067

Note: (1) Data covers the Greeley, CO Metropolitan Statistical Area. The values shown are the composite ozone concentration averages among trend sites based on the highest fourth daily maximum 8-hour concentration in parts per million. These trends are based on sites having an adequate record of monitoring data during the trend period. Data from exceptional events are included.
Source: U.S. Environmental Protection Agency, Air Quality Monitoring Information, "Air Quality Trends by City, 1990-2021"

Air Quality Index

Area	Percent of Days when Air Quality was...[2]					AQI Statistics[2]	
	Good	Moderate	Unhealthy for Sensitive Groups	Unhealthy	Very Unhealthy	Maximum	Median
MSA[1]	54.5	36.2	9.0	0.3	0.0	154	49

Note: (1) Data covers the Greeley, CO Metropolitan Statistical Area; (2) Based on 365 days with AQI data in 2021. Air Quality Index (AQI) is an index for reporting daily air quality. EPA calculates the AQI for five major air pollutants regulated by the Clean Air Act: ground-level ozone, particle pollution (aka particulate matter), carbon monoxide, sulfur dioxide, and nitrogen dioxide. The AQI runs from 0 to 500. The higher the AQI value, the greater the level of air pollution and the greater the health concern. There are six AQI categories: "Good" AQI is between 0 and 50. Air quality is considered satisfactory; "Moderate" AQI is between 51 and 100. Air quality is acceptable; "Unhealthy for Sensitive Groups" When AQI values are between 101 and 150, members of sensitive groups may experience health effects; "Unhealthy" When AQI values are between 151 and 200 everyone may begin to experience health effects; "Very Unhealthy" AQI values between 201 and 300 trigger a health alert; "Hazardous" AQI values over 300 trigger warnings of emergency conditions (not shown).
Source: U.S. Environmental Protection Agency, Air Quality Index Report, 2021

Air Quality Index Pollutants

Area	Percent of Days when AQI Pollutant was...[2]					
	Carbon Monoxide	Nitrogen Dioxide	Ozone	Sulfur Dioxide	Particulate Matter 2.5	Particulate Matter 10
MSA[1]	0.0	0.3	78.6	(3)	21.1	0.0

Note: (1) Data covers the Greeley, CO Metropolitan Statistical Area; (2) Based on 365 days with AQI data in 2021. The Air Quality Index (AQI) is an index for reporting daily air quality. EPA calculates the AQI for five major air pollutants regulated by the Clean Air Act: ground-level ozone, particle pollution (also known as particulate matter), carbon monoxide, sulfur dioxide, and nitrogen dioxide. The AQI runs from 0 to 500. The higher the AQI value, the greater the level of air pollution and the greater the health concern; (3) Sulfur dioxide is no longer included in this table (as of December 8, 2021) because SO_2 concentrations tend to be very localized and not necessarily representative of broad geographical areas like counties and CBSAs.
Source: U.S. Environmental Protection Agency, Air Quality Index Report, 2021

Maximum Air Pollutant Concentrations: Particulate Matter, Ozone, CO and Lead

	Particulate Matter 10 (ug/m^3)	Particulate Matter 2.5 Wtd AM (ug/m^3)	Particulate Matter 2.5 24-Hr (ug/m^3)	Ozone (ppm)	Carbon Monoxide (ppm)	Lead (ug/m^3)
MSA[1] Level	n/a	9.8	31	0.083	1	n/a
NAAQS[2]	150	15	35	0.075	9	0.15
Met NAAQS[2]	n/a	Yes	Yes	No	Yes	n/a

Note: (1) Data covers the Greeley, CO Metropolitan Statistical Area; Data from exceptional events are included; (2) National Ambient Air Quality Standards; ppm = parts per million; ug/m^3 = micrograms per cubic meter; n/a not available.
Concentrations: Particulate Matter 10 (coarse particulate)—highest second maximum 24-hour concentration; Particulate Matter 2.5 Wtd AM (fine particulate)—highest weighted annual mean concentration; Particulate Matter 2.5 24-Hour (fine particulate)—highest 98th percentile 24-hour concentration; Ozone—highest fourth daily maximum 8-hour concentration; Carbon Monoxide—highest second maximum non-overlapping 8-hour concentration; Lead—maximum running 3-month average
Source: U.S. Environmental Protection Agency, Air Quality Monitoring Information, "Air Quality Statistics by City, 2021"

Maximum Air Pollutant Concentrations: Nitrogen Dioxide and Sulfur Dioxide

	Nitrogen Dioxide AM (ppb)	Nitrogen Dioxide 1-Hr (ppb)	Sulfur Dioxide AM (ppb)	Sulfur Dioxide 1-Hr (ppb)	Sulfur Dioxide 24-Hr (ppb)
MSA[1] Level	6	42	n/a	n/a	n/a
NAAQS[2]	53	100	30	75	140
Met NAAQS[2]	Yes	Yes	n/a	n/a	n/a

Note: (1) Data covers the Greeley, CO Metropolitan Statistical Area; Data from exceptional events are included; (2) National Ambient Air Quality Standards; ppm = parts per million; ug/m^3 = micrograms per cubic meter; n/a not available.
Concentrations: Nitrogen Dioxide AM—highest arithmetic mean concentration; Nitrogen Dioxide 1-Hr—highest 98th percentile 1-hour daily maximum concentration; Sulfur Dioxide AM—highest annual mean concentration; Sulfur Dioxide 1-Hr—highest 99th percentile 1-hour daily maximum concentration; Sulfur Dioxide 24-Hr—highest second maximum 24-hour concentration
Source: U.S. Environmental Protection Agency, Air Quality Monitoring Information, "Air Quality Statistics by City, 2021"

Honolulu, Hawaii

Background

Honolulu, whose name means "sheltered harbor," is the capital of Hawaii and the seat of Honolulu County. The city sits in one of the most famously attractive areas of the world, on the island of Oahu, home to the extinct volcano Diamond Head, Waikiki Beach, and two mountain ranges, the Koolau and the Waianae. Honolulu is the economic hub of Hawaii and a major seaport. Tourism has continued to increase in recent years, after a drop during the pandemic.

Traditionally home to fishing and horticultural tribal groups, the Hawaiian Islands were politically united under the reign of King Kamehameha I, who first moved his triumphant court to Waikiki and subsequently to a site in what is now downtown Honolulu (1804). It was during his time that the port became a center for the sandalwood trade, thus establishing the region as an international presence even before the political interventions of non-Hawaiians.

European activity dates from 1794, when the English sea captain William Brown entered Honolulu, dubbing it Fair Harbor. Two decades later, the first missionaries arrived. American Congregationalists were followed by French Catholics and, later, Mormons and Anglicans. By the end of the nineteenth century, non-Hawaiians owned most of the land. In 1898 Hawaii was annexed by the U.S.

As is true for many strategically located cities, the events of World War II had a profound effect on Honolulu. The Japanese attack on December 7, 1941, forever etched the name of Pearl Harbor into the national memory. During the war, existing military bases were expanded, and new bases built, providing considerable economic stimuli. The Vietnam War also had a dramatic effect on Honolulu and by the end of the twentieth century, military families accounted for 10 percent of the population.

Today, the U.S. military employs more than 45,000 throughout the state. Fruit, primarily pineapple, processing and light manufacturing are also important to the economy. Aquaculture, which includes cultivated species of shellfish, finfish, and algae, has grown in recent years, as has biotechnology.

Tourism, however, has been the private-sector mainstay of Honolulu's economy, with most of the millions of tourists who visit Hawaii annually coming through its port or airport. Honolulu is a required stop for any holiday ship cruising these waters, and it is also the center for the inter-island air services that ferry tourists to various resort locations. The Hawaii Tourism Authority is actively implementing a strategic plan, launched in 2020, to support tourism through 2025.

The center of Honolulu's downtown district is dominated by the Iolani Palace, once home to Hawaii's original royal family. Nearby are the State Capitol Building and the State Supreme Court Building, known as Ali'iolani Hall. The Aloha Tower Development Corporation has recently modernized the mixed-use space in and around the Aloha Tower Complex along the city's piers.

Construction of the Honolulu High-Capacity Transit Corridor Project, including a new rail line connecting Kapolei in West Oahu to the University of Hawaii at Manoa was completed in 2018.

Honolulu, as it has grown along the southern coast of Oahu, has established a mix of residential zones, with single-family dwellings and relatively small multi-unit buildings. The result is that large parts of what is a major metropolitan area feel like cozy neighborhoods. In fact, Honolulu is governed in part through a Neighborhood Board System, which insures maximal local input with regard to planning decisions and city services.

Cultural amenities include the Bishop Museum, the Honolulu Academy of Arts, and the Contemporary Museum, which together offer world-class collections in Polynesian art and artifacts, Japanese, Chinese, and Korean art, and modern art from the world over. Honolulu also hosts a symphony orchestra, the oldest U.S. symphony orchestra west of the Rocky Mountains, which performs at the Neal S. Blaisdell Center.

Barack Obama, the United States' 44th president, is the first president from Hawaii. Obama was born in Honolulu, causing the city a fair amount of attention during the 2008 presidential election.

Honolulu's weather is subtropical, with temperatures moderated by the surrounding ocean and the trade winds. There are only slight variations in temperature from summer to winter. Rain is moderate, though heavier in summer, when it sometimes comes in the form of quick showers while the sun is shining—known locally as "liquid sunshine."

Rankings

General Rankings

- For its "Best for Vets: Places to Live 2019" rankings, *Military Times* evaluated 599 cities (83 large, 234 medium, 282 small) and compared the locations across three broad categories: veteran and military culture/services; economic indicators; and livability factors such as health, crime, traffic, and school quality. Honolulu ranked #5 out of the top 25, in the large city category (population of more than 250,000). Data points more specific to veterans and the military weighed more heavily than others. *rebootcamp.militarytimes.com, "Military Times Best Places to Live 2019," September 10, 2018*

- The human resources consulting firm Mercer ranked 231 major cities worldwide in terms of overall quality of life. Honolulu ranked #37. Criteria: political, social, economic, and socio-cultural factors; medical and health considerations; schools and education; public services and transportation; recreation; consumer goods; housing; and natural environment. *Mercer, "Mercer 2019 Quality of Living Survey," March 13, 2019*

- Honolulu appeared on *Travel + Leisure's* list of "The 15 Best Cities in the United States." The city was ranked #5. Criteria: sights/landmarks; culture; food; friendliness; shopping; and overall value. *Travel + Leisure, "The World's Best Awards 2022" July 12, 2022*

- For its 35th annual "Readers' Choice Awards" survey, *Condé Nast Traveler* ranked its readers' favorite cities in the U.S. Whether it be a longed-for visit or a first on the list, these are the places that inspired a return to travel. The list was broken into large cities and cities under 250,000. Honolulu ranked #2 in the big city category. *Condé Nast Traveler, Readers' Choice Awards 2022, "Best Big Cities in the U.S." October 4, 2022*

Business/Finance Rankings

- The Brookings Institution ranked the nation's largest cities based on income inequality. Honolulu was ranked #54 (#1 = greatest inequality). Criteria: the "95/20 ratio," a figure representing the income at which a household earns more than 95 percent of all other households, divided by the income at which a household earns more than only 20 percent of all other households. *Brookings Institution, "Household Income Inequality, Largest Cities of 97 Large U.S. Metro Areas, 2014-2016," February 5, 2018*

- The Brookings Institution ranked the 100 largest metro areas in the U.S. based on income inequality. Honolulu was ranked #79 (#1 = greatest inequality). Criteria: the "95/20 ratio," a figure representing the income at which a household earns more than 95 percent of all other households, divided by the income at which a household earns more than only 20 percent of all other households. *Brookings Institution, "Household Income Inequality, 100 Largest U.S. Metro Areas, 2014-2016," February 5, 2018*

- For its annual survey of the "Most Expensive U.S. Cities to Live In," Kiplinger applied Cost of Living Index statistics developed by the Council for Community and Economic Research to U.S. Census Bureau population and median household income data for 265 urban areas. Honolulu ranked #2 among the most expensive in the country. *Kiplinger.com, "The 11 Most Expensive Cities to Live in the U.S.," April 15, 2023*

- The Honolulu metro area appeared on the Milken Institute "2022 Best Performing Cities" list. Rank: #191 out of 200 large metro areas (population over 250,000). Criteria: job growth; wage and salary growth; high-tech output growth; housing affordability; household broadband access. *Milken Institute, "Best-Performing Cities 2022," March 28, 2022*

- *Forbes* ranked the 200 most populous metro areas to determine the nation's "Best Places for Business and Careers." The Honolulu metro area was ranked #162. Criteria: costs (business and living); job growth (past and projected); income growth; quality of life; educational attainment (college and high school); projected economic growth; cultural and leisure opportunities; workplace tolerance laws; net migration patterns. *Forbes, "The Best Places for Business and Careers 2019: Seattle Still On Top," October 30, 2019*

- Mercer Human Resources Consulting ranked 227 cities worldwide in terms of cost-of-living. Honolulu ranked #20 (the lower the ranking, the higher the cost-of-living). The survey measured the comparative cost of over 200 items (such as housing, food, clothing, domestic supplies, transportation, and recreation/entertainment) in each location. *Mercer, "2022 Cost of Living City Ranking," June 29, 2022*

Education Rankings

- Personal finance website *WalletHub* analyzed the 150 largest U.S. metropolitan statistical areas to determine where the most educated Americans are putting their degrees to work. Criteria: education levels; percentage of workers with degrees; education quality and attainment gap; public school quality rankings; quality and enrollment of each metro area's universities. Honolulu was ranked #29 (#1 = most educated city). *www.WalletHub.com, "Most & Least Educated Cities in America," July 18, 2022*

- Honolulu was selected as one of America's most literate cities. The city ranked #30 out of the 84 largest U.S. cities. Criteria: number of booksellers; library resources; Internet resources; educational attainment; periodical publishing resources; newspaper circulation. *Central Connecticut State University, "America's Most Literate Cities, 2018," February 2019*

Environmental Rankings

- Honolulu was highlighted as one of the cleanest metro areas for ozone air pollution in the U.S. during 2019 through 2021. The list represents cities with no monitored ozone air pollution in unhealthful ranges. *American Lung Association, "State of the Air 2023," April 19, 2023*

- Honolulu was highlighted as one of the top 25 cleanest metro areas for year-round particle pollution (Annual PM 2.5) in the U.S. during 2019 through 2021. The area ranked #1. *American Lung Association, "State of the Air 2023," April 19, 2023*

- Honolulu was highlighted as one of the top 59 cleanest metro areas for short-term particle pollution (24-hour PM 2.5) in the U.S. during 2019 through 2021. Monitors in these cities reported no days with unhealthful PM 2.5 levels. *American Lung Association, "State of the Air 2023," April 19, 2023*

Health/Fitness Rankings

- For each of the 100 largest cities in the United States, the American Fitness Index®, compiled in partnership between the American College of Sports Medicine and the Elevance Health Foundation, evaluated community infrastructure and 34 health behaviors including preventive health, levels of chronic disease conditions, food insecurity, sleep quality, pedestrian safety, air quality, and community/environment resources that support physical activity. Honolulu ranked #22 for "community fitness." *americanfitnessindex.org, "2022 ACSM American Fitness Index Summary Report," July 12, 2022*

- The Sharecare Community Well-Being Index evaluates 10 individual and social health factors in order to measure what matters to Americans in the communities in which they live. The Honolulu metro area ranked #6 in the top 10 across all 10 domains. Criteria: access to healthcare, food, and community resources; housng and transportation; economic security; feeling of purpose; physical, financial, social, and community well-being. *www.sharecare.com, "Community Well-Being Index: 2020 Metro Area & County Rankings Report," August 30, 2021*

Real Estate Rankings

- *WalletHub* compared the most populated U.S. cities to determine which had the best markets for real estate agents. Honolulu ranked #41 where demand was high and pay was the best. Criteria: sales per agent; annual median wage for real-estate agents; monthly average starting salary for real estate agents; real estate job density and competition; unemployment rate; home turnover rate; housing-market health index; and other relevant metrics. *www.WalletHub.com, "2021 Best Places to Be a Real Estate Agent," May 12, 2021*

- The Honolulu metro area was identified as one of the 20 least affordable housing markets in the U.S. in 2022. The area ranked #183 out of 186 markets. Criteria: qualification for a mortgage loan with a 10 percent down payment on a typical home. *National Association of Realtors®, Qualifying Income Based on Sales Price of Existing Single-Family Homes for Metropolitan Areas, 2022*

- Honolulu was ranked #166 out of 235 metro areas in terms of housing affordability in 2022 by the National Association of Home Builders (#1 = most affordable). Criteria: the share of homes sold in that area affordable to a family earning the local median income, based on standard mortgage underwriting criteria. *National Association of Home Builders®, NAHB-Wells Fargo Housing Opportunity Index, 4th Quarter 2022*

Safety Rankings

- Allstate ranked the 200 largest cities in America in terms of driver safety. Honolulu ranked #94. Criteria: internal property damage claims over a two-year period from January 2016 to December 2017. The report helps increase the importance of safety and awareness behind the wheel. *Allstate, "Allstate America's Best Drivers Report, 2019" June 24, 2019*

- The National Insurance Crime Bureau ranked 390 metro areas in the U.S. in terms of per capita rates of vehicle theft. The Honolulu metro area ranked #78 (#1 = highest rate). Criteria: number of vehicle theft offenses per 100,000 inhabitants in 2021. *National Insurance Crime Bureau, "Hot Spots 2021," September 1, 2022*

Seniors/Retirement Rankings

- From its Best Cities for Successful Aging indexes, the Milken Institute generated rankings for metropolitan areas, weighing data in nine categories—health care, wellness, living arrangements, transportation and convenience, financial characteristics, education, employment, community engagement, and overall livability. The Honolulu metro area was ranked #24 overall in the large metro area category. *Milken Institute, "Best Cities for Successful Aging, 2017" March 14, 2017*

Transportation Rankings

- Honolulu was identified as one of the most congested metro areas in the U.S. The area ranked #7 out of 10. Criteria: yearly delay per auto commuter in hours. *Texas A&M Transportation Institute, "2021 Urban Mobility Report," June 2021*

Women/Minorities Rankings

- Personal finance website *WalletHub* compared more than 180 U.S. cities across two key dimensions, "Hispanic Business-Friendliness" and "Hispanic Purchasing Power," to arrive at the most favorable conditions for Hispanic entrepreneurs. Honolulu was ranked #151 out of 182. Criteria includes: share of Hispanic-Owned Businesses; Hispanic entrepreneurship rate to median annual income of Hispanics; Small Business-Friendliness score; cost of living; and number of Hispanics with at least a bachelor's degree. *WalletHub.com, "2019's Best Cities for Hispanic Entrepreneurs," May 1, 2019*

Miscellaneous Rankings

- *MoveHub* ranked 446 hipster cities across 20 countries, using its new and improved *alternative* Hipster Index and Honolulu came out as #45 among the top 50. Criteria: population over 150,000; number of vintage boutiques; density of tattoo parlors; vegan places to eat; coffee shops; and density of vinyl record stores. *www.movehub.com, "The Hipster Index: Brighton Pips Portland to Global Top Spot," July 28, 2021*

- In *Condé Nast Traveler* magazine's 2022 Readers' Choice Survey, Honolulu made the top ten list of friendliest American cities. Honolulu ranked #4. *www.cntraveler.com, "The 10 Friendliest Cities in the U.S.," December 20, 2022*

- The financial planning site SmartAsset has compiled its annual study on the best places for Halloween in the U.S. for 2022. 146 cities were compared to determine that Honolulu ranked #28 out of 35 for still being able to enjoy the festivities despite COVID-19. Metrics included: safety, family-friendliness, percentage of children in the population, concentration of candy and costume shops, weather and COVID infection rates. *www.smartasset.com, "2022 Edition-Best Places to Celebrate Halloween," October 19, 2022*

- Honolulu was selected as one of "America's Friendliest Cities." The city ranked #19 in the "Friendliest" category. Respondents to an online survey were asked to rate 38 top urban destinations in the United States as to general friendliness, as well as manners, politeness and warm disposition. *Travel + Leisure, "America's Friendliest Cities," October 20, 2017*

Business Environment

DEMOGRAPHICS

Population Growth

Area	1990 Census	2000 Census	2010 Census	2020 Census	Population Growth (%) 1990-2020	Population Growth (%) 2010-2020
City	376,465	371,657	337,256	350,964	-6.8	4.1
MSA[1]	836,231	876,156	953,207	1,016,508	21.6	6.6
U.S.	248,709,873	281,421,906	308,745,538	331,449,281	33.3	7.4

Note: (1) Figures cover the Urban Honolulu, HI Metropolitan Statistical Area
Source: U.S. Census Bureau, 1990 Census, 2000 Census, 2010 Census, 2020 Census

Race

Area	White Alone[2] (%)	Black Alone[2] (%)	Asian Alone[2] (%)	AIAN[3] Alone[2] (%)	NHOPI[4] Alone[2] (%)	Other Race Alone[2] (%)	Two or More Races (%)
City	16.4	1.7	52.9	0.2	9.2	1.3	18.2
MSA[1]	18.5	2.0	43.0	0.2	10.0	1.7	24.5
U.S.	61.6	12.4	6.0	1.1	0.2	8.4	10.2

Note: (1) Figures cover the Urban Honolulu, HI Metropolitan Statistical Area; (2) Alone is defined as not being in combination with one or more other races; (3) American Indian and Alaska Native; (4) Native Hawaiian and Other Pacific Islander
Source: U.S. Census Bureau, 2020 Census

Hispanic or Latino Origin

Area	Total (%)	Mexican (%)	Puerto Rican (%)	Cuban (%)	Other (%)
City	7.2	2.2	2.0	0.1	2.8
MSA[1]	10.2	3.2	3.5	0.1	3.5
U.S.	18.4	11.2	1.8	0.7	4.7

Note: Persons of Hispanic or Latino origin can be of any race; (1) Figures cover the Urban Honolulu, HI Metropolitan Statistical Area
Source: U.S. Census Bureau, 2017-2021 American Community Survey 5-Year Estimates

Age

Area	Under Age 5	Age 5–19	Age 20–34	Age 35–44	Age 45–54	Age 55–64	Age 65–74	Age 75–84	Age 85+	Median Age
City	4.5	14.3	20.5	13.0	12.7	13.7	11.5	6.0	3.6	42.9
MSA[1]	5.4	17.3	21.1	12.6	12.2	12.9	10.4	5.4	2.8	39.8
U.S.	5.6	19.2	20.2	12.7	12.4	13.1	10.0	4.9	1.9	38.8

Note: (1) Figures cover the Urban Honolulu, HI Metropolitan Statistical Area
Source: U.S. Census Bureau, 2020 Census

Disability by Age

Area	All Ages	Under 18 Years Old	18 to 64 Years Old	65 Years and Over
City	11.5	3.1	6.9	32.4
MSA[1]	11.2	3.0	7.5	33.0
U.S.	12.6	4.4	10.3	33.4

Note: Figures show percent of the civilian noninstitutionalized population that reported having a disability. Disability status is determined from six types of difficulty: vision, hearing, cognitive, ambulatory, self-care, and independent living. For children under 5 years old, hearing and vision difficulty are used to determine disability status. For children between the ages of 5 and 14, disability status is determined from hearing, vision, cognitive, ambulatory, and self-care difficulties. For people aged 15 years and older, they are considered to have a disability if they have difficulty with any one of the six difficulty types; Note: (1) Figures cover the Urban Honolulu, HI Metropolitan Statistical Area
Source: U.S. Census Bureau, 2017-2021 American Community Survey 5-Year Estimates

Ancestry

Area	German	Irish	English	American	Italian	Polish	French[2]	Scottish	Dutch
City	4.4	3.1	3.2	1.4	1.7	0.8	0.8	0.6	0.2
MSA[1]	5.2	3.9	3.7	1.3	1.9	0.8	1.1	0.8	0.4
U.S.	12.8	9.6	8.1	5.7	5.0	2.7	2.2	1.6	1.1

Note: Figures are the percentage of the total population reporting a particular ancestry. The nine most commonly reported ancestries in the U.S. are shown. Figures include multiple ancestries (e.g. if a person reported being Irish and Italian, they were included in both columns); (1) Figures cover the Urban Honolulu, HI Metropolitan Statistical Area; (2) Excludes Basque
Source: U.S. Census Bureau, 2017-2021 American Community Survey 5-Year Estimates

Foreign-born Population

Area	Percent of Population Born in								
	Any Foreign Country	Asia	Mexico	Europe	Caribbean	Central America[2]	South America	Africa	Canada
City	27.5	22.9	0.2	0.9	0.2	0.1	0.2	0.2	0.2
MSA[1]	19.5	15.7	0.2	0.7	0.2	0.1	0.2	0.2	0.2
U.S.	13.6	4.2	3.3	1.5	1.4	1.1	1.1	0.8	0.2

Note: (1) Figures cover the Urban Honolulu, HI Metropolitan Statistical Area; (2) Excludes Mexico.
Source: U.S. Census Bureau, 2017-2021 American Community Survey 5-Year Estimates

Household Size

Area	Persons in Household (%)							Average Household Size
	One	Two	Three	Four	Five	Six	Seven or More	
City	34.9	30.5	14.1	10.6	5.0	2.2	2.8	2.50
MSA[1]	24.6	30.5	16.6	13.4	7.2	3.8	4.0	3.00
U.S.	28.1	33.8	15.5	12.9	6.0	2.3	1.4	2.60

Note: (1) Figures cover the Urban Honolulu, HI Metropolitan Statistical Area
Source: U.S. Census Bureau, 2017-2021 American Community Survey 5-Year Estimates

Household Relationships

Area	House-holder	Opposite-sex Spouse	Same-sex Spouse	Opposite-sex Unmarried Partner	Same-sex Unmarried Partner	Child[2]	Grand-child	Other Relatives	Non-relatives
City	39.1	15.0	0.3	2.4	0.2	22.2	3.1	9.1	5.6
MSA[1]	33.1	16.3	0.2	1.9	0.1	26.2	4.5	9.2	4.9
U.S.	38.3	17.5	0.2	2.5	0.2	28.3	2.4	4.8	3.4

Note: Figures are percent of the total population; (1) Figures cover the Urban Honolulu, HI Metropolitan Statistical Area; (2) Includes biological, adopted, and stepchildren of the householder
Source: U.S. Census Bureau, 2020 Census

Gender

Area	Males	Females	Males per 100 Females
City	172,783	178,181	97.0
MSA[1]	509,569	506,939	100.5
U.S.	162,685,811	168,763,470	96.4

Note: (1) Figures cover the Urban Honolulu, HI Metropolitan Statistical Area
Source: U.S. Census Bureau, 2020 Census

Marital Status

Area	Never Married	Now Married[2]	Separated	Widowed	Divorced
City	37.5	44.7	1.1	6.7	10.0
MSA[1]	34.4	49.7	1.2	6.0	8.7
U.S.	33.8	48.0	1.8	5.6	10.8

Note: Figures are percentages and cover the population 15 years of age and older; (1) Figures cover the Urban Honolulu, HI Metropolitan Statistical Area; (2) Excludes separated
Source: U.S. Census Bureau, 2017-2021 American Community Survey 5-Year Estimates

Religious Groups by Family

Area	Catholic	Baptist	Methodist	LDS[2]	Pentecostal	Lutheran	Islam	Adventist	Other
MSA[1]	18.0	1.4	0.5	4.1	2.6	0.2	<0.1	1.9	9.8
U.S.	18.7	7.3	3.0	2.0	1.8	1.7	1.3	1.3	11.6

Note: Figures are the number of adherents as a percentage of the total population and cover the eight largest religious groups in the U.S; (1) Figures cover the Urban Honolulu, HI Metropolitan Statistical Area; (2) Church of Jesus Christ of Latter-day Saints
Sources: 2020 U.S. Religion Census, Association of Statisticians of American Religious Bodies; The Association of Religion Data Archives (ARDA)

Religious Groups by Tradition

Area	Catholic	Evangelical Protestant	Mainline Protestant	Black Protestant	Islam	Judaism	Hinduism	Orthodox	Buddhism
MSA[1]	18.0	8.1	2.3	0.2	<0.1	0.1	0.2	<0.1	4.0
U.S.	18.7	16.5	5.2	2.3	1.3	0.6	0.4	0.4	0.3

Note: Figures are the number of adherents as a percentage of the total population; (1) Figures cover the Urban Honolulu, HI Metropolitan Statistical Area
Sources: 2020 U.S. Religion Census, Association of Statisticians of American Religious Bodies; The Association of Religion Data Archives (ARDA)

ECONOMY

Gross Metropolitan Product

Area	2020	2021	2022	2023	Rank[2]
MSA[1]	62.1	66.8	74.3	80.2	56

Note: Figures are in billions of dollars; (1) Figures cover the Urban Honolulu, HI Metropolitan Statistical Area; (2) Rank is based on 2021 data and ranges from 1 to 381
Source: U.S. Conference of Mayors, U.S. Metro Economies: U.S. Metros Compared to Global and State Economies, June 2022

Economic Growth

Area	2018-20 (%)	2021 (%)	2022 (%)	2023 (%)	Rank[2]
MSA[1]	-5.4	3.6	5.2	4.6	376
U.S.	-0.6	5.7	3.1	2.9	–

Note: Figures are real gross metropolitan product (GMP) growth rates and represent average annual percent change; (1) Figures cover the Urban Honolulu, HI Metropolitan Statistical Area; (2) Rank is based on 2020 2-year average annual percent change and ranges from 1 to 381
Source: U.S. Conference of Mayors, U.S. Metro Economies: U.S. Metros Compared to Global and State Economies, June 2022

Metropolitan Area Exports

Area	2016	2017	2018	2019	2020	2021	Rank[2]
MSA[1]	330.3	393.6	438.9	308.6	169.0	164.3	319

Note: Figures are in millions of dollars; (1) Figures cover the Urban Honolulu, HI Metropolitan Statistical Area; (2) Rank is based on 2021 data and ranges from 1 to 388
Source: U.S. Department of Commerce, International Trade Administration, Office of Trade and Economic Analysis, Industry and Analysis, Exports by Metropolitan Area, data extracted March 16, 2023

Building Permits

Area	Single-Family			Multi-Family			Total		
	2021	2022	Pct. Chg.	2021	2022	Pct. Chg.	2021	2022	Pct. Chg.
City	n/a	n/a	n/a	n/a	n/a	n/a	n/a	n/a	n/a
MSA[1]	938	652	-30.5	500	1,901	280.2	1,438	2,553	77.5
U.S.	1,115,400	975,600	-12.5	621,600	689,500	10.9	1,737,000	1,665,100	-4.1

Note: (1) Figures cover the Urban Honolulu, HI Metropolitan Statistical Area; Figures represent new, privately-owned housing units authorized (unadjusted data); All permit data are based on estimates with imputation
Source: U.S. Census Bureau, Manufacturing, Mining, and Construction Statistics, Building Permits, 2021, 2022

Bankruptcy Filings

Area	Business Filings			Nonbusiness Filings		
	2021	2022	% Chg.	2021	2022	% Chg.
Honolulu County	28	35	25.0	830	671	-19.2
U.S.	14,347	13,481	-6.0	399,269	374,240	-6.3

Note: Business filings include Chapter 7, Chapter 9, Chapter 11, Chapter 12, Chapter 13, Chapter 15, and Section 304; Nonbusiness filings include Chapter 7, Chapter 11, and Chapter 13
Source: Administrative Office of the U.S. Courts, Business and Nonbusiness Bankruptcy, County Cases Commenced by Chapter of the Bankruptcy Code, During the 12-Month Period Ending December 31, 2021 and Business and Nonbusiness Bankruptcy, County Cases Commenced by Chapter of the Bankruptcy Code, During the 12-Month Period Ending December 31, 2022

Housing Vacancy Rates

Area	Gross Vacancy Rate[2] (%)			Year-Round Vacancy Rate[3] (%)			Rental Vacancy Rate[4] (%)			Homeowner Vacancy Rate[5] (%)		
	2020	2021	2022	2020	2021	2022	2020	2021	2022	2020	2021	2022
MSA[1]	10.0	10.6	10.6	9.6	10.1	10.0	5.5	5.1	5.7	1.0	0.6	0.6
U.S.	10.6	10.8	10.5	8.2	8.4	8.2	6.3	6.1	5.8	1.0	0.9	0.8

Note: (1) Figures cover the Urban Honolulu, HI Metropolitan Statistical Area; (2) The percentage of the total housing inventory that is vacant; (3) The percentage of the housing inventory (excluding seasonal units) that is year-round vacant; (4) The percentage of rental inventory that is vacant for rent; (5) The percentage of homeowner inventory that is vacant for sale
Source: U.S. Census Bureau, Housing Vacancies and Homeownership Annual Statistics: 2020, 2021, 2022

INCOME

Income

Area	Per Capita ($)	Median Household ($)	Average Household ($)
City	41,571	76,495	105,724
MSA[1]	40,339	92,600	118,470
U.S.	37,638	69,021	97,196

Note: (1) Figures cover the Urban Honolulu, HI Metropolitan Statistical Area
Source: U.S. Census Bureau, 2017-2021 American Community Survey 5-Year Estimates

Household Income Distribution

Area	Percent of Households Earning							
	Under $15,000	$15,000 -$24,999	$25,000 -$34,999	$35,000 -$49,999	$50,000 -$74,999	$75,000 -$99,999	$100,000 -$149,999	$150,000 and up
City	9.1	6.3	6.1	11.0	16.5	13.2	17.1	20.6
MSA[1]	6.5	4.5	5.4	9.0	14.7	13.5	20.0	26.3
U.S.	9.4	7.8	8.2	11.4	16.8	12.8	16.3	17.3

Note: (1) Figures cover the Urban Honolulu, HI Metropolitan Statistical Area
Source: U.S. Census Bureau, 2017-2021 American Community Survey 5-Year Estimates

Poverty Rate

Area	All Ages	Under 18 Years Old	18 to 64 Years Old	65 Years and Over
City	11.0	13.3	10.4	10.8
MSA[1]	8.6	11.0	7.9	8.0
U.S.	12.6	17.0	11.8	9.6

Note: Figures are percentage of people whose income during the past 12 months was below the poverty level;
(1) Figures cover the Urban Honolulu, HI Metropolitan Statistical Area
Source: U.S. Census Bureau, 2017-2021 American Community Survey 5-Year Estimates

EMPLOYMENT

Labor Force and Employment

Area	Civilian Labor Force			Workers Employed		
	Dec. 2021	Dec. 2022	% Chg.	Dec. 2021	Dec. 2022	% Chg.
City	459,370	457,096	-0.5	440,467	441,407	0.2
MSA[1]	459,370	457,096	-0.5	440,467	441,407	0.2
U.S.	161,696,000	164,224,000	1.6	155,732,000	158,872,000	2.0

Note: Data is not seasonally adjusted and covers workers 16 years of age and older; (1) Figures cover the
Urban Honolulu, HI Metropolitan Statistical Area
Source: Bureau of Labor Statistics, Local Area Unemployment Statistics

Unemployment Rate

Area	2022											
	Jan.	Feb.	Mar.	Apr.	May	Jun.	Jul.	Aug.	Sep.	Oct.	Nov.	Dec.
City	3.7	3.5	3.2	3.3	3.4	3.9	3.5	3.4	3.3	3.4	3.8	3.4
MSA[1]	3.7	3.5	3.2	3.3	3.4	3.9	3.5	3.4	3.3	3.4	3.8	3.4
U.S.	4.4	4.1	3.8	3.3	3.4	3.8	3.8	3.8	3.3	3.4	3.4	3.3

Note: Data is not seasonally adjusted and covers workers 16 years of age and older; (1) Figures cover the
Urban Honolulu, HI Metropolitan Statistical Area
Source: Bureau of Labor Statistics, Local Area Unemployment Statistics

Average Wages

Occupation	$/Hr.	Occupation	$/Hr.
Accountants and Auditors	35.01	Maintenance and Repair Workers	25.25
Automotive Mechanics	25.53	Marketing Managers	59.72
Bookkeepers	23.01	Network and Computer Systems Admin.	44.72
Carpenters	40.03	Nurses, Licensed Practical	27.07
Cashiers	15.19	Nurses, Registered	55.38
Computer Programmers	40.35	Nursing Assistants	19.29
Computer Systems Analysts	44.09	Office Clerks, General	20.72
Computer User Support Specialists	29.83	Physical Therapists	49.00
Construction Laborers	32.93	Physicians	132.28
Cooks, Restaurant	19.44	Plumbers, Pipefitters and Steamfitters	37.07
Customer Service Representatives	20.16	Police and Sheriff's Patrol Officers	43.41
Dentists	n/a	Postal Service Mail Carriers	26.72
Electricians	43.15	Real Estate Sales Agents	26.75
Engineers, Electrical	50.24	Retail Salespersons	17.85
Fast Food and Counter Workers	13.92	Sales Representatives, Technical/Scientific	54.70
Financial Managers	65.00	Secretaries, Exc. Legal/Medical/Executive	23.30
First-Line Supervisors of Office Workers	29.47	Security Guards	17.09
General and Operations Managers	57.59	Surgeons	205.79
Hairdressers/Cosmetologists	15.94	Teacher Assistants, Exc. Postsecondary*	16.06
Home Health and Personal Care Aides	15.75	Teachers, Secondary School, Exc. Sp. Ed.*	29.35
Janitors and Cleaners	16.29	Telemarketers	16.92
Landscaping/Groundskeeping Workers	19.21	Truck Drivers, Heavy/Tractor-Trailer	26.64
Lawyers	50.95	Truck Drivers, Light/Delivery Services	21.01
Maids and Housekeeping Cleaners	23.06	Waiters and Waitresses	16.89

Note: Wage data covers the Urban Honolulu, HI Metropolitan Statistical Area; (*) Hourly wages were
calculated from annual wage data based on a 40 hour work week; n/a not available.
Source: Bureau of Labor Statistics, Metro Area Occupational Employment & Wage Estimates, May 2022

Employment by Industry

Sector	MSA[1]		U.S.
	Number of Employees	Percent of Total	Percent of Total
Construction, Mining, and Logging	28,500	6.2	5.4
Private Education and Health Services	66,400	14.5	16.1
Financial Activities	21,500	4.7	5.9
Government	96,200	21.0	14.5
Information	7,400	1.6	2.0
Leisure and Hospitality	70,000	15.3	10.3
Manufacturing	9,400	2.1	8.4
Other Services	20,300	4.4	3.7
Professional and Business Services	56,100	12.2	14.7
Retail Trade	44,300	9.7	10.2
Transportation, Warehousing, and Utilities	24,800	5.4	4.9
Wholesale Trade	13,600	3.0	3.9

Note: Figures are non-farm employment as of December 2022. Figures are not seasonally adjusted and include workers 16 years of age and older; (1) Figures cover the Urban Honolulu, HI Metropolitan Statistical Area
Source: Bureau of Labor Statistics, Current Employment Statistics, Employment, Hours, and Earnings

Employment by Occupation

Occupation Classification	City (%)	MSA[1] (%)	U.S. (%)
Management, Business, Science, and Arts	39.3	38.5	40.3
Natural Resources, Construction, and Maintenance	6.1	8.6	8.7
Production, Transportation, and Material Moving	8.8	9.2	13.1
Sales and Office	23.5	23.2	20.9
Service	22.3	20.6	17.0

Note: Figures cover employed civilians 16 years of age and older; (1) Figures cover the Urban Honolulu, HI Metropolitan Statistical Area
Source: U.S. Census Bureau, 2017-2021 American Community Survey 5-Year Estimates

Occupations with Greatest Projected Employment Growth: 2021 – 2023

Occupation[1]	2021 Employment	2023 Projected Employment	Numeric Employment Change	Percent Employment Change
Maids and Housekeeping Cleaners	8,640	12,800	4,160	48.1
Waiters and Waitresses	12,200	16,160	3,960	32.5
Fast Food and Counter Workers	15,100	18,160	3,060	20.3
Cooks, Restaurant	7,110	9,750	2,640	37.1
Retail Salespersons	19,600	22,020	2,420	12.3
First-Line Supervisors of Food Preparation and Serving Workers	5,130	6,410	1,280	25.0
Food Preparation Workers	7,590	8,870	1,280	16.9
Security Guards	7,830	9,040	1,210	15.5
Dining Room and Cafeteria Attendants and Bartender Helpers	2,850	4,020	1,170	41.1
Maintenance and Repair Workers, General	5,940	7,110	1,170	19.7

Note: Projections cover Hawaii; Projections for 2022-2024 were not available at time of publication; (1) Sorted by numeric employment change
Source: www.projectionscentral.com, State Occupational Projections, 2021–2023 Short-Term Projections

Fastest-Growing Occupations: 2021 – 2023

Occupation[1]	2021 Employment	2023 Projected Employment	Numeric Employment Change	Percent Employment Change
Hotel, Motel, and Resort Desk Clerks	1,550	2,680	1,130	72.9
Locker Room, Coatroom, and Dressing Room Attendants	110	180	70	63.6
Baggage Porters and Bellhops	780	1,270	490	62.8
Concierges	540	820	280	51.9
Lodging Managers	340	510	170	50.0
Maids and Housekeeping Cleaners	8,640	12,800	4,160	48.1
Passenger Vehicle Drivers, Except Bus Drivers, Transit and Intercity	1,780	2,560	780	43.8
Captains, Mates, and Pilots of Water Vessels	400	570	170	42.5
Dining Room and Cafeteria Attendants and Bartender Helpers	2,850	4,020	1,170	41.1
Bartenders	2,080	2,890	810	38.9

Note: Projections cover Hawaii; Projections for 2022-2024 were not available at time of publication; (1) Sorted by percent employment change and excludes occupations with numeric employment change less than 50
Source: www.projectionscentral.com, State Occupational Projections, 2021–2023 Short-Term Projections

CITY FINANCES

City Government Finances

Component	2020 ($000)	2020 ($ per capita)
Total Revenues	3,528,224	3,533
Total Expenditures	3,728,253	3,733
Debt Outstanding	6,587,227	6,596
Cash and Securities[1]	3,432,255	3,437

Note: (1) Cash and security holdings of a government at the close of its fiscal year, including those of its dependent agencies, utilities, and liquor stores.
Source: U.S. Census Bureau, State & Local Government Finances 2020

City Government Revenue by Source

Source	2020 ($000)	2020 ($ per capita)	2020 (%)
General Revenue			
From Federal Government	162,127	162	4.6
From State Government	178,690	179	5.1
From Local Governments	3,157	3	0.1
Taxes			
Property	1,426,467	1,428	40.4
Sales and Gross Receipts	458,439	459	13.0
Personal Income	0	0	0.0
Corporate Income	0	0	0.0
Motor Vehicle License	177,650	178	5.0
Other Taxes	33,436	33	0.9
Current Charges	662,874	664	18.8
Liquor Store	0	0	0.0
Utility	278,553	279	7.9

Source: U.S. Census Bureau, State & Local Government Finances 2020

City Government Expenditures by Function

Function	2020 ($000)	2020 ($ per capita)	2020 (%)
General Direct Expenditures			
Air Transportation	0	0	0.0
Corrections	0	0	0.0
Education	0	0	0.0
Employment Security Administration	0	0	0.0
Financial Administration	49,003	49	1.3
Fire Protection	145,206	145	3.9
General Public Buildings	37,586	37	1.0
Governmental Administration, Other	89,768	89	2.4
Health	40,718	40	1.1
Highways	111,131	111	3.0
Hospitals	0	0	0.0
Housing and Community Development	118,299	118	3.2
Interest on General Debt	213,608	213	5.7
Judicial and Legal	32,527	32	0.9
Libraries	0	0	0.0
Parking	950	1	0.0
Parks and Recreation	147,313	147	4.0
Police Protection	323,419	323	8.7
Public Welfare	9,836	9	0.3
Sewerage	434,508	435	11.7
Solid Waste Management	247,353	247	6.6
Veterans' Services	0	0	0.0
Liquor Store	0	0	0.0
Utility	1,436,777	1,438	38.5

Source: U.S. Census Bureau, State & Local Government Finances 2020

TAXES

State Corporate Income Tax Rates

State	Tax Rate (%)	Income Brackets ($)	Num. of Brackets	Financial Institution Tax Rate (%)[a]	Federal Income Tax Ded.
Hawaii	4.4 - 6.4 (e)	25,000 - 100,001	3	7.92 (e)	No

Note: Tax rates as of January 1, 2023; (a) Rates listed are the corporate income tax rate applied to financial institutions or excise taxes based on income. Some states have other taxes based upon the value of deposits or shares; (e) Hawaii taxes capital gains at 4%. Financial institutions pay a franchise tax of 7.92% of taxable income (in lieu of the corporate income tax and general excise taxes).
Source: Federation of Tax Administrators, State Corporate Income Tax Rates, January 1, 2023

State Individual Income Tax Rates

State	Tax Rate (%)	Income Brackets ($)	Personal Exemptions ($)			Standard Ded. ($)	
			Single	Married	Depend.	Single	Married
Hawaii	1.4 - 11.0	2,400 - 200,000 (b)	1,144	2,288	1,144	2,200	4,400

Note: Tax rates as of January 1, 2023; Local- and county-level taxes are not included; Federal income tax is not deductible on state income tax returns; (b) For joint returns, taxes are twice the tax on half the couple's income.
Source: Federation of Tax Administrators, State Individual Income Tax Rates, January 1, 2023

Various State Sales and Excise Tax Rates

State	State Sales Tax (%)	Gasoline[1] ($/gal.)	Cigarette[2] ($/pack)	Spirits[3] ($/gal.)	Wine[4] ($/gal.)	Beer[5] ($/gal.)	Recreational Marijuana (%)
Hawaii	4	0.5535	3.20	5.98	1.38	0.93	Not legal

Note: All tax rates as of January 1, 2023; (1) The American Petroleum Institute has developed a methodology for determining the average tax rate on a gallon of fuel. Rates may include any of the following: excise taxes, environmental fees, storage tank fees, other fees or taxes, general sales tax, and local taxes; (2) The federal excise tax of $1.0066 per pack and local taxes are not included; (3) Rates are those applicable to off-premise sales of 40% alcohol by volume (a.b.v.) distilled spirits in 750ml containers. Local excise taxes are excluded; (4) Rates are those applicable to off-premise sales of 11% a.b.v. non-carbonated wine in 750ml containers; (5) Rates are those applicable to off-premise sales of 4.7% a.b.v. beer in 12 ounce containers.
Source: Tax Foundation, 2023 Facts & Figures: How Does Your State Compare?

State Business Tax Climate Index Rankings

State	Overall Rank	Corporate Tax Rank	Individual Income Tax Rank	Sales Tax Rank	Property Tax Rank	Unemployment Insurance Tax Rank
Hawaii	43	19	46	27	32	30

Note: The index is a measure of how each state's tax laws affect economic performance. The lower the rank, the more favorable a state's tax system is for business. States without a given tax are given a ranking of 1. The scores/rankings for the District of Columbia do not affect other states. The 2023 index represents the tax climate as of July 1, 2022.
Source: Tax Foundation, State Business Tax Climate Index 2023

TRANSPORTATION

Means of Transportation to Work

Area	Car/Truck/Van		Public Transportation			Bicycle	Walked	Other Means	Worked at Home
	Drove Alone	Car-pooled	Bus	Subway	Railroad				
City	57.7	13.1	9.4	0.0	0.0	1.6	8.2	3.6	6.4
MSA[1]	65.4	13.2	6.3	0.0	0.0	0.9	5.2	2.5	6.4
U.S.	73.2	8.6	2.0	1.6	0.5	0.5	2.5	1.5	9.7

Note: Figures are percentages and cover workers 16 years of age and older; (1) Figures cover the Urban Honolulu, HI Metropolitan Statistical Area
Source: U.S. Census Bureau, 2017-2021 American Community Survey 5-Year Estimates

Travel Time to Work

Area	Less Than 10 Minutes	10 to 19 Minutes	20 to 29 Minutes	30 to 44 Minutes	45 to 59 Minutes	60 to 89 Minutes	90 Minutes or More
City	8.7	38.2	22.6	20.6	5.0	3.6	1.2
MSA[1]	9.8	26.1	19.9	24.9	9.4	7.3	2.6
U.S.	12.4	28.5	21.0	20.9	8.2	6.2	2.9

Note: Note: Figures are percentages and include workers 16 years old and over; (1) Figures cover the Urban Honolulu, HI Metropolitan Statistical Area
Source: U.S. Census Bureau, 2017-2021 American Community Survey 5-Year Estimates

Key Congestion Measures

Measure	1990	2000	2010	2015	2020
Annual Hours of Delay, Total (000)	11,789	18,787	27,593	32,628	13,365
Annual Hours of Delay, Per Auto Commuter	31	44	55	60	24
Annual Congestion Cost, Per Auto Commuter ($)	849	1,023	1,191	1,302	562

Note: Covers the Honolulu HI urban area
Source: Texas A&M Transportation Institute, 2021 Urban Mobility Report

Freeway Travel Time Index

Measure	1985	1990	1995	2000	2005	2010	2015	2020
Urban Area Index[1]	1.18	1.23	1.28	1.32	1.37	1.38	1.40	1.11
Urban Area Rank[1,2]	8	4	4	4	3	3	4	20

Note: Freeway Travel Time Index—the ratio of travel time in the peak period to the travel time at free-flow conditions. For example, a value of 1.30 indicates a 20-minute free-flow trip takes 26 minutes in the peak (20 minutes x 1.30 = 26 minutes); (1) Covers the Honolulu HI urban area; (2) Rank is based on 101 larger urban areas (#1 = highest travel time index)
Source: Texas A&M Transportation Institute, 2021 Urban Mobility Report

Public Transportation

Agency Name / Mode of Transportation	Vehicles Operated in Maximum Service[1]	Annual Unlinked Passenger Trips[2] (in thous.)	Annual Passenger Miles[3] (in thous.)
City and County of Honolulu Dept. of Transportation Services (DTS)			
Bus (purchased transportation)	364	27,814.6	122,372.7
Demand Response (purchased transportation)	182	679.2	6,139.8
Demand Response - Taxi	79	47.5	357.0
Vanpool (purchased transportation)	58	173.3	4,161.6

Note: (1) Number of revenue vehicles operated by the given mode and type of service to meet the annual maximum service requirement. This is the revenue vehicle count during the peak season of the year; on the week and day that maximum service is provided. Vehicles operated in maximum service (VOMS) exclude atypical days and one-time special events; (2) Number of passengers who boarded public transportation vehicles. Passengers are counted each time they board a vehicle no matter how many vehicles they use to travel from their origin to their destination. (3) Sum of the distances ridden by all passengers during the entire fiscal year.
Source: Federal Transit Administration, National Transit Database, 2021

Air Transportation

Airport Name and Code / Type of Service	Passenger Airlines[1]	Passenger Enplanements	Freight Carriers[2]	Freight (lbs)
Honolulu International (HNL)				
Domestic service (U.S. carriers - 2022)	14	8,120,619	16	406,111,193
International service (U.S. carriers - 2021)	4	25,232	8	152,947,370

Note: (1) Includes all U.S.-based major, minor and commuter airlines that carried at least one passenger during the year; (2) Includes all U.S.-based airlines and freight carriers that transported at least one pound of freight during the year.
Source: Bureau of Transportation Statistics, The Intermodal Transportation Database, Air Carriers: T-100 Domestic Market (U.S. Carriers), 2022; Bureau of Transportation Statistics, The Intermodal Transportation Database, Air Carriers: T-100 International Market (U.S. Carriers), 2021

BUSINESSES

Major Business Headquarters

Company Name	Industry	Rankings	
		Fortune[1]	Forbes[2]
No companies listed	-	-	-

Note: (1) Companies that produce a 10-K are ranked 1 to 500 based on 2021 revenue; (2) All private companies with at least $2 billion in annual revenue through the end of their most current fiscal year are ranked 1 to 246; companies listed are headquartered in the city; dashes indicate no ranking
Source: Fortune, "Fortune 500," 2022; Forbes, "America's Largest Private Companies," 2022

Fastest-Growing Businesses

According to *Inc.*, Honolulu is home to one of America's 500 fastest-growing private companies: **Malama Solar** (#41). Criteria: must be an independent, privately-held, for-profit, U.S. corporation, proprietorship or partnership as of December 31, 2021; revenues must be at least $100,000 in 2018 and $2 million in 2021; must have four-year operating/sales history. *Inc., "America's 500 Fastest-Growing Private Companies," 2022*

Living Environment

COST OF LIVING

Cost of Living Index

Composite Index	Groceries	Housing	Utilities	Trans-portation	Health Care	Misc. Goods/Services
184.1	149.9	314.3	142.1	125.5	117.6	127.3

Note: The Cost of Living Index measures regional differences in the cost of consumer goods and services, excluding taxes and non-consumer expenditures, for professional and managerial households in the top income quintile. It is based on more than 50,000 prices covering almost 60 different items for which prices are collected three times a year by chambers of commerce, economic development organizations or university applied economic centers in each participating urban area. The numbers shown should be read as a percentage above or below the national average of 100. For example, a value of 115.4 in the groceries column indicates that grocery prices are 15.4% higher than the national average. Small differences in the index numbers should not be interpreted as significant; Figures cover the Honolulu HI urban area.
Source: The Council for Community and Economic Research, Cost of Living Index, 2022

Grocery Prices

Area[1]	T-Bone Steak ($/pound)	Frying Chicken ($/pound)	Whole Milk ($/half gal.)	Eggs ($/dozen)	Orange Juice ($/64 oz.)	Coffee ($/11.5 oz.)
City[2]	18.12	2.74	4.32	4.32	5.31	8.59
Avg.	13.81	1.59	2.43	2.25	3.85	4.95
Min.	10.17	0.90	1.51	1.30	2.90	3.46
Max.	19.35	3.30	4.32	4.32	5.31	8.59

*Note: (1) Values for the local area are compared with the average, minimum and maximum values for all 286 areas in the Cost of Living Index; (2) Figures cover the Honolulu HI urban area; **T-Bone Steak** (price per pound); **Frying Chicken** (price per pound, whole fryer); **Whole Milk** (half gallon carton); **Eggs** (price per dozen, Grade A, large); **Orange Juice** (64 oz. Tropicana or Florida Natural); **Coffee** (11.5 oz. can, vacuum-packed, Maxwell House, Hills Bros, or Folgers).*
Source: The Council for Community and Economic Research, Cost of Living Index, 2022

Housing and Utility Costs

Area[1]	New Home Price ($)	Apartment Rent ($/month)	All Electric ($/month)	Part Electric ($/month)	Other Energy ($/month)	Telephone ($/month)
City[2]	1,605,915	3,589	309.47	-	-	182.54
Avg.	450,913	1,371	176.41	99.93	76.96	190.22
Min.	229,283	546	100.84	31.56	27.15	174.27
Max.	2,434,977	4,569	356.86	249.59	272.24	208.31

*Note: (1) Values for the local area are compared with the average, minimum and maximum values for all 286 areas in the Cost of Living Index; (2) Figures cover the Honolulu HI urban area; **New Home Price** (2,400 sf living area, 8,000 sf lot, in urban area with full utilities); **Apartment Rent** (950 sf 2 bedroom/1.5 or 2 bath, unfurnished, all utilities except water); **All Electric** (average monthly cost for an all-electric home); **Part Electric** (average monthly cost for a part-electric home); **Other Energy** (average monthly cost for natural gas, fuel oil, coal, wood, and any other forms of energy except electricity); **Telephone** (price includes the base monthly rate plus taxes and fees for three lines of mobile phone service).*
Source: The Council for Community and Economic Research, Cost of Living Index, 2022

Health Care, Transportation, and Other Costs

Area[1]	Doctor ($/visit)	Dentist ($/visit)	Optometrist ($/visit)	Gasoline ($/gallon)	Beauty Salon ($/visit)	Men's Shirt ($)
City[2]	168.32	97.93	209.95	5.03	75.67	53.63
Avg.	124.91	107.77	117.66	3.86	43.31	34.21
Min.	36.61	58.25	51.79	2.90	22.18	13.05
Max.	250.21	162.58	371.96	5.54	85.61	63.54

*Note: (1) Values for the local area are compared with the average, minimum and maximum values for all 286 areas in the Cost of Living Index; (2) Figures cover the Honolulu HI urban area; **Doctor** (general practitioners routine exam of an established patient); **Dentist** (adult teeth cleaning and periodic oral examination); **Optometrist** (full vision eye exam for established adult patient); **Gasoline** (one gallon regular unleaded, national brand, including all taxes, cash price at self-service pump if available); **Beauty Salon** (woman's shampoo, trim, and blow-dry); **Men's Shirt** (cotton/polyester dress shirt, pinpoint weave, long sleeves).*
Source: The Council for Community and Economic Research, Cost of Living Index, 2022

HOUSING

Homeownership Rate

Area	2015 (%)	2016 (%)	2017 (%)	2018 (%)	2019 (%)	2020 (%)	2021 (%)	2022 (%)
MSA[1]	59.6	57.9	53.8	57.7	59.0	56.9	55.9	57.7
U.S.	63.7	63.4	63.9	64.4	64.6	66.6	65.5	65.8

Note: (1) Figures cover the Urban Honolulu, HI Metropolitan Statistical Area
Source: U.S. Census Bureau, Housing Vacancies and Homeownership Annual Statistics: 2015-2022

House Price Index (HPI)

Area	National Ranking[2]	Quarterly Change (%)	One-Year Change (%)	Five-Year Change (%)	Since 1991Q1 (%)
MSA[1]	122	-5.39	11.51	33.52	222.93
U.S.[3]	–	0.34	8.41	58.44	289.08

Note: The HPI is a weighted repeat sales index. It measures average price changes in repeat sales or refinancings on the same properties. This information is obtained by reviewing repeat mortgage transactions on single-family properties whose mortgages have been purchased or securitized by Fannie Mae or Freddie Mac since January 1975; (1) Figures cover the Urban Honolulu, HI Metropolitan Statistical Area; (2) Rankings are based on annual percentage change for all metro areas containing at least 15,000 transactions over the last 10 years and ranges from 1 to 257; (3) figures based on a weighted average of Census Division estimates using a seasonally adjusted, purchase-only index; all figures are for the period ending December 31, 2022
Source: Federal Housing Finance Agency, Change in FHFA Metropolitan Area House Price Indexes, 2022Q4

Median Single-Family Home Prices

Area	2020	2021	2022[p]	Percent Change 2021 to 2022
MSA[1]	851.5	996.2	1,126.7	13.1
U.S. Average	300.2	357.1	392.6	9.9

Note: Figures are median sales prices of existing single-family homes in thousands of dollars; (p) preliminary; (1) Figures cover the Urban Honolulu, HI Metropolitan Statistical Area
Source: National Association of Realtors, Median Sales Price of Existing Single-Family Homes for Metropolitan Areas, 4th Quarter 2022

Qualifying Income Based on Median Sales Price of Existing Single-Family Homes

Area	With 5% Down ($)	With 10% Down ($)	With 20% Down ($)
MSA[1]	326,170	309,003	274,670
U.S. Average	112,234	106,237	94,513

Note: Figures are preliminary; Qualifying income is based on a mortgage rate of 6.77%. Monthly principal and interest payment is limited to 25% of income; (1) Figures cover the Urban Honolulu, HI Metropolitan Statistical Area
Source: National Association of Realtors, Qualifying Income Based on Median Sales Price of Existing Single-Family Homes for Metropolitan Areas, 4th Quarter 2022

Home Value

Area	Under $100,000	$100,000 -$199,999	$200,000 -$299,999	$300,000 -$399,999	$400,000 -$499,999	$500,000 -$999,999	$1,000,000 or more	Median ($)
City	1.6	1.6	5.5	11.7	10.7	41.2	27.6	726,000
MSA[1]	1.6	1.6	3.6	8.3	9.7	53.8	21.5	726,800
U.S.	16.2	24.2	20.1	13.6	8.3	13.6	4.1	244,900

Note: Figures are percentages except for median and cover owner-occupied housing units; (1) Figures cover the Urban Honolulu, HI Metropolitan Statistical Area
Source: U.S. Census Bureau, 2017-2021 American Community Survey 5-Year Estimates

Year Housing Structure Built

Area	2020 or Later	2010 -2019	2000 -2009	1990 -1999	1980 -1989	1970 -1979	1960 -1969	1950 -1959	1940 -1949	Before 1940	Median Year
City	0.1	6.0	6.8	8.2	9.8	26.1	21.0	11.9	5.2	5.0	1973
MSA[1]	0.1	6.7	9.7	11.8	12.4	24.3	17.9	10.1	3.8	3.1	1976
U.S.	0.2	7.3	13.6	13.6	13.2	14.8	10.3	10.0	4.7	12.2	1979

Note: Figures are percentages except for Median Year; Note: (1) Figures cover the Urban Honolulu, HI Metropolitan Statistical Area
Source: U.S. Census Bureau, 2017-2021 American Community Survey 5-Year Estimates

Gross Monthly Rent

Area	Under $500	$500 -$999	$1,000 -$1,499	$1,500 -$1,999	$2,000 -$2,499	$2,500 -$2,999	$3,000 and up	Median ($)
City	6.7	10.1	27.5	24.0	13.2	7.9	10.7	1,620
MSA[1]	5.4	8.4	20.9	20.8	15.0	12.0	17.6	1,870
U.S.	8.1	30.5	30.8	16.8	7.3	3.1	3.5	1,163

Note: Figures are percentages except for median; Gross rent is the contract rent plus the estimated average monthly cost of utilities (electricity, gas, and water and sewer) and fuels (oil, coal, kerosene, wood, etc.) if these are paid by the renter (or paid for the renter by someone else); (1) Figures cover the Urban Honolulu, HI Metropolitan Statistical Area
Source: U.S. Census Bureau, 2017-2021 American Community Survey 5-Year Estimates

HEALTH

Health Risk Factors

Category	MSA[1] (%)	U.S. (%)
Adults aged 18–64 who have any kind of health care coverage	n/a	90.9
Adults who reported being in good or better health	n/a	85.2
Adults who have been told they have high blood cholesterol	n/a	35.7
Adults who have been told they have high blood pressure	n/a	32.4
Adults who are current smokers	n/a	14.4
Adults who currently use e-cigarettes	n/a	6.7
Adults who currently use chewing tobacco, snuff, or snus	n/a	3.5
Adults who are heavy drinkers[2]	n/a	6.3
Adults who are binge drinkers[3]	n/a	15.4
Adults who are overweight (BMI 25.0 - 29.9)	n/a	34.4
Adults who are obese (BMI 30.0 - 99.8)	n/a	33.9
Adults who participated in any physical activities in the past month	n/a	76.3

Note: (1) Figures for the Urban Honolulu, HI Metropolitan Statistical Area were not available.
(2) Heavy drinkers are classified as adult men having more than 14 drinks per week and adult women having more than 7 drinks per week; (3) Binge drinkers are classified as males having five or more drinks on one occasion or females having four or more drinks on one occasion
Source: Centers for Disease Control and Prevention, Behavioral Risk Factor Surveillance System, SMART: Selected Metropolitan Area Risk Trends, 2021

Acute and Chronic Health Conditions

Category	MSA[1] (%)	U.S. (%)
Adults who have ever been told they had a heart attack	n/a	4.0
Adults who have ever been told they have angina or coronary heart disease	n/a	3.8
Adults who have ever been told they had a stroke	n/a	3.0
Adults who have ever been told they have asthma	n/a	14.9
Adults who have ever been told they have arthritis	n/a	25.8
Adults who have ever been told they have diabetes[2]	n/a	10.9
Adults who have ever been told they had skin cancer	n/a	6.6
Adults who have ever been told they had any other types of cancer	n/a	7.5
Adults who have ever been told they have COPD	n/a	6.1
Adults who have ever been told they have kidney disease	n/a	3.0
Adults who have ever been told they have a form of depression	n/a	20.5

Note: (1) Figures for the Urban Honolulu, HI Metropolitan Statistical Area were not available.
(2) Figures do not include pregnancy-related, borderline, or pre-diabetes
Source: Centers for Disease Control and Prevention, Behaviorial Risk Factor Surveillance System, SMART: Selected Metropolitan Area Risk Trends, 2021

Health Screening and Vaccination Rates

Category	MSA[1] (%)	U.S. (%)
Adults who have ever been tested for HIV	n/a	34.9
Adults who have had their blood cholesterol checked within the last five years	n/a	85.2
Adults aged 65+ who have had flu shot within the past year	n/a	68.6
Adults aged 65+ who have ever had a pneumonia vaccination	n/a	71.0

Note: (1) Figures for the Urban Honolulu, HI Metropolitan Statistical Area were not available.
Source: Centers for Disease Control and Prevention, Behaviorial Risk Factor Surveillance System, SMART: Selected Metropolitan Area Risk Trends, 2021

Disability Status

Category	MSA[1] (%)	U.S. (%)
Adults who reported being deaf	n/a	7.2
Are you blind or have serious difficulty seeing, even when wearing glasses?	n/a	4.8
Are you limited in any way in any of your usual activities due to arthritis?	n/a	11.1
Do you have difficulty doing errands alone?	n/a	7.0
Do you have difficulty dressing or bathing?	n/a	3.6
Do you have serious difficulty concentrating/remembering/making decisions?	n/a	12.1
Do you have serious difficulty walking or climbing stairs?	n/a	12.8

Note: (1) Figures for the Urban Honolulu, HI Metropolitan Statistical Area were not available.
Source: Centers for Disease Control and Prevention, Behaviorial Risk Factor Surveillance System, SMART: Selected Metropolitan Area Risk Trends, 2021

Mortality Rates for the Top 10 Causes of Death in the U.S.

ICD-10[a] Sub-Chapter	ICD-10[a] Code	Crude Mortality Rate[1] per 100,000 population	
		County[2]	U.S.
Malignant neoplasms	C00-C97	171.2	182.6
Ischaemic heart diseases	I20-I25	89.1	113.1
Other forms of heart disease	I30-I51	58.4	64.4
Other degenerative diseases of the nervous system	G30-G31	45.8	51.0
Cerebrovascular diseases	I60-I69	60.1	47.8
Other external causes of accidental injury	W00-X59	39.6	46.4
Chronic lower respiratory diseases	J40-J47	22.5	45.7
Organic, including symptomatic, mental disorders	F01-F09	61.4	35.9
Hypertensive diseases	I10-I15	34.5	35.0
Diabetes mellitus	E10-E14	23.1	29.6

Note: (a) ICD-10 = International Classification of Diseases 10th Revision; (1) Crude mortality rates are a three-year average covering 2019-2021; (2) Figures cover Honolulu County.
Source: Centers for Disease Control and Prevention, National Center for Health Statistics. National Vital Statistics System, Mortality 2018-2021 on CDC WONDER Online Database

Mortality Rates for Selected Causes of Death

ICD-10[a] Sub-Chapter	ICD-10[a] Code	Crude Mortality Rate[1] per 100,000 population	
		County[2]	U.S.
Assault	X85-Y09	3.0	7.0
Diseases of the liver	K70-K76	11.5	19.8
Human immunodeficiency virus (HIV) disease	B20-B24	0.8	1.5
Influenza and pneumonia	J09-J18	20.4	14.7
Intentional self-harm	X60-X84	12.1	14.3
Malnutrition	E40-E46	1.0	4.3
Obesity and other hyperalimentation	E65-E68	1.3	3.0
Renal failure	N17-N19	16.9	15.7
Transport accidents	V01-V99	6.4	13.6
Viral hepatitis	B15-B19	1.3	1.2

Note: (a) ICD-10 = International Classification of Diseases 10th Revision; (1) Crude mortality rates are a three-year average covering 2019-2021; (2) Figures cover Honolulu County; Data are suppressed when the data meet the criteria for confidentiality constraints; Crude mortality rates are flagged as unreliable when the rate would be calculated with a numerator of 20 or less.
Source: Centers for Disease Control and Prevention, National Center for Health Statistics. National Vital Statistics System, Mortality 2018-2021 on CDC WONDER Online Database

Health Insurance Coverage

Area	With Health Insurance	With Private Health Insurance	With Public Health Insurance	Without Health Insurance	Population Under Age 19 Without Health Insurance
City	96.0	76.9	36.2	4.0	1.9
MSA[1]	96.5	79.2	34.3	3.5	2.3
U.S.	91.2	67.8	35.4	8.8	5.3

Note: Figures are percentages that cover the civilian noninstitutionalized population; (1) Figures cover the Urban Honolulu, HI Metropolitan Statistical Area
Source: U.S. Census Bureau, 2017-2021 American Community Survey 5-Year Estimates

Number of Medical Professionals

Area	MDs[3]	DOs[3,4]	Dentists	Podiatrists	Chiropractors	Optometrists
County[1] (number)	3,560	164	972	36	204	248
County[1] (rate[2])	351.4	16.2	97.1	3.6	20.4	24.8
U.S. (rate[2])	289.3	23.5	72.5	6.2	28.7	17.4

Note: Data as of 2021 unless noted; (1) Data covers Honolulu County; (2) Rate per 100,000 population; (3) Data as of 2020 and includes all active, non-federal physicians; (4) Doctor of Osteopathic Medicine
Source: U.S. Department of Health and Human Services, Health Resources and Services Administration, Bureau of Health Professions, Area Resource File (ARF) 2021-2022

Best Hospitals

According to *U.S. News,* the Urban Honolulu, HI metro area is home to one of the best hospitals in the U.S.: **Queen's Medical Center** (3 adult specialties). The hospital listed was nationally ranked in at least one of 15 adult or 10 pediatric specialties. The number of specialties shown cover the parent hospital. Only 164 U.S. hospitals performed well enough to be nationally ranked in one or more specialties. Twenty hospitals in the U.S. made the Honor Roll. The Best Hospitals Honor Roll takes both the national rankings and the procedure and condition ratings into account. Hospitals received points if they were nationally ranked in one of the 15 adult specialties—the higher they ranked, the more points they got—and how many ratings of "high performing" they earned in the 17 procedures and conditions. *U.S. News Online, "America's Best Hospitals 2022-23"*

EDUCATION

Public School District Statistics

District Name	Schls	Pupils	Pupil/ Teacher Ratio	Minority Pupils[1] (%)	LEP/ELL[2] (%)	IEP[3] (%)
Hawaii Department of Education	294	173,178	14.4	88.7	9.1	11.1

Note: Table includes school districts with 2,000 or more students; (1) Percentage of students that are not non-Hispanic white; (2) Percentage of students that are Limited English Proficient or English Language Learners (2018-19); (3) Percentage of students that have an Individualized Education Program (2019-20). Source: U.S. Department of Education, National Center for Education Statistics, Common Core of Data, Local Education Agency (School District) Universe Survey: School Year 2021-2022

Highest Level of Education

Area	Less than H.S.	H.S. Diploma	Some College, No Deg.	Associate Degree	Bachelor's Degree	Master's Degree	Prof. School Degree	Doctorate Degree
City	9.6	23.1	18.1	10.8	24.0	9.1	3.1	2.1
MSA[1]	7.3	25.6	19.8	11.1	23.2	8.9	2.5	1.6
U.S.	11.1	26.5	20.0	8.7	20.6	9.3	2.2	1.5

Note: Figures cover persons age 25 and over; (1) Figures cover the Urban Honolulu, HI Metropolitan Statistical Area Source: U.S. Census Bureau, 2017-2021 American Community Survey 5-Year Estimates

Educational Attainment by Race

Area	High School Graduate or Higher (%)					Bachelor's Degree or Higher (%)				
	Total	White	Black	Asian	Hisp.[2]	Total	White	Black	Asian	Hisp.[2]
City	90.4	97.9	94.5	87.4	93.9	38.4	54.2	31.3	37.9	31.6
MSA[1]	92.7	97.6	97.1	90.3	95.1	36.2	50.0	33.8	37.4	28.7
U.S.	88.9	91.4	87.2	87.6	71.2	33.7	35.5	23.3	55.6	18.4

Note: Figures shown cover persons 25 years old and over; (1) Figures cover the Urban Honolulu, HI Metropolitan Statistical Area; (2) People of Hispanic origin can be of any race Source: U.S. Census Bureau, 2017-2021 American Community Survey 5-Year Estimates

School Enrollment by Grade and Control

Area	Preschool (%)		Kindergarten (%)		Grades 1 - 4 (%)		Grades 5 - 8 (%)		Grades 9 - 12 (%)	
	Public	Private	Public	Private	Public	Private	Public	Private	Public	Private
City	40.2	59.8	73.5	26.5	79.4	20.6	75.4	24.6	71.9	28.1
MSA[1]	38.4	61.6	78.3	21.7	82.6	17.4	79.3	20.7	75.9	24.1
U.S.	58.8	41.2	86.3	13.7	88.3	11.7	88.6	11.4	89.4	10.6

Note: Figures shown cover persons 3 years old and over; (1) Figures cover the Urban Honolulu, HI Metropolitan Statistical Area Source: U.S. Census Bureau, 2017-2021 American Community Survey 5-Year Estimates

Higher Education

Four-Year Colleges			Two-Year Colleges			Medical Schools[1]	Law Schools[2]	Voc/ Tech[3]
Public	Private Non-profit	Private For-profit	Public	Private Non-profit	Private For-profit			
2	4	2	4	0	2	0	0	2

Note: Figures cover institutions located within the Urban Honolulu, HI Metropolitan Statistical Area and include main campuses only; (1) includes schools accredited by the Liaison Committee on Medical Education and the American Osteopathic Association's Commission on Osteopathic College Accreditation; (2) includes ABA-accredited schools, schools with provisional ABA accreditation, and state accredited schools; (3) includes all schools with programs that are less than 2 years. Source: National Center for Education Statistics, Integrated Postsecondary Education System (IPEDS), 2021-22; Wikipedia, List of Medical Schools in the United States, accessed April 10, 2023; Wikipedia, List of Law Schools in the United States, accessed April 10, 2023

EMPLOYERS

Major Employers

Company Name	Industry
City and County of Honolulu	Civil service/commission government
First Hawaiin Bank	State commercial banks
Hawaii Dept of Health	Administration of public health programs
Hawaii Dept of Transportation	Administration of transportation
Hawaii Mediacal Services Assoc	Hospital & medical services plans
Hawaii Pacific Health	General medical & surgical hospitals
Hawaiian Telecom	Local & long distance telephone
KYO YA Hotels and Resorts	Hotels & motels
Mormon Church	Misc denominational church
OAHU transit Services	Bus line operations
St. Francis Healthcare Sys of Hawaii	Skilled nursing facility
State of Hawaii	State government
The Boeing Company	Airplanes, fixed or rotary wing
The Queens Medical Center	General medical & surgical hospitals
Trustess of the Estate of Bernice Bishop	Private elementary/secondary schools
University of Hawaii System	Colleges & universities

Note: Companies shown are located within the Urban Honolulu, HI Metropolitan Statistical Area.
Source: Hoovers.com; Wikipedia

PUBLIC SAFETY

Crime Rate

Area	Total Crime	Violent Crime Rate				Property Crime Rate		
		Murder	Rape[3]	Robbery	Aggrav. Assault	Burglary	Larceny -Theft	Motor Vehicle Theft
City	3,272.2	2.8	34.9	97.9	135.1	396.3	2,211.7	393.6
Suburbs[1]	n/a	n/a	n/a	n/a	n/a	n/a	n/a	n/a
Metro[2]	n/a	n/a	n/a	n/a	n/a	n/a	n/a	n/a
U.S.	2,510.4	5.1	42.6	81.8	250.4	340.5	1,569.2	220.8

Note: Figures are crimes per 100,000 population; (1) All areas within the metro area that are located outside the city limits; (2) Figures cover the Urban Honolulu, HI Metropolitan Statistical Area; n/a not available; (3) All figures shown were reported using the revised Uniform Crime Reporting (UCR) definition of rape; Due to the transition to the National Incident-Based Reporting System (NIBRS), limited city and metro area data was released for 2021.
Source: FBI Uniform Crime Reports, 2019 (data for 2020 was not available)

Hate Crimes

Area	Number of Quarters Reported	Number of Incidents per Bias Motivation					
		Race/Ethnicity/ Ancestry	Religion	Sexual Orientation	Disability	Gender	Gender Identity
City	4	31	0	5	0	0	0
U.S.	4	5,227	1,244	1,110	130	75	266

Note: Due to the transition to the National Incident-Based Reporting System (NIBRS), limited crime data was released for 2021.
Source: Federal Bureau of Investigation, Hate Crime Statistics 2020

Identity Theft Consumer Reports

Area	Reports	Reports per 100,000 Population	Rank[2]
MSA[1]	1,319	135	286
U.S.	1,108,609	339	-

Note: (1) Figures cover the Urban Honolulu, HI Metropolitan Statistical Area; (2) Rank ranges from 1 to 391 where 1 indicates greatest number of identity theft reports per 100,000 population
Source: Federal Trade Commission, Consumer Sentinel Network Data Book 2022

Fraud and Other Consumer Reports

Area	Reports	Reports per 100,000 Population	Rank[2]
MSA[1]	7,547	770	241
U.S.	4,064,520	1,245	-

Note: (1) Figures cover the Urban Honolulu, HI Metropolitan Statistical Area; (2) Rank ranges from 1 to 391 where 1 indicates greatest number of fraud and other consumer reports per 100,000 population
Source: Federal Trade Commission, Consumer Sentinel Network Data Book 2022

POLITICS

2020 Presidential Election Results

Area	Biden	Trump	Jorgensen	Hawkins	Other
Honolulu County	62.5	35.7	0.9	0.6	0.4
U.S.	51.3	46.8	1.2	0.3	0.5

Note: Results are percentages and may not add to 100% due to rounding
Source: Dave Leip's Atlas of U.S. Presidential Elections

SPORTS

Professional Sports Teams

Team Name	League	Year Established
No teams are located in the metro area		

Source: Wikipedia, Major Professional Sports Teams of the United States and Canada, April 12, 2023

CLIMATE

Average and Extreme Temperatures

Temperature	Jan	Feb	Mar	Apr	May	Jun	Jul	Aug	Sep	Oct	Nov	Dec	Yr.
Extreme High (°F)	87	88	89	89	93	92	92	93	94	94	93	89	94
Average High (°F)	80	80	81	82	84	86	87	88	88	86	84	81	84
Average Temp. (°F)	73	73	74	76	77	79	80	81	81	79	77	74	77
Average Low (°F)	66	66	67	69	70	72	73	74	73	72	70	67	70
Extreme Low (°F)	52	53	55	56	60	65	66	67	66	64	57	54	52

Note: Figures cover the years 1949-1990
Source: National Climatic Data Center, International Station Meteorological Climate Summary, 9/96

Average Precipitation/Snowfall/Humidity

Precip./Humidity	Jan	Feb	Mar	Apr	May	Jun	Jul	Aug	Sep	Oct	Nov	Dec	Yr.
Avg. Precip. (in.)	3.7	2.5	2.8	1.4	1.0	0.4	0.5	0.6	0.7	2.0	2.8	3.7	22.4
Avg. Snowfall (in.)	0	0	0	0	0	0	0	0	0	0	0	0	0
Avg. Rel. Hum. 5am (%)	82	80	78	77	76	75	75	75	76	78	79	80	78
Avg. Rel. Hum. 5pm (%)	66	64	62	61	60	58	58	58	60	63	66	66	62

Note: Figures cover the years 1949-1990; Tr = Trace amounts (<0.05 in. of rain; <0.5 in. of snow)
Source: National Climatic Data Center, International Station Meteorological Climate Summary, 9/96

Weather Conditions

Temperature			Daytime Sky			Precipitation		
32°F & below	45°F & below	90°F & above	Clear	Partly cloudy	Cloudy	0.01 inch or more precip.	0.1 inch or more snow/ice	Thunder-storms
0	0	23	25	286	54	98	0	7

Note: Figures are average number of days per year and cover the years 1949-1990
Source: National Climatic Data Center, International Station Meteorological Climate Summary, 9/96

HAZARDOUS WASTE

Superfund Sites

The Urban Honolulu, HI metro area is home to three sites on the EPA's Superfund National Priorities List: **Del Monte Corp. (Oahu Plantation)** (final); **Naval Computer and Telecommunications Area Master Station Eastern Pacific** (final); **Pearl Harbor Naval Complex** (final). There are a total of 1,165 Superfund sites with a status of proposed or final on the list in the U.S. *U.S. Environmental Protection Agency, National Priorities List, April 12, 2023*

AIR QUALITY

Air Quality Trends: Ozone

	1990	1995	2000	2005	2010	2015	2018	2019	2020	2021
MSA[1]	0.034	0.049	0.044	0.042	0.046	0.048	0.046	0.053	0.044	0.045
U.S.	0.087	0.089	0.081	0.080	0.072	0.067	0.069	0.065	0.065	0.067

Note: (1) Data covers the Urban Honolulu, HI Metropolitan Statistical Area. The values shown are the composite ozone concentration averages among trend sites based on the highest fourth daily maximum 8-hour concentration in parts per million. These trends are based on sites having an adequate record of monitoring data during the trend period. Data from exceptional events are included.
Source: U.S. Environmental Protection Agency, Air Quality Monitoring Information, "Air Quality Trends by City, 1990-2021"

Air Quality Index

Area	Percent of Days when Air Quality was...[2]					AQI Statistics[2]	
	Good	Moderate	Unhealthy for Sensitive Groups	Unhealthy	Very Unhealthy	Maximum	Median
MSA[1]	99.7	0.3	0.0	0.0	0.0	52	26

Note: (1) Data covers the Urban Honolulu, HI Metropolitan Statistical Area; (2) Based on 365 days with AQI data in 2021. Air Quality Index (AQI) is an index for reporting daily air quality. EPA calculates the AQI for five major air pollutants regulated by the Clean Air Act: ground-level ozone, particle pollution (aka particulate matter), carbon monoxide, sulfur dioxide, and nitrogen dioxide. The AQI runs from 0 to 500. The higher the AQI value, the greater the level of air pollution and the greater the health concern. There are six AQI categories: "Good" AQI is between 0 and 50. Air quality is considered satisfactory; "Moderate" AQI is between 51 and 100. Air quality is acceptable; "Unhealthy for Sensitive Groups" When AQI values are between 101 and 150, members of sensitive groups may experience health effects; "Unhealthy" When AQI values are between 151 and 200 everyone may begin to experience health effects; "Very Unhealthy" AQI values between 201 and 300 trigger a health alert; "Hazardous" AQI values over 300 trigger warnings of emergency conditions (not shown).
Source: U.S. Environmental Protection Agency, Air Quality Index Report, 2021

Air Quality Index Pollutants

Area	Percent of Days when AQI Pollutant was...[2]					
	Carbon Monoxide	Nitrogen Dioxide	Ozone	Sulfur Dioxide	Particulate Matter 2.5	Particulate Matter 10
MSA[1]	0.3	0.8	83.8	(3)	11.5	3.6

Note: (1) Data covers the Urban Honolulu, HI Metropolitan Statistical Area; (2) Based on 365 days with AQI data in 2021. The Air Quality Index (AQI) is an index for reporting daily air quality. EPA calculates the AQI for five major air pollutants regulated by the Clean Air Act: ground-level ozone, particle pollution (also known as particulate matter), carbon monoxide, sulfur dioxide, and nitrogen dioxide. The AQI runs from 0 to 500. The higher the AQI value, the greater the level of air pollution and the greater the health concern; (3) Sulfur dioxide is no longer included in this table (as of December 8, 2021) because SO_2 concentrations tend to be very localized and not necessarily representative of broad geographical areas like counties and CBSAs.
Source: U.S. Environmental Protection Agency, Air Quality Index Report, 2021

Maximum Air Pollutant Concentrations: Particulate Matter, Ozone, CO and Lead

	Particulate Matter 10 (ug/m^3)	Particulate Matter 2.5 Wtd AM (ug/m^3)	Particulate Matter 2.5 24-Hr (ug/m^3)	Ozone (ppm)	Carbon Monoxide (ppm)	Lead (ug/m^3)
MSA[1] Level	34	3.3	6	0.047	2	n/a
NAAQS[2]	150	15	35	0.075	9	0.15
Met NAAQS[2]	Yes	Yes	Yes	Yes	Yes	n/a

Note: (1) Data covers the Urban Honolulu, HI Metropolitan Statistical Area; Data from exceptional events are included; (2) National Ambient Air Quality Standards; ppm = parts per million; ug/m³ = micrograms per cubic meter; n/a not available.
Concentrations: Particulate Matter 10 (coarse particulate)—highest second maximum 24-hour concentration; Particulate Matter 2.5 Wtd AM (fine particulate)—highest weighted annual mean concentration; Particulate Matter 2.5 24-Hour (fine particulate)—highest 98th percentile 24-hour concentration; Ozone—highest fourth daily maximum 8-hour concentration; Carbon Monoxide—highest second maximum non-overlapping 8-hour concentration; Lead—maximum running 3-month average
Source: U.S. Environmental Protection Agency, Air Quality Monitoring Information, "Air Quality Statistics by City, 2021"

Maximum Air Pollutant Concentrations: Nitrogen Dioxide and Sulfur Dioxide

	Nitrogen Dioxide AM (ppb)	Nitrogen Dioxide 1-Hr (ppb)	Sulfur Dioxide AM (ppb)	Sulfur Dioxide 1-Hr (ppb)	Sulfur Dioxide 24-Hr (ppb)
MSA[1] Level	3	22	n/a	44	n/a
NAAQS[2]	53	100	30	75	140
Met NAAQS[2]	Yes	Yes	n/a	Yes	n/a

Note: (1) Data covers the Urban Honolulu, HI Metropolitan Statistical Area; Data from exceptional events are included; (2) National Ambient Air Quality Standards; ppm = parts per million; ug/m³ = micrograms per cubic meter; n/a not available.
Concentrations: Nitrogen Dioxide AM—highest arithmetic mean concentration; Nitrogen Dioxide 1-Hr—highest 98th percentile 1-hour daily maximum concentration; Sulfur Dioxide AM—highest annual mean concentration; Sulfur Dioxide 1-Hr—highest 99th percentile 1-hour daily maximum concentration; Sulfur Dioxide 24-Hr—highest second maximum 24-hour concentration
Source: U.S. Environmental Protection Agency, Air Quality Monitoring Information, "Air Quality Statistics by City, 2021"

Las Cruces, New Mexico

Background

"People helping people" is the motto of the city of Las Cruces which is also known as "City of Crosses." The seat of Doña Ana County, Las Cruces has experienced a rich history filled with war, growth, and renewal. Like other sunbelt communities, its economy is booming, mainly due to its major research university, an abundance of government jobs, and popularity with retirees. With a younger-than-national-average median age, the city has a prime, mostly bilingual labor force.

Las Cruces was officially founded in 1849 when the US Army laid out the town plans. It sits 3,908 feet above sea level, 225 miles south of Albuquerque, with Doña Ana Mountains to the north and the Organ Mountains to the east. West of Las Cruces is the Rio Grande River, which supplies irrigation water for the extensive agriculture in the region.

Las Cruces is part of the Borderplex Region which, together with El Paso, TX and Ciudad Juarez, Mexico represent the seventh largest manufacturing center in North America. The city is a top aerospace research, testing, and development center and home to divisions of Boeing, General Dynamics, Honeywell, Raytheon, and NASA. The nation's first purpose-built commercial space facility, Spaceport America, is just north of the city and has completed several successful manned, sub-orbital space flights; Virgin Galactic is the spaceport's anchor tenant and neighbors with other top commercial space and research firms.

The city's major research institution New Mexico State University (NMSU) is home to The Physical Science Laboratory—an aerospace and defense-oriented organization that provides cutting-edge research. Long standing government organizations—White Sands Missile Range providing research and experiment support, and White Sands Test Facility providing testing of spacecraft materials and propulsion systems—provide many NMSU graduates with high-paying jobs. Other significant areas of concentration at NMSU include creative media and agriculture.

The city is also home to other major employers including Las Cruces Public Schools, Memorial Medical Center, and NASA. Renewable energy from biofuels and solar energy generation is a growing industry in the region, which is in the nation's top-rated solar resource aera for flat-plate solar energy collectors.

Ongoing planned development in the city's east side provides multiple living and recreational options, and its historic downtown offers museums, art galleries, restaurants, and theaters up and down Main Street. Las Cruces hosts a variety of annual cultural events, including celebrations of the Day of the Dead and Cinco de Mayo—a testament to the city's Spanish roots.

Due to its stunning physical location, many films have been set in Las Cruces including *Hang 'Em High* (1968), *Lost in America* (1985), *Due Date* (2010), *Captain Fantastic* (2016), *The Mule* (2018), and *All the World Is Sleeping* (2021).

Las Cruces offers an arid climate, with mild winters and hot summers. Winter frost with light snow dusting can occur, usually only for a few hours. Summers often see extended periods of 100-plus degrees, with high humidity and frequent afternoon thunderstorms late in the season. The wettest single day in Las Cruces was in 1935, with 6.49 inches of rain.

Rankings

Business/Finance Rankings

- The Las Cruces metro area appeared on the Milken Institute "2022 Best Performing Cities" list. Rank: #66 out of 201 small metro areas (population over 60,000). Criteria: job growth; wage and salary growth; high-tech output growth; housing affordability; household broadband access. *Milken Institute, "Best-Performing Cities 2022," March 28, 2022*

- *Forbes* ranked 203 smaller metro areas (population under 268,000) to determine the nation's "Best Small Places for Business and Careers." The Las Cruces metro area was ranked #122. Criteria: costs (business and living); job growth (past and projected); income growth; quality of life; educational attainment (college and high school); projected economic growth; cultural and leisure opportunities; workplace tolerance laws; net migration patterns. *Forbes, "The Best Small Places for Business and Careers 2019," October 30, 2019*

Children/Family Rankings

- Las Cruces was selected as one of the most playful cities in the U.S. by KaBOOM! The organization's Playful City USA initiative honors cities and towns across the nation that have made their communities more playable. Criteria: pledging to integrate play as a solution to challenges in their communities; making it easy for children to get active and balanced play; creating more family-friendly and innovative communities as a result. *KaBOOM! National Campaign for Play, "2017 Playful City USA Communities"*

Culture/Performing Arts Rankings

- Las Cruces was selected as one of the ten best small North American cities and towns for moviemakers. Of cities with smaller populations, the area ranked #7. As with the 2023 list for bigger cities, the philosophy of freedom to pursue filmmaking dreams were highly factored in. Other criteria: film community and culture; access to equipment and facilities; affordability; tax incentives; and quality of life. *MovieMaker Magazine, "Best Places to Live and Work as a Moviemaker, 2023," January 18, 2023*

Health/Fitness Rankings

- The Sharecare Community Well-Being Index evaluates 10 individual and social health factors in order to measure what matters to Americans in the communities in which they live. The Las Cruces metro area ranked #380 in the bottom 10 across all 10 domains. Criteria: access to healthcare, food, and community resources; housng and transportation; economic security; feeling of purpose; physical, financial, social, and community well-being. *www.sharecare.com, "Community Well-Being Index: 2020 Metro Area & County Rankings Report," August 30, 2021*

Real Estate Rankings

- *WalletHub* compared the most populated U.S. cities to determine which had the best markets for real estate agents. Las Cruces ranked #178 where demand was high and pay was the best. Criteria: sales per agent; annual median wage for real-estate agents; monthly average starting salary for real estate agents; real estate job density and competition; unemployment rate; home turnover rate; housing-market health index; and other relevant metrics. *www.WalletHub.com, "2021 Best Places to Be a Real Estate Agent," May 12, 2021*

Safety Rankings

- The National Insurance Crime Bureau ranked 390 metro areas in the U.S. in terms of per capita rates of vehicle theft. The Las Cruces metro area ranked #59 (#1 = highest rate). Criteria: number of vehicle theft offenses per 100,000 inhabitants in 2021. *National Insurance Crime Bureau, "Hot Spots 2021," September 1, 2022*

Seniors/Retirement Rankings

- From its Best Cities for Successful Aging indexes, the Milken Institute generated rankings for metropolitan areas, weighing data in nine categories—health care, wellness, living arrangements, transportation and convenience, financial characteristics, education, employment, community engagement, and overall livability. The Las Cruces metro area was ranked #227 overall in the small metro area category. *Milken Institute, "Best Cities for Successful Aging, 2017" March 14, 2017*

- Las Cruces was identified as #3 of 20 most captivating places to retire in the U.S. by *Topretirements.com*. After consulting its visitor logs, the list primarily reflects the 20 cities that members are most interested in for retirement, based on which reviews were visited the most. *Topretirements.com, "20 Most Captivating Places to Retire for 2022," January 12, 2022*

- Las Cruces was identified as #5 of 20 most popular places to retire in the Southwest region by *Topretirements.com*. The site separated its annual "Best Places to Retire" list by major U.S. regions for 2019. The list reflects the 20 cities that visitors to the website are most interested in for retirement, based on the number of times a city's review was viewed on the website. *Topretirements.com, "20 Most Popular Places to Retire in the Southwest for 2019," October 2, 2019*

Women/Minorities Rankings

- Personal finance website *WalletHub* compared more than 180 U.S. cities across two key dimensions, "Hispanic Business-Friendliness" and "Hispanic Purchasing Power," to arrive at the most favorable conditions for Hispanic entrepreneurs. Las Cruces was ranked #45 out of 182. Criteria includes: share of Hispanic-Owned Businesses; Hispanic entrepreneurship rate to median annual income of Hispanics; Small Business-Friendliness score; cost of living; and number of Hispanics with at least a bachelor's degree. *WalletHub.com, "2019's Best Cities for Hispanic Entrepreneurs," May 1, 2019*

Miscellaneous Rankings

- *WalletHub* compared the 150 most populated U.S. cities to determine their operating efficiency. A "Quality of Services" score was constructed for each city and then divided by the total budget per capita to reveal which were managed the best. Las Cruces ranked #7. Criteria: financial stability; economy; education; safety; health; infrastructure and pollution. *www.WalletHub.com, "2022's Best- & Worst-Run Cities in America," June 21, 2022*

Business Environment

DEMOGRAPHICS

Population Growth

Area	1990 Census	2000 Census	2010 Census	2020 Census	Population Growth (%) 1990-2020	Population Growth (%) 2010-2020
City	63,267	74,267	97,618	111,385	76.1	14.1
MSA[1]	135,510	174,682	209,233	219,561	62.0	4.9
U.S.	248,709,873	281,421,906	308,745,538	331,449,281	33.3	7.4

Note: (1) Figures cover the Las Cruces, NM Metropolitan Statistical Area
Source: U.S. Census Bureau, 1990 Census, 2000 Census, 2010 Census, 2020 Census

Race

Area	White Alone[2] (%)	Black Alone[2] (%)	Asian Alone[2] (%)	AIAN[3] Alone[2] (%)	NHOPI[4] Alone[2] (%)	Other Race Alone[2] (%)	Two or More Races (%)
City	51.9	2.7	1.9	2.3	0.1	16.6	24.5
MSA[1]	47.5	1.9	1.2	1.9	0.1	20.1	27.4
U.S.	61.6	12.4	6.0	1.1	0.2	8.4	10.2

Note: (1) Figures cover the Las Cruces, NM Metropolitan Statistical Area; (2) Alone is defined as not being in combination with one or more other races; (3) American Indian and Alaska Native; (4) Native Hawaiian and Other Pacific Islander
Source: U.S. Census Bureau, 2020 Census

Hispanic or Latino Origin

Area	Total (%)	Mexican (%)	Puerto Rican (%)	Cuban (%)	Other (%)
City	61.8	51.1	0.6	0.2	9.9
MSA[1]	68.9	60.8	0.4	0.1	7.6
U.S.	18.4	11.2	1.8	0.7	4.7

Note: Persons of Hispanic or Latino origin can be of any race; (1) Figures cover the Las Cruces, NM Metropolitan Statistical Area
Source: U.S. Census Bureau, 2017-2021 American Community Survey 5-Year Estimates

Age

Area	Under Age 5	Age 5–19	Age 20–34	Age 35–44	Age 45–54	Age 55–64	Age 65–74	Age 75–84	Age 85+	Median Age
City	5.8	20.1	23.5	11.9	10.0	11.2	10.0	5.4	2.1	35.5
MSA[1]	5.8	21.3	21.6	11.4	10.6	12.2	10.2	5.2	1.9	36.0
U.S.	5.6	19.2	20.2	12.7	12.4	13.1	10.0	4.9	1.9	38.8

Note: (1) Figures cover the Las Cruces, NM Metropolitan Statistical Area
Source: U.S. Census Bureau, 2020 Census

Disability by Age

Area	All Ages	Under 18 Years Old	18 to 64 Years Old	65 Years and Over
City	15.9	7.9	13.6	38.0
MSA[1]	15.2	6.6	13.4	35.7
U.S.	12.6	4.4	10.3	33.4

Note: Figures show percent of the civilian noninstitutionalized population that reported having a disability. Disability status is determined from six types of difficulty: vision, hearing, cognitive, ambulatory, self-care, and independent living. For children under 5 years old, hearing and vision difficulty are used to determine disability status. For children between the ages of 5 and 14, disability status is determined from hearing, vision, cognitive, ambulatory, and self-care difficulties. For people aged 15 years and older, they are considered to have a disability if they have difficulty with any one of the six difficulty types; Note: (1) Figures cover the Las Cruces, NM Metropolitan Statistical Area
Source: U.S. Census Bureau, 2017-2021 American Community Survey 5-Year Estimates

Ancestry

Area	German	Irish	English	American	Italian	Polish	French[2]	Scottish	Dutch
City	7.0	5.8	6.4	2.6	1.9	1.0	1.2	1.1	0.8
MSA[1]	6.5	4.7	5.3	2.5	1.6	0.7	1.1	1.1	0.7
U.S.	12.8	9.6	8.1	5.7	5.0	2.7	2.2	1.6	1.1

Note: Figures are the percentage of the total population reporting a particular ancestry. The nine most commonly reported ancestries in the U.S. are shown. Figures include multiple ancestries (e.g. if a person reported being Irish and Italian, they were included in both columns); (1) Figures cover the Las Cruces, NM Metropolitan Statistical Area; (2) Excludes Basque
Source: U.S. Census Bureau, 2017-2021 American Community Survey 5-Year Estimates

Foreign-born Population

Area	Any Foreign Country	\<center\>Percent of Population Born in							
		Asia	Mexico	Europe	Caribbean	Central America[2]	South America	Africa	Canada
City	11.0	2.3	7.0	0.8	0.1	0.1	0.2	0.4	0.1
MSA[1]	16.0	1.4	13.3	0.6	0.1	0.1	0.1	0.2	0.1
U.S.	13.6	4.2	3.3	1.5	1.4	1.1	1.1	0.8	0.2

Note: (1) Figures cover the Las Cruces, NM Metropolitan Statistical Area; (2) Excludes Mexico.
Source: U.S. Census Bureau, 2017-2021 American Community Survey 5-Year Estimates

Household Size

Area	Persons in Household (%)							Average Household Size
	One	Two	Three	Four	Five	Six	Seven or More	
City	32.0	31.5	15.9	12.7	5.6	1.7	0.8	2.50
MSA[1]	27.3	33.3	15.7	13.5	6.5	2.1	1.6	2.70
U.S.	28.1	33.8	15.5	12.9	6.0	2.3	1.4	2.60

Note: (1) Figures cover the Las Cruces, NM Metropolitan Statistical Area
Source: U.S. Census Bureau, 2017-2021 American Community Survey 5-Year Estimates

Household Relationships

Area	House-holder	Opposite-sex Spouse	Same-sex Spouse	Opposite-sex Unmarried Partner	Same-sex Unmarried Partner	Child[2]	Grand-child	Other Relatives	Non-relatives
City	41.1	14.9	0.2	3.4	0.3	28.5	2.5	4.5	3.6
MSA[1]	37.5	15.9	0.2	2.7	0.2	30.0	3.6	5.1	2.7
U.S.	38.3	17.5	0.2	2.5	0.2	28.3	2.4	4.8	3.4

Note: Figures are percent of the total population; (1) Figures cover the Las Cruces, NM Metropolitan Statistical Area; (2) Includes biological, adopted, and stepchildren of the householder
Source: U.S. Census Bureau, 2020 Census

Gender

Area	Males	Females	Males per 100 Females
City	53,571	57,814	92.7
MSA[1]	107,150	112,411	95.3
U.S.	162,685,811	168,763,470	96.4

Note: (1) Figures cover the Las Cruces, NM Metropolitan Statistical Area
Source: U.S. Census Bureau, 2020 Census

Marital Status

Area	Never Married	Now Married[2]	Separated	Widowed	Divorced
City	41.9	39.4	1.7	4.7	12.4
MSA[1]	38.8	43.7	2.0	4.9	10.7
U.S.	33.8	48.0	1.8	5.6	10.8

Note: Figures are percentages and cover the population 15 years of age and older; (1) Figures cover the Las Cruces, NM Metropolitan Statistical Area; (2) Excludes separated
Source: U.S. Census Bureau, 2017-2021 American Community Survey 5-Year Estimates

Religious Groups by Family

Area	Catholic	Baptist	Methodist	LDS[2]	Pentecostal	Lutheran	Islam	Adventist	Other
MSA[1]	19.3	4.1	1.6	2.5	2.5	0.4	0.6	2.2	4.2
U.S.	18.7	7.3	3.0	2.0	1.8	1.7	1.3	1.3	11.6

Note: Figures are the number of adherents as a percentage of the total population and cover the eight largest religious groups in the U.S; (1) Figures cover the Las Cruces, NM Metropolitan Statistical Area; (2) Church of Jesus Christ of Latter-day Saints
Sources: 2020 U.S. Religion Census, Association of Statisticians of American Religious Bodies; The Association of Religion Data Archives (ARDA)

Religious Groups by Tradition

Area	Catholic	Evangelical Protestant	Mainline Protestant	Black Protestant	Islam	Judaism	Hinduism	Orthodox	Buddhism
MSA[1]	19.3	9.8	2.4	0.2	0.6	0.1	0.2	<0.1	n/a
U.S.	18.7	16.5	5.2	2.3	1.3	0.6	0.4	0.4	0.3

Note: Figures are the number of adherents as a percentage of the total population; (1) Figures cover the Las Cruces, NM Metropolitan Statistical Area
Sources: 2020 U.S. Religion Census, Association of Statisticians of American Religious Bodies; The Association of Religion Data Archives (ARDA)

ECONOMY

Gross Metropolitan Product

Area	2020	2021	2022	2023	Rank[2]
MSA[1]	7.6	8.5	9.6	10.0	258

Note: Figures are in billions of dollars; (1) Figures cover the Las Cruces, NM Metropolitan Statistical Area; (2) Rank is based on 2021 data and ranges from 1 to 381
Source: U.S. Conference of Mayors, U.S. Metro Economies: U.S. Metros Compared to Global and State Economies, June 2022

Economic Growth

Area	2018-20 (%)	2021 (%)	2022 (%)	2023 (%)	Rank[2]
MSA[1]	-1.8	6.3	7.3	3.2	273
U.S.	-0.6	5.7	3.1	2.9	–

Note: Figures are real gross metropolitan product (GMP) growth rates and represent average annual percent change; (1) Figures cover the Las Cruces, NM Metropolitan Statistical Area; (2) Rank is based on 2020 2-year average annual percent change and ranges from 1 to 381
Source: U.S. Conference of Mayors, U.S. Metro Economies: U.S. Metros Compared to Global and State Economies, June 2022

Metropolitan Area Exports

Area	2016	2017	2018	2019	2020	2021	Rank[2]
MSA[1]	1,568.6	1,390.2	1,467.5	n/a	2,149.5	2,408.2	95

Note: Figures are in millions of dollars; (1) Figures cover the Las Cruces, NM Metropolitan Statistical Area; (2) Rank is based on 2021 data and ranges from 1 to 388
Source: U.S. Department of Commerce, International Trade Administration, Office of Trade and Economic Analysis, Industry and Analysis, Exports by Metropolitan Area, data extracted March 16, 2023

Building Permits

Area	Single-Family			Multi-Family			Total		
	2021	2022	Pct. Chg.	2021	2022	Pct. Chg.	2021	2022	Pct. Chg.
City	763	685	-10.2	99	26	-73.7	862	711	-17.5
MSA[1]	1,239	1,079	-12.9	99	26	-73.7	1,338	1,105	-17.4
U.S.	1,115,400	975,600	-12.5	621,600	689,500	10.9	1,737,000	1,665,100	-4.1

Note: (1) Figures cover the Las Cruces, NM Metropolitan Statistical Area; Figures represent new, privately-owned housing units authorized (unadjusted data); All permit data are based on estimates with imputation
Source: U.S. Census Bureau, Manufacturing, Mining, and Construction Statistics, Building Permits, 2021, 2022

Bankruptcy Filings

Area	Business Filings			Nonbusiness Filings		
	2021	2022	% Chg.	2021	2022	% Chg.
Dona Ana County	8	4	-50.0	187	178	-4.8
U.S.	14,347	13,481	-6.0	399,269	374,240	-6.3

Note: Business filings include Chapter 7, Chapter 9, Chapter 11, Chapter 12, Chapter 13, Chapter 15, and Section 304; Nonbusiness filings include Chapter 7, Chapter 11, and Chapter 13
Source: Administrative Office of the U.S. Courts, Business and Nonbusiness Bankruptcy, County Cases Commenced by Chapter of the Bankruptcy Code, During the 12-Month Period Ending December 31, 2021 and Business and Nonbusiness Bankruptcy, County Cases Commenced by Chapter of the Bankruptcy Code, During the 12-Month Period Ending December 31, 2022

Housing Vacancy Rates

Area	Gross Vacancy Rate[2] (%)			Year-Round Vacancy Rate[3] (%)			Rental Vacancy Rate[4] (%)			Homeowner Vacancy Rate[5] (%)		
	2020	2021	2022	2020	2021	2022	2020	2021	2022	2020	2021	2022
MSA[1]	n/a	n/a	n/a	n/a	n/a	n/a	n/a	n/a	n/a	n/a	n/a	n/a
U.S.	10.6	10.8	10.5	8.2	8.4	8.2	6.3	6.1	5.8	1.0	0.9	0.8

Note: (1) Figures cover the Las Cruces, NM Metropolitan Statistical Area; (2) The percentage of the total housing inventory that is vacant; (3) The percentage of the housing inventory (excluding seasonal units) that is year-round vacant; (4) The percentage of rental inventory that is vacant for rent; (5) The percentage of homeowner inventory that is vacant for sale; n/a not available
Source: U.S. Census Bureau, Housing Vacancies and Homeownership Annual Statistics: 2020, 2021, 2022

INCOME

Income

Area	Per Capita ($)	Median Household ($)	Average Household ($)
City	26,290	47,722	64,425
MSA[1]	24,645	47,151	65,405
U.S.	37,638	69,021	97,196

Note: (1) Figures cover the Las Cruces, NM Metropolitan Statistical Area
Source: U.S. Census Bureau, 2017-2021 American Community Survey 5-Year Estimates

Household Income Distribution

Area	Percent of Households Earning							
	Under $15,000	$15,000 -$24,999	$25,000 -$34,999	$35,000 -$49,999	$50,000 -$74,999	$75,000 -$99,999	$100,000 -$149,999	$150,000 and up
City	17.5	12.3	10.4	12.2	17.4	9.8	13.1	7.4
MSA[1]	16.8	12.7	10.8	12.2	17.7	9.5	12.9	7.3
U.S.	9.4	7.8	8.2	11.4	16.8	12.8	16.3	17.3

Note: (1) Figures cover the Las Cruces, NM Metropolitan Statistical Area
Source: U.S. Census Bureau, 2017-2021 American Community Survey 5-Year Estimates

Poverty Rate

Area	All Ages	Under 18 Years Old	18 to 64 Years Old	65 Years and Over
City	21.8	26.9	22.4	11.5
MSA[1]	23.2	30.9	22.2	14.7
U.S.	12.6	17.0	11.8	9.6

Note: Figures are percentage of people whose income during the past 12 months was below the poverty level;
(1) Figures cover the Las Cruces, NM Metropolitan Statistical Area
Source: U.S. Census Bureau, 2017-2021 American Community Survey 5-Year Estimates

EMPLOYMENT

Labor Force and Employment

Area	Civilian Labor Force			Workers Employed		
	Dec. 2021	Dec. 2022	% Chg.	Dec. 2021	Dec. 2022	% Chg.
City	48,477	48,211	-0.5	46,260	46,735	1.0
MSA[1]	99,600	99,107	-0.5	94,429	95,399	1.0
U.S.	161,696,000	164,224,000	1.6	155,732,000	158,872,000	2.0

Note: Data is not seasonally adjusted and covers workers 16 years of age and older; (1) Figures cover the Las Cruces, NM Metropolitan Statistical Area
Source: Bureau of Labor Statistics, Local Area Unemployment Statistics

Unemployment Rate

Area	2022											
	Jan.	Feb.	Mar.	Apr.	May	Jun.	Jul.	Aug.	Sep.	Oct.	Nov.	Dec.
City	4.8	3.9	3.6	3.5	3.4	4.9	4.7	4.6	4.5	3.8	3.4	3.1
MSA[1]	5.7	5.1	4.8	4.8	4.4	5.3	5.0	4.6	4.8	4.2	4.0	3.7
U.S.	4.4	4.1	3.8	3.3	3.4	3.8	3.8	3.8	3.3	3.4	3.4	3.3

Note: Data is not seasonally adjusted and covers workers 16 years of age and older; (1) Figures cover the Las Cruces, NM Metropolitan Statistical Area
Source: Bureau of Labor Statistics, Local Area Unemployment Statistics

Average Wages

Occupation	$/Hr.	Occupation	$/Hr.
Accountants and Auditors	31.08	Maintenance and Repair Workers	18.02
Automotive Mechanics	19.52	Marketing Managers	n/a
Bookkeepers	19.12	Network and Computer Systems Admin.	41.48
Carpenters	19.82	Nurses, Licensed Practical	27.19
Cashiers	12.79	Nurses, Registered	37.30
Computer Programmers	32.88	Nursing Assistants	14.84
Computer Systems Analysts	40.51	Office Clerks, General	15.58
Computer User Support Specialists	22.91	Physical Therapists	40.75
Construction Laborers	17.03	Physicians	135.79
Cooks, Restaurant	14.13	Plumbers, Pipefitters and Steamfitters	22.92
Customer Service Representatives	15.26	Police and Sheriff's Patrol Officers	27.37
Dentists	76.28	Postal Service Mail Carriers	25.66
Electricians	25.44	Real Estate Sales Agents	22.91
Engineers, Electrical	44.62	Retail Salespersons	13.98
Fast Food and Counter Workers	12.21	Sales Representatives, Technical/Scientific	n/a
Financial Managers	46.68	Secretaries, Exc. Legal/Medical/Executive	18.37
First-Line Supervisors of Office Workers	25.64	Security Guards	15.27
General and Operations Managers	50.87	Surgeons	n/a
Hairdressers/Cosmetologists	13.04	Teacher Assistants, Exc. Postsecondary*	14.06
Home Health and Personal Care Aides	12.29	Teachers, Secondary School, Exc. Sp. Ed.*	33.00
Janitors and Cleaners	13.56	Telemarketers	n/a
Landscaping/Groundskeeping Workers	15.38	Truck Drivers, Heavy/Tractor-Trailer	21.52
Lawyers	53.03	Truck Drivers, Light/Delivery Services	17.37
Maids and Housekeeping Cleaners	12.60	Waiters and Waitresses	15.04

Note: Wage data covers the Las Cruces, NM Metropolitan Statistical Area; (*) Hourly wages were calculated from annual wage data based on a 40 hour work week; n/a not available.
Source: Bureau of Labor Statistics, Metro Area Occupational Employment & Wage Estimates, May 2022

Employment by Industry

Sector	MSA[1]		U.S.
	Number of Employees	Percent of Total	Percent of Total
Construction, Mining, and Logging	3,700	4.7	5.4
Private Education and Health Services	17,700	22.7	16.1
Financial Activities	2,400	3.1	5.9
Government	20,800	26.7	14.5
Information	600	0.8	2.0
Leisure and Hospitality	8,900	11.4	10.3
Manufacturing	3,400	4.4	8.4
Other Services	1,600	2.1	3.7
Professional and Business Services	7,100	9.1	14.7
Retail Trade	7,700	9.9	10.2
Transportation, Warehousing, and Utilities	2,500	3.2	4.9
Wholesale Trade	1,500	1.9	3.9

Note: Figures are non-farm employment as of December 2022. Figures are not seasonally adjusted and include workers 16 years of age and older; (1) Figures cover the Las Cruces, NM Metropolitan Statistical Area
Source: Bureau of Labor Statistics, Current Employment Statistics, Employment, Hours, and Earnings

Employment by Occupation

Occupation Classification	City (%)	MSA[1] (%)	U.S. (%)
Management, Business, Science, and Arts	41.7	36.7	40.3
Natural Resources, Construction, and Maintenance	8.8	11.0	8.7
Production, Transportation, and Material Moving	5.1	8.7	13.1
Sales and Office	22.4	21.3	20.9
Service	22.0	22.3	17.0

Note: Figures cover employed civilians 16 years of age and older; (1) Figures cover the Las Cruces, NM Metropolitan Statistical Area
Source: U.S. Census Bureau, 2017-2021 American Community Survey 5-Year Estimates

Occupations with Greatest Projected Employment Growth: 2022 – 2024

Occupation[1]	2022 Employment	2024 Projected Employment	Numeric Employment Change	Percent Employment Change
Home Health and Personal Care Aides	35,710	37,830	2,120	5.9
Construction Laborers	14,780	15,630	850	5.8
Cooks, Restaurant	8,140	8,950	810	10.0
Fast Food and Counter Workers	21,760	22,500	740	3.4
Heavy and Tractor-Trailer Truck Drivers	12,510	13,190	680	5.4
Stockers and Order Fillers	14,010	14,680	670	4.8
Waiters and Waitresses	11,520	12,090	570	4.9
Maids and Housekeeping Cleaners	6,690	7,240	550	8.2
Registered Nurses	18,320	18,850	530	2.9
Laborers and Freight, Stock, and Material Movers, Hand	8,870	9,400	530	6.0

Note: Projections cover New Mexico; (1) Sorted by numeric employment change
Source: www.projectionscentral.com, State Occupational Projections, 2022–2024 Short-Term Projections

Fastest-Growing Occupations: 2022 – 2024

Occupation[1]	2022 Employment	2024 Projected Employment	Numeric Employment Change	Percent Employment Change
Fitness Trainers and Aerobics Instructors	1,690	2,000	310	18.3
Amusement and Recreation Attendants	840	990	150	17.9
Gaming Change Persons and Booth Cashiers	440	500	60	13.6
Lodging Managers	460	520	60	13.0
Hotel, Motel, and Resort Desk Clerks	3,620	4,030	410	11.3
Nurse Practitioners	1,370	1,520	150	10.9
Roustabouts, Oil and Gas	2,780	3,070	290	10.4
Industrial Truck and Tractor Operators	1,770	1,950	180	10.2
Cooks, Restaurant	8,140	8,950	810	10.0
Insurance Sales Agents	1,890	2,060	170	9.0

Note: Projections cover New Mexico; (1) Sorted by percent employment change and excludes occupations with numeric employment change less than 50
Source: www.projectionscentral.com, State Occupational Projections, 2022–2024 Short-Term Projections

CITY FINANCES

City Government Finances

Component	2020 ($000)	2020 ($ per capita)
Total Revenues	251,232	2,429
Total Expenditures	203,414	1,967
Debt Outstanding	283,941	2,745
Cash and Securities[1]	306,494	2,963

Note: (1) Cash and security holdings of a government at the close of its fiscal year, including those of its dependent agencies, utilities, and liquor stores.
Source: U.S. Census Bureau, State & Local Government Finances 2020

City Government Revenue by Source

Source	2020 ($000)	2020 ($ per capita)	2020 (%)
General Revenue			
From Federal Government	7,576	73	3.0
From State Government	11,363	110	4.5
From Local Governments	4,867	47	1.9
Taxes			
Property	24,725	239	9.8
Sales and Gross Receipts	105,774	1,023	42.1
Personal Income	0	0	0.0
Corporate Income	0	0	0.0
Motor Vehicle License	482	5	0.2
Other Taxes	3,608	35	1.4
Current Charges	43,707	423	17.4
Liquor Store	0	0	0.0
Utility	40,454	391	16.1

Source: U.S. Census Bureau, State & Local Government Finances 2020

City Government Expenditures by Function

Function	2020 ($000)	2020 ($ per capita)	2020 (%)
General Direct Expenditures			
Air Transportation	0	0	0.0
Corrections	0	0	0.0
Education	0	0	0.0
Employment Security Administration	0	0	0.0
Financial Administration	3,991	38	2.0
Fire Protection	23,594	228	11.6
General Public Buildings	11,083	107	5.4
Governmental Administration, Other	473	4	0.2
Health	1,522	14	0.7
Highways	2,405	23	1.2
Hospitals	0	0	0.0
Housing and Community Development	1,511	14	0.7
Interest on General Debt	5,871	56	2.9
Judicial and Legal	74	< 1	< 0.1
Libraries	745	7	0.4
Parking	0	0	0.0
Parks and Recreation	12,199	117	6.0
Police Protection	30,509	295	15.0
Public Welfare	0	0	0.0
Sewerage	16,530	159	8.1
Solid Waste Management	16,536	159	8.1
Veterans' Services	0	0	0.0
Liquor Store	0	0	0.0
Utility	43,257	418	21.3

Source: U.S. Census Bureau, State & Local Government Finances 2020

TAXES

State Corporate Income Tax Rates

State	Tax Rate (%)	Income Brackets ($)	Num. of Brackets	Financial Institution Tax Rate (%)[a]	Federal Income Tax Ded.
New Mexico	4.8 - 5.9	500,000	2	4.8 - 5.9	No

Note: Tax rates as of January 1, 2023; (a) Rates listed are the corporate income tax rate applied to financial institutions or excise taxes based on income. Some states have other taxes based upon the value of deposits or shares.
Source: Federation of Tax Administrators, State Corporate Income Tax Rates, January 1, 2023

State Individual Income Tax Rates

State	Tax Rate (%)	Income Brackets ($)	Personal Exemptions ($)			Standard Ded. ($)	
			Single	Married	Depend.	Single	Married
New Mexico	1.7 - 5.9	5,500 - 210,000 (r)	(d)	(d)	(d)	13,850	27,700 (d)

Note: Tax rates as of January 1, 2023; Local- and county-level taxes are not included; Federal income tax is not deductible on state income tax returns; (d) These states use the personal exemption/standard deduction amounts provided in the federal Internal Revenue Code; (r) The income brackets reported for New Mexico are for single individuals. For married couples filing jointly, the same tax rates apply to income brackets ranging from $8,000 to $315,000.
Source: Federation of Tax Administrators, State Individual Income Tax Rates, January 1, 2023

Various State Sales and Excise Tax Rates

State	State Sales Tax (%)	Gasoline[1] ($/gal.)	Cigarette[2] ($/pack)	Spirits[3] ($/gal.)	Wine[4] ($/gal.)	Beer[5] ($/gal.)	Recreational Marijuana (%)
New Mexico	5	0.19	2.00	6.06	1.70	0.41	(n)

Note: All tax rates as of January 1, 2023; (1) The American Petroleum Institute has developed a methodology for determining the average tax rate on a gallon of fuel. Rates may include any of the following: excise taxes, environmental fees, storage tank fees, other fees or taxes, general sales tax, and local taxes; (2) The federal excise tax of $1.0066 per pack and local taxes are not included; (3) Rates are those applicable to off-premise sales of 40% alcohol by volume (a.b.v.) distilled spirits in 750ml containers. Local excise taxes are excluded; (4) Rates are those applicable to off-premise sales of 11% a.b.v. non-carbonated wine in 750ml containers; (5) Rates are those applicable to off-premise sales of 4.7% a.b.v. beer in 12 ounce containers; (n) 12% excise tax (retail price)
Source: Tax Foundation, 2023 Facts & Figures: How Does Your State Compare?

State Business Tax Climate Index Rankings

State	Overall Rank	Corporate Tax Rank	Individual Income Tax Rank	Sales Tax Rank	Property Tax Rank	Unemployment Insurance Tax Rank
New Mexico	22	12	36	35	1	9

Note: The index is a measure of how each state's tax laws affect economic performance. The lower the rank, the more favorable a state's tax system is for business. States without a given tax are given a ranking of 1. The scores/rankings for the District of Columbia do not affect other states. The 2023 index represents the tax climate as of July 1, 2022.
Source: Tax Foundation, State Business Tax Climate Index 2023

TRANSPORTATION

Means of Transportation to Work

Area	Car/Truck/Van		Public Transportation			Bicycle	Walked	Other Means	Worked at Home
	Drove Alone	Car-pooled	Bus	Subway	Railroad				
City	74.3	13.2	0.5	0.0	0.0	1.6	1.7	1.4	7.4
MSA[1]	76.4	12.3	0.4	0.0	0.0	0.9	1.7	1.3	7.1
U.S.	73.2	8.6	2.0	1.6	0.5	0.5	2.5	1.5	9.7

Note: Figures are percentages and cover workers 16 years of age and older; (1) Figures cover the Las Cruces, NM Metropolitan Statistical Area
Source: U.S. Census Bureau, 2017-2021 American Community Survey 5-Year Estimates

Travel Time to Work

Area	Less Than 10 Minutes	10 to 19 Minutes	20 to 29 Minutes	30 to 44 Minutes	45 to 59 Minutes	60 to 89 Minutes	90 Minutes or More
City	16.2	49.2	16.2	9.5	3.5	4.8	0.7
MSA[1]	13.9	40.3	20.0	14.2	5.2	4.8	1.7
U.S.	12.4	28.5	21.0	20.9	8.2	6.2	2.9

Note: Note: Figures are percentages and include workers 16 years old and over; (1) Figures cover the Las Cruces, NM Metropolitan Statistical Area
Source: U.S. Census Bureau, 2017-2021 American Community Survey 5-Year Estimates

Key Congestion Measures

Measure	1990	2000	2010	2015	2020
Annual Hours of Delay, Total (000)	n/a	n/a	n/a	2,651	1,236
Annual Hours of Delay, Per Auto Commuter	n/a	n/a	n/a	18	8
Annual Congestion Cost, Per Auto Commuter ($)	n/a	n/a	n/a	383	187

Note: n/a not available
Source: Texas A&M Transportation Institute, 2021 Urban Mobility Report

Freeway Travel Time Index

Measure	1985	1990	1995	2000	2005	2010	2015	2020
Urban Area Index[1]	n/a	n/a	n/a	n/a	n/a	n/a	1.07	1.04
Urban Area Rank[1,2]	n/a	n/a	n/a	n/a	n/a	n/a	n/a	n/a

Note: Freeway Travel Time Index—the ratio of travel time in the peak period to the travel time at free-flow conditions. For example, a value of 1.30 indicates a 20-minute free-flow trip takes 26 minutes in the peak (20 minutes x 1.30 = 26 minutes); (1) Covers the Las Cruces NM urban area; (2) Rank is based on 101 larger urban areas (#1 = highest travel time index); n/a not available
Source: Texas A&M Transportation Institute, 2021 Urban Mobility Report

Public Transportation

Agency Name / Mode of Transportation	Vehicles Operated in Maximum Service[1]	Annual Unlinked Passenger Trips[2] (in thous.)	Annual Passenger Miles[3] (in thous.)
Las Cruces Area Transit			
Bus (directly operated)	11	281.6	n/a
Demand Response (directly operated)	15	24.7	n/a

Note: (1) Number of revenue vehicles operated by the given mode and type of service to meet the annual maximum service requirement. This is the revenue vehicle count during the peak season of the year; on the week and day that maximum service is provided. Vehicles operated in maximum service (VOMS) exclude atypical days and one-time special events; (2) Number of passengers who boarded public transportation vehicles. Passengers are counted each time they board a vehicle no matter how many vehicles they use to travel from their origin to their destination. (3) Sum of the distances ridden by all passengers during the entire fiscal year.
Source: Federal Transit Administration, National Transit Database, 2021

Air Transportation

Airport Name and Code / Type of Service	Passenger Airlines[1]	Passenger Enplanements	Freight Carriers[2]	Freight (lbs)
El Paso International (52 miles) (ELP)				
Domestic service (U.S. carriers - 2022)	25	1,929,158	20	99,385,532
International service (U.S. carriers - 2021)	2	2,571	7	719,648

Note: (1) Includes all U.S.-based major, minor and commuter airlines that carried at least one passenger during the year; (2) Includes all U.S.-based airlines and freight carriers that transported at least one pound of freight during the year.
Source: Bureau of Transportation Statistics, The Intermodal Transportation Database, Air Carriers: T-100 Domestic Market (U.S. Carriers), 2022; Bureau of Transportation Statistics, The Intermodal Transportation Database, Air Carriers: T-100 International Market (U.S. Carriers), 2021

BUSINESSES

Major Business Headquarters

Company Name	Industry	Rankings	
		Fortune[1]	Forbes[2]
No companies listed	-	-	-

Note: (1) Companies that produce a 10-K are ranked 1 to 500 based on 2021 revenue; (2) All private companies with at least $2 billion in annual revenue through the end of their most current fiscal year are ranked 1 to 246; companies listed are headquartered in the city; dashes indicate no ranking
Source: Fortune, "Fortune 500," 2022; Forbes, "America's Largest Private Companies," 2022

Living Environment

COST OF LIVING

Cost of Living Index

Composite Index	Groceries	Housing	Utilities	Trans-portation	Health Care	Misc. Goods/ Services
92.0	102.3	78.9	86.7	100.6	105.3	95.5

Note: The Cost of Living Index measures regional differences in the cost of consumer goods and services, excluding taxes and non-consumer expenditures, for professional and managerial households in the top income quintile. It is based on more than 50,000 prices covering almost 60 different items for which prices are collected three times a year by chambers of commerce, economic development organizations or university applied economic centers in each participating urban area. The numbers shown should be read as a percentage above or below the national average of 100. For example, a value of 115.4 in the groceries column indicates that grocery prices are 15.4% higher than the national average. Small differences in the index numbers should not be interpreted as significant; Figures cover the Las Cruces NM urban area.
Source: The Council for Community and Economic Research, Cost of Living Index, 2022

Grocery Prices

Area[1]	T-Bone Steak ($/pound)	Frying Chicken ($/pound)	Whole Milk ($/half gal.)	Eggs ($/dozen)	Orange Juice ($/64 oz.)	Coffee ($/11.5 oz.)
City[2]	13.28	1.47	2.51	2.47	3.97	5.37
Avg.	13.81	1.59	2.43	2.25	3.85	4.95
Min.	10.17	0.90	1.51	1.30	2.90	3.46
Max.	19.35	3.30	4.32	4.32	5.31	8.59

Note: (1) Values for the local area are compared with the average, minimum and maximum values for all 286 areas in the Cost of Living Index; (2) Figures cover the Las Cruces NM urban area; **T-Bone Steak** (price per pound); **Frying Chicken** (price per pound, whole fryer); **Whole Milk** (half gallon carton); **Eggs** (price per dozen, Grade A, large); **Orange Juice** (64 oz. Tropicana or Florida Natural); **Coffee** (11.5 oz. can, vacuum-packed, Maxwell House, Hills Bros, or Folgers).
Source: The Council for Community and Economic Research, Cost of Living Index, 2022

Housing and Utility Costs

Area[1]	New Home Price ($)	Apartment Rent ($/month)	All Electric ($/month)	Part Electric ($/month)	Other Energy ($/month)	Telephone ($/month)
City[2]	364,513	926	-	95.18	40.12	192.31
Avg.	450,913	1,371	176.41	99.93	76.96	190.22
Min.	229,283	546	100.84	31.56	27.15	174.27
Max.	2,434,977	4,569	356.86	249.59	272.24	208.31

Note: (1) Values for the local area are compared with the average, minimum and maximum values for all 286 areas in the Cost of Living Index; (2) Figures cover the Las Cruces NM urban area; **New Home Price** (2,400 sf living area, 8,000 sf lot, in urban area with full utilities); **Apartment Rent** (950 sf 2 bedroom/1.5 or 2 bath, unfurnished, excluding all utilities except water); **All Electric** (average monthly cost for an all-electric home); **Part Electric** (average monthly cost for a part-electric home); **Other Energy** (average monthly cost for natural gas, fuel oil, coal, wood, and any other forms of energy except electricity); **Telephone** (price includes the base monthly rate plus taxes and fees for three lines of mobile phone service).
Source: The Council for Community and Economic Research, Cost of Living Index, 2022

Health Care, Transportation, and Other Costs

Area[1]	Doctor ($/visit)	Dentist ($/visit)	Optometrist ($/visit)	Gasoline ($/gallon)	Beauty Salon ($/visit)	Men's Shirt ($)
City[2]	114.46	118.68	146.98	3.89	41.11	36.87
Avg.	124.91	107.77	117.66	3.86	43.31	34.21
Min.	36.61	58.25	51.79	2.90	22.18	13.05
Max.	250.21	162.58	371.96	5.54	85.61	63.54

Note: (1) Values for the local area are compared with the average, minimum and maximum values for all 286 areas in the Cost of Living Index; (2) Figures cover the Las Cruces NM urban area; **Doctor** (general practitioners routine exam of an established patient); **Dentist** (adult teeth cleaning and periodic oral examination); **Optometrist** (full vision eye exam for established adult patient); **Gasoline** (one gallon regular unleaded, national brand, including all taxes, cash price at self-service pump if available); **Beauty Salon** (woman's shampoo, trim, and blow-dry); **Men's Shirt** (cotton/polyester dress shirt, pinpoint weave, long sleeves).
Source: The Council for Community and Economic Research, Cost of Living Index, 2022

HOUSING

Homeownership Rate

Area	2015 (%)	2016 (%)	2017 (%)	2018 (%)	2019 (%)	2020 (%)	2021 (%)	2022 (%)
MSA[1]	n/a	n/a	n/a	n/a	n/a	n/a	n/a	n/a
U.S.	63.7	63.4	63.9	64.4	64.6	66.6	65.5	65.8

Note: (1) Figures cover the Las Cruces, NM Metropolitan Statistical Area; n/a not available
Source: U.S. Census Bureau, Housing Vacancies and Homeownership Annual Statistics: 2015-2022

House Price Index (HPI)

Area	National Ranking[2]	Quarterly Change (%)	One-Year Change (%)	Five-Year Change (%)	Since 1991Q1 (%)
MSA[1]	n/a	n/a	n/a	n/a	n/a
U.S.[3]	–	0.34	8.41	58.44	289.08

Note: The HPI is a weighted repeat sales index. It measures average price changes in repeat sales or refinancings on the same properties. This information is obtained by reviewing repeat mortgage transactions on single-family properties whose mortgages have been purchased or securitized by Fannie Mae or Freddie Mac since January 1975; (1) Figures cover the , Metropolitan Statistical Area; (2) Rankings are based on annual percentage change for all metro areas containing at least 15,000 transactions over the last 10 years and ranges from 1 to 257; (3) figures based on a weighted average of Census Division estimates using a seasonally adjusted, purchase-only index; all figures are for the period ending December 31, 2022; n/a not available
Source: Federal Housing Finance Agency, Change in FHFA Metropolitan Area House Price Indexes, 2022Q4

Median Single-Family Home Prices

Area	2020	2021	2022p	Percent Change 2021 to 2022
MSA[1]	n/a	n/a	n/a	n/a
U.S. Average	300.2	357.1	392.6	9.9

Note: Figures are median sales prices of existing single-family homes in thousands of dollars; (p) preliminary; n/a not available; (1) Figures cover the Las Cruces, NM Metropolitan Statistical Area
Source: National Association of Realtors, Median Sales Price of Existing Single-Family Homes for Metropolitan Areas, 4th Quarter 2022

Qualifying Income Based on Median Sales Price of Existing Single-Family Homes

Area	With 5% Down ($)	With 10% Down ($)	With 20% Down ($)
MSA[1]	n/a	n/a	n/a
U.S. Average	112,234	106,237	94,513

Note: Figures are preliminary; Qualifying income is based on a mortgage rate of 6.77%. Monthly principal and interest payment is limited to 25% of income; n/a not available; (1) Figures cover the Las Cruces, NM Metropolitan Statistical Area
Source: National Association of Realtors, Qualifying Income Based on Median Sales Price of Existing Single-Family Homes for Metropolitan Areas, 4th Quarter 2022

Home Value

Area	Under $100,000	$100,000 -$199,999	$200,000 -$299,999	$300,000 -$399,999	$400,000 -$499,999	$500,000 -$999,999	$1,000,000 or more	Median ($)
City	17.4	49.1	21.5	7.7	1.5	2.5	0.3	167,800
MSA[1]	26.6	38.7	19.7	7.3	3.9	3.4	0.4	162,200
U.S.	16.2	24.2	20.1	13.6	8.3	13.6	4.1	244,900

Note: Figures are percentages except for median and cover owner-occupied housing units; (1) Figures cover the Las Cruces, NM Metropolitan Statistical Area
Source: U.S. Census Bureau, 2017-2021 American Community Survey 5-Year Estimates

Year Housing Structure Built

Area	2020 or Later	2010 -2019	2000 -2009	1990 -1999	1980 -1989	1970 -1979	1960 -1969	1950 -1959	1940 -1949	Before 1940	Median Year
City	0.3	10.7	19.9	15.0	16.9	15.5	8.1	8.9	2.1	2.6	1988
MSA[1]	0.2	11.0	17.9	19.3	18.3	15.3	7.0	6.3	1.9	2.7	1989
U.S.	0.2	7.3	13.6	13.6	13.2	14.8	10.3	10.0	4.7	12.2	1979

Note: Figures are percentages except for Median Year; Note: (1) Figures cover the Las Cruces, NM Metropolitan Statistical Area
Source: U.S. Census Bureau, 2017-2021 American Community Survey 5-Year Estimates

Gross Monthly Rent

Area	Under $500	$500 -$999	$1,000 -$1,499	$1,500 -$1,999	$2,000 -$2,499	$2,500 -$2,999	$3,000 and up	Median ($)
City	13.0	56.6	25.0	4.0	1.0	0.1	0.4	824
MSA[1]	16.4	55.8	22.5	3.8	1.2	0.1	0.3	785
U.S.	8.1	30.5	30.8	16.8	7.3	3.1	3.5	1,163

Note: Figures are percentages except for median; Gross rent is the contract rent plus the estimated average monthly cost of utilities (electricity, gas, and water and sewer) and fuels (oil, coal, kerosene, wood, etc.) if these are paid by the renter (or paid for the renter by someone else); (1) Figures cover the Las Cruces, NM Metropolitan Statistical Area
Source: U.S. Census Bureau, 2017-2021 American Community Survey 5-Year Estimates

HEALTH

Health Risk Factors

Category	MSA[1] (%)	U.S. (%)
Adults aged 18–64 who have any kind of health care coverage	n/a	90.9
Adults who reported being in good or better health	n/a	85.2
Adults who have been told they have high blood cholesterol	n/a	35.7
Adults who have been told they have high blood pressure	n/a	32.4
Adults who are current smokers	n/a	14.4
Adults who currently use e-cigarettes	n/a	6.7
Adults who currently use chewing tobacco, snuff, or snus	n/a	3.5
Adults who are heavy drinkers[2]	n/a	6.3
Adults who are binge drinkers[3]	n/a	15.4
Adults who are overweight (BMI 25.0 - 29.9)	n/a	34.4
Adults who are obese (BMI 30.0 - 99.8)	n/a	33.9
Adults who participated in any physical activities in the past month	n/a	76.3

Note: (1) Figures for the Las Cruces, NM Metropolitan Statistical Area were not available.
(2) Heavy drinkers are classified as adult men having more than 14 drinks per week and adult women having more than 7 drinks per week; (3) Binge drinkers are classified as males having five or more drinks on one occasion or females having four or more drinks on one occasion
Source: Centers for Disease Control and Prevention, Behaviorial Risk Factor Surveillance System, SMART: Selected Metropolitan Area Risk Trends, 2021

Acute and Chronic Health Conditions

Category	MSA[1] (%)	U.S. (%)
Adults who have ever been told they had a heart attack	n/a	4.0
Adults who have ever been told they have angina or coronary heart disease	n/a	3.8
Adults who have ever been told they had a stroke	n/a	3.0
Adults who have ever been told they have asthma	n/a	14.9
Adults who have ever been told they have arthritis	n/a	25.8
Adults who have ever been told they have diabetes[2]	n/a	10.9
Adults who have ever been told they had skin cancer	n/a	6.6
Adults who have ever been told they had any other types of cancer	n/a	7.5
Adults who have ever been told they have COPD	n/a	6.1
Adults who have ever been told they have kidney disease	n/a	3.0
Adults who have ever been told they have a form of depression	n/a	20.5

Note: (1) Figures for the Las Cruces, NM Metropolitan Statistical Area were not available.
(2) Figures do not include pregnancy-related, borderline, or pre-diabetes
Source: Centers for Disease Control and Prevention, Behaviorial Risk Factor Surveillance System, SMART: Selected Metropolitan Area Risk Trends, 2021

Health Screening and Vaccination Rates

Category	MSA[1] (%)	U.S. (%)
Adults who have ever been tested for HIV	n/a	34.9
Adults who have had their blood cholesterol checked within the last five years	n/a	85.2
Adults aged 65+ who have had flu shot within the past year	n/a	68.6
Adults aged 65+ who have ever had a pneumonia vaccination	n/a	71.0

Note: (1) Figures for the Las Cruces, NM Metropolitan Statistical Area were not available.
Source: Centers for Disease Control and Prevention, Behaviorial Risk Factor Surveillance System, SMART: Selected Metropolitan Area Risk Trends, 2021

Disability Status

Category	MSA[1] (%)	U.S. (%)
Adults who reported being deaf	n/a	7.2
Are you blind or have serious difficulty seeing, even when wearing glasses?	n/a	4.8
Are you limited in any way in any of your usual activities due to arthritis?	n/a	11.1
Do you have difficulty doing errands alone?	n/a	7.0
Do you have difficulty dressing or bathing?	n/a	3.6
Do you have serious difficulty concentrating/remembering/making decisions?	n/a	12.1
Do you have serious difficulty walking or climbing stairs?	n/a	12.8

Note: (1) Figures for the Las Cruces, NM Metropolitan Statistical Area were not available.
Source: Centers for Disease Control and Prevention, Behaviorial Risk Factor Surveillance System, SMART: Selected Metropolitan Area Risk Trends, 2021

Mortality Rates for the Top 10 Causes of Death in the U.S.

ICD-10[a] Sub-Chapter	ICD-10[a] Code	Crude Mortality Rate[1] per 100,000 population	
		County[2]	U.S.
Malignant neoplasms	C00-C97	158.9	182.6
Ischaemic heart diseases	I20-I25	113.2	113.1
Other forms of heart disease	I30-I51	41.5	64.4
Other degenerative diseases of the nervous system	G30-G31	40.4	51.0
Cerebrovascular diseases	I60-I69	48.7	47.8
Other external causes of accidental injury	W00-X59	43.9	46.4
Chronic lower respiratory diseases	J40-J47	40.2	45.7
Organic, including symptomatic, mental disorders	F01-F09	44.0	35.9
Hypertensive diseases	I10-I15	18.9	35.0
Diabetes mellitus	E10-E14	34.0	29.6

Note: (a) ICD-10 = International Classification of Diseases 10th Revision; (1) Crude mortality rates are a three-year average covering 2019-2021; (2) Figures cover Dona Ana County.
Source: Centers for Disease Control and Prevention, National Center for Health Statistics. National Vital Statistics System, Mortality 2018-2021 on CDC WONDER Online Database

Mortality Rates for Selected Causes of Death

ICD-10[a] Sub-Chapter	ICD-10[a] Code	Crude Mortality Rate[1] per 100,000 population	
		County[2]	U.S.
Assault	X85-Y09	6.4	7.0
Diseases of the liver	K70-K76	30.7	19.8
Human immunodeficiency virus (HIV) disease	B20-B24	Unreliable	1.5
Influenza and pneumonia	J09-J18	17.9	14.7
Intentional self-harm	X60-X84	16.9	14.3
Malnutrition	E40-E46	3.3	4.3
Obesity and other hyperalimentation	E65-E68	3.0	3.0
Renal failure	N17-N19	23.9	15.7
Transport accidents	V01-V99	14.4	13.6
Viral hepatitis	B15-B19	Unreliable	1.2

Note: (a) ICD-10 = International Classification of Diseases 10th Revision; (1) Crude mortality rates are a three-year average covering 2019-2021; (2) Figures cover Dona Ana County; Data are suppressed when the data meet the criteria for confidentiality constraints; Crude mortality rates are flagged as unreliable when the rate would be calculated with a numerator of 20 or less.
Source: Centers for Disease Control and Prevention, National Center for Health Statistics. National Vital Statistics System, Mortality 2018-2021 on CDC WONDER Online Database

Health Insurance Coverage

Area	With Health Insurance	With Private Health Insurance	With Public Health Insurance	Without Health Insurance	Population Under Age 19 Without Health Insurance
City	92.0	54.9	50.8	8.0	2.2
MSA[1]	89.4	48.3	52.6	10.6	4.8
U.S.	91.2	67.8	35.4	8.8	5.3

Note: Figures are percentages that cover the civilian noninstitutionalized population; (1) Figures cover the Las Cruces, NM Metropolitan Statistical Area
Source: U.S. Census Bureau, 2017-2021 American Community Survey 5-Year Estimates

Number of Medical Professionals

Area	MDs[3]	DOs[3,4]	Dentists	Podiatrists	Chiropractors	Optometrists
County[1] (number)	365	30	131	14	41	19
County[1] (rate[2])	166.0	13.6	59.1	6.3	18.5	8.6
U.S. (rate[2])	289.3	23.5	72.5	6.2	28.7	17.4

Note: Data as of 2021 unless noted; (1) Data covers Dona Ana County; (2) Rate per 100,000 population; (3) Data as of 2020 and includes all active, non-federal physicians; (4) Doctor of Osteopathic Medicine
Source: U.S. Department of Health and Human Services, Health Resources and Services Administration, Bureau of Health Professions, Area Resource File (ARF) 2021-2022

EDUCATION

Public School District Statistics

District Name	Schls	Pupils	Pupil/ Teacher Ratio	Minority Pupils[1] (%)	LEP/ELL[2] (%)	IEP[3] (%)
Las Cruces Public Schools	40	23,771	15.9	82.9	12.9	15.3

Note: Table includes school districts with 2,000 or more students; (1) Percentage of students that are not non-Hispanic white; (2) Percentage of students that are Limited English Proficient or English Language Learners (2018-19); (3) Percentage of students that have an Individualized Education Program (2019-20).
Source: U.S. Department of Education, National Center for Education Statistics, Common Core of Data, Local Education Agency (School District) Universe Survey: School Year 2021-2022

Highest Level of Education

Area	Less than H.S.	H.S. Diploma	Some College, No Deg.	Associate Degree	Bachelor's Degree	Master's Degree	Prof. School Degree	Doctorate Degree
City	12.5	19.8	22.0	9.3	20.5	11.7	2.2	2.0
MSA[1]	19.3	21.5	20.9	8.3	17.5	9.2	1.7	1.7
U.S.	11.1	26.5	20.0	8.7	20.6	9.3	2.2	1.5

Note: Figures cover persons age 25 and over; (1) Figures cover the Las Cruces, NM Metropolitan Statistical Area
Source: U.S. Census Bureau, 2017-2021 American Community Survey 5-Year Estimates

Educational Attainment by Race

Area	High School Graduate or Higher (%)					Bachelor's Degree or Higher (%)				
	Total	White	Black	Asian	Hisp.[2]	Total	White	Black	Asian	Hisp.[2]
City	87.5	90.4	83.9	85.3	83.2	36.4	38.7	47.4	63.0	24.8
MSA[1]	80.7	83.8	84.8	88.6	73.5	30.0	32.5	44.9	60.3	19.8
U.S.	88.9	91.4	87.2	87.6	71.2	33.7	35.5	23.3	55.6	18.4

Note: Figures shown cover persons 25 years old and over; (1) Figures cover the Las Cruces, NM Metropolitan Statistical Area; (2) People of Hispanic origin can be of any race
Source: U.S. Census Bureau, 2017-2021 American Community Survey 5-Year Estimates

School Enrollment by Grade and Control

Area	Preschool (%)		Kindergarten (%)		Grades 1 - 4 (%)		Grades 5 - 8 (%)		Grades 9 - 12 (%)	
	Public	Private	Public	Private	Public	Private	Public	Private	Public	Private
City	84.8	15.2	91.5	8.5	92.9	7.1	96.6	3.4	96.2	3.8
MSA[1]	83.3	16.7	92.7	7.3	90.3	9.7	96.5	3.5	94.7	5.3
U.S.	58.8	41.2	86.3	13.7	88.3	11.7	88.6	11.4	89.4	10.6

Note: Figures shown cover persons 3 years old and over; (1) Figures cover the Las Cruces, NM Metropolitan Statistical Area
Source: U.S. Census Bureau, 2017-2021 American Community Survey 5-Year Estimates

Higher Education

Four-Year Colleges			Two-Year Colleges			Medical Schools[1]	Law Schools[2]	Voc/ Tech[3]
Public	Private Non-profit	Private For-profit	Public	Private Non-profit	Private For-profit			
1	0	1	1	0	0	1	0	1

Note: Figures cover institutions located within the Las Cruces, NM Metropolitan Statistical Area and include main campuses only; (1) includes schools accredited by the Liaison Committee on Medical Education and the American Osteopathic Association's Commission on Osteopathic College Accreditation; (2) includes ABA-accredited schools, schools with provisional ABA accreditation, and state accredited schools; (3) includes all schools with programs that are less than 2 years.
Source: National Center for Education Statistics, Integrated Postsecondary Education System (IPEDS), 2021-22; Wikipedia, List of Medical Schools in the United States, accessed April 10, 2023; Wikipedia, List of Law Schools in the United States, accessed April 10, 2023

EMPLOYERS

Major Employers

Company Name	Industry
City of Las Cruces	Municipal government
Doña Ana Co. Independent School Districts	School districts
Doña Ana Community College	Community college
Doña Ana County	County government
Memorial Medical Center	Medical center
Mountain View Regional Medical Center	Medical center
NASA White Sands Test Facility	Government test facility
New Mexico State University	State universities
SiTel/Client Logic	Telemarketing
State of New Mexico	State government
Tresco	Early intervention services
U.S. Postal Service	Mail and package delivery
Wal-Mart Stores	Retail

Note: Companies shown are located within the Las Cruces, NM Metropolitan Statistical Area.
Source: Hoovers.com; Wikipedia

PUBLIC SAFETY

Crime Rate

Area	Total Crime	Violent Crime Rate				Property Crime Rate		
		Murder	Rape[3]	Robbery	Aggrav. Assault	Burglary	Larceny -Theft	Motor Vehicle Theft
City	4,077.5	9.7	61.8	55.1	370.0	631.8	2,652.6	296.6
Suburbs[1]	1,781.8	1.7	52.3	10.5	546.8	362.8	699.5	108.1
Metro[2]	2,871.0	5.5	56.8	31.6	462.9	490.4	1,626.2	197.5
U.S.	2,510.4	5.1	42.6	81.8	250.4	340.5	1,569.2	220.8

Note: Figures are crimes per 100,000 population; (1) All areas within the metro area that are located outside the city limits; (2) Figures cover the Las Cruces, NM Metropolitan Statistical Area; (3) All figures shown were reported using the revised Uniform Crime Reporting (UCR) definition of rape; Due to the transition to the National Incident-Based Reporting System (NIBRS), limited city and metro area data was released for 2021.
Source: FBI Uniform Crime Reports, 2019 (data for 2020 was not available)

Hate Crimes

Area	Number of Quarters Reported	Number of Incidents per Bias Motivation					
		Race/Ethnicity/ Ancestry	Religion	Sexual Orientation	Disability	Gender	Gender Identity
City	4	0	0	0	0	0	0
U.S.	4	5,227	1,244	1,110	130	75	266

Note: Due to the transition to the National Incident-Based Reporting System (NIBRS), limited crime data was released for 2021.
Source: Federal Bureau of Investigation, Hate Crime Statistics 2020

Identity Theft Consumer Reports

Area	Reports	Reports per 100,000 Population	Rank[2]
MSA[1]	364	167	212
U.S.	1,108,609	339	-

Note: (1) Figures cover the Las Cruces, NM Metropolitan Statistical Area; (2) Rank ranges from 1 to 391 where 1 indicates greatest number of identity theft reports per 100,000 population
Source: Federal Trade Commission, Consumer Sentinel Network Data Book 2022

Fraud and Other Consumer Reports

Area	Reports	Reports per 100,000 Population	Rank[2]
MSA[1]	1,845	848	180
U.S.	4,064,520	1,245	-

Note: (1) Figures cover the Las Cruces, NM Metropolitan Statistical Area; (2) Rank ranges from 1 to 391 where 1 indicates greatest number of fraud and other consumer reports per 100,000 population
Source: Federal Trade Commission, Consumer Sentinel Network Data Book 2022

POLITICS

2020 Presidential Election Results

Area	Biden	Trump	Jorgensen	Hawkins	Other
Dona Ana County	58.0	39.7	1.4	0.5	0.4
U.S.	51.3	46.8	1.2	0.3	0.5

Note: Results are percentages and may not add to 100% due to rounding
Source: Dave Leip's Atlas of U.S. Presidential Elections

SPORTS

Professional Sports Teams

Team Name	League	Year Established

No teams are located in the metro area
Source: Wikipedia, Major Professional Sports Teams of the United States and Canada, April 12, 2023

CLIMATE

Average and Extreme Temperatures

Temperature	Jan	Feb	Mar	Apr	May	Jun	Jul	Aug	Sep	Oct	Nov	Dec	Yr.
Extreme High (°F)	80	83	89	98	104	114	112	108	104	96	87	80	114
Average High (°F)	57	63	70	79	87	96	95	93	88	79	66	58	78
Average Temp. (°F)	44	49	56	64	73	81	83	81	75	65	52	45	64
Average Low (°F)	31	35	41	49	58	66	70	68	62	50	38	32	50
Extreme Low (°F)	-8	8	14	23	31	46	57	56	42	25	1	5	-8

Note: Figures cover the years 1948-1995
Source: National Climatic Data Center, International Station Meteorological Climate Summary, 9/96

Average Precipitation/Snowfall/Humidity

Precip./Humidity	Jan	Feb	Mar	Apr	May	Jun	Jul	Aug	Sep	Oct	Nov	Dec	Yr.
Avg. Precip. (in.)	0.4	0.4	0.3	0.2	0.3	0.7	1.6	1.5	1.4	0.7	0.3	0.6	8.6
Avg. Snowfall (in.)	1	1	Tr	Tr	0	0	0	0	0	Tr	1	2	6
Avg. Rel. Hum. 6am (%)	68	60	50	43	44	46	63	69	72	66	63	68	59
Avg. Rel. Hum. 3pm (%)	34	27	21	17	17	17	28	30	32	29	30	36	26

Note: Figures cover the years 1948-1995; Tr = Trace amounts (<0.05 in. of rain; <0.5 in. of snow)
Source: National Climatic Data Center, International Station Meteorological Climate Summary, 9/96

Weather Conditions

Temperature			Daytime Sky			Precipitation		
10°F & below	32°F & below	90°F & above	Clear	Partly cloudy	Cloudy	0.01 inch or more precip.	0.1 inch or more snow/ice	Thunder-storms
1	59	106	147	164	54	49	3	35

Note: Figures are average number of days per year and cover the years 1948-1995
Source: National Climatic Data Center, International Station Meteorological Climate Summary, 9/96

HAZARDOUS WASTE

Superfund Sites

The Las Cruces, NM metro area has no sites on the EPA's Superfund Final National Priorities List. There are a total of 1,165 Superfund sites with a status of proposed or final on the list in the U.S. *U.S. Environmental Protection Agency, National Priorities List, April 12, 2023*

AIR QUALITY

Air Quality Trends: Ozone

	1990	1995	2000	2005	2010	2015	2018	2019	2020	2021
MSA[1]	0.073	0.075	0.075	0.070	0.060	0.070	0.072	0.068	0.071	0.079
U.S.	0.087	0.089	0.081	0.080	0.072	0.067	0.069	0.065	0.065	0.067

Note: (1) Data covers the Las Cruces, NM Metropolitan Statistical Area. The values shown are the composite ozone concentration averages among trend sites based on the highest fourth daily maximum 8-hour concentration in parts per million. These trends are based on sites having an adequate record of monitoring data during the trend period. Data from exceptional events are included.
Source: U.S. Environmental Protection Agency, Air Quality Monitoring Information, "Air Quality Trends by City, 1990-2021"

Air Quality Index

Area	Percent of Days when Air Quality was...[2]					AQI Statistics[2]	
	Good	Moderate	Unhealthy for Sensitive Groups	Unhealthy	Very Unhealthy	Maximum	Median
MSA[1]	38.4	53.2	5.5	2.2	0.3	665	55

Note: (1) Data covers the Las Cruces, NM Metropolitan Statistical Area; (2) Based on 365 days with AQI data in 2021. Air Quality Index (AQI) is an index for reporting daily air quality. EPA calculates the AQI for five major air pollutants regulated by the Clean Air Act: ground-level ozone, particle pollution (aka particulate matter), carbon monoxide, sulfur dioxide, and nitrogen dioxide. The AQI runs from 0 to 500. The higher the AQI value, the greater the level of air pollution and the greater the health concern. There are six AQI categories: "Good" AQI is between 0 and 50. Air quality is considered satisfactory; "Moderate" AQI is between 51 and 100. Air quality is acceptable; "Unhealthy for Sensitive Groups" When AQI values are between 101 and 150, members of sensitive groups may experience health effects; "Unhealthy" When AQI values are between 151 and 200 everyone may begin to experience health effects; "Very Unhealthy" AQI values between 201 and 300 trigger a health alert; "Hazardous" AQI values over 300 trigger warnings of emergency conditions (not shown).
Source: U.S. Environmental Protection Agency, Air Quality Index Report, 2021

Air Quality Index Pollutants

Area	Percent of Days when AQI Pollutant was...[2]					
	Carbon Monoxide	Nitrogen Dioxide	Ozone	Sulfur Dioxide	Particulate Matter 2.5	Particulate Matter 10
MSA[1]	0.0	2.5	58.1	(3)	6.3	33.2

Note: (1) Data covers the Las Cruces, NM Metropolitan Statistical Area; (2) Based on 365 days with AQI data in 2021. The Air Quality Index (AQI) is an index for reporting daily air quality. EPA calculates the AQI for five major air pollutants regulated by the Clean Air Act: ground-level ozone, particle pollution (also known as particulate matter), carbon monoxide, sulfur dioxide, and nitrogen dioxide. The AQI runs from 0 to 500. The higher the AQI value, the greater the level of air pollution and the greater the health concern; (3) Sulfur dioxide is no longer included in this table (as of December 8, 2021) because SO_2 concentrations tend to be very localized and not necessarily representative of broad geographical areas like counties and CBSAs.
Source: U.S. Environmental Protection Agency, Air Quality Index Report, 2021

Maximum Air Pollutant Concentrations: Particulate Matter, Ozone, CO and Lead

	Particulate Matter 10 (ug/m³)	Particulate Matter 2.5 Wtd AM (ug/m³)	Particulate Matter 2.5 24-Hr (ug/m³)	Ozone (ppm)	Carbon Monoxide (ppm)	Lead (ug/m³)
MSA[1] Level	439	9.3	26	0.086	n/a	n/a
NAAQS[2]	150	15	35	0.075	9	0.15
Met NAAQS[2]	No	Yes	Yes	No	n/a	n/a

Note: (1) Data covers the Las Cruces, NM Metropolitan Statistical Area; Data from exceptional events are included; (2) National Ambient Air Quality Standards; ppm = parts per million; ug/m³ = micrograms per cubic meter; n/a not available.
Concentrations: Particulate Matter 10 (coarse particulate)—highest second maximum 24-hour concentration; Particulate Matter 2.5 Wtd AM (fine particulate)—highest weighted annual mean concentration; Particulate Matter 2.5 24-Hour (fine particulate)—highest 98th percentile 24-hour concentration; Ozone—highest fourth daily maximum 8-hour concentration; Carbon Monoxide—highest second maximum non-overlapping 8-hour concentration; Lead—maximum running 3-month average
Source: U.S. Environmental Protection Agency, Air Quality Monitoring Information, "Air Quality Statistics by City, 2021"

Maximum Air Pollutant Concentrations: Nitrogen Dioxide and Sulfur Dioxide

	Nitrogen Dioxide AM (ppb)	Nitrogen Dioxide 1-Hr (ppb)	Sulfur Dioxide AM (ppb)	Sulfur Dioxide 1-Hr (ppb)	Sulfur Dioxide 24-Hr (ppb)
MSA[1] Level	8	48	n/a	n/a	n/a
NAAQS[2]	53	100	30	75	140
Met NAAQS[2]	Yes	Yes	n/a	n/a	n/a

Note: (1) Data covers the Las Cruces, NM Metropolitan Statistical Area; Data from exceptional events are included; (2) National Ambient Air Quality Standards; ppm = parts per million; ug/m³ = micrograms per cubic meter; n/a not available.
Concentrations: Nitrogen Dioxide AM—highest arithmetic mean concentration; Nitrogen Dioxide 1-Hr—highest 98th percentile 1-hour daily maximum concentration; Sulfur Dioxide AM—highest annual mean concentration; Sulfur Dioxide 1-Hr—highest 99th percentile 1-hour daily maximum concentration; Sulfur Dioxide 24-Hr—highest second maximum 24-hour concentration
Source: U.S. Environmental Protection Agency, Air Quality Monitoring Information, "Air Quality Statistics by City, 2021"

Las Vegas, Nevada

Upright citizens can accuse Las Vegas of many vices, but not of hypocrisy. Back in 1931, the city officials of this desert town, located 225 miles northeast of Los Angeles, saw gambling to be a growing popular pastime. To capitalize upon that trend, the city simply legalized it. Gambling, combined with spectacular, neon-lit entertainment, lured more than 36.4 million visitors annually during pre-COVID years; 2021 saw 32.2 million. Numbers increased in 2022, with the city still working to fill its 143,000 hotel rooms and 60 casinos in its Strip area.

Before celebrities and tourists flocked to Las Vegas, it was a temporary stopping place for a diverse group of people. In the early 1880s, Las Vegas was a watering hole for those on the trail to California. Areas of the Las Vegas Valley contained artesian wells that supported extensive green meadows, or *vega* in Spanish, hence the name Las Vegas. In 1855 the area was settled by Mormon missionaries, but they left two years later. In the late 1800s the land was used for ranching.

In the beginning of the twentieth century, the seeds of the present Las Vegas began to sprout. In 1905 the arrival of the Union Pacific Railroad came with businesses, saloons, and gambling houses sprinkled along it tracks and the city was formally founded on May 15, 1905.

During the Great Depression, men working on the nearby Hoover Dam spent much of their earnings in the city's establishments, and gambling was quickly legalized. Hydroelectric power from the Hoover Dam lit the city in neon, and hotels began to compete for the brightest stars and the plushest surroundings. Las Vegas was an overnight success, luring many people with get-rich-quick dreams. The dream has thus far endured, and in 2005 the city celebrated its centennial with a suitably festive media blitz, special events, and the world's largest, 130,000-pound, birthday cake.

Las Vegas is home to the World Series of Poker, which consists of 101 events. Winners have pocketed more than $12 million.

For the past 25 years, senior citizens have constituted the fastest-growing segment of the Las Vegas population, taking advantage of the dry climate, reasonably priced housing, low property taxes, no sales tax, and plenty of entertainment. Nevada continues to lead the nation in growth of its senior citizen population. Many programs exist to ensure their comfort and welfare, including quality economic, legal, and medical plans.

The city's World Market Center, a furniture wholesale showroom and marketplace, was built to compete with current furniture market capital of High Point, North Carolina. Megahotels and smaller projects continue to be developed. Billions have been spent have on hotel and casino construction. At its peak, some 3,000 people moved to the city each month, most of them in construction and casino-related work. The Durango Drive Improvement project has helped to ease traffic congestion with new ramps, a trails system underpass, new auxiliary lanes, and a new traffic signal system.

Since 2012, hundreds of millions of dollars' worth of projects have been completed. They include The Smith Center for the Performing Arts and DISCOVERY Children's Museum, Mob Museum, Neon Museum, City Hall complex and a new Zappos.com corporate headquarters in the old City Hall building.

Las Vegas valley is home to three major professional sports teams: Vegas Golden Knights (NHL); Las Vegas Raiders (NFL); and Las Vegas Aces (WNBA).

One of the more serious problems facing the fast-growing city is its diminishing water supply. It's estimated that Las Vegas gets up to 90 percent of its water from Lake Mead, whose levels are falling, not only due to usage (219 gallons daily person, more than most U.S. cities), but also due to climate change. The city employs reuse and recycle programs and encourages conservation by homeowners and businesses through desert landscaping.

The city made national headlines in October 2017 when a gunman opened fire on a crowd of concert goers on Las Vegas Boulevard, killing 58 people and injuring 800. This mass shooting, and others in recent years, contributed to the ongoing national debate on gun control.

Las Vegas is located near the center of a broad desert valley, which is nearly surrounded by mountains ranging from 2,000 to 10,000 feet. The four seasons are well defined. Summers display desert conditions with extreme high temperatures, but nights are relatively cool due to the closeness of the mountains. For about two weeks almost every summer, warm, moist air predominates, causing higher-than-average humidity and scattered, severe thunderstorms. Winters are generally mild and pleasant with clear skies prevailing. Strong winds, associated with major storms, usually reach the valley from the southwest or through the pass from the northwest. Winds over 50 miles per hour are infrequent but troublesome because of the dust and sand they stir up.

Rankings

General Rankings

- *Insider* listed 23 places in the U.S. that travel industry trends reveal would be popular destinations in 2023. This year the list trends towards cultural and historical happenings, sports events, wellness experiences and invigorating outdoor escapes. According to the website insider.com Las Vegas is a place to visit in 2023. *Insider, "23 of the Best Places You Should Travel to in the U.S. in 2023," December 17, 2022*

- The Las Vegas metro area was identified as one of America's fastest-growing areas in terms of population and business growth by *MagnifyMoney*. The area ranked #26 out of 35. The 100 most populous metro areas in the U.S. were evaluated on their change from 2011 to 2016 in the following categories: people and housing; workforce and employment opportunities; growing industry. *www.businessinsider.com, "The 35 Cities in the US with the Biggest Influx of People, the Most Work Opportunities, and the Hottest Business Growth," August 12, 2018*

- The Las Vegas metro area was identified as one of America's fastest-growing areas in terms of population and economy by *Forbes*. The area ranked #6 out of 25. The 100 most populous metro areas in the U.S. were evaluated on the following criteria: estimated population growth; employment; economic output; wages; home values. *Forbes, "America's Fastest-Growing Cities 2018," February 28, 2018*

Business/Finance Rankings

- The Brookings Institution ranked the nation's largest cities based on income inequality. Las Vegas was ranked #80 (#1 = greatest inequality). Criteria: the "95/20 ratio," a figure representing the income at which a household earns more than 95 percent of all other households, divided by the income at which a household earns more than only 20 percent of all other households. *Brookings Institution, "Household Income Inequality, Largest Cities of 97 Large U.S. Metro Areas, 2014-2016," February 5, 2018*

- The Brookings Institution ranked the 100 largest metro areas in the U.S. based on income inequality. Las Vegas was ranked #86 (#1 = greatest inequality). Criteria: the "95/20 ratio," a figure representing the income at which a household earns more than 95 percent of all other households, divided by the income at which a household earns more than only 20 percent of all other households. *Brookings Institution, "Household Income Inequality, 100 Largest U.S. Metro Areas, 2014-2016," February 5, 2018*

- Las Vegas was identified as one of America's most frugal metro areas by *Coupons.com*. The city ranked #21 out of 25. Criteria: digital coupon usage. *Coupons.com, "America's Most Frugal Cities of 2017," March 22, 2018*

- The Las Vegas metro area appeared on the Milken Institute "2022 Best Performing Cities" list. Rank: #149 out of 200 large metro areas (population over 250,000). Criteria: job growth; wage and salary growth; high-tech output growth; housing affordability; household broadband access. *Milken Institute, "Best-Performing Cities 2022," March 28, 2022*

- *Forbes* ranked the 200 most populous metro areas to determine the nation's "Best Places for Business and Careers." The Las Vegas metro area was ranked #49. Criteria: costs (business and living); job growth (past and projected); income growth; quality of life; educational attainment (college and high school); projected economic growth; cultural and leisure opportunities; workplace tolerance laws; net migration patterns. *Forbes, "The Best Places for Business and Careers 2019: Seattle Still On Top," October 30, 2019*

Culture/Performing Arts Rankings

- Las Vegas was selected as one of "America's Favorite Cities." The city ranked #13 in the "Architecture" category. Respondents to an online survey were asked to rate their favorite place (population over 100,000) in over 65 categories. *Travelandleisure.com, "America's Favorite Cities for Architecture 2016," March 2, 2017*

Dating/Romance Rankings

- Las Vegas was selected as one of America's best cities for singles by the readers of *Travel + Leisure* in their annual "America's Favorite Cities" survey. Criteria included good-looking locals, cool shopping, an active bar scene and hipster-magnet coffee bars. *Travel + Leisure, "Best Cities in America for Singles," July 21, 2017*

- Las Vegas was selected as one of the nation's most romantic cities with 100,000 or more residents by Amazon.com. The city ranked #17 of 20. Criteria: per capita sales of romance novels, relationship books, romantic comedy movies, romantic music, and sexual wellness products. *Amazon.com, "Top 20 Most Romantic Cities in the U.S.," February 1, 2017*

Education Rankings

- Personal finance website *WalletHub* analyzed the 150 largest U.S. metropolitan statistical areas to determine where the most educated Americans are putting their degrees to work. Criteria: education levels; percentage of workers with degrees; education quality and attainment gap; public school quality rankings; quality and enrollment of each metro area's universities. Las Vegas was ranked #122 (#1 = most educated city). *www.WalletHub.com, "Most & Least Educated Cities in America," July 18, 2022*

- Las Vegas was selected as one of America's most literate cities. The city ranked #54 out of the 84 largest U.S. cities. Criteria: number of booksellers; library resources; Internet resources; educational attainment; periodical publishing resources; newspaper circulation. *Central Connecticut State University, "America's Most Literate Cities, 2018," February 2019*

Environmental Rankings

- Las Vegas was highlighted as one of the 25 most ozone-polluted metro areas in the U.S. during 2019 through 2021. The area ranked #15. *American Lung Association, "State of the Air 2023," April 19, 2023*

Health/Fitness Rankings

- For each of the 100 largest cities in the United States, the American Fitness Index®, compiled in partnership between the American College of Sports Medicine and the Elevance Health Foundation, evaluated community infrastructure and 34 health behaviors including preventive health, levels of chronic disease conditions, food insecurity, sleep quality, pedestrian safety, air quality, and community/environment resources that support physical activity. Las Vegas ranked #95 for "community fitness." *americanfitnessindex.org, "2022 ACSM American Fitness Index Summary Report," July 12, 2022*

- Las Vegas was identified as a "2022 Spring Allergy Capital." The area ranked #22 out of 100. Three groups of factors were used to identify the most challenging cities for people with allergies during the spring season: annual spring pollen scores; over the counter allergy medicine use; number of board-certified allergy specialists. *Asthma and Allergy Foundation of America, "Spring Allergy Capitals 2022," March 2, 2022*

- Las Vegas was identified as a "2022 Fall Allergy Capital." The area ranked #20 out of 100. Three groups of factors were used to identify the most challenging cities for people with allergies during the fall season: annual fall pollen scores; over the counter allergy medicine use; number of board-certified allergy specialists. *Asthma and Allergy Foundation of America, "Fall Allergy Capitals 2022," March 2, 2022*

- Las Vegas was identified as a "2022 Asthma Capital." The area ranked #37 out of the nation's 100 largest metropolitan areas. Criteria: estimated asthma prevalence; asthma-related mortality; and ER visits due to asthma. Risk factors analyzed but not factored in the rankings: annual pollen score; annual air quality; public smoking laws; access to board-certified asthma specialists; rescue and controller medication use; uninsured rate; poverty rate. *Asthma and Allergy Foundation of America, "Asthma Capitals 2022: The Most Challenging Places to Live With Asthma," September 14, 2022*

Real Estate Rankings

- *WalletHub* compared the most populated U.S. cities to determine which had the best markets for real estate agents. Las Vegas ranked #87 where demand was high and pay was the best. Criteria: sales per agent; annual median wage for real-estate agents; monthly average starting salary for real estate agents; real estate job density and competition; unemployment rate; home turnover rate; housing-market health index; and other relevant metrics. *www.WalletHub.com, "2021 Best Places to Be a Real Estate Agent," May 12, 2021*

- According to Penske Truck Rental, the Las Vegas metro area was named the #2 moving destination in 2022, based on one-way consumer truck rental reservations made through Penske's website, rental locations, and reservations call center. *gopenske.com/blog, "Penske Truck Rental's 2022 Top Moving Destinations," April 27, 2023*

- Las Vegas was ranked #197 out of 235 metro areas in terms of housing affordability in 2022 by the National Association of Home Builders (#1 = most affordable). Criteria: the share of homes sold in that area affordable to a family earning the local median income, based on standard mortgage underwriting criteria. *National Association of Home Builders®, NAHB-Wells Fargo Housing Opportunity Index, 4th Quarter 2022*

- The nation's largest metro areas were analyzed in terms of the percentage of households entering some stage of foreclosure in 2022. The Las Vegas metro area ranked #7 out of 8 (#1 = highest foreclosure rate). *ATTOM Data Solutions, "2022 Year-End U.S. Foreclosure Market Report™," January 12, 2023*

Safety Rankings

- Allstate ranked the 200 largest cities in America in terms of driver safety. Las Vegas ranked #129. Criteria: internal property damage claims over a two-year period from January 2016 to December 2017. The report helps increase the importance of safety and awareness behind the wheel. *Allstate, "Allstate America's Best Drivers Report, 2019" June 24, 2019*

- The National Insurance Crime Bureau ranked 390 metro areas in the U.S. in terms of per capita rates of vehicle theft. The Las Vegas metro area ranked #27 (#1 = highest rate). Criteria: number of vehicle theft offenses per 100,000 inhabitants in 2021. *National Insurance Crime Bureau, "Hot Spots 2021," September 1, 2022*

Seniors/Retirement Rankings

- From its Best Cities for Successful Aging indexes, the Milken Institute generated rankings for metropolitan areas, weighing data in nine categories—health care, wellness, living arrangements, transportation and convenience, financial characteristics, education, employment, community engagement, and overall livability. The Las Vegas metro area was ranked #77 overall in the large metro area category. *Milken Institute, "Best Cities for Successful Aging, 2017" March 14, 2017*

Transportation Rankings

- According to the INRIX "2022 Global Traffic Scorecard," Las Vegas was identified as one of the most congested metro areas in the U.S. The area ranked #22 out of 25. Criteria: average annual time spent in traffic and average cost of congestion per motorist. *Inrix.com, "Return to Work, Higher Gas Prices & Inflation Drove Americans to Spend Hundreds More in Time and Money Commuting," January 10, 2023*

Women/Minorities Rankings

- *Travel + Leisure* listed the best cities in and around the U.S. for a memorable and fun girls' trip, even on a budget. Whether it is for a special occasion, to make new memories or just to get away, Las Vegas is sure to have something for all the ladies in your tribe. *Travel + Leisure, "25 Affordable Girls Weekend Getaways That Won't Break the Bank," November 25, 2022*

- The *Houston Chronicle* listed the Las Vegas metro area as #15 in top places for young Latinos to live in the U.S. Research was largely based on housing and occupational data from the largest metropolitan areas performed by *Forbes* and NBC Universo. Criteria: percentage of 18-34 year-olds; Latino college grad rates; and diversity. *blog.chron.com, "The 15 Best Big Cities for Latino Millenials," January 26, 2016*

- Personal finance website *WalletHub* compared more than 180 U.S. cities across two key dimensions, "Hispanic Business-Friendliness" and "Hispanic Purchasing Power," to arrive at the most favorable conditions for Hispanic entrepreneurs. Las Vegas was ranked #78 out of 182. Criteria includes: share of Hispanic-Owned Businesses; Hispanic entrepreneurship rate to median annual income of Hispanics; Small Business-Friendliness score; cost of living; and number of Hispanics with at least a bachelor's degree. *WalletHub.com, "2019's Best Cities for Hispanic Entrepreneurs," May 1, 2019*

Miscellaneous Rankings

- *MoveHub* ranked 446 hipster cities across 20 countries, using its new and improved *alternative* Hipster Index and Las Vegas came out as #19 among the top 50. Criteria: population over 150,000; number of vintage boutiques; density of tattoo parlors; vegan places to eat; coffee shops; and density of vinyl record stores. *www.movehub.com, "The Hipster Index: Brighton Pips Portland to Global Top Spot," July 28, 2021*

- The financial planning site SmartAsset has compiled its annual study on the best places for Halloween in the U.S. for 2022. 146 cities were compared to determine that Las Vegas ranked #6 out of 35 for still being able to enjoy the festivities despite COVID-19. Metrics included: safety, family-friendliness, percentage of children in the population, concentration of candy and costume shops, weather and COVID infection rates. *www.smartasset.com, "2022 Edition-Best Places to Celebrate Halloween," October 19, 2022*

- *WalletHub* compared the 150 most populated U.S. cities to determine their operating efficiency. A "Quality of Services" score was constructed for each city and then divided by the total budget per capita to reveal which were managed the best. Las Vegas ranked #46. Criteria: financial stability; economy; education; safety; health; infrastructure and pollution. *www.WalletHub.com, "2022's Best- & Worst-Run Cities in America," June 21, 2022*

Business Environment

DEMOGRAPHICS

Population Growth

Area	1990 Census	2000 Census	2010 Census	2020 Census	Population Growth (%) 1990-2020	Population Growth (%) 2010-2020
City	261,374	478,434	583,756	641,903	145.6	10.0
MSA[1]	741,459	1,375,765	1,951,269	2,265,461	205.5	16.1
U.S.	248,709,873	281,421,906	308,745,538	331,449,281	33.3	7.4

Note: (1) Figures cover the Las Vegas-Henderson-Paradise, NV Metropolitan Statistical Area
Source: U.S. Census Bureau, 1990 Census, 2000 Census, 2010 Census, 2020 Census

Race

Area	White Alone[2] (%)	Black Alone[2] (%)	Asian Alone[2] (%)	AIAN[3] Alone[2] (%)	NHOPI[4] Alone[2] (%)	Other Race Alone[2] (%)	Two or More Races (%)
City	46.0	12.9	7.2	1.1	0.7	17.0	15.0
MSA[1]	44.9	12.7	10.5	1.0	0.9	15.4	14.7
U.S.	61.6	12.4	6.0	1.1	0.2	8.4	10.2

Note: (1) Figures cover the Las Vegas-Henderson-Paradise, NV Metropolitan Statistical Area; (2) Alone is defined as not being in combination with one or more other races; (3) American Indian and Alaska Native; (4) Native Hawaiian and Other Pacific Islander
Source: U.S. Census Bureau, 2020 Census

Hispanic or Latino Origin

Area	Total (%)	Mexican (%)	Puerto Rican (%)	Cuban (%)	Other (%)
City	34.1	24.9	1.2	1.4	6.5
MSA[1]	31.8	23.3	1.1	1.5	5.9
U.S.	18.4	11.2	1.8	0.7	4.7

Note: Persons of Hispanic or Latino origin can be of any race; (1) Figures cover the Las Vegas-Henderson-Paradise, NV Metropolitan Statistical Area
Source: U.S. Census Bureau, 2017-2021 American Community Survey 5-Year Estimates

Age

Area	Under Age 5	Age 5–19	Age 20–34	Age 35–44	Age 45–54	Age 55–64	Age 65–74	Age 75–84	Age 85+	Median Age
City	5.7	20.0	20.0	13.5	13.1	12.1	9.4	4.7	1.5	38.0
MSA[1]	5.7	19.4	20.6	13.9	13.1	12.1	9.5	4.6	1.3	38.0
U.S.	5.6	19.2	20.2	12.7	12.4	13.1	10.0	4.9	1.9	38.8

Note: (1) Figures cover the Las Vegas-Henderson-Paradise, NV Metropolitan Statistical Area
Source: U.S. Census Bureau, 2020 Census

Disability by Age

Area	All Ages	Under 18 Years Old	18 to 64 Years Old	65 Years and Over
City	12.5	4.0	10.4	34.8
MSA[1]	12.1	4.0	9.9	33.9
U.S.	12.6	4.4	10.3	33.4

Note: Figures show percent of the civilian noninstitutionalized population that reported having a disability. Disability status is determined from six types of difficulty: vision, hearing, cognitive, ambulatory, self-care, and independent living. For children under 5 years old, hearing and vision difficulty are used to determine disability status. For children between the ages of 5 and 14, disability status is determined from hearing, vision, cognitive, ambulatory, and self-care difficulties. For people aged 15 years and older, they are considered to have a disability if they have difficulty with any one of the six difficulty types; Note: (1) Figures cover the Las Vegas-Henderson-Paradise, NV Metropolitan Statistical Area
Source: U.S. Census Bureau, 2017-2021 American Community Survey 5-Year Estimates

Ancestry

Area	German	Irish	English	American	Italian	Polish	French[2]	Scottish	Dutch
City	8.5	7.3	6.2	3.2	5.2	1.8	1.6	1.3	0.7
MSA[1]	8.2	6.9	6.3	3.0	4.9	1.8	1.5	1.2	0.6
U.S.	12.8	9.6	8.1	5.7	5.0	2.7	2.2	1.6	1.1

Note: Figures are the percentage of the total population reporting a particular ancestry. The nine most commonly reported ancestries in the U.S. are shown. Figures include multiple ancestries (e.g. if a person reported being Irish and Italian, they were included in both columns); (1) Figures cover the Las Vegas-Henderson-Paradise, NV Metropolitan Statistical Area; (2) Excludes Basque
Source: U.S. Census Bureau, 2017-2021 American Community Survey 5-Year Estimates

Foreign-born Population

Area	Any Foreign Country	Percent of Population Born in							
		Asia	Mexico	Europe	Caribbean	Central America[2]	South America	Africa	Canada
City	20.8	5.3	8.8	1.6	1.1	2.4	0.8	0.4	0.4
MSA[1]	22.0	7.3	7.8	1.5	1.2	2.0	0.9	0.8	0.4
U.S.	13.6	4.2	3.3	1.5	1.4	1.1	1.1	0.8	0.2

Note: (1) Figures cover the Las Vegas-Henderson-Paradise, NV Metropolitan Statistical Area; (2) Excludes Mexico.
Source: U.S. Census Bureau, 2017-2021 American Community Survey 5-Year Estimates

Household Size

Area	Persons in Household (%)							Average Household Size
	One	Two	Three	Four	Five	Six	Seven or More	
City	30.2	31.4	15.5	12.2	6.1	2.8	1.8	2.70
MSA[1]	28.0	32.8	15.5	12.3	6.8	2.8	1.8	2.70
U.S.	28.1	33.8	15.5	12.9	6.0	2.3	1.4	2.60

Note: (1) Figures cover the Las Vegas-Henderson-Paradise, NV Metropolitan Statistical Area
Source: U.S. Census Bureau, 2017-2021 American Community Survey 5-Year Estimates

Household Relationships

Area	House-holder	Opposite-sex Spouse	Same-sex Spouse	Opposite-sex Unmarried Partner	Same-sex Unmarried Partner	Child[2]	Grand-child	Other Relatives	Non-relatives
City	37.5	15.2	0.3	2.9	0.2	29.3	2.7	6.7	4.3
MSA[1]	37.3	15.5	0.3	3.0	0.2	28.7	2.6	7.0	4.4
U.S.	38.3	17.5	0.2	2.5	0.2	28.3	2.4	4.8	3.4

Note: Figures are percent of the total population; (1) Figures cover the Las Vegas-Henderson-Paradise, NV Metropolitan Statistical Area; (2) Includes biological, adopted, and stepchildren of the householder
Source: U.S. Census Bureau, 2020 Census

Gender

Area	Males	Females	Males per 100 Females
City	317,700	324,203	98.0
MSA[1]	1,126,444	1,139,017	98.9
U.S.	162,685,811	168,763,470	96.4

Note: (1) Figures cover the Las Vegas-Henderson-Paradise, NV Metropolitan Statistical Area
Source: U.S. Census Bureau, 2020 Census

Marital Status

Area	Never Married	Now Married[2]	Separated	Widowed	Divorced
City	35.6	43.7	2.0	5.2	13.5
MSA[1]	35.2	44.3	2.1	5.0	13.4
U.S.	33.8	48.0	1.8	5.6	10.8

Note: Figures are percentages and cover the population 15 years of age and older; (1) Figures cover the Las Vegas-Henderson-Paradise, NV Metropolitan Statistical Area; (2) Excludes separated
Source: U.S. Census Bureau, 2017-2021 American Community Survey 5-Year Estimates

Religious Groups by Family

Area	Catholic	Baptist	Methodist	LDS[2]	Pentecostal	Lutheran	Islam	Adventist	Other
MSA[1]	26.2	1.9	0.3	5.8	1.5	0.6	0.3	1.3	5.5
U.S.	18.7	7.3	3.0	2.0	1.8	1.7	1.3	1.3	11.6

Note: Figures are the number of adherents as a percentage of the total population and cover the eight largest religious groups in the U.S; (1) Figures cover the Las Vegas-Henderson-Paradise, NV Metropolitan Statistical Area; (2) Church of Jesus Christ of Latter-day Saints
Sources: 2020 U.S. Religion Census, Association of Statisticians of American Religious Bodies; The Association of Religion Data Archives (ARDA)

Religious Groups by Tradition

Area	Catholic	Evangelical Protestant	Mainline Protestant	Black Protestant	Islam	Judaism	Hinduism	Orthodox	Buddhism
MSA[1]	26.2	6.6	1.0	0.5	0.3	0.3	0.2	0.6	0.7
U.S.	18.7	16.5	5.2	2.3	1.3	0.6	0.4	0.4	0.3

Note: Figures are the number of adherents as a percentage of the total population; (1) Figures cover the Las Vegas-Henderson-Paradise, NV Metropolitan Statistical Area
Sources: 2020 U.S. Religion Census, Association of Statisticians of American Religious Bodies; The Association of Religion Data Archives (ARDA)

ECONOMY

Gross Metropolitan Product

Area	2020	2021	2022	2023	Rank[2]
MSA[1]	119.4	134.8	151.1	164.0	36

Note: Figures are in billions of dollars; (1) Figures cover the Las Vegas-Henderson-Paradise, NV Metropolitan Statistical Area; (2) Rank is based on 2021 data and ranges from 1 to 381
Source: U.S. Conference of Mayors, U.S. Metro Economies: U.S. Metros Compared to Global and State Economies, June 2022

Economic Growth

Area	2018-20 (%)	2021 (%)	2022 (%)	2023 (%)	Rank[2]
MSA[1]	-3.4	7.7	5.7	5.1	349
U.S.	-0.6	5.7	3.1	2.9	–

Note: Figures are real gross metropolitan product (GMP) growth rates and represent average annual percent change; (1) Figures cover the Las Vegas-Henderson-Paradise, NV Metropolitan Statistical Area; (2) Rank is based on 2020 2-year average annual percent change and ranges from 1 to 381
Source: U.S. Conference of Mayors, U.S. Metro Economies: U.S. Metros Compared to Global and State Economies, June 2022

Metropolitan Area Exports

Area	2016	2017	2018	2019	2020	2021	Rank[2]
MSA[1]	2,312.3	2,710.6	2,240.6	2,430.8	1,705.9	1,866.2	115

Note: Figures are in millions of dollars; (1) Figures cover the Las Vegas-Henderson-Paradise, NV Metropolitan Statistical Area; (2) Rank is based on 2021 data and ranges from 1 to 388
Source: U.S. Department of Commerce, International Trade Administration, Office of Trade and Economic Analysis, Industry and Analysis, Exports by Metropolitan Area, data extracted March 16, 2023

Building Permits

Area	Single-Family			Multi-Family			Total		
	2021	2022	Pct. Chg.	2021	2022	Pct. Chg.	2021	2022	Pct. Chg.
City	2,700	3,001	11.1	1,048	1,024	-2.3	3,748	4,025	7.4
MSA[1]	12,156	9,199	-24.3	4,151	3,867	-6.8	16,307	13,066	-19.9
U.S.	1,115,400	975,600	-12.5	621,600	689,500	10.9	1,737,000	1,665,100	-4.1

Note: (1) Figures cover the Las Vegas-Henderson-Paradise, NV Metropolitan Statistical Area; Figures represent new, privately-owned housing units authorized (unadjusted data); All permit data are based on estimates with imputation
Source: U.S. Census Bureau, Manufacturing, Mining, and Construction Statistics, Building Permits, 2021, 2022

Bankruptcy Filings

Area	Business Filings			Nonbusiness Filings		
	2021	2022	% Chg.	2021	2022	% Chg.
Clark County	181	163	-9.9	5,825	4,525	-22.3
U.S.	14,347	13,481	-6.0	399,269	374,240	-6.3

Note: Business filings include Chapter 7, Chapter 9, Chapter 11, Chapter 12, Chapter 13, Chapter 15, and Section 304; Nonbusiness filings include Chapter 7, Chapter 11, and Chapter 13
Source: Administrative Office of the U.S. Courts, Business and Nonbusiness Bankruptcy, County Cases Commenced by Chapter of the Bankruptcy Code, During the 12-Month Period Ending December 31, 2021 and Business and Nonbusiness Bankruptcy, County Cases Commenced by Chapter of the Bankruptcy Code, During the 12-Month Period Ending December 31, 2022

Housing Vacancy Rates

Area	Gross Vacancy Rate[2] (%)			Year-Round Vacancy Rate[3] (%)			Rental Vacancy Rate[4] (%)			Homeowner Vacancy Rate[5] (%)		
	2020	2021	2022	2020	2021	2022	2020	2021	2022	2020	2021	2022
MSA[1]	7.8	7.7	9.2	7.1	7.1	8.3	5.0	3.7	5.7	1.1	0.9	0.9
U.S.	10.6	10.8	10.5	8.2	8.4	8.2	6.3	6.1	5.8	1.0	0.9	0.8

Note: (1) Figures cover the Las Vegas-Henderson-Paradise, NV Metropolitan Statistical Area; (2) The percentage of the total housing inventory that is vacant; (3) The percentage of the housing inventory (excluding seasonal units) that is year-round vacant; (4) The percentage of rental inventory that is vacant for rent; (5) The percentage of homeowner inventory that is vacant for sale
Source: U.S. Census Bureau, Housing Vacancies and Homeownership Annual Statistics: 2020, 2021, 2022

INCOME

Income

Area	Per Capita ($)	Median Household ($)	Average Household ($)
City	33,363	61,356	86,008
MSA[1]	33,461	64,210	87,879
U.S.	37,638	69,021	97,196

Note: (1) Figures cover the Las Vegas-Henderson-Paradise, NV Metropolitan Statistical Area
Source: U.S. Census Bureau, 2017-2021 American Community Survey 5-Year Estimates

Household Income Distribution

Area	Percent of Households Earning							
	Under $15,000	$15,000 -$24,999	$25,000 -$34,999	$35,000 -$49,999	$50,000 -$74,999	$75,000 -$99,999	$100,000 -$149,999	$150,000 and up
City	11.6	8.1	8.7	12.9	17.3	13.1	15.2	13.0
MSA[1]	9.7	7.7	8.8	12.8	18.2	13.4	15.7	13.6
U.S.	9.4	7.8	8.2	11.4	16.8	12.8	16.3	17.3

Note: (1) Figures cover the Las Vegas-Henderson-Paradise, NV Metropolitan Statistical Area
Source: U.S. Census Bureau, 2017-2021 American Community Survey 5-Year Estimates

Poverty Rate

Area	All Ages	Under 18 Years Old	18 to 64 Years Old	65 Years and Over
City	14.9	20.8	13.6	11.3
MSA[1]	13.6	19.0	12.5	9.8
U.S.	12.6	17.0	11.8	9.6

Note: Figures are percentage of people whose income during the past 12 months was below the poverty level;
(1) Figures cover the Las Vegas-Henderson-Paradise, NV Metropolitan Statistical Area
Source: U.S. Census Bureau, 2017-2021 American Community Survey 5-Year Estimates

EMPLOYMENT

Labor Force and Employment

Area	Civilian Labor Force			Workers Employed		
	Dec. 2021	Dec. 2022	% Chg.	Dec. 2021	Dec. 2022	% Chg.
City	301,290	316,801	5.1	286,123	299,424	4.6
MSA[1]	1,093,227	1,149,504	5.1	1,039,029	1,087,331	4.6
U.S.	161,696,000	164,224,000	1.6	155,732,000	158,872,000	2.0

Note: Data is not seasonally adjusted and covers workers 16 years of age and older; (1) Figures cover the Las Vegas-Henderson-Paradise, NV Metropolitan Statistical Area
Source: Bureau of Labor Statistics, Local Area Unemployment Statistics

Unemployment Rate

Area	2022											
	Jan.	Feb.	Mar.	Apr.	May	Jun.	Jul.	Aug.	Sep.	Oct.	Nov.	Dec.
City	5.9	5.4	5.2	5.2	5.4	5.8	5.7	5.8	5.4	5.8	5.7	5.5
MSA[1]	5.8	5.3	5.0	5.0	5.2	5.7	5.6	5.7	5.3	5.6	5.6	5.4
U.S.	4.4	4.1	3.8	3.3	3.4	3.8	3.8	3.8	3.3	3.4	3.4	3.3

Note: Data is not seasonally adjusted and covers workers 16 years of age and older; (1) Figures cover the Las Vegas-Henderson-Paradise, NV Metropolitan Statistical Area
Source: Bureau of Labor Statistics, Local Area Unemployment Statistics

Average Wages

Occupation	$/Hr.	Occupation	$/Hr.
Accountants and Auditors	32.32	Maintenance and Repair Workers	23.05
Automotive Mechanics	23.93	Marketing Managers	51.14
Bookkeepers	22.52	Network and Computer Systems Admin.	49.43
Carpenters	31.29	Nurses, Licensed Practical	30.50
Cashiers	12.95	Nurses, Registered	46.96
Computer Programmers	46.77	Nursing Assistants	19.90
Computer Systems Analysts	45.39	Office Clerks, General	19.84
Computer User Support Specialists	25.53	Physical Therapists	51.20
Construction Laborers	21.97	Physicians	126.98
Cooks, Restaurant	17.17	Plumbers, Pipefitters and Steamfitters	31.07
Customer Service Representatives	18.68	Police and Sheriff's Patrol Officers	36.94
Dentists	n/a	Postal Service Mail Carriers	26.97
Electricians	33.87	Real Estate Sales Agents	38.35
Engineers, Electrical	42.86	Retail Salespersons	16.82
Fast Food and Counter Workers	12.19	Sales Representatives, Technical/Scientific	41.45
Financial Managers	58.11	Secretaries, Exc. Legal/Medical/Executive	21.22
First-Line Supervisors of Office Workers	29.10	Security Guards	15.06
General and Operations Managers	60.12	Surgeons	n/a
Hairdressers/Cosmetologists	13.20	Teacher Assistants, Exc. Postsecondary*	16.36
Home Health and Personal Care Aides	15.34	Teachers, Secondary School, Exc. Sp. Ed.*	30.96
Janitors and Cleaners	15.69	Telemarketers	15.02
Landscaping/Groundskeeping Workers	17.85	Truck Drivers, Heavy/Tractor-Trailer	24.98
Lawyers	82.94	Truck Drivers, Light/Delivery Services	20.79
Maids and Housekeeping Cleaners	17.87	Waiters and Waitresses	13.18

Note: Wage data covers the Las Vegas-Henderson-Paradise, NV Metropolitan Statistical Area; (*) Hourly wages were calculated from annual wage data based on a 40 hour work week; n/a not available.
Source: Bureau of Labor Statistics, Metro Area Occupational Employment & Wage Estimates, May 2022

Employment by Industry

Sector	MSA[1]		U.S.
	Number of Employees	Percent of Total	Percent of Total
Construction	81,000	7.3	5.0
Private Education and Health Services	120,300	10.8	16.1
Financial Activities	59,700	5.4	5.9
Government	111,600	10.0	14.5
Information	13,600	1.2	2.0
Leisure and Hospitality	288,900	25.9	10.3
Manufacturing	29,000	2.6	8.4
Mining and Logging	400	<0.1	0.4
Other Services	32,200	2.9	3.7
Professional and Business Services	164,900	14.8	14.7
Retail Trade	115,500	10.4	10.2
Transportation, Warehousing, and Utilities	71,200	6.4	4.9
Wholesale Trade	26,500	2.4	3.9

Note: Figures are non-farm employment as of December 2022. Figures are not seasonally adjusted and include workers 16 years of age and older; (1) Figures cover the Las Vegas-Henderson-Paradise, NV Metropolitan Statistical Area
Source: Bureau of Labor Statistics, Current Employment Statistics, Employment, Hours, and Earnings

Employment by Occupation

Occupation Classification	City (%)	MSA[1] (%)	U.S. (%)
Management, Business, Science, and Arts	31.4	30.9	40.3
Natural Resources, Construction, and Maintenance	9.1	8.3	8.7
Production, Transportation, and Material Moving	10.8	11.4	13.1
Sales and Office	22.9	22.9	20.9
Service	25.8	26.5	17.0

Note: Figures cover employed civilians 16 years of age and older; (1) Figures cover the Las Vegas-Henderson-Paradise, NV Metropolitan Statistical Area
Source: U.S. Census Bureau, 2017-2021 American Community Survey 5-Year Estimates

Occupations with Greatest Projected Employment Growth: 2022 – 2024

Occupation[1]	2022 Employment	2024 Projected Employment	Numeric Employment Change	Percent Employment Change
Cooks, Restaurant	21,370	23,140	1,770	8.3
Retail Salespersons	45,170	46,620	1,450	3.2
Waiters and Waitresses	33,630	35,050	1,420	4.2
Fast Food and Counter Workers	48,110	49,490	1,380	2.9
Laborers and Freight, Stock, and Material Movers, Hand	40,790	42,090	1,300	3.2
Gaming Dealers	17,690	18,870	1,180	6.7
Stockers and Order Fillers	25,590	26,760	1,170	4.6
Carpenters	18,390	19,350	960	5.2
Construction Laborers	16,070	16,910	840	5.2
General and Operations Managers	23,480	24,240	760	3.2

Note: Projections cover Nevada; (1) Sorted by numeric employment change
Source: www.projectionscentral.com, State Occupational Projections, 2022–2024 Short-Term Projections

Fastest-Growing Occupations: 2022 – 2024

Occupation[1]	2022 Employment	2024 Projected Employment	Numeric Employment Change	Percent Employment Change
Nurse Practitioners	1,480	1,640	160	10.8
Flight Attendants	3,500	3,850	350	10.0
Refuse and Recyclable Material Collectors	1,340	1,460	120	9.0
Logisticians	680	740	60	8.8
Cutting and Slicing Machine Setters, Operators, and Tenders	690	750	60	8.7
Printing Press Operators	1,660	1,800	140	8.4
Cooks, Restaurant	21,370	23,140	1,770	8.3
Plasterers and Stucco Masons	1,590	1,720	130	8.2
Nonfarm Animal Caretakers	2,470	2,670	200	8.1
Molders, Shapers, and Casters, Except Metal and Plastic	780	840	60	7.7

Note: Projections cover Nevada; (1) Sorted by percent employment change and excludes occupations with numeric employment change less than 50
Source: www.projectionscentral.com, State Occupational Projections, 2022–2024 Short-Term Projections

CITY FINANCES

City Government Finances

Component	2020 ($000)	2020 ($ per capita)
Total Revenues	1,018,421	1,564
Total Expenditures	1,090,099	1,674
Debt Outstanding	753,381	1,157
Cash and Securities[1]	1,114,816	1,712

Note: (1) Cash and security holdings of a government at the close of its fiscal year, including those of its dependent agencies, utilities, and liquor stores.
Source: U.S. Census Bureau, State & Local Government Finances 2020

City Government Revenue by Source

Source	2020 ($000)	2020 ($ per capita)	2020 (%)
General Revenue			
From Federal Government	70,777	109	6.9
From State Government	321,439	494	31.6
From Local Governments	134,979	207	13.3
Taxes			
Property	137,139	211	13.5
Sales and Gross Receipts	79,934	123	7.8
Personal Income	0	0	0.0
Corporate Income	0	0	0.0
Motor Vehicle License	0	0	0.0
Other Taxes	56,413	87	5.5
Current Charges	157,580	242	15.5
Liquor Store	0	0	0.0
Utility	87	0	0.0

Source: U.S. Census Bureau, State & Local Government Finances 2020

City Government Expenditures by Function

Function	2020 ($000)	2020 ($ per capita)	2020 (%)
General Direct Expenditures			
Air Transportation	0	0	0.0
Corrections	66,712	102	6.1
Education	0	0	0.0
Employment Security Administration	0	0	0.0
Financial Administration	10,033	15	0.9
Fire Protection	163,653	251	15.0
General Public Buildings	39,734	61	3.6
Governmental Administration, Other	35,240	54	3.2
Health	5,184	8	0.5
Highways	172,526	264	15.8
Hospitals	0	0	0.0
Housing and Community Development	21,230	32	1.9
Interest on General Debt	31,114	47	2.9
Judicial and Legal	35,181	54	3.2
Libraries	0	0	0.0
Parking	10,456	16	1.0
Parks and Recreation	53,684	82	4.9
Police Protection	15,100	23	1.4
Public Welfare	0	0	0.0
Sewerage	63,986	98	5.9
Solid Waste Management	7,709	11	0.7
Veterans' Services	0	0	0.0
Liquor Store	0	0	0.0
Utility	0	0	0.0

Source: U.S. Census Bureau, State & Local Government Finances 2020

TAXES

State Corporate Income Tax Rates

State	Tax Rate (%)	Income Brackets ($)	Num. of Brackets	Financial Institution Tax Rate (%)[a]	Federal Income Tax Ded.
Nevada	None	–	–	–	

Note: Tax rates as of January 1, 2023; (a) Rates listed are the corporate income tax rate applied to financial institutions or excise taxes based on income. Some states have other taxes based upon the value of deposits or shares.
Source: Federation of Tax Administrators, State Corporate Income Tax Rates, January 1, 2023

State Individual Income Tax Rates

State	Tax Rate (%)	Income Brackets ($)	Personal Exemptions ($)			Standard Ded. ($)	
			Single	Married	Depend.	Single	Married
Nevada					– No state income tax –		

Note: Tax rates as of January 1, 2023; Local- and county-level taxes are not included
Source: Federation of Tax Administrators, State Individual Income Tax Rates, January 1, 2023

Various State Sales and Excise Tax Rates

State	State Sales Tax (%)	Gasoline[1] ($/gal.)	Cigarette[2] ($/pack)	Spirits[3] ($/gal.)	Wine[4] ($/gal.)	Beer[5] ($/gal.)	Recreational Marijuana (%)
Nevada	6.85	0.5228	1.80	3.60	0.70	0.16	(l)

Note: All tax rates as of January 1, 2023; (1) The American Petroleum Institute has developed a methodology for determining the average tax rate on a gallon of fuel. Rates may include any of the following: excise taxes, environmental fees, storage tank fees, other fees or taxes, general sales tax, and local taxes; (2) The federal excise tax of $1.0066 per pack and local taxes are not included; (3) Rates are those applicable to off-premise sales of 40% alcohol by volume (a.b.v.) distilled spirits in 750ml containers. Local excise taxes are excluded; (4) Rates are those applicable to off-premise sales of 11% a.b.v. non-carbonated wine in 750ml containers; (5) Rates are those applicable to off-premise sales of 4.7% a.b.v. beer in 12 ounce containers; (l) 15% excise tax (fair market value at wholesale); 10% excise tax (retail price)
Source: Tax Foundation, 2023 Facts & Figures: How Does Your State Compare?

State Business Tax Climate Index Rankings

State	Overall Rank	Corporate Tax Rank	Individual Income Tax Rank	Sales Tax Rank	Property Tax Rank	Unemployment Insurance Tax Rank
Nevada	7	25	5	44	5	46

Note: The index is a measure of how each state's tax laws affect economic performance. The lower the rank, the more favorable a state's tax system is for business. States without a given tax are given a ranking of 1. The scores/rankings for the District of Columbia do not affect other states. The 2023 index represents the tax climate as of July 1, 2022.
Source: Tax Foundation, State Business Tax Climate Index 2023

TRANSPORTATION

Means of Transportation to Work

Area	Car/Truck/Van		Public Transportation			Bicycle	Walked	Other Means	Worked at Home
	Drove Alone	Car-pooled	Bus	Subway	Railroad				
City	75.5	9.8	2.8	0.0	0.0	0.2	1.3	2.9	7.4
MSA[1]	75.8	10.1	2.6	0.0	0.0	0.2	1.3	2.5	7.4
U.S.	73.2	8.6	2.0	1.6	0.5	0.5	2.5	1.5	9.7

Note: Figures are percentages and cover workers 16 years of age and older; (1) Figures cover the Las Vegas-Henderson-Paradise, NV Metropolitan Statistical Area
Source: U.S. Census Bureau, 2017-2021 American Community Survey 5-Year Estimates

Travel Time to Work

Area	Less Than 10 Minutes	10 to 19 Minutes	20 to 29 Minutes	30 to 44 Minutes	45 to 59 Minutes	60 to 89 Minutes	90 Minutes or More
City	7.3	24.0	30.6	27.4	6.2	2.7	1.9
MSA[1]	7.8	27.5	29.4	25.4	5.4	2.6	1.9
U.S.	12.4	28.5	21.0	20.9	8.2	6.2	2.9

Note: Note: Figures are percentages and include workers 16 years old and over; (1) Figures cover the Las Vegas-Henderson-Paradise, NV Metropolitan Statistical Area
Source: U.S. Census Bureau, 2017-2021 American Community Survey 5-Year Estimates

Key Congestion Measures

Measure	1990	2000	2010	2015	2020
Annual Hours of Delay, Total (000)	9,793	31,658	48,936	56,055	21,702
Annual Hours of Delay, Per Auto Commuter	28	41	44	49	18
Annual Congestion Cost, Per Auto Commuter ($)	291	708	871	922	363

Note: Covers the Las Vegas-Henderson NV urban area
Source: Texas A&M Transportation Institute, 2021 Urban Mobility Report

Freeway Travel Time Index

Measure	1985	1990	1995	2000	2005	2010	2015	2020
Urban Area Index[1]	1.10	1.16	1.21	1.24	1.27	1.25	1.24	1.07
Urban Area Rank[1,2]	27	19	16	18	18	21	26	57

Note: Freeway Travel Time Index—the ratio of travel time in the peak period to the travel time at free-flow conditions. For example, a value of 1.30 indicates a 20-minute free-flow trip takes 26 minutes in the peak (20 minutes x 1.30 = 26 minutes); (1) Covers the Las Vegas-Henderson NV urban area; (2) Rank is based on 101 larger urban areas (#1 = highest travel time index)
Source: Texas A&M Transportation Institute, 2021 Urban Mobility Report

Public Transportation

Agency Name / Mode of Transportation	Vehicles Operated in Maximum Service[1]	Annual Unlinked Passenger Trips[2] (in thous.)	Annual Passenger Miles[3] (in thous.)
Regional Transportation Commission of Southern Nevada (RTC)			
Bus (purchased transportation)	230	33,427.3	132,526.2
Demand Response (purchased transportation)	293	915.1	8,579.5

Note: (1) Number of revenue vehicles operated by the given mode and type of service to meet the annual maximum service requirement. This is the revenue vehicle count during the peak season of the year; on the week and day that maximum service is provided. Vehicles operated in maximum service (VOMS) exclude atypical days and one-time special events; (2) Number of passengers who boarded public transportation vehicles. Passengers are counted each time they board a vehicle no matter how many vehicles they use to travel from their origin to their destination. (3) Sum of the distances ridden by all passengers during the entire fiscal year.
Source: Federal Transit Administration, National Transit Database, 2021

Air Transportation

Airport Name and Code / Type of Service	Passenger Airlines[1]	Passenger Enplanements	Freight Carriers[2]	Freight (lbs)
McCarran International (LAS)				
Domestic service (U.S. carriers - 2022)	28	24,148,074	15	107,743,312
International service (U.S. carriers - 2021)	8	23,572	1	44,776

Note: (1) Includes all U.S.-based major, minor and commuter airlines that carried at least one passenger during the year; (2) Includes all U.S.-based airlines and freight carriers that transported at least one pound of freight during the year.
Source: Bureau of Transportation Statistics, The Intermodal Transportation Database, Air Carriers: T-100 Domestic Market (U.S. Carriers), 2022; Bureau of Transportation Statistics, The Intermodal Transportation Database, Air Carriers: T-100 International Market (U.S. Carriers), 2021

BUSINESSES

Major Business Headquarters

Company Name	Industry	Rankings	
		Fortune[1]	Forbes[2]
No companies listed	-	-	-

Note: (1) Companies that produce a 10-K are ranked 1 to 500 based on 2021 revenue; (2) All private companies with at least $2 billion in annual revenue through the end of their most current fiscal year are ranked 1 to 246; companies listed are headquartered in the city; dashes indicate no ranking
Source: Fortune, "Fortune 500," 2022; Forbes, "America's Largest Private Companies," 2022

Fastest-Growing Businesses

According to *Inc.*, Las Vegas is home to three of America's 500 fastest-growing private companies: **Fohse** (#19); **Neato** (#39); **Macros** (#480). Criteria: must be an independent, privately-held, for-profit, U.S. corporation, proprietorship or partnership as of December 31, 2021; revenues must be at least $100,000 in 2018 and $2 million in 2021; must have four-year operating/sales history. *Inc., "America's 500 Fastest-Growing Private Companies," 2022*

According to Deloitte, Las Vegas is home to one of North America's 500 fastest-growing high-technology companies: **Remark Holdings** (#341). Companies are ranked by percentage growth in revenue over a four-year period. Criteria for inclusion: company must be headquartered within North America; must own proprietary intellectual property or technology that is sold to customers in products that contributes to a significant portion of the company's operating revenue; must have been in business for a minumum of four years with 2018 operating revenues of at least $50,000 USD/CD and 2021 operating revenues of at least $5 million USD/CD. *Deloitte, 2022 Technology Fast 500*™

Living Environment

COST OF LIVING

Cost of Living Index

Composite Index	Groceries	Housing	Utilities	Trans-portation	Health Care	Misc. Goods/ Services
101.0	102.8	110.3	102.3	113.3	92.8	90.1

Note: The Cost of Living Index measures regional differences in the cost of consumer goods and services, excluding taxes and non-consumer expenditures, for professional and managerial households in the top income quintile. It is based on more than 50,000 prices covering almost 60 different items for which prices are collected three times a year by chambers of commerce, economic development organizations or university applied economic centers in each participating urban area. The numbers shown should be read as a percentage above or below the national average of 100. For example, a value of 115.4 in the groceries column indicates that grocery prices are 15.4% higher than the national average. Small differences in the index numbers should not be interpreted as significant; Figures cover the Las Vegas NV urban area.
Source: The Council for Community and Economic Research, Cost of Living Index, 2022

Grocery Prices

Area[1]	T-Bone Steak ($/pound)	Frying Chicken ($/pound)	Whole Milk ($/half gal.)	Eggs ($/dozen)	Orange Juice ($/64 oz.)	Coffee ($/11.5 oz.)
City[2]	14.35	1.87	2.51	2.43	4.05	5.47
Avg.	13.81	1.59	2.43	2.25	3.85	4.95
Min.	10.17	0.90	1.51	1.30	2.90	3.46
Max.	19.35	3.30	4.32	4.32	5.31	8.59

*Note: (1) Values for the local area are compared with the average, minimum and maximum values for all 286 areas in the Cost of Living Index; (2) Figures cover the Las Vegas NV urban area; **T-Bone Steak** (price per pound); **Frying Chicken** (price per pound, whole fryer); **Whole Milk** (half gallon carton); **Eggs** (price per dozen, Grade A, large); **Orange Juice** (64 oz. Tropicana or Florida Natural); **Coffee** (11.5 oz. can, vacuum-packed, Maxwell House, Hills Bros, or Folgers).*
Source: The Council for Community and Economic Research, Cost of Living Index, 2022

Housing and Utility Costs

Area[1]	New Home Price ($)	Apartment Rent ($/month)	All Electric ($/month)	Part Electric ($/month)	Other Energy ($/month)	Telephone ($/month)
City[2]	491,447	1,600	-	121.78	57.89	196.21
Avg.	450,913	1,371	176.41	99.93	76.96	190.22
Min.	229,283	546	100.84	31.56	27.15	174.27
Max.	2,434,977	4,569	356.86	249.59	272.24	208.31

*Note: (1) Values for the local area are compared with the average, minimum and maximum values for all 286 areas in the Cost of Living Index; (2) Figures cover the Las Vegas NV urban area; **New Home Price** (2,400 sf living area, 8,000 sf lot, in urban area with full utilities); **Apartment Rent** (950 sf 2 bedroom/1.5 or 2 bath, unfurnished, excluding all utilities except water); **All Electric** (average monthly cost for an all-electric home); **Part Electric** (average monthly cost for a part-electric home); **Other Energy** (average monthly cost for natural gas, fuel oil, coal, wood, and any other forms of energy except electricity); **Telephone** (price includes the base monthly rate plus taxes and fees for three lines of mobile phone service).*
Source: The Council for Community and Economic Research, Cost of Living Index, 2022

Health Care, Transportation, and Other Costs

Area[1]	Doctor ($/visit)	Dentist ($/visit)	Optometrist ($/visit)	Gasoline ($/gallon)	Beauty Salon ($/visit)	Men's Shirt ($)
City[2]	108.58	98.81	101.71	4.55	46.52	20.35
Avg.	124.91	107.77	117.66	3.86	43.31	34.21
Min.	36.61	58.25	51.79	2.90	22.18	13.05
Max.	250.21	162.58	371.96	5.54	85.61	63.54

*Note: (1) Values for the local area are compared with the average, minimum and maximum values for all 286 areas in the Cost of Living Index; (2) Figures cover the Las Vegas NV urban area; **Doctor** (general practitioners routine exam of an established patient); **Dentist** (adult teeth cleaning and periodic oral examination); **Optometrist** (full vision eye exam for established adult patient); **Gasoline** (one gallon regular unleaded, national brand, including all taxes, cash price at self-service pump if available); **Beauty Salon** (woman's shampoo, trim, and blow-dry); **Men's Shirt** (cotton/polyester dress shirt, pinpoint weave, long sleeves).*
Source: The Council for Community and Economic Research, Cost of Living Index, 2022

HOUSING

Homeownership Rate

Area	2015 (%)	2016 (%)	2017 (%)	2018 (%)	2019 (%)	2020 (%)	2021 (%)	2022 (%)
MSA[1]	52.1	51.3	54.4	58.1	56.0	57.3	57.7	58.7
U.S.	63.7	63.4	63.9	64.4	64.6	66.6	65.5	65.8

Note: (1) Figures cover the Las Vegas-Henderson-Paradise, NV Metropolitan Statistical Area
Source: U.S. Census Bureau, Housing Vacancies and Homeownership Annual Statistics: 2015-2022

House Price Index (HPI)

Area	National Ranking[2]	Quarterly Change (%)	One-Year Change (%)	Five-Year Change (%)	Since 1991Q1 (%)
MSA[1]	157	-3.37	10.38	70.87	260.78
U.S.[3]	–	0.34	8.41	58.44	289.08

Note: The HPI is a weighted repeat sales index. It measures average price changes in repeat sales or refinancings on the same properties. This information is obtained by reviewing repeat mortgage transactions on single-family properties whose mortgages have been purchased or securitized by Fannie Mae or Freddie Mac since January 1975; (1) Figures cover the Las Vegas-Henderson-Paradise, NV Metropolitan Statistical Area; (2) Rankings are based on annual percentage change for all metro areas containing at least 15,000 transactions over the last 10 years and ranges from 1 to 257; (3) figures based on a weighted average of Census Division estimates using a seasonally adjusted, purchase-only index; all figures are for the period ending December 31, 2022
Source: Federal Housing Finance Agency, Change in FHFA Metropolitan Area House Price Indexes, 2022Q4

Median Single-Family Home Prices

Area	2020	2021	2022[p]	Percent Change 2021 to 2022
MSA[1]	331.0	397.0	466.4	17.5
U.S. Average	300.2	357.1	392.6	9.9

Note: Figures are median sales prices of existing single-family homes in thousands of dollars; (p) preliminary; (1) Figures cover the Las Vegas-Henderson-Paradise, NV Metropolitan Statistical Area
Source: National Association of Realtors, Median Sales Price of Existing Single-Family Homes for Metropolitan Areas, 4th Quarter 2022

Qualifying Income Based on Median Sales Price of Existing Single-Family Homes

Area	With 5% Down ($)	With 10% Down ($)	With 20% Down ($)
MSA[1]	132,030	125,081	111,183
U.S. Average	112,234	106,237	94,513

Note: Figures are preliminary; Qualifying income is based on a mortgage rate of 6.77%. Monthly principal and interest payment is limited to 25% of income; (1) Figures cover the Las Vegas-Henderson-Paradise, NV Metropolitan Statistical Area
Source: National Association of Realtors, Qualifying Income Based on Median Sales Price of Existing Single-Family Homes for Metropolitan Areas, 4th Quarter 2022

Home Value

Area	Under $100,000	$100,000 -$199,999	$200,000 -$299,999	$300,000 -$399,999	$400,000 -$499,999	$500,000 -$999,999	$1,000,000 or more	Median ($)
City	4.3	14.0	31.2	23.5	11.7	13.1	2.2	302,100
MSA[1]	5.6	12.8	29.4	25.2	12.4	12.3	2.3	308,800
U.S.	16.2	24.2	20.1	13.6	8.3	13.6	4.1	244,900

Note: Figures are percentages except for median and cover owner-occupied housing units; (1) Figures cover the Las Vegas-Henderson-Paradise, NV Metropolitan Statistical Area
Source: U.S. Census Bureau, 2017-2021 American Community Survey 5-Year Estimates

Year Housing Structure Built

Area	2020 or Later	2010 -2019	2000 -2009	1990 -1999	1980 -1989	1970 -1979	1960 -1969	1950 -1959	1940 -1949	Before 1940	Median Year
City	0.2	7.1	21.8	31.0	16.3	10.1	7.6	4.2	1.1	0.5	1993
MSA[1]	0.3	10.0	29.1	27.6	14.2	10.6	4.9	2.1	0.7	0.4	1996
U.S.	0.2	7.3	13.6	13.6	13.2	14.8	10.3	10.0	4.7	12.2	1979

Note: Figures are percentages except for Median Year; Note: (1) Figures cover the Las Vegas-Henderson-Paradise, NV Metropolitan Statistical Area
Source: U.S. Census Bureau, 2017-2021 American Community Survey 5-Year Estimates

Gross Monthly Rent

Area	Under $500	$500 -$999	$1,000 -$1,499	$1,500 -$1,999	$2,000 -$2,499	$2,500 -$2,999	$3,000 and up	Median ($)
City	4.0	25.7	42.9	20.6	4.9	1.0	0.9	1,219
MSA[1]	2.3	24.0	42.7	23.4	5.6	1.2	0.8	1,257
U.S.	8.1	30.5	30.8	16.8	7.3	3.1	3.5	1,163

Note: Figures are percentages except for median; Gross rent is the contract rent plus the estimated average monthly cost of utilities (electricity, gas, and water and sewer) and fuels (oil, coal, kerosene, wood, etc.) if these are paid by the renter (or paid for the renter by someone else); (1) Figures cover the Las Vegas-Henderson-Paradise, NV Metropolitan Statistical Area
Source: U.S. Census Bureau, 2017-2021 American Community Survey 5-Year Estimates

HEALTH

Health Risk Factors

Category	MSA[1] (%)	U.S. (%)
Adults aged 18–64 who have any kind of health care coverage	n/a	90.9
Adults who reported being in good or better health	n/a	85.2
Adults who have been told they have high blood cholesterol	n/a	35.7
Adults who have been told they have high blood pressure	n/a	32.4
Adults who are current smokers	n/a	14.4
Adults who currently use e-cigarettes	n/a	6.7
Adults who currently use chewing tobacco, snuff, or snus	n/a	3.5
Adults who are heavy drinkers[2]	n/a	6.3
Adults who are binge drinkers[3]	n/a	15.4
Adults who are overweight (BMI 25.0 - 29.9)	n/a	34.4
Adults who are obese (BMI 30.0 - 99.8)	n/a	33.9
Adults who participated in any physical activities in the past month	n/a	76.3

Note: (1) Figures for the Las Vegas-Henderson-Paradise, NV Metropolitan Statistical Area were not available.
(2) Heavy drinkers are classified as adult men having more than 14 drinks per week and adult women having more than 7 drinks per week; (3) Binge drinkers are classified as males having five or more drinks on one occasion or females having four or more drinks on one occasion
Source: Centers for Disease Control and Prevention, Behaviorial Risk Factor Surveillance System, SMART: Selected Metropolitan Area Risk Trends, 2021

Acute and Chronic Health Conditions

Category	MSA[1] (%)	U.S. (%)
Adults who have ever been told they had a heart attack	n/a	4.0
Adults who have ever been told they have angina or coronary heart disease	n/a	3.8
Adults who have ever been told they had a stroke	n/a	3.0
Adults who have ever been told they have asthma	n/a	14.9
Adults who have ever been told they have arthritis	n/a	25.8
Adults who have ever been told they have diabetes[2]	n/a	10.9
Adults who have ever been told they had skin cancer	n/a	6.6
Adults who have ever been told they had any other types of cancer	n/a	7.5
Adults who have ever been told they have COPD	n/a	6.1
Adults who have ever been told they have kidney disease	n/a	3.0
Adults who have ever been told they have a form of depression	n/a	20.5

Note: (1) Figures for the Las Vegas-Henderson-Paradise, NV Metropolitan Statistical Area were not available.
(2) Figures do not include pregnancy-related, borderline, or pre-diabetes
Source: Centers for Disease Control and Prevention, Behaviorial Risk Factor Surveillance System, SMART: Selected Metropolitan Area Risk Trends, 2021

Health Screening and Vaccination Rates

Category	MSA[1] (%)	U.S. (%)
Adults who have ever been tested for HIV	n/a	34.9
Adults who have had their blood cholesterol checked within the last five years	n/a	85.2
Adults aged 65+ who have had flu shot within the past year	n/a	68.6
Adults aged 65+ who have ever had a pneumonia vaccination	n/a	71.0

Note: (1) Figures for the Las Vegas-Henderson-Paradise, NV Metropolitan Statistical Area were not available.
Source: Centers for Disease Control and Prevention, Behaviorial Risk Factor Surveillance System, SMART: Selected Metropolitan Area Risk Trends, 2021

Disability Status

Category	MSA[1] (%)	U.S. (%)
Adults who reported being deaf	n/a	7.2
Are you blind or have serious difficulty seeing, even when wearing glasses?	n/a	4.8
Are you limited in any way in any of your usual activities due to arthritis?	n/a	11.1
Do you have difficulty doing errands alone?	n/a	7.0
Do you have difficulty dressing or bathing?	n/a	3.6
Do you have serious difficulty concentrating/remembering/making decisions?	n/a	12.1
Do you have serious difficulty walking or climbing stairs?	n/a	12.8

Note: (1) Figures for the Las Vegas-Henderson-Paradise, NV Metropolitan Statistical Area were not available.
Source: Centers for Disease Control and Prevention, Behaviorial Risk Factor Surveillance System, SMART: Selected Metropolitan Area Risk Trends, 2021

Mortality Rates for the Top 10 Causes of Death in the U.S.

ICD-10[a] Sub-Chapter	ICD-10[a] Code	Crude Mortality Rate[1] per 100,000 population	
		County[2]	U.S.
Malignant neoplasms	C00-C97	164.3	182.6
Ischaemic heart diseases	I20-I25	105.9	113.1
Other forms of heart disease	I30-I51	74.7	64.4
Other degenerative diseases of the nervous system	G30-G31	47.2	51.0
Cerebrovascular diseases	I60-I69	40.5	47.8
Other external causes of accidental injury	W00-X59	39.6	46.4
Chronic lower respiratory diseases	J40-J47	44.4	45.7
Organic, including symptomatic, mental disorders	F01-F09	16.3	35.9
Hypertensive diseases	I10-I15	48.8	35.0
Diabetes mellitus	E10-E14	25.9	29.6

Note: (a) ICD-10 = International Classification of Diseases 10th Revision; (1) Crude mortality rates are a three-year average covering 2019-2021; (2) Figures cover Clark County.
Source: Centers for Disease Control and Prevention, National Center for Health Statistics. National Vital Statistics System, Mortality 2018-2021 on CDC WONDER Online Database

Mortality Rates for Selected Causes of Death

ICD-10[a] Sub-Chapter	ICD-10[a] Code	Crude Mortality Rate[1] per 100,000 population	
		County[2]	U.S.
Assault	X85-Y09	7.3	7.0
Diseases of the liver	K70-K76	20.0	19.8
Human immunodeficiency virus (HIV) disease	B20-B24	2.1	1.5
Influenza and pneumonia	J09-J18	14.7	14.7
Intentional self-harm	X60-X84	18.2	14.3
Malnutrition	E40-E46	5.3	4.3
Obesity and other hyperalimentation	E65-E68	2.8	3.0
Renal failure	N17-N19	8.9	15.7
Transport accidents	V01-V99	10.3	13.6
Viral hepatitis	B15-B19	1.7	1.2

Note: (a) ICD-10 = International Classification of Diseases 10th Revision; (1) Crude mortality rates are a three-year average covering 2019-2021; (2) Figures cover Clark County; Data are suppressed when the data meet the criteria for confidentiality constraints; Crude mortality rates are flagged as unreliable when the rate would be calculated with a numerator of 20 or less.
Source: Centers for Disease Control and Prevention, National Center for Health Statistics. National Vital Statistics System, Mortality 2018-2021 on CDC WONDER Online Database

Health Insurance Coverage

Area	With Health Insurance	With Private Health Insurance	With Public Health Insurance	Without Health Insurance	Population Under Age 19 Without Health Insurance
City	87.1	60.7	36.0	12.9	8.6
MSA[1]	88.1	63.3	34.7	11.9	8.0
U.S.	91.2	67.8	35.4	8.8	5.3

Note: Figures are percentages that cover the civilian noninstitutionalized population; (1) Figures cover the Las Vegas-Henderson-Paradise, NV Metropolitan Statistical Area
Source: U.S. Census Bureau, 2017-2021 American Community Survey 5-Year Estimates

Number of Medical Professionals

Area	MDs[3]	DOs[3,4]	Dentists	Podiatrists	Chiropractors	Optometrists
County[1] (number)	4,157	818	1,499	104	469	323
County[1] (rate[2])	182.9	36.0	65.4	4.5	20.5	14.1
U.S. (rate[2])	289.3	23.5	72.5	6.2	28.7	17.4

Note: Data as of 2021 unless noted; (1) Data covers Clark County; (2) Rate per 100,000 population; (3) Data as of 2020 and includes all active, non-federal physicians; (4) Doctor of Osteopathic Medicine
Source: U.S. Department of Health and Human Services, Health Resources and Services Administration, Bureau of Health Professions, Area Resource File (ARF) 2021-2022

EDUCATION

Public School District Statistics

District Name	Schls	Pupils	Pupil/ Teacher Ratio	Minority Pupils[1] (%)	LEP/ELL[2] (%)	IEP[3] (%)
Clark County School District	380	315,787	n/a	78.4	16.9	12.9

Note: Table includes school districts with 2,000 or more students; (1) Percentage of students that are not non-Hispanic white; (2) Percentage of students that are Limited English Proficient or English Language Learners (2018-19); (3) Percentage of students that have an Individualized Education Program (2019-20).
Source: U.S. Department of Education, National Center for Education Statistics, Common Core of Data, Local Education Agency (School District) Universe Survey: School Year 2021-2022

Best High Schools

According to *U.S. News,* Las Vegas is home to two of the top 500 high schools in the U.S.: **Advanced Technologies Academy** (#147); **West Career and Technical Academy** (#402). Nearly 18,000 public, magnet and charter schools were ranked based on their performance on state assessments and how well they prepare students for college. *U.S. News & World Report, "Best High Schools 2022"*

Highest Level of Education

Area	Less than H.S.	H.S. Diploma	Some College, No Deg.	Associate Degree	Bachelor's Degree	Master's Degree	Prof. School Degree	Doctorate Degree
City	14.6	27.4	24.0	8.0	16.7	6.4	1.9	0.9
MSA[1]	13.6	28.0	24.3	8.3	17.1	6.2	1.7	0.9
U.S.	11.1	26.5	20.0	8.7	20.6	9.3	2.2	1.5

Note: Figures cover persons age 25 and over; (1) Figures cover the Las Vegas-Henderson-Paradise, NV Metropolitan Statistical Area
Source: U.S. Census Bureau, 2017-2021 American Community Survey 5-Year Estimates

Educational Attainment by Race

Area	High School Graduate or Higher (%)					Bachelor's Degree or Higher (%)				
	Total	White	Black	Asian	Hisp.[2]	Total	White	Black	Asian	Hisp.[2]
City	85.4	89.5	88.3	91.9	66.0	25.9	29.4	18.8	43.3	11.6
MSA[1]	86.4	90.0	89.9	90.6	68.4	25.8	28.3	19.8	41.0	11.9
U.S.	88.9	91.4	87.2	87.6	71.2	33.7	35.5	23.3	55.6	18.4

Note: Figures shown cover persons 25 years old and over; (1) Figures cover the Las Vegas-Henderson-Paradise, NV Metropolitan Statistical Area; (2) People of Hispanic origin can be of any race
Source: U.S. Census Bureau, 2017-2021 American Community Survey 5-Year Estimates

School Enrollment by Grade and Control

Area	Preschool (%)		Kindergarten (%)		Grades 1 - 4 (%)		Grades 5 - 8 (%)		Grades 9 - 12 (%)	
	Public	Private	Public	Private	Public	Private	Public	Private	Public	Private
City	63.4	36.6	88.2	11.8	90.3	9.7	91.1	8.9	92.5	7.5
MSA[1]	60.9	39.1	88.6	11.4	91.5	8.5	92.4	7.6	92.7	7.3
U.S.	58.8	41.2	86.3	13.7	88.3	11.7	88.6	11.4	89.4	10.6

Note: Figures shown cover persons 3 years old and over; (1) Figures cover the Las Vegas-Henderson-Paradise, NV Metropolitan Statistical Area
Source: U.S. Census Bureau, 2017-2021 American Community Survey 5-Year Estimates

Higher Education

Four-Year Colleges			Two-Year Colleges			Medical Schools[1]	Law Schools[2]	Voc/ Tech[3]
Public	Private Non-profit	Private For-profit	Public	Private Non-profit	Private For-profit			
3	3	5	0	0	5	2	1	12

Note: Figures cover institutions located within the Las Vegas-Henderson-Paradise, NV Metropolitan Statistical Area and include main campuses only; (1) includes schools accredited by the Liaison Committee on Medical Education and the American Osteopathic Association's Commission on Osteopathic College Accreditation; (2) includes ABA-accredited schools, schools with provisional ABA accreditation, and state accredited schools; (3) includes all schools with programs that are less than 2 years.
Source: National Center for Education Statistics, Integrated Postsecondary Education System (IPEDS), 2021-22; Wikipedia, List of Medical Schools in the United States, accessed April 10, 2023; Wikipedia, List of Law Schools in the United States, accessed April 10, 2023

According to *U.S. News & World Report,* the Las Vegas-Henderson-Paradise, NV metro area is home to one of the top 100 law schools in the U.S.: **University of Nevada—Las Vegas (Boyd)** (#67 tie). The rankings are based on a weighted average of 12 measures of quality: peer assessment score; assessment score by lawyers/judges; median LSAT scores; median undergrad GPA; acceptance rate; employment rates for graduates; placement success; bar passage rate; faculty resources; expenditures per student; student/faculty ratio; and library resources. *U.S. News & World Report, "America's Best Graduate Schools, Law, 2023"*

EMPLOYERS

Major Employers

Company Name	Industry
American Casino & Entertainment	Hospitality
Blackstone Group	Hospitality
Boyd Gaming Corporation	Hospitality
Caesars Entertainment	Hospitality
Cannery Casino Resorts	Hospitality
City of Henderson	Municipal government
City of Las Vegas	Municipal government
Clark County	County government
Clark County School District	K-12 public education
Dignity Health	Health care
Landry's	Hospitality
Las Vegas Metropolitan Police Department	Police protection
Las Vegas Sands Corporation	Hospitality
MGM Resorts International	Hospitality
Nellis & Creech AFB	National security
Southwest Airlines	Air transportation, scheduled
Stations Casinos	Hospitality
Sunrise Health System	Health care
University Medical Center	Health care
University of Nevada Las Vegas	Higher education
Valley Health System	Health care
Wynn Resorts	Hospitality
Yellow Checker Star Transportation	Taxi/limo service

Note: Companies shown are located within the Las Vegas-Henderson-Paradise, NV Metropolitan Statistical Area.
Source: Hoovers.com; Wikipedia

PUBLIC SAFETY

Crime Rate

Area	Total Crime	Violent Crime Rate				Property Crime Rate		
		Murder	Rape[3]	Robbery	Aggrav. Assault	Burglary	Larceny -Theft	Motor Vehicle Theft
City	2,738.2	5.7	63.1	100.8	358.1	416.8	1,390.7	403.0
Suburbs[1]	1,944.4	5.0	31.6	99.0	209.5	261.9	1,057.0	280.4
Metro[2]	2,525.2	5.5	54.6	100.3	318.2	375.2	1,301.2	370.1
U.S.	2,356.7	6.5	38.4	73.9	279.7	314.2	1,398.0	246.0

Note: Figures are crimes per 100,000 population; (1) All areas within the metro area that are located outside the city limits; (2) Figures cover the Las Vegas-Henderson-Paradise, NV Metropolitan Statistical Area; (3) All figures shown were reported using the revised Uniform Crime Reporting (UCR) definition of rape; Due to the transition to the National Incident-Based Reporting System (NIBRS), limited city and metro area data was released for 2021.
Source: FBI Uniform Crime Reports, 2020

Hate Crimes

Area	Number of Quarters Reported	Number of Incidents per Bias Motivation					
		Race/Ethnicity/ Ancestry	Religion	Sexual Orientation	Disability	Gender	Gender Identity
City	4	27	1	9	1	0	1
U.S.	4	5,227	1,244	1,110	130	75	266

Note: Due to the transition to the National Incident-Based Reporting System (NIBRS), limited crime data was released for 2021.
Source: Federal Bureau of Investigation, Hate Crime Statistics 2020

Identity Theft Consumer Reports

Area	Reports	Reports per 100,000 Population	Rank[2]
MSA[1]	11,219	503	18
U.S.	1,108,609	339	-

Note: (1) Figures cover the Las Vegas-Henderson-Paradise, NV Metropolitan Statistical Area; (2) Rank ranges from 1 to 391 where 1 indicates greatest number of identity theft reports per 100,000 population
Source: Federal Trade Commission, Consumer Sentinel Network Data Book 2022

Fraud and Other Consumer Reports

Area	Reports	Reports per 100,000 Population	Rank[2]
MSA[1]	36,173	1,623	4
U.S.	4,064,520	1,245	-

Note: (1) Figures cover the Las Vegas-Henderson-Paradise, NV Metropolitan Statistical Area; (2) Rank ranges from 1 to 391 where 1 indicates greatest number of fraud and other consumer reports per 100,000 population
Source: Federal Trade Commission, Consumer Sentinel Network Data Book 2022

POLITICS

2020 Presidential Election Results

Area	Biden	Trump	Jorgensen	Hawkins	Other
Clark County	53.7	44.3	0.9	0.0	1.1
U.S.	51.3	46.8	1.2	0.3	0.5

Note: Results are percentages and may not add to 100% due to rounding
Source: Dave Leip's Atlas of U.S. Presidential Elections

SPORTS

Professional Sports Teams

Team Name	League	Year Established
Las Vegas Raiders	National Football League (NFL)	2020
Vegas Golden Nights	National Hockey League (NHL)	2017

Note: Includes teams located in the Las Vegas-Henderson-Paradise, NV Metropolitan Statistical Area.
Source: Wikipedia, Major Professional Sports Teams of the United States and Canada, April 12, 2023

CLIMATE

Average and Extreme Temperatures

Temperature	Jan	Feb	Mar	Apr	May	Jun	Jul	Aug	Sep	Oct	Nov	Dec	Yr.
Extreme High (°F)	77	87	91	99	109	115	116	116	113	103	87	77	116
Average High (°F)	56	62	69	78	88	99	104	102	94	81	66	57	80
Average Temp. (°F)	45	50	56	65	74	84	90	88	80	68	54	46	67
Average Low (°F)	33	38	43	51	60	69	76	74	66	54	41	34	53
Extreme Low (°F)	8	16	23	31	40	49	60	56	43	26	21	11	8

Note: Figures cover the years 1948-1990
Source: National Climatic Data Center, International Station Meteorological Climate Summary, 9/96

Average Precipitation/Snowfall/Humidity

Precip./Humidity	Jan	Feb	Mar	Apr	May	Jun	Jul	Aug	Sep	Oct	Nov	Dec	Yr.
Avg. Precip. (in.)	0.5	0.4	0.4	0.2	0.2	0.1	0.4	0.5	0.3	0.2	0.4	0.3	4.0
Avg. Snowfall (in.)	1	Tr	Tr	Tr	0	0	0	0	0	0	Tr	Tr	1
Avg. Rel. Hum. 7am (%)	59	52	41	31	26	20	26	31	30	36	47	56	38
Avg. Rel. Hum. 4pm (%)	32	25	20	15	13	10	14	16	16	18	26	31	20

Note: Figures cover the years 1948-1990; Tr = Trace amounts (<0.05 in. of rain; <0.5 in. of snow)
Source: National Climatic Data Center, International Station Meteorological Climate Summary, 9/96

Weather Conditions

Temperature			Daytime Sky			Precipitation		
10°F & below	32°F & below	90°F & above	Clear	Partly cloudy	Cloudy	0.01 inch or more precip.	0.1 inch or more snow/ice	Thunder-storms
<1	37	134	185	132	48	27	2	13

Note: Figures are average number of days per year and cover the years 1948-1990
Source: National Climatic Data Center, International Station Meteorological Climate Summary, 9/96

HAZARDOUS WASTE

Superfund Sites

The Las Vegas-Henderson-Paradise, NV metro area has no sites on the EPA's Superfund Final National Priorities List. There are a total of 1,165 Superfund sites with a status of proposed or final on the list in the U.S. *U.S. Environmental Protection Agency, National Priorities List, April 12, 2023*

AIR QUALITY

Air Quality Trends: Ozone

	1990	1995	2000	2005	2010	2015	2018	2019	2020	2021
MSA[1]	n/a	n/a	n/a	n/a	n/a	n/a	n/a	n/a	n/a	n/a
U.S.	0.087	0.089	0.081	0.080	0.072	0.067	0.069	0.065	0.065	0.067

Note: (1) Data covers the Las Vegas-Henderson-Paradise, NV Metropolitan Statistical Area; n/a not available. The values shown are the composite ozone concentration averages among trend sites based on the highest fourth daily maximum 8-hour concentration in parts per million. These trends are based on sites having an adequate record of monitoring data during the trend period. Data from exceptional events are included.
Source: U.S. Environmental Protection Agency, Air Quality Monitoring Information, "Air Quality Trends by City, 1990-2021"

Air Quality Index

Area	Percent of Days when Air Quality was...[2]					AQI Statistics[2]	
	Good	Moderate	Unhealthy for Sensitive Groups	Unhealthy	Very Unhealthy	Maximum	Median
MSA[1]	32.6	58.1	8.5	0.8	0.0	174	59

Note: (1) Data covers the Las Vegas-Henderson-Paradise, NV Metropolitan Statistical Area; (2) Based on 365 days with AQI data in 2021. Air Quality Index (AQI) is an index for reporting daily air quality. EPA calculates the AQI for five major air pollutants regulated by the Clean Air Act: ground-level ozone, particle pollution (aka particulate matter), carbon monoxide, sulfur dioxide, and nitrogen dioxide. The AQI runs from 0 to 500. The higher the AQI value, the greater the level of air pollution and the greater the health concern. There are six AQI categories: "Good" AQI is between 0 and 50. Air quality is considered satisfactory; "Moderate" AQI is between 51 and 100. Air quality is acceptable; "Unhealthy for Sensitive Groups" When AQI values are between 101 and 150, members of sensitive groups may experience health effects; "Unhealthy" When AQI values are between 151 and 200 everyone may begin to experience health effects; "Very Unhealthy" AQI values between 201 and 300 trigger a health alert; "Hazardous" AQI values over 300 trigger warnings of emergency conditions (not shown).
Source: U.S. Environmental Protection Agency, Air Quality Index Report, 2021

Air Quality Index Pollutants

Area	Percent of Days when AQI Pollutant was...[2]					
	Carbon Monoxide	Nitrogen Dioxide	Ozone	Sulfur Dioxide	Particulate Matter 2.5	Particulate Matter 10
MSA[1]	0.0	1.6	66.6	(3)	24.9	6.8

Note: (1) Data covers the Las Vegas-Henderson-Paradise, NV Metropolitan Statistical Area; (2) Based on 365 days with AQI data in 2021. The Air Quality Index (AQI) is an index for reporting daily air quality. EPA calculates the AQI for five major air pollutants regulated by the Clean Air Act: ground-level ozone, particle pollution (also known as particulate matter), carbon monoxide, sulfur dioxide, and nitrogen dioxide. The AQI runs from 0 to 500. The higher the AQI value, the greater the level of air pollution and the greater the health concern; (3) Sulfur dioxide is no longer included in this table (as of December 8, 2021) because SO_2 concentrations tend to be very localized and not necessarily representative of broad geographical areas like counties and CBSAs.
Source: U.S. Environmental Protection Agency, Air Quality Index Report, 2021

Maximum Air Pollutant Concentrations: Particulate Matter, Ozone, CO and Lead

	Particulate Matter 10 (ug/m^3)	Particulate Matter 2.5 Wtd AM (ug/m^3)	Particulate Matter 2.5 24-Hr (ug/m^3)	Ozone (ppm)	Carbon Monoxide (ppm)	Lead (ug/m^3)
MSA[1] Level	176	9.9	33	0.076	2	n/a
NAAQS[2]	150	15	35	0.075	9	0.15
Met NAAQS[2]	No	Yes	Yes	No	Yes	n/a

Note: (1) Data covers the Las Vegas-Henderson-Paradise, NV Metropolitan Statistical Area; Data from exceptional events are included; (2) National Ambient Air Quality Standards; ppm = parts per million; ug/m^3 = micrograms per cubic meter; n/a not available.
Concentrations: Particulate Matter 10 (coarse particulate)—highest second maximum 24-hour concentration; Particulate Matter 2.5 Wtd AM (fine particulate)—highest weighted annual mean concentration; Particulate Matter 2.5 24-Hour (fine particulate)—highest 98th percentile 24-hour concentration; Ozone—highest fourth daily maximum 8-hour concentration; Carbon Monoxide—highest second maximum non-overlapping 8-hour concentration; Lead—maximum running 3-month average
Source: U.S. Environmental Protection Agency, Air Quality Monitoring Information, "Air Quality Statistics by City, 2021"

Maximum Air Pollutant Concentrations: Nitrogen Dioxide and Sulfur Dioxide

	Nitrogen Dioxide AM (ppb)	Nitrogen Dioxide 1-Hr (ppb)	Sulfur Dioxide AM (ppb)	Sulfur Dioxide 1-Hr (ppb)	Sulfur Dioxide 24-Hr (ppb)
MSA[1] Level	22	53	n/a	3	n/a
NAAQS[2]	53	100	30	75	140
Met NAAQS[2]	Yes	Yes	n/a	Yes	n/a

Note: (1) Data covers the Las Vegas-Henderson-Paradise, NV Metropolitan Statistical Area; Data from exceptional events are included; (2) National Ambient Air Quality Standards; ppm = parts per million; ug/m^3 = micrograms per cubic meter; n/a not available.
Concentrations: Nitrogen Dioxide AM—highest arithmetic mean concentration; Nitrogen Dioxide 1-Hr—highest 98th percentile 1-hour daily maximum concentration; Sulfur Dioxide AM—highest annual mean concentration; Sulfur Dioxide 1-Hr—highest 99th percentile 1-hour daily maximum concentration; Sulfur Dioxide 24-Hr—highest second maximum 24-hour concentration
Source: U.S. Environmental Protection Agency, Air Quality Monitoring Information, "Air Quality Statistics by City, 2021"

Los Angeles, California

Background

There is as much to say about Los Angeles as there are municipalities under its jurisdiction. The city is immense, and as the saying goes, "If you want a life in LA, you need a car."

Los Angeles acquired its many neighborhoods and communities such as Hollywood, Glendale, Burbank, and Alhambra when those cities wanted to share in the water piped into Los Angeles from the Owens River. To obtain it, the cities were required to join the Los Angeles municipal system. Due to those annexations, Los Angeles is now one of the largest U.S. cities in both acreage and population. It is also one of the most racially diverse.

The city's communities are connected through a complex system of freeways which gives Los Angeles its reputation as a congested, car-oriented culture, where people must schedule their days around the three-hour rush hour.

Despite these challenges, Los Angeles is a city with a diversified economy and an average of 325 days of sunshine a year. What was founded in 1781 as a sleepy pueblo of 44 people, with chickens roaming the footpaths, is now a city leading the nation in commerce, transportation, finance, and, especially, entertainment—with most of all motion pictures made in the United States still produced in the Los Angeles area, and headquarters of such major studios as MGM and Universal located in "municipalities" unto themselves.

Playa Vista, the first new community to be established on the west side of Los Angeles in more than 50 years, was built in 2002 on the former site of the Hughes Aircraft Company. It is home to Electronic Arts, the world's leading video game publisher, Belkin, and others. Lincoln Properties built office buildings totaling more than 820,000 square feet in the eastern portion of Playa Vista community known as "The Campus at Playa Vista." The National Basketball Association Clippers has a training facility at the Campus, which is also home to a basketball-themed public park, a fitting way to celebrate the 2011 NBA champion Lakers.

The arts are center stage in Los Angeles. The Getty Center and Museum, an architectural masterpiece designed by Richard Meier built on a commanding hill, is a dramatic venue for visual arts and other events. The Los Angeles Opera, under the direction of Placido Domingo, offers a lively season of operas as well as recitals by such luminaries as Cecilia Bartoli and Renee Fleming. The Los Angeles Philharmonic performs in the Walt Disney Concert Hall, designed by Frank Gehry, famous as the architect of the Guggenheim Museum at Bilbao. The city's iconic music venue, The Hollywood Bowl, celebrated its 100th anniversary in 2022.

The downtown's first modern industrial park, Los Angeles World Trade Center, is a 20-acre project that is downtown's only foreign trade zone.

Los Angeles has hosted the Olympic and Paralympic Games twice and will again in 2028. Los Angeles will be the third city after London and Paris to host the Olympic Games three times. Major league baseball's Los Angeles Dodgers won the World Series in 2020, ending a 32-year drought. In 2022, the Los Angeles Rams won Super Bowl LVI at their new SoFi Stadium in neighboring Inglewood.

Inland and up foothill slopes, both high and low temperatures become more extreme and the relative humidity, which is frequently high near the coast, drops. Most rain falls November through March, while the summers are very dry. Destructive flash floods occasionally develop in and below some mountain canyons. Snow is often visible on the nearby mountains in the winter but is extremely rare in the coastal basin. Thunderstorms are infrequent.

The climate of Los Angeles is normally pleasant and mild throughout the year, with unusual differences in temperature, humidity, cloudiness, fog, rain, and sunshine over short distances in the metro area. Low clouds are common at night and in the morning along the coast during spring and summer. Near the foothills, clouds form later in the day and clear a short time later. Annual percentages of fog and cloudiness are greatest near the ocean. Sunshine totals are highest on the inland side of the city.

At times, high concentrations of air pollution affect the Los Angeles coastal basin and adjacent areas, when lack of air movement combines with an atmospheric inversion. In fall and winter, the Santa Ana winds pick up considerable amounts of dust and can blow strongly in the northern and eastern sections of the city and in outlying areas in the north and east, increasing the threat of wildfires in the region. The Woolsey Fire in 2018 burned 96,949 acres of land in Los Angeles and Ventura Counties.

Rankings

General Rankings

- *Insider* listed 23 places in the U.S. that travel industry trends reveal would be popular destinations in 2023. This year the list trends towards cultural and historical happenings, sports events, wellness experiences and invigorating outdoor escapes. According to the website insider.com Los Angeles is a place to visit in 2023. *Insider, "23 of the Best Places You Should Travel to in the U.S. in 2023," December 17, 2022*

- The human resources consulting firm Mercer ranked 231 major cities worldwide in terms of overall quality of life. Los Angeles ranked #66. Criteria: political, social, economic, and socio-cultural factors; medical and health considerations; schools and education; public services and transportation; recreation; consumer goods; housing; and natural environment. *Mercer, "Mercer 2019 Quality of Living Survey," March 13, 2019*

- Los Angeles was selected as an "All-America City" by the National Civic League. The All-America City Award recognizes civic excellence and in 2022 honored 10 communities that best exemplify the spirit of grassroots citizen involvement and cross-sector collaborative problem solving to collectively tackle pressing and complex issues. This year's theme was: "Housing as a Platform to Promote Early School Success and Equitable Learning Recovery." *National Civic League, "2022 All-America City Awards," July 21, 2022*

Business/Finance Rankings

- According to *Business Insider*, the Los Angeles metro area is a prime place to run a startup or move an existing business to. The area ranked #9. More than 300 metro areas were analyzed for factors that were of top concern to new business owners. Data was based on the 2019 U.S. Census Bureau American Community Survey, statistics from the CDC, Bureau of Labor Statistics employment report, and University of Chicago analysis. Criteria: business formations; percentage of vaccinated population; percentage of households with internet subscriptions; median household income; and share of work that can be done from home. *www.businessinsider.com, "The 20 Best Cities for Starting a Business in 2022 Include Baltimore, Boulder, and Boston," January 5, 2022*

- The Brookings Institution ranked the nation's largest cities based on income inequality. Los Angeles was ranked #15 (#1 = greatest inequality). Criteria: the "95/20 ratio," a figure representing the income at which a household earns more than 95 percent of all other households, divided by the income at which a household earns more than only 20 percent of all other households. *Brookings Institution, "Household Income Inequality, Largest Cities of 97 Large U.S. Metro Areas, 2014-2016," February 5, 2018*

- The Brookings Institution ranked the 100 largest metro areas in the U.S. based on income inequality. Los Angeles was ranked #4 (#1 = greatest inequality). Criteria: the "95/20 ratio," a figure representing the income at which a household earns more than 95 percent of all other households, divided by the income at which a household earns more than only 20 percent of all other households. *Brookings Institution, "Household Income Inequality, 100 Largest U.S. Metro Areas, 2014-2016," February 5, 2018*

- Payscale.com ranked the 32 largest metro areas in terms of wage growth. The Los Angeles metro area ranked #15. Criteria: quarterly changes in private industry employee and education professional wage growth from the previous year. *PayScale, "Wage Trends by Metro Area-1st Quarter," April 20, 2023*

- The Los Angeles metro area was identified as one of the most debt-ridden places in America by the finance site Credit.com. The metro area was ranked #13. Criteria: residents' average credit card debt as well as median income. *Credit.com, "25 Cities With the Most Credit Card Debt," February 28, 2018*

- For its annual survey of the "Most Expensive U.S. Cities to Live In," Kiplinger applied Cost of Living Index statistics developed by the Council for Community and Economic Research to U.S. Census Bureau population and median household income data for 265 urban areas. Los Angeles ranked #7 among the most expensive in the country. *Kiplinger.com, "The 11 Most Expensive Cities to Live in the U.S.," April 15, 2023*

- Los Angeles was cited as one of America's top metros for total corporate facility investment in 2022. The area ranked #5 in the large metro area category (population over 1 million). *Site Selection, "Top Metros of 2022," March 2023*

- The Los Angeles metro area appeared on the Milken Institute "2022 Best Performing Cities" list. Rank: #87 out of 200 large metro areas (population over 250,000). Criteria: job growth; wage and salary growth; high-tech output growth; housing affordability; household broadband access. *Milken Institute, "Best-Performing Cities 2022," March 28, 2022*

- *Forbes* ranked the 200 most populous metro areas to determine the nation's "Best Places for Business and Careers." The Los Angeles metro area was ranked #113. Criteria: costs (business and living); job growth (past and projected); income growth; quality of life; educational attainment (college and high school); projected economic growth; cultural and leisure opportunities; workplace tolerance laws; net migration patterns. *Forbes, "The Best Places for Business and Careers 2019: Seattle Still On Top," October 30, 2019*

- Mercer Human Resources Consulting ranked 227 cities worldwide in terms of cost-of-living. Los Angeles ranked #17 (the lower the ranking, the higher the cost-of-living). The survey measured the comparative cost of over 200 items (such as housing, food, clothing, domestic supplies, transportation, and recreation/entertainment) in each location. *Mercer, "2022 Cost of Living City Ranking," June 29, 2022*

Education Rankings

- Personal finance website *WalletHub* analyzed the 150 largest U.S. metropolitan statistical areas to determine where the most educated Americans are putting their degrees to work. Criteria: education levels; percentage of workers with degrees; education quality and attainment gap; public school quality rankings; quality and enrollment of each metro area's universities. Los Angeles was ranked #89 (#1 = most educated city). *www.WalletHub.com, "Most & Least Educated Cities in America," July 18, 2022*

- Los Angeles was selected as one of America's most literate cities. The city ranked #62 out of the 84 largest U.S. cities. Criteria: number of booksellers; library resources; Internet resources; educational attainment; periodical publishing resources; newspaper circulation. *Central Connecticut State University, "America's Most Literate Cities, 2018," February 2019*

Environmental Rankings

- The U.S. Environmental Protection Agency (EPA) released its list of U.S. metropolitan areas with the most ENERGY STAR certified buildings in 2022. The Los Angeles metro area was ranked #1 out of 25. *U.S. Environmental Protection Agency, "2023 Energy Star Top Cities," April 26, 2023*

- Los Angeles was highlighted as one of the 25 most ozone-polluted metro areas in the U.S. during 2019 through 2021. The area ranked #1. *American Lung Association, "State of the Air 2023," April 19, 2023*

- Los Angeles was highlighted as one of the 25 metro areas most polluted by year-round particle pollution (Annual PM 2.5) in the U.S. during 2019 through 2021. The area ranked #4. *American Lung Association, "State of the Air 2023," April 19, 2023*

- Los Angeles was highlighted as one of the 25 metro areas most polluted by short-term particle pollution (24-hour PM 2.5) in the U.S. during 2019 through 2021. The area ranked #9. *American Lung Association, "State of the Air 2023," April 19, 2023*

Food/Drink Rankings

- The U.S. Chamber of Commerce Foundation conducted an in-depth study on local food truck regulations, surveyed 288 food truck owners, and ranked 20 major American cities based on how friendly they are for operating a food truck. The compiled index assessed the following: procedures for obtaining permits and licenses; complying with restrictions; and financial obligations associated with operating a food truck. Los Angeles ranked #8 overall (1 being the best). *www.foodtrucknation.us, "Food Truck Nation," March 20, 2018*

- Los Angeles was identified as one of the cities in America ordering the most vegan food options by GrubHub.com. The city ranked #1 out of 5. Criteria: percentage of vegan, vegetarian and plant-based food orders compared to the overall number of orders. *GrubHub.com, "State of the Plate Report 2021: Top Cities for Vegans," June 20, 2021*

- Dodger stadium was selected as one of PETA's "Top 10 Vegan-Friendly Ballparks" for 2019. The park ranked #7. *People for the Ethical Treatment of Animals, "Top 10 Vegan-Friendly Ballparks," May 23, 2019*

Health/Fitness Rankings

- For each of the 100 largest cities in the United States, the American Fitness Index®, compiled in partnership between the American College of Sports Medicine and the Elevance Health Foundation, evaluated community infrastructure and 34 health behaviors including preventive health, levels of chronic disease conditions, food insecurity, sleep quality, pedestrian safety, air quality, and community/environment resources that support physical activity. Los Angeles ranked #52 for "community fitness." *americanfitnessindex.org, "2022 ACSM American Fitness Index Summary Report," July 12, 2022*

- Los Angeles was identified as a "2022 Spring Allergy Capital." The area ranked #67 out of 100. Three groups of factors were used to identify the most challenging cities for people with allergies during the spring season: annual spring pollen scores; over the counter allergy medicine use; number of board-certified allergy specialists. *Asthma and Allergy Foundation of America, "Spring Allergy Capitals 2022," March 2, 2022*

- Los Angeles was identified as a "2022 Fall Allergy Capital." The area ranked #66 out of 100. Three groups of factors were used to identify the most challenging cities for people with allergies during the fall season: annual fall pollen scores; over the counter allergy medicine use; number of board-certified allergy specialists. *Asthma and Allergy Foundation of America, "Fall Allergy Capitals 2022," March 2, 2022*

- Los Angeles was identified as a "2022 Asthma Capital." The area ranked #62 out of the nation's 100 largest metropolitan areas. Criteria: estimated asthma prevalence; asthma-related mortality; and ER visits due to asthma. Risk factors analyzed but not factored in the rankings: annual pollen score; annual air quality; public smoking laws; access to board-certified asthma specialists; rescue and controller medication use; uninsured rate; poverty rate. *Asthma and Allergy Foundation of America, "Asthma Capitals 2022: The Most Challenging Places to Live With Asthma," September 14, 2022*

Real Estate Rankings

- *WalletHub* compared the most populated U.S. cities to determine which had the best markets for real estate agents. Los Angeles ranked #40 where demand was high and pay was the best. Criteria: sales per agent; annual median wage for real-estate agents; monthly average starting salary for real estate agents; real estate job density and competition; unemployment rate; home turnover rate; housing-market health index; and other relevant metrics. *www.WalletHub.com, "2021 Best Places to Be a Real Estate Agent," May 12, 2021*

- The Los Angeles metro area was identified as one of the 20 worst housing markets in the U.S. in 2022. The area ranked #173 out of 187 markets. Criteria: year-over-year change of median sales price of existing single-family homes between the 4th quarter of 2021 and the 4th quarter of 2022. *National Association of Realtors®, Median Sales Price of Existing Single-Family Homes for Metropolitan Areas, 4th Quarter 2022*

- The Los Angeles metro area was identified as one of the 10 worst condo markets in the U.S. in 2022. The area ranked #57 out of 63 markets. Criteria: year-over-year change of median sales price of existing apartment condo-coop homes between the 4th quarter of 2021 and the 4th quarter of 2022. *National Association of Realtors®, Median Sales Price of Existing Apartment Condo-Coops Homes for Metropolitan Areas, 4th Quarter 2022*

- The Los Angeles metro area was identified as one of the 20 least affordable housing markets in the U.S. in 2022. The area ranked #181 out of 186 markets. Criteria: qualification for a mortgage loan with a 10 percent down payment on a typical home. *National Association of Realtors®, Qualifying Income Based on Sales Price of Existing Single-Family Homes for Metropolitan Areas, 2022*

- Los Angeles was ranked #235 out of 235 metro areas in terms of housing affordability in 2022 by the National Association of Home Builders (#1 = most affordable). Criteria: the share of homes sold in that area affordable to a family earning the local median income, based on standard mortgage underwriting criteria. *National Association of Home Builders®, NAHB-Wells Fargo Housing Opportunity Index, 4th Quarter 2022*

Safety Rankings

- Allstate ranked the 200 largest cities in America in terms of driver safety. Los Angeles ranked #195. Criteria: internal property damage claims over a two-year period from January 2016 to December 2017. The report helps increase the importance of safety and awareness behind the wheel. *Allstate, "Allstate America's Best Drivers Report, 2019" June 24, 2019*

- The National Insurance Crime Bureau ranked 390 metro areas in the U.S. in terms of per capita rates of vehicle theft. The Los Angeles metro area ranked #12 (#1 = highest rate). Criteria: number of vehicle theft offenses per 100,000 inhabitants in 2021. *National Insurance Crime Bureau, "Hot Spots 2021," September 1, 2022*

Seniors/Retirement Rankings

- From its Best Cities for Successful Aging indexes, the Milken Institute generated rankings for metropolitan areas, weighing data in nine categories—health care, wellness, living arrangements, transportation and convenience, financial characteristics, education, employment, community engagement, and overall livability. The Los Angeles metro area was ranked #56 overall in the large metro area category. *Milken Institute, "Best Cities for Successful Aging, 2017" March 14, 2017*

Transportation Rankings

- Los Angeles was identified as one of the most congested metro areas in the U.S. The area ranked #1 out of 10. Criteria: yearly delay per auto commuter in hours. *Texas A&M Transportation Institute, "2021 Urban Mobility Report," June 2021*

- According to the INRIX "2022 Global Traffic Scorecard," Los Angeles was identified as one of the most congested metro areas in the U.S. The area ranked #6 out of 25. Criteria: average annual time spent in traffic and average cost of congestion per motorist. *Inrix.com, "Return to Work, Higher Gas Prices & Inflation Drove Americans to Spend Hundreds More in Time and Money Commuting," January 10, 2023*

Women/Minorities Rankings

- The *Houston Chronicle* listed the Los Angeles metro area as #6 in top places for young Latinos to live in the U.S. Research was largely based on housing and occupational data from the largest metropolitan areas performed by *Forbes* and NBC Universo. Criteria: percentage of 18-34 year-olds; Latino college grad rates; and diversity. *blog.chron.com, "The 15 Best Big Cities for Latino Millenials," January 26, 2016*

- Personal finance website *WalletHub* compared more than 180 U.S. cities across two key dimensions, "Hispanic Business-Friendliness" and "Hispanic Purchasing Power," to arrive at the most favorable conditions for Hispanic entrepreneurs. Los Angeles was ranked #123 out of 182. Criteria includes: share of Hispanic-Owned Businesses; Hispanic entrepreneurship rate to median annual income of Hispanics; Small Business-Friendliness score; cost of living; and number of Hispanics with at least a bachelor's degree. *WalletHub.com, "2019's Best Cities for Hispanic Entrepreneurs," May 1, 2019*

Miscellaneous Rankings

- Los Angeles was selected as a 2022 Digital Cities Survey winner. The city ranked #2 in the large city (500,000 or more population) category. The survey examined and assessed how city governments are utilizing technology to continue innovation, engage with residents, and persevere through the challenges of the pandemic. Survey questions focused on ten initiatives: cybersecurity; citizen experience; disaster recovery; business intelligence; IT personnel; data governance; business automation; IT governance; infrastructure modernization; and broadband connectivity. *Center for Digital Government, "2022 Digital Cities Survey," November 10, 2022*

- The watchdog site, Charity Navigator, conducted a study of charities in major markets both to analyze statistical differences in their financial, accountability, and transparency practices and to track year-to-year variations in individual philanthropic communities. The Los Angeles metro area was ranked #14 among the 30 metro markets in the rating category of Overall Score. *www.charitynavigator.org, "2017 Metro Market Study," May 1, 2017*

- *WalletHub* compared the 150 most populated U.S. cities to determine their operating efficiency. A "Quality of Services" score was constructed for each city and then divided by the total budget per capita to reveal which were managed the best. Los Angeles ranked #129. Criteria: financial stability; economy; education; safety; health; infrastructure and pollution. *www.WalletHub.com, "2022's Best- & Worst-Run Cities in America," June 21, 2022*

- The National Alliance to End Homelessness listed the 25 most populous metro areas with the highest rate of homelessness. The Los Angeles metro area had a high rate of homelessness. Criteria: number of homeless people per 10,000 population in 2016. *National Alliance to End Homelessness, "Homelessness in the 25 Most Populous U.S. Metro Areas," September 1, 2017*

Business Environment

DEMOGRAPHICS

Population Growth

Area	1990 Census	2000 Census	2010 Census	2020 Census	Population Growth (%) 1990-2020	Population Growth (%) 2010-2020
City	3,487,671	3,694,820	3,792,621	3,898,747	11.8	2.8
MSA[1]	11,273,720	12,365,627	12,828,837	13,200,998	17.1	2.9
U.S.	248,709,873	281,421,906	308,745,538	331,449,281	33.3	7.4

Note: (1) Figures cover the Los Angeles-Long Beach-Anaheim, CA Metropolitan Statistical Area
Source: U.S. Census Bureau, 1990 Census, 2000 Census, 2010 Census, 2020 Census

Race

Area	White Alone[2] (%)	Black Alone[2] (%)	Asian Alone[2] (%)	AIAN[3] Alone[2] (%)	NHOPI[4] Alone[2] (%)	Other Race Alone[2] (%)	Two or More Races (%)
City	34.9	8.6	11.9	1.7	0.2	29.5	13.3
MSA[1]	35.2	6.4	16.7	1.5	0.3	25.2	14.7
U.S.	61.6	12.4	6.0	1.1	0.2	8.4	10.2

Note: (1) Figures cover the Los Angeles-Long Beach-Anaheim, CA Metropolitan Statistical Area; (2) Alone is defined as not being in combination with one or more other races; (3) American Indian and Alaska Native; (4) Native Hawaiian and Other Pacific Islander
Source: U.S. Census Bureau, 2020 Census

Hispanic or Latino Origin

Area	Total (%)	Mexican (%)	Puerto Rican (%)	Cuban (%)	Other (%)
City	48.4	31.5	0.5	0.4	16.1
MSA[1]	45.2	34.5	0.5	0.4	9.8
U.S.	18.4	11.2	1.8	0.7	4.7

Note: Persons of Hispanic or Latino origin can be of any race; (1) Figures cover the Los Angeles-Long Beach-Anaheim, CA Metropolitan Statistical Area
Source: U.S. Census Bureau, 2017-2021 American Community Survey 5-Year Estimates

Age

Area	Under Age 5	Age 5–19	Age 20–34	Age 35–44	Age 45–54	Age 55–64	Age 65–74	Age 75–84	Age 85+	Median Age
City	4.9	17.0	25.6	14.6	12.9	11.5	8.0	3.9	1.7	36.5
MSA[1]	5.0	18.3	22.5	13.7	13.3	12.4	8.6	4.4	1.9	37.9
U.S.	5.6	19.2	20.2	12.7	12.4	13.1	10.0	4.9	1.9	38.8

Note: (1) Figures cover the Los Angeles-Long Beach-Anaheim, CA Metropolitan Statistical Area
Source: U.S. Census Bureau, 2020 Census

Disability by Age

Area	All Ages	Under 18 Years Old	18 to 64 Years Old	65 Years and Over
City	10.3	3.1	7.5	36.6
MSA[1]	9.8	3.2	7.0	33.0
U.S.	12.6	4.4	10.3	33.4

Note: Figures show percent of the civilian noninstitutionalized population that reported having a disability. Disability status is determined from six types of difficulty: vision, hearing, cognitive, ambulatory, self-care, and independent living. For children under 5 years old, hearing and vision difficulty are used to determine disability status. For children between the ages of 5 and 14, disability status is determined from hearing, vision, cognitive, ambulatory, and self-care difficulties. For people aged 15 years and older, they are considered to have a disability if they have difficulty with any one of the six difficulty types; Note: (1) Figures cover the Los Angeles-Long Beach-Anaheim, CA Metropolitan Statistical Area
Source: U.S. Census Bureau, 2017-2021 American Community Survey 5-Year Estimates

Ancestry

Area	German	Irish	English	American	Italian	Polish	French[2]	Scottish	Dutch
City	3.8	3.6	3.1	3.9	2.7	1.4	1.1	0.7	0.4
MSA[1]	5.1	4.3	4.1	3.5	2.9	1.2	1.2	0.8	0.5
U.S.	12.8	9.6	8.1	5.7	5.0	2.7	2.2	1.6	1.1

Note: Figures are the percentage of the total population reporting a particular ancestry. The nine most commonly reported ancestries in the U.S. are shown. Figures include multiple ancestries (e.g. if a person reported being Irish and Italian, they were included in both columns); (1) Figures cover the Los Angeles-Long Beach-Anaheim, CA Metropolitan Statistical Area; (2) Excludes Basque
Source: U.S. Census Bureau, 2017-2021 American Community Survey 5-Year Estimates

Foreign-born Population

Area	Any Foreign Country	Asia	Mexico	Europe	Caribbean	Central America[2]	South America	Africa	Canada
City	36.2	10.9	12.0	2.4	0.3	8.4	1.1	0.7	0.4
MSA[1]	32.5	12.7	11.5	1.7	0.3	4.3	1.0	0.6	0.3
U.S.	13.6	4.2	3.3	1.5	1.4	1.1	1.1	0.8	0.2

Note: (1) Figures cover the Los Angeles-Long Beach-Anaheim, CA Metropolitan Statistical Area; (2) Excludes Mexico.
Source: U.S. Census Bureau, 2017-2021 American Community Survey 5-Year Estimates

Household Size

Area	Persons in Household (%)							Average Household Size
	One	Two	Three	Four	Five	Six	Seven or More	
City	30.6	28.6	15.5	13.1	6.8	2.9	2.5	2.80
MSA[1]	24.7	28.7	17.1	15.5	7.9	3.4	2.8	3.00
U.S.	28.1	33.8	15.5	12.9	6.0	2.3	1.4	2.60

Note: (1) Figures cover the Los Angeles-Long Beach-Anaheim, CA Metropolitan Statistical Area
Source: U.S. Census Bureau, 2017-2021 American Community Survey 5-Year Estimates

Household Relationships

Area	House-holder	Opposite-sex Spouse	Same-sex Spouse	Opposite-sex Unmarried Partner	Same-sex Unmarried Partner	Child[2]	Grand-child	Other Relatives	Non-relatives
City	36.2	13.1	0.3	2.8	0.3	26.5	2.8	9.0	6.3
MSA[1]	34.0	15.2	0.2	2.3	0.2	29.0	3.0	9.1	5.1
U.S.	38.3	17.5	0.2	2.5	0.2	28.3	2.4	4.8	3.4

Note: Figures are percent of the total population; (1) Figures cover the Los Angeles-Long Beach-Anaheim, CA Metropolitan Statistical Area; (2) Includes biological, adopted, and stepchildren of the householder
Source: U.S. Census Bureau, 2020 Census

Gender

Area	Males	Females	Males per 100 Females
City	1,925,675	1,973,072	97.6
MSA[1]	6,469,965	6,731,033	96.1
U.S.	162,685,811	168,763,470	96.4

Note: (1) Figures cover the Los Angeles-Long Beach-Anaheim, CA Metropolitan Statistical Area
Source: U.S. Census Bureau, 2020 Census

Marital Status

Area	Never Married	Now Married[2]	Separated	Widowed	Divorced
City	46.1	38.9	2.5	4.4	8.1
MSA[1]	40.3	44.5	2.0	4.7	8.4
U.S.	33.8	48.0	1.8	5.6	10.8

Note: Figures are percentages and cover the population 15 years of age and older; (1) Figures cover the Los Angeles-Long Beach-Anaheim, CA Metropolitan Statistical Area; (2) Excludes separated
Source: U.S. Census Bureau, 2017-2021 American Community Survey 5-Year Estimates

Religious Groups by Family

Area	Catholic	Baptist	Methodist	LDS[2]	Pentecostal	Lutheran	Islam	Adventist	Other
MSA[1]	31.1	2.6	0.8	1.5	2.4	0.4	1.4	1.5	9.1
U.S.	18.7	7.3	3.0	2.0	1.8	1.7	1.3	1.3	11.6

Note: Figures are the number of adherents as a percentage of the total population and cover the eight largest religious groups in the U.S; (1) Figures cover the Los Angeles-Long Beach-Anaheim, CA Metropolitan Statistical Area; (2) Church of Jesus Christ of Latter-day Saints
Sources: 2020 U.S. Religion Census, Association of Statisticians of American Religious Bodies; The Association of Religion Data Archives (ARDA)

Religious Groups by Tradition

Area	Catholic	Evangelical Protestant	Mainline Protestant	Black Protestant	Islam	Judaism	Hinduism	Orthodox	Buddhism
MSA[1]	31.1	9.3	1.5	1.7	1.4	0.8	0.4	0.9	0.9
U.S.	18.7	16.5	5.2	2.3	1.3	0.6	0.4	0.4	0.3

Note: Figures are the number of adherents as a percentage of the total population; (1) Figures cover the Los Angeles-Long Beach-Anaheim, CA Metropolitan Statistical Area
Sources: 2020 U.S. Religion Census, Association of Statisticians of American Religious Bodies; The Association of Religion Data Archives (ARDA)

ECONOMY

Gross Metropolitan Product

Area	2020	2021	2022	2023	Rank[2]
MSA[1]	1,007.0	1,129.4	1,226.9	1,295.5	2

Note: Figures are in billions of dollars; (1) Figures cover the Los Angeles-Long Beach-Anaheim, CA Metropolitan Statistical Area; (2) Rank is based on 2021 data and ranges from 1 to 381
Source: U.S. Conference of Mayors, U.S. Metro Economies: U.S. Metros Compared to Global and State Economies, June 2022

Economic Growth

Area	2018-20 (%)	2021 (%)	2022 (%)	2023 (%)	Rank[2]
MSA[1]	-1.6	8.8	3.3	2.6	256
U.S.	-0.6	5.7	3.1	2.9	–

Note: Figures are real gross metropolitan product (GMP) growth rates and represent average annual percent change; (1) Figures cover the Los Angeles-Long Beach-Anaheim, CA Metropolitan Statistical Area; (2) Rank is based on 2020 2-year average annual percent change and ranges from 1 to 381
Source: U.S. Conference of Mayors, U.S. Metro Economies: U.S. Metros Compared to Global and State Economies, June 2022

Metropolitan Area Exports

Area	2016	2017	2018	2019	2020	2021	Rank[2]
MSA[1]	61,245.7	63,752.9	64,814.6	61,041.1	50,185.4	58,588.4	3

Note: Figures are in millions of dollars; (1) Figures cover the Los Angeles-Long Beach-Anaheim, CA Metropolitan Statistical Area; (2) Rank is based on 2021 data and ranges from 1 to 388
Source: U.S. Department of Commerce, International Trade Administration, Office of Trade and Economic Analysis, Industry and Analysis, Exports by Metropolitan Area, data extracted March 16, 2023

Building Permits

Area	Single-Family			Multi-Family			Total		
	2021	2022	Pct. Chg.	2021	2022	Pct. Chg.	2021	2022	Pct. Chg.
City	2,475	3,182	28.6	11,613	13,525	16.5	14,088	16,707	18.6
MSA[1]	11,090	11,184	0.8	20,061	21,326	6.3	31,151	32,510	4.4
U.S.	1,115,400	975,600	-12.5	621,600	689,500	10.9	1,737,000	1,665,100	-4.1

Note: (1) Figures cover the Los Angeles-Long Beach-Anaheim, CA Metropolitan Statistical Area; Figures represent new, privately-owned housing units authorized (unadjusted data); All permit data are based on estimates with imputation
Source: U.S. Census Bureau, Manufacturing, Mining, and Construction Statistics, Building Permits, 2021, 2022

Bankruptcy Filings

Area	Business Filings			Nonbusiness Filings		
	2021	2022	% Chg.	2021	2022	% Chg.
Los Angeles County	672	626	-6.8	11,316	8,314	-26.5
U.S.	14,347	13,481	-6.0	399,269	374,240	-6.3

Note: Business filings include Chapter 7, Chapter 9, Chapter 11, Chapter 12, Chapter 13, Chapter 15, and Section 304; Nonbusiness filings include Chapter 7, Chapter 11, and Chapter 13
Source: Administrative Office of the U.S. Courts, Business and Nonbusiness Bankruptcy, County Cases Commenced by Chapter of the Bankruptcy Code, During the 12-Month Period Ending December 31, 2021 and Business and Nonbusiness Bankruptcy, County Cases Commenced by Chapter of the Bankruptcy Code, During the 12-Month Period Ending December 31, 2022

Housing Vacancy Rates

Area	Gross Vacancy Rate[2] (%)			Year-Round Vacancy Rate[3] (%)			Rental Vacancy Rate[4] (%)			Homeowner Vacancy Rate[5] (%)		
	2020	2021	2022	2020	2021	2022	2020	2021	2022	2020	2021	2022
MSA[1]	5.5	6.4	5.9	4.8	5.9	5.5	3.6	4.6	4.1	0.6	0.7	0.5
U.S.	10.6	10.8	10.5	8.2	8.4	8.2	6.3	6.1	5.8	1.0	0.9	0.8

Note: (1) Figures cover the Los Angeles-Long Beach-Anaheim, CA Metropolitan Statistical Area; (2) The percentage of the total housing inventory that is vacant; (3) The percentage of the housing inventory (excluding seasonal units) that is year-round vacant; (4) The percentage of rental inventory that is vacant for rent; (5) The percentage of homeowner inventory that is vacant for sale
Source: U.S. Census Bureau, Housing Vacancies and Homeownership Annual Statistics: 2020, 2021, 2022

INCOME

Income

Area	Per Capita ($)	Median Household ($)	Average Household ($)
City	39,378	69,778	106,931
MSA[1]	39,895	81,652	115,584
U.S.	37,638	69,021	97,196

Note: (1) Figures cover the Los Angeles-Long Beach-Anaheim, CA Metropolitan Statistical Area
Source: U.S. Census Bureau, 2017-2021 American Community Survey 5-Year Estimates

Household Income Distribution

Area	Percent of Households Earning							
	Under $15,000	$15,000 -$24,999	$25,000 -$34,999	$35,000 -$49,999	$50,000 -$74,999	$75,000 -$99,999	$100,000 -$149,999	$150,000 and up
City	11.6	7.8	7.8	10.4	15.1	11.7	15.4	20.1
MSA[1]	9.0	6.4	6.8	9.5	14.8	12.3	17.4	23.8
U.S.	9.4	7.8	8.2	11.4	16.8	12.8	16.3	17.3

Note: (1) Figures cover the Los Angeles-Long Beach-Anaheim, CA Metropolitan Statistical Area
Source: U.S. Census Bureau, 2017-2021 American Community Survey 5-Year Estimates

Poverty Rate

Area	All Ages	Under 18 Years Old	18 to 64 Years Old	65 Years and Over
City	16.6	22.9	14.7	16.3
MSA[1]	12.9	17.2	11.6	12.4
U.S.	12.6	17.0	11.8	9.6

Note: Figures are percentage of people whose income during the past 12 months was below the poverty level;
(1) Figures cover the Los Angeles-Long Beach-Anaheim, CA Metropolitan Statistical Area
Source: U.S. Census Bureau, 2017-2021 American Community Survey 5-Year Estimates

EMPLOYMENT

Labor Force and Employment

Area	Civilian Labor Force			Workers Employed		
	Dec. 2021	Dec. 2022	% Chg.	Dec. 2021	Dec. 2022	% Chg.
City	2,047,789	2,027,026	-1.0	1,931,445	1,935,875	0.2
MD[1]	5,001,852	4,965,511	-0.7	4,701,620	4,747,043	1.0
U.S.	161,696,000	164,224,000	1.6	155,732,000	158,872,000	2.0

Note: Data is not seasonally adjusted and covers workers 16 years of age and older; (1) Figures cover the Los Angeles-Long Beach-Glendale, CA Metropolitan Division
Source: Bureau of Labor Statistics, Local Area Unemployment Statistics

Unemployment Rate

Area	2022											
	Jan.	Feb.	Mar.	Apr.	May	Jun.	Jul.	Aug.	Sep.	Oct.	Nov.	Dec.
City	6.3	5.5	5.0	4.9	4.6	5.3	5.2	5.1	4.6	4.6	4.6	4.5
MD[1]	6.5	5.8	5.2	4.8	4.5	4.9	4.9	4.7	4.3	4.5	4.5	4.4
U.S.	4.4	4.1	3.8	3.3	3.4	3.8	3.8	3.8	3.3	3.4	3.4	3.3

Note: Data is not seasonally adjusted and covers workers 16 years of age and older; (1) Figures cover the Los Angeles-Long Beach-Glendale, CA Metropolitan Division
Source: Bureau of Labor Statistics, Local Area Unemployment Statistics

Average Wages

Occupation	$/Hr.	Occupation	$/Hr.
Accountants and Auditors	44.41	Maintenance and Repair Workers	24.86
Automotive Mechanics	27.03	Marketing Managers	81.73
Bookkeepers	25.38	Network and Computer Systems Admin.	49.56
Carpenters	32.48	Nurses, Licensed Practical	32.95
Cashiers	16.40	Nurses, Registered	60.26
Computer Programmers	52.39	Nursing Assistants	20.49
Computer Systems Analysts	56.78	Office Clerks, General	21.66
Computer User Support Specialists	33.66	Physical Therapists	52.02
Construction Laborers	25.96	Physicians	113.43
Cooks, Restaurant	18.92	Plumbers, Pipefitters and Steamfitters	34.45
Customer Service Representatives	22.21	Police and Sheriff's Patrol Officers	50.13
Dentists	n/a	Postal Service Mail Carriers	28.35
Electricians	37.09	Real Estate Sales Agents	35.65
Engineers, Electrical	65.13	Retail Salespersons	18.93
Fast Food and Counter Workers	16.43	Sales Representatives, Technical/Scientific	52.61
Financial Managers	87.66	Secretaries, Exc. Legal/Medical/Executive	24.22
First-Line Supervisors of Office Workers	34.56	Security Guards	18.19
General and Operations Managers	67.77	Surgeons	n/a
Hairdressers/Cosmetologists	22.18	Teacher Assistants, Exc. Postsecondary*	20.58
Home Health and Personal Care Aides	15.68	Teachers, Secondary School, Exc. Sp. Ed.*	43.33
Janitors and Cleaners	18.46	Telemarketers	18.39
Landscaping/Groundskeeping Workers	19.81	Truck Drivers, Heavy/Tractor-Trailer	26.10
Lawyers	93.69	Truck Drivers, Light/Delivery Services	22.77
Maids and Housekeeping Cleaners	18.69	Waiters and Waitresses	18.08

Note: Wage data covers the Los Angeles-Long Beach-Anaheim, CA Metropolitan Statistical Area; (*) Hourly wages were calculated from annual wage data based on a 40 hour work week; n/a not available.
Source: Bureau of Labor Statistics, Metro Area Occupational Employment & Wage Estimates, May 2022

Employment by Industry

Sector	MD[1]		U.S.
	Number of Employees	Percent of Total	Percent of Total
Construction	147,400	3.2	5.0
Private Education and Health Services	899,400	19.4	16.1
Financial Activities	219,300	4.7	5.9
Government	569,800	12.3	14.5
Information	231,900	5.0	2.0
Leisure and Hospitality	525,700	11.4	10.3
Manufacturing	320,900	6.9	8.4
Mining and Logging	1,600	<0.1	0.4
Other Services	157,500	3.4	3.7
Professional and Business Services	689,100	14.9	14.7
Retail Trade	423,300	9.2	10.2
Transportation, Warehousing, and Utilities	235,300	5.1	4.9
Wholesale Trade	203,000	4.4	3.9

Note: Figures are non-farm employment as of December 2022. Figures are not seasonally adjusted and include workers 16 years of age and older; (1) Figures cover the Los Angeles-Long Beach-Glendale, CA Metropolitan Division
Source: Bureau of Labor Statistics, Current Employment Statistics, Employment, Hours, and Earnings

Employment by Occupation

Occupation Classification	City (%)	MSA[1] (%)	U.S. (%)
Management, Business, Science, and Arts	40.9	40.8	40.3
Natural Resources, Construction, and Maintenance	7.7	7.3	8.7
Production, Transportation, and Material Moving	11.8	12.5	13.1
Sales and Office	19.8	21.5	20.9
Service	19.8	17.8	17.0

Note: Figures cover employed civilians 16 years of age and older; (1) Figures cover the Los Angeles-Long Beach-Anaheim, CA Metropolitan Statistical Area
Source: U.S. Census Bureau, 2017-2021 American Community Survey 5-Year Estimates

Occupations with Greatest Projected Employment Growth: 2022 – 2024

Occupation[1]	2022 Employment	2024 Projected Employment	Numeric Employment Change	Percent Employment Change
Home Health and Personal Care Aides	811,300	858,600	47,300	5.8
Fast Food and Counter Workers	422,000	444,100	22,100	5.2
Cooks, Restaurant	154,300	172,000	17,700	11.5
Software Developers and Software Quality Assurance Analysts and Testers	337,600	352,100	14,500	4.3
Waiters and Waitresses	205,800	219,200	13,400	6.5
Laborers and Freight, Stock, and Material Movers, Hand	391,100	403,100	12,000	3.1
Stockers and Order Fillers	268,000	277,500	9,500	3.5
General and Operations Managers	308,500	317,600	9,100	2.9
First-Line Supervisors of Food Preparation and Serving Workers	118,100	126,000	7,900	6.7
Project Management Specialists and Business Operations Specialists, All Other	332,400	339,800	7,400	2.2

Note: Projections cover California; (1) Sorted by numeric employment change
Source: www.projectionscentral.com, State Occupational Projections, 2022–2024 Short-Term Projections

Fastest-Growing Occupations: 2022 – 2024

Occupation[1]	2022 Employment	2024 Projected Employment	Numeric Employment Change	Percent Employment Change
Fitness Trainers and Aerobics Instructors	40,700	46,300	5,600	13.8
Nurse Practitioners	18,300	20,500	2,200	12.0
Cooks, Restaurant	154,300	172,000	17,700	11.5
Airfield Operations Specialists	3,700	4,100	400	10.8
Solar Photovoltaic Installers	6,600	7,300	700	10.6
Ushers, Lobby Attendants, and Ticket Takers	7,800	8,600	800	10.3
Amusement and Recreation Attendants	47,500	52,300	4,800	10.1
Sociologists	1,000	1,100	100	10.0
Paperhangers	1,000	1,100	100	10.0
Avionics Technicians	2,000	2,200	200	10.0

Note: Projections cover California; (1) Sorted by percent employment change and excludes occupations with numeric employment change less than 50
Source: www.projectionscentral.com, State Occupational Projections, 2022–2024 Short-Term Projections

CITY FINANCES

City Government Finances

Component	2020 ($000)	2020 ($ per capita)
Total Revenues	17,950,024	4,511
Total Expenditures	17,319,889	4,352
Debt Outstanding	31,912,333	8,019
Cash and Securities[1]	8,306,533	2,087

Note: (1) Cash and security holdings of a government at the close of its fiscal year, including those of its dependent agencies, utilities, and liquor stores.
Source: U.S. Census Bureau, State & Local Government Finances 2020

City Government Revenue by Source

Source	2020 ($000)	2020 ($ per capita)	2020 (%)
General Revenue			
From Federal Government	502,819	126	2.8
From State Government	761,992	191	4.2
From Local Governments	40,166	10	0.2
Taxes			
Property	2,339,099	588	13.0
Sales and Gross Receipts	1,913,745	481	10.7
Personal Income	0	0	0.0
Corporate Income	0	0	0.0
Motor Vehicle License	0	0	0.0
Other Taxes	1,094,610	275	6.1
Current Charges	4,610,772	1,159	25.7
Liquor Store	0	0	0.0
Utility	5,201,951	1,307	29.0

Source: U.S. Census Bureau, State & Local Government Finances 2020

City Government Expenditures by Function

Function	2020 ($000)	2020 ($ per capita)	2020 (%)
General Direct Expenditures			
Air Transportation	2,489,592	625	14.4
Corrections	0	0	0.0
Education	0	0	0.0
Employment Security Administration	0	0	0.0
Financial Administration	173,750	43	1.0
Fire Protection	559,883	140	3.2
General Public Buildings	0	0	0.0
Governmental Administration, Other	196,810	49	1.1
Health	431,294	108	2.5
Highways	811,397	203	4.7
Hospitals	0	0	0.0
Housing and Community Development	269,916	67	1.6
Interest on General Debt	676,298	169	3.9
Judicial and Legal	0	0	0.0
Libraries	202,753	50	1.2
Parking	36,223	9	0.2
Parks and Recreation	610,456	153	3.5
Police Protection	2,547,793	640	14.7
Public Welfare	0	0	0.0
Sewerage	795,706	199	4.6
Solid Waste Management	518,257	130	3.0
Veterans' Services	0	0	0.0
Liquor Store	0	0	0.0
Utility	5,449,123	1,369	31.5

Source: U.S. Census Bureau, State & Local Government Finances 2020

TAXES

State Corporate Income Tax Rates

State	Tax Rate (%)	Income Brackets ($)	Num. of Brackets	Financial Institution Tax Rate (%)[a]	Federal Income Tax Ded.
California	8.84 (b)	Flat rate	1	10.84 (b)	No

Note: Tax rates as of January 1, 2023; (a) Rates listed are the corporate income tax rate applied to financial institutions or excise taxes based on income. Some states have other taxes based upon the value of deposits or shares; (b) Minimum tax is $800 in California, $250 in District of Columbia, $50 in Arizona and North Dakota (banks), $400 ($100 banks) in Rhode Island, $200 per location in South Dakota (banks), $100 in Utah, $300 in Vermont.
Source: Federation of Tax Administrators, State Corporate Income Tax Rates, January 1, 2023

State Individual Income Tax Rates

State	Tax Rate (%)	Income Brackets ($)	Personal Exemptions ($)			Standard Ded. ($)	
			Single	Married	Depend.	Single	Married
California (a)	1.0 - 12.3 (g)	10,099 - 677,275 (b)	140	280	433 (c)	5,202	10,404 (a)

Note: Tax rates as of January 1, 2023; Local- and county-level taxes are not included; Federal income tax is not deductible on state income tax returns; (a) 16 states have statutory provision for automatically adjusting to the rate of inflation the dollar values of the income tax brackets, standard deductions, and/or personal exemptions. Oregon does not index the income brackets for $125,000 and over; (b) For joint returns, taxes are twice the tax on half the couple's income; (c) The personal exemption takes the form of a tax credit instead of a deduction; (g) California imposes an additional 1% tax on taxable income over $1 million, making the maximum rate 13.3% over $1 million.
Source: Federation of Tax Administrators, State Individual Income Tax Rates, January 1, 2023

Various State Sales and Excise Tax Rates

State	State Sales Tax (%)	Gasoline[1] ($/gal.)	Cigarette[2] ($/pack)	Spirits[3] ($/gal.)	Wine[4] ($/gal.)	Beer[5] ($/gal.)	Recreational Marijuana (%)
California	7.25	0.7766	2.87	3.30	0.20	0.20	(c)

Note: All tax rates as of January 1, 2023; (1) The American Petroleum Institute has developed a methodology for determining the average tax rate on a gallon of fuel. Rates may include any of the following: excise taxes, environmental fees, storage tank fees, other fees or taxes, general sales tax, and local taxes; (2) The federal excise tax of $1.0066 per pack and local taxes are not included; (3) Rates are those applicable to off-premise sales of 40% alcohol by volume (a.b.v.) distilled spirits in 750ml containers. Local excise taxes are excluded; (4) Rates are those applicable to off-premise sales of 11% a.b.v. non-carbonated wine in 750ml containers; (5) Rates are those applicable to off-premise sales of 4.7% a.b.v. beer in 12 ounce containers; (c) 15% excise tax (levied on wholesale at average market rate); $10.08/oz. flowers & $3/oz. leaves cultivation tax; $1.41/oz fresh cannabis plant
Source: Tax Foundation, 2023 Facts & Figures: How Does Your State Compare?

State Business Tax Climate Index Rankings

State	Overall Rank	Corporate Tax Rank	Individual Income Tax Rank	Sales Tax Rank	Property Tax Rank	Unemployment Insurance Tax Rank
California	48	46	49	47	19	24

Note: The index is a measure of how each state's tax laws affect economic performance. The lower the rank, the more favorable a state's tax system is for business. States without a given tax are given a ranking of 1. The scores/rankings for the District of Columbia do not affect other states. The 2023 index represents the tax climate as of July 1, 2022.
Source: Tax Foundation, State Business Tax Climate Index 2023

TRANSPORTATION

Means of Transportation to Work

Area	Car/Truck/Van		Public Transportation			Bicycle	Walked	Other Means	Worked at Home
	Drove Alone	Car-pooled	Bus	Subway	Railroad				
City	65.2	8.9	6.6	0.8	0.1	0.7	3.2	2.1	12.4
MSA[1]	70.9	9.3	3.4	0.4	0.2	0.6	2.3	1.8	11.2
U.S.	73.2	8.6	2.0	1.6	0.5	0.5	2.5	1.5	9.7

Note: Figures are percentages and cover workers 16 years of age and older; (1) Figures cover the Los Angeles-Long Beach-Anaheim, CA Metropolitan Statistical Area
Source: U.S. Census Bureau, 2017-2021 American Community Survey 5-Year Estimates

Travel Time to Work

Area	Less Than 10 Minutes	10 to 19 Minutes	20 to 29 Minutes	30 to 44 Minutes	45 to 59 Minutes	60 to 89 Minutes	90 Minutes or More
City	5.9	22.2	19.3	28.5	10.5	10.1	3.6
MSA[1]	7.1	24.8	19.9	25.4	9.9	9.3	3.5
U.S.	12.4	28.5	21.0	20.9	8.2	6.2	2.9

Note: Note: Figures are percentages and include workers 16 years old and over; (1) Figures cover the Los Angeles-Long Beach-Anaheim, CA Metropolitan Statistical Area
Source: U.S. Census Bureau, 2017-2021 American Community Survey 5-Year Estimates

Key Congestion Measures

Measure	1990	2000	2010	2015	2020
Annual Hours of Delay, Total (000)	472,274	673,878	812,204	924,196	365,543
Annual Hours of Delay, Per Auto Commuter	70	84	97	113	46
Annual Congestion Cost, Per Auto Commuter ($)	2,423	2,596	2,487	2,688	1,142

Note: Covers the Los Angeles-Long Beach-Anaheim CA urban area
Source: Texas A&M Transportation Institute, 2021 Urban Mobility Report

Freeway Travel Time Index

Measure	1985	1990	1995	2000	2005	2010	2015	2020
Urban Area Index[1]	1.31	1.34	1.38	1.41	1.45	1.45	1.49	1.16
Urban Area Rank[1,2]	1	1	1	1	1	1	1	2

Note: Freeway Travel Time Index—the ratio of travel time in the peak period to the travel time at free-flow conditions. For example, a value of 1.30 indicates a 20-minute free-flow trip takes 26 minutes in the peak (20 minutes x 1.30 = 26 minutes); (1) Covers the Los Angeles-Long Beach-Anaheim CA urban area; (2) Rank is based on 101 larger urban areas (#1 = highest travel time index)
Source: Texas A&M Transportation Institute, 2021 Urban Mobility Report

Public Transportation

Agency Name / Mode of Transportation	Vehicles Operated in Maximum Service[1]	Annual Unlinked Passenger Trips[2] (in thous.)	Annual Passenger Miles[3] (in thous.)
Los Angeles Co. Metro Transportation Authority (LACMTA)			
Bus (directly operated)	1,399	142,272.8	406,992.0
Bus (purchased transportation)	109	6,559.6	24,874.0
Bus Rapid Transit (directly operated)	15	2,949.4	17,257.0
Demand Response (directly operated)	41	42.1	104.9
Heavy Rail (directly operated)	54	18,888.6	99,058.4
Light Rail (directly operated)	110	22,871.1	151,162.5
Vanpool (purchased transportation)	813	1,136.2	53,378.2
City of Los Angeles Department of Transportation (LADOT)			
Bus (purchased transportation)	171	8,830.4	10,479.4
Commuter Bus (purchased transportation)	87	343.6	3,748.5
Demand Response (purchased transportation)	81	139.8	533.1
Demand Response - Taxi	9	86.8	206.7

Note: (1) Number of revenue vehicles operated by the given mode and type of service to meet the annual maximum service requirement. This is the revenue vehicle count during the peak season of the year; on the week and day that maximum service is provided. Vehicles operated in maximum service (VOMS) exclude atypical days and one-time special events; (2) Number of passengers who boarded public transportation vehicles. Passengers are counted each time they board a vehicle no matter how many vehicles they use to travel from their origin to their destination. (3) Sum of the distances ridden by all passengers during the entire fiscal year.
Source: Federal Transit Administration, National Transit Database, 2021

Air Transportation

Airport Name and Code / Type of Service	Passenger Airlines[1]	Passenger Enplanements	Freight Carriers[2]	Freight (lbs)
Los Angeles International (LAX)				
Domestic service (U.S. carriers - 2022)	27	24,454,101	20	891,900,984
International service (U.S. carriers - 2021)	14	1,425,765	13	382,637,851

Note: (1) Includes all U.S.-based major, minor and commuter airlines that carried at least one passenger during the year; (2) Includes all U.S.-based airlines and freight carriers that transported at least one pound of freight during the year.
Source: Bureau of Transportation Statistics, The Intermodal Transportation Database, Air Carriers: T-100 Domestic Market (U.S. Carriers), 2022; Bureau of Transportation Statistics, The Intermodal Transportation Database, Air Carriers: T-100 International Market (U.S. Carriers), 2021

BUSINESSES

Major Business Headquarters

Company Name	Industry	Rankings	
		Fortune[1]	Forbes[2]
AECOM	Engineering, construction	260	-
CBRE Group	Real estate	126	-
Capital Group Companies	Diversified financials	-	63
Gibson, Dunn & Crutcher	Services	-	218
Reliance Steel & Aluminum	Metals	261	-
The Wonderful Company	Multicompany	-	110

Note: (1) Companies that produce a 10-K are ranked 1 to 500 based on 2021 revenue; (2) All private companies with at least $2 billion in annual revenue through the end of their most current fiscal year are ranked 1 to 246; companies listed are headquartered in the city; dashes indicate no ranking
Source: Fortune, "Fortune 500," 2022; Forbes, "America's Largest Private Companies," 2022

Fastest-Growing Businesses

According to *Inc.*, Los Angeles is home to 11 of America's 500 fastest-growing private companies: **MUD\WTR** (#30); **Generation Genius** (#88); **Vegamour** (#152); **Lettuce Grow** (#183); **AVM Consulting** (#194); **Fernish** (#250); **WeeCare** (#292); **Birdy Grey** (#305); **Sunbit** (#306); **American Hartford Gold** (#415); **MaryRuth's** (#469). Criteria: must be an independent, privately-held, for-profit, U.S. corporation, proprietorship or partnership as of December 31, 2021; revenues must be at least $100,000 in 2018 and $2 million in 2021; must have four-year operating/sales history. *Inc., "America's 500 Fastest-Growing Private Companies," 2022*

According to *Initiative for a Competitive Inner City (ICIC)*, Los Angeles is home to three of America's 100 fastest-growing "inner city" companies: **The Spirit Guild** (#54); **City Design Studio** (#62); **Giroux Glass** (#90). Criteria for inclusion: company must be headquartered in or have 51 percent or more of its physical operations in an economically distressed urban area; must be an independent, for-profit corporation, partnership or proprietorship; must have 10 or more employees and have a five-year sales history that includes sales of at least $200,000 in the base year and at least $1 million in the current year with no decrease in sales over the two most recent years. Companies were ranked overall by revenue growth over the five-year period between 2017 and 2021. *Initiative for a Competitive Inner City (ICIC), "Inner City 100 Companies," 2022*

According to Deloitte, Los Angeles is home to five of North America's 500 fastest-growing high-technology companies: **Boulevard** (#54); **Sunbit** (#87); **Xos** (#102); **AdQuick** (#349); **Emburse** (#493). Companies are ranked by percentage growth in revenue over a four-year period. Criteria for inclusion: company must be headquartered within North America; must own proprietary intellectual property or technology that is sold to customers in products that contributes to a significant portion of the company's operating revenue; must have been in business for a minumum of four years with 2018 operating revenues of at least $50,000 USD/CD and 2021 operating revenues of at least $5 million USD/CD. *Deloitte, 2022 Technology Fast 500*[TM]

Living Environment

COST OF LIVING

Cost of Living Index

Composite Index	Groceries	Housing	Utilities	Trans-portation	Health Care	Misc. Goods/Services
150.7	111.2	240.4	110.8	128.3	111.6	116.5

Note: The Cost of Living Index measures regional differences in the cost of consumer goods and services, excluding taxes and non-consumer expenditures, for professional and managerial households in the top income quintile. It is based on more than 50,000 prices covering almost 60 different items for which prices are collected three times a year by chambers of commerce, economic development organizations or university applied economic centers in each participating urban area. The numbers shown should be read as a percentage above or below the national average of 100. For example, a value of 115.4 in the groceries column indicates that grocery prices are 15.4% higher than the national average. Small differences in the index numbers should not be interpreted as significant; Figures cover the Los Angeles-Long Beach CA urban area.
Source: The Council for Community and Economic Research, Cost of Living Index, 2022

Grocery Prices

Area[1]	T-Bone Steak ($/pound)	Frying Chicken ($/pound)	Whole Milk ($/half gal.)	Eggs ($/dozen)	Orange Juice ($/64 oz.)	Coffee ($/11.5 oz.)
City[2]	14.79	1.77	2.76	3.66	4.20	6.21
Avg.	13.81	1.59	2.43	2.25	3.85	4.95
Min.	10.17	0.90	1.51	1.30	2.90	3.46
Max.	19.35	3.30	4.32	4.32	5.31	8.59

*Note: (1) Values for the local area are compared with the average, minimum and maximum values for all 286 areas in the Cost of Living Index; (2) Figures cover the Los Angeles-Long Beach CA urban area; **T-Bone Steak** (price per pound); **Frying Chicken** (price per pound, whole fryer); **Whole Milk** (half gallon carton); **Eggs** (price per dozen, Grade A, large); **Orange Juice** (64 oz. Tropicana or Florida Natural); **Coffee** (11.5 oz. can, vacuum-packed, Maxwell House, Hills Bros, or Folgers).*
Source: The Council for Community and Economic Research, Cost of Living Index, 2022

Housing and Utility Costs

Area[1]	New Home Price ($)	Apartment Rent ($/month)	All Electric ($/month)	Part Electric ($/month)	Other Energy ($/month)	Telephone ($/month)
City[2]	1,098,874	3,182	-	123.99	84.34	192.21
Avg.	450,913	1,371	176.41	99.93	76.96	190.22
Min.	229,283	546	100.84	31.56	27.15	174.27
Max.	2,434,977	4,569	356.86	249.59	272.24	208.31

*Note: (1) Values for the local area are compared with the average, minimum and maximum values for all 286 areas in the Cost of Living Index; (2) Figures cover the Los Angeles-Long Beach CA urban area; **New Home Price** (2,400 sf living area, 8,000 sf lot, in urban area with full utilities); **Apartment Rent** (950 sf 2 bedroom/1.5 or 2 bath, unfurnished, excluding all utilities except water); **All Electric** (average monthly cost for an all-electric home); **Part Electric** (average monthly cost for a part-electric home); **Other Energy** (average monthly cost for natural gas, fuel oil, coal, wood, and any other forms of energy except electricity); **Telephone** (price includes the base monthly rate plus taxes and fees for three lines of mobile phone service).*
Source: The Council for Community and Economic Research, Cost of Living Index, 2022

Health Care, Transportation, and Other Costs

Area[1]	Doctor ($/visit)	Dentist ($/visit)	Optometrist ($/visit)	Gasoline ($/gallon)	Beauty Salon ($/visit)	Men's Shirt ($)
City[2]	130.00	128.20	132.27	5.54	82.67	36.49
Avg.	124.91	107.77	117.66	3.86	43.31	34.21
Min.	36.61	58.25	51.79	2.90	22.18	13.05
Max.	250.21	162.58	371.96	5.54	85.61	63.54

*Note: (1) Values for the local area are compared with the average, minimum and maximum values for all 286 areas in the Cost of Living Index; (2) Figures cover the Los Angeles-Long Beach CA urban area; **Doctor** (general practitioners routine exam of an established patient); **Dentist** (adult teeth cleaning and periodic oral examination); **Optometrist** (full vision eye exam for established adult patient); **Gasoline** (one gallon regular unleaded, national brand, including all taxes, cash price at self-service pump if available); **Beauty Salon** (woman's shampoo, trim, and blow-dry); **Men's Shirt** (cotton/polyester dress shirt, pinpoint weave, long sleeves).*
Source: The Council for Community and Economic Research, Cost of Living Index, 2022

HOUSING

Homeownership Rate

Area	2015 (%)	2016 (%)	2017 (%)	2018 (%)	2019 (%)	2020 (%)	2021 (%)	2022 (%)
MSA[1]	49.1	47.1	49.1	49.5	48.2	48.5	47.9	48.3
U.S.	63.7	63.4	63.9	64.4	64.6	66.6	65.5	65.8

Note: (1) Figures cover the Los Angeles-Long Beach-Anaheim, CA Metropolitan Statistical Area
Source: U.S. Census Bureau, Housing Vacancies and Homeownership Annual Statistics: 2015-2022

House Price Index (HPI)

Area	National Ranking[2]	Quarterly Change (%)	One-Year Change (%)	Five-Year Change (%)	Since 1991Q1 (%)
MD[1]	200	-1.90	8.62	46.01	298.97
U.S.[3]	–	0.34	8.41	58.44	289.08

Note: The HPI is a weighted repeat sales index. It measures average price changes in repeat sales or refinancings on the same properties. This information is obtained by reviewing repeat mortgage transactions on single-family properties whose mortgages have been purchased or securitized by Fannie Mae or Freddie Mac since January 1975; (1) Figures cover the Los Angeles-Long Beach-Glendale, CA Metropolitan Division; (2) Rankings are based on annual percentage change for all metro areas containing at least 15,000 transactions over the last 10 years and ranges from 1 to 257; (3) figures based on a weighted average of Census Division estimates using a seasonally adjusted, purchase-only index; all figures are for the period ending December 31, 2022
Source: Federal Housing Finance Agency, Change in FHFA Metropolitan Area House Price Indexes, 2022Q4

Median Single-Family Home Prices

Area	2020	2021	2022[p]	Percent Change 2021 to 2022
MD[1]	673.1	801.3	849.4	6.0
U.S. Average	300.2	357.1	392.6	9.9

Note: Figures are median sales prices of existing single-family homes in thousands of dollars; (p) preliminary; (1) Figures cover the Los Angeles-Long Beach-Glendale, CA Metropolitan Division
Source: National Association of Realtors, Median Sales Price of Existing Single-Family Homes for Metropolitan Areas, 4th Quarter 2022

Qualifying Income Based on Median Sales Price of Existing Single-Family Homes

Area	With 5% Down ($)	With 10% Down ($)	With 20% Down ($)
MD[1]	248,053	234,998	208,887
U.S. Average	112,234	106,237	94,513

Note: Figures are preliminary; Qualifying income is based on a mortgage rate of 6.77%. Monthly principal and interest payment is limited to 25% of income; (1) Figures cover the Los Angeles-Long Beach-Glendale, CA Metropolitan Division
Source: National Association of Realtors, Qualifying Income Based on Median Sales Price of Existing Single-Family Homes for Metropolitan Areas, 4th Quarter 2022

Home Value

Area	Under $100,000	$100,000 -$199,999	$200,000 -$299,999	$300,000 -$399,999	$400,000 -$499,999	$500,000 -$999,999	$1,000,000 or more	Median ($)
City	2.2	1.3	2.4	6.2	11.3	50.1	26.6	705,900
MSA[1]	3.2	1.7	3.2	7.0	11.9	52.3	20.7	671,700
U.S.	16.2	24.2	20.1	13.6	8.3	13.6	4.1	244,900

Note: Figures are percentages except for median and cover owner-occupied housing units; (1) Figures cover the Los Angeles-Long Beach-Anaheim, CA Metropolitan Statistical Area
Source: U.S. Census Bureau, 2017-2021 American Community Survey 5-Year Estimates

Year Housing Structure Built

Area	2020 or Later	2010 -2019	2000 -2009	1990 -1999	1980 -1989	1970 -1979	1960 -1969	1950 -1959	1940 -1949	Before 1940	Median Year
City	0.1	4.8	5.5	6.0	10.6	13.4	13.6	16.8	9.3	19.7	1963
MSA[1]	0.1	4.2	6.1	7.7	12.4	16.1	15.5	18.2	8.0	11.7	1968
U.S.	0.2	7.3	13.6	13.6	13.2	14.8	10.3	10.0	4.7	12.2	1979

Note: Figures are percentages except for Median Year; Note: (1) Figures cover the Los Angeles-Long Beach-Anaheim, CA Metropolitan Statistical Area
Source: U.S. Census Bureau, 2017-2021 American Community Survey 5-Year Estimates

Gross Monthly Rent

Area	Under $500	$500 -$999	$1,000 -$1,499	$1,500 -$1,999	$2,000 -$2,499	$2,500 -$2,999	$3,000 and up	Median ($)
City	4.9	11.1	27.1	24.6	15.1	8.1	9.2	1,641
MSA[1]	3.8	8.7	24.8	26.8	17.5	8.9	9.5	1,737
U.S.	8.1	30.5	30.8	16.8	7.3	3.1	3.5	1,163

Note: Figures are percentages except for median; Gross rent is the contract rent plus the estimated average monthly cost of utilities (electricity, gas, and water and sewer) and fuels (oil, coal, kerosene, wood, etc.) if these are paid by the renter (or paid for the renter by someone else); (1) Figures cover the Los Angeles-Long Beach-Anaheim, CA Metropolitan Statistical Area
Source: U.S. Census Bureau, 2017-2021 American Community Survey 5-Year Estimates

HEALTH

Health Risk Factors

Category	MSA[1] (%)	U.S. (%)
Adults aged 18–64 who have any kind of health care coverage	87.6	90.9
Adults who reported being in good or better health	83.4	85.2
Adults who have been told they have high blood cholesterol	35.0	35.7
Adults who have been told they have high blood pressure	27.0	32.4
Adults who are current smokers	7.4	14.4
Adults who currently use e-cigarettes	5.5	6.7
Adults who currently use chewing tobacco, snuff, or snus	1.6	3.5
Adults who are heavy drinkers[2]	5.6	6.3
Adults who are binge drinkers[3]	14.4	15.4
Adults who are overweight (BMI 25.0 - 29.9)	37.1	34.4
Adults who are obese (BMI 30.0 - 99.8)	26.8	33.9
Adults who participated in any physical activities in the past month	79.5	76.3

Note: (1) Figures cover the Los Angeles-Long Beach-Anaheim, CA Metropolitan Statistical Area; (2) Heavy drinkers are classified as adult men having more than 14 drinks per week and adult women having more than 7 drinks per week; (3) Binge drinkers are classified as males having five or more drinks on one occasion or females having four or more drinks on one occasion
Source: Centers for Disease Control and Prevention, Behaviorial Risk Factor Surveillance System, SMART: Selected Metropolitan Area Risk Trends, 2021

Acute and Chronic Health Conditions

Category	MSA[1] (%)	U.S. (%)
Adults who have ever been told they had a heart attack	2.2	4.0
Adults who have ever been told they have angina or coronary heart disease	2.7	3.8
Adults who have ever been told they had a stroke	2.1	3.0
Adults who have ever been told they have asthma	14.3	14.9
Adults who have ever been told they have arthritis	18.4	25.8
Adults who have ever been told they have diabetes[2]	12.2	10.9
Adults who have ever been told they had skin cancer	3.7	6.6
Adults who have ever been told they had any other types of cancer	4.5	7.5
Adults who have ever been told they have COPD	3.8	6.1
Adults who have ever been told they have kidney disease	2.2	3.0
Adults who have ever been told they have a form of depression	13.6	20.5

Note: (1) Figures cover the Los Angeles-Long Beach-Anaheim, CA Metropolitan Statistical Area; (2) Figures do not include pregnancy-related, borderline, or pre-diabetes
Source: Centers for Disease Control and Prevention, Behaviorial Risk Factor Surveillance System, SMART: Selected Metropolitan Area Risk Trends, 2021

Health Screening and Vaccination Rates

Category	MSA[1] (%)	U.S. (%)
Adults who have ever been tested for HIV	40.7	34.9
Adults who have had their blood cholesterol checked within the last five years	88.7	85.2
Adults aged 65+ who have had flu shot within the past year	63.7	68.6
Adults aged 65+ who have ever had a pneumonia vaccination	64.5	71.0

Note: (1) Figures cover the Los Angeles-Long Beach-Anaheim, CA Metropolitan Statistical Area.
Source: Centers for Disease Control and Prevention, Behaviorial Risk Factor Surveillance System, SMART: Selected Metropolitan Area Risk Trends, 2021

Disability Status

Category	MSA[1] (%)	U.S. (%)
Adults who reported being deaf	5.3	7.2
Are you blind or have serious difficulty seeing, even when wearing glasses?	4.9	4.8
Are you limited in any way in any of your usual activities due to arthritis?	8.2	11.1
Do you have difficulty doing errands alone?	5.4	7.0
Do you have difficulty dressing or bathing?	3.5	3.6
Do you have serious difficulty concentrating/remembering/making decisions?	9.6	12.1
Do you have serious difficulty walking or climbing stairs?	11.7	12.8

Note: (1) Figures cover the Los Angeles-Long Beach-Anaheim, CA Metropolitan Statistical Area.
Source: Centers for Disease Control and Prevention, Behaviorial Risk Factor Surveillance System, SMART: Selected Metropolitan Area Risk Trends, 2021

Mortality Rates for the Top 10 Causes of Death in the U.S.

ICD-10[a] Sub-Chapter	ICD-10[a] Code	Crude Mortality Rate[1] per 100,000 population	
		County[2]	U.S.
Malignant neoplasms	C00-C97	145.3	182.6
Ischaemic heart diseases	I20-I25	116.4	113.1
Other forms of heart disease	I30-I51	38.7	64.4
Other degenerative diseases of the nervous system	G30-G31	50.5	51.0
Cerebrovascular diseases	I60-I69	39.6	47.8
Other external causes of accidental injury	W00-X59	26.7	46.4
Chronic lower respiratory diseases	J40-J47	28.4	45.7
Organic, including symptomatic, mental disorders	F01-F09	12.3	35.9
Hypertensive diseases	I10-I15	33.8	35.0
Diabetes mellitus	E10-E14	33.6	29.6

Note: (a) ICD-10 = International Classification of Diseases 10th Revision; (1) Crude mortality rates are a three-year average covering 2019-2021; (2) Figures cover Los Angeles County.
Source: Centers for Disease Control and Prevention, National Center for Health Statistics. National Vital Statistics System, Mortality 2018-2021 on CDC WONDER Online Database

Mortality Rates for Selected Causes of Death

ICD-10[a] Sub-Chapter	ICD-10[a] Code	Crude Mortality Rate[1] per 100,000 population	
		County[2]	U.S.
Assault	X85-Y09	6.7	7.0
Diseases of the liver	K70-K76	18.3	19.8
Human immunodeficiency virus (HIV) disease	B20-B24	2.1	1.5
Influenza and pneumonia	J09-J18	19.1	14.7
Intentional self-harm	X60-X84	8.5	14.3
Malnutrition	E40-E46	1.4	4.3
Obesity and other hyperalimentation	E65-E68	2.7	3.0
Renal failure	N17-N19	14.7	15.7
Transport accidents	V01-V99	10.4	13.6
Viral hepatitis	B15-B19	1.3	1.2

Note: (a) ICD-10 = International Classification of Diseases 10th Revision; (1) Crude mortality rates are a three-year average covering 2019-2021; (2) Figures cover Los Angeles County; Data are suppressed when the data meet the criteria for confidentiality constraints; Crude mortality rates are flagged as unreliable when the rate would be calculated with a numerator of 20 or less.
Source: Centers for Disease Control and Prevention, National Center for Health Statistics. National Vital Statistics System, Mortality 2018-2021 on CDC WONDER Online Database

Health Insurance Coverage

Area	With Health Insurance	With Private Health Insurance	With Public Health Insurance	Without Health Insurance	Population Under Age 19 Without Health Insurance
City	89.3	55.1	40.8	10.7	3.8
MSA[1]	91.4	61.2	37.6	8.6	3.6
U.S.	91.2	67.8	35.4	8.8	5.3

Note: Figures are percentages that cover the civilian noninstitutionalized population; (1) Figures cover the Los Angeles-Long Beach-Anaheim, CA Metropolitan Statistical Area
Source: U.S. Census Bureau, 2017-2021 American Community Survey 5-Year Estimates

Number of Medical Professionals

Area	MDs[3]	DOs[3,4]	Dentists	Podiatrists	Chiropractors	Optometrists
County[1] (number)	31,470	1,461	9,258	642	3,013	1,939
County[1] (rate[2])	315.0	14.6	94.2	6.5	30.7	19.7
U.S. (rate[2])	289.3	23.5	72.5	6.2	28.7	17.4

Note: Data as of 2021 unless noted; (1) Data covers Los Angeles County; (2) Rate per 100,000 population; (3) Data as of 2020 and includes all active, non-federal physicians; (4) Doctor of Osteopathic Medicine
Source: U.S. Department of Health and Human Services, Health Resources and Services Administration, Bureau of Health Professions, Area Resource File (ARF) 2021-2022

Best Hospitals

According to *U.S. News,* the Los Angeles-Long Beach-Glendale, CA metro area is home to 13 of the best hospitals in the U.S.: **Cedars-Sinai Medical Center** (Honor Roll/11 adult specialties); **City of Hope Comprehensive Cancer Center** (1 adult specialty); **Kaiser Permanente Los Angeles Medical Center** (1 adult specialty); **Keck Medical Center of USC** (8 adult specialties); **MemorialCare Long Beach Medical Center** (1 adult specialty); **Providence Little Company of Mary Medical Center San Pedro** (1 adult specialty); **Rancho Los Amigos National Rehabilitation Center** (1 adult specialty); **Resnick Neuropsychiatric Hospital at UCLA** (1 adult specialty); **Santa Monica-UCLA Medical Center and Orthopedic Hospital** (1 adult specialty); **Stein and Doheny Eye Institute at UCLA Medical Center** (Honor Roll/14 adult specialties and 7 pediatric specialties);

Torrance Memorial Medical Center (1 adult specialty); **UCLA Medical Center** (Honor Roll/14 adult specialties and 7 pediatric specialties); **USC Norris Cancer Hospital-Keck Medical Center of USC** (1 adult specialty). The hospitals listed were nationally ranked in at least one of 15 adult or 10 pediatric specialties. The number of specialties shown cover the parent hospital. Only 164 U.S. hospitals performed well enough to be nationally ranked in one or more specialties. Twenty hospitals in the U.S. made the Honor Roll. The Best Hospitals Honor Roll takes both the national rankings and the procedure and condition ratings into account. Hospitals received points if they were nationally ranked in one of the 15 adult specialties—the higher they ranked, the more points they got—and how many ratings of "high performing" they earned in the 17 procedures and conditions. *U.S. News Online, "America's Best Hospitals 2022-23"*

According to *U.S. News,* the Los Angeles-Long Beach-Glendale, CA metro area is home to two of the best children's hospitals in the U.S.: **Children's Hospital Los Angeles** (Honor Roll/10 pediatric specialties); **UCLA Mattel Children's Hospital** (7 pediatric specialties). The hospitals listed were highly ranked in at least one of 10 pediatric specialties. Eighty-six children's hospitals in the U.S. were nationally ranked in at least one specialty. Hospitals received points for being ranked in a specialty, and the 10 hospitals with the most points across the 10 specialties make up the Honor Roll. *U.S. News Online, "America's Best Children's Hospitals 2022-23"*

EDUCATION

Public School District Statistics

District Name	Schls	Pupils	Pupil/ Teacher Ratio	Minority Pupils[1] (%)	LEP/ELL[2] (%)	IEP[3] (%)
Los Angeles Unified	778	435,958	19.9	90.0	20.6	16.1

Note: Table includes school districts with 2,000 or more students; (1) Percentage of students that are not non-Hispanic white; (2) Percentage of students that are Limited English Proficient or English Language Learners (2018-19); (3) Percentage of students that have an Individualized Education Program (2019-20).
Source: U.S. Department of Education, National Center for Education Statistics, Common Core of Data, Local Education Agency (School District) Universe Survey: School Year 2021-2022

Best High Schools

According to *U.S. News,* Los Angeles is home to seven of the top 500 high schools in the U.S.: **Harbor Teacher Preparation Academy** (#62); **Downtown Business High School** (#194); **Los Angeles Center for Enriched Studies** (#225); **Alliance Gertz-Ressler Richard Merkin 6-12 Complex** (#300); **Alliance Marc and Eva Stern Math and Science** (#369); **Francisco Bravo Medical Magnet High School** (#389); **Alliance Ted K. Tajima High School** (#444). Nearly 18,000 public, magnet and charter schools were ranked based on their performance on state assessments and how well they prepare students for college. *U.S. News & World Report, "Best High Schools 2022"*

Highest Level of Education

Area	Less than H.S.	H.S. Diploma	Some College, No Deg.	Associate Degree	Bachelor's Degree	Master's Degree	Prof. School Degree	Doctorate Degree
City	21.6	18.8	17.2	6.3	23.7	8.1	3.0	1.5
MSA[1]	18.4	19.6	18.8	7.2	23.2	8.6	2.7	1.5
U.S.	11.1	26.5	20.0	8.7	20.6	9.3	2.2	1.5

Note: Figures cover persons age 25 and over; (1) Figures cover the Los Angeles-Long Beach-Anaheim, CA Metropolitan Statistical Area
Source: U.S. Census Bureau, 2017-2021 American Community Survey 5-Year Estimates

Educational Attainment by Race

Area	High School Graduate or Higher (%)					Bachelor's Degree or Higher (%)				
	Total	White	Black	Asian	Hisp.[2]	Total	White	Black	Asian	Hisp.[2]
City	78.4	84.6	89.3	90.9	58.3	36.2	44.9	29.3	56.8	14.0
MSA[1]	81.6	86.5	90.5	88.8	64.5	36.0	40.8	29.5	54.5	15.1
U.S.	88.9	91.4	87.2	87.6	71.2	33.7	35.5	23.3	55.6	18.4

Note: Figures shown cover persons 25 years old and over; (1) Figures cover the Los Angeles-Long Beach-Anaheim, CA Metropolitan Statistical Area; (2) People of Hispanic origin can be of any race
Source: U.S. Census Bureau, 2017-2021 American Community Survey 5-Year Estimates

School Enrollment by Grade and Control

Area	Preschool (%)		Kindergarten (%)		Grades 1 - 4 (%)		Grades 5 - 8 (%)		Grades 9 - 12 (%)	
	Public	Private	Public	Private	Public	Private	Public	Private	Public	Private
City	57.1	42.9	85.7	14.3	88.0	12.0	87.6	12.4	89.1	10.9
MSA[1]	55.8	44.2	86.9	13.1	90.0	10.0	90.1	9.9	91.1	8.9
U.S.	58.8	41.2	86.3	13.7	88.3	11.7	88.6	11.4	89.4	10.6

Note: Figures shown cover persons 3 years old and over; (1) Figures cover the Los Angeles-Long Beach-Anaheim, CA Metropolitan Statistical Area
Source: U.S. Census Bureau, 2017-2021 American Community Survey 5-Year Estimates

Higher Education

Four-Year Colleges			Two-Year Colleges			Medical Schools[1]	Law Schools[2]	Voc/Tech[3]
Public	Private Non-profit	Private For-profit	Public	Private Non-profit	Private For-profit			
14	78	36	28	1	29	6	22	75

Note: Figures cover institutions located within the Los Angeles-Long Beach-Anaheim, CA Metropolitan Statistical Area and include main campuses only; (1) includes schools accredited by the Liaison Committee on Medical Education and the American Osteopathic Association's Commission on Osteopathic College Accreditation; (2) includes ABA-accredited schools, schools with provisional ABA accreditation, and state accredited schools; (3) includes all schools with programs that are less than 2 years.
Source: National Center for Education Statistics, Integrated Postsecondary Education System (IPEDS), 2021-22; Wikipedia, List of Medical Schools in the United States, accessed April 10, 2023; Wikipedia, List of Law Schools in the United States, accessed April 10, 2023

According to *U.S. News & World Report,* the Los Angeles-Long Beach-Glendale, CA metro division is home to eight of the top 200 national universities in the U.S.: **California Institute of Technology** (#9); **University of California—Los Angeles** (#20 tie); **University of Southern California** (#25 tie); **Pepperdine University** (#55 tie); **Loyola Marymount University** (#77 tie); **California State University—Long Beach** (#137 tie); **University of La Verne** (#151 tie); **Biola University** (#194 tie). The indicators used to capture academic quality fall into a number of categories: assessment by administrators at peer institutions; retention of students; faculty resources; student selectivity; financial resources; alumni giving; high school counselor ratings of colleges; and graduation rate. *U.S. News & World Report, "America's Best Colleges 2023"*

According to *U.S. News & World Report,* the Los Angeles-Long Beach-Glendale, CA metro division is home to six of the top 100 liberal arts colleges in the U.S.: **Pomona College** (#3); **Claremont McKenna College** (#9 tie); **Harvey Mudd College** (#29 tie); **Pitzer College** (#33 tie); **Scripps College** (#33 tie); **Occidental College** (#37 tie). The indicators used to capture academic quality fall into a number of categories: assessment by administrators at peer institutions; retention of students; faculty resources; student selectivity; financial resources; alumni giving; high school counselor ratings of colleges; and graduation rate. *U.S. News & World Report, "America's Best Colleges 2023"*

According to *U.S. News & World Report,* the Los Angeles-Long Beach-Glendale, CA metro division is home to four of the top 100 law schools in the U.S.: **University of California—Los Angeles** (#15); **University of Southern California (Gould)** (#20); **Pepperdine University (Caruso)** (#52 tie); **Loyola Marymount University** (#67 tie). The rankings are based on a weighted average of 12 measures of quality: peer assessment score; assessment score by lawyers/judges; median LSAT scores; median undergrad GPA; acceptance rate; employment rates for graduates; placement success; bar passage rate; faculty resources; expenditures per student; student/faculty ratio; and library resources. *U.S. News & World Report, "America's Best Graduate Schools, Law, 2023"*

According to *U.S. News & World Report,* the Los Angeles-Long Beach-Glendale, CA metro division is home to two of the top 75 medical schools for research in the U.S.: **University of California—Los Angeles (Geffen)** (#19); **University of Southern California (Keck)** (#28). The rankings are based on a weighted average of 11 measures of quality: quality assessment; peer assessment score; assessment score by residency directors; research activity; total research activity; average research activity per faculty member; student selectivity; median MCAT total score; median undergraduate GPA; acceptance rate; and faculty resources. *U.S. News & World Report, "America's Best Graduate Schools, Medical, 2023"*

According to *U.S. News & World Report,* the Los Angeles-Long Beach-Glendale, CA metro division is home to two of the top 75 business schools in the U.S.: **University of California—Los Angeles (Anderson)** (#17); **University of Southern California (Marshall)** (#19 tie). The rankings are based on a weighted average of the following nine measures: quality assessment; peer assessment; recruiter assessment; placement success; mean starting salary and bonus; student selectivity; mean GMAT and GRE scores; mean undergraduate GPA; and acceptance rate. *U.S. News & World Report, "America's Best Graduate Schools, Business, 2023"*

EMPLOYERS

Major Employers

Company Name	Industry
City of Los Angeles	Municipal government
County of Los Angeles	County government
Decton	Employment agencies
Disney Enterprises	Motion picture production & distribution
Disney Worldwide Services	Telecommunication equipment repair, excl telephones
Electronic Arts	Home entertainment computer software
King Holding Corporation	Bolts, nuts, rivets, & washers
Securitas Security Services USA	Security guard service
Team-One Employment Specialists	Employment agencies
The Boeing Company	Aircraft
The Walt Disney Company	Television broadcasting stations
UCLA Health System	Home health care services
UCLA Medical Group	Medical centers
University of California, Irvine	University
University of Southern California	Colleges & universities
Veterans Health Administration	Administration of veterans' affairs
Warner Bros. Entertainment	Motion picture production & distribution

Note: Companies shown are located within the Los Angeles-Long Beach-Anaheim, CA Metropolitan Statistical Area.
Source: Hoovers.com; Wikipedia

Best Companies to Work For

Boulevard, headquartered in Los Angeles, is among "Fortune's Best Workplaces for Women." To pick the best companies, *Fortune* partnered with the Great Place to Work Institute. To be considered for the list, companies must be Great Place To Work-Certified. Companies must also employ at least 50 women, at least 20% of their non-executive managers must be female, and at least one executive must be female. To determine the Best Workplaces for Women, Great Place To Work measured the differences in women's survey responses to those of their peers and assesses the impact of demographics and roles on the quality and consistency of women's experiences. Great Place To Work also analyzed the gender balance of each workplace, how it compared to each company's industry, and patterns in representation as women rise from front-line positions to the board of directors. *Fortune, "Best Workplaces for Women," 2022*

Skilled Wound Care, headquartered in Los Angeles, is among "Best Workplaces in Health Care." To determine the Best Workplaces in Health Care list, Great Place To Work analyzed the survey responses of over 161,000 employees from Great Place To Work-Certified companies in the health care industry. Survey data analysis and company-provided datapoints are then factored into a combined score to compare and rank the companies that create the most consistently positive experience for all employees in this industry. *Fortune, "Best Workplaces in Health Care," 2022*

Riot Games, headquartered in Los Angeles, is among "Fortune's Best Workplaces for Parents." To pick the best companies, *Fortune* partnered with the Great Place to Work Institute. To be considered for the list, companies must be Great Place To Work-Certified and have at least 50 responses from parents in the US. The survey enables employees to share confidential quantitative and qualitative feedback about their organization's culture by responding to 60 statements on a 5-point scale and answering two open-ended questions. Collectively, these statements describe a great employee experience, defined by high levels of trust, respect, credibility, fairness, pride, and camaraderie. In addition, companies provide organizational data like size, location, industry, demographics, roles, and levels; and provide information about parental leave, adoption, flexible schedule, childcare and dependent health care benefits. *Fortune, "Best Workplaces for Parents," 2022*

Cedars-Sinai, headquartered in Los Angeles, is among the "100 Best Places to Work in IT." To qualify, companies had to have a minimum of 100 total employees and five IT employees. The best places to work were selected based on DEI (diversity, equity, and inclusion) practices; IT turnover, promotions, and growth; IT retention and engagement programs; remote/hybrid working; benefits and perks (such as elder care and child care, flextime, and reimbursement for college tuition); and training and career development opportunities. *Computerworld, "Best Places to Work in IT," 2023*

PUBLIC SAFETY

Crime Rate

Area	Total Crime	Violent Crime Rate				Property Crime Rate		
		Murder	Rape[3]	Robbery	Aggrav. Assault	Burglary	Larceny -Theft	Motor Vehicle Theft
City	2,869.9	8.8	49.6	200.3	463.3	344.3	1,274.6	529.1
Suburbs[1]	2,435.2	4.2	28.0	102.7	228.4	355.9	1,303.4	412.7
Metro[2]	2,567.7	5.6	34.6	132.5	300.0	352.3	1,294.6	448.2
U.S.	2,356.7	6.5	38.4	73.9	279.7	314.2	1,398.0	246.0

Note: Figures are crimes per 100,000 population; (1) All areas within the metro area that are located outside the city limits; (2) Figures cover the Los Angeles-Long Beach-Glendale, CA Metropolitan Division; (3) All figures shown were reported using the revised Uniform Crime Reporting (UCR) definition of rape; Due to the transition to the National Incident-Based Reporting System (NIBRS), limited city and metro area data was released for 2021.
Source: FBI Uniform Crime Reports, 2020

Hate Crimes

Area	Number of Quarters Reported	Number of Incidents per Bias Motivation					
		Race/Ethnicity/ Ancestry	Religion	Sexual Orientation	Disability	Gender	Gender Identity
City[1]	4	187	67	81	1	2	31
U.S.	4	5,227	1,244	1,110	130	75	266

Note: (1) Figures include one incident reported with more than one bias motivation; Due to the transition to the National Incident-Based Reporting System (NIBRS), limited crime data was released for 2021.
Source: Federal Bureau of Investigation, Hate Crime Statistics 2020

Identity Theft Consumer Reports

Area	Reports	Reports per 100,000 Population	Rank[2]
MSA[1]	63,962	484	20
U.S.	1,108,609	339	-

Note: (1) Figures cover the Los Angeles-Long Beach-Anaheim, CA Metropolitan Statistical Area; (2) Rank ranges from 1 to 391 where 1 indicates greatest number of identity theft reports per 100,000 population
Source: Federal Trade Commission, Consumer Sentinel Network Data Book 2022

Fraud and Other Consumer Reports

Area	Reports	Reports per 100,000 Population	Rank[2]
MSA[1]	133,883	1,013	92
U.S.	4,064,520	1,245	-

Note: (1) Figures cover the Los Angeles-Long Beach-Anaheim, CA Metropolitan Statistical Area; (2) Rank ranges from 1 to 391 where 1 indicates greatest number of fraud and other consumer reports per 100,000 population
Source: Federal Trade Commission, Consumer Sentinel Network Data Book 2022

POLITICS

2020 Presidential Election Results

Area	Biden	Trump	Jorgensen	Hawkins	Other
Los Angeles County	71.0	26.9	0.8	0.5	0.8
U.S.	51.3	46.8	1.2	0.3	0.5

Note: Results are percentages and may not add to 100% due to rounding
Source: Dave Leip's Atlas of U.S. Presidential Elections

SPORTS

Professional Sports Teams

Team Name	League	Year Established
Anaheim Ducks	National Hockey League (NHL)	1993
C.D. Chivas USA	Major League Soccer (MLS)	2004
Los Angeles Angels of Anaheim	Major League Baseball (MLB)	1961
Los Angeles Chargers	National Football League (NFL)	2017
Los Angeles Clippers	National Basketball Association (NBA)	1984
Los Angeles Dodgers	Major League Baseball (MLB)	1958
Los Angeles FC	Major League Soccer (MLS)	2018
Los Angeles Galaxy	Major League Soccer (MLS)	1996
Los Angeles Kings	National Hockey League (NHL)	1967
Los Angeles Lakers	National Basketball Association (NBA)	1960
Los Angeles Rams	National Football League (NFL)	2016

Note: Includes teams located in the Los Angeles-Long Beach-Anaheim, CA Metropolitan Statistical Area.
Source: Wikipedia, Major Professional Sports Teams of the United States and Canada, April 12, 2023

CLIMATE

Average and Extreme Temperatures

Temperature	Jan	Feb	Mar	Apr	May	Jun	Jul	Aug	Sep	Oct	Nov	Dec	Yr.
Extreme High (°F)	88	92	95	102	97	104	97	98	110	106	101	94	110
Average High (°F)	65	66	65	67	69	72	75	76	76	74	71	66	70
Average Temp. (°F)	56	57	58	60	63	66	69	70	70	67	62	57	63
Average Low (°F)	47	49	50	53	56	59	63	64	63	59	52	48	55
Extreme Low (°F)	27	34	37	43	45	48	52	51	47	43	38	32	27

Note: Figures cover the years 1947-1990
Source: National Climatic Data Center, International Station Meteorological Climate Summary, 9/96

Average Precipitation/Snowfall/Humidity

Precip./Humidity	Jan	Feb	Mar	Apr	May	Jun	Jul	Aug	Sep	Oct	Nov	Dec	Yr.
Avg. Precip. (in.)	2.6	2.3	1.8	0.8	0.1	Tr	Tr	0.1	0.2	0.3	1.5	1.5	11.3
Avg. Snowfall (in.)	Tr	0	0	0	0	0	0	0	0	0	0	0	Tr
Avg. Rel. Hum. 7am (%)	69	72	76	76	77	80	80	81	80	76	69	67	75
Avg. Rel. Hum. 4pm (%)	60	62	64	64	66	67	67	68	67	66	61	60	64

Note: Figures cover the years 1947-1990; Tr = Trace amounts (<0.05 in. of rain; <0.5 in. of snow)
Source: National Climatic Data Center, International Station Meteorological Climate Summary, 9/96

Weather Conditions

Temperature			Daytime Sky			Precipitation		
10°F & below	32°F & below	90°F & above	Clear	Partly cloudy	Cloudy	0.01 inch or more precip.	0.1 inch or more snow/ice	Thunder-storms
0	<1	5	131	125	109	34	0	1

Note: Figures are average number of days per year and cover the years 1947-1990
Source: National Climatic Data Center, International Station Meteorological Climate Summary, 9/96

HAZARDOUS WASTE

Superfund Sites

The Los Angeles-Long Beach-Glendale, CA metro division is home to 15 sites on the EPA's Superfund National Priorities List: **Cooper Drum Co.** (final); **Del Amo** (final); **Jervis B. Webb Co.** (final); **Jet Propulsion Laboratory (NASA)** (final); **Montrose Chemical Corp.** (final); **Omega Chemical Corporation** (final); **Operating Industries, Inc., Landfill** (final); **Pemaco Maywood** (final); **San Fernando Valley (Area 1)** (final); **San Fernando Valley (Area 2)** (final); **San Fernando Valley (Area 4)** (final); **San Gabriel Valley (Area 1)** (final); **San Gabriel Valley (Area 2)** (final); **San Gabriel Valley (Area 3)** (final); **San Gabriel Valley (Area 4)** (final). There are a total of 1,165 Superfund sites with a status of proposed or final on the list in the U.S. *U.S. Environmental Protection Agency, National Priorities List, April 12, 2023*

AIR QUALITY

Air Quality Trends: Ozone

	1990	1995	2000	2005	2010	2015	2018	2019	2020	2021
MSA[1]	0.128	0.109	0.090	0.086	0.074	0.082	0.082	0.080	0.096	0.076
U.S.	0.087	0.089	0.081	0.080	0.072	0.067	0.069	0.065	0.065	0.067

Note: (1) Data covers the Los Angeles-Long Beach-Anaheim, CA Metropolitan Statistical Area. The values shown are the composite ozone concentration averages among trend sites based on the highest fourth daily maximum 8-hour concentration in parts per million. These trends are based on sites having an adequate record of monitoring data during the trend period. Data from exceptional events are included.
Source: U.S. Environmental Protection Agency, Air Quality Monitoring Information, "Air Quality Trends by City, 1990-2021"

Air Quality Index

Area	Percent of Days when Air Quality was...[2]					AQI Statistics[2]	
	Good	Moderate	Unhealthy for Sensitive Groups	Unhealthy	Very Unhealthy	Maximum	Median
MSA[1]	10.7	62.5	19.5	7.1	0.3	281	77

Note: (1) Data covers the Los Angeles-Long Beach-Anaheim, CA Metropolitan Statistical Area; (2) Based on 365 days with AQI data in 2021. Air Quality Index (AQI) is an index for reporting daily air quality. EPA calculates the AQI for five major air pollutants regulated by the Clean Air Act: ground-level ozone, particle pollution (aka particulate matter), carbon monoxide, sulfur dioxide, and nitrogen dioxide. The AQI runs from 0 to 500. The higher the AQI value, the greater the level of air pollution and the greater the health concern. There are six AQI categories: "Good" AQI is between 0 and 50. Air quality is considered satisfactory; "Moderate" AQI is between 51 and 100. Air quality is acceptable; "Unhealthy for Sensitive Groups" When AQI values are between 101 and 150, members of sensitive groups may experience health effects; "Unhealthy" When AQI values are between 151 and 200 everyone may begin to experience health effects; "Very Unhealthy" AQI values between 201 and 300 trigger a health alert; "Hazardous" AQI values over 300 trigger warnings of emergency conditions (not shown).
Source: U.S. Environmental Protection Agency, Air Quality Index Report, 2021

Air Quality Index Pollutants

Area	Percent of Days when AQI Pollutant was...[2]					
	Carbon Monoxide	Nitrogen Dioxide	Ozone	Sulfur Dioxide	Particulate Matter 2.5	Particulate Matter 10
MSA[1]	0.0	6.6	46.0	(3)	45.2	2.2

Note: (1) Data covers the Los Angeles-Long Beach-Anaheim, CA Metropolitan Statistical Area; (2) Based on 365 days with AQI data in 2021. The Air Quality Index (AQI) is an index for reporting daily air quality. EPA calculates the AQI for five major air pollutants regulated by the Clean Air Act: ground-level ozone, particle pollution (also known as particulate matter), carbon monoxide, sulfur dioxide, and nitrogen dioxide. The AQI runs from 0 to 500. The higher the AQI value, the greater the level of air pollution and the greater the health concern; (3) Sulfur dioxide is no longer included in this table (as of December 8, 2021) because SO_2 concentrations tend to be very localized and not necessarily representative of broad geographical areas like counties and CBSAs.
Source: U.S. Environmental Protection Agency, Air Quality Index Report, 2021

Maximum Air Pollutant Concentrations: Particulate Matter, Ozone, CO and Lead

	Particulate Matter 10 (ug/m^3)	Particulate Matter 2.5 Wtd AM (ug/m^3)	Particulate Matter 2.5 24-Hr (ug/m^3)	Ozone (ppm)	Carbon Monoxide (ppm)	Lead (ug/m^3)
MSA[1] Level	113	13.4	48	0.097	3	0.06
NAAQS[2]	150	15	35	0.075	9	0.15
Met NAAQS[2]	Yes	Yes	No	No	Yes	Yes

Note: (1) Data covers the Los Angeles-Long Beach-Anaheim, CA Metropolitan Statistical Area; Data from exceptional events are included; (2) National Ambient Air Quality Standards; ppm = parts per million; ug/m^3 = micrograms per cubic meter; n/a not available.
Concentrations: Particulate Matter 10 (coarse particulate)—highest second maximum 24-hour concentration; Particulate Matter 2.5 Wtd AM (fine particulate)—highest weighted annual mean concentration; Particulate Matter 2.5 24-Hour (fine particulate)—highest 98th percentile 24-hour concentration; Ozone—highest fourth daily maximum 8-hour concentration; Carbon Monoxide—highest second maximum non-overlapping 8-hour concentration; Lead—maximum running 3-month average
Source: U.S. Environmental Protection Agency, Air Quality Monitoring Information, "Air Quality Statistics by City, 2021"

Maximum Air Pollutant Concentrations: Nitrogen Dioxide and Sulfur Dioxide

	Nitrogen Dioxide AM (ppb)	Nitrogen Dioxide 1-Hr (ppb)	Sulfur Dioxide AM (ppb)	Sulfur Dioxide 1-Hr (ppb)	Sulfur Dioxide 24-Hr (ppb)
MSA[1] Level	25	76	n/a	4	n/a
NAAQS[2]	53	100	30	75	140
Met NAAQS[2]	Yes	Yes	n/a	Yes	n/a

Note: (1) Data covers the Los Angeles-Long Beach-Anaheim, CA Metropolitan Statistical Area; Data from exceptional events are included; (2) National Ambient Air Quality Standards; ppm = parts per million; ug/m^3 = micrograms per cubic meter; n/a not available.
Concentrations: Nitrogen Dioxide AM—highest arithmetic mean concentration; Nitrogen Dioxide 1-Hr—highest 98th percentile 1-hour daily maximum concentration; Sulfur Dioxide AM—highest annual mean concentration; Sulfur Dioxide 1-Hr—highest 99th percentile 1-hour daily maximum concentration; Sulfur Dioxide 24-Hr—highest second maximum 24-hour concentration
Source: U.S. Environmental Protection Agency, Air Quality Monitoring Information, "Air Quality Statistics by City, 2021"

Phoenix, Arizona

Background

Phoenix, the arid "Valley of the Sun," and the capital of Arizona, was named by the English soldier and prospector, "Lord Darell" Duppa for the mythical bird of ancient Greek/Phoenician lore. According to the legend, the Phoenix was a beautiful bird that destroyed itself with its own flames. When nothing remained but embers, it would rise again from the ashes, more awesome and beautiful than before. Like the romantic tale, Duppa hoped that his city of Phoenix would rise again from the mysteriously abandoned Hohokam village which occupied the Phoenix area for 2,000 years.

Many might agree that Phoenix fulfilled Duppa's wish. Within 15 years after its second founding in 1867, Phoenix had grown to be an important supply point for the mining districts of north-central Arizona, as well as an important trading site for farmers, cattlemen, and prospectors.

Around this time, Phoenix entered its Wild West phase, complete with stagecoaches, saloons, gambling houses, soldiers, cowboys, miners, and the pungent air of outlawry. Two public hangings near the end of the 1800s set a dramatic example and helped turn the tide.

Today, Phoenix is just as exciting as ever, but more law-abiding, and many continue to be attracted to Phoenix's natural beauty. Despite occasional sprawling suburbs and shopping malls, the sophisticated blend of Spanish, Native American, and cowboy culture is obvious in the city's architecture, arts, and crafts. Downtown Phoenix underwent a major renaissance in the 1990s with the completion of a history museum, expanded art museum, new central library, Arizona Science Center, and a renovated concert hall. Today it also features the 20,000-square-foot Musical Instrument Museum featuring musical instruments from around the world. More than 300 arts and entertainment venues are in the Phoenix region, as well as five professional sports teams. Phoenix Concept 2000 split the city into 15 urban villages, each with its own building height and density permits, further shaping the city's free-market development culture.

Phoenix is the country's fifth-largest city, with more than one million people, while the Phoenix metro area population has grown to nearly four million. This increase in population continues to make Phoenix an attractive location for companies that are expanding in the fields of electronics and communications. Renewable energy, biomedicine, advanced business services, manufacturing and distribution, aerospace and aviation, and emerging technologies from start-ups are key industries in the region, as are insurance, healthcare, and technology.

Phoenix is home to several professional sports franchises. The Phoenix Suns of the NBA and the Phoenix Mercury of the WNBA both play at Talking Stick Resort Arena. The Mercury have won the WNBA championships three times: in 2007, 2009, and 2014. The Arizona Diamondbacks of Major League Baseball play their home games in Chase Field, the second-highest stadium in the country, and defeated the New York Yankees in 2001 to claim the World Series title. The Arizona Cardinals is the oldest continuously run professional football franchise in the nation, though they originated in Chicago. They play at the University of Phoenix Stadium in Glendale, 20 miles from Phoenix, which hosted Super Bowl in 2008, 2015, and 2023.

The Valley Metro Rail light rail eco-friendly transit system's 60-mile expansion is nearly complete.

In 1981, Phoenix resident Sandra Day O'Connor broke the gender barrier on the U.S. Supreme Court when she was sworn in as the first female justice. The influx of refugees—most recently about 450 Afghans—has resulted in more than 100 languages being spoken in local schools.

Temperatures in Phoenix are mild in winter and very hot in summer. The low humidity makes the summer heat somewhat more bearable than one might expect. Rainfall is slight and comes in two seasons: winter rain comes on winds from the Pacific, ending by April; summer rain with severe thunderstorms come from the southeast.

Rankings

General Rankings

- For its "Best for Vets: Places to Live 2019" rankings, *Military Times* evaluated 599 cities (83 large, 234 medium, 282 small) and compared the locations across three broad categories: veteran and military culture/services; economic indicators; and livability factors such as health, crime, traffic, and school quality. Phoenix ranked #21 out of the top 25, in the large city category (population of more than 250,000). Data points more specific to veterans and the military weighed more heavily than others. *rebootcamp.militarytimes.com, "Military Times Best Places to Live 2019," September 10, 2018*

- *Insider* listed 23 places in the U.S. that travel industry trends reveal would be popular destinations in 2023. This year the list trends towards cultural and historical happenings, sports events, wellness experiences and invigorating outdoor escapes. According to the website insider.com Phoenix is a place to visit in 2023. *Insider, "23 of the Best Places You Should Travel to in the U.S. in 2023," December 17, 2022*

- The Phoenix metro area was identified as one of America's fastest-growing areas in terms of population and business growth by *MagnifyMoney*. The area ranked #28 out of 35. The 100 most populous metro areas in the U.S. were evaluated on their change from 2011 to 2016 in the following categories: people and housing; workforce and employment opportunities; growing industry. *www.businessinsider.com, "The 35 Cities in the US with the Biggest Influx of People, the Most Work Opportunities, and the Hottest Business Growth," August 12, 2018*

- The Phoenix metro area was identified as one of America's fastest-growing areas in terms of population and economy by *Forbes*. The area ranked #11 out of 25. The 100 most populous metro areas in the U.S. were evaluated on the following criteria: estimated population growth; employment; economic output; wages; home values. *Forbes, "America's Fastest-Growing Cities 2018," February 28, 2018*

- Phoenix was selected as an "All-America City" by the National Civic League. The All-America City Award recognizes civic excellence and in 2022 honored 10 communities that best exemplify the spirit of grassroots citizen involvement and cross-sector collaborative problem solving to collectively tackle pressing and complex issues. This year's theme was: "Housing as a Platform to Promote Early School Success and Equitable Learning Recovery." *National Civic League, "2022 All-America City Awards," July 21, 2022*

Business/Finance Rankings

- The Brookings Institution ranked the nation's largest cities based on income inequality. Phoenix was ranked #62 (#1 = greatest inequality). Criteria: the "95/20 ratio," a figure representing the income at which a household earns more than 95 percent of all other households, divided by the income at which a household earns more than only 20 percent of all other households. *Brookings Institution, "Household Income Inequality, Largest Cities of 97 Large U.S. Metro Areas, 2014-2016," February 5, 2018*

- The Brookings Institution ranked the 100 largest metro areas in the U.S. based on income inequality. Phoenix was ranked #61 (#1 = greatest inequality). Criteria: the "95/20 ratio," a figure representing the income at which a household earns more than 95 percent of all other households, divided by the income at which a household earns more than only 20 percent of all other households. *Brookings Institution, "Household Income Inequality, 100 Largest U.S. Metro Areas, 2014-2016," February 5, 2018*

- Payscale.com ranked the 32 largest metro areas in terms of wage growth. The Phoenix metro area ranked #5. Criteria: quarterly changes in private industry employee and education professional wage growth from the previous year. *PayScale, "Wage Trends by Metro Area-1st Quarter," April 20, 2023*

- The Phoenix metro area was identified as one of the most debt-ridden places in America by the finance site Credit.com. The metro area was ranked #17. Criteria: residents' average credit card debt as well as median income. *Credit.com, "25 Cities With the Most Credit Card Debt," February 28, 2018*

- Phoenix was identified as one of America's most frugal metro areas by *Coupons.com*. The city ranked #16 out of 25. Criteria: digital coupon usage. *Coupons.com, "America's Most Frugal Cities of 2017," March 22, 2018*

- Phoenix was identified as one of the happiest cities to work in by CareerBliss.com, an online community for career advancement. The city ranked #4 out of 10. Criteria: an employee's relationship with his or her boss and co-workers; daily tasks; general work environment; compensation; opportunities for advancement; company culture and job reputation; and resources. *Businesswire.com, "CareerBliss Happiest Cities to Work 2019," February 12, 2019*

- The Phoenix metro area appeared on the Milken Institute "2022 Best Performing Cities" list. Rank: #4 out of 200 large metro areas (population over 250,000). Criteria: job growth; wage and salary growth; high-tech output growth; housing affordability; household broadband access. *Milken Institute, "Best-Performing Cities 2022," March 28, 2022*

- *Forbes* ranked the 200 most populous metro areas to determine the nation's "Best Places for Business and Careers." The Phoenix metro area was ranked #26. Criteria: costs (business and living); job growth (past and projected); income growth; quality of life; educational attainment (college and high school); projected economic growth; cultural and leisure opportunities; workplace tolerance laws; net migration patterns. *Forbes, "The Best Places for Business and Careers 2019: Seattle Still On Top," October 30, 2019*

Education Rankings

- Personal finance website *WalletHub* analyzed the 150 largest U.S. metropolitan statistical areas to determine where the most educated Americans are putting their degrees to work. Criteria: education levels; percentage of workers with degrees; education quality and attainment gap; public school quality rankings; quality and enrollment of each metro area's universities. Phoenix was ranked #72 (#1 = most educated city). *www.WalletHub.com, "Most & Least Educated Cities in America," July 18, 2022*

- Phoenix was selected as one of America's most literate cities. The city ranked #74 out of the 84 largest U.S. cities. Criteria: number of booksellers; library resources; Internet resources; educational attainment; periodical publishing resources; newspaper circulation. *Central Connecticut State University, "America's Most Literate Cities, 2018," February 2019*

Environmental Rankings

- Sperling's BestPlaces assessed the 50 largest metropolitan areas of the United States for the likelihood of dangerously extreme weather events or earthquakes. In general the Southeast and South-Central regions have the highest risk of weather extremes and earthquakes, while the Pacific Northwest enjoys the lowest risk. Of the most risky metropolitan areas, the Phoenix metro area was ranked #9. *www.bestplaces.net, "Avoid Natural Disasters: BestPlaces Reveals The Top 10 Safest Places to Live," October 25, 2017*

- The U.S. Environmental Protection Agency (EPA) released its list of U.S. metropolitan areas with the most ENERGY STAR certified buildings in 2022. The Phoenix metro area was ranked #17 out of 25. *U.S. Environmental Protection Agency, "2023 Energy Star Top Cities," April 26, 2023*

- Phoenix was highlighted as one of the 25 most ozone-polluted metro areas in the U.S. during 2019 through 2021. The area ranked #5. *American Lung Association, "State of the Air 2023," April 19, 2023*

- Phoenix was highlighted as one of the 25 metro areas most polluted by year-round particle pollution (Annual PM 2.5) in the U.S. during 2019 through 2021. The area ranked #7. *American Lung Association, "State of the Air 2023," April 19, 2023*

- Phoenix was highlighted as one of the 25 metro areas most polluted by short-term particle pollution (24-hour PM 2.5) in the U.S. during 2019 through 2021. The area ranked #13. *American Lung Association, "State of the Air 2023," April 19, 2023*

Food/Drink Rankings

- The U.S. Chamber of Commerce Foundation conducted an in-depth study on local food truck regulations, surveyed 288 food truck owners, and ranked 20 major American cities based on how friendly they are for operating a food truck. The compiled index assessed the following: procedures for obtaining permits and licenses; complying with restrictions; and financial obligations associated with operating a food truck. Phoenix ranked #14 overall (1 being the best). *www.foodtrucknation.us, "Food Truck Nation," March 20, 2018*

- Chase Field was selected as one of PETA's "Top 10 Vegan-Friendly Ballparks" for 2019. The park ranked #10. *People for the Ethical Treatment of Animals, "Top 10 Vegan-Friendly Ballparks," May 23, 2019*

Health/Fitness Rankings

- For each of the 100 largest cities in the United States, the American Fitness Index®, compiled in partnership between the American College of Sports Medicine and the Elevance Health Foundation, evaluated community infrastructure and 34 health behaviors including preventive health, levels of chronic disease conditions, food insecurity, sleep quality, pedestrian safety, air quality, and community/environment resources that support physical activity. Phoenix ranked #66 for "community fitness." *americanfitnessindex.org, "2022 ACSM American Fitness Index Summary Report," July 12, 2022*

- Phoenix was identified as a "2022 Spring Allergy Capital." The area ranked #97 out of 100. Three groups of factors were used to identify the most challenging cities for people with allergies during the spring season: annual spring pollen scores; over the counter allergy medicine use; number of board-certified allergy specialists. *Asthma and Allergy Foundation of America, "Spring Allergy Capitals 2022," March 2, 2022*

- Phoenix was identified as a "2022 Fall Allergy Capital." The area ranked #90 out of 100. Three groups of factors were used to identify the most challenging cities for people with allergies during the fall season: annual fall pollen scores; over the counter allergy medicine use; number of board-certified allergy specialists. *Asthma and Allergy Foundation of America, "Fall Allergy Capitals 2022," March 2, 2022*

- Phoenix was identified as a "2022 Asthma Capital." The area ranked #34 out of the nation's 100 largest metropolitan areas. Criteria: estimated asthma prevalence; asthma-related mortality; and ER visits due to asthma. Risk factors analyzed but not factored in the rankings: annual pollen score; annual air quality; public smoking laws; access to board-certified asthma specialists; rescue and controller medication use; uninsured rate; poverty rate. *Asthma and Allergy Foundation of America, "Asthma Capitals 2022: The Most Challenging Places to Live With Asthma," September 14, 2022*

Real Estate Rankings

- *WalletHub* compared the most populated U.S. cities to determine which had the best markets for real estate agents. Phoenix ranked #45 where demand was high and pay was the best. Criteria: sales per agent; annual median wage for real-estate agents; monthly average starting salary for real estate agents; real estate job density and competition; unemployment rate; home turnover rate; housing-market health index; and other relevant metrics. *www.WalletHub.com, "2021 Best Places to Be a Real Estate Agent," May 12, 2021*

- According to Penske Truck Rental, the Phoenix metro area was named the #4 moving destination in 2022, based on one-way consumer truck rental reservations made through Penske's website, rental locations, and reservations call center. *gopenske.com/blog, "Penske Truck Rental's 2022 Top Moving Destinations," April 27, 2023*

- The Phoenix metro area was identified as one of the 10 worst condo markets in the U.S. in 2022. The area ranked #54 out of 63 markets. Criteria: year-over-year change of median sales price of existing apartment condo-coop homes between the 4th quarter of 2021 and the 4th quarter of 2022. *National Association of Realtors®, Median Sales Price of Existing Apartment Condo-Coops Homes for Metropolitan Areas, 4th Quarter 2022*

- Phoenix was ranked #190 out of 235 metro areas in terms of housing affordability in 2022 by the National Association of Home Builders (#1 = most affordable). Criteria: the share of homes sold in that area affordable to a family earning the local median income, based on standard mortgage underwriting criteria. *National Association of Home Builders®, NAHB-Wells Fargo Housing Opportunity Index, 4th Quarter 2022*

Safety Rankings

- Allstate ranked the 200 largest cities in America in terms of driver safety. Phoenix ranked #84. Criteria: internal property damage claims over a two-year period from January 2016 to December 2017. The report helps increase the importance of safety and awareness behind the wheel. *Allstate, "Allstate America's Best Drivers Report, 2019" June 24, 2019*

- The National Insurance Crime Bureau ranked 390 metro areas in the U.S. in terms of per capita rates of vehicle theft. The Phoenix metro area ranked #89 (#1 = highest rate). Criteria: number of vehicle theft offenses per 100,000 inhabitants in 2021. *National Insurance Crime Bureau, "Hot Spots 2021," September 1, 2022*

Seniors/Retirement Rankings

- From its Best Cities for Successful Aging indexes, the Milken Institute generated rankings for metropolitan areas, weighing data in nine categories—health care, wellness, living arrangements, transportation and convenience, financial characteristics, education, employment, community engagement, and overall livability. The Phoenix metro area was ranked #88 overall in the large metro area category. *Milken Institute, "Best Cities for Successful Aging, 2017" March 14, 2017*

Women/Minorities Rankings

- The *Houston Chronicle* listed the Phoenix metro area as #5 in top places for young Latinos to live in the U.S. Research was largely based on housing and occupational data from the largest metropolitan areas performed by *Forbes* and NBC Universo. Criteria: percentage of 18-34 year-olds; Latino college grad rates; and diversity. *blog.chron.com, "The 15 Best Big Cities for Latino Millenials," January 26, 2016*

- *Women's Health*, together with the site Yelp, identified the 15 "Wellthiest" spots in the U.S. Phoenix appeared among the top for happiest, healthiest, outdoorsiest and Zen-iest. *Women's Health, "The 15 Wellthiest Cities in the U.S." July 5, 2017*

- Personal finance website *WalletHub* compared more than 180 U.S. cities across two key dimensions, "Hispanic Business-Friendliness" and "Hispanic Purchasing Power," to arrive at the most favorable conditions for Hispanic entrepreneurs. Phoenix was ranked #77 out of 182. Criteria includes: share of Hispanic-Owned Businesses; Hispanic entrepreneurship rate to median annual income of Hispanics; Small Business-Friendliness score; cost of living; and number of Hispanics with at least a bachelor's degree. *WalletHub.com, "2019's Best Cities for Hispanic Entrepreneurs," May 1, 2019*

Miscellaneous Rankings

- Despite the freedom to now travel internationally, plugged-in travel influencers and experts continue to rediscover their local regions. Phoenix appeared on a *Forbes* list of places in the U.S. that provide solace as well as local inspiration. Whether it be quirky things to see and do, delicious take out, outdoor exploring and daytrips, these places are must-see destinations. *Forbes, "The Best Places To Travel In The U.S. In 2023, According To The Experts," April 13, 2023*

- Phoenix was selected as a 2022 Digital Cities Survey winner. The city ranked #6 in the large city (500,000 or more population) category. The survey examined and assessed how city governments are utilizing technology to continue innovation, engage with residents, and persevere through the challenges of the pandemic. Survey questions focused on ten initiatives: cybersecurity; citizen experience; disaster recovery; business intelligence; IT personnel; data governance; business automation; IT governance; infrastructure modernization; and broadband connectivity. *Center for Digital Government, "2022 Digital Cities Survey," November 10, 2022*

- The watchdog site, Charity Navigator, conducted a study of charities in major markets both to analyze statistical differences in their financial, accountability, and transparency practices and to track year-to-year variations in individual philanthropic communities. The Phoenix metro area was ranked #12 among the 30 metro markets in the rating category of Overall Score. *www.charitynavigator.org, "2017 Metro Market Study," May 1, 2017*

- The financial planning site SmartAsset has compiled its annual study on the best places for Halloween in the U.S. for 2022. 146 cities were compared to determine that Phoenix ranked #27 out of 35 for still being able to enjoy the festivities despite COVID-19. Metrics included: safety, family-friendliness, percentage of children in the population, concentration of candy and costume shops, weather and COVID infection rates. *www.smartasset.com, "2022 Edition-Best Places to Celebrate Halloween," October 19, 2022*

- *WalletHub* compared the 150 most populated U.S. cities to determine their operating efficiency. A "Quality of Services" score was constructed for each city and then divided by the total budget per capita to reveal which were managed the best. Phoenix ranked #34. Criteria: financial stability; economy; education; safety; health; infrastructure and pollution. *www.WalletHub.com, "2022's Best- & Worst-Run Cities in America," June 21, 2022*

- The National Alliance to End Homelessness listed the 25 most populous metro areas with the highest rate of homelessness. The Phoenix metro area had a high rate of homelessness. Criteria: number of homeless people per 10,000 population in 2016. *National Alliance to End Homelessness, "Homelessness in the 25 Most Populous U.S. Metro Areas," September 1, 2017*

Business Environment

DEMOGRAPHICS

Population Growth

Area	1990 Census	2000 Census	2010 Census	2020 Census	Population Growth (%) 1990-2020	Population Growth (%) 2010-2020
City	989,873	1,321,045	1,445,632	1,608,139	62.5	11.2
MSA[1]	2,238,480	3,251,876	4,192,887	4,845,832	116.5	15.6
U.S.	248,709,873	281,421,906	308,745,538	331,449,281	33.3	7.4

Note: (1) Figures cover the Phoenix-Mesa-Chandler, AZ Metropolitan Statistical Area
Source: U.S. Census Bureau, 1990 Census, 2000 Census, 2010 Census, 2020 Census

Race

Area	White Alone[2] (%)	Black Alone[2] (%)	Asian Alone[2] (%)	AIAN[3] Alone[2] (%)	NHOPI[4] Alone[2] (%)	Other Race Alone[2] (%)	Two or More Races (%)
City	49.7	7.8	4.1	2.6	0.2	20.1	15.5
MSA[1]	60.2	5.8	4.3	2.5	0.3	13.4	13.5
U.S.	61.6	12.4	6.0	1.1	0.2	8.4	10.2

Note: (1) Figures cover the Phoenix-Mesa-Chandler, AZ Metropolitan Statistical Area; (2) Alone is defined as not being in combination with one or more other races; (3) American Indian and Alaska Native; (4) Native Hawaiian and Other Pacific Islander
Source: U.S. Census Bureau, 2020 Census

Hispanic or Latino Origin

Area	Total (%)	Mexican (%)	Puerto Rican (%)	Cuban (%)	Other (%)
City	42.7	37.9	0.7	0.4	3.8
MSA[1]	31.5	27.1	0.7	0.3	3.4
U.S.	18.4	11.2	1.8	0.7	4.7

Note: Persons of Hispanic or Latino origin can be of any race; (1) Figures cover the Phoenix-Mesa-Chandler, AZ Metropolitan Statistical Area
Source: U.S. Census Bureau, 2017-2021 American Community Survey 5-Year Estimates

Age

Area	Under Age 5	Age 5–19	Age 20–34	Age 35–44	Age 45–54	Age 55–64	Age 65–74	Age 75–84	Age 85+	Median Age
City	6.3	21.6	22.9	13.7	12.4	11.3	7.5	3.2	1.1	34.5
MSA[1]	5.7	20.5	20.5	12.8	12.1	11.9	9.8	5.1	1.7	37.5
U.S.	5.6	19.2	20.2	12.7	12.4	13.1	10.0	4.9	1.9	38.8

Note: (1) Figures cover the Phoenix-Mesa-Chandler, AZ Metropolitan Statistical Area
Source: U.S. Census Bureau, 2020 Census

Disability by Age

Area	All Ages	Under 18 Years Old	18 to 64 Years Old	65 Years and Over
City	10.8	4.2	9.7	32.9
MSA[1]	11.8	4.3	9.7	31.4
U.S.	12.6	4.4	10.3	33.4

Note: Figures show percent of the civilian noninstitutionalized population that reported having a disability. Disability status is determined from six types of difficulty: vision, hearing, cognitive, ambulatory, self-care, and independent living. For children under 5 years old, hearing and vision difficulty are used to determine disability status. For children between the ages of 5 and 14, disability status is determined from hearing, vision, cognitive, ambulatory, and self-care difficulties. For people aged 15 years and older, they are considered to have a disability if they have difficulty with any one of the six difficulty types; Note: (1) Figures cover the Phoenix-Mesa-Chandler, AZ Metropolitan Statistical Area
Source: U.S. Census Bureau, 2017-2021 American Community Survey 5-Year Estimates

Ancestry

Area	German	Irish	English	American	Italian	Polish	French[2]	Scottish	Dutch
City	9.8	7.4	6.3	2.8	3.8	1.8	1.6	1.2	0.8
MSA[1]	12.5	8.6	8.6	3.8	4.4	2.3	1.9	1.6	1.0
U.S.	12.8	9.6	8.1	5.7	5.0	2.7	2.2	1.6	1.1

Note: Figures are the percentage of the total population reporting a particular ancestry. The nine most commonly reported ancestries in the U.S. are shown. Figures include multiple ancestries (e.g. if a person reported being Irish and Italian, they were included in both columns); (1) Figures cover the Phoenix-Mesa-Chandler, AZ Metropolitan Statistical Area; (2) Excludes Basque
Source: U.S. Census Bureau, 2017-2021 American Community Survey 5-Year Estimates

Foreign-born Population

Area	Percent of Population Born in								
	Any Foreign Country	Asia	Mexico	Europe	Caribbean	Central America[2]	South America	Africa	Canada
City	19.2	3.2	11.7	1.4	0.4	0.9	0.4	0.8	0.4
MSA[1]	14.0	3.2	7.0	1.3	0.3	0.6	0.4	0.6	0.6
U.S.	13.6	4.2	3.3	1.5	1.4	1.1	1.1	0.8	0.2

Note: (1) Figures cover the Phoenix-Mesa-Chandler, AZ Metropolitan Statistical Area; (2) Excludes Mexico.
Source: U.S. Census Bureau, 2017-2021 American Community Survey 5-Year Estimates

Household Size

Area	Persons in Household (%)							Average Household Size
	One	Two	Three	Four	Five	Six	Seven or More	
City	28.0	30.0	15.3	13.0	7.4	3.6	2.7	2.70
MSA[1]	25.9	34.5	14.7	12.7	6.9	3.1	2.2	2.70
U.S.	28.1	33.8	15.5	12.9	6.0	2.3	1.4	2.60

Note: (1) Figures cover the Phoenix-Mesa-Chandler, AZ Metropolitan Statistical Area
Source: U.S. Census Bureau, 2017-2021 American Community Survey 5-Year Estimates

Household Relationships

Area	House-holder	Opposite-sex Spouse	Same-sex Spouse	Opposite-sex Unmarried Partner	Same-sex Unmarried Partner	Child[2]	Grand-child	Other Relatives	Non-relatives
City	36.3	14.4	0.3	3.1	0.3	30.2	2.9	6.6	4.2
MSA[1]	36.9	17.2	0.2	2.8	0.2	29.0	2.5	5.4	3.7
U.S.	38.3	17.5	0.2	2.5	0.2	28.3	2.4	4.8	3.4

Note: Figures are percent of the total population; (1) Figures cover the Phoenix-Mesa-Chandler, AZ Metropolitan Statistical Area; (2) Includes biological, adopted, and stepchildren of the householder
Source: U.S. Census Bureau, 2020 Census

Gender

Area	Males	Females	Males per 100 Females
City	799,456	808,683	98.9
MSA[1]	2,395,320	2,450,512	97.7
U.S.	162,685,811	168,763,470	96.4

Note: (1) Figures cover the Phoenix-Mesa-Chandler, AZ Metropolitan Statistical Area
Source: U.S. Census Bureau, 2020 Census

Marital Status

Area	Never Married	Now Married[2]	Separated	Widowed	Divorced
City	39.1	42.5	2.1	4.0	12.2
MSA[1]	33.7	48.2	1.6	4.8	11.7
U.S.	33.8	48.0	1.8	5.6	10.8

Note: Figures are percentages and cover the population 15 years of age and older; (1) Figures cover the Phoenix-Mesa-Chandler, AZ Metropolitan Statistical Area; (2) Excludes separated
Source: U.S. Census Bureau, 2017-2021 American Community Survey 5-Year Estimates

Religious Groups by Family

Area	Catholic	Baptist	Methodist	LDS[2]	Pentecostal	Lutheran	Islam	Adventist	Other
MSA[1]	22.9	1.7	0.6	6.2	1.5	1.0	1.9	1.5	9.3
U.S.	18.7	7.3	3.0	2.0	1.8	1.7	1.3	1.3	11.6

Note: Figures are the number of adherents as a percentage of the total population and cover the eight largest religious groups in the U.S; (1) Figures cover the Phoenix-Mesa-Chandler, AZ Metropolitan Statistical Area; (2) Church of Jesus Christ of Latter-day Saints
Sources: 2020 U.S. Religion Census, Association of Statisticians of American Religious Bodies; The Association of Religion Data Archives (ARDA)

Religious Groups by Tradition

Area	Catholic	Evangelical Protestant	Mainline Protestant	Black Protestant	Islam	Judaism	Hinduism	Orthodox	Buddhism
MSA[1]	22.9	11.0	1.6	0.3	1.9	0.3	0.5	0.4	0.2
U.S.	18.7	16.5	5.2	2.3	1.3	0.6	0.4	0.4	0.3

Note: Figures are the number of adherents as a percentage of the total population; (1) Figures cover the Phoenix-Mesa-Chandler, AZ Metropolitan Statistical Area
Sources: 2020 U.S. Religion Census, Association of Statisticians of American Religious Bodies; The Association of Religion Data Archives (ARDA)

ECONOMY

Gross Metropolitan Product

Area	2020	2021	2022	2023	Rank[2]
MSA[1]	281.0	310.1	336.3	358.7	14

Note: Figures are in billions of dollars; (1) Figures cover the Phoenix-Mesa-Chandler, AZ Metropolitan Statistical Area; (2) Rank is based on 2021 data and ranges from 1 to 381
Source: U.S. Conference of Mayors, U.S. Metro Economies: U.S. Metros Compared to Global and State Economies, June 2022

Economic Growth

Area	2018-20 (%)	2021 (%)	2022 (%)	2023 (%)	Rank[2]
MSA[1]	1.9	5.8	2.7	3.4	39
U.S.	-0.6	5.7	3.1	2.9	–

Note: Figures are real gross metropolitan product (GMP) growth rates and represent average annual percent change; (1) Figures cover the Phoenix-Mesa-Chandler, AZ Metropolitan Statistical Area; (2) Rank is based on 2020 2-year average annual percent change and ranges from 1 to 381
Source: U.S. Conference of Mayors, U.S. Metro Economies: U.S. Metros Compared to Global and State Economies, June 2022

Metropolitan Area Exports

Area	2016	2017	2018	2019	2020	2021	Rank[2]
MSA[1]	12,838.2	13,223.1	13,614.9	15,136.6	11,073.9	14,165.1	27

Note: Figures are in millions of dollars; (1) Figures cover the Phoenix-Mesa-Chandler, AZ Metropolitan Statistical Area; (2) Rank is based on 2021 data and ranges from 1 to 388
Source: U.S. Department of Commerce, International Trade Administration, Office of Trade and Economic Analysis, Industry and Analysis, Exports by Metropolitan Area, data extracted March 16, 2023

Building Permits

Area	Single-Family			Multi-Family			Total		
	2021	2022	Pct. Chg.	2021	2022	Pct. Chg.	2021	2022	Pct. Chg.
City	4,922	3,982	-19.1	6,570	10,616	61.6	11,492	14,598	27.0
MSA[1]	34,347	26,857	-21.8	16,234	20,410	25.7	50,581	47,267	-6.6
U.S.	1,115,400	975,600	-12.5	621,600	689,500	10.9	1,737,000	1,665,100	-4.1

Note: (1) Figures cover the Phoenix-Mesa-Chandler, AZ Metropolitan Statistical Area; Figures represent new, privately-owned housing units authorized (unadjusted data); All permit data are based on estimates with imputation
Source: U.S. Census Bureau, Manufacturing, Mining, and Construction Statistics, Building Permits, 2021, 2022

Bankruptcy Filings

Area	Business Filings			Nonbusiness Filings		
	2021	2022	% Chg.	2021	2022	% Chg.
Maricopa County	223	172	-22.9	6,402	5,811	-9.2
U.S.	14,347	13,481	-6.0	399,269	374,240	-6.3

Note: Business filings include Chapter 7, Chapter 9, Chapter 11, Chapter 12, Chapter 13, Chapter 15, and Section 304; Nonbusiness filings include Chapter 7, Chapter 11, and Chapter 13
Source: Administrative Office of the U.S. Courts, Business and Nonbusiness Bankruptcy, County Cases Commenced by Chapter of the Bankruptcy Code, During the 12-Month Period Ending December 31, 2021 and Business and Nonbusiness Bankruptcy, County Cases Commenced by Chapter of the Bankruptcy Code, During the 12-Month Period Ending December 31, 2022

Housing Vacancy Rates

Area	Gross Vacancy Rate[2] (%)			Year-Round Vacancy Rate[3] (%)			Rental Vacancy Rate[4] (%)			Homeowner Vacancy Rate[5] (%)		
	2020	2021	2022	2020	2021	2022	2020	2021	2022	2020	2021	2022
MSA[1]	8.9	9.0	10.9	5.3	5.6	6.7	4.9	4.9	6.4	0.7	0.6	0.9
U.S.	10.6	10.8	10.5	8.2	8.4	8.2	6.3	6.1	5.8	1.0	0.9	0.8

Note: (1) Figures cover the Phoenix-Mesa-Chandler, AZ Metropolitan Statistical Area; (2) The percentage of the total housing inventory that is vacant; (3) The percentage of the housing inventory (excluding seasonal units) that is year-round vacant; (4) The percentage of rental inventory that is vacant for rent; (5) The percentage of homeowner inventory that is vacant for sale
Source: U.S. Census Bureau, Housing Vacancies and Homeownership Annual Statistics: 2020, 2021, 2022

INCOME

Income

Area	Per Capita ($)	Median Household ($)	Average Household ($)
City	33,718	64,927	90,481
MSA[1]	36,842	72,211	97,412
U.S.	37,638	69,021	97,196

Note: (1) Figures cover the Phoenix-Mesa-Chandler, AZ Metropolitan Statistical Area
Source: U.S. Census Bureau, 2017-2021 American Community Survey 5-Year Estimates

Household Income Distribution

Area	Percent of Households Earning							
	Under $15,000	$15,000 -$24,999	$25,000 -$34,999	$35,000 -$49,999	$50,000 -$74,999	$75,000 -$99,999	$100,000 -$149,999	$150,000 and up
City	8.4	7.6	8.8	13.5	18.2	13.5	15.3	14.8
MSA[1]	7.4	6.6	7.7	12.0	18.1	13.9	17.7	16.7
U.S.	9.4	7.8	8.2	11.4	16.8	12.8	16.3	17.3

Note: (1) Figures cover the Phoenix-Mesa-Chandler, AZ Metropolitan Statistical Area
Source: U.S. Census Bureau, 2017-2021 American Community Survey 5-Year Estimates

Poverty Rate

Area	All Ages	Under 18 Years Old	18 to 64 Years Old	65 Years and Over
City	15.4	22.7	13.3	10.5
MSA[1]	12.0	16.9	11.0	8.3
U.S.	12.6	17.0	11.8	9.6

Note: Figures are percentage of people whose income during the past 12 months was below the poverty level;
(1) Figures cover the Phoenix-Mesa-Chandler, AZ Metropolitan Statistical Area
Source: U.S. Census Bureau, 2017-2021 American Community Survey 5-Year Estimates

EMPLOYMENT

Labor Force and Employment

Area	Civilian Labor Force			Workers Employed		
	Dec. 2021	Dec. 2022	% Chg.	Dec. 2021	Dec. 2022	% Chg.
City	865,943	889,029	2.7	842,267	864,868	2.7
MSA[1]	2,518,007	2,590,356	2.9	2,453,226	2,520,303	2.7
U.S.	161,696,000	164,224,000	1.6	155,732,000	158,872,000	2.0

Note: Data is not seasonally adjusted and covers workers 16 years of age and older; (1) Figures cover the Phoenix-Mesa-Chandler, AZ Metropolitan Statistical Area
Source: Bureau of Labor Statistics, Local Area Unemployment Statistics

Unemployment Rate

Area	2022											
	Jan.	Feb.	Mar.	Apr.	May	Jun.	Jul.	Aug.	Sep.	Oct.	Nov.	Dec.
City	3.4	3.3	2.5	2.8	3.0	3.4	3.4	3.5	3.6	3.5	3.0	2.7
MSA[1]	3.2	3.1	2.4	2.7	2.9	3.4	3.3	3.4	3.5	3.5	3.0	2.7
U.S.	4.4	4.1	3.8	3.3	3.4	3.8	3.8	3.8	3.3	3.4	3.4	3.3

Note: Data is not seasonally adjusted and covers workers 16 years of age and older; (1) Figures cover the Phoenix-Mesa-Chandler, AZ Metropolitan Statistical Area
Source: Bureau of Labor Statistics, Local Area Unemployment Statistics

Average Wages

Occupation	$/Hr.	Occupation	$/Hr.
Accountants and Auditors	40.79	Maintenance and Repair Workers	22.41
Automotive Mechanics	24.61	Marketing Managers	68.83
Bookkeepers	23.11	Network and Computer Systems Admin.	45.37
Carpenters	24.95	Nurses, Licensed Practical	30.07
Cashiers	14.93	Nurses, Registered	42.03
Computer Programmers	42.27	Nursing Assistants	18.44
Computer Systems Analysts	50.03	Office Clerks, General	21.73
Computer User Support Specialists	29.29	Physical Therapists	48.80
Construction Laborers	21.22	Physicians	98.99
Cooks, Restaurant	18.08	Plumbers, Pipefitters and Steamfitters	28.48
Customer Service Representatives	19.49	Police and Sheriff's Patrol Officers	35.65
Dentists	87.37	Postal Service Mail Carriers	27.93
Electricians	25.61	Real Estate Sales Agents	29.19
Engineers, Electrical	49.97	Retail Salespersons	17.07
Fast Food and Counter Workers	15.53	Sales Representatives, Technical/Scientific	46.98
Financial Managers	76.99	Secretaries, Exc. Legal/Medical/Executive	21.31
First-Line Supervisors of Office Workers	30.64	Security Guards	17.03
General and Operations Managers	54.46	Surgeons	n/a
Hairdressers/Cosmetologists	20.15	Teacher Assistants, Exc. Postsecondary*	15.19
Home Health and Personal Care Aides	15.17	Teachers, Secondary School, Exc. Sp. Ed.*	30.07
Janitors and Cleaners	15.82	Telemarketers	17.98
Landscaping/Groundskeeping Workers	17.31	Truck Drivers, Heavy/Tractor-Trailer	25.42
Lawyers	72.30	Truck Drivers, Light/Delivery Services	22.85
Maids and Housekeeping Cleaners	16.08	Waiters and Waitresses	22.24

Note: Wage data covers the Phoenix-Mesa-Chandler, AZ Metropolitan Statistical Area; (*) Hourly wages were calculated from annual wage data based on a 40 hour work week; n/a not available.
Source: Bureau of Labor Statistics, Metro Area Occupational Employment & Wage Estimates, May 2022

Employment by Industry

Sector	MSA[1]		U.S.
	Number of Employees	Percent of Total	Percent of Total
Construction	153,100	6.4	5.0
Private Education and Health Services	379,300	15.9	16.1
Financial Activities	222,400	9.3	5.9
Government	241,600	10.2	14.5
Information	43,600	1.8	2.0
Leisure and Hospitality	241,400	10.1	10.3
Manufacturing	151,600	6.4	8.4
Mining and Logging	3,100	0.1	0.4
Other Services	73,100	3.1	3.7
Professional and Business Services	403,600	17.0	14.7
Retail Trade	249,200	10.5	10.2
Transportation, Warehousing, and Utilities	121,200	5.1	4.9
Wholesale Trade	96,300	4.0	3.9

Note: Figures are non-farm employment as of December 2022. Figures are not seasonally adjusted and include workers 16 years of age and older; (1) Figures cover the Phoenix-Mesa-Chandler, AZ Metropolitan Statistical Area
Source: Bureau of Labor Statistics, Current Employment Statistics, Employment, Hours, and Earnings

Employment by Occupation

Occupation Classification	City (%)	MSA[1] (%)	U.S. (%)
Management, Business, Science, and Arts	37.2	39.9	40.3
Natural Resources, Construction, and Maintenance	9.8	8.5	8.7
Production, Transportation, and Material Moving	12.2	11.0	13.1
Sales and Office	22.9	23.9	20.9
Service	17.9	16.7	17.0

Note: Figures cover employed civilians 16 years of age and older; (1) Figures cover the Phoenix-Mesa-Chandler, AZ Metropolitan Statistical Area
Source: U.S. Census Bureau, 2017-2021 American Community Survey 5-Year Estimates

Occupations with Greatest Projected Employment Growth: 2022 – 2024

Occupation[1]	2022 Employment	2024 Projected Employment	Numeric Employment Change	Percent Employment Change
Home Health and Personal Care Aides	71,650	75,090	3,440	4.8
Laborers and Freight, Stock, and Material Movers, Hand	63,960	67,090	3,130	4.9
General and Operations Managers	82,890	85,760	2,870	3.5
Stockers and Order Fillers	56,490	59,310	2,820	5.0
Cooks, Restaurant	29,560	32,170	2,610	8.8
Heavy and Tractor-Trailer Truck Drivers	43,800	45,870	2,070	4.7
Fast Food and Counter Workers	57,520	59,510	1,990	3.5
Waiters and Waitresses	50,910	52,850	1,940	3.8
Software Developers	38,570	40,370	1,800	4.7
Industrial Truck and Tractor Operators	18,980	20,500	1,520	8.0

Note: Projections cover Arizona; (1) Sorted by numeric employment change
Source: www.projectionscentral.com, State Occupational Projections, 2022–2024 Short-Term Projections

Fastest-Growing Occupations: 2022 – 2024

Occupation[1]	2022 Employment	2024 Projected Employment	Numeric Employment Change	Percent Employment Change
Ushers, Lobby Attendants, and Ticket Takers	1,080	1,370	290	26.9
Media and Communication Workers, All Other	450	520	70	15.6
Paper Goods Machine Setters, Operators, and Tenders	800	900	100	12.5
Molders, Shapers, and Casters, Except Metal and Plastic	570	640	70	12.3
Nurse Practitioners	5,570	6,220	650	11.7
Chemical Equipment Operators and Tenders	1,380	1,540	160	11.6
Cooks, All Other	800	890	90	11.3
Packaging and Filling Machine Operators and Tenders	3,500	3,880	380	10.9
Logisticians	3,730	4,120	390	10.5
Solar Photovoltaic Installers	1,180	1,300	120	10.2

Note: Projections cover Arizona; (1) Sorted by percent employment change and excludes occupations with numeric employment change less than 50
Source: www.projectionscentral.com, State Occupational Projections, 2022–2024 Short-Term Projections

CITY FINANCES

City Government Finances

Component	2020 ($000)	2020 ($ per capita)
Total Revenues	4,101,169	2,440
Total Expenditures	3,900,909	2,321
Debt Outstanding	8,211,370	4,885
Cash and Securities[1]	6,639,380	3,950

Note: (1) Cash and security holdings of a government at the close of its fiscal year, including those of its dependent agencies, utilities, and liquor stores.
Source: U.S. Census Bureau, State & Local Government Finances 2020

City Government Revenue by Source

Source	2020 ($000)	2020 ($ per capita)	2020 (%)
General Revenue			
From Federal Government	258,466	154	6.3
From State Government	749,802	446	18.3
From Local Governments	33,402	20	0.8
Taxes			
Property	277,252	165	6.8
Sales and Gross Receipts	956,709	569	23.3
Personal Income	0	0	0.0
Corporate Income	0	0	0.0
Motor Vehicle License	0	0	0.0
Other Taxes	111,639	66	2.7
Current Charges	907,462	540	22.1
Liquor Store	0	0	0.0
Utility	479,687	285	11.7

Source: U.S. Census Bureau, State & Local Government Finances 2020

City Government Expenditures by Function

Function	2020 ($000)	2020 ($ per capita)	2020 (%)
General Direct Expenditures			
Air Transportation	693,960	412	17.8
Corrections	0	0	0.0
Education	722	< 1	< 0.1
Employment Security Administration	0	0	0.0
Financial Administration	51,499	30	1.3
Fire Protection	347,541	206	8.9
General Public Buildings	6,499	3	0.2
Governmental Administration, Other	37,624	22	1.0
Health	0	0	0.0
Highways	173,875	103	4.5
Hospitals	0	0	0.0
Housing and Community Development	183,360	109	4.7
Interest on General Debt	281,370	167	7.2
Judicial and Legal	58,824	35	1.5
Libraries	38,519	22	1.0
Parking	1,103	< 1	< 0.1
Parks and Recreation	223,601	133	5.7
Police Protection	783,690	466	20.1
Public Welfare	469	< 1	< 0.1
Sewerage	105,262	62	2.7
Solid Waste Management	137,925	82	3.5
Veterans' Services	0	0	0.0
Liquor Store	0	0	0.0
Utility	570,339	339	14.6

Source: U.S. Census Bureau, State & Local Government Finances 2020

TAXES

State Corporate Income Tax Rates

State	Tax Rate (%)	Income Brackets ($)	Num. of Brackets	Financial Institution Tax Rate (%)[a]	Federal Income Tax Ded.
Arizona	4.9 (b)	Flat rate	1	4.9 (b)	No

Note: Tax rates as of January 1, 2023; (a) Rates listed are the corporate income tax rate applied to financial institutions or excise taxes based on income. Some states have other taxes based upon the value of deposits or shares; (b) Minimum tax is $800 in California, $250 in District of Columbia, $50 in Arizona and North Dakota (banks), $400 ($100 banks) in Rhode Island, $200 per location in South Dakota (banks), $100 in Utah, $300 in Vermont.
Source: Federation of Tax Administrators, State Corporate Income Tax Rates, January 1, 2023

State Individual Income Tax Rates

State	Tax Rate (%)	Income Brackets ($)	Personal Exemptions ($)			Standard Ded. ($)	
			Single	Married	Depend.	Single	Married
Arizona	2.5	27,808 - 166,843 (b)	–	–	100 (c)	12,950	25,900

Note: Tax rates as of January 1, 2023; Local- and county-level taxes are not included; Federal income tax is not deductible on state income tax returns; (b) For joint returns, taxes are twice the tax on half the couple's income; (c) The personal exemption takes the form of a tax credit instead of a deduction
Source: Federation of Tax Administrators, State Individual Income Tax Rates, January 1, 2023

Various State Sales and Excise Tax Rates

State	State Sales Tax (%)	Gasoline[1] ($/gal.)	Cigarette[2] ($/pack)	Spirits[3] ($/gal.)	Wine[4] ($/gal.)	Beer[5] ($/gal.)	Recreational Marijuana (%)
Arizona	5.6	0.19	2.00	3.00	0.84	0.16	(b)

Note: All tax rates as of January 1, 2023; (1) The American Petroleum Institute has developed a methodology for determining the average tax rate on a gallon of fuel. Rates may include any of the following: excise taxes, environmental fees, storage tank fees, other fees or taxes, general sales tax, and local taxes; (2) The federal excise tax of $1.0066 per pack and local taxes are not included; (3) Rates are those applicable to off-premise sales of 40% alcohol by volume (a.b.v.) distilled spirits in 750ml containers. Local excise taxes are excluded; (4) Rates are those applicable to off-premise sales of 11% a.b.v. non-carbonated wine in 750ml containers; (5) Rates are those applicable to off-premise sales of 4.7% a.b.v. beer in 12 ounce containers; (b) 16% excise tax (retail price)
Source: Tax Foundation, 2023 Facts & Figures: How Does Your State Compare?

State Business Tax Climate Index Rankings

State	Overall Rank	Corporate Tax Rank	Individual Income Tax Rank	Sales Tax Rank	Property Tax Rank	Unemployment Insurance Tax Rank
Arizona	19	23	16	41	11	14

Note: The index is a measure of how each state's tax laws affect economic performance. The lower the rank, the more favorable a state's tax system is for business. States without a given tax are given a ranking of 1. The scores/rankings for the District of Columbia do not affect other states. The 2023 index represents the tax climate as of July 1, 2022.
Source: Tax Foundation, State Business Tax Climate Index 2023

TRANSPORTATION

Means of Transportation to Work

Area	Car/Truck/Van		Public Transportation			Bicycle	Walked	Other Means	Worked at Home
	Drove Alone	Car-pooled	Bus	Subway	Railroad				
City	70.8	11.5	2.1	0.0	0.0	0.5	1.5	1.9	11.5
MSA[1]	71.6	10.3	1.3	0.0	0.0	0.6	1.4	1.8	13.0
U.S.	73.2	8.6	2.0	1.6	0.5	0.5	2.5	1.5	9.7

Note: Figures are percentages and cover workers 16 years of age and older; (1) Figures cover the Phoenix-Mesa-Chandler, AZ Metropolitan Statistical Area
Source: U.S. Census Bureau, 2017-2021 American Community Survey 5-Year Estimates

Travel Time to Work

Area	Less Than 10 Minutes	10 to 19 Minutes	20 to 29 Minutes	30 to 44 Minutes	45 to 59 Minutes	60 to 89 Minutes	90 Minutes or More
City	8.6	26.6	26.6	24.5	7.4	4.5	1.8
MSA[1]	9.9	26.1	24.0	23.6	8.9	5.6	1.9
U.S.	12.4	28.5	21.0	20.9	8.2	6.2	2.9

Note: Note: Figures are percentages and include workers 16 years old and over; (1) Figures cover the Phoenix-Mesa-Chandler, AZ Metropolitan Statistical Area
Source: U.S. Census Bureau, 2017-2021 American Community Survey 5-Year Estimates

Key Congestion Measures

Measure	1990	2000	2010	2015	2020
Annual Hours of Delay, Total (000)	42,716	86,505	133,493	156,520	68,645
Annual Hours of Delay, Per Auto Commuter	41	45	50	59	25
Annual Congestion Cost, Per Auto Commuter ($)	544	829	1,017	1,102	489

Note: Covers the Phoenix-Mesa AZ urban area
Source: Texas A&M Transportation Institute, 2021 Urban Mobility Report

Freeway Travel Time Index

Measure	1985	1990	1995	2000	2005	2010	2015	2020
Urban Area Index[1]	1.20	1.21	1.22	1.25	1.28	1.28	1.27	1.08
Urban Area Rank[1,2]	5	7	13	16	14	16	20	44

Note: Freeway Travel Time Index—the ratio of travel time in the peak period to the travel time at free-flow conditions. For example, a value of 1.30 indicates a 20-minute free-flow trip takes 26 minutes in the peak (20 minutes x 1.30 = 26 minutes); (1) Covers the Phoenix-Mesa AZ urban area; (2) Rank is based on 101 larger urban areas (#1 = highest travel time index)
Source: Texas A&M Transportation Institute, 2021 Urban Mobility Report

Public Transportation

Agency Name / Mode of Transportation	Vehicles Operated in Maximum Service[1]	Annual Unlinked Passenger Trips[2] (in thous.)	Annual Passenger Miles[3] (in thous.)
City of Phoenix Public Transit Dept. (Valley Metro)			
Bus (purchased transportation)	421	38,414.1	134,736.6
Demand Response (purchased transportation)	121	273.5	2,250.7

Note: (1) Number of revenue vehicles operated by the given mode and type of service to meet the annual maximum service requirement. This is the revenue vehicle count during the peak season of the year; on the week and day that maximum service is provided. Vehicles operated in maximum service (VOMS) exclude atypical days and one-time special events; (2) Number of passengers who boarded public transportation vehicles. Passengers are counted each time they board a vehicle no matter how many vehicles they use to travel from their origin to their destination. (3) Sum of the distances ridden by all passengers during the entire fiscal year.
Source: Federal Transit Administration, National Transit Database, 2021

Air Transportation

Airport Name and Code / Type of Service	Passenger Airlines[1]	Passenger Enplanements	Freight Carriers[2]	Freight (lbs)
Phoenix Sky Harbor International (PHX)				
Domestic service (U.S. carriers - 2022)	33	20,793,157	20	355,213,276
International service (U.S. carriers - 2021)	6	481,230	2	148,367

Note: (1) Includes all U.S.-based major, minor and commuter airlines that carried at least one passenger during the year; (2) Includes all U.S.-based airlines and freight carriers that transported at least one pound of freight during the year.
Source: Bureau of Transportation Statistics, The Intermodal Transportation Database, Air Carriers: T-100 Domestic Market (U.S. Carriers), 2022; Bureau of Transportation Statistics, The Intermodal Transportation Database, Air Carriers: T-100 International Market (U.S. Carriers), 2021

BUSINESSES

Major Business Headquarters

Company Name	Industry	Rankings	
		Fortune[1]	Forbes[2]
Avnet	Wholesalers, electronics and office equipment	180	-
Freeport-McMoRan	Mining, crude-oil production	157	-
ON Semiconductor	Semiconductors and other electronic components	483	-
Republic Services	Waste management	329	-
Shamrock Foods	Food, drink & tobacco	-	89

Note: (1) Companies that produce a 10-K are ranked 1 to 500 based on 2021 revenue; (2) All private companies with at least $2 billion in annual revenue through the end of their most current fiscal year are ranked 1 to 246; companies listed are headquartered in the city; dashes indicate no ranking
Source: Fortune, "Fortune 500," 2022; Forbes, "America's Largest Private Companies," 2022

Fastest-Growing Businesses

According to *Inc.*, Phoenix is home to two of America's 500 fastest-growing private companies: **Zenernet** (#162); **HireRising** (#454). Criteria: must be an independent, privately-held, for-profit, U.S. corporation, proprietorship or partnership as of December 31, 2021; revenues must be at least $100,000 in 2018 and $2 million in 2021; must have four-year operating/sales history. *Inc., "America's 500 Fastest-Growing Private Companies," 2022*

According to Deloitte, Phoenix is home to one of North America's 500 fastest-growing high-technology companies: **MedAvail Holdings** (#368). Companies are ranked by percentage growth in revenue over a four-year period. Criteria for inclusion: company must be headquartered within North America; must own proprietary intellectual property or technology that is sold to customers in products that contributes to a significant portion of the company's operating revenue; must have been in business for a minumum of four years with 2018 operating revenues of at least $50,000 USD/CD and 2021 operating revenues of at least $5 million USD/CD. *Deloitte, 2022 Technology Fast 500™*

Living Environment

COST OF LIVING

Cost of Living Index

Composite Index	Groceries	Housing	Utilities	Trans-portation	Health Care	Misc. Goods/ Services
104.3	99.5	124.0	102.7	106.5	93.4	91.7

Note: The Cost of Living Index measures regional differences in the cost of consumer goods and services, excluding taxes and non-consumer expenditures, for professional and managerial households in the top income quintile. It is based on more than 50,000 prices covering almost 60 different items for which prices are collected three times a year by chambers of commerce, economic development organizations or university applied economic centers in each participating urban area. The numbers shown should be read as a percentage above or below the national average of 100. For example, a value of 115.4 in the groceries column indicates that grocery prices are 15.4% higher than the national average. Small differences in the index numbers should not be interpreted as significant; Figures cover the Phoenix AZ urban area.
Source: The Council for Community and Economic Research, Cost of Living Index, 2022

Grocery Prices

Area[1]	T-Bone Steak ($/pound)	Frying Chicken ($/pound)	Whole Milk ($/half gal.)	Eggs ($/dozen)	Orange Juice ($/64 oz.)	Coffee ($/11.5 oz.)
City[2]	14.66	1.65	2.06	2.51	4.00	5.82
Avg.	13.81	1.59	2.43	2.25	3.85	4.95
Min.	10.17	0.90	1.51	1.30	2.90	3.46
Max.	19.35	3.30	4.32	4.32	5.31	8.59

*Note: (1) Values for the local area are compared with the average, minimum and maximum values for all 286 areas in the Cost of Living Index; (2) Figures cover the Phoenix AZ urban area; **T-Bone Steak** (price per pound); **Frying Chicken** (price per pound, whole fryer); **Whole Milk** (half gallon carton); **Eggs** (price per dozen, Grade A, large); **Orange Juice** (64 oz. Tropicana or Florida Natural); **Coffee** (11.5 oz. can, vacuum-packed, Maxwell House, Hills Bros, or Folgers).*
Source: The Council for Community and Economic Research, Cost of Living Index, 2022

Housing and Utility Costs

Area[1]	New Home Price ($)	Apartment Rent ($/month)	All Electric ($/month)	Part Electric ($/month)	Other Energy ($/month)	Telephone ($/month)
City[2]	497,561	2,083	187.70	-	-	185.99
Avg.	450,913	1,371	176.41	99.93	76.96	190.22
Min.	229,283	546	100.84	31.56	27.15	174.27
Max.	2,434,977	4,569	356.86	249.59	272.24	208.31

*Note: (1) Values for the local area are compared with the average, minimum and maximum values for all 286 areas in the Cost of Living Index; (2) Figures cover the Phoenix AZ urban area; **New Home Price** (2,400 sf living area, 8,000 sf lot, in urban area with full utilities); **Apartment Rent** (950 sf 2 bedroom/1.5 or 2 bath, unfurnished, excluding all utilities except water); **All Electric** (average monthly cost for an all-electric home); **Part Electric** (average monthly cost for a part-electric home); **Other Energy** (average monthly cost for natural gas, fuel oil, coal, wood, and any other forms of energy except electricity); **Telephone** (price includes the base monthly rate plus taxes and fees for three lines of mobile phone service).*
Source: The Council for Community and Economic Research, Cost of Living Index, 2022

Health Care, Transportation, and Other Costs

Area[1]	Doctor ($/visit)	Dentist ($/visit)	Optometrist ($/visit)	Gasoline ($/gallon)	Beauty Salon ($/visit)	Men's Shirt ($)
City[2]	99.00	99.00	117.08	4.30	50.83	19.04
Avg.	124.91	107.77	117.66	3.86	43.31	34.21
Min.	36.61	58.25	51.79	2.90	22.18	13.05
Max.	250.21	162.58	371.96	5.54	85.61	63.54

*Note: (1) Values for the local area are compared with the average, minimum and maximum values for all 286 areas in the Cost of Living Index; (2) Figures cover the Phoenix AZ urban area; **Doctor** (general practitioners routine exam of an established patient); **Dentist** (adult teeth cleaning and periodic oral examination); **Optometrist** (full vision eye exam for established adult patient); **Gasoline** (one gallon regular unleaded, national brand, including all taxes, cash price at self-service pump if available); **Beauty Salon** (woman's shampoo, trim, and blow-dry); **Men's Shirt** (cotton/polyester dress shirt, pinpoint weave, long sleeves).*
Source: The Council for Community and Economic Research, Cost of Living Index, 2022

HOUSING

Homeownership Rate

Area	2015 (%)	2016 (%)	2017 (%)	2018 (%)	2019 (%)	2020 (%)	2021 (%)	2022 (%)
MSA[1]	61.0	62.6	64.0	65.3	65.9	67.9	65.2	68.0
U.S.	63.7	63.4	63.9	64.4	64.6	66.6	65.5	65.8

Note: (1) Figures cover the Phoenix-Mesa-Chandler, AZ Metropolitan Statistical Area
Source: U.S. Census Bureau, Housing Vacancies and Homeownership Annual Statistics: 2015-2022

House Price Index (HPI)

Area	National Ranking[2]	Quarterly Change (%)	One-Year Change (%)	Five-Year Change (%)	Since 1991Q1 (%)
MSA[1]	144	-4.25	10.82	83.46	453.06
U.S.[3]	–	0.34	8.41	58.44	289.08

Note: The HPI is a weighted repeat sales index. It measures average price changes in repeat sales or refinancings on the same properties. This information is obtained by reviewing repeat mortgage transactions on single-family properties whose mortgages have been purchased or securitized by Fannie Mae or Freddie Mac since January 1975; (1) Figures cover the Phoenix-Mesa-Scottsdale, AZ Metropolitan Statistical Area; (2) Rankings are based on annual percentage change for all metro areas containing at least 15,000 transactions over the last 10 years and ranges from 1 to 257; (3) figures based on a weighted average of Census Division estimates using a seasonally adjusted, purchase-only index; all figures are for the period ending December 31, 2022
Source: Federal Housing Finance Agency, Change in FHFA Metropolitan Area House Price Indexes, 2022Q4

Median Single-Family Home Prices

Area	2020	2021	2022[p]	Percent Change 2021 to 2022
MSA[1]	333.0	415.4	477.9	15.0
U.S. Average	300.2	357.1	392.6	9.9

Note: Figures are median sales prices of existing single-family homes in thousands of dollars; (p) preliminary; (1) Figures cover the Phoenix-Mesa-Chandler, AZ Metropolitan Statistical Area
Source: National Association of Realtors, Median Sales Price of Existing Single-Family Homes for Metropolitan Areas, 4th Quarter 2022

Qualifying Income Based on Median Sales Price of Existing Single-Family Homes

Area	With 5% Down ($)	With 10% Down ($)	With 20% Down ($)
MSA[1]	134,752	127,660	113,476
U.S. Average	112,234	106,237	94,513

Note: Figures are preliminary; Qualifying income is based on a mortgage rate of 6.77%. Monthly principal and interest payment is limited to 25% of income; (1) Figures cover the Phoenix-Mesa-Chandler, AZ Metropolitan Statistical Area
Source: National Association of Realtors, Qualifying Income Based on Median Sales Price of Existing Single-Family Homes for Metropolitan Areas, 4th Quarter 2022

Home Value

Area	Under $100,000	$100,000 -$199,999	$200,000 -$299,999	$300,000 -$399,999	$400,000 -$499,999	$500,000 -$999,999	$1,000,000 or more	Median ($)
City	7.3	19.8	28.5	18.6	9.6	13.8	2.4	277,700
MSA[1]	8.3	15.9	27.3	20.3	11.4	13.9	2.9	294,700
U.S.	16.2	24.2	20.1	13.6	8.3	13.6	4.1	244,900

Note: Figures are percentages except for median and cover owner-occupied housing units; (1) Figures cover the Phoenix-Mesa-Chandler, AZ Metropolitan Statistical Area
Source: U.S. Census Bureau, 2017-2021 American Community Survey 5-Year Estimates

Year Housing Structure Built

Area	2020 or Later	2010 -2019	2000 -2009	1990 -1999	1980 -1989	1970 -1979	1960 -1969	1950 -1959	1940 -1949	Before 1940	Median Year
City	0.2	6.4	16.3	15.4	17.5	19.4	11.0	9.6	2.4	1.9	1983
MSA[1]	0.3	9.8	24.5	19.4	16.8	15.4	6.9	4.8	1.2	0.9	1992
U.S.	0.2	7.3	13.6	13.6	13.2	14.8	10.3	10.0	4.7	12.2	1979

Note: Figures are percentages except for Median Year; Note: (1) Figures cover the Phoenix-Mesa-Chandler, AZ Metropolitan Statistical Area
Source: U.S. Census Bureau, 2017-2021 American Community Survey 5-Year Estimates

Gross Monthly Rent

Area	Under $500	$500 -$999	$1,000 -$1,499	$1,500 -$1,999	$2,000 -$2,499	$2,500 -$2,999	$3,000 and up	Median ($)
City	3.8	28.5	43.3	18.5	4.2	0.9	0.8	1,175
MSA[1]	3.0	23.1	41.3	22.9	6.3	1.7	1.7	1,268
U.S.	8.1	30.5	30.8	16.8	7.3	3.1	3.5	1,163

Note: Figures are percentages except for median; Gross rent is the contract rent plus the estimated average monthly cost of utilities (electricity, gas, and water and sewer) and fuels (oil, coal, kerosene, wood, etc.) if these are paid by the renter (or paid for the renter by someone else); (1) Figures cover the Phoenix-Mesa-Chandler, AZ Metropolitan Statistical Area
Source: U.S. Census Bureau, 2017-2021 American Community Survey 5-Year Estimates

HEALTH

Health Risk Factors

Category	MSA[1] (%)	U.S. (%)
Adults aged 18–64 who have any kind of health care coverage	87.4	90.9
Adults who reported being in good or better health	84.4	85.2
Adults who have been told they have high blood cholesterol	35.1	35.7
Adults who have been told they have high blood pressure	29.4	32.4
Adults who are current smokers	12.9	14.4
Adults who currently use e-cigarettes	8.6	6.7
Adults who currently use chewing tobacco, snuff, or snus	2.6	3.5
Adults who are heavy drinkers[2]	6.2	6.3
Adults who are binge drinkers[3]	16.5	15.4
Adults who are overweight (BMI 25.0 - 29.9)	37.8	34.4
Adults who are obese (BMI 30.0 - 99.8)	30.4	33.9
Adults who participated in any physical activities in the past month	78.2	76.3

Note: (1) Figures cover the Phoenix-Mesa-Scottsdale, AZ Metropolitan Statistical Area; (2) Heavy drinkers are classified as adult men having more than 14 drinks per week and adult women having more than 7 drinks per week; (3) Binge drinkers are classified as males having five or more drinks on one occasion or females having four or more drinks on one occasion
Source: Centers for Disease Control and Prevention, Behaviorial Risk Factor Surveillance System, SMART: Selected Metropolitan Area Risk Trends, 2021

Acute and Chronic Health Conditions

Category	MSA[1] (%)	U.S. (%)
Adults who have ever been told they had a heart attack	4.0	4.0
Adults who have ever been told they have angina or coronary heart disease	3.8	3.8
Adults who have ever been told they had a stroke	2.7	3.0
Adults who have ever been told they have asthma	14.8	14.9
Adults who have ever been told they have arthritis	22.9	25.8
Adults who have ever been told they have diabetes[2]	10.6	10.9
Adults who have ever been told they had skin cancer	8.7	6.6
Adults who have ever been told they had any other types of cancer	7.3	7.5
Adults who have ever been told they have COPD	5.4	6.1
Adults who have ever been told they have kidney disease	3.8	3.0
Adults who have ever been told they have a form of depression	16.9	20.5

Note: (1) Figures cover the Phoenix-Mesa-Scottsdale, AZ Metropolitan Statistical Area; (2) Figures do not include pregnancy-related, borderline, or pre-diabetes
Source: Centers for Disease Control and Prevention, Behaviorial Risk Factor Surveillance System, SMART: Selected Metropolitan Area Risk Trends, 2021

Health Screening and Vaccination Rates

Category	MSA[1] (%)	U.S. (%)
Adults who have ever been tested for HIV	35.5	34.9
Adults who have had their blood cholesterol checked within the last five years	86.0	85.2
Adults aged 65+ who have had flu shot within the past year	63.7	68.6
Adults aged 65+ who have ever had a pneumonia vaccination	70.3	71.0

Note: (1) Figures cover the Phoenix-Mesa-Scottsdale, AZ Metropolitan Statistical Area.
Source: Centers for Disease Control and Prevention, Behaviorial Risk Factor Surveillance System, SMART: Selected Metropolitan Area Risk Trends, 2021

Disability Status

Category	MSA[1] (%)	U.S. (%)
Adults who reported being deaf	7.2	7.2
Are you blind or have serious difficulty seeing, even when wearing glasses?	4.3	4.8
Are you limited in any way in any of your usual activities due to arthritis?	9.3	11.1
Do you have difficulty doing errands alone?	6.5	7.0
Do you have difficulty dressing or bathing?	3.4	3.6
Do you have serious difficulty concentrating/remembering/making decisions?	12.6	12.1
Do you have serious difficulty walking or climbing stairs?	12.5	12.8

Note: (1) Figures cover the Phoenix-Mesa-Scottsdale, AZ Metropolitan Statistical Area.
Source: Centers for Disease Control and Prevention, Behaviorial Risk Factor Surveillance System, SMART: Selected Metropolitan Area Risk Trends, 2021

Mortality Rates for the Top 10 Causes of Death in the U.S.

ICD-10[a] Sub-Chapter	ICD-10[a] Code	Crude Mortality Rate[1] per 100,000 population	
		County[2]	U.S.
Malignant neoplasms	C00-C97	151.3	182.6
Ischaemic heart diseases	I20-I25	95.4	113.1
Other forms of heart disease	I30-I51	40.3	64.4
Other degenerative diseases of the nervous system	G30-G31	63.9	51.0
Cerebrovascular diseases	I60-I69	37.9	47.8
Other external causes of accidental injury	W00-X59	53.2	46.4
Chronic lower respiratory diseases	J40-J47	41.1	45.7
Organic, including symptomatic, mental disorders	F01-F09	16.0	35.9
Hypertensive diseases	I10-I15	38.6	35.0
Diabetes mellitus	E10-E14	29.2	29.6

Note: (a) ICD-10 = International Classification of Diseases 10th Revision; (1) Crude mortality rates are a three-year average covering 2019-2021; (2) Figures cover Maricopa County.
Source: Centers for Disease Control and Prevention, National Center for Health Statistics. National Vital Statistics System, Mortality 2018-2021 on CDC WONDER Online Database

Mortality Rates for Selected Causes of Death

ICD-10[a] Sub-Chapter	ICD-10[a] Code	Crude Mortality Rate[1] per 100,000 population	
		County[2]	U.S.
Assault	X85-Y09	6.7	7.0
Diseases of the liver	K70-K76	19.0	19.8
Human immunodeficiency virus (HIV) disease	B20-B24	1.2	1.5
Influenza and pneumonia	J09-J18	11.8	14.7
Intentional self-harm	X60-X84	16.1	14.3
Malnutrition	E40-E46	4.6	4.3
Obesity and other hyperalimentation	E65-E68	3.1	3.0
Renal failure	N17-N19	7.8	15.7
Transport accidents	V01-V99	13.6	13.6
Viral hepatitis	B15-B19	1.2	1.2

Note: (a) ICD-10 = International Classification of Diseases 10th Revision; (1) Crude mortality rates are a three-year average covering 2019-2021; (2) Figures cover Maricopa County; Data are suppressed when the data meet the criteria for confidentiality constraints; Crude mortality rates are flagged as unreliable when the rate would be calculated with a numerator of 20 or less.
Source: Centers for Disease Control and Prevention, National Center for Health Statistics. National Vital Statistics System, Mortality 2018-2021 on CDC WONDER Online Database

Health Insurance Coverage

Area	With Health Insurance	With Private Health Insurance	With Public Health Insurance	Without Health Insurance	Population Under Age 19 Without Health Insurance
City	85.5	57.9	35.0	14.5	10.0
MSA[1]	89.2	65.8	34.2	10.8	8.6
U.S.	91.2	67.8	35.4	8.8	5.3

Note: Figures are percentages that cover the civilian noninstitutionalized population; (1) Figures cover the Phoenix-Mesa-Chandler, AZ Metropolitan Statistical Area
Source: U.S. Census Bureau, 2017-2021 American Community Survey 5-Year Estimates

Number of Medical Professionals

Area	MDs[3]	DOs[3,4]	Dentists	Podiatrists	Chiropractors	Optometrists
County[1] (number)	11,333	1,473	3,199	314	1,526	753
County[1] (rate[2])	255.3	33.2	71.1	7.0	33.9	16.7
U.S. (rate[2])	289.3	23.5	72.5	6.2	28.7	17.4

Note: Data as of 2021 unless noted; (1) Data covers Maricopa County; (2) Rate per 100,000 population; (3) Data as of 2020 and includes all active, non-federal physicians; (4) Doctor of Osteopathic Medicine
Source: U.S. Department of Health and Human Services, Health Resources and Services Administration, Bureau of Health Professions, Area Resource File (ARF) 2021-2022

Best Hospitals

According to *U.S. News,* the Phoenix-Mesa-Chandler, AZ metro area is home to two of the best hospitals in the U.S.: **Barrow Neurological Institute** (2 adult specialties); **Mayo Clinic-Phoenix** (Honor Roll/10 adult specialties). The hospitals listed were nationally ranked in at least one of 15 adult or 10 pediatric specialties. The number of specialties shown cover the parent hospital. Only 164 U.S. hospitals performed well enough to be nationally ranked in one or more specialties. Twenty hospitals in the U.S. made the Honor Roll. The Best Hospitals Honor Roll takes both the national rankings and the procedure and condition ratings into account. Hospitals received points if they were nationally ranked in one of the 15 adult specialties—the higher they ranked, the more points they got—and how many ratings of "high performing" they earned in the 17 procedures and conditions. *U.S. News Online, "America's Best Hospitals 2022-23"*

According to *U.S. News,* the Phoenix-Mesa-Chandler, AZ metro area is home to one of the best children's hospitals in the U.S.: **Phoenix Children's Hospital** (8 pediatric specialties). The hospital listed was highly ranked in at least one of 10 pediatric specialties. Eighty-six children's hospitals in the U.S. were nationally ranked in at least one specialty. Hospitals received points for being ranked in a specialty, and the 10 hospitals with the most points across the 10 specialties make up the Honor Roll. *U.S. News Online, "America's Best Children's Hospitals 2022-23"*

EDUCATION

Public School District Statistics

District Name	Schls	Pupils	Pupil/ Teacher Ratio	Minority Pupils[1] (%)	LEP/ELL[2] (%)	IEP[3] (%)
Alhambra Elementary District	18	10,256	18.4	95.4	21.0	11.5
Balsz Elementary District	6	2,278	18.8	95.0	23.2	15.2
Cartwright Elementary District	23	14,826	19.7	97.3	23.4	10.7
Creighton Elementary District	11	5,308	17.5	94.1	24.2	12.2
Deer Valley Unified District	40	33,353	17.6	34.6	2.2	12.6
Fowler Elementary District	8	3,759	19.0	95.3	18.2	10.9
Isaac Elementary District	13	5,272	20.8	98.6	33.4	13.4
Madison Elementary District	9	5,802	19.7	54.8	4.4	9.2
Osborn Elementary District	7	2,651	15.0	88.2	13.1	16.0
Paradise Valley Unified District	45	28,707	15.2	46.9	6.0	11.2
Pendergast Elementary District	12	8,017	18.1	89.4	11.1	13.9
Phoenix Elementary District	15	5,415	14.3	93.3	15.2	12.9
Phoenix Union High SD	19	27,890	19.1	95.8	9.9	11.5
Portable Practical Ed. Prep.	2	7,004	n/a	60.4	1.0	17.7
Roosevelt Elementary District	20	7,333	7.6	97.3	20.8	14.2

Note: Table includes school districts with 2,000 or more students; (1) Percentage of students that are not non-Hispanic white; (2) Percentage of students that are Limited English Proficient or English Language Learners (2018-19); (3) Percentage of students that have an Individualized Education Program (2019-20).
Source: U.S. Department of Education, National Center for Education Statistics, Common Core of Data, Local Education Agency (School District) Universe Survey: School Year 2021-2022

Best High Schools

According to *U.S. News,* Phoenix is home to three of the top 500 high schools in the U.S.: **BASIS Ahwatukee** (#56); **BASIS Phoenix** (#58); **Phoenix Union Bioscience High School** (#209). Nearly 18,000 public, magnet and charter schools were ranked based on their performance on state assessments and how well they prepare students for college. *U.S. News & World Report, "Best High Schools 2022"*

Highest Level of Education

Area	Less than H.S.	H.S. Diploma	Some College, No Deg.	Associate Degree	Bachelor's Degree	Master's Degree	Prof. School Degree	Doctorate Degree
City	16.5	22.9	22.1	8.0	19.1	8.2	2.1	1.2
MSA[1]	11.3	22.8	23.8	9.0	20.9	9.0	2.0	1.3
U.S.	11.1	26.5	20.0	8.7	20.6	9.3	2.2	1.5

Note: Figures cover persons age 25 and over; (1) Figures cover the Phoenix-Mesa-Chandler, AZ Metropolitan Statistical Area
Source: U.S. Census Bureau, 2017-2021 American Community Survey 5-Year Estimates

Educational Attainment by Race

Area	High School Graduate or Higher (%)					Bachelor's Degree or Higher (%)				
	Total	White	Black	Asian	Hisp.[2]	Total	White	Black	Asian	Hisp.[2]
City	83.5	87.0	89.8	86.8	65.5	30.6	33.8	25.9	60.2	12.0
MSA[1]	88.7	91.3	91.7	89.3	71.8	33.1	35.2	28.2	59.7	14.9
U.S.	88.9	91.4	87.2	87.6	71.2	33.7	35.5	23.3	55.6	18.4

Note: Figures shown cover persons 25 years old and over; (1) Figures cover the Phoenix-Mesa-Chandler, AZ Metropolitan Statistical Area; (2) People of Hispanic origin can be of any race
Source: U.S. Census Bureau, 2017-2021 American Community Survey 5-Year Estimates

School Enrollment by Grade and Control

Area	Preschool (%)		Kindergarten (%)		Grades 1 - 4 (%)		Grades 5 - 8 (%)		Grades 9 - 12 (%)	
	Public	Private	Public	Private	Public	Private	Public	Private	Public	Private
City	61.2	38.8	86.5	13.5	90.6	9.4	91.6	8.4	93.1	6.9
MSA[1]	61.7	38.3	86.0	14.0	89.6	10.4	91.1	8.9	92.7	7.3
U.S.	58.8	41.2	86.3	13.7	88.3	11.7	88.6	11.4	89.4	10.6

Note: Figures shown cover persons 3 years old and over; (1) Figures cover the Phoenix-Mesa-Chandler, AZ Metropolitan Statistical Area
Source: U.S. Census Bureau, 2017-2021 American Community Survey 5-Year Estimates

Higher Education

Four-Year Colleges			Two-Year Colleges			Medical Schools[1]	Law Schools[2]	Voc/ Tech[3]
Public	Private Non-profit	Private For-profit	Public	Private Non-profit	Private For-profit			
2	8	14	12	0	13	3	1	25

Note: Figures cover institutions located within the Phoenix-Mesa-Chandler, AZ Metropolitan Statistical Area and include main campuses only; (1) includes schools accredited by the Liaison Committee on Medical Education and the American Osteopathic Association's Commission on Osteopathic College Accreditation; (2) includes ABA-accredited schools, schools with provisional ABA accreditation, and state accredited schools; (3) includes all schools with programs that are less than 2 years.
Source: National Center for Education Statistics, Integrated Postsecondary Education System (IPEDS), 2021-22; Wikipedia, List of Medical Schools in the United States, accessed April 10, 2023; Wikipedia, List of Law Schools in the United States, accessed April 10, 2023

According to *U.S. News & World Report,* the Phoenix-Mesa-Chandler, AZ metro area is home to one of the top 200 national universities in the U.S.: **Arizona State University** (#121 tie). The indicators used to capture academic quality fall into a number of categories: assessment by administrators at peer institutions; retention of students; faculty resources; student selectivity; financial resources; alumni giving; high school counselor ratings of colleges; and graduation rate. *U.S. News & World Report, "America's Best Colleges 2023"*

According to *U.S. News & World Report,* the Phoenix-Mesa-Chandler, AZ metro area is home to one of the top 100 law schools in the U.S.: **Arizona State University (O'Connor)** (#30 tie). The rankings are based on a weighted average of 12 measures of quality: peer assessment score; assessment score by lawyers/judges; median LSAT scores; median undergrad GPA; acceptance rate; employment rates for graduates; placement success; bar passage rate; faculty resources; expenditures per student; student/faculty ratio; and library resources. *U.S. News & World Report, "America's Best Graduate Schools, Law, 2023"*

According to *U.S. News & World Report,* the Phoenix-Mesa-Chandler, AZ metro area is home to one of the top 75 business schools in the U.S.: **Arizona State University (W.P. Carey)** (#29 tie). The rankings are based on a weighted average of the following nine measures: quality assessment; peer assessment; recruiter assessment; placement success; mean starting salary and bonus; student selectivity; mean GMAT and GRE scores; mean undergraduate GPA; and acceptance rate. *U.S. News & World Report, "America's Best Graduate Schools, Business, 2023"*

EMPLOYERS

Major Employers

Company Name	Industry
Arizona Dept of Transportation	Regulation, administration of transportation
Arizona State University	University
Avnet	Electronic parts & equipment, nec
Carter & Burgess	Engineering services
Chase Bankcard Services	State commercial banks
City of Mesa	Municipal government
City of Phoenix	Municipal government
General Dynamics C4 Systems	Communications equipment, nec
Grand Canyon Education	Colleges & universities
Honeywell International	Aircraft engines & engine parts
Lockheed Martin Corporation	Search & navigation equipment
Paramount Building Solutions	Janitorial service, contract basis
Salt River Pima-Maricopa Indian Community	Casino resort
Scottsdale Healthcare Osborn Med Ctr	General medical & surgical hospitals
Swift Transportation Company	Trucking, except local
The Boeing Company	Helicopters
Veterans Health Administration	General medical & surgical hospitals

Note: Companies shown are located within the Phoenix-Mesa-Chandler, AZ Metropolitan Statistical Area.
Source: Hoovers.com; Wikipedia

Best Companies to Work For

Banner Health; DriveTime, headquartered in Phoenix, are among the "100 Best Places to Work in IT." To qualify, companies had to have a minimum of 100 total employees and five IT employees.

The best places to work were selected based on DEI (diversity, equity, and inclusion) practices; IT turnover, promotions, and growth; IT retention and engagement programs; remote/hybrid working; benefits and perks (such as elder care and child care, flextime, and reimbursement for college tuition); and training and career development opportunities. *Computerworld, "Best Places to Work in IT," 2023*

PUBLIC SAFETY

Crime Rate

Area	Total Crime	Violent Crime Rate				Property Crime Rate		
		Murder	Rape[3]	Robbery	Aggrav. Assault	Burglary	Larceny -Theft	Motor Vehicle Theft
City	3,788.0	10.9	62.5	191.8	533.2	433.4	2,121.4	434.7
Suburbs[1]	2,118.2	3.8	35.2	43.8	211.2	276.5	1,380.4	167.3
Metro[2]	2,681.7	6.2	44.4	93.8	319.9	329.5	1,630.4	257.5
U.S.	2,356.7	6.5	38.4	73.9	279.7	314.2	1,398.0	246.0

Note: Figures are crimes per 100,000 population; (1) All areas within the metro area that are located outside the city limits; (2) Figures cover the Phoenix-Mesa-Scottsdale, AZ Metropolitan Statistical Area; (3) All figures shown were reported using the revised Uniform Crime Reporting (UCR) definition of rape; Due to the transition to the National Incident-Based Reporting System (NIBRS), limited city and metro area data was released for 2021.
Source: FBI Uniform Crime Reports, 2020

Hate Crimes

Area	Number of Quarters Reported	Number of Incidents per Bias Motivation					
		Race/Ethnicity/ Ancestry	Religion	Sexual Orientation	Disability	Gender	Gender Identity
City[1]	4	140	17	28	0	1	3
U.S.	4	5,227	1,244	1,110	130	75	266

Note: (1) Figures include one incident reported with more than one bias motivation; Due to the transition to the National Incident-Based Reporting System (NIBRS), limited crime data was released for 2021.
Source: Federal Bureau of Investigation, Hate Crime Statistics 2020

Identity Theft Consumer Reports

Area	Reports	Reports per 100,000 Population	Rank[2]
MSA[1]	15,488	319	56
U.S.	1,108,609	339	-

Note: (1) Figures cover the Phoenix-Mesa-Chandler, AZ Metropolitan Statistical Area; (2) Rank ranges from 1 to 391 where 1 indicates greatest number of identity theft reports per 100,000 population
Source: Federal Trade Commission, Consumer Sentinel Network Data Book 2022

Fraud and Other Consumer Reports

Area	Reports	Reports per 100,000 Population	Rank[2]
MSA[1]	54,856	1,129	58
U.S.	4,064,520	1,245	-

Note: (1) Figures cover the Phoenix-Mesa-Chandler, AZ Metropolitan Statistical Area; (2) Rank ranges from 1 to 391 where 1 indicates greatest number of fraud and other consumer reports per 100,000 population
Source: Federal Trade Commission, Consumer Sentinel Network Data Book 2022

POLITICS

2020 Presidential Election Results

Area	Biden	Trump	Jorgensen	Hawkins	Other
Maricopa County	50.1	48.0	1.5	0.0	0.3
U.S.	51.3	46.8	1.2	0.3	0.5

Note: Results are percentages and may not add to 100% due to rounding
Source: Dave Leip's Atlas of U.S. Presidential Elections

SPORTS

Professional Sports Teams

Team Name	League	Year Established
Arizona Cardinals	National Football League (NFL)	1988
Arizona Diamondbacks	Major League Baseball (MLB)	1998
Phoenix Coyotes	National Hockey League (NHL)	1996
Phoenix Suns	National Basketball Association (NBA)	1968

Note: Includes teams located in the Phoenix-Mesa-Chandler, AZ Metropolitan Statistical Area.
Source: Wikipedia, Major Professional Sports Teams of the United States and Canada, April 12, 2023

CLIMATE

Average and Extreme Temperatures

Temperature	Jan	Feb	Mar	Apr	May	Jun	Jul	Aug	Sep	Oct	Nov	Dec	Yr.
Extreme High (°F)	88	92	100	105	113	122	118	116	118	107	93	88	122
Average High (°F)	66	70	75	84	93	103	105	103	99	88	75	67	86
Average Temp. (°F)	53	57	62	70	78	88	93	91	85	74	62	54	72
Average Low (°F)	40	44	48	55	63	72	80	78	72	60	48	41	59
Extreme Low (°F)	17	22	25	37	40	51	66	61	47	34	27	22	17

Note: Figures cover the years 1948-1990
Source: National Climatic Data Center, International Station Meteorological Climate Summary, 9/96

Average Precipitation/Snowfall/Humidity

Precip./Humidity	Jan	Feb	Mar	Apr	May	Jun	Jul	Aug	Sep	Oct	Nov	Dec	Yr.
Avg. Precip. (in.)	0.7	0.6	0.8	0.3	0.1	0.1	0.8	1.0	0.7	0.6	0.6	0.9	7.3
Avg. Snowfall (in.)	Tr	Tr	0	0	0	0	0	0	0	0	0	Tr	Tr
Avg. Rel. Hum. 5am (%)	68	63	56	45	37	33	47	53	50	53	59	66	53
Avg. Rel. Hum. 5pm (%)	34	28	24	17	14	12	21	24	23	24	28	34	24

Note: Figures cover the years 1948-1990; Tr = Trace amounts (<0.05 in. of rain; <0.5 in. of snow)
Source: National Climatic Data Center, International Station Meteorological Climate Summary, 9/96

Weather Conditions

Temperature			Daytime Sky			Precipitation		
10°F & below	32°F & below	90°F & above	Clear	Partly cloudy	Cloudy	0.01 inch or more precip.	0.1 inch or more snow/ice	Thunder-storms
0	10	167	186	125	54	37	< 1	23

Note: Figures are average number of days per year and cover the years 1948-1990
Source: National Climatic Data Center, International Station Meteorological Climate Summary, 9/96

HAZARDOUS WASTE

Superfund Sites

The Phoenix-Mesa-Chandler, AZ metro area is home to four sites on the EPA's Superfund National Priorities List: **Hassayampa Landfill** (final); **Indian Bend Wash Area** (final); **Motorola, Inc. (52nd Street Plant)** (final); **Phoenix-Goodyear Airport Area** (final). There are a total of 1,165 Superfund sites with a status of proposed or final on the list in the U.S. *U.S. Environmental Protection Agency, National Priorities List, April 12, 2023*

AIR QUALITY

Air Quality Trends: Ozone

	1990	1995	2000	2005	2010	2015	2018	2019	2020	2021
MSA[1]	0.080	0.086	0.082	0.077	0.075	0.072	0.073	0.071	0.079	0.079
U.S.	0.087	0.089	0.081	0.080	0.072	0.067	0.069	0.065	0.065	0.067

Note: (1) Data covers the Phoenix-Mesa-Chandler, AZ Metropolitan Statistical Area. The values shown are the composite ozone concentration averages among trend sites based on the highest fourth daily maximum 8-hour concentration in parts per million. These trends are based on sites having an adequate record of monitoring data during the trend period. Data from exceptional events are included.
Source: U.S. Environmental Protection Agency, Air Quality Monitoring Information, "Air Quality Trends by City, 1990-2021"

Air Quality Index

Area	Percent of Days when Air Quality was...[2]					AQI Statistics[2]	
	Good	Moderate	Unhealthy for Sensitive Groups	Unhealthy	Very Unhealthy	Maximum	Median
MSA[1]	3.0	32.1	28.2	16.7	20.0	272	123

Note: (1) Data covers the Phoenix-Mesa-Chandler, AZ Metropolitan Statistical Area; (2) Based on 365 days with AQI data in 2021. Air Quality Index (AQI) is an index for reporting daily air quality. EPA calculates the AQI for five major air pollutants regulated by the Clean Air Act: ground-level ozone, particle pollution (aka particulate matter), carbon monoxide, sulfur dioxide, and nitrogen dioxide. The AQI runs from 0 to 500. The higher the AQI value, the greater the level of air pollution and the greater the health concern. There are six AQI categories: "Good" AQI is between 0 and 50. Air quality is considered satisfactory; "Moderate" AQI is between 51 and 100. Air quality is acceptable; "Unhealthy for Sensitive Groups" When AQI values are between 101 and 150, members of sensitive groups may experience health effects; "Unhealthy" When AQI values are between 151 and 200 everyone may begin to experience health effects; "Very Unhealthy" AQI values between 201 and 300 trigger a health alert; "Hazardous" AQI values over 300 trigger warnings of emergency conditions (not shown).
Source: U.S. Environmental Protection Agency, Air Quality Index Report, 2021

Air Quality Index Pollutants

Area	Percent of Days when AQI Pollutant was...[2]					
	Carbon Monoxide	Nitrogen Dioxide	Ozone	Sulfur Dioxide	Particulate Matter 2.5	Particulate Matter 10
MSA[1]	0.0	0.0	75.3	(3)	6.3	18.4

Note: (1) Data covers the Phoenix-Mesa-Chandler, AZ Metropolitan Statistical Area; (2) Based on 365 days with AQI data in 2021. The Air Quality Index (AQI) is an index for reporting daily air quality. EPA calculates the AQI for five major air pollutants regulated by the Clean Air Act: ground-level ozone, particle pollution (also known as particulate matter), carbon monoxide, sulfur dioxide, and nitrogen dioxide. The AQI runs from 0 to 500. The higher the AQI value, the greater the level of air pollution and the greater the health concern; (3) Sulfur dioxide is no longer included in this table (as of December 8, 2021) because SO_2 concentrations tend to be very localized and not necessarily representative of broad geographical areas like counties and CBSAs.
Source: U.S. Environmental Protection Agency, Air Quality Index Report, 2021

Maximum Air Pollutant Concentrations: Particulate Matter, Ozone, CO and Lead

	Particulate Matter 10 (ug/m^3)	Particulate Matter 2.5 Wtd AM (ug/m^3)	Particulate Matter 2.5 24-Hr (ug/m^3)	Ozone (ppm)	Carbon Monoxide (ppm)	Lead (ug/m^3)
MSA[1] Level	225	12.7	36	0.083	3	n/a
NAAQS[2]	150	15	35	0.075	9	0.15
Met NAAQS[2]	No	Yes	No	No	Yes	n/a

Note: (1) Data covers the Phoenix-Mesa-Chandler, AZ Metropolitan Statistical Area; Data from exceptional events are included; (2) National Ambient Air Quality Standards; ppm = parts per million; ug/m^3 = micrograms per cubic meter; n/a not available.
Concentrations: Particulate Matter 10 (coarse particulate)—highest second maximum 24-hour concentration; Particulate Matter 2.5 Wtd AM (fine particulate)—highest weighted annual mean concentration; Particulate Matter 2.5 24-Hour (fine particulate)—highest 98th percentile 24-hour concentration; Ozone—highest fourth daily maximum 8-hour concentration; Carbon Monoxide—highest second maximum non-overlapping 8-hour concentration; Lead—maximum running 3-month average
Source: U.S. Environmental Protection Agency, Air Quality Monitoring Information, "Air Quality Statistics by City, 2021"

Maximum Air Pollutant Concentrations: Nitrogen Dioxide and Sulfur Dioxide

	Nitrogen Dioxide AM (ppb)	Nitrogen Dioxide 1-Hr (ppb)	Sulfur Dioxide AM (ppb)	Sulfur Dioxide 1-Hr (ppb)	Sulfur Dioxide 24-Hr (ppb)
MSA[1] Level	26	59	n/a	7	n/a
NAAQS[2]	53	100	30	75	140
Met NAAQS[2]	Yes	Yes	n/a	Yes	n/a

Note: (1) Data covers the Phoenix-Mesa-Chandler, AZ Metropolitan Statistical Area; Data from exceptional events are included; (2) National Ambient Air Quality Standards; ppm = parts per million; ug/m^3 = micrograms per cubic meter; n/a not available.
Concentrations: Nitrogen Dioxide AM—highest arithmetic mean concentration; Nitrogen Dioxide 1-Hr—highest 98th percentile 1-hour daily maximum concentration; Sulfur Dioxide AM—highest annual mean concentration; Sulfur Dioxide 1-Hr—highest 99th percentile 1-hour daily maximum concentration; Sulfur Dioxide 24-Hr—highest second maximum 24-hour concentration
Source: U.S. Environmental Protection Agency, Air Quality Monitoring Information, "Air Quality Statistics by City, 2021"

Portland, Oregon

Background

Portland is the kind of city that inspires civic pride and the desire to preserve. It offers magnificent views of the Cascade Mountains, a mild climate, and an attractive combination of historical brick structures and contemporary architecture.

Nature is the undisputed queen of Portland and embodied in Portlandia, the city's statue of an earth mother kneeling among her animal children. The number of activities, such as fishing, skiing, and hunting, as well as the number of outdoor zoological gardens, attest to the mindset of the typical Portlander.

Portland is a major industrial and commercial center that boasts clean air and water within its city limits, as many of the factories use the electricity generated by mountain rivers; thus, little soot or smoke is belched out. Manufacturing specializing in high-tech electronics and specialty metal fabrication is leading industry in the city, and major employers include Intel, NIKE, US Bank, and Precision Castparts. Health services and the highly-rated University of Portland also make a significant impact in the city.

The city is a major cultural center, with art museums such as the Portland Art Museum and the Oregon Museum of Science and Industry, and educational institutions including Reed College and the University of Portland. In 2001, Portland's PGE Park sports stadium had a multi-million-dollar facelift, with a field level bar and grill and pavilion suites, all state-of-the-art and seismic code compliant.

The Portland area's metro region includes 24 cities and parts of three counties. Established in the late 1970s, it is the nation's first and only elected regional government. It attempts to control growth by using its authority over land use, transportation, and the environment. This experiment in urban planning is designed to protect farms, forests, and open space. Portland today has a downtown area that caters to pedestrians and includes a heavily used city park. Visible from the air is a clear line against sprawl—with cities on one side and open spaces on the other.

Portland is Oregon's biggest city, and is a shining example of effective sprawl control, a "role model for twenty-first century urban development." The city's well-organized mass-transit system makes living there more enjoyable, and Portland Streetcar continues to add track, streetcars, and additional improvements.

In 2000, the Portland Art Museum completed its "Program for the Millennium," a multi-stage expansion program that brought total exhibition space to 240,000 square feet. In 2005, restoration of the North Building, a former Masonic Temple, was completed. While preserving the historical integrity, the restoration provides space for the Portland Art Museum's Center for Modern and Contemporary Art.

The Portland metropolitan area had a significant LGBTQ population throughout the late 20th and early 21st century. In 2015, it had the second highest percentage of LGBTQ residents in the United States, at 5.4 percent, second only to San Francisco. The city held its first pride festival in 1975 on the Portland State University campus.

Many films have been shot in Portland, from independents to big-budget productions. The city has been featured in various television programs, most notably the comedy series *Portlandia*, which ran 2011 to 2018. Shot on location in Portland, it lovingly satirized the city as a hub of liberal politics, organic food, alternative lifestyles, and anti-establishment attitudes.

Portland has a very definite winter rainfall climate, with the most rain falling October through May in relatively mild temperatures. Summer produces pleasant, mild temperatures with very little precipitation. Fall and spring are transitional. Fall and early winter bring the most frequent fog. Destructive storms are infrequent, with thunderstorms occurring once a month through the spring and summer.

Rankings

General Rankings

- *US News & World Report* conducted a survey of more than 3,600 people and analyzed the 150 largest metropolitan areas to determine what matters most when selecting where to settle down. Portland ranked #22 out of the top 25 as having the best combination of desirable factors. Criteria: cost of living; quality of life and education; net migration; job market; desirability; and other factors. *money.usnews.com, "The 25 Best Places to Live in the U.S. in 2022-2023," May 17, 2022*

- *Insider* listed 23 places in the U.S. that travel industry trends reveal would be popular destinations in 2023. This year the list trends towards cultural and historical happenings, sports events, wellness experiences and invigorating outdoor escapes. According to the website insider.com Portland is a place to visit in 2023. *Insider, "23 of the Best Places You Should Travel to in the U.S. in 2023," December 17, 2022*

- The Portland metro area was identified as one of America's fastest-growing areas in terms of population and business growth by *MagnifyMoney*. The area ranked #21 out of 35. The 100 most populous metro areas in the U.S. were evaluated on their change from 2011 to 2016 in the following categories: people and housing; workforce and employment opportunities; growing industry. *www.businessinsider.com, "The 35 Cities in the US with the Biggest Influx of People, the Most Work Opportunities, and the Hottest Business Growth," August 12, 2018*

- The Portland metro area was identified as one of America's fastest-growing areas in terms of population and economy by *Forbes*. The area ranked #17 out of 25. The 100 most populous metro areas in the U.S. were evaluated on the following criteria: estimated population growth; employment; economic output; wages; home values. *Forbes, "America's Fastest-Growing Cities 2018," February 28, 2018*

Business/Finance Rankings

- The Brookings Institution ranked the nation's largest cities based on income inequality. Portland was ranked #48 (#1 = greatest inequality). Criteria: the "95/20 ratio," a figure representing the income at which a household earns more than 95 percent of all other households, divided by the income at which a household earns more than only 20 percent of all other households. *Brookings Institution, "Household Income Inequality, Largest Cities of 97 Large U.S. Metro Areas, 2014-2016," February 5, 2018*

- The Brookings Institution ranked the 100 largest metro areas in the U.S. based on income inequality. Portland was ranked #83 (#1 = greatest inequality). Criteria: the "95/20 ratio," a figure representing the income at which a household earns more than 95 percent of all other households, divided by the income at which a household earns more than only 20 percent of all other households. *Brookings Institution, "Household Income Inequality, 100 Largest U.S. Metro Areas, 2014-2016," February 5, 2018*

- Payscale.com ranked the 32 largest metro areas in terms of wage growth. The Portland metro area ranked #9. Criteria: quarterly changes in private industry employee and education professional wage growth from the previous year. *PayScale, "Wage Trends by Metro Area-1st Quarter," April 20, 2023*

- The Portland metro area was identified as one of the most debt-ridden places in America by the finance site Credit.com. The metro area was ranked #21. Criteria: residents' average credit card debt as well as median income. *Credit.com, "25 Cities With the Most Credit Card Debt," February 28, 2018*

- The Portland metro area appeared on the Milken Institute "2022 Best Performing Cities" list. Rank: #34 out of 200 large metro areas (population over 250,000). Criteria: job growth; wage and salary growth; high-tech output growth; housing affordability; household broadband access. *Milken Institute, "Best-Performing Cities 2022," March 28, 2022*

- *Forbes* ranked the 200 most populous metro areas to determine the nation's "Best Places for Business and Careers." The Portland metro area was ranked #5. Criteria: costs (business and living); job growth (past and projected); income growth; quality of life; educational attainment (college and high school); projected economic growth; cultural and leisure opportunities; workplace tolerance laws; net migration patterns. *Forbes, "The Best Places for Business and Careers 2019: Seattle Still On Top," October 30, 2019*

- Mercer Human Resources Consulting ranked 227 cities worldwide in terms of cost-of-living. Portland ranked #91 (the lower the ranking, the higher the cost-of-living). The survey measured the comparative cost of over 200 items (such as housing, food, clothing, domestic supplies, transportation, and recreation/entertainment) in each location. *Mercer, "2022 Cost of Living City Ranking," June 29, 2022*

Dating/Romance Rankings

- Portland was selected as one of the nation's most romantic cities with 100,000 or more residents by Amazon.com. The city ranked #18 of 20. Criteria: per capita sales of romance novels, relationship books, romantic comedy movies, romantic music, and sexual wellness products. *Amazon.com, "Top 20 Most Romantic Cities in the U.S.," February 1, 2017*

Education Rankings

- Personal finance website *WalletHub* analyzed the 150 largest U.S. metropolitan statistical areas to determine where the most educated Americans are putting their degrees to work. Criteria: education levels; percentage of workers with degrees; education quality and attainment gap; public school quality rankings; quality and enrollment of each metro area's universities. Portland was ranked #17 (#1 = most educated city). *www.WalletHub.com, "Most & Least Educated Cities in America," July 18, 2022*

- Portland was selected as one of America's most literate cities. The city ranked #5 out of the 84 largest U.S. cities. Criteria: number of booksellers; library resources; Internet resources; educational attainment; periodical publishing resources; newspaper circulation. *Central Connecticut State University, "America's Most Literate Cities, 2018," February 2019*

Environmental Rankings

- Sperling's BestPlaces assessed the 50 largest metropolitan areas of the United States for the likelihood of dangerously extreme weather events or earthquakes. In general the Southeast and South-Central regions have the highest risk of weather extremes and earthquakes, while the Pacific Northwest enjoys the lowest risk. Of the least risky metropolitan areas, the Portland metro area was ranked #1. *www.bestplaces.net, "Avoid Natural Disasters: BestPlaces Reveals The Top 10 Safest Places to Live," October 25, 2017*

- The U.S. Environmental Protection Agency (EPA) released its list of U.S. metropolitan areas with the most ENERGY STAR certified buildings in 2022. The Portland metro area was ranked #24 out of 25. *U.S. Environmental Protection Agency, "2023 Energy Star Top Cities," April 26, 2023*

Food/Drink Rankings

- The U.S. Chamber of Commerce Foundation conducted an in-depth study on local food truck regulations, surveyed 288 food truck owners, and ranked 20 major American cities based on how friendly they are for operating a food truck. The compiled index assessed the following: procedures for obtaining permits and licenses; complying with restrictions; and financial obligations associated with operating a food truck. Portland ranked #1 overall (1 being the best). *www.foodtrucknation.us, "Food Truck Nation," March 20, 2018*

- Portland was identified as one of the cities in America ordering the most vegan food options by GrubHub.com. The city ranked #3 out of 5. Criteria: percentage of vegan, vegetarian and plant-based food orders compared to the overall number of orders. *GrubHub.com, "State of the Plate Report 2021: Top Cities for Vegans," June 20, 2021*

Health/Fitness Rankings

- For each of the 100 largest cities in the United States, the American Fitness Index®, compiled in partnership between the American College of Sports Medicine and the Elevance Health Foundation, evaluated community infrastructure and 34 health behaviors including preventive health, levels of chronic disease conditions, food insecurity, sleep quality, pedestrian safety, air quality, and community/environment resources that support physical activity. Portland ranked #7 for "community fitness." *americanfitnessindex.org, "2022 ACSM American Fitness Index Summary Report," July 12, 2022*

- Portland was identified as a "2022 Spring Allergy Capital." The area ranked #91 out of 100. Three groups of factors were used to identify the most challenging cities for people with allergies during the spring season: annual spring pollen scores; over the counter allergy medicine use; number of board-certified allergy specialists. *Asthma and Allergy Foundation of America, "Spring Allergy Capitals 2022," March 2, 2022*

- Portland was identified as a "2022 Fall Allergy Capital." The area ranked #95 out of 100. Three groups of factors were used to identify the most challenging cities for people with allergies during the fall season: annual fall pollen scores; over the counter allergy medicine use; number of board-certified allergy specialists. *Asthma and Allergy Foundation of America, "Fall Allergy Capitals 2022," March 2, 2022*

- Portland was identified as a "2022 Asthma Capital." The area ranked #83 out of the nation's 100 largest metropolitan areas. Criteria: estimated asthma prevalence; asthma-related mortality; and ER visits due to asthma. Risk factors analyzed but not factored in the rankings: annual pollen score; annual air quality; public smoking laws; access to board-certified asthma specialists; rescue and controller medication use; uninsured rate; poverty rate. *Asthma and Allergy Foundation of America, "Asthma Capitals 2022: The Most Challenging Places to Live With Asthma," September 14, 2022*

Real Estate Rankings

- *WalletHub* compared the most populated U.S. cities to determine which had the best markets for real estate agents. Portland ranked #16 where demand was high and pay was the best. Criteria: sales per agent; annual median wage for real-estate agents; monthly average starting salary for real estate agents; real estate job density and competition; unemployment rate; home turnover rate; housing-market health index; and other relevant metrics. *www.WalletHub.com, "2021 Best Places to Be a Real Estate Agent," May 12, 2021*

- The Portland metro area was identified as one of the 20 least affordable housing markets in the U.S. in 2022. The area ranked #169 out of 186 markets. Criteria: qualification for a mortgage loan with a 10 percent down payment on a typical home. *National Association of Realtors®, Qualifying Income Based on Sales Price of Existing Single-Family Homes for Metropolitan Areas, 2022*

- Portland was ranked #204 out of 235 metro areas in terms of housing affordability in 2022 by the National Association of Home Builders (#1 = most affordable). Criteria: the share of homes sold in that area affordable to a family earning the local median income, based on standard mortgage underwriting criteria. *National Association of Home Builders®, NAHB-Wells Fargo Housing Opportunity Index, 4th Quarter 2022*

Safety Rankings

- Allstate ranked the 200 largest cities in America in terms of driver safety. Portland ranked #181. Criteria: internal property damage claims over a two-year period from January 2016 to December 2017. The report helps increase the importance of safety and awareness behind the wheel. *Allstate, "Allstate America's Best Drivers Report, 2019" June 24, 2019*

Seniors/Retirement Rankings

- From its Best Cities for Successful Aging indexes, the Milken Institute generated rankings for metropolitan areas, weighing data in nine categories—health care, wellness, living arrangements, transportation and convenience, financial characteristics, education, employment, community engagement, and overall livability. The Portland metro area was ranked #40 overall in the large metro area category. *Milken Institute, "Best Cities for Successful Aging, 2017" March 14, 2017*

Sports/Recreation Rankings

- Portland was chosen as one of America's best cities for bicycling. The city ranked #5 out of 50. Criteria: cycling infrastructure that is safe and friendly for all ages; energy and bike culture. The editors evaluated cities with populations of 100,000 or more. *Bicycling, "The 50 Best Bike Cities in America," October 10, 2018*

Transportation Rankings

- Business Insider presented an AllTransit Performance Score ranking of public transportation in major U.S. cities and towns, with populations over 250,000, in which Portland earned the #13-ranked "Transit Score," awarded for frequency of service, access to jobs, quality and number of stops, and affordability. *www.businessinsider.com, "The 17 Major U.S. Cities with the Best Public Transportation," April 17, 2018*

- According to the INRIX "2022 Global Traffic Scorecard," Portland was identified as one of the most congested metro areas in the U.S. The area ranked #12 out of 25. Criteria: average annual time spent in traffic and average cost of congestion per motorist. *Inrix.com, "Return to Work, Higher Gas Prices & Inflation Drove Americans to Spend Hundreds More in Time and Money Commuting," January 10, 2023*

Women/Minorities Rankings

- *Women's Health*, together with the site Yelp, identified the 15 "Wellthiest" spots in the U.S. Portland appeared among the top for happiest, healthiest, outdoorsiest and Zen-iest. *Women's Health, "The 15 Wellthiest Cities in the U.S." July 5, 2017*

- Personal finance website *WalletHub* compared more than 180 U.S. cities across two key dimensions, "Hispanic Business-Friendliness" and "Hispanic Purchasing Power," to arrive at the most favorable conditions for Hispanic entrepreneurs. Portland was ranked #95 out of 182. Criteria includes: share of Hispanic-Owned Businesses; Hispanic entrepreneurship rate to median annual income of Hispanics; Small Business-Friendliness score; cost of living; and number of Hispanics with at least a bachelor's degree. *WalletHub.com, "2019's Best Cities for Hispanic Entrepreneurs," May 1, 2019*

Miscellaneous Rankings

- Despite the freedom to now travel internationally, plugged-in travel influencers and experts continue to rediscover their local regions. Portland appeared on a *Forbes* list of places in the U.S. that provide solace as well as local inspiration. Whether it be quirky things to see and do, delicious take out, outdoor exploring and daytrips, these places are must-see destinations. *Forbes, "The Best Places To Travel In The U.S. In 2023, According To The Experts," April 13, 2023*

- *MoveHub* ranked 446 hipster cities across 20 countries, using its new and improved *alternative* Hipster Index and Portland came out as #2 among the top 50. Criteria: population over 150,000; number of vintage boutiques; density of tattoo parlors; vegan places to eat; coffee shops; and density of vinyl record stores. *www.movehub.com, "The Hipster Index: Brighton Pips Portland to Global Top Spot," July 28, 2021*

- The watchdog site, Charity Navigator, conducted a study of charities in major markets both to analyze statistical differences in their financial, accountability, and transparency practices and to track year-to-year variations in individual philanthropic communities. The Portland metro area was ranked #10 among the 30 metro markets in the rating category of Overall Score. *www.charitynavigator.org, "2017 Metro Market Study," May 1, 2017*

- *WalletHub* compared the 150 most populated U.S. cities to determine their operating efficiency. A "Quality of Services" score was constructed for each city and then divided by the total budget per capita to reveal which were managed the best. Portland ranked #67. Criteria: financial stability; economy; education; safety; health; infrastructure and pollution. *www.WalletHub.com, "2022's Best- & Worst-Run Cities in America," June 21, 2022*

- The National Alliance to End Homelessness listed the 25 most populous metro areas with the highest rate of homelessness. The Portland metro area had a high rate of homelessness. Criteria: number of homeless people per 10,000 population in 2016. *National Alliance to End Homelessness, "Homelessness in the 25 Most Populous U.S. Metro Areas," September 1, 2017*

Business Environment

DEMOGRAPHICS

Population Growth

Area	1990 Census	2000 Census	2010 Census	2020 Census	Population Growth (%) 1990-2020	Population Growth (%) 2010-2020
City	485,833	529,121	583,776	652,503	34.3	11.8
MSA[1]	1,523,741	1,927,881	2,226,009	2,512,859	64.9	12.9
U.S.	248,709,873	281,421,906	308,745,538	331,449,281	33.3	7.4

Note: (1) Figures cover the Portland-Vancouver-Hillsboro, OR-WA Metropolitan Statistical Area
Source: U.S. Census Bureau, 1990 Census, 2000 Census, 2010 Census, 2020 Census

Race

Area	White Alone[2] (%)	Black Alone[2] (%)	Asian Alone[2] (%)	AIAN[3] Alone[2] (%)	NHOPI[4] Alone[2] (%)	Other Race Alone[2] (%)	Two or More Races (%)
City	68.8	5.9	8.1	1.1	0.6	4.8	10.7
MSA[1]	71.5	3.0	7.1	1.1	0.6	6.0	10.7
U.S.	61.6	12.4	6.0	1.1	0.2	8.4	10.2

Note: (1) Figures cover the Portland-Vancouver-Hillsboro, OR-WA Metropolitan Statistical Area; (2) Alone is defined as not being in combination with one or more other races; (3) American Indian and Alaska Native; (4) Native Hawaiian and Other Pacific Islander
Source: U.S. Census Bureau, 2020 Census

Hispanic or Latino Origin

Area	Total (%)	Mexican (%)	Puerto Rican (%)	Cuban (%)	Other (%)
City	10.3	7.0	0.5	0.4	2.3
MSA[1]	12.5	9.4	0.4	0.3	2.4
U.S.	18.4	11.2	1.8	0.7	4.7

Note: Persons of Hispanic or Latino origin can be of any race; (1) Figures cover the Portland-Vancouver-Hillsboro, OR-WA Metropolitan Statistical Area
Source: U.S. Census Bureau, 2017-2021 American Community Survey 5-Year Estimates

Age

Area	Under Age 5	Age 5–19	Age 20–34	Age 35–44	Age 45–54	Age 55–64	Age 65–74	Age 75–84	Age 85+	Median Age
City	4.5	14.6	25.8	17.2	13.1	10.8	8.9	3.7	1.4	37.6
MSA[1]	5.2	18.3	21.0	14.8	12.8	12.0	9.8	4.4	1.6	38.6
U.S.	5.6	19.2	20.2	12.7	12.4	13.1	10.0	4.9	1.9	38.8

Note: (1) Figures cover the Portland-Vancouver-Hillsboro, OR-WA Metropolitan Statistical Area
Source: U.S. Census Bureau, 2020 Census

Disability by Age

Area	All Ages	Under 18 Years Old	18 to 64 Years Old	65 Years and Over
City	12.1	4.8	9.9	33.4
MSA[1]	12.1	4.1	10.0	32.3
U.S.	12.6	4.4	10.3	33.4

Note: Figures show percent of the civilian noninstitutionalized population that reported having a disability. Disability status is determined from six types of difficulty: vision, hearing, cognitive, ambulatory, self-care, and independent living. For children under 5 years old, hearing and vision difficulty are used to determine disability status. For children between the ages of 5 and 14, disability status is determined from hearing, vision, cognitive, ambulatory, and self-care difficulties. For people aged 15 years and older, they are considered to have a disability if they have difficulty with any one of the six difficulty types; Note: (1) Figures cover the Portland-Vancouver-Hillsboro, OR-WA Metropolitan Statistical Area
Source: U.S. Census Bureau, 2017-2021 American Community Survey 5-Year Estimates

Ancestry

Area	German	Irish	English	American	Italian	Polish	French[2]	Scottish	Dutch
City	15.3	11.2	11.9	4.5	4.5	2.3	2.8	2.9	1.7
MSA[1]	16.4	10.5	11.7	4.6	3.7	1.8	2.7	2.7	1.7
U.S.	12.8	9.6	8.1	5.7	5.0	2.7	2.2	1.6	1.1

Note: Figures are the percentage of the total population reporting a particular ancestry. The nine most commonly reported ancestries in the U.S. are shown. Figures include multiple ancestries (e.g. if a person reported being Irish and Italian, they were included in both columns); (1) Figures cover the Portland-Vancouver-Hillsboro, OR-WA Metropolitan Statistical Area; (2) Excludes Basque
Source: U.S. Census Bureau, 2017-2021 American Community Survey 5-Year Estimates

Foreign-born Population

Area	Any Foreign Country	Percent of Population Born in							
		Asia	Mexico	Europe	Caribbean	Central America[2]	South America	Africa	Canada
City	13.1	6.0	1.9	2.5	0.2	0.4	0.3	0.9	0.5
MSA[1]	12.7	5.1	2.9	2.4	0.2	0.5	0.3	0.6	0.4
U.S.	13.6	4.2	3.3	1.5	1.4	1.1	1.1	0.8	0.2

Note: (1) Figures cover the Portland-Vancouver-Hillsboro, OR-WA Metropolitan Statistical Area; (2) Excludes Mexico.
Source: U.S. Census Bureau, 2017-2021 American Community Survey 5-Year Estimates

Household Size

Area	Persons in Household (%)							Average Household Size
	One	Two	Three	Four	Five	Six	Seven or More	
City	35.0	35.2	13.7	10.4	3.6	1.3	0.8	2.30
MSA[1]	26.9	35.6	15.5	13.3	5.3	2.0	1.3	2.50
U.S.	28.1	33.8	15.5	12.9	6.0	2.3	1.4	2.60

Note: (1) Figures cover the Portland-Vancouver-Hillsboro, OR-WA Metropolitan Statistical Area
Source: U.S. Census Bureau, 2017-2021 American Community Survey 5-Year Estimates

Household Relationships

Area	House-holder	Opposite-sex Spouse	Same-sex Spouse	Opposite-sex Unmarried Partner	Same-sex Unmarried Partner	Child[2]	Grand-child	Other Relatives	Non-relatives
City	43.2	14.9	0.7	4.4	0.6	21.2	1.1	3.7	7.2
MSA[1]	39.0	18.1	0.4	3.2	0.3	26.7	1.6	4.2	4.9
U.S.	38.3	17.5	0.2	2.5	0.2	28.3	2.4	4.8	3.4

Note: Figures are percent of the total population; (1) Figures cover the Portland-Vancouver-Hillsboro, OR-WA Metropolitan Statistical Area; (2) Includes biological, adopted, and stepchildren of the householder
Source: U.S. Census Bureau, 2020 Census

Gender

Area	Males	Females	Males per 100 Females
City	322,690	329,813	97.8
MSA[1]	1,240,947	1,271,912	97.6
U.S.	162,685,811	168,763,470	96.4

Note: (1) Figures cover the Portland-Vancouver-Hillsboro, OR-WA Metropolitan Statistical Area
Source: U.S. Census Bureau, 2020 Census

Marital Status

Area	Never Married	Now Married[2]	Separated	Widowed	Divorced
City	41.6	41.1	1.3	3.6	12.4
MSA[1]	32.8	49.6	1.3	4.3	12.0
U.S.	33.8	48.0	1.8	5.6	10.8

Note: Figures are percentages and cover the population 15 years of age and older; (1) Figures cover the Portland-Vancouver-Hillsboro, OR-WA Metropolitan Statistical Area; (2) Excludes separated
Source: U.S. Census Bureau, 2017-2021 American Community Survey 5-Year Estimates

Religious Groups by Family

Area	Catholic	Baptist	Methodist	LDS[2]	Pentecostal	Lutheran	Islam	Adventist	Other
MSA[1]	11.8	0.8	0.6	3.3	1.4	1.1	0.2	2.0	14.4
U.S.	18.7	7.3	3.0	2.0	1.8	1.7	1.3	1.3	11.6

Note: Figures are the number of adherents as a percentage of the total population and cover the eight largest religious groups in the U.S; (1) Figures cover the Portland-Vancouver-Hillsboro, OR-WA Metropolitan Statistical Area; (2) Church of Jesus Christ of Latter-day Saints
Sources: 2020 U.S. Religion Census, Association of Statisticians of American Religious Bodies; The Association of Religion Data Archives (ARDA)

Religious Groups by Tradition

Area	Catholic	Evangelical Protestant	Mainline Protestant	Black Protestant	Islam	Judaism	Hinduism	Orthodox	Buddhism
MSA[1]	11.8	14.6	2.3	0.4	0.2	0.3	0.7	0.3	0.4
U.S.	18.7	16.5	5.2	2.3	1.3	0.6	0.4	0.4	0.3

Note: Figures are the number of adherents as a percentage of the total population; (1) Figures cover the Portland-Vancouver-Hillsboro, OR-WA Metropolitan Statistical Area
Sources: 2020 U.S. Religion Census, Association of Statisticians of American Religious Bodies; The Association of Religion Data Archives (ARDA)

ECONOMY

Gross Metropolitan Product

Area	2020	2021	2022	2023	Rank[2]
MSA[1]	168.4	184.1	201.8	214.4	25

Note: Figures are in billions of dollars; (1) Figures cover the Portland-Vancouver-Hillsboro, OR-WA Metropolitan Statistical Area; (2) Rank is based on 2021 data and ranges from 1 to 381
Source: U.S. Conference of Mayors, U.S. Metro Economies: U.S. Metros Compared to Global and State Economies, June 2022

Economic Growth

Area	2018-20 (%)	2021 (%)	2022 (%)	2023 (%)	Rank[2]
MSA[1]	-0.6	5.8	4.2	2.9	179
U.S.	-0.6	5.7	3.1	2.9	—

Note: Figures are real gross metropolitan product (GMP) growth rates and represent average annual percent change; (1) Figures cover the Portland-Vancouver-Hillsboro, OR-WA Metropolitan Statistical Area; (2) Rank is based on 2020 2-year average annual percent change and ranges from 1 to 381
Source: U.S. Conference of Mayors, U.S. Metro Economies: U.S. Metros Compared to Global and State Economies, June 2022

Metropolitan Area Exports

Area	2016	2017	2018	2019	2020	2021	Rank[2]
MSA[1]	20,256.8	20,788.8	21,442.9	23,761.9	27,824.7	33,787.5	10

Note: Figures are in millions of dollars; (1) Figures cover the Portland-Vancouver-Hillsboro, OR-WA Metropolitan Statistical Area; (2) Rank is based on 2021 data and ranges from 1 to 388
Source: U.S. Department of Commerce, International Trade Administration, Office of Trade and Economic Analysis, Industry and Analysis, Exports by Metropolitan Area, data extracted March 16, 2023

Building Permits

Area	Single-Family			Multi-Family			Total		
	2021	2022	Pct. Chg.	2021	2022	Pct. Chg.	2021	2022	Pct. Chg.
City	474	489	3.2	2,554	1,708	-33.1	3,028	2,197	-27.4
MSA[1]	8,008	6,029	-24.7	7,015	6,949	-0.9	15,023	12,978	-13.6
U.S.	1,115,400	975,600	-12.5	621,600	689,500	10.9	1,737,000	1,665,100	-4.1

Note: (1) Figures cover the Portland-Vancouver-Hillsboro, OR-WA Metropolitan Statistical Area; Figures represent new, privately-owned housing units authorized (unadjusted data); All permit data are based on estimates with imputation
Source: U.S. Census Bureau, Manufacturing, Mining, and Construction Statistics, Building Permits, 2021, 2022

Bankruptcy Filings

Area	Business Filings			Nonbusiness Filings		
	2021	2022	% Chg.	2021	2022	% Chg.
Multnomah County	33	17	-48.5	802	749	-6.6
U.S.	14,347	13,481	-6.0	399,269	374,240	-6.3

Note: Business filings include Chapter 7, Chapter 9, Chapter 11, Chapter 12, Chapter 13, Chapter 15, and Section 304; Nonbusiness filings include Chapter 7, Chapter 11, and Chapter 13
Source: Administrative Office of the U.S. Courts, Business and Nonbusiness Bankruptcy, County Cases Commenced by Chapter of the Bankruptcy Code, During the 12-Month Period Ending December 31, 2021 and Business and Nonbusiness Bankruptcy, County Cases Commenced by Chapter of the Bankruptcy Code, During the 12-Month Period Ending December 31, 2022

Housing Vacancy Rates

Area	Gross Vacancy Rate[2] (%)			Year-Round Vacancy Rate[3] (%)			Rental Vacancy Rate[4] (%)			Homeowner Vacancy Rate[5] (%)		
	2020	2021	2022	2020	2021	2022	2020	2021	2022	2020	2021	2022
MSA[1]	5.5	6.0	5.4	4.9	5.6	5.1	4.3	5.2	4.0	0.8	0.9	1.2
U.S.	10.6	10.8	10.5	8.2	8.4	8.2	6.3	6.1	5.8	1.0	0.9	0.8

Note: (1) Figures cover the Portland-Vancouver-Hillsboro, OR-WA Metropolitan Statistical Area; (2) The percentage of the total housing inventory that is vacant; (3) The percentage of the housing inventory (excluding seasonal units) that is year-round vacant; (4) The percentage of rental inventory that is vacant for rent; (5) The percentage of homeowner inventory that is vacant for sale
Source: U.S. Census Bureau, Housing Vacancies and Homeownership Annual Statistics: 2020, 2021, 2022

INCOME

Income

Area	Per Capita ($)	Median Household ($)	Average Household ($)
City	47,289	78,476	106,948
MSA[1]	42,946	82,901	108,110
U.S.	37,638	69,021	97,196

Note: (1) Figures cover the Portland-Vancouver-Hillsboro, OR-WA Metropolitan Statistical Area
Source: U.S. Census Bureau, 2017-2021 American Community Survey 5-Year Estimates

Household Income Distribution

| Area | Percent of Households Earning | | | | | | | |
	Under $15,000	$15,000 -$24,999	$25,000 -$34,999	$35,000 -$49,999	$50,000 -$74,999	$75,000 -$99,999	$100,000 -$149,999	$150,000 and up
City	9.8	6.3	6.7	9.7	15.7	12.6	17.5	21.8
MSA[1]	7.2	5.7	6.3	10.0	16.3	13.6	19.5	21.5
U.S.	9.4	7.8	8.2	11.4	16.8	12.8	16.3	17.3

Note: (1) Figures cover the Portland-Vancouver-Hillsboro, OR-WA Metropolitan Statistical Area
Source: U.S. Census Bureau, 2017-2021 American Community Survey 5-Year Estimates

Poverty Rate

Area	All Ages	Under 18 Years Old	18 to 64 Years Old	65 Years and Over
City	12.6	13.5	12.7	10.6
MSA[1]	9.9	11.3	9.8	8.2
U.S.	12.6	17.0	11.8	9.6

Note: Figures are percentage of people whose income during the past 12 months was below the poverty level;
(1) Figures cover the Portland-Vancouver-Hillsboro, OR-WA Metropolitan Statistical Area
Source: U.S. Census Bureau, 2017-2021 American Community Survey 5-Year Estimates

EMPLOYMENT

Labor Force and Employment

| Area | Civilian Labor Force | | | Workers Employed | | |
	Dec. 2021	Dec. 2022	% Chg.	Dec. 2021	Dec. 2022	% Chg.
City	387,410	393,179	1.5	373,537	376,724	0.9
MSA[1]	1,369,607	1,391,563	1.6	1,322,133	1,334,787	1.0
U.S.	161,696,000	164,224,000	1.6	155,732,000	158,872,000	2.0

Note: Data is not seasonally adjusted and covers workers 16 years of age and older; (1) Figures cover the
Portland-Vancouver-Hillsboro, OR-WA Metropolitan Statistical Area
Source: Bureau of Labor Statistics, Local Area Unemployment Statistics

Unemployment Rate

| Area | 2022 | | | | | | | | | | | |
	Jan.	Feb.	Mar.	Apr.	May	Jun.	Jul.	Aug.	Sep.	Oct.	Nov.	Dec.
City	4.5	3.9	3.9	3.4	3.0	3.5	3.7	4.1	3.8	3.8	4.1	4.2
MSA[1]	4.4	3.9	3.9	3.4	3.1	3.5	3.6	4.0	3.7	3.7	3.9	4.1
U.S.	4.4	4.1	3.8	3.3	3.4	3.8	3.8	3.8	3.3	3.4	3.4	3.3

Note: Data is not seasonally adjusted and covers workers 16 years of age and older; (1) Figures cover the
Portland-Vancouver-Hillsboro, OR-WA Metropolitan Statistical Area
Source: Bureau of Labor Statistics, Local Area Unemployment Statistics

Average Wages

Occupation	$/Hr.	Occupation	$/Hr.
Accountants and Auditors	40.08	Maintenance and Repair Workers	24.55
Automotive Mechanics	26.62	Marketing Managers	66.94
Bookkeepers	24.24	Network and Computer Systems Admin.	48.17
Carpenters	30.98	Nurses, Licensed Practical	33.26
Cashiers	16.34	Nurses, Registered	53.66
Computer Programmers	54.65	Nursing Assistants	21.15
Computer Systems Analysts	56.22	Office Clerks, General	21.40
Computer User Support Specialists	30.08	Physical Therapists	46.36
Construction Laborers	25.00	Physicians	111.11
Cooks, Restaurant	18.56	Plumbers, Pipefitters and Steamfitters	40.51
Customer Service Representatives	21.22	Police and Sheriff's Patrol Officers	40.50
Dentists	91.21	Postal Service Mail Carriers	27.17
Electricians	41.15	Real Estate Sales Agents	28.64
Engineers, Electrical	51.53	Retail Salespersons	19.03
Fast Food and Counter Workers	15.88	Sales Representatives, Technical/Scientific	56.64
Financial Managers	75.43	Secretaries, Exc. Legal/Medical/Executive	24.16
First-Line Supervisors of Office Workers	32.27	Security Guards	18.14
General and Operations Managers	56.83	Surgeons	n/a
Hairdressers/Cosmetologists	18.86	Teacher Assistants, Exc. Postsecondary*	19.64
Home Health and Personal Care Aides	17.48	Teachers, Secondary School, Exc. Sp. Ed.*	41.94
Janitors and Cleaners	18.11	Telemarketers	19.08
Landscaping/Groundskeeping Workers	20.88	Truck Drivers, Heavy/Tractor-Trailer	28.25
Lawyers	73.57	Truck Drivers, Light/Delivery Services	22.77
Maids and Housekeeping Cleaners	17.60	Waiters and Waitresses	18.37

Note: Wage data covers the Portland-Vancouver-Hillsboro, OR-WA Metropolitan Statistical Area; (*) Hourly
wages were calculated from annual wage data based on a 40 hour work week; n/a not available.
Source: Bureau of Labor Statistics, Metro Area Occupational Employment & Wage Estimates, May 2022

Employment by Industry

| Sector | MSA[1] | | U.S. |
	Number of Employees	Percent of Total	Percent of Total
Construction	82,500	6.6	5.0
Private Education and Health Services	187,300	15.0	16.1
Financial Activities	77,400	6.2	5.9
Government	153,300	12.2	14.5
Information	28,300	2.3	2.0
Leisure and Hospitality	117,400	9.4	10.3
Manufacturing	127,300	10.2	8.4
Mining and Logging	1,100	0.1	0.4
Other Services	42,000	3.4	3.7
Professional and Business Services	202,900	16.2	14.7
Retail Trade	120,900	9.7	10.2
Transportation, Warehousing, and Utilities	54,400	4.3	4.9
Wholesale Trade	57,400	4.6	3.9

Note: Figures are non-farm employment as of December 2022. Figures are not seasonally adjusted and include workers 16 years of age and older; (1) Figures cover the Portland-Vancouver-Hillsboro, OR-WA Metropolitan Statistical Area
Source: Bureau of Labor Statistics, Current Employment Statistics, Employment, Hours, and Earnings

Employment by Occupation

Occupation Classification	City (%)	MSA[1] (%)	U.S. (%)
Management, Business, Science, and Arts	52.0	44.7	40.3
Natural Resources, Construction, and Maintenance	5.0	7.6	8.7
Production, Transportation, and Material Moving	9.7	12.2	13.1
Sales and Office	17.9	20.1	20.9
Service	15.4	15.5	17.0

Note: Figures cover employed civilians 16 years of age and older; (1) Figures cover the Portland-Vancouver-Hillsboro, OR-WA Metropolitan Statistical Area
Source: U.S. Census Bureau, 2017-2021 American Community Survey 5-Year Estimates

Occupations with Greatest Projected Employment Growth: 2022 – 2024

Occupation[1]	2022 Employment	2024 Projected Employment	Numeric Employment Change	Percent Employment Change
Fast Food and Counter Workers	66,590	76,330	9,740	14.6
Waiters and Waitresses	26,060	30,030	3,970	15.2
Cooks, Restaurant	20,600	24,040	3,440	16.7
Home Health and Personal Care Aides	31,660	34,200	2,540	8.0
Maids and Housekeeping Cleaners	16,400	18,280	1,880	11.5
First-Line Supervisors of Food Preparation and Serving Workers	13,120	14,930	1,810	13.8
Bartenders	8,410	9,990	1,580	18.8
General and Operations Managers	36,530	37,990	1,460	4.0
Stockers and Order Fillers	39,960	41,380	1,420	3.6
Retail Salespersons	58,520	59,830	1,310	2.2

Note: Projections cover Oregon; (1) Sorted by numeric employment change
Source: www.projectionscentral.com, State Occupational Projections, 2022–2024 Short-Term Projections

Fastest-Growing Occupations: 2022 – 2024

Occupation[1]	2022 Employment	2024 Projected Employment	Numeric Employment Change	Percent Employment Change
First-Line Supervisors of Gambling Services Workers	220	280	60	27.3
Gaming Dealers	310	390	80	25.8
Film and Video Editors	390	480	90	23.1
Multimedia Artists and Animators	820	990	170	20.7
Tour and Travel Guides	560	670	110	19.6
Fine Artists, Including Painters, Sculptors, and Illustrators	620	740	120	19.4
Bartenders	8,410	9,990	1,580	18.8
Ushers, Lobby Attendants, and Ticket Takers	610	720	110	18.0
Hotel, Motel, and Resort Desk Clerks	3,650	4,300	650	17.8
Fitness Trainers and Aerobics Instructors	4,800	5,650	850	17.7

Note: Projections cover Oregon; (1) Sorted by percent employment change and excludes occupations with numeric employment change less than 50
Source: www.projectionscentral.com, State Occupational Projections, 2022–2024 Short-Term Projections

CITY FINANCES

City Government Finances

Component	2020 ($000)	2020 ($ per capita)
Total Revenues	2,233,651	3,412
Total Expenditures	2,043,421	3,121
Debt Outstanding	3,393,833	5,183
Cash and Securities[1]	1,998,821	3,053

Note: (1) Cash and security holdings of a government at the close of its fiscal year, including those of its dependent agencies, utilities, and liquor stores.
Source: U.S. Census Bureau, State & Local Government Finances 2020

City Government Revenue by Source

Source	2020 ($000)	2020 ($ per capita)	2020 (%)
General Revenue			
From Federal Government	39,568	60	1.8
From State Government	77,272	118	3.5
From Local Governments	122,702	187	5.5
Taxes			
Property	628,695	960	28.1
Sales and Gross Receipts	244,829	374	11.0
Personal Income	0	0	0.0
Corporate Income	0	0	0.0
Motor Vehicle License	0	0	0.0
Other Taxes	244,540	373	10.9
Current Charges	592,722	905	26.5
Liquor Store	0	0	0.0
Utility	204,858	313	9.2

Source: U.S. Census Bureau, State & Local Government Finances 2020

City Government Expenditures by Function

Function	2020 ($000)	2020 ($ per capita)	2020 (%)
General Direct Expenditures			
Air Transportation	0	0	0.0
Corrections	0	0	0.0
Education	0	0	0.0
Employment Security Administration	0	0	0.0
Financial Administration	64,514	98	3.2
Fire Protection	133,080	203	6.5
General Public Buildings	31,428	48	1.5
Governmental Administration, Other	52,067	79	2.5
Health	0	0	0.0
Highways	265,183	405	13.0
Hospitals	0	0	0.0
Housing and Community Development	130,161	198	6.4
Interest on General Debt	118,335	180	5.8
Judicial and Legal	14,245	21	0.7
Libraries	0	0	0.0
Parking	14,572	22	0.7
Parks and Recreation	153,364	234	7.5
Police Protection	230,653	352	11.3
Public Welfare	0	0	0.0
Sewerage	314,413	480	15.4
Solid Waste Management	6,233	9	0.3
Veterans' Services	0	0	0.0
Liquor Store	0	0	0.0
Utility	278,603	425	13.6

Source: U.S. Census Bureau, State & Local Government Finances 2020

TAXES

State Corporate Income Tax Rates

State	Tax Rate (%)	Income Brackets ($)	Num. of Brackets	Financial Institution Tax Rate (%)[a]	Federal Income Tax Ded.
Oregon	6.6 - 7.6 (s)	1 million	2	6.6 - 7.6 (s)	No

Note: Tax rates as of January 1, 2023; (a) Rates listed are the corporate income tax rate applied to financial institutions or excise taxes based on income. Some states have other taxes based upon the value of deposits or shares; (s) Oregon's minimum tax for C corporations depends on the Oregon sales of the filing group. The minimum tax ranges from $150 for corporations with sales under $500,000, up to $100,000 for companies with sales of $100 million or above. Oregon also imposes Corporate Activity Tax [CAT] of $250 plus 0.57% of activity in excess of $1 million.
Source: Federation of Tax Administrators, State Corporate Income Tax Rates, January 1, 2023

State Individual Income Tax Rates

State	Tax Rate (%)	Income Brackets ($)	Personal Exemptions ($)			Standard Ded. ($)	
			Single	Married	Depend.	Single	Married
Oregon (a)	4.75 - 9.9	4,050 -125,000 (b)	236	472	236 (c)	2,605	5,210

Note: Tax rates as of January 1, 2023; Local- and county-level taxes are not included; (a) 16 states have statutory provision for automatically adjusting to the rate of inflation the dollar values of the income tax brackets, standard deductions, and/or personal exemptions. Oregon does not index the income brackets for $125,000 and over; (b) For joint returns, taxes are twice the tax on half the couple's income; (c) The personal exemption takes the form of a tax credit instead of a deduction
Source: Federation of Tax Administrators, State Individual Income Tax Rates, January 1, 2023

Various State Sales and Excise Tax Rates

State	State Sales Tax (%)	Gasoline[1] ($/gal.)	Cigarette[2] ($/pack)	Spirits[3] ($/gal.)	Wine[4] ($/gal.)	Beer[5] ($/gal.)	Recreational Marijuana (%)
Oregon	None	0.3883	3.33	22.86	0.67	0.08	(p)

Note: All tax rates as of January 1, 2023; (1) The American Petroleum Institute has developed a methodology for determining the average tax rate on a gallon of fuel. Rates may include any of the following: excise taxes, environmental fees, storage tank fees, other fees or taxes, general sales tax, and local taxes; (2) The federal excise tax of $1.0066 per pack and local taxes are not included; (3) Rates are those applicable to off-premise sales of 40% alcohol by volume (a.b.v.) distilled spirits in 750ml containers. Local excise taxes are excluded; (4) Rates are those applicable to off-premise sales of 11% a.b.v. non-carbonated wine in 750ml containers; (5) Rates are those applicable to off-premise sales of 4.7% a.b.v. beer in 12 ounce containers; (p) 17% excise tax (retail price)
Source: Tax Foundation, 2023 Facts & Figures: How Does Your State Compare?

State Business Tax Climate Index Rankings

State	Overall Rank	Corporate Tax Rank	Individual Income Tax Rank	Sales Tax Rank	Property Tax Rank	Unemployment Insurance Tax Rank
Oregon	24	49	42	4	20	36

Note: The index is a measure of how each state's tax laws affect economic performance. The lower the rank, the more favorable a state's tax system is for business. States without a given tax are given a ranking of 1. The scores/rankings for the District of Columbia do not affect other states. The 2023 index represents the tax climate as of July 1, 2022.
Source: Tax Foundation, State Business Tax Climate Index 2023

TRANSPORTATION

Means of Transportation to Work

Area	Car/Truck/Van		Public Transportation			Bicycle	Walked	Other Means	Worked at Home
	Drove Alone	Car-pooled	Bus	Subway	Railroad				
City	53.8	7.4	7.2	0.5	0.2	4.7	5.1	3.2	18.0
MSA[1]	66.2	8.4	3.6	0.4	0.2	1.7	3.1	2.0	14.4
U.S.	73.2	8.6	2.0	1.6	0.5	0.5	2.5	1.5	9.7

Note: Figures are percentages and cover workers 16 years of age and older; (1) Figures cover the Portland-Vancouver-Hillsboro, OR-WA Metropolitan Statistical Area
Source: U.S. Census Bureau, 2017-2021 American Community Survey 5-Year Estimates

Travel Time to Work

Area	Less Than 10 Minutes	10 to 19 Minutes	20 to 29 Minutes	30 to 44 Minutes	45 to 59 Minutes	60 to 89 Minutes	90 Minutes or More
City	8.3	28.2	26.8	24.0	7.1	4.1	1.5
MSA[1]	10.8	27.5	23.0	22.7	8.9	5.1	2.0
U.S.	12.4	28.5	21.0	20.9	8.2	6.2	2.9

Note: Note: Figures are percentages and include workers 16 years old and over; (1) Figures cover the Portland-Vancouver-Hillsboro, OR-WA Metropolitan Statistical Area
Source: U.S. Census Bureau, 2017-2021 American Community Survey 5-Year Estimates

Key Congestion Measures

Measure	1990	2000	2010	2015	2020
Annual Hours of Delay, Total (000)	16,712	37,832	57,165	71,704	36,065
Annual Hours of Delay, Per Auto Commuter	28	44	51	62	31
Annual Congestion Cost, Per Auto Commuter ($)	553	941	1,130	1,308	690

Note: Covers the Portland OR-WA urban area
Source: Texas A&M Transportation Institute, 2021 Urban Mobility Report

Freeway Travel Time Index

Measure	1985	1990	1995	2000	2005	2010	2015	2020
Urban Area Index[1]	1.16	1.19	1.25	1.30	1.32	1.32	1.36	1.10
Urban Area Rank[1,2]	10	12	6	5	8	8	6	29

Note: Freeway Travel Time Index—the ratio of travel time in the peak period to the travel time at free-flow conditions. For example, a value of 1.30 indicates a 20-minute free-flow trip takes 26 minutes in the peak (20 minutes x 1.30 = 26 minutes); (1) Covers the Portland OR-WA urban area; (2) Rank is based on 101 larger urban areas (#1 = highest travel time index)
Source: Texas A&M Transportation Institute, 2021 Urban Mobility Report

Public Transportation

Agency Name / Mode of Transportation	Vehicles Operated in Maximum Service[1]	Annual Unlinked Passenger Trips[2] (in thous.)	Annual Passenger Miles[3] (in thous.)
Tri-County Metropolitan Transportation District of Oregon (Tri-Met)			
Bus (directly operated)	512	25,138.0	98,687.2
Demand Response (purchased transportation)	100	244.8	1,812.1
Demand Response - Taxi	18	23.5	279.2
Hybrid Rail (purchased transportation)	4	84.7	676.0
Light Rail (directly operated)	102	14,817.5	77,158.0
Ride Connection, Inc.			
Bus (directly operated)	7	61.9	199.2
Demand Response (directly operated)	22	27.9	275.8
Demand Response - Taxi	41	48.5	288.8
City of Portland			
Streetcar Rail (purchased transportation)	12	1,564.3	2,080.6
Special Mobility Services			
Bus (directly operated)	5	4.9	n/a
Demand Response (directly operated)	1	2.0	n/a

Note: (1) Number of revenue vehicles operated by the given mode and type of service to meet the annual maximum service requirement. This is the revenue vehicle count during the peak season of the year; on the week and day that maximum service is provided. Vehicles operated in maximum service (VOMS) exclude atypical days and one-time special events; (2) Number of passengers who boarded public transportation vehicles. Passengers are counted each time they board a vehicle no matter how many vehicles they use to travel from their origin to their destination. (3) Sum of the distances ridden by all passengers during the entire fiscal year.
Source: Federal Transit Administration, National Transit Database, 2021

Air Transportation

Airport Name and Code / Type of Service	Passenger Airlines[1]	Passenger Enplanements	Freight Carriers[2]	Freight (lbs)
Portland International (PDX)				
Domestic service (U.S. carriers - 2022)	27	6,967,743	17	317,498,801
International service (U.S. carriers - 2021)	4	38,432	4	128,847

Note: (1) Includes all U.S.-based major, minor and commuter airlines that carried at least one passenger during the year; (2) Includes all U.S.-based airlines and freight carriers that transported at least one pound of freight during the year.
Source: Bureau of Transportation Statistics, The Intermodal Transportation Database, Air Carriers: T-100 Domestic Market (U.S. Carriers), 2022; Bureau of Transportation Statistics, The Intermodal Transportation Database, Air Carriers: T-100 International Market (U.S. Carriers), 2021

BUSINESSES

Major Business Headquarters

Company Name	Industry	Rankings	
		Fortune[1]	Forbes[2]
No companies listed	-	-	-

Note: (1) Companies that produce a 10-K are ranked 1 to 500 based on 2021 revenue; (2) All private companies with at least $2 billion in annual revenue through the end of their most current fiscal year are ranked 1 to 246; companies listed are headquartered in the city; dashes indicate no ranking
Source: Fortune, "Fortune 500," 2022; Forbes, "America's Largest Private Companies," 2022

Fastest-Growing Businesses

According to *Initiative for a Competitive Inner City (ICIC)*, Portland is home to two of America's 100 fastest-growing "inner city" companies: **Above The Fray** (#2); **Pepper Foster Consulting** (#10). Criteria for inclusion: company must be headquartered in or have 51 percent or more of its physical operations in an economically distressed urban area; must be an independent, for-profit corporation, partnership or proprietorship; must have 10 or more employees and have a five-year sales history that includes sales of at least $200,000 in the base year and at least $1 million in the current year with no decrease in sales over the two most recent years. Companies were ranked overall by revenue growth over the five-year period between 2017 and 2021. *Initiative for a Competitive Inner City (ICIC), "Inner City 100 Companies," 2022*

According to Deloitte, Portland is home to one of North America's 500 fastest-growing high-technology companies: **Brandlive** (#458). Companies are ranked by percentage growth in revenue over a four-year period. Criteria for inclusion: company must be headquartered within North America; must own proprietary intellectual property or technology that is sold to customers in products that contributes to a significant portion of the company's operating revenue; must have been in business for a minumum of four years with 2018 operating revenues of at least $50,000 USD/CD and 2021 operating revenues of at least $5 million USD/CD. *Deloitte, 2022 Technology Fast 500*[TM]

Living Environment

COST OF LIVING

Cost of Living Index

Composite Index	Groceries	Housing	Utilities	Trans-portation	Health Care	Misc. Goods/ Services
124.3	107.9	161.8	91.6	122.0	106.1	112.7

Note: The Cost of Living Index measures regional differences in the cost of consumer goods and services, excluding taxes and non-consumer expenditures, for professional and managerial households in the top income quintile. It is based on more than 50,000 prices covering almost 60 different items for which prices are collected three times a year by chambers of commerce, economic development organizations or university applied economic centers in each participating urban area. The numbers shown should be read as a percentage above or below the national average of 100. For example, a value of 115.4 in the groceries column indicates that grocery prices are 15.4% higher than the national average. Small differences in the index numbers should not be interpreted as significant; Figures cover the Portland OR urban area.
Source: The Council for Community and Economic Research, Cost of Living Index, 2022

Grocery Prices

Area[1]	T-Bone Steak ($/pound)	Frying Chicken ($/pound)	Whole Milk ($/half gal.)	Eggs ($/dozen)	Orange Juice ($/64 oz.)	Coffee ($/11.5 oz.)
City[2]	12.15	1.28	2.88	2.75	4.10	6.48
Avg.	13.81	1.59	2.43	2.25	3.85	4.95
Min.	10.17	0.90	1.51	1.30	2.90	3.46
Max.	19.35	3.30	4.32	4.32	5.31	8.59

*Note: (1) Values for the local area are compared with the average, minimum and maximum values for all 286 areas in the Cost of Living Index; (2) Figures cover the Portland OR urban area; **T-Bone Steak** (price per pound); **Frying Chicken** (price per pound, whole fryer); **Whole Milk** (half gallon carton); **Eggs** (price per dozen, Grade A, large); **Orange Juice** (64 oz. Tropicana or Florida Natural); **Coffee** (11.5 oz. can, vacuum-packed, Maxwell House, Hills Bros, or Folgers).*
Source: The Council for Community and Economic Research, Cost of Living Index, 2022

Housing and Utility Costs

Area[1]	New Home Price ($)	Apartment Rent ($/month)	All Electric ($/month)	Part Electric ($/month)	Other Energy ($/month)	Telephone ($/month)
City[2]	661,664	2,636	-	80.74	76.64	181.33
Avg.	450,913	1,371	176.41	99.93	76.96	190.22
Min.	229,283	546	100.84	31.56	27.15	174.27
Max.	2,434,977	4,569	356.86	249.59	272.24	208.31

*Note: (1) Values for the local area are compared with the average, minimum and maximum values for all 286 areas in the Cost of Living Index; (2) Figures cover the Portland OR urban area; **New Home Price** (2,400 sf living area, 8,000 sf lot, in urban area with full utilities); **Apartment Rent** (950 sf 2 bedroom/1.5 or 2 bath, unfurnished, excluding all utilities except water); **All Electric** (average monthly cost for an all-electric home); **Part Electric** (average monthly cost for a part-electric home); **Other Energy** (average monthly cost for natural gas, fuel oil, coal, wood, and any other forms of energy except electricity); **Telephone** (price includes the base monthly rate plus taxes and fees for three lines of mobile phone service).*
Source: The Council for Community and Economic Research, Cost of Living Index, 2022

Health Care, Transportation, and Other Costs

Area[1]	Doctor ($/visit)	Dentist ($/visit)	Optometrist ($/visit)	Gasoline ($/gallon)	Beauty Salon ($/visit)	Men's Shirt ($)
City[2]	142.04	113.83	122.48	4.72	56.61	32.88
Avg.	124.91	107.77	117.66	3.86	43.31	34.21
Min.	36.61	58.25	51.79	2.90	22.18	13.05
Max.	250.21	162.58	371.96	5.54	85.61	63.54

*Note: (1) Values for the local area are compared with the average, minimum and maximum values for all 286 areas in the Cost of Living Index; (2) Figures cover the Portland OR urban area; **Doctor** (general practitioners routine exam of an established patient); **Dentist** (adult teeth cleaning and periodic oral examination); **Optometrist** (full vision eye exam for established adult patient); **Gasoline** (one gallon regular unleaded, national brand, including all taxes, cash price at self-service pump if available); **Beauty Salon** (woman's shampoo, trim, and blow-dry); **Men's Shirt** (cotton/polyester dress shirt, pinpoint weave, long sleeves).*
Source: The Council for Community and Economic Research, Cost of Living Index, 2022

HOUSING

Homeownership Rate

Area	2015 (%)	2016 (%)	2017 (%)	2018 (%)	2019 (%)	2020 (%)	2021 (%)	2022 (%)
MSA[1]	58.9	61.8	61.1	59.2	60.0	62.5	64.1	65.2
U.S.	63.7	63.4	63.9	64.6	64.4	64.6	65.5	65.8

Note: (1) Figures cover the Portland-Vancouver-Hillsboro, OR-WA Metropolitan Statistical Area
Source: U.S. Census Bureau, Housing Vacancies and Homeownership Annual Statistics: 2015-2022

House Price Index (HPI)

Area	National Ranking[2]	Quarterly Change (%)	One-Year Change (%)	Five-Year Change (%)	Since 1991Q1 (%)
MSA[1]	247	-2.87	4.63	43.13	493.76
U.S.[3]	—	0.34	8.41	58.44	289.08

Note: The HPI is a weighted repeat sales index. It measures average price changes in repeat sales or refinancings on the same properties. This information is obtained by reviewing repeat mortgage transactions on single-family properties whose mortgages have been purchased or securitized by Fannie Mae or Freddie Mac since January 1975; (1) Figures cover the Portland-Vancouver-Hillsboro, OR-WA Metropolitan Statistical Area; (2) Rankings are based on annual percentage change for all metro areas containing at least 15,000 transactions over the last 10 years and ranges from 1 to 257; (3) figures based on a weighted average of Census Division estimates using a seasonally adjusted, purchase-only index; all figures are for the period ending December 31, 2022
Source: Federal Housing Finance Agency, Change in FHFA Metropolitan Area House Price Indexes, 2022Q4

Median Single-Family Home Prices

Area	2020	2021	2022[p]	Percent Change 2021 to 2022
MSA[1]	451.0	536.4	591.0	10.2
U.S. Average	300.2	357.1	392.6	9.9

Note: Figures are median sales prices of existing single-family homes in thousands of dollars; (p) preliminary; (1) Figures cover the Portland-Vancouver-Hillsboro, OR-WA Metropolitan Statistical Area
Source: National Association of Realtors, Median Sales Price of Existing Single-Family Homes for Metropolitan Areas, 4th Quarter 2022

Qualifying Income Based on Median Sales Price of Existing Single-Family Homes

Area	With 5% Down ($)	With 10% Down ($)	With 20% Down ($)
MSA[1]	169,787	160,851	142,978
U.S. Average	112,234	106,237	94,513

Note: Figures are preliminary; Qualifying income is based on a mortgage rate of 6.77%. Monthly principal and interest payment is limited to 25% of income; (1) Figures cover the Portland-Vancouver-Hillsboro, OR-WA Metropolitan Statistical Area
Source: National Association of Realtors, Qualifying Income Based on Median Sales Price of Existing Single-Family Homes for Metropolitan Areas, 4th Quarter 2022

Home Value

Area	Under $100,000	$100,000 -$199,999	$200,000 -$299,999	$300,000 -$399,999	$400,000 -$499,999	$500,000 -$999,999	$1,000,000 or more	Median ($)
City	2.6	2.8	9.9	21.8	20.5	38.3	4.1	462,800
MSA[1]	4.2	3.7	12.4	25.2	21.3	29.7	3.5	421,300
U.S.	16.2	24.2	20.1	13.6	8.3	13.6	4.1	244,900

Note: Figures are percentages except for median and cover owner-occupied housing units; (1) Figures cover the Portland-Vancouver-Hillsboro, OR-WA Metropolitan Statistical Area
Source: U.S. Census Bureau, 2017-2021 American Community Survey 5-Year Estimates

Year Housing Structure Built

Area	2020 or Later	2010 -2019	2000 -2009	1990 -1999	1980 -1989	1970 -1979	1960 -1969	1950 -1959	1940 -1949	Before 1940	Median Year
City	0.2	8.9	9.9	7.9	6.8	10.8	8.6	11.4	7.8	27.7	1964
MSA[1]	0.3	9.2	14.0	17.3	11.3	16.7	8.2	6.9	4.5	11.7	1982
U.S.	0.2	7.3	13.6	13.6	13.2	14.8	10.3	10.0	4.7	12.2	1979

Note: Figures are percentages except for Median Year; Note: (1) Figures cover the Portland-Vancouver-Hillsboro, OR-WA Metropolitan Statistical Area
Source: U.S. Census Bureau, 2017-2021 American Community Survey 5-Year Estimates

Gross Monthly Rent

Area	Under $500	$500 -$999	$1,000 -$1,499	$1,500 -$1,999	$2,000 -$2,499	$2,500 -$2,999	$3,000 and up	Median ($)
City	5.6	14.2	37.6	25.6	10.8	3.9	2.3	1,406
MSA[1]	4.1	12.6	38.8	28.4	10.8	3.2	2.0	1,434
U.S.	8.1	30.5	30.8	16.8	7.3	3.5	3.1	1,163

Note: Figures are percentages except for median; Gross rent is the contract rent plus the estimated average monthly cost of utilities (electricity, gas, and water and sewer) and fuels (oil, coal, kerosene, wood, etc.) if these are paid by the renter (or paid for the renter by someone else); (1) Figures cover the Portland-Vancouver-Hillsboro, OR-WA Metropolitan Statistical Area
Source: U.S. Census Bureau, 2017-2021 American Community Survey 5-Year Estimates

HEALTH

Health Risk Factors

Category	MSA[1] (%)	U.S. (%)
Adults aged 18–64 who have any kind of health care coverage	93.5	90.9
Adults who reported being in good or better health	86.5	85.2
Adults who have been told they have high blood cholesterol	31.1	35.7
Adults who have been told they have high blood pressure	27.3	32.4
Adults who are current smokers	10.5	14.4
Adults who currently use e-cigarettes	6.6	6.7
Adults who currently use chewing tobacco, snuff, or snus	3.2	3.5
Adults who are heavy drinkers[2]	8.7	6.3
Adults who are binge drinkers[3]	17.7	15.4
Adults who are overweight (BMI 25.0 - 29.9)	35.4	34.4
Adults who are obese (BMI 30.0 - 99.8)	28.8	33.9
Adults who participated in any physical activities in the past month	82.9	76.3

Note: (1) Figures cover the Portland-Vancouver-Hillsboro, OR-WA Metropolitan Statistical Area; (2) Heavy drinkers are classified as adult men having more than 14 drinks per week and adult women having more than 7 drinks per week; (3) Binge drinkers are classified as males having five or more drinks on one occasion or females having four or more drinks on one occasion
Source: Centers for Disease Control and Prevention, Behaviorial Risk Factor Surveillance System, SMART: Selected Metropolitan Area Risk Trends, 2021

Acute and Chronic Health Conditions

Category	MSA[1] (%)	U.S. (%)
Adults who have ever been told they had a heart attack	3.2	4.0
Adults who have ever been told they have angina or coronary heart disease	3.5	3.8
Adults who have ever been told they had a stroke	2.3	3.0
Adults who have ever been told they have asthma	16.2	14.9
Adults who have ever been told they have arthritis	23.0	25.8
Adults who have ever been told they have diabetes[2]	8.4	10.9
Adults who have ever been told they had skin cancer	7.5	6.6
Adults who have ever been told they had any other types of cancer	7.5	7.5
Adults who have ever been told they have COPD	5.2	6.1
Adults who have ever been told they have kidney disease	2.7	3.0
Adults who have ever been told they have a form of depression	23.9	20.5

Note: (1) Figures cover the Portland-Vancouver-Hillsboro, OR-WA Metropolitan Statistical Area; (2) Figures do not include pregnancy-related, borderline, or pre-diabetes
Source: Centers for Disease Control and Prevention, Behaviorial Risk Factor Surveillance System, SMART: Selected Metropolitan Area Risk Trends, 2021

Health Screening and Vaccination Rates

Category	MSA[1] (%)	U.S. (%)
Adults who have ever been tested for HIV	37.1	34.9
Adults who have had their blood cholesterol checked within the last five years	84.5	85.2
Adults aged 65+ who have had flu shot within the past year	68.5	68.6
Adults aged 65+ who have ever had a pneumonia vaccination	75.3	71.0

Note: (1) Figures cover the Portland-Vancouver-Hillsboro, OR-WA Metropolitan Statistical Area.
Source: Centers for Disease Control and Prevention, Behaviorial Risk Factor Surveillance System, SMART: Selected Metropolitan Area Risk Trends, 2021

Disability Status

Category	MSA[1] (%)	U.S. (%)
Adults who reported being deaf	5.7	7.2
Are you blind or have serious difficulty seeing, even when wearing glasses?	3.1	4.8
Are you limited in any way in any of your usual activities due to arthritis?	9.2	11.1
Do you have difficulty doing errands alone?	5.8	7.0
Do you have difficulty dressing or bathing?	2.6	3.6
Do you have serious difficulty concentrating/remembering/making decisions?	12.3	12.1
Do you have serious difficulty walking or climbing stairs?	10.3	12.8

Note: (1) Figures cover the Portland-Vancouver-Hillsboro, OR-WA Metropolitan Statistical Area.
Source: Centers for Disease Control and Prevention, Behaviorial Risk Factor Surveillance System, SMART: Selected Metropolitan Area Risk Trends, 2021

Mortality Rates for the Top 10 Causes of Death in the U.S.

ICD-10[a] Sub-Chapter	ICD-10[a] Code	Crude Mortality Rate[1] per 100,000 population	
		County[2]	U.S.
Malignant neoplasms	C00-C97	155.6	182.6
Ischaemic heart diseases	I20-I25	60.7	113.1
Other forms of heart disease	I30-I51	56.4	64.4
Other degenerative diseases of the nervous system	G30-G31	44.1	51.0
Cerebrovascular diseases	I60-I69	43.3	47.8
Other external causes of accidental injury	W00-X59	53.5	46.4
Chronic lower respiratory diseases	J40-J47	30.0	45.7
Organic, including symptomatic, mental disorders	F01-F09	32.2	35.9
Hypertensive diseases	I10-I15	28.1	35.0
Diabetes mellitus	E10-E14	27.9	29.6

Note: (a) ICD-10 = International Classification of Diseases 10th Revision; (1) Crude mortality rates are a three-year average covering 2019-2021; (2) Figures cover Multnomah County.
Source: Centers for Disease Control and Prevention, National Center for Health Statistics. National Vital Statistics System, Mortality 2018-2021 on CDC WONDER Online Database

Mortality Rates for Selected Causes of Death

ICD-10[a] Sub-Chapter	ICD-10[a] Code	Crude Mortality Rate[1] per 100,000 population	
		County[2]	U.S.
Assault	X85-Y09	6.4	7.0
Diseases of the liver	K70-K76	19.4	19.8
Human immunodeficiency virus (HIV) disease	B20-B24	2.4	1.5
Influenza and pneumonia	J09-J18	8.9	14.7
Intentional self-harm	X60-X84	18.5	14.3
Malnutrition	E40-E46	2.7	4.3
Obesity and other hyperalimentation	E65-E68	2.9	3.0
Renal failure	N17-N19	7.3	15.7
Transport accidents	V01-V99	10.2	13.6
Viral hepatitis	B15-B19	2.4	1.2

Note: (a) ICD-10 = International Classification of Diseases 10th Revision; (1) Crude mortality rates are a three-year average covering 2019-2021; (2) Figures cover Multnomah County; Data are suppressed when the data meet the criteria for confidentiality constraints; Crude mortality rates are flagged as unreliable when the rate would be calculated with a numerator of 20 or less.
Source: Centers for Disease Control and Prevention, National Center for Health Statistics. National Vital Statistics System, Mortality 2018-2021 on CDC WONDER Online Database

Health Insurance Coverage

Area	With Health Insurance	With Private Health Insurance	With Public Health Insurance	Without Health Insurance	Population Under Age 19 Without Health Insurance
City	93.9	72.1	31.8	6.1	2.3
MSA[1]	93.9	73.0	32.9	6.1	3.1
U.S.	91.2	67.8	35.4	8.8	5.3

Note: Figures are percentages that cover the civilian noninstitutionalized population; (1) Figures cover the Portland-Vancouver-Hillsboro, OR-WA Metropolitan Statistical Area
Source: U.S. Census Bureau, 2017-2021 American Community Survey 5-Year Estimates

Number of Medical Professionals

Area	MDs[3]	DOs[3,4]	Dentists	Podiatrists	Chiropractors	Optometrists
County[1] (number)	5,276	263	816	41	613	199
County[1] (rate[2])	646.7	32.2	101.6	5.1	76.3	24.8
U.S. (rate[2])	289.3	23.5	101.6	6.2	28.7	17.4

Note: Data as of 2021 unless noted; (1) Data covers Multnomah County; (2) Rate per 100,000 population; (3) Data as of 2020 and includes all active, non-federal physicians; (4) Doctor of Osteopathic Medicine
Source: U.S. Department of Health and Human Services, Health Resources and Services Administration, Bureau of Health Professions, Area Resource File (ARF) 2021-2022

Best Hospitals

According to *U.S. News,* the Portland-Vancouver-Hillsboro, OR-WA metro area is home to three of the best hospitals in the U.S.: **Legacy Good Samaritan Medical Center** (1 adult specialty); **OHSU Hospital** (6 adult specialties and 7 pediatric specialties); **OHSU Hospital-Knight Cancer Institute** (6 adult specialties and 7 pediatric specialties). The hospitals listed were nationally ranked in at least one of 15 adult or 10 pediatric specialties. The number of specialties shown cover the parent hospital. Only 164 U.S. hospitals performed well enough to be nationally ranked in one or more specialties. Twenty hospitals in the U.S. made the Honor Roll. The Best Hospitals Honor Roll takes both the national rankings and the procedure and condition ratings into account. Hospitals received points if they were nationally ranked in one of the 15 adult specialties—the higher they ranked, the more points they got—and how many ratings of "high performing" they earned in the 17 procedures and conditions. *U.S. News Online, "America's Best Hospitals 2022-23"*

According to *U.S. News,* the Portland-Vancouver-Hillsboro, OR-WA metro area is home to one of the best children's hospitals in the U.S.: **Doernbecher Children's Hospital at Oregon Health and Science University** (7 pediatric specialties). The hospital listed was highly ranked in at least one of 10 pediatric specialties. Eighty-six children's hospitals in the U.S. were nationally ranked in at least one specialty. Hospitals received points for being ranked in a specialty, and the 10 hospitals with the most points across the 10 specialties make up the Honor Roll. *U.S. News Online, "America's Best Children's Hospitals 2022-23"*

EDUCATION

Public School District Statistics

District Name	Schls	Pupils	Pupil/ Teacher Ratio	Minority Pupils[1] (%)	LEP/ELL[2] (%)	IEP[3] (%)
Centennial SD 28J	9	5,528	19.9	62.8	19.4	16.1
David Douglas SD 40	14	8,807	17.7	67.6	20.4	13.7
Parkrose SD 3	6	2,802	17.5	70.0	14.4	18.6
Portland SD 1J	86	45,171	16.3	44.5	7.3	17.6
Reynolds SD 7	19	10,010	17.4	71.4	25.5	18.4

Note: Table includes school districts with 2,000 or more students; (1) Percentage of students that are not non-Hispanic white; (2) Percentage of students that are Limited English Proficient or English Language Learners (2018-19); (3) Percentage of students that have an Individualized Education Program (2019-20).
Source: U.S. Department of Education, National Center for Education Statistics, Common Core of Data, Local Education Agency (School District) Universe Survey: School Year 2021-2022

Highest Level of Education

Area	Less than H.S.	H.S. Diploma	Some College, No Deg.	Associate Degree	Bachelor's Degree	Master's Degree	Prof. School Degree	Doctorate Degree
City	6.7	15.1	19.4	6.9	31.2	13.9	4.3	2.4
MSA[1]	7.2	20.1	22.9	8.9	25.5	10.8	2.7	2.0
U.S.	11.1	26.5	20.0	8.7	20.6	9.3	2.2	1.5

Note: Figures cover persons age 25 and over; (1) Figures cover the Portland-Vancouver-Hillsboro, OR-WA Metropolitan Statistical Area
Source: U.S. Census Bureau, 2017-2021 American Community Survey 5-Year Estimates

Educational Attainment by Race

Area	High School Graduate or Higher (%)					Bachelor's Degree or Higher (%)				
	Total	White	Black	Asian	Hisp.[2]	Total	White	Black	Asian	Hisp.[2]
City	93.3	95.7	89.2	79.9	79.1	51.9	56.1	26.6	43.6	34.5
MSA[1]	92.8	94.6	90.8	87.6	73.2	41.0	41.6	31.3	54.0	22.1
U.S.	88.9	91.4	87.2	87.6	71.2	33.7	35.5	23.3	55.6	18.4

Note: Figures shown cover persons 25 years old and over; (1) Figures cover the Portland-Vancouver-Hillsboro, OR-WA Metropolitan Statistical Area; (2) People of Hispanic origin can be of any race
Source: U.S. Census Bureau, 2017-2021 American Community Survey 5-Year Estimates

School Enrollment by Grade and Control

Area	Preschool (%)		Kindergarten (%)		Grades 1 - 4 (%)		Grades 5 - 8 (%)		Grades 9 - 12 (%)	
	Public	Private	Public	Private	Public	Private	Public	Private	Public	Private
City	37.9	62.1	84.9	15.1	87.2	12.8	88.2	11.8	87.1	12.9
MSA[1]	41.3	58.7	85.1	14.9	87.5	12.5	89.1	10.9	90.2	9.8
U.S.	58.8	41.2	86.3	13.7	88.3	11.7	88.6	11.4	89.4	10.6

Note: Figures shown cover persons 3 years old and over; (1) Figures cover the Portland-Vancouver-Hillsboro, OR-WA Metropolitan Statistical Area
Source: U.S. Census Bureau, 2017-2021 American Community Survey 5-Year Estimates

Higher Education

Four-Year Colleges			Two-Year Colleges			Medical Schools[1]	Law Schools[2]	Voc/ Tech[3]
Public	Private Non-profit	Private For-profit	Public	Private Non-profit	Private For-profit			
3	17	3	3	1	8	1	2	5

Note: Figures cover institutions located within the Portland-Vancouver-Hillsboro, OR-WA Metropolitan Statistical Area and include main campuses only; (1) includes schools accredited by the Liaison Committee on Medical Education and the American Osteopathic Association's Commission on Osteopathic College Accreditation; (2) includes ABA-accredited schools, schools with provisional ABA accreditation, and state accredited schools; (3) includes all schools with programs that are less than 2 years.
Source: National Center for Education Statistics, Integrated Postsecondary Education System (IPEDS), 2021-22; Wikipedia, List of Medical Schools in the United States, accessed April 10, 2023; Wikipedia, List of Law Schools in the United States, accessed April 10, 2023

According to *U.S. News & World Report,* the Portland-Vancouver-Hillsboro, OR-WA metro area is home to one of the top 200 national universities in the U.S.: **Pacific University** (#194 tie). The indicators used to capture academic quality fall into a number of categories: assessment by administrators at peer institutions; retention of students; faculty resources; student selectivity; financial resources; alumni giving; high school counselor ratings of colleges; and graduation rate. *U.S. News & World Report, "America's Best Colleges 2023"*

According to *U.S. News & World Report,* the Portland-Vancouver-Hillsboro, OR-WA metro area is home to two of the top 100 liberal arts colleges in the U.S.: **Reed College** (#72 tie); **Lewis & Clark College** (#94 tie). The indicators used to capture academic quality fall into a number of categories: assessment by administrators at peer institutions; retention of students; faculty resources; student selectivity; financial resources; alumni giving; high school counselor ratings of colleges; and graduation rate. *U.S. News & World Report, "America's Best Colleges 2023"*

According to *U.S. News & World Report,* the Portland-Vancouver-Hillsboro, OR-WA metro area is home to one of the top 100 law schools in the U.S.: **Lewis & Clark College (Northwestern)** (#88 tie). The rankings are based on a weighted average of 12 measures of quality: peer assessment score; assessment score by lawyers/judges; median LSAT scores; median undergrad GPA; acceptance rate; employment rates for graduates; placement success; bar passage rate; faculty resources; expenditures per student; student/faculty ratio; and library resources. *U.S. News & World Report, "America's Best Graduate Schools, Law, 2023"*

According to *U.S. News & World Report,* the Portland-Vancouver-Hillsboro, OR-WA metro area is home to one of the top 75 medical schools for research in the U.S.: **Oregon Health and Science University** (#32 tie). The rankings are based on a weighted average of 11 measures of quality: quality assessment; peer assessment score; assessment score by residency directors; research activity; total research activity; average research activity per faculty member; student selectivity; median MCAT total score; median undergraduate GPA; acceptance rate; and faculty resources. *U.S. News & World Report, "America's Best Graduate Schools, Medical, 2023"*

EMPLOYERS

Major Employers

Company Name	Industry
Children's Creative Learning Center	Child day care services
Clackamas Community College	Community college
Coho Distributing	Liquor
Con-Way Enterprise Services	Accounting, auditing, & bookkeeping
Legacy Emanuel Hospital and Health Center	General medical & surgical hospitals
Nike	Rubber & plastics footwear
Oregon Health & Science University	Colleges & universities
PCC Structurals	Aircraft parts & equipment, nec
Portland Adventist Medical Center	General medical & surgical hospitals
Portland Community College	Community college
Portland State University	Colleges & universities
Providence Health & Services - Oregon	Skilled nursing facility
School Dist 1 Multnomah County	Public elementary & secondary schools
Shilo Management Corp.	Hotels & motels
Southwest Washington Medical Center	General medical & surgical hospitals
Stancorp Mortgage Investors	Life insurance
SW Washington Hospital	General medical & surgical hospitals
Tektronix	Instruments to measure elasticity
The Evergreen Aviation and Space Museum	Museums & art galleries
Veterans Health Administration	Administration of veterans' affairs

Note: Companies shown are located within the Portland-Vancouver-Hillsboro, OR-WA Metropolitan Statistical Area.
Source: Hoovers.com; Wikipedia

Best Companies to Work For

Propeller, headquartered in Portland, is among "Fortune's Best Workplaces for Parents." To pick the best companies, *Fortune* partnered with the Great Place to Work Institute. To be considered for the list, companies must be Great Place To Work-Certified and have at least 50 responses from parents in the US. The survey enables employees to share confidential quantitative and qualitative feedback about their organization's culture by responding to 60 statements on a 5-point scale and answering two open-ended questions. Collectively, these statements describe a great employee experience, defined by high levels of trust, respect, credibility, fairness, pride, and camaraderie. In addition, companies provide organizational data like size, location, industry, demographics, roles, and levels; and provide information about parental leave, adoption, flexible schedule, childcare and dependent health care benefits. *Fortune, "Best Workplaces for Parents," 2022*

Portland State University, headquartered in Portland, is among the "100 Best Places to Work in IT." To qualify, companies had to have a minimum of 100 total employees and five IT employees. The best places to work were selected based on DEI (diversity, equity, and inclusion) practices; IT turnover, promotions, and growth; IT retention and engagement programs; remote/hybrid working; benefits and perks (such as elder care and child care, flextime, and reimbursement for college tuition); and training and career development opportunities. *Computerworld, "Best Places to Work in IT," 2023*

PUBLIC SAFETY

Crime Rate

Area	Total Crime	Violent Crime Rate				Property Crime Rate		
		Murder	Rape[3]	Robbery	Aggrav. Assault	Burglary	Larceny -Theft	Motor Vehicle Theft
City	5,261.6	8.0	39.5	121.7	353.4	567.0	3,211.0	960.9
Suburbs[1]	n/a	n/a	41.7	37.9	150.0	262.3	1,381.0	296.2
Metro[2]	n/a	n/a	41.1	60.0	203.7	342.7	1,864.0	471.6
U.S.	2,356.7	6.5	38.4	73.9	279.7	314.2	1,398.0	246.0

Note: Figures are crimes per 100,000 population; (1) All areas within the metro area that are located outside the city limits; (2) Figures cover the Portland-Vancouver-Hillsboro, OR-WA Metropolitan Statistical Area; (3) All figures shown were reported using the revised Uniform Crime Reporting (UCR) definition of rape; Due to the transition to the National Incident-Based Reporting System (NIBRS), limited city and metro area data was released for 2021.
Source: FBI Uniform Crime Reports, 2020

Hate Crimes

Area	Number of Quarters Reported	Number of Incidents per Bias Motivation					
		Race/Ethnicity/ Ancestry	Religion	Sexual Orientation	Disability	Gender	Gender Identity
City[1]	4	28	2	9	0	1	0
U.S.	4	5,227	1,244	1,110	130	75	266

Note: (1) Figures include one incident reported with more than one bias motivation; Due to the transition to the National Incident-Based Reporting System (NIBRS), limited crime data was released for 2021.
Source: Federal Bureau of Investigation, Hate Crime Statistics 2020

Identity Theft Consumer Reports

Area	Reports	Reports per 100,000 Population	Rank[2]
MSA[1]	4,181	169	207
U.S.	1,108,609	339	-

Note: (1) Figures cover the Portland-Vancouver-Hillsboro, OR-WA Metropolitan Statistical Area; (2) Rank ranges from 1 to 391 where 1 indicates greatest number of identity theft reports per 100,000 population
Source: Federal Trade Commission, Consumer Sentinel Network Data Book 2022

Fraud and Other Consumer Reports

Area	Reports	Reports per 100,000 Population	Rank[2]
MSA[1]	24,896	1,007	95
U.S.	4,064,520	1,245	-

Note: (1) Figures cover the Portland-Vancouver-Hillsboro, OR-WA Metropolitan Statistical Area; (2) Rank ranges from 1 to 391 where 1 indicates greatest number of fraud and other consumer reports per 100,000 population
Source: Federal Trade Commission, Consumer Sentinel Network Data Book 2022

POLITICS

2020 Presidential Election Results

Area	Biden	Trump	Jorgensen	Hawkins	Other
Multnomah County	79.2	17.9	1.2	0.6	1.0
U.S.	51.3	46.8	1.2	0.3	0.5

Note: Results are percentages and may not add to 100% due to rounding
Source: Dave Leip's Atlas of U.S. Presidential Elections

SPORTS

Professional Sports Teams

Team Name	League	Year Established
Portland Timbers	Major League Soccer (MLS)	2011
Portland Trail Blazers	National Basketball Association (NBA)	1970

Note: Includes teams located in the Portland-Vancouver-Hillsboro, OR-WA Metropolitan Statistical Area.
Source: Wikipedia, Major Professional Sports Teams of the United States and Canada, April 12, 2023

CLIMATE

Average and Extreme Temperatures

Temperature	Jan	Feb	Mar	Apr	May	Jun	Jul	Aug	Sep	Oct	Nov	Dec	Yr.
Extreme High (°F)	65	71	83	93	100	102	107	107	105	92	73	64	107
Average High (°F)	45	50	56	61	68	73	80	79	74	64	53	46	62
Average Temp. (°F)	39	43	48	52	58	63	68	68	63	55	46	41	54
Average Low (°F)	34	36	39	42	48	53	57	57	52	46	40	36	45
Extreme Low (°F)	-2	-3	19	29	29	39	43	44	34	26	13	6	-3

Note: Figures cover the years 1926-1992
Source: National Climatic Data Center, International Station Meteorological Climate Summary, 9/96

Average Precipitation/Snowfall/Humidity

Precip./Humidity	Jan	Feb	Mar	Apr	May	Jun	Jul	Aug	Sep	Oct	Nov	Dec	Yr.
Avg. Precip. (in.)	5.5	4.2	3.8	2.4	2.0	1.5	0.5	0.9	1.7	3.0	5.5	6.6	37.5
Avg. Snowfall (in.)	3	1	1	Tr	Tr	0	0	0	0	0	1	2	7
Avg. Rel. Hum. 7am (%)	85	86	86	84	80	78	77	81	87	90	88	87	84
Avg. Rel. Hum. 4pm (%)	75	67	60	55	53	50	45	45	49	61	74	79	59

Note: Figures cover the years 1926-1992; Tr = Trace amounts (<0.05 in. of rain; <0.5 in. of snow)
Source: National Climatic Data Center, International Station Meteorological Climate Summary, 9/96

Weather Conditions

Temperature			Daytime Sky			Precipitation		
5°F & below	32°F & below	90°F & above	Clear	Partly cloudy	Cloudy	0.01 inch or more precip.	0.1 inch or more snow/ice	Thunder-storms
< 1	37	11	67	116	182	152	4	7

Note: Figures are average number of days per year and cover the years 1926-1992
Source: National Climatic Data Center, International Station Meteorological Climate Summary, 9/96

HAZARDOUS WASTE

Superfund Sites

The Portland-Vancouver-Hillsboro, OR-WA metro area is home to six sites on the EPA's Superfund National Priorities List: **Boomsnub/Airco** (final); **Bradford Island** (final); **McCormick & Baxter Creosoting Co. (Portland Plant)** (final); **Northwest Pipe & Casing/Hall Process Company** (final); **Portland Harbor** (final); **Reynolds Metals Company** (final). There are a total of 1,165 Superfund sites with a status of proposed or final on the list in the U.S. *U.S. Environmental Protection Agency, National Priorities List, April 12, 2023*

AIR QUALITY

Air Quality Trends: Ozone

	1990	1995	2000	2005	2010	2015	2018	2019	2020	2021
MSA[1]	0.081	0.065	0.059	0.059	0.056	0.064	0.062	0.058	0.058	0.058
U.S.	0.087	0.089	0.081	0.080	0.072	0.067	0.069	0.065	0.065	0.067

Note: (1) Data covers the Portland-Vancouver-Hillsboro, OR-WA Metropolitan Statistical Area. The values shown are the composite ozone concentration averages among trend sites based on the highest fourth daily maximum 8-hour concentration in parts per million. These trends are based on sites having an adequate record of monitoring data during the trend period. Data from exceptional events are included.
Source: U.S. Environmental Protection Agency, Air Quality Monitoring Information, "Air Quality Trends by City, 1990-2021"

Air Quality Index

Area	Percent of Days when Air Quality was...[2]					AQI Statistics[2]	
	Good	Moderate	Unhealthy for Sensitive Groups	Unhealthy	Very Unhealthy	Maximum	Median
MSA[1]	79.7	20.0	0.0	0.3	0.0	161	37

Note: (1) Data covers the Portland-Vancouver-Hillsboro, OR-WA Metropolitan Statistical Area; (2) Based on 365 days with AQI data in 2021. Air Quality Index (AQI) is an index for reporting daily air quality. EPA calculates the AQI for five major air pollutants regulated by the Clean Air Act: ground-level ozone, particle pollution (aka particulate matter), carbon monoxide, sulfur dioxide, and nitrogen dioxide. The AQI runs from 0 to 500. The higher the AQI value, the greater the level of air pollution and the greater the health concern. There are six AQI categories: "Good" AQI is between 0 and 50. Air quality is considered satisfactory; "Moderate" AQI is between 51 and 100. Air quality is acceptable; "Unhealthy for Sensitive Groups" When AQI values are between 101 and 150, members of sensitive groups may experience health effects; "Unhealthy" When AQI values are between 151 and 200 everyone may begin to experience health effects; "Very Unhealthy" AQI values between 201 and 300 trigger a health alert; "Hazardous" AQI values over 300 trigger warnings of emergency conditions (not shown).
Source: U.S. Environmental Protection Agency, Air Quality Index Report, 2021

Air Quality Index Pollutants

| Area | Percent of Days when AQI Pollutant was...[2] | | | | | |
	Carbon Monoxide	Nitrogen Dioxide	Ozone	Sulfur Dioxide	Particulate Matter 2.5	Particulate Matter 10
MSA[1]	0.0	0.5	61.1	(3)	38.4	0.0

Note: (1) Data covers the Portland-Vancouver-Hillsboro, OR-WA Metropolitan Statistical Area; (2) Based on 365 days with AQI data in 2021. The Air Quality Index (AQI) is an index for reporting daily air quality. EPA calculates the AQI for five major air pollutants regulated by the Clean Air Act: ground-level ozone, particle pollution (also known as particulate matter), carbon monoxide, sulfur dioxide, and nitrogen dioxide. The AQI runs from 0 to 500. The higher the AQI value, the greater the level of air pollution and the greater the health concern; (3) Sulfur dioxide is no longer included in this table (as of December 8, 2021) because SO_2 concentrations tend to be very localized and not necessarily representative of broad geographical areas like counties and CBSAs.
Source: U.S. Environmental Protection Agency, Air Quality Index Report, 2021

Maximum Air Pollutant Concentrations: Particulate Matter, Ozone, CO and Lead

	Particulate Matter 10 (ug/m³)	Particulate Matter 2.5 Wtd AM (ug/m³)	Particulate Matter 2.5 24-Hr (ug/m³)	Ozone (ppm)	Carbon Monoxide (ppm)	Lead (ug/m³)
MSA[1] Level	29	6.4	16	0.062	1	n/a
NAAQS[2]	150	15	35	0.075	9	0.15
Met NAAQS[2]	Yes	Yes	Yes	Yes	Yes	n/a

Note: (1) Data covers the Portland-Vancouver-Hillsboro, OR-WA Metropolitan Statistical Area; Data from exceptional events are included; (2) National Ambient Air Quality Standards; ppm = parts per million; ug/m³ = micrograms per cubic meter; n/a not available.
Concentrations: Particulate Matter 10 (coarse particulate)—highest second maximum 24-hour concentration; Particulate Matter 2.5 Wtd AM (fine particulate)—highest weighted annual mean concentration; Particulate Matter 2.5 24-Hour (fine particulate)—highest 98th percentile 24-hour concentration; Ozone—highest fourth daily maximum 8-hour concentration; Carbon Monoxide—highest second maximum non-overlapping 8-hour concentration; Lead—maximum running 3-month average
Source: U.S. Environmental Protection Agency, Air Quality Monitoring Information, "Air Quality Statistics by City, 2021"

Maximum Air Pollutant Concentrations: Nitrogen Dioxide and Sulfur Dioxide

	Nitrogen Dioxide AM (ppb)	Nitrogen Dioxide 1-Hr (ppb)	Sulfur Dioxide AM (ppb)	Sulfur Dioxide 1-Hr (ppb)	Sulfur Dioxide 24-Hr (ppb)
MSA[1] Level	9	31	n/a	3	n/a
NAAQS[2]	53	100	30	75	140
Met NAAQS[2]	Yes	Yes	n/a	Yes	n/a

Note: (1) Data covers the Portland-Vancouver-Hillsboro, OR-WA Metropolitan Statistical Area; Data from exceptional events are included; (2) National Ambient Air Quality Standards; ppm = parts per million; ug/m³ = micrograms per cubic meter; n/a not available.
Concentrations: Nitrogen Dioxide AM—highest arithmetic mean concentration; Nitrogen Dioxide 1-Hr—highest 98th percentile 1-hour daily maximum concentration; Sulfur Dioxide AM—highest annual mean concentration; Sulfur Dioxide 1-Hr—highest 99th percentile 1-hour daily maximum concentration; Sulfur Dioxide 24-Hr—highest second maximum 24-hour concentration
Source: U.S. Environmental Protection Agency, Air Quality Monitoring Information, "Air Quality Statistics by City, 2021"

Provo, Utah

Background

Provo is situated on the Provo River at a site that was, prehistorically, under the waters of Lake Bonneville. Today, Provo enjoys one of the country's highest employment rates, a growing high-tech economy, a low crime rate, and a magnificent natural environment. The seat of Utah County, it lies at the base of the steep Wasatch Mountains, with Provo Peak rising to a height of 11,054 feet just east of the city, making Provo convenient to many of Utah's famed ski areas and to the Uinta National Forest.

Spanish missionaries Francisco Silvestre Velez de Escalante and Francisco Atanasio Dominguez, exploring for a more direct route from present-day New Mexico to California, were likely the first Europeans to view the area. They did not establish a permanent mission but did note that the area could easily be irrigated and developed into an important agricultural settlement. Etienne Prevot, a Canadian trapper and explorer, likewise visited but did not settle, though he too remarked on the beauty and potential of the site. These early explorers also met, and conflicted with, the area's original inhabitants, the Ute Indians, who held an important fish festival on the river every spring.

Permanent European settlement of Provo is strongly linked to Mormon history. In 1849, John S. Higbee, with 30 families in a wagon train, left the larger Salt Lake City community to move north. As they arrived in the region, they confronted a group of Ute, with whom white settlers had already been in some conflict. A short-lived peace agreement gave way to further conflict and a series of battles, after which the Indians agreed to resettlement. Peace ensued, and Provo was subject to long periods of peaceful relations with the Indians, different from many other young Western towns.

Irrigation has been central to Provo's success, and in the very year of Higbee's arrival, two large canals were dug, taking water from the Provo River. Grain mills were constructed to serve the needs of nearby farmers, and important rail links were completed in the 1870s connecting Provo to Salt Lake City and to the Union Pacific System, giving impetus to the region's agricultural and mining industries.

Provo's growth took off, with an electric generating plant built in 1890, and an interurban commuter rail service between Provo and Salt Lake City in 1914. The town had become a major regional industrial center, with ironworks, flourmills, and brickyards. Today, the area has the second largest concentration of software technology companies in the country and the third concentration of high-tech companies. Also important to the economy of the region are biotech companies, Nestle Frozen Foods, and NuSkin Enterprises.

Provo's industrial dynamism and creativity is reflected in the careers of two of its favorite sons. Dr. Harvey Fletcher, of Bell Laboratories, was the inventor of aids to the deaf and hearing-impaired, and an important early leader of the National Acoustic Association. Philo T. Farnsworth, born in Beaver but raised in Provo, developed the fundamental concepts of television in 1924 at the age of 18.

Provo is home to Farnsworth's alma mater, Brigham Young University (BYU), a private university operated by The Church of Jesus Christ of Latter-day Saints (LDS). Founded in 1875 it has earned national respect for everything from football and undergraduate liberal arts programs to its graduate programs in business and law. The Provo Tabernacle, destroyed by fire in 2010, was rebuilt as the Provo City Center Temple in 2016, making Provo the second city in the LDS Church to have two temples.

In 2001, Provo resident Larry H. Miller donated the Larry H. Miller Field to Brigham Young University, which is currently used as a training and competitive facility by various teams, including the Brigham Young Cougars. In 2009, the city of Provo implemented CITYWATCH, a city-wide emergency notification system. The Utah Valley Convention Center was completed in early 2012.

Provo hosts the annual America's Freedom Festival, a private, non-profit, non-political event, and one of the largest and longest (May to July) patriotic celebrations in the country. It's not without controversy, as it has prevented certain entities, namely Mormons and LGBTQ groups, from participating over the years.

The festivities have featured such notable figures as Bob Hope, David Hasselhoff, Reba McEntire, Mandy Moore, Huey Lewis and the News, Toby Keith, Sean Hannity, Fred Willard, Taylor Hicks, Journey, Olivia Holt, Marie Osmond, and Tim McGraw.

The climate of Provo is semi-arid continental. Summers are generally hot and dry. Winters are cold but not severe. Precipitation is generally light, with most of the rain falling in the spring.

Rankings

General Rankings

- The Provo metro area was identified as one of America's fastest-growing areas in terms of population and business growth by *MagnifyMoney*. The area ranked #2 out of 35. The 100 most populous metro areas in the U.S. were evaluated on their change from 2011 to 2016 in the following categories: people and housing; workforce and employment opportunities; growing industry. *www.businessinsider.com, "The 35 Cities in the US with the Biggest Influx of People, the Most Work Opportunities, and the Hottest Business Growth," August 12, 2018*

- In their ninth annual survey, Livability.com looked at data for more than 2,300 mid-sized U.S. cities to determine the rankings for Livability's "Top 100 Best Places to Live" in 2022. Provo ranked #87. Criteria: housing and economy; social and civic engagement; education; demographics; health care options; transportation & infrastructure; and community amenities. *Livability.com, "Top 100 Best Places to Live 2022" July 19, 2022*

Business/Finance Rankings

- The Brookings Institution ranked the nation's largest cities based on income inequality. Provo was ranked #63 (#1 = greatest inequality). Criteria: the "95/20 ratio," a figure representing the income at which a household earns more than 95 percent of all other households, divided by the income at which a household earns more than only 20 percent of all other households. *Brookings Institution, "Household Income Inequality, Largest Cities of 97 Large U.S. Metro Areas, 2014-2016," February 5, 2018*

- The Brookings Institution ranked the 100 largest metro areas in the U.S. based on income inequality. Provo was ranked #99 (#1 = greatest inequality). Criteria: the "95/20 ratio," a figure representing the income at which a household earns more than 95 percent of all other households, divided by the income at which a household earns more than only 20 percent of all other households. *Brookings Institution, "Household Income Inequality, 100 Largest U.S. Metro Areas, 2014-2016," February 5, 2018*

- The Provo metro area appeared on the Milken Institute "2022 Best Performing Cities" list. Rank: #1 out of 200 large metro areas (population over 250,000). Criteria: job growth; wage and salary growth; high-tech output growth; housing affordability; household broadband access. *Milken Institute, "Best-Performing Cities 2022," March 28, 2022*

- *Forbes* ranked the 200 most populous metro areas to determine the nation's "Best Places for Business and Careers." The Provo metro area was ranked #6. Criteria: costs (business and living); job growth (past and projected); income growth; quality of life; educational attainment (college and high school); projected economic growth; cultural and leisure opportunities; workplace tolerance laws; net migration patterns. *Forbes, "The Best Places for Business and Careers 2019: Seattle Still On Top," October 30, 2019*

Education Rankings

- Personal finance website *WalletHub* analyzed the 150 largest U.S. metropolitan statistical areas to determine where the most educated Americans are putting their degrees to work. Criteria: education levels; percentage of workers with degrees; education quality and attainment gap; public school quality rankings; quality and enrollment of each metro area's universities. Provo was ranked #12 (#1 = most educated city). *www.WalletHub.com, "Most & Least Educated Cities in America," July 18, 2022*

Environmental Rankings

- Niche compiled a list of the nation's snowiest cities, based on the National Oceanic and Atmospheric Administration's 30-year average snowfall data. Among cities with a population of at least 50,000, Provo ranked #20. *Niche.com, Top 25 Snowiest Cities in America, December 10, 2018*

- The U.S. Environmental Protection Agency (EPA) released its list of mid-size U.S. metropolitan areas with the most ENERGY STAR certified buildings in 2022. The Provo metro area was ranked #3 out of 10. *U.S. Environmental Protection Agency, "2023 Energy Star Top Cities," April 26, 2023*

Health/Fitness Rankings

- Provo was identified as a "2022 Spring Allergy Capital." The area ranked #96 out of 100. Three groups of factors were used to identify the most challenging cities for people with allergies during the spring season: annual spring pollen scores; over the counter allergy medicine use; number of board-certified allergy specialists. *Asthma and Allergy Foundation of America, "Spring Allergy Capitals 2022," March 2, 2022*

- Provo was identified as a "2022 Fall Allergy Capital." The area ranked #93 out of 100. Three groups of factors were used to identify the most challenging cities for people with allergies during the fall season: annual fall pollen scores; over the counter allergy medicine use; number of board-certified allergy specialists. *Asthma and Allergy Foundation of America, "Fall Allergy Capitals 2022," March 2, 2022*

- Provo was identified as a "2022 Asthma Capital." The area ranked #100 out of the nation's 100 largest metropolitan areas. Criteria: estimated asthma prevalence; asthma-related mortality; and ER visits due to asthma. Risk factors analyzed but not factored in the rankings: annual pollen score; annual air quality; public smoking laws; access to board-certified asthma specialists; rescue and controller medication use; uninsured rate; poverty rate. *Asthma and Allergy Foundation of America, "Asthma Capitals 2022: The Most Challenging Places to Live With Asthma," September 14, 2022*

Real Estate Rankings

- Provo was ranked #202 out of 235 metro areas in terms of housing affordability in 2022 by the National Association of Home Builders (#1 = most affordable). Criteria: the share of homes sold in that area affordable to a family earning the local median income, based on standard mortgage underwriting criteria. *National Association of Home Builders®, NAHB-Wells Fargo Housing Opportunity Index, 4th Quarter 2022*

Safety Rankings

- The National Insurance Crime Bureau ranked 390 metro areas in the U.S. in terms of per capita rates of vehicle theft. The Provo metro area ranked #310 (#1 = highest rate). Criteria: number of vehicle theft offenses per 100,000 inhabitants in 2021. *National Insurance Crime Bureau, "Hot Spots 2021," September 1, 2022*

Seniors/Retirement Rankings

- *AARP the Magazine* selected Provo as one of the great places in the United States for seniors, as well as younger generations, that represent "a place to call home." For the list, the magazine recognized the change in criteria due to the pandemic, and looked for cities with easy access to exercise/outdoors, quality healthcare, sense of community, relatively affordable housing costs, job markets that accommodate working from home, and reliable internet access. *www.aarp.org/magazine, "Best Places to Live and Retire Now," November 29, 2021*

- From its Best Cities for Successful Aging indexes, the Milken Institute generated rankings for metropolitan areas, weighing data in nine categories—health care, wellness, living arrangements, transportation and convenience, financial characteristics, education, employment, community engagement, and overall livability. The Provo metro area was ranked #1 overall in the large metro area category. *Milken Institute, "Best Cities for Successful Aging, 2017" March 14, 2017*

Miscellaneous Rankings

- *WalletHub* compared the 150 most populated U.S. cities to determine their operating efficiency. A "Quality of Services" score was constructed for each city and then divided by the total budget per capita to reveal which were managed the best. Provo ranked #15. Criteria: financial stability; economy; education; safety; health; infrastructure and pollution. *www.WalletHub.com, "2022's Best- & Worst-Run Cities in America," June 21, 2022*

Business Environment

DEMOGRAPHICS

Population Growth

Area	1990 Census	2000 Census	2010 Census	2020 Census	Population Growth (%)	
					1990-2020	2010-2020
City	87,148	105,166	112,488	115,162	32.1	2.4
MSA[1]	269,407	376,774	526,810	671,185	149.1	27.4
U.S.	248,709,873	281,421,906	308,745,538	331,449,281	33.3	7.4

Note: (1) Figures cover the Provo-Orem, UT Metropolitan Statistical Area
Source: U.S. Census Bureau, 1990 Census, 2000 Census, 2010 Census, 2020 Census

Race

Area	White Alone[2] (%)	Black Alone[2] (%)	Asian Alone[2] (%)	AIAN[3] Alone[2] (%)	NHOPI[4] Alone[2] (%)	Other Race Alone[2] (%)	Two or More Races (%)
City	74.6	0.9	2.5	1.0	1.5	8.2	11.3
MSA[1]	81.8	0.7	1.6	0.7	1.0	5.4	8.9
U.S.	61.6	12.4	6.0	1.1	0.2	8.4	10.2

Note: (1) Figures cover the Provo-Orem, UT Metropolitan Statistical Area; (2) Alone is defined as not being in combination with one or more other races; (3) American Indian and Alaska Native; (4) Native Hawaiian and Other Pacific Islander
Source: U.S. Census Bureau, 2020 Census

Hispanic or Latino Origin

Area	Total (%)	Mexican (%)	Puerto Rican (%)	Cuban (%)	Other (%)
City	17.8	11.3	0.7	0.2	5.6
MSA[1]	12.1	7.5	0.3	0.1	4.1
U.S.	18.4	11.2	1.8	0.7	4.7

Note: Persons of Hispanic or Latino origin can be of any race; (1) Figures cover the Provo-Orem, UT Metropolitan Statistical Area
Source: U.S. Census Bureau, 2017-2021 American Community Survey 5-Year Estimates

Age

Area	Under Age 5	Age 5–19	Age 20–34	Age 35–44	Age 45–54	Age 55–64	Age 65–74	Age 75–84	Age 85+	Median Age
City	7.1	21.4	44.5	8.3	6.1	5.4	3.8	2.2	1.1	23.8
MSA[1]	8.9	27.9	26.5	12.8	8.9	6.9	4.9	2.5	0.9	25.9
U.S.	5.6	19.2	20.2	12.7	12.4	13.1	10.0	4.9	1.9	38.8

Note: (1) Figures cover the Provo-Orem, UT Metropolitan Statistical Area
Source: U.S. Census Bureau, 2020 Census

Disability by Age

Area	All Ages	Under 18 Years Old	18 to 64 Years Old	65 Years and Over
City	9.6	4.9	8.1	41.8
MSA[1]	8.3	3.6	8.0	31.9
U.S.	12.6	4.4	10.3	33.4

Note: Figures show percent of the civilian noninstitutionalized population that reported having a disability. Disability status is determined from six types of difficulty: vision, hearing, cognitive, ambulatory, self-care, and independent living. For children under 5 years old, hearing and vision difficulty are used to determine disability status. For children between the ages of 5 and 14, disability status is determined from hearing, vision, cognitive, ambulatory, and self-care difficulties. For people aged 15 years and older, they are considered to have a disability if they have difficulty with any one of the six difficulty types; Note: (1) Figures cover the Provo-Orem, UT Metropolitan Statistical Area
Source: U.S. Census Bureau, 2017-2021 American Community Survey 5-Year Estimates

Ancestry

Area	German	Irish	English	American	Italian	Polish	French[2]	Scottish	Dutch
City	9.9	5.2	25.3	2.6	1.8	0.7	1.4	4.1	1.7
MSA[1]	10.0	4.9	29.5	4.2	2.2	0.5	1.6	4.3	1.5
U.S.	12.8	9.6	8.1	5.7	5.0	2.7	2.2	1.6	1.1

Note: Figures are the percentage of the total population reporting a particular ancestry. The nine most commonly reported ancestries in the U.S. are shown. Figures include multiple ancestries (e.g. if a person reported being Irish and Italian, they were included in both columns); (1) Figures cover the Provo-Orem, UT Metropolitan Statistical Area; (2) Excludes Basque
Source: U.S. Census Bureau, 2017-2021 American Community Survey 5-Year Estimates

Foreign-born Population

Area	Any Foreign Country	Percent of Population Born in							
		Asia	Mexico	Europe	Caribbean	Central America[2]	South America	Africa	Canada
City	11.3	1.9	4.3	0.4	0.4	0.9	2.4	0.4	0.4
MSA[1]	7.2	1.0	2.5	0.5	0.2	0.6	1.6	0.2	0.3
U.S.	13.6	4.2	3.3	1.5	1.4	1.1	1.1	0.8	0.2

Note: (1) Figures cover the Provo-Orem, UT Metropolitan Statistical Area; (2) Excludes Mexico.
Source: U.S. Census Bureau, 2017-2021 American Community Survey 5-Year Estimates

Household Size

Area	Persons in Household (%)							Average Household Size
	One	Two	Three	Four	Five	Six	Seven or More	
City	15.2	34.9	17.3	15.0	7.2	7.0	3.5	3.10
MSA[1]	12.4	28.7	15.5	16.0	12.5	9.0	5.9	3.50
U.S.	28.1	33.8	15.5	12.9	6.0	2.3	1.4	2.60

Note: (1) Figures cover the Provo-Orem, UT Metropolitan Statistical Area
Source: U.S. Census Bureau, 2017-2021 American Community Survey 5-Year Estimates

Household Relationships

Area	House-holder	Opposite-sex Spouse	Same-sex Spouse	Opposite-sex Unmarried Partner	Same-sex Unmarried Partner	Child[2]	Grand-child	Other Relatives	Non-relatives
City	29.6	15.9	0.1	0.6	0.0	25.7	1.6	4.0	12.7
MSA[1]	28.0	18.8	0.1	0.7	0.0	39.0	2.1	4.0	4.8
U.S.	38.3	17.5	0.2	2.5	0.2	28.3	2.4	4.8	3.4

Note: Figures are percent of the total population; (1) Figures cover the Provo-Orem, UT Metropolitan Statistical Area; (2) Includes biological, adopted, and stepchildren of the householder
Source: U.S. Census Bureau, 2020 Census

Gender

Area	Males	Females	Males per 100 Females
City	56,944	58,218	97.8
MSA[1]	336,952	334,233	100.8
U.S.	162,685,811	168,763,470	96.4

Note: (1) Figures cover the Provo-Orem, UT Metropolitan Statistical Area
Source: U.S. Census Bureau, 2020 Census

Marital Status

Area	Never Married	Now Married[2]	Separated	Widowed	Divorced
City	48.8	43.8	0.9	2.2	4.3
MSA[1]	33.0	58.1	0.8	2.5	5.5
U.S.	33.8	48.0	1.8	5.6	10.8

Note: Figures are percentages and cover the population 15 years of age and older; (1) Figures cover the Provo-Orem, UT Metropolitan Statistical Area; (2) Excludes separated
Source: U.S. Census Bureau, 2017-2021 American Community Survey 5-Year Estimates

Religious Groups by Family

Area	Catholic	Baptist	Methodist	LDS[2]	Pentecostal	Lutheran	Islam	Adventist	Other
MSA[1]	4.9	0.1	<0.1	82.6	0.1	<0.1	0.3	0.3	0.4
U.S.	18.7	7.3	3.0	2.0	1.8	1.7	1.3	1.3	11.6

Note: Figures are the number of adherents as a percentage of the total population and cover the eight largest religious groups in the U.S; (1) Figures cover the Provo-Orem, UT Metropolitan Statistical Area; (2) Church of Jesus Christ of Latter-day Saints
Sources: 2020 U.S. Religion Census, Association of Statisticians of American Religious Bodies; The Association of Religion Data Archives (ARDA)

Religious Groups by Tradition

Area	Catholic	Evangelical Protestant	Mainline Protestant	Black Protestant	Islam	Judaism	Hinduism	Orthodox	Buddhism
MSA[1]	4.9	0.4	<0.1	n/a	0.3	n/a	0.1	n/a	n/a
U.S.	18.7	16.5	5.2	2.3	1.3	0.6	0.4	0.4	0.3

Note: Figures are the number of adherents as a percentage of the total population; (1) Figures cover the Provo-Orem, UT Metropolitan Statistical Area
Sources: 2020 U.S. Religion Census, Association of Statisticians of American Religious Bodies; The Association of Religion Data Archives (ARDA)

ECONOMY

Gross Metropolitan Product

Area	2020	2021	2022	2023	Rank[2]
MSA[1]	31.9	36.5	40.2	43.1	91

Note: Figures are in billions of dollars; (1) Figures cover the Provo-Orem, UT Metropolitan Statistical Area; (2) Rank is based on 2021 data and ranges from 1 to 381
Source: U.S. Conference of Mayors, U.S. Metro Economies: U.S. Metros Compared to Global and State Economies, June 2022

Economic Growth

Area	2018-20 (%)	2021 (%)	2022 (%)	2023 (%)	Rank[2]
MSA[1]	5.1	10.9	6.1	4.3	3
U.S.	-0.6	5.7	3.1	2.9	—

Note: Figures are real gross metropolitan product (GMP) growth rates and represent average annual percent change; (1) Figures cover the Provo-Orem, UT Metropolitan Statistical Area; (2) Rank is based on 2020 2-year average annual percent change and ranges from 1 to 381
Source: U.S. Conference of Mayors, U.S. Metro Economies: U.S. Metros Compared to Global and State Economies, June 2022

Metropolitan Area Exports

Area	2016	2017	2018	2019	2020	2021	Rank[2]
MSA[1]	1,894.8	2,065.3	1,788.1	1,783.7	1,888.5	2,053.8	108

Note: Figures are in millions of dollars; (1) Figures cover the Provo-Orem, UT Metropolitan Statistical Area; (2) Rank is based on 2021 data and ranges from 1 to 388
Source: U.S. Department of Commerce, International Trade Administration, Office of Trade and Economic Analysis, Industry and Analysis, Exports by Metropolitan Area, data extracted March 16, 2023

Building Permits

Area	Single-Family			Multi-Family			Total		
	2021	2022	Pct. Chg.	2021	2022	Pct. Chg.	2021	2022	Pct. Chg.
City	98	134	36.7	617	327	-47.0	715	461	-35.5
MSA[1]	7,562	5,153	-31.9	3,613	3,134	-13.3	11,175	8,287	-25.8
U.S.	1,115,400	975,600	-12.5	621,600	689,500	10.9	1,737,000	1,665,100	-4.1

Note: (1) Figures cover the Provo-Orem, UT Metropolitan Statistical Area; Figures represent new, privately-owned housing units authorized (unadjusted data); All permit data are based on estimates with imputation
Source: U.S. Census Bureau, Manufacturing, Mining, and Construction Statistics, Building Permits, 2021, 2022

Bankruptcy Filings

Area	Business Filings			Nonbusiness Filings		
	2021	2022	% Chg.	2021	2022	% Chg.
Utah County	22	19	-13.6	814	790	-2.9
U.S.	14,347	13,481	-6.0	399,269	374,240	-6.3

Note: Business filings include Chapter 7, Chapter 9, Chapter 11, Chapter 12, Chapter 13, Chapter 15, and Section 304; Nonbusiness filings include Chapter 7, Chapter 11, and Chapter 13
Source: Administrative Office of the U.S. Courts, Business and Nonbusiness Bankruptcy, County Cases Commenced by Chapter of the Bankruptcy Code, During the 12-Month Period Ending December 31, 2021 and Business and Nonbusiness Bankruptcy, County Cases Commenced by Chapter of the Bankruptcy Code, During the 12-Month Period Ending December 31, 2022

Housing Vacancy Rates

Area	Gross Vacancy Rate[2] (%)			Year-Round Vacancy Rate[3] (%)			Rental Vacancy Rate[4] (%)			Homeowner Vacancy Rate[5] (%)		
	2020	2021	2022	2020	2021	2022	2020	2021	2022	2020	2021	2022
MSA[1]	n/a	n/a	n/a	n/a	n/a	n/a	n/a	n/a	n/a	n/a	n/a	n/a
U.S.	10.6	10.8	10.5	8.2	8.4	8.2	6.3	6.1	5.8	1.0	0.9	0.8

Note: (1) Figures cover the Provo-Orem, UT Metropolitan Statistical Area; (2) The percentage of the total housing inventory that is vacant; (3) The percentage of the housing inventory (excluding seasonal units) that is year-round vacant; (4) The percentage of rental inventory that is vacant for rent; (5) The percentage of homeowner inventory that is vacant for sale; n/a not available
Source: U.S. Census Bureau, Housing Vacancies and Homeownership Annual Statistics: 2020, 2021, 2022

INCOME

Income

Area	Per Capita ($)	Median Household ($)	Average Household ($)
City	23,440	53,572	76,163
MSA[1]	29,817	82,742	105,296
U.S.	37,638	69,021	97,196

Note: (1) Figures cover the Provo-Orem, UT Metropolitan Statistical Area
Source: U.S. Census Bureau, 2017-2021 American Community Survey 5-Year Estimates

Household Income Distribution

Area	Percent of Households Earning							
	Under $15,000	$15,000 -$24,999	$25,000 -$34,999	$35,000 -$49,999	$50,000 -$74,999	$75,000 -$99,999	$100,000 -$149,999	$150,000 and up
City	11.4	10.2	11.3	14.1	19.1	12.7	10.7	10.5
MSA[1]	5.1	5.0	6.4	10.4	17.9	15.7	20.8	18.6
U.S.	9.4	7.8	8.2	11.4	16.8	12.8	16.3	17.3

Note: (1) Figures cover the Provo-Orem, UT Metropolitan Statistical Area
Source: U.S. Census Bureau, 2017-2021 American Community Survey 5-Year Estimates

Poverty Rate

Area	All Ages	Under 18 Years Old	18 to 64 Years Old	65 Years and Over
City	24.6	17.7	28.2	10.0
MSA[1]	9.3	7.9	10.7	5.2
U.S.	12.6	17.0	11.8	9.6

Note: Figures are percentage of people whose income during the past 12 months was below the poverty level;
(1) Figures cover the Provo-Orem, UT Metropolitan Statistical Area
Source: U.S. Census Bureau, 2017-2021 American Community Survey 5-Year Estimates

EMPLOYMENT

Labor Force and Employment

Area	Civilian Labor Force			Workers Employed		
	Dec. 2021	Dec. 2022	% Chg.	Dec. 2021	Dec. 2022	% Chg.
City	70,289	73,861	5.1	69,267	72,590	4.8
MSA[1]	345,721	363,397	5.1	340,264	356,597	4.8
U.S.	161,696,000	164,224,000	1.6	155,732,000	158,872,000	2.0

Note: Data is not seasonally adjusted and covers workers 16 years of age and older; (1) Figures cover the
Provo-Orem, UT Metropolitan Statistical Area
Source: Bureau of Labor Statistics, Local Area Unemployment Statistics

Unemployment Rate

Area	2022											
	Jan.	Feb.	Mar.	Apr.	May	Jun.	Jul.	Aug.	Sep.	Oct.	Nov.	Dec.
City	1.8	1.5	1.6	1.7	2.0	2.4	1.8	1.8	1.6	1.8	1.8	1.7
MSA[1]	2.0	1.8	1.8	1.8	2.0	2.3	1.8	1.9	1.7	1.9	1.9	1.9
U.S.	4.4	4.1	3.8	3.3	3.4	3.8	3.8	3.8	3.3	3.4	3.4	3.3

Note: Data is not seasonally adjusted and covers workers 16 years of age and older; (1) Figures cover the
Provo-Orem, UT Metropolitan Statistical Area
Source: Bureau of Labor Statistics, Local Area Unemployment Statistics

Average Wages

Occupation	$/Hr.	Occupation	$/Hr.
Accountants and Auditors	36.53	Maintenance and Repair Workers	21.46
Automotive Mechanics	24.47	Marketing Managers	62.12
Bookkeepers	21.59	Network and Computer Systems Admin.	43.16
Carpenters	22.45	Nurses, Licensed Practical	25.28
Cashiers	13.70	Nurses, Registered	34.96
Computer Programmers	50.42	Nursing Assistants	15.59
Computer Systems Analysts	42.69	Office Clerks, General	18.82
Computer User Support Specialists	28.02	Physical Therapists	43.16
Construction Laborers	21.54	Physicians	82.30
Cooks, Restaurant	15.72	Plumbers, Pipefitters and Steamfitters	25.73
Customer Service Representatives	18.34	Police and Sheriff's Patrol Officers	28.90
Dentists	65.12	Postal Service Mail Carriers	27.30
Electricians	26.76	Real Estate Sales Agents	27.88
Engineers, Electrical	56.26	Retail Salespersons	16.90
Fast Food and Counter Workers	12.33	Sales Representatives, Technical/Scientific	43.62
Financial Managers	68.82	Secretaries, Exc. Legal/Medical/Executive	19.25
First-Line Supervisors of Office Workers	29.37	Security Guards	15.75
General and Operations Managers	47.51	Surgeons	n/a
Hairdressers/Cosmetologists	18.44	Teacher Assistants, Exc. Postsecondary*	13.34
Home Health and Personal Care Aides	15.63	Teachers, Secondary School, Exc. Sp. Ed.*	31.61
Janitors and Cleaners	13.80	Telemarketers	17.82
Landscaping/Groundskeeping Workers	18.30	Truck Drivers, Heavy/Tractor-Trailer	25.28
Lawyers	72.07	Truck Drivers, Light/Delivery Services	20.06
Maids and Housekeeping Cleaners	14.71	Waiters and Waitresses	17.18

Note: Wage data covers the Provo-Orem, UT Metropolitan Statistical Area; (*) Hourly wages were calculated
from annual wage data based on a 40 hour work week; n/a not available.
Source: Bureau of Labor Statistics, Metro Area Occupational Employment & Wage Estimates, May 2022

Employment by Industry

Sector	MSA[1]		U.S.
	Number of Employees	Percent of Total	Percent of Total
Construction, Mining, and Logging	30,900	10.0	5.4
Private Education and Health Services	61,100	19.8	16.1
Financial Activities	13,000	4.2	5.9
Government	36,000	11.7	14.5
Information	14,600	4.7	2.0
Leisure and Hospitality	26,600	8.6	10.3
Manufacturing	23,700	7.7	8.4
Other Services	7,000	2.3	3.7
Professional and Business Services	46,300	15.0	14.7
Retail Trade	36,100	11.7	10.2
Transportation, Warehousing, and Utilities	5,700	1.8	4.9
Wholesale Trade	7,800	2.5	3.9

Note: Figures are non-farm employment as of December 2022. Figures are not seasonally adjusted and include workers 16 years of age and older; (1) Figures cover the Provo-Orem, UT Metropolitan Statistical Area
Source: Bureau of Labor Statistics, Current Employment Statistics, Employment, Hours, and Earnings

Employment by Occupation

Occupation Classification	City (%)	MSA[1] (%)	U.S. (%)
Management, Business, Science, and Arts	42.2	43.3	40.3
Natural Resources, Construction, and Maintenance	5.9	8.0	8.7
Production, Transportation, and Material Moving	9.6	10.4	13.1
Sales and Office	23.5	23.8	20.9
Service	18.8	14.5	17.0

Note: Figures cover employed civilians 16 years of age and older; (1) Figures cover the Provo-Orem, UT Metropolitan Statistical Area
Source: U.S. Census Bureau, 2017-2021 American Community Survey 5-Year Estimates

Occupations with Greatest Projected Employment Growth: 2022 – 2024

Occupation[1]	2022 Employment	2024 Projected Employment	Numeric Employment Change	Percent Employment Change
General and Operations Managers	60,740	63,930	3,190	5.3
Software Developers and Software Quality Assurance Analysts and Testers	24,170	26,830	2,660	11.0
Fast Food and Counter Workers	50,960	52,790	1,830	3.6
Project Management Specialists and Business Operations Specialists, All Other	27,030	28,520	1,490	5.5
Construction Laborers	27,740	29,230	1,490	5.4
Electricians	11,880	13,160	1,280	10.8
Janitors and Cleaners, Except Maids and Housekeeping Cleaners	25,040	26,230	1,190	4.8
Laborers and Freight, Stock, and Material Movers, Hand	25,040	26,190	1,150	4.6
Cooks, Restaurant	12,460	13,590	1,130	9.1
Registered Nurses	25,490	26,600	1,110	4.4

Note: Projections cover Utah; (1) Sorted by numeric employment change
Source: www.projectionscentral.com, State Occupational Projections, 2022–2024 Short-Term Projections

Fastest-Growing Occupations: 2022 – 2024

Occupation[1]	2022 Employment	2024 Projected Employment	Numeric Employment Change	Percent Employment Change
Solar Photovoltaic Installers	430	510	80	18.6
Physical Therapist Aides	1,220	1,440	220	18.0
Chiropractors	570	660	90	15.8
Information Security Analysts (SOC 2018)	1,610	1,840	230	14.3
Architects, Except Landscape and Naval	1,600	1,820	220	13.8
Nurse Practitioners	3,010	3,420	410	13.6
Aerospace Engineers	1,110	1,260	150	13.5
Physical Therapist Assistants	740	840	100	13.5
Preschool Teachers, Except Special Education	4,360	4,910	550	12.6
Data Scientists and Mathematical Science Occupations, All Other	3,610	4,050	440	12.2

Note: Projections cover Utah; (1) Sorted by percent employment change and excludes occupations with numeric employment change less than 50
Source: www.projectionscentral.com, State Occupational Projections, 2022–2024 Short-Term Projections

CITY FINANCES

City Government Finances

Component	2020 ($000)	2020 ($ per capita)
Total Revenues	214,466	1,839
Total Expenditures	204,141	1,751
Debt Outstanding	166,983	1,432
Cash and Securities[1]	190,427	1,633

Note: (1) Cash and security holdings of a government at the close of its fiscal year, including those of its dependent agencies, utilities, and liquor stores.
Source: U.S. Census Bureau, State & Local Government Finances 2020

City Government Revenue by Source

Source	2020 ($000)	2020 ($ per capita)	2020 (%)
General Revenue			
From Federal Government	4,220	36	2.0
From State Government	13,316	114	6.2
From Local Governments	4,423	38	2.1
Taxes			
Property	19,641	168	9.2
Sales and Gross Receipts	28,086	241	13.1
Personal Income	0	0	0.0
Corporate Income	0	0	0.0
Motor Vehicle License	0	0	0.0
Other Taxes	2,270	19	1.1
Current Charges	37,391	321	17.4
Liquor Store	0	0	0.0
Utility	88,021	755	41.0

Source: U.S. Census Bureau, State & Local Government Finances 2020

City Government Expenditures by Function

Function	2020 ($000)	2020 ($ per capita)	2020 (%)
General Direct Expenditures			
Air Transportation	7,031	60	3.4
Corrections	0	0	0.0
Education	0	0	0.0
Employment Security Administration	0	0	0.0
Financial Administration	1,958	16	1.0
Fire Protection	10,016	85	4.9
General Public Buildings	0	0	0.0
Governmental Administration, Other	5,385	46	2.6
Health	0	0	0.0
Highways	6,586	56	3.2
Hospitals	0	0	0.0
Housing and Community Development	5,377	46	2.6
Interest on General Debt	3,238	27	1.6
Judicial and Legal	2,659	22	1.3
Libraries	3,701	31	1.8
Parking	0	0	0.0
Parks and Recreation	16,611	142	8.1
Police Protection	16,353	140	8.0
Public Welfare	0	0	0.0
Sewerage	21,845	187	10.7
Solid Waste Management	0	0	0.0
Veterans' Services	0	0	0.0
Liquor Store	0	0	0.0
Utility	70,761	606	34.7

Source: U.S. Census Bureau, State & Local Government Finances 2020

TAXES

State Corporate Income Tax Rates

State	Tax Rate (%)	Income Brackets ($)	Num. of Brackets	Financial Institution Tax Rate (%)[a]	Federal Income Tax Ded.
Utah	4.65 (b)	Flat rate	–	4.65 (b)	No

Note: Tax rates as of January 1, 2023; (a) Rates listed are the corporate income tax rate applied to financial institutions or excise taxes based on income. Some states have other taxes based upon the value of deposits or shares; (b) Minimum tax is $800 in California, $250 in District of Columbia, $50 in Arizona and North Dakota (banks), $400 ($100 banks) in Rhode Island, $200 per location in South Dakota (banks), $100 in Utah, $300 in Vermont.
Source: Federation of Tax Administrators, State Corporate Income Tax Rates, January 1, 2023

State Individual Income Tax Rates

State	Tax Rate (%)	Income Brackets ($)	Personal Exemptions ($)			Standard Ded. ($)	
			Single	Married	Depend.	Single	Married
Utah	4.85	Flat rate	None	None	None	(w)	(w)

Note: Tax rates as of January 1, 2023; Local- and county-level taxes are not included; Federal income tax is not deductible on state income tax returns; (w) Utah provides a tax credit equal to 6% of the federal personal exemption amounts (and applicable standard deduction).
Source: Federation of Tax Administrators, State Individual Income Tax Rates, January 1, 2023

Various State Sales and Excise Tax Rates

State	State Sales Tax (%)	Gasoline[1] ($/gal.)	Cigarette[2] ($/pack)	Spirits[3] ($/gal.)	Wine[4] ($/gal.)	Beer[5] ($/gal.)	Recreational Marijuana (%)
Utah	6.1	0.3641	1.70	15.92	—	0.41	Not legal

Note: All tax rates as of January 1, 2023; (1) The American Petroleum Institute has developed a methodology for determining the average tax rate on a gallon of fuel. Rates may include any of the following: excise taxes, environmental fees, storage tank fees, other fees or taxes, general sales tax, and local taxes; (2) The federal excise tax of $1.0066 per pack and local taxes are not included; (3) Rates are those applicable to off-premise sales of 40% alcohol by volume (a.b.v.) distilled spirits in 750ml containers. Local excise taxes are excluded; (4) Rates are those applicable to off-premise sales of 11% a.b.v. non-carbonated wine in 750ml containers; (5) Rates are those applicable to off-premise sales of 4.7% a.b.v. beer in 12 ounce containers.
Source: Tax Foundation, 2023 Facts & Figures: How Does Your State Compare?

State Business Tax Climate Index Rankings

State	Overall Rank	Corporate Tax Rank	Individual Income Tax Rank	Sales Tax Rank	Property Tax Rank	Unemployment Insurance Tax Rank
Utah	8	14	10	22	8	16

Note: The index is a measure of how each state's tax laws affect economic performance. The lower the rank, the more favorable a state's tax system is for business. States without a given tax are given a ranking of 1. The scores/rankings for the District of Columbia do not affect other states. The 2023 index represents the tax climate as of July 1, 2022.
Source: Tax Foundation, State Business Tax Climate Index 2023

TRANSPORTATION

Means of Transportation to Work

Area	Car/Truck/Van		Public Transportation			Bicycle	Walked	Other Means	Worked at Home
	Drove Alone	Car-pooled	Bus	Subway	Railroad				
City	59.2	11.2	3.2	0.1	0.9	2.0	11.8	1.0	10.5
MSA[1]	70.1	10.3	1.0	0.1	0.7	0.7	3.3	1.0	12.8
U.S.	73.2	8.6	2.0	1.6	0.5	0.5	2.5	1.5	9.7

Note: Figures are percentages and cover workers 16 years of age and older; (1) Figures cover the Provo-Orem, UT Metropolitan Statistical Area
Source: U.S. Census Bureau, 2017-2021 American Community Survey 5-Year Estimates

Travel Time to Work

Area	Less Than 10 Minutes	10 to 19 Minutes	20 to 29 Minutes	30 to 44 Minutes	45 to 59 Minutes	60 to 89 Minutes	90 Minutes or More
City	21.4	44.2	16.8	9.8	3.5	3.1	1.2
MSA[1]	17.1	34.7	20.2	16.5	6.2	3.9	1.5
U.S.	12.4	28.5	21.0	20.9	8.2	6.2	2.9

Note: Note: Figures are percentages and include workers 16 years old and over; (1) Figures cover the Provo-Orem, UT Metropolitan Statistical Area
Source: U.S. Census Bureau, 2017-2021 American Community Survey 5-Year Estimates

Key Congestion Measures

Measure	1990	2000	2010	2015	2020
Annual Hours of Delay, Total (000)	1,961	4,001	6,075	8,107	5,275
Annual Hours of Delay, Per Auto Commuter	12	18	21	23	15
Annual Congestion Cost, Per Auto Commuter ($)	203	311	379	466	309

Note: Covers the Provo-Orem UT urban area
Source: Texas A&M Transportation Institute, 2021 Urban Mobility Report

Freeway Travel Time Index

Measure	1985	1990	1995	2000	2005	2010	2015	2020
Urban Area Index[1]	1.05	1.07	1.08	1.10	1.12	1.11	1.11	1.05
Urban Area Rank[1,2]	64	74	84	85	86	93	96	85

Note: Freeway Travel Time Index—the ratio of travel time in the peak period to the travel time at free-flow conditions. For example, a value of 1.30 indicates a 20-minute free-flow trip takes 26 minutes in the peak (20 minutes x 1.30 = 26 minutes); (1) Covers the Provo-Orem UT urban area; (2) Rank is based on 101 larger urban areas (#1 = highest travel time index)
Source: Texas A&M Transportation Institute, 2021 Urban Mobility Report

Public Transportation

Agency Name / Mode of Transportation	Vehicles Operated in Maximum Service[1]	Annual Unlinked Passenger Trips[2] (in thous.)	Annual Passenger Miles[3] (in thous.)
Utah Transit Authority (UT)			
Bus (directly operated)	338	12,114.6	49,332.4
Bus (purchased transportation)	7	73.0	280.2
Commuter Bus (directly operated)	58	429.3	6,440.5
Commuter Rail (directly operated)	45	2,062.3	54,462.1
Demand Response (directly operated)	52	156.3	1,493.8
Demand Response (purchased transportation)	63	145.2	1,333.1
Light Rail (directly operated)	81	8,403.9	37,900.6
Vanpool (directly operated)	372	587.7	25,403.5

Note: (1) Number of revenue vehicles operated by the given mode and type of service to meet the annual maximum service requirement. This is the revenue vehicle count during the peak season of the year; on the week and day that maximum service is provided. Vehicles operated in maximum service (VOMS) exclude atypical days and one-time special events; (2) Number of passengers who boarded public transportation vehicles. Passengers are counted each time they board a vehicle no matter how many vehicles they use to travel from their origin to their destination. (3) Sum of the distances ridden by all passengers during the entire fiscal year.
Source: Federal Transit Administration, National Transit Database, 2021

Air Transportation

Airport Name and Code / Type of Service	Passenger Airlines[1]	Passenger Enplanements	Freight Carriers[2]	Freight (lbs)
Salt Lake City International (50 miles) (SLC)				
Domestic service (U.S. carriers - 2022)	27	11,832,407	16	194,442,064
International service (U.S. carriers - 2021)	5	279,638	3	1,061,618

Note: (1) Includes all U.S.-based major, minor and commuter airlines that carried at least one passenger during the year; (2) Includes all U.S.-based airlines and freight carriers that transported at least one pound of freight during the year.
Source: Bureau of Transportation Statistics, The Intermodal Transportation Database, Air Carriers: T-100 Domestic Market (U.S. Carriers), 2022; Bureau of Transportation Statistics, The Intermodal Transportation Database, Air Carriers: T-100 International Market (U.S. Carriers), 2021

BUSINESSES

Major Business Headquarters

Company Name	Industry	Rankings	
		Fortune[1]	Forbes[2]
No companies listed	-	-	-

Note: (1) Companies that produce a 10-K are ranked 1 to 500 based on 2021 revenue; (2) All private companies with at least $2 billion in annual revenue through the end of their most current fiscal year are ranked 1 to 246; companies listed are headquartered in the city; dashes indicate no ranking
Source: Fortune, "Fortune 500," 2022; Forbes, "America's Largest Private Companies," 2022

Living Environment

COST OF LIVING

Cost of Living Index

Composite Index	Groceries	Housing	Utilities	Trans-portation	Health Care	Misc. Goods/ Services
104.4	100.5	111.6	89.0	106.5	92.2	105.5

Note: The Cost of Living Index measures regional differences in the cost of consumer goods and services, excluding taxes and non-consumer expenditures, for professional and managerial households in the top income quintile. It is based on more than 50,000 prices covering almost 60 different items for which prices are collected three times a year by chambers of commerce, economic development organizations or university applied economic centers in each participating urban area. The numbers shown should be read as a percentage above or below the national average of 100. For example, a value of 115.4 in the groceries column indicates that grocery prices are 15.4% higher than the national average. Small differences in the index numbers should not be interpreted as significant; Figures cover the Provo-Orem UT urban area.
Source: The Council for Community and Economic Research, Cost of Living Index, 2022

Grocery Prices

Area[1]	T-Bone Steak ($/pound)	Frying Chicken ($/pound)	Whole Milk ($/half gal.)	Eggs ($/dozen)	Orange Juice ($/64 oz.)	Coffee ($/11.5 oz.)
City[2]	14.23	1.44	2.04	2.18	4.02	5.39
Avg.	13.81	1.59	2.43	2.25	3.85	4.95
Min.	10.17	0.90	1.51	1.30	2.90	3.46
Max.	19.35	3.30	4.32	4.32	5.31	8.59

*Note: (1) Values for the local area are compared with the average, minimum and maximum values for all 286 areas in the Cost of Living Index; (2) Figures cover the Provo-Orem UT urban area; **T-Bone Steak** (price per pound); **Frying Chicken** (price per pound, whole fryer); **Whole Milk** (half gallon carton); **Eggs** (price per dozen, Grade A, large); **Orange Juice** (64 oz. Tropicana or Florida Natural); **Coffee** (11.5 oz. can, vacuum-packed, Maxwell House, Hills Bros, or Folgers).*
Source: The Council for Community and Economic Research, Cost of Living Index, 2022

Housing and Utility Costs

Area[1]	New Home Price ($)	Apartment Rent ($/month)	All Electric ($/month)	Part Electric ($/month)	Other Energy ($/month)	Telephone ($/month)
City[2]	532,268	1,449	-	67.96	72.66	194.35
Avg.	450,913	1,371	176.41	99.93	76.96	190.22
Min.	229,283	546	100.84	31.56	27.15	174.27
Max.	2,434,977	4,569	356.86	249.59	272.24	208.31

*Note: (1) Values for the local area are compared with the average, minimum and maximum values for all 286 areas in the Cost of Living Index; (2) Figures cover the Provo-Orem UT urban area; **New Home Price** (2,400 sf living area, 8,000 sf lot, in urban area with full utilities); **Apartment Rent** (950 sf 2 bedroom/1.5 or 2 bath, unfurnished, excluding all utilities except water); **All Electric** (average monthly cost for an all-electric home); **Part Electric** (average monthly cost for a part-electric home); **Other Energy** (average monthly cost for natural gas, fuel oil, coal, wood, and any other forms of energy except electricity); **Telephone** (price includes the base monthly rate plus taxes and fees for three lines of mobile phone service).*
Source: The Council for Community and Economic Research, Cost of Living Index, 2022

Health Care, Transportation, and Other Costs

Area[1]	Doctor ($/visit)	Dentist ($/visit)	Optometrist ($/visit)	Gasoline ($/gallon)	Beauty Salon ($/visit)	Men's Shirt ($)
City[2]	105.44	95.74	116.76	4.24	40.94	46.89
Avg.	124.91	107.77	117.66	3.86	43.31	34.21
Min.	36.61	58.25	51.79	2.90	22.18	13.05
Max.	250.21	162.58	371.96	5.54	85.61	63.54

*Note: (1) Values for the local area are compared with the average, minimum and maximum values for all 286 areas in the Cost of Living Index; (2) Figures cover the Provo-Orem UT urban area; **Doctor** (general practitioners routine exam of an established patient); **Dentist** (adult teeth cleaning and periodic oral examination); **Optometrist** (full vision eye exam for established adult patient); **Gasoline** (one gallon regular unleaded, national brand, including all taxes, cash price at self-service pump if available); **Beauty Salon** (woman's shampoo, trim, and blow-dry); **Men's Shirt** (cotton/polyester dress shirt, pinpoint weave, long sleeves).*
Source: The Council for Community and Economic Research, Cost of Living Index, 2022

HOUSING

Homeownership Rate

Area	2015 (%)	2016 (%)	2017 (%)	2018 (%)	2019 (%)	2020 (%)	2021 (%)	2022 (%)
MSA[1]	n/a	n/a	n/a	n/a	n/a	n/a	n/a	n/a
U.S.	63.7	63.4	63.9	64.4	64.6	66.6	65.5	65.8

Note: (1) Figures cover the Provo-Orem, UT Metropolitan Statistical Area; n/a not available
Source: U.S. Census Bureau, Housing Vacancies and Homeownership Annual Statistics: 2015-2022

House Price Index (HPI)

Area	National Ranking[2]	Quarterly Change (%)	One-Year Change (%)	Five-Year Change (%)	Since 1991Q1 (%)
MSA[1]	206	-3.27	8.39	75.92	514.28
U.S.[3]	–	0.34	8.41	58.44	289.08

Note: The HPI is a weighted repeat sales index. It measures average price changes in repeat sales or refinancings on the same properties. This information is obtained by reviewing repeat mortgage transactions on single-family properties whose mortgages have been purchased or securitized by Fannie Mae or Freddie Mac since January 1975; (1) Figures cover the Provo-Orem, UT Metropolitan Statistical Area; (2) Rankings are based on annual percentage change for all metro areas containing at least 15,000 transactions over the last 10 years and ranges from 1 to 257; (3) figures based on a weighted average of Census Division estimates using a seasonally adjusted, purchase-only index; all figures are for the period ending December 31, 2022
Source: Federal Housing Finance Agency, Change in FHFA Metropolitan Area House Price Indexes, 2022Q4

Median Single-Family Home Prices

Area	2020	2021	2022p	Percent Change 2021 to 2022
MSA[1]	n/a	n/a	n/a	n/a
U.S. Average	300.2	357.1	392.6	9.9

Note: Figures are median sales prices of existing single-family homes in thousands of dollars; (p) preliminary; n/a not available; (1) Figures cover the Provo-Orem, UT Metropolitan Statistical Area
Source: National Association of Realtors, Median Sales Price of Existing Single-Family Homes for Metropolitan Areas, 4th Quarter 2022

Qualifying Income Based on Median Sales Price of Existing Single-Family Homes

Area	With 5% Down ($)	With 10% Down ($)	With 20% Down ($)
MSA[1]	n/a	n/a	n/a
U.S. Average	112,234	106,237	94,513

Note: Figures are preliminary; Qualifying income is based on a mortgage rate of 6.77%. Monthly principal and interest payment is limited to 25% of income; n/a not available; (1) Figures cover the Provo-Orem, UT Metropolitan Statistical Area
Source: National Association of Realtors, Qualifying Income Based on Median Sales Price of Existing Single-Family Homes for Metropolitan Areas, 4th Quarter 2022

Home Value

Area	Under $100,000	$100,000 -$199,999	$200,000 -$299,999	$300,000 -$399,999	$400,000 -$499,999	$500,000 -$999,999	$1,000,000 or more	Median ($)
City	5.3	9.2	27.9	26.4	12.3	16.1	2.7	328,500
MSA[1]	3.1	6.2	22.3	28.1	17.5	20.2	2.6	365,500
U.S.	16.2	24.2	20.1	13.6	8.3	13.6	4.1	244,900

Note: Figures are percentages except for median and cover owner-occupied housing units; (1) Figures cover the Provo-Orem, UT Metropolitan Statistical Area
Source: U.S. Census Bureau, 2017-2021 American Community Survey 5-Year Estimates

Year Housing Structure Built

Area	2020 or Later	2010 -2019	2000 -2009	1990 -1999	1980 -1989	1970 -1979	1960 -1969	1950 -1959	1940 -1949	Before 1940	Median Year
City	0.4	6.9	10.7	18.8	14.4	18.5	9.9	7.8	5.0	7.6	1981
MSA[1]	0.4	19.6	24.2	17.6	8.9	12.7	4.7	5.0	2.7	4.2	1997
U.S.	0.2	7.3	13.6	13.6	13.2	14.8	10.3	10.0	4.7	12.2	1979

Note: Figures are percentages except for Median Year; Note: (1) Figures cover the Provo-Orem, UT Metropolitan Statistical Area
Source: U.S. Census Bureau, 2017-2021 American Community Survey 5-Year Estimates

Gross Monthly Rent

Area	Under $500	$500 -$999	$1,000 -$1,499	$1,500 -$1,999	$2,000 -$2,499	$2,500 -$2,999	$3,000 and up	Median ($)
City	9.1	44.7	29.6	11.4	4.1	0.5	0.6	973
MSA[1]	4.6	31.0	36.2	20.0	6.2	1.0	1.1	1,193
U.S.	8.1	30.5	30.8	16.8	7.3	3.1	3.5	1,163

Note: Figures are percentages except for median; Gross rent is the contract rent plus the estimated average monthly cost of utilities (electricity, gas, and water and sewer) and fuels (oil, coal, kerosene, wood, etc.) if these are paid by the renter (or paid for the renter by someone else); (1) Figures cover the Provo-Orem, UT Metropolitan Statistical Area
Source: U.S. Census Bureau, 2017-2021 American Community Survey 5-Year Estimates

HEALTH

Health Risk Factors

Category	MSA[1] (%)	U.S. (%)
Adults aged 18–64 who have any kind of health care coverage	90.2	90.9
Adults who reported being in good or better health	90.0	85.2
Adults who have been told they have high blood cholesterol	28.8	35.7
Adults who have been told they have high blood pressure	21.6	32.4
Adults who are current smokers	4.1	14.4
Adults who currently use e-cigarettes	5.1	6.7
Adults who currently use chewing tobacco, snuff, or snus	2.4	3.5
Adults who are heavy drinkers[2]	2.1	6.3
Adults who are binge drinkers[3]	7.5	15.4
Adults who are overweight (BMI 25.0 - 29.9)	33.1	34.4
Adults who are obese (BMI 30.0 - 99.8)	27.5	33.9
Adults who participated in any physical activities in the past month	85.6	76.3

Note: (1) Figures cover the Provo-Orem, UT Metropolitan Statistical Area; (2) Heavy drinkers are classified as adult men having more than 14 drinks per week and adult women having more than 7 drinks per week; (3) Binge drinkers are classified as males having five or more drinks on one occasion or females having four or more drinks on one occasion
Source: Centers for Disease Control and Prevention, Behaviorial Risk Factor Surveillance System, SMART: Selected Metropolitan Area Risk Trends, 2021

Acute and Chronic Health Conditions

Category	MSA[1] (%)	U.S. (%)
Adults who have ever been told they had a heart attack	2.4	4.0
Adults who have ever been told they have angina or coronary heart disease	1.5	3.8
Adults who have ever been told they had a stroke	1.9	3.0
Adults who have ever been told they have asthma	15.2	14.9
Adults who have ever been told they have arthritis	16.5	25.8
Adults who have ever been told they have diabetes[2]	7.1	10.9
Adults who have ever been told they had skin cancer	6.2	6.6
Adults who have ever been told they had any other types of cancer	5.1	7.5
Adults who have ever been told they have COPD	2.7	6.1
Adults who have ever been told they have kidney disease	2.4	3.0
Adults who have ever been told they have a form of depression	24.4	20.5

Note: (1) Figures cover the Provo-Orem, UT Metropolitan Statistical Area; (2) Figures do not include pregnancy-related, borderline, or pre-diabetes
Source: Centers for Disease Control and Prevention, Behaviorial Risk Factor Surveillance System, SMART: Selected Metropolitan Area Risk Trends, 2021

Health Screening and Vaccination Rates

Category	MSA[1] (%)	U.S. (%)
Adults who have ever been tested for HIV	23.2	34.9
Adults who have had their blood cholesterol checked within the last five years	80.2	85.2
Adults aged 65+ who have had flu shot within the past year	69.8	68.6
Adults aged 65+ who have ever had a pneumonia vaccination	76.6	71.0

Note: (1) Figures cover the Provo-Orem, UT Metropolitan Statistical Area.
Source: Centers for Disease Control and Prevention, Behaviorial Risk Factor Surveillance System, SMART: Selected Metropolitan Area Risk Trends, 2021

Disability Status

Category	MSA[1] (%)	U.S. (%)
Adults who reported being deaf	4.0	7.2
Are you blind or have serious difficulty seeing, even when wearing glasses?	2.3	4.8
Are you limited in any way in any of your usual activities due to arthritis?	7.2	11.1
Do you have difficulty doing errands alone?	4.9	7.0
Do you have difficulty dressing or bathing?	1.5	3.6
Do you have serious difficulty concentrating/remembering/making decisions?	12.0	12.1
Do you have serious difficulty walking or climbing stairs?	6.4	12.8

Note: (1) Figures cover the Provo-Orem, UT Metropolitan Statistical Area.
Source: Centers for Disease Control and Prevention, Behaviorial Risk Factor Surveillance System, SMART: Selected Metropolitan Area Risk Trends, 2021

Mortality Rates for the Top 10 Causes of Death in the U.S.

ICD-10[a] Sub-Chapter	ICD-10[a] Code	Crude Mortality Rate[1] per 100,000 population	
		County[2]	U.S.
Malignant neoplasms	C00-C97	70.3	182.6
Ischaemic heart diseases	I20-I25	36.7	113.1
Other forms of heart disease	I30-I51	45.8	64.4
Other degenerative diseases of the nervous system	G30-G31	30.8	51.0
Cerebrovascular diseases	I60-I69	20.1	47.8
Other external causes of accidental injury	W00-X59	24.7	46.4
Chronic lower respiratory diseases	J40-J47	11.2	45.7
Organic, including symptomatic, mental disorders	F01-F09	17.8	35.9
Hypertensive diseases	I10-I15	12.1	35.0
Diabetes mellitus	E10-E14	16.3	29.6

Note: (a) ICD-10 = International Classification of Diseases 10th Revision; (1) Crude mortality rates are a three-year average covering 2019-2021; (2) Figures cover Utah County.
Source: Centers for Disease Control and Prevention, National Center for Health Statistics. National Vital Statistics System, Mortality 2018-2021 on CDC WONDER Online Database

Mortality Rates for Selected Causes of Death

ICD-10[a] Sub-Chapter	ICD-10[a] Code	Crude Mortality Rate[1] per 100,000 population	
		County[2]	U.S.
Assault	X85-Y09	1.0	7.0
Diseases of the liver	K70-K76	6.0	19.8
Human immunodeficiency virus (HIV) disease	B20-B24	Suppressed	1.5
Influenza and pneumonia	J09-J18	6.6	14.7
Intentional self-harm	X60-X84	15.3	14.3
Malnutrition	E40-E46	6.6	4.3
Obesity and other hyperalimentation	E65-E68	2.1	3.0
Renal failure	N17-N19	8.5	15.7
Transport accidents	V01-V99	7.3	13.6
Viral hepatitis	B15-B19	Suppressed	1.2

Note: (a) ICD-10 = International Classification of Diseases 10th Revision; (1) Crude mortality rates are a three-year average covering 2019-2021; (2) Figures cover Utah County; Data are suppressed when the data meet the criteria for confidentiality constraints; Crude mortality rates are flagged as unreliable when the rate would be calculated with a numerator of 20 or less.
Source: Centers for Disease Control and Prevention, National Center for Health Statistics. National Vital Statistics System, Mortality 2018-2021 on CDC WONDER Online Database

Health Insurance Coverage

Area	With Health Insurance	With Private Health Insurance	With Public Health Insurance	Without Health Insurance	Population Under Age 19 Without Health Insurance
City	89.3	78.1	17.5	10.7	10.8
MSA[1]	92.2	82.4	17.0	7.8	6.2
U.S.	91.2	67.8	35.4	8.8	5.3

Note: Figures are percentages that cover the civilian noninstitutionalized population; (1) Figures cover the Provo-Orem, UT Metropolitan Statistical Area
Source: U.S. Census Bureau, 2017-2021 American Community Survey 5-Year Estimates

Number of Medical Professionals

Area	MDs[3]	DOs[3,4]	Dentists	Podiatrists	Chiropractors	Optometrists
County[1] (number)	792	138	406	32	181	80
County[1] (rate[2])	119.4	20.8	59.3	4.7	26.4	11.7
U.S. (rate[2])	289.3	23.5	72.5	6.2	28.7	17.4

Note: Data as of 2021 unless noted; (1) Data covers Utah County; (2) Rate per 100,000 population; (3) Data as of 2020 and includes all active, non-federal physicians; (4) Doctor of Osteopathic Medicine
Source: U.S. Department of Health and Human Services, Health Resources and Services Administration, Bureau of Health Professions, Area Resource File (ARF) 2021-2022

EDUCATION

Public School District Statistics

District Name	Schls	Pupils	Pupil/ Teacher Ratio	Minority Pupils[1] (%)	LEP/ELL[2] (%)	IEP[3] (%)
Provo District	23	13,983	20.1	41.3	13.6	10.8

Note: Table includes school districts with 2,000 or more students; (1) Percentage of students that are not non-Hispanic white; (2) Percentage of students that are Limited English Proficient or English Language Learners (2018-19); (3) Percentage of students that have an Individualized Education Program (2019-20).
Source: U.S. Department of Education, National Center for Education Statistics, Common Core of Data, Local Education Agency (School District) Universe Survey: School Year 2021-2022

Highest Level of Education

Area	Less than H.S.	H.S. Diploma	Some College, No Deg.	Associate Degree	Bachelor's Degree	Master's Degree	Prof. School Degree	Doctorate Degree
City	7.3	14.4	25.3	8.6	31.6	8.7	1.6	2.4
MSA[1]	4.9	17.2	25.6	10.4	29.0	9.4	1.7	1.7
U.S.	11.1	26.5	20.0	8.7	20.6	9.3	2.2	1.5

Note: Figures cover persons age 25 and over; (1) Figures cover the Provo-Orem, UT Metropolitan Statistical Area
Source: U.S. Census Bureau, 2017-2021 American Community Survey 5-Year Estimates

Educational Attainment by Race

Area	High School Graduate or Higher (%)					Bachelor's Degree or Higher (%)				
	Total	White	Black	Asian	Hisp.[2]	Total	White	Black	Asian	Hisp.[2]
City	92.7	94.5	95.3	84.4	73.5	44.3	46.4	17.0	47.4	19.3
MSA[1]	95.1	95.8	95.1	93.1	79.7	41.9	42.6	34.1	54.0	24.9
U.S.	88.9	91.4	87.2	87.6	71.2	33.7	35.5	23.3	55.6	18.4

Note: Figures shown cover persons 25 years old and over; (1) Figures cover the Provo-Orem, UT Metropolitan Statistical Area; (2) People of Hispanic origin can be of any race
Source: U.S. Census Bureau, 2017-2021 American Community Survey 5-Year Estimates

School Enrollment by Grade and Control

Area	Preschool (%)		Kindergarten (%)		Grades 1 - 4 (%)		Grades 5 - 8 (%)		Grades 9 - 12 (%)	
	Public	Private	Public	Private	Public	Private	Public	Private	Public	Private
City	63.9	36.1	91.4	8.6	92.1	7.9	95.5	4.5	90.2	9.8
MSA[1]	54.2	45.8	89.1	10.9	91.5	8.5	93.7	6.3	94.4	5.6
U.S.	58.8	41.2	86.3	13.7	88.3	11.7	88.6	11.4	89.4	10.6

Note: Figures shown cover persons 3 years old and over; (1) Figures cover the Provo-Orem, UT Metropolitan Statistical Area
Source: U.S. Census Bureau, 2017-2021 American Community Survey 5-Year Estimates

Higher Education

Four-Year Colleges			Two-Year Colleges			Medical Schools[1]	Law Schools[2]	Voc/ Tech[3]
Public	Private Non-profit	Private For-profit	Public	Private Non-profit	Private For-profit			
1	1	3	0	0	0	1	1	8

Note: Figures cover institutions located within the Provo-Orem, UT Metropolitan Statistical Area and include main campuses only; (1) includes schools accredited by the Liaison Committee on Medical Education and the American Osteopathic Association's Commission on Osteopathic College Accreditation; (2) includes ABA-accredited schools, schools with provisional ABA accreditation, and state accredited schools; (3) includes all schools with programs that are less than 2 years.
Source: National Center for Education Statistics, Integrated Postsecondary Education System (IPEDS), 2021-22; Wikipedia, List of Medical Schools in the United States, accessed April 10, 2023; Wikipedia, List of Law Schools in the United States, accessed April 10, 2023

According to *U.S. News & World Report,* the Provo-Orem, UT metro area is home to one of the top 200 national universities in the U.S.: **Brigham Young University—Provo** (#89 tie). The indicators used to capture academic quality fall into a number of categories: assessment by administrators at peer institutions; retention of students; faculty resources; student selectivity; financial resources; alumni giving; high school counselor ratings of colleges; and graduation rate. *U.S. News & World Report, "America's Best Colleges 2023"*

According to *U.S. News & World Report,* the Provo-Orem, UT metro area is home to one of the top 100 law schools in the U.S.: **Brigham Young University (Clark)** (#23 tie). The rankings are based on a weighted average of 12 measures of quality: peer assessment score; assessment score by lawyers/judges; median LSAT scores; median undergrad GPA; acceptance rate; employment rates for graduates; placement success; bar passage rate; faculty resources; expenditures per student; student/faculty ratio; and library resources. *U.S. News & World Report, "America's Best Graduate Schools, Law, 2023"*

According to *U.S. News & World Report,* the Provo-Orem, UT metro area is home to one of the top 75 business schools in the U.S.: **Brigham Young University (Marriott)** (#36 tie). The rankings are based on a weighted average of the following nine measures: quality assessment; peer assessment; recruiter assessment; placement success; mean starting salary and bonus; student selectivity; mean GMAT and GRE scores; mean undergraduate GPA; and acceptance rate. *U.S. News & World Report, "America's Best Graduate Schools, Business, 2023"*

EMPLOYERS

Major Employers

Company Name	Industry
About Time Technologies	Movements, clock or watch
Ancestry.com	Communication services, nec
Brigham Young University	Colleges & universities
City of Provo	Municipal government
Intermountain Health Care	General medical & surgical hospitals
Morinda Holdings	Bottled & canned soft drinks
Novell	Prepackaged software
Nu Skin Enterprises United States	Drugs, proprietaries, & sundries
Nu Skin International	Toilet preparations
Phone Directories Company	Directories, phone: publish only, not printed on site
RBM Services	Building cleaning service
TPUSA	Telemarketing services
Utah Dept of Human Services	Mental hospital, except for the mentally retarded
Utah Valley University	Colleges & universities
Wal-Mart Stores	Department stores, discount
Wasatch Summit	Management consulting services
Xango	Drugs, proprietaries, & sundries

Note: Companies shown are located within the Provo-Orem, UT Metropolitan Statistical Area.
Source: Hoovers.com; Wikipedia

Best Companies to Work For

Qualtrics, headquartered in Provo, is among "The 100 Best Companies to Work For." To pick the best companies, *Fortune* partnered with the Great Place to Work Institute. Two-thirds of a company's score is based on the results of the Institute's Trust Index survey, which is sent to a random sample of employees from each company. The questions related to attitudes about management's credibility, job satisfaction, and camaraderie. The other third of the scoring is based on the company's responses to the Institute's Culture Audit, which includes detailed questions about pay and benefit programs, and a series of open-ended questions about hiring practices, internal communication, training, recognition programs, and diversity efforts. Any company that is at least five years old with more than 1,000 U.S. employees is eligible. *Fortune, "The 100 Best Companies to Work For," 2023*

PUBLIC SAFETY

Crime Rate

Area	Total Crime	Violent Crime Rate				Property Crime Rate		
		Murder	Rape[3]	Robbery	Aggrav. Assault	Burglary	Larceny -Theft	Motor Vehicle Theft
City	1,623.0	0.9	37.5	11.1	65.7	139.1	1,259.5	109.2
Suburbs[1]	1,312.0	1.1	30.2	7.2	46.1	131.5	1,018.1	77.8
Metro[2]	1,368.4	1.1	31.6	7.9	49.6	132.9	1,061.8	83.5
U.S.	2,510.4	5.1	42.6	81.8	250.4	340.5	1,569.2	220.8

Note: Figures are crimes per 100,000 population; (1) All areas within the metro area that are located outside the city limits; (2) Figures cover the Provo-Orem, UT Metropolitan Statistical Area; (3) All figures shown were reported using the revised Uniform Crime Reporting (UCR) definition of rape; Due to the transition to the National Incident-Based Reporting System (NIBRS), limited city and metro area data was released for 2021.
Source: FBI Uniform Crime Reports, 2019 (data for 2020 was not available)

Hate Crimes

Area	Number of Quarters Reported	Number of Incidents per Bias Motivation					
		Race/Ethnicity/Ancestry	Religion	Sexual Orientation	Disability	Gender	Gender Identity
City	1	0	0	0	0	0	0
U.S.	4	5,227	1,244	1,110	130	75	266

Note: Due to the transition to the National Incident-Based Reporting System (NIBRS), limited crime data was released for 2021.
Source: Federal Bureau of Investigation, Hate Crime Statistics 2020

Identity Theft Consumer Reports

Area	Reports	Reports per 100,000 Population	Rank[2]
MSA[1]	952	150	254
U.S.	1,108,609	339	-

Note: (1) Figures cover the Provo-Orem, UT Metropolitan Statistical Area; (2) Rank ranges from 1 to 391 where 1 indicates greatest number of identity theft reports per 100,000 population
Source: Federal Trade Commission, Consumer Sentinel Network Data Book 2022

Fraud and Other Consumer Reports

Area	Reports	Reports per 100,000 Population	Rank[2]
MSA[1]	4,381	692	299
U.S.	4,064,520	1,245	-

Note: (1) Figures cover the Provo-Orem, UT Metropolitan Statistical Area; (2) Rank ranges from 1 to 391 where 1 indicates greatest number of fraud and other consumer reports per 100,000 population
Source: Federal Trade Commission, Consumer Sentinel Network Data Book 2022

POLITICS

2020 Presidential Election Results

Area	Biden	Trump	Jorgensen	Hawkins	Other
Utah County	26.3	66.7	3.6	0.3	3.1
U.S.	51.3	46.8	1.2	0.3	0.5

Note: Results are percentages and may not add to 100% due to rounding
Source: Dave Leip's Atlas of U.S. Presidential Elections

SPORTS

Professional Sports Teams

Team Name	League	Year Established

No teams are located in the metro area
Source: Wikipedia, Major Professional Sports Teams of the United States and Canada, April 12, 2023

CLIMATE

Average and Extreme Temperatures

Temperature	Jan	Feb	Mar	Apr	May	Jun	Jul	Aug	Sep	Oct	Nov	Dec	Yr.
Extreme High (°F)	62	69	78	85	93	104	107	104	100	89	75	67	107
Average High (°F)	37	43	52	62	72	83	93	90	80	66	50	38	64
Average Temp. (°F)	28	34	41	50	59	69	78	76	65	53	40	30	52
Average Low (°F)	19	24	31	38	46	54	62	61	51	40	30	22	40
Extreme Low (°F)	-22	-14	2	15	25	35	40	37	27	16	-14	-15	-22

Note: Figures cover the years 1948-1990
Source: National Climatic Data Center, International Station Meteorological Climate Summary, 9/96

Average Precipitation/Snowfall/Humidity

Precip./Humidity	Jan	Feb	Mar	Apr	May	Jun	Jul	Aug	Sep	Oct	Nov	Dec	Yr.
Avg. Precip. (in.)	1.3	1.2	1.8	2.0	1.7	0.9	0.8	0.9	1.1	1.3	1.3	1.4	15.6
Avg. Snowfall (in.)	13	10	11	6	1	Tr	0	0	Tr	2	6	13	63
Avg. Rel. Hum. 5am (%)	79	77	71	67	66	60	53	54	60	68	75	79	67
Avg. Rel. Hum. 5pm (%)	69	59	47	38	33	26	22	23	28	40	59	71	43

Note: Figures cover the years 1948-1990; Tr = Trace amounts (<0.05 in. of rain; <0.5 in. of snow)
Source: National Climatic Data Center, International Station Meteorological Climate Summary, 9/96

Weather Conditions

Temperature			Daytime Sky			Precipitation		
5°F & below	32°F & below	90°F & above	Clear	Partly cloudy	Cloudy	0.01 inch or more precip.	0.1 inch or more snow/ice	Thunder-storms
7	128	56	94	152	119	92	38	38

Note: Figures are average number of days per year and cover the years 1948-1990
Source: National Climatic Data Center, International Station Meteorological Climate Summary, 9/96

HAZARDOUS WASTE

Superfund Sites

The Provo-Orem, UT metro area has no sites on the EPA's Superfund Final National Priorities List. There are a total of 1,165 Superfund sites with a status of proposed or final on the list in the U.S. *U.S. Environmental Protection Agency, National Priorities List, April 12, 2023*

AIR QUALITY

Air Quality Trends: Ozone

	1990	1995	2000	2005	2010	2015	2018	2019	2020	2021
MSA[1]	n/a	n/a	n/a	n/a	n/a	n/a	n/a	n/a	n/a	n/a
U.S.	0.087	0.089	0.081	0.080	0.072	0.067	0.069	0.065	0.065	0.067

Note: (1) Data covers the Provo-Orem, UT Metropolitan Statistical Area; n/a not available. The values shown are the composite ozone concentration averages among trend sites based on the highest fourth daily maximum 8-hour concentration in parts per million. These trends are based on sites having an adequate record of monitoring data during the trend period. Data from exceptional events are included.
Source: U.S. Environmental Protection Agency, Air Quality Monitoring Information, "Air Quality Trends by City, 1990-2021"

Air Quality Index

Area	Percent of Days when Air Quality was...[2]					AQI Statistics[2]	
	Good	Moderate	Unhealthy for Sensitive Groups	Unhealthy	Very Unhealthy	Maximum	Median
MSA[1]	60.0	35.3	4.7	0.0	0.0	144	46

Note: (1) Data covers the Provo-Orem, UT Metropolitan Statistical Area; (2) Based on 365 days with AQI data in 2021. Air Quality Index (AQI) is an index for reporting daily air quality. EPA calculates the AQI for five major air pollutants regulated by the Clean Air Act: ground-level ozone, particle pollution (aka particulate matter), carbon monoxide, sulfur dioxide, and nitrogen dioxide. The AQI runs from 0 to 500. The higher the AQI value, the greater the level of air pollution and the greater the health concern. There are six AQI categories: "Good" AQI is between 0 and 50. Air quality is considered satisfactory; "Moderate" AQI is between 51 and 100. Air quality is acceptable; "Unhealthy for Sensitive Groups" When AQI values are between 101 and 150, members of sensitive groups may experience health effects; "Unhealthy" When AQI values are between 151 and 200 everyone may begin to experience health effects; "Very Unhealthy" AQI values between 201 and 300 trigger a health alert; "Hazardous" AQI values over 300 trigger warnings of emergency conditions (not shown).
Source: U.S. Environmental Protection Agency, Air Quality Index Report, 2021

Air Quality Index Pollutants

Area	Percent of Days when AQI Pollutant was...[2]					
	Carbon Monoxide	Nitrogen Dioxide	Ozone	Sulfur Dioxide	Particulate Matter 2.5	Particulate Matter 10
MSA[1]	0.0	3.3	78.9	(3)	16.4	1.4

Note: (1) Data covers the Provo-Orem, UT Metropolitan Statistical Area; (2) Based on 365 days with AQI data in 2021. The Air Quality Index (AQI) is an index for reporting daily air quality. EPA calculates the AQI for five major air pollutants regulated by the Clean Air Act: ground-level ozone, particle pollution (also known as particulate matter), carbon monoxide, sulfur dioxide, and nitrogen dioxide. The AQI runs from 0 to 500. The higher the AQI value, the greater the level of air pollution and the greater the health concern; (3) Sulfur dioxide is no longer included in this table (as of December 8, 2021) because SO_2 concentrations tend to be very localized and not necessarily representative of broad geographical areas like counties and CBSAs.
Source: U.S. Environmental Protection Agency, Air Quality Index Report, 2021

Maximum Air Pollutant Concentrations: Particulate Matter, Ozone, CO and Lead

	Particulate Matter 10 (ug/m^3)	Particulate Matter 2.5 Wtd AM (ug/m^3)	Particulate Matter 2.5 24-Hr (ug/m^3)	Ozone (ppm)	Carbon Monoxide (ppm)	Lead (ug/m^3)
MSA[1] Level	100	7.7	31	0.077	1	n/a
NAAQS[2]	150	15	35	0.075	9	0.15
Met NAAQS[2]	Yes	Yes	Yes	No	Yes	n/a

Note: (1) Data covers the Provo-Orem, UT Metropolitan Statistical Area; Data from exceptional events are included; (2) National Ambient Air Quality Standards; ppm = parts per million; ug/m^3 = micrograms per cubic meter; n/a not available.
Concentrations: Particulate Matter 10 (coarse particulate)—highest second maximum 24-hour concentration; Particulate Matter 2.5 Wtd AM (fine particulate)—highest weighted annual mean concentration; Particulate Matter 2.5 24-Hour (fine particulate)—highest 98th percentile 24-hour concentration; Ozone—highest fourth daily maximum 8-hour concentration; Carbon Monoxide—highest second maximum non-overlapping 8-hour concentration; Lead—maximum running 3-month average
Source: U.S. Environmental Protection Agency, Air Quality Monitoring Information, "Air Quality Statistics by City, 2021"

Maximum Air Pollutant Concentrations: Nitrogen Dioxide and Sulfur Dioxide

	Nitrogen Dioxide AM (ppb)	Nitrogen Dioxide 1-Hr (ppb)	Sulfur Dioxide AM (ppb)	Sulfur Dioxide 1-Hr (ppb)	Sulfur Dioxide 24-Hr (ppb)
MSA[1] Level	9	42	n/a	n/a	n/a
NAAQS[2]	53	100	30	75	140
Met NAAQS[2]	Yes	Yes	n/a	n/a	n/a

Note: (1) Data covers the Provo-Orem, UT Metropolitan Statistical Area; Data from exceptional events are included; (2) National Ambient Air Quality Standards; ppm = parts per million; ug/m^3 = micrograms per cubic meter; n/a not available.
Concentrations: Nitrogen Dioxide AM—highest arithmetic mean concentration; Nitrogen Dioxide 1-Hr—highest 98th percentile 1-hour daily maximum concentration; Sulfur Dioxide AM—highest annual mean concentration; Sulfur Dioxide 1-Hr—highest 99th percentile 1-hour daily maximum concentration; Sulfur Dioxide 24-Hr—highest second maximum 24-hour concentration
Source: U.S. Environmental Protection Agency, Air Quality Monitoring Information, "Air Quality Statistics by City, 2021"

Reno, Nevada

Background

Dubbed the "Biggest Little City in the World," Reno is known as a mecca for tourists who want to gamble, but it is so much more. Native American Washoes and Paiutes roamed the area before white explorers led by the famed John C. Fremont arrived in the nineteenth century. Due to the Truckee River running through it, the area became a stopping point for people hurrying to California to take advantage of the 1849 gold rush. In 1859, prospectors discovered the Comstock Lode—a massive vein of gold and silver forty miles to the south of the Truckee.

Shrewd entrepreneur Charles Fuller built a hotel and a toll bridge across the river for prospectors desperate to reach the lode. Floods kept destroying Fuller's bridge, and he sold the land to Myron Lake in 1861, who constructed another bridge around which a settlement grew. Lake turned over to the Central Pacific Railroad several dozen acres of his land, on the condition that half of the transcontinental railroad would run through the area. Here, the town of Reno was founded in 1868 and named after Jesse Lee Reno, a valiant Union officer killed during the Civil War. Reno became an important shipping point for the mines of the Comstock Lode.

By 1900, the lode was in decline and Reno had to look to other commercial ventures. One was the quick divorce—a six weeks' residency requirement was approved by the state legislature in 1931. In a continuing effort to jumpstart the state's economy during the Great Depression, Nevada legalized gambling in 1931. As the number of gambling houses increased in Reno, so did its population.

The Reno Arch, emblazoned with the city's nickname—Biggest Little City in the World—welcomes tourists to an array of glittering casinos and hotels. The tourist and gambling industries are still quite important to the area's commerce, but other commercial ventures have been attracted to Reno's business-friendly environment, which includes no corporate or personal income taxes, and no inventory or franchise taxes. Key industries throughout the Greater Reno-Sparks-Tahoe area include manufacturing; distribution/logistics/internet fulfillment; back office/business support; financial and intangible assets; clean energy; and aerospace/aviation/defense. Companies with distribution and fulfillment operations in the city include Walmart, PetSmart, Urban Outfitters, and Barnes & Noble. Major employers include Amazon, Tesla, Wells Fargo, Target, and Home Depot.

The University of Nevada at Reno opened its Earthquake Engineering Laboratory in 2014, the largest seismic stimulation facility in the country and the second largest in the world. The city boasts significant renovated meeting space at both the Reno-Sparks Convention Center and Reno Events Center, a premier venue for concerts, community events, tradeshows, and sporting events. Reno is home to the National Bowling Stadium and the Reno-Sparks Livestock Events Center, which, this year, is undergoing a major renovation. The Reno Aces play ball under the flag of the MLB-affiliated Pacific Coast League. The city hosts ArtTown, in which music, visual arts, film, dance, theater and historical tours are highlighted every year in July, for one of the country's largest visual and performing arts festivals.

Skiing and snowboarding are popular winter sports and draw many tourists. There are 18 ski resorts within a 98-mile radius of the Reno-Tahoe International Airport. In 2018, the city changed its flag to a colorful mountain graphic. Other popular winter activities include snowshoeing, ice skating, and snowmobiling, with many bike paths for summertime fun.

Located on a semi-arid plateau to the east of the Sierra Nevada mountains, Reno offers short, hot summers and relatively mild winters. Temperatures can vary widely from day to night. More than half of the city's precipitation falls as a rain-snow mixture during winter. Located at the edge of the Sierra Nevada, snow can pile up but tends to melt within a few days. Reno sees relatively little rain.

Rankings

General Rankings

- In their ninth annual survey, Livability.com looked at data for more than 2,300 mid-sized U.S. cities to determine the rankings for Livability's "Top 100 Best Places to Live" in 2022. Reno ranked #50. Criteria: housing and economy; social and civic engagement; education; demographics; health care options; transportation & infrastructure; and community amenities. *Livability.com, "Top 100 Best Places to Live 2022" July 19, 2022*

Business/Finance Rankings

- The Reno metro area appeared on the Milken Institute "2022 Best Performing Cities" list. Rank: #20 out of 200 large metro areas (population over 250,000). Criteria: job growth; wage and salary growth; high-tech output growth; housing affordability; household broadband access. *Milken Institute, "Best-Performing Cities 2022," March 28, 2022*

- *Forbes* ranked the 200 most populous metro areas to determine the nation's "Best Places for Business and Careers." The Reno metro area was ranked #11. Criteria: costs (business and living); job growth (past and projected); income growth; quality of life; educational attainment (college and high school); projected economic growth; cultural and leisure opportunities; workplace tolerance laws; net migration patterns. *Forbes, "The Best Places for Business and Careers 2019: Seattle Still On Top," October 30, 2019*

Dating/Romance Rankings

- Reno was ranked #21 out of 25 cities that stood out for inspiring romance and attracting diners on the website OpenTable.com. Criteria: percentage of people who dined out on Valentine's Day in 2018; percentage of romantic restaurants as rated by OpenTable diner reviews; and percentage of tables seated for two. *OpenTable, "25 Most Romantic Cities in America for 2019," February 7, 2019*

Education Rankings

- Personal finance website *WalletHub* analyzed the 150 largest U.S. metropolitan statistical areas to determine where the most educated Americans are putting their degrees to work. Criteria: education levels; percentage of workers with degrees; education quality and attainment gap; public school quality rankings; quality and enrollment of each metro area's universities. Reno was ranked #63 (#1 = most educated city). *www.WalletHub.com, "Most & Least Educated Cities in America," July 18, 2022*

Environmental Rankings

- Reno was highlighted as one of the 25 most ozone-polluted metro areas in the U.S. during 2019 through 2021. The area ranked #19. *American Lung Association, "State of the Air 2023," April 19, 2023*

- Reno was highlighted as one of the 25 metro areas most polluted by short-term particle pollution (24-hour PM 2.5) in the U.S. during 2019 through 2021. The area ranked #5. *American Lung Association, "State of the Air 2023," April 19, 2023*

Health/Fitness Rankings

- For each of the 100 largest cities in the United States, the American Fitness Index®, compiled in partnership between the American College of Sports Medicine and the Elevance Health Foundation, evaluated community infrastructure and 34 health behaviors including preventive health, levels of chronic disease conditions, food insecurity, sleep quality, pedestrian safety, air quality, and community/environment resources that support physical activity. Reno ranked #50 for "community fitness." *americanfitnessindex.org, "2022 ACSM American Fitness Index Summary Report," July 12, 2022*

Real Estate Rankings

- *WalletHub* compared the most populated U.S. cities to determine which had the best markets for real estate agents. Reno ranked #12 where demand was high and pay was the best. Criteria: sales per agent; annual median wage for real-estate agents; monthly average starting salary for real estate agents; real estate job density and competition; unemployment rate; home turnover rate; housing-market health index; and other relevant metrics. *www.WalletHub.com, "2021 Best Places to Be a Real Estate Agent," May 12, 2021*

- The Reno metro area was identified as one of the 20 worst housing markets in the U.S. in 2022. The area ranked #169 out of 187 markets. Criteria: year-over-year change of median sales price of existing single-family homes between the 4th quarter of 2021 and the 4th quarter of 2022. *National Association of Realtors®, Median Sales Price of Existing Single-Family Homes for Metropolitan Areas, 4th Quarter 2022*

- The Reno metro area was identified as one of the 20 least affordable housing markets in the U.S. in 2022. The area ranked #168 out of 186 markets. Criteria: qualification for a mortgage loan with a 10 percent down payment on a typical home. *National Association of Realtors®, Qualifying Income Based on Sales Price of Existing Single-Family Homes for Metropolitan Areas, 2022*

- Reno was ranked #211 out of 235 metro areas in terms of housing affordability in 2022 by the National Association of Home Builders (#1 = most affordable). Criteria: the share of homes sold in that area affordable to a family earning the local median income, based on standard mortgage underwriting criteria. *National Association of Home Builders®, NAHB-Wells Fargo Housing Opportunity Index, 4th Quarter 2022*

Safety Rankings

- Allstate ranked the 200 largest cities in America in terms of driver safety. Reno ranked #25. Criteria: internal property damage claims over a two-year period from January 2016 to December 2017. The report helps increase the importance of safety and awareness behind the wheel. *Allstate, "Allstate America's Best Drivers Report, 2019" June 24, 2019*

- The National Insurance Crime Bureau ranked 390 metro areas in the U.S. in terms of per capita rates of vehicle theft. The Reno metro area ranked #61 (#1 = highest rate). Criteria: number of vehicle theft offenses per 100,000 inhabitants in 2021. *National Insurance Crime Bureau, "Hot Spots 2021," September 1, 2022*

Seniors/Retirement Rankings

- From its Best Cities for Successful Aging indexes, the Milken Institute generated rankings for metropolitan areas, weighing data in nine categories—health care, wellness, living arrangements, transportation and convenience, financial characteristics, education, employment, community engagement, and overall livability. The Reno metro area was ranked #101 overall in the small metro area category. *Milken Institute, "Best Cities for Successful Aging, 2017" March 14, 2017*

- Reno was identified as #15 of 20 most popular places to retire in the Western region by *Topretirements.com*. The site separated its annual "Best Places to Retire" list by major U.S. regions for 2019. The list reflects the 20 cities that visitors to the website are most interested in for retirement, based on the number of times a city's review was viewed on the website. *Topretirements.com, "20 Best Places to Retire in the West-2019," November 11, 2019*

Women/Minorities Rankings

- Personal finance website *WalletHub* compared more than 180 U.S. cities across two key dimensions, "Hispanic Business-Friendliness" and "Hispanic Purchasing Power," to arrive at the most favorable conditions for Hispanic entrepreneurs. Reno was ranked #102 out of 182. Criteria includes: share of Hispanic-Owned Businesses; Hispanic entrepreneurship rate to median annual income of Hispanics; Small Business-Friendliness score; cost of living; and number of Hispanics with at least a bachelor's degree. *WalletHub.com, "2019's Best Cities for Hispanic Entrepreneurs," May 1, 2019*

Miscellaneous Rankings

- *WalletHub* compared the 150 most populated U.S. cities to determine their operating efficiency. A "Quality of Services" score was constructed for each city and then divided by the total budget per capita to reveal which were managed the best. Reno ranked #47. Criteria: financial stability; economy; education; safety; health; infrastructure and pollution. *www.WalletHub.com, "2022's Best- & Worst-Run Cities in America," June 21, 2022*

Business Environment

DEMOGRAPHICS

Population Growth

Area	1990 Census	2000 Census	2010 Census	2020 Census	Population Growth (%) 1990-2020	Population Growth (%) 2010-2020
City	139,950	180,480	225,221	264,165	88.8	17.3
MSA[1]	257,193	342,885	425,417	490,596	90.8	15.3
U.S.	248,709,873	281,421,906	308,745,538	331,449,281	33.3	7.4

Note: (1) Figures cover the Reno, NV Metropolitan Statistical Area
Source: U.S. Census Bureau, 1990 Census, 2000 Census, 2010 Census, 2020 Census

Race

Area	White Alone[2] (%)	Black Alone[2] (%)	Asian Alone[2] (%)	AIAN[3] Alone[2] (%)	NHOPI[4] Alone[2] (%)	Other Race Alone[2] (%)	Two or More Races (%)
City	62.7	3.1	7.1	1.4	0.8	12.0	13.0
MSA[1]	64.2	2.5	5.9	1.8	0.7	11.8	13.0
U.S.	61.6	12.4	6.0	1.1	0.2	8.4	10.2

Note: (1) Figures cover the Reno, NV Metropolitan Statistical Area; (2) Alone is defined as not being in combination with one or more other races; (3) American Indian and Alaska Native; (4) Native Hawaiian and Other Pacific Islander
Source: U.S. Census Bureau, 2020 Census

Hispanic or Latino Origin

Area	Total (%)	Mexican (%)	Puerto Rican (%)	Cuban (%)	Other (%)
City	23.3	17.8	0.7	0.3	4.6
MSA[1]	25.1	19.3	0.7	0.4	4.6
U.S.	18.4	11.2	1.8	0.7	4.7

Note: Persons of Hispanic or Latino origin can be of any race; (1) Figures cover the Reno, NV Metropolitan Statistical Area
Source: U.S. Census Bureau, 2017-2021 American Community Survey 5-Year Estimates

Age

Area	Under Age 5	Age 5–19	Age 20–34	Age 35–44	Age 45–54	Age 55–64	Age 65–74	Age 75–84	Age 85+	Median Age
City	5.5	18.0	24.5	12.7	11.3	11.9	9.9	4.6	1.5	36.3
MSA[1]	5.4	18.5	21.4	12.3	11.8	13.1	10.9	5.0	1.5	38.5
U.S.	5.6	19.2	20.2	12.7	12.4	13.1	10.0	4.9	1.9	38.8

Note: (1) Figures cover the Reno, NV Metropolitan Statistical Area
Source: U.S. Census Bureau, 2020 Census

Disability by Age

Area	All Ages	Under 18 Years Old	18 to 64 Years Old	65 Years and Over
City	11.2	3.2	9.0	31.1
MSA[1]	11.7	4.0	9.2	30.9
U.S.	12.6	4.4	10.3	33.4

Note: Figures show percent of the civilian noninstitutionalized population that reported having a disability. Disability status is determined from six types of difficulty: vision, hearing, cognitive, ambulatory, self-care, and independent living. For children under 5 years old, hearing and vision difficulty are used to determine disability status. For children between the ages of 5 and 14, disability status is determined from hearing, vision, cognitive, ambulatory, and self-care difficulties. For people aged 15 years and older, they are considered to have a disability if they have difficulty with any one of the six difficulty types; Note: (1) Figures cover the Reno, NV Metropolitan Statistical Area
Source: U.S. Census Bureau, 2017-2021 American Community Survey 5-Year Estimates

Ancestry

Area	German	Irish	English	American	Italian	Polish	French[2]	Scottish	Dutch
City	12.0	10.6	10.5	4.2	5.7	1.9	2.4	2.0	1.2
MSA[1]	12.5	10.6	10.9	3.8	6.2	1.8	2.6	2.0	1.2
U.S.	12.8	9.6	8.1	5.7	5.0	2.7	2.2	1.6	1.1

Note: Figures are the percentage of the total population reporting a particular ancestry. The nine most commonly reported ancestries in the U.S. are shown. Figures include multiple ancestries (e.g. if a person reported being Irish and Italian, they were included in both columns); (1) Figures cover the Reno, NV Metropolitan Statistical Area; (2) Excludes Basque
Source: U.S. Census Bureau, 2017-2021 American Community Survey 5-Year Estimates

Foreign-born Population

Area	Any Foreign Country	Percent of Population Born in							
		Asia	Mexico	Europe	Caribbean	Central America[2]	South America	Africa	Canada
City	15.6	5.4	5.1	1.4	0.2	1.7	0.4	0.6	0.4
MSA[1]	14.0	4.0	5.7	1.2	0.2	1.4	0.4	0.4	0.4
U.S.	13.6	4.2	3.3	1.5	1.4	1.1	1.1	0.8	0.2

Note: (1) Figures cover the Reno, NV Metropolitan Statistical Area; (2) Excludes Mexico.
Source: U.S. Census Bureau, 2017-2021 American Community Survey 5-Year Estimates

Household Size

Area	Persons in Household (%)							Average Household Size
	One	Two	Three	Four	Five	Six	Seven or More	
City	31.9	34.0	14.6	11.3	5.4	1.5	1.3	2.40
MSA[1]	27.5	34.9	15.6	12.6	5.8	2.1	1.5	2.50
U.S.	28.1	33.8	15.5	12.9	6.0	2.3	1.4	2.60

Note: (1) Figures cover the Reno, NV Metropolitan Statistical Area
Source: U.S. Census Bureau, 2017-2021 American Community Survey 5-Year Estimates

Household Relationships

Area	House-holder	Opposite-sex Spouse	Same-sex Spouse	Opposite-sex Unmarried Partner	Same-sex Unmarried Partner	Child[2]	Grand-child	Other Relatives	Non-relatives
City	41.1	15.2	0.3	3.8	0.2	24.8	1.7	4.7	5.7
MSA[1]	39.5	17.2	0.2	3.4·	0.2	26.1	2.1	5.0	4.9
U.S.	38.3	17.5	0.2	2.5	0.2	28.3	2.4	4.8	3.4

Note: Figures are percent of the total population; (1) Figures cover the Reno, NV Metropolitan Statistical Area; (2) Includes biological, adopted, and stepchildren of the householder
Source: U.S. Census Bureau, 2020 Census

Gender

Area	Males	Females	Males per 100 Females
City	134,002	130,163	102.9
MSA[1]	247,924	242,672	102.2
U.S.	162,685,811	168,763,470	96.4

Note: (1) Figures cover the Reno, NV Metropolitan Statistical Area
Source: U.S. Census Bureau, 2020 Census

Marital Status

Area	Never Married	Now Married[2]	Separated	Widowed	Divorced
City	36.5	42.1	1.9	4.9	14.8
MSA[1]	32.4	47.4	1.7	4.9	13.7
U.S.	33.8	48.0	1.8	5.6	10.8

Note: Figures are percentages and cover the population 15 years of age and older; (1) Figures cover the Reno, NV Metropolitan Statistical Area; (2) Excludes separated
Source: U.S. Census Bureau, 2017-2021 American Community Survey 5-Year Estimates

Religious Groups by Family

Area	Catholic	Baptist	Methodist	LDS[2]	Pentecostal	Lutheran	Islam	Adventist	Other
MSA[1]	24.4	1.4	0.5	4.0	0.9	0.5	0.3	1.4	5.3
U.S.	18.7	7.3	3.0	1.8	2.0	1.7	1.3	1.3	11.6

Note: Figures are the number of adherents as a percentage of the total population and cover the eight largest religious groups in the U.S; (1) Figures cover the Reno, NV Metropolitan Statistical Area; (2) Church of Jesus Christ of Latter-day Saints
Sources: 2020 U.S. Religion Census, Association of Statisticians of American Religious Bodies; The Association of Religion Data Archives (ARDA)

Religious Groups by Tradition

Area	Catholic	Evangelical Protestant	Mainline Protestant	Black Protestant	Islam	Judaism	Hinduism	Orthodox	Buddhism
MSA[1]	24.4	6.8	1.3	0.2	0.3	0.1	0.1	0.1	0.2
U.S.	18.7	16.5	5.2	2.3	1.3	0.6	0.4	0.4	0.3

Note: Figures are the number of adherents as a percentage of the total population; (1) Figures cover the Reno, NV Metropolitan Statistical Area
Sources: 2020 U.S. Religion Census, Association of Statisticians of American Religious Bodies; The Association of Religion Data Archives (ARDA)

ECONOMY

Gross Metropolitan Product

Area	2020	2021	2022	2023	Rank[2]
MSA[1]	31.8	35.9	39.3	41.9	92

Note: Figures are in billions of dollars; (1) Figures cover the Reno, NV Metropolitan Statistical Area; (2) Rank is based on 2021 data and ranges from 1 to 381
Source: U.S. Conference of Mayors, U.S. Metro Economies: U.S. Metros Compared to Global and State Economies, June 2022

Economic Growth

Area	2018-20 (%)	2021 (%)	2022 (%)	2023 (%)	Rank[2]
MSA[1]	2.1	7.5	2.8	3.2	31
U.S.	-0.6	5.7	3.1	2.9	—

Note: Figures are real gross metropolitan product (GMP) growth rates and represent average annual percent change; (1) Figures cover the Reno, NV Metropolitan Statistical Area; (2) Rank is based on 2020 2-year average annual percent change and ranges from 1 to 381
Source: U.S. Conference of Mayors, U.S. Metro Economies: U.S. Metros Compared to Global and State Economies, June 2022

Metropolitan Area Exports

Area	2016	2017	2018	2019	2020	2021	Rank[2]
MSA[1]	2,382.1	2,517.3	2,631.7	2,598.3	4,553.3	4,503.0	66

Note: Figures are in millions of dollars; (1) Figures cover the Reno, NV Metropolitan Statistical Area; (2) Rank is based on 2021 data and ranges from 1 to 388
Source: U.S. Department of Commerce, International Trade Administration, Office of Trade and Economic Analysis, Industry and Analysis, Exports by Metropolitan Area, data extracted March 16, 2023

Building Permits

Area	Single-Family			Multi-Family			Total		
	2021	2022	Pct. Chg.	2021	2022	Pct. Chg.	2021	2022	Pct. Chg.
City	1,414	1,158	-18.1	2,539	2,535	-0.2	3,953	3,693	-6.6
MSA[1]	2,717	2,184	-19.6	2,620	3,628	38.5	5,337	5,812	8.9
U.S.	1,115,400	975,600	-12.5	621,600	689,500	10.9	1,737,000	1,665,100	-4.1

Note: (1) Figures cover the Reno, NV Metropolitan Statistical Area; Figures represent new, privately-owned housing units authorized (unadjusted data); All permit data are based on estimates with imputation
Source: U.S. Census Bureau, Manufacturing, Mining, and Construction Statistics, Building Permits, 2021, 2022

Bankruptcy Filings

Area	Business Filings			Nonbusiness Filings		
	2021	2022	% Chg.	2021	2022	% Chg.
Washoe County	25	26	4.0	592	467	-21.1
U.S.	14,347	13,481	-6.0	399,269	374,240	-6.3

Note: Business filings include Chapter 7, Chapter 9, Chapter 11, Chapter 12, Chapter 13, Chapter 15, and Section 304; Nonbusiness filings include Chapter 7, Chapter 11, and Chapter 13
Source: Administrative Office of the U.S. Courts, Business and Nonbusiness Bankruptcy, County Cases Commenced by Chapter of the Bankruptcy Code, During the 12-Month Period Ending December 31, 2021 and Business and Nonbusiness Bankruptcy, County Cases Commenced by Chapter of the Bankruptcy Code, During the 12-Month Period Ending December 31, 2022

Housing Vacancy Rates

Area	Gross Vacancy Rate[2] (%)			Year-Round Vacancy Rate[3] (%)			Rental Vacancy Rate[4] (%)			Homeowner Vacancy Rate[5] (%)		
	2020	2021	2022	2020	2021	2022	2020	2021	2022	2020	2021	2022
MSA[1]	n/a	n/a	n/a	n/a	n/a	n/a	n/a	n/a	n/a	n/a	n/a	n/a
U.S.	10.6	10.8	10.5	8.2	8.4	8.2	6.3	6.1	5.8	1.0	0.9	0.8

Note: (1) Figures cover the Reno, NV Metropolitan Statistical Area; (2) The percentage of the total housing inventory that is vacant; (3) The percentage of the housing inventory (excluding seasonal units) that is year-round vacant; (4) The percentage of rental inventory that is vacant for rent; (5) The percentage of homeowner inventory that is vacant for sale; n/a not available
Source: U.S. Census Bureau, Housing Vacancies and Homeownership Annual Statistics: 2020, 2021, 2022

INCOME

Income

Area	Per Capita ($)	Median Household ($)	Average Household ($)
City	39,104	67,557	93,306
MSA[1]	40,299	74,216	100,824
U.S.	37,638	69,021	97,196

Note: (1) Figures cover the Reno, NV Metropolitan Statistical Area
Source: U.S. Census Bureau, 2017-2021 American Community Survey 5-Year Estimates

Household Income Distribution

Area	Percent of Households Earning							
	Under $15,000	$15,000 -$24,999	$25,000 -$34,999	$35,000 -$49,999	$50,000 -$74,999	$75,000 -$99,999	$100,000 -$149,999	$150,000 and up
City	8.6	7.7	8.6	11.5	18.1	13.4	16.7	15.3
MSA[1]	7.2	6.7	7.8	10.8	18.0	14.0	18.3	17.2
U.S.	9.4	7.8	8.2	11.4	16.8	12.8	16.3	17.3

Note: (1) Figures cover the Reno, NV Metropolitan Statistical Area
Source: U.S. Census Bureau, 2017-2021 American Community Survey 5-Year Estimates

Poverty Rate

Area	All Ages	Under 18 Years Old	18 to 64 Years Old	65 Years and Over
City	12.6	13.6	12.4	11.8
MSA[1]	11.0	12.8	10.6	9.9
U.S.	12.6	17.0	11.8	9.6

Note: Figures are percentage of people whose income during the past 12 months was below the poverty level;
(1) Figures cover the Reno, NV Metropolitan Statistical Area
Source: U.S. Census Bureau, 2017-2021 American Community Survey 5-Year Estimates

EMPLOYMENT

Labor Force and Employment

Area	Civilian Labor Force			Workers Employed		
	Dec. 2021	Dec. 2022	% Chg.	Dec. 2021	Dec. 2022	% Chg.
City	134,416	141,155	5.0	131,188	136,416	4.0
MSA[1]	249,159	261,626	5.0	243,158	252,847	4.0
U.S.	161,696,000	164,224,000	1.6	155,732,000	158,872,000	2.0

Note: Data is not seasonally adjusted and covers workers 16 years of age and older; (1) Figures cover the Reno, NV Metropolitan Statistical Area
Source: Bureau of Labor Statistics, Local Area Unemployment Statistics

Unemployment Rate

Area	2022											
	Jan.	Feb.	Mar.	Apr.	May	Jun.	Jul.	Aug.	Sep.	Oct.	Nov.	Dec.
City	3.1	2.8	2.5	2.7	2.9	3.3	3.2	3.5	3.1	3.6	3.5	3.4
MSA[1]	3.2	2.8	2.6	2.7	2.9	3.3	3.2	3.5	3.1	3.5	3.5	3.4
U.S.	4.4	4.1	3.8	3.3	3.4	3.8	3.8	3.8	3.3	3.4	3.4	3.3

Note: Data is not seasonally adjusted and covers workers 16 years of age and older; (1) Figures cover the Reno, NV Metropolitan Statistical Area
Source: Bureau of Labor Statistics, Local Area Unemployment Statistics

Average Wages

Occupation	$/Hr.	Occupation	$/Hr.
Accountants and Auditors	36.36	Maintenance and Repair Workers	23.76
Automotive Mechanics	26.22	Marketing Managers	64.64
Bookkeepers	23.68	Network and Computer Systems Admin.	55.57
Carpenters	30.24	Nurses, Licensed Practical	32.19
Cashiers	13.43	Nurses, Registered	44.85
Computer Programmers	47.35	Nursing Assistants	19.69
Computer Systems Analysts	51.99	Office Clerks, General	21.19
Computer User Support Specialists	26.75	Physical Therapists	49.42
Construction Laborers	25.44	Physicians	142.69
Cooks, Restaurant	17.06	Plumbers, Pipefitters and Steamfitters	32.67
Customer Service Representatives	19.43	Police and Sheriff's Patrol Officers	35.21
Dentists	56.35	Postal Service Mail Carriers	27.69
Electricians	32.25	Real Estate Sales Agents	24.89
Engineers, Electrical	48.35	Retail Salespersons	17.26
Fast Food and Counter Workers	12.62	Sales Representatives, Technical/Scientific	42.94
Financial Managers	59.63	Secretaries, Exc. Legal/Medical/Executive	22.47
First-Line Supervisors of Office Workers	29.96	Security Guards	16.07
General and Operations Managers	61.79	Surgeons	n/a
Hairdressers/Cosmetologists	16.20	Teacher Assistants, Exc. Postsecondary*	18.08
Home Health and Personal Care Aides	17.81	Teachers, Secondary School, Exc. Sp. Ed.*	36.23
Janitors and Cleaners	15.57	Telemarketers	n/a
Landscaping/Groundskeeping Workers	18.37	Truck Drivers, Heavy/Tractor-Trailer	26.51
Lawyers	72.00	Truck Drivers, Light/Delivery Services	21.26
Maids and Housekeeping Cleaners	16.74	Waiters and Waitresses	13.12

Note: Wage data covers the Reno, NV Metropolitan Statistical Area; (*) Hourly wages were calculated from annual wage data based on a 40 hour work week; n/a not available.
Source: Bureau of Labor Statistics, Metro Area Occupational Employment & Wage Estimates, May 2022

Employment by Industry

Sector	MSA[1]		U.S.
	Number of Employees	Percent of Total	Percent of Total
Construction	22,300	8.3	5.0
Private Education and Health Services	29,800	11.1	16.1
Financial Activities	11,900	4.4	5.9
Government	32,500	12.1	14.5
Information	3,700	1.4	2.0
Leisure and Hospitality	38,700	14.4	10.3
Manufacturing	29,000	10.8	8.4
Mining and Logging	400	0.1	0.4
Other Services	6,400	2.4	3.7
Professional and Business Services	34,100	12.7	14.7
Retail Trade	25,100	9.3	10.2
Transportation, Warehousing, and Utilities	25,200	9.4	4.9
Wholesale Trade	10,400	3.9	3.9

Note: Figures are non-farm employment as of December 2022. Figures are not seasonally adjusted and include workers 16 years of age and older; (1) Figures cover the Reno, NV Metropolitan Statistical Area
Source: Bureau of Labor Statistics, Current Employment Statistics, Employment, Hours, and Earnings

Employment by Occupation

Occupation Classification	City (%)	MSA[1] (%)	U.S. (%)
Management, Business, Science, and Arts	36.9	35.9	40.3
Natural Resources, Construction, and Maintenance	7.9	9.2	8.7
Production, Transportation, and Material Moving	13.5	14.3	13.1
Sales and Office	21.7	21.8	20.9
Service	20.0	18.8	17.0

Note: Figures cover employed civilians 16 years of age and older; (1) Figures cover the Reno, NV Metropolitan Statistical Area
Source: U.S. Census Bureau, 2017-2021 American Community Survey 5-Year Estimates

Occupations with Greatest Projected Employment Growth: 2022 – 2024

Occupation[1]	2022 Employment	2024 Projected Employment	Numeric Employment Change	Percent Employment Change
Cooks, Restaurant	21,370	23,140	1,770	8.3
Retail Salespersons	45,170	46,620	1,450	3.2
Waiters and Waitresses	33,630	35,050	1,420	4.2
Fast Food and Counter Workers	48,110	49,490	1,380	2.9
Laborers and Freight, Stock, and Material Movers, Hand	40,790	42,090	1,300	3.2
Gaming Dealers	17,690	18,870	1,180	6.7
Stockers and Order Fillers	25,590	26,760	1,170	4.6
Carpenters	18,390	19,350	960	5.2
Construction Laborers	16,070	16,910	840	5.2
General and Operations Managers	23,480	24,240	760	3.2

Note: Projections cover Nevada; (1) Sorted by numeric employment change
Source: www.projectionscentral.com, State Occupational Projections, 2022–2024 Short-Term Projections

Fastest-Growing Occupations: 2022 – 2024

Occupation[1]	2022 Employment	2024 Projected Employment	Numeric Employment Change	Percent Employment Change
Nurse Practitioners	1,480	1,640	160	10.8
Flight Attendants	3,500	3,850	350	10.0
Refuse and Recyclable Material Collectors	1,340	1,460	120	9.0
Logisticians	680	740	60	8.8
Cutting and Slicing Machine Setters, Operators, and Tenders	690	750	60	8.7
Printing Press Operators	1,660	1,800	140	8.4
Cooks, Restaurant	21,370	23,140	1,770	8.3
Plasterers and Stucco Masons	1,590	1,720	130	8.2
Nonfarm Animal Caretakers	2,470	2,670	200	8.1
Molders, Shapers, and Casters, Except Metal and Plastic	780	840	60	7.7

Note: Projections cover Nevada; (1) Sorted by percent employment change and excludes occupations with numeric employment change less than 50
Source: www.projectionscentral.com, State Occupational Projections, 2022–2024 Short-Term Projections

CITY FINANCES

City Government Finances

Component	2020 ($000)	2020 ($ per capita)
Total Revenues	494,502	1,935
Total Expenditures	463,629	1,814
Debt Outstanding	635,914	2,488
Cash and Securities[1]	546,290	2,137

Note: (1) Cash and security holdings of a government at the close of its fiscal year, including those of its dependent agencies, utilities, and liquor stores.
Source: U.S. Census Bureau, State & Local Government Finances 2020

City Government Revenue by Source

Source	2020 ($000)	2020 ($ per capita)	2020 (%)
General Revenue			
From Federal Government	25,419	99	5.1
From State Government	94,685	370	19.1
From Local Governments	9,412	37	1.9
Taxes			
Property	76,415	299	15.5
Sales and Gross Receipts	39,644	155	8.0
Personal Income	0	0	0.0
Corporate Income	0	0	0.0
Motor Vehicle License	0	0	0.0
Other Taxes	37,046	145	7.5
Current Charges	136,360	533	27.6
Liquor Store	0	0	0.0
Utility	0	0	0.0

Source: U.S. Census Bureau, State & Local Government Finances 2020

City Government Expenditures by Function

Function	2020 ($000)	2020 ($ per capita)	2020 (%)
General Direct Expenditures			
Air Transportation	0	0	0.0
Corrections	0	0	0.0
Education	0	0	0.0
Employment Security Administration	0	0	0.0
Financial Administration	4,152	16	0.9
Fire Protection	58,241	227	12.6
General Public Buildings	0	0	0.0
Governmental Administration, Other	19,891	77	4.3
Health	0	0	0.0
Highways	37,452	146	8.1
Hospitals	0	0	0.0
Housing and Community Development	23,886	93	5.2
Interest on General Debt	23,439	91	5.1
Judicial and Legal	11,960	46	2.6
Libraries	0	0	0.0
Parking	445	1	0.1
Parks and Recreation	16,726	65	3.6
Police Protection	85,555	334	18.5
Public Welfare	0	0	0.0
Sewerage	104,570	409	22.6
Solid Waste Management	0	0	0.0
Veterans' Services	0	0	0.0
Liquor Store	0	0	0.0
Utility	0	0	0.0

Source: U.S. Census Bureau, State & Local Government Finances 2020

TAXES

State Corporate Income Tax Rates

State	Tax Rate (%)	Income Brackets ($)	Num. of Brackets	Financial Institution Tax Rate (%)[a]	Federal Income Tax Ded.
Nevada	None	–	–	–	–

Note: Tax rates as of January 1, 2023; (a) Rates listed are the corporate income tax rate applied to financial institutions or excise taxes based on income. Some states have other taxes based upon the value of deposits or shares.
Source: Federation of Tax Administrators, State Corporate Income Tax Rates, January 1, 2023

State Individual Income Tax Rates

State	Tax Rate (%)	Income Brackets ($)	Personal Exemptions ($)			Standard Ded. ($)	
			Single	Married	Depend.	Single	Married
Nevada			– No state income tax –				

Note: Tax rates as of January 1, 2023; Local- and county-level taxes are not included
Source: Federation of Tax Administrators, State Individual Income Tax Rates, January 1, 2023

Various State Sales and Excise Tax Rates

State	State Sales Tax (%)	Gasoline[1] ($/gal.)	Cigarette[2] ($/pack)	Spirits[3] ($/gal.)	Wine[4] ($/gal.)	Beer[5] ($/gal.)	Recreational Marijuana (%)
Nevada	6.85	0.5228	1.80	3.60	0.70	0.16	(l)

Note: All tax rates as of January 1, 2023; (1) The American Petroleum Institute has developed a methodology for determining the average tax rate on a gallon of fuel. Rates may include any of the following: excise taxes, environmental fees, storage tank fees, other fees or taxes, general sales tax, and local taxes; (2) The federal excise tax of $1.0066 per pack and local taxes are not included; (3) Rates are those applicable to off-premise sales of 40% alcohol by volume (a.b.v.) distilled spirits in 750ml containers. Local excise taxes are excluded; (4) Rates are those applicable to off-premise sales of 11% a.b.v. non-carbonated wine in 750ml containers; (5) Rates are those applicable to off-premise sales of 4.7% a.b.v. beer in 12 ounce containers; (l) 15% excise tax (fair market value at wholesale); 10% excise tax (retail price)
Source: Tax Foundation, 2023 Facts & Figures: How Does Your State Compare?

State Business Tax Climate Index Rankings

State	Overall Rank	Corporate Tax Rank	Individual Income Tax Rank	Sales Tax Rank	Property Tax Rank	Unemployment Insurance Tax Rank
Nevada	7	25	5	44	5	46

Note: The index is a measure of how each state's tax laws affect economic performance. The lower the rank, the more favorable a state's tax system is for business. States without a given tax are given a ranking of 1. The scores/rankings for the District of Columbia do not affect other states. The 2023 index represents the tax climate as of July 1, 2022.
Source: Tax Foundation, State Business Tax Climate Index 2023

TRANSPORTATION

Means of Transportation to Work

Area	Car/Truck/Van		Public Transportation			Bicycle	Walked	Other Means	Worked at Home
	Drove Alone	Car-pooled	Bus	Subway	Railroad				
City	71.1	12.0	2.7	0.0	0.0	0.7	2.8	2.5	8.3
MSA[1]	73.1	12.0	2.0	0.0	0.0	0.5	2.0	2.0	8.3
U.S.	73.2	8.6	2.0	1.6	0.5	0.5	2.5	1.5	9.7

Note: Figures are percentages and cover workers 16 years of age and older; (1) Figures cover the Reno, NV Metropolitan Statistical Area
Source: U.S. Census Bureau, 2017-2021 American Community Survey 5-Year Estimates

Travel Time to Work

Area	Less Than 10 Minutes	10 to 19 Minutes	20 to 29 Minutes	30 to 44 Minutes	45 to 59 Minutes	60 to 89 Minutes	90 Minutes or More
City	15.6	40.3	22.8	12.5	4.7	2.7	1.4
MSA[1]	13.0	35.6	24.5	17.2	5.2	2.9	1.6
U.S.	12.4	28.5	21.0	20.9	8.2	6.2	2.9

Note: Note: Figures are percentages and include workers 16 years old and over; (1) Figures cover the Reno, NV Metropolitan Statistical Area
Source: U.S. Census Bureau, 2017-2021 American Community Survey 5-Year Estimates

Key Congestion Measures

Measure	1990	2000	2010	2015	2020
Annual Hours of Delay, Total (000)	n/a	n/a	n/a	10,688	4,936
Annual Hours of Delay, Per Auto Commuter	n/a	n/a	n/a	26	11
Annual Congestion Cost, Per Auto Commuter ($)	n/a	n/a	n/a	539	263

Note: n/a not available
Source: Texas A&M Transportation Institute, 2021 Urban Mobility Report

Freeway Travel Time Index

Measure	1985	1990	1995	2000	2005	2010	2015	2020
Urban Area Index[1]	n/a	n/a	n/a	n/a	n/a	n/a	1.13	1.07
Urban Area Rank[1,2]	n/a	n/a	n/a	n/a	n/a	n/a	n/a	n/a

Note: Freeway Travel Time Index—the ratio of travel time in the peak period to the travel time at free-flow conditions. For example, a value of 1.30 indicates a 20-minute free-flow trip takes 26 minutes in the peak (20 minutes x 1.30 = 26 minutes); (1) Covers the Reno NV-CA urban area; (2) Rank is based on 101 larger urban areas (#1 = highest travel time index); n/a not available
Source: Texas A&M Transportation Institute, 2021 Urban Mobility Report

Public Transportation

Agency Name / Mode of Transportation	Vehicles Operated in Maximum Service[1]	Annual Unlinked Passenger Trips[2] (in thous.)	Annual Passenger Miles[3] (in thous.)
Regional Transportation Commission of Washoe County (RTC)			
Bus (purchased transportation)	55	5,167.7	20,983.0
Commuter Bus (purchased transportation)	3	17.1	437.7
Demand Response (purchased transportation)	37	121.5	796.6
Vanpool (purchased transportation)	265	507.1	18,007.6

Note: (1) Number of revenue vehicles operated by the given mode and type of service to meet the annual maximum service requirement. This is the revenue vehicle count during the peak season of the year; on the week and day that maximum service is provided. Vehicles operated in maximum service (VOMS) exclude atypical days and one-time special events; (2) Number of passengers who boarded public transportation vehicles. Passengers are counted each time they board a vehicle no matter how many vehicles they use to travel from their origin to their destination. (3) Sum of the distances ridden by all passengers during the entire fiscal year.
Source: Federal Transit Administration, National Transit Database, 2021

Air Transportation

Airport Name and Code / Type of Service	Passenger Airlines[1]	Passenger Enplanements	Freight Carriers[2]	Freight (lbs)
Reno-Tahoe International (RNO)				
Domestic service (U.S. carriers - 2022)	25	2,103,374	9	84,350,506
International service (U.S. carriers - 2021)	2	21	1	8,143

Note: (1) Includes all U.S.-based major, minor and commuter airlines that carried at least one passenger during the year; (2) Includes all U.S.-based airlines and freight carriers that transported at least one pound of freight during the year.
Source: Bureau of Transportation Statistics, The Intermodal Transportation Database, Air Carriers: T-100 Domestic Market (U.S. Carriers), 2022; Bureau of Transportation Statistics, The Intermodal Transportation Database, Air Carriers: T-100 International Market (U.S. Carriers), 2021

BUSINESSES

Major Business Headquarters

Company Name	Industry	Rankings Fortune[1]	Rankings Forbes[2]
Caesars Entertainment	Gaming and hospitality	335	-

Note: (1) Companies that produce a 10-K ranked 1 to 500 based on 2021 revenue; (2) All private companies with at least $2 billion in annual revenue through the end of their most current fiscal year are ranked 1 to 246; companies listed are headquartered in the city; dashes indicate no ranking
Source: Fortune, "Fortune 500," 2022; Forbes, "America's Largest Private Companies," 2022

Fastest-Growing Businesses

According to *Inc.*, Reno is home to two of America's 500 fastest-growing private companies: **Gold Alliance Capital** (#71); **BiOptimizers** (#245). Criteria: must be an independent, privately-held, for-profit, U.S. corporation, proprietorship or partnership as of December 31, 2021; revenues must be at least $100,000 in 2018 and $2 million in 2021; must have four-year operating/sales history. *Inc., "America's 500 Fastest-Growing Private Companies," 2022*

Living Environment

COST OF LIVING

Cost of Living Index

Composite Index	Groceries	Housing	Utilities	Trans-portation	Health Care	Misc. Goods/ Services
105.4	105.4	121.2	87.6	116.7	99.3	94.9

Note: The Cost of Living Index measures regional differences in the cost of consumer goods and services, excluding taxes and non-consumer expenditures, for professional and managerial households in the top income quintile. It is based on more than 50,000 prices covering almost 60 different items for which prices are collected three times a year by chambers of commerce, economic development organizations or university applied economic centers in each participating urban area. The numbers shown should be read as a percentage above or below the national average of 100. For example, a value of 115.4 in the groceries column indicates that grocery prices are 15.4% higher than the national average. Small differences in the index numbers should not be interpreted as significant; Figures cover the Reno-Sparks NV urban area.
Source: The Council for Community and Economic Research, Cost of Living Index, 2022

Grocery Prices

Area[1]	T-Bone Steak ($/pound)	Frying Chicken ($/pound)	Whole Milk ($/half gal.)	Eggs ($/dozen)	Orange Juice ($/64 oz.)	Coffee ($/11.5 oz.)
City[2]	13.35	1.68	2.82	2.46	3.75	5.69
Avg.	13.81	1.59	2.43	2.25	3.85	4.95
Min.	10.17	0.90	1.51	1.30	2.90	3.46
Max.	19.35	3.30	4.32	4.32	5.31	8.59

Note: (1) Values for the local area are compared with the average, minimum and maximum values for all 286 areas in the Cost of Living Index; (2) Figures cover the Reno-Sparks NV urban area; T-Bone Steak (price per pound); Frying Chicken (price per pound, whole fryer); Whole Milk (half gallon carton); Eggs (price per dozen, Grade A, large); Orange Juice (64 oz. Tropicana or Florida Natural); Coffee (11.5 oz. can, vacuum-packed, Maxwell House, Hills Bros, or Folgers).
Source: The Council for Community and Economic Research, Cost of Living Index, 2022

Housing and Utility Costs

Area[1]	New Home Price ($)	Apartment Rent ($/month)	All Electric ($/month)	Part Electric ($/month)	Other Energy ($/month)	Telephone ($/month)
City[2]	576,610	1,515	-	97.93	44.46	185.65
Avg.	450,913	1,371	176.41	99.93	76.96	190.22
Min.	229,283	546	100.84	31.56	27.15	174.27
Max.	2,434,977	4,569	356.86	249.59	272.24	208.31

Note: (1) Values for the local area are compared with the average, minimum and maximum values for all 286 areas in the Cost of Living Index; (2) Figures cover the Reno-Sparks NV urban area; New Home Price (2,400 sf living area, 8,000 sf lot, in urban area with full utilities); Apartment Rent (950 sf 2 bedroom/1.5 or 2 bath, unfurnished, excluding all utilities except water); All Electric (average monthly cost for an all-electric home); Part Electric (average monthly cost for a part-electric home); Other Energy (average monthly cost for natural gas, fuel oil, coal, wood, and any other forms of energy except electricity); Telephone (price includes the base monthly rate plus taxes and fees for three lines of mobile phone service).
Source: The Council for Community and Economic Research, Cost of Living Index, 2022

Health Care, Transportation, and Other Costs

Area[1]	Doctor ($/visit)	Dentist ($/visit)	Optometrist ($/visit)	Gasoline ($/gallon)	Beauty Salon ($/visit)	Men's Shirt ($)
City[2]	124.83	110.67	109.50	4.63	36.67	21.59
Avg.	124.91	107.77	117.66	3.86	43.31	34.21
Min.	36.61	58.25	51.79	2.90	22.18	13.05
Max.	250.21	162.58	371.96	5.54	85.61	63.54

Note: (1) Values for the local area are compared with the average, minimum and maximum values for all 286 areas in the Cost of Living Index; (2) Figures cover the Reno-Sparks NV urban area; Doctor (general practitioners routine exam of an established patient); Dentist (adult teeth cleaning and periodic oral examination); Optometrist (full vision eye exam for established adult patient); Gasoline (one gallon regular unleaded, national brand, including all taxes, cash price at self-service pump if available); Beauty Salon (woman's shampoo, trim, and blow-dry); Men's Shirt (cotton/polyester dress shirt, pinpoint weave, long sleeves).
Source: The Council for Community and Economic Research, Cost of Living Index, 2022

HOUSING

Homeownership Rate

Area	2015 (%)	2016 (%)	2017 (%)	2018 (%)	2019 (%)	2020 (%)	2021 (%)	2022 (%)
MSA[1]	n/a	n/a	n/a	n/a	n/a	n/a	n/a	n/a
U.S.	63.7	63.4	63.9	64.4	64.6	66.6	65.5	65.8

Note: (1) Figures cover the Reno, NV Metropolitan Statistical Area; n/a not available
Source: U.S. Census Bureau, Housing Vacancies and Homeownership Annual Statistics: 2015-2022

House Price Index (HPI)

Area	National Ranking[2]	Quarterly Change (%)	One-Year Change (%)	Five-Year Change (%)	Since 1991Q1 (%)
MSA[1]	244	-1.71	5.01	60.21	333.43
U.S.[3]	–	0.34	8.41	58.44	289.08

Note: The HPI is a weighted repeat sales index. It measures average price changes in repeat sales or refinancings on the same properties. This information is obtained by reviewing repeat mortgage transactions on single-family properties whose mortgages have been purchased or securitized by Fannie Mae or Freddie Mac since January 1975; (1) Figures cover the Reno, NV Metropolitan Statistical Area; (2) Rankings are based on annual percentage change for all metro areas containing at least 15,000 transactions over the last 10 years and ranges from 1 to 257; (3) figures based on a weighted average of Census Division estimates using a seasonally adjusted, purchase-only index; all figures are for the period ending December 31, 2022
Source: Federal Housing Finance Agency, Change in FHFA Metropolitan Area House Price Indexes, 2022Q4

Median Single-Family Home Prices

Area	2020	2021	2022[p]	Percent Change 2021 to 2022
MSA[1]	440.8	531.8	596.6	12.2
U.S. Average	300.2	357.1	392.6	9.9

Note: Figures are median sales prices of existing single-family homes in thousands of dollars; (p) preliminary; (1) Figures cover the Reno, NV Metropolitan Statistical Area
Source: National Association of Realtors, Median Sales Price of Existing Single-Family Homes for Metropolitan Areas, 4th Quarter 2022

Qualifying Income Based on Median Sales Price of Existing Single-Family Homes

Area	With 5% Down ($)	With 10% Down ($)	With 20% Down ($)
MSA[1]	168,171	159,320	141,618
U.S. Average	112,234	106,237	94,513

Note: Figures are preliminary; Qualifying income is based on a mortgage rate of 6.77%. Monthly principal and interest payment is limited to 25% of income; (1) Figures cover the Reno, NV Metropolitan Statistical Area
Source: National Association of Realtors, Qualifying Income Based on Median Sales Price of Existing Single-Family Homes for Metropolitan Areas, 4th Quarter 2022

Home Value

Area	Under $100,000	$100,000 -$199,999	$200,000 -$299,999	$300,000 -$399,999	$400,000 -$499,999	$500,000 -$999,999	$1,000,000 or more	Median ($)
City	5.9	5.9	14.6	25.8	20.2	24.1	3.5	391,500
MSA[1]	5.5	6.4	16.4	25.0	18.1	22.9	5.9	387,400
U.S.	16.2	24.2	20.1	13.6	8.3	13.6	4.1	244,900

Note: Figures are percentages except for median and cover owner-occupied housing units; (1) Figures cover the Reno, NV Metropolitan Statistical Area
Source: U.S. Census Bureau, 2017-2021 American Community Survey 5-Year Estimates

Year Housing Structure Built

Area	2020 or Later	2010 -2019	2000 -2009	1990 -1999	1980 -1989	1970 -1979	1960 -1969	1950 -1959	1940 -1949	Before 1940	Median Year
City	1.0	9.8	19.0	17.3	13.8	18.0	8.8	6.1	3.1	3.1	1988
MSA[1]	0.7	8.8	20.1	18.8	14.8	18.9	8.6	4.7	2.3	2.3	1989
U.S.	0.2	7.3	13.6	13.6	13.2	14.8	10.3	10.0	4.7	12.2	1979

Note: Figures are percentages except for Median Year; Note: (1) Figures cover the Reno, NV Metropolitan Statistical Area
Source: U.S. Census Bureau, 2017-2021 American Community Survey 5-Year Estimates

Gross Monthly Rent

Area	Under $500	$500 -$999	$1,000 -$1,499	$1,500 -$1,999	$2,000 -$2,499	$2,500 -$2,999	$3,000 and up	Median ($)
City	5.7	27.4	37.5	21.1	6.4	1.0	1.0	1,213
MSA[1]	4.8	26.6	36.7	22.2	6.7	1.5	1.5	1,250
U.S.	8.1	30.5	30.8	16.8	7.3	3.1	3.5	1,163

Note: Figures are percentages except for median; Gross rent is the contract rent plus the estimated average monthly cost of utilities (electricity, gas, and water and sewer) and fuels (oil, coal, kerosene, wood, etc.) if these are paid by the renter (or paid for the renter by someone else); (1) Figures cover the Reno, NV Metropolitan Statistical Area
Source: U.S. Census Bureau, 2017-2021 American Community Survey 5-Year Estimates

HEALTH

Health Risk Factors

Category	MSA[1] (%)	U.S. (%)
Adults aged 18–64 who have any kind of health care coverage	92.9	90.9
Adults who reported being in good or better health	84.0	85.2
Adults who have been told they have high blood cholesterol	36.9	35.7
Adults who have been told they have high blood pressure	31.4	32.4
Adults who are current smokers	16.3	14.4
Adults who currently use e-cigarettes	7.3	6.7
Adults who currently use chewing tobacco, snuff, or snus	3.5	3.5
Adults who are heavy drinkers[2]	8.6	6.3
Adults who are binge drinkers[3]	19.9	15.4
Adults who are overweight (BMI 25.0 - 29.9)	36.5	34.4
Adults who are obese (BMI 30.0 - 99.8)	27.4	33.9
Adults who participated in any physical activities in the past month	74.9	76.3

Note: (1) Figures cover the Reno, NV Metropolitan Statistical Area; (2) Heavy drinkers are classified as adult men having more than 14 drinks per week and adult women having more than 7 drinks per week; (3) Binge drinkers are classified as males having five or more drinks on one occasion or females having four or more drinks on one occasion
Source: Centers for Disease Control and Prevention, Behaviorial Risk Factor Surveillance System, SMART: Selected Metropolitan Area Risk Trends, 2021

Acute and Chronic Health Conditions

Category	MSA[1] (%)	U.S. (%)
Adults who have ever been told they had a heart attack	4.9	4.0
Adults who have ever been told they have angina or coronary heart disease	4.8	3.8
Adults who have ever been told they had a stroke	2.9	3.0
Adults who have ever been told they have asthma	12.8	14.9
Adults who have ever been told they have arthritis	26.8	25.8
Adults who have ever been told they have diabetes[2]	10.8	10.9
Adults who have ever been told they had skin cancer	11.8	6.6
Adults who have ever been told they had any other types of cancer	8.4	7.5
Adults who have ever been told they have COPD	8.4	6.1
Adults who have ever been told they have kidney disease	3.6	3.0
Adults who have ever been told they have a form of depression	18.3	20.5

Note: (1) Figures cover the Reno, NV Metropolitan Statistical Area; (2) Figures do not include pregnancy-related, borderline, or pre-diabetes
Source: Centers for Disease Control and Prevention, Behaviorial Risk Factor Surveillance System, SMART: Selected Metropolitan Area Risk Trends, 2021

Health Screening and Vaccination Rates

Category	MSA[1] (%)	U.S. (%)
Adults who have ever been tested for HIV	42.2	34.9
Adults who have had their blood cholesterol checked within the last five years	81.3	85.2
Adults aged 65+ who have had flu shot within the past year	67.1	68.6
Adults aged 65+ who have ever had a pneumonia vaccination	75.8	71.0

Note: (1) Figures cover the Reno, NV Metropolitan Statistical Area.
Source: Centers for Disease Control and Prevention, Behaviorial Risk Factor Surveillance System, SMART: Selected Metropolitan Area Risk Trends, 2021

Disability Status

Category	MSA[1] (%)	U.S. (%)
Adults who reported being deaf	10.2	7.2
Are you blind or have serious difficulty seeing, even when wearing glasses?	4.8	4.8
Are you limited in any way in any of your usual activities due to arthritis?	11.4	11.1
Do you have difficulty doing errands alone?	9.0	7.0
Do you have difficulty dressing or bathing?	4.3	3.6
Do you have serious difficulty concentrating/remembering/making decisions?	13.2	12.1
Do you have serious difficulty walking or climbing stairs?	14.9	12.8

Note: (1) Figures cover the Reno, NV Metropolitan Statistical Area.
Source: Centers for Disease Control and Prevention, Behaviorial Risk Factor Surveillance System, SMART: Selected Metropolitan Area Risk Trends, 2021

Mortality Rates for the Top 10 Causes of Death in the U.S.

ICD-10[a] Sub-Chapter	ICD-10[a] Code	Crude Mortality Rate[1] per 100,000 population	
		County[2]	U.S.
Malignant neoplasms	C00-C97	166.9	182.6
Ischaemic heart diseases	I20-I25	129.4	113.1
Other forms of heart disease	I30-I51	46.6	64.4
Other degenerative diseases of the nervous system	G30-G31	34.5	51.0
Cerebrovascular diseases	I60-I69	53.7	47.8
Other external causes of accidental injury	W00-X59	55.8	46.4
Chronic lower respiratory diseases	J40-J47	50.8	45.7
Organic, including symptomatic, mental disorders	F01-F09	20.8	35.9
Hypertensive diseases	I10-I15	33.8	35.0
Diabetes mellitus	E10-E14	26.4	29.6

Note: (a) ICD-10 = International Classification of Diseases 10th Revision; (1) Crude mortality rates are a three-year average covering 2019-2021; (2) Figures cover Washoe County.
Source: Centers for Disease Control and Prevention, National Center for Health Statistics. National Vital Statistics System, Mortality 2018-2021 on CDC WONDER Online Database

Mortality Rates for Selected Causes of Death

ICD-10[a] Sub-Chapter	ICD-10[a] Code	Crude Mortality Rate[1] per 100,000 population	
		County[2]	U.S.
Assault	X85-Y09	6.3	7.0
Diseases of the liver	K70-K76	23.3	19.8
Human immunodeficiency virus (HIV) disease	B20-B24	1.4	1.5
Influenza and pneumonia	J09-J18	12.1	14.7
Intentional self-harm	X60-X84	22.1	14.3
Malnutrition	E40-E46	6.2	4.3
Obesity and other hyperalimentation	E65-E68	3.8	3.0
Renal failure	N17-N19	9.9	15.7
Transport accidents	V01-V99	12.5	13.6
Viral hepatitis	B15-B19	Unreliable	1.2

Note: (a) ICD-10 = International Classification of Diseases 10th Revision; (1) Crude mortality rates are a three-year average covering 2019-2021; (2) Figures cover Washoe County; Data are suppressed when the data meet the criteria for confidentiality constraints; Crude mortality rates are flagged as unreliable when the rate would be calculated with a numerator of 20 or less.
Source: Centers for Disease Control and Prevention, National Center for Health Statistics. National Vital Statistics System, Mortality 2018-2021 on CDC WONDER Online Database

Health Insurance Coverage

Area	With Health Insurance	With Private Health Insurance	With Public Health Insurance	Without Health Insurance	Population Under Age 19 Without Health Insurance
City	90.0	69.1	30.5	10.0	8.4
MSA[1]	90.2	69.8	31.2	9.8	7.8
U.S.	91.2	67.8	35.4	8.8	5.3

Note: Figures are percentages that cover the civilian noninstitutionalized population; (1) Figures cover the Reno, NV Metropolitan Statistical Area
Source: U.S. Census Bureau, 2017-2021 American Community Survey 5-Year Estimates

Number of Medical Professionals

Area	MDs[3]	DOs[3,4]	Dentists	Podiatrists	Chiropractors	Optometrists
County[1] (number)	1,453	100	343	19	143	118
County[1] (rate[2])	298.1	20.5	69.5	3.9	29.0	23.9
U.S. (rate[2])	289.3	23.5	72.5	6.2	28.7	17.4

Note: Data as of 2021 unless noted; (1) Data covers Washoe County; (2) Rate per 100,000 population; (3) Data as of 2020 and includes all active, non-federal physicians; (4) Doctor of Osteopathic Medicine
Source: U.S. Department of Health and Human Services, Health Resources and Services Administration, Bureau of Health Professions, Area Resource File (ARF) 2021-2022

EDUCATION

Public School District Statistics

District Name	Schls	Pupils	Pupil/ Teacher Ratio	Minority Pupils[1] (%)	LEP/ELL[2] (%)	IEP[3] (%)
Washoe County School District	114	65,538	n/a	57.7	15.0	14.2

Note: Table includes school districts with 2,000 or more students; (1) Percentage of students that are not non-Hispanic white; (2) Percentage of students that are Limited English Proficient or English Language Learners (2018-19); (3) Percentage of students that have an Individualized Education Program (2019-20).
Source: U.S. Department of Education, National Center for Education Statistics, Common Core of Data, Local Education Agency (School District) Universe Survey: School Year 2021-2022

Best High Schools

According to *U.S. News,* Reno is home to two of the top 500 high schools in the U.S.: **The Davidson Academy of Nevada** (#6); **Coral Academy High School** (#275). Nearly 18,000 public, magnet and charter schools were ranked based on their performance on state assessments and how well they prepare students for college. *U.S. News & World Report, "Best High Schools 2022"*

Highest Level of Education

Area	Less than H.S.	H.S. Diploma	Some College, No Deg.	Associate Degree	Bachelor's Degree	Master's Degree	Prof. School Degree	Doctorate Degree
City	10.2	22.7	23.3	8.3	21.6	9.2	2.5	2.3
MSA[1]	11.4	23.8	23.9	8.6	19.8	8.5	2.2	1.8
U.S.	11.1	26.5	20.0	8.7	20.6	9.3	2.2	1.5

Note: Figures cover persons age 25 and over; (1) Figures cover the Reno, NV Metropolitan Statistical Area
Source: U.S. Census Bureau, 2017-2021 American Community Survey 5-Year Estimates

Educational Attainment by Race

Area	High School Graduate or Higher (%)					Bachelor's Degree or Higher (%)				
	Total	White	Black	Asian	Hisp.[2]	Total	White	Black	Asian	Hisp.[2]
City	89.8	93.9	90.8	92.4	66.3	35.5	38.3	31.1	49.5	13.5
MSA[1]	88.6	92.8	90.7	92.0	64.2	32.3	34.9	28.0	47.1	13.2
U.S.	88.9	91.4	87.2	87.6	71.2	33.7	35.5	23.3	55.6	18.4

Note: Figures shown cover persons 25 years old and over; (1) Figures cover the Reno, NV Metropolitan Statistical Area; (2) People of Hispanic origin can be of any race
Source: U.S. Census Bureau, 2017-2021 American Community Survey 5-Year Estimates

School Enrollment by Grade and Control

Area	Preschool (%)		Kindergarten (%)		Grades 1 - 4 (%)		Grades 5 - 8 (%)		Grades 9 - 12 (%)	
	Public	Private	Public	Private	Public	Private	Public	Private	Public	Private
City	59.8	40.2	92.4	7.6	94.3	5.7	92.0	8.0	93.1	6.9
MSA[1]	54.1	45.9	89.2	10.8	93.0	7.0	92.3	7.7	92.1	7.9
U.S.	58.8	41.2	86.3	13.7	88.3	11.7	88.6	11.4	89.4	10.6

Note: Figures shown cover persons 3 years old and over; (1) Figures cover the Reno, NV Metropolitan Statistical Area
Source: U.S. Census Bureau, 2017-2021 American Community Survey 5-Year Estimates

Higher Education

Four-Year Colleges			Two-Year Colleges			Medical Schools[1]	Law Schools[2]	Voc/ Tech[3]
Public	Private Non-profit	Private For-profit	Public	Private Non-profit	Private For-profit			
2	1	0	2	0	2	1	0	4

Note: Figures cover institutions located within the Reno, NV Metropolitan Statistical Area and include main campuses only; (1) includes schools accredited by the Liaison Committee on Medical Education and the American Osteopathic Association's Commission on Osteopathic College Accreditation; (2) includes ABA-accredited schools, schools with provisional ABA accreditation, and state accredited schools; (3) includes all schools with programs that are less than 2 years.
Source: National Center for Education Statistics, Integrated Postsecondary Education System (IPEDS), 2021-22; Wikipedia, List of Medical Schools in the United States, accessed April 10, 2023; Wikipedia, List of Law Schools in the United States, accessed April 10, 2023

EMPLOYERS

Major Employers

Company Name	Industry
Atlantis Casino Resort	Casino hotels
Bellagio	Casino hotels
Circus Circus Casinos - Reno	Casino hotels
City of Reno	Municipal government
Desert Palace	Casino hotels
Eldorado Hotel & Casino	Casino hotels
Grand Sierra Resort & Casino	Casino hotels
Harrahs Reno	Casino hotels
IGT	All other miscellaneous manufacturing
Integrity Staffing Solutions	Temporary help services
Mandalay Corp	Casino hotels
Peppermill Hotel Casino - Reno	Casino hotels
Renown Regional Medical Center	General medical & surgical hospitals
Saint Marys	General medical & surgical hospitals
Sierra Nevada Healthcare System	General medical & surgical hospitals
Silver Legacy Resort Casino	Casino hotels
Sparks Nugget	Casino hotels
Truckee Meadows Community Coll	Junior colleges
United Parcel Service	Package delivery services
University of Nevada-Reno	Colleges & universities
Washoe County Comptroller	Executive & legislative offices combined
Washoe County School District	Elementary & secondary schools
West Business Solutions	Telemarketing bureaus

Note: Companies shown are located within the Reno, NV Metropolitan Statistical Area.
Source: Hoovers.com; Wikipedia

PUBLIC SAFETY

Crime Rate

Area	Total Crime	Violent Crime Rate				Property Crime Rate		
		Murder	Rape[3]	Robbery	Aggrav. Assault	Burglary	Larceny-Theft	Motor Vehicle Theft
City	2,710.2	6.6	108.4	110.4	338.0	426.4	1,345.1	375.4
Suburbs[1]	1,808.3	4.5	59.7	39.2	243.4	304.1	959.0	198.4
Metro[2]	2,291.8	5.6	85.8	77.4	294.1	369.6	1,165.9	293.3
U.S.	2,356.7	6.5	38.4	73.9	279.7	314.2	1,398.0	246.0

Note: Figures are crimes per 100,000 population; (1) All areas within the metro area that are located outside the city limits; (2) Figures cover the Reno, NV Metropolitan Statistical Area; (3) All figures shown were reported using the revised Uniform Crime Reporting (UCR) definition of rape; Due to the transition to the National Incident-Based Reporting System (NIBRS), limited city and metro area data was released for 2021.
Source: FBI Uniform Crime Reports, 2020

Hate Crimes

Area	Number of Quarters Reported	Number of Incidents per Bias Motivation					
		Race/Ethnicity/ Ancestry	Religion	Sexual Orientation	Disability	Gender	Gender Identity
City	4	30	3	1	0	2	0
U.S.	4	5,227	1,244	1,110	130	75	266

Note: Due to the transition to the National Incident-Based Reporting System (NIBRS), limited crime data was released for 2021.
Source: Federal Bureau of Investigation, Hate Crime Statistics 2020

Identity Theft Consumer Reports

Area	Reports	Reports per 100,000 Population	Rank[2]
MSA[1]	882	188	186
U.S.	1,108,609	339	-

Note: (1) Figures cover the Reno, NV Metropolitan Statistical Area; (2) Rank ranges from 1 to 391 where 1 indicates greatest number of identity theft reports per 100,000 population
Source: Federal Trade Commission, Consumer Sentinel Network Data Book 2022

Fraud and Other Consumer Reports

Area	Reports	Reports per 100,000 Population	Rank[2]
MSA[1]	4,582	978	106
U.S.	4,064,520	1,245	-

Note: (1) Figures cover the Reno, NV Metropolitan Statistical Area; (2) Rank ranges from 1 to 391 where 1 indicates greatest number of fraud and other consumer reports per 100,000 population
Source: Federal Trade Commission, Consumer Sentinel Network Data Book 2022

POLITICS

2020 Presidential Election Results

Area	Biden	Trump	Jorgensen	Hawkins	Other
Washoe County	50.8	46.3	1.4	0.0	1.5
U.S.	51.3	46.8	1.2	0.3	0.5

Note: Results are percentages and may not add to 100% due to rounding
Source: Dave Leip's Atlas of U.S. Presidential Elections

SPORTS

Professional Sports Teams

Team Name	League	Year Established

No teams are located in the metro area
Source: Wikipedia, Major Professional Sports Teams of the United States and Canada, April 12, 2023

CLIMATE

Average and Extreme Temperatures

Temperature	Jan	Feb	Mar	Apr	May	Jun	Jul	Aug	Sep	Oct	Nov	Dec	Yr.
Extreme High (°F)	70	75	83	89	96	103	104	105	101	91	77	70	105
Average High (°F)	45	51	56	64	73	82	91	89	81	70	55	46	67
Average Temp. (°F)	32	38	41	48	56	63	70	68	61	51	40	33	50
Average Low (°F)	19	23	26	31	38	44	49	47	40	32	25	20	33
Extreme Low (°F)	-16	-16	0	13	18	25	33	24	20	8	1	-16	-16

Note: Figures cover the years 1949-1992
Source: National Climatic Data Center, International Station Meteorological Climate Summary, 9/96

Average Precipitation/Snowfall/Humidity

Precip./Humidity	Jan	Feb	Mar	Apr	May	Jun	Jul	Aug	Sep	Oct	Nov	Dec	Yr.
Avg. Precip. (in.)	1.0	0.9	0.7	0.4	0.7	0.4	0.3	0.2	0.3	0.4	0.8	1.0	7.2
Avg. Snowfall (in.)	6	5	4	1	1	Tr	0	0	Tr	Tr	2	4	24
Avg. Rel. Hum. 7am (%)	79	77	71	61	55	51	49	55	64	72	78	80	66
Avg. Rel. Hum. 4pm (%)	51	41	34	27	26	22	19	19	22	27	41	51	32

Note: Figures cover the years 1949-1992; Tr = Trace amounts (<0.05 in. of rain; <0.5 in. of snow)
Source: National Climatic Data Center, International Station Meteorological Climate Summary, 9/96

Weather Conditions

Temperature			Daytime Sky			Precipitation		
10°F & below	32°F & below	90°F & above	Clear	Partly cloudy	Cloudy	0.01 inch or more precip.	0.1 inch or more snow/ice	Thunder-storms
14	178	50	143	139	83	50	17	14

Note: Figures are average number of days per year and cover the years 1949-1992
Source: National Climatic Data Center, International Station Meteorological Climate Summary, 9/96

HAZARDOUS WASTE

Superfund Sites

The Reno, NV metro area has no sites on the EPA's Superfund Final National Priorities List. There are a total of 1,165 Superfund sites with a status of proposed or final on the list in the U.S. *U.S. Environmental Protection Agency, National Priorities List, April 12, 2023*

AIR QUALITY

Air Quality Trends: Ozone

	1990	1995	2000	2005	2010	2015	2018	2019	2020	2021
MSA[1]	0.074	0.069	0.067	0.069	0.068	0.071	0.077	0.063	0.073	0.078
U.S.	0.087	0.089	0.081	0.080	0.072	0.067	0.069	0.065	0.065	0.067

Note: (1) Data covers the Reno, NV Metropolitan Statistical Area. The values shown are the composite ozone concentration averages among trend sites based on the highest fourth daily maximum 8-hour concentration in parts per million. These trends are based on sites having an adequate record of monitoring data during the trend period. Data from exceptional events are included.
Source: U.S. Environmental Protection Agency, Air Quality Monitoring Information, "Air Quality Trends by City, 1990-2021"

Air Quality Index

Area	Percent of Days when Air Quality was...[2]					AQI Statistics[2]	
	Good	Moderate	Unhealthy for Sensitive Groups	Unhealthy	Very Unhealthy	Maximum	Median
MSA[1]	54.2	36.2	4.4	4.4	0.8	291	49

Note: (1) Data covers the Reno, NV Metropolitan Statistical Area; (2) Based on 365 days with AQI data in 2021. Air Quality Index (AQI) is an index for reporting daily air quality. EPA calculates the AQI for five major air pollutants regulated by the Clean Air Act: ground-level ozone, particle pollution (aka particulate matter), carbon monoxide, sulfur dioxide, and nitrogen dioxide. The AQI runs from 0 to 500. The higher the AQI value, the greater the level of air pollution and the greater the health concern. There are six AQI categories: "Good" AQI is between 0 and 50. Air quality is considered satisfactory; "Moderate" AQI is between 51 and 100. Air quality is acceptable; "Unhealthy for Sensitive Groups" When AQI values are between 101 and 150, members of sensitive groups may experience health effects; "Unhealthy" When AQI values are between 151 and 200 everyone may begin to experience health effects; "Very Unhealthy" AQI values between 201 and 300 trigger a health alert; "Hazardous" AQI values over 300 trigger warnings of emergency conditions (not shown).
Source: U.S. Environmental Protection Agency, Air Quality Index Report, 2021

Air Quality Index Pollutants

Area	Percent of Days when AQI Pollutant was...[2]					
	Carbon Monoxide	Nitrogen Dioxide	Ozone	Sulfur Dioxide	Particulate Matter 2.5	Particulate Matter 10
MSA[1]	0.0	1.4	72.6	(3)	24.9	1.1

Note: (1) Data covers the Reno, NV Metropolitan Statistical Area; (2) Based on 365 days with AQI data in 2021. The Air Quality Index (AQI) is an index for reporting daily air quality. EPA calculates the AQI for five major air pollutants regulated by the Clean Air Act: ground-level ozone, particle pollution (also known as particulate matter), carbon monoxide, sulfur dioxide, and nitrogen dioxide. The AQI runs from 0 to 500. The higher the AQI value, the greater the level of air pollution and the greater the health concern; (3) Sulfur dioxide is no longer included in this table (as of December 8, 2021) because SO_2 concentrations tend to be very localized and not necessarily representative of broad geographical areas like counties and CBSAs.
Source: U.S. Environmental Protection Agency, Air Quality Index Report, 2021

Maximum Air Pollutant Concentrations: Particulate Matter, Ozone, CO and Lead

	Particulate Matter 10 (ug/m³)	Particulate Matter 2.5 Wtd AM (ug/m³)	Particulate Matter 2.5 24-Hr (ug/m³)	Ozone (ppm)	Carbon Monoxide (ppm)	Lead (ug/m³)
MSA[1] Level	284	12.4	105	0.08	2	n/a
NAAQS[2]	150	15	35	0.075	9	0.15
Met NAAQS[2]	No	Yes	No	No	Yes	n/a

Note: (1) Data covers the Reno, NV Metropolitan Statistical Area; Data from exceptional events are included; (2) National Ambient Air Quality Standards; ppm = parts per million; ug/m³ = micrograms per cubic meter; n/a not available.
Concentrations: Particulate Matter 10 (coarse particulate)—highest second maximum 24-hour concentration; Particulate Matter 2.5 Wtd AM (fine particulate)—highest weighted annual mean concentration; Particulate Matter 2.5 24-Hour (fine particulate)—highest 98th percentile 24-hour concentration; Ozone—highest fourth daily maximum 8-hour concentration; Carbon Monoxide—highest second maximum non-overlapping 8-hour concentration; Lead—maximum running 3-month average
Source: U.S. Environmental Protection Agency, Air Quality Monitoring Information, "Air Quality Statistics by City, 2021"

Maximum Air Pollutant Concentrations: Nitrogen Dioxide and Sulfur Dioxide

	Nitrogen Dioxide AM (ppb)	Nitrogen Dioxide 1-Hr (ppb)	Sulfur Dioxide AM (ppb)	Sulfur Dioxide 1-Hr (ppb)	Sulfur Dioxide 24-Hr (ppb)
MSA[1] Level	12	47	n/a	3	n/a
NAAQS[2]	53	100	30	75	140
Met NAAQS[2]	Yes	Yes	n/a	Yes	n/a

Note: (1) Data covers the Reno, NV Metropolitan Statistical Area; Data from exceptional events are included; (2) National Ambient Air Quality Standards; ppm = parts per million; ug/m³ = micrograms per cubic meter; n/a not available.
Concentrations: Nitrogen Dioxide AM—highest arithmetic mean concentration; Nitrogen Dioxide 1-Hr—highest 98th percentile 1-hour daily maximum concentration; Sulfur Dioxide AM—highest annual mean concentration; Sulfur Dioxide 1-Hr—highest 99th percentile 1-hour daily maximum concentration; Sulfur Dioxide 24-Hr—highest second maximum 24-hour concentration
Source: U.S. Environmental Protection Agency, Air Quality Monitoring Information, "Air Quality Statistics by City, 2021"

Sacramento, California

Background

Sacramento is the capital of California, the seat of Sacramento County, and the sixth-largest city in the state. It was named after the Sacramento River which derived its name from the Catholic sacrament of the Holy Eucharist. It lies at the juncture of the Sacramento and American rivers.

A Swiss soldier, Captain John Augustus Sutter, settled Sacramento in 1839, when he received permission from the Mexican government to establish a new colony which became known as New Helvetia. The 50,000-acre land grant included a wide swath of the rich and fertile valley between the two rivers, and Sutter's ranch, trading post, and agricultural projects were soon productive and profitable. When, in 1846, American troops occupied the area, Sutter was well-positioned to take advantage, and his trade soon extended well up the northern coast.

In 1848, one of Sutter's employees, a carpenter named James W. Marshall, discovered gold at what became known as "Sutter's Mill" in the settlement of Coloma. The discovery brought an onslaught of prospectors and the beginning of the California Gold Rush. The prospectors overwhelmed New Helvetia resources and the havoc that followed destroyed the economic foundation of the town. The newcomers overran Sutter's land and claimed it as their own. Sutter tried to expand his business to include mining supplies but was only meagerly rewarded. He ceded land along the Sacramento River to his son, who founded the town that became the city we know today.

Sacramento supported miners with housing, food, banking, transportation and necessary mining equipment. One of Sacramento's most famous entrepreneurs is Levi Strauss who sold the ultimate mining pants known as "Levi's." Sacramento's economy was booming, but plagued by floods, fire, and a cholera epidemic. Today, flooding that is endemic to the area is controlled by a series of dams, which also supply a large amount of electricity to the area.

On April 3, 1860, the legendary Pony Express carried mail from Sacramento to St. Joseph, Missouri on horseback in record time. The ten-day journey of nearly 1,800 miles was unprofitable but caught the attention of the federal government and helped launch our current postal system.

In the years since, the city has grown rapidly, passing 400,000 in 2000 and 500,000 in 2020. As befitting a state capital, government (state, county, and local) is the largest employer in the city, followed by the health industry, including UC David Health and Kaiser Permanente. Other notable companies located in the area include Sutter Health, Blue Diamond Growers, Aerojet Rocketdyne, and the McClatchey Company.

Sutter's Fort State Historical Monument features a restoration of John Sutter's original ranch and trading post, and a designated Old Sacramento Historical Area preserves many buildings from the gold rush period and thereafter. At the city's Crocker Art Museum, visitors can view an extensive collection of works by Michelangelo, Rembrandt, and Leonardo da Vinci. In October 2010, the Crocker completed a 100,000-ft. expansion that more than tripled its size.

Sacramento has been called America's most diverse city and the most hipster city in California.

The Wells Fargo Museum is a monument to the history of the Pony Express and the era of the gold rush. Housed in the original bank building that managed the Pony Express, its staff conducts tours dressed in period attire. The museum displays include tools, gold nuggets, documents, and other relevant artifacts.

The Woodland Opera House opened in 1896 in nearby Woodland, California. It closed in 1913, when motion pictures took hold of the public's interest and the building stayed dormant until 1971 when Yolo County Historic Society saved it from demolition. They gave it to the state in 1980 and it underwent a total renovation in 1982. Today it is a major entertainment venue and on the National Register of Historic Places.

Since 1985, Sacramento has hosted NBA basketball when the Kings relocated from Kansas City. The city fields a professional soccer team, the Sacramento Republic FC of the USL Championship League, and a minor league baseball team, the River Cats, the AAA affiliate of the San Francisco Giants. Golden1 Center sports arena opened in 2016.

Sacramento has a mild climate with abundant sunshine. A nearly cloud-free sky prevails throughout the summer months, which are usually dry, with warm to hot afternoons and mostly mild nights.

Rankings

General Rankings

- Sacramento was selected as one of the best places to live in America by *Outside Magazine*. Criteria centered on diversity; sustainability; outdoor equity; and affordability. Local experts shared highlights from hands-on experience in each location. *Outside Magazine, "The 20 Most Livable Towns and Cities in America," October 15, 2021*

- Sacramento was selected as an "All-America City" by the National Civic League. The All-America City Award recognizes civic excellence and in 2022 honored 10 communities that best exemplify the spirit of grassroots citizen involvement and cross-sector collaborative problem solving to collectively tackle pressing and complex issues. This year's theme was: "Housing as a Platform to Promote Early School Success and Equitable Learning Recovery." *National Civic League, "2022 All-America City Awards," July 21, 2022*

Business/Finance Rankings

- The Brookings Institution ranked the nation's largest cities based on income inequality. Sacramento was ranked #71 (#1 = greatest inequality). Criteria: the "95/20 ratio," a figure representing the income at which a household earns more than 95 percent of all other households, divided by the income at which a household earns more than only 20 percent of all other households. *Brookings Institution, "Household Income Inequality, Largest Cities of 97 Large U.S. Metro Areas, 2014-2016," February 5, 2018*

- The Brookings Institution ranked the 100 largest metro areas in the U.S. based on income inequality. Sacramento was ranked #33 (#1 = greatest inequality). Criteria: the "95/20 ratio," a figure representing the income at which a household earns more than 95 percent of all other households, divided by the income at which a household earns more than only 20 percent of all other households. *Brookings Institution, "Household Income Inequality, 100 Largest U.S. Metro Areas, 2014-2016," February 5, 2018*

- The Sacramento metro area appeared on the Milken Institute "2022 Best Performing Cities" list. Rank: #44 out of 200 large metro areas (population over 250,000). Criteria: job growth; wage and salary growth; high-tech output growth; housing affordability; household broadband access. *Milken Institute, "Best-Performing Cities 2022," March 28, 2022*

- *Forbes* ranked the 200 most populous metro areas to determine the nation's "Best Places for Business and Careers." The Sacramento metro area was ranked #56. Criteria: costs (business and living); job growth (past and projected); income growth; quality of life; educational attainment (college and high school); projected economic growth; cultural and leisure opportunities; workplace tolerance laws; net migration patterns. *Forbes, "The Best Places for Business and Careers 2019: Seattle Still On Top," October 30, 2019*

Education Rankings

- Personal finance website *WalletHub* analyzed the 150 largest U.S. metropolitan statistical areas to determine where the most educated Americans are putting their degrees to work. Criteria: education levels; percentage of workers with degrees; education quality and attainment gap; public school quality rankings; quality and enrollment of each metro area's universities. Sacramento was ranked #49 (#1 = most educated city). *www.WalletHub.com, "Most & Least Educated Cities in America," July 18, 2022*

- Sacramento was selected as one of America's most literate cities. The city ranked #42 out of the 84 largest U.S. cities. Criteria: number of booksellers; library resources; Internet resources; educational attainment; periodical publishing resources; newspaper circulation. *Central Connecticut State University, "America's Most Literate Cities, 2018," February 2019*

Environmental Rankings

- Sperling's BestPlaces assessed the 50 largest metropolitan areas of the United States for the likelihood of dangerously extreme weather events or earthquakes. In general the Southeast and South-Central regions have the highest risk of weather extremes and earthquakes, while the Pacific Northwest enjoys the lowest risk. Of the least risky metropolitan areas, the Sacramento metro area was ranked #3. *www.bestplaces.net, "Avoid Natural Disasters: BestPlaces Reveals The Top 10 Safest Places to Live," October 25, 2017*

- The U.S. Environmental Protection Agency (EPA) released its list of U.S. metropolitan areas with the most ENERGY STAR certified buildings in 2022. The Sacramento metro area was ranked #21 out of 25. *U.S. Environmental Protection Agency, "2023 Energy Star Top Cities," April 26, 2023*

- Sacramento was highlighted as one of the 25 most ozone-polluted metro areas in the U.S. during 2019 through 2021. The area ranked #7. *American Lung Association, "State of the Air 2023," April 19, 2023*

- Sacramento was highlighted as one of the 25 metro areas most polluted by year-round particle pollution (Annual PM 2.5) in the U.S. during 2019 through 2021. The area ranked #6. *American Lung Association, "State of the Air 2023," April 19, 2023*

- Sacramento was highlighted as one of the 25 metro areas most polluted by short-term particle pollution (24-hour PM 2.5) in the U.S. during 2019 through 2021. The area ranked #8. *American Lung Association, "State of the Air 2023," April 19, 2023*

Health/Fitness Rankings

- For each of the 100 largest cities in the United States, the American Fitness Index®, compiled in partnership between the American College of Sports Medicine and the Elevance Health Foundation, evaluated community infrastructure and 34 health behaviors including preventive health, levels of chronic disease conditions, food insecurity, sleep quality, pedestrian safety, air quality, and community/environment resources that support physical activity. Sacramento ranked #28 for "community fitness." *americanfitnessindex.org, "2022 ACSM American Fitness Index Summary Report," July 12, 2022*

- Sacramento was identified as a "2022 Spring Allergy Capital." The area ranked #90 out of 100. Three groups of factors were used to identify the most challenging cities for people with allergies during the spring season: annual spring pollen scores; over the counter allergy medicine use; number of board-certified allergy specialists. *Asthma and Allergy Foundation of America, "Spring Allergy Capitals 2022," March 2, 2022*

- Sacramento was identified as a "2022 Fall Allergy Capital." The area ranked #97 out of 100. Three groups of factors were used to identify the most challenging cities for people with allergies during the fall season: annual fall pollen scores; over the counter allergy medicine use; number of board-certified allergy specialists. *Asthma and Allergy Foundation of America, "Fall Allergy Capitals 2022," March 2, 2022*

- Sacramento was identified as a "2022 Asthma Capital." The area ranked #43 out of the nation's 100 largest metropolitan areas. Criteria: estimated asthma prevalence; asthma-related mortality; and ER visits due to asthma. Risk factors analyzed but not factored in the rankings: annual pollen score; annual air quality; public smoking laws; access to board-certified asthma specialists; rescue and controller medication use; uninsured rate; poverty rate. *Asthma and Allergy Foundation of America, "Asthma Capitals 2022: The Most Challenging Places to Live With Asthma," September 14, 2022*

Real Estate Rankings

- *WalletHub* compared the most populated U.S. cities to determine which had the best markets for real estate agents. Sacramento ranked #3 where demand was high and pay was the best. Criteria: sales per agent; annual median wage for real-estate agents; monthly average starting salary for real estate agents; real estate job density and competition; unemployment rate; home turnover rate; housing-market health index; and other relevant metrics. *www.WalletHub.com, "2021 Best Places to Be a Real Estate Agent," May 12, 2021*

- The Sacramento metro area was identified as one of the 20 worst housing markets in the U.S. in 2022. The area ranked #181 out of 187 markets. Criteria: year-over-year change of median sales price of existing single-family homes between the 4th quarter of 2021 and the 4th quarter of 2022. *National Association of Realtors®, Median Sales Price of Existing Single-Family Homes for Metropolitan Areas, 4th Quarter 2022*

- The Sacramento metro area was identified as one of the 10 worst condo markets in the U.S. in 2022. The area ranked #58 out of 63 markets. Criteria: year-over-year change of median sales price of existing apartment condo-coop homes between the 4th quarter of 2021 and the 4th quarter of 2022. *National Association of Realtors®, Median Sales Price of Existing Apartment Condo-Coops Homes for Metropolitan Areas, 4th Quarter 2022*

- Sacramento was ranked #216 out of 235 metro areas in terms of housing affordability in 2022 by the National Association of Home Builders (#1 = most affordable). Criteria: the share of homes sold in that area affordable to a family earning the local median income, based on standard mortgage underwriting criteria. *National Association of Home Builders®, NAHB-Wells Fargo Housing Opportunity Index, 4th Quarter 2022*

Safety Rankings

■ Allstate ranked the 200 largest cities in America in terms of driver safety. Sacramento ranked #163. Criteria: internal property damage claims over a two-year period from January 2016 to December 2017. The report helps increase the importance of safety and awareness behind the wheel. *Allstate, "Allstate America's Best Drivers Report, 2019" June 24, 2019*

■ The National Insurance Crime Bureau ranked 390 metro areas in the U.S. in terms of per capita rates of vehicle theft. The Sacramento metro area ranked #51 (#1 = highest rate). Criteria: number of vehicle theft offenses per 100,000 inhabitants in 2021. *National Insurance Crime Bureau, "Hot Spots 2021," September 1, 2022*

Seniors/Retirement Rankings

■ From its Best Cities for Successful Aging indexes, the Milken Institute generated rankings for metropolitan areas, weighing data in nine categories—health care, wellness, living arrangements, transportation and convenience, financial characteristics, education, employment, community engagement, and overall livability. The Sacramento metro area was ranked #82 overall in the large metro area category. *Milken Institute, "Best Cities for Successful Aging, 2017" March 14, 2017*

Sports/Recreation Rankings

■ Sacramento was chosen as one of America's best cities for bicycling. The city ranked #32 out of 50. Criteria: cycling infrastructure that is safe and friendly for all ages; energy and bike culture. The editors evaluated cities with populations of 100,000 or more. *Bicycling, "The 50 Best Bike Cities in America," October 10, 2018*

Transportation Rankings

■ According to the INRIX "2022 Global Traffic Scorecard," Sacramento was identified as one of the most congested metro areas in the U.S. The area ranked #25 out of 25. Criteria: average annual time spent in traffic and average cost of congestion per motorist. *Inrix.com, "Return to Work, Higher Gas Prices & Inflation Drove Americans to Spend Hundreds More in Time and Money Commuting," January 10, 2023*

Women/Minorities Rankings

■ Personal finance website *WalletHub* compared more than 180 U.S. cities across two key dimensions, "Hispanic Business-Friendliness" and "Hispanic Purchasing Power," to arrive at the most favorable conditions for Hispanic entrepreneurs. Sacramento was ranked #125 out of 182. Criteria includes: share of Hispanic-Owned Businesses; Hispanic entrepreneurship rate to median annual income of Hispanics; Small Business-Friendliness score; cost of living; and number of Hispanics with at least a bachelor's degree. *WalletHub.com, "2019's Best Cities for Hispanic Entrepreneurs," May 1, 2019*

Miscellaneous Rankings

■ *MoveHub* ranked 446 hipster cities across 20 countries, using its new and improved *alternative* Hipster Index and Sacramento came out as #35 among the top 50. Criteria: population over 150,000; number of vintage boutiques; density of tattoo parlors; vegan places to eat; coffee shops; and density of vinyl record stores. *www.movehub.com, "The Hipster Index: Brighton Pips Portland to Global Top Spot," July 28, 2021*

■ *WalletHub* compared the 150 most populated U.S. cities to determine their operating efficiency. A "Quality of Services" score was constructed for each city and then divided by the total budget per capita to reveal which were managed the best. Sacramento ranked #115. Criteria: financial stability; economy; education; safety; health; infrastructure and pollution. *www.WalletHub.com, "2022's Best-& Worst-Run Cities in America," June 21, 2022*

Business Environment

DEMOGRAPHICS

Population Growth

Area	1990 Census	2000 Census	2010 Census	2020 Census	Population Growth (%) 1990-2020	Population Growth (%) 2010-2020
City	368,923	407,018	466,488	524,943	42.3	12.5
MSA[1]	1,481,126	1,796,857	2,149,127	2,397,382	61.9	11.6
U.S.	248,709,873	281,421,906	308,745,538	331,449,281	33.3	7.4

Note: (1) Figures cover the Sacramento-Roseville-Folsom, CA Metropolitan Statistical Area
Source: U.S. Census Bureau, 1990 Census, 2000 Census, 2010 Census, 2020 Census

Race

Area	White Alone[2] (%)	Black Alone[2] (%)	Asian Alone[2] (%)	AIAN[3] Alone[2] (%)	NHOPI[4] Alone[2] (%)	Other Race Alone[2] (%)	Two or More Races (%)
City	34.8	13.2	19.9	1.4	1.6	15.3	13.8
MSA[1]	52.5	7.0	14.9	1.1	0.9	10.4	13.2
U.S.	61.6	12.4	6.0	1.1	0.2	8.4	10.2

Note: (1) Figures cover the Sacramento-Roseville-Folsom, CA Metropolitan Statistical Area; (2) Alone is defined as not being in combination with one or more other races; (3) American Indian and Alaska Native; (4) Native Hawaiian and Other Pacific Islander
Source: U.S. Census Bureau, 2020 Census

Hispanic or Latino Origin

Area	Total (%)	Mexican (%)	Puerto Rican (%)	Cuban (%)	Other (%)
City	28.9	24.1	0.9	0.2	3.7
MSA[1]	22.2	17.8	0.7	0.2	3.5
U.S.	18.4	11.2	1.8	0.7	4.7

Note: Persons of Hispanic or Latino origin can be of any race; (1) Figures cover the Sacramento-Roseville-Folsom, CA Metropolitan Statistical Area
Source: U.S. Census Bureau, 2017-2021 American Community Survey 5-Year Estimates

Age

Area	Under Age 5	Age 5–19	Age 20–34	Age 35–44	Age 45–54	Age 55–64	Age 65–74	Age 75–84	Age 85+	Median Age
City	5.9	18.8	24.6	14.1	11.5	11.2	8.5	3.7	1.6	35.4
MSA[1]	5.6	19.8	20.3	13.2	12.1	12.7	9.8	4.8	2.0	38.2
U.S.	5.6	19.2	20.2	12.7	12.4	13.1	10.0	4.9	1.9	38.8

Note: (1) Figures cover the Sacramento-Roseville-Folsom, CA Metropolitan Statistical Area
Source: U.S. Census Bureau, 2020 Census

Disability by Age

Area	All Ages	Under 18 Years Old	18 to 64 Years Old	65 Years and Over
City	11.8	3.3	9.6	36.7
MSA[1]	11.5	3.4	9.0	33.7
U.S.	12.6	4.4	10.3	33.4

Note: Figures show percent of the civilian noninstitutionalized population that reported having a disability. Disability status is determined from six types of difficulty: vision, hearing, cognitive, ambulatory, self-care, and independent living. For children under 5 years old, hearing and vision difficulty are used to determine disability status. For children between the ages of 5 and 14, disability status is determined from hearing, vision, cognitive, ambulatory, and self-care difficulties. For people aged 15 years and older, they are considered to have a disability if they have difficulty with any one of the six difficulty types; Note: (1) Figures cover the Sacramento-Roseville-Folsom, CA Metropolitan Statistical Area
Source: U.S. Census Bureau, 2017-2021 American Community Survey 5-Year Estimates

Ancestry

Area	German	Irish	English	American	Italian	Polish	French[2]	Scottish	Dutch
City	6.6	5.9	5.5	1.8	3.5	1.0	1.5	1.1	0.6
MSA[1]	10.1	7.9	8.7	2.6	4.7	1.2	1.9	1.6	0.9
U.S.	12.8	9.6	8.1	5.7	5.0	2.7	2.2	1.6	1.1

Note: Figures are the percentage of the total population reporting a particular ancestry. The nine most commonly reported ancestries in the U.S. are shown. Figures include multiple ancestries (e.g. if a person reported being Irish and Italian, they were included in both columns); (1) Figures cover the Sacramento-Roseville-Folsom, CA Metropolitan Statistical Area; (2) Excludes Basque
Source: U.S. Census Bureau, 2017-2021 American Community Survey 5-Year Estimates

Foreign-born Population

Area	Percent of Population Born in								
	Any Foreign Country	Asia	Mexico	Europe	Caribbean	Central America[2]	South America	Africa	Canada
City	20.9	10.3	5.8	1.4	0.1	0.7	0.4	0.5	0.2
MSA[1]	18.6	9.1	4.3	2.7	0.1	0.7	0.4	0.4	0.3
U.S.	13.6	4.2	3.3	1.5	1.4	1.1	1.1	0.8	0.2

Note: (1) Figures cover the Sacramento-Roseville-Folsom, CA Metropolitan Statistical Area; (2) Excludes Mexico.
Source: U.S. Census Bureau, 2017-2021 American Community Survey 5-Year Estimates

Household Size

Area	Persons in Household (%)							Average Household Size
	One	Two	Three	Four	Five	Six	Seven or More	
City	30.6	30.3	14.6	13.0	6.2	2.9	2.4	2.60
MSA[1]	24.7	33.0	16.0	14.8	6.9	2.8	1.9	2.70
U.S.	28.1	33.8	15.5	12.9	6.0	2.3	1.4	2.60

Note: (1) Figures cover the Sacramento-Roseville-Folsom, CA Metropolitan Statistical Area
Source: U.S. Census Bureau, 2017-2021 American Community Survey 5-Year Estimates

Household Relationships

Area	House-holder	Opposite-sex Spouse	Same-sex Spouse	Opposite-sex Unmarried Partner	Same-sex Unmarried Partner	Child[2]	Grand-child	Other Relatives	Non-relatives
City	36.7	13.5	0.4	3.0	0.3	28.0	2.6	7.5	4.7
MSA[1]	36.2	17.1	0.3	2.4	0.2	29.4	2.2	6.0	4.2
U.S.	38.3	17.5	0.2	2.5	0.2	28.3	2.4	4.8	3.4

Note: Figures are percent of the total population; (1) Figures cover the Sacramento-Roseville-Folsom, CA Metropolitan Statistical Area; (2) Includes biological, adopted, and stepchildren of the householder
Source: U.S. Census Bureau, 2020 Census

Gender

Area	Males	Females	Males per 100 Females
City	255,987	268,956	95.2
MSA[1]	1,170,850	1,226,532	95.5
U.S.	162,685,811	168,763,470	96.4

Note: (1) Figures cover the Sacramento-Roseville-Folsom, CA Metropolitan Statistical Area
Source: U.S. Census Bureau, 2020 Census

Marital Status

Area	Never Married	Now Married[2]	Separated	Widowed	Divorced
City	40.5	41.1	2.6	4.8	11.2
MSA[1]	33.9	48.6	2.0	4.9	10.6
U.S.	33.8	48.0	1.8	5.6	10.8

Note: Figures are percentages and cover the population 15 years of age and older; (1) Figures cover the Sacramento-Roseville-Folsom, CA Metropolitan Statistical Area; (2) Excludes separated
Source: U.S. Census Bureau, 2017-2021 American Community Survey 5-Year Estimates

Religious Groups by Family

Area	Catholic	Baptist	Methodist	LDS[2]	Pentecostal	Lutheran	Islam	Adventist	Other
MSA[1]	17.1	1.9	1.1	3.1	2.2	0.6	1.9	1.9	8.2
U.S.	18.7	7.3	3.0	2.0	1.8	1.7	1.3	1.3	11.6

Note: Figures are the number of adherents as a percentage of the total population and cover the eight largest religious groups in the U.S; (1) Figures cover the Sacramento-Roseville-Folsom, CA Metropolitan Statistical Area; (2) Church of Jesus Christ of Latter-day Saints
Sources: 2020 U.S. Religion Census, Association of Statisticians of American Religious Bodies; The Association of Religion Data Archives (ARDA)

Religious Groups by Tradition

Area	Catholic	Evangelical Protestant	Mainline Protestant	Black Protestant	Islam	Judaism	Hinduism	Orthodox	Buddhism
MSA[1]	17.1	10.4	1.4	1.1	1.9	0.2	0.4	0.3	0.5
U.S.	18.7	16.5	5.2	2.3	1.3	0.6	0.4	0.4	0.3

Note: Figures are the number of adherents as a percentage of the total population; (1) Figures cover the Sacramento-Roseville-Folsom, CA Metropolitan Statistical Area
Sources: 2020 U.S. Religion Census, Association of Statisticians of American Religious Bodies; The Association of Religion Data Archives (ARDA)

ECONOMY

Gross Metropolitan Product

Area	2020	2021	2022	2023	Rank[2]
MSA[1]	145.4	161.7	176.8	188.8	29

Note: Figures are in billions of dollars; (1) Figures cover the Sacramento-Roseville-Folsom, CA Metropolitan Statistical Area; (2) Rank is based on 2021 data and ranges from 1 to 381
Source: U.S. Conference of Mayors, U.S. Metro Economies: U.S. Metros Compared to Global and State Economies, June 2022

Economic Growth

Area	2018-20 (%)	2021 (%)	2022 (%)	2023 (%)	Rank[2]
MSA[1]	0.0	7.4	3.6	3.6	142
U.S.	-0.6	5.7	3.1	2.9	–

Note: Figures are real gross metropolitan product (GMP) growth rates and represent average annual percent change; (1) Figures cover the Sacramento-Roseville-Folsom, CA Metropolitan Statistical Area; (2) Rank is based on 2020 2-year average annual percent change and ranges from 1 to 381
Source: U.S. Conference of Mayors, U.S. Metro Economies: U.S. Metros Compared to Global and State Economies, June 2022

Metropolitan Area Exports

Area	2016	2017	2018	2019	2020	2021	Rank[2]
MSA[1]	7,032.1	6,552.6	6,222.8	5,449.2	4,980.9	5,682.3	54

Note: Figures are in millions of dollars; (1) Figures cover the Sacramento-Roseville-Folsom, CA Metropolitan Statistical Area; (2) Rank is based on 2021 data and ranges from 1 to 388
Source: U.S. Department of Commerce, International Trade Administration, Office of Trade and Economic Analysis, Industry and Analysis, Exports by Metropolitan Area, data extracted March 16, 2023

Building Permits

Area	Single-Family			Multi-Family			Total		
	2021	2022	Pct. Chg.	2021	2022	Pct. Chg.	2021	2022	Pct. Chg.
City	1,004	905	-9.9	2,079	1,149	-44.7	3,083	2,054	-33.4
MSA[1]	9,390	8,170	-13.0	3,044	2,630	-13.6	12,434	10,800	-13.1
U.S.	1,115,400	975,600	-12.5	621,600	689,500	10.9	1,737,000	1,665,100	-4.1

Note: (1) Figures cover the Sacramento-Roseville-Folsom, CA Metropolitan Statistical Area; Figures represent new, privately-owned housing units authorized (unadjusted data); All permit data are based on estimates with imputation
Source: U.S. Census Bureau, Manufacturing, Mining, and Construction Statistics, Building Permits, 2021, 2022

Bankruptcy Filings

Area	Business Filings			Nonbusiness Filings		
	2021	2022	% Chg.	2021	2022	% Chg.
Sacramento County	80	61	-23.8	1,731	1,275	-26.3
U.S.	14,347	13,481	-6.0	399,269	374,240	-6.3

Note: Business filings include Chapter 7, Chapter 9, Chapter 11, Chapter 12, Chapter 13, Chapter 15, and Section 304; Nonbusiness filings include Chapter 7, Chapter 11, and Chapter 13
Source: Administrative Office of the U.S. Courts, Business and Nonbusiness Bankruptcy, County Cases Commenced by Chapter of the Bankruptcy Code, During the 12-Month Period Ending December 31, 2021 and Business and Nonbusiness Bankruptcy, County Cases Commenced by Chapter of the Bankruptcy Code, During the 12-Month Period Ending December 31, 2022

Housing Vacancy Rates

Area	Gross Vacancy Rate[2] (%)			Year-Round Vacancy Rate[3] (%)			Rental Vacancy Rate[4] (%)			Homeowner Vacancy Rate[5] (%)		
	2020	2021	2022	2020	2021	2022	2020	2021	2022	2020	2021	2022
MSA[1]	6.1	6.7	6.3	5.8	6.5	6.1	4.2	3.6	2.3	1.0	0.7	0.6
U.S.	10.6	10.8	10.5	8.2	8.4	8.2	6.3	6.1	5.8	1.0	0.9	0.8

Note: (1) Figures cover the Sacramento-Roseville-Folsom, CA Metropolitan Statistical Area; (2) The percentage of the total housing inventory that is vacant; (3) The percentage of the housing inventory (excluding seasonal units) that is year-round vacant; (4) The percentage of rental inventory that is vacant for rent; (5) The percentage of homeowner inventory that is vacant for sale
Source: U.S. Census Bureau, Housing Vacancies and Homeownership Annual Statistics: 2020, 2021, 2022

INCOME

Income

Area	Per Capita ($)	Median Household ($)	Average Household ($)
City	35,793	71,074	93,320
MSA[1]	39,510	81,264	107,069
U.S.	37,638	69,021	97,196

Note: (1) Figures cover the Sacramento-Roseville-Folsom, CA Metropolitan Statistical Area
Source: U.S. Census Bureau, 2017-2021 American Community Survey 5-Year Estimates

Household Income Distribution

Area	Percent of Households Earning							
	Under $15,000	$15,000 -$24,999	$25,000 -$34,999	$35,000 -$49,999	$50,000 -$74,999	$75,000 -$99,999	$100,000 -$149,999	$150,000 and up
City	10.5	6.9	7.2	10.4	17.3	13.8	17.2	16.7
MSA[1]	8.3	6.1	6.7	9.5	15.9	13.2	18.3	22.1
U.S.	9.4	7.8	8.2	11.4	16.8	12.8	16.3	17.3

Note: (1) Figures cover the Sacramento-Roseville-Folsom, CA Metropolitan Statistical Area
Source: U.S. Census Bureau, 2017-2021 American Community Survey 5-Year Estimates

Poverty Rate

Area	All Ages	Under 18 Years Old	18 to 64 Years Old	65 Years and Over
City	14.8	18.5	14.1	12.1
MSA[1]	12.2	14.9	12.0	8.8
U.S.	12.6	17.0	11.8	9.6

Note: Figures are percentage of people whose income during the past 12 months was below the poverty level;
(1) Figures cover the Sacramento-Roseville-Folsom, CA Metropolitan Statistical Area
Source: U.S. Census Bureau, 2017-2021 American Community Survey 5-Year Estimates

EMPLOYMENT

Labor Force and Employment

Area	Civilian Labor Force			Workers Employed		
	Dec. 2021	Dec. 2022	% Chg.	Dec. 2021	Dec. 2022	% Chg.
City	237,842	239,915	0.9	226,017	231,146	2.3
MSA[1]	1,102,380	1,115,511	1.2	1,055,002	1,078,900	2.3
U.S.	161,696,000	164,224,000	1.6	155,732,000	158,872,000	2.0

Note: Data is not seasonally adjusted and covers workers 16 years of age and older; (1) Figures cover the
Sacramento-Roseville-Folsom, CA Metropolitan Statistical Area
Source: Bureau of Labor Statistics, Local Area Unemployment Statistics

Unemployment Rate

Area	2022											
	Jan.	Feb.	Mar.	Apr.	May	Jun.	Jul.	Aug.	Sep.	Oct.	Nov.	Dec.
City	5.7	4.9	4.3	3.7	3.3	3.8	3.8	4.1	3.8	3.9	4.2	3.7
MSA[1]	5.0	4.4	3.7	3.3	2.9	3.4	3.3	3.6	3.3	3.4	3.7	3.3
U.S.	4.4	4.1	3.8	3.3	3.4	3.8	3.8	3.8	3.3	3.4	3.4	3.3

Note: Data is not seasonally adjusted and covers workers 16 years of age and older; (1) Figures cover the
Sacramento-Roseville-Folsom, CA Metropolitan Statistical Area
Source: Bureau of Labor Statistics, Local Area Unemployment Statistics

Average Wages

Occupation	$/Hr.	Occupation	$/Hr.
Accountants and Auditors	41.27	Maintenance and Repair Workers	24.95
Automotive Mechanics	28.35	Marketing Managers	77.80
Bookkeepers	25.70	Network and Computer Systems Admin.	43.18
Carpenters	32.41	Nurses, Licensed Practical	34.27
Cashiers	16.67	Nurses, Registered	69.82
Computer Programmers	54.48	Nursing Assistants	21.17
Computer Systems Analysts	52.53	Office Clerks, General	21.97
Computer User Support Specialists	44.86	Physical Therapists	58.89
Construction Laborers	26.69	Physicians	145.43
Cooks, Restaurant	18.68	Plumbers, Pipefitters and Steamfitters	33.87
Customer Service Representatives	22.15	Police and Sheriff's Patrol Officers	48.52
Dentists	81.12	Postal Service Mail Carriers	28.15
Electricians	35.93	Real Estate Sales Agents	32.19
Engineers, Electrical	59.48	Retail Salespersons	19.11
Fast Food and Counter Workers	16.46	Sales Representatives, Technical/Scientific	58.98
Financial Managers	79.36	Secretaries, Exc. Legal/Medical/Executive	23.74
First-Line Supervisors of Office Workers	35.50	Security Guards	18.43
General and Operations Managers	67.53	Surgeons	n/a
Hairdressers/Cosmetologists	21.69	Teacher Assistants, Exc. Postsecondary*	19.35
Home Health and Personal Care Aides	15.29	Teachers, Secondary School, Exc. Sp. Ed.*	41.56
Janitors and Cleaners	18.34	Telemarketers	18.78
Landscaping/Groundskeeping Workers	20.30	Truck Drivers, Heavy/Tractor-Trailer	26.24
Lawyers	79.67	Truck Drivers, Light/Delivery Services	23.03
Maids and Housekeeping Cleaners	20.36	Waiters and Waitresses	17.51

Note: Wage data covers the Sacramento-Roseville-Folsom, CA Metropolitan Statistical Area; (*) Hourly wages
were calculated from annual wage data based on a 40 hour work week; n/a not available.
Source: Bureau of Labor Statistics, Metro Area Occupational Employment & Wage Estimates, May 2022

Employment by Industry

Sector	MSA[1]		U.S.
	Number of Employees	Percent of Total	Percent of Total
Construction	72,700	6.8	5.0
Private Education and Health Services	181,700	16.9	16.1
Financial Activities	52,800	4.9	5.9
Government	244,000	22.7	14.5
Information	10,600	1.0	2.0
Leisure and Hospitality	111,000	10.3	10.3
Manufacturing	40,300	3.7	8.4
Mining and Logging	500	<0.1	0.4
Other Services	37,700	3.5	3.7
Professional and Business Services	150,800	14.0	14.7
Retail Trade	103,200	9.6	10.2
Transportation, Warehousing, and Utilities	42,800	4.0	4.9
Wholesale Trade	28,400	2.6	3.9

Note: Figures are non-farm employment as of December 2022. Figures are not seasonally adjusted and include workers 16 years of age and older; (1) Figures cover the Sacramento-Roseville-Folsom, CA Metropolitan Statistical Area
Source: Bureau of Labor Statistics, Current Employment Statistics, Employment, Hours, and Earnings

Employment by Occupation

Occupation Classification	City (%)	MSA[1] (%)	U.S. (%)
Management, Business, Science, and Arts	41.9	42.7	40.3
Natural Resources, Construction, and Maintenance	7.6	7.8	8.7
Production, Transportation, and Material Moving	11.7	10.2	13.1
Sales and Office	21.3	21.5	20.9
Service	17.4	17.8	17.0

Note: Figures cover employed civilians 16 years of age and older; (1) Figures cover the Sacramento-Roseville-Folsom, CA Metropolitan Statistical Area
Source: U.S. Census Bureau, 2017-2021 American Community Survey 5-Year Estimates

Occupations with Greatest Projected Employment Growth: 2022 – 2024

Occupation[1]	2022 Employment	2024 Projected Employment	Numeric Employment Change	Percent Employment Change
Home Health and Personal Care Aides	811,300	858,600	47,300	5.8
Fast Food and Counter Workers	422,000	444,100	22,100	5.2
Cooks, Restaurant	154,300	172,000	17,700	11.5
Software Developers and Software Quality Assurance Analysts and Testers	337,600	352,100	14,500	4.3
Waiters and Waitresses	205,800	219,200	13,400	6.5
Laborers and Freight, Stock, and Material Movers, Hand	391,100	403,100	12,000	3.1
Stockers and Order Fillers	268,000	277,500	9,500	3.5
General and Operations Managers	308,500	317,600	9,100	2.9
First-Line Supervisors of Food Preparation and Serving Workers	118,100	126,000	7,900	6.7
Project Management Specialists and Business Operations Specialists, All Other	332,400	339,800	7,400	2.2

Note: Projections cover California; (1) Sorted by numeric employment change
Source: www.projectionscentral.com, State Occupational Projections, 2022–2024 Short-Term Projections

Fastest-Growing Occupations: 2022 – 2024

Occupation[1]	2022 Employment	2024 Projected Employment	Numeric Employment Change	Percent Employment Change
Fitness Trainers and Aerobics Instructors	40,700	46,300	5,600	13.8
Nurse Practitioners	18,300	20,500	2,200	12.0
Cooks, Restaurant	154,300	172,000	17,700	11.5
Airfield Operations Specialists	3,700	4,100	400	10.8
Solar Photovoltaic Installers	6,600	7,300	700	10.6
Ushers, Lobby Attendants, and Ticket Takers	7,800	8,600	800	10.3
Amusement and Recreation Attendants	47,500	52,300	4,800	10.1
Sociologists	1,000	1,100	100	10.0
Paperhangers	1,000	1,100	100	10.0
Avionics Technicians	2,000	2,200	200	10.0

Note: Projections cover California; (1) Sorted by percent employment change and excludes occupations with numeric employment change less than 50
Source: www.projectionscentral.com, State Occupational Projections, 2022–2024 Short-Term Projections

CITY FINANCES

City Government Finances

Component	2020 ($000)	2020 ($ per capita)
Total Revenues	1,392,031	2,710
Total Expenditures	1,279,442	2,491
Debt Outstanding	2,291,894	4,462
Cash and Securities[1]	2,258,294	4,397

Note: (1) Cash and security holdings of a government at the close of its fiscal year, including those of its dependent agencies, utilities, and liquor stores.
Source: U.S. Census Bureau, State & Local Government Finances 2020

City Government Revenue by Source

Source	2020 ($000)	2020 ($ per capita)	2020 (%)
General Revenue			
From Federal Government	40,459	79	2.9
From State Government	73,426	143	5.3
From Local Governments	4,953	10	0.4
Taxes			
Property	187,767	366	13.5
Sales and Gross Receipts	279,356	544	20.1
Personal Income	0	0	0.0
Corporate Income	0	0	0.0
Motor Vehicle License	0	0	0.0
Other Taxes	70,002	136	5.0
Current Charges	390,548	760	28.1
Liquor Store	0	0	0.0
Utility	142,041	277	10.2

Source: U.S. Census Bureau, State & Local Government Finances 2020

City Government Expenditures by Function

Function	2020 ($000)	2020 ($ per capita)	2020 (%)
General Direct Expenditures			
Air Transportation	0	0	0.0
Corrections	0	0	0.0
Education	0	0	0.0
Employment Security Administration	0	0	0.0
Financial Administration	0	0	0.0
Fire Protection	140,202	273	11.0
General Public Buildings	0	0	0.0
Governmental Administration, Other	135,484	263	10.6
Health	26,487	51	2.1
Highways	65,075	126	5.1
Hospitals	0	0	0.0
Housing and Community Development	77,003	149	6.0
Interest on General Debt	103,674	201	8.1
Judicial and Legal	0	0	0.0
Libraries	19,076	37	1.5
Parking	19,259	37	1.5
Parks and Recreation	97,899	190	7.7
Police Protection	213,270	415	16.7
Public Welfare	5,506	10	0.4
Sewerage	63,561	123	5.0
Solid Waste Management	57,392	111	4.5
Veterans' Services	0	0	0.0
Liquor Store	0	0	0.0
Utility	107,131	208	8.4

Source: U.S. Census Bureau, State & Local Government Finances 2020

TAXES

State Corporate Income Tax Rates

State	Tax Rate (%)	Income Brackets ($)	Num. of Brackets	Financial Institution Tax Rate (%)[a]	Federal Income Tax Ded.
California	8.84 (b)	Flat rate	1	10.84 (b)	No

Note: Tax rates as of January 1, 2023; (a) Rates listed are the corporate income tax rate applied to financial institutions or excise taxes based on income. Some states have other taxes based upon the value of deposits or shares; (b) Minimum tax is $800 in California, $250 in District of Columbia, $50 in Arizona and North Dakota (banks), $400 ($100 banks) in Rhode Island, $200 per location in South Dakota (banks), $100 in Utah, $300 in Vermont.
Source: Federation of Tax Administrators, State Corporate Income Tax Rates, January 1, 2023

State Individual Income Tax Rates

State	Tax Rate (%)	Income Brackets ($)	Personal Exemptions ($)			Standard Ded. ($)	
			Single	Married	Depend.	Single	Married
California (a)	1.0 - 12.3 (g)	10,099 - 677,275 (b)	140	280	433 (c)	5,202	10,404 (a)

Note: Tax rates as of January 1, 2023; Local- and county-level taxes are not included; Federal income tax is not deductible on state income tax returns; (a) 16 states have statutory provision for automatically adjusting to the rate of inflation the dollar values of the income tax brackets, standard deductions, and/or personal exemptions. Oregon does not index the income brackets for $125,000 and over; (b) For joint returns, taxes are twice the tax on half the couple's income; (c) The personal exemption takes the form of a tax credit instead of a deduction; (g) California imposes an additional 1% tax on taxable income over $1 million, making the maximum rate 13.3% over $1 million.
Source: Federation of Tax Administrators, State Individual Income Tax Rates, January 1, 2023

Various State Sales and Excise Tax Rates

State	State Sales Tax (%)	Gasoline[1] ($/gal.)	Cigarette[2] ($/pack)	Spirits[3] ($/gal.)	Wine[4] ($/gal.)	Beer[5] ($/gal.)	Recreational Marijuana (%)
California	7.25	0.7766	2.87	3.30	0.20	0.20	(c)

Note: All tax rates as of January 1, 2023; (1) The American Petroleum Institute has developed a methodology for determining the average tax rate on a gallon of fuel. Rates may include any of the following: excise taxes, environmental fees, storage tank fees, other fees or taxes, general sales tax, and local taxes; (2) The federal excise tax of $1.0066 per pack and local taxes are not included; (3) Rates are those applicable to off-premise sales of 40% alcohol by volume (a.b.v.) distilled spirits in 750ml containers. Local excise taxes are excluded; (4) Rates are those applicable to off-premise sales of 11% a.b.v. non-carbonated wine in 750ml containers; (5) Rates are those applicable to off-premise sales of 4.7% a.b.v. beer in 12 ounce containers; (c) 15% excise tax (levied on wholesale at average market rate); $10.08/oz. flowers & $3/oz. leaves cultivation tax; $1.41/oz fresh cannabis plant
Source: Tax Foundation, 2023 Facts & Figures: How Does Your State Compare?

State Business Tax Climate Index Rankings

State	Overall Rank	Corporate Tax Rank	Individual Income Tax Rank	Sales Tax Rank	Property Tax Rank	Unemployment Insurance Tax Rank
California	48	46	49	47	19	24

Note: The index is a measure of how each state's tax laws affect economic performance. The lower the rank, the more favorable a state's tax system is for business. States without a given tax are given a ranking of 1. The scores/rankings for the District of Columbia do not affect other states. The 2023 index represents the tax climate as of July 1, 2022.
Source: Tax Foundation, State Business Tax Climate Index 2023

TRANSPORTATION

Means of Transportation to Work

Area	Car/Truck/Van		Public Transportation			Bicycle	Walked	Other Means	Worked at Home
	Drove Alone	Car-pooled	Bus	Subway	Railroad				
City	68.9	9.6	1.7	0.2	0.3	1.6	2.9	2.2	12.6
MSA[1]	72.1	8.8	1.3	0.1	0.2	1.1	1.6	1.7	13.1
U.S.	73.2	8.6	2.0	1.6	0.5	0.5	2.5	1.5	9.7

Note: Figures are percentages and cover workers 16 years of age and older; (1) Figures cover the Sacramento-Roseville-Folsom, CA Metropolitan Statistical Area
Source: U.S. Census Bureau, 2017-2021 American Community Survey 5-Year Estimates

Travel Time to Work

Area	Less Than 10 Minutes	10 to 19 Minutes	20 to 29 Minutes	30 to 44 Minutes	45 to 59 Minutes	60 to 89 Minutes	90 Minutes or More
City	8.4	31.3	24.9	22.4	5.6	4.2	3.1
MSA[1]	9.9	28.3	22.4	23.1	7.9	4.7	3.7
U.S.	12.4	28.5	21.0	20.9	8.2	6.2	2.9

Note: Note: Figures are percentages and include workers 16 years old and over; (1) Figures cover the Sacramento-Roseville-Folsom, CA Metropolitan Statistical Area
Source: U.S. Census Bureau, 2017-2021 American Community Survey 5-Year Estimates

Key Congestion Measures

Measure	1990	2000	2010	2015	2020
Annual Hours of Delay, Total (000)	17,833	37,073	59,264	68,922	47,492
Annual Hours of Delay, Per Auto Commuter	26	37	46	55	38
Annual Congestion Cost, Per Auto Commuter ($)	519	812	1,032	1,108	800

Note: Covers the Sacramento CA urban area
Source: Texas A&M Transportation Institute, 2021 Urban Mobility Report

Freeway Travel Time Index

Measure	1985	1990	1995	2000	2005	2010	2015	2020
Urban Area Index[1]	1.10	1.14	1.17	1.20	1.23	1.24	1.27	1.11
Urban Area Rank[1,2]	27	26	29	29	28	24	20	20

Note: Freeway Travel Time Index—the ratio of travel time in the peak period to the travel time at free-flow conditions. For example, a value of 1.30 indicates a 20-minute free-flow trip takes 26 minutes in the peak (20 minutes x 1.30 = 26 minutes); (1) Covers the Sacramento CA urban area; (2) Rank is based on 101 larger urban areas (#1 = highest travel time index)
Source: Texas A&M Transportation Institute, 2021 Urban Mobility Report

Public Transportation

Agency Name / Mode of Transportation	Vehicles Operated in Maximum Service[1]	Annual Unlinked Passenger Trips[2] (in thous.)	Annual Passenger Miles[3] (in thous.)
Sacramento Regional Transit District (Sacramento RT)			
Bus (directly operated)	159	3,928.7	14,647.3
Demand Response (directly operated)	106	305.4	1,777.9
Light Rail (directly operated)	35	3,841.4	22,188.8

Note: (1) Number of revenue vehicles operated by the given mode and type of service to meet the annual maximum service requirement. This is the revenue vehicle count during the peak season of the year; on the week and day that maximum service is provided. Vehicles operated in maximum service (VOMS) exclude atypical days and one-time special events; (2) Number of passengers who boarded public transportation vehicles. Passengers are counted each time they board a vehicle no matter how many vehicles they use to travel from their origin to their destination. (3) Sum of the distances ridden by all passengers during the entire fiscal year.
Source: Federal Transit Administration, National Transit Database, 2021

Air Transportation

Airport Name and Code / Type of Service	Passenger Airlines[1]	Passenger Enplanements	Freight Carriers[2]	Freight (lbs)
Sacramento International (SMF)				
Domestic service (U.S. carriers - 2022)	20	5,862,571	12	119,098,425
International service (U.S. carriers - 2021)	6	26,751	0	0

Note: (1) Includes all U.S.-based major, minor and commuter airlines that carried at least one passenger during the year; (2) Includes all U.S.-based airlines and freight carriers that transported at least one pound of freight during the year.
Source: Bureau of Transportation Statistics, The Intermodal Transportation Database, Air Carriers: T-100 Domestic Market (U.S. Carriers), 2022; Bureau of Transportation Statistics, The Intermodal Transportation Database, Air Carriers: T-100 International Market (U.S. Carriers), 2021

BUSINESSES

Major Business Headquarters

Company Name	Industry	Rankings	
		Fortune[1]	Forbes[2]
No companies listed	-	-	-

Note: (1) Companies that produce a 10-K are ranked 1 to 500 based on 2021 revenue; (2) All private companies with at least $2 billion in annual revenue through the end of their most current fiscal year are ranked 1 to 246; companies listed are headquartered in the city; dashes indicate no ranking
Source: Fortune, "Fortune 500," 2022; Forbes, "America's Largest Private Companies," 2022

Fastest-Growing Businesses

According to *Inc.*, Sacramento is home to one of America's 500 fastest-growing private companies: **RCG LOGISTICS** (#448). Criteria: must be an independent, privately-held, for-profit, U.S. corporation, proprietorship or partnership as of December 31, 2021; revenues must be at least $100,000 in 2018 and $2 million in 2021; must have four-year operating/sales history. *Inc., "America's 500 Fastest-Growing Private Companies," 2022*

Living Environment

COST OF LIVING

Cost of Living Index

Composite Index	Groceries	Housing	Utilities	Transportation	Health Care	Misc. Goods/ Services
118.7	105.5	142.9	106.2	124.0	114.1	107.5

Note: The Cost of Living Index measures regional differences in the cost of consumer goods and services, excluding taxes and non-consumer expenditures, for professional and managerial households in the top income quintile. It is based on more than 50,000 prices covering almost 60 different items for which prices are collected three times a year by chambers of commerce, economic development organizations or university applied economic centers in each participating urban area. The numbers shown should be read as a percentage above or below the national average of 100. For example, a value of 115.4 in the groceries column indicates that grocery prices are 15.4% higher than the national average. Small differences in the index numbers should not be interpreted as significant; Figures cover the Sacramento CA urban area.
Source: The Council for Community and Economic Research, Cost of Living Index, 2022

Grocery Prices

Area[1]	T-Bone Steak ($/pound)	Frying Chicken ($/pound)	Whole Milk ($/half gal.)	Eggs ($/dozen)	Orange Juice ($/64 oz.)	Coffee ($/11.5 oz.)
City[2]	12.12	1.51	3.08	3.34	4.02	5.25
Avg.	13.81	1.59	2.43	2.25	3.85	4.95
Min.	10.17	0.90	1.51	1.30	2.90	3.46
Max.	19.35	3.30	4.32	4.32	5.31	8.59

*Note: (1) Values for the local area are compared with the average, minimum and maximum values for all 286 areas in the Cost of Living Index; (2) Figures cover the Sacramento CA urban area; **T-Bone Steak** (price per pound); **Frying Chicken** (price per pound, whole fryer); **Whole Milk** (half gallon carton); **Eggs** (price per dozen, Grade A, large); **Orange Juice** (64 oz. Tropicana or Florida Natural); **Coffee** (11.5 oz. can, vacuum-packed, Maxwell House, Hills Bros, or Folgers).*
Source: The Council for Community and Economic Research, Cost of Living Index, 2022

Housing and Utility Costs

Area[1]	New Home Price ($)	Apartment Rent ($/month)	All Electric ($/month)	Part Electric ($/month)	Other Energy ($/month)	Telephone ($/month)
City[2]	582,334	2,402	-	152.89	43.30	189.21
Avg.	450,913	1,371	176.41	99.93	76.96	190.22
Min.	229,283	546	100.84	31.56	27.15	174.27
Max.	2,434,977	4,569	356.86	249.59	272.24	208.31

*Note: (1) Values for the local area are compared with the average, minimum and maximum values for all 286 areas in the Cost of Living Index; (2) Figures cover the Sacramento CA urban area; **New Home Price** (2,400 sf living area, 8,000 sf lot, in urban area with full utilities); **Apartment Rent** (950 sf 2 bedroom/1.5 or 2 bath, unfurnished, excluding all utilities except water); **All Electric** (average monthly cost for an all-electric home); **Part Electric** (average monthly cost for a part-electric home); **Other Energy** (average monthly cost for natural gas, fuel oil, coal, wood, and any other forms of energy except electricity); **Telephone** (price includes the base monthly rate plus taxes and fees for three lines of mobile phone service).*
Source: The Council for Community and Economic Research, Cost of Living Index, 2022

Health Care, Transportation, and Other Costs

Area[1]	Doctor ($/visit)	Dentist ($/visit)	Optometrist ($/visit)	Gasoline ($/gallon)	Beauty Salon ($/visit)	Men's Shirt ($)
City[2]	176.26	109.67	149.00	5.48	57.08	33.30
Avg.	124.91	107.77	117.66	3.86	43.31	34.21
Min.	36.61	58.25	51.79	2.90	22.18	13.05
Max.	250.21	162.58	371.96	5.54	85.61	63.54

*Note: (1) Values for the local area are compared with the average, minimum and maximum values for all 286 areas in the Cost of Living Index; (2) Figures cover the Sacramento CA urban area; **Doctor** (general practitioners routine exam of an established patient); **Dentist** (adult teeth cleaning and periodic oral examination); **Optometrist** (full vision eye exam for established adult patient); **Gasoline** (one gallon regular unleaded, national brand, including all taxes, cash price at self-service pump if available); **Beauty Salon** (woman's shampoo, trim, and blow-dry); **Men's Shirt** (cotton/polyester dress shirt, pinpoint weave, long sleeves).*
Source: The Council for Community and Economic Research, Cost of Living Index, 2022

HOUSING

Homeownership Rate

Area	2015 (%)	2016 (%)	2017 (%)	2018 (%)	2019 (%)	2020 (%)	2021 (%)	2022 (%)
MSA[1]	60.8	60.5	60.1	64.1	61.6	63.4	63.2	63.5
U.S.	63.7	63.4	63.9	64.4	64.6	66.6	65.5	65.8

Note: (1) Figures cover the Sacramento-Roseville-Folsom, CA Metropolitan Statistical Area
Source: U.S. Census Bureau, Housing Vacancies and Homeownership Annual Statistics: 2015-2022

House Price Index (HPI)

Area	National Ranking[2]	Quarterly Change (%)	One-Year Change (%)	Five-Year Change (%)	Since 1991Q1 (%)
MSA[1]	253	-3.63	3.17	45.83	234.41
U.S.[3]	–	0.34	8.41	58.44	289.08

Note: The HPI is a weighted repeat sales index. It measures average price changes in repeat sales or refinancings on the same properties. This information is obtained by reviewing repeat mortgage transactions on single-family properties whose mortgages have been purchased or securitized by Fannie Mae or Freddie Mac since January 1975; (1) Figures cover the Sacramento—Roseville—Arden-Arcade, CA Metropolitan Statistical Area; (2) Rankings are based on annual percentage change for all metro areas containing at least 15,000 transactions over the last 10 years and ranges from 1 to 257; (3) figures based on a weighted average of Census Division estimates using a seasonally adjusted, purchase-only index; all figures are for the period ending December 31, 2022
Source: Federal Housing Finance Agency, Change in FHFA Metropolitan Area House Price Indexes, 2022Q4

Median Single-Family Home Prices

Area	2020	2021	2022[p]	Percent Change 2021 to 2022
MSA[1]	421.0	500.0	541.0	8.2
U.S. Average	300.2	357.1	392.6	9.9

Note: Figures are median sales prices of existing single-family homes in thousands of dollars; (p) preliminary; (1) Figures cover the Sacramento-Roseville-Folsom, CA Metropolitan Statistical Area
Source: National Association of Realtors, Median Sales Price of Existing Single-Family Homes for Metropolitan Areas, 4th Quarter 2022

Qualifying Income Based on Median Sales Price of Existing Single-Family Homes

Area	With 5% Down ($)	With 10% Down ($)	With 20% Down ($)
MSA[1]	149,592	141,719	125,972
U.S. Average	112,234	106,237	94,513

Note: Figures are preliminary; Qualifying income is based on a mortgage rate of 6.77%. Monthly principal and interest payment is limited to 25% of income; (1) Figures cover the Sacramento-Roseville-Folsom, CA Metropolitan Statistical Area
Source: National Association of Realtors, Qualifying Income Based on Median Sales Price of Existing Single-Family Homes for Metropolitan Areas, 4th Quarter 2022

Home Value

Area	Under $100,000	$100,000 -$199,999	$200,000 -$299,999	$300,000 -$399,999	$400,000 -$499,999	$500,000 -$999,999	$1,000,000 or more	Median ($)
City	4.0	5.0	19.4	25.1	19.3	24.0	3.0	385,500
MSA[1]	4.1	3.6	11.7	22.0	20.6	33.7	4.4	441,800
U.S.	16.2	24.2	20.1	13.6	8.3	13.6	4.1	244,900

Note: Figures are percentages except for median and cover owner-occupied housing units; (1) Figures cover the Sacramento-Roseville-Folsom, CA Metropolitan Statistical Area
Source: U.S. Census Bureau, 2017-2021 American Community Survey 5-Year Estimates

Year Housing Structure Built

Area	2020 or Later	2010 -2019	2000 -2009	1990 -1999	1980 -1989	1970 -1979	1960 -1969	1950 -1959	1940 -1949	Before 1940	Median Year
City	0.1	4.6	14.5	8.7	15.6	14.2	11.4	12.3	7.3	11.3	1975
MSA[1]	0.2	5.3	16.9	14.9	16.7	18.0	10.6	9.7	3.4	4.2	1982
U.S.	0.2	7.3	13.6	13.6	13.2	14.8	10.3	10.0	4.7	12.2	1979

Note: Figures are percentages except for Median Year; Note: (1) Figures cover the Sacramento-Roseville-Folsom, CA Metropolitan Statistical Area
Source: U.S. Census Bureau, 2017-2021 American Community Survey 5-Year Estimates

Gross Monthly Rent

Area	Under $500	$500 -$999	$1,000 -$1,499	$1,500 -$1,999	$2,000 -$2,499	$2,500 -$2,999	$3,000 and up	Median ($)
City	5.5	16.1	33.0	30.1	11.3	2.5	1.6	1,434
MSA[1]	4.3	14.1	34.2	27.8	13.3	3.9	2.5	1,465
U.S.	8.1	30.5	30.8	16.8	7.3	3.1	3.5	1,163

Note: Figures are percentages except for median; Gross rent is the contract rent plus the estimated average monthly cost of utilities (electricity, gas, and water and sewer) and fuels (oil, coal, kerosene, wood, etc.) if these are paid by the renter (or paid for the renter by someone else); (1) Figures cover the Sacramento-Roseville-Folsom, CA Metropolitan Statistical Area
Source: U.S. Census Bureau, 2017-2021 American Community Survey 5-Year Estimates

HEALTH

Health Risk Factors

Category	MSA[1] (%)	U.S. (%)
Adults aged 18–64 who have any kind of health care coverage	94.8	90.9
Adults who reported being in good or better health	88.2	85.2
Adults who have been told they have high blood cholesterol	30.0	35.7
Adults who have been told they have high blood pressure	30.9	32.4
Adults who are current smokers	8.9	14.4
Adults who currently use e-cigarettes	6.4	6.7
Adults who currently use chewing tobacco, snuff, or snus	1.8	3.5
Adults who are heavy drinkers[2]	7.5	6.3
Adults who are binge drinkers[3]	14.2	15.4
Adults who are overweight (BMI 25.0 - 29.9)	35.8	34.4
Adults who are obese (BMI 30.0 - 99.8)	28.2	33.9
Adults who participated in any physical activities in the past month	83.0	76.3

Note: (1) Figures cover the Sacramento—Roseville—Arden-Arcade, CA Metropolitan Statistical Area;
(2) Heavy drinkers are classified as adult men having more than 14 drinks per week and adult women having
more than 7 drinks per week; (3) Binge drinkers are classified as males having five or more drinks on one
occasion or females having four or more drinks on one occasion
Source: Centers for Disease Control and Prevention, Behavioral Risk Factor Surveillance System, SMART:
Selected Metropolitan Area Risk Trends, 2021

Acute and Chronic Health Conditions

Category	MSA[1] (%)	U.S. (%)
Adults who have ever been told they had a heart attack	4.4	4.0
Adults who have ever been told they have angina or coronary heart disease	3.7	3.8
Adults who have ever been told they had a stroke	2.6	3.0
Adults who have ever been told they have asthma	18.5	14.9
Adults who have ever been told they have arthritis	21.5	25.8
Adults who have ever been told they have diabetes[2]	9.6	10.9
Adults who have ever been told they had skin cancer	6.8	6.6
Adults who have ever been told they had any other types of cancer	4.4	7.5
Adults who have ever been told they have COPD	5.5	6.1
Adults who have ever been told they have kidney disease	n/a	3.0
Adults who have ever been told they have a form of depression	17.1	20.5

Note: (1) Figures cover the Sacramento—Roseville—Arden-Arcade, CA Metropolitan Statistical Area; (2)
Figures do not include pregnancy-related, borderline, or pre-diabetes
Source: Centers for Disease Control and Prevention, Behavioral Risk Factor Surveillance System, SMART:
Selected Metropolitan Area Risk Trends, 2021

Health Screening and Vaccination Rates

Category	MSA[1] (%)	U.S. (%)
Adults who have ever been tested for HIV	33.6	34.9
Adults who have had their blood cholesterol checked within the last five years	87.8	85.2
Adults aged 65+ who have had flu shot within the past year	65.8	68.6
Adults aged 65+ who have ever had a pneumonia vaccination	66.6	71.0

Note: (1) Figures cover the Sacramento—Roseville—Arden-Arcade, CA Metropolitan Statistical Area.
Source: Centers for Disease Control and Prevention, Behavioral Risk Factor Surveillance System, SMART:
Selected Metropolitan Area Risk Trends, 2021

Disability Status

Category	MSA[1] (%)	U.S. (%)
Adults who reported being deaf	6.1	7.2
Are you blind or have serious difficulty seeing, even when wearing glasses?	n/a	4.8
Are you limited in any way in any of your usual activities due to arthritis?	10.1	11.1
Do you have difficulty doing errands alone?	7.8	7.0
Do you have difficulty dressing or bathing?	3.7	3.6
Do you have serious difficulty concentrating/remembering/making decisions?	11.9	12.1
Do you have serious difficulty walking or climbing stairs?	12.0	12.8

Note: (1) Figures cover the Sacramento—Roseville—Arden-Arcade, CA Metropolitan Statistical Area.
Source: Centers for Disease Control and Prevention, Behavioral Risk Factor Surveillance System, SMART:
Selected Metropolitan Area Risk Trends, 2021

Mortality Rates for the Top 10 Causes of Death in the U.S.

ICD-10[a] Sub-Chapter	ICD-10[a] Code	Crude Mortality Rate[1] per 100,000 population	
		County[2]	U.S.
Malignant neoplasms	C00-C97	166.0	182.6
Ischaemic heart diseases	I20-I25	90.4	113.1
Other forms of heart disease	I30-I51	45.6	64.4
Other degenerative diseases of the nervous system	G30-G31	57.8	51.0
Cerebrovascular diseases	I60-I69	52.6	47.8
Other external causes of accidental injury	W00-X59	37.4	46.4
Chronic lower respiratory diseases	J40-J47	34.6	45.7
Organic, including symptomatic, mental disorders	F01-F09	25.0	35.9
Hypertensive diseases	I10-I15	34.7	35.0
Diabetes mellitus	E10-E14	32.1	29.6

Note: (a) ICD-10 = International Classification of Diseases 10th Revision; (1) Crude mortality rates are a three-year average covering 2019-2021; (2) Figures cover Sacramento County.
Source: Centers for Disease Control and Prevention, National Center for Health Statistics. National Vital Statistics System, Mortality 2018-2021 on CDC WONDER Online Database

Mortality Rates for Selected Causes of Death

ICD-10[a] Sub-Chapter	ICD-10[a] Code	Crude Mortality Rate[1] per 100,000 population	
		County[2]	U.S.
Assault	X85-Y09	6.8	7.0
Diseases of the liver	K70-K76	18.4	19.8
Human immunodeficiency virus (HIV) disease	B20-B24	1.3	1.5
Influenza and pneumonia	J09-J18	13.0	14.7
Intentional self-harm	X60-X84	12.2	14.3
Malnutrition	E40-E46	4.5	4.3
Obesity and other hyperalimentation	E65-E68	3.3	3.0
Renal failure	N17-N19	6.1	15.7
Transport accidents	V01-V99	14.3	13.6
Viral hepatitis	B15-B19	2.3	1.2

Note: (a) ICD-10 = International Classification of Diseases 10th Revision; (1) Crude mortality rates are a three-year average covering 2019-2021; (2) Figures cover Sacramento County; Data are suppressed when the data meet the criteria for confidentiality constraints; Crude mortality rates are flagged as unreliable when the rate would be calculated with a numerator of 20 or less.
Source: Centers for Disease Control and Prevention, National Center for Health Statistics. National Vital Statistics System, Mortality 2018-2021 on CDC WONDER Online Database

Health Insurance Coverage

Area	With Health Insurance	With Private Health Insurance	With Public Health Insurance	Without Health Insurance	Population Under Age 19 Without Health Insurance
City	94.3	64.2	40.8	5.7	2.4
MSA[1]	95.1	70.1	38.0	4.9	2.6
U.S.	91.2	67.8	35.4	8.8	5.3

Note: Figures are percentages that cover the civilian noninstitutionalized population; (1) Figures cover the Sacramento-Roseville-Folsom, CA Metropolitan Statistical Area
Source: U.S. Census Bureau, 2017-2021 American Community Survey 5-Year Estimates

Number of Medical Professionals

Area	MDs[3]	DOs[3,4]	Dentists	Podiatrists	Chiropractors	Optometrists
County[1] (number)	5,223	264	1,283	73	346	293
County[1] (rate[2])	329.3	16.6	80.7	4.6	21.8	18.4
U.S. (rate[2])	289.3	23.5	72.5	6.2	28.7	17.4

Note: Data as of 2021 unless noted; (1) Data covers Sacramento County; (2) Rate per 100,000 population; (3) Data as of 2020 and includes all active, non-federal physicians; (4) Doctor of Osteopathic Medicine
Source: U.S. Department of Health and Human Services, Health Resources and Services Administration, Bureau of Health Professions, Area Resource File (ARF) 2021-2022

Best Hospitals

According to *U.S. News,* the Sacramento-Roseville-Folsom, CA metro area is home to one of the best hospitals in the U.S.: **UC Davis Medical Center** (9 adult specialties and 5 pediatric specialties). The hospital listed was nationally ranked in at least one of 15 adult or 10 pediatric specialties. The number of specialties shown cover the parent hospital. Only 164 U.S. hospitals performed well enough to be nationally ranked in one or more specialties. Twenty hospitals in the U.S. made the Honor Roll. The Best Hospitals Honor Roll takes both the national rankings and the procedure and condition ratings into account. Hospitals received points if they were nationally ranked in one of the 15 adult specialties—the higher they ranked, the more points they got—and how many ratings of "high performing" they earned in the 17 procedures and conditions. *U.S. News Online, "America's Best Hospitals 2022-23"*

According to *U.S. News,* the Sacramento-Roseville-Folsom, CA metro area is home to one of the best children's hospitals in the U.S.: **UC Davis Children's Hospital** (5 pediatric specialties). The hospital listed was highly ranked in at least one of 10 pediatric specialties. Eighty-six children's hospitals in the U.S. were nationally ranked in at least one specialty. Hospitals received points for being ranked in a specialty, and the 10 hospitals with the most points across the 10 specialties make up the Honor Roll. *U.S. News Online, "America's Best Children's Hospitals 2022-23"*

EDUCATION

Public School District Statistics

District Name	Schls	Pupils	Pupil/ Teacher Ratio	Minority Pupils[1] (%)	LEP/ELL[2] (%)	IEP[3] (%)
Natomas Unified	19	14,197	21.8	86.3	13.1	12.0
Sacramento City Unified	73	39,711	22.8	83.2	19.0	14.0

Note: Table includes school districts with 2,000 or more students; (1) Percentage of students that are not non-Hispanic white; (2) Percentage of students that are Limited English Proficient or English Language Learners (2018-19); (3) Percentage of students that have an Individualized Education Program (2019-20).
Source: U.S. Department of Education, National Center for Education Statistics, Common Core of Data, Local Education Agency (School District) Universe Survey: School Year 2021-2022

Best High Schools

According to *U.S. News,* Sacramento is home to one of the top 500 high schools in the U.S.: **West Campus High School** (#199). Nearly 18,000 public, magnet and charter schools were ranked based on their performance on state assessments and how well they prepare students for college. *U.S. News & World Report, "Best High Schools 2022"*

Highest Level of Education

Area	Less than H.S.	H.S. Diploma	Some College, No Deg.	Associate Degree	Bachelor's Degree	Master's Degree	Prof. School Degree	Doctorate Degree
City	13.6	20.3	22.6	8.4	22.2	8.4	3.2	1.4
MSA[1]	10.2	20.8	24.1	9.9	22.3	8.3	2.8	1.5
U.S.	11.1	26.5	20.0	8.7	20.6	9.3	2.2	1.5

Note: Figures cover persons age 25 and over; (1) Figures cover the Sacramento-Roseville-Folsom, CA Metropolitan Statistical Area
Source: U.S. Census Bureau, 2017-2021 American Community Survey 5-Year Estimates

Educational Attainment by Race

Area	High School Graduate or Higher (%)					Bachelor's Degree or Higher (%)				
	Total	White	Black	Asian	Hisp.[2]	Total	White	Black	Asian	Hisp.[2]
City	86.4	91.5	91.3	81.6	75.4	35.1	42.6	24.8	39.3	21.6
MSA[1]	89.8	93.2	91.2	84.7	76.7	35.0	36.8	25.5	44.8	20.1
U.S.	88.9	91.4	87.2	87.6	71.2	33.7	35.5	23.3	55.6	18.4

Note: Figures shown cover persons 25 years old and over; (1) Figures cover the Sacramento-Roseville-Folsom, CA Metropolitan Statistical Area; (2) People of Hispanic origin can be of any race
Source: U.S. Census Bureau, 2017-2021 American Community Survey 5-Year Estimates

School Enrollment by Grade and Control

Area	Preschool (%)		Kindergarten (%)		Grades 1 - 4 (%)		Grades 5 - 8 (%)		Grades 9 - 12 (%)	
	Public	Private	Public	Private	Public	Private	Public	Private	Public	Private
City	65.0	35.0	91.0	9.0	93.1	6.9	91.5	8.5	90.9	9.1
MSA[1]	59.9	40.1	90.0	10.0	91.7	8.3	91.9	8.1	91.7	8.3
U.S.	58.8	41.2	86.3	13.7	88.3	11.7	88.6	11.4	89.4	10.6

Note: Figures shown cover persons 3 years old and over; (1) Figures cover the Sacramento-Roseville-Folsom, CA Metropolitan Statistical Area
Source: U.S. Census Bureau, 2017-2021 American Community Survey 5-Year Estimates

Higher Education

Four-Year Colleges			Two-Year Colleges			Medical Schools[1]	Law Schools[2]	Voc/ Tech[3]
Public	Private Non-profit	Private For-profit	Public	Private Non-profit	Private For-profit			
2	3	2	7	0	7	2	4	14

Note: Figures cover institutions located within the Sacramento-Roseville-Folsom, CA Metropolitan Statistical Area and include main campuses only; (1) includes schools accredited by the Liaison Committee on Medical Education and the American Osteopathic Association's Commission on Osteopathic College Accreditation; (2) includes ABA-accredited schools, schools with provisional ABA accreditation, and state accredited schools; (3) includes all schools with programs that are less than 2 years.
Source: National Center for Education Statistics, Integrated Postsecondary Education System (IPEDS), 2021-22; Wikipedia, List of Medical Schools in the United States, accessed April 10, 2023; Wikipedia, List of Law Schools in the United States, accessed April 10, 2023

According to *U.S. News & World Report,* the Sacramento-Roseville-Folsom, CA metro area is home to one of the top 200 national universities in the U.S.: **University of California—Davis** (#38 tie). The indicators used to capture academic quality fall into a number of categories: assessment by administrators at peer institutions; retention of students; faculty resources; student selectivity; financial resources; alumni giving; high school counselor ratings of colleges; and graduation rate. *U.S. News & World Report, "America's Best Colleges 2023"*

According to *U.S. News & World Report,* the Sacramento-Roseville-Folsom, CA metro area is home to one of the top 100 law schools in the U.S.: **University of California—Davis** (#37 tie). The rankings are based on a weighted average of 12 measures of quality: peer assessment score; assessment score by lawyers/judges; median LSAT scores; median undergrad GPA; acceptance rate; employment rates for graduates; placement success; bar passage rate; faculty resources; expenditures per student; student/faculty ratio; and library resources. *U.S. News & World Report, "America's Best Graduate Schools, Law, 2023"*

According to *U.S. News & World Report,* the Sacramento-Roseville-Folsom, CA metro area is home to one of the top 75 medical schools for research in the U.S.: **University of California—Davis** (#51 tie). The rankings are based on a weighted average of 11 measures of quality: quality assessment; peer assessment score; assessment score by residency directors; research activity; total research activity; average research activity per faculty member; student selectivity; median MCAT total score; median undergraduate GPA; acceptance rate; and faculty resources. *U.S. News & World Report, "America's Best Graduate Schools, Medical, 2023"*

According to *U.S. News & World Report,* the Sacramento-Roseville-Folsom, CA metro area is home to one of the top 75 business schools in the U.S.: **University of California—Davis** (#52). The rankings are based on a weighted average of the following nine measures: quality assessment; peer assessment; recruiter assessment; placement success; mean starting salary and bonus; student selectivity; mean GMAT and GRE scores; mean undergraduate GPA; and acceptance rate. *U.S. News & World Report, "America's Best Graduate Schools, Business, 2023"*

EMPLOYERS

Major Employers

Company Name	Industry
Aerojet Rocketdyne	Aerospace industries, mfg
Agreeya Solutions	Information technology services
Ampac Fine Chemicals	Electronic equipment & supplies, mfg
Apple Distribution Center	Distribution centers, wholesale
California Department of Corrections	State govt-correctional institutions
California Prison Ind Auth	Government offices-state
California State Univercity-Sacramento	Schools-universities & colleges academic
Department of Transportation	Government offices-state
Disabled American Veterans	Veterans' & military organizations
Division of Fiscal Services	Services nec
Employment Development Dept	Government offices-state
Environmental Protection Agency	State government-environmental programs
Intel Corp	Semiconductor devices, mfg
Kaiser Permanente South	Hospitals
L A Care Health Plan	Health plans
Mercy General Hospital	Hospitals
Mercy San Juan Medical Center	Hospitals
Sacramento Municipal Utility	Electric contractors
Securitas Security Services USA	Security guard & patrol services
SMUD	Electric companies
State Compensation Insurance Fund	Insurance
Sutter Medical Center-Sacramento	Hospitals
United Loan Corp	Real estate
Water Resource Dept	Government offices-state

Note: Companies shown are located within the Sacramento-Roseville-Folsom, CA Metropolitan Statistical Area.
Source: Hoovers.com; Wikipedia

PUBLIC SAFETY

Crime Rate

Area	Total Crime	Violent Crime Rate				Property Crime Rate		
		Murder	Rape[3]	Robbery	Aggrav. Assault	Burglary	Larceny -Theft	Motor Vehicle Theft
City	3,428.4	8.1	24.1	169.3	481.8	546.0	1,715.2	483.8
Suburbs[1]	2,102.6	3.8	27.9	64.5	196.3	323.1	1,274.4	212.6
Metro[2]	2,393.6	4.8	27.0	87.5	259.0	372.0	1,371.2	272.1
U.S.	2,356.7	6.5	38.4	73.9	279.7	314.2	1,398.0	246.0

Note: Figures are crimes per 100,000 population; (1) All areas within the metro area that are located outside the city limits; (2) Figures cover the Sacramento—Arden-Arcade—Roseville, CA Metropolitan Statistical Area; (3) All figures shown were reported using the revised Uniform Crime Reporting (UCR) definition of rape; Due to the transition to the National Incident-Based Reporting System (NIBRS), limited city and metro area data was released for 2021.
Source: FBI Uniform Crime Reports, 2020

Hate Crimes

Area	Number of Quarters Reported	Number of Incidents per Bias Motivation					
		Race/Ethnicity/ Ancestry	Religion	Sexual Orientation	Disability	Gender	Gender Identity
City	4	8	0	2	0	0	0
U.S.	4	5,227	1,244	1,110	130	75	266

Note: Due to the transition to the National Incident-Based Reporting System (NIBRS), limited crime data was released for 2021.
Source: Federal Bureau of Investigation, Hate Crime Statistics 2020

Identity Theft Consumer Reports

Area	Reports	Reports per 100,000 Population	Rank[2]
MSA[1]	6,491	278	83
U.S.	1,108,609	339	-

Note: (1) Figures cover the Sacramento-Roseville-Folsom, CA Metropolitan Statistical Area; (2) Rank ranges from 1 to 391 where 1 indicates greatest number of identity theft reports per 100,000 population
Source: Federal Trade Commission, Consumer Sentinel Network Data Book 2022

Fraud and Other Consumer Reports

Area	Reports	Reports per 100,000 Population	Rank[2]
MSA[1]	24,805	1,061	73
U.S.	4,064,520	1,245	-

Note: (1) Figures cover the Sacramento-Roseville-Folsom, CA Metropolitan Statistical Area; (2) Rank ranges from 1 to 391 where 1 indicates greatest number of fraud and other consumer reports per 100,000 population
Source: Federal Trade Commission, Consumer Sentinel Network Data Book 2022

POLITICS

2020 Presidential Election Results

Area	Biden	Trump	Jorgensen	Hawkins	Other
Sacramento County	61.4	36.1	1.4	0.5	0.7
U.S.	51.3	46.8	1.2	0.3	0.5

Note: Results are percentages and may not add to 100% due to rounding
Source: Dave Leip's Atlas of U.S. Presidential Elections

SPORTS

Professional Sports Teams

Team Name	League	Year Established
Sacramento Kings	National Basketball Association (NBA)	1985
Sacramento Republic FC	Major League Soccer (MLS)	2023

Note: Includes teams located in the Sacramento-Roseville-Folsom, CA Metropolitan Statistical Area.
Source: Wikipedia, Major Professional Sports Teams of the United States and Canada, April 12, 2023

CLIMATE

Average and Extreme Temperatures

Temperature	Jan	Feb	Mar	Apr	May	Jun	Jul	Aug	Sep	Oct	Nov	Dec	Yr.
Extreme High (°F)	70	76	88	93	105	115	114	109	108	101	87	72	115
Average High (°F)	53	60	64	71	80	87	93	91	87	78	63	53	73
Average Temp. (°F)	45	51	54	59	65	72	76	75	72	64	53	46	61
Average Low (°F)	38	41	43	46	50	55	58	58	56	50	43	38	48
Extreme Low (°F)	20	23	26	32	34	41	48	48	43	35	26	18	18

Note: Figures cover the years 1947-1990
Source: National Climatic Data Center, International Station Meteorological Climate Summary, 9/96

Average Precipitation/Snowfall/Humidity

Precip./Humidity	Jan	Feb	Mar	Apr	May	Jun	Jul	Aug	Sep	Oct	Nov	Dec	Yr.
Avg. Precip. (in.)	3.6	2.8	2.4	1.3	0.4	0.1	Tr	0.1	0.3	1.0	2.4	2.8	17.3
Avg. Snowfall (in.)	Tr	Tr	Tr	Tr	0	0	0	0	0	0	0	Tr	Tr
Avg. Rel. Hum. 7am (%)	90	88	84	78	71	67	68	73	75	80	87	90	79
Avg. Rel. Hum. 4pm (%)	70	59	51	43	36	31	28	29	31	39	57	70	45

Note: Figures cover the years 1947-1990; Tr = Trace amounts (<0.05 in. of rain; <0.5 in. of snow)
Source: National Climatic Data Center, International Station Meteorological Climate Summary, 9/96

Weather Conditions

Temperature			Daytime Sky			Precipitation		
10°F & below	32°F & below	90°F & above	Clear	Partly cloudy	Cloudy	0.01 inch or more precip.	0.1 inch or more snow/ice	Thunder-storms
0	21	73	175	111	79	58	< 1	2

Note: Figures are average number of days per year and cover the years 1947-1990
Source: National Climatic Data Center, International Station Meteorological Climate Summary, 9/96

HAZARDOUS WASTE

Superfund Sites

The Sacramento-Roseville-Folsom, CA metro area is home to five sites on the EPA's Superfund National Priorities List: **Aerojet General Corp.** (final); **Frontier Fertilizer** (final); **Mather Air Force Base (AC&W Disposal Site)** (final); **McClellan Air Force Base (Ground Water Contamination)** (final); **Sacramento Army Depot** (final). There are a total of 1,165 Superfund sites with a status of proposed or final on the list in the U.S. *U.S. Environmental Protection Agency, National Priorities List, April 12, 2023*

AIR QUALITY

Air Quality Trends: Ozone

	1990	1995	2000	2005	2010	2015	2018	2019	2020	2021
MSA[1]	0.087	0.092	0.085	0.084	0.072	0.073	0.074	0.067	0.072	0.073
U.S.	0.087	0.089	0.081	0.080	0.072	0.067	0.069	0.065	0.065	0.067

Note: (1) Data covers the Sacramento-Roseville-Folsom, CA Metropolitan Statistical Area. The values shown are the composite ozone concentration averages among trend sites based on the highest fourth daily maximum 8-hour concentration in parts per million. These trends are based on sites having an adequate record of monitoring data during the trend period. Data from exceptional events are included.
Source: U.S. Environmental Protection Agency, Air Quality Monitoring Information, "Air Quality Trends by City, 1990-2021"

Air Quality Index

Area	Percent of Days when Air Quality was...[2]					AQI Statistics[2]	
	Good	Moderate	Unhealthy for Sensitive Groups	Unhealthy	Very Unhealthy	Maximum	Median
MSA[1]	37.8	46.3	10.4	3.3	1.4	448	62

Note: (1) Data covers the Sacramento-Roseville-Folsom, CA Metropolitan Statistical Area; (2) Based on 365 days with AQI data in 2021. Air Quality Index (AQI) is an index for reporting daily air quality. EPA calculates the AQI for five major air pollutants regulated by the Clean Air Act: ground-level ozone, particle pollution (aka particulate matter), carbon monoxide, sulfur dioxide, and nitrogen dioxide. The AQI runs from 0 to 500. The higher the AQI value, the greater the level of air pollution and the greater the health concern. There are six AQI categories: "Good" AQI is between 0 and 50. Air quality is considered satisfactory; "Moderate" AQI is between 51 and 100. Air quality is acceptable; "Unhealthy for Sensitive Groups" When AQI values are between 101 and 150, members of sensitive groups may experience health effects; "Unhealthy" When AQI values are between 151 and 200 everyone may begin to experience health effects; "Very Unhealthy" AQI values between 201 and 300 trigger a health alert; "Hazardous" AQI values over 300 trigger warnings of emergency conditions (not shown).
Source: U.S. Environmental Protection Agency, Air Quality Index Report, 2021

Air Quality Index Pollutants

Area	Percent of Days when AQI Pollutant was...[2]					
	Carbon Monoxide	Nitrogen Dioxide	Ozone	Sulfur Dioxide	Particulate Matter 2.5	Particulate Matter 10
MSA[1]	0.0	0.0	66.0	(3)	33.4	0.5

Note: (1) Data covers the Sacramento-Roseville-Folsom, CA Metropolitan Statistical Area; (2) Based on 365 days with AQI data in 2021. The Air Quality Index (AQI) is an index for reporting daily air quality. EPA calculates the AQI for five major air pollutants regulated by the Clean Air Act: ground-level ozone, particle pollution (also known as particulate matter), carbon monoxide, sulfur dioxide, and nitrogen dioxide. The AQI runs from 0 to 500. The higher the AQI value, the greater the level of air pollution and the greater the health concern; (3) Sulfur dioxide is no longer included in this table (as of December 8, 2021) because SO_2 concentrations tend to be very localized and not necessarily representative of broad geographical areas like counties and CBSAs.
Source: U.S. Environmental Protection Agency, Air Quality Index Report, 2021

Maximum Air Pollutant Concentrations: Particulate Matter, Ozone, CO and Lead

	Particulate Matter 10 (ug/m^3)	Particulate Matter 2.5 Wtd AM (ug/m^3)	Particulate Matter 2.5 24-Hr (ug/m^3)	Ozone (ppm)	Carbon Monoxide (ppm)	Lead (ug/m^3)
MSA[1] Level	406	11.3	57	0.085	1	n/a
NAAQS[2]	150	15	35	0.075	9	0.15
Met NAAQS[2]	No	Yes	No	No	Yes	n/a

Note: (1) Data covers the Sacramento-Roseville-Folsom, CA Metropolitan Statistical Area; Data from exceptional events are included; (2) National Ambient Air Quality Standards; ppm = parts per million; ug/m^3 = micrograms per cubic meter; n/a not available.
Concentrations: Particulate Matter 10 (coarse particulate)—highest second maximum 24-hour concentration; Particulate Matter 2.5 Wtd AM (fine particulate)—highest weighted annual mean concentration; Particulate Matter 2.5 24-Hour (fine particulate)—highest 98th percentile 24-hour concentration; Ozone—highest fourth daily maximum 8-hour concentration; Carbon Monoxide—highest second maximum non-overlapping 8-hour concentration; Lead—maximum running 3-month average
Source: U.S. Environmental Protection Agency, Air Quality Monitoring Information, "Air Quality Statistics by City, 2021"

Maximum Air Pollutant Concentrations: Nitrogen Dioxide and Sulfur Dioxide

	Nitrogen Dioxide AM (ppb)	Nitrogen Dioxide 1-Hr (ppb)	Sulfur Dioxide AM (ppb)	Sulfur Dioxide 1-Hr (ppb)	Sulfur Dioxide 24-Hr (ppb)
MSA[1] Level	7	41	n/a	n/a	n/a
NAAQS[2]	53	100	30	75	140
Met NAAQS[2]	Yes	Yes	n/a	n/a	n/a

Note: (1) Data covers the Sacramento-Roseville-Folsom, CA Metropolitan Statistical Area; Data from exceptional events are included; (2) National Ambient Air Quality Standards; ppm = parts per million; ug/m^3 = micrograms per cubic meter; n/a not available.
Concentrations: Nitrogen Dioxide AM—highest arithmetic mean concentration; Nitrogen Dioxide 1-Hr—highest 98th percentile 1-hour daily maximum concentration; Sulfur Dioxide AM—highest annual mean concentration; Sulfur Dioxide 1-Hr—highest 99th percentile 1-hour daily maximum concentration; Sulfur Dioxide 24-Hr—highest second maximum 24-hour concentration
Source: U.S. Environmental Protection Agency, Air Quality Monitoring Information, "Air Quality Statistics by City, 2021"

Salem, Oregon

Background

The first civilization to occupy the Willamette Valley, the area surrounding Salem, were the Kalapuya Native Americans, who resided there seasonally for over 5,000 years. The Kalapuya were semi-nomadic, subsisting on wild game and vegetation, and were master canoe-builders who traveled the intricate web of rivers and streams flowing through the Willamette countryside. In the early 19th century, sailors from distant shores brought devastating diseases to the region and the native population declined rapidly.

The first non-native settlers to call Salem home were Methodist ministers who established the Willamette Mission, ten miles north of Salem. The Methodist Mission would later become the Oregon Institute, the first "white settlers" school west of the Missouri River. The whole community became known as the "Institute" and the institute would become Willamette University.

By 1843, a new influx of settlers arrived in wagons with the fervor of manifest destiny. They brought an agrarian lifestyle, planting wheat, raising sheep, and building mills for lumber. By 1851, the steamboat "Hoosier" traveled the Willamette River south to Eugene, and north to Oregon City (near Portland), providing trade and transportation to the entire Willamette Valley. Oregon achieved statehood in 1859, and Salem was the new state capital. Although Oregon was a "free" state, it was illegal for black people to live there. One of the initial candidates for Oregon's first governor was Abraham Lincoln, who turned down the job because his wife, Mary, had no interest in moving west.

The population tripled in the years between 1900 and 1920. In 1903, Salem won the moniker "The Cherry City" in recognition of its food processing industry. In 1920, the Oregon Pulp and Paper Company began operations, and Salem General Hospital opened its doors. By the time of its centennial in 1940, Salem's population topped 30,900.

After a disastrous flood in 1964, Salem began reconstructing the downtown, and in 1970 Chemeketa Community College opened its doors. In the 1990s, Salem's roots as a lumber producer gradually waned and high-technology industry took root. The city is home to Kettle Foods.

In 1962 movie producers filmed the Oscar Award-winning movie, *One Flew Over the Cuckoo's Nest,* in the Oregon State Mental Hospital. Now listed in the National Register of Historic Places, the hospital is now the Oregon State Hospital Museum of Mental Health. In 2005, Oregonian writer Sarah Kershaw won a Pulitzer for her series about the discovery of 5,000 copper urns in the hospital, containing the cremated remains of hospital patients. The annual Capital Pride festival is hosted by Aundrea Smith, author of the 2019 *Your Local Queer*.

Salem is the capital of Oregon, one hour west of the Cascade Mountains, and one hour east of the Pacific Ocean. In addition to the Oregon State Fair, Salem hosts numerous festivals and tours including the annual jazz and winefest at the historic Deepwood Estate. Salem has been awarded "Tree City USA" status by the National Arbor Day Foundation for 30 consecutive years for its dedication to urban forestry. Salem was the first city in Oregon to receive the award.

Peter Courtney pedestrian and bicycle bridge was completed in 2018, and the city counciul recently agreeed to a multi-billion dollar improvement project for Salem's airport.

Like most of the Willamette Valley area, Salem has a Marine West Coast climate with some distinct characteristics of the Mediterranean climate. Rain is heaviest in late fall and throughout winter, but precipitation is spread from October until May, with a dry season from June through September. Light snowfall occurs in winter, but major snows are rare. Mostly cloudy skies, and low cloud ceilings are commonplace during the rainy season. Salem's mean annual temperature is 53.0 °F, annual precipitation is 39.64 inches, including an average 3.5 inches of snow.

Rankings

Business/Finance Rankings

- The Salem metro area appeared on the Milken Institute "2022 Best Performing Cities" list. Rank: #33 out of 200 large metro areas (population over 250,000). Criteria: job growth; wage and salary growth; high-tech output growth; housing affordability; household broadband access. *Milken Institute, "Best-Performing Cities 2022," March 28, 2022*

- *Forbes* ranked the 200 most populous metro areas to determine the nation's "Best Places for Business and Careers." The Salem metro area was ranked #78. Criteria: costs (business and living); job growth (past and projected); income growth; quality of life; educational attainment (college and high school); projected economic growth; cultural and leisure opportunities; workplace tolerance laws; net migration patterns. *Forbes, "The Best Places for Business and Careers 2019: Seattle Still On Top," October 30, 2019*

Education Rankings

- Personal finance website *WalletHub* analyzed the 150 largest U.S. metropolitan statistical areas to determine where the most educated Americans are putting their degrees to work. Criteria: education levels; percentage of workers with degrees; education quality and attainment gap; public school quality rankings; quality and enrollment of each metro area's universities. Salem was ranked #116 (#1 = most educated city). *www.WalletHub.com, "Most & Least Educated Cities in America," July 18, 2022*

Real Estate Rankings

- *WalletHub* compared the most populated U.S. cities to determine which had the best markets for real estate agents. Salem ranked #64 where demand was high and pay was the best. Criteria: sales per agent; annual median wage for real-estate agents; monthly average starting salary for real estate agents; real estate job density and competition; unemployment rate; home turnover rate; housing-market health index; and other relevant metrics. *www.WalletHub.com, "2021 Best Places to Be a Real Estate Agent," May 12, 2021*

- Salem was ranked #198 out of 235 metro areas in terms of housing affordability in 2022 by the National Association of Home Builders (#1 = most affordable). Criteria: the share of homes sold in that area affordable to a family earning the local median income, based on standard mortgage underwriting criteria. *National Association of Home Builders®, NAHB-Wells Fargo Housing Opportunity Index, 4th Quarter 2022*

Safety Rankings

- Allstate ranked the 200 largest cities in America in terms of driver safety. Salem ranked #102. Criteria: internal property damage claims over a two-year period from January 2016 to December 2017. The report helps increase the importance of safety and awareness behind the wheel. *Allstate, "Allstate America's Best Drivers Report, 2019" June 24, 2019*

- The National Insurance Crime Bureau ranked 390 metro areas in the U.S. in terms of per capita rates of vehicle theft. The Salem metro area ranked #42 (#1 = highest rate). Criteria: number of vehicle theft offenses per 100,000 inhabitants in 2021. *National Insurance Crime Bureau, "Hot Spots 2021," September 1, 2022*

Seniors/Retirement Rankings

- From its Best Cities for Successful Aging indexes, the Milken Institute generated rankings for metropolitan areas, weighing data in nine categories—health care, wellness, living arrangements, transportation and convenience, financial characteristics, education, employment, community engagement, and overall livability. The Salem metro area was ranked #252 overall in the small metro area category. *Milken Institute, "Best Cities for Successful Aging, 2017" March 14, 2017*

Women/Minorities Rankings

- Personal finance website *WalletHub* compared more than 180 U.S. cities across two key dimensions, "Hispanic Business-Friendliness" and "Hispanic Purchasing Power," to arrive at the most favorable conditions for Hispanic entrepreneurs. Salem was ranked #153 out of 182. Criteria includes: share of Hispanic-Owned Businesses; Hispanic entrepreneurship rate to median annual income of Hispanics; Small Business-Friendliness score; cost of living; and number of Hispanics with at least a bachelor's degree. *WalletHub.com, "2019's Best Cities for Hispanic Entrepreneurs," May 1, 2019*

Miscellaneous Rankings

■ *WalletHub* compared the 150 most populated U.S. cities to determine their operating efficiency. A "Quality of Services" score was constructed for each city and then divided by the total budget per capita to reveal which were managed the best. Salem ranked #18. Criteria: financial stability; economy; education; safety; health; infrastructure and pollution. *www.WalletHub.com, "2022's Best-& Worst-Run Cities in America," June 21, 2022*

Business Environment

DEMOGRAPHICS

Population Growth

Area	1990 Census	2000 Census	2010 Census	2020 Census	Population Growth (%) 1990-2020	Population Growth (%) 2010-2020
City	112,046	136,924	154,637	175,535	56.7	13.5
MSA[1]	278,024	347,214	390,738	433,353	55.9	10.9
U.S.	248,709,873	281,421,906	308,745,538	331,449,281	33.3	7.4

Note: (1) Figures cover the Salem, OR Metropolitan Statistical Area
Source: U.S. Census Bureau, 1990 Census, 2000 Census, 2010 Census, 2020 Census

Race

Area	White Alone[2] (%)	Black Alone[2] (%)	Asian Alone[2] (%)	AIAN[3] Alone[2] (%)	NHOPI[4] Alone[2] (%)	Other Race Alone[2] (%)	Two or More Races (%)
City	69.1	1.7	3.2	1.7	1.4	10.9	12.1
MSA[1]	69.6	1.1	2.1	2.0	1.0	12.2	12.0
U.S.	61.6	12.4	6.0	1.1	0.2	8.4	10.2

Note: (1) Figures cover the Salem, OR Metropolitan Statistical Area; (2) Alone is defined as not being in combination with one or more other races; (3) American Indian and Alaska Native; (4) Native Hawaiian and Other Pacific Islander
Source: U.S. Census Bureau, 2020 Census

Hispanic or Latino Origin

Area	Total (%)	Mexican (%)	Puerto Rican (%)	Cuban (%)	Other (%)
City	22.4	19.5	0.6	0.1	2.2
MSA[1]	24.9	22.1	0.4	0.1	2.3
U.S.	18.4	11.2	1.8	0.7	4.7

Note: Persons of Hispanic or Latino origin can be of any race; (1) Figures cover the Salem, OR Metropolitan Statistical Area
Source: U.S. Census Bureau, 2017-2021 American Community Survey 5-Year Estimates

Age

Area	Under Age 5	Age 5–19	Age 20–34	Age 35–44	Age 45–54	Age 55–64	Age 65–74	Age 75–84	Age 85+	Median Age
City	5.9	20.3	21.7	13.6	11.5	11.2	9.6	4.5	1.8	36.3
MSA[1]	5.9	20.8	20.0	12.7	11.3	11.9	10.4	5.1	1.9	37.4
U.S.	5.6	19.2	20.2	12.7	12.4	13.1	10.0	4.9	1.9	38.8

Note: (1) Figures cover the Salem, OR Metropolitan Statistical Area
Source: U.S. Census Bureau, 2020 Census

Disability by Age

Area	All Ages	Under 18 Years Old	18 to 64 Years Old	65 Years and Over
City	15.2	6.3	13.9	35.5
MSA[1]	14.9	5.3	13.0	36.5
U.S.	12.6	4.4	10.3	33.4

Note: Figures show percent of the civilian noninstitutionalized population that reported having a disability. Disability status is determined from six types of difficulty: vision, hearing, cognitive, ambulatory, self-care, and independent living. For children under 5 years old, hearing and vision difficulty are used to determine disability status. For children between the ages of 5 and 14, disability status is determined from hearing, vision, cognitive, ambulatory, and self-care difficulties. For people aged 15 years and older, they are considered to have a disability if they have difficulty with any one of the six difficulty types; Note: (1) Figures cover the Salem, OR Metropolitan Statistical Area
Source: U.S. Census Bureau, 2017-2021 American Community Survey 5-Year Estimates

Ancestry

Area	German	Irish	English	American	Italian	Polish	French[2]	Scottish	Dutch
City	16.9	9.3	11.1	3.6	2.9	1.4	2.7	2.5	1.8
MSA[1]	16.9	9.0	10.6	3.7	2.8	1.2	2.6	2.3	1.8
U.S.	12.8	9.6	8.1	5.7	5.0	2.7	2.2	1.6	1.1

Note: Figures are the percentage of the total population reporting a particular ancestry. The nine most commonly reported ancestries in the U.S. are shown. Figures include multiple ancestries (e.g. if a person reported being Irish and Italian, they were included in both columns); (1) Figures cover the Salem, OR Metropolitan Statistical Area; (2) Excludes Basque
Source: U.S. Census Bureau, 2017-2021 American Community Survey 5-Year Estimates

Foreign-born Population

Area	Percent of Population Born in								
	Any Foreign Country	Asia	Mexico	Europe	Caribbean	Central America[2]	South America	Africa	Canada
City	11.3	2.4	5.8	1.1	0.1	0.4	0.2	0.2	0.2
MSA[1]	11.5	1.5	7.2	1.1	0.1	0.5	0.3	0.1	0.2
U.S.	13.6	4.2	3.3	1.5	1.4	1.1	1.1	0.8	0.2

Note: (1) Figures cover the Salem, OR Metropolitan Statistical Area; (2) Excludes Mexico.
Source: U.S. Census Bureau, 2017-2021 American Community Survey 5-Year Estimates

Household Size

Area	Persons in Household (%)							Average Household Size
	One	Two	Three	Four	Five	Six	Seven or More	
City	29.7	33.2	14.8	11.0	6.5	2.8	2.0	2.60
MSA[1]	25.3	34.2	15.3	12.4	7.5	3.3	2.0	2.70
U.S.	28.1	33.8	15.5	12.9	6.0	2.3	1.4	2.60

Note: (1) Figures cover the Salem, OR Metropolitan Statistical Area
Source: U.S. Census Bureau, 2017-2021 American Community Survey 5-Year Estimates

Household Relationships

Area	House-holder	Opposite-sex Spouse	Same-sex Spouse	Opposite-sex Unmarried Partner	Same-sex Unmarried Partner	Child[2]	Grand-child	Other Relatives	Non-relatives
City	36.6	16.0	0.2	3.1	0.2	28.1	1.9	4.6	4.2
MSA[1]	35.7	17.6	0.2	2.7	0.1	29.3	2.3	5.0	4.1
U.S.	38.3	17.5	0.2	2.5	0.2	28.3	2.4	4.8	3.4

Note: Figures are percent of the total population; (1) Figures cover the Salem, OR Metropolitan Statistical Area; (2) Includes biological, adopted, and stepchildren of the householder
Source: U.S. Census Bureau, 2020 Census

Gender

Area	Males	Females	Males per 100 Females
City	87,574	87,961	99.6
MSA[1]	214,703	218,650	98.2
U.S.	162,685,811	168,763,470	96.4

Note: (1) Figures cover the Salem, OR Metropolitan Statistical Area
Source: U.S. Census Bureau, 2020 Census

Marital Status

Area	Never Married	Now Married[2]	Separated	Widowed	Divorced
City	34.6	45.1	1.6	5.2	13.4
MSA[1]	31.8	48.7	1.7	5.3	12.6
U.S.	33.8	48.0	1.8	5.6	10.8

Note: Figures are percentages and cover the population 15 years of age and older; (1) Figures cover the Salem, OR Metropolitan Statistical Area; (2) Excludes separated
Source: U.S. Census Bureau, 2017-2021 American Community Survey 5-Year Estimates

Religious Groups by Family

Area	Catholic	Baptist	Methodist	LDS[2]	Pentecostal	Lutheran	Islam	Adventist	Other
MSA[1]	19.5	0.5	0.6	3.8	2.9	1.2	n/a	2.5	10.7
U.S.	18.7	7.3	3.0	2.0	1.8	1.7	1.3	1.3	11.6

Note: Figures are the number of adherents as a percentage of the total population and cover the eight largest religious groups in the U.S; (1) Figures cover the Salem, OR Metropolitan Statistical Area; (2) Church of Jesus Christ of Latter-day Saints
Sources: 2020 U.S. Religion Census, Association of Statisticians of American Religious Bodies; The Association of Religion Data Archives (ARDA)

Religious Groups by Tradition

Area	Catholic	Evangelical Protestant	Mainline Protestant	Black Protestant	Islam	Judaism	Hinduism	Orthodox	Buddhism
MSA[1]	19.5	14.4	2.0	0.2	n/a	0.1	<0.1	<0.1	<0.1
U.S.	18.7	16.5	5.2	2.3	1.3	0.6	0.4	0.4	0.3

Note: Figures are the number of adherents as a percentage of the total population; (1) Figures cover the Salem, OR Metropolitan Statistical Area
Sources: 2020 U.S. Religion Census, Association of Statisticians of American Religious Bodies; The Association of Religion Data Archives (ARDA)

ECONOMY

Gross Metropolitan Product

Area	2020	2021	2022	2023	Rank[2]
MSA[1]	19.2	21.0	22.9	24.2	144

Note: Figures are in billions of dollars; (1) Figures cover the Salem, OR Metropolitan Statistical Area; (2) Rank is based on 2021 data and ranges from 1 to 381
Source: U.S. Conference of Mayors, U.S. Metro Economies: U.S. Metros Compared to Global and State Economies, June 2022

Economic Growth

Area	2018-20 (%)	2021 (%)	2022 (%)	2023 (%)	Rank[2]
MSA[1]	0.3	5.6	4.2	2.6	119
U.S.	-0.6	5.7	3.1	2.9	–

Note: Figures are real gross metropolitan product (GMP) growth rates and represent average annual percent change; (1) Figures cover the Salem, OR Metropolitan Statistical Area; (2) Rank is based on 2020 2-year average annual percent change and ranges from 1 to 381
Source: U.S. Conference of Mayors, U.S. Metro Economies: U.S. Metros Compared to Global and State Economies, June 2022

Metropolitan Area Exports

Area	2016	2017	2018	2019	2020	2021	Rank[2]
MSA[1]	358.2	339.0	410.2	405.7	350.5	372.0	244

Note: Figures are in millions of dollars; (1) Figures cover the Salem, OR Metropolitan Statistical Area; (2) Rank is based on 2021 data and ranges from 1 to 388
Source: U.S. Department of Commerce, International Trade Administration, Office of Trade and Economic Analysis, Industry and Analysis, Exports by Metropolitan Area, data extracted March 16, 2023

Building Permits

Area	Single-Family			Multi-Family			Total		
	2021	2022	Pct. Chg.	2021	2022	Pct. Chg.	2021	2022	Pct. Chg.
City	447	318	-28.9	399	851	113.3	846	1,169	38.2
MSA[1]	1,368	874	-36.1	786	1,943	147.2	2,154	2,817	30.8
U.S.	1,115,400	975,600	-12.5	621,600	689,500	10.9	1,737,000	1,665,100	-4.1

Note: (1) Figures cover the Salem, OR Metropolitan Statistical Area; Figures represent new, privately-owned housing units authorized (unadjusted data); All permit data are based on estimates with imputation
Source: U.S. Census Bureau, Manufacturing, Mining, and Construction Statistics, Building Permits, 2021, 2022

Bankruptcy Filings

Area	Business Filings			Nonbusiness Filings		
	2021	2022	% Chg.	2021	2022	% Chg.
Marion County	7	4	-42.9	489	439	-10.2
U.S.	14,347	13,481	-6.0	399,269	374,240	-6.3

Note: Business filings include Chapter 7, Chapter 9, Chapter 11, Chapter 12, Chapter 13, Chapter 15, and Section 304; Nonbusiness filings include Chapter 7, Chapter 11, and Chapter 13
Source: Administrative Office of the U.S. Courts, Business and Nonbusiness Bankruptcy, County Cases Commenced by Chapter of the Bankruptcy Code, During the 12-Month Period Ending December 31, 2021 and Business and Nonbusiness Bankruptcy, County Cases Commenced by Chapter of the Bankruptcy Code, During the 12-Month Period Ending December 31, 2022

Housing Vacancy Rates

Area	Gross Vacancy Rate[2] (%)			Year-Round Vacancy Rate[3] (%)			Rental Vacancy Rate[4] (%)			Homeowner Vacancy Rate[5] (%)		
	2020	2021	2022	2020	2021	2022	2020	2021	2022	2020	2021	2022
MSA[1]	n/a	n/a	n/a	n/a	n/a	n/a	n/a	n/a	n/a	n/a	n/a	n/a
U.S.	10.6	10.8	10.5	8.2	8.4	8.2	6.3	6.1	5.8	1.0	0.9	0.8

Note: (1) Figures cover the Salem, OR Metropolitan Statistical Area; (2) The percentage of the total housing inventory that is vacant; (3) The percentage of the housing inventory (excluding seasonal units) that is year-round vacant; (4) The percentage of rental inventory that is vacant for rent; (5) The percentage of homeowner inventory that is vacant for sale; n/a not available
Source: U.S. Census Bureau, Housing Vacancies and Homeownership Annual Statistics: 2020, 2021, 2022

INCOME

Income

Area	Per Capita ($)	Median Household ($)	Average Household ($)
City	31,610	62,185	82,450
MSA[1]	31,447	65,881	85,642
U.S.	37,638	69,021	97,196

Note: (1) Figures cover the Salem, OR Metropolitan Statistical Area
Source: U.S. Census Bureau, 2017-2021 American Community Survey 5-Year Estimates

Household Income Distribution

Area	Percent of Households Earning							
	Under $15,000	$15,000 -$24,999	$25,000 -$34,999	$35,000 -$49,999	$50,000 -$74,999	$75,000 -$99,999	$100,000 -$149,999	$150,000 and up
City	9.9	8.3	8.7	12.8	19.4	13.0	16.6	11.3
MSA[1]	8.5	7.8	8.7	12.3	18.9	13.8	17.5	12.3
U.S.	9.4	7.8	8.2	11.4	16.8	12.8	16.3	17.3

Note: (1) Figures cover the Salem, OR Metropolitan Statistical Area
Source: U.S. Census Bureau, 2017-2021 American Community Survey 5-Year Estimates

Poverty Rate

Area	All Ages	Under 18 Years Old	18 to 64 Years Old	65 Years and Over
City	14.7	18.0	14.5	10.2
MSA[1]	13.1	16.8	12.8	8.8
U.S.	12.6	17.0	11.8	9.6

Note: Figures are percentage of people whose income during the past 12 months was below the poverty level;
(1) Figures cover the Salem, OR Metropolitan Statistical Area
Source: U.S. Census Bureau, 2017-2021 American Community Survey 5-Year Estimates

EMPLOYMENT

Labor Force and Employment

Area	Civilian Labor Force			Workers Employed		
	Dec. 2021	Dec. 2022	% Chg.	Dec. 2021	Dec. 2022	% Chg.
City	84,706	83,973	-0.9	81,711	80,171	-1.9
MSA[1]	210,043	208,341	-0.8	202,733	198,916	-1.9
U.S.	161,696,000	164,224,000	1.6	155,732,000	158,872,000	2.0

Note: Data is not seasonally adjusted and covers workers 16 years of age and older; (1) Figures cover the Salem, OR Metropolitan Statistical Area
Source: Bureau of Labor Statistics, Local Area Unemployment Statistics

Unemployment Rate

Area	2022											
	Jan.	Feb.	Mar.	Apr.	May	Jun.	Jul.	Aug.	Sep.	Oct.	Nov.	Dec.
City	4.4	4.0	4.0	3.7	3.1	3.8	4.2	4.5	4.1	4.2	4.3	4.5
MSA[1]	4.5	3.9	3.9	3.6	3.1	3.7	4.0	4.4	4.0	4.2	4.3	4.5
U.S.	4.4	4.1	3.8	3.3	3.4	3.8	3.8	3.8	3.3	3.4	3.4	3.3

Note: Data is not seasonally adjusted and covers workers 16 years of age and older; (1) Figures cover the Salem, OR Metropolitan Statistical Area
Source: Bureau of Labor Statistics, Local Area Unemployment Statistics

Average Wages

Occupation	$/Hr.	Occupation	$/Hr.
Accountants and Auditors	37.81	Maintenance and Repair Workers	22.28
Automotive Mechanics	26.17	Marketing Managers	52.32
Bookkeepers	23.29	Network and Computer Systems Admin.	46.22
Carpenters	27.37	Nurses, Licensed Practical	30.83
Cashiers	15.07	Nurses, Registered	46.17
Computer Programmers	43.99	Nursing Assistants	21.59
Computer Systems Analysts	48.05	Office Clerks, General	20.38
Computer User Support Specialists	29.88	Physical Therapists	45.54
Construction Laborers	23.00	Physicians	158.13
Cooks, Restaurant	17.44	Plumbers, Pipefitters and Steamfitters	34.34
Customer Service Representatives	19.55	Police and Sheriff's Patrol Officers	37.37
Dentists	94.78	Postal Service Mail Carriers	26.44
Electricians	37.27	Real Estate Sales Agents	29.11
Engineers, Electrical	52.49	Retail Salespersons	17.64
Fast Food and Counter Workers	14.60	Sales Representatives, Technical/Scientific	53.51
Financial Managers	64.50	Secretaries, Exc. Legal/Medical/Executive	22.97
First-Line Supervisors of Office Workers	30.14	Security Guards	18.21
General and Operations Managers	46.82	Surgeons	n/a
Hairdressers/Cosmetologists	18.25	Teacher Assistants, Exc. Postsecondary*	19.13
Home Health and Personal Care Aides	17.28	Teachers, Secondary School, Exc. Sp. Ed.*	39.59
Janitors and Cleaners	17.05	Telemarketers	16.13
Landscaping/Groundskeeping Workers	19.59	Truck Drivers, Heavy/Tractor-Trailer	26.69
Lawyers	67.46	Truck Drivers, Light/Delivery Services	21.33
Maids and Housekeeping Cleaners	16.44	Waiters and Waitresses	16.15

Note: Wage data covers the Salem, OR Metropolitan Statistical Area; (*) Hourly wages were calculated from annual wage data based on a 40 hour work week; n/a not available.
Source: Bureau of Labor Statistics, Metro Area Occupational Employment & Wage Estimates, May 2022

Employment by Industry

Sector	MSA[1]		U.S.
	Number of Employees	Percent of Total	Percent of Total
Construction	13,100	7.3	5.0
Private Education and Health Services	32,000	17.8	16.1
Financial Activities	6,800	3.8	5.9
Government	44,200	24.5	14.5
Information	1,700	0.9	2.0
Leisure and Hospitality	15,900	8.8	10.3
Manufacturing	12,000	6.7	8.4
Mining and Logging	600	0.3	0.4
Other Services	5,400	3.0	3.7
Professional and Business Services	17,200	9.5	14.7
Retail Trade	19,800	11.0	10.2
Transportation, Warehousing, and Utilities	7,300	4.1	4.9
Wholesale Trade	4,200	2.3	3.9

Note: Figures are non-farm employment as of December 2022. Figures are not seasonally adjusted and include workers 16 years of age and older; (1) Figures cover the Salem, OR Metropolitan Statistical Area
Source: Bureau of Labor Statistics, Current Employment Statistics, Employment, Hours, and Earnings

Employment by Occupation

Occupation Classification	City (%)	MSA[1] (%)	U.S. (%)
Management, Business, Science, and Arts	36.5	33.4	40.3
Natural Resources, Construction, and Maintenance	9.3	12.5	8.7
Production, Transportation, and Material Moving	12.1	13.5	13.1
Sales and Office	21.9	21.5	20.9
Service	20.1	19.2	17.0

Note: Figures cover employed civilians 16 years of age and older; (1) Figures cover the Salem, OR Metropolitan Statistical Area
Source: U.S. Census Bureau, 2017-2021 American Community Survey 5-Year Estimates

Occupations with Greatest Projected Employment Growth: 2022 – 2024

Occupation[1]	2022 Employment	2024 Projected Employment	Numeric Employment Change	Percent Employment Change
Fast Food and Counter Workers	66,590	76,330	9,740	14.6
Waiters and Waitresses	26,060	30,030	3,970	15.2
Cooks, Restaurant	20,600	24,040	3,440	16.7
Home Health and Personal Care Aides	31,660	34,200	2,540	8.0
Maids and Housekeeping Cleaners	16,400	18,280	1,880	11.5
First-Line Supervisors of Food Preparation and Serving Workers	13,120	14,930	1,810	13.8
Bartenders	8,410	9,990	1,580	18.8
General and Operations Managers	36,530	37,990	1,460	4.0
Stockers and Order Fillers	39,960	41,380	1,420	3.6
Retail Salespersons	58,520	59,830	1,310	2.2

Note: Projections cover Oregon; (1) Sorted by numeric employment change
Source: www.projectionscentral.com, State Occupational Projections, 2022–2024 Short-Term Projections

Fastest-Growing Occupations: 2022 – 2024

Occupation[1]	2022 Employment	2024 Projected Employment	Numeric Employment Change	Percent Employment Change
First-Line Supervisors of Gambling Services Workers	220	280	60	27.3
Gaming Dealers	310	390	80	25.8
Film and Video Editors	390	480	90	23.1
Multimedia Artists and Animators	820	990	170	20.7
Tour and Travel Guides	560	670	110	19.6
Fine Artists, Including Painters, Sculptors, and Illustrators	620	740	120	19.4
Bartenders	8,410	9,990	1,580	18.8
Ushers, Lobby Attendants, and Ticket Takers	610	720	110	18.0
Hotel, Motel, and Resort Desk Clerks	3,650	4,300	650	17.8
Fitness Trainers and Aerobics Instructors	4,800	5,650	850	17.7

Note: Projections cover Oregon; (1) Sorted by percent employment change and excludes occupations with numeric employment change less than 50
Source: www.projectionscentral.com, State Occupational Projections, 2022–2024 Short-Term Projections

CITY FINANCES

City Government Finances

Component	2020 ($000)	2020 ($ per capita)
Total Revenues	403,307	2,313
Total Expenditures	413,037	2,369
Debt Outstanding	897,081	5,145
Cash and Securities[1]	1,600,460	9,179

Note: (1) Cash and security holdings of a government at the close of its fiscal year, including those of its dependent agencies, utilities, and liquor stores.
Source: U.S. Census Bureau, State & Local Government Finances 2020

City Government Revenue by Source

Source	2020 ($000)	2020 ($ per capita)	2020 (%)
General Revenue			
From Federal Government	22,395	128	5.6
From State Government	51,080	293	12.7
From Local Governments	11,815	68	2.9
Taxes			
Property	101,928	585	25.3
Sales and Gross Receipts	26,043	149	6.5
Personal Income	0	0	0.0
Corporate Income	0	0	0.0
Motor Vehicle License	0	0	0.0
Other Taxes	19,233	110	4.8
Current Charges	81,885	470	20.3
Liquor Store	0	0	0.0
Utility	39,226	225	9.7

Source: U.S. Census Bureau, State & Local Government Finances 2020

City Government Expenditures by Function

Function	2020 ($000)	2020 ($ per capita)	2020 (%)
General Direct Expenditures			
Air Transportation	1,250	7	0.3
Corrections	0	0	0.0
Education	0	0	0.0
Employment Security Administration	0	0	0.0
Financial Administration	3,604	20	0.9
Fire Protection	35,558	203	8.6
General Public Buildings	4,075	23	1.0
Governmental Administration, Other	2,804	16	0.7
Health	997	5	0.2
Highways	62,665	359	15.2
Hospitals	0	0	0.0
Housing and Community Development	41,904	240	10.1
Interest on General Debt	27,451	157	6.6
Judicial and Legal	4,287	24	1.0
Libraries	4,597	26	1.1
Parking	1,525	8	0.4
Parks and Recreation	12,698	72	3.1
Police Protection	45,626	261	11.0
Public Welfare	0	0	0.0
Sewerage	67,211	385	16.3
Solid Waste Management	0	0	0.0
Veterans' Services	0	0	0.0
Liquor Store	0	0	0.0
Utility	39,637	227	9.6

Source: U.S. Census Bureau, State & Local Government Finances 2020

TAXES

State Corporate Income Tax Rates

State	Tax Rate (%)	Income Brackets ($)	Num. of Brackets	Financial Institution Tax Rate (%)[a]	Federal Income Tax Ded.
Oregon	6.6 - 7.6 (s)	1 million	2	6.6 - 7.6 (s)	No

Note: Tax rates as of January 1, 2023; (a) Rates listed are the corporate income tax rate applied to financial institutions or excise taxes based on income. Some states have other taxes based upon the value of deposits or shares; (s) Oregon's minimum tax for C corporations depends on the Oregon sales of the filing group. The minimum tax ranges from $150 for corporations with sales under $500,000, up to $100,000 for companies with sales of $100 million or above. Oregon also imposes Corporate Activity Tax [CAT] of $250 plus 0.57% of activity in excess of $1 million.
Source: Federation of Tax Administrators, State Corporate Income Tax Rates, January 1, 2023

State Individual Income Tax Rates

State	Tax Rate (%)	Income Brackets ($)	Personal Exemptions ($)			Standard Ded. ($)	
			Single	Married	Depend.	Single	Married
Oregon (a)	4.75 - 9.9	4,050 -125,000 (b)	236	472	236 (c)	2,605	5,210

Note: Tax rates as of January 1, 2023; Local- and county-level taxes are not included; (a) 16 states have statutory provision for automatically adjusting to the rate of inflation the dollar values of the income tax brackets, standard deductions, and/or personal exemptions. Oregon does not index the income brackets for $125,000 and over; (b) For joint returns, taxes are twice the tax on half the couple's income; (c) The personal exemption takes the form of a tax credit instead of a deduction
Source: Federation of Tax Administrators, State Individual Income Tax Rates, January 1, 2023

Various State Sales and Excise Tax Rates

State	State Sales Tax (%)	Gasoline[1] ($/gal.)	Cigarette[2] ($/pack)	Spirits[3] ($/gal.)	Wine[4] ($/gal.)	Beer[5] ($/gal.)	Recreational Marijuana (%)
Oregon	None	0.3883	3.33	22.86	0.67	0.08	(p)

Note: All tax rates as of January 1, 2023; (1) The American Petroleum Institute has developed a methodology for determining the average tax rate on a gallon of fuel. Rates may include any of the following: excise taxes, environmental fees, storage tank fees, other fees or taxes, general sales tax, and local taxes; (2) The federal excise tax of $1.0066 per pack and local taxes are not included; (3) Rates are those applicable to off-premise sales of 40% alcohol by volume (a.b.v.) distilled spirits in 750ml containers. Local excise taxes are excluded; (4) Rates are those applicable to off-premise sales of 11% a.b.v. non-carbonated wine in 750ml containers; (5) Rates are those applicable to off-premise sales of 4.7% a.b.v. beer in 12 ounce containers; (p) 17% excise tax (retail price)
Source: Tax Foundation, 2023 Facts & Figures: How Does Your State Compare?

State Business Tax Climate Index Rankings

State	Overall Rank	Corporate Tax Rank	Individual Income Tax Rank	Sales Tax Rank	Property Tax Rank	Unemployment Insurance Tax Rank
Oregon	24	49	42	4	20	36

Note: The index is a measure of how each state's tax laws affect economic performance. The lower the rank, the more favorable a state's tax system is for business. States without a given tax are given a ranking of 1. The scores/rankings for the District of Columbia do not affect other states. The 2023 index represents the tax climate as of July 1, 2022.
Source: Tax Foundation, State Business Tax Climate Index 2023

TRANSPORTATION

Means of Transportation to Work

Area	Car/Truck/Van		Public Transportation			Bicycle	Walked	Other Means	Worked at Home
	Drove Alone	Car-pooled	Bus	Subway	Railroad				
City	71.7	9.5	2.2	0.0	0.0	1.4	3.4	1.2	10.5
MSA[1]	74.3	10.1	1.3	0.0	0.0	0.8	2.6	1.1	9.8
U.S.	73.2	8.6	2.0	1.6	0.5	0.5	2.5	1.5	9.7

Note: Figures are percentages and cover workers 16 years of age and older; (1) Figures cover the Salem, OR Metropolitan Statistical Area
Source: U.S. Census Bureau, 2017-2021 American Community Survey 5-Year Estimates

Travel Time to Work

Area	Less Than 10 Minutes	10 to 19 Minutes	20 to 29 Minutes	30 to 44 Minutes	45 to 59 Minutes	60 to 89 Minutes	90 Minutes or More
City	13.0	41.0	19.7	12.7	6.0	6.0	1.6
MSA[1]	13.7	32.6	20.9	16.9	7.6	6.3	2.0
U.S.	12.4	28.5	21.0	20.9	8.2	6.2	2.9

Note: Note: Figures are percentages and include workers 16 years old and over; (1) Figures cover the Salem, OR Metropolitan Statistical Area
Source: U.S. Census Bureau, 2017-2021 American Community Survey 5-Year Estimates

Key Congestion Measures

Measure	1990	2000	2010	2015	2020
Annual Hours of Delay, Total (000)	1,927	3,677	5,706	6,319	2,541
Annual Hours of Delay, Per Auto Commuter	21	31	37	39	15
Annual Congestion Cost, Per Auto Commuter ($)	415	578	717	731	302

Note: Covers the Salem OR urban area
Source: Texas A&M Transportation Institute, 2021 Urban Mobility Report

Freeway Travel Time Index

Measure	1985	1990	1995	2000	2005	2010	2015	2020
Urban Area Index[1]	1.04	1.10	1.12	1.15	1.19	1.17	1.15	1.05
Urban Area Rank[1,2]	81	47	57	53	38	41	67	85

Note: Freeway Travel Time Index—the ratio of travel time in the peak period to the travel time at free-flow conditions. For example, a value of 1.30 indicates a 20-minute free-flow trip takes 26 minutes in the peak (20 minutes x 1.30 = 26 minutes); (1) Covers the Salem OR urban area; (2) Rank is based on 101 larger urban areas (#1 = highest travel time index)
Source: Texas A&M Transportation Institute, 2021 Urban Mobility Report

Public Transportation

Agency Name / Mode of Transportation	Vehicles Operated in Maximum Service[1]	Annual Unlinked Passenger Trips[2] (in thous.)	Annual Passenger Miles[3] (in thous.)
Salem Area Mass Transit District			
Bus (directly operated)	53	1,718.9	5,259.8
Bus (purchased transportation)	8	56.9	845.2
Demand Response (purchased transportation)	40	58.2	301.7
Vanpool (purchased transportation)	15	22.5	698.1

Note: (1) Number of revenue vehicles operated by the given mode and type of service to meet the annual maximum service requirement. This is the revenue vehicle count during the peak season of the year; on the week and day that maximum service is provided. Vehicles operated in maximum service (VOMS) exclude atypical days and one-time special events; (2) Number of passengers who boarded public transportation vehicles. Passengers are counted each time they board a vehicle no matter how many vehicles they use to travel from their origin to their destination. (3) Sum of the distances ridden by all passengers during the entire fiscal year.
Source: Federal Transit Administration, National Transit Database, 2021

Air Transportation

Airport Name and Code / Type of Service	Passenger Airlines[1]	Passenger Enplanements	Freight Carriers[2]	Freight (lbs)
Portland International Airport (60 miles) (PDX)				
Domestic service (U.S. carriers - 2022)	27	6,967,743	17	317,498,801
International service (U.S. carriers - 2021)	4	38,432	4	128,847

Note: (1) Includes all U.S.-based major, minor and commuter airlines that carried at least one passenger during the year; (2) Includes all U.S.-based airlines and freight carriers that transported at least one pound of freight during the year.
Source: Bureau of Transportation Statistics, The Intermodal Transportation Database, Air Carriers: T-100 Domestic Market (U.S. Carriers), 2022; Bureau of Transportation Statistics, The Intermodal Transportation Database, Air Carriers: T-100 International Market (U.S. Carriers), 2021

BUSINESSES

Major Business Headquarters

Company Name	Industry	Rankings	
		Fortune[1]	Forbes[2]
No companies listed	-	-	-

Note: (1) Companies that produce a 10-K are ranked 1 to 500 based on 2021 revenue; (2) All private companies with at least $2 billion in annual revenue through the end of their most current fiscal year are ranked 1 to 246; companies listed are headquartered in the city; dashes indicate no ranking
Source: Fortune, "Fortune 500," 2022; Forbes, "America's Largest Private Companies," 2022

Living Environment

COST OF LIVING

Cost of Living Index

Composite Index	Groceries	Housing	Utilities	Trans-portation	Health Care	Misc. Goods/ Services
n/a	n/a	n/a	n/a	n/a	n/a	n/a

Note: The Cost of Living Index measures regional differences in the cost of consumer goods and services, excluding taxes and non-consumer expenditures, for professional and managerial households in the top income quintile. It is based on more than 50,000 prices covering almost 60 different items for which prices are collected three times a year by chambers of commerce, economic development organizations or university applied economic centers in each participating urban area. The numbers shown should be read as a percentage above or below the national average of 100. For example, a value of 115.4 in the groceries column indicates that grocery prices are 15.4% higher than the national average. Small differences in the index numbers should not be interpreted as significant; n/a not available.
Source: The Council for Community and Economic Research, Cost of Living Index, 2022

Grocery Prices

Area[1]	T-Bone Steak ($/pound)	Frying Chicken ($/pound)	Whole Milk ($/half gal.)	Eggs ($/dozen)	Orange Juice ($/64 oz.)	Coffee ($/11.5 oz.)
City[2]	n/a	n/a	n/a	n/a	n/a	n/a
Avg.	13.81	1.59	2.43	2.25	3.85	4.95
Min.	10.17	0.90	1.51	1.30	2.90	3.46
Max.	19.35	3.30	4.32	4.32	5.31	8.59

*Note: (1) Values for the local area are compared with the average, minimum and maximum values for all 286 areas in the Cost of Living Index; (2) Figures cover the Salem OR urban area; n/a not available; **T-Bone Steak** (price per pound); **Frying Chicken** (price per pound, whole fryer); **Whole Milk** (half gallon carton); **Eggs** (price per dozen, Grade A, large); **Orange Juice** (64 oz. Tropicana or Florida Natural); **Coffee** (11.5 oz. can, vacuum-packed, Maxwell House, Hills Bros, or Folgers).*
Source: The Council for Community and Economic Research, Cost of Living Index, 2022

Housing and Utility Costs

Area[1]	New Home Price ($)	Apartment Rent ($/month)	All Electric ($/month)	Part Electric ($/month)	Other Energy ($/month)	Telephone ($/month)
City[2]	n/a	n/a	n/a	n/a	n/a	n/a
Avg.	450,913	1,371	176.41	99.93	76.96	190.22
Min.	229,283	546	100.84	31.56	27.15	174.27
Max.	2,434,977	4,569	356.86	249.59	272.24	208.31

*Note: (1) Values for the local area are compared with the average, minimum and maximum values for all 286 areas in the Cost of Living Index; (2) Figures cover the Salem OR urban area; n/a not available; **New Home Price** (2,400 sf living area, 8,000 sf lot, in urban area with full utilities); **Apartment Rent** (950 sf 2 bedroom/1.5 or 2 bath, unfurnished, excluding all utilities except water); **All Electric** (average monthly cost for an all-electric home); **Part Electric** (average monthly cost for a part-electric home); **Other Energy** (average monthly cost for natural gas, fuel oil, coal, wood, and any other forms of energy except electricity); **Telephone** (price includes the base monthly rate plus taxes and fees for three lines of mobile phone service).*
Source: The Council for Community and Economic Research, Cost of Living Index, 2022

Health Care, Transportation, and Other Costs

Area[1]	Doctor ($/visit)	Dentist ($/visit)	Optometrist ($/visit)	Gasoline ($/gallon)	Beauty Salon ($/visit)	Men's Shirt ($)
City[2]	n/a	n/a	n/a	n/a	n/a	n/a
Avg.	124.91	107.77	117.66	3.86	43.31	34.21
Min.	36.61	58.25	51.79	2.90	22.18	13.05
Max.	250.21	162.58	371.96	5.54	85.61	63.54

*Note: (1) Values for the local area are compared with the average, minimum and maximum values for all 286 areas in the Cost of Living Index; (2) Figures cover the Salem OR urban area; n/a not available; **Doctor** (general practitioners routine exam of an established patient); **Dentist** (adult teeth cleaning and periodic oral examination); **Optometrist** (full vision eye exam for established adult patient); **Gasoline** (one gallon regular unleaded, national brand, including all taxes, cash price at self-service pump if available); **Beauty Salon** (woman's shampoo, trim, and blow-dry); **Men's Shirt** (cotton/polyester dress shirt, pinpoint weave, long sleeves).*
Source: The Council for Community and Economic Research, Cost of Living Index, 2022

HOUSING

Homeownership Rate

Area	2015 (%)	2016 (%)	2017 (%)	2018 (%)	2019 (%)	2020 (%)	2021 (%)	2022 (%)
MSA[1]	n/a	n/a	n/a	n/a	n/a	n/a	n/a	n/a
U.S.	63.7	63.4	63.9	64.4	64.6	66.6	65.5	65.8

Note: (1) Figures cover the Salem, OR Metropolitan Statistical Area; n/a not available
Source: U.S. Census Bureau, Housing Vacancies and Homeownership Annual Statistics: 2015-2022

House Price Index (HPI)

Area	National Ranking[2]	Quarterly Change (%)	One-Year Change (%)	Five-Year Change (%)	Since 1991Q1 (%)
MSA[1]	204	-1.19	8.51	62.82	461.52
U.S.[3]	–	0.34	8.41	58.44	289.08

Note: The HPI is a weighted repeat sales index. It measures average price changes in repeat sales or refinancings on the same properties. This information is obtained by reviewing repeat mortgage transactions on single-family properties whose mortgages have been purchased or securitized by Fannie Mae or Freddie Mac since January 1975; (1) Figures cover the Salem, OR Metropolitan Statistical Area; (2) Rankings are based on annual percentage change for all metro areas containing at least 15,000 transactions over the last 10 years and ranges from 1 to 257; (3) figures based on a weighted average of Census Division estimates using a seasonally adjusted, purchase-only index; all figures are for the period ending December 31, 2022
Source: Federal Housing Finance Agency, Change in FHFA Metropolitan Area House Price Indexes, 2022Q4

Median Single-Family Home Prices

Area	2020	2021	2022[p]	Percent Change 2021 to 2022
MSA[1]	353.6	411.1	451.7	9.9
U.S. Average	300.2	357.1	392.6	9.9

Note: Figures are median sales prices of existing single-family homes in thousands of dollars; (p) preliminary; (1) Figures cover the Salem, OR Metropolitan Statistical Area
Source: National Association of Realtors, Median Sales Price of Existing Single-Family Homes for Metropolitan Areas, 4th Quarter 2022

Qualifying Income Based on Median Sales Price of Existing Single-Family Homes

Area	With 5% Down ($)	With 10% Down ($)	With 20% Down ($)
MSA[1]	132,718	125,733	111,762
U.S. Average	112,234	106,237	94,513

Note: Figures are preliminary; Qualifying income is based on a mortgage rate of 6.77%. Monthly principal and interest payment is limited to 25% of income; (1) Figures cover the Salem, OR Metropolitan Statistical Area
Source: National Association of Realtors, Qualifying Income Based on Median Sales Price of Existing Single-Family Homes for Metropolitan Areas, 4th Quarter 2022

Home Value

Area	Under $100,000	$100,000 -$199,999	$200,000 -$299,999	$300,000 -$399,999	$400,000 -$499,999	$500,000 -$999,999	$1,000,000 or more	Median ($)
City	7.5	13.6	32.7	26.7	11.1	7.9	0.5	289,500
MSA[1]	8.1	12.8	29.6	24.3	12.1	12.1	1.0	298,400
U.S.	16.2	24.2	20.1	13.6	8.3	13.6	4.1	244,900

Note: Figures are percentages except for median and cover owner-occupied housing units; (1) Figures cover the Salem, OR Metropolitan Statistical Area
Source: U.S. Census Bureau, 2017-2021 American Community Survey 5-Year Estimates

Year Housing Structure Built

Area	2020 or Later	2010 -2019	2000 -2009	1990 -1999	1980 -1989	1970 -1979	1960 -1969	1950 -1959	1940 -1949	Before 1940	Median Year
City	0.2	6.9	12.5	16.8	9.7	19.9	9.5	10.6	4.9	9.0	1978
MSA[1]	0.2	6.5	13.4	17.3	9.7	22.3	10.3	8.0	4.0	8.4	1979
U.S.	0.2	7.3	13.6	13.6	13.2	14.8	10.3	10.0	4.7	12.2	1979

Note: Figures are percentages except for Median Year; Note: (1) Figures cover the Salem, OR Metropolitan Statistical Area
Source: U.S. Census Bureau, 2017-2021 American Community Survey 5-Year Estimates

Gross Monthly Rent

Area	Under $500	$500 -$999	$1,000 -$1,499	$1,500 -$1,999	$2,000 -$2,499	$2,500 -$2,999	$3,000 and up	Median ($)
City	6.3	30.7	43.7	15.2	2.8	0.6	0.7	1,125
MSA[1]	5.9	30.4	45.3	14.0	2.9	1.0	0.5	1,128
U.S.	8.1	30.5	30.8	16.8	7.3	3.1	3.5	1,163

Note: Figures are percentages except for median; Gross rent is the contract rent plus the estimated average monthly cost of utilities (electricity, gas, and water and sewer) and fuels (oil, coal, kerosene, wood, etc.) if these are paid by the renter (or paid for the renter by someone else); (1) Figures cover the Salem, OR Metropolitan Statistical Area
Source: U.S. Census Bureau, 2017-2021 American Community Survey 5-Year Estimates

HEALTH

Health Risk Factors

Category	MSA[1] (%)	U.S. (%)
Adults aged 18–64 who have any kind of health care coverage	86.1	90.9
Adults who reported being in good or better health	81.1	85.2
Adults who have been told they have high blood cholesterol	37.0	35.7
Adults who have been told they have high blood pressure	35.4	32.4
Adults who are current smokers	16.2	14.4
Adults who currently use e-cigarettes	7.2	6.7
Adults who currently use chewing tobacco, snuff, or snus	3.0	3.5
Adults who are heavy drinkers[2]	7.2	6.3
Adults who are binge drinkers[3]	12.2	15.4
Adults who are overweight (BMI 25.0 - 29.9)	32.0	34.4
Adults who are obese (BMI 30.0 - 99.8)	38.1	33.9
Adults who participated in any physical activities in the past month	70.8	76.3

Note: (1) Figures cover the Salem, OR Metropolitan Statistical Area; (2) Heavy drinkers are classified as adult men having more than 14 drinks per week and adult women having more than 7 drinks per week; (3) Binge drinkers are classified as males having five or more drinks on one occasion or females having four or more drinks on one occasion
Source: Centers for Disease Control and Prevention, Behaviorial Risk Factor Surveillance System, SMART: Selected Metropolitan Area Risk Trends, 2021

Acute and Chronic Health Conditions

Category	MSA[1] (%)	U.S. (%)
Adults who have ever been told they had a heart attack	3.2	4.0
Adults who have ever been told they have angina or coronary heart disease	3.5	3.8
Adults who have ever been told they had a stroke	4.3	3.0
Adults who have ever been told they have asthma	18.2	14.9
Adults who have ever been told they have arthritis	25.5	25.8
Adults who have ever been told they have diabetes[2]	14.0	10.9
Adults who have ever been told they had skin cancer	6.5	6.6
Adults who have ever been told they had any other types of cancer	9.1	7.5
Adults who have ever been told they have COPD	6.6	6.1
Adults who have ever been told they have kidney disease	3.5	3.0
Adults who have ever been told they have a form of depression	27.9	20.5

Note: (1) Figures cover the Salem, OR Metropolitan Statistical Area; (2) Figures do not include pregnancy-related, borderline, or pre-diabetes
Source: Centers for Disease Control and Prevention, Behaviorial Risk Factor Surveillance System, SMART: Selected Metropolitan Area Risk Trends, 2021

Health Screening and Vaccination Rates

Category	MSA[1] (%)	U.S. (%)
Adults who have ever been tested for HIV	34.7	34.9
Adults who have had their blood cholesterol checked within the last five years	79.8	85.2
Adults aged 65+ who have had flu shot within the past year	68.4	68.6
Adults aged 65+ who have ever had a pneumonia vaccination	82.4	71.0

Note: (1) Figures cover the Salem, OR Metropolitan Statistical Area.
Source: Centers for Disease Control and Prevention, Behaviorial Risk Factor Surveillance System, SMART: Selected Metropolitan Area Risk Trends, 2021

Disability Status

Category	MSA[1] (%)	U.S. (%)
Adults who reported being deaf	8.8	7.2
Are you blind or have serious difficulty seeing, even when wearing glasses?	5.2	4.8
Are you limited in any way in any of your usual activities due to arthritis?	11.8	11.1
Do you have difficulty doing errands alone?	9.3	7.0
Do you have difficulty dressing or bathing?	6.0	3.6
Do you have serious difficulty concentrating/remembering/making decisions?	17.1	12.1
Do you have serious difficulty walking or climbing stairs?	17.0	12.8

Note: (1) Figures cover the Salem, OR Metropolitan Statistical Area.
Source: Centers for Disease Control and Prevention, Behaviorial Risk Factor Surveillance System, SMART: Selected Metropolitan Area Risk Trends, 2021

Mortality Rates for the Top 10 Causes of Death in the U.S.

ICD-10[a] Sub-Chapter	ICD-10[a] Code	Crude Mortality Rate[1] per 100,000 population County[2]	U.S.
Malignant neoplasms	C00-C97	179.8	182.6
Ischaemic heart diseases	I20-I25	71.4	113.1
Other forms of heart disease	I30-I51	63.8	64.4
Other degenerative diseases of the nervous system	G30-G31	44.7	51.0
Cerebrovascular diseases	I60-I69	48.5	47.8
Other external causes of accidental injury	W00-X59	44.3	46.4
Chronic lower respiratory diseases	J40-J47	44.7	45.7
Organic, including symptomatic, mental disorders	F01-F09	58.2	35.9
Hypertensive diseases	I10-I15	28.2	35.0
Diabetes mellitus	E10-E14	33.3	29.6

Note: (a) ICD-10 = International Classification of Diseases 10th Revision; (1) Crude mortality rates are a three-year average covering 2019-2021; (2) Figures cover Marion County.
Source: Centers for Disease Control and Prevention, National Center for Health Statistics. National Vital Statistics System, Mortality 2018-2021 on CDC WONDER Online Database

Mortality Rates for Selected Causes of Death

ICD-10[a] Sub-Chapter	ICD-10[a] Code	Crude Mortality Rate[1] per 100,000 population County[2]	U.S.
Assault	X85-Y09	2.9	7.0
Diseases of the liver	K70-K76	22.9	19.8
Human immunodeficiency virus (HIV) disease	B20-B24	Unreliable	1.5
Influenza and pneumonia	J09-J18	11.1	14.7
Intentional self-harm	X60-X84	16.3	14.3
Malnutrition	E40-E46	3.2	4.3
Obesity and other hyperalimentation	E65-E68	3.0	3.0
Renal failure	N17-N19	9.4	15.7
Transport accidents	V01-V99	15.8	13.6
Viral hepatitis	B15-B19	2.4	1.2

Note: (a) ICD-10 = International Classification of Diseases 10th Revision; (1) Crude mortality rates are a three-year average covering 2019-2021; (2) Figures cover Marion County; Data are suppressed when the data meet the criteria for confidentiality constraints; Crude mortality rates are flagged as unreliable when the rate would be calculated with a numerator of 20 or less.
Source: Centers for Disease Control and Prevention, National Center for Health Statistics. National Vital Statistics System, Mortality 2018-2021 on CDC WONDER Online Database

Health Insurance Coverage

Area	With Health Insurance	With Private Health Insurance	With Public Health Insurance	Without Health Insurance	Population Under Age 19 Without Health Insurance
City	92.9	64.7	41.5	7.1	2.1
MSA[1]	92.2	63.8	41.9	7.8	3.1
U.S.	91.2	67.8	35.4	8.8	5.3

Note: Figures are percentages that cover the civilian noninstitutionalized population; (1) Figures cover the Salem, OR Metropolitan Statistical Area
Source: U.S. Census Bureau, 2017-2021 American Community Survey 5-Year Estimates

Number of Medical Professionals

Area	MDs[3]	DOs[3,4]	Dentists	Podiatrists	Chiropractors	Optometrists
County[1] (number)	630	52	293	20	118	57
County[1] (rate[2])	182.0	15.0	84.4	5.8	34.0	16.4
U.S. (rate[2])	289.3	23.5	72.5	6.2	28.7	17.4

Note: Data as of 2021 unless noted; (1) Data covers Marion County; (2) Rate per 100,000 population; (3) Data as of 2020 and includes all active, non-federal physicians; (4) Doctor of Osteopathic Medicine
Source: U.S. Department of Health and Human Services, Health Resources and Services Administration, Bureau of Health Professions, Area Resource File (ARF) 2021-2022

EDUCATION

Public School District Statistics

District Name	Schls	Pupils	Pupil/ Teacher Ratio	Minority Pupils[1] (%)	LEP/ELL[2] (%)	IEP[3] (%)
SALEM-KEIZER SD 24J	65	39,507	19.1	58.2	17.2	17.7

Note: Table includes school districts with 2,000 or more students; (1) Percentage of students that are not non-Hispanic white; (2) Percentage of students that are Limited English Proficient or English Language Learners (2018-19); (3) Percentage of students that have an Individualized Education Program (2019-20).
Source: U.S. Department of Education, National Center for Education Statistics, Common Core of Data, Local Education Agency (School District) Universe Survey: School Year 2021-2022

Highest Level of Education

Area	Less than H.S.	H.S. Diploma	Some College, No Deg.	Associate Degree	Bachelor's Degree	Master's Degree	Prof. School Degree	Doctorate Degree
City	11.6	23.2	25.8	9.4	18.4	8.4	1.8	1.4
MSA[1]	13.2	25.1	26.3	9.7	16.7	6.8	1.3	1.0
U.S.	11.1	26.5	20.0	8.7	20.6	9.3	2.2	1.5

Note: Figures cover persons age 25 and over; (1) Figures cover the Salem, OR Metropolitan Statistical Area
Source: U.S. Census Bureau, 2017-2021 American Community Survey 5-Year Estimates

Educational Attainment by Race

Area	High School Graduate or Higher (%)					Bachelor's Degree or Higher (%)				
	Total	White	Black	Asian	Hisp.[2]	Total	White	Black	Asian	Hisp.[2]
City	88.4	92.3	95.0	84.5	61.8	30.0	32.6	27.1	44.4	11.1
MSA[1]	86.8	90.9	92.8	81.5	60.7	25.7	28.0	25.2	37.3	10.0
U.S.	88.9	91.4	87.2	87.6	71.2	33.7	35.5	23.3	55.6	18.4

Note: Figures shown cover persons 25 years old and over; (1) Figures cover the Salem, OR Metropolitan Statistical Area; (2) People of Hispanic origin can be of any race
Source: U.S. Census Bureau, 2017-2021 American Community Survey 5-Year Estimates

School Enrollment by Grade and Control

Area	Preschool (%)		Kindergarten (%)		Grades 1 - 4 (%)		Grades 5 - 8 (%)		Grades 9 - 12 (%)	
	Public	Private	Public	Private	Public	Private	Public	Private	Public	Private
City	61.3	38.7	87.8	12.2	90.0	10.0	93.3	6.7	96.5	3.5
MSA[1]	59.7	40.3	86.9	13.1	89.6	10.4	91.7	8.3	93.9	6.1
U.S.	58.8	41.2	86.3	13.7	88.3	11.7	88.6	11.4	89.4	10.6

Note: Figures shown cover persons 3 years old and over; (1) Figures cover the Salem, OR Metropolitan Statistical Area
Source: U.S. Census Bureau, 2017-2021 American Community Survey 5-Year Estimates

Higher Education

Four-Year Colleges			Two-Year Colleges			Medical Schools[1]	Law Schools[2]	Voc/ Tech[3]
Public	Private Non-profit	Private For-profit	Public	Private Non-profit	Private For-profit			
1	3	0	1	0	2	0	1	2

Note: Figures cover institutions located within the Salem, OR Metropolitan Statistical Area and include main campuses only; (1) includes schools accredited by the Liaison Committee on Medical Education and the American Osteopathic Association's Commission on Osteopathic College Accreditation; (2) includes ABA-accredited schools, schools with provisional ABA accreditation, and state accredited schools; (3) includes all schools with programs that are less than 2 years.
Source: National Center for Education Statistics, Integrated Postsecondary Education System (IPEDS), 2021-22; Wikipedia, List of Medical Schools in the United States, accessed April 10, 2023; Wikipedia, List of Law Schools in the United States, accessed April 10, 2023

According to *U.S. News & World Report,* the Salem, OR metro area is home to one of the top 100 liberal arts colleges in the U.S.: **Willamette University** (#76 tie). The indicators used to capture academic quality fall into a number of categories: assessment by administrators at peer institutions; retention of students; faculty resources; student selectivity; financial resources; alumni giving; high school counselor ratings of colleges; and graduation rate. *U.S. News & World Report, "America's Best Colleges 2023"*

EMPLOYERS

Major Employers

Company Name	Industry
Chemeketa Community College	Colleges & universities
City of Salem	Municipal government
Kaiser Permanente	Integrated managed care consortium
Liberty Tax Service	Accounting, auditing, & bookkeeping
Marion County	County government
NORPAC Foods	Farm cooperative
Safeway	Grocery stores
Salem Health Laboratories	Laboratory services
Salem Hospital	Health care
Salem-Keizer School District	School districts
Spirit Mountain Casino	Casinos
State Accident Insurance Fund	Insurance
State of Oregon	State government
T-Mobile USA	Telecomunications

Note: Companies shown are located within the Salem, OR Metropolitan Statistical Area.
Source: Hoovers.com; Wikipedia

PUBLIC SAFETY

Crime Rate

Area	Total Crime	Violent Crime Rate				Property Crime Rate		
		Murder	Rape[3]	Robbery	Aggrav. Assault	Burglary	Larceny -Theft	Motor Vehicle Theft
City	4,187.2	1.1	15.9	83.8	294.4	383.8	2,780.4	627.9
Suburbs[1]	2,400.4	1.9	29.2	29.6	123.4	258.0	1,578.0	380.3
Metro[2]	3,123.1	1.6	23.8	51.5	192.6	308.9	2,064.3	480.4
U.S.	2,356.7	6.5	38.4	73.9	279.7	314.2	1,398.0	246.0

Note: Figures are crimes per 100,000 population; (1) All areas within the metro area that are located outside the city limits; (2) Figures cover the Salem, OR Metropolitan Statistical Area; (3) All figures shown were reported using the revised Uniform Crime Reporting (UCR) definition of rape; Due to the transition to the National Incident-Based Reporting System (NIBRS), limited city and metro area data was released for 2021.
Source: FBI Uniform Crime Reports, 2020

Hate Crimes

Area	Number of Quarters Reported	Number of Incidents per Bias Motivation					
		Race/Ethnicity/ Ancestry	Religion	Sexual Orientation	Disability	Gender	Gender Identity
City	4	21	2	5	0	0	2
U.S.	4	5,227	1,244	1,110	130	75	266

Note: Due to the transition to the National Incident-Based Reporting System (NIBRS), limited crime data was released for 2021.
Source: Federal Bureau of Investigation, Hate Crime Statistics 2020

Identity Theft Consumer Reports

Area	Reports	Reports per 100,000 Population	Rank[2]
MSA[1]	550	128	301
U.S.	1,108,609	339	-

Note: (1) Figures cover the Salem, OR Metropolitan Statistical Area; (2) Rank ranges from 1 to 391 where 1 indicates greatest number of identity theft reports per 100,000 population
Source: Federal Trade Commission, Consumer Sentinel Network Data Book 2022

Fraud and Other Consumer Reports

Area	Reports	Reports per 100,000 Population	Rank[2]
MSA[1]	3,213	750	260
U.S.	4,064,520	1,245	-

Note: (1) Figures cover the Salem, OR Metropolitan Statistical Area; (2) Rank ranges from 1 to 391 where 1 indicates greatest number of fraud and other consumer reports per 100,000 population
Source: Federal Trade Commission, Consumer Sentinel Network Data Book 2022

POLITICS

2020 Presidential Election Results

Area	Biden	Trump	Jorgensen	Hawkins	Other
Marion County	48.9	47.7	2.0	0.5	0.9
U.S.	51.3	46.8	1.2	0.3	0.5

Note: Results are percentages and may not add to 100% due to rounding
Source: Dave Leip's Atlas of U.S. Presidential Elections

SPORTS

Professional Sports Teams

Team Name	League	Year Established

No teams are located in the metro area
Source: Wikipedia, Major Professional Sports Teams of the United States and Canada, April 12, 2023

CLIMATE

Average and Extreme Temperatures

Temperature	Jan	Feb	Mar	Apr	May	Jun	Jul	Aug	Sep	Oct	Nov	Dec	Yr.
Extreme High (°F)	65	72	75	88	100	102	106	108	104	93	72	66	108
Average High (°F)	46	51	55	61	67	74	82	81	76	64	53	47	63
Average Temp. (°F)	39	43	46	50	55	61	66	67	62	53	45	41	52
Average Low (°F)	32	34	36	38	43	48	51	51	47	41	37	34	41
Extreme Low (°F)	-10	-4	12	23	25	32	37	36	26	23	9	-12	-12

Note: Figures cover the years 1948-1990
Source: National Climatic Data Center, International Station Meteorological Climate Summary, 9/96

Average Precipitation/Snowfall/Humidity

Precip./Humidity	Jan	Feb	Mar	Apr	May	Jun	Jul	Aug	Sep	Oct	Nov	Dec	Yr.
Avg. Precip. (in.)	6.5	4.9	4.3	2.4	2.0	1.4	0.5	0.7	1.5	3.3	6.1	6.8	40.2
Avg. Snowfall (in.)	3	1	1	Tr	Tr	0	0	0	0	Tr	Tr	2	7
Avg. Rel. Hum. 7am (%)	87	89	89	85	81	77	75	79	86	92	90	89	85
Avg. Rel. Hum. 4pm (%)	76	70	62	56	53	50	40	40	45	61	76	81	59

Note: Figures cover the years 1948-1990; Tr = Trace amounts (<0.05 in. of rain; <0.5 in. of snow)
Source: National Climatic Data Center, International Station Meteorological Climate Summary, 9/96

Weather Conditions

Temperature			Daytime Sky			Precipitation		
5°F & below	32°F & below	90°F & above	Clear	Partly cloudy	Cloudy	0.01 inch or more precip.	0.1 inch or more snow/ice	Thunder-storms
< 1	66	16	78	118	169	146	6	5

Note: Figures are average number of days per year and cover the years 1948-1990
Source: National Climatic Data Center, International Station Meteorological Climate Summary, 9/96

HAZARDOUS WASTE

Superfund Sites

The Salem, OR metro area has no sites on the EPA's Superfund Final National Priorities List. There are a total of 1,165 Superfund sites with a status of proposed or final on the list in the U.S. *U.S. Environmental Protection Agency, National Priorities List, April 12, 2023*

AIR QUALITY

Air Quality Trends: Ozone

	1990	1995	2000	2005	2010	2015	2018	2019	2020	2021
MSA[1]	n/a	n/a	n/a	n/a	n/a	n/a	n/a	n/a	n/a	n/a
U.S.	0.087	0.089	0.081	0.080	0.072	0.067	0.069	0.065	0.065	0.067

Note: (1) Data covers the Salem, OR Metropolitan Statistical Area; n/a not available. The values shown are the composite ozone concentration averages among trend sites based on the highest fourth daily maximum 8-hour concentration in parts per million. These trends are based on sites having an adequate record of monitoring data during the trend period. Data from exceptional events are included.
Source: U.S. Environmental Protection Agency, Air Quality Monitoring Information, "Air Quality Trends by City, 1990-2021"

Air Quality Index

Area	Percent of Days when Air Quality was...[2]					AQI Statistics[2]	
	Good	Moderate	Unhealthy for Sensitive Groups	Unhealthy	Very Unhealthy	Maximum	Median
MSA[1]	87.1	12.9	0.0	0.0	0.0	93	33

Note: (1) Data covers the Salem, OR Metropolitan Statistical Area; (2) Based on 363 days with AQI data in 2021. Air Quality Index (AQI) is an index for reporting daily air quality. EPA calculates the AQI for five major air pollutants regulated by the Clean Air Act: ground-level ozone, particle pollution (aka particulate matter), carbon monoxide, sulfur dioxide, and nitrogen dioxide. The AQI runs from 0 to 500. The higher the AQI value, the greater the level of air pollution and the greater the health concern. There are six AQI categories: "Good" AQI is between 0 and 50. Air quality is considered satisfactory; "Moderate" AQI is between 51 and 100. Air quality is acceptable; "Unhealthy for Sensitive Groups" When AQI values are between 101 and 150, members of sensitive groups may experience health effects; "Unhealthy" When AQI values are between 151 and 200 everyone may begin to experience health effects; "Very Unhealthy" AQI values between 201 and 300 trigger a health alert; "Hazardous" AQI values over 300 trigger warnings of emergency conditions (not shown).
Source: U.S. Environmental Protection Agency, Air Quality Index Report, 2021

Air Quality Index Pollutants

Area	Percent of Days when AQI Pollutant was...[2]					
	Carbon Monoxide	Nitrogen Dioxide	Ozone	Sulfur Dioxide	Particulate Matter 2.5	Particulate Matter 10
MSA[1]	0.0	0.0	39.7	(3)	60.3	0.0

Note: (1) Data covers the Salem, OR Metropolitan Statistical Area; (2) Based on 363 days with AQI data in 2021. The Air Quality Index (AQI) is an index for reporting daily air quality. EPA calculates the AQI for five major air pollutants regulated by the Clean Air Act: ground-level ozone, particle pollution (also known as particulate matter), carbon monoxide, sulfur dioxide, and nitrogen dioxide. The AQI runs from 0 to 500. The higher the AQI value, the greater the level of air pollution and the greater the health concern; (3) Sulfur dioxide is no longer included in this table (as of December 8, 2021) because SO_2 concentrations tend to be very localized and not necessarily representative of broad geographical areas like counties and CBSAs.
Source: U.S. Environmental Protection Agency, Air Quality Index Report, 2021

Maximum Air Pollutant Concentrations: Particulate Matter, Ozone, CO and Lead

	Particulate Matter 10 (ug/m³)	Particulate Matter 2.5 Wtd AM (ug/m³)	Particulate Matter 2.5 24-Hr (ug/m³)	Ozone (ppm)	Carbon Monoxide (ppm)	Lead (ug/m³)
MSA[1] Level	n/a	n/a	n/a	0.063	n/a	n/a
NAAQS[2]	150	15	35	0.075	9	0.15
Met NAAQS[2]	n/a	n/a	n/a	Yes	n/a	n/a

Note: (1) Data covers the Salem, OR Metropolitan Statistical Area; Data from exceptional events are included; (2) National Ambient Air Quality Standards; ppm = parts per million; ug/m³ = micrograms per cubic meter; n/a not available.
Concentrations: Particulate Matter 10 (coarse particulate)—highest second maximum 24-hour concentration; Particulate Matter 2.5 Wtd AM (fine particulate)—highest weighted annual mean concentration; Particulate Matter 2.5 24-Hour (fine particulate)—highest 98th percentile 24-hour concentration; Ozone—highest fourth daily maximum 8-hour concentration; Carbon Monoxide—highest second maximum non-overlapping 8-hour concentration; Lead—maximum running 3-month average
Source: U.S. Environmental Protection Agency, Air Quality Monitoring Information, "Air Quality Statistics by City, 2021"

Maximum Air Pollutant Concentrations: Nitrogen Dioxide and Sulfur Dioxide

	Nitrogen Dioxide AM (ppb)	Nitrogen Dioxide 1-Hr (ppb)	Sulfur Dioxide AM (ppb)	Sulfur Dioxide 1-Hr (ppb)	Sulfur Dioxide 24-Hr (ppb)
MSA[1] Level	n/a	n/a	n/a	n/a	n/a
NAAQS[2]	53	100	30	75	140
Met NAAQS[2]	n/a	n/a	n/a	n/a	n/a

Note: (1) Data covers the Salem, OR Metropolitan Statistical Area; Data from exceptional events are included; (2) National Ambient Air Quality Standards; ppm = parts per million; ug/m³ = micrograms per cubic meter; n/a not available.
Concentrations: Nitrogen Dioxide AM—highest arithmetic mean concentration; Nitrogen Dioxide 1-Hr—highest 98th percentile 1-hour daily maximum concentration; Sulfur Dioxide AM—highest annual mean concentration; Sulfur Dioxide 1-Hr—highest 99th percentile 1-hour daily maximum concentration; Sulfur Dioxide 24-Hr—highest second maximum 24-hour concentration
Source: U.S. Environmental Protection Agency, Air Quality Monitoring Information, "Air Quality Statistics by City, 2021"

Salt Lake City, Utah

Background

Salt Lake City, Utah's largest city and state capital, is known for its Mormon, or Church of Jesus Christ of Latter-day Saints, origins. The city was founded by Brigham Young on July 24, 1847, as a place of refuge from mainstream ostracism for the Mormon's polygamous lifestyle.

Brigham Young led his people to a "land that nobody wanted," so they could exercise their form of worship in peace. Two scouts, Orson Pratt and Erastus Snow located the site for Brigham Young, who declared: "This is the place." The site that was to be called Salt Lake City was breathtaking, bordered on the east and southwest by the dramatic peaks of the Wasatch Range, and on the northwest by the Great Salt Lake.

The land was too dry and hard for traditional farming, but Mormon industry diverted the flow of mountain streams to irrigate the land, and the valley turned into a prosperous agricultural region. More than 10 years after its incorporation as a city, the U.S. government was still suspicious of its Mormon residents. Fort Douglas, founded in 1862, was manned by federal troops to keep an eye on the Mormons and their polygamous practices. In 1869, the completion of the Transcontinental Railroad brought mining, industry, and other non-Mormon interests to Salt Lake City. As for polygamy, the Mormon Church made it illegal in 1890.

While mining played a major role in the early development of Salt Lake City, major industry sectors today include construction, trade, transportation, communications, finance, insurance, and real estate. The University of Utah Research Park, also known at Bionic Valley, is on the campus of the university and houses 48 companies, 18 university departments, and employs more than 14,000. Updates to Research Park are progressing, including additional student housing, research innovation hub and additional locations for businesses.

Major efforts to revitalize the downtown area have included the $1 billion, 20-acre City Creek Center with residences, offices, and a mall; Salt Lake City Redevelopment Agency renovated retail space that is part of the Utah Theater, a former 1918 vaudeville theater on Main Street; Utah Performing Arts Center costing $116 million and holding 2,500.

The Utah Pride Festival is held in June each year. Since 1983, it has grown dramatically to a three-day festival with attendance over 20,000 and is one of the largest festivals in the country comprising hundreds of vendors, food, musical performers, a 5k run, a dyke and trans march, as well as an interfaith service by the Utah Pride Interfaith Coalition.

Redevelopment at Salt Lake City International Airport is ongoing. Recently completed Phase 1 incudes a new concourse and terminal. Phase 2, which will be complete in 2025, includes more shops, restaurants, and gates, and a Central Tunnel with an art installation called The River Tunnel.

Salt Lake City was designated as a Silver-level Bicycle Friendly Community in 2010 by the League of American Bicyclists. Many streets in the city have bike lanes, and the city has published a bicycle map.

The NBA's Utah Jazz plays at the EnergySolutions Arena. The city is also home to Real Salt Lake of Major League Soccer.

The nearby mountain ranges and the Great Salt Lake greatly influence climatic conditions. Temperatures are moderated by the lake in winter, and storm activity is enhanced by both the lake and the mountains. Salt Lake City has a semi-arid continental climate with four well-defined seasons. Summers are hot and dry, while winters are cold, but not severe due to the mountains to the north and east that barricade the cold air. Periods of heavy fog can develop in winter and persist for several days.

Rankings

General Rankings

- *US News & World Report* conducted a survey of more than 3,600 people and analyzed the 150 largest metropolitan areas to determine what matters most when selecting where to settle down. Salt Lake City ranked #23 out of the top 25 as having the best combination of desirable factors. Criteria: cost of living; quality of life and education; net migration; job market; desirability; and other factors. *money.usnews.com, "The 25 Best Places to Live in the U.S. in 2022-2023," May 17, 2022*

- The Salt Lake City metro area was identified as one of America's fastest-growing areas in terms of population and business growth by *MagnifyMoney*. The area ranked #18 out of 35. The 100 most populous metro areas in the U.S. were evaluated on their change from 2011 to 2016 in the following categories: people and housing; workforce and employment opportunities; growing industry. *www.businessinsider.com, "The 35 Cities in the US with the Biggest Influx of People, the Most Work Opportunities, and the Hottest Business Growth," August 12, 2018*

- The Salt Lake City metro area was identified as one of America's fastest-growing areas in terms of population and economy by *Forbes*. The area ranked #24 out of 25. The 100 most populous metro areas in the U.S. were evaluated on the following criteria: estimated population growth; employment; economic output; wages; home values. *Forbes, "America's Fastest-Growing Cities 2018," February 28, 2018*

- Salt Lake City was selected as one of the best places to live in the United States by *Money* magazine. The city ranked #41 out of 50. This year's list focused on cities that would be welcoming to a broader group of people and with populations of at least 20,000. Beginning with a pool of 1,370 candidates, editors looked at 350 data points, organized into the these nine categories: income and personal finance, cost of living, economic opportunity, housing market, fun and amenities, health and safety, education, diversity, and quality of life. *Money, "The 50 Best Places to Live in the U.S. in 2022-2023" September 29, 2022*

- In their ninth annual survey, Livability.com looked at data for more than 2,300 mid-sized U.S. cities to determine the rankings for Livability's "Top 100 Best Places to Live" in 2022. Salt Lake City ranked #8. Criteria: housing and economy; social and civic engagement; education; demographics; health care options; transportation & infrastructure; and community amenities. *Livability.com, "Top 100 Best Places to Live 2022" July 19, 2022*

Business/Finance Rankings

- According to *Business Insider*, the Salt Lake City metro area is a prime place to run a startup or move an existing business to. The area ranked #19. More than 300 metro areas were analyzed for factors that were of top concern to new business owners. Data was based on the 2019 U.S. Census Bureau American Community Survey, statistics from the CDC, Bureau of Labor Statistics employment report, and University of Chicago analysis. Criteria: business formations; percentage of vaccinated population; percentage of households with internet subscriptions; median household income; and share of work that can be done from home. *www.businessinsider.com, "The 20 Best Cities for Starting a Business in 2022 Include Baltimore, Boulder, and Boston," January 5, 2022*

- The Brookings Institution ranked the nation's largest cities based on income inequality. Salt Lake City was ranked #57 (#1 = greatest inequality). Criteria: the "95/20 ratio," a figure representing the income at which a household earns more than 95 percent of all other households, divided by the income at which a household earns more than only 20 percent of all other households. *Brookings Institution, "Household Income Inequality, Largest Cities of 97 Large U.S. Metro Areas, 2014-2016," February 5, 2018*

- The Brookings Institution ranked the 100 largest metro areas in the U.S. based on income inequality. Salt Lake City was ranked #98 (#1 = greatest inequality). Criteria: the "95/20 ratio," a figure representing the income at which a household earns more than 95 percent of all other households, divided by the income at which a household earns more than only 20 percent of all other households. *Brookings Institution, "Household Income Inequality, 100 Largest U.S. Metro Areas, 2014-2016," February 5, 2018*

- The Salt Lake City metro area appeared on the Milken Institute "2022 Best Performing Cities" list. Rank: #3 out of 200 large metro areas (population over 250,000). Criteria: job growth; wage and salary growth; high-tech output growth; housing affordability; household broadband access. *Milken Institute, "Best-Performing Cities 2022," March 28, 2022*

- *Forbes* ranked the 200 most populous metro areas to determine the nation's "Best Places for Business and Careers." The Salt Lake City metro area was ranked #21. Criteria: costs (business and living); job growth (past and projected); income growth; quality of life; educational attainment (college and high school); projected economic growth; cultural and leisure opportunities; workplace tolerance laws; net migration patterns. *Forbes, "The Best Places for Business and Careers 2019: Seattle Still On Top," October 30, 2019*

Culture/Performing Arts Rankings

- Salt Lake City was selected as one of the 25 best cities for moviemakers in North America. Great film cities are places where filmmaking dreams can come true, that offer more creative space, lower costs, and great outdoor locations. NYC & LA were intentionally excluded. Criteria: longstanding reputations as film-friendly communities; film community and culture; affordability; and quality of life. The city was ranked #15. *MovieMaker Magazine, "Best Places to Live and Work as a Moviemaker, 2023," January 18, 2023*

Dating/Romance Rankings

- Salt Lake City was ranked #22 out of 25 cities that stood out for inspiring romance and attracting diners on the website OpenTable.com. Criteria: percentage of people who dined out on Valentine's Day in 2018; percentage of romantic restaurants as rated by OpenTable diner reviews; and percentage of tables seated for two. *OpenTable, "25 Most Romantic Cities in America for 2019," February 7, 2019*

- Salt Lake City was selected as one of the nation's most romantic cities with 100,000 or more residents by Amazon.com. The city ranked #5 of 20. Criteria: per capita sales of romance novels, relationship books, romantic comedy movies, romantic music, and sexual wellness products. *Amazon.com, "Top 20 Most Romantic Cities in the U.S.," February 1, 2017*

Education Rankings

- Personal finance website *WalletHub* analyzed the 150 largest U.S. metropolitan statistical areas to determine where the most educated Americans are putting their degrees to work. Criteria: education levels; percentage of workers with degrees; education quality and attainment gap; public school quality rankings; quality and enrollment of each metro area's universities. Salt Lake City was ranked #35 (#1 = most educated city). *www.WalletHub.com, "Most & Least Educated Cities in America," July 18, 2022*

Environmental Rankings

- Sperling's BestPlaces assessed the 50 largest metropolitan areas of the United States for the likelihood of dangerously extreme weather events or earthquakes. In general the Southeast and South-Central regions have the highest risk of weather extremes and earthquakes, while the Pacific Northwest enjoys the lowest risk. Of the least risky metropolitan areas, the Salt Lake City metro area was ranked #2. *www.bestplaces.net, "Avoid Natural Disasters: BestPlaces Reveals The Top 10 Safest Places to Live," October 25, 2017*

- The U.S. Environmental Protection Agency (EPA) released its list of mid-size U.S. metropolitan areas with the most ENERGY STAR certified buildings in 2022. The Salt Lake City metro area was ranked #5 out of 10. *U.S. Environmental Protection Agency, "2023 Energy Star Top Cities," April 26, 2023*

- Salt Lake City was highlighted as one of the 25 most ozone-polluted metro areas in the U.S. during 2019 through 2021. The area ranked #10. *American Lung Association, "State of the Air 2023," April 19, 2023*

- Salt Lake City was highlighted as one of the 25 metro areas most polluted by short-term particle pollution (24-hour PM 2.5) in the U.S. during 2019 through 2021. The area ranked #19. *American Lung Association, "State of the Air 2023," April 19, 2023*

Health/Fitness Rankings

- Trulia analyzed the 100 largest U.S. metro areas to identify the nation's best cities for weight loss, based on the percentage of adults who bike or walk to work, sporting goods stores, grocery stores, access to outdoor activities, weight-loss centers, gyms, and average space reserved for parks. Salt Lake City ranked #1. *Trulia.com, "Where to Live to Get in Shape in the New Year," January 4, 2018*

- Salt Lake City was identified as a "2022 Spring Allergy Capital." The area ranked #93 out of 100. Three groups of factors were used to identify the most challenging cities for people with allergies during the spring season: annual spring pollen scores; over the counter allergy medicine use; number of board-certified allergy specialists. *Asthma and Allergy Foundation of America, "Spring Allergy Capitals 2022," March 2, 2022*

- Salt Lake City was identified as a "2022 Fall Allergy Capital." The area ranked #89 out of 100. Three groups of factors were used to identify the most challenging cities for people with allergies during the fall season: annual fall pollen scores; over the counter allergy medicine use; number of board-certified allergy specialists. *Asthma and Allergy Foundation of America, "Fall Allergy Capitals 2022," March 2, 2022*

- Salt Lake City was identified as a "2022 Asthma Capital." The area ranked #94 out of the nation's 100 largest metropolitan areas. Criteria: estimated asthma prevalence; asthma-related mortality; and ER visits due to asthma. Risk factors analyzed but not factored in the rankings: annual pollen score; annual air quality; public smoking laws; access to board-certified asthma specialists; rescue and controller medication use; uninsured rate; poverty rate. *Asthma and Allergy Foundation of America, "Asthma Capitals 2022: The Most Challenging Places to Live With Asthma," September 14, 2022*

Real Estate Rankings

- *WalletHub* compared the most populated U.S. cities to determine which had the best markets for real estate agents. Salt Lake City ranked #4 where demand was high and pay was the best. Criteria: sales per agent; annual median wage for real-estate agents; monthly average starting salary for real estate agents; real estate job density and competition; unemployment rate; home turnover rate; housing-market health index; and other relevant metrics. *www.WalletHub.com, "2021 Best Places to Be a Real Estate Agent," May 12, 2021*

- Salt Lake City was ranked #187 out of 235 metro areas in terms of housing affordability in 2022 by the National Association of Home Builders (#1 = most affordable). Criteria: the share of homes sold in that area affordable to a family earning the local median income, based on standard mortgage underwriting criteria. *National Association of Home Builders®, NAHB-Wells Fargo Housing Opportunity Index, 4th Quarter 2022*

Safety Rankings

- Statistics drawn from the FBI's Uniform Crime Report were used to rank the cities where violent crime rose the most year over year from 2019 to 2020. Only cities with 25,000 or more residents were included. *24/7 Wall St.* found that Salt Lake City placed #26 of those with a notable surge in incidents of violent crime. *247wallst.com, "American Cities Where Crime Is Soaring," March 4, 2022*

- Allstate ranked the 200 largest cities in America in terms of driver safety. Salt Lake City ranked #67. Criteria: internal property damage claims over a two-year period from January 2016 to December 2017. The report helps increase the importance of safety and awareness behind the wheel. *Allstate, "Allstate America's Best Drivers Report, 2019" June 24, 2019*

- Salt Lake City was identified as one of the most dangerous cities in America by NeighborhoodScout. The city ranked #78 out of 100 (#1 = most dangerous). Criteria: number of violent crimes per 1,000 residents. The editors evaluated cities with 25,000 or more residents. *NeighborhoodScout.com, "2023 Top 100 Most Dangerous Cities in the U.S.," January 12, 2023*

- The National Insurance Crime Bureau ranked 390 metro areas in the U.S. in terms of per capita rates of vehicle theft. The Salt Lake City metro area ranked #28 (#1 = highest rate). Criteria: number of vehicle theft offenses per 100,000 inhabitants in 2021. *National Insurance Crime Bureau, "Hot Spots 2021," September 1, 2022*

Seniors/Retirement Rankings

- From its Best Cities for Successful Aging indexes, the Milken Institute generated rankings for metropolitan areas, weighing data in nine categories—health care, wellness, living arrangements, transportation and convenience, financial characteristics, education, employment, community engagement, and overall livability. The Salt Lake City metro area was ranked #4 overall in the large metro area category. *Milken Institute, "Best Cities for Successful Aging, 2017" March 14, 2017*

Sports/Recreation Rankings

- Salt Lake City was chosen as one of America's best cities for bicycling. The city ranked #16 out of 50. Criteria: cycling infrastructure that is safe and friendly for all ages; energy and bike culture. The editors evaluated cities with populations of 100,000 or more. *Bicycling, "The 50 Best Bike Cities in America," October 10, 2018*

Women/Minorities Rankings

- Personal finance website *WalletHub* compared more than 180 U.S. cities across two key dimensions, "Hispanic Business-Friendliness" and "Hispanic Purchasing Power," to arrive at the most favorable conditions for Hispanic entrepreneurs. Salt Lake City was ranked #55 out of 182. Criteria includes: share of Hispanic-Owned Businesses; Hispanic entrepreneurship rate to median annual income of Hispanics; Small Business-Friendliness score; cost of living; and number of Hispanics with at least a bachelor's degree. *WalletHub.com, "2019's Best Cities for Hispanic Entrepreneurs," May 1, 2019*

Miscellaneous Rankings

- *MoveHub* ranked 446 hipster cities across 20 countries, using its new and improved *alternative* Hipster Index and Salt Lake City came out as #3 among the top 50. Criteria: population over 150,000; number of vintage boutiques; density of tattoo parlors; vegan places to eat; coffee shops; and density of vinyl record stores. *www.movehub.com, "The Hipster Index: Brighton Pips Portland to Global Top Spot," July 28, 2021*

- *WalletHub* compared the 150 most populated U.S. cities to determine their operating efficiency. A "Quality of Services" score was constructed for each city and then divided by the total budget per capita to reveal which were managed the best. Salt Lake City ranked #89. Criteria: financial stability; economy; education; safety; health; infrastructure and pollution. *www.WalletHub.com, "2022's Best-& Worst-Run Cities in America," June 21, 2022*

Business Environment

DEMOGRAPHICS

Population Growth

Area	1990 Census	2000 Census	2010 Census	2020 Census	Population Growth (%) 1990-2020	Population Growth (%) 2010-2020
City	159,796	181,743	186,440	199,723	25.0	7.1
MSA[1]	768,075	968,858	1,124,197	1,257,936	63.8	11.9
U.S.	248,709,873	281,421,906	308,745,538	331,449,281	33.3	7.4

Note: (1) Figures cover the Salt Lake City, UT Metropolitan Statistical Area
Source: U.S. Census Bureau, 1990 Census, 2000 Census, 2010 Census, 2020 Census

Race

Area	White Alone[2] (%)	Black Alone[2] (%)	Asian Alone[2] (%)	AIAN[3] Alone[2] (%)	NHOPI[4] Alone[2] (%)	Other Race Alone[2] (%)	Two or More Races (%)
City	68.4	2.9	5.5	1.4	2.1	9.7	9.9
MSA[1]	72.3	1.9	4.1	1.1	1.8	9.1	9.8
U.S.	61.6	12.4	6.0	1.1	0.2	8.4	10.2

Note: (1) Figures cover the Salt Lake City, UT Metropolitan Statistical Area; (2) Alone is defined as not being in combination with one or more other races; (3) American Indian and Alaska Native; (4) Native Hawaiian and Other Pacific Islander
Source: U.S. Census Bureau, 2020 Census

Hispanic or Latino Origin

Area	Total (%)	Mexican (%)	Puerto Rican (%)	Cuban (%)	Other (%)
City	19.9	14.2	0.4	0.3	5.0
MSA[1]	18.5	13.1	0.5	0.2	4.7
U.S.	18.4	11.2	1.8	0.7	4.7

Note: Persons of Hispanic or Latino origin can be of any race; (1) Figures cover the Salt Lake City, UT Metropolitan Statistical Area
Source: U.S. Census Bureau, 2017-2021 American Community Survey 5-Year Estimates

Age

Area	Under Age 5	Age 5–19	Age 20–34	Age 35–44	Age 45–54	Age 55–64	Age 65–74	Age 75–84	Age 85+	Median Age
City	5.1	16.7	33.3	14.1	10.3	9.2	7.0	2.9	1.3	32.1
MSA[1]	6.7	22.8	23.7	14.7	11.1	9.7	7.0	3.1	1.1	32.8
U.S.	5.6	19.2	20.2	12.7	12.4	13.1	10.0	4.9	1.9	38.8

Note: (1) Figures cover the Salt Lake City, UT Metropolitan Statistical Area
Source: U.S. Census Bureau, 2020 Census

Disability by Age

Area	All Ages	Under 18 Years Old	18 to 64 Years Old	65 Years and Over
City	11.0	4.0	9.4	32.6
MSA[1]	9.5	3.9	8.4	30.0
U.S.	12.6	4.4	10.3	33.4

Note: Figures show percent of the civilian noninstitutionalized population that reported having a disability. Disability status is determined from six types of difficulty: vision, hearing, cognitive, ambulatory, self-care, and independent living. For children under 5 years old, hearing and vision difficulty are used to determine disability status. For children between the ages of 5 and 14, disability status is determined from hearing, vision, cognitive, ambulatory, and self-care difficulties. For people aged 15 years and older, they are considered to have a disability if they have difficulty with any one of the six difficulty types; Note: (1) Figures cover the Salt Lake City, UT Metropolitan Statistical Area
Source: U.S. Census Bureau, 2017-2021 American Community Survey 5-Year Estimates

Ancestry

Area	German	Irish	English	American	Italian	Polish	French[2]	Scottish	Dutch
City	10.9	6.9	17.7	3.2	4.1	1.4	2.1	3.5	1.8
MSA[1]	9.7	5.7	21.7	4.0	2.9	0.9	1.9	3.6	1.7
U.S.	12.8	9.6	8.1	5.7	5.0	2.7	2.2	1.6	1.1

Note: Figures are the percentage of the total population reporting a particular ancestry. The nine most commonly reported ancestries in the U.S. are shown. Figures include multiple ancestries (e.g. if a person reported being Irish and Italian, they were included in both columns); (1) Figures cover the Salt Lake City, UT Metropolitan Statistical Area; (2) Excludes Basque
Source: U.S. Census Bureau, 2017-2021 American Community Survey 5-Year Estimates

Foreign-born Population

Area	Any Foreign Country	Asia	Mexico	Europe	Caribbean	Central America[2]	South America	Africa	Canada
City	15.3	4.1	4.9	1.9	0.2	0.7	1.3	1.0	0.4
MSA[1]	12.4	3.1	4.3	1.3	0.1	0.6	1.5	0.6	0.3
U.S.	13.6	4.2	3.3	1.5	1.4	1.1	1.1	0.8	0.2

Note: (1) Figures cover the Salt Lake City, UT Metropolitan Statistical Area; (2) Excludes Mexico.
Source: U.S. Census Bureau, 2017-2021 American Community Survey 5-Year Estimates

Household Size

Area	One	Two	Three	Four	Five	Six	Seven or More	Average Household Size
City	38.3	32.7	11.9	9.4	4.1	1.9	1.7	2.30
MSA[1]	23.2	30.9	15.7	13.9	8.5	4.7	3.1	2.90
U.S.	28.1	33.8	15.5	12.9	6.0	2.3	1.4	2.60

Note: (1) Figures cover the Salt Lake City, UT Metropolitan Statistical Area
Source: U.S. Census Bureau, 2017-2021 American Community Survey 5-Year Estimates

Household Relationships

Area	House-holder	Opposite-sex Spouse	Same-sex Spouse	Opposite-sex Unmarried Partner	Same-sex Unmarried Partner	Child[2]	Grand-child	Other Relatives	Non-relatives
City	42.3	13.9	0.5	3.4	0.4	22.1	1.7	4.2	7.6
MSA[1]	34.0	17.4	0.3	2.1	0.2	32.4	2.5	5.3	4.4
U.S.	38.3	17.5	0.2	2.5	0.2	28.3	2.4	4.8	3.4

Note: Figures are percent of the total population; (1) Figures cover the Salt Lake City, UT Metropolitan Statistical Area; (2) Includes biological, adopted, and stepchildren of the householder
Source: U.S. Census Bureau, 2020 Census

Gender

Area	Males	Females	Males per 100 Females
City	102,530	97,193	105.5
MSA[1]	632,295	625,641	101.1
U.S.	162,685,811	168,763,470	96.4

Note: (1) Figures cover the Salt Lake City, UT Metropolitan Statistical Area
Source: U.S. Census Bureau, 2020 Census

Marital Status

Area	Never Married	Now Married[2]	Separated	Widowed	Divorced
City	44.4	40.3	1.3	3.1	10.8
MSA[1]	32.7	52.3	1.4	3.6	10.1
U.S.	33.8	48.0	1.8	5.6	10.8

Note: Figures are percentages and cover the population 15 years of age and older; (1) Figures cover the Salt Lake City, UT Metropolitan Statistical Area; (2) Excludes separated
Source: U.S. Census Bureau, 2017-2021 American Community Survey 5-Year Estimates

Religious Groups by Family

Area	Catholic	Baptist	Methodist	LDS[2]	Pentecostal	Lutheran	Islam	Adventist	Other
MSA[1]	9.0	0.6	0.2	52.0	0.7	0.2	1.6	0.7	2.6
U.S.	18.7	7.3	3.0	2.0	1.8	1.7	1.3	1.3	11.6

Note: Figures are the number of adherents as a percentage of the total population and cover the eight largest religious groups in the U.S; (1) Figures cover the Salt Lake City, UT Metropolitan Statistical Area; (2) Church of Jesus Christ of Latter-day Saints
Sources: 2020 U.S. Religion Census, Association of Statisticians of American Religious Bodies; The Association of Religion Data Archives (ARDA)

Religious Groups by Tradition

Area	Catholic	Evangelical Protestant	Mainline Protestant	Black Protestant	Islam	Judaism	Hinduism	Orthodox	Buddhism
MSA[1]	9.0	2.4	0.7	0.1	1.6	0.1	0.3	0.4	0.3
U.S.	18.7	16.5	5.2	2.3	1.3	0.6	0.4	0.4	0.3

Note: Figures are the number of adherents as a percentage of the total population; (1) Figures cover the Salt Lake City, UT Metropolitan Statistical Area
Sources: 2020 U.S. Religion Census, Association of Statisticians of American Religious Bodies; The Association of Religion Data Archives (ARDA)

ECONOMY

Gross Metropolitan Product

Area	2020	2021	2022	2023	Rank[2]
MSA[1]	103.9	114.9	124.5	132.3	37

Note: Figures are in billions of dollars; (1) Figures cover the Salt Lake City, UT Metropolitan Statistical Area; (2) Rank is based on 2021 data and ranges from 1 to 381
Source: U.S. Conference of Mayors, U.S. Metro Economies: U.S. Metros Compared to Global and State Economies, June 2022

Economic Growth

Area	2018-20 (%)	2021 (%)	2022 (%)	2023 (%)	Rank[2]
MSA[1]	1.9	6.1	2.7	3.1	38
U.S.	-0.6	5.7	3.1	2.9	–

Note: Figures are real gross metropolitan product (GMP) growth rates and represent average annual percent change; (1) Figures cover the Salt Lake City, UT Metropolitan Statistical Area; (2) Rank is based on 2020 2-year average annual percent change and ranges from 1 to 381
Source: U.S. Conference of Mayors, U.S. Metro Economies: U.S. Metros Compared to Global and State Economies, June 2022

Metropolitan Area Exports

Area	2016	2017	2018	2019	2020	2021	Rank[2]
MSA[1]	8,653.7	7,916.9	9,748.6	13,273.9	13,565.5	13,469.1	28

Note: Figures are in millions of dollars; (1) Figures cover the Salt Lake City, UT Metropolitan Statistical Area; (2) Rank is based on 2021 data and ranges from 1 to 388
Source: U.S. Department of Commerce, International Trade Administration, Office of Trade and Economic Analysis, Industry and Analysis, Exports by Metropolitan Area, data extracted March 16, 2023

Building Permits

Area	Single-Family			Multi-Family			Total		
	2021	2022	Pct. Chg.	2021	2022	Pct. Chg.	2021	2022	Pct. Chg.
City	172	144	-16.3	3,519	3,489	-0.9	3,691	3,633	-1.6
MSA[1]	5,338	3,992	-25.2	6,304	6,110	-3.1	11,642	10,102	-13.2
U.S.	1,115,400	975,600	-12.5	621,600	689,500	10.9	1,737,000	1,665,100	-4.1

Note: (1) Figures cover the Salt Lake City, UT Metropolitan Statistical Area; Figures represent new, privately-owned housing units authorized (unadjusted data); All permit data are based on estimates with imputation
Source: U.S. Census Bureau, Manufacturing, Mining, and Construction Statistics, Building Permits, 2021, 2022

Bankruptcy Filings

Area	Business Filings			Nonbusiness Filings		
	2021	2022	% Chg.	2021	2022	% Chg.
Salt Lake County	27	23	-14.8	2,389	2,147	-10.1
U.S.	14,347	13,481	-6.0	399,269	374,240	-6.3

Note: Business filings include Chapter 7, Chapter 9, Chapter 11, Chapter 12, Chapter 13, Chapter 15, and Section 304; Nonbusiness filings include Chapter 7, Chapter 11, and Chapter 13
Source: Administrative Office of the U.S. Courts, Business and Nonbusiness Bankruptcy, County Cases Commenced by Chapter of the Bankruptcy Code, During the 12-Month Period Ending December 31, 2021 and Business and Nonbusiness Bankruptcy, County Cases Commenced by Chapter of the Bankruptcy Code, During the 12-Month Period Ending December 31, 2022

Housing Vacancy Rates

Area	Gross Vacancy Rate[2] (%)			Year-Round Vacancy Rate[3] (%)			Rental Vacancy Rate[4] (%)			Homeowner Vacancy Rate[5] (%)		
	2020	2021	2022	2020	2021	2022	2020	2021	2022	2020	2021	2022
MSA[1]	5.7	4.1	5.1	5.6	3.9	4.5	6.2	4.1	4.6	0.3	0.8	0.6
U.S.	10.6	10.8	10.5	8.2	8.4	8.2	6.3	6.1	5.8	1.0	0.9	0.8

Note: (1) Figures cover the Salt Lake City, UT Metropolitan Statistical Area; (2) The percentage of the total housing inventory that is vacant; (3) The percentage of the housing inventory (excluding seasonal units) that is year-round vacant; (4) The percentage of rental inventory that is vacant for rent; (5) The percentage of homeowner inventory that is vacant for sale
Source: U.S. Census Bureau, Housing Vacancies and Homeownership Annual Statistics: 2020, 2021, 2022

INCOME

Income

Area	Per Capita ($)	Median Household ($)	Average Household ($)
City	42,081	65,880	97,628
MSA[1]	36,688	82,506	105,669
U.S.	37,638	69,021	97,196

Note: (1) Figures cover the Salt Lake City, UT Metropolitan Statistical Area
Source: U.S. Census Bureau, 2017-2021 American Community Survey 5-Year Estimates

Household Income Distribution

Area	Percent of Households Earning							
	Under $15,000	$15,000 -$24,999	$25,000 -$34,999	$35,000 -$49,999	$50,000 -$74,999	$75,000 -$99,999	$100,000 -$149,999	$150,000 and up
City	11.2	6.9	8.6	10.9	18.1	13.1	15.0	16.2
MSA[1]	6.0	4.8	6.3	10.2	17.9	14.8	20.6	19.3
U.S.	9.4	7.8	8.2	11.4	16.8	12.8	16.3	17.3

Note: (1) Figures cover the Salt Lake City, UT Metropolitan Statistical Area
Source: U.S. Census Bureau, 2017-2021 American Community Survey 5-Year Estimates

Poverty Rate

Area	All Ages	Under 18 Years Old	18 to 64 Years Old	65 Years and Over
City	14.7	15.4	15.2	10.3
MSA[1]	8.2	9.2	8.0	6.5
U.S.	12.6	17.0	11.8	9.6

Note: Figures are percentage of people whose income during the past 12 months was below the poverty level;
(1) Figures cover the Salt Lake City, UT Metropolitan Statistical Area
Source: U.S. Census Bureau, 2017-2021 American Community Survey 5-Year Estimates

EMPLOYMENT

Labor Force and Employment

Area	Civilian Labor Force			Workers Employed		
	Dec. 2021	Dec. 2022	% Chg.	Dec. 2021	Dec. 2022	% Chg.
City	121,702	125,773	3.3	119,545	123,299	3.1
MSA[1]	699,196	722,471	3.3	686,309	707,898	3.1
U.S.	161,696,000	164,224,000	1.6	155,732,000	158,872,000	2.0

Note: Data is not seasonally adjusted and covers workers 16 years of age and older; (1) Figures cover the Salt Lake City, UT Metropolitan Statistical Area
Source: Bureau of Labor Statistics, Local Area Unemployment Statistics

Unemployment Rate

Area	2022											
	Jan.	Feb.	Mar.	Apr.	May	Jun.	Jul.	Aug.	Sep.	Oct.	Nov.	Dec.
City	2.4	2.1	2.0	2.1	2.1	2.3	2.1	2.1	1.9	2.1	2.0	2.0
MSA[1]	2.4	2.2	2.1	2.1	2.2	2.4	2.1	2.1	1.9	2.1	2.0	2.0
U.S.	4.4	4.1	3.8	3.3	3.4	3.8	3.8	3.8	3.3	3.4	3.4	3.3

Note: Data is not seasonally adjusted and covers workers 16 years of age and older; (1) Figures cover the Salt Lake City, UT Metropolitan Statistical Area
Source: Bureau of Labor Statistics, Local Area Unemployment Statistics

Average Wages

Occupation	$/Hr.	Occupation	$/Hr.
Accountants and Auditors	38.26	Maintenance and Repair Workers	23.79
Automotive Mechanics	24.06	Marketing Managers	65.16
Bookkeepers	23.32	Network and Computer Systems Admin.	45.48
Carpenters	24.89	Nurses, Licensed Practical	29.02
Cashiers	13.79	Nurses, Registered	38.16
Computer Programmers	48.36	Nursing Assistants	16.66
Computer Systems Analysts	47.68	Office Clerks, General	19.23
Computer User Support Specialists	30.53	Physical Therapists	45.74
Construction Laborers	20.17	Physicians	120.76
Cooks, Restaurant	16.82	Plumbers, Pipefitters and Steamfitters	30.62
Customer Service Representatives	20.02	Police and Sheriff's Patrol Officers	32.06
Dentists	64.38	Postal Service Mail Carriers	28.08
Electricians	28.08	Real Estate Sales Agents	26.96
Engineers, Electrical	58.74	Retail Salespersons	18.75
Fast Food and Counter Workers	13.19	Sales Representatives, Technical/Scientific	57.43
Financial Managers	69.34	Secretaries, Exc. Legal/Medical/Executive	20.26
First-Line Supervisors of Office Workers	30.21	Security Guards	17.09
General and Operations Managers	53.16	Surgeons	219.11
Hairdressers/Cosmetologists	19.62	Teacher Assistants, Exc. Postsecondary*	14.52
Home Health and Personal Care Aides	16.45	Teachers, Secondary School, Exc. Sp. Ed.*	33.46
Janitors and Cleaners	14.30	Telemarketers	15.85
Landscaping/Groundskeeping Workers	18.82	Truck Drivers, Heavy/Tractor-Trailer	26.89
Lawyers	65.12	Truck Drivers, Light/Delivery Services	21.89
Maids and Housekeeping Cleaners	16.12	Waiters and Waitresses	17.80

Note: Wage data covers the Salt Lake City, UT Metropolitan Statistical Area; (*) Hourly wages were calculated from annual wage data based on a 40 hour work week; n/a not available.
Source: Bureau of Labor Statistics, Metro Area Occupational Employment & Wage Estimates, May 2022

Employment by Industry

Sector	MSA[1]		U.S.
	Number of Employees	Percent of Total	Percent of Total
Construction, Mining, and Logging	57,500	7.0	5.4
Private Education and Health Services	94,100	11.5	16.1
Financial Activities	62,200	7.6	5.9
Government	111,300	13.6	14.5
Information	26,100	3.2	2.0
Leisure and Hospitality	67,800	8.3	10.3
Manufacturing	63,800	7.8	8.4
Other Services	23,300	2.8	3.7
Professional and Business Services	145,900	17.8	14.7
Retail Trade	80,800	9.9	10.2
Transportation, Warehousing, and Utilities	47,800	5.8	4.9
Wholesale Trade	37,100	4.5	3.9

Note: Figures are non-farm employment as of December 2022. Figures are not seasonally adjusted and include workers 16 years of age and older; (1) Figures cover the Salt Lake City, UT Metropolitan Statistical Area
Source: Bureau of Labor Statistics, Current Employment Statistics, Employment, Hours, and Earnings

Employment by Occupation

Occupation Classification	City (%)	MSA[1] (%)	U.S. (%)
Management, Business, Science, and Arts	49.4	41.6	40.3
Natural Resources, Construction, and Maintenance	6.3	8.7	8.7
Production, Transportation, and Material Moving	11.1	13.0	13.1
Sales and Office	18.7	23.1	20.9
Service	14.5	13.7	17.0

Note: Figures cover employed civilians 16 years of age and older; (1) Figures cover the Salt Lake City, UT Metropolitan Statistical Area
Source: U.S. Census Bureau, 2017-2021 American Community Survey 5-Year Estimates

Occupations with Greatest Projected Employment Growth: 2022 – 2024

Occupation[1]	2022 Employment	2024 Projected Employment	Numeric Employment Change	Percent Employment Change
General and Operations Managers	60,740	63,930	3,190	5.3
Software Developers and Software Quality Assurance Analysts and Testers	24,170	26,830	2,660	11.0
Fast Food and Counter Workers	50,960	52,790	1,830	3.6
Project Management Specialists and Business Operations Specialists, All Other	27,030	28,520	1,490	5.5
Construction Laborers	27,740	29,230	1,490	5.4
Electricians	11,880	13,160	1,280	10.8
Janitors and Cleaners, Except Maids and Housekeeping Cleaners	25,040	26,230	1,190	4.8
Laborers and Freight, Stock, and Material Movers, Hand	25,040	26,190	1,150	4.6
Cooks, Restaurant	12,460	13,590	1,130	9.1
Registered Nurses	25,490	26,600	1,110	4.4

Note: Projections cover Utah; (1) Sorted by numeric employment change
Source: www.projectionscentral.com, State Occupational Projections, 2022–2024 Short-Term Projections

Fastest-Growing Occupations: 2022 – 2024

Occupation[1]	2022 Employment	2024 Projected Employment	Numeric Employment Change	Percent Employment Change
Solar Photovoltaic Installers	430	510	80	18.6
Physical Therapist Aides	1,220	1,440	220	18.0
Chiropractors	570	660	90	15.8
Information Security Analysts (SOC 2018)	1,610	1,840	230	14.3
Architects, Except Landscape and Naval	1,600	1,820	220	13.8
Nurse Practitioners	3,010	3,420	410	13.6
Aerospace Engineers	1,110	1,260	150	13.5
Physical Therapist Assistants	740	840	100	13.5
Preschool Teachers, Except Special Education	4,360	4,910	550	12.6
Data Scientists and Mathematical Science Occupations, All Other	3,610	4,050	440	12.2

Note: Projections cover Utah; (1) Sorted by percent employment change and excludes occupations with numeric employment change less than 50
Source: www.projectionscentral.com, State Occupational Projections, 2022–2024 Short-Term Projections

CITY FINANCES

City Government Finances

Component	2020 ($000)	2020 ($ per capita)
Total Revenues	899,629	4,485
Total Expenditures	1,628,745	8,121
Debt Outstanding	2,259,554	11,266
Cash and Securities[1]	859,849	4,287

Note: (1) Cash and security holdings of a government at the close of its fiscal year, including those of its dependent agencies, utilities, and liquor stores.
Source: U.S. Census Bureau, State & Local Government Finances 2020

City Government Revenue by Source

Source	2020 ($000)	2020 ($ per capita)	2020 (%)
General Revenue			
From Federal Government	19,227	96	2.1
From State Government	10,740	54	1.2
From Local Governments	12,967	65	1.4
Taxes			
Property	171,761	856	19.1
Sales and Gross Receipts	124,427	620	13.8
Personal Income	0	0	0.0
Corporate Income	0	0	0.0
Motor Vehicle License	0	0	0.0
Other Taxes	16,610	83	1.8
Current Charges	396,956	1,979	44.1
Liquor Store	0	0	0.0
Utility	78,073	389	8.7

Source: U.S. Census Bureau, State & Local Government Finances 2020

City Government Expenditures by Function

Function	2020 ($000)	2020 ($ per capita)	2020 (%)
General Direct Expenditures			
Air Transportation	882,061	4,397	54.2
Corrections	0	0	0.0
Education	3,257	16	0.2
Employment Security Administration	0	0	0.0
Financial Administration	7,833	39	0.5
Fire Protection	45,062	224	2.8
General Public Buildings	847	4	0.1
Governmental Administration, Other	11,436	57	0.7
Health	52,556	262	3.2
Highways	30,947	154	1.9
Hospitals	0	0	0.0
Housing and Community Development	10,739	53	0.7
Interest on General Debt	110,756	552	6.8
Judicial and Legal	13,153	65	0.8
Libraries	14,975	74	0.9
Parking	2	< 1	< 0.1
Parks and Recreation	19,203	95	1.2
Police Protection	87,486	436	5.4
Public Welfare	101	< 1	< 0.1
Sewerage	64,916	323	4.0
Solid Waste Management	16,634	82	1.0
Veterans' Services	0	0	0.0
Liquor Store	0	0	0.0
Utility	108,068	538	6.6

Source: U.S. Census Bureau, State & Local Government Finances 2020

TAXES

State Corporate Income Tax Rates

State	Tax Rate (%)	Income Brackets ($)	Num. of Brackets	Financial Institution Tax Rate (%)[a]	Federal Income Tax Ded.
Utah	4.65 (b)	Flat rate	–	4.65 (b)	No

Note: Tax rates as of January 1, 2023; (a) Rates listed are the corporate income tax rate applied to financial institutions or excise taxes based on income. Some states have other taxes based upon the value of deposits or shares; (b) Minimum tax is $800 in California, $250 in District of Columbia, $50 in Arizona and North Dakota (banks), $400 ($100 banks) in Rhode Island, $200 per location in South Dakota (banks), $100 in Utah, $300 in Vermont.
Source: Federation of Tax Administrators, State Corporate Income Tax Rates, January 1, 2023

State Individual Income Tax Rates

State	Tax Rate (%)	Income Brackets ($)	Personal Exemptions ($)			Standard Ded. ($)	
			Single	Married	Depend.	Single	Married
Utah	4.85	Flat rate	None	None	None	(w)	(w)

Note: Tax rates as of January 1, 2023; Local- and county-level taxes are not included; Federal income tax is not deductible on state income tax returns; (w) Utah provides a tax credit equal to 6% of the federal personal exemption amounts (and applicable standard deduction).
Source: Federation of Tax Administrators, State Individual Income Tax Rates, January 1, 2023

Various State Sales and Excise Tax Rates

State	State Sales Tax (%)	Gasoline[1] ($/gal.)	Cigarette[2] ($/pack)	Spirits[3] ($/gal.)	Wine[4] ($/gal.)	Beer[5] ($/gal.)	Recreational Marijuana (%)
Utah	6.1	0.3641	1.70	15.92	—	0.41	Not legal

Note: All tax rates as of January 1, 2023; (1) The American Petroleum Institute has developed a methodology for determining the average tax rate on a gallon of fuel. Rates may include any of the following: excise taxes, environmental fees, storage tank fees, other fees or taxes, general sales tax, and local taxes; (2) The federal excise tax of $1.0066 per pack and local taxes are not included; (3) Rates are those applicable to off-premise sales of 40% alcohol by volume (a.b.v.) distilled spirits in 750ml containers. Local excise taxes are excluded; (4) Rates are those applicable to off-premise sales of 11% a.b.v. non-carbonated wine in 750ml containers; (5) Rates are those applicable to off-premise sales of 4.7% a.b.v. beer in 12 ounce containers.
Source: Tax Foundation, 2023 Facts & Figures: How Does Your State Compare?

State Business Tax Climate Index Rankings

State	Overall Rank	Corporate Tax Rank	Individual Income Tax Rank	Sales Tax Rank	Property Tax Rank	Unemployment Insurance Tax Rank
Utah	8	14	10	22	8	16

Note: The index is a measure of how each state's tax laws affect economic performance. The lower the rank, the more favorable a state's tax system is for business. States without a given tax are given a ranking of 1. The scores/rankings for the District of Columbia do not affect other states. The 2023 index represents the tax climate as of July 1, 2022.
Source: Tax Foundation, State Business Tax Climate Index 2023

TRANSPORTATION

Means of Transportation to Work

Area	Car/Truck/Van		Public Transportation			Bicycle	Walked	Other Means	Worked at Home
	Drove Alone	Car-pooled	Bus	Subway	Railroad				
City	63.1	8.8	3.8	0.3	0.6	2.1	4.8	3.2	13.2
MSA[1]	71.0	10.3	1.5	0.2	0.4	0.6	1.9	1.7	12.5
U.S.	73.2	8.6	2.0	1.6	0.5	0.5	2.5	1.5	9.7

Note: Figures are percentages and cover workers 16 years of age and older; (1) Figures cover the Salt Lake City, UT Metropolitan Statistical Area
Source: U.S. Census Bureau, 2017-2021 American Community Survey 5-Year Estimates

Travel Time to Work

Area	Less Than 10 Minutes	10 to 19 Minutes	20 to 29 Minutes	30 to 44 Minutes	45 to 59 Minutes	60 to 89 Minutes	90 Minutes or More
City	14.1	45.1	21.4	12.6	3.5	2.2	1.2
MSA[1]	10.8	33.5	26.9	19.2	5.5	3.0	1.2
U.S.	12.4	28.5	21.0	20.9	8.2	6.2	2.9

Note: Note: Figures are percentages and include workers 16 years old and over; (1) Figures cover the Salt Lake City, UT Metropolitan Statistical Area
Source: U.S. Census Bureau, 2017-2021 American Community Survey 5-Year Estimates

Key Congestion Measures

Measure	1990	2000	2010	2015	2020
Annual Hours of Delay, Total (000)	6,374	14,974	22,524	27,472	17,124
Annual Hours of Delay, Per Auto Commuter	15	28	36	43	26
Annual Congestion Cost, Per Auto Commuter ($)	352	623	746	840	544

Note: Covers the Salt Lake City-West Valley City UT urban area
Source: Texas A&M Transportation Institute, 2021 Urban Mobility Report

Freeway Travel Time Index

Measure	1985	1990	1995	2000	2005	2010	2015	2020
Urban Area Index[1]	1.06	1.07	1.10	1.14	1.17	1.17	1.18	1.06
Urban Area Rank[1,2]	53	74	72	62	49	41	41	75

Note: Freeway Travel Time Index—the ratio of travel time in the peak period to the travel time at free-flow conditions. For example, a value of 1.30 indicates a 20-minute free-flow trip takes 26 minutes in the peak (20 minutes x 1.30 = 26 minutes); (1) Covers the Salt Lake City-West Valley City UT urban area; (2) Rank is based on 101 larger urban areas (#1 = highest travel time index)
Source: Texas A&M Transportation Institute, 2021 Urban Mobility Report

Public Transportation

Agency Name / Mode of Transportation	Vehicles Operated in Maximum Service[1]	Annual Unlinked Passenger Trips[2] (in thous.)	Annual Passenger Miles[3] (in thous.)
Utah Transit Authority (UTA)			
Bus (directly operated)	338	12,114.6	49,332.4
Bus (purchased transportation)	7	73.0	280.2
Commuter Bus (directly operated)	58	429.3	6,440.5
Commuter Rail (directly operated)	45	2,062.3	54,462.1
Demand Response (directly operated)	52	156.3	1,493.8
Demand Response (purchased transportation)	63	145.2	1,333.1
Light Rail (directly operated)	81	8,403.9	37,900.6
Vanpool (directly operated)	372	587.7	25,403.5

Note: (1) Number of revenue vehicles operated by the given mode and type of service to meet the annual maximum service requirement. This is the revenue vehicle count during the peak season of the year; on the week and day that maximum service is provided. Vehicles operated in maximum service (VOMS) exclude atypical days and one-time special events; (2) Number of passengers who boarded public transportation vehicles. Passengers are counted each time they board a vehicle no matter how many vehicles they use to travel from their origin to their destination. (3) Sum of the distances ridden by all passengers during the entire fiscal year.
Source: Federal Transit Administration, National Transit Database, 2021

Air Transportation

Airport Name and Code / Type of Service	Passenger Airlines[1]	Passenger Enplanements	Freight Carriers[2]	Freight (lbs)
Salt Lake City International (SLC)				
Domestic service (U.S. carriers - 2022)	27	11,832,407	16	194,442,064
International service (U.S. carriers - 2021)	5	279,638	3	1,061,618

Note: (1) Includes all U.S.-based major, minor and commuter airlines that carried at least one passenger during the year; (2) Includes all U.S.-based airlines and freight carriers that transported at least one pound of freight during the year.
Source: Bureau of Transportation Statistics, The Intermodal Transportation Database, Air Carriers: T-100 Domestic Market (U.S. Carriers), 2022; Bureau of Transportation Statistics, The Intermodal Transportation Database, Air Carriers: T-100 International Market (U.S. Carriers), 2021

BUSINESSES

Major Business Headquarters

Company Name	Industry	Rankings	
		Fortune[1]	Forbes[2]
Huntsman	Chemicals	410	-

Note: (1) Companies that produce a 10-K are ranked 1 to 500 based on 2021 revenue; (2) All private companies with at least $2 billion in annual revenue through the end of their most current fiscal year are ranked 1 to 246; companies listed are headquartered in the city; dashes indicate no ranking
Source: Fortune, "Fortune 500," 2022; Forbes, "America's Largest Private Companies," 2022

Fastest-Growing Businesses

According to *Inc.*, Salt Lake City is home to three of America's 500 fastest-growing private companies: **IMAGE Studios** (#238); **Izzard Ink Publishing** (#467); **Ivy City Co.** (#492). Criteria: must be an independent, privately-held, for-profit, U.S. corporation, proprietorship or partnership as of December 31, 2021; revenues must be at least $100,000 in 2018 and $2 million in 2021; must have four-year operating/sales history. *Inc., "America's 500 Fastest-Growing Private Companies," 2022*

According to *Initiative for a Competitive Inner City (ICIC)*, Salt Lake City is home to one of America's 100 fastest-growing "inner city" companies: **Brand Aid** (#45). Criteria for inclusion: company must be headquartered in or have 51 percent or more of its physical operations in an economically distressed urban area; must be an independent, for-profit corporation, partnership or proprietorship; must have 10 or more employees and have a five-year sales history that includes sales of at least $200,000 in the base year and at least $1 million in the current year with no decrease in sales over the two most recent years. Companies were ranked overall by revenue growth over the five-year period between 2017 and 2021. *Initiative for a Competitive Inner City (ICIC), "Inner City 100 Companies," 2022*

According to Deloitte, Salt Lake City is home to one of North America's 500 fastest-growing high-technology companies: **Filevine** (#167). Companies are ranked by percentage growth in revenue over a four-year period. Criteria for inclusion: company must be headquartered within North America; must own proprietary intellectual property or technology that is sold to customers in products that contributes to a significant portion of the company's operating revenue; must have been in business for a minumum of four years with 2018 operating revenues of at least $50,000 USD/CD and 2021 operating revenues of at least $5 million USD/CD. *Deloitte, 2022 Technology Fast 500*™

Living Environment

COST OF LIVING

Cost of Living Index

Composite Index	Groceries	Housing	Utilities	Trans- portation	Health Care	Misc. Goods/ Services
108.3	104.0	122.4	92.9	109.9	95.5	104.2

Note: The Cost of Living Index measures regional differences in the cost of consumer goods and services, excluding taxes and non-consumer expenditures, for professional and managerial households in the top income quintile. It is based on more than 50,000 prices covering almost 60 different items for which prices are collected three times a year by chambers of commerce, economic development organizations or university applied economic centers in each participating urban area. The numbers shown should be read as a percentage above or below the national average of 100. For example, a value of 115.4 in the groceries column indicates that grocery prices are 15.4% higher than the national average. Small differences in the index numbers should not be interpreted as significant; Figures cover the Salt Lake City UT urban area.
Source: The Council for Community and Economic Research, Cost of Living Index, 2022

Grocery Prices

Area[1]	T-Bone Steak ($/pound)	Frying Chicken ($/pound)	Whole Milk ($/half gal.)	Eggs ($/dozen)	Orange Juice ($/64 oz.)	Coffee ($/11.5 oz.)
City[2]	13.19	1.85	2.28	2.25	4.46	5.46
Avg.	13.81	1.59	2.43	2.25	3.85	4.95
Min.	10.17	0.90	1.51	1.30	2.90	3.46
Max.	19.35	3.30	4.32	4.32	5.31	8.59

*Note: (1) Values for the local area are compared with the average, minimum and maximum values for all 286 areas in the Cost of Living Index; (2) Figures cover the Salt Lake City UT urban area; **T-Bone Steak** (price per pound); **Frying Chicken** (price per pound, whole fryer); **Whole Milk** (half gallon carton); **Eggs** (price per dozen, Grade A, large); **Orange Juice** (64 oz. Tropicana or Florida Natural); **Coffee** (11.5 oz. can, vacuum-packed, Maxwell House, Hills Bros, or Folgers).*
Source: The Council for Community and Economic Research, Cost of Living Index, 2022

Housing and Utility Costs

Area[1]	New Home Price ($)	Apartment Rent ($/month)	All Electric ($/month)	Part Electric ($/month)	Other Energy ($/month)	Telephone ($/month)
City[2]	575,689	1,609	-	77.74	74.42	194.94
Avg.	450,913	1,371	176.41	99.93	76.96	190.22
Min.	229,283	546	100.84	31.56	27.15	174.27
Max.	2,434,977	4,569	356.86	249.59	272.24	208.31

*Note: (1) Values for the local area are compared with the average, minimum and maximum values for all 286 areas in the Cost of Living Index; (2) Figures cover the Salt Lake City UT urban area; **New Home Price** (2,400 sf living area, 8,000 sf lot, in urban area with full utilities); **Apartment Rent** (950 sf 2 bedroom/1.5 or 2 bath, unfurnished, excluding all utilities except water); **All Electric** (average monthly cost for an all-electric home); **Part Electric** (average monthly cost for a part-electric home); **Other Energy** (average monthly cost for natural gas, fuel oil, coal, wood, and any other forms of energy except electricity); **Telephone** (price includes the base monthly rate plus taxes and fees for three lines of mobile phone service).*
Source: The Council for Community and Economic Research, Cost of Living Index, 2022

Health Care, Transportation, and Other Costs

Area[1]	Doctor ($/visit)	Dentist ($/visit)	Optometrist ($/visit)	Gasoline ($/gallon)	Beauty Salon ($/visit)	Men's Shirt ($)
City[2]	114.47	93.33	109.59	4.14	39.28	46.00
Avg.	124.91	107.77	117.66	3.86	43.31	34.21
Min.	36.61	58.25	51.79	2.90	22.18	13.05
Max.	250.21	162.58	371.96	5.54	85.61	63.54

*Note: (1) Values for the local area are compared with the average, minimum and maximum values for all 286 areas in the Cost of Living Index; (2) Figures cover the Salt Lake City UT urban area; **Doctor** (general practitioners routine exam of an established patient); **Dentist** (adult teeth cleaning and periodic oral examination); **Optometrist** (full vision eye exam for established adult patient); **Gasoline** (one gallon regular unleaded, national brand, including all taxes, cash price at self-service pump if available); **Beauty Salon** (woman's shampoo, trim, and blow-dry); **Men's Shirt** (cotton/polyester dress shirt, pinpoint weave, long sleeves).*
Source: The Council for Community and Economic Research, Cost of Living Index, 2022

HOUSING

Homeownership Rate

Area	2015 (%)	2016 (%)	2017 (%)	2018 (%)	2019 (%)	2020 (%)	2021 (%)	2022 (%)
MSA[1]	69.1	69.2	68.1	69.5	69.2	68.0	64.1	66.6
U.S.	63.7	63.4	63.9	64.4	64.6	66.6	65.5	65.8

Note: (1) Figures cover the Salt Lake City, UT Metropolitan Statistical Area
Source: U.S. Census Bureau, Housing Vacancies and Homeownership Annual Statistics: 2015-2022

House Price Index (HPI)

Area	National Ranking[2]	Quarterly Change (%)	One-Year Change (%)	Five-Year Change (%)	Since 1991Q1 (%)
MSA[1]	197	-2.92	8.70	74.37	596.70
U.S.[3]	—	0.34	8.41	58.44	289.08

Note: The HPI is a weighted repeat sales index. It measures average price changes in repeat sales or refinancings on the same properties. This information is obtained by reviewing repeat mortgage transactions on single-family properties whose mortgages have been purchased or securitized by Fannie Mae or Freddie Mac since January 1975; (1) Figures cover the Salt Lake City, UT Metropolitan Statistical Area; (2) Rankings are based on annual percentage change for all metro areas containing at least 15,000 transactions over the last 10 years and ranges from 1 to 257; (3) figures based on a weighted average of Census Division estimates using a seasonally adjusted, purchase-only index; all figures are for the period ending December 31, 2022
Source: Federal Housing Finance Agency, Change in FHFA Metropolitan Area House Price Indexes, 2022Q4

Median Single-Family Home Prices

Area	2020	2021	2022[p]	Percent Change 2021 to 2022
MSA[1]	391.0	486.1	569.1	17.1
U.S. Average	300.2	357.1	392.6	9.9

Note: Figures are median sales prices of existing single-family homes in thousands of dollars; (p) preliminary; (1) Figures cover the Salt Lake City, UT Metropolitan Statistical Area
Source: National Association of Realtors, Median Sales Price of Existing Single-Family Homes for Metropolitan Areas, 4th Quarter 2022

Qualifying Income Based on Median Sales Price of Existing Single-Family Homes

Area	With 5% Down ($)	With 10% Down ($)	With 20% Down ($)
MSA[1]	157,012	148,748	132,220
U.S. Average	112,234	106,237	94,513

Note: Figures are preliminary; Qualifying income is based on a mortgage rate of 6.77%. Monthly principal and interest payment is limited to 25% of income; (1) Figures cover the Salt Lake City, UT Metropolitan Statistical Area
Source: National Association of Realtors, Qualifying Income Based on Median Sales Price of Existing Single-Family Homes for Metropolitan Areas, 4th Quarter 2022

Home Value

Area	Under $100,000	$100,000 -$199,999	$200,000 -$299,999	$300,000 -$399,999	$400,000 -$499,999	$500,000 -$999,999	$1,000,000 or more	Median ($)
City	3.8	10.8	19.8	19.3	14.6	26.2	5.3	380,200
MSA[1]	3.8	8.2	22.9	24.5	16.6	21.1	2.9	361,600
U.S.	16.2	24.2	20.1	13.6	8.3	13.6	4.1	244,900

Note: Figures are percentages except for median and cover owner-occupied housing units; (1) Figures cover the Salt Lake City, UT Metropolitan Statistical Area
Source: U.S. Census Bureau, 2017-2021 American Community Survey 5-Year Estimates

Year Housing Structure Built

Area	2020 or Later	2010 -2019	2000 -2009	1990 -1999	1980 -1989	1970 -1979	1960 -1969	1950 -1959	1940 -1949	Before 1940	Median Year
City	0.2	8.1	6.8	6.4	7.6	11.3	9.8	12.8	9.2	27.8	1960
MSA[1]	0.2	12.6	14.8	15.1	11.9	17.4	8.6	8.3	3.5	7.5	1984
U.S.	0.2	7.3	13.6	13.6	13.2	14.8	10.3	10.0	4.7	12.2	1979

Note: Figures are percentages except for Median Year; Note: (1) Figures cover the Salt Lake City, UT Metropolitan Statistical Area
Source: U.S. Census Bureau, 2017-2021 American Community Survey 5-Year Estimates

Gross Monthly Rent

Area	Under $500	$500 -$999	$1,000 -$1,499	$1,500 -$1,999	$2,000 -$2,499	$2,500 -$2,999	$3,000 and up	Median ($)
City	8.0	30.3	36.6	17.7	5.4	1.2	0.8	1,141
MSA[1]	4.6	21.7	43.4	22.2	6.0	1.1	0.9	1,253
U.S.	8.1	30.5	30.8	16.8	7.3	3.1	3.5	1,163

Note: Figures are percentages except for median; Gross rent is the contract rent plus the estimated average monthly cost of utilities (electricity, gas, and water and sewer) and fuels (oil, coal, kerosene, wood, etc.) if these are paid by the renter (or paid for the renter by someone else); (1) Figures cover the Salt Lake City, UT Metropolitan Statistical Area
Source: U.S. Census Bureau, 2017-2021 American Community Survey 5-Year Estimates

HEALTH

Health Risk Factors

Category	MSA[1] (%)	U.S. (%)
Adults aged 18–64 who have any kind of health care coverage	89.1	90.9
Adults who reported being in good or better health	87.5	85.2
Adults who have been told they have high blood cholesterol	31.1	35.7
Adults who have been told they have high blood pressure	27.4	32.4
Adults who are current smokers	8.0	14.4
Adults who currently use e-cigarettes	8.2	6.7
Adults who currently use chewing tobacco, snuff, or snus	2.0	3.5
Adults who are heavy drinkers[2]	5.5	6.3
Adults who are binge drinkers[3]	15.6	15.4
Adults who are overweight (BMI 25.0 - 29.9)	33.2	34.4
Adults who are obese (BMI 30.0 - 99.8)	30.8	33.9
Adults who participated in any physical activities in the past month	81.2	76.3

Note: (1) Figures cover the Salt Lake City, UT Metropolitan Statistical Area; (2) Heavy drinkers are classified as adult men having more than 14 drinks per week and adult women having more than 7 drinks per week; (3) Binge drinkers are classified as males having five or more drinks on one occasion or females having four or more drinks on one occasion
Source: Centers for Disease Control and Prevention, Behaviorial Risk Factor Surveillance System, SMART: Selected Metropolitan Area Risk Trends, 2021

Acute and Chronic Health Conditions

Category	MSA[1] (%)	U.S. (%)
Adults who have ever been told they had a heart attack	2.8	4.0
Adults who have ever been told they have angina or coronary heart disease	2.3	3.8
Adults who have ever been told they had a stroke	2.1	3.0
Adults who have ever been told they have asthma	14.4	14.9
Adults who have ever been told they have arthritis	20.0	25.8
Adults who have ever been told they have diabetes[2]	8.6	10.9
Adults who have ever been told they had skin cancer	7.4	6.6
Adults who have ever been told they had any other types of cancer	6.6	7.5
Adults who have ever been told they have COPD	4.6	6.1
Adults who have ever been told they have kidney disease	2.5	3.0
Adults who have ever been told they have a form of depression	25.4	20.5

Note: (1) Figures cover the Salt Lake City, UT Metropolitan Statistical Area; (2) Figures do not include pregnancy-related, borderline, or pre-diabetes
Source: Centers for Disease Control and Prevention, Behaviorial Risk Factor Surveillance System, SMART: Selected Metropolitan Area Risk Trends, 2021

Health Screening and Vaccination Rates

Category	MSA[1] (%)	U.S. (%)
Adults who have ever been tested for HIV	32.1	34.9
Adults who have had their blood cholesterol checked within the last five years	82.2	85.2
Adults aged 65+ who have had flu shot within the past year	73.9	68.6
Adults aged 65+ who have ever had a pneumonia vaccination	75.7	71.0

Note: (1) Figures cover the Salt Lake City, UT Metropolitan Statistical Area.
Source: Centers for Disease Control and Prevention, Behaviorial Risk Factor Surveillance System, SMART: Selected Metropolitan Area Risk Trends, 2021

Disability Status

Category	MSA[1] (%)	U.S. (%)
Adults who reported being deaf	5.1	7.2
Are you blind or have serious difficulty seeing, even when wearing glasses?	3.3	4.8
Are you limited in any way in any of your usual activities due to arthritis?	8.2	11.1
Do you have difficulty doing errands alone?	7.1	7.0
Do you have difficulty dressing or bathing?	2.6	3.6
Do you have serious difficulty concentrating/remembering/making decisions?	12.8	12.1
Do you have serious difficulty walking or climbing stairs?	9.1	12.8

Note: (1) Figures cover the Salt Lake City, UT Metropolitan Statistical Area.
Source: Centers for Disease Control and Prevention, Behaviorial Risk Factor Surveillance System, SMART: Selected Metropolitan Area Risk Trends, 2021

Mortality Rates for the Top 10 Causes of Death in the U.S.

ICD-10[a] Sub-Chapter	ICD-10[a] Code	Crude Mortality Rate[1] per 100,000 population	
		County[2]	U.S.
Malignant neoplasms	C00-C97	106.4	182.6
Ischaemic heart diseases	I20-I25	55.8	113.1
Other forms of heart disease	I30-I51	49.7	64.4
Other degenerative diseases of the nervous system	G30-G31	39.4	51.0
Cerebrovascular diseases	I60-I69	27.0	47.8
Other external causes of accidental injury	W00-X59	36.1	46.4
Chronic lower respiratory diseases	J40-J47	27.2	45.7
Organic, including symptomatic, mental disorders	F01-F09	25.2	35.9
Hypertensive diseases	I10-I15	19.9	35.0
Diabetes mellitus	E10-E14	24.5	29.6

Note: (a) ICD-10 = International Classification of Diseases 10th Revision; (1) Crude mortality rates are a three-year average covering 2019-2021; (2) Figures cover Salt Lake County.
Source: Centers for Disease Control and Prevention, National Center for Health Statistics. National Vital Statistics System, Mortality 2018-2021 on CDC WONDER Online Database

Mortality Rates for Selected Causes of Death

ICD-10[a] Sub-Chapter	ICD-10[a] Code	Crude Mortality Rate[1] per 100,000 population	
		County[2]	U.S.
Assault	X85-Y09	4.3	7.0
Diseases of the liver	K70-K76	14.7	19.8
Human immunodeficiency virus (HIV) disease	B20-B24	0.7	1.5
Influenza and pneumonia	J09-J18	6.3	14.7
Intentional self-harm	X60-X84	20.8	14.3
Malnutrition	E40-E46	12.4	4.3
Obesity and other hyperalimentation	E65-E68	3.8	3.0
Renal failure	N17-N19	8.5	15.7
Transport accidents	V01-V99	9.8	13.6
Viral hepatitis	B15-B19	0.9	1.2

Note: (a) ICD-10 = International Classification of Diseases 10th Revision; (1) Crude mortality rates are a three-year average covering 2019-2021; (2) Figures cover Salt Lake County; Data are suppressed when the data meet the criteria for confidentiality constraints; Crude mortality rates are flagged as unreliable when the rate would be calculated with a numerator of 20 or less.
Source: Centers for Disease Control and Prevention, National Center for Health Statistics. National Vital Statistics System, Mortality 2018-2021 on CDC WONDER Online Database

Health Insurance Coverage

Area	With Health Insurance	With Private Health Insurance	With Public Health Insurance	Without Health Insurance	Population Under Age 19 Without Health Insurance
City	88.9	74.0	22.7	11.1	9.9
MSA[1]	90.2	77.7	20.2	9.8	8.2
U.S.	91.2	67.8	35.4	8.8	5.3

Note: Figures are percentages that cover the civilian noninstitutionalized population; (1) Figures cover the Salt Lake City, UT Metropolitan Statistical Area
Source: U.S. Census Bureau, 2017-2021 American Community Survey 5-Year Estimates

Number of Medical Professionals

Area	MDs[3]	DOs[3,4]	Dentists	Podiatrists	Chiropractors	Optometrists
County[1] (number)	4,595	222	943	76	335	167
County[1] (rate[2])	387.4	18.7	79.5	6.4	28.2	14.1
U.S. (rate[2])	289.3	23.5	72.5	6.2	28.7	17.4

Note: Data as of 2021 unless noted; (1) Data covers Salt Lake County; (2) Rate per 100,000 population; (3) Data as of 2020 and includes all active, non-federal physicians; (4) Doctor of Osteopathic Medicine
Source: U.S. Department of Health and Human Services, Health Resources and Services Administration, Bureau of Health Professions, Area Resource File (ARF) 2021-2022

Best Hospitals

According to *U.S. News,* the Salt Lake City, UT metro area is home to three of the best hospitals in the U.S.: **Craig H. Neilsen Rehabilitation Hospital** (3 adult specialties); **Huntsman Cancer Institute at the University of Utah** (3 adult specialties); **John A. Moran Eye Center at University of Utah Hospitals and Clinics** (3 adult specialties). The hospitals listed were nationally ranked in at least one of 15 adult or 10 pediatric specialties. The number of specialties shown cover the parent hospital. Only 164 U.S. hospitals performed well enough to be nationally ranked in one or more specialties. Twenty hospitals in the U.S. made the Honor Roll. The Best Hospitals Honor Roll takes both the national rankings and the procedure and condition ratings into account. Hospitals received points if they were nationally ranked in one of the 15 adult specialties—the higher they ranked, the more points they got—and how many ratings of "high performing" they earned in the 17 procedures and conditions. *U.S. News Online, "America's Best Hospitals 2022-23"*

According to *U.S. News,* the Salt Lake City, UT metro area is home to one of the best children's hospitals in the U.S.: **Intermountain Primary Children's Hospital-University of Utah** (8 pediatric specialties). The hospital listed was highly ranked in at least one of 10 pediatric specialties. Eighty-six children's hospitals in the U.S. were nationally ranked in at least one specialty. Hospitals received points for being ranked in a specialty, and the 10 hospitals with the most points across the 10 specialties make up the Honor Roll. *U.S. News Online, "America's Best Children's Hospitals 2022-23"*

EDUCATION

Public School District Statistics

District Name	Schls	Pupils	Pupil/ Teacher Ratio	Minority Pupils[1] (%)	LEP/ELL[2] (%)	IEP[3] (%)
Granite District	92	62,544	22.5	53.5	21.8	12.6
Salt Lake District	43	20,239	17.9	59.1	20.8	13.1

Note: Table includes school districts with 2,000 or more students; (1) Percentage of students that are not non-Hispanic white; (2) Percentage of students that are Limited English Proficient or English Language Learners (2018-19); (3) Percentage of students that have an Individualized Education Program (2019-20).
Source: U.S. Department of Education, National Center for Education Statistics, Common Core of Data, Local Education Agency (School District) Universe Survey: School Year 2021-2022

Highest Level of Education

Area	Less than H.S.	H.S. Diploma	Some College, No Deg.	Associate Degree	Bachelor's Degree	Master's Degree	Prof. School Degree	Doctorate Degree
City	8.9	16.6	17.9	6.7	28.3	13.4	4.6	3.5
MSA[1]	8.2	22.8	23.5	9.2	23.4	9.3	2.2	1.5
U.S.	11.1	26.5	20.0	8.7	20.6	9.3	2.2	1.5

Note: Figures cover persons age 25 and over; (1) Figures cover the Salt Lake City, UT Metropolitan Statistical Area
Source: U.S. Census Bureau, 2017-2021 American Community Survey 5-Year Estimates

Educational Attainment by Race

Area	High School Graduate or Higher (%)					Bachelor's Degree or Higher (%)				
	Total	White	Black	Asian	Hisp.[2]	Total	White	Black	Asian	Hisp.[2]
City	91.1	95.3	84.5	83.1	69.3	49.8	54.8	32.1	57.8	21.2
MSA[1]	91.8	94.9	84.6	86.6	73.5	36.4	38.9	25.4	49.1	17.1
U.S.	88.9	91.4	87.2	87.6	71.2	33.7	35.5	23.3	55.6	18.4

Note: Figures shown cover persons 25 years old and over; (1) Figures cover the Salt Lake City, UT Metropolitan Statistical Area; (2) People of Hispanic origin can be of any race
Source: U.S. Census Bureau, 2017-2021 American Community Survey 5-Year Estimates

School Enrollment by Grade and Control

Area	Preschool (%)		Kindergarten (%)		Grades 1 - 4 (%)		Grades 5 - 8 (%)		Grades 9 - 12 (%)	
	Public	Private	Public	Private	Public	Private	Public	Private	Public	Private
City	42.5	57.5	86.4	13.6	88.6	11.4	91.0	9.0	94.8	5.2
MSA[1]	55.1	44.9	86.9	13.1	90.6	9.4	93.7	6.3	93.7	6.3
U.S.	58.8	41.2	86.3	13.7	88.3	11.7	88.6	11.4	89.4	10.6

Note: Figures shown cover persons 3 years old and over; (1) Figures cover the Salt Lake City, UT Metropolitan Statistical Area
Source: U.S. Census Bureau, 2017-2021 American Community Survey 5-Year Estimates

Higher Education

Four-Year Colleges			Two-Year Colleges			Medical Schools[1]	Law Schools[2]	Voc/ Tech[3]
Public	Private Non-profit	Private For-profit	Public	Private Non-profit	Private For-profit			
1	4	6	1	0	1	1	1	13

Note: Figures cover institutions located within the Salt Lake City, UT Metropolitan Statistical Area and include main campuses only; (1) includes schools accredited by the Liaison Committee on Medical Education and the American Osteopathic Association's Commission on Osteopathic College Accreditation; (2) includes ABA-accredited schools, schools with provisional ABA accreditation, and state accredited schools; (3) includes all schools with programs that are less than 2 years.
Source: National Center for Education Statistics, Integrated Postsecondary Education System (IPEDS), 2021-22; Wikipedia, List of Medical Schools in the United States, accessed April 10, 2023; Wikipedia, List of Law Schools in the United States, accessed April 10, 2023

According to *U.S. News & World Report,* the Salt Lake City, UT metro area is home to one of the top 200 national universities in the U.S.: **University of Utah** (#105 tie). The indicators used to capture academic quality fall into a number of categories: assessment by administrators at peer institutions;

retention of students; faculty resources; student selectivity; financial resources; alumni giving; high school counselor ratings of colleges; and graduation rate. *U.S. News & World Report, "America's Best Colleges 2023"*

According to *U.S. News & World Report,* the Salt Lake City, UT metro area is home to one of the top 100 law schools in the U.S.: **University of Utah (Quinney)** (#37 tie). The rankings are based on a weighted average of 12 measures of quality: peer assessment score; assessment score by lawyers/judges; median LSAT scores; median undergrad GPA; acceptance rate; employment rates for graduates; placement success; bar passage rate; faculty resources; expenditures per student; student/faculty ratio; and library resources. *U.S. News & World Report, "America's Best Graduate Schools, Law, 2023"*

According to *U.S. News & World Report,* the Salt Lake City, UT metro area is home to one of the top 75 medical schools for research in the U.S.: **University of Utah** (#35 tie). The rankings are based on a weighted average of 11 measures of quality: quality assessment; peer assessment score; assessment score by residency directors; research activity; total research activity; average research activity per faculty member; student selectivity; median MCAT total score; median undergraduate GPA; acceptance rate; and faculty resources. *U.S. News & World Report, "America's Best Graduate Schools, Medical, 2023"*

According to *U.S. News & World Report,* the Salt Lake City, UT metro area is home to one of the top 75 business schools in the U.S.: **University of Utah (Eccles)** (#40). The rankings are based on a weighted average of the following nine measures: quality assessment; peer assessment; recruiter assessment; placement success; mean starting salary and bonus; student selectivity; mean GMAT and GRE scores; mean undergraduate GPA; and acceptance rate. *U.S. News & World Report, "America's Best Graduate Schools, Business, 2023"*

EMPLOYERS

Major Employers

Company Name	Industry
ACS Commercial Solutions	Data entry service
Alsco	Laundry & garment services, nec
Boart Longyear Company	Test boring for nonmetallic minerals
Church of Jesus Christ of LDS	Mormon church
Comenity Capital Bank	State commercial banks
County of Salt Lake	County government
EnergySolutions	Nonresidential construction, nec
Executive Office of the State of Utah	Executive offices
Granite School District Aid Association	Public elementary & secondary schools
Huntsman Corporation	Plastics materials & resins
Huntsman Holdings	Polystyrene resins
Intermountain Health Care	General medical & surgical hospitals
Jordan School District	Public elementary & secondary schools
Longyear Holdings	Test boring for nonmetallic minerals
Sinclair Oil Corporation	Petroleum refining
Smith's Food & Drug Centers	Grocery stores
Sportsman's Warehouse Holdings	Hunting equipment
State of Utah	State government
The University of Utah	Colleges & universities
TPUSA	Telemarketing services
University of Utah Hospitals & Clinics	General medical & surgical hospitals
Utah Department of Human Services	Administration of social & manpower programs
Zions Bancorporation	Bank holding companies

Note: Companies shown are located within the Salt Lake City, UT Metropolitan Statistical Area.
Source: Hoovers.com; Wikipedia

PUBLIC SAFETY

Crime Rate

Area	Total Crime	Violent Crime Rate				Property Crime Rate		
		Murder	Rape[3]	Robbery	Aggrav. Assault	Burglary	Larceny -Theft	Motor Vehicle Theft
City	8,274.5	8.4	137.0	240.9	536.1	764.1	5,503.8	1,084.1
Suburbs[1]	3,411.8	4.1	53.4	45.4	176.7	364.6	2,327.6	439.9
Metro[2]	4,200.7	4.8	67.0	77.1	235.0	429.5	2,842.9	544.4
U.S.	2,356.7	6.5	38.4	73.9	279.7	314.2	1,398.0	246.0

Note: Figures are crimes per 100,000 population; (1) All areas within the metro area that are located outside the city limits; (2) Figures cover the Salt Lake City, UT Metropolitan Statistical Area; (3) All figures shown were reported using the revised Uniform Crime Reporting (UCR) definition of rape; Due to the transition to the National Incident-Based Reporting System (NIBRS), limited city and metro area data was released for 2021.
Source: FBI Uniform Crime Reports, 2020

Hate Crimes

Area	Number of Quarters Reported	Number of Incidents per Bias Motivation					
		Race/Ethnicity/ Ancestry	Religion	Sexual Orientation	Disability	Gender	Gender Identity
City[1]	4	1	0	2	0	0	0
U.S.	4	5,227	1,244	1,110	130	75	266

Note: (1) Figures include one incident reported with more than one bias motivation; Due to the transition to the National Incident-Based Reporting System (NIBRS), limited crime data was released for 2021.
Source: Federal Bureau of Investigation, Hate Crime Statistics 2020

Identity Theft Consumer Reports

Area	Reports	Reports per 100,000 Population	Rank[2]
MSA[1]	2,620	215	141
U.S.	1,108,609	339	-

Note: (1) Figures cover the Salt Lake City, UT Metropolitan Statistical Area; (2) Rank ranges from 1 to 391 where 1 indicates greatest number of identity theft reports per 100,000 population
Source: Federal Trade Commission, Consumer Sentinel Network Data Book 2022

Fraud and Other Consumer Reports

Area	Reports	Reports per 100,000 Population	Rank[2]
MSA[1]	10,458	860	174
U.S.	4,064,520	1,245	-

Note: (1) Figures cover the Salt Lake City, UT Metropolitan Statistical Area; (2) Rank ranges from 1 to 391 where 1 indicates greatest number of fraud and other consumer reports per 100,000 population
Source: Federal Trade Commission, Consumer Sentinel Network Data Book 2022

POLITICS

2020 Presidential Election Results

Area	Biden	Trump	Jorgensen	Hawkins	Other
Salt Lake County	53.0	42.1	2.2	0.4	2.2
U.S.	51.3	46.8	1.2	0.3	0.5

Note: Results are percentages and may not add to 100% due to rounding
Source: Dave Leip's Atlas of U.S. Presidential Elections

SPORTS

Professional Sports Teams

Team Name	League	Year Established
Real Salt Lake	Major League Soccer (MLS)	2005
Utah Jazz	National Basketball Association (NBA)	1979

Note: Includes teams located in the Salt Lake City, UT Metropolitan Statistical Area.
Source: Wikipedia, Major Professional Sports Teams of the United States and Canada, April 12, 2023

CLIMATE

Average and Extreme Temperatures

Temperature	Jan	Feb	Mar	Apr	May	Jun	Jul	Aug	Sep	Oct	Nov	Dec	Yr.
Extreme High (°F)	62	69	78	85	93	104	107	104	100	89	75	67	107
Average High (°F)	37	43	52	62	72	83	93	90	80	66	50	38	64
Average Temp. (°F)	28	34	41	50	59	69	78	76	65	53	40	30	52
Average Low (°F)	19	24	31	38	46	54	62	61	51	40	30	22	40
Extreme Low (°F)	-22	-14	2	15	25	35	40	37	27	16	-14	-15	-22

Note: Figures cover the years 1948-1990
Source: National Climatic Data Center, International Station Meteorological Climate Summary, 9/96

Average Precipitation/Snowfall/Humidity

Precip./Humidity	Jan	Feb	Mar	Apr	May	Jun	Jul	Aug	Sep	Oct	Nov	Dec	Yr.
Avg. Precip. (in.)	1.3	1.2	1.8	2.0	1.7	0.9	0.8	0.9	1.1	1.3	1.3	1.4	15.6
Avg. Snowfall (in.)	13	10	11	6	1	Tr	0	0	Tr	2	6	13	63
Avg. Rel. Hum. 5am (%)	79	77	71	67	66	60	53	54	60	68	75	79	67
Avg. Rel. Hum. 5pm (%)	69	59	47	38	33	26	22	23	28	40	59	71	43

Note: Figures cover the years 1948-1990; Tr = Trace amounts (<0.05 in. of rain; <0.5 in. of snow)
Source: National Climatic Data Center, International Station Meteorological Climate Summary, 9/96

Weather Conditions

Temperature			Daytime Sky			Precipitation		
5°F & below	32°F & below	90°F & above	Clear	Partly cloudy	Cloudy	0.01 inch or more precip.	0.1 inch or more snow/ice	Thunder-storms
7	128	56	94	152	119	92	38	38

Note: Figures are average number of days per year and cover the years 1948-1990
Source: National Climatic Data Center, International Station Meteorological Climate Summary, 9/96

HAZARDOUS WASTE

Superfund Sites

The Salt Lake City, UT metro area is home to five sites on the EPA's Superfund National Priorities List: **700 South 1600 East Pce Plume** (final); **Jacobs Smelter** (final); **Kennecott (North Zone)** (proposed); **Murray Smelter** (proposed); **Portland Cement (Kiln Dust 2 & 3)** (final). There are a total of 1,165 Superfund sites with a status of proposed or final on the list in the U.S. *U.S. Environmental Protection Agency, National Priorities List, April 12, 2023*

AIR QUALITY

Air Quality Trends: Ozone

	1990	1995	2000	2005	2010	2015	2018	2019	2020	2021
MSA[1]	n/a	n/a	n/a	n/a	n/a	n/a	n/a	n/a	n/a	n/a
U.S.	0.087	0.089	0.081	0.080	0.072	0.067	0.069	0.065	0.065	0.067

Note: (1) Data covers the Salt Lake City, UT Metropolitan Statistical Area; n/a not available. The values shown are the composite ozone concentration averages among trend sites based on the highest fourth daily maximum 8-hour concentration in parts per million. These trends are based on sites having an adequate record of monitoring data during the trend period. Data from exceptional events are included.
Source: U.S. Environmental Protection Agency, Air Quality Monitoring Information, "Air Quality Trends by City, 1990-2021"

Air Quality Index

Area	Percent of Days when Air Quality was...[2]					AQI Statistics[2]	
	Good	Moderate	Unhealthy for Sensitive Groups	Unhealthy	Very Unhealthy	Maximum	Median
MSA[1]	47.4	39.5	10.7	2.5	0.0	177	52

Note: (1) Data covers the Salt Lake City, UT Metropolitan Statistical Area; (2) Based on 365 days with AQI data in 2021. Air Quality Index (AQI) is an index for reporting daily air quality. EPA calculates the AQI for five major air pollutants regulated by the Clean Air Act: ground-level ozone, particle pollution (aka particulate matter), carbon monoxide, sulfur dioxide, and nitrogen dioxide. The AQI runs from 0 to 500. The higher the AQI value, the greater the level of air pollution and the greater the health concern. There are six AQI categories: "Good" AQI is between 0 and 50. Air quality is considered satisfactory; "Moderate" AQI is between 51 and 100. Air quality is acceptable; "Unhealthy for Sensitive Groups" When AQI values are between 101 and 150, members of sensitive groups may experience health effects; "Unhealthy" When AQI values are between 151 and 200 everyone may begin to experience health effects; "Very Unhealthy" AQI values between 201 and 300 trigger a health alert; "Hazardous" AQI values over 300 trigger warnings of emergency conditions (not shown).
Source: U.S. Environmental Protection Agency, Air Quality Index Report, 2021

Air Quality Index Pollutants

Area	Percent of Days when AQI Pollutant was...[2]					
	Carbon Monoxide	Nitrogen Dioxide	Ozone	Sulfur Dioxide	Particulate Matter 2.5	Particulate Matter 10
MSA[1]	0.0	7.9	64.4	(3)	24.1	3.6

Note: (1) Data covers the Salt Lake City, UT Metropolitan Statistical Area; (2) Based on 365 days with AQI data in 2021. The Air Quality Index (AQI) is an index for reporting daily air quality. EPA calculates the AQI for five major air pollutants regulated by the Clean Air Act: ground-level ozone, particle pollution (also known as particulate matter), carbon monoxide, sulfur dioxide, and nitrogen dioxide. The AQI runs from 0 to 500. The higher the AQI value, the greater the level of air pollution and the greater the health concern; (3) Sulfur dioxide is no longer included in this table (as of December 8, 2021) because SO$_2$ concentrations tend to be very localized and not necessarily representative of broad geographical areas like counties and CBSAs.
Source: U.S. Environmental Protection Agency, Air Quality Index Report, 2021

Maximum Air Pollutant Concentrations: Particulate Matter, Ozone, CO and Lead

	Particulate Matter 10 (ug/m³)	Particulate Matter 2.5 Wtd AM (ug/m³)	Particulate Matter 2.5 24-Hr (ug/m³)	Ozone (ppm)	Carbon Monoxide (ppm)	Lead (ug/m³)
MSA[1] Level	103	10.3	43	0.087	1	n/a
NAAQS[2]	150	15	35	0.075	9	0.15
Met NAAQS[2]	Yes	Yes	No	No	Yes	n/a

Note: (1) Data covers the Salt Lake City, UT Metropolitan Statistical Area; Data from exceptional events are included; (2) National Ambient Air Quality Standards; ppm = parts per million; ug/m³ = micrograms per cubic meter; n/a not available.
Concentrations: Particulate Matter 10 (coarse particulate)—highest second maximum 24-hour concentration; Particulate Matter 2.5 Wtd AM (fine particulate)—highest weighted annual mean concentration; Particulate Matter 2.5 24-Hour (fine particulate)—highest 98th percentile 24-hour concentration; Ozone—highest fourth daily maximum 8-hour concentration; Carbon Monoxide—highest second maximum non-overlapping 8-hour concentration; Lead—maximum running 3-month average
Source: U.S. Environmental Protection Agency, Air Quality Monitoring Information, "Air Quality Statistics by City, 2021"

Maximum Air Pollutant Concentrations: Nitrogen Dioxide and Sulfur Dioxide

	Nitrogen Dioxide AM (ppb)	Nitrogen Dioxide 1-Hr (ppb)	Sulfur Dioxide AM (ppb)	Sulfur Dioxide 1-Hr (ppb)	Sulfur Dioxide 24-Hr (ppb)
MSA[1] Level	16	51	n/a	7	n/a
NAAQS[2]	53	100	30	75	140
Met NAAQS[2]	Yes	Yes	n/a	Yes	n/a

Note: (1) Data covers the Salt Lake City, UT Metropolitan Statistical Area; Data from exceptional events are included; (2) National Ambient Air Quality Standards; ppm = parts per million; ug/m³ = micrograms per cubic meter; n/a not available.
Concentrations: Nitrogen Dioxide AM—highest arithmetic mean concentration; Nitrogen Dioxide 1-Hr—highest 98th percentile 1-hour daily maximum concentration; Sulfur Dioxide AM—highest annual mean concentration; Sulfur Dioxide 1-Hr—highest 99th percentile 1-hour daily maximum concentration; Sulfur Dioxide 24-Hr—highest second maximum 24-hour concentration
Source: U.S. Environmental Protection Agency, Air Quality Monitoring Information, "Air Quality Statistics by City, 2021"

San Diego, California

Background

San Diego is the archetypal southern California City. Located 100 miles south of Los Angeles, near the Mexican border, San Diego is characterized by sunny days, an excellent harbor, a populous citizenry influenced by its Spanish heritage, and recreational activities based on ideal weather conditions.

San Diego was first claimed in 1542 for Spain by Juan Rodríguez Cabrillo, a Portuguese navigator in the service of the Spanish crown. The site remained uneventful until 1769, when Spanish colonizer, Gaspar de Portola, established the first European settlement in California. Accompanying de Portola was a Franciscan monk named Junipero Serra, who established the Mission Basilica San Diego de Alcala, the first of a chain of missions along the California coast.

After San Diego fell under the U.S. flag during the Mexican War of 1846, the city existed in relative isolation, deferring status and importance to its sister cities in the north, Los Angeles and San Francisco. Even when San Francisco businessman Alonzo Horton bought 1,000 acres of land near the harbor to establish a downtown there, San Diego remained secondary to both these cities, and saw a decrease in population from 40,000 in 1880 to 17,000 at the turn of the century.

World War II repopulated the city, when the Navy moved one of its bases from Pearl Harbor to San Diego. The naval base brought personnel and several related industries, such as nuclear and oceanographic research, and aviation development. In celebration of this past, the famed *Midway*, a 1,000-foot World War II aircraft carrier, has undergone a $6.5 million reconstruction and has been moved to Navy Pier, where it opened in 2004 as a floating museum.

Today, San Diego is the second most populous city in California, with plenty of outdoor activities, jobs, fine educational institutions, theaters, and museums. Its downtown redevelopment agency has transformed what was largely an abandoned downtown into a glittering showcase of waterfront skyscrapers, live-work loft developments, five-star hotels, cafes, restaurants, and shops. The once-industrial East Village adjacent to PETCO ballpark is now the new frontier in San Diego's downtown urban renewal.

The western part of the U.S., from Seattle to the Silicon Valley, and from San Diego to Denver, is the center for hot growth industries, including telecommunications, biomedical products, software, and financial services. San Diego also leads the country in biotechnology companies.

The San Diego Convention Center underwent expansion in 2001, increasing exhibit space from 250,000 to 615,000 square feet. The water supply system, always a significant issue in this part of California, has been upgraded and improved in recent years.

Expansion of the city's trolley service was completed in 2021 and that same year renovations to San Diego International Airport began, promising a new terminal with 30 new gates, a new parking garage, and a new three-lane airport access road by 2030.

San Diego is a LGBTQ-friendly city, with the seventh-highest percentage of gay residents in the U.S. Additionally, San Diego State University (SDSU), one of the city's prominent universities, has been named one of the top LGBTQ-friendly campuses in the nation.

The city's Windansea Beach is known for its reef break and iconic palm frond shack, attracting some of the best surfers in the world. Windansea was the inspiration for the popular "Beach Party" movies in the 1960s. Today, the Windansea Surf Club continues to compete in surf contests and combines community involvement with its competitive heritage. Windansea's surf shack, originally built in 1946, has been rebuilt by surfers numerous times after storms destroyed it. Designated a Historical Landmark in 1998, it remains a symbol of San Diego's surfing heritage and Hawaiian roots.

San Diego summers are cool, and winters are warm in comparison with other locations along the same general latitude, due to the Pacific Ocean. A marked feature of the climate is the wide variation in temperature. In nearby valleys, for example, daytime temperatures are much warmer in summer and noticeably cooler on winter nights than in the city proper. As is usual on the Pacific Coast, nighttime and early morning cloudiness is the norm. Considerable fog occurs along the coast, especially during the winter months.

Rankings

General Rankings

- For its "Best for Vets: Places to Live 2019" rankings, *Military Times* evaluated 599 cities (83 large, 234 medium, 282 small) and compared the locations across three broad categories: veteran and military culture/services; economic indicators; and livability factors such as health, crime, traffic, and school quality. San Diego ranked #4 out of the top 25, in the large city category (population of more than 250,000). Data points more specific to veterans and the military weighed more heavily than others. *rebootcamp.militarytimes.com, "Military Times Best Places to Live 2019," September 10, 2018*

- San Diego was selected as one of the best places to live in the United States by *Money* magazine. The city ranked #22 out of 50. This year's list focused on cities that would be welcoming to a broader group of people and with populations of at least 20,000. Beginning with a pool of 1,370 candidates, editors looked at 350 data points, organized into the these nine categories: income and personal finance, cost of living, economic opportunity, housing market, fun and amenities, health and safety, education, diversity, and quality of life. *Money, "The 50 Best Places to Live in the U.S. in 2022-2023" September 29, 2022*

- San Diego appeared on *Travel + Leisure's* list of "The 15 Best Cities in the United States." The city was ranked #14. Criteria: sights/landmarks; culture; food; friendliness; shopping; and overall value. *Travel + Leisure, "The World's Best Awards 2022" July 12, 2022*

- For its 35th annual "Readers' Choice Awards" survey, *Condé Nast Traveler* ranked its readers' favorite cities in the U.S. Whether it be a longed-for visit or a first on the list, these are the places that inspired a return to travel. The list was broken into large cities and cities under 250,000. San Diego ranked #3 in the big city category. *Condé Nast Traveler, Readers' Choice Awards 2022, "Best Big Cities in the U.S." October 4, 2022*

Business/Finance Rankings

- The Brookings Institution ranked the nation's largest cities based on income inequality. San Diego was ranked #68 (#1 = greatest inequality). Criteria: the "95/20 ratio," a figure representing the income at which a household earns more than 95 percent of all other households, divided by the income at which a household earns more than only 20 percent of all other households. *Brookings Institution, "Household Income Inequality, Largest Cities of 97 Large U.S. Metro Areas, 2014-2016," February 5, 2018*

- The Brookings Institution ranked the 100 largest metro areas in the U.S. based on income inequality. San Diego was ranked #51 (#1 = greatest inequality). Criteria: the "95/20 ratio," a figure representing the income at which a household earns more than 95 percent of all other households, divided by the income at which a household earns more than only 20 percent of all other households. *Brookings Institution, "Household Income Inequality, 100 Largest U.S. Metro Areas, 2014-2016," February 5, 2018*

- Payscale.com ranked the 32 largest metro areas in terms of wage growth. The San Diego metro area ranked #4. Criteria: quarterly changes in private industry employee and education professional wage growth from the previous year. *PayScale, "Wage Trends by Metro Area-1st Quarter," April 20, 2023*

- The San Diego metro area was identified as one of the most debt-ridden places in America by the finance site Credit.com. The metro area was ranked #8. Criteria: residents' average credit card debt as well as median income. *Credit.com, "25 Cities With the Most Credit Card Debt," February 28, 2018*

- For its annual survey of the "Most Expensive U.S. Cities to Live In," Kiplinger applied Cost of Living Index statistics developed by the Council for Community and Economic Research to U.S. Census Bureau population and median household income data for 265 urban areas. San Diego ranked #11 among the most expensive in the country. *Kiplinger.com, "The 11 Most Expensive Cities to Live in the U.S.," April 15, 2023*

- The San Diego metro area appeared on the Milken Institute "2022 Best Performing Cities" list. Rank: #42 out of 200 large metro areas (population over 250,000). Criteria: job growth; wage and salary growth; high-tech output growth; housing affordability; household broadband access. *Milken Institute, "Best-Performing Cities 2022," March 28, 2022*

- *Forbes* ranked the 200 most populous metro areas to determine the nation's "Best Places for Business and Careers." The San Diego metro area was ranked #45. Criteria: costs (business and living); job growth (past and projected); income growth; quality of life; educational attainment (college and high school); projected economic growth; cultural and leisure opportunities; workplace tolerance laws; net migration patterns. *Forbes, "The Best Places for Business and Careers 2019: Seattle Still On Top," October 30, 2019*

Children/Family Rankings

- San Diego was selected as one of the best cities for newlyweds by *Rent.com*. The city ranked #9 of 15. Criteria: cost of living; availability of affordable rental inventory; annual household income; activities and restaurant options; percentage of married couples; concentration of millennials; safety. *Rent.com, "The 15 Best Cities for Newlyweds," December 11, 2018*

Dating/Romance Rankings

- *Apartment List* conducted its Annual Renter Satisfaction Survey and asked renters "how satisfied are you with opportunities for dating in your current city." The cities were ranked from highest to lowest based on their satisfaction scores. San Diego ranked #4 out of 85 cities. *Apartment List, "Best Cities for Dating 2022 with Local Dating Insights from Bumble," February 7, 2022*

- San Diego was selected as one of America's best cities for singles by the readers of *Travel + Leisure* in their annual "America's Favorite Cities" survey. Criteria included good-looking locals, cool shopping, an active bar scene and hipster-magnet coffee bars. *Travel + Leisure, "Best Cities in America for Singles," July 21, 2017*

Education Rankings

- Personal finance website *WalletHub* analyzed the 150 largest U.S. metropolitan statistical areas to determine where the most educated Americans are putting their degrees to work. Criteria: education levels; percentage of workers with degrees; education quality and attainment gap; public school quality rankings; quality and enrollment of each metro area's universities. San Diego was ranked #22 (#1 = most educated city). *www.WalletHub.com, "Most & Least Educated Cities in America," July 18, 2022*

- San Diego was selected as one of America's most literate cities. The city ranked #31 out of the 84 largest U.S. cities. Criteria: number of booksellers; library resources; Internet resources; educational attainment; periodical publishing resources; newspaper circulation. *Central Connecticut State University, "America's Most Literate Cities, 2018," February 2019*

Environmental Rankings

- The U.S. Environmental Protection Agency (EPA) released its list of U.S. metropolitan areas with the most ENERGY STAR certified buildings in 2022. The San Diego metro area was ranked #14 out of 25. *U.S. Environmental Protection Agency, "2023 Energy Star Top Cities," April 26, 2023*

- San Diego was highlighted as one of the 25 most ozone-polluted metro areas in the U.S. during 2019 through 2021. The area ranked #8. *American Lung Association, "State of the Air 2023," April 19, 2023*

- San Diego was highlighted as one of the 25 metro areas most polluted by short-term particle pollution (24-hour PM 2.5) in the U.S. during 2019 through 2021. The area ranked #16. *American Lung Association, "State of the Air 2023," April 19, 2023*

Health/Fitness Rankings

- For each of the 100 largest cities in the United States, the American Fitness Index®, compiled in partnership between the American College of Sports Medicine and the Elevance Health Foundation, evaluated community infrastructure and 34 health behaviors including preventive health, levels of chronic disease conditions, food insecurity, sleep quality, pedestrian safety, air quality, and community/environment resources that support physical activity. San Diego ranked #23 for "community fitness." *americanfitnessindex.org, "2022 ACSM American Fitness Index Summary Report," July 12, 2022*

- Trulia analyzed the 100 largest U.S. metro areas to identify the nation's best cities for weight loss, based on the percentage of adults who bike or walk to work, sporting goods stores, grocery stores, access to outdoor activities, weight-loss centers, gyms, and average space reserved for parks. San Diego ranked #9. *Trulia.com, "Where to Live to Get in Shape in the New Year," January 4, 2018*

- San Diego was identified as a "2022 Spring Allergy Capital." The area ranked #88 out of 100. Three groups of factors were used to identify the most challenging cities for people with allergies during the spring season: annual spring pollen scores; over the counter allergy medicine use; number of board-certified allergy specialists. *Asthma and Allergy Foundation of America, "Spring Allergy Capitals 2022," March 2, 2022*

- San Diego was identified as a "2022 Fall Allergy Capital." The area ranked #88 out of 100. Three groups of factors were used to identify the most challenging cities for people with allergies during the fall season: annual fall pollen scores; over the counter allergy medicine use; number of board-certified allergy specialists. *Asthma and Allergy Foundation of America, "Fall Allergy Capitals 2022," March 2, 2022*

- San Diego was identified as a "2022 Asthma Capital." The area ranked #71 out of the nation's 100 largest metropolitan areas. Criteria: estimated asthma prevalence; asthma-related mortality; and ER visits due to asthma. Risk factors analyzed but not factored in the rankings: annual pollen score; annual air quality; public smoking laws; access to board-certified asthma specialists; rescue and controller medication use; uninsured rate; poverty rate. *Asthma and Allergy Foundation of America, "Asthma Capitals 2022: The Most Challenging Places to Live With Asthma," September 14, 2022*

Real Estate Rankings

- *WalletHub* compared the most populated U.S. cities to determine which had the best markets for real estate agents. San Diego ranked #17 where demand was high and pay was the best. Criteria: sales per agent; annual median wage for real-estate agents; monthly average starting salary for real estate agents; real estate job density and competition; unemployment rate; home turnover rate; housing-market health index; and other relevant metrics. *www.WalletHub.com, "2021 Best Places to Be a Real Estate Agent," May 12, 2021*

- The San Diego metro area was identified as one of the 20 least affordable housing markets in the U.S. in 2022. The area ranked #182 out of 186 markets. Criteria: qualification for a mortgage loan with a 10 percent down payment on a typical home. *National Association of Realtors®, Qualifying Income Based on Sales Price of Existing Single-Family Homes for Metropolitan Areas, 2022*

- San Diego was ranked #232 out of 235 metro areas in terms of housing affordability in 2022 by the National Association of Home Builders (#1 = most affordable). Criteria: the share of homes sold in that area affordable to a family earning the local median income, based on standard mortgage underwriting criteria. *National Association of Home Builders®, NAHB-Wells Fargo Housing Opportunity Index, 4th Quarter 2022*

Safety Rankings

- Allstate ranked the 200 largest cities in America in terms of driver safety. San Diego ranked #119. Criteria: internal property damage claims over a two-year period from January 2016 to December 2017. The report helps increase the importance of safety and awareness behind the wheel. *Allstate, "Allstate America's Best Drivers Report, 2019" June 24, 2019*

- The National Insurance Crime Bureau ranked 390 metro areas in the U.S. in terms of per capita rates of vehicle theft. The San Diego metro area ranked #54 (#1 = highest rate). Criteria: number of vehicle theft offenses per 100,000 inhabitants in 2021. *National Insurance Crime Bureau, "Hot Spots 2021," September 1, 2022*

Seniors/Retirement Rankings

- From its Best Cities for Successful Aging indexes, the Milken Institute generated rankings for metropolitan areas, weighing data in nine categories—health care, wellness, living arrangements, transportation and convenience, financial characteristics, education, employment, community engagement, and overall livability. The San Diego metro area was ranked #22 overall in the large metro area category. *Milken Institute, "Best Cities for Successful Aging, 2017" March 14, 2017*

Transportation Rankings

- San Diego was identified as one of the most congested metro areas in the U.S. The area ranked #9 out of 10. Criteria: yearly delay per auto commuter in hours. *Texas A&M Transportation Institute, "2021 Urban Mobility Report," June 2021*

- According to the INRIX "2022 Global Traffic Scorecard," San Diego was identified as one of the most congested metro areas in the U.S. The area ranked #16 out of 25. Criteria: average annual time spent in traffic and average cost of congestion per motorist. *Inrix.com, "Return to Work, Higher Gas Prices & Inflation Drove Americans to Spend Hundreds More in Time and Money Commuting," January 10, 2023*

Women/Minorities Rankings

- *Travel + Leisure* listed the best cities in and around the U.S. for a memorable and fun girls' trip, even on a budget. Whether it is for a special occasion, to make new memories or just to get away, San Diego is sure to have something for all the ladies in your tribe. *Travel + Leisure, "25 Affordable Girls Weekend Getaways That Won't Break the Bank," November 25, 2022*

- The *Houston Chronicle* listed the San Diego metro area as #9 in top places for young Latinos to live in the U.S. Research was largely based on housing and occupational data from the largest metropolitan areas performed by *Forbes* and NBC Universo. Criteria: percentage of 18-34 year-olds; Latino college grad rates; and diversity. *blog.chron.com, "The 15 Best Big Cities for Latino Millenials," January 26, 2016*

- Personal finance website *WalletHub* compared more than 180 U.S. cities across two key dimensions, "Hispanic Business-Friendliness" and "Hispanic Purchasing Power," to arrive at the most favorable conditions for Hispanic entrepreneurs. San Diego was ranked #120 out of 182. Criteria includes: share of Hispanic-Owned Businesses; Hispanic entrepreneurship rate to median annual income of Hispanics; Small Business-Friendliness score; cost of living; and number of Hispanics with at least a bachelor's degree. *WalletHub.com, "2019's Best Cities for Hispanic Entrepreneurs," May 1, 2019*

Miscellaneous Rankings

- San Diego was selected as a 2022 Digital Cities Survey winner. The city ranked #1 in the large city (500,000 or more population) category. The survey examined and assessed how city governments are utilizing technology to continue innovation, engage with residents, and persevere through the challenges of the pandemic. Survey questions focused on ten initiatives: cybersecurity; citizen experience; disaster recovery; business intelligence; IT personnel; data governance; business automation; IT governance; infrastructure modernization; and broadband connectivity. *Center for Digital Government, "2022 Digital Cities Survey," November 10, 2022*

- In its roundup of St. Patrick's Day parades "Gayot" listed the best festivals and parades of all things Irish. The festivities in San Diego as among the best in North America. *www.gayot.com, "Best St. Patrick's Day Parades," March 2023*

- The watchdog site, Charity Navigator, conducted a study of charities in major markets both to analyze statistical differences in their financial, accountability, and transparency practices and to track year-to-year variations in individual philanthropic communities. The San Diego metro area was ranked #1 among the 30 metro markets in the rating category of Overall Score. *www.charitynavigator.org, "2017 Metro Market Study," May 1, 2017*

- The financial planning site SmartAsset has compiled its annual study on the best places for Halloween in the U.S. for 2022. 146 cities were compared to determine that San Diego ranked #16 out of 35 for still being able to enjoy the festivities despite COVID-19. Metrics included: safety, family-friendliness, percentage of children in the population, concentration of candy and costume shops, weather and COVID infection rates. *www.smartasset.com, "2022 Edition-Best Places to Celebrate Halloween," October 19, 2022*

- *WalletHub* compared the 150 most populated U.S. cities to determine their operating efficiency. A "Quality of Services" score was constructed for each city and then divided by the total budget per capita to reveal which were managed the best. San Diego ranked #59. Criteria: financial stability; economy; education; safety; health; infrastructure and pollution. *www.WalletHub.com, "2022's Best- & Worst-Run Cities in America," June 21, 2022*

- The National Alliance to End Homelessness listed the 25 most populous metro areas with the highest rate of homelessness. The San Diego metro area had a high rate of homelessness. Criteria: number of homeless people per 10,000 population in 2016. *National Alliance to End Homelessness, "Homelessness in the 25 Most Populous U.S. Metro Areas," September 1, 2017*

Business Environment

DEMOGRAPHICS

Population Growth

Area	1990 Census	2000 Census	2010 Census	2020 Census	Population Growth (%) 1990-2020	Population Growth (%) 2010-2020
City	1,111,048	1,223,400	1,307,402	1,386,932	24.8	6.1
MSA[1]	2,498,016	2,813,833	3,095,313	3,298,634	32.1	6.6
U.S.	248,709,873	281,421,906	308,745,538	331,449,281	33.3	7.4

Note: (1) Figures cover the San Diego-Chula Vista-Carlsbad, CA Metropolitan Statistical Area
Source: U.S. Census Bureau, 1990 Census, 2000 Census, 2010 Census, 2020 Census

Race

Area	White Alone[2] (%)	Black Alone[2] (%)	Asian Alone[2] (%)	AIAN[3] Alone[2] (%)	NHOPI[4] Alone[2] (%)	Other Race Alone[2] (%)	Two or More Races (%)
City	46.4	5.9	17.9	0.9	0.4	14.1	14.4
MSA[1]	49.5	4.7	12.5	1.2	0.5	15.8	15.8
U.S.	61.6	12.4	6.0	1.1	0.2	8.4	10.2

Note: (1) Figures cover the San Diego-Chula Vista-Carlsbad, CA Metropolitan Statistical Area; (2) Alone is defined as not being in combination with one or more other races; (3) American Indian and Alaska Native; (4) Native Hawaiian and Other Pacific Islander
Source: U.S. Census Bureau, 2020 Census

Hispanic or Latino Origin

Area	Total (%)	Mexican (%)	Puerto Rican (%)	Cuban (%)	Other (%)
City	30.1	25.6	0.8	0.3	3.4
MSA[1]	34.3	29.9	0.8	0.2	3.4
U.S.	18.4	11.2	1.8	0.7	4.7

Note: Persons of Hispanic or Latino origin can be of any race; (1) Figures cover the San Diego-Chula Vista-Carlsbad, CA Metropolitan Statistical Area
Source: U.S. Census Bureau, 2017-2021 American Community Survey 5-Year Estimates

Age

Area	Under Age 5	Age 5–19	Age 20–34	Age 35–44	Age 45–54	Age 55–64	Age 65–74	Age 75–84	Age 85+	Median Age
City	5.0	16.8	26.7	14.2	11.9	11.3	8.3	4.0	1.7	35.8
MSA[1]	5.3	18.5	23.2	13.4	12.2	12.2	9.0	4.3	1.9	37.1
U.S.	5.6	19.2	20.2	12.7	12.4	13.1	10.0	4.9	1.9	38.8

Note: (1) Figures cover the San Diego-Chula Vista-Carlsbad, CA Metropolitan Statistical Area
Source: U.S. Census Bureau, 2020 Census

Disability by Age

Area	All Ages	Under 18 Years Old	18 to 64 Years Old	65 Years and Over
City	9.2	3.3	6.5	31.3
MSA[1]	10.0	3.3	7.4	31.7
U.S.	12.6	4.4	10.3	33.4

Note: Figures show percent of the civilian noninstitutionalized population that reported having a disability. Disability status is determined from six types of difficulty: vision, hearing, cognitive, ambulatory, self-care, and independent living. For children under 5 years old, hearing and vision difficulty are used to determine disability status. For children between the ages of 5 and 14, disability status is determined from hearing, vision, cognitive, ambulatory, and self-care difficulties. For people aged 15 years and older, they are considered to have a disability if they have difficulty with any one of the six difficulty types; Note: (1) Figures cover the San Diego-Chula Vista-Carlsbad, CA Metropolitan Statistical Area
Source: U.S. Census Bureau, 2017-2021 American Community Survey 5-Year Estimates

Ancestry

Area	German	Irish	English	American	Italian	Polish	French[2]	Scottish	Dutch
City	8.3	7.1	6.2	2.3	4.2	1.8	1.7	1.4	0.7
MSA[1]	8.9	7.4	6.7	2.7	4.1	1.7	1.8	1.4	0.8
U.S.	12.8	9.6	8.1	5.7	5.0	2.7	2.2	1.6	1.1

Note: Figures are the percentage of the total population reporting a particular ancestry. The nine most commonly reported ancestries in the U.S. are shown. Figures include multiple ancestries (e.g. if a person reported being Irish and Italian, they were included in both columns); (1) Figures cover the San Diego-Chula Vista-Carlsbad, CA Metropolitan Statistical Area; (2) Excludes Basque
Source: U.S. Census Bureau, 2017-2021 American Community Survey 5-Year Estimates

Foreign-born Population

Area	Any Foreign Country	Asia	Mexico	Europe	Caribbean	Central America[2]	South America	Africa	Canada
City	25.1	11.8	8.2	2.2	0.2	0.5	0.9	0.9	0.4
MSA[1]	22.7	8.8	9.6	1.8	0.2	0.6	0.7	0.6	0.4
U.S.	13.6	4.2	3.3	1.5	1.4	1.1	1.1	0.8	0.2

Note: (1) Figures cover the San Diego-Chula Vista-Carlsbad, CA Metropolitan Statistical Area; (2) Excludes Mexico.
Source: U.S. Census Bureau, 2017-2021 American Community Survey 5-Year Estimates

Household Size

Area	One	Two	Three	Four	Five	Six	Seven or More	Average Household Size
City	27.9	34.1	15.8	12.9	5.6	2.2	1.6	2.60
MSA[1]	24.0	32.9	16.9	14.6	6.9	2.7	2.0	2.80
U.S.	28.1	33.8	15.5	12.9	6.0	2.3	1.4	2.60

Note: (1) Figures cover the San Diego-Chula Vista-Carlsbad, CA Metropolitan Statistical Area
Source: U.S. Census Bureau, 2017-2021 American Community Survey 5-Year Estimates

Household Relationships

Area	House-holder	Opposite-sex Spouse	Same-sex Spouse	Opposite-sex Unmarried Partner	Same-sex Unmarried Partner	Child[2]	Grand-child	Other Relatives	Non-relatives
City	37.2	15.7	0.4	2.6	0.3	25.0	2.0	6.2	6.1
MSA[1]	35.1	16.9	0.3	2.3	0.2	27.8	2.3	6.6	5.1
U.S.	38.3	17.5	0.2	2.5	0.2	28.3	2.4	4.8	3.4

Note: Figures are percent of the total population; (1) Figures cover the San Diego-Chula Vista-Carlsbad, CA Metropolitan Statistical Area; (2) Includes biological, adopted, and stepchildren of the householder
Source: U.S. Census Bureau, 2020 Census

Gender

Area	Males	Females	Males per 100 Females
City	694,107	692,825	100.2
MSA[1]	1,642,796	1,655,838	99.2
U.S.	162,685,811	168,763,470	96.4

Note: (1) Figures cover the San Diego-Chula Vista-Carlsbad, CA Metropolitan Statistical Area
Source: U.S. Census Bureau, 2020 Census

Marital Status

Area	Never Married	Now Married[2]	Separated	Widowed	Divorced
City	40.1	44.8	1.6	4.0	9.5
MSA[1]	36.2	47.9	1.6	4.4	9.8
U.S.	33.8	48.0	1.8	5.6	10.8

Note: Figures are percentages and cover the population 15 years of age and older; (1) Figures cover the San Diego-Chula Vista-Carlsbad, CA Metropolitan Statistical Area; (2) Excludes separated
Source: U.S. Census Bureau, 2017-2021 American Community Survey 5-Year Estimates

Religious Groups by Family

Area	Catholic	Baptist	Methodist	LDS[2]	Pentecostal	Lutheran	Islam	Adventist	Other
MSA[1]	22.9	1.5	0.6	2.1	1.0	0.6	1.5	1.9	9.4
U.S.	18.7	7.3	3.0	2.0	1.8	1.7	1.3	1.3	11.6

Note: Figures are the number of adherents as a percentage of the total population and cover the eight largest religious groups in the U.S; (1) Figures cover the San Diego-Chula Vista-Carlsbad, CA Metropolitan Statistical Area; (2) Church of Jesus Christ of Latter-day Saints
Sources: 2020 U.S. Religion Census, Association of Statisticians of American Religious Bodies; The Association of Religion Data Archives (ARDA)

Religious Groups by Tradition

Area	Catholic	Evangelical Protestant	Mainline Protestant	Black Protestant	Islam	Judaism	Hinduism	Orthodox	Buddhism
MSA[1]	22.9	9.5	1.5	0.6	1.5	0.4	0.3	0.4	0.7
U.S.	18.7	16.5	5.2	2.3	1.3	0.6	0.4	0.4	0.3

Note: Figures are the number of adherents as a percentage of the total population; (1) Figures cover the San Diego-Chula Vista-Carlsbad, CA Metropolitan Statistical Area
Sources: 2020 U.S. Religion Census, Association of Statisticians of American Religious Bodies; The Association of Religion Data Archives (ARDA)

ECONOMY

Gross Metropolitan Product

Area	2020	2021	2022	2023	Rank[2]
MSA[1]	240.4	269.0	294.4	313.2	17

Note: Figures are in billions of dollars; (1) Figures cover the San Diego-Chula Vista-Carlsbad, CA Metropolitan Statistical Area; (2) Rank is based on 2021 data and ranges from 1 to 381
Source: U.S. Conference of Mayors, U.S. Metro Economies: U.S. Metros Compared to Global and State Economies, June 2022

Economic Growth

Area	2018-20 (%)	2021 (%)	2022 (%)	2023 (%)	Rank[2]
MSA[1]	-0.5	8.2	3.9	3.3	174
U.S.	-0.6	5.7	3.1	2.9	—

Note: Figures are real gross metropolitan product (GMP) growth rates and represent average annual percent change; (1) Figures cover the San Diego-Chula Vista-Carlsbad, CA Metropolitan Statistical Area; (2) Rank is based on 2020 2-year average annual percent change and ranges from 1 to 381
Source: U.S. Conference of Mayors, U.S. Metro Economies: U.S. Metros Compared to Global and State Economies, June 2022

Metropolitan Area Exports

Area	2016	2017	2018	2019	2020	2021	Rank[2]
MSA[1]	18,086.6	18,637.1	20,156.8	19,774.1	18,999.7	23,687.8	18

Note: Figures are in millions of dollars; (1) Figures cover the San Diego-Chula Vista-Carlsbad, CA Metropolitan Statistical Area; (2) Rank is based on 2021 data and ranges from 1 to 388
Source: U.S. Department of Commerce, International Trade Administration, Office of Trade and Economic Analysis, Industry and Analysis, Exports by Metropolitan Area, data extracted March 16, 2023

Building Permits

Area	Single-Family			Multi-Family			Total		
	2021	2022	Pct. Chg.	2021	2022	Pct. Chg.	2021	2022	Pct. Chg.
City	539	506	-6.1	4,249	3,916	-7.8	4,788	4,422	-7.6
MSA[1]	3,227	3,517	9.0	6,821	5,829	-14.5	10,048	9,346	-7.0
U.S.	1,115,400	975,600	-12.5	621,600	689,500	10.9	1,737,000	1,665,100	-4.1

Note: (1) Figures cover the San Diego-Chula Vista-Carlsbad, CA Metropolitan Statistical Area; Figures represent new, privately-owned housing units authorized (unadjusted data); All permit data are based on estimates with imputation
Source: U.S. Census Bureau, Manufacturing, Mining, and Construction Statistics, Building Permits, 2021, 2022

Bankruptcy Filings

Area	Business Filings			Nonbusiness Filings		
	2021	2022	% Chg.	2021	2022	% Chg.
San Diego County	194	158	-18.6	4,533	3,136	-30.8
U.S.	14,347	13,481	-6.0	399,269	374,240	-6.3

Note: Business filings include Chapter 7, Chapter 9, Chapter 11, Chapter 12, Chapter 13, Chapter 15, and Section 304; Nonbusiness filings include Chapter 7, Chapter 11, and Chapter 13
Source: Administrative Office of the U.S. Courts, Business and Nonbusiness Bankruptcy, County Cases Commenced by Chapter of the Bankruptcy Code, During the 12-Month Period Ending December 31, 2021 and Business and Nonbusiness Bankruptcy, County Cases Commenced by Chapter of the Bankruptcy Code, During the 12-Month Period Ending December 31, 2022

Housing Vacancy Rates

Area	Gross Vacancy Rate[2] (%)			Year-Round Vacancy Rate[3] (%)			Rental Vacancy Rate[4] (%)			Homeowner Vacancy Rate[5] (%)		
	2020	2021	2022	2020	2021	2022	2020	2021	2022	2020	2021	2022
MSA[1]	6.0	6.9	6.9	5.6	6.7	6.6	3.9	3.1	3.6	0.8	0.7	0.6
U.S.	10.6	10.8	10.5	8.2	8.4	8.2	6.3	6.1	5.8	1.0	0.9	0.8

Note: (1) Figures cover the San Diego-Chula Vista-Carlsbad, CA Metropolitan Statistical Area; (2) The percentage of the total housing inventory that is vacant; (3) The percentage of the housing inventory (excluding seasonal units) that is year-round vacant; (4) The percentage of rental inventory that is vacant for rent; (5) The percentage of homeowner inventory that is vacant for sale
Source: U.S. Census Bureau, Housing Vacancies and Homeownership Annual Statistics: 2020, 2021, 2022

INCOME

Income

Area	Per Capita ($)	Median Household ($)	Average Household ($)
City	46,460	89,457	121,230
MSA[1]	42,696	88,240	118,474
U.S.	37,638	69,021	97,196

Note: (1) Figures cover the San Diego-Chula Vista-Carlsbad, CA Metropolitan Statistical Area
Source: U.S. Census Bureau, 2017-2021 American Community Survey 5-Year Estimates

Household Income Distribution

Area	Percent of Households Earning							
	Under $15,000	$15,000 -$24,999	$25,000 -$34,999	$35,000 -$49,999	$50,000 -$74,999	$75,000 -$99,999	$100,000 -$149,999	$150,000 and up
City	7.3	5.4	5.9	8.6	15.2	12.6	19.0	26.0
MSA[1]	6.9	5.7	6.3	9.1	15.0	12.6	18.9	25.5
U.S.	9.4	7.8	8.2	11.4	16.8	12.8	16.3	17.3

Note: (1) Figures cover the San Diego-Chula Vista-Carlsbad, CA Metropolitan Statistical Area
Source: U.S. Census Bureau, 2017-2021 American Community Survey 5-Year Estimates

Poverty Rate

Area	All Ages	Under 18 Years Old	18 to 64 Years Old	65 Years and Over
City	11.6	13.9	11.3	9.4
MSA[1]	10.7	13.2	10.3	8.9
U.S.	12.6	17.0	11.8	9.6

Note: Figures are percentage of people whose income during the past 12 months was below the poverty level;
(1) Figures cover the San Diego-Chula Vista-Carlsbad, CA Metropolitan Statistical Area
Source: U.S. Census Bureau, 2017-2021 American Community Survey 5-Year Estimates

EMPLOYMENT

Labor Force and Employment

Area	Civilian Labor Force			Workers Employed		
	Dec. 2021	Dec. 2022	% Chg.	Dec. 2021	Dec. 2022	% Chg.
City	711,954	721,000	1.3	684,180	701,197	2.5
MSA[1]	1,570,184	1,588,968	1.2	1,505,925	1,543,381	2.5
U.S.	161,696,000	164,224,000	1.6	155,732,000	158,872,000	2.0

Note: Data is not seasonally adjusted and covers workers 16 years of age and older; (1) Figures cover the San Diego-Chula Vista-Carlsbad, CA Metropolitan Statistical Area
Source: Bureau of Labor Statistics, Local Area Unemployment Statistics

Unemployment Rate

Area	2022											
	Jan.	Feb.	Mar.	Apr.	May	Jun.	Jul.	Aug.	Sep.	Oct.	Nov.	Dec.
City	4.5	3.9	3.3	2.9	2.6	3.0	2.9	3.2	2.9	3.0	3.2	2.7
MSA[1]	4.7	4.0	3.4	3.0	2.7	3.2	3.1	3.4	3.1	3.2	3.3	2.9
U.S.	4.4	4.1	3.8	3.3	3.4	3.8	3.8	3.8	3.3	3.4	3.4	3.3

Note: Data is not seasonally adjusted and covers workers 16 years of age and older; (1) Figures cover the San Diego-Chula Vista-Carlsbad, CA Metropolitan Statistical Area
Source: Bureau of Labor Statistics, Local Area Unemployment Statistics

Average Wages

Occupation	$/Hr.	Occupation	$/Hr.
Accountants and Auditors	43.86	Maintenance and Repair Workers	24.59
Automotive Mechanics	27.06	Marketing Managers	84.68
Bookkeepers	25.51	Network and Computer Systems Admin.	49.31
Carpenters	32.52	Nurses, Licensed Practical	32.57
Cashiers	16.54	Nurses, Registered	56.65
Computer Programmers	61.76	Nursing Assistants	20.39
Computer Systems Analysts	55.08	Office Clerks, General	21.38
Computer User Support Specialists	31.80	Physical Therapists	52.92
Construction Laborers	26.98	Physicians	125.61
Cooks, Restaurant	18.75	Plumbers, Pipefitters and Steamfitters	34.09
Customer Service Representatives	22.23	Police and Sheriff's Patrol Officers	47.51
Dentists	70.37	Postal Service Mail Carriers	27.48
Electricians	33.63	Real Estate Sales Agents	41.65
Engineers, Electrical	61.94	Retail Salespersons	18.69
Fast Food and Counter Workers	16.37	Sales Representatives, Technical/Scientific	57.24
Financial Managers	83.73	Secretaries, Exc. Legal/Medical/Executive	23.50
First-Line Supervisors of Office Workers	33.77	Security Guards	18.37
General and Operations Managers	n/a	Surgeons	n/a
Hairdressers/Cosmetologists	21.87	Teacher Assistants, Exc. Postsecondary*	19.50
Home Health and Personal Care Aides	16.23	Teachers, Secondary School, Exc. Sp. Ed.*	47.51
Janitors and Cleaners	18.06	Telemarketers	17.68
Landscaping/Groundskeeping Workers	19.61	Truck Drivers, Heavy/Tractor-Trailer	25.83
Lawyers	89.63	Truck Drivers, Light/Delivery Services	22.99
Maids and Housekeeping Cleaners	18.37	Waiters and Waitresses	17.49

Note: Wage data covers the San Diego-Chula Vista-Carlsbad, CA Metropolitan Statistical Area; (*) Hourly wages were calculated from annual wage data based on a 40 hour work week; n/a not available.
Source: Bureau of Labor Statistics, Metro Area Occupational Employment & Wage Estimates, May 2022

Employment by Industry

| Sector | MSA[1] | | U.S. |
	Number of Employees	Percent of Total	Percent of Total
Construction	88,200	5.6	5.0
Private Education and Health Services	235,000	15.0	16.1
Financial Activities	76,000	4.8	5.9
Government	249,500	15.9	14.5
Information	22,200	1.4	2.0
Leisure and Hospitality	200,900	12.8	10.3
Manufacturing	118,500	7.6	8.4
Mining and Logging	400	<0.1	0.4
Other Services	56,600	3.6	3.7
Professional and Business Services	291,700	18.6	14.7
Retail Trade	143,000	9.1	10.2
Transportation, Warehousing, and Utilities	42,200	2.7	4.9
Wholesale Trade	43,500	2.8	3.9

Note: Figures are non-farm employment as of December 2022. Figures are not seasonally adjusted and include workers 16 years of age and older; (1) Figures cover the San Diego-Chula Vista-Carlsbad, CA Metropolitan Statistical Area
Source: Bureau of Labor Statistics, Current Employment Statistics, Employment, Hours, and Earnings

Employment by Occupation

Occupation Classification	City (%)	MSA[1] (%)	U.S. (%)
Management, Business, Science, and Arts	50.4	44.3	40.3
Natural Resources, Construction, and Maintenance	5.3	7.4	8.7
Production, Transportation, and Material Moving	8.8	9.8	13.1
Sales and Office	18.3	20.3	20.9
Service	17.2	18.2	17.0

Note: Figures cover employed civilians 16 years of age and older; (1) Figures cover the San Diego-Chula Vista-Carlsbad, CA Metropolitan Statistical Area
Source: U.S. Census Bureau, 2017-2021 American Community Survey 5-Year Estimates

Occupations with Greatest Projected Employment Growth: 2022 – 2024

Occupation[1]	2022 Employment	2024 Projected Employment	Numeric Employment Change	Percent Employment Change
Home Health and Personal Care Aides	811,300	858,600	47,300	5.8
Fast Food and Counter Workers	422,000	444,100	22,100	5.2
Cooks, Restaurant	154,300	172,000	17,700	11.5
Software Developers and Software Quality Assurance Analysts and Testers	337,600	352,100	14,500	4.3
Waiters and Waitresses	205,800	219,200	13,400	6.5
Laborers and Freight, Stock, and Material Movers, Hand	391,100	403,100	12,000	3.1
Stockers and Order Fillers	268,000	277,500	9,500	3.5
General and Operations Managers	308,500	317,600	9,100	2.9
First-Line Supervisors of Food Preparation and Serving Workers	118,100	126,000	7,900	6.7
Project Management Specialists and Business Operations Specialists, All Other	332,400	339,800	7,400	2.2

Note: Projections cover California; (1) Sorted by numeric employment change
Source: www.projectionscentral.com, State Occupational Projections, 2022–2024 Short-Term Projections

Fastest-Growing Occupations: 2022 – 2024

Occupation[1]	2022 Employment	2024 Projected Employment	Numeric Employment Change	Percent Employment Change
Fitness Trainers and Aerobics Instructors	40,700	46,300	5,600	13.8
Nurse Practitioners	18,300	20,500	2,200	12.0
Cooks, Restaurant	154,300	172,000	17,700	11.5
Airfield Operations Specialists	3,700	4,100	400	10.8
Solar Photovoltaic Installers	6,600	7,300	700	10.6
Ushers, Lobby Attendants, and Ticket Takers	7,800	8,600	800	10.3
Amusement and Recreation Attendants	47,500	52,300	4,800	10.1
Sociologists	1,000	1,100	100	10.0
Paperhangers	1,000	1,100	100	10.0
Avionics Technicians	2,000	2,200	200	10.0

Note: Projections cover California; (1) Sorted by percent employment change and excludes occupations with numeric employment change less than 50
Source: www.projectionscentral.com, State Occupational Projections, 2022–2024 Short-Term Projections

CITY FINANCES

City Government Finances

Component	2020 ($000)	2020 ($ per capita)
Total Revenues	4,244,700	2,981
Total Expenditures	3,791,989	2,663
Debt Outstanding	5,129,104	3,602
Cash and Securities[1]	2,358,319	1,656

Note: (1) Cash and security holdings of a government at the close of its fiscal year, including those of its dependent agencies, utilities, and liquor stores.
Source: U.S. Census Bureau, State & Local Government Finances 2020

City Government Revenue by Source

Source	2020 ($000)	2020 ($ per capita)	2020 (%)
General Revenue			
From Federal Government	455,721	320	10.7
From State Government	151,105	106	3.6
From Local Governments	2,727	2	0.1
Taxes			
Property	622,207	437	14.7
Sales and Gross Receipts	668,215	469	15.7
Personal Income	0	0	0.0
Corporate Income	0	0	0.0
Motor Vehicle License	0	0	0.0
Other Taxes	97,460	68	2.3
Current Charges	1,334,569	937	31.4
Liquor Store	0	0	0.0
Utility	564,213	396	13.3

Source: U.S. Census Bureau, State & Local Government Finances 2020

City Government Expenditures by Function

Function	2020 ($000)	2020 ($ per capita)	2020 (%)
General Direct Expenditures			
Air Transportation	5,787	4	0.2
Corrections	0	0	0.0
Education	0	0	0.0
Employment Security Administration	0	0	0.0
Financial Administration	59,469	41	1.6
Fire Protection	205,534	144	5.4
General Public Buildings	79,818	56	2.1
Governmental Administration, Other	41,659	29	1.1
Health	45,052	31	1.2
Highways	307,642	216	8.1
Hospitals	0	0	0.0
Housing and Community Development	389,250	273	10.3
Interest on General Debt	229,290	161	6.0
Judicial and Legal	61,844	43	1.6
Libraries	47,391	33	1.2
Parking	0	0	0.0
Parks and Recreation	373,819	262	9.9
Police Protection	399,076	280	10.5
Public Welfare	0	0	0.0
Sewerage	355,221	249	9.4
Solid Waste Management	53,451	37	1.4
Veterans' Services	0	0	0.0
Liquor Store	0	0	0.0
Utility	743,445	522	19.6

Source: U.S. Census Bureau, State & Local Government Finances 2020

TAXES

State Corporate Income Tax Rates

State	Tax Rate (%)	Income Brackets ($)	Num. of Brackets	Financial Institution Tax Rate (%)[a]	Federal Income Tax Ded.
California	8.84 (b)	Flat rate	1	10.84 (b)	No

Note: Tax rates as of January 1, 2023; (a) Rates listed are the corporate income tax rate applied to financial institutions or excise taxes based on income. Some states have other taxes based upon the value of deposits or shares; (b) Minimum tax is $800 in California, $250 in District of Columbia, $50 in Arizona and North Dakota (banks), $400 ($100 banks) in Rhode Island, $200 per location in South Dakota (banks), $100 in Utah, $300 in Vermont.
Source: Federation of Tax Administrators, State Corporate Income Tax Rates, January 1, 2023

State Individual Income Tax Rates

State	Tax Rate (%)	Income Brackets ($)	Personal Exemptions ($)			Standard Ded. ($)	
			Single	Married	Depend.	Single	Married
California (a)	1.0 - 12.3 (g)	10,099 - 677,275 (b)	140	280	433 (c)	5,202	10,404 (a)

Note: Tax rates as of January 1, 2023; Local- and county-level taxes are not included; Federal income tax is not deductible on state income tax returns; (a) 16 states have statutory provision for automatically adjusting to the rate of inflation the dollar values of the income tax brackets, standard deductions, and/or personal exemptions. Oregon does not index the income brackets for $125,000 and over; (b) For joint returns, taxes are twice the tax on half the couple's income; (c) The personal exemption takes the form of a tax credit instead of a deduction; (g) California imposes an additional 1% tax on taxable income over $1 million, making the maximum rate 13.3% over $1 million.
Source: Federation of Tax Administrators, State Individual Income Tax Rates, January 1, 2023

Various State Sales and Excise Tax Rates

State	State Sales Tax (%)	Gasoline[1] ($/gal.)	Cigarette[2] ($/pack)	Spirits[3] ($/gal.)	Wine[4] ($/gal.)	Beer[5] ($/gal.)	Recreational Marijuana (%)
California	7.25	0.7766	2.87	3.30	0.20	0.20	(c)

Note: All tax rates as of January 1, 2023; (1) The American Petroleum Institute has developed a methodology for determining the average tax rate on a gallon of fuel. Rates may include any of the following: excise taxes, environmental fees, storage tank fees, other fees or taxes, general sales tax, and local taxes; (2) The federal excise tax of $1.0066 per pack and local taxes are not included; (3) Rates are those applicable to off-premise sales of 40% alcohol by volume (a.b.v.) distilled spirits in 750ml containers. Local excise taxes are excluded; (4) Rates are those applicable to off-premise sales of 11% a.b.v. non-carbonated wine in 750ml containers; (5) Rates are those applicable to off-premise sales of 4.7% a.b.v. beer in 12 ounce containers; (c) 15% excise tax (levied on wholesale at average market rate); $10.08/oz. flowers & $3/oz. leaves cultivation tax; $1.41/oz fresh cannabis plant
Source: Tax Foundation, 2023 Facts & Figures: How Does Your State Compare?

State Business Tax Climate Index Rankings

State	Overall Rank	Corporate Tax Rank	Individual Income Tax Rank	Sales Tax Rank	Property Tax Rank	Unemployment Insurance Tax Rank
California	48	46	49	47	19	24

Note: The index is a measure of how each state's tax laws affect economic performance. The lower the rank, the more favorable a state's tax system is for business. States without a given tax are given a ranking of 1. The scores/rankings for the District of Columbia do not affect other states. The 2023 index represents the tax climate as of July 1, 2022.
Source: Tax Foundation, State Business Tax Climate Index 2023

TRANSPORTATION

Means of Transportation to Work

Area	Car/Truck/Van		Public Transportation			Bicycle	Walked	Other Means	Worked at Home
	Drove Alone	Car-pooled	Bus	Subway	Railroad				
City	68.9	8.2	2.8	0.1	0.1	0.7	3.2	2.0	14.0
MSA[1]	71.6	8.4	2.0	0.1	0.1	0.5	2.9	2.0	12.5
U.S.	73.2	8.6	2.0	1.6	0.5	0.5	2.5	1.5	9.7

Note: Figures are percentages and cover workers 16 years of age and older; (1) Figures cover the San Diego-Chula Vista-Carlsbad, CA Metropolitan Statistical Area
Source: U.S. Census Bureau, 2017-2021 American Community Survey 5-Year Estimates

Travel Time to Work

Area	Less Than 10 Minutes	10 to 19 Minutes	20 to 29 Minutes	30 to 44 Minutes	45 to 59 Minutes	60 to 89 Minutes	90 Minutes or More
City	7.7	32.9	27.5	20.9	5.7	3.6	1.7
MSA[1]	8.1	29.4	24.5	23.5	7.5	5.0	2.1
U.S.	12.4	28.5	21.0	20.9	8.2	6.2	2.9

Note: Note: Figures are percentages and include workers 16 years old and over; (1) Figures cover the San Diego-Chula Vista-Carlsbad, CA Metropolitan Statistical Area
Source: U.S. Census Bureau, 2017-2021 American Community Survey 5-Year Estimates

Key Congestion Measures

Measure	1990	2000	2010	2015	2020
Annual Hours of Delay, Total (000)	41,751	85,177	115,240	138,187	55,433
Annual Hours of Delay, Per Auto Commuter	29	41	54	63	24
Annual Congestion Cost, Per Auto Commuter ($)	864	1,324	1,426	1,577	665

Note: Covers the San Diego CA urban area
Source: Texas A&M Transportation Institute, 2021 Urban Mobility Report

Freeway Travel Time Index

Measure	1985	1990	1995	2000	2005	2010	2015	2020
Urban Area Index[1]	1.10	1.14	1.16	1.22	1.27	1.30	1.34	1.10
Urban Area Rank[1,2]	27	26	32	24	18	12	9	29

Note: Freeway Travel Time Index—the ratio of travel time in the peak period to the travel time at free-flow conditions. For example, a value of 1.30 indicates a 20-minute free-flow trip takes 26 minutes in the peak (20 minutes x 1.30 = 26 minutes); (1) Covers the San Diego CA urban area; (2) Rank is based on 101 larger urban areas (#1 = highest travel time index)
Source: Texas A&M Transportation Institute, 2021 Urban Mobility Report

Public Transportation

Agency Name / Mode of Transportation	Vehicles Operated in Maximum Service[1]	Annual Unlinked Passenger Trips[2] (in thous.)	Annual Passenger Miles[3] (in thous.)
San Diego Metropolitan Transit System (MTS)			
Bus (directly operated)	225	8,604.0	45,773.7
Bus (purchased transportation)	290	10,953.3	42,281.4
Commuter Bus (purchased transportation)	9	34.0	887.8
Demand Response (purchased transportation)	41	92.4	928.0
Demand Response - Taxi	30	14.8	178.4
Light Rail (directly operated)	96	19,516.3	123,388.9
North San Diego County Transit District (NCTD)			
Bus (purchased transportation)	135	3,012.2	13,062.6
Commuter Rail (purchased transportation)	24	162.7	4,302.6
Demand Response (purchased transportation)	16	57.4	774.3
Hybrid Rail (purchased transportation)	8	1,225.4	8,938.9
San Diego Association of Governments (SANDAG)			
Vanpool (purchased transportation)	389	861.9	47,500.4

Note: (1) Number of revenue vehicles operated by the given mode and type of service to meet the annual maximum service requirement. This is the revenue vehicle count during the peak season of the year; on the week and day that maximum service is provided. Vehicles operated in maximum service (VOMS) exclude atypical days and one-time special events; (2) Number of passengers who boarded public transportation vehicles. Passengers are counted each time they board a vehicle no matter how many vehicles they use to travel from their origin to their destination. (3) Sum of the distances ridden by all passengers during the entire fiscal year.
Source: Federal Transit Administration, National Transit Database, 2021

Air Transportation

Airport Name and Code / Type of Service	Passenger Airlines[1]	Passenger Enplanements	Freight Carriers[2]	Freight (lbs)
San Diego International-Lindbergh Field (SAN)				
Domestic service (U.S. carriers - 2022)	26	10,802,011	11	129,277,364
International service (U.S. carriers - 2021)	6	83,109	2	2,314,855

Note: (1) Includes all U.S.-based major, minor and commuter airlines that carried at least one passenger during the year; (2) Includes all U.S.-based airlines and freight carriers that transported at least one pound of freight during the year.
Source: Bureau of Transportation Statistics, The Intermodal Transportation Database, Air Carriers: T-100 Domestic Market (U.S. Carriers), 2022; Bureau of Transportation Statistics, The Intermodal Transportation Database, Air Carriers: T-100 International Market (U.S. Carriers), 2021

BUSINESSES

Major Business Headquarters

Company Name	Industry	Rankings	
		Fortune[1]	Forbes[2]
LPL Financial Holdings	Securities	442	-
Qualcomm	Network and other communications equipment	107	-
Sempra	Electric and gas utilities	288	-

Note: (1) Companies that produce a 10-K are ranked 1 to 500 based on 2021 revenue; (2) All private companies with at least $2 billion in annual revenue through the end of their most current fiscal year are ranked 1 to 246; companies listed are headquartered in the city; dashes indicate no ranking
Source: Fortune, "Fortune 500," 2022; Forbes, "America's Largest Private Companies," 2022

Fastest-Growing Businesses

According to *Inc.*, San Diego is home to five of America's 500 fastest-growing private companies: **The San Diego Home Buyer** (#192); **Limelight Media** (#332); **Paint the Town** (#338); **BriteVox** (#383); **CFO Hub** (#419). Criteria: must be an independent, privately-held, for-profit, U.S. corporation, proprietorship or partnership as of December 31, 2021; revenues must be at least $100,000 in 2018 and $2 million in 2021; must have four-year operating/sales history. *Inc., "America's 500 Fastest-Growing Private Companies," 2022*

According to Deloitte, San Diego is home to 11 of North America's 500 fastest-growing high-technology companies: **ClickUp** (#14); **Avidity Biosciences** (#72); **MEI Pharma** (#82); **Anaptysbio** (#124); **Fate Therapeutics** (#135); **Maravai LifeSciences Holdings** (#270); **Mirati Therapeutics** (#315); **DermTech** (#361); **Cordial** (#398); **Tandem Diabetes Care** (#444); **SOCi** (#445). Companies are ranked by percentage growth in revenue over a four-year period. Criteria for inclusion: company must be headquartered within North America; must own proprietary intellectual property or technology that is sold to customers in products that contributes to a significant portion of the company's operating revenue; must have been in business for a minumum of four years with 2018 operating revenues of at least $50,000 USD/CD and 2021 operating revenues of at least $5 million USD/CD. *Deloitte, 2022 Technology Fast 500*^{TM}

Living Environment

COST OF LIVING

Cost of Living Index

Composite Index	Groceries	Housing	Utilities	Trans-portation	Health Care	Misc. Goods/Services
143.8	111.9	222.8	113.0	131.5	104.4	109.9

Note: The Cost of Living Index measures regional differences in the cost of consumer goods and services, excluding taxes and non-consumer expenditures, for professional and managerial households in the top income quintile. It is based on more than 50,000 prices covering almost 60 different items for which prices are collected three times a year by chambers of commerce, economic development organizations or university applied economic centers in each participating urban area. The numbers shown should be read as a percentage above or below the national average of 100. For example, a value of 115.4 in the groceries column indicates that grocery prices are 15.4% higher than the national average. Small differences in the index numbers should not be interpreted as significant; Figures cover the San Diego CA urban area.
Source: The Council for Community and Economic Research, Cost of Living Index, 2022

Grocery Prices

Area[1]	T-Bone Steak ($/pound)	Frying Chicken ($/pound)	Whole Milk ($/half gal.)	Eggs ($/dozen)	Orange Juice ($/64 oz.)	Coffee ($/11.5 oz.)
City[2]	14.80	1.85	2.70	3.71	4.32	5.91
Avg.	13.81	1.59	2.43	2.25	3.85	4.95
Min.	10.17	0.90	1.51	1.30	2.90	3.46
Max.	19.35	3.30	4.32	4.32	5.31	8.59

*Note: (1) Values for the local area are compared with the average, minimum and maximum values for all 286 areas in the Cost of Living Index; (2) Figures cover the San Diego CA urban area; **T-Bone Steak** (price per pound); **Frying Chicken** (price per pound, whole fryer); **Whole Milk** (half gallon carton); **Eggs** (price per dozen, Grade A, large); **Orange Juice** (64 oz. Tropicana or Florida Natural); **Coffee** (11.5 oz. can, vacuum-packed, Maxwell House, Hills Bros, or Folgers).*
Source: The Council for Community and Economic Research, Cost of Living Index, 2022

Housing and Utility Costs

Area[1]	New Home Price ($)	Apartment Rent ($/month)	All Electric ($/month)	Part Electric ($/month)	Other Energy ($/month)	Telephone ($/month)
City[2]	1,001,748	3,057	-	145.75	74.47	183.97
Avg.	450,913	1,371	176.41	99.93	76.96	190.22
Min.	229,283	546	100.84	31.56	27.15	174.27
Max.	2,434,977	4,569	356.86	249.59	272.24	208.31

*Note: (1) Values for the local area are compared with the average, minimum and maximum values for all 286 areas in the Cost of Living Index; (2) Figures cover the San Diego CA urban area; **New Home Price** (2,400 sf living area, 8,000 sf lot, in urban area with full utilities); **Apartment Rent** (950 sf 2 bedroom/1.5 or 2 bath, unfurnished, excluding all utilities except water); **All Electric** (average monthly cost for an all-electric home); **Part Electric** (average monthly cost for a part-electric home); **Other Energy** (average monthly cost for natural gas, fuel oil, coal, wood, and any other forms of energy except electricity); **Telephone** (price includes the base monthly rate plus taxes and fees for three lines of mobile phone service).*
Source: The Council for Community and Economic Research, Cost of Living Index, 2022

Health Care, Transportation, and Other Costs

Area[1]	Doctor ($/visit)	Dentist ($/visit)	Optometrist ($/visit)	Gasoline ($/gallon)	Beauty Salon ($/visit)	Men's Shirt ($)
City[2]	116.25	118.33	126.18	5.50	66.33	36.49
Avg.	124.91	107.77	117.66	3.86	43.31	34.21
Min.	36.61	58.25	51.79	2.90	22.18	13.05
Max.	250.21	162.58	371.96	5.54	85.61	63.54

*Note: (1) Values for the local area are compared with the average, minimum and maximum values for all 286 areas in the Cost of Living Index; (2) Figures cover the San Diego CA urban area; **Doctor** (general practitioners routine exam of an established patient); **Dentist** (adult teeth cleaning and periodic oral examination); **Optometrist** (full vision eye exam for established adult patient); **Gasoline** (one gallon regular unleaded, national brand, including all taxes, cash price at self-service pump if available); **Beauty Salon** (woman's shampoo, trim, and blow-dry); **Men's Shirt** (cotton/polyester dress shirt, pinpoint weave, long sleeves).*
Source: The Council for Community and Economic Research, Cost of Living Index, 2022

HOUSING

Homeownership Rate

Area	2015 (%)	2016 (%)	2017 (%)	2018 (%)	2019 (%)	2020 (%)	2021 (%)	2022 (%)
MSA[1]	51.8	53.3	56.0	56.1	56.7	57.8	52.6	51.6
U.S.	63.7	63.4	63.9	64.4	64.6	66.6	65.5	65.8

Note: (1) Figures cover the San Diego-Chula Vista-Carlsbad, CA Metropolitan Statistical Area
Source: U.S. Census Bureau, Housing Vacancies and Homeownership Annual Statistics: 2015-2022

House Price Index (HPI)

Area	National Ranking[2]	Quarterly Change (%)	One-Year Change (%)	Five-Year Change (%)	Since 1991Q1 (%)
MSA[1]	181	-2.11	9.62	51.34	344.82
U.S.[3]	–	0.34	8.41	58.44	289.08

Note: The HPI is a weighted repeat sales index. It measures average price changes in repeat sales or refinancings on the same properties. This information is obtained by reviewing repeat mortgage transactions on single-family properties whose mortgages have been purchased or securitized by Fannie Mae or Freddie Mac since January 1975; (1) Figures cover the San Diego-Carlsbad, CA Metropolitan Statistical Area; (2) Rankings are based on annual percentage change for all metro areas containing at least 15,000 transactions over the last 10 years and ranges from 1 to 257; (3) figures based on a weighted average of Census Division estimates using a seasonally adjusted, purchase-only index; all figures are for the period ending December 31, 2022
Source: Federal Housing Finance Agency, Change in FHFA Metropolitan Area House Price Indexes, 2022Q4

Median Single-Family Home Prices

Area	2020	2021	2022[p]	Percent Change 2021 to 2022
MSA[1]	710.0	830.0	911.0	9.8
U.S. Average	300.2	357.1	392.6	9.9

Note: Figures are median sales prices of existing single-family homes in thousands of dollars; (p) preliminary; (1) Figures cover the San Diego-Chula Vista-Carlsbad, CA Metropolitan Statistical Area
Source: National Association of Realtors, Median Sales Price of Existing Single-Family Homes for Metropolitan Areas, 4th Quarter 2022

Qualifying Income Based on Median Sales Price of Existing Single-Family Homes

Area	With 5% Down ($)	With 10% Down ($)	With 20% Down ($)
MSA[1]	256,401	242,906	215,916
U.S. Average	112,234	106,237	94,513

Note: Figures are preliminary; Qualifying income is based on a mortgage rate of 6.77%. Monthly principal and interest payment is limited to 25% of income; (1) Figures cover the San Diego-Chula Vista-Carlsbad, CA Metropolitan Statistical Area
Source: National Association of Realtors, Qualifying Income Based on Median Sales Price of Existing Single-Family Homes for Metropolitan Areas, 4th Quarter 2022

Home Value

Area	Under $100,000	$100,000 -$199,999	$200,000 -$299,999	$300,000 -$399,999	$400,000 -$499,999	$500,000 -$999,999	$1,000,000 or more	Median ($)
City	2.6	1.4	3.1	8.1	13.7	51.4	19.8	664,000
MSA[1]	4.2	2.2	3.5	7.9	14.3	52.3	15.7	627,200
U.S.	16.2	24.2	20.1	13.6	8.3	13.6	4.1	244,900

Note: Figures are percentages except for median and cover owner-occupied housing units; (1) Figures cover the San Diego-Chula Vista-Carlsbad, CA Metropolitan Statistical Area
Source: U.S. Census Bureau, 2017-2021 American Community Survey 5-Year Estimates

Year Housing Structure Built

Area	2020 or Later	2010 -2019	2000 -2009	1990 -1999	1980 -1989	1970 -1979	1960 -1969	1950 -1959	1940 -1949	Before 1940	Median Year
City	0.2	5.7	10.2	11.0	17.5	20.7	12.5	11.5	4.1	6.7	1977
MSA[1]	0.2	5.1	11.8	12.2	18.6	22.2	11.9	10.5	3.4	4.2	1979
U.S.	0.2	7.3	13.6	13.6	13.2	14.8	10.3	10.0	4.7	12.2	1979

Note: Figures are percentages except for Median Year; Note: (1) Figures cover the San Diego-Chula Vista-Carlsbad, CA Metropolitan Statistical Area
Source: U.S. Census Bureau, 2017-2021 American Community Survey 5-Year Estimates

Gross Monthly Rent

Area	Under $500	$500 -$999	$1,000 -$1,499	$1,500 -$1,999	$2,000 -$2,499	$2,500 -$2,999	$3,000 and up	Median ($)
City	2.7	6.1	19.8	27.8	21.3	11.6	10.7	1,885
MSA[1]	2.9	5.9	21.1	29.4	19.7	10.6	10.4	1,842
U.S.	8.1	30.5	30.8	16.8	7.3	3.1	3.5	1,163

Note: Figures are percentages except for median; Gross rent is the contract rent plus the estimated average monthly cost of utilities (electricity, gas, and water and sewer) and fuels (oil, coal, kerosene, wood, etc.) if these are paid by the renter (or paid for the renter by someone else); (1) Figures cover the San Diego-Chula Vista-Carlsbad, CA Metropolitan Statistical Area
Source: U.S. Census Bureau, 2017-2021 American Community Survey 5-Year Estimates

HEALTH

Health Risk Factors

Category	MSA[1] (%)	U.S. (%)
Adults aged 18–64 who have any kind of health care coverage	n/a	90.9
Adults who reported being in good or better health	n/a	85.2
Adults who have been told they have high blood cholesterol	n/a	35.7
Adults who have been told they have high blood pressure	n/a	32.4
Adults who are current smokers	n/a	14.4
Adults who currently use e-cigarettes	n/a	6.7
Adults who currently use chewing tobacco, snuff, or snus	n/a	3.5
Adults who are heavy drinkers[2]	n/a	6.3
Adults who are binge drinkers[3]	n/a	15.4
Adults who are overweight (BMI 25.0 - 29.9)	n/a	34.4
Adults who are obese (BMI 30.0 - 99.8)	n/a	33.9
Adults who participated in any physical activities in the past month	n/a	76.3

Note: (1) Figures for the San Diego-Chula Vista-Carlsbad, CA Metropolitan Statistical Area were not available.
(2) Heavy drinkers are classified as adult men having more than 14 drinks per week and adult women having more than 7 drinks per week; (3) Binge drinkers are classified as males having five or more drinks on one occasion or females having four or more drinks on one occasion
Source: Centers for Disease Control and Prevention, Behaviorial Risk Factor Surveillance System, SMART: Selected Metropolitan Area Risk Trends, 2021

Acute and Chronic Health Conditions

Category	MSA[1] (%)	U.S. (%)
Adults who have ever been told they had a heart attack	n/a	4.0
Adults who have ever been told they have angina or coronary heart disease	n/a	3.8
Adults who have ever been told they had a stroke	n/a	3.0
Adults who have ever been told they have asthma	n/a	14.9
Adults who have ever been told they have arthritis	n/a	25.8
Adults who have ever been told they have diabetes[2]	n/a	10.9
Adults who have ever been told they had skin cancer	n/a	6.6
Adults who have ever been told they had any other types of cancer	n/a	7.5
Adults who have ever been told they have COPD	n/a	6.1
Adults who have ever been told they have kidney disease	n/a	3.0
Adults who have ever been told they have a form of depression	n/a	20.5

Note: (1) Figures for the San Diego-Chula Vista-Carlsbad, CA Metropolitan Statistical Area were not available.
(2) Figures do not include pregnancy-related, borderline, or pre-diabetes
Source: Centers for Disease Control and Prevention, Behaviorial Risk Factor Surveillance System, SMART: Selected Metropolitan Area Risk Trends, 2021

Health Screening and Vaccination Rates

Category	MSA[1] (%)	U.S. (%)
Adults who have ever been tested for HIV	n/a	34.9
Adults who have had their blood cholesterol checked within the last five years	n/a	85.2
Adults aged 65+ who have had flu shot within the past year	n/a	68.6
Adults aged 65+ who have ever had a pneumonia vaccination	n/a	71.0

Note: (1) Figures for the San Diego-Chula Vista-Carlsbad, CA Metropolitan Statistical Area were not available.
Source: Centers for Disease Control and Prevention, Behaviorial Risk Factor Surveillance System, SMART: Selected Metropolitan Area Risk Trends, 2021

Disability Status

Category	MSA[1] (%)	U.S. (%)
Adults who reported being deaf	n/a	7.2
Are you blind or have serious difficulty seeing, even when wearing glasses?	n/a	4.8
Are you limited in any way in any of your usual activities due to arthritis?	n/a	11.1
Do you have difficulty doing errands alone?	n/a	7.0
Do you have difficulty dressing or bathing?	n/a	3.6
Do you have serious difficulty concentrating/remembering/making decisions?	n/a	12.1
Do you have serious difficulty walking or climbing stairs?	n/a	12.8

Note: (1) Figures for the San Diego-Chula Vista-Carlsbad, CA Metropolitan Statistical Area were not available.
Source: Centers for Disease Control and Prevention, Behaviorial Risk Factor Surveillance System, SMART: Selected Metropolitan Area Risk Trends, 2021

Mortality Rates for the Top 10 Causes of Death in the U.S.

ICD-10[a] Sub-Chapter	ICD-10[a] Code	Crude Mortality Rate[1] per 100,000 population	
		County[2]	U.S.
Malignant neoplasms	C00-C97	151.6	182.6
Ischaemic heart diseases	I20-I25	77.7	113.1
Other forms of heart disease	I30-I51	50.4	64.4
Other degenerative diseases of the nervous system	G30-G31	58.7	51.0
Cerebrovascular diseases	I60-I69	51.0	47.8
Other external causes of accidental injury	W00-X59	36.6	46.4
Chronic lower respiratory diseases	J40-J47	28.5	45.7
Organic, including symptomatic, mental disorders	F01-F09	19.1	35.9
Hypertensive diseases	I10-I15	29.1	35.0
Diabetes mellitus	E10-E14	25.3	29.6

Note: (a) ICD-10 = International Classification of Diseases 10th Revision; (1) Crude mortality rates are a three-year average covering 2019-2021; (2) Figures cover San Diego County.
Source: Centers for Disease Control and Prevention, National Center for Health Statistics. National Vital Statistics System, Mortality 2018-2021 on CDC WONDER Online Database

Mortality Rates for Selected Causes of Death

ICD-10[a] Sub-Chapter	ICD-10[a] Code	Crude Mortality Rate[1] per 100,000 population	
		County[2]	U.S.
Assault	X85-Y09	3.1	7.0
Diseases of the liver	K70-K76	14.7	19.8
Human immunodeficiency virus (HIV) disease	B20-B24	1.3	1.5
Influenza and pneumonia	J09-J18	7.6	14.7
Intentional self-harm	X60-X84	11.9	14.3
Malnutrition	E40-E46	3.8	4.3
Obesity and other hyperalimentation	E65-E68	2.0	3.0
Renal failure	N17-N19	3.6	15.7
Transport accidents	V01-V99	10.0	13.6
Viral hepatitis	B15-B19	1.5	1.2

Note: (a) ICD-10 = International Classification of Diseases 10th Revision; (1) Crude mortality rates are a three-year average covering 2019-2021; (2) Figures cover San Diego County; Data are suppressed when the data meet the criteria for confidentiality constraints; Crude mortality rates are flagged as unreliable when the rate would be calculated with a numerator of 20 or less.
Source: Centers for Disease Control and Prevention, National Center for Health Statistics. National Vital Statistics System, Mortality 2018-2021 on CDC WONDER Online Database

Health Insurance Coverage

Area	With Health Insurance	With Private Health Insurance	With Public Health Insurance	Without Health Insurance	Population Under Age 19 Without Health Insurance
City	92.8	71.1	31.1	7.2	3.7
MSA[1]	92.5	69.4	33.6	7.5	3.9
U.S.	91.2	67.8	35.4	8.8	5.3

Note: Figures are percentages that cover the civilian noninstitutionalized population; (1) Figures cover the San Diego-Chula Vista-Carlsbad, CA Metropolitan Statistical Area
Source: U.S. Census Bureau, 2017-2021 American Community Survey 5-Year Estimates

Number of Medical Professionals

Area	MDs[3]	DOs[3,4]	Dentists	Podiatrists	Chiropractors	Optometrists
County[1] (number)	11,417	649	3,165	153	1,166	670
County[1] (rate[2])	346.3	19.7	96.3	4.7	35.5	20.4
U.S. (rate[2])	289.3	23.5	72.5	6.2	28.7	17.4

Note: Data as of 2021 unless noted; (1) Data covers San Diego County; (2) Rate per 100,000 population; (3) Data as of 2020 and includes all active, non-federal physicians; (4) Doctor of Osteopathic Medicine
Source: U.S. Department of Health and Human Services, Health Resources and Services Administration, Bureau of Health Professions, Area Resource File (ARF) 2021-2022

Best Hospitals

According to *U.S. News,* the San Diego-Chula Vista-Carlsbad, CA metro area is home to five of the best hospitals in the U.S.: **Scripps La Jolla Hospitals** (5 adult specialties); **Sharp Memorial Hospital** (2 adult specialties); **UC San Diego Health-Cardiovascular Institute** (10 adult specialties); **UC San Diego Health-La Jolla and Hillcrest Hospitals** (10 adult specialties); **UC San Diego Health-Moores Cancer Center** (10 adult specialties). The hospitals listed were nationally ranked in at least one of 15 adult or 10 pediatric specialties. The number of specialties shown cover the parent hospital. Only 164 U.S. hospitals performed well enough to be nationally ranked in one or more specialties. Twenty hospitals in the U.S. made the Honor Roll. The Best Hospitals Honor Roll takes both the national rankings and the procedure and condition ratings into account. Hospitals received points if they were nationally ranked in one of the 15 adult specialties—the higher they ranked, the more points they got—and how many ratings of "high performing" they earned in the 17 procedures and conditions. *U.S. News Online, "America's Best Hospitals 2022-23"*

According to *U.S. News,* the San Diego-Chula Vista-Carlsbad, CA metro area is home to one of the best children's hospitals in the U.S.: **Rady Children's Hospital** (10 pediatric specialties). The hospital listed was highly ranked in at least one of 10 pediatric specialties. Eighty-six children's hospitals in the U.S. were nationally ranked in at least one specialty. Hospitals received points for being ranked in a specialty, and the 10 hospitals with the most points across the 10 specialties make up the Honor Roll. *U.S. News Online, "America's Best Children's Hospitals 2022-23"*

EDUCATION

Public School District Statistics

District Name	Schls	Pupils	Pupil/ Teacher Ratio	Minority Pupils[1] (%)	LEP/ELL[2] (%)	IEP[3] (%)
Del Mar Union Elementary	8	3,895	19.8	55.5	11.8	14.4
Poway Unified	38	35,192	23.4	60.5	11.1	13.0
San Diego Unified	176	95,233	22.2	76.4	20.9	14.8

Note: Table includes school districts with 2,000 or more students; (1) Percentage of students that are not non-Hispanic white; (2) Percentage of students that are Limited English Proficient or English Language Learners (2018-19); (3) Percentage of students that have an Individualized Education Program (2019-20).
Source: U.S. Department of Education, National Center for Education Statistics, Common Core of Data, Local Education Agency (School District) Universe Survey: School Year 2021-2022

Best High Schools

According to *U.S. News,* San Diego is home to four of the top 500 high schools in the U.S.: **Preuss School UCSD** (#71); **Canyon Crest Academy** (#156); **Del Norte High School** (#314); **Westview High School** (#421). Nearly 18,000 public, magnet and charter schools were ranked based on their performance on state assessments and how well they prepare students for college. *U.S. News & World Report, "Best High Schools 2022"*

Highest Level of Education

Area	Less than H.S.	H.S. Diploma	Some College, No Deg.	Associate Degree	Bachelor's Degree	Master's Degree	Prof. School Degree	Doctorate Degree
City	10.7	15.4	18.6	7.7	27.9	12.8	3.6	3.4
MSA[1]	11.7	18.2	21.5	8.4	24.5	10.5	2.9	2.3
U.S.	11.1	26.5	20.0	8.7	20.6	9.3	2.2	1.5

Note: Figures cover persons age 25 and over; (1) Figures cover the San Diego-Chula Vista-Carlsbad, CA Metropolitan Statistical Area
Source: U.S. Census Bureau, 2017-2021 American Community Survey 5-Year Estimates

Educational Attainment by Race

Area	High School Graduate or Higher (%)					Bachelor's Degree or Higher (%)				
	Total	White	Black	Asian	Hisp.[2]	Total	White	Black	Asian	Hisp.[2]
City	89.3	91.8	91.2	89.2	73.4	47.6	52.0	28.3	55.1	22.6
MSA[1]	88.3	90.8	91.6	90.0	73.1	40.3	43.2	27.4	53.0	19.6
U.S.	88.9	91.4	87.2	87.6	71.2	33.7	35.5	23.3	55.6	18.4

Note: Figures shown cover persons 25 years old and over; (1) Figures cover the San Diego-Chula Vista-Carlsbad, CA Metropolitan Statistical Area; (2) People of Hispanic origin can be of any race
Source: U.S. Census Bureau, 2017-2021 American Community Survey 5-Year Estimates

School Enrollment by Grade and Control

Area	Preschool (%)		Kindergarten (%)		Grades 1 - 4 (%)		Grades 5 - 8 (%)		Grades 9 - 12 (%)	
	Public	Private	Public	Private	Public	Private	Public	Private	Public	Private
City	46.8	53.2	89.4	10.6	90.4	9.6	91.7	8.3	91.2	8.8
MSA[1]	49.0	51.0	89.7	10.3	90.8	9.2	91.8	8.2	92.3	7.7
U.S.	58.8	41.2	86.3	13.7	88.3	11.7	88.6	11.4	89.4	10.6

Note: Figures shown cover persons 3 years old and over; (1) Figures cover the San Diego-Chula Vista-Carlsbad, CA Metropolitan Statistical Area
Source: U.S. Census Bureau, 2017-2021 American Community Survey 5-Year Estimates

Higher Education

Four-Year Colleges			Two-Year Colleges			Medical Schools[1]	Law Schools[2]	Voc/ Tech[3]
Public	Private Non-profit	Private For-profit	Public	Private Non-profit	Private For-profit			
5	16	12	6	0	10	1	4	15

Note: Figures cover institutions located within the San Diego-Chula Vista-Carlsbad, CA Metropolitan Statistical Area and include main campuses only; (1) includes schools accredited by the Liaison Committee on Medical Education and the American Osteopathic Association's Commission on Osteopathic College Accreditation; (2) includes ABA-accredited schools, schools with provisional ABA accreditation, and state accredited schools; (3) includes all schools with programs that are less than 2 years.
Source: National Center for Education Statistics, Integrated Postsecondary Education System (IPEDS), 2021-22; Wikipedia, List of Medical Schools in the United States, accessed April 10, 2023; Wikipedia, List of Law Schools in the United States, accessed April 10, 2023

According to *U.S. News & World Report,* the San Diego-Chula Vista-Carlsbad, CA metro area is home to three of the top 200 national universities in the U.S.: **University of California—San Diego** (#34 tie); **University of San Diego** (#97 tie); **San Diego State University** (#151 tie). The indicators used to capture academic quality fall into a number of categories: assessment by administrators at peer institutions; retention of students; faculty resources; student selectivity; financial resources; alumni giving; high school counselor ratings of colleges; and graduation rate. *U.S. News & World Report, "America's Best Colleges 2023"*

According to *U.S. News & World Report,* the San Diego-Chula Vista-Carlsbad, CA metro area is home to one of the top 100 law schools in the U.S.: **University of San Diego** (#64 tie). The rankings are based on a weighted average of 12 measures of quality: peer assessment score; assessment score by lawyers/judges; median LSAT scores; median undergrad GPA; acceptance rate; employment rates for graduates; placement success; bar passage rate; faculty resources; expenditures per student; student/faculty ratio; and library resources. *U.S. News & World Report, "America's Best Graduate Schools, Law, 2023"*

According to *U.S. News & World Report,* the San Diego-Chula Vista-Carlsbad, CA metro area is home to one of the top 75 medical schools for research in the U.S.: **University of California—San Diego** (#20 tie). The rankings are based on a weighted average of 11 measures of quality: quality assessment; peer assessment score; assessment score by residency directors; research activity; total research activity; average research activity per faculty member; student selectivity; median MCAT total score; median undergraduate GPA; acceptance rate; and faculty resources. *U.S. News & World Report, "America's Best Graduate Schools, Medical, 2023"*

EMPLOYERS

Major Employers

Company Name	Industry
Barona Resort & Casino	Resort hotels
CA Dept of Forestry and Fire Protection	Fire department, not including volunteer
CA Dept of Housing & Comm Dev	Housing agency, government
City of San Diego	Municipal government
Elite Show Services	Help supply services
Go-Staff	Temporary help services
Kaiser Foundation Hospitals	Trusts, nec
Palomar Community College District	Junior colleges
Qualcomm International	Patent buying, licensing, leasing
Risk Management Strategies	Employee programs administration
San Diego State University	Colleges & universities
Sharp Memorial Hospital	General medical & surgical hospitals
Solar Turbines Incorporated	Turbines & turbine generator sets
U.S. Marine Corps	Marine corps
U.S. Navy	U.S. military
University of California, San Diego	General medical & surgical hospitals
Veterans Health Administration	Administration of veterans' affairs

Note: Companies shown are located within the San Diego-Chula Vista-Carlsbad, CA Metropolitan Statistical Area.
Source: Hoovers.com; Wikipedia

Best Companies to Work For

Scripps Health, headquartered in San Diego, is among "The 100 Best Companies to Work For." To pick the best companies, *Fortune* partnered with the Great Place to Work Institute. Two-thirds of a company's score is based on the results of the Institute's Trust Index survey, which is sent to a random sample of employees from each company. The questions related to attitudes about management's credibility, job satisfaction, and camaraderie. The other third of the scoring is based on the company's responses to the Institute's Culture Audit, which includes detailed questions about pay and benefit programs, and a series of open-ended questions about hiring practices, internal communication, training, recognition programs, and diversity efforts. Any company that is at least five years old with more than 1,000 U.S. employees is eligible. *Fortune, "The 100 Best Companies to Work For," 2023*

Aya Healthcare; Scripps Health, headquartered in San Diego, are among "Best Workplaces in Health Care." To determine the Best Workplaces in Health Care list, Great Place To Work analyzed the survey responses of over 161,000 employees from Great Place To Work-Certified companies in the health care industry. Survey data analysis and company-provided datapoints are then factored into a combined score to compare and rank the companies that create the most consistently positive experience for all employees in this industry. *Fortune, "Best Workplaces in Health Care," 2022*

Seismic Software; WestPac Wealth Partners, headquartered in San Diego, are among "Fortune's Best Workplaces for Parents." To pick the best companies, *Fortune* partnered with the Great Place to Work Institute. To be considered for the list, companies must be Great Place To Work-Certified and have at least 50 responses from parents in the US. The survey enables employees to share confidential quantitative and qualitative feedback about their organization's culture by responding to 60 statements on a 5-point scale and answering two open-ended questions. Collectively, these statements describe a great employee experience, defined by high levels of trust, respect, credibility, fairness, pride, and camaraderie. In addition, companies provide organizational data like size, location, industry, demographics, roles, and levels; and provide information about parental leave, adoption, flexible schedule, childcare and dependent health care benefits. *Fortune, "Best Workplaces for Parents," 2022*

San Diego Gas & Electric and Southern California Gas Company, headquartered in San Diego, is among the "100 Best Places to Work in IT." To qualify, companies had to have a minimum of 100 total employees and five IT employees. The best places to work were selected based on DEI (diversity, equity, and inclusion) practices; IT turnover, promotions, and growth; IT retention and engagement programs; remote/hybrid working; benefits and perks (such as elder care and child care, flextime, and reimbursement for college tuition); and training and career development opportunities. *Computerworld, "Best Places to Work in IT," 2023*

PUBLIC SAFETY

Crime Rate

Area	Total Crime	Violent Crime Rate				Property Crime Rate		
		Murder	Rape[3]	Robbery	Aggrav. Assault	Burglary	Larceny -Theft	Motor Vehicle Theft
City	2,060.6	3.9	33.7	84.0	247.3	231.2	1,116.0	344.5
Suburbs[1]	1,655.8	3.1	25.4	69.7	229.9	210.0	887.9	229.9
Metro[2]	1,830.5	3.4	29.0	75.8	237.4	219.1	986.3	279.3
U.S.	2,356.7	6.5	38.4	73.9	279.7	314.2	1,398.0	246.0

Note: Figures are crimes per 100,000 population; (1) All areas within the metro area that are located outside the city limits; (2) Figures cover the San Diego-Carlsbad, CA Metropolitan Statistical Area; (3) All figures shown were reported using the revised Uniform Crime Reporting (UCR) definition of rape; Due to the transition to the National Incident-Based Reporting System (NIBRS), limited city and metro area data was released for 2021.
Source: FBI Uniform Crime Reports, 2020

Hate Crimes

Area	Number of Quarters Reported	Number of Incidents per Bias Motivation					
		Race/Ethnicity/ Ancestry	Religion	Sexual Orientation	Disability	Gender	Gender Identity
City	4	17	1	7	0	0	1
U.S.	4	5,227	1,244	1,110	130	75	266

Note: Due to the transition to the National Incident-Based Reporting System (NIBRS), limited crime data was released for 2021.
Source: Federal Bureau of Investigation, Hate Crime Statistics 2020

Identity Theft Consumer Reports

Area	Reports	Reports per 100,000 Population	Rank[2]
MSA[1]	8,412	253	103
U.S.	1,108,609	339	-

Note: (1) Figures cover the San Diego-Chula Vista-Carlsbad, CA Metropolitan Statistical Area; (2) Rank ranges from 1 to 391 where 1 indicates greatest number of identity theft reports per 100,000 population
Source: Federal Trade Commission, Consumer Sentinel Network Data Book 2022

Fraud and Other Consumer Reports

Area	Reports	Reports per 100,000 Population	Rank[2]
MSA[1]	34,142	1,027	86
U.S.	4,064,520	1,245	-

Note: (1) Figures cover the San Diego-Chula Vista-Carlsbad, CA Metropolitan Statistical Area; (2) Rank ranges from 1 to 391 where 1 indicates greatest number of fraud and other consumer reports per 100,000 population
Source: Federal Trade Commission, Consumer Sentinel Network Data Book 2022

POLITICS

2020 Presidential Election Results

Area	Biden	Trump	Jorgensen	Hawkins	Other
San Diego County	60.2	37.5	1.3	0.5	0.5
U.S.	51.3	46.8	1.2	0.3	0.5

Note: Results are percentages and may not add to 100% due to rounding
Source: Dave Leip's Atlas of U.S. Presidential Elections

SPORTS

Professional Sports Teams

Team Name	League	Year Established
San Diego Padres	Major League Baseball (MLB)	1969

Note: Includes teams located in the San Diego-Chula Vista-Carlsbad, CA Metropolitan Statistical Area.
Source: Wikipedia, Major Professional Sports Teams of the United States and Canada, April 12, 2023

CLIMATE

Average and Extreme Temperatures

Temperature	Jan	Feb	Mar	Apr	May	Jun	Jul	Aug	Sep	Oct	Nov	Dec	Yr.
Extreme High (°F)	88	88	93	98	96	101	95	98	111	107	97	88	111
Average High (°F)	65	66	66	68	69	72	76	77	77	74	71	66	71
Average Temp. (°F)	57	58	59	62	64	67	71	72	71	67	62	58	64
Average Low (°F)	48	50	52	55	58	61	65	66	65	60	53	49	57
Extreme Low (°F)	29	36	39	44	48	51	55	58	51	43	38	34	29

Note: Figures cover the years 1948-1990
Source: National Climatic Data Center, International Station Meteorological Climate Summary, 9/96

Average Precipitation/Snowfall/Humidity

Precip./Humidity	Jan	Feb	Mar	Apr	May	Jun	Jul	Aug	Sep	Oct	Nov	Dec	Yr.
Avg. Precip. (in.)	1.9	1.4	1.7	0.8	0.2	0.1	Tr	0.1	0.2	0.4	1.2	1.4	9.5
Avg. Snowfall (in.)	Tr	0	0	0	0	0	0	0	0	0	0	Tr	Tr
Avg. Rel. Hum. 7am (%)	70	72	73	72	73	77	79	79	78	74	69	68	74
Avg. Rel. Hum. 4pm (%)	57	58	59	59	63	66	65	66	65	63	60	58	62

Note: Figures cover the years 1948-1990; Tr = Trace amounts (<0.05 in. of rain; <0.5 in. of snow)
Source: National Climatic Data Center, International Station Meteorological Climate Summary, 9/96

Weather Conditions

Temperature			Daytime Sky			Precipitation		
10°F & below	32°F & below	90°F & above	Clear	Partly cloudy	Cloudy	0.01 inch or more precip.	0.1 inch or more snow/ice	Thunder-storms
0	< 1	4	115	126	124	40	0	5

Note: Figures are average number of days per year and cover the years 1948-1990
Source: National Climatic Data Center, International Station Meteorological Climate Summary, 9/96

HAZARDOUS WASTE

Superfund Sites

The San Diego-Chula Vista-Carlsbad, CA metro area is home to one site on the EPA's Superfund National Priorities List: **Camp Pendleton Marine Corps Base** (final). There are a total of 1,165 Superfund sites with a status of proposed or final on the list in the U.S. *U.S. Environmental Protection Agency, National Priorities List, April 12, 2023*

AIR QUALITY

Air Quality Trends: Ozone

	1990	1995	2000	2005	2010	2015	2018	2019	2020	2021
MSA[1]	0.110	0.085	0.079	0.074	0.073	0.068	0.069	0.069	0.078	0.068
U.S.	0.087	0.089	0.081	0.080	0.072	0.067	0.069	0.065	0.065	0.067

Note: (1) Data covers the San Diego-Chula Vista-Carlsbad, CA Metropolitan Statistical Area. The values shown are the composite ozone concentration averages among trend sites based on the highest fourth daily maximum 8-hour concentration in parts per million. These trends are based on sites having an adequate record of monitoring data during the trend period. Data from exceptional events are included.
Source: U.S. Environmental Protection Agency, Air Quality Monitoring Information, "Air Quality Trends by City, 1990-2021"

Air Quality Index

Area	Percent of Days when Air Quality was...[2]					AQI Statistics[2]	
	Good	Moderate	Unhealthy for Sensitive Groups	Unhealthy	Very Unhealthy	Maximum	Median
MSA[1]	26.8	68.8	4.4	0.0	0.0	133	64

Note: (1) Data covers the San Diego-Chula Vista-Carlsbad, CA Metropolitan Statistical Area; (2) Based on 365 days with AQI data in 2021. Air Quality Index (AQI) is an index for reporting daily air quality. EPA calculates the AQI for five major air pollutants regulated by the Clean Air Act: ground-level ozone, particle pollution (aka particulate matter), carbon monoxide, sulfur dioxide, and nitrogen dioxide. The AQI runs from 0 to 500. The higher the AQI value, the greater the level of air pollution and the greater the health concern. There are six AQI categories: "Good" AQI is between 0 and 50. Air quality is considered satisfactory; "Moderate" AQI is between 51 and 100. Air quality is acceptable; "Unhealthy for Sensitive Groups" When AQI values are between 101 and 150, members of sensitive groups may experience health effects; "Unhealthy" When AQI values are between 151 and 200 everyone may begin to experience health effects; "Very Unhealthy" AQI values between 201 and 300 trigger a health alert; "Hazardous" AQI values over 300 trigger warnings of emergency conditions (not shown).
Source: U.S. Environmental Protection Agency, Air Quality Index Report, 2021

Air Quality Index Pollutants

Area	Percent of Days when AQI Pollutant was...[2]					
	Carbon Monoxide	Nitrogen Dioxide	Ozone	Sulfur Dioxide	Particulate Matter 2.5	Particulate Matter 10
MSA[1]	0.0	1.1	59.5	(3)	38.6	0.8

Note: (1) Data covers the San Diego-Chula Vista-Carlsbad, CA Metropolitan Statistical Area; (2) Based on 365 days with AQI data in 2021. The Air Quality Index (AQI) is an index for reporting daily air quality. EPA calculates the AQI for five major air pollutants regulated by the Clean Air Act: ground-level ozone, particle pollution (also known as particulate matter), carbon monoxide, sulfur dioxide, and nitrogen dioxide. The AQI runs from 0 to 500. The higher the AQI value, the greater the level of air pollution and the greater the health concern; (3) Sulfur dioxide is no longer included in this table (as of December 8, 2021) because SO_2 concentrations tend to be very localized and not necessarily representative of broad geographical areas like counties and CBSAs.
Source: U.S. Environmental Protection Agency, Air Quality Index Report, 2021

Maximum Air Pollutant Concentrations: Particulate Matter, Ozone, CO and Lead

	Particulate Matter 10 (ug/m^3)	Particulate Matter 2.5 Wtd AM (ug/m^3)	Particulate Matter 2.5 24-Hr (ug/m^3)	Ozone (ppm)	Carbon Monoxide (ppm)	Lead (ug/m^3)
MSA[1] Level	119	11.2	24	0.078	1	0.02
NAAQS[2]	150	15	35	0.075	9	0.15
Met NAAQS[2]	Yes	Yes	Yes	No	Yes	Yes

Note: (1) Data covers the San Diego-Chula Vista-Carlsbad, CA Metropolitan Statistical Area; Data from exceptional events are included; (2) National Ambient Air Quality Standards; ppm = parts per million; ug/m^3 = micrograms per cubic meter; n/a not available.
Concentrations: Particulate Matter 10 (coarse particulate)—highest second maximum 24-hour concentration; Particulate Matter 2.5 Wtd AM (fine particulate)—highest weighted annual mean concentration; Particulate Matter 2.5 24-Hour (fine particulate)—highest 98th percentile 24-hour concentration; Ozone—highest fourth daily maximum 8-hour concentration; Carbon Monoxide—highest second maximum non-overlapping 8-hour concentration; Lead—maximum running 3-month average
Source: U.S. Environmental Protection Agency, Air Quality Monitoring Information, "Air Quality Statistics by City, 2021"

Maximum Air Pollutant Concentrations: Nitrogen Dioxide and Sulfur Dioxide

	Nitrogen Dioxide AM (ppb)	Nitrogen Dioxide 1-Hr (ppb)	Sulfur Dioxide AM (ppb)	Sulfur Dioxide 1-Hr (ppb)	Sulfur Dioxide 24-Hr (ppb)
MSA[1] Level	13	54	n/a	1	n/a
NAAQS[2]	53	100	30	75	140
Met NAAQS[2]	Yes	Yes	n/a	Yes	n/a

Note: (1) Data covers the San Diego-Chula Vista-Carlsbad, CA Metropolitan Statistical Area; Data from exceptional events are included; (2) National Ambient Air Quality Standards; ppm = parts per million; ug/m^3 = micrograms per cubic meter; n/a not available.
Concentrations: Nitrogen Dioxide AM—highest arithmetic mean concentration; Nitrogen Dioxide 1-Hr—highest 98th percentile 1-hour daily maximum concentration; Sulfur Dioxide AM—highest annual mean concentration; Sulfur Dioxide 1-Hr—highest 99th percentile 1-hour daily maximum concentration; Sulfur Dioxide 24-Hr—highest second maximum 24-hour concentration
Source: U.S. Environmental Protection Agency, Air Quality Monitoring Information, "Air Quality Statistics by City, 2021"

San Francisco, California

Background

San Francisco is one of the most beautiful cities in the world. It is blessed with a mild climate, one of the best landlocked harbors in the world, and a strong sense of civic pride shaped by its unique history.

The hilly peninsula known today as San Francisco and its bay was largely ignored by explorers during the sixteenth and seventeenth centuries. Until the 1760s, Europeans had not seen the "Golden Gate" or the narrow strip of water leading into what was to become one of the greatest harbors in the world. San Francisco remained a quiet and pastoral settlement for nearly 90 years, until the discovery of gold in the Sierra Nevada foothills in 1848, which changed San Francisco forever. Every hopeful adventurer from around the world docked in San Francisco, aspiring to make his fortune, creating a rowdy, frontier, gold-prospecting town, with plenty of gambling houses and saloons.

When the supply of gold dwindled around 1855, many gold miners went back to their native countries. Those that stayed continued to live in the ethnic neighborhoods they had created—neighborhoods that still exist today, such as Chinatown, the Italian District, and Japan Center.

The present-day charm of San Francisco lies in its cosmopolitan, yet cohesive, flavor. The city has long embraced a significant gay community, and was home to the first lesbian-rights organization in the United States, Daughters of Bilitis; the first openly gay person to run for public office in the United States, José Sarria; the first openly gay man to be elected to public office in California, Harvey Milk; the first openly lesbian judge appointed in the U.S., Mary C. Morgan; and the first transgender police commissioner, Theresa Sparks.

The San Francisco Bay Area is part of the Silicon Valley—the region in Northern California that serves as a global center for high technology and innovation. As such, it is one of the major economic regions of the United States, with one of the highest percentages of college-educated adults and per-capita income in the nation. The Bay Area is home to seven Fortune 500 companies, and major employers include Lyft, Securitize, Wells Fargo, and Wanda. Twenty percent of California's environmental companies live in San Francisco, which has the largest concentration of biotech companies in the state. A former warehouse district in San Francisco has become the center for nearly 400 multimedia and technology companies. Silicon Valley accounts for about one-third of the nation's high-technology exports.

AT&T Park, home of the San Francisco Giants major league baseball team, was completed in 2000; the Giants won the World Series in 2010, 2012, and 2014, and the Golden State Warriors won the 2022 NBA championship. The city offers excellent convention facilities with its Moscone Center, which comprises 770,000 square feet of exhibit space. The center was named for Mayor George Moscone, who championed controversial causes and who was murdered in office in 1978, along with gay activist Harvey Milk. The film, *The Times of Harvey Milk* won the 2008 Academy Award for best picture.

The Fine Arts Museums of San Francisco include the de Young, the city's oldest museum, and the Legion of Honor, home to Rodin's *Thinker*. In 2005, the de Young reopened in a new space in Golden Gate Park, replacing a structure damaged by the 1989 earthquake.

Also damaged in that quake was the main facility of the California Academy of Sciences, which oversees the Steinhart Aquarium, the Morrison Planetarium, and the Natural History Museum and which also reopened in Golden Gate Park in 2008. Architect Renzo Piano designed the building to be seismically safe, green, and sustainable, which allows outside views from nearly anywhere inside.

San Francisco is known as the "Air-Conditioned City" with cool pleasant summers and mild winters. It has greater climatic variability than any other urban area of the same size in the country. Sea fogs and associated low stratus clouds are most common in the summertime.

Rankings

General Rankings

- *US News & World Report* conducted a survey of more than 3,600 people and analyzed the 150 largest metropolitan areas to determine what matters most when selecting where to settle down. San Francisco ranked #10 out of the top 25 as having the best combination of desirable factors. Criteria: cost of living; quality of life and education; net migration; job market; desirability; and other factors. *money.usnews.com, "The 25 Best Places to Live in the U.S. in 2022-2023," May 17, 2022*

- *Insider* listed 23 places in the U.S. that travel industry trends reveal would be popular destinations in 2023. This year the list trends towards cultural and historical happenings, sports events, wellness experiences and invigorating outdoor escapes. According to the website insider.com San Francisco is a place to visit in 2023. *Insider, "23 of the Best Places You Should Travel to in the U.S. in 2023," December 17, 2022*

- The San Francisco metro area was identified as one of America's fastest-growing areas in terms of population and business growth by *MagnifyMoney*. The area ranked #22 out of 35. The 100 most populous metro areas in the U.S. were evaluated on their change from 2011 to 2016 in the following categories: people and housing; workforce and employment opportunities; growing industry. *www.businessinsider.com, "The 35 Cities in the US with the Biggest Influx of People, the Most Work Opportunities, and the Hottest Business Growth," August 12, 2018*

- San Francisco was selected as one of the best places in the world that are "under the radar, ahead of the curve, and ready for exploring" by *National Geographic Travel* editors. The list reflects 25 of the most extraordinary and inspiring destinations that also support local communities and ecosystems. These timeless must-see sites for 2023, are framed by the five categories of Culture, Family, Adventure, Community, and Nature. *www.nationalgeographic.com/travel, "Best of the World, 25 Breathtaking Places And Experiences for 2023," October 26, 2022*

- The human resources consulting firm Mercer ranked 231 major cities worldwide in terms of overall quality of life. San Francisco ranked #34. Criteria: political, social, economic, and socio-cultural factors; medical and health considerations; schools and education; public services and transportation; recreation; consumer goods; housing; and natural environment. *Mercer, "Mercer 2019 Quality of Living Survey," March 13, 2019*

- For its 35th annual "Readers' Choice Awards" survey, *Condé Nast Traveler* ranked its readers' favorite cities in the U.S. Whether it be a longed-for visit or a first on the list, these are the places that inspired a return to travel. The list was broken into large cities and cities under 250,000. San Francisco ranked #7 in the big city category. *Condé Nast Traveler, Readers' Choice Awards 2022, "Best Big Cities in the U.S." October 4, 2022*

Business/Finance Rankings

- According to *Business Insider*, the San Francisco metro area is a prime place to run a startup or move an existing business to. The area ranked #2. More than 300 metro areas were analyzed for factors that were of top concern to new business owners. Data was based on the 2019 U.S. Census Bureau American Community Survey, statistics from the CDC, Bureau of Labor Statistics employment report, and University of Chicago analysis. Criteria: business formations; percentage of vaccinated population; percentage of households with internet subscriptions; median household income; and share of work that can be done from home. *www.businessinsider.com, "The 20 Best Cities for Starting a Business in 2022 Include Baltimore, Boulder, and Boston," January 5, 2022*

- The Brookings Institution ranked the nation's largest cities based on income inequality. San Francisco was ranked #6 (#1 = greatest inequality). Criteria: the "95/20 ratio," a figure representing the income at which a household earns more than 95 percent of all other households, divided by the income at which a household earns more than only 20 percent of all other households. *Brookings Institution, "Household Income Inequality, Largest Cities of 97 Large U.S. Metro Areas, 2014-2016," February 5, 2018*

- The Brookings Institution ranked the 100 largest metro areas in the U.S. based on income inequality. San Francisco was ranked #3 (#1 = greatest inequality). Criteria: the "95/20 ratio," a figure representing the income at which a household earns more than 95 percent of all other households, divided by the income at which a household earns more than only 20 percent of all other households. *Brookings Institution, "Household Income Inequality, 100 Largest U.S. Metro Areas, 2014-2016," February 5, 2018*

- Payscale.com ranked the 32 largest metro areas in terms of wage growth. The San Francisco metro area ranked #31. Criteria: quarterly changes in private industry employee and education professional wage growth from the previous year. *PayScale, "Wage Trends by Metro Area-1st Quarter," April 20, 2023*

- The San Francisco metro area was identified as one of the most debt-ridden places in America by the finance site Credit.com. The metro area was ranked #15. Criteria: residents' average credit card debt as well as median income. *Credit.com, "25 Cities With the Most Credit Card Debt," February 28, 2018*

- For its annual survey of the "Most Expensive U.S. Cities to Live In," Kiplinger applied Cost of Living Index statistics developed by the Council for Community and Economic Research to U.S. Census Bureau population and median household income data for 265 urban areas. San Francisco ranked #3 among the most expensive in the country. *Kiplinger.com, "The 11 Most Expensive Cities to Live in the U.S.," April 15, 2023*

- San Francisco was identified as one of America's most frugal metro areas by *Coupons.com*. The city ranked #14 out of 25. Criteria: digital coupon usage. *Coupons.com, "America's Most Frugal Cities of 2017," March 22, 2018*

- San Francisco was identified as one of the happiest cities to work in by CareerBliss.com, an online community for career advancement. The city ranked #1 out of 10. Criteria: an employee's relationship with his or her boss and co-workers; daily tasks; general work environment; compensation; opportunities for advancement; company culture and job reputation; and resources. *Businesswire.com, "CareerBliss Happiest Cities to Work 2019," February 12, 2019*

- The San Francisco metro area appeared on the Milken Institute "2022 Best Performing Cities" list. Rank: #35 out of 200 large metro areas (population over 250,000). Criteria: job growth; wage and salary growth; high-tech output growth; housing affordability; household broadband access. *Milken Institute, "Best-Performing Cities 2022," March 28, 2022*

- *Forbes* ranked the 200 most populous metro areas to determine the nation's "Best Places for Business and Careers." The San Francisco metro area was ranked #18. Criteria: costs (business and living); job growth (past and projected); income growth; quality of life; educational attainment (college and high school); projected economic growth; cultural and leisure opportunities; workplace tolerance laws; net migration patterns. *Forbes, "The Best Places for Business and Careers 2019: Seattle Still On Top," October 30, 2019*

- Mercer Human Resources Consulting ranked 227 cities worldwide in terms of cost-of-living. San Francisco ranked #19 (the lower the ranking, the higher the cost-of-living). The survey measured the comparative cost of over 200 items (such as housing, food, clothing, domestic supplies, transportation, and recreation/entertainment) in each location. *Mercer, "2022 Cost of Living City Ranking," June 29, 2022*

Children/Family Rankings

- San Francisco was selected as one of the most playful cities in the U.S. by KaBOOM! The organization's Playful City USA initiative honors cities and towns across the nation that have made their communities more playable. Criteria: pledging to integrate play as a solution to challenges in their communities; making it easy for children to get active and balanced play; creating more family-friendly and innovative communities as a result. *KaBOOM! National Campaign for Play, "2017 Playful City USA Communities"*

Education Rankings

- Personal finance website *WalletHub* analyzed the 150 largest U.S. metropolitan statistical areas to determine where the most educated Americans are putting their degrees to work. Criteria: education levels; percentage of workers with degrees; education quality and attainment gap; public school quality rankings; quality and enrollment of each metro area's universities. San Francisco was ranked #5 (#1 = most educated city). *www.WalletHub.com, "Most & Least Educated Cities in America," July 18, 2022*

- San Francisco was selected as one of America's most literate cities. The city ranked #3 out of the 84 largest U.S. cities. Criteria: number of booksellers; library resources; Internet resources; educational attainment; periodical publishing resources; newspaper circulation. *Central Connecticut State University, "America's Most Literate Cities, 2018," February 2019*

Environmental Rankings

- Sperling's BestPlaces assessed the 50 largest metropolitan areas of the United States for the likelihood of dangerously extreme weather events or earthquakes. In general the Southeast and South-Central regions have the highest risk of weather extremes and earthquakes, while the Pacific Northwest enjoys the lowest risk. Of the least risky metropolitan areas, the San Francisco metro area was ranked #4. *www.bestplaces.net, "Avoid Natural Disasters: BestPlaces Reveals The Top 10 Safest Places to Live," October 25, 2017*

- The U.S. Environmental Protection Agency (EPA) released its list of U.S. metropolitan areas with the most ENERGY STAR certified buildings in 2022. The San Francisco metro area was ranked #4 out of 25. *U.S. Environmental Protection Agency, "2023 Energy Star Top Cities," April 26, 2023*

Food/Drink Rankings

- The U.S. Chamber of Commerce Foundation conducted an in-depth study on local food truck regulations, surveyed 288 food truck owners, and ranked 20 major American cities based on how friendly they are for operating a food truck. The compiled index assessed the following: procedures for obtaining permits and licenses; complying with restrictions; and financial obligations associated with operating a food truck. San Francisco ranked #18 overall (1 being the best). *www.foodtrucknation.us, "Food Truck Nation," March 20, 2018*

- Oracle Park was selected as one of PETA's "Top 10 Vegan-Friendly Ballparks" for 2019. The park ranked #4. *People for the Ethical Treatment of Animals, "Top 10 Vegan-Friendly Ballparks," May 23, 2019*

Health/Fitness Rankings

- For each of the 100 largest cities in the United States, the American Fitness Index®, compiled in partnership between the American College of Sports Medicine and the Elevance Health Foundation, evaluated community infrastructure and 34 health behaviors including preventive health, levels of chronic disease conditions, food insecurity, sleep quality, pedestrian safety, air quality, and community/environment resources that support physical activity. San Francisco ranked #14 for "community fitness." *americanfitnessindex.org, "2022 ACSM American Fitness Index Summary Report," July 12, 2022*

- San Francisco was identified as one of the 10 most walkable cities in the U.S. by Walk Score. The city ranked #2. Walk Score measures walkability by analyzing hundreds of walking routes to nearby amenities, and also measures pedestrian friendliness by analyzing population density and road metrics such as block length and intersection density. *WalkScore.com, April 13, 2021*

- The San Francisco metro area was identified as one of the worst cities for bed bugs in America by pest control company Orkin. The area ranked #22 out of 50 based on the number of bed bug treatments Orkin performed from December 2021 to November 2022. *Orkin, "The Windy City Can't Blow Bed Bugs Away: Chicago Ranks #1 For Third Consecutive Year On Orkin's Bed Bug Cities List," January 9, 2023*

- San Francisco was identified as a "2022 Spring Allergy Capital." The area ranked #94 out of 100. Three groups of factors were used to identify the most challenging cities for people with allergies during the spring season: annual spring pollen scores; over the counter allergy medicine use; number of board-certified allergy specialists. *Asthma and Allergy Foundation of America, "Spring Allergy Capitals 2022," March 2, 2022*

- San Francisco was identified as a "2022 Fall Allergy Capital." The area ranked #99 out of 100. Three groups of factors were used to identify the most challenging cities for people with allergies during the fall season: annual fall pollen scores; over the counter allergy medicine use; number of board-certified allergy specialists. *Asthma and Allergy Foundation of America, "Fall Allergy Capitals 2022," March 2, 2022*

- San Francisco was identified as a "2022 Asthma Capital." The area ranked #70 out of the nation's 100 largest metropolitan areas. Criteria: estimated asthma prevalence; asthma-related mortality; and ER visits due to asthma. Risk factors analyzed but not factored in the rankings: annual pollen score; annual air quality; public smoking laws; access to board-certified asthma specialists; rescue and controller medication use; uninsured rate; poverty rate. *Asthma and Allergy Foundation of America, "Asthma Capitals 2022: The Most Challenging Places to Live With Asthma," September 14, 2022*

- The Sharecare Community Well-Being Index evaluates 10 individual and social health factors in order to measure what matters to Americans in the communities in which they live. The San Francisco metro area ranked #1 in the top 10 across all 10 domains. Criteria: access to healthcare, food, and community resources; housng and transportation; economic security; feeling of purpose; physical, financial, social, and community well-being. *www.sharecare.com, "Community Well-Being Index: 2020 Metro Area & County Rankings Report," August 30, 2021*

Real Estate Rankings

- *WalletHub* compared the most populated U.S. cities to determine which had the best markets for real estate agents. San Francisco ranked #24 where demand was high and pay was the best. Criteria: sales per agent; annual median wage for real-estate agents; monthly average starting salary for real estate agents; real estate job density and competition; unemployment rate; home turnover rate; housing-market health index; and other relevant metrics. *www.WalletHub.com, "2021 Best Places to Be a Real Estate Agent," May 12, 2021*

- The San Francisco metro area was identified as one of the 20 worst housing markets in the U.S. in 2022. The area ranked #187 out of 187 markets. Criteria: year-over-year change of median sales price of existing single-family homes between the 4th quarter of 2021 and the 4th quarter of 2022. *National Association of Realtors®, Median Sales Price of Existing Single-Family Homes for Metropolitan Areas, 4th Quarter 2022*

- The San Francisco metro area was identified as one of the 10 worst condo markets in the U.S. in 2022. The area ranked #56 out of 63 markets. Criteria: year-over-year change of median sales price of existing apartment condo-coop homes between the 4th quarter of 2021 and the 4th quarter of 2022. *National Association of Realtors®, Median Sales Price of Existing Apartment Condo-Coops Homes for Metropolitan Areas, 4th Quarter 2022*

- The San Francisco metro area was identified as one of the 20 least affordable housing markets in the U.S. in 2022. The area ranked #185 out of 186 markets. Criteria: qualification for a mortgage loan with a 10 percent down payment on a typical home. *National Association of Realtors®, Qualifying Income Based on Sales Price of Existing Single-Family Homes for Metropolitan Areas, 2022*

- San Francisco was ranked #232 out of 235 metro areas in terms of housing affordability in 2022 by the National Association of Home Builders (#1 = most affordable). Criteria: the share of homes sold in that area affordable to a family earning the local median income, based on standard mortgage underwriting criteria. *National Association of Home Builders®, NAHB-Wells Fargo Housing Opportunity Index, 4th Quarter 2022*

Safety Rankings

- Allstate ranked the 200 largest cities in America in terms of driver safety. San Francisco ranked #189. Criteria: internal property damage claims over a two-year period from January 2016 to December 2017. The report helps increase the importance of safety and awareness behind the wheel. *Allstate, "Allstate America's Best Drivers Report, 2019" June 24, 2019*

- The National Insurance Crime Bureau ranked 390 metro areas in the U.S. in terms of per capita rates of vehicle theft. The San Francisco metro area ranked #6 (#1 = highest rate). Criteria: number of vehicle theft offenses per 100,000 inhabitants in 2021. *National Insurance Crime Bureau, "Hot Spots 2021," September 1, 2022*

Seniors/Retirement Rankings

- From its Best Cities for Successful Aging indexes, the Milken Institute generated rankings for metropolitan areas, weighing data in nine categories—health care, wellness, living arrangements, transportation and convenience, financial characteristics, education, employment, community engagement, and overall livability. The San Francisco metro area was ranked #11 overall in the large metro area category. *Milken Institute, "Best Cities for Successful Aging, 2017" March 14, 2017*

Sports/Recreation Rankings

- San Francisco was chosen as one of America's best cities for bicycling. The city ranked #2 out of 50. Criteria: cycling infrastructure that is safe and friendly for all ages; energy and bike culture. The editors evaluated cities with populations of 100,000 or more. *Bicycling, "The 50 Best Bike Cities in America," October 10, 2018*

Transportation Rankings

- Business Insider presented an AllTransit Performance Score ranking of public transportation in major U.S. cities and towns, with populations over 250,000, in which San Francisco earned the #1-ranked "Transit Score," awarded for frequency of service, access to jobs, quality and number of stops, and affordability. *www.businessinsider.com, "The 17 Major U.S. Cities with the Best Public Transportation," April 17, 2018*

- The business website *24/7 Wall St.* reviewed U.S. Census data to identify the 25 cities where the largest share of households do not own a vehicle. San Francisco held the #10 position. *247wallst.com, "Cities Where No One Wants to Drive," January 12, 2020*

- San Francisco was identified as one of the most congested metro areas in the U.S. The area ranked #3 out of 10. Criteria: yearly delay per auto commuter in hours. *Texas A&M Transportation Institute, "2021 Urban Mobility Report," June 2021*

- According to the INRIX "2022 Global Traffic Scorecard," San Francisco was identified as one of the most congested metro areas in the U.S. The area ranked #7 out of 25. Criteria: average annual time spent in traffic and average cost of congestion per motorist. *Inrix.com, "Return to Work, Higher Gas Prices & Inflation Drove Americans to Spend Hundreds More in Time and Money Commuting," January 10, 2023*

Women/Minorities Rankings

- *24/7 Wall St.* compared median annual earnings for men and women who worked full-time, year-round, female employment in management roles, bachelor's degree attainment among women, female life expectancy, uninsured rates, and preschool enrollment to identify the best cities for women. The U.S. metropolitan area, San Francisco was ranked #4 in pay disparity and other gender gaps. *24/7 Wall St., "The Easiest (and Toughest) Cities to Be a Woman," January 11, 2020*

- San Francisco was selected as one of the queerest cities in America by *The Advocate*. The city ranked #17 out of 25. Criteria, among many: Trans Pride parades/festivals; gay rugby teams; lesbian bars; LGBTQ centers; theater screenings of "Moonlight"; LGBTQ-inclusive nondiscrimination ordinances; and gay bowling teams. *The Advocate, "Queerest Cities in America 2017" January 12, 2017*

- Personal finance website *WalletHub* compared more than 180 U.S. cities across two key dimensions, "Hispanic Business-Friendliness" and "Hispanic Purchasing Power," to arrive at the most favorable conditions for Hispanic entrepreneurs. San Francisco was ranked #87 out of 182. Criteria includes: share of Hispanic-Owned Businesses; Hispanic entrepreneurship rate to median annual income of Hispanics; Small Business-Friendliness score; cost of living; and number of Hispanics with at least a bachelor's degree. *WalletHub.com, "2019's Best Cities for Hispanic Entrepreneurs," May 1, 2019*

Miscellaneous Rankings

- Despite the freedom to now travel internationally, plugged-in travel influencers and experts continue to rediscover their local regions. San Francisco appeared on a *Forbes* list of places in the U.S. that provide solace as well as local inspiration. Whether it be quirky things to see and do, delicious take out, outdoor exploring and daytrips, these places are must-see destinations. *Forbes, "The Best Places To Travel In The U.S. In 2023, According To The Experts," April 13, 2023*

- *MoveHub* ranked 446 hipster cities across 20 countries, using its new and improved *alternative* Hipster Index and San Francisco came out as #15 among the top 50. Criteria: population over 150,000; number of vintage boutiques; density of tattoo parlors; vegan places to eat; coffee shops; and density of vinyl record stores. *www.movehub.com, "The Hipster Index: Brighton Pips Portland to Global Top Spot," July 28, 2021*

- San Francisco was selected as a 2022 Digital Cities Survey winner. The city ranked #4 in the large city (500,000 or more population) category. The survey examined and assessed how city governments are utilizing technology to continue innovation, engage with residents, and persevere through the challenges of the pandemic. Survey questions focused on ten initiatives: cybersecurity; citizen experience; disaster recovery; business intelligence; IT personnel; data governance; business automation; IT governance; infrastructure modernization; and broadband connectivity. *Center for Digital Government, "2022 Digital Cities Survey," November 10, 2022*

- In its roundup of St. Patrick's Day parades "Gayot" listed the best festivals and parades of all things Irish. The festivities in San Francisco as among the best in North America. *www.gayot.com, "Best St. Patrick's Day Parades," March 2023*

- The watchdog site, Charity Navigator, conducted a study of charities in major markets both to analyze statistical differences in their financial, accountability, and transparency practices and to track year-to-year variations in individual philanthropic communities. The San Francisco metro area was ranked #16 among the 30 metro markets in the rating category of Overall Score. *www.charitynavigator.org, "2017 Metro Market Study," May 1, 2017*

- *WalletHub* compared the 150 most populated U.S. cities to determine their operating efficiency. A "Quality of Services" score was constructed for each city and then divided by the total budget per capita to reveal which were managed the best. San Francisco ranked #149. Criteria: financial stability; economy; education; safety; health; infrastructure and pollution. *www.WalletHub.com, "2022's Best-& Worst-Run Cities in America," June 21, 2022*

- The National Alliance to End Homelessness listed the 25 most populous metro areas with the highest rate of homelessness. The San Francisco metro area had a high rate of homelessness. Criteria: number of homeless people per 10,000 population in 2016. *National Alliance to End Homelessness, "Homelessness in the 25 Most Populous U.S. Metro Areas," September 1, 2017*

Business Environment

DEMOGRAPHICS

Population Growth

Area	1990 Census	2000 Census	2010 Census	2020 Census	Population Growth (%) 1990-2020	Population Growth (%) 2010-2020
City	723,959	776,733	805,235	873,965	20.7	8.5
MSA[1]	3,686,592	4,123,740	4,335,391	4,749,008	28.8	9.5
U.S.	248,709,873	281,421,906	308,745,538	331,449,281	33.3	7.4

Note: (1) Figures cover the San Francisco-Oakland-Berkeley, CA Metropolitan Statistical Area
Source: U.S. Census Bureau, 1990 Census, 2000 Census, 2010 Census, 2020 Census

Race

Area	White Alone[2] (%)	Black Alone[2] (%)	Asian Alone[2] (%)	AIAN[3] Alone[2] (%)	NHOPI[4] Alone[2] (%)	Other Race Alone[2] (%)	Two or More Races (%)
City	41.3	5.3	33.9	0.7	0.4	8.4	9.9
MSA[1]	39.3	7.1	27.5	1.0	0.7	12.7	11.7
U.S.	61.6	12.4	6.0	1.1	0.2	8.4	10.2

Note: (1) Figures cover the San Francisco-Oakland-Berkeley, CA Metropolitan Statistical Area; (2) Alone is defined as not being in combination with one or more other races; (3) American Indian and Alaska Native; (4) Native Hawaiian and Other Pacific Islander
Source: U.S. Census Bureau, 2020 Census

Hispanic or Latino Origin

Area	Total (%)	Mexican (%)	Puerto Rican (%)	Cuban (%)	Other (%)
City	15.4	7.8	0.7	0.3	6.7
MSA[1]	22.0	14.1	0.7	0.2	7.0
U.S.	18.4	11.2	1.8	0.7	4.7

Note: Persons of Hispanic or Latino origin can be of any race; (1) Figures cover the San Francisco-Oakland-Berkeley, CA Metropolitan Statistical Area
Source: U.S. Census Bureau, 2017-2021 American Community Survey 5-Year Estimates

Age

Area	Under Age 5	Age 5–19	Age 20–34	Age 35–44	Age 45–54	Age 55–64	Age 65–74	Age 75–84	Age 85+	Median Age
	Percent of Population									
City	4.0	10.5	29.3	15.8	12.5	11.4	9.2	4.6	2.4	38.2
MSA[1]	5.0	16.8	21.7	14.7	13.3	12.4	9.3	4.7	2.0	39.1
U.S.	5.6	19.2	20.2	12.7	12.4	13.1	10.0	4.9	1.9	38.8

Note: (1) Figures cover the San Francisco-Oakland-Berkeley, CA Metropolitan Statistical Area
Source: U.S. Census Bureau, 2020 Census

Disability by Age

Area	All Ages	Under 18 Years Old	18 to 64 Years Old	65 Years and Over
City	10.1	2.6	6.3	33.5
MSA[1]	9.6	3.1	6.7	30.0
U.S.	12.6	4.4	10.3	33.4

Note: Figures show percent of the civilian noninstitutionalized population that reported having a disability. Disability status is determined from six types of difficulty: vision, hearing, cognitive, ambulatory, self-care, and independent living. For children under 5 years old, hearing and vision difficulty are used to determine disability status. For children between the ages of 5 and 14, disability status is determined from hearing, vision, cognitive, ambulatory, and self-care difficulties. For people aged 15 years and older, they are considered to have a disability if they have difficulty with any one of the six difficulty types; Note: (1) Figures cover the San Francisco-Oakland-Berkeley, CA Metropolitan Statistical Area
Source: U.S. Census Bureau, 2017-2021 American Community Survey 5-Year Estimates

Ancestry

Area	German	Irish	English	American	Italian	Polish	French[2]	Scottish	Dutch
City	6.9	7.6	5.5	2.5	4.6	1.8	2.1	1.3	0.7
MSA[1]	7.3	7.0	6.2	2.3	4.4	1.4	1.8	1.4	0.7
U.S.	12.8	9.6	8.1	5.7	5.0	2.7	2.2	1.6	1.1

Note: Figures are the percentage of the total population reporting a particular ancestry. The nine most commonly reported ancestries in the U.S. are shown. Figures include multiple ancestries (e.g. if a person reported being Irish and Italian, they were included in both columns); (1) Figures cover the San Francisco-Oakland-Berkeley, CA Metropolitan Statistical Area; (2) Excludes Basque
Source: U.S. Census Bureau, 2017-2021 American Community Survey 5-Year Estimates

Foreign-born Population

Area	Percent of Population Born in								
	Any Foreign Country	Asia	Mexico	Europe	Caribbean	Central America[2]	South America	Africa	Canada
City	34.1	22.0	2.4	4.5	0.2	2.4	1.1	0.5	0.6
MSA[1]	30.7	17.8	4.7	2.8	0.2	2.5	1.1	0.9	0.5
U.S.	13.6	4.2	3.3	1.5	1.4	1.1	1.1	0.8	0.2

Note: (1) Figures cover the San Francisco-Oakland-Berkeley, CA Metropolitan Statistical Area; (2) Excludes Mexico.
Source: U.S. Census Bureau, 2017-2021 American Community Survey 5-Year Estimates

Household Size

Area	Persons in Household (%)							Average Household Size
	One	Two	Three	Four	Five	Six	Seven or More	
City	36.6	32.9	13.9	10.2	3.6	1.4	1.4	2.30
MSA[1]	26.4	31.9	16.8	14.9	6.1	2.2	1.7	2.70
U.S.	28.1	33.8	15.5	12.9	6.0	2.3	1.4	2.60

Note: (1) Figures cover the San Francisco-Oakland-Berkeley, CA Metropolitan Statistical Area
Source: U.S. Census Bureau, 2017-2021 American Community Survey 5-Year Estimates

Household Relationships

Area	House-holder	Opposite-sex Spouse	Same-sex Spouse	Opposite-sex Unmarried Partner	Same-sex Unmarried Partner	Child[2]	Grand-child	Other Relatives	Non-relatives
City	42.6	13.6	0.8	3.3	0.6	17.6	1.3	6.8	10.3
MSA[1]	36.7	17.0	0.4	2.3	0.3	26.3	1.8	6.9	5.9
U.S.	38.3	17.5	0.2	2.5	0.2	28.3	2.4	4.8	3.4

Note: Figures are percent of the total population; (1) Figures cover the San Francisco-Oakland-Berkeley, CA Metropolitan Statistical Area; (2) Includes biological, adopted, and stepchildren of the householder
Source: U.S. Census Bureau, 2020 Census

Gender

Area	Males	Females	Males per 100 Females
City	446,144	427,821	104.3
MSA[1]	2,344,775	2,404,233	97.5
U.S.	162,685,811	168,763,470	96.4

Note: (1) Figures cover the San Francisco-Oakland-Berkeley, CA Metropolitan Statistical Area
Source: U.S. Census Bureau, 2020 Census

Marital Status

Area	Never Married	Now Married[2]	Separated	Widowed	Divorced
City	46.0	40.1	1.4	4.5	8.0
MSA[1]	36.6	48.6	1.4	4.6	8.7
U.S.	33.8	48.0	1.8	5.6	10.8

Note: Figures are percentages and cover the population 15 years of age and older; (1) Figures cover the San Francisco-Oakland-Berkeley, CA Metropolitan Statistical Area; (2) Excludes separated
Source: U.S. Census Bureau, 2017-2021 American Community Survey 5-Year Estimates

Religious Groups by Family

Area	Catholic	Baptist	Methodist	LDS[2]	Pentecostal	Lutheran	Islam	Adventist	Other
MSA[1]	21.5	2.2	0.9	1.5	1.4	0.4	2.0	1.0	7.7
U.S.	18.7	7.3	3.0	2.0	1.8	1.7	1.3	1.3	11.6

Note: Figures are the number of adherents as a percentage of the total population and cover the eight largest religious groups in the U.S.; (1) Figures cover the San Francisco-Oakland-Berkeley, CA Metropolitan Statistical Area; (2) Church of Jesus Christ of Latter-day Saints
Sources: 2020 U.S. Religion Census, Association of Statisticians of American Religious Bodies; The Association of Religion Data Archives (ARDA)

Religious Groups by Tradition

Area	Catholic	Evangelical Protestant	Mainline Protestant	Black Protestant	Islam	Judaism	Hinduism	Orthodox	Buddhism
MSA[1]	21.5	5.2	2.2	1.8	2.0	0.7	1.1	0.7	1.1
U.S.	18.7	16.5	5.2	2.3	1.3	0.6	0.4	0.4	0.3

Note: Figures are the number of adherents as a percentage of the total population; (1) Figures cover the San Francisco-Oakland-Berkeley, CA Metropolitan Statistical Area
Sources: 2020 U.S. Religion Census, Association of Statisticians of American Religious Bodies; The Association of Religion Data Archives (ARDA)

ECONOMY

Gross Metropolitan Product

Area	2020	2021	2022	2023	Rank[2]
MSA[1]	588.3	652.7	713.1	748.9	4

Note: Figures are in billions of dollars; (1) Figures cover the San Francisco-Oakland-Berkeley, CA Metropolitan Statistical Area; (2) Rank is based on 2021 data and ranges from 1 to 381
Source: U.S. Conference of Mayors, U.S. Metro Economies: U.S. Metros Compared to Global and State Economies, June 2022

Economic Growth

Area	2018-20 (%)	2021 (%)	2022 (%)	2023 (%)	Rank[2]
MSA[1]	1.2	7.1	4.0	1.9	60
U.S.	-0.6	5.7	3.1	2.9	–

Note: Figures are real gross metropolitan product (GMP) growth rates and represent average annual percent change; (1) Figures cover the San Francisco-Oakland-Berkeley, CA Metropolitan Statistical Area; (2) Rank is based on 2020 2-year average annual percent change and ranges from 1 to 381
Source: U.S. Conference of Mayors, U.S. Metro Economies: U.S. Metros Compared to Global and State Economies, June 2022

Metropolitan Area Exports

Area	2016	2017	2018	2019	2020	2021	Rank[2]
MSA[1]	24,506.3	29,103.8	27,417.0	28,003.8	23,864.5	29,972.0	13

Note: Figures are in millions of dollars; (1) Figures cover the San Francisco-Oakland-Berkeley, CA Metropolitan Statistical Area; (2) Rank is based on 2021 data and ranges from 1 to 388
Source: U.S. Department of Commerce, International Trade Administration, Office of Trade and Economic Analysis, Industry and Analysis, Exports by Metropolitan Area, data extracted March 16, 2023

Building Permits

Area	Single-Family			Multi-Family			Total		
	2021	2022	Pct. Chg.	2021	2022	Pct. Chg.	2021	2022	Pct. Chg.
City	33	38	15.2	2,486	2,006	-19.3	2,519	2,044	-18.9
MSA[1]	4,301	3,370	-21.6	9,305	7,834	-15.8	13,606	11,204	-17.7
U.S.	1,115,400	975,600	-12.5	621,600	689,500	10.9	1,737,000	1,665,100	-4.1

Note: (1) Figures cover the San Francisco-Oakland-Berkeley, CA Metropolitan Statistical Area; Figures represent new, privately-owned housing units authorized (unadjusted data); All permit data are based on estimates with imputation
Source: U.S. Census Bureau, Manufacturing, Mining, and Construction Statistics, Building Permits, 2021, 2022

Bankruptcy Filings

Area	Business Filings			Nonbusiness Filings		
	2021	2022	% Chg.	2021	2022	% Chg.
San Francisco County	65	55	-15.4	334	342	2.4
U.S.	14,347	13,481	-6.0	399,269	374,240	-6.3

Note: Business filings include Chapter 7, Chapter 9, Chapter 11, Chapter 12, Chapter 13, Chapter 15, and Section 304; Nonbusiness filings include Chapter 7, Chapter 11, and Chapter 13
Source: Administrative Office of the U.S. Courts, Business and Nonbusiness Bankruptcy, County Cases Commenced by Chapter of the Bankruptcy Code, During the 12-Month Period Ending December 31, 2021 and Business and Nonbusiness Bankruptcy, County Cases Commenced by Chapter of the Bankruptcy Code, During the 12-Month Period Ending December 31, 2022

Housing Vacancy Rates

Area	Gross Vacancy Rate[2] (%)			Year-Round Vacancy Rate[3] (%)			Rental Vacancy Rate[4] (%)			Homeowner Vacancy Rate[5] (%)		
	2020	2021	2022	2020	2021	2022	2020	2021	2022	2020	2021	2022
MSA[1]	6.4	7.6	7.9	6.2	7.3	7.7	5.3	6.5	5.4	0.5	1.1	1.3
U.S.	10.6	10.8	10.5	8.2	8.4	8.2	6.3	6.1	5.8	1.0	0.9	0.8

Note: (1) Figures cover the San Francisco-Oakland-Berkeley, CA Metropolitan Statistical Area; (2) The percentage of the total housing inventory that is vacant; (3) The percentage of the housing inventory (excluding seasonal units) that is year-round vacant; (4) The percentage of rental inventory that is vacant for rent; (5) The percentage of homeowner inventory that is vacant for sale
Source: U.S. Census Bureau, Housing Vacancies and Homeownership Annual Statistics: 2020, 2021, 2022

INCOME

Income

Area	Per Capita ($)	Median Household ($)	Average Household ($)
City	77,267	126,187	178,742
MSA[1]	62,070	118,547	165,749
U.S.	37,638	69,021	97,196

Note: (1) Figures cover the San Francisco-Oakland-Berkeley, CA Metropolitan Statistical Area
Source: U.S. Census Bureau, 2017-2021 American Community Survey 5-Year Estimates

Household Income Distribution

Area	Percent of Households Earning							
	Under $15,000	$15,000 -$24,999	$25,000 -$34,999	$35,000 -$49,999	$50,000 -$74,999	$75,000 -$99,999	$100,000 -$149,999	$150,000 and up
City	9.2	4.9	4.5	6.0	9.1	8.3	14.9	43.2
MSA[1]	6.7	4.3	4.5	6.4	10.8	10.0	17.1	40.0
U.S.	9.4	7.8	8.2	11.4	16.8	12.8	16.3	17.3

Note: (1) Figures cover the San Francisco-Oakland-Berkeley, CA Metropolitan Statistical Area
Source: U.S. Census Bureau, 2017-2021 American Community Survey 5-Year Estimates

Poverty Rate

Area	All Ages	Under 18 Years Old	18 to 64 Years Old	65 Years and Over
City	10.3	10.1	9.4	14.4
MSA[1]	8.4	9.1	8.1	9.1
U.S.	12.6	17.0	11.8	9.6

Note: Figures are percentage of people whose income during the past 12 months was below the poverty level;
(1) Figures cover the San Francisco-Oakland-Berkeley, CA Metropolitan Statistical Area
Source: U.S. Census Bureau, 2017-2021 American Community Survey 5-Year Estimates

EMPLOYMENT

Labor Force and Employment

Area	Civilian Labor Force			Workers Employed		
	Dec. 2021	Dec. 2022	% Chg.	Dec. 2021	Dec. 2022	% Chg.
City	560,450	578,421	3.2	543,659	566,695	4.2
MD[1]	1,003,772	1,035,986	3.2	974,872	1,015,702	4.2
U.S.	161,696,000	164,224,000	1.6	155,732,000	158,872,000	2.0

Note: Data is not seasonally adjusted and covers workers 16 years of age and older; (1) Figures cover the San Francisco-San Mateo-Redwood City, CA Metropolitan Division
Source: Bureau of Labor Statistics, Local Area Unemployment Statistics

Unemployment Rate

Area	2022											
	Jan.	Feb.	Mar.	Apr.	May	Jun.	Jul.	Aug.	Sep.	Oct.	Nov.	Dec.
City	3.5	3.0	2.5	2.2	1.9	2.2	2.1	2.3	2.1	2.2	2.3	2.0
MD[1]	3.3	2.9	2.4	2.1	1.8	2.1	2.1	2.3	2.1	2.1	2.3	2.0
U.S.	4.4	4.1	3.8	3.3	3.4	3.8	3.8	3.8	3.3	3.4	3.4	3.3

Note: Data is not seasonally adjusted and covers workers 16 years of age and older; (1) Figures cover the San Francisco-San Mateo-Redwood City, CA Metropolitan Division
Source: Bureau of Labor Statistics, Local Area Unemployment Statistics

Average Wages

Occupation	$/Hr.	Occupation	$/Hr.
Accountants and Auditors	54.83	Maintenance and Repair Workers	29.95
Automotive Mechanics	31.95	Marketing Managers	100.73
Bookkeepers	30.30	Network and Computer Systems Admin.	61.21
Carpenters	38.33	Nurses, Licensed Practical	38.69
Cashiers	18.96	Nurses, Registered	79.21
Computer Programmers	64.89	Nursing Assistants	25.13
Computer Systems Analysts	70.44	Office Clerks, General	26.29
Computer User Support Specialists	40.10	Physical Therapists	60.61
Construction Laborers	31.48	Physicians	114.31
Cooks, Restaurant	20.39	Plumbers, Pipefitters and Steamfitters	44.23
Customer Service Representatives	25.95	Police and Sheriff's Patrol Officers	57.43
Dentists	98.09	Postal Service Mail Carriers	29.20
Electricians	46.31	Real Estate Sales Agents	39.87
Engineers, Electrical	77.67	Retail Salespersons	21.47
Fast Food and Counter Workers	18.38	Sales Representatives, Technical/Scientific	60.73
Financial Managers	107.34	Secretaries, Exc. Legal/Medical/Executive	28.82
First-Line Supervisors of Office Workers	40.24	Security Guards	21.09
General and Operations Managers	80.86	Surgeons	75.20
Hairdressers/Cosmetologists	23.34	Teacher Assistants, Exc. Postsecondary*	22.38
Home Health and Personal Care Aides	16.61	Teachers, Secondary School, Exc. Sp. Ed.*	44.23
Janitors and Cleaners	21.39	Telemarketers	22.03
Landscaping/Groundskeeping Workers	23.72	Truck Drivers, Heavy/Tractor-Trailer	30.83
Lawyers	115.06	Truck Drivers, Light/Delivery Services	25.29
Maids and Housekeeping Cleaners	22.92	Waiters and Waitresses	18.52

Note: Wage data covers the San Francisco-Oakland-Berkeley, CA Metropolitan Statistical Area; (*) Hourly wages were calculated from annual wage data based on a 40 hour work week; n/a not available.
Source: Bureau of Labor Statistics, Metro Area Occupational Employment & Wage Estimates, May 2022

Employment by Industry

Sector	MD[1]		U.S.
	Number of Employees	Percent of Total	Percent of Total
Construction	40,800	3.4	5.0
Private Education and Health Services	158,400	13.1	16.1
Financial Activities	89,600	7.4	5.9
Government	131,200	10.9	14.5
Information	127,700	10.6	2.0
Leisure and Hospitality	122,500	10.2	10.3
Manufacturing	39,200	3.3	8.4
Mining and Logging	100	<0.1	0.4
Other Services	38,800	3.2	3.7
Professional and Business Services	316,400	26.3	14.7
Retail Trade	68,800	5.7	10.2
Transportation, Warehousing, and Utilities	48,800	4.1	4.9
Wholesale Trade	22,500	1.9	3.9

Note: Figures are non-farm employment as of December 2022. Figures are not seasonally adjusted and include workers 16 years of age and older; (1) Figures cover the San Francisco-San Mateo-Redwood City, CA Metropolitan Division
Source: Bureau of Labor Statistics, Current Employment Statistics, Employment, Hours, and Earnings

Employment by Occupation

Occupation Classification	City (%)	MSA[1] (%)	U.S. (%)
Management, Business, Science, and Arts	60.4	53.0	40.3
Natural Resources, Construction, and Maintenance	2.9	5.6	8.7
Production, Transportation, and Material Moving	5.7	8.2	13.1
Sales and Office	16.9	18.1	20.9
Service	14.2	15.1	17.0

Note: Figures cover employed civilians 16 years of age and older; (1) Figures cover the San Francisco-Oakland-Berkeley, CA Metropolitan Statistical Area
Source: U.S. Census Bureau, 2017-2021 American Community Survey 5-Year Estimates

Occupations with Greatest Projected Employment Growth: 2022 – 2024

Occupation[1]	2022 Employment	2024 Projected Employment	Numeric Employment Change	Percent Employment Change
Home Health and Personal Care Aides	811,300	858,600	47,300	5.8
Fast Food and Counter Workers	422,000	444,100	22,100	5.2
Cooks, Restaurant	154,300	172,000	17,700	11.5
Software Developers and Software Quality Assurance Analysts and Testers	337,600	352,100	14,500	4.3
Waiters and Waitresses	205,800	219,200	13,400	6.5
Laborers and Freight, Stock, and Material Movers, Hand	391,100	403,100	12,000	3.1
Stockers and Order Fillers	268,000	277,500	9,500	3.5
General and Operations Managers	308,500	317,600	9,100	2.9
First-Line Supervisors of Food Preparation and Serving Workers	118,100	126,000	7,900	6.7
Project Management Specialists and Business Operations Specialists, All Other	332,400	339,800	7,400	2.2

Note: Projections cover California; (1) Sorted by numeric employment change
Source: www.projectionscentral.com, State Occupational Projections, 2022–2024 Short-Term Projections

Fastest-Growing Occupations: 2022 – 2024

Occupation[1]	2022 Employment	2024 Projected Employment	Numeric Employment Change	Percent Employment Change
Fitness Trainers and Aerobics Instructors	40,700	46,300	5,600	13.8
Nurse Practitioners	18,300	20,500	2,200	12.0
Cooks, Restaurant	154,300	172,000	17,700	11.5
Airfield Operations Specialists	3,700	4,100	400	10.8
Solar Photovoltaic Installers	6,600	7,300	700	10.6
Ushers, Lobby Attendants, and Ticket Takers	7,800	8,600	800	10.3
Amusement and Recreation Attendants	47,500	52,300	4,800	10.1
Sociologists	1,000	1,100	100	10.0
Paperhangers	1,000	1,100	100	10.0
Avionics Technicians	2,000	2,200	200	10.0

Note: Projections cover California; (1) Sorted by percent employment change and excludes occupations with numeric employment change less than 50
Source: www.projectionscentral.com, State Occupational Projections, 2022–2024 Short-Term Projections

CITY FINANCES

City Government Finances

Component	2020 ($000)	2020 ($ per capita)
Total Revenues	14,179,105	16,084
Total Expenditures	15,147,509	17,183
Debt Outstanding	21,155,583	23,998
Cash and Securities[1]	9,566,977	10,852

Note: (1) Cash and security holdings of a government at the close of its fiscal year, including those of its dependent agencies, utilities, and liquor stores.
Source: U.S. Census Bureau, State & Local Government Finances 2020

City Government Revenue by Source

Source	2020 ($000)	2020 ($ per capita)	2020 (%)
General Revenue			
From Federal Government	879,165	997	6.2
From State Government	2,047,301	2,322	14.4
From Local Governments	754,453	856	5.3
Taxes			
Property	2,835,239	3,216	20.0
Sales and Gross Receipts	1,003,418	1,138	7.1
Personal Income	0	0	0.0
Corporate Income	0	0	0.0
Motor Vehicle License	4,016	5	0.0
Other Taxes	1,265,366	1,435	8.9
Current Charges	3,236,337	3,671	22.8
Liquor Store	0	0	0.0
Utility	1,096,559	1,244	7.7

Source: U.S. Census Bureau, State & Local Government Finances 2020

City Government Expenditures by Function

Function	2020 ($000)	2020 ($ per capita)	2020 (%)
General Direct Expenditures			
Air Transportation	1,626,504	1,845	10.7
Corrections	259,992	294	1.7
Education	0	0	0.0
Employment Security Administration	0	0	0.0
Financial Administration	79,739	90	0.5
Fire Protection	329,075	373	2.2
General Public Buildings	0	0	0.0
Governmental Administration, Other	461,695	523	3.0
Health	2,232,187	2,532	14.7
Highways	252,326	286	1.7
Hospitals	1,136,686	1,289	7.5
Housing and Community Development	559,372	634	3.7
Interest on General Debt	672,482	762	4.4
Judicial and Legal	150,512	170	1.0
Libraries	132,871	150	0.9
Parking	203,830	231	1.3
Parks and Recreation	349,997	397	2.3
Police Protection	608,840	690	4.0
Public Welfare	1,628,999	1,847	10.8
Sewerage	523,247	593	3.5
Solid Waste Management	0	0	0.0
Veterans' Services	0	0	0.0
Liquor Store	0	0	0.0
Utility	2,537,905	2,878	16.8

Source: U.S. Census Bureau, State & Local Government Finances 2020

TAXES

State Corporate Income Tax Rates

State	Tax Rate (%)	Income Brackets ($)	Num. of Brackets	Financial Institution Tax Rate (%)[a]	Federal Income Tax Ded.
California	8.84 (b)	Flat rate	1	10.84 (b)	No

Note: Tax rates as of January 1, 2023; (a) Rates listed are the corporate income tax rate applied to financial institutions or excise taxes based on income. Some states have other taxes based upon the value of deposits or shares; (b) Minimum tax is $800 in California, $250 in District of Columbia, $50 in Arizona and North Dakota (banks), $400 ($100 banks) in Rhode Island, $200 per location in South Dakota (banks), $100 in Utah, $300 in Vermont.
Source: Federation of Tax Administrators, State Corporate Income Tax Rates, January 1, 2023

State Individual Income Tax Rates

State	Tax Rate (%)	Income Brackets ($)	Personal Exemptions ($) Single	Married	Depend.	Standard Ded. ($) Single	Married
California (a)	1.0 - 12.3 (g)	10,099 - 677,275 (b)	140	280	433 (c)	5,202	10,404 (a)

Note: Tax rates as of January 1, 2023; Local- and county-level taxes are not included; Federal income tax is not deductible on state income tax returns; (a) 16 states have statutory provision for automatically adjusting to the rate of inflation the dollar values of the income tax brackets, standard deductions, and/or personal exemptions. Oregon does not index the income brackets for $125,000 and over; (b) For joint returns, taxes are twice the tax on half the couple's income; (c) The personal exemption takes the form of a tax credit instead of a deduction; (g) California imposes an additional 1% tax on taxable income over $1 million, making the maximum rate 13.3% over $1 million.
Source: Federation of Tax Administrators, State Individual Income Tax Rates, January 1, 2023

Various State Sales and Excise Tax Rates

State	State Sales Tax (%)	Gasoline[1] ($/gal.)	Cigarette[2] ($/pack)	Spirits[3] ($/gal.)	Wine[4] ($/gal.)	Beer[5] ($/gal.)	Recreational Marijuana (%)
California	7.25	0.7766	2.87	3.30	0.20	0.20	(c)

Note: All tax rates as of January 1, 2023; (1) The American Petroleum Institute has developed a methodology for determining the average tax rate on a gallon of fuel. Rates may include any of the following: excise taxes, environmental fees, storage tank fees, other fees or taxes, general sales tax, and local taxes; (2) The federal excise tax of $1.0066 per pack and local taxes are not included; (3) Rates are those applicable to off-premise sales of 40% alcohol by volume (a.b.v.) distilled spirits in 750ml containers. Local excise taxes are excluded; (4) Rates are those applicable to off-premise sales of 11% a.b.v. non-carbonated wine in 750ml containers; (5) Rates are those applicable to off-premise sales of 4.7% a.b.v. beer in 12 ounce containers; (c) 15% excise tax (levied on wholesale at average market rate); $10.08/oz. flowers & $3/oz. leaves cultivation tax; $1.41/oz fresh cannabis plant
Source: Tax Foundation, 2023 Facts & Figures: How Does Your State Compare?

State Business Tax Climate Index Rankings

State	Overall Rank	Corporate Tax Rank	Individual Income Tax Rank	Sales Tax Rank	Property Tax Rank	Unemployment Insurance Tax Rank
California	48	46	49	47	19	24

Note: The index is a measure of how each state's tax laws affect economic performance. The lower the rank, the more favorable a state's tax system is for business. States without a given tax are given a ranking of 1. The scores/rankings for the District of Columbia do not affect other states. The 2023 index represents the tax climate as of July 1, 2022.
Source: Tax Foundation, State Business Tax Climate Index 2023

TRANSPORTATION

Means of Transportation to Work

Area	Car/Truck/Van Drove Alone	Car-pooled	Public Transportation Bus	Subway	Railroad	Bicycle	Walked	Other Means	Worked at Home
City	29.4	6.5	17.8	7.0	1.3	3.3	11.0	5.6	18.0
MSA[1]	53.4	8.6	6.1	5.7	1.2	1.6	4.3	2.8	16.3
U.S.	73.2	8.6	2.0	1.6	0.5	0.5	2.5	1.5	9.7

Note: Figures are percentages and cover workers 16 years of age and older; (1) Figures cover the San Francisco-Oakland-Berkeley, CA Metropolitan Statistical Area
Source: U.S. Census Bureau, 2017-2021 American Community Survey 5-Year Estimates

Travel Time to Work

Area	Less Than 10 Minutes	10 to 19 Minutes	20 to 29 Minutes	30 to 44 Minutes	45 to 59 Minutes	60 to 89 Minutes	90 Minutes or More
City	4.5	19.3	21.4	29.5	11.6	10.1	3.7
MSA[1]	7.0	22.9	17.8	23.6	11.9	12.0	4.9
U.S.	12.4	28.5	21.0	20.9	8.2	6.2	2.9

Note: Note: Figures are percentages and include workers 16 years old and over; (1) Figures cover the San Francisco-Oakland-Berkeley, CA Metropolitan Statistical Area
Source: U.S. Census Bureau, 2017-2021 American Community Survey 5-Year Estimates

Key Congestion Measures

Measure	1990	2000	2010	2015	2020
Annual Hours of Delay, Total (000)	131,150	182,881	208,286	245,689	112,507
Annual Hours of Delay, Per Auto Commuter	68	79	90	101	46
Annual Congestion Cost, Per Auto Commuter ($)	2,590	2,713	2,456	2,675	1,301

Note: Covers the San Francisco-Oakland CA urban area
Source: Texas A&M Transportation Institute, 2021 Urban Mobility Report

Freeway Travel Time Index

Measure	1985	1990	1995	2000	2005	2010	2015	2020
Urban Area Index[1]	1.30	1.32	1.36	1.38	1.40	1.41	1.49	1.16
Urban Area Rank[1,2]	2	2	2	2	2	2	1	2

Note: Freeway Travel Time Index—the ratio of travel time in the peak period to the travel time at free-flow conditions. For example, a value of 1.30 indicates a 20-minute free-flow trip takes 26 minutes in the peak (20 minutes x 1.30 = 26 minutes); (1) Covers the San Francisco-Oakland CA urban area; (2) Rank is based on 101 larger urban areas (#1 = highest travel time index)
Source: Texas A&M Transportation Institute, 2021 Urban Mobility Report

Public Transportation

Agency Name / Mode of Transportation	Vehicles Operated in Maximum Service[1]	Annual Unlinked Passenger Trips[2] (in thous.)	Annual Passenger Miles[3] (in thous.)
San Francisco Municipal Railway (MUNI)			
Bus (directly operated)	398	40,938.4	82,487.6
Demand Response (purchased transportation)	66	114.9	776.5
Light Rail (directly operated)	112	3,596.0	2,668.1
Streetcar Rail (directly operated)	12	0.0	n/a
Trolleybus (directly operated)	158	17,107.4	26,226.6
San Francisco Bay Area Rapid Transit District (BART)			
Heavy Rail (directly operated)	496	17,125.3	233,787.8
Hybrid Rail (directly operated)	14	601.4	4,123.1
Monorail and Automated Guideway (purchased transportation)	2	113.0	359.3

Note: (1) Number of revenue vehicles operated by the given mode and type of service to meet the annual maximum service requirement. This is the revenue vehicle count during the peak season of the year; on the week and day that maximum service is provided. Vehicles operated in maximum service (VOMS) exclude atypical days and one-time special events; (2) Number of passengers who boarded public transportation vehicles. Passengers are counted each time they board a vehicle no matter how many vehicles they use to travel from their origin to their destination. (3) Sum of the distances ridden by all passengers during the entire fiscal year.
Source: Federal Transit Administration, National Transit Database, 2021

Air Transportation

Airport Name and Code / Type of Service	Passenger Airlines[1]	Passenger Enplanements	Freight Carriers[2]	Freight (lbs)
San Francisco International (SFO)				
Domestic service (U.S. carriers - 2022)	24	15,604,040	14	192,078,697
International service (U.S. carriers - 2021)	6	685,890	4	83,977,700

Note: (1) Includes all U.S.-based major, minor and commuter airlines that carried at least one passenger during the year; (2) Includes all U.S.-based airlines and freight carriers that transported at least one pound of freight during the year.
Source: Bureau of Transportation Statistics, The Intermodal Transportation Database, Air Carriers: T-100 Domestic Market (U.S. Carriers), 2022; Bureau of Transportation Statistics, The Intermodal Transportation Database, Air Carriers: T-100 International Market (U.S. Carriers), 2021

BUSINESSES

Major Business Headquarters

Company Name	Industry	Rankings	
		Fortune[1]	Forbes[2]
Block	Consumer credit card and related services	208	-
Charles Schwab	Securities	188	-
Flexport	Transportation	-	165
Gap	Specialty retailers, apparel	220	-
McKesson	Wholesalers, health care	9	-
Opendoor Technologies	Real estate	425	-
PG&E	Utilities, gas and electric	168	-
Salesforce	Computer software	136	-
Stripe	Business services & supplies	-	222
Swinerton	Construction	-	126
Twitter	It software & services	-	104
Uber Technologies	Internet services and retailing	210	-
Wells Fargo	Commercial banks	41	-
Wilbur-Ellis	Chemicals	-	151
Williams-Sonoma	Specialty retailers, other	420	-

Note: (1) Companies that produce a 10-K are ranked 1 to 500 based on 2021 revenue; (2) All private companies with at least $2 billion in annual revenue through the end of their most current fiscal year are ranked 1 to 246; companies listed are headquartered in the city; dashes indicate no ranking
Source: Fortune, "Fortune 500," 2022; Forbes, "America's Largest Private Companies," 2022

Fastest-Growing Businesses

According to *Inc.*, San Francisco is home to six of America's 500 fastest-growing private companies: **Vanta** (#25); **Empower** (#55); **ArtsAI** (#56); **Truework** (#64); **Varo Bank** (#191); **Instawork** (#456). Criteria: must be an independent, privately-held, for-profit, U.S. corporation, proprietorship or partnership as of December 31, 2021; revenues must be at least $100,000 in 2018 and $2 million in 2021; must have four-year operating/sales history. *Inc., "America's 500 Fastest-Growing Private Companies," 2022*

According to Deloitte, San Francisco is home to 44 of North America's 500 fastest-growing high-technology companies: **Vir Biotechnology** (#1); **Evisort** (#16); **Truework** (#27); **Super (fka Snapcommerce)** (#35); **Samsara** (#63); **Discord** (#77); **MDalgorithms** (#122); **6sense** (#130); **Lattice** (#145); **SaaS Labs** (#151); **Pipefy** (#153); **Sigmoid** (#157); **Apollo GraphQL** (#166); **Upgrade** (#169); **Domino Data Lab** (#200); **Premise** (#210); **Kong** (#211); **Enable** (#228); **Skillz** (#230); **Qualio** (#241); **Innovaccer** (#243); **Alto Pharmacy** (#262); **Sense** (#266); **Sentry** (#280); **Sysdig** (#297); **Aurora Solar** (#304); **Block** (#324); **Mursion** (#326); **GoodTime** (#329); **Nozomi Networks** (#333); **Karbon** (#352); **Blueshift** (#366); **Nylas** (#380); **Twilio** (#389); **15Five** (#411); **Mindtickle** (#415); **PandaDoc** (#423); **CircleCI** (#463); **Onfleet** (#471); **Groove** (#475); **Fountain** (#479); **Ease** (#482); **Pinterest** (#498); **Cloudflare** (#500). Companies are ranked by percentage growth in revenue over a four-year period. Criteria for inclusion: company must be headquartered within North America; must own proprietary intellectual property or technology that is sold to customers in products that contributes to a significant portion of the company's operating revenue; must have been in business for a minumum of four years with 2018 operating revenues of at least $50,000 USD/CD and 2021 operating revenues of at least $5 million USD/CD. *Deloitte, 2022 Technology Fast 500*™

Living Environment

COST OF LIVING

Cost of Living Index

Composite Index	Groceries	Housing	Utilities	Trans-portation	Health Care	Misc. Goods/Services
178.8	131.2	307.4	132.4	138.2	131.0	123.4

Note: The Cost of Living Index measures regional differences in the cost of consumer goods and services, excluding taxes and non-consumer expenditures, for professional and managerial households in the top income quintile. It is based on more than 50,000 prices covering almost 60 different items for which prices are collected three times a year by chambers of commerce, economic development organizations or university applied economic centers in each participating urban area. The numbers shown should be read as a percentage above or below the national average of 100. For example, a value of 115.4 in the groceries column indicates that grocery prices are 15.4% higher than the national average. Small differences in the index numbers should not be interpreted as significant; Figures cover the San Francisco CA urban area.
Source: The Council for Community and Economic Research, Cost of Living Index, 2022

Grocery Prices

Area[1]	T-Bone Steak ($/pound)	Frying Chicken ($/pound)	Whole Milk ($/half gal.)	Eggs ($/dozen)	Orange Juice ($/64 oz.)	Coffee ($/11.5 oz.)
City[2]	18.36	1.95	3.38	3.83	4.48	7.00
Avg.	13.81	1.59	2.43	2.25	3.85	4.95
Min.	10.17	0.90	1.51	1.30	2.90	3.46
Max.	19.35	3.30	4.32	4.32	5.31	8.59

*Note: (1) Values for the local area are compared with the average, minimum and maximum values for all 286 areas in the Cost of Living Index; (2) Figures cover the San Francisco CA urban area; **T-Bone Steak** (price per pound); **Frying Chicken** (price per pound, whole fryer); **Whole Milk** (half gallon carton); **Eggs** (price per dozen, Grade A, large); **Orange Juice** (64 oz. Tropicana or Florida Natural); **Coffee** (11.5 oz. can, vacuum-packed, Maxwell House, Hills Bros, or Folgers).*
Source: The Council for Community and Economic Research, Cost of Living Index, 2022

Housing and Utility Costs

Area[1]	New Home Price ($)	Apartment Rent ($/month)	All Electric ($/month)	Part Electric ($/month)	Other Energy ($/month)	Telephone ($/month)
City[2]	1,502,557	3,585	-	172.31	95.33	201.38
Avg.	450,913	1,371	176.41	99.93	76.96	190.22
Min.	229,283	546	100.84	31.56	27.15	174.27
Max.	2,434,977	4,569	356.86	249.59	272.24	208.31

*Note: (1) Values for the local area are compared with the average, minimum and maximum values for all 286 areas in the Cost of Living Index; (2) Figures cover the San Francisco CA urban area; **New Home Price** (2,400 sf living area, 8,000 sf lot, in urban area with full utilities); **Apartment Rent** (950 sf 2 bedroom/1.5 or 2 bath, unfurnished, excluding all utilities except water); **All Electric** (average monthly cost for an all-electric home); **Part Electric** (average monthly cost for a part-electric home); **Other Energy** (average monthly cost for natural gas, fuel oil, coal, wood, and any other forms of energy except electricity); **Telephone** (price includes the base monthly rate plus taxes and fees for three lines of mobile phone service).*
Source: The Council for Community and Economic Research, Cost of Living Index, 2022

Health Care, Transportation, and Other Costs

Area[1]	Doctor ($/visit)	Dentist ($/visit)	Optometrist ($/visit)	Gasoline ($/gallon)	Beauty Salon ($/visit)	Men's Shirt ($)
City[2]	174.07	148.07	154.96	5.42	85.61	50.77
Avg.	124.91	107.77	117.66	3.86	43.31	34.21
Min.	36.61	58.25	51.79	2.90	22.18	13.05
Max.	250.21	162.58	371.96	5.54	85.61	63.54

*Note: (1) Values for the local area are compared with the average, minimum and maximum values for all 286 areas in the Cost of Living Index; (2) Figures cover the San Francisco CA urban area; **Doctor** (general practitioners routine exam of an established patient); **Dentist** (adult teeth cleaning and periodic oral examination); **Optometrist** (full vision eye exam for established adult patient); **Gasoline** (one gallon regular unleaded, national brand, including all taxes, cash price at self-service pump if available); **Beauty Salon** (woman's shampoo, trim, and blow-dry); **Men's Shirt** (cotton/polyester dress shirt, pinpoint weave, long sleeves).*
Source: The Council for Community and Economic Research, Cost of Living Index, 2022

HOUSING

Homeownership Rate

Area	2015 (%)	2016 (%)	2017 (%)	2018 (%)	2019 (%)	2020 (%)	2021 (%)	2022 (%)
MSA[1]	56.3	55.8	55.7	55.6	52.8	53.0	54.7	56.4
U.S.	63.7	63.4	63.9	64.4	64.6	66.6	65.5	65.8

Note: (1) Figures cover the San Francisco-Oakland-Berkeley, CA Metropolitan Statistical Area
Source: U.S. Census Bureau, Housing Vacancies and Homeownership Annual Statistics: 2015-2022

House Price Index (HPI)

Area	National Ranking[2]	Quarterly Change (%)	One-Year Change (%)	Five-Year Change (%)	Since 1991Q1 (%)
MD[1]	177	3.28	9.77	19.08	360.06
U.S.[3]	–	0.34	8.41	58.44	289.08

Note: The HPI is a weighted repeat sales index. It measures average price changes in repeat sales or refinancings on the same properties. This information is obtained by reviewing repeat mortgage transactions on single-family properties whose mortgages have been purchased or securitized by Fannie Mae or Freddie Mac since January 1975; (1) Figures cover the San Francisco-Redwood City-South San Francisco, CA Metropolitan Division; (2) Rankings are based on annual percentage change for all metro areas containing at least 15,000 transactions over the last 10 years and ranges from 1 to 257; (3) figures based on a weighted average of Census Division estimates using a seasonally adjusted, purchase-only index; all figures are for the period ending December 31, 2022
Source: Federal Housing Finance Agency, Change in FHFA Metropolitan Area House Price Indexes, 2022Q4

Median Single-Family Home Prices

Area	2020	2021	2022p	Percent Change 2021 to 2022
MSA[1]	1,100.0	1,320.0	1,375.0	4.2
U.S. Average	300.2	357.1	392.6	9.9

Note: Figures are median sales prices of existing single-family homes in thousands of dollars; (p) preliminary; (1) Figures cover the San Francisco-Oakland-Berkeley, CA Metropolitan Statistical Area
Source: National Association of Realtors, Median Sales Price of Existing Single-Family Homes for Metropolitan Areas, 4th Quarter 2022

Qualifying Income Based on Median Sales Price of Existing Single-Family Homes

Area	With 5% Down ($)	With 10% Down ($)	With 20% Down ($)
MSA[1]	367,996	348,628	309,891
U.S. Average	112,234	106,237	94,513

Note: Figures are preliminary; Qualifying income is based on a mortgage rate of 6.77%. Monthly principal and interest payment is limited to 25% of income; (1) Figures cover the San Francisco-Oakland-Berkeley, CA Metropolitan Statistical Area
Source: National Association of Realtors, Qualifying Income Based on Median Sales Price of Existing Single-Family Homes for Metropolitan Areas, 4th Quarter 2022

Home Value

Area	Under $100,000	$100,000 -$199,999	$200,000 -$299,999	$300,000 -$399,999	$400,000 -$499,999	$500,000 -$999,999	$1,000,000 or more	Median ($)
City	1.5	0.8	1.0	1.9	1.6	26.1	67.1	1,194,500
MSA[1]	2.0	1.4	1.7	3.8	5.9	40.7	44.4	933,300
U.S.	16.2	24.2	20.1	13.6	8.3	13.6	4.1	244,900

Note: Figures are percentages except for median and cover owner-occupied housing units; (1) Figures cover the San Francisco-Oakland-Berkeley, CA Metropolitan Statistical Area
Source: U.S. Census Bureau, 2017-2021 American Community Survey 5-Year Estimates

Year Housing Structure Built

Area	2020 or Later	2010 -2019	2000 -2009	1990 -1999	1980 -1989	1970 -1979	1960 -1969	1950 -1959	1940 -1949	Before 1940	Median Year
City	0.1	5.4	6.3	4.2	5.4	7.2	7.9	8.6	8.8	46.2	1944
MSA[1]	0.1	4.6	7.6	8.1	10.9	14.7	13.1	13.6	7.7	19.7	1967
U.S.	0.2	7.3	13.6	13.6	13.2	14.8	10.3	10.0	4.7	12.2	1979

Note: Figures are percentages except for Median Year; Note: (1) Figures cover the San Francisco-Oakland-Berkeley, CA Metropolitan Statistical Area
Source: U.S. Census Bureau, 2017-2021 American Community Survey 5-Year Estimates

Gross Monthly Rent

Area	Under $500	$500 -$999	$1,000 -$1,499	$1,500 -$1,999	$2,000 -$2,499	$2,500 -$2,999	$3,000 and up	Median ($)
City	8.6	10.0	13.7	14.1	13.3	11.6	28.5	2,130
MSA[1]	5.6	7.0	13.2	18.3	19.2	14.0	22.8	2,155
U.S.	8.1	30.5	30.8	16.8	7.3	3.1	3.5	1,163

Note: Figures are percentages except for median; Gross rent is the contract rent plus the estimated average monthly cost of utilities (electricity, gas, and water and sewer) and fuels (oil, coal, kerosene, wood, etc.) if these are paid by the renter (or paid for the renter by someone else); (1) Figures cover the San Francisco-Oakland-Berkeley, CA Metropolitan Statistical Area
Source: U.S. Census Bureau, 2017-2021 American Community Survey 5-Year Estimates

HEALTH

Health Risk Factors

Category	MSA[1] (%)	U.S. (%)
Adults aged 18–64 who have any kind of health care coverage	n/a	90.9
Adults who reported being in good or better health	n/a	85.2
Adults who have been told they have high blood cholesterol	n/a	35.7
Adults who have been told they have high blood pressure	n/a	32.4
Adults who are current smokers	n/a	14.4
Adults who currently use e-cigarettes	n/a	6.7
Adults who currently use chewing tobacco, snuff, or snus	n/a	3.5
Adults who are heavy drinkers[2]	n/a	6.3
Adults who are binge drinkers[3]	n/a	15.4
Adults who are overweight (BMI 25.0 - 29.9)	n/a	34.4
Adults who are obese (BMI 30.0 - 99.8)	n/a	33.9
Adults who participated in any physical activities in the past month	n/a	76.3

Note: (1) Figures for the San Francisco-Oakland-Berkeley, CA Metropolitan Statistical Area were not available.
(2) Heavy drinkers are classified as adult men having more than 14 drinks per week and adult women having more than 7 drinks per week; (3) Binge drinkers are classified as males having five or more drinks on one occasion or females having four or more drinks on one occasion
Source: Centers for Disease Control and Prevention, Behaviorial Risk Factor Surveillance System, SMART: Selected Metropolitan Area Risk Trends, 2021

Acute and Chronic Health Conditions

Category	MSA[1] (%)	U.S. (%)
Adults who have ever been told they had a heart attack	n/a	4.0
Adults who have ever been told they have angina or coronary heart disease	n/a	3.8
Adults who have ever been told they had a stroke	n/a	3.0
Adults who have ever been told they have asthma	n/a	14.9
Adults who have ever been told they have arthritis	n/a	25.8
Adults who have ever been told they have diabetes[2]	n/a	10.9
Adults who have ever been told they had skin cancer	n/a	6.6
Adults who have ever been told they had any other types of cancer	n/a	7.5
Adults who have ever been told they have COPD	n/a	6.1
Adults who have ever been told they have kidney disease	n/a	3.0
Adults who have ever been told they have a form of depression	n/a	20.5

Note: (1) Figures for the San Francisco-Oakland-Berkeley, CA Metropolitan Statistical Area were not available.
(2) Figures do not include pregnancy-related, borderline, or pre-diabetes
Source: Centers for Disease Control and Prevention, Behaviorial Risk Factor Surveillance System, SMART: Selected Metropolitan Area Risk Trends, 2021

Health Screening and Vaccination Rates

Category	MSA[1] (%)	U.S. (%)
Adults who have ever been tested for HIV	n/a	34.9
Adults who have had their blood cholesterol checked within the last five years	n/a	85.2
Adults aged 65+ who have had flu shot within the past year	n/a	68.6
Adults aged 65+ who have ever had a pneumonia vaccination	n/a	71.0

Note: (1) Figures for the San Francisco-Oakland-Berkeley, CA Metropolitan Statistical Area were not available.
Source: Centers for Disease Control and Prevention, Behaviorial Risk Factor Surveillance System, SMART: Selected Metropolitan Area Risk Trends, 2021

Disability Status

Category	MSA[1] (%)	U.S. (%)
Adults who reported being deaf	n/a	7.2
Are you blind or have serious difficulty seeing, even when wearing glasses?	n/a	4.8
Are you limited in any way in any of your usual activities due to arthritis?	n/a	11.1
Do you have difficulty doing errands alone?	n/a	7.0
Do you have difficulty dressing or bathing?	n/a	3.6
Do you have serious difficulty concentrating/remembering/making decisions?	n/a	12.1
Do you have serious difficulty walking or climbing stairs?	n/a	12.8

Note: (1) Figures for the San Francisco-Oakland-Berkeley, CA Metropolitan Statistical Area were not available.
Source: Centers for Disease Control and Prevention, Behaviorial Risk Factor Surveillance System, SMART: Selected Metropolitan Area Risk Trends, 2021

Mortality Rates for the Top 10 Causes of Death in the U.S.

ICD-10[a] Sub-Chapter	ICD-10[a] Code	Crude Mortality Rate[1] per 100,000 population	
		County[2]	U.S.
Malignant neoplasms	C00-C97	147.1	182.6
Ischaemic heart diseases	I20-I25	88.7	113.1
Other forms of heart disease	I30-I51	45.5	64.4
Other degenerative diseases of the nervous system	G30-G31	40.7	51.0
Cerebrovascular diseases	I60-I69	45.1	47.8
Other external causes of accidental injury	W00-X59	70.9	46.4
Chronic lower respiratory diseases	J40-J47	21.1	45.7
Organic, including symptomatic, mental disorders	F01-F09	26.6	35.9
Hypertensive diseases	I10-I15	32.9	35.0
Diabetes mellitus	E10-E14	18.0	29.6

Note: (a) ICD-10 = International Classification of Diseases 10th Revision; (1) Crude mortality rates are a three-year average covering 2019-2021; (2) Figures cover San Francisco County.
Source: Centers for Disease Control and Prevention, National Center for Health Statistics. National Vital Statistics System, Mortality 2018-2021 on CDC WONDER Online Database

Mortality Rates for Selected Causes of Death

ICD-10[a] Sub-Chapter	ICD-10[a] Code	Crude Mortality Rate[1] per 100,000 population	
		County[2]	U.S.
Assault	X85-Y09	4.7	7.0
Diseases of the liver	K70-K76	12.2	19.8
Human immunodeficiency virus (HIV) disease	B20-B24	4.4	1.5
Influenza and pneumonia	J09-J18	9.9	14.7
Intentional self-harm	X60-X84	9.5	14.3
Malnutrition	E40-E46	1.6	4.3
Obesity and other hyperalimentation	E65-E68	0.8	3.0
Renal failure	N17-N19	11.0	15.7
Transport accidents	V01-V99	5.4	13.6
Viral hepatitis	B15-B19	2.0	1.2

Note: (a) ICD-10 = International Classification of Diseases 10th Revision; (1) Crude mortality rates are a three-year average covering 2019-2021; (2) Figures cover San Francisco County; Data are suppressed when the data meet the criteria for confidentiality constraints; Crude mortality rates are flagged as unreliable when the rate would be calculated with a numerator of 20 or less.
Source: Centers for Disease Control and Prevention, National Center for Health Statistics. National Vital Statistics System, Mortality 2018-2021 on CDC WONDER Online Database

Health Insurance Coverage

Area	With Health Insurance	With Private Health Insurance	With Public Health Insurance	Without Health Insurance	Population Under Age 19 Without Health Insurance
City	96.4	76.2	29.5	3.6	1.9
MSA[1]	95.9	76.0	30.5	4.1	2.3
U.S.	91.2	67.8	35.4	8.8	5.3

Note: Figures are percentages that cover the civilian noninstitutionalized population; (1) Figures cover the San Francisco-Oakland-Berkeley, CA Metropolitan Statistical Area
Source: U.S. Census Bureau, 2017-2021 American Community Survey 5-Year Estimates

Number of Medical Professionals

Area	MDs[3]	DOs[3,4]	Dentists	Podiatrists	Chiropractors	Optometrists
County[1] (number)	7,262	114	1,394	96	351	259
County[1] (rate[2])	834.7	13.1	171.0	11.8	43.1	31.8
U.S. (rate[2])	289.3	23.5	72.5	6.2	28.7	17.4

Note: Data as of 2021 unless noted; (1) Data covers San Francisco County; (2) Rate per 100,000 population; (3) Data as of 2020 and includes all active, non-federal physicians; (4) Doctor of Osteopathic Medicine
Source: U.S. Department of Health and Human Services, Health Resources and Services Administration, Bureau of Health Professions, Area Resource File (ARF) 2021-2022

Best Hospitals

According to *U.S. News,* the San Francisco-San Mateo-Redwood City, CA metro area is home to one of the best hospitals in the U.S.: **UCSF Health-UCSF Medical Center** (Honor Roll/14 adult specialties and 10 pediatric specialties). The hospital listed was nationally ranked in at least one of 15 adult or 10 pediatric specialties. The number of specialties shown cover the parent hospital. Only 164 U.S. hospitals performed well enough to be nationally ranked in one or more specialties. Twenty hospitals in the U.S. made the Honor Roll. The Best Hospitals Honor Roll takes both the national rankings and the procedure and condition ratings into account. Hospitals received points if they were nationally ranked in one of the 15 adult specialties—the higher they ranked, the more points they got—and how many ratings of "high performing" they earned in the 17 procedures and conditions. *U.S. News Online, "America's Best Hospitals 2022-23"*

According to *U.S. News,* the San Francisco-San Mateo-Redwood City, CA metro area is home to one of the best children's hospitals in the U.S.: **UCSF Benioff Children's Hospitals** (10 pediatric specialties). The hospital listed was highly ranked in at least one of 10 pediatric specialties. Eighty-six children's hospitals in the U.S. were nationally ranked in at least one specialty. Hospitals received points for being ranked in a specialty, and the 10 hospitals with the most points across the 10 specialties make up the Honor Roll. *U.S. News Online, "America's Best Children's Hospitals 2022-23"*

EDUCATION

Public School District Statistics

District Name	Schls	Pupils	Pupil/ Teacher Ratio	Minority Pupils[1] (%)	LEP/ELL[2] (%)	IEP[3] (%)
Five Keys Independence HSD	1	2,352	46.3	91.5	28.4	2.8
San Francisco Unified	113	49,204	19.3	86.2	28.6	12.4

Note: Table includes school districts with 2,000 or more students; (1) Percentage of students that are not non-Hispanic white; (2) Percentage of students that are Limited English Proficient or English Language Learners (2018-19); (3) Percentage of students that have an Individualized Education Program (2019-20).
Source: U.S. Department of Education, National Center for Education Statistics, Common Core of Data, Local Education Agency (School District) Universe Survey: School Year 2021-2022

Best High Schools

According to *U.S. News,* San Francisco is home to two of the top 500 high schools in the U.S.: **Lowell High School** (#82); **KIPP San Francisco College Preparatory** (#407). Nearly 18,000 public, magnet and charter schools were ranked based on their performance on state assessments and how well they prepare students for college. *U.S. News & World Report, "Best High Schools 2022"*

Highest Level of Education

Area	Less than H.S.	H.S. Diploma	Some College, No Deg.	Associate Degree	Bachelor's Degree	Master's Degree	Prof. School Degree	Doctorate Degree
City	11.2	11.4	12.7	5.2	35.4	16.0	5.1	3.0
MSA[1]	10.3	15.1	16.5	6.7	29.9	14.5	3.9	3.1
U.S.	11.1	26.5	20.0	8.7	20.6	9.3	2.2	1.5

Note: Figures cover persons age 25 and over; (1) Figures cover the San Francisco-Oakland-Berkeley, CA Metropolitan Statistical Area
Source: U.S. Census Bureau, 2017-2021 American Community Survey 5-Year Estimates

Educational Attainment by Race

Area	High School Graduate or Higher (%)					Bachelor's Degree or Higher (%)				
	Total	White	Black	Asian	Hisp.[2]	Total	White	Black	Asian	Hisp.[2]
City	88.8	97.3	87.3	80.4	79.2	59.5	75.4	31.5	48.9	38.1
MSA[1]	89.7	95.0	91.3	88.1	73.1	51.4	58.7	31.6	57.6	23.9
U.S.	88.9	91.4	87.2	87.6	71.2	33.7	35.5	23.3	55.6	18.4

Note: Figures shown cover persons 25 years old and over; (1) Figures cover the San Francisco-Oakland-Berkeley, CA Metropolitan Statistical Area; (2) People of Hispanic origin can be of any race
Source: U.S. Census Bureau, 2017-2021 American Community Survey 5-Year Estimates

School Enrollment by Grade and Control

Area	Preschool (%)		Kindergarten (%)		Grades 1 - 4 (%)		Grades 5 - 8 (%)		Grades 9 - 12 (%)	
	Public	Private	Public	Private	Public	Private	Public	Private	Public	Private
City	34.0	66.0	67.4	32.6	71.0	29.0	66.6	33.4	75.5	24.5
MSA[1]	40.5	59.5	83.1	16.9	85.1	14.9	84.7	15.3	86.2	13.8
U.S.	58.8	41.2	86.3	13.7	88.3	11.7	88.6	11.4	89.4	10.6

Note: Figures shown cover persons 3 years old and over; (1) Figures cover the San Francisco-Oakland-Berkeley, CA Metropolitan Statistical Area
Source: U.S. Census Bureau, 2017-2021 American Community Survey 5-Year Estimates

Higher Education

Four-Year Colleges			Two-Year Colleges			Medical Schools[1]	Law Schools[2]	Voc/ Tech[3]
Public	Private Non-profit	Private For-profit	Public	Private Non-profit	Private For-profit			
6	32	5	14	0	6	1	7	14

Note: Figures cover institutions located within the San Francisco-Oakland-Berkeley, CA Metropolitan Statistical Area and include main campuses only; (1) includes schools accredited by the Liaison Committee on Medical Education and the American Osteopathic Association's Commission on Osteopathic College Accreditation; (2) includes ABA-accredited schools, schools with provisional ABA accreditation, and state accredited schools; (3) includes all schools with programs that are less than 2 years.
Source: National Center for Education Statistics, Integrated Postsecondary Education System (IPEDS), 2021-22; Wikipedia, List of Medical Schools in the United States, accessed April 10, 2023; Wikipedia, List of Law Schools in the United States, accessed April 10, 2023

According to *U.S. News & World Report,* the San Francisco-San Mateo-Redwood City, CA metro division is home to one of the top 200 national universities in the U.S.: **University of San Francisco** (#105 tie). The indicators used to capture academic quality fall into a number of categories: assessment by administrators at peer institutions; retention of students; faculty resources; student selectivity; financial resources; alumni giving; high school counselor ratings of colleges; and graduation rate. *U.S. News & World Report, "America's Best Colleges 2023"*

According to *U.S. News & World Report,* the San Francisco-San Mateo-Redwood City, CA metro division is home to one of the top 100 law schools in the U.S.: **University of California College of the Law—San Francisco** (#51). The rankings are based on a weighted average of 12 measures of quality: peer assessment score; assessment score by lawyers/judges; median LSAT scores; median undergrad GPA; acceptance rate; employment rates for graduates; placement success; bar passage rate; faculty resources; expenditures per student; student/faculty ratio; and library resources. *U.S. News & World Report, "America's Best Graduate Schools, Law, 2023"*

According to *U.S. News & World Report,* the San Francisco-San Mateo-Redwood City, CA metro division is home to one of the top 75 medical schools for research in the U.S.: **University of California—San Francisco** (#3 tie). The rankings are based on a weighted average of 11 measures of quality: quality assessment; peer assessment score; assessment score by residency directors; research activity; total research activity; average research activity per faculty member; student selectivity; median MCAT total score; median undergraduate GPA; acceptance rate; and faculty resources. *U.S. News & World Report, "America's Best Graduate Schools, Medical, 2023"*

EMPLOYERS

Major Employers

Company Name	Industry
All Hallows Preservation	Apartment building operators
AT&T	Telephone communication, except radio
AT&T Services	Telephone communication, except radio
California Pacific Medical Center	General medical & surgical hospitals
City & County of San Francisco	Public welfare administration: nonoperating, govt.
Edy's Grand Ice Cream	Ice cream & other frozen treats
Franklin Templeton Services	Investment advice
Lawrence Livermore National Laboratory	Noncommercial research organizations
Menlo Worldwide Forwarding	Letter delivery, private air
Oracle America	Minicomputers
Oracle Systems Corporation	Prepackaged software
Pacific Gas and Electric Company	Electric & other services combined
PACPIZZA	Pizzeria, chain
San Francisco Community College District	Colleges & universities
University of California, Berkeley	University
Veterans Health Administration	Administration of veterans' affairs
Wells Fargo	National commercial banks

Note: Companies shown are located within the San Francisco-Oakland-Berkeley, CA Metropolitan Statistical Area.
Source: Hoovers.com; Wikipedia

Best Companies to Work For

Atlassian; Kimpton Hotels & Restaurants; Orrick; Salesforce, headquartered in San Francisco, are among "The 100 Best Companies to Work For." To pick the best companies, *Fortune* partnered with the Great Place to Work Institute. Two-thirds of a company's score is based on the results of the Institute's Trust Index survey, which is sent to a random sample of employees from each company. The questions related to attitudes about management's credibility, job satisfaction, and camaraderie. The other third of the scoring is based on the company's responses to the Institute's Culture Audit, which includes detailed questions about pay and benefit programs, and a series of open-ended questions about hiring practices, internal communication, training, recognition programs, and diversity efforts. Any company that is at least five years old with more than 1,000 U.S. employees is eligible. *Fortune, "The 100 Best Companies to Work For," 2023*

6sense; Asana; Atlassian; Gem; HashiCorp; Kimpton Hotels & Restaurants; Lattice; NerdWallet; Opendoor Technologies; Orrick; PagerDuty; Real Chemistry; Salesforce; Splunk; Twilio; Udemy; WorkRamp, headquartered in San Francisco, are among "Fortune's Best Workplaces for Women." To pick the best companies, *Fortune* partnered with the Great Place to Work Institute. To be considered for the list, companies must be Great Place To Work-Certified. Companies must also employ at least 50 women, at least 20% of their non-executive managers must be female, and at least one executive must be female. To determine the Best Workplaces for Women, Great Place To Work measured the differences in women's survey responses to those of their peers and assesses the impact of demographics and roles on the quality and consistency of women's experiences. Great Place To Work also analyzed the gender balance of each workplace, how it compared to each company's industry, and patterns in representation as women rise from front-line positions to the board of directors. *Fortune, "Best Workplaces for Women," 2022*

Virta Health, headquartered in San Francisco, is among "Best Workplaces in Health Care." To determine the Best Workplaces in Health Care list, Great Place To Work analyzed the survey responses of over 161,000 employees from Great Place To Work-Certified companies in the health care industry. Survey data analysis and company-provided datapoints are then factored into a combined score to compare and rank the companies that create the most consistently positive experience for all employees in this industry. *Fortune, "Best Workplaces in Health Care," 2022*

Asana; Atlassian; Demandbase; HashiCorp; Ironclad; Kimpton Hotels & Restaurants; Lattice; NextRoll; Okta; Opendoor Technologies; Orrick; Ripple; Salesforce; Splunk; Thumbtack; Turo; Twilio; Udemy, headquartered in San Francisco, are among "Fortune's Best Workplaces for Parents." To pick the best companies, *Fortune* partnered with the Great Place To Work Institute. To be considered for the list, companies must be Great Place To Work-Certified and have at least 50 responses from parents in the US. The survey enables employees to share confidential quantitative and qualitative feedback about their organization's culture by responding to 60 statements on a 5-point scale and answering two open-ended questions. Collectively, these statements describe a great employee experience, defined by high levels of trust, respect, credibility, fairness, pride, and camaraderie. In addition, companies provide organizational data like size, location, industry, demographics, roles, and levels; and provide information about parental leave, adoption, flexible schedule, childcare and dependent health care benefits. *Fortune, "Best Workplaces for Parents," 2022*

PUBLIC SAFETY

Crime Rate

Area	Total Crime	Violent Crime Rate				Property Crime Rate		
		Murder	Rape[3]	Robbery	Aggrav. Assault	Burglary	Larceny -Theft	Motor Vehicle Theft
City	4,938.4	5.4	22.5	270.9	245.3	845.4	2,872.2	676.8
Suburbs[1]	3,106.9	5.3	33.9	157.3	219.7	345.9	1,757.2	587.6
Metro[2]	3,448.3	5.3	31.8	178.5	224.5	439.0	1,965.0	604.2
U.S.	2,356.7	6.5	38.4	73.9	279.7	314.2	1,398.0	246.0

Note: Figures are crimes per 100,000 population; (1) All areas within the metro area that are located outside the city limits; (2) Figures cover the San Francisco-Redwood City-South San Francisco, CA Metropolitan Division; (3) All figures shown were reported using the revised Uniform Crime Reporting (UCR) definition of rape; Due to the transition to the National Incident-Based Reporting System (NIBRS), limited city and metro area data was released for 2021.
Source: FBI Uniform Crime Reports, 2020

Hate Crimes

Area	Number of Quarters Reported	Number of Incidents per Bias Motivation						
		Race/Ethnicity/ Ancestry	Religion	Sexual Orientation	Disability	Gender	Gender Identity
City	4	37	7	8	0	0	2
U.S.	4	5,227	1,244	1,110	130	75	266

Note: Due to the transition to the National Incident-Based Reporting System (NIBRS), limited crime data was released for 2021.
Source: Federal Bureau of Investigation, Hate Crime Statistics 2020

Identity Theft Consumer Reports

Area	Reports	Reports per 100,000 Population	Rank[2]
MSA[1]	10,154	216	140
U.S.	1,108,609	339	-

Note: (1) Figures cover the San Francisco-Oakland-Berkeley, CA Metropolitan Statistical Area; (2) Rank ranges from 1 to 391 where 1 indicates greatest number of identity theft reports per 100,000 population
Source: Federal Trade Commission, Consumer Sentinel Network Data Book 2022

Fraud and Other Consumer Reports

Area	Reports	Reports per 100,000 Population	Rank[2]
MSA[1]	45,227	960	115
U.S.	4,064,520	1,245	-

Note: (1) Figures cover the San Francisco-Oakland-Berkeley, CA Metropolitan Statistical Area; (2) Rank ranges from 1 to 391 where 1 indicates greatest number of fraud and other consumer reports per 100,000 population
Source: Federal Trade Commission, Consumer Sentinel Network Data Book 2022

POLITICS

2020 Presidential Election Results

Area	Biden	Trump	Jorgensen	Hawkins	Other
San Francisco County	85.3	12.7	0.7	0.6	0.7
U.S.	51.3	46.8	1.2	0.3	0.5

Note: Results are percentages and may not add to 100% due to rounding
Source: Dave Leip's Atlas of U.S. Presidential Elections

SPORTS

Professional Sports Teams

Team Name	League	Year Established
Golden State Warriors	National Basketball Association (NBA)	1962
Oakland Athletics	Major League Baseball (MLB)	1968
San Francisco 49ers	National Football League (NFL)	1946
San Francisco Giants	Major League Baseball (MLB)	1958

Note: Includes teams located in the San Francisco-Oakland-Berkeley, CA Metropolitan Statistical Area.
Source: Wikipedia, Major Professional Sports Teams of the United States and Canada, April 12, 2023

CLIMATE

Average and Extreme Temperatures

Temperature	Jan	Feb	Mar	Apr	May	Jun	Jul	Aug	Sep	Oct	Nov	Dec	Yr.
Extreme High (°F)	72	77	85	92	97	106	105	98	103	99	85	75	106
Average High (°F)	56	59	61	64	66	70	71	72	73	70	63	56	65
Average Temp. (°F)	49	52	53	56	58	61	63	63	64	61	55	50	57
Average Low (°F)	42	44	45	47	49	52	53	54	54	51	47	42	49
Extreme Low (°F)	26	30	31	36	39	43	44	45	41	37	31	24	24

Note: Figures cover the years 1948-1990
Source: National Climatic Data Center, International Station Meteorological Climate Summary, 9/96

Average Precipitation/Snowfall/Humidity

Precip./Humidity	Jan	Feb	Mar	Apr	May	Jun	Jul	Aug	Sep	Oct	Nov	Dec	Yr.
Avg. Precip. (in.)	4.3	3.1	2.9	1.4	0.3	0.1	Tr	Tr	0.2	1.0	2.5	3.4	19.3
Avg. Snowfall (in.)	Tr	Tr	Tr	0	0	0	0	0	0	0	0	Tr	Tr
Avg. Rel. Hum. 7am (%)	86	85	82	79	78	77	81	83	83	83	85	86	82
Avg. Rel. Hum. 4pm (%)	67	65	63	61	61	60	60	62	60	60	64	68	63

Note: Figures cover the years 1948-1990; Tr = Trace amounts (<0.05 in. of rain; <0.5 in. of snow)
Source: National Climatic Data Center, International Station Meteorological Climate Summary, 9/96

Weather Conditions

Temperature			Daytime Sky			Precipitation		
10°F & below	32°F & below	90°F & above	Clear	Partly cloudy	Cloudy	0.01 inch or more precip.	0.1 inch or more snow/ice	Thunder-storms
0	6	4	136	130	99	63	< 1	5

Note: Figures are average number of days per year and cover the years 1948-1990
Source: National Climatic Data Center, International Station Meteorological Climate Summary, 9/96

HAZARDOUS WASTE

Superfund Sites

The San Francisco-San Mateo-Redwood City, CA metro division is home to one site on the EPA's Superfund National Priorities List: **Treasure Island Naval Station-Hunters Point Annex** (final). There are a total of 1,165 Superfund sites with a status of proposed or final on the list in the U.S. *U.S. Environmental Protection Agency, National Priorities List, April 12, 2023*

AIR QUALITY

Air Quality Trends: Ozone

	1990	1995	2000	2005	2010	2015	2018	2019	2020	2021
MSA[1]	0.062	0.077	0.060	0.060	0.063	0.064	0.056	0.062	0.062	0.064
U.S.	0.087	0.089	0.081	0.080	0.072	0.067	0.069	0.065	0.065	0.067

Note: (1) Data covers the San Francisco-Oakland-Berkeley, CA Metropolitan Statistical Area. The values shown are the composite ozone concentration averages among trend sites based on the highest fourth daily maximum 8-hour concentration in parts per million. These trends are based on sites having an adequate record of monitoring data during the trend period. Data from exceptional events are included.
Source: U.S. Environmental Protection Agency, Air Quality Monitoring Information, "Air Quality Trends by City, 1990-2021"

Air Quality Index

Area	Percent of Days when Air Quality was...[2]					AQI Statistics[2]	
	Good	Moderate	Unhealthy for Sensitive Groups	Unhealthy	Very Unhealthy	Maximum	Median
MSA[1]	58.1	39.2	2.5	0.3	0.0	151	46

Note: (1) Data covers the San Francisco-Oakland-Berkeley, CA Metropolitan Statistical Area; (2) Based on 365 days with AQI data in 2021. Air Quality Index (AQI) is an index for reporting daily air quality. EPA calculates the AQI for five major air pollutants regulated by the Clean Air Act: ground-level ozone, particle pollution (aka particulate matter), carbon monoxide, sulfur dioxide, and nitrogen dioxide. The AQI runs from 0 to 500. The higher the AQI value, the greater the level of air pollution and the greater the health concern. There are six AQI categories: "Good" AQI is between 0 and 50. Air quality is considered satisfactory; "Moderate" AQI is between 51 and 100. Air quality is acceptable; "Unhealthy for Sensitive Groups" When AQI values are between 101 and 150, members of sensitive groups may experience health effects; "Unhealthy" When AQI values are between 151 and 200 everyone may begin to experience health effects; "Very Unhealthy" AQI values between 201 and 300 trigger a health alert; "Hazardous" AQI values over 300 trigger warnings of emergency conditions (not shown).
Source: U.S. Environmental Protection Agency, Air Quality Index Report, 2021

Air Quality Index Pollutants

Area	Percent of Days when AQI Pollutant was...[2]					
	Carbon Monoxide	Nitrogen Dioxide	Ozone	Sulfur Dioxide	Particulate Matter 2.5	Particulate Matter 10
MSA[1]	0.0	1.1	47.9	(3)	51.0	0.0

Note: (1) Data covers the San Francisco-Oakland-Berkeley, CA Metropolitan Statistical Area; (2) Based on 365 days with AQI data in 2021. The Air Quality Index (AQI) is an index for reporting daily air quality. EPA calculates the AQI for five major air pollutants regulated by the Clean Air Act: ground-level ozone, particle pollution (also known as particulate matter), carbon monoxide, sulfur dioxide, and nitrogen dioxide. The AQI runs from 0 to 500. The higher the AQI value, the greater the level of air pollution and the greater the health concern; (3) Sulfur dioxide is no longer included in this table (as of December 8, 2021) because SO_2 concentrations tend to be very localized and not necessarily representative of broad geographical areas like counties and CBSAs.
Source: U.S. Environmental Protection Agency, Air Quality Index Report, 2021

Maximum Air Pollutant Concentrations: Particulate Matter, Ozone, CO and Lead

	Particulate Matter 10 (ug/m³)	Particulate Matter 2.5 Wtd AM (ug/m³)	Particulate Matter 2.5 24-Hr (ug/m³)	Ozone (ppm)	Carbon Monoxide (ppm)	Lead (ug/m³)
MSA[1] Level	35	9.1	23	0.074	2	n/a
NAAQS[2]	150	15	35	0.075	9	0.15
Met NAAQS[2]	Yes	Yes	Yes	Yes	Yes	n/a

Note: (1) Data covers the San Francisco-Oakland-Berkeley, CA Metropolitan Statistical Area; Data from exceptional events are included; (2) National Ambient Air Quality Standards; ppm = parts per million; ug/m³ = micrograms per cubic meter; n/a not available.
Concentrations: Particulate Matter 10 (coarse particulate)—highest second maximum 24-hour concentration; Particulate Matter 2.5 Wtd AM (fine particulate)—highest weighted annual mean concentration; Particulate Matter 2.5 24-Hour (fine particulate)—highest 98th percentile 24-hour concentration; Ozone—highest fourth daily maximum 8-hour concentration; Carbon Monoxide—highest second maximum non-overlapping 8-hour concentration; Lead—maximum running 3-month average
Source: U.S. Environmental Protection Agency, Air Quality Monitoring Information, "Air Quality Statistics by City, 2021"

Maximum Air Pollutant Concentrations: Nitrogen Dioxide and Sulfur Dioxide

	Nitrogen Dioxide AM (ppb)	Nitrogen Dioxide 1-Hr (ppb)	Sulfur Dioxide AM (ppb)	Sulfur Dioxide 1-Hr (ppb)	Sulfur Dioxide 24-Hr (ppb)
MSA[1] Level	12	40	n/a	11	n/a
NAAQS[2]	53	100	30	75	140
Met NAAQS[2]	Yes	Yes	n/a	Yes	n/a

Note: (1) Data covers the San Francisco-Oakland-Berkeley, CA Metropolitan Statistical Area; Data from exceptional events are included; (2) National Ambient Air Quality Standards; ppm = parts per million; ug/m^3 = micrograms per cubic meter; n/a not available.
Concentrations: Nitrogen Dioxide AM—highest arithmetic mean concentration; Nitrogen Dioxide 1-Hr—highest 98th percentile 1-hour daily maximum concentration; Sulfur Dioxide AM—highest annual mean concentration; Sulfur Dioxide 1-Hr—highest 99th percentile 1-hour daily maximum concentration; Sulfur Dioxide 24-Hr—highest second maximum 24-hour concentration
Source: U.S. Environmental Protection Agency, Air Quality Monitoring Information, "Air Quality Statistics by City, 2021"

San Jose, California

Background

Like many cities in the valleys of northern California, San Jose is an abundant cornucopia of wine grapes and produce. It is part of the famed, high-tech Silicon Valley, and situated only seven miles from the southernmost tip of San Francisco Bay, San Jose is flanked by the Santa Cruz Mountains to the west, and the Mount Hamilton arm of the Diablo Range to the east. The Coyote and Guadalupe rivers gently cut through this landscape, carrying water only in the spring.

San Jose was founded on November 29, 1777, by Spanish colonizers, and can rightfully claim to be the oldest civic settlement in California. San Jose was established by the Spanish to be a produce and cattle supplier to the nearby communities and presidios of San Francisco and Monterey, a role that it still enjoys today.

After U.S. troops wrested the territory of California from Mexican rule, San Jose became its state capital. At the same time, the city served as a supply base to gold prospectors.

Today, San Jose retains much of its history, still a major shipping and processing center for agricultural produce, and the city produces some of the best table wines in the country. A replica of the Mission of Santa Clara stands on the grounds of the University of Santa Clara—a reminder of its Spanish heritage.

Due to annexation of surrounding communities after World War II, the population of San Jose increased more than tenfold, attracting residents with industries that included NASA research, electronic components, and motors production. San Jose rapidly became a family-oriented community of housing developments and shopping malls.

During the 1990s, San Jose was home to more than half of Silicon Valley's leading semiconductor, networking, and telecommunications companies, earning the nickname "Capital of Silicon Valley." The renovated downtown is headquarters for a number of major software developers.

At the turn of the 21st century, San Jose suffered from a downturn in electronics and computer industries, but the city has since rebounded, with lower unemployment numbers and plans to ensure that the city's economic future remains bright. The region has been cited as the happiest place to work in the United States, noting that technology jobs typically offer a high salary and opportunity for growth, and that tech companies usually provide a fun and innovative work environment.

The HP Pavilion, home of the San Jose Sharks hockey team, is one of the most active venues for non-sporting events in the world.

Public art is an evolving attraction in the city. The city was one of the first to adopt a public art ordinance at 2 percent of capital improvement building project budgets, a commitment that has affected the visual landscape of the city, with a considerable number of public art projects throughout the downtown area, and a growing collection in the newer civic locations in neighborhoods including libraries, parks, and fire stations. Of note, San Jose's Mineta Airport has incorporated a program of Art & Technology that includes a series of platforms for projection-based, digital and data-driven artwork throughout the airport, designed to be changed over time in keeping up with technological advances.

San Jose enjoys a Mediterranean, or dry summer subtropical, climate. The rain that does fall comes mostly November through March. Severe winter storms with gale winds and heavy rain occur occasionally. The summer weather is dominated by night and morning stratus clouds along with sea breezes blowing from the cold waters of the bay. During the winter months fog is common, causing difficult flying conditions.

Rankings

General Rankings

- *US News & World Report* conducted a survey of more than 3,600 people and analyzed the 150 largest metropolitan areas to determine what matters most when selecting where to settle down. San Jose ranked #5 out of the top 25 as having the best combination of desirable factors. Criteria: cost of living; quality of life and education; net migration; job market; desirability; and other factors. *money.usnews.com, "The 25 Best Places to Live in the U.S. in 2022-2023," May 17, 2022*

- The San Jose metro area was identified as one of America's fastest-growing areas in terms of population and business growth by *MagnifyMoney*. The area ranked #19 out of 35. The 100 most populous metro areas in the U.S. were evaluated on their change from 2011 to 2016 in the following categories: people and housing; workforce and employment opportunities; growing industry. *www.businessinsider.com, "The 35 Cities in the US with the Biggest Influx of People, the Most Work Opportunities, and the Hottest Business Growth," August 12, 2018*

- San Jose was selected as one of the best places to live in the United States by *Money* magazine. The city ranked #25 out of 50. This year's list focused on cities that would be welcoming to a broader group of people and with populations of at least 20,000. Beginning with a pool of 1,370 candidates, editors looked at 350 data points, organized into the these nine categories: income and personal finance, cost of living, economic opportunity, housing market, fun and amenities, health and safety, education, diversity, and quality of life. *Money, "The 50 Best Places to Live in the U.S. in 2022-2023" September 29, 2022*

Business/Finance Rankings

- According to *Business Insider*, the San Jose metro area is a prime place to run a startup or move an existing business to. The area ranked #1. More than 300 metro areas were analyzed for factors that were of top concern to new business owners. Data was based on the 2019 U.S. Census Bureau American Community Survey, statistics from the CDC, Bureau of Labor Statistics employment report, and University of Chicago analysis. Criteria: business formations; percentage of vaccinated population; percentage of households with internet subscriptions; median household income; and share of work that can be done from home. *www.businessinsider.com, "The 20 Best Cities for Starting a Business in 2022 Include Baltimore, Boulder, and Boston," January 5, 2022*

- *24/7 Wall St.* used metro data from the Bureau of Labor Statistics' Occupational Employment database to identify the cities with the highest percentage of those employed in jobs requiring knowledge in the science, technology, engineering, and math (STEM) fields as well as average wages for STEM jobs. The San Jose metro area was #11. *247wallst.com, "15 Cities with the Most High-Tech Jobs," January 11, 2020*

- Based on metro area social media reviews, the employment opinion group Glassdoor surveyed 50 of the most populous U.S. metro areas and equally weighed cost of living, hiring opportunity, and job satisfaction to compose a list of "25 Best Cities for Jobs." Median pay and home value, and number of active job openings were also factored in. The San Jose metro area was ranked #16 in overall job satisfaction. *www.glassdoor.com, "Best Cities for Jobs," February 25, 2020*

- The Brookings Institution ranked the nation's largest cities based on income inequality. San Jose was ranked #56 (#1 = greatest inequality). Criteria: the "95/20 ratio," a figure representing the income at which a household earns more than 95 percent of all other households, divided by the income at which a household earns more than only 20 percent of all other households. *Brookings Institution, "Household Income Inequality, Largest Cities of 97 Large U.S. Metro Areas, 2014-2016," February 5, 2018*

- The Brookings Institution ranked the 100 largest metro areas in the U.S. based on income inequality. San Jose was ranked #6 (#1 = greatest inequality). Criteria: the "95/20 ratio," a figure representing the income at which a household earns more than 95 percent of all other households, divided by the income at which a household earns more than only 20 percent of all other households. *Brookings Institution, "Household Income Inequality, 100 Largest U.S. Metro Areas, 2014-2016," February 5, 2018*

- Payscale.com ranked the 32 largest metro areas in terms of wage growth. The San Jose metro area ranked #32. Criteria: quarterly changes in private industry employee and education professional wage growth from the previous year. *PayScale, "Wage Trends by Metro Area-1st Quarter," April 20, 2023*

- The San Jose metro area appeared on the Milken Institute "2022 Best Performing Cities" list. Rank: #7 out of 200 large metro areas (population over 250,000). Criteria: job growth; wage and salary growth; high-tech output growth; housing affordability; household broadband access. *Milken Institute, "Best-Performing Cities 2022," March 28, 2022*

- *Forbes* ranked the 200 most populous metro areas to determine the nation's "Best Places for Business and Careers." The San Jose metro area was ranked #42. Criteria: costs (business and living); job growth (past and projected); income growth; quality of life; educational attainment (college and high school); projected economic growth; cultural and leisure opportunities; workplace tolerance laws; net migration patterns. *Forbes, "The Best Places for Business and Careers 2019: Seattle Still On Top," October 30, 2019*

Education Rankings

- Personal finance website *WalletHub* analyzed the 150 largest U.S. metropolitan statistical areas to determine where the most educated Americans are putting their degrees to work. Criteria: education levels; percentage of workers with degrees; education quality and attainment gap; public school quality rankings; quality and enrollment of each metro area's universities. San Jose was ranked #2 (#1 = most educated city). *www.WalletHub.com, "Most & Least Educated Cities in America," July 18, 2022*

- San Jose was selected as one of America's most literate cities. The city ranked #50 out of the 84 largest U.S. cities. Criteria: number of booksellers; library resources; Internet resources; educational attainment; periodical publishing resources; newspaper circulation. *Central Connecticut State University, "America's Most Literate Cities, 2018," February 2019*

Environmental Rankings

- Sperling's BestPlaces assessed the 50 largest metropolitan areas of the United States for the likelihood of dangerously extreme weather events or earthquakes. In general the Southeast and South-Central regions have the highest risk of weather extremes and earthquakes, while the Pacific Northwest enjoys the lowest risk. Of the least risky metropolitan areas, the San Jose metro area was ranked #6. *www.bestplaces.net, "Avoid Natural Disasters: BestPlaces Reveals The Top 10 Safest Places to Live," October 25, 2017*

- The U.S. Environmental Protection Agency (EPA) released its list of U.S. metropolitan areas with the most ENERGY STAR certified buildings in 2022. The San Jose metro area was ranked #18 out of 25. *U.S. Environmental Protection Agency, "2023 Energy Star Top Cities," April 26, 2023*

- San Jose was highlighted as one of the 25 most ozone-polluted metro areas in the U.S. during 2019 through 2021. The area ranked #11. *American Lung Association, "State of the Air 2023," April 19, 2023*

- San Jose was highlighted as one of the 25 metro areas most polluted by year-round particle pollution (Annual PM 2.5) in the U.S. during 2019 through 2021. The area ranked #7. *American Lung Association, "State of the Air 2023," April 19, 2023*

- San Jose was highlighted as one of the 25 metro areas most polluted by short-term particle pollution (24-hour PM 2.5) in the U.S. during 2019 through 2021. The area ranked #6. *American Lung Association, "State of the Air 2023," April 19, 2023*

Health/Fitness Rankings

- For each of the 100 largest cities in the United States, the American Fitness Index®, compiled in partnership between the American College of Sports Medicine and the Elevance Health Foundation, evaluated community infrastructure and 34 health behaviors including preventive health, levels of chronic disease conditions, food insecurity, sleep quality, pedestrian safety, air quality, and community/environment resources that support physical activity. San Jose ranked #20 for "community fitness." *americanfitnessindex.org, "2022 ACSM American Fitness Index Summary Report," July 12, 2022*

- Trulia analyzed the 100 largest U.S. metro areas to identify the nation's best cities for weight loss, based on the percentage of adults who bike or walk to work, sporting goods stores, grocery stores, access to outdoor activities, weight-loss centers, gyms, and average space reserved for parks. San Jose ranked #10. *Trulia.com, "Where to Live to Get in Shape in the New Year," January 4, 2018*

- San Jose was identified as a "2022 Spring Allergy Capital." The area ranked #92 out of 100. Three groups of factors were used to identify the most challenging cities for people with allergies during the spring season: annual spring pollen scores; over the counter allergy medicine use; number of board-certified allergy specialists. *Asthma and Allergy Foundation of America, "Spring Allergy Capitals 2022," March 2, 2022*

- San Jose was identified as a "2022 Fall Allergy Capital." The area ranked #96 out of 100. Three groups of factors were used to identify the most challenging cities for people with allergies during the fall season: annual fall pollen scores; over the counter allergy medicine use; number of board-certified allergy specialists. *Asthma and Allergy Foundation of America, "Fall Allergy Capitals 2022," March 2, 2022*

- San Jose was identified as a "2022 Asthma Capital." The area ranked #79 out of the nation's 100 largest metropolitan areas. Criteria: estimated asthma prevalence; asthma-related mortality; and ER visits due to asthma. Risk factors analyzed but not factored in the rankings: annual pollen score; annual air quality; public smoking laws; access to board-certified asthma specialists; rescue and controller medication use; uninsured rate; poverty rate. *Asthma and Allergy Foundation of America, "Asthma Capitals 2022: The Most Challenging Places to Live With Asthma," September 14, 2022*

- The Sharecare Community Well-Being Index evaluates 10 individual and social health factors in order to measure what matters to Americans in the communities in which they live. The San Jose metro area ranked #2 in the top 10 across all 10 domains. Criteria: access to healthcare, food, and community resources; housng and transportation; economic security; feeling of purpose; physical, financial, social, and community well-being. *www.sharecare.com, "Community Well-Being Index: 2020 Metro Area & County Rankings Report," August 30, 2021*

Real Estate Rankings

- *WalletHub* compared the most populated U.S. cities to determine which had the best markets for real estate agents. San Jose ranked #10 where demand was high and pay was the best. Criteria: sales per agent; annual median wage for real-estate agents; monthly average starting salary for real estate agents; real estate job density and competition; unemployment rate; home turnover rate; housing-market health index; and other relevant metrics. *www.WalletHub.com, "2021 Best Places to Be a Real Estate Agent," May 12, 2021*

- The San Jose metro area was identified as one of the top 5 housing markets to invest in for 2022 by *Forbes*. Criteria: ratio of sales-to-list price; days on the market; available inventory; median sales prices; and other factors. *Forbes.com, "The Hottest Housing Markets Going Into 2022," November 29, 2021*

- The San Jose metro area was identified as one of the 20 worst housing markets in the U.S. in 2022. The area ranked #186 out of 187 markets. Criteria: year-over-year change of median sales price of existing single-family homes between the 4th quarter of 2021 and the 4th quarter of 2022. *National Association of Realtors®, Median Sales Price of Existing Single-Family Homes for Metropolitan Areas, 4th Quarter 2022*

- The San Jose metro area was identified as one of the 20 least affordable housing markets in the U.S. in 2022. The area ranked #186 out of 186 markets. Criteria: qualification for a mortgage loan with a 10 percent down payment on a typical home. *National Association of Realtors®, Qualifying Income Based on Sales Price of Existing Single-Family Homes for Metropolitan Areas, 2022*

- San Jose was ranked #227 out of 235 metro areas in terms of housing affordability in 2022 by the National Association of Home Builders (#1 = most affordable). Criteria: the share of homes sold in that area affordable to a family earning the local median income, based on standard mortgage underwriting criteria. *National Association of Home Builders®, NAHB-Wells Fargo Housing Opportunity Index, 4th Quarter 2022*

Safety Rankings

- Allstate ranked the 200 largest cities in America in terms of driver safety. San Jose ranked #170. Criteria: internal property damage claims over a two-year period from January 2016 to December 2017. The report helps increase the importance of safety and awareness behind the wheel. *Allstate, "Allstate America's Best Drivers Report, 2019" June 24, 2019*

- The National Insurance Crime Bureau ranked 390 metro areas in the U.S. in terms of per capita rates of vehicle theft. The San Jose metro area ranked #17 (#1 = highest rate). Criteria: number of vehicle theft offenses per 100,000 inhabitants in 2021. *National Insurance Crime Bureau, "Hot Spots 2021," September 1, 2022*

Seniors/Retirement Rankings

- From its Best Cities for Successful Aging indexes, the Milken Institute generated rankings for metropolitan areas, weighing data in nine categories—health care, wellness, living arrangements, transportation and convenience, financial characteristics, education, employment, community engagement, and overall livability. The San Jose metro area was ranked #10 overall in the large metro area category. *Milken Institute, "Best Cities for Successful Aging, 2017" March 14, 2017*

Sports/Recreation Rankings

- San Jose was chosen as a bicycle friendly community by the League of American Bicyclists. A "Bicycle Friendly Community" welcomes cyclists by providing safe and supportive accommodation for cycling and encouraging people to bike for transportation and recreation. There are five award levels: Diamond; Platinum; Gold; Silver; and Bronze. The community achieved an award level of Silver. *League of American Bicyclists, "Fall 2022 Awards-New & Renewing Bicycle Friendly Communities List," December 14, 2022*

- San Jose was chosen as one of America's best cities for bicycling. The city ranked #43 out of 50. Criteria: cycling infrastructure that is safe and friendly for all ages; energy and bike culture. The editors evaluated cities with populations of 100,000 or more. *Bicycling, "The 50 Best Bike Cities in America," October 10, 2018*

Transportation Rankings

- San Jose was identified as one of the most congested metro areas in the U.S. The area ranked #4 out of 10. Criteria: yearly delay per auto commuter in hours. *Texas A&M Transportation Institute, "2021 Urban Mobility Report," June 2021*

Women/Minorities Rankings

- The *Houston Chronicle* listed the San Jose metro area as #12 in top places for young Latinos to live in the U.S. Research was largely based on housing and occupational data from the largest metropolitan areas performed by *Forbes* and NBC Universo. Criteria: percentage of 18-34 year-olds; Latino college grad rates; and diversity. *blog.chron.com, "The 15 Best Big Cities for Latino Millenials," January 26, 2016*

- Personal finance website *WalletHub* compared more than 180 U.S. cities across two key dimensions, "Hispanic Business-Friendliness" and "Hispanic Purchasing Power," to arrive at the most favorable conditions for Hispanic entrepreneurs. San Jose was ranked #103 out of 182. Criteria includes: share of Hispanic-Owned Businesses; Hispanic entrepreneurship rate to median annual income of Hispanics; Small Business-Friendliness score; cost of living; and number of Hispanics with at least a bachelor's degree. *WalletHub.com, "2019's Best Cities for Hispanic Entrepreneurs," May 1, 2019*

Miscellaneous Rankings

- San Jose was selected as a 2022 Digital Cities Survey winner. The city ranked #3 in the large city (500,000 or more population) category. The survey examined and assessed how city governments are utilizing technology to continue innovation, engage with residents, and persevere through the challenges of the pandemic. Survey questions focused on ten initiatives: cybersecurity; citizen experience; disaster recovery; business intelligence; IT personnel; data governance; business automation; IT governance; infrastructure modernization; and broadband connectivity. *Center for Digital Government, "2022 Digital Cities Survey," November 10, 2022*

- *WalletHub* compared the 150 most populated U.S. cities to determine their operating efficiency. A "Quality of Services" score was constructed for each city and then divided by the total budget per capita to reveal which were managed the best. San Jose ranked #94. Criteria: financial stability; economy; education; safety; health; infrastructure and pollution. *www.WalletHub.com, "2022's Best- & Worst-Run Cities in America," June 21, 2022*

- The National Alliance to End Homelessness listed the 25 most populous metro areas with the highest rate of homelessness. The San Jose metro area had a high rate of homelessness. Criteria: number of homeless people per 10,000 population in 2016. *National Alliance to End Homelessness, "Homelessness in the 25 Most Populous U.S. Metro Areas," September 1, 2017*

Business Environment

DEMOGRAPHICS

Population Growth

Area	1990 Census	2000 Census	2010 Census	2020 Census	Population Growth (%) 1990-2020	Population Growth (%) 2010-2020
City	784,324	894,943	945,942	1,013,240	29.2	7.1
MSA[1]	1,534,280	1,735,819	1,836,911	2,000,468	30.4	8.9
U.S.	248,709,873	281,421,906	308,745,538	331,449,281	33.3	7.4

Note: (1) Figures cover the San Jose-Sunnyvale-Santa Clara, CA Metropolitan Statistical Area
Source: U.S. Census Bureau, 1990 Census, 2000 Census, 2010 Census, 2020 Census

Race

Area	White Alone[2] (%)	Black Alone[2] (%)	Asian Alone[2] (%)	AIAN[3] Alone[2] (%)	NHOPI[4] Alone[2] (%)	Other Race Alone[2] (%)	Two or More Races (%)
City	27.3	2.9	38.5	1.4	0.4	18.2	11.2
MSA[1]	32.5	2.3	38.1	1.2	0.4	14.6	11.0
U.S.	61.6	12.4	6.0	1.1	0.2	8.4	10.2

Note: (1) Figures cover the San Jose-Sunnyvale-Santa Clara, CA Metropolitan Statistical Area; (2) Alone is defined as not being in combination with one or more other races; (3) American Indian and Alaska Native; (4) Native Hawaiian and Other Pacific Islander
Source: U.S. Census Bureau, 2020 Census

Hispanic or Latino Origin

Area	Total (%)	Mexican (%)	Puerto Rican (%)	Cuban (%)	Other (%)
City	31.0	26.0	0.5	0.2	4.3
MSA[1]	26.2	21.5	0.5	0.2	4.1
U.S.	18.4	11.2	1.8	0.7	4.7

Note: Persons of Hispanic or Latino origin can be of any race; (1) Figures cover the San Jose-Sunnyvale-Santa Clara, CA Metropolitan Statistical Area
Source: U.S. Census Bureau, 2017-2021 American Community Survey 5-Year Estimates

Age

Area	Under Age 5	Age 5–19	Age 20–34	Age 35–44	Age 45–54	Age 55–64	Age 65–74	Age 75–84	Age 85+	Median Age
City	5.3	18.5	22.2	14.7	13.9	12.2	7.7	4.0	1.6	37.6
MSA[1]	5.3	18.4	22.4	14.6	13.6	12.0	7.7	4.2	1.9	37.5
U.S.	5.6	19.2	20.2	12.7	12.4	13.1	10.0	4.9	1.9	38.8

Note: (1) Figures cover the San Jose-Sunnyvale-Santa Clara, CA Metropolitan Statistical Area
Source: U.S. Census Bureau, 2020 Census

Disability by Age

Area	All Ages	Under 18 Years Old	18 to 64 Years Old	65 Years and Over
City	8.9	3.1	6.0	33.1
MSA[1]	8.3	2.7	5.5	30.7
U.S.	12.6	4.4	10.3	33.4

Note: Figures show percent of the civilian noninstitutionalized population that reported having a disability. Disability status is determined from six types of difficulty: vision, hearing, cognitive, ambulatory, self-care, and independent living. For children under 5 years old, hearing and vision difficulty are used to determine disability status. For children between the ages of 5 and 14, disability status is determined from hearing, vision, cognitive, ambulatory, and self-care difficulties. For people aged 15 years and older, they are considered to have a disability if they have difficulty with any one of the six difficulty types; Note: (1) Figures cover the San Jose-Sunnyvale-Santa Clara, CA Metropolitan Statistical Area
Source: U.S. Census Bureau, 2017-2021 American Community Survey 5-Year Estimates

Ancestry

Area	German	Irish	English	American	Italian	Polish	French[2]	Scottish	Dutch
City	4.6	4.0	3.8	1.8	3.3	0.8	1.1	0.8	0.5
MSA[1]	5.8	4.7	4.7	2.0	3.7	1.1	1.3	0.9	0.6
U.S.	12.8	9.6	8.1	5.7	5.0	2.7	2.2	1.6	1.1

Note: Figures are the percentage of the total population reporting a particular ancestry. The nine most commonly reported ancestries in the U.S. are shown. Figures include multiple ancestries (e.g. if a person reported being Irish and Italian, they were included in both columns); (1) Figures cover the San Jose-Sunnyvale-Santa Clara, CA Metropolitan Statistical Area; (2) Excludes Basque
Source: U.S. Census Bureau, 2017-2021 American Community Survey 5-Year Estimates

Foreign-born Population

Area	Any Foreign Country	Asia	Mexico	Europe	Caribbean	Central America[2]	South America	Africa	Canada
City	40.7	26.4	8.6	2.3	0.1	1.2	0.7	0.8	0.3
MSA[1]	39.3	26.2	6.7	3.1	0.1	1.0	0.8	0.7	0.5
U.S.	13.6	4.2	3.3	1.4	1.4	1.1	1.1	0.8	0.2

Note: (1) Figures cover the San Jose-Sunnyvale-Santa Clara, CA Metropolitan Statistical Area; (2) Excludes Mexico.
Source: U.S. Census Bureau, 2017-2021 American Community Survey 5-Year Estimates

Household Size

Area	Persons in Household (%)							Average Household Size
	One	Two	Three	Four	Five	Six	Seven or More	
City	19.7	28.9	18.9	18.0	8.0	3.2	3.2	3.10
MSA[1]	20.5	30.5	19.1	17.7	7.2	2.7	2.3	2.90
U.S.	28.1	33.8	15.5	12.9	6.0	2.3	1.4	2.60

Note: (1) Figures cover the San Jose-Sunnyvale-Santa Clara, CA Metropolitan Statistical Area
Source: U.S. Census Bureau, 2017-2021 American Community Survey 5-Year Estimates

Household Relationships

Area	House-holder	Opposite-sex Spouse	Same-sex Spouse	Opposite-sex Unmarried Partner	Same-sex Unmarried Partner	Child[2]	Grand-child	Other Relatives	Non-relatives
City	32.4	17.1	0.2	1.9	0.1	28.6	2.3	9.8	6.1
MSA[1]	33.8	18.4	0.2	1.8	0.1	28.3	1.9	7.9	5.6
U.S.	38.3	17.5	0.2	2.5	0.2	28.3	2.4	4.8	3.4

Note: Figures are percent of the total population; (1) Figures cover the San Jose-Sunnyvale-Santa Clara, CA Metropolitan Statistical Area; (2) Includes biological, adopted, and stepchildren of the householder
Source: U.S. Census Bureau, 2020 Census

Gender

Area	Males	Females	Males per 100 Females
City	509,260	503,980	101.0
MSA[1]	1,007,254	993,214	101.4
U.S.	162,685,811	168,763,470	96.4

Note: (1) Figures cover the San Jose-Sunnyvale-Santa Clara, CA Metropolitan Statistical Area
Source: U.S. Census Bureau, 2020 Census

Marital Status

Area	Never Married	Now Married[2]	Separated	Widowed	Divorced
City	36.2	50.3	1.5	4.2	7.8
MSA[1]	34.4	52.7	1.4	4.1	7.4
U.S.	33.8	48.0	1.8	5.6	10.8

Note: Figures are percentages and cover the population 15 years of age and older; (1) Figures cover the San Jose-Sunnyvale-Santa Clara, CA Metropolitan Statistical Area; (2) Excludes separated
Source: U.S. Census Bureau, 2017-2021 American Community Survey 5-Year Estimates

Religious Groups by Family

Area	Catholic	Baptist	Methodist	LDS[2]	Pentecostal	Lutheran	Islam	Adventist	Other
MSA[1]	27.2	1.2	0.6	1.4	0.9	0.4	2.0	1.3	11.4
U.S.	18.7	7.3	3.0	2.0	1.8	1.7	1.3	1.3	11.6

Note: Figures are the number of adherents as a percentage of the total population and cover the eight largest religious groups in the U.S; (1) Figures cover the San Jose-Sunnyvale-Santa Clara, CA Metropolitan Statistical Area; (2) Church of Jesus Christ of Latter-day Saints
Sources: 2020 U.S. Religion Census, Association of Statisticians of American Religious Bodies; The Association of Religion Data Archives (ARDA)

Religious Groups by Tradition

Area	Catholic	Evangelical Protestant	Mainline Protestant	Black Protestant	Islam	Judaism	Hinduism	Orthodox	Buddhism
MSA[1]	27.2	8.4	1.4	0.3	2.0	0.6	2.4	0.6	1.2
U.S.	18.7	16.5	5.2	2.3	1.3	0.6	0.4	0.4	0.3

Note: Figures are the number of adherents as a percentage of the total population; (1) Figures cover the San Jose-Sunnyvale-Santa Clara, CA Metropolitan Statistical Area
Sources: 2020 U.S. Religion Census, Association of Statisticians of American Religious Bodies; The Association of Religion Data Archives (ARDA)

ECONOMY

Gross Metropolitan Product

Area	2020	2021	2022	2023	Rank[2]
MSA[1]	360.5	400.1	431.2	450.9	13

Note: Figures are in billions of dollars; (1) Figures cover the San Jose-Sunnyvale-Santa Clara, CA Metropolitan Statistical Area; (2) Rank is based on 2021 data and ranges from 1 to 381
Source: U.S. Conference of Mayors, U.S. Metro Economies: U.S. Metros Compared to Global and State Economies, June 2022

Economic Growth

Area	2018-20 (%)	2021 (%)	2022 (%)	2023 (%)	Rank[2]
MSA[1]	5.2	8.6	3.3	1.6	2
U.S.	-0.6	5.7	3.1	2.9	–

Note: Figures are real gross metropolitan product (GMP) growth rates and represent average annual percent change; (1) Figures cover the San Jose-Sunnyvale-Santa Clara, CA Metropolitan Statistical Area; (2) Rank is based on 2020 2-year average annual percent change and ranges from 1 to 381
Source: U.S. Conference of Mayors, U.S. Metro Economies: U.S. Metros Compared to Global and State Economies, June 2022

Metropolitan Area Exports

Area	2016	2017	2018	2019	2020	2021	Rank[2]
MSA[1]	21,716.8	21,464.7	22,224.2	20,909.4	19,534.5	22,293.6	20

Note: Figures are in millions of dollars; (1) Figures cover the San Jose-Sunnyvale-Santa Clara, CA Metropolitan Statistical Area; (2) Rank is based on 2021 data and ranges from 1 to 388
Source: U.S. Department of Commerce, International Trade Administration, Office of Trade and Economic Analysis, Industry and Analysis, Exports by Metropolitan Area, data extracted March 16, 2023

Building Permits

Area	Single-Family			Multi-Family			Total		
	2021	2022	Pct. Chg.	2021	2022	Pct. Chg.	2021	2022	Pct. Chg.
City	299	553	84.9	359	1,450	303.9	658	2,003	204.4
MSA[1]	2,400	3,899	62.5	2,129	4,308	102.3	4,529	8,207	81.2
U.S.	1,115,400	975,600	-12.5	621,600	689,500	10.9	1,737,000	1,665,100	-4.1

Note: (1) Figures cover the San Jose-Sunnyvale-Santa Clara, CA Metropolitan Statistical Area; Figures represent new, privately-owned housing units authorized (unadjusted data); All permit data are based on estimates with imputation
Source: U.S. Census Bureau, Manufacturing, Mining, and Construction Statistics, Building Permits, 2021, 2022

Bankruptcy Filings

Area	Business Filings			Nonbusiness Filings		
	2021	2022	% Chg.	2021	2022	% Chg.
Santa Clara County	80	77	-3.8	868	655	-24.5
U.S.	14,347	13,481	-6.0	399,269	374,240	-6.3

Note: Business filings include Chapter 7, Chapter 9, Chapter 11, Chapter 12, Chapter 13, Chapter 15, and Section 304; Nonbusiness filings include Chapter 7, Chapter 11, and Chapter 13
Source: Administrative Office of the U.S. Courts, Business and Nonbusiness Bankruptcy, County Cases Commenced by Chapter of the Bankruptcy Code, During the 12-Month Period Ending December 31, 2021 and Business and Nonbusiness Bankruptcy, County Cases Commenced by Chapter of the Bankruptcy Code, During the 12-Month Period Ending December 31, 2022

Housing Vacancy Rates

Area	Gross Vacancy Rate[2] (%)			Year-Round Vacancy Rate[3] (%)			Rental Vacancy Rate[4] (%)			Homeowner Vacancy Rate[5] (%)		
	2020	2021	2022	2020	2021	2022	2020	2021	2022	2020	2021	2022
MSA[1]	4.7	5.9	5.8	4.7	5.6	5.8	4.4	6.6	4.7	0.0	0.4	0.4
U.S.	10.6	10.8	10.5	8.2	8.4	8.2	6.3	6.1	5.8	1.0	0.9	0.8

Note: (1) Figures cover the San Jose-Sunnyvale-Santa Clara, CA Metropolitan Statistical Area; (2) The percentage of the total housing inventory that is vacant; (3) The percentage of the housing inventory (excluding seasonal units) that is year-round vacant; (4) The percentage of rental inventory that is vacant for rent; (5) The percentage of homeowner inventory that is vacant for sale
Source: U.S. Census Bureau, Housing Vacancies and Homeownership Annual Statistics: 2020, 2021, 2022

INCOME

Income

Area	Per Capita ($)	Median Household ($)	Average Household ($)
City	53,574	125,075	162,521
MSA[1]	64,169	138,370	187,324
U.S.	37,638	69,021	97,196

Note: (1) Figures cover the San Jose-Sunnyvale-Santa Clara, CA Metropolitan Statistical Area
Source: U.S. Census Bureau, 2017-2021 American Community Survey 5-Year Estimates

Household Income Distribution

Area	Percent of Households Earning							
	Under $15,000	$15,000 -$24,999	$25,000 -$34,999	$35,000 -$49,999	$50,000 -$74,999	$75,000 -$99,999	$100,000 -$149,999	$150,000 and up
City	5.2	4.2	4.2	6.3	10.9	9.9	17.7	41.6
MSA[1]	4.9	3.6	3.7	5.5	9.9	9.2	16.8	46.6
U.S.	9.4	7.8	8.2	11.4	16.8	12.8	16.3	17.3

Note: (1) Figures cover the San Jose-Sunnyvale-Santa Clara, CA Metropolitan Statistical Area
Source: U.S. Census Bureau, 2017-2021 American Community Survey 5-Year Estimates

Poverty Rate

Area	All Ages	Under 18 Years Old	18 to 64 Years Old	65 Years and Over
City	7.7	8.2	7.1	9.5
MSA[1]	6.7	6.8	6.3	8.2
U.S.	12.6	17.0	11.8	9.6

Note: Figures are percentage of people whose income during the past 12 months was below the poverty level;
(1) Figures cover the San Jose-Sunnyvale-Santa Clara, CA Metropolitan Statistical Area
Source: U.S. Census Bureau, 2017-2021 American Community Survey 5-Year Estimates

EMPLOYMENT

Labor Force and Employment

Area	Civilian Labor Force			Workers Employed		
	Dec. 2021	Dec. 2022	% Chg.	Dec. 2021	Dec. 2022	% Chg.
City	546,462	558,687	2.2	529,424	546,728	3.3
MSA[1]	1,067,389	1,093,480	2.4	1,036,363	1,070,252	3.3
U.S.	161,696,000	164,224,000	1.6	155,732,000	158,872,000	2.0

Note: Data is not seasonally adjusted and covers workers 16 years of age and older; (1) Figures cover the San Jose-Sunnyvale-Santa Clara, CA Metropolitan Statistical Area
Source: Bureau of Labor Statistics, Local Area Unemployment Statistics

Unemployment Rate

Area	2022											
	Jan.	Feb.	Mar.	Apr.	May	Jun.	Jul.	Aug.	Sep.	Oct.	Nov.	Dec.
City	3.5	3.1	2.6	2.3	2.0	2.4	2.3	2.5	2.2	2.3	2.5	2.1
MSA[1]	3.4	3.0	2.5	2.2	1.9	2.3	2.2	2.4	2.2	2.2	2.4	2.1
U.S.	4.4	4.1	3.8	3.3	3.4	3.8	3.8	3.8	3.3	3.4	3.4	3.3

Note: Data is not seasonally adjusted and covers workers 16 years of age and older; (1) Figures cover the San Jose-Sunnyvale-Santa Clara, CA Metropolitan Statistical Area
Source: Bureau of Labor Statistics, Local Area Unemployment Statistics

Average Wages

Occupation	$/Hr.	Occupation	$/Hr.
Accountants and Auditors	55.92	Maintenance and Repair Workers	30.88
Automotive Mechanics	37.42	Marketing Managers	113.98
Bookkeepers	29.94	Network and Computer Systems Admin.	72.84
Carpenters	37.76	Nurses, Licensed Practical	38.75
Cashiers	19.15	Nurses, Registered	76.94
Computer Programmers	70.63	Nursing Assistants	24.81
Computer Systems Analysts	79.75	Office Clerks, General	25.56
Computer User Support Specialists	39.13	Physical Therapists	64.33
Construction Laborers	30.35	Physicians	124.09
Cooks, Restaurant	21.53	Plumbers, Pipefitters and Steamfitters	46.57
Customer Service Representatives	26.29	Police and Sheriff's Patrol Officers	62.36
Dentists	103.12	Postal Service Mail Carriers	29.08
Electricians	47.71	Real Estate Sales Agents	36.25
Engineers, Electrical	n/a	Retail Salespersons	21.34
Fast Food and Counter Workers	18.80	Sales Representatives, Technical/Scientific	78.03
Financial Managers	103.92	Secretaries, Exc. Legal/Medical/Executive	28.34
First-Line Supervisors of Office Workers	41.82	Security Guards	21.24
General and Operations Managers	90.32	Surgeons	n/a
Hairdressers/Cosmetologists	20.99	Teacher Assistants, Exc. Postsecondary*	22.29
Home Health and Personal Care Aides	17.24	Teachers, Secondary School, Exc. Sp. Ed.*	46.64
Janitors and Cleaners	20.64	Telemarketers	20.56
Landscaping/Groundskeeping Workers	24.14	Truck Drivers, Heavy/Tractor-Trailer	29.99
Lawyers	128.77	Truck Drivers, Light/Delivery Services	24.72
Maids and Housekeeping Cleaners	22.48	Waiters and Waitresses	19.37

Note: Wage data covers the San Jose-Sunnyvale-Santa Clara, CA Metropolitan Statistical Area; (*) Hourly wages were calculated from annual wage data based on a 40 hour work week; n/a not available.
Source: Bureau of Labor Statistics, Metro Area Occupational Employment & Wage Estimates, May 2022

Employment by Industry

Sector	MSA[1]		U.S.
	Number of Employees	Percent of Total	Percent of Total
Construction	56,400	4.7	5.0
Private Education and Health Services	193,300	16.3	16.1
Financial Activities	38,800	3.3	5.9
Government	98,400	8.3	14.5
Information	108,000	9.1	2.0
Leisure and Hospitality	101,200	8.5	10.3
Manufacturing	183,400	15.4	8.4
Mining and Logging	200	<0.1	0.4
Other Services	24,700	2.1	3.7
Professional and Business Services	257,700	21.7	14.7
Retail Trade	76,200	6.4	10.2
Transportation, Warehousing, and Utilities	21,000	1.8	4.9
Wholesale Trade	29,100	2.4	3.9

Note: Figures are non-farm employment as of December 2022. Figures are not seasonally adjusted and include workers 16 years of age and older; (1) Figures cover the San Jose-Sunnyvale-Santa Clara, CA Metropolitan Statistical Area
Source: Bureau of Labor Statistics, Current Employment Statistics, Employment, Hours, and Earnings

Employment by Occupation

Occupation Classification	City (%)	MSA[1] (%)	U.S. (%)
Management, Business, Science, and Arts	49.3	55.8	40.3
Natural Resources, Construction, and Maintenance	6.9	6.1	8.7
Production, Transportation, and Material Moving	9.5	8.0	13.1
Sales and Office	17.3	16.0	20.9
Service	17.0	14.0	17.0

Note: Figures cover employed civilians 16 years of age and older; (1) Figures cover the San Jose-Sunnyvale-Santa Clara, CA Metropolitan Statistical Area
Source: U.S. Census Bureau, 2017-2021 American Community Survey 5-Year Estimates

Occupations with Greatest Projected Employment Growth: 2022 – 2024

Occupation[1]	2022 Employment	2024 Projected Employment	Numeric Employment Change	Percent Employment Change
Home Health and Personal Care Aides	811,300	858,600	47,300	5.8
Fast Food and Counter Workers	422,000	444,100	22,100	5.2
Cooks, Restaurant	154,300	172,000	17,700	11.5
Software Developers and Software Quality Assurance Analysts and Testers	337,600	352,100	14,500	4.3
Waiters and Waitresses	205,800	219,200	13,400	6.5
Laborers and Freight, Stock, and Material Movers, Hand	391,100	403,100	12,000	3.1
Stockers and Order Fillers	268,000	277,500	9,500	3.5
General and Operations Managers	308,500	317,600	9,100	2.9
First-Line Supervisors of Food Preparation and Serving Workers	118,100	126,000	7,900	6.7
Project Management Specialists and Business Operations Specialists, All Other	332,400	339,800	7,400	2.2

Note: Projections cover California; (1) Sorted by numeric employment change
Source: www.projectionscentral.com, State Occupational Projections, 2022–2024 Short-Term Projections

Fastest-Growing Occupations: 2022 – 2024

Occupation[1]	2022 Employment	2024 Projected Employment	Numeric Employment Change	Percent Employment Change
Fitness Trainers and Aerobics Instructors	40,700	46,300	5,600	13.8
Nurse Practitioners	18,300	20,500	2,200	12.0
Cooks, Restaurant	154,300	172,000	17,700	11.5
Airfield Operations Specialists	3,700	4,100	400	10.8
Solar Photovoltaic Installers	6,600	7,300	700	10.6
Ushers, Lobby Attendants, and Ticket Takers	7,800	8,600	800	10.3
Amusement and Recreation Attendants	47,500	52,300	4,800	10.1
Sociologists	1,000	1,100	100	10.0
Paperhangers	1,000	1,100	100	10.0
Avionics Technicians	2,000	2,200	200	10.0

Note: Projections cover California; (1) Sorted by percent employment change and excludes occupations with numeric employment change less than 50
Source: www.projectionscentral.com, State Occupational Projections, 2022–2024 Short-Term Projections

CITY FINANCES

City Government Finances

Component	2020 ($000)	2020 ($ per capita)
Total Revenues	3,190,656	3,123
Total Expenditures	2,188,213	2,142
Debt Outstanding	5,461,977	5,345
Cash and Securities[1]	3,116,182	3,050

Note: (1) Cash and security holdings of a government at the close of its fiscal year, including those of its dependent agencies, utilities, and liquor stores.
Source: U.S. Census Bureau, State & Local Government Finances 2020

City Government Revenue by Source

Source	2020 ($000)	2020 ($ per capita)	2020 (%)
General Revenue			
From Federal Government	93,464	91	2.9
From State Government	130,141	127	4.1
From Local Governments	6,640	6	0.2
Taxes			
Property	578,099	566	18.1
Sales and Gross Receipts	472,072	462	14.8
Personal Income	0	0	0.0
Corporate Income	0	0	0.0
Motor Vehicle License	0	0	0.0
Other Taxes	328,400	321	10.3
Current Charges	806,016	789	25.3
Liquor Store	0	0	0.0
Utility	388,802	381	12.2

Source: U.S. Census Bureau, State & Local Government Finances 2020

City Government Expenditures by Function

Function	2020 ($000)	2020 ($ per capita)	2020 (%)
General Direct Expenditures			
Air Transportation	101,820	99	4.7
Corrections	0	0	0.0
Education	0	0	0.0
Employment Security Administration	0	0	0.0
Financial Administration	0	0	0.0
Fire Protection	111,113	108	5.1
General Public Buildings	0	0	0.0
Governmental Administration, Other	180,082	176	8.2
Health	245	< 1	< 0.1
Highways	239,765	234	11.0
Hospitals	0	0	0.0
Housing and Community Development	43,204	42	2.0
Interest on General Debt	212,254	207	9.7
Judicial and Legal	0	0	0.0
Libraries	36,808	36	1.7
Parking	20,845	20	1.0
Parks and Recreation	186,331	182	8.5
Police Protection	312,462	305	14.3
Public Welfare	0	0	0.0
Sewerage	209,604	205	9.6
Solid Waste Management	133,129	130	6.1
Veterans' Services	0	0	0.0
Liquor Store	0	0	0.0
Utility	343,307	336	15.7

Source: U.S. Census Bureau, State & Local Government Finances 2020

TAXES

State Corporate Income Tax Rates

State	Tax Rate (%)	Income Brackets ($)	Num. of Brackets	Financial Institution Tax Rate (%)[a]	Federal Income Tax Ded.
California	8.84 (b)	Flat rate	1	10.84 (b)	No

Note: Tax rates as of January 1, 2023; (a) Rates listed are the corporate income tax rate applied to financial institutions or excise taxes based on income. Some states have other taxes based upon the value of deposits or shares; (b) Minimum tax is $800 in California, $250 in District of Columbia, $50 in Arizona and North Dakota (banks), $400 ($100 banks) in Rhode Island, $200 per location in South Dakota (banks), $100 in Utah, $300 in Vermont.
Source: Federation of Tax Administrators, State Corporate Income Tax Rates, January 1, 2023

State Individual Income Tax Rates

State	Tax Rate (%)	Income Brackets ($)	Personal Exemptions ($)			Standard Ded. ($)	
			Single	Married	Depend.	Single	Married
California (a)	1.0 - 12.3 (g)	10,099 - 677,275 (b)	140	280	433 (c)	5,202	10,404 (a)

Note: Tax rates as of January 1, 2023; Local- and county-level taxes are not included; Federal income tax is not deductible on state income tax returns; (a) 16 states have statutory provision for automatically adjusting to the rate of inflation the dollar values of the income tax brackets, standard deductions, and/or personal exemptions. Oregon does not index the income brackets for $125,000 and over; (b) For joint returns, taxes are twice the tax on half the couple's income; (c) The personal exemption takes the form of a tax credit instead of a deduction; (g) California imposes an additional 1% tax on taxable income over $1 million, making the maximum rate 13.3% over $1 million.
Source: Federation of Tax Administrators, State Individual Income Tax Rates, January 1, 2023

Various State Sales and Excise Tax Rates

State	State Sales Tax (%)	Gasoline[1] ($/gal.)	Cigarette[2] ($/pack)	Spirits[3] ($/gal.)	Wine[4] ($/gal.)	Beer[5] ($/gal.)	Recreational Marijuana (%)
California	7.25	0.7766	2.87	3.30	0.20	0.20	(c)

Note: All tax rates as of January 1, 2023; (1) The American Petroleum Institute has developed a methodology for determining the average tax rate on a gallon of fuel. Rates may include any of the following: excise taxes, environmental fees, storage tank fees, other fees or taxes, general sales tax, and local taxes; (2) The federal excise tax of $1.0066 per pack and local taxes are not included; (3) Rates are those applicable to off-premise sales of 40% alcohol by volume (a.b.v.) distilled spirits in 750ml containers. Local excise taxes are excluded; (4) Rates are those applicable to off-premise sales of 11% a.b.v. non-carbonated wine in 750ml containers; (5) Rates are those applicable to off-premise sales of 4.7% a.b.v. beer in 12 ounce containers; (c) 15% excise tax (levied on wholesale at average market rate); $10.08/oz. flowers & $3/oz. leaves cultivation tax; $1.41/oz fresh cannabis plant
Source: Tax Foundation, 2023 Facts & Figures: How Does Your State Compare?

State Business Tax Climate Index Rankings

State	Overall Rank	Corporate Tax Rank	Individual Income Tax Rank	Sales Tax Rank	Property Tax Rank	Unemployment Insurance Tax Rank
California	48	46	49	47	19	24

Note: The index is a measure of how each state's tax laws affect economic performance. The lower the rank, the more favorable a state's tax system is for business. States without a given tax are given a ranking of 1. The scores/rankings for the District of Columbia do not affect other states. The 2023 index represents the tax climate as of July 1, 2022.
Source: Tax Foundation, State Business Tax Climate Index 2023

TRANSPORTATION

Means of Transportation to Work

Area	Car/Truck/Van		Public Transportation			Bicycle	Walked	Other Means	Worked at Home
	Drove Alone	Car-pooled	Bus	Subway	Railroad				
City	69.2	10.5	2.0	0.3	0.9	0.6	1.9	1.8	13.0
MSA[1]	67.1	9.4	1.8	0.3	1.0	1.4	2.1	1.6	15.3
U.S.	73.2	8.6	2.0	1.6	0.5	0.5	2.5	1.5	9.7

Note: Figures are percentages and cover workers 16 years of age and older; (1) Figures cover the San Jose-Sunnyvale-Santa Clara, CA Metropolitan Statistical Area
Source: U.S. Census Bureau, 2017-2021 American Community Survey 5-Year Estimates

Travel Time to Work

Area	Less Than 10 Minutes	10 to 19 Minutes	20 to 29 Minutes	30 to 44 Minutes	45 to 59 Minutes	60 to 89 Minutes	90 Minutes or More
City	5.6	24.6	23.2	26.1	10.1	7.5	3.0
MSA[1]	7.0	26.5	23.0	24.3	9.1	7.0	3.1
U.S.	12.4	28.5	21.0	20.9	8.2	6.2	2.9

Note: Note: Figures are percentages and include workers 16 years old and over; (1) Figures cover the San Jose-Sunnyvale-Santa Clara, CA Metropolitan Statistical Area
Source: U.S. Census Bureau, 2017-2021 American Community Survey 5-Year Estimates

Key Congestion Measures

Measure	1990	2000	2010	2015	2020
Annual Hours of Delay, Total (000)	33,232	59,026	87,229	114,375	46,377
Annual Hours of Delay, Per Auto Commuter	37	49	63	78	31
Annual Congestion Cost, Per Auto Commuter ($)	859	1,147	1,347	1,630	712

Note: Covers the San Jose CA urban area
Source: Texas A&M Transportation Institute, 2021 Urban Mobility Report

Freeway Travel Time Index

Measure	1985	1990	1995	2000	2005	2010	2015	2020
Urban Area Index[1]	1.15	1.21	1.23	1.28	1.32	1.34	1.43	1.12
Urban Area Rank[1,2]	15	7	8	9	8	6	3	10

Note: Freeway Travel Time Index—the ratio of travel time in the peak period to the travel time at free-flow conditions. For example, a value of 1.30 indicates a 20-minute free-flow trip takes 26 minutes in the peak (20 minutes x 1.30 = 26 minutes); (1) Covers the San Jose CA urban area; (2) Rank is based on 101 larger urban areas (#1 = highest travel time index)
Source: Texas A&M Transportation Institute, 2021 Urban Mobility Report

Public Transportation

Agency Name / Mode of Transportation	Vehicles Operated in Maximum Service[1]	Annual Unlinked Passenger Trips[2] (in thous.)	Annual Passenger Miles[3] (in thous.)
Santa Clara Valley Transportation Authority (VTA)			
Bus (directly operated)	319	9,687.3	48,473.1
Bus (purchased transportation)	12	27.1	121.7
Demand Response (purchased transportation)	138	173.3	1,400.0
Light Rail (directly operated)	46	2,168.1	13,970.9

Note: (1) Number of revenue vehicles operated by the given mode and type of service to meet the annual maximum service requirement. This is the revenue vehicle count during the peak season of the year; on the week and day that maximum service is provided. Vehicles operated in maximum service (VOMS) exclude atypical days and one-time special events; (2) Number of passengers who boarded public transportation vehicles. Passengers are counted each time they board a vehicle no matter how many vehicles they use to travel from their origin to their destination. (3) Sum of the distances ridden by all passengers during the entire fiscal year.
Source: Federal Transit Administration, National Transit Database, 2021

Air Transportation

Airport Name and Code / Type of Service	Passenger Airlines[1]	Passenger Enplanements	Freight Carriers[2]	Freight (lbs)
San Jose International (SJC)				
Domestic service (U.S. carriers - 2022)	25	5,345,937	10	40,737,866
International service (U.S. carriers - 2021)	6	71,624	1	24,033

Note: (1) Includes all U.S.-based major, minor and commuter airlines that carried at least one passenger during the year; (2) Includes all U.S.-based airlines and freight carriers that transported at least one pound of freight during the year.
Source: Bureau of Transportation Statistics, The Intermodal Transportation Database, Air Carriers: T-100 Domestic Market (U.S. Carriers), 2022; Bureau of Transportation Statistics, The Intermodal Transportation Database, Air Carriers: T-100 International Market (U.S. Carriers), 2021

BUSINESSES

Major Business Headquarters

Company Name	Industry	Rankings	
		Fortune[1]	Forbes[2]
Adobe	Computer software	235	-
Broadcom	Semiconductors and other electronic components	128	-
Cisco Systems	Network and other communications equipment	74	-
Ma Labs	Technology hardware & equipment	-	244
PayPal Holdings	Financial data services	143	-
Sanmina	Semiconductors and other electronic components	482	-
eBay	Internet services and retailing	301	-

Note: (1) Companies that produce a 10-K are ranked 1 to 500 based on 2021 revenue; (2) All private companies with at least $2 billion in annual revenue through the end of their most current fiscal year are ranked 1 to 246; companies listed are headquartered in the city; dashes indicate no ranking
Source: Fortune, "Fortune 500," 2022; Forbes, "America's Largest Private Companies," 2022

Fastest-Growing Businesses

According to Deloitte, San Jose is home to 10 of North America's 500 fastest-growing high-technology companies: **Outset Medical** (#33); **Zoom Video Communications** (#97); **Mezmo** (#164); **Kami Vision Incorporated** (#181); **BrightInsight** (#217); **Whatfix** (#261); **Roku** (#456); **Bill.com Holdings** (#464); **Zscaler** (#476); **Peraso** (#483). Companies are ranked by percentage growth in revenue over a four-year period. Criteria for inclusion: company must be headquartered within North America; must own proprietary intellectual property or technology that is sold to customers in products that contributes to a significant portion of the company's operating revenue; must have been in business for a minumum of four years with 2018 operating revenues of at least $50,000 USD/CD and 2021 operating revenues of at least $5 million USD/CD. *Deloitte, 2022 Technology Fast 500*[TM]

Living Environment

COST OF LIVING

Cost of Living Index

Composite Index	Groceries	Housing	Utilities	Trans-portation	Health Care	Misc. Goods/ Services
n/a	n/a	n/a	n/a	n/a	n/a	n/a

Note: The Cost of Living Index measures regional differences in the cost of consumer goods and services, excluding taxes and non-consumer expenditures, for professional and managerial households in the top income quintile. It is based on more than 50,000 prices covering almost 60 different items for which prices are collected three times a year by chambers of commerce, economic development organizations or university applied economic centers in each participating urban area. The numbers shown should be read as a percentage above or below the national average of 100. For example, a value of 115.4 in the groceries column indicates that grocery prices are 15.4% higher than the national average. Small differences in the index numbers should not be interpreted as significant; n/a not available.
Source: The Council for Community and Economic Research, Cost of Living Index, 2022

Grocery Prices

Area[1]	T-Bone Steak ($/pound)	Frying Chicken ($/pound)	Whole Milk ($/half gal.)	Eggs ($/dozen)	Orange Juice ($/64 oz.)	Coffee ($/11.5 oz.)
City[2]	n/a	n/a	n/a	n/a	n/a	n/a
Avg.	13.81	1.59	2.43	2.25	3.85	4.95
Min.	10.17	0.90	1.51	1.30	2.90	3.46
Max.	19.35	3.30	4.32	4.32	5.31	8.59

*Note: (1) Values for the local area are compared with the average, minimum and maximum values for all 286 areas in the Cost of Living Index; (2) Figures cover the San Jose CA urban area; n/a not available; **T-Bone Steak** (price per pound); **Frying Chicken** (price per pound, whole fryer); **Whole Milk** (half gallon carton); **Eggs** (price per dozen, Grade A, large); **Orange Juice** (64 oz. Tropicana or Florida Natural); **Coffee** (11.5 oz. can, vacuum-packed, Maxwell House, Hills Bros, or Folgers).*
Source: The Council for Community and Economic Research, Cost of Living Index, 2022

Housing and Utility Costs

Area[1]	New Home Price ($)	Apartment Rent ($/month)	All Electric ($/month)	Part Electric ($/month)	Other Energy ($/month)	Telephone ($/month)
City[2]	n/a	n/a	n/a	n/a	n/a	n/a
Avg.	450,913	1,371	176.41	99.93	76.96	190.22
Min.	229,283	546	100.84	31.56	27.15	174.27
Max.	2,434,977	4,569	356.86	249.59	272.24	208.31

*Note: (1) Values for the local area are compared with the average, minimum and maximum values for all 286 areas in the Cost of Living Index; (2) Figures cover the San Jose CA urban area; n/a not available; **New Home Price** (2,400 sf living area, 8,000 sf lot, in urban area with full utilities); **Apartment Rent** (950 sf 2 bedroom/1.5 or 2 bath, unfurnished, excluding all utilities except water); **All Electric** (average monthly cost for an all-electric home); **Part Electric** (average monthly cost for a part-electric home); **Other Energy** (average monthly cost for natural gas, fuel oil, coal, wood, and any other forms of energy except electricity); **Telephone** (price includes the base monthly rate plus taxes and fees for three lines of mobile phone service).*
Source: The Council for Community and Economic Research, Cost of Living Index, 2022

Health Care, Transportation, and Other Costs

Area[1]	Doctor ($/visit)	Dentist ($/visit)	Optometrist ($/visit)	Gasoline ($/gallon)	Beauty Salon ($/visit)	Men's Shirt ($)
City[2]	n/a	n/a	n/a	n/a	n/a	n/a
Avg.	124.91	107.77	117.66	3.86	43.31	34.21
Min.	36.61	58.25	51.79	2.90	22.18	13.05
Max.	250.21	162.58	371.96	5.54	85.61	63.54

*Note: (1) Values for the local area are compared with the average, minimum and maximum values for all 286 areas in the Cost of Living Index; (2) Figures cover the San Jose CA urban area; n/a not available; **Doctor** (general practitioners routine exam of an established patient); **Dentist** (adult teeth cleaning and periodic oral examination); **Optometrist** (full vision eye exam for established adult patient); **Gasoline** (one gallon regular unleaded, national brand, including all taxes, cash price at self-service pump if available); **Beauty Salon** (woman's shampoo, trim, and blow-dry); **Men's Shirt** (cotton/polyester dress shirt, pinpoint weave, long sleeves).*
Source: The Council for Community and Economic Research, Cost of Living Index, 2022

HOUSING

Homeownership Rate

Area	2015 (%)	2016 (%)	2017 (%)	2018 (%)	2019 (%)	2020 (%)	2021 (%)	2022 (%)
MSA[1]	50.7	49.9	50.4	50.4	52.4	52.6	48.4	53.1
U.S.	63.7	63.4	63.9	64.4	64.6	66.6	65.5	65.8

Note: (1) Figures cover the San Jose-Sunnyvale-Santa Clara, CA Metropolitan Statistical Area
Source: U.S. Census Bureau, Housing Vacancies and Homeownership Annual Statistics: 2015-2022

House Price Index (HPI)

Area	National Ranking[2]	Quarterly Change (%)	One-Year Change (%)	Five-Year Change (%)	Since 1991Q1 (%)
MSA[1]	101	1.47	12.23	31.21	389.33
U.S.[3]	–	0.34	8.41	58.44	289.08

Note: The HPI is a weighted repeat sales index. It measures average price changes in repeat sales or refinancings on the same properties. This information is obtained by reviewing repeat mortgage transactions on single-family properties whose mortgages have been purchased or securitized by Fannie Mae or Freddie Mac since January 1975; (1) Figures cover the San Jose-Sunnyvale-Santa Clara, CA Metropolitan Statistical Area; (2) Rankings are based on annual percentage change for all metro areas containing at least 15,000 transactions over the last 10 years and ranges from 1 to 257; (3) figures based on a weighted average of Census Division estimates using a seasonally adjusted, purchase-only index; all figures are for the period ending December 31, 2022
Source: Federal Housing Finance Agency, Change in FHFA Metropolitan Area House Price Indexes, 2022Q4

Median Single-Family Home Prices

Area	2020	2021	2022[p]	Percent Change 2021 to 2022
MSA[1]	1,385.0	1,640.0	1,797.8	9.6
U.S. Average	300.2	357.1	392.6	9.9

Note: Figures are median sales prices of existing single-family homes in thousands of dollars; (p) preliminary; (1) Figures cover the San Jose-Sunnyvale-Santa Clara, CA Metropolitan Statistical Area
Source: National Association of Realtors, Median Sales Price of Existing Single-Family Homes for Metropolitan Areas, 4th Quarter 2022

Qualifying Income Based on Median Sales Price of Existing Single-Family Homes

Area	With 5% Down ($)	With 10% Down ($)	With 20% Down ($)
MSA[1]	471,962	447,122	397,442
U.S. Average	112,234	106,237	94,513

Note: Figures are preliminary; Qualifying income is based on a mortgage rate of 6.77%. Monthly principal and interest payment is limited to 25% of income; (1) Figures cover the San Jose-Sunnyvale-Santa Clara, CA Metropolitan Statistical Area
Source: National Association of Realtors, Qualifying Income Based on Median Sales Price of Existing Single-Family Homes for Metropolitan Areas, 4th Quarter 2022

Home Value

Area	Under $100,000	$100,000 -$199,999	$200,000 -$299,999	$300,000 -$399,999	$400,000 -$499,999	$500,000 -$999,999	$1,000,000 or more	Median ($)
City	2.3	2.5	2.0	1.6	2.6	40.3	48.6	986,700
MSA[1]	2.1	2.0	1.7	1.6	2.3	32.2	58.0	1,113,700
U.S.	16.2	24.2	20.1	13.6	8.3	13.6	4.1	244,900

Note: Figures are percentages except for median and cover owner-occupied housing units; (1) Figures cover the San Jose-Sunnyvale-Santa Clara, CA Metropolitan Statistical Area
Source: U.S. Census Bureau, 2017-2021 American Community Survey 5-Year Estimates

Year Housing Structure Built

Area	2020 or Later	2010 -2019	2000 -2009	1990 -1999	1980 -1989	1970 -1979	1960 -1969	1950 -1959	1940 -1949	Before 1940	Median Year
City	0.2	6.4	9.2	10.1	12.5	24.3	18.0	11.1	2.8	5.3	1975
MSA[1]	0.2	7.5	8.9	10.0	12.1	21.3	17.6	13.9	3.5	5.0	1975
U.S.	0.2	7.3	13.6	13.6	13.2	14.8	10.3	10.0	4.7	12.2	1979

Note: Figures are percentages except for Median Year; Note: (1) Figures cover the San Jose-Sunnyvale-Santa Clara, CA Metropolitan Statistical Area
Source: U.S. Census Bureau, 2017-2021 American Community Survey 5-Year Estimates

Gross Monthly Rent

Area	Under $500	$500 -$999	$1,000 -$1,499	$1,500 -$1,999	$2,000 -$2,499	$2,500 -$2,999	$3,000 and up	Median ($)
City	3.7	5.6	9.3	17.0	19.6	18.0	26.7	2,366
MSA[1]	3.0	4.7	7.8	14.7	19.4	18.5	31.9	2,511
U.S.	8.1	30.5	30.8	16.8	7.3	3.1	3.5	1,163

Note: Figures are percentages except for median; Gross rent is the contract rent plus the estimated average monthly cost of utilities (electricity, gas, and water and sewer) and fuels (oil, coal, kerosene, wood, etc.) if these are paid by the renter (or paid for the renter by someone else); (1) Figures cover the San Jose-Sunnyvale-Santa Clara, CA Metropolitan Statistical Area
Source: U.S. Census Bureau, 2017-2021 American Community Survey 5-Year Estimates

HEALTH

Health Risk Factors

Category	MSA[1] (%)	U.S. (%)
Adults aged 18–64 who have any kind of health care coverage	n/a	90.9
Adults who reported being in good or better health	n/a	85.2
Adults who have been told they have high blood cholesterol	n/a	35.7
Adults who have been told they have high blood pressure	n/a	32.4
Adults who are current smokers	n/a	14.4
Adults who currently use e-cigarettes	n/a	6.7
Adults who currently use chewing tobacco, snuff, or snus	n/a	3.5
Adults who are heavy drinkers[2]	n/a	6.3
Adults who are binge drinkers[3]	n/a	15.4
Adults who are overweight (BMI 25.0 - 29.9)	n/a	34.4
Adults who are obese (BMI 30.0 - 99.8)	n/a	33.9
Adults who participated in any physical activities in the past month	n/a	76.3

Note: (1) Figures for the San Jose-Sunnyvale-Santa Clara, CA Metropolitan Statistical Area were not available.
(2) Heavy drinkers are classified as adult men having more than 14 drinks per week and adult women having more than 7 drinks per week; (3) Binge drinkers are classified as males having five or more drinks on one occasion or females having four or more drinks on one occasion
Source: Centers for Disease Control and Prevention, Behaviorial Risk Factor Surveillance System, SMART: Selected Metropolitan Area Risk Trends, 2021

Acute and Chronic Health Conditions

Category	MSA[1] (%)	U.S. (%)
Adults who have ever been told they had a heart attack	n/a	4.0
Adults who have ever been told they have angina or coronary heart disease	n/a	3.8
Adults who have ever been told they had a stroke	n/a	3.0
Adults who have ever been told they have asthma	n/a	14.9
Adults who have ever been told they have arthritis	n/a	25.8
Adults who have ever been told they have diabetes[2]	n/a	10.9
Adults who have ever been told they had skin cancer	n/a	6.6
Adults who have ever been told they had any other types of cancer	n/a	7.5
Adults who have ever been told they have COPD	n/a	6.1
Adults who have ever been told they have kidney disease	n/a	3.0
Adults who have ever been told they have a form of depression	n/a	20.5

Note: (1) Figures for the San Jose-Sunnyvale-Santa Clara, CA Metropolitan Statistical Area were not available.
(2) Figures do not include pregnancy-related, borderline, or pre-diabetes
Source: Centers for Disease Control and Prevention, Behaviorial Risk Factor Surveillance System, SMART: Selected Metropolitan Area Risk Trends, 2021

Health Screening and Vaccination Rates

Category	MSA[1] (%)	U.S. (%)
Adults who have ever been tested for HIV	n/a	34.9
Adults who have had their blood cholesterol checked within the last five years	n/a	85.2
Adults aged 65+ who have had flu shot within the past year	n/a	68.6
Adults aged 65+ who have ever had a pneumonia vaccination	n/a	71.0

Note: (1) Figures for the San Jose-Sunnyvale-Santa Clara, CA Metropolitan Statistical Area were not available.
Source: Centers for Disease Control and Prevention, Behaviorial Risk Factor Surveillance System, SMART: Selected Metropolitan Area Risk Trends, 2021

Disability Status

Category	MSA[1] (%)	U.S. (%)
Adults who reported being deaf	n/a	7.2
Are you blind or have serious difficulty seeing, even when wearing glasses?	n/a	4.8
Are you limited in any way in any of your usual activities due to arthritis?	n/a	11.1
Do you have difficulty doing errands alone?	n/a	7.0
Do you have difficulty dressing or bathing?	n/a	3.6
Do you have serious difficulty concentrating/remembering/making decisions?	n/a	12.1
Do you have serious difficulty walking or climbing stairs?	n/a	12.8

Note: (1) Figures for the San Jose-Sunnyvale-Santa Clara, CA Metropolitan Statistical Area were not available.
Source: Centers for Disease Control and Prevention, Behaviorial Risk Factor Surveillance System, SMART: Selected Metropolitan Area Risk Trends, 2021

Mortality Rates for the Top 10 Causes of Death in the U.S.

ICD-10[a] Sub-Chapter	ICD-10[a] Code	Crude Mortality Rate[1] per 100,000 population	
		County[2]	U.S.
Malignant neoplasms	C00-C97	123.6	182.6
Ischaemic heart diseases	I20-I25	60.4	113.1
Other forms of heart disease	I30-I51	24.7	64.4
Other degenerative diseases of the nervous system	G30-G31	61.7	51.0
Cerebrovascular diseases	I60-I69	35.7	47.8
Other external causes of accidental injury	W00-X59	25.6	46.4
Chronic lower respiratory diseases	J40-J47	15.5	45.7
Organic, including symptomatic, mental disorders	F01-F09	3.3	35.9
Hypertensive diseases	I10-I15	41.8	35.0
Diabetes mellitus	E10-E14	25.5	29.6

Note: (a) ICD-10 = International Classification of Diseases 10th Revision; (1) Crude mortality rates are a three-year average covering 2019-2021; (2) Figures cover Santa Clara County.
Source: Centers for Disease Control and Prevention, National Center for Health Statistics. National Vital Statistics System, Mortality 2018-2021 on CDC WONDER Online Database

Mortality Rates for Selected Causes of Death

ICD-10[a] Sub-Chapter	ICD-10[a] Code	Crude Mortality Rate[1] per 100,000 population	
		County[2]	U.S.
Assault	X85-Y09	2.6	7.0
Diseases of the liver	K70-K76	10.5	19.8
Human immunodeficiency virus (HIV) disease	B20-B24	0.4	1.5
Influenza and pneumonia	J09-J18	8.5	14.7
Intentional self-harm	X60-X84	8.7	14.3
Malnutrition	E40-E46	0.9	4.3
Obesity and other hyperalimentation	E65-E68	1.7	3.0
Renal failure	N17-N19	3.8	15.7
Transport accidents	V01-V99	7.9	13.6
Viral hepatitis	B15-B19	1.2	1.2

Note: (a) ICD-10 = International Classification of Diseases 10th Revision; (1) Crude mortality rates are a three-year average covering 2019-2021; (2) Figures cover Santa Clara County; Data are suppressed when the data meet the criteria for confidentiality constraints; Crude mortality rates are flagged as unreliable when the rate would be calculated with a numerator of 20 or less.
Source: Centers for Disease Control and Prevention, National Center for Health Statistics. National Vital Statistics System, Mortality 2018-2021 on CDC WONDER Online Database

Health Insurance Coverage

Area	With Health Insurance	With Private Health Insurance	With Public Health Insurance	Without Health Insurance	Population Under Age 19 Without Health Insurance
City	94.9	72.9	29.9	5.1	2.1
MSA[1]	95.8	77.5	26.7	4.2	1.9
U.S.	91.2	67.8	35.4	8.8	5.3

Note: Figures are percentages that cover the civilian noninstitutionalized population; (1) Figures cover the San Jose-Sunnyvale-Santa Clara, CA Metropolitan Statistical Area
Source: U.S. Census Bureau, 2017-2021 American Community Survey 5-Year Estimates

Number of Medical Professionals

Area	MDs[3]	DOs[3,4]	Dentists	Podiatrists	Chiropractors	Optometrists
County[1] (number)	8,608	232	2,342	131	849	543
County[1] (rate[2])	445.9	12.0	124.2	6.9	45.0	28.8
U.S. (rate[2])	289.3	23.5	72.5	6.2	28.7	17.4

Note: Data as of 2021 unless noted; (1) Data covers Santa Clara County; (2) Rate per 100,000 population; (3) Data as of 2020 and includes all active, non-federal physicians; (4) Doctor of Osteopathic Medicine
Source: U.S. Department of Health and Human Services, Health Resources and Services Administration, Bureau of Health Professions, Area Resource File (ARF) 2021-2022

Best Hospitals

According to *U.S. News,* the San Jose-Sunnyvale-Santa Clara, CA metro area is home to three of the best hospitals in the U.S.: **Providence St. Joseph Medical Center-Burbank** (1 adult specialty); **Santa Clara Valley Medical Center** (1 adult specialty); **Stanford Health Care-Stanford Hospital** (Honor Roll/11 adult specialties). The hospitals listed were nationally ranked in at least one of 15 adult or 10 pediatric specialties. The number of specialties shown cover the parent hospital. Only 164 U.S. hospitals performed well enough to be nationally ranked in one or more specialties. Twenty hospitals in the U.S. made the Honor Roll. The Best Hospitals Honor Roll takes both the national rankings and the procedure and condition ratings into account. Hospitals received points if they were nationally ranked in one of the 15 adult specialties—the higher they ranked, the more points they got—and how many ratings of "high performing" they earned in the 17 procedures and conditions. *U.S. News Online, "America's Best Hospitals 2022-23"*

According to *U.S. News,* the San Jose-Sunnyvale-Santa Clara, CA metro area is home to one of the best children's hospitals in the U.S.: **Lucile Packard Children's Hospital Stanford** (Honor Roll/10 pediatric specialties). The hospital listed was highly ranked in at least one of 10 pediatric specialties. Eighty-six children's hospitals in the U.S. were nationally ranked in at least one specialty. Hospitals received points for being ranked in a specialty, and the 10 hospitals with the most points across the 10 specialties make up the Honor Roll. *U.S. News Online, "America's Best Children's Hospitals 2022-23"*

EDUCATION

Public School District Statistics

District Name	Schls	Pupils	Pupil/ Teacher Ratio	Minority Pupils[1] (%)	LEP/ELL[2] (%)	IEP[3] (%)
Alum Rock Union Elementary	22	8,000	20.3	98.5	40.5	12.7
Berryessa Union Elementary	14	6,258	23.6	95.4	33.5	10.8
Cambrian	6	2,985	22.2	65.7	13.1	12.5
Campbell Union High	6	8,583	22.1	67.4	6.7	13.2
East Side Union High	16	21,844	22.6	94.7	15.5	10.9
Evergreen Elementary	16	9,165	22.9	95.6	24.3	9.4
Franklin-Mckinley Elementary	16	6,196	19.3	97.8	45.3	13.2
Moreland	7	4,043	21.8	79.5	28.9	11.5
Oak Grove Elementary	18	8,860	23.0	86.1	25.2	13.5
San Jose Unified	42	25,677	22.0	77.3	22.2	12.2
Union Elementary	8	5,447	23.9	63.1	11.9	9.9

Note: Table includes school districts with 2,000 or more students; (1) Percentage of students that are not non-Hispanic white; (2) Percentage of students that are Limited English Proficient or English Language Learners (2018-19); (3) Percentage of students that have an Individualized Education Program (2019-20). Source: U.S. Department of Education, National Center for Education Statistics, Common Core of Data, Local Education Agency (School District) Universe Survey: School Year 2021-2022

Best High Schools

According to *U.S. News,* San Jose is home to three of the top 500 high schools in the U.S.: **Lynbrook High School** (#101); **KIPP San Jose Collegiate** (#349); **Leland High School** (#481). Nearly 18,000 public, magnet and charter schools were ranked based on their performance on state assessments and how well they prepare students for college. *U.S. News & World Report, "Best High Schools 2022"*

Highest Level of Education

Area	Less than H.S.	H.S. Diploma	Some College, No Deg.	Associate Degree	Bachelor's Degree	Master's Degree	Prof. School Degree	Doctorate Degree
City	14.5	16.3	16.2	7.6	26.0	14.5	2.2	2.8
MSA[1]	11.0	14.1	14.7	6.9	27.5	18.7	2.8	4.4
U.S.	11.1	26.5	20.0	8.7	20.6	9.3	2.2	1.5

Note: Figures cover persons age 25 and over; (1) Figures cover the San Jose-Sunnyvale-Santa Clara, CA Metropolitan Statistical Area Source: U.S. Census Bureau, 2017-2021 American Community Survey 5-Year Estimates

Educational Attainment by Race

Area	High School Graduate or Higher (%)					Bachelor's Degree or Higher (%)				
	Total	White	Black	Asian	Hisp.[2]	Total	White	Black	Asian	Hisp.[2]
City	85.5	90.9	91.4	87.6	69.6	45.4	48.2	38.3	57.5	16.6
MSA[1]	89.0	92.7	92.4	91.4	71.9	53.4	53.4	41.7	67.5	19.0
U.S.	88.9	91.4	87.6	87.6	71.2	33.7	35.5	23.3	55.6	18.4

Note: Figures shown cover persons 25 years old and over; (1) Figures cover the San Jose-Sunnyvale-Santa Clara, CA Metropolitan Statistical Area; (2) People of Hispanic origin can be of any race Source: U.S. Census Bureau, 2017-2021 American Community Survey 5-Year Estimates

School Enrollment by Grade and Control

Area	Preschool (%)		Kindergarten (%)		Grades 1 - 4 (%)		Grades 5 - 8 (%)		Grades 9 - 12 (%)	
	Public	Private	Public	Private	Public	Private	Public	Private	Public	Private
City	43.4	56.6	81.8	18.2	87.0	13.0	87.6	12.4	85.9	14.1
MSA[1]	36.0	64.0	78.9	21.1	85.4	14.6	86.0	14.0	85.9	14.1
U.S.	58.8	41.2	86.3	13.7	88.3	11.7	88.6	11.4	89.4	10.6

Note: Figures shown cover persons 3 years old and over; (1) Figures cover the San Jose-Sunnyvale-Santa Clara, CA Metropolitan Statistical Area Source: U.S. Census Bureau, 2017-2021 American Community Survey 5-Year Estimates

Higher Education

Four-Year Colleges			Two-Year Colleges			Medical Schools[1]	Law Schools[2]	Voc/ Tech[3]
Public	Private Non-profit	Private For-profit	Public	Private Non-profit	Private For-profit			
2	4	3	6	0	2	1	3	3

Note: Figures cover institutions located within the San Jose-Sunnyvale-Santa Clara, CA Metropolitan Statistical Area and include main campuses only; (1) includes schools accredited by the Liaison Committee on Medical Education and the American Osteopathic Association's Commission on Osteopathic College Accreditation; (2) includes ABA-accredited schools, schools with provisional ABA accreditation, and state accredited schools; (3) includes all schools with programs that are less than 2 years.
Source: National Center for Education Statistics, Integrated Postsecondary Education System (IPEDS), 2021-22; Wikipedia, List of Medical Schools in the United States, accessed April 10, 2023; Wikipedia, List of Law Schools in the United States, accessed April 10, 2023

According to *U.S. News & World Report*, the San Jose-Sunnyvale-Santa Clara, CA metro area is home to two of the top 200 national universities in the U.S.: **Stanford University** (#3 tie); **Santa Clara University** (#55 tie). The indicators used to capture academic quality fall into a number of categories: assessment by administrators at peer institutions; retention of students; faculty resources; student selectivity; financial resources; alumni giving; high school counselor ratings of colleges; and graduation rate. *U.S. News & World Report, "America's Best Colleges 2023"*

According to *U.S. News & World Report*, the San Jose-Sunnyvale-Santa Clara, CA metro area is home to one of the top 100 law schools in the U.S.: **Stanford University** (#2). The rankings are based on a weighted average of 12 measures of quality: peer assessment score; assessment score by lawyers/judges; median LSAT scores; median undergrad GPA; acceptance rate; employment rates for graduates; placement success; bar passage rate; faculty resources; expenditures per student; student/faculty ratio; and library resources. *U.S. News & World Report, "America's Best Graduate Schools, Law, 2023"*

According to *U.S. News & World Report*, the San Jose-Sunnyvale-Santa Clara, CA metro area is home to one of the top 75 medical schools for research in the U.S.: **Stanford University** (#8). The rankings are based on a weighted average of 11 measures of quality: quality assessment; peer assessment score; assessment score by residency directors; research activity; total research activity; average research activity per faculty member; student selectivity; median MCAT total score; median undergraduate GPA; acceptance rate; and faculty resources. *U.S. News & World Report, "America's Best Graduate Schools, Medical, 2023"*

According to *U.S. News & World Report*, the San Jose-Sunnyvale-Santa Clara, CA metro area is home to one of the top 75 business schools in the U.S.: **Stanford University** (#3 tie). The rankings are based on a weighted average of the following nine measures: quality assessment; peer assessment; recruiter assessment; placement success; mean starting salary and bonus; student selectivity; mean GMAT and GRE scores; mean undergraduate GPA; and acceptance rate. *U.S. News & World Report, "America's Best Graduate Schools, Business, 2023"*

EMPLOYERS

Major Employers

Company Name	Industry
Adobe Systems Inc	Publishers-computer software, mfg
Advanced Micro Devices Inc	Semiconductor devices, mfg
Apple Inc	Computers-electronic-manufacturers
Applied Materials	Semiconductor manufacturing equip, mfg
Bon Appetit-Cafe Adobe	Restaurant management
California's Great America	Amusement & theme parks
Christopher Ranch	Garlic manufacturers
Cisco Systems Inc	Computer peripherals
Ebay	E-commerce
Flextronics	Solar energy equipment-manufacturers
General Motors Advanced Tech	Automobile manufacturing
Hewlett-Packard Co.	Computers-electronic-manufacturers
Intel Corporation	Semiconductor devices, mfg
Kaiser Permanente Medical Ctr	General medical & surgical hospitals
Lockheed Martin Space Systems	Satellite equipment & systems, mfg
Microsoft	Computer software-manufacturers
NASA	Government offices, federal
Net App Inc	Computer storage devices

Note: Companies shown are located within the San Jose-Sunnyvale-Santa Clara, CA Metropolitan Statistical Area.
Source: Hoovers.com; Wikipedia

Best Companies to Work For

Adobe Systems; Cadence; Cisco, headquartered in San Jose, are among "The 100 Best Companies to Work For." To pick the best companies, *Fortune* partnered with the Great Place to Work Institute. Two-thirds of a company's score is based on the results of the Institute's Trust Index survey, which is sent to a random sample of employees from each company. The questions related to attitudes about management's credibility, job satisfaction, and camaraderie. The other third of the scoring is based on the company's responses to the Institute's Culture Audit, which includes detailed questions about pay and benefit programs, and a series of open-ended questions about hiring practices, internal communication, training, recognition programs, and diversity efforts. Any company that is at least five years old with more than 1,000 U.S. employees is eligible. *Fortune, "The 100 Best Companies to Work For," 2023*

Cisco, headquartered in San Jose, is among "Fortune's Best Workplaces for Women." To pick the best companies, *Fortune* partnered with the Great Place to Work Institute. To be considered for the list, companies must be Great Place To Work-Certified. Companies must also employ at least 50 women, at least 20% of their non-executive managers must be female, and at least one executive must be female. To determine the Best Workplaces for Women, Great Place To Work measured the differences in women's survey responses to those of their peers and assesses the impact of demographics and roles on the quality and consistency of women's experiences. Great Place To Work also analyzed the gender balance of each workplace, how it compared to each company's industry, and patterns in representation as women rise from front-line positions to the board of directors. *Fortune, "Best Workplaces for Women," 2022*

Adobe Systems; Cisco, headquartered in San Jose, are among "Fortune's Best Workplaces for Parents." To pick the best companies, *Fortune* partnered with the Great Place to Work Institute. To be considered for the list, companies must be Great Place To Work-Certified and have at least 50 responses from parents in the US. The survey enables employees to share confidential quantitative and qualitative feedback about their organization's culture by responding to 60 statements on a 5-point scale and answering two open-ended questions. Collectively, these statements describe a great employee experience, defined by high levels of trust, respect, credibility, fairness, pride, and camaraderie. In addition, companies provide organizational data like size, location, industry, demographics, roles, and levels; and provide information about parental leave, adoption, flexible schedule, childcare and dependent health care benefits. *Fortune, "Best Workplaces for Parents," 2022*

Align Technology; Extreme Networks, headquartered in San Jose, are among the "100 Best Places to Work in IT." To qualify, companies had to have a minimum of 100 total employees and five IT employees. The best places to work were selected based on DEI (diversity, equity, and inclusion) practices; IT turnover, promotions, and growth; IT retention and engagement programs; remote/hybrid working; benefits and perks (such as elder care and child care, flextime, and reimbursement for college tuition); and training and career development opportunities. *Computerworld, "Best Places to Work in IT," 2023*

PUBLIC SAFETY

Crime Rate

Area	Total Crime	Violent Crime Rate				Property Crime Rate		
		Murder	Rape[3]	Robbery	Aggrav. Assault	Burglary	Larceny -Theft	Motor Vehicle Theft
City	2,741.2	3.9	55.0	115.1	251.0	392.9	1,237.2	686.2
Suburbs[1]	2,331.9	1.7	27.1	56.1	116.6	343.6	1,474.4	312.3
Metro[2]	2,543.9	2.8	41.6	86.7	186.2	369.1	1,351.5	506.0
U.S.	2,356.7	6.5	38.4	73.9	279.7	314.2	1,398.0	246.0

Note: Figures are crimes per 100,000 population; (1) All areas within the metro area that are located outside the city limits; (2) Figures cover the San Jose-Sunnyvale-Santa Clara, CA Metropolitan Statistical Area; (3) All figures shown were reported using the revised Uniform Crime Reporting (UCR) definition of rape; Due to the transition to the National Incident-Based Reporting System (NIBRS), limited city and metro area data was released for 2021.
Source: FBI Uniform Crime Reports, 2020

Hate Crimes

Area	Number of Quarters Reported	Number of Incidents per Bias Motivation					
		Race/Ethnicity/ Ancestry	Religion	Sexual Orientation	Disability	Gender	Gender Identity
City	4	75	9	9	0	0	1
U.S.	4	5,227	1,244	1,110	130	75	266

Note: Due to the transition to the National Incident-Based Reporting System (NIBRS), limited crime data was released for 2021.
Source: Federal Bureau of Investigation, Hate Crime Statistics 2020

Identity Theft Consumer Reports

Area	Reports	Reports per 100,000 Population	Rank[2]
MSA[1]	4,274	215	143
U.S.	1,108,609	339	-

Note: (1) Figures cover the San Jose-Sunnyvale-Santa Clara, CA Metropolitan Statistical Area; (2) Rank ranges from 1 to 391 where 1 indicates greatest number of identity theft reports per 100,000 population
Source: Federal Trade Commission, Consumer Sentinel Network Data Book 2022

Fraud and Other Consumer Reports

Area	Reports	Reports per 100,000 Population	Rank[2]
MSA[1]	17,906	902	146
U.S.	4,064,520	1,245	-

Note: (1) Figures cover the San Jose-Sunnyvale-Santa Clara, CA Metropolitan Statistical Area; (2) Rank ranges from 1 to 391 where 1 indicates greatest number of fraud and other consumer reports per 100,000 population
Source: Federal Trade Commission, Consumer Sentinel Network Data Book 2022

POLITICS

2020 Presidential Election Results

Area	Biden	Trump	Jorgensen	Hawkins	Other
Santa Clara County	72.6	25.2	1.1	0.5	0.6
U.S.	51.3	46.8	1.2	0.3	0.5

Note: Results are percentages and may not add to 100% due to rounding
Source: Dave Leip's Atlas of U.S. Presidential Elections

SPORTS

Professional Sports Teams

Team Name	League	Year Established
San Jose Earthquakes	Major League Soccer (MLS)	1996
San Jose Sharks	National Hockey League (NHL)	1991

Note: Includes teams located in the San Jose-Sunnyvale-Santa Clara, CA Metropolitan Statistical Area.
Source: Wikipedia, Major Professional Sports Teams of the United States and Canada, April 12, 2023

CLIMATE

Average and Extreme Temperatures

Temperature	Jan	Feb	Mar	Apr	May	Jun	Jul	Aug	Sep	Oct	Nov	Dec	Yr.
Extreme High (°F)	76	82	83	95	103	104	105	101	105	100	87	76	105
Average High (°F)	57	61	63	67	70	74	75	75	76	72	65	58	68
Average Temp. (°F)	50	53	55	58	61	65	66	67	66	63	56	50	59
Average Low (°F)	42	45	46	48	51	55	57	58	57	53	47	42	50
Extreme Low (°F)	21	26	30	32	38	43	45	47	41	33	29	23	21

Note: Figures cover the years 1945-1993
Source: National Climatic Data Center, International Station Meteorological Climate Summary, 9/96

Average Precipitation/Snowfall/Humidity

Precip./Humidity	Jan	Feb	Mar	Apr	May	Jun	Jul	Aug	Sep	Oct	Nov	Dec	Yr.
Avg. Precip. (in.)	2.7	2.3	2.2	0.9	0.3	0.1	Tr	Tr	0.2	0.7	1.7	2.3	13.5
Avg. Snowfall (in.)	Tr	Tr	Tr	0	0	0	0	0	0	0	0	Tr	Tr
Avg. Rel. Hum. 7am (%)	82	82	80	76	74	73	77	79	79	79	81	82	79
Avg. Rel. Hum. 4pm (%)	62	59	56	52	53	54	58	58	55	54	59	63	57

Note: Figures cover the years 1945-1993; Tr = Trace amounts (<0.05 in. of rain; <0.5 in. of snow)
Source: National Climatic Data Center, International Station Meteorological Climate Summary, 9/96

Weather Conditions

Temperature			Daytime Sky			Precipitation		
10°F & below	32°F & below	90°F & above	Clear	Partly cloudy	Cloudy	0.01 inch or more precip.	0.1 inch or more snow/ice	Thunder-storms
0	5	5	106	180	79	57	< 1	6

Note: Figures are average number of days per year and cover the years 1945-1993
Source: National Climatic Data Center, International Station Meteorological Climate Summary, 9/96

HAZARDOUS WASTE

Superfund Sites

The San Jose-Sunnyvale-Santa Clara, CA metro area is home to 17 sites on the EPA's Superfund National Priorities List: **Advanced Micro Devices, Inc.** (final); **Advanced Micro Devices, Inc. (Building 915)** (final); **Applied Materials** (final); **CTS Printex, Inc.** (final); **Fairchild Semiconductor Corp. (Mountain View Plant)** (final); **Fairchild Semiconductor Corp. (South San Jose Plant)** (final); **Hewlett-Packard (620-640 Page Mill Road)** (final); **Intel Corp. (Mountain View Plant)** (final); **Intel Magnetics** (final); **Intersil Inc./Siemens Components** (final); **Lorentz Barrel & Drum Co.** (final); **Moffett Field Naval Air Station** (final); **Monolithic Memories** (final); **National Semiconductor Corp.** (final); **New Idria Mercury Mine** (final); **Raytheon Corp.** (final); **South Bay Asbestos Area** (final). There are a total of 1,165 Superfund sites with a status of proposed or final on the list in the U.S. *U.S. Environmental Protection Agency, National Priorities List, April 12, 2023*

AIR QUALITY

Air Quality Trends: Ozone

	1990	1995	2000	2005	2010	2015	2018	2019	2020	2021
MSA[1]	0.078	0.084	0.065	0.063	0.072	0.067	0.059	0.061	0.066	0.067
U.S.	0.087	0.089	0.081	0.080	0.072	0.067	0.069	0.065	0.065	0.067

Note: (1) Data covers the San Jose-Sunnyvale-Santa Clara, CA Metropolitan Statistical Area. The values shown are the composite ozone concentration averages among trend sites based on the highest fourth daily maximum 8-hour concentration in parts per million. These trends are based on sites having an adequate record of monitoring data during the trend period. Data from exceptional events are included.
Source: U.S. Environmental Protection Agency, Air Quality Monitoring Information, "Air Quality Trends by City, 1990-2021"

Air Quality Index

Area	Percent of Days when Air Quality was...[2]					AQI Statistics[2]	
	Good	Moderate	Unhealthy for Sensitive Groups	Unhealthy	Very Unhealthy	Maximum	Median
MSA[1]	60.5	37.5	1.9	0.0	0.0	147	46

Note: (1) Data covers the San Jose-Sunnyvale-Santa Clara, CA Metropolitan Statistical Area; (2) Based on 365 days with AQI data in 2021. Air Quality Index (AQI) is an index for reporting daily air quality. EPA calculates the AQI for five major air pollutants regulated by the Clean Air Act: ground-level ozone, particle pollution (aka particulate matter), carbon monoxide, sulfur dioxide, and nitrogen dioxide. The AQI runs from 0 to 500. The higher the AQI value, the greater the level of air pollution and the greater the health concern. There are six AQI categories: "Good" AQI is between 0 and 50. Air quality is considered satisfactory; "Moderate" AQI is between 51 and 100. Air quality is acceptable; "Unhealthy for Sensitive Groups" When AQI values are between 101 and 150, members of sensitive groups may experience health effects; "Unhealthy" When AQI values are between 151 and 200 everyone may begin to experience health effects; "Very Unhealthy" AQI values between 201 and 300 trigger a health alert; "Hazardous" AQI values over 300 trigger warnings of emergency conditions (not shown).
Source: U.S. Environmental Protection Agency, Air Quality Index Report, 2021

Air Quality Index Pollutants

Area	Percent of Days when AQI Pollutant was...[2]					
	Carbon Monoxide	Nitrogen Dioxide	Ozone	Sulfur Dioxide	Particulate Matter 2.5	Particulate Matter 10
MSA[1]	0.0	0.0	54.8	(3)	44.1	1.1

Note: (1) Data covers the San Jose-Sunnyvale-Santa Clara, CA Metropolitan Statistical Area; (2) Based on 365 days with AQI data in 2021. The Air Quality Index (AQI) is an index for reporting daily air quality. EPA calculates the AQI for five major air pollutants regulated by the Clean Air Act: ground-level ozone, particle pollution (also known as particulate matter), carbon monoxide, sulfur dioxide, and nitrogen dioxide. The AQI runs from 0 to 500. The higher the AQI value, the greater the level of air pollution and the greater the health concern; (3) Sulfur dioxide is no longer included in this table (as of December 8, 2021) because SO_2 concentrations tend to be very localized and not necessarily representative of broad geographical areas like counties and CBSAs.
Source: U.S. Environmental Protection Agency, Air Quality Index Report, 2021

Maximum Air Pollutant Concentrations: Particulate Matter, Ozone, CO and Lead

	Particulate Matter 10 (ug/m³)	Particulate Matter 2.5 Wtd AM (ug/m³)	Particulate Matter 2.5 24-Hr (ug/m³)	Ozone (ppm)	Carbon Monoxide (ppm)	Lead (ug/m³)
MSA[1] Level	76	10.9	25	0.074	1	n/a
NAAQS[2]	150	15	35	0.075	9	0.15
Met NAAQS[2]	Yes	Yes	Yes	Yes	Yes	n/a

Note: (1) Data covers the San Jose-Sunnyvale-Santa Clara, CA Metropolitan Statistical Area; Data from exceptional events are included; (2) National Ambient Air Quality Standards; ppm = parts per million; ug/m³ = micrograms per cubic meter; n/a not available.
Concentrations: Particulate Matter 10 (coarse particulate)—highest second maximum 24-hour concentration; Particulate Matter 2.5 Wtd AM (fine particulate)—highest weighted annual mean concentration; Particulate Matter 2.5 24-Hour (fine particulate)—highest 98th percentile 24-hour concentration; Ozone—highest fourth daily maximum 8-hour concentration; Carbon Monoxide—highest second maximum non-overlapping 8-hour concentration; Lead—maximum running 3-month average
Source: U.S. Environmental Protection Agency, Air Quality Monitoring Information, "Air Quality Statistics by City, 2021"

Maximum Air Pollutant Concentrations: Nitrogen Dioxide and Sulfur Dioxide

	Nitrogen Dioxide AM (ppb)	Nitrogen Dioxide 1-Hr (ppb)	Sulfur Dioxide AM (ppb)	Sulfur Dioxide 1-Hr (ppb)	Sulfur Dioxide 24-Hr (ppb)
MSA[1] Level	12	39	n/a	2	n/a
NAAQS[2]	53	100	30	75	140
Met NAAQS[2]	Yes	Yes	n/a	Yes	n/a

Note: (1) Data covers the San Jose-Sunnyvale-Santa Clara, CA Metropolitan Statistical Area; Data from exceptional events are included; (2) National Ambient Air Quality Standards; ppm = parts per million; ug/m³ = micrograms per cubic meter; n/a not available.
Concentrations: Nitrogen Dioxide AM—highest arithmetic mean concentration; Nitrogen Dioxide 1-Hr—highest 98th percentile 1-hour daily maximum concentration; Sulfur Dioxide AM—highest annual mean concentration; Sulfur Dioxide 1-Hr—highest 99th percentile 1-hour daily maximum concentration; Sulfur Dioxide 24-Hr—highest second maximum 24-hour concentration
Source: U.S. Environmental Protection Agency, Air Quality Monitoring Information, "Air Quality Statistics by City, 2021"

Santa Rosa, California

Background

Santa Rosa is located 55 miles north of San Francisco in the county seat of Sonoma County and home to one-third of the county's residents. The city is part of both the San Francisco Bay Area and the region known as California wine country. The popularity of the vineyards, especially among tourists, has helped the city evolve from a small farming town during the California gold rush to a thriving, modern city known for its climate, location, and natural beauty.

During the early days of European exploration, the area that is now Santa Rosa was a homestead for wealthy and prominent families, both under Mexican and Spanish rule. In 1852, the Mexican American War ended, and the territory of California became part of the United States. Around this time, the California Gold Rush brought large numbers of new settlers to the area. As the gold rush waned, explorers found they could make more money farming than they could digging for gold. The community began to grow, and the city was officially incorporated 1868. That same year, the first railroad line reached the city helping Santa Rosa's population to increase tenfold in just seven years.

During the twentieth century, population began to level off, and Santa Rosa settled into a medium-sized city that affords residents the benefits of a larger urban center.

Population began increasing rapidly at the end of the twentieth century. The city is planning for future growth via the *Santa Rosa 2030 Vision* and in 2017 annexed the community of Roseland in its quest for more land.

The city has two Sonoma-Marin Area Rail transit (SMART) stations—one downtown and the other in North Santa Rosa—enhancing pedestrian-friendly neighborhoods.

Downtown Santa Rosa, including the central Old Courthouse Square and historic Railroad Square is an area of shopping, restaurants, nightclubs, and theaters. The city's health care facilities include a Kaiser Permanente medical hub, and Sutter Medical Center.

Largely because of the city's natural beauty and highly regarded vineyards, Santa Rosa is a popular destination for tourists and wine enthusiasts. In addition to wine production, major attractions in Santa Rosa include the Luther Burbank Home and Gardens, Redwood Empire Ice Arena, Sonoma County Museum, and 6th Street Playhouse. The city is also home to the Charles M. Schulz Museum and Research Center, which celebrates the life and work of the Peanuts comic strip and its creator, who lived in Santa Rosa for over 30 years. In 2000, the city renamed its airport "Charles M. Schulz Sonoma County Airport," which is served by Alaska Airlines, with destinations that include San Diego, Los Angeles, Portland, and Seattle.

Institutions of higher learning in the city include the University of San Francisco Santa Rosa, Empire College, and Santa Rosa Junior College.

The city has the same comfortable northern California climate as other Bay Area cities with hot average temperatures and low humidity, ideal for wine grape production. Most of the city's precipitation falls during the spring and winter months, when temperatures are generally much cooler. Summer and fall hold potential for wildfires, and the October 2017 firestorm in the region was the most destructive and third deadliest in California history.

Rankings

Business/Finance Rankings

- According to *Business Insider*, the Santa Rosa metro area is a prime place to run a startup or move an existing business to. The area ranked #8. More than 300 metro areas were analyzed for factors that were of top concern to new business owners. Data was based on the 2019 U.S. Census Bureau American Community Survey, statistics from the CDC, Bureau of Labor Statistics employment report, and University of Chicago analysis. Criteria: business formations; percentage of vaccinated population; percentage of households with internet subscriptions; median household income; and share of work that can be done from home. *www.businessinsider.com, "The 20 Best Cities for Starting a Business in 2022 Include Baltimore, Boulder, and Boston," January 5, 2022*

- The Santa Rosa metro area appeared on the Milken Institute "2022 Best Performing Cities" list. Rank: #68 out of 200 large metro areas (population over 250,000). Criteria: job growth; wage and salary growth; high-tech output growth; housing affordability; household broadband access. *Milken Institute, "Best-Performing Cities 2022," March 28, 2022*

- *Forbes* ranked the 200 most populous metro areas to determine the nation's "Best Places for Business and Careers." The Santa Rosa metro area was ranked #110. Criteria: costs (business and living); job growth (past and projected); income growth; quality of life; educational attainment (college and high school); projected economic growth; cultural and leisure opportunities; workplace tolerance laws; net migration patterns. *Forbes, "The Best Places for Business and Careers 2019: Seattle Still On Top," October 30, 2019*

Education Rankings

- Personal finance website *WalletHub* analyzed the 150 largest U.S. metropolitan statistical areas to determine where the most educated Americans are putting their degrees to work. Criteria: education levels; percentage of workers with degrees; education quality and attainment gap; public school quality rankings; quality and enrollment of each metro area's universities. Santa Rosa was ranked #34 (#1 = most educated city). *www.WalletHub.com, "Most & Least Educated Cities in America," July 18, 2022*

Real Estate Rankings

- *WalletHub* compared the most populated U.S. cities to determine which had the best markets for real estate agents. Santa Rosa ranked #43 where demand was high and pay was the best. Criteria: sales per agent; annual median wage for real-estate agents; monthly average starting salary for real estate agents; real estate job density and competition; unemployment rate; home turnover rate; housing-market health index; and other relevant metrics. *www.WalletHub.com, "2021 Best Places to Be a Real Estate Agent," May 12, 2021*

- Santa Rosa was ranked #225 out of 235 metro areas in terms of housing affordability in 2022 by the National Association of Home Builders (#1 = most affordable). Criteria: the share of homes sold in that area affordable to a family earning the local median income, based on standard mortgage underwriting criteria. *National Association of Home Builders®, NAHB-Wells Fargo Housing Opportunity Index, 4th Quarter 2022*

Safety Rankings

- Allstate ranked the 200 largest cities in America in terms of driver safety. Santa Rosa ranked #90. Criteria: internal property damage claims over a two-year period from January 2016 to December 2017. The report helps increase the importance of safety and awareness behind the wheel. *Allstate, "Allstate America's Best Drivers Report, 2019" June 24, 2019*

- The National Insurance Crime Bureau ranked 390 metro areas in the U.S. in terms of per capita rates of vehicle theft. The Santa Rosa metro area ranked #149 (#1 = highest rate). Criteria: number of vehicle theft offenses per 100,000 inhabitants in 2021. *National Insurance Crime Bureau, "Hot Spots 2021," September 1, 2022*

Seniors/Retirement Rankings

- From its Best Cities for Successful Aging indexes, the Milken Institute generated rankings for metropolitan areas, weighing data in nine categories—health care, wellness, living arrangements, transportation and convenience, financial characteristics, education, employment, community engagement, and overall livability. The Santa Rosa metro area was ranked #148 overall in the small metro area category. *Milken Institute, "Best Cities for Successful Aging, 2017" March 14, 2017*

Women/Minorities Rankings

- Personal finance website *WalletHub* compared more than 180 U.S. cities across two key dimensions, "Hispanic Business-Friendliness" and "Hispanic Purchasing Power," to arrive at the most favorable conditions for Hispanic entrepreneurs. Santa Rosa was ranked #114 out of 182. Criteria includes: share of Hispanic-Owned Businesses; Hispanic entrepreneurship rate to median annual income of Hispanics; Small Business-Friendliness score; cost of living; and number of Hispanics with at least a bachelor's degree. *WalletHub.com, "2019's Best Cities for Hispanic Entrepreneurs," May 1, 2019*

Business Environment

DEMOGRAPHICS

Population Growth

Area	1990 Census	2000 Census	2010 Census	2020 Census	Population Growth (%) 1990-2020	Population Growth (%) 2010-2020
City	123,297	147,595	167,815	178,127	44.5	6.1
MSA[1]	388,222	458,614	483,878	488,863	25.9	1.0
U.S.	248,709,873	281,421,906	308,745,538	331,449,281	33.3	7.4

Note: (1) Figures cover the Santa Rosa-Petaluma, CA Metropolitan Statistical Area
Source: U.S. Census Bureau, 1990 Census, 2000 Census, 2010 Census, 2020 Census

Race

Area	White Alone[2] (%)	Black Alone[2] (%)	Asian Alone[2] (%)	AIAN[3] Alone[2] (%)	NHOPI[4] Alone[2] (%)	Other Race Alone[2] (%)	Two or More Races (%)
City	55.7	2.3	6.1	2.3	0.6	19.1	13.9
MSA[1]	62.7	1.6	4.7	1.8	0.4	15.3	13.5
U.S.	61.6	12.4	6.0	1.1	0.2	8.4	10.2

Note: (1) Figures cover the Santa Rosa-Petaluma, CA Metropolitan Statistical Area; (2) Alone is defined as not being in combination with one or more other races; (3) American Indian and Alaska Native; (4) Native Hawaiian and Other Pacific Islander
Source: U.S. Census Bureau, 2020 Census

Hispanic or Latino Origin

Area	Total (%)	Mexican (%)	Puerto Rican (%)	Cuban (%)	Other (%)
City	34.0	29.3	0.5	0.1	4.1
MSA[1]	27.5	22.7	0.4	0.2	4.2
U.S.	18.4	11.2	1.8	0.7	4.7

Note: Persons of Hispanic or Latino origin can be of any race; (1) Figures cover the Santa Rosa-Petaluma, CA Metropolitan Statistical Area
Source: U.S. Census Bureau, 2017-2021 American Community Survey 5-Year Estimates

Age

Area	Under Age 5	Age 5–19	Age 20–34	Age 35–44	Age 45–54	Age 55–64	Age 65–74	Age 75–84	Age 85+	Median Age
City	5.1	18.5	19.4	13.7	12.1	12.5	10.9	5.4	2.5	39.9
MSA[1]	4.6	17.3	18.2	12.9	12.2	14.2	12.7	5.8	2.3	42.6
U.S.	5.6	19.2	20.2	12.7	12.4	13.1	10.0	4.9	1.9	38.8

Note: (1) Figures cover the Santa Rosa-Petaluma, CA Metropolitan Statistical Area
Source: U.S. Census Bureau, 2020 Census

Disability by Age

Area	All Ages	Under 18 Years Old	18 to 64 Years Old	65 Years and Over
City	11.7	3.2	9.5	29.7
MSA[1]	11.6	3.4	8.8	28.4
U.S.	12.6	4.4	10.3	33.4

Note: Figures show percent of the civilian noninstitutionalized population that reported having a disability. Disability status is determined from six types of difficulty: vision, hearing, cognitive, ambulatory, self-care, and independent living. For children under 5 years old, hearing and vision difficulty are used to determine disability status. For children between the ages of 5 and 14, disability status is determined from hearing, vision, cognitive, ambulatory, and self-care difficulties. For people aged 15 years and older, they are considered to have a disability if they have difficulty with any one of the six difficulty types; Note: (1) Figures cover the Santa Rosa-Petaluma, CA Metropolitan Statistical Area
Source: U.S. Census Bureau, 2017-2021 American Community Survey 5-Year Estimates

Ancestry

Area	German	Irish	English	American	Italian	Polish	French[2]	Scottish	Dutch
City	11.1	9.8	9.6	2.5	6.6	1.6	2.8	1.7	1.1
MSA[1]	12.8	12.2	10.9	2.5	8.3	1.7	3.1	2.5	1.2
U.S.	12.8	9.6	8.1	5.7	5.0	2.7	2.2	1.6	1.1

Note: Figures are the percentage of the total population reporting a particular ancestry. The nine most commonly reported ancestries in the U.S. are shown. Figures include multiple ancestries (e.g. if a person reported being Irish and Italian, they were included in both columns); (1) Figures cover the Santa Rosa-Petaluma, CA Metropolitan Statistical Area; (2) Excludes Basque
Source: U.S. Census Bureau, 2017-2021 American Community Survey 5-Year Estimates

Foreign-born Population

Area	Any Foreign Country	Percent of Population Born in							
		Asia	Mexico	Europe	Caribbean	Central America[2]	South America	Africa	Canada
City	21.1	4.6	11.9	1.9	0.0	1.1	0.3	0.6	0.4
MSA[1]	16.3	3.1	8.9	1.9	0.1	0.9	0.4	0.3	0.4
U.S.	13.6	4.2	3.3	1.9	1.4	1.1	0.4	0.8	0.2

Note: (1) Figures cover the Santa Rosa-Petaluma, CA Metropolitan Statistical Area; (2) Excludes Mexico.
Source: U.S. Census Bureau, 2017-2021 American Community Survey 5-Year Estimates

Household Size

Area	Persons in Household (%)							Average Household Size
	One	Two	Three	Four	Five	Six	Seven or More	
City	28.4	32.5	15.1	13.9	6.7	2.1	1.4	2.60
MSA[1]	27.0	35.1	14.8	13.8	6.2	2.0	1.1	2.60
U.S.	28.1	33.8	15.5	12.9	6.0	2.3	1.4	2.60

Note: (1) Figures cover the Santa Rosa-Petaluma, CA Metropolitan Statistical Area
Source: U.S. Census Bureau, 2017-2021 American Community Survey 5-Year Estimates

Household Relationships

Area	House-holder	Opposite-sex Spouse	Same-sex Spouse	Opposite-sex Unmarried Partner	Same-sex Unmarried Partner	Child[2]	Grand-child	Other Relatives	Non-relatives
City	37.6	16.2	0.4	3.0	0.2	27.3	1.8	6.2	5.5
MSA[1]	38.4	17.6	0.4	2.9	0.2	26.1	1.9	5.2	5.5
U.S.	38.3	17.5	0.2	2.5	0.2	28.3	2.4	4.8	3.4

Note: Figures are percent of the total population; (1) Figures cover the Santa Rosa-Petaluma, CA Metropolitan Statistical Area; (2) Includes biological, adopted, and stepchildren of the householder
Source: U.S. Census Bureau, 2020 Census

Gender

Area	Males	Females	Males per 100 Females
City	86,767	91,360	95.0
MSA[1]	238,535	250,328	95.3
U.S.	162,685,811	168,763,470	96.4

Note: (1) Figures cover the Santa Rosa-Petaluma, CA Metropolitan Statistical Area
Source: U.S. Census Bureau, 2020 Census

Marital Status

Area	Never Married	Now Married[2]	Separated	Widowed	Divorced
City	33.8	46.4	2.0	5.4	12.3
MSA[1]	32.3	48.7	1.5	5.1	12.5
U.S.	33.8	48.0	1.8	5.6	10.8

Note: Figures are percentages and cover the population 15 years of age and older; (1) Figures cover the Santa Rosa-Petaluma, CA Metropolitan Statistical Area; (2) Excludes separated
Source: U.S. Census Bureau, 2017-2021 American Community Survey 5-Year Estimates

Religious Groups by Family

Area	Catholic	Baptist	Methodist	LDS[2]	Pentecostal	Lutheran	Islam	Adventist	Other
MSA[1]	23.5	1.1	0.5	1.4	0.5	0.5	0.2	1.8	6.9
U.S.	18.7	7.3	3.0	2.0	1.8	1.7	1.3	1.3	11.6

Note: Figures are the number of adherents as a percentage of the total population and cover the eight largest religious groups in the U.S.; (1) Figures cover the Santa Rosa-Petaluma, CA Metropolitan Statistical Area; (2) Church of Jesus Christ of Latter-day Saints
Sources: 2020 U.S. Religion Census, Association of Statisticians of American Religious Bodies; The Association of Religion Data Archives (ARDA)

Religious Groups by Tradition

Area	Catholic	Evangelical Protestant	Mainline Protestant	Black Protestant	Islam	Judaism	Hinduism	Orthodox	Buddhism
MSA[1]	23.5	5.3	1.5	<0.1	0.2	0.4	0.3	0.4	1.7
U.S.	18.7	16.5	5.2	2.3	1.3	0.6	0.4	0.4	0.3

Note: Figures are the number of adherents as a percentage of the total population; (1) Figures cover the Santa Rosa-Petaluma, CA Metropolitan Statistical Area
Sources: 2020 U.S. Religion Census, Association of Statisticians of American Religious Bodies; The Association of Religion Data Archives (ARDA)

ECONOMY

Gross Metropolitan Product

Area	2020	2021	2022	2023	Rank[2]
MSA[1]	31.2	35.6	39.1	41.5	93

Note: Figures are in billions of dollars; (1) Figures cover the Santa Rosa-Petaluma, CA Metropolitan Statistical Area; (2) Rank is based on 2021 data and ranges from 1 to 381
Source: U.S. Conference of Mayors, U.S. Metro Economies: U.S. Metros Compared to Global and State Economies, June 2022

Economic Growth

Area	2018-20 (%)	2021 (%)	2022 (%)	2023 (%)	Rank[2]
MSA[1]	-1.8	9.7	5.0	3.1	269
U.S.	-0.6	5.7	3.1	2.9	–

Note: Figures are real gross metropolitan product (GMP) growth rates and represent average annual percent change; (1) Figures cover the Santa Rosa-Petaluma, CA Metropolitan Statistical Area; (2) Rank is based on 2020 2-year average annual percent change and ranges from 1 to 381
Source: U.S. Conference of Mayors, U.S. Metro Economies: U.S. Metros Compared to Global and State Economies, June 2022

Metropolitan Area Exports

Area	2016	2017	2018	2019	2020	2021	Rank[2]
MSA[1]	1,194.3	1,168.2	1,231.7	1,234.5	1,131.4	1,301.8	137

Note: Figures are in millions of dollars; (1) Figures cover the Santa Rosa-Petaluma, CA Metropolitan Statistical Area; (2) Rank is based on 2021 data and ranges from 1 to 388
Source: U.S. Department of Commerce, International Trade Administration, Office of Trade and Economic Analysis, Industry and Analysis, Exports by Metropolitan Area, data extracted March 16, 2023

Building Permits

Area	Single-Family			Multi-Family			Total		
	2021	2022	Pct. Chg.	2021	2022	Pct. Chg.	2021	2022	Pct. Chg.
City	420	286	-31.9	1,031	911	-11.6	1,451	1,197	-17.5
MSA[1]	1,227	954	-22.2	1,391	1,310	-5.8	2,618	2,264	-13.5
U.S.	1,115,400	975,600	-12.5	621,600	689,500	10.9	1,737,000	1,665,100	-4.1

Note: (1) Figures cover the Santa Rosa-Petaluma, CA Metropolitan Statistical Area; Figures represent new, privately-owned housing units authorized (unadjusted data); All permit data are based on estimates with imputation
Source: U.S. Census Bureau, Manufacturing, Mining, and Construction Statistics, Building Permits, 2021, 2022

Bankruptcy Filings

Area	Business Filings			Nonbusiness Filings		
	2021	2022	% Chg.	2021	2022	% Chg.
Sonoma County	23	29	26.1	329	278	-15.5
U.S.	14,347	13,481	-6.0	399,269	374,240	-6.3

Note: Business filings include Chapter 7, Chapter 9, Chapter 11, Chapter 12, Chapter 13, Chapter 15, and Section 304; Nonbusiness filings include Chapter 7, Chapter 11, and Chapter 13
Source: Administrative Office of the U.S. Courts, Business and Nonbusiness Bankruptcy, County Cases Commenced by Chapter of the Bankruptcy Code, During the 12-Month Period Ending December 31, 2021 and Business and Nonbusiness Bankruptcy, County Cases Commenced by Chapter of the Bankruptcy Code, During the 12-Month Period Ending December 31, 2022

Housing Vacancy Rates

Area	Gross Vacancy Rate[2] (%)			Year-Round Vacancy Rate[3] (%)			Rental Vacancy Rate[4] (%)			Homeowner Vacancy Rate[5] (%)		
	2020	2021	2022	2020	2021	2022	2020	2021	2022	2020	2021	2022
MSA[1]	n/a	n/a	n/a	n/a	n/a	n/a	n/a	n/a	n/a	n/a	n/a	n/a
U.S.	10.6	10.8	10.5	8.2	8.4	8.2	6.3	6.1	5.8	1.0	0.9	0.8

Note: (1) Figures cover the Santa Rosa-Petaluma, CA Metropolitan Statistical Area; (2) The percentage of the total housing inventory that is vacant; (3) The percentage of the housing inventory (excluding seasonal units) that is year-round vacant; (4) The percentage of rental inventory that is vacant for rent; (5) The percentage of homeowner inventory that is vacant for sale; n/a not available
Source: U.S. Census Bureau, Housing Vacancies and Homeownership Annual Statistics: 2020, 2021, 2022

INCOME

Income

Area	Per Capita ($)	Median Household ($)	Average Household ($)
City	41,880	84,823	108,164
MSA[1]	47,580	91,607	121,206
U.S.	37,638	69,021	97,196

Note: (1) Figures cover the Santa Rosa-Petaluma, CA Metropolitan Statistical Area
Source: U.S. Census Bureau, 2017-2021 American Community Survey 5-Year Estimates

Household Income Distribution

Area	Percent of Households Earning							
	Under $15,000	$15,000 -$24,999	$25,000 -$34,999	$35,000 -$49,999	$50,000 -$74,999	$75,000 -$99,999	$100,000 -$149,999	$150,000 and up
City	7.3	4.9	6.0	10.1	15.6	13.8	20.2	22.1
MSA[1]	6.5	5.0	5.9	9.0	14.3	13.4	19.6	26.3
U.S.	9.4	7.8	8.2	11.4	16.8	12.8	16.3	17.3

Note: (1) Figures cover the Santa Rosa-Petaluma, CA Metropolitan Statistical Area
Source: U.S. Census Bureau, 2017-2021 American Community Survey 5-Year Estimates

Poverty Rate

Area	All Ages	Under 18 Years Old	18 to 64 Years Old	65 Years and Over
City	9.8	12.9	9.0	9.0
MSA[1]	8.7	10.3	8.6	7.4
U.S.	12.6	17.0	11.8	9.6

Note: Figures are percentage of people whose income during the past 12 months was below the poverty level;
(1) Figures cover the Santa Rosa-Petaluma, CA Metropolitan Statistical Area
Source: U.S. Census Bureau, 2017-2021 American Community Survey 5-Year Estimates

EMPLOYMENT

Labor Force and Employment

Area	Civilian Labor Force			Workers Employed		
	Dec. 2021	Dec. 2022	% Chg.	Dec. 2021	Dec. 2022	% Chg.
City	85,496	86,918	1.7	82,307	84,605	2.8
MSA[1]	243,938	248,408	1.8	235,525	242,101	2.8
U.S.	161,696,000	164,224,000	1.6	155,732,000	158,872,000	2.0

Note: Data is not seasonally adjusted and covers workers 16 years of age and older; (1) Figures cover the
Santa Rosa-Petaluma, CA Metropolitan Statistical Area
Source: Bureau of Labor Statistics, Local Area Unemployment Statistics

Unemployment Rate

Area	2022											
	Jan.	Feb.	Mar.	Apr.	May	Jun.	Jul.	Aug.	Sep.	Oct.	Nov.	Dec.
City	4.3	3.8	3.3	2.7	2.4	2.8	2.7	2.9	2.7	2.8	3.1	2.7
MSA[1]	4.0	3.5	3.0	2.6	2.3	2.7	2.6	2.8	2.6	2.6	2.9	2.5
U.S.	4.4	4.1	3.8	3.3	3.4	3.8	3.8	3.8	3.3	3.4	3.4	3.3

Note: Data is not seasonally adjusted and covers workers 16 years of age and older; (1) Figures cover the
Santa Rosa-Petaluma, CA Metropolitan Statistical Area
Source: Bureau of Labor Statistics, Local Area Unemployment Statistics

Average Wages

Occupation	$/Hr.	Occupation	$/Hr.
Accountants and Auditors	44.48	Maintenance and Repair Workers	26.12
Automotive Mechanics	28.50	Marketing Managers	75.37
Bookkeepers	27.43	Network and Computer Systems Admin.	46.00
Carpenters	37.66	Nurses, Licensed Practical	36.88
Cashiers	17.71	Nurses, Registered	72.67
Computer Programmers	51.79	Nursing Assistants	20.99
Computer Systems Analysts	53.46	Office Clerks, General	22.86
Computer User Support Specialists	34.14	Physical Therapists	60.31
Construction Laborers	28.67	Physicians	112.97
Cooks, Restaurant	19.90	Plumbers, Pipefitters and Steamfitters	36.74
Customer Service Representatives	23.15	Police and Sheriff's Patrol Officers	49.57
Dentists	79.52	Postal Service Mail Carriers	27.31
Electricians	36.36	Real Estate Sales Agents	39.25
Engineers, Electrical	60.81	Retail Salespersons	19.94
Fast Food and Counter Workers	17.13	Sales Representatives, Technical/Scientific	53.84
Financial Managers	81.95	Secretaries, Exc. Legal/Medical/Executive	25.29
First-Line Supervisors of Office Workers	34.88	Security Guards	19.11
General and Operations Managers	64.13	Surgeons	n/a
Hairdressers/Cosmetologists	21.59	Teacher Assistants, Exc. Postsecondary*	20.52
Home Health and Personal Care Aides	16.52	Teachers, Secondary School, Exc. Sp. Ed.*	43.10
Janitors and Cleaners	22.75	Telemarketers	n/a
Landscaping/Groundskeeping Workers	21.42	Truck Drivers, Heavy/Tractor-Trailer	27.66
Lawyers	88.92	Truck Drivers, Light/Delivery Services	24.22
Maids and Housekeeping Cleaners	20.35	Waiters and Waitresses	18.13

Note: Wage data covers the Santa Rosa-Petaluma, CA Metropolitan Statistical Area; (*) Hourly wages were
calculated from annual wage data based on a 40 hour work week; n/a not available.
Source: Bureau of Labor Statistics, Metro Area Occupational Employment & Wage Estimates, May 2022

Employment by Industry

| Sector | MSA[1] | | U.S. |
	Number of Employees	Percent of Total	Percent of Total
Construction	16,200	7.8	5.0
Private Education and Health Services	36,000	17.3	16.1
Financial Activities	8,200	4.0	5.9
Government	26,300	12.7	14.5
Information	2,600	1.3	2.0
Leisure and Hospitality	25,800	12.4	10.3
Manufacturing	23,800	11.5	8.4
Mining and Logging	200	0.1	0.4
Other Services	7,400	3.6	3.7
Professional and Business Services	25,400	12.2	14.7
Retail Trade	23,600	11.4	10.2
Transportation, Warehousing, and Utilities	4,800	2.3	4.9
Wholesale Trade	7,200	3.5	3.9

Note: Figures are non-farm employment as of December 2022. Figures are not seasonally adjusted and include workers 16 years of age and older; (1) Figures cover the Santa Rosa-Petaluma, CA Metropolitan Statistical Area
Source: Bureau of Labor Statistics, Current Employment Statistics, Employment, Hours, and Earnings

Employment by Occupation

Occupation Classification	City (%)	MSA[1] (%)	U.S. (%)
Management, Business, Science, and Arts	37.4	40.3	40.3
Natural Resources, Construction, and Maintenance	10.6	10.2	8.7
Production, Transportation, and Material Moving	12.4	10.4	13.1
Sales and Office	20.7	20.4	20.9
Service	19.0	18.7	17.0

Note: Figures cover employed civilians 16 years of age and older; (1) Figures cover the Santa Rosa-Petaluma, CA Metropolitan Statistical Area
Source: U.S. Census Bureau, 2017-2021 American Community Survey 5-Year Estimates

Occupations with Greatest Projected Employment Growth: 2022 – 2024

Occupation[1]	2022 Employment	2024 Projected Employment	Numeric Employment Change	Percent Employment Change
Home Health and Personal Care Aides	811,300	858,600	47,300	5.8
Fast Food and Counter Workers	422,000	444,100	22,100	5.2
Cooks, Restaurant	154,300	172,000	17,700	11.5
Software Developers and Software Quality Assurance Analysts and Testers	337,600	352,100	14,500	4.3
Waiters and Waitresses	205,800	219,200	13,400	6.5
Laborers and Freight, Stock, and Material Movers, Hand	391,100	403,100	12,000	3.1
Stockers and Order Fillers	268,000	277,500	9,500	3.5
General and Operations Managers	308,500	317,600	9,100	2.9
First-Line Supervisors of Food Preparation and Serving Workers	118,100	126,000	7,900	6.7
Project Management Specialists and Business Operations Specialists, All Other	332,400	339,800	7,400	2.2

Note: Projections cover California; (1) Sorted by numeric employment change
Source: www.projectionscentral.com, State Occupational Projections, 2022–2024 Short-Term Projections

Fastest-Growing Occupations: 2022 – 2024

Occupation[1]	2022 Employment	2024 Projected Employment	Numeric Employment Change	Percent Employment Change
Fitness Trainers and Aerobics Instructors	40,700	46,300	5,600	13.8
Nurse Practitioners	18,300	20,500	2,200	12.0
Cooks, Restaurant	154,300	172,000	17,700	11.5
Airfield Operations Specialists	3,700	4,100	400	10.8
Solar Photovoltaic Installers	6,600	7,300	700	10.6
Ushers, Lobby Attendants, and Ticket Takers	7,800	8,600	800	10.3
Amusement and Recreation Attendants	47,500	52,300	4,800	10.1
Sociologists	1,000	1,100	100	10.0
Paperhangers	1,000	1,100	100	10.0
Avionics Technicians	2,000	2,200	200	10.0

Note: Projections cover California; (1) Sorted by percent employment change and excludes occupations with numeric employment change less than 50
Source: www.projectionscentral.com, State Occupational Projections, 2022–2024 Short-Term Projections

CITY FINANCES

City Government Finances

Component	2020 ($000)	2020 ($ per capita)
Total Revenues	415,891	2,353
Total Expenditures	373,877	2,115
Debt Outstanding	293,917	1,663
Cash and Securities[1]	141,361	800

Note: (1) Cash and security holdings of a government at the close of its fiscal year, including those of its dependent agencies, utilities, and liquor stores.
Source: U.S. Census Bureau, State & Local Government Finances 2020

City Government Revenue by Source

Source	2020 ($000)	2020 ($ per capita)	2020 (%)
General Revenue			
From Federal Government	17,070	97	4.1
From State Government	34,757	197	8.4
From Local Governments	7,587	43	1.8
Taxes			
Property	45,218	256	10.9
Sales and Gross Receipts	64,587	365	15.5
Personal Income	0	0	0.0
Corporate Income	0	0	0.0
Motor Vehicle License	0	0	0.0
Other Taxes	45,863	259	11.0
Current Charges	113,078	640	27.2
Liquor Store	0	0	0.0
Utility	48,987	277	11.8

Source: U.S. Census Bureau, State & Local Government Finances 2020

City Government Expenditures by Function

Function	2020 ($000)	2020 ($ per capita)	2020 (%)
General Direct Expenditures			
Air Transportation	0	0	0.0
Corrections	0	0	0.0
Education	0	0	0.0
Employment Security Administration	0	0	0.0
Financial Administration	0	0	0.0
Fire Protection	47,054	266	12.6
General Public Buildings	0	0	0.0
Governmental Administration, Other	35,562	201	9.5
Health	2,603	14	0.7
Highways	15,348	86	4.1
Hospitals	0	0	0.0
Housing and Community Development	23,362	132	6.2
Interest on General Debt	11,272	63	3.0
Judicial and Legal	0	0	0.0
Libraries	0	0	0.0
Parking	5,534	31	1.5
Parks and Recreation	15,969	90	4.3
Police Protection	65,063	368	17.4
Public Welfare	0	0	0.0
Sewerage	66,219	374	17.7
Solid Waste Management	0	0	0.0
Veterans' Services	0	0	0.0
Liquor Store	0	0	0.0
Utility	75,915	429	20.3

Source: U.S. Census Bureau, State & Local Government Finances 2020

TAXES

State Corporate Income Tax Rates

State	Tax Rate (%)	Income Brackets ($)	Num. of Brackets	Financial Institution Tax Rate (%)[a]	Federal Income Tax Ded.
California	8.84 (b)	Flat rate	1	10.84 (b)	No

Note: Tax rates as of January 1, 2023; (a) Rates listed are the corporate income tax rate applied to financial institutions or excise taxes based on income. Some states have other taxes based upon the value of deposits or shares; (b) Minimum tax is $800 in California, $250 in District of Columbia, $50 in Arizona and North Dakota (banks), $400 ($100 banks) in Rhode Island, $200 per location in South Dakota (banks), $100 in Utah, $300 in Vermont.
Source: Federation of Tax Administrators, State Corporate Income Tax Rates, January 1, 2023

State Individual Income Tax Rates

State	Tax Rate (%)	Income Brackets ($)	Personal Exemptions ($)			Standard Ded. ($)	
			Single	Married	Depend.	Single	Married
California (a)	1.0 - 12.3 (g)	10,099 - 677,275 (b)	140	280	433 (c)	5,202	10,404 (a)

Note: Tax rates as of January 1, 2023; Local- and county-level taxes are not included; Federal income tax is not deductible on state income tax returns; (a) 16 states have statutory provision for automatically adjusting to the rate of inflation the dollar values of the income tax brackets, standard deductions, and/or personal exemptions. Oregon does not index the income brackets for $125,000 and over; (b) For joint returns, taxes are twice the tax on half the couple's income; (c) The personal exemption takes the form of a tax credit instead of a deduction; (g) California imposes an additional 1% tax on taxable income over $1 million, making the maximum rate 13.3% over $1 million.
Source: Federation of Tax Administrators, State Individual Income Tax Rates, January 1, 2023

Various State Sales and Excise Tax Rates

State	State Sales Tax (%)	Gasoline[1] ($/gal.)	Cigarette[2] ($/pack)	Spirits[3] ($/gal.)	Wine[4] ($/gal.)	Beer[5] ($/gal.)	Recreational Marijuana (%)
California	7.25	0.7766	2.87	3.30	0.20	0.20	(c)

Note: All tax rates as of January 1, 2023; (1) The American Petroleum Institute has developed a methodology for determining the average tax rate on a gallon of fuel. Rates may include any of the following: excise taxes, environmental fees, storage tank fees, other fees or taxes, general sales tax, and local taxes; (2) The federal excise tax of $1.0066 per pack and local taxes are not included; (3) Rates are those applicable to off-premise sales of 40% alcohol by volume (a.b.v.) distilled spirits in 750ml containers. Local excise taxes are excluded; (4) Rates are those applicable to off-premise sales of 11% a.b.v. non-carbonated wine in 750ml containers; (5) Rates are those applicable to off-premise sales of 4.7% a.b.v. beer in 12 ounce containers; (c) 15% excise tax (levied on wholesale at average market rate); $10.08/oz. flowers & $3/oz. leaves cultivation tax; $1.41/oz fresh cannabis plant
Source: Tax Foundation, 2023 Facts & Figures: How Does Your State Compare?

State Business Tax Climate Index Rankings

State	Overall Rank	Corporate Tax Rank	Individual Income Tax Rank	Sales Tax Rank	Property Tax Rank	Unemployment Insurance Tax Rank
California	48	46	49	47	19	24

Note: The index is a measure of how each state's tax laws affect economic performance. The lower the rank, the more favorable a state's tax system is for business. States without a given tax are given a ranking of 1. The scores/rankings for the District of Columbia do not affect other states. The 2023 index represents the tax climate as of July 1, 2022.
Source: Tax Foundation, State Business Tax Climate Index 2023

TRANSPORTATION

Means of Transportation to Work

Area	Car/Truck/Van		Public Transportation			Bicycle	Walked	Other Means	Worked at Home
	Drove Alone	Car-pooled	Bus	Subway	Railroad				
City	76.1	10.3	1.4	0.1	0.1	0.8	1.8	1.4	7.9
MSA[1]	72.8	10.0	1.2	0.1	0.2	0.6	2.3	1.5	11.3
U.S.	73.2	8.6	2.0	1.6	0.5	0.5	2.5	1.5	9.7

Note: Figures are percentages and cover workers 16 years of age and older; (1) Figures cover the Santa Rosa-Petaluma, CA Metropolitan Statistical Area
Source: U.S. Census Bureau, 2017-2021 American Community Survey 5-Year Estimates

Travel Time to Work

Area	Less Than 10 Minutes	10 to 19 Minutes	20 to 29 Minutes	30 to 44 Minutes	45 to 59 Minutes	60 to 89 Minutes	90 Minutes or More
City	12.6	40.1	21.3	14.4	4.3	4.0	3.3
MSA[1]	14.0	32.4	20.4	17.1	6.4	6.0	3.8
U.S.	12.4	28.5	21.0	20.9	8.2	6.2	2.9

Note: Note: Figures are percentages and include workers 16 years old and over; (1) Figures cover the Santa Rosa-Petaluma, CA Metropolitan Statistical Area
Source: U.S. Census Bureau, 2017-2021 American Community Survey 5-Year Estimates

Key Congestion Measures

Measure	1990	2000	2010	2015	2020
Annual Hours of Delay, Total (000)	n/a	n/a	n/a	18,462	7,830
Annual Hours of Delay, Per Auto Commuter	n/a	n/a	n/a	53	22
Annual Congestion Cost, Per Auto Commuter ($)	n/a	n/a	n/a	1,100	512

Note: n/a not available
Source: Texas A&M Transportation Institute, 2021 Urban Mobility Report

Freeway Travel Time Index

Measure	1985	1990	1995	2000	2005	2010	2015	2020
Urban Area Index[1]	n/a	n/a	n/a	n/a	n/a	n/a	1.22	1.11
Urban Area Rank[1,2]	n/a	n/a	n/a	n/a	n/a	n/a	n/a	n/a

Note: Freeway Travel Time Index—the ratio of travel time in the peak period to the travel time at free-flow conditions. For example, a value of 1.30 indicates a 20-minute free-flow trip takes 26 minutes in the peak (20 minutes x 1.30 = 26 minutes); (1) Covers the Santa Rosa CA urban area; (2) Rank is based on 101 larger urban areas (#1 = highest travel time index); n/a not available
Source: Texas A&M Transportation Institute, 2021 Urban Mobility Report

Public Transportation

Agency Name / Mode of Transportation	Vehicles Operated in Maximum Service[1]	Annual Unlinked Passenger Trips[2] (in thous.)	Annual Passenger Miles[3] (in thous.)
City of Santa Rosa (Santa Rosa CityBus)			
Bus (directly operated)	17	766.9	2,109.0
Bus (purchased transportation)	1	4.2	15.1
Demand Response (purchased transportation)	7	17.5	69.8
Sonoma County Transit			
Bus (purchased transportation)	27	345.7	2,878.8
Demand Response (purchased transportation)	17	23.2	282.1

Note: (1) Number of revenue vehicles operated by the given mode and type of service to meet the annual maximum service requirement. This is the revenue vehicle count during the peak season of the year; on the week and day that maximum service is provided. Vehicles operated in maximum service (VOMS) exclude atypical days and one-time special events; (2) Number of passengers who boarded public transportation vehicles. Passengers are counted each time they board a vehicle no matter how many vehicles they use to travel from their origin to their destination. (3) Sum of the distances ridden by all passengers during the entire fiscal year.
Source: Federal Transit Administration, National Transit Database, 2021

Air Transportation

Airport Name and Code / Type of Service	Passenger Airlines[1]	Passenger Enplanements	Freight Carriers[2]	Freight (lbs)
San Francisco International (SFO)				
Domestic service (U.S. carriers - 2022)	24	15,604,040	14	192,078,697
International service (U.S. carriers - 2021)	6	685,890	4	83,977,700

Note: (1) Includes all U.S.-based major, minor and commuter airlines that carried at least one passenger during the year; (2) Includes all U.S.-based airlines and freight carriers that transported at least one pound of freight during the year.
Source: Bureau of Transportation Statistics, The Intermodal Transportation Database, Air Carriers: T-100 Domestic Market (U.S. Carriers), 2022; Bureau of Transportation Statistics, The Intermodal Transportation Database, Air Carriers: T-100 International Market (U.S. Carriers), 2021

BUSINESSES

Major Business Headquarters

Company Name	Industry	Rankings	
		Fortune[1]	Forbes[2]
No companies listed	-	-	-

Note: (1) Companies that produce a 10-K are ranked 1 to 500 based on 2021 revenue; (2) All private companies with at least $2 billion in annual revenue through the end of their most current fiscal year are ranked 1 to 246; companies listed are headquartered in the city; dashes indicate no ranking
Source: Fortune, "Fortune 500," 2022; Forbes, "America's Largest Private Companies," 2022

Living Environment

COST OF LIVING

Cost of Living Index

Composite Index	Groceries	Housing	Utilities	Trans-portation	Health Care	Misc. Goods/ Services
n/a	n/a	n/a	n/a	n/a	n/a	n/a

Note: The Cost of Living Index measures regional differences in the cost of consumer goods and services, excluding taxes and non-consumer expenditures, for professional and managerial households in the top income quintile. It is based on more than 50,000 prices covering almost 60 different items for which prices are collected three times a year by chambers of commerce, economic development organizations or university applied economic centers in each participating urban area. The numbers shown should be read as a percentage above or below the national average of 100. For example, a value of 115.4 in the groceries column indicates that grocery prices are 15.4% higher than the national average. Small differences in the index numbers should not be interpreted as significant; n/a not available.
Source: The Council for Community and Economic Research, Cost of Living Index, 2022

Grocery Prices

Area[1]	T-Bone Steak ($/pound)	Frying Chicken ($/pound)	Whole Milk ($/half gal.)	Eggs ($/dozen)	Orange Juice ($/64 oz.)	Coffee ($/11.5 oz.)
City[2]	n/a	n/a	n/a	n/a	n/a	n/a
Avg.	13.81	1.59	2.43	2.25	3.85	4.95
Min.	10.17	0.90	1.51	1.30	2.90	3.46
Max.	19.35	3.30	4.32	4.32	5.31	8.59

*Note: (1) Values for the local area are compared with the average, minimum and maximum values for all 286 areas in the Cost of Living Index; (2) Figures cover the Santa Rosa CA urban area; n/a not available; **T-Bone Steak** (price per pound); **Frying Chicken** (price per pound, whole fryer); **Whole Milk** (half gallon carton); **Eggs** (price per dozen, Grade A, large); **Orange Juice** (64 oz. Tropicana or Florida Natural); **Coffee** (11.5 oz. can, vacuum-packed, Maxwell House, Hills Bros, or Folgers).*
Source: The Council for Community and Economic Research, Cost of Living Index, 2022

Housing and Utility Costs

Area[1]	New Home Price ($)	Apartment Rent ($/month)	All Electric ($/month)	Part Electric ($/month)	Other Energy ($/month)	Telephone ($/month)
City[2]	n/a	n/a	n/a	n/a	n/a	n/a
Avg.	450,913	1,371	176.41	99.93	76.96	190.22
Min.	229,283	546	100.84	31.56	27.15	174.27
Max.	2,434,977	4,569	356.86	249.59	272.24	208.31

*Note: (1) Values for the local area are compared with the average, minimum and maximum values for all 286 areas in the Cost of Living Index; (2) Figures cover the Santa Rosa CA urban area; n/a not available; **New Home Price** (2,400 sf living area, 8,000 sf lot, in urban area with full utilities); **Apartment Rent** (950 sf 2 bedroom/1.5 or 2 bath, unfurnished, excluding all utilities except water); **All Electric** (average monthly cost for an all-electric home); **Part Electric** (average monthly cost for a part-electric home); **Other Energy** (average monthly cost for natural gas, fuel oil, coal, wood, and any other forms of energy except electricity); **Telephone** (price includes the base monthly rate plus taxes and fees for three lines of mobile phone service).*
Source: The Council for Community and Economic Research, Cost of Living Index, 2022

Health Care, Transportation, and Other Costs

Area[1]	Doctor ($/visit)	Dentist ($/visit)	Optometrist ($/visit)	Gasoline ($/gallon)	Beauty Salon ($/visit)	Men's Shirt ($)
City[2]	n/a	n/a	n/a	n/a	n/a	n/a
Avg.	124.91	107.77	117.66	3.86	43.31	34.21
Min.	36.61	58.25	51.79	2.90	22.18	13.05
Max.	250.21	162.58	371.96	5.54	85.61	63.54

*Note: (1) Values for the local area are compared with the average, minimum and maximum values for all 286 areas in the Cost of Living Index; (2) Figures cover the Santa Rosa CA urban area; n/a not available; **Doctor** (general practitioners routine exam of an established patient); **Dentist** (adult teeth cleaning and periodic oral examination); **Optometrist** (full vision eye exam for established adult patient); **Gasoline** (one gallon regular unleaded, national brand, including all taxes, cash price at self-service pump if available); **Beauty Salon** (woman's shampoo, trim, and blow-dry); **Men's Shirt** (cotton/polyester dress shirt, pinpoint weave, long sleeves).*
Source: The Council for Community and Economic Research, Cost of Living Index, 2022

HOUSING

Homeownership Rate

Area	2015 (%)	2016 (%)	2017 (%)	2018 (%)	2019 (%)	2020 (%)	2021 (%)	2022 (%)
MSA[1]	n/a	n/a	n/a	n/a	n/a	n/a	n/a	n/a
U.S.	63.7	63.4	63.9	64.4	64.6	66.6	65.5	65.8

Note: (1) Figures cover the Santa Rosa-Petaluma, CA Metropolitan Statistical Area; n/a not available
Source: U.S. Census Bureau, Housing Vacancies and Homeownership Annual Statistics: 2015-2022

House Price Index (HPI)

Area	National Ranking[2]	Quarterly Change (%)	One-Year Change (%)	Five-Year Change (%)	Since 1991Q1 (%)
MSA[1]	250	-4.80	3.50	26.56	276.48
U.S.[3]	—	0.34	8.41	58.44	289.08

Note: The HPI is a weighted repeat sales index. It measures average price changes in repeat sales or refinancings on the same properties. This information is obtained by reviewing repeat mortgage transactions on single-family properties whose mortgages have been purchased or securitized by Fannie Mae or Freddie Mac since January 1975; (1) Figures cover the Santa Rosa, CA Metropolitan Statistical Area; (2) Rankings are based on annual percentage change for all metro areas containing at least 15,000 transactions over the last 10 years and ranges from 1 to 257; (3) figures based on a weighted average of Census Division estimates using a seasonally adjusted, purchase-only index; all figures are for the period ending December 31, 2022
Source: Federal Housing Finance Agency, Change in FHFA Metropolitan Area House Price Indexes, 2022Q4

Median Single-Family Home Prices

Area	2020	2021	2022p	Percent Change 2021 to 2022
MSA[1]	n/a	n/a	n/a	n/a
U.S. Average	300.2	357.1	392.6	9.9

Note: Figures are median sales prices of existing single-family homes in thousands of dollars; (p) preliminary; n/a not available; (1) Figures cover the Santa Rosa-Petaluma, CA Metropolitan Statistical Area
Source: National Association of Realtors, Median Sales Price of Existing Single-Family Homes for Metropolitan Areas, 4th Quarter 2022

Qualifying Income Based on Median Sales Price of Existing Single-Family Homes

Area	With 5% Down ($)	With 10% Down ($)	With 20% Down ($)
MSA[1]	n/a	n/a	n/a
U.S. Average	112,234	106,237	94,513

Note: Figures are preliminary; Qualifying income is based on a mortgage rate of 6.77%. Monthly principal and interest payment is limited to 25% of income; n/a not available; (1) Figures cover the Santa Rosa-Petaluma, CA Metropolitan Statistical Area
Source: National Association of Realtors, Qualifying Income Based on Median Sales Price of Existing Single-Family Homes for Metropolitan Areas, 4th Quarter 2022

Home Value

Area	Under $100,000	$100,000 -$199,999	$200,000 -$299,999	$300,000 -$399,999	$400,000 -$499,999	$500,000 -$999,999	$1,000,000 or more	Median ($)
City	4.1	2.6	4.0	7.3	13.6	60.0	8.4	598,700
MSA[1]	3.9	2.9	2.9	5.1	9.9	58.1	17.2	665,800
U.S.	16.2	24.2	20.1	13.6	8.3	13.6	4.1	244,900

Note: Figures are percentages except for median and cover owner-occupied housing units; (1) Figures cover the Santa Rosa-Petaluma, CA Metropolitan Statistical Area
Source: U.S. Census Bureau, 2017-2021 American Community Survey 5-Year Estimates

Year Housing Structure Built

Area	2020 or Later	2010 -2019	2000 -2009	1990 -1999	1980 -1989	1970 -1979	1960 -1969	1950 -1959	1940 -1949	Before 1940	Median Year
City	0.5	4.6	12.5	13.2	17.9	21.1	12.0	8.1	4.7	5.5	1979
MSA[1]	0.3	4.0	10.3	13.7	18.2	20.6	11.6	8.9	4.4	8.0	1978
U.S.	0.2	7.3	13.6	13.6	13.2	14.8	10.3	10.0	4.7	12.2	1979

Note: Figures are percentages except for Median Year; Note: (1) Figures cover the Santa Rosa-Petaluma, CA Metropolitan Statistical Area
Source: U.S. Census Bureau, 2017-2021 American Community Survey 5-Year Estimates

Gross Monthly Rent

Area	Under $500	$500 -$999	$1,000 -$1,499	$1,500 -$1,999	$2,000 -$2,499	$2,500 -$2,999	$3,000 and up	Median ($)
City	4.9	5.3	21.2	27.5	21.2	11.7	8.1	1,837
MSA[1]	4.8	7.8	19.2	25.6	21.0	11.3	10.3	1,856
U.S.	8.1	30.5	30.8	16.8	7.3	3.1	3.5	1,163

Note: Figures are percentages except for median; Gross rent is the contract rent plus the estimated average monthly cost of utilities (electricity, gas, and water and sewer) and fuels (oil, coal, kerosene, wood, etc.) if these are paid by the renter (or paid for the renter by someone else); (1) Figures cover the Santa Rosa-Petaluma, CA Metropolitan Statistical Area
Source: U.S. Census Bureau, 2017-2021 American Community Survey 5-Year Estimates

HEALTH

Health Risk Factors

Category	MSA[1] (%)	U.S. (%)
Adults aged 18–64 who have any kind of health care coverage	n/a	90.9
Adults who reported being in good or better health	n/a	85.2
Adults who have been told they have high blood cholesterol	n/a	35.7
Adults who have been told they have high blood pressure	n/a	32.4
Adults who are current smokers	n/a	14.4
Adults who currently use e-cigarettes	n/a	6.7
Adults who currently use chewing tobacco, snuff, or snus	n/a	3.5
Adults who are heavy drinkers[2]	n/a	6.3
Adults who are binge drinkers[3]	n/a	15.4
Adults who are overweight (BMI 25.0 - 29.9)	n/a	34.4
Adults who are obese (BMI 30.0 - 99.8)	n/a	33.9
Adults who participated in any physical activities in the past month	n/a	76.3

Note: (1) Figures for the Santa Rosa-Petaluma, CA Metropolitan Statistical Area were not available.
(2) Heavy drinkers are classified as adult men having more than 14 drinks per week and adult women having more than 7 drinks per week; (3) Binge drinkers are classified as males having five or more drinks on one occasion or females having four or more drinks on one occasion
Source: Centers for Disease Control and Prevention, Behaviorial Risk Factor Surveillance System, SMART: Selected Metropolitan Area Risk Trends, 2021

Acute and Chronic Health Conditions

Category	MSA[1] (%)	U.S. (%)
Adults who have ever been told they had a heart attack	n/a	4.0
Adults who have ever been told they have angina or coronary heart disease	n/a	3.8
Adults who have ever been told they had a stroke	n/a	3.0
Adults who have ever been told they have asthma	n/a	14.9
Adults who have ever been told they have arthritis	n/a	25.8
Adults who have ever been told they have diabetes[2]	n/a	10.9
Adults who have ever been told they had skin cancer	n/a	6.6
Adults who have ever been told they had any other types of cancer	n/a	7.5
Adults who have ever been told they have COPD	n/a	6.1
Adults who have ever been told they have kidney disease	n/a	3.0
Adults who have ever been told they have a form of depression	n/a	20.5

Note: (1) Figures for the Santa Rosa-Petaluma, CA Metropolitan Statistical Area were not available.
(2) Figures do not include pregnancy-related, borderline, or pre-diabetes
Source: Centers for Disease Control and Prevention, Behaviorial Risk Factor Surveillance System, SMART: Selected Metropolitan Area Risk Trends, 2021

Health Screening and Vaccination Rates

Category	MSA[1] (%)	U.S. (%)
Adults who have ever been tested for HIV	n/a	34.9
Adults who have had their blood cholesterol checked within the last five years	n/a	85.2
Adults aged 65+ who have had flu shot within the past year	n/a	68.6
Adults aged 65+ who have ever had a pneumonia vaccination	n/a	71.0

Note: (1) Figures for the Santa Rosa-Petaluma, CA Metropolitan Statistical Area were not available.
Source: Centers for Disease Control and Prevention, Behaviorial Risk Factor Surveillance System, SMART: Selected Metropolitan Area Risk Trends, 2021

Disability Status

Category	MSA[1] (%)	U.S. (%)
Adults who reported being deaf	n/a	7.2
Are you blind or have serious difficulty seeing, even when wearing glasses?	n/a	4.8
Are you limited in any way in any of your usual activities due to arthritis?	n/a	11.1
Do you have difficulty doing errands alone?	n/a	7.0
Do you have difficulty dressing or bathing?	n/a	3.6
Do you have serious difficulty concentrating/remembering/making decisions?	n/a	12.1
Do you have serious difficulty walking or climbing stairs?	n/a	12.8

Note: (1) Figures for the Santa Rosa-Petaluma, CA Metropolitan Statistical Area were not available.
Source: Centers for Disease Control and Prevention, Behaviorial Risk Factor Surveillance System, SMART: Selected Metropolitan Area Risk Trends, 2021

Mortality Rates for the Top 10 Causes of Death in the U.S.

ICD-10[a] Sub-Chapter	ICD-10[a] Code	Crude Mortality Rate[1] per 100,000 population	
		County[2]	U.S.
Malignant neoplasms	C00-C97	199.5	182.6
Ischaemic heart diseases	I20-I25	91.1	113.1
Other forms of heart disease	I30-I51	61.6	64.4
Other degenerative diseases of the nervous system	G30-G31	60.7	51.0
Cerebrovascular diseases	I60-I69	52.6	47.8
Other external causes of accidental injury	W00-X59	38.8	46.4
Chronic lower respiratory diseases	J40-J47	36.2	45.7
Organic, including symptomatic, mental disorders	F01-F09	38.3	35.9
Hypertensive diseases	I10-I15	28.2	35.0
Diabetes mellitus	E10-E14	24.6	29.6

Note: (a) ICD-10 = International Classification of Diseases 10th Revision; (1) Crude mortality rates are a three-year average covering 2019-2021; (2) Figures cover Sonoma County.
Source: Centers for Disease Control and Prevention, National Center for Health Statistics. National Vital Statistics System, Mortality 2018-2021 on CDC WONDER Online Database

Mortality Rates for Selected Causes of Death

ICD-10[a] Sub-Chapter	ICD-10[a] Code	Crude Mortality Rate[1] per 100,000 population	
		County[2]	U.S.
Assault	X85-Y09	2.3	7.0
Diseases of the liver	K70-K76	19.3	19.8
Human immunodeficiency virus (HIV) disease	B20-B24	Unreliable	1.5
Influenza and pneumonia	J09-J18	10.1	14.7
Intentional self-harm	X60-X84	15.2	14.3
Malnutrition	E40-E46	5.6	4.3
Obesity and other hyperalimentation	E65-E68	3.1	3.0
Renal failure	N17-N19	6.8	15.7
Transport accidents	V01-V99	9.9	13.6
Viral hepatitis	B15-B19	1.7	1.2

Note: (a) ICD-10 = International Classification of Diseases 10th Revision; (1) Crude mortality rates are a three-year average covering 2019-2021; (2) Figures cover Sonoma County; Data are suppressed when the data meet the criteria for confidentiality constraints; Crude mortality rates are flagged as unreliable when the rate would be calculated with a numerator of 20 or less.
Source: Centers for Disease Control and Prevention, National Center for Health Statistics. National Vital Statistics System, Mortality 2018-2021 on CDC WONDER Online Database

Health Insurance Coverage

Area	With Health Insurance	With Private Health Insurance	With Public Health Insurance	Without Health Insurance	Population Under Age 19 Without Health Insurance
City	92.4	68.5	36.9	7.6	5.5
MSA[1]	94.1	72.5	36.2	5.9	3.5
U.S.	91.2	67.8	35.4	8.8	5.3

Note: Figures are percentages that cover the civilian noninstitutionalized population; (1) Figures cover the Santa Rosa-Petaluma, CA Metropolitan Statistical Area
Source: U.S. Census Bureau, 2017-2021 American Community Survey 5-Year Estimates

Number of Medical Professionals

Area	MDs[3]	DOs[3,4]	Dentists	Podiatrists	Chiropractors	Optometrists
County[1] (number)	1,389	93	470	36	209	89
County[1] (rate[2])	284.4	19.0	96.7	7.4	43.0	18.3
U.S. (rate[2])	289.3	23.5	72.5	6.2	28.7	17.4

Note: Data as of 2021 unless noted; (1) Data covers Sonoma County; (2) Rate per 100,000 population; (3) Data as of 2020 and includes all active, non-federal physicians; (4) Doctor of Osteopathic Medicine
Source: U.S. Department of Health and Human Services, Health Resources and Services Administration, Bureau of Health Professions, Area Resource File (ARF) 2021-2022

EDUCATION

Public School District Statistics

District Name	Schls	Pupils	Pupil/ Teacher Ratio	Minority Pupils[1] (%)	LEP/ELL[2] (%)	IEP[3] (%)
Rincon Valley Union Elementary	9	3,020	20.7	48.8	13.3	13.0
Santa Rosa Elementary	13	4,846	21.2	77.3	40.6	14.4
Santa Rosa High	12	10,394	22.6	68.4	13.6	16.9

Note: Table includes school districts with 2,000 or more students; (1) Percentage of students that are not non-Hispanic white; (2) Percentage of students that are Limited English Proficient or English Language Learners (2018-19); (3) Percentage of students that have an Individualized Education Program (2019-20).
Source: U.S. Department of Education, National Center for Education Statistics, Common Core of Data, Local Education Agency (School District) Universe Survey: School Year 2021-2022

Highest Level of Education

Area	Less than H.S.	H.S. Diploma	Some College, No Deg.	Associate Degree	Bachelor's Degree	Master's Degree	Prof. School Degree	Doctorate Degree
City	14.5	18.0	23.2	10.0	21.3	8.7	3.0	1.3
MSA[1]	10.8	18.3	24.2	9.5	23.2	9.2	3.3	1.5
U.S.	11.1	26.5	20.0	8.7	20.6	9.3	2.2	1.5

Note: Figures cover persons age 25 and over; (1) Figures cover the Santa Rosa-Petaluma, CA Metropolitan Statistical Area
Source: U.S. Census Bureau, 2017-2021 American Community Survey 5-Year Estimates

Educational Attainment by Race

Area	High School Graduate or Higher (%)					Bachelor's Degree or Higher (%)				
	Total	White	Black	Asian	Hisp.[2]	Total	White	Black	Asian	Hisp.[2]
City	85.5	92.6	83.5	86.8	62.4	34.3	40.0	27.4	48.4	14.4
MSA[1]	89.2	94.2	87.2	88.3	66.1	37.1	41.5	32.1	48.5	15.9
U.S.	88.9	91.4	87.2	87.6	71.2	33.7	35.5	23.3	55.6	18.4

Note: Figures shown cover persons 25 years old and over; (1) Figures cover the Santa Rosa-Petaluma, CA Metropolitan Statistical Area; (2) People of Hispanic origin can be of any race
Source: U.S. Census Bureau, 2017-2021 American Community Survey 5-Year Estimates

School Enrollment by Grade and Control

Area	Preschool (%)		Kindergarten (%)		Grades 1 - 4 (%)		Grades 5 - 8 (%)		Grades 9 - 12 (%)	
	Public	Private	Public	Private	Public	Private	Public	Private	Public	Private
City	53.7	46.3	86.2	13.8	92.9	7.1	89.1	10.9	93.8	6.2
MSA[1]	48.2	51.8	87.3	12.7	92.4	7.6	89.8	10.2	92.0	8.0
U.S.	58.8	41.2	86.3	13.7	88.3	11.7	88.6	11.4	89.4	10.6

Note: Figures shown cover persons 3 years old and over; (1) Figures cover the Santa Rosa-Petaluma, CA Metropolitan Statistical Area
Source: U.S. Census Bureau, 2017-2021 American Community Survey 5-Year Estimates

Higher Education

Four-Year Colleges			Two-Year Colleges			Medical Schools[1]	Law Schools[2]	Voc/ Tech[3]
Public	Private Non-profit	Private For-profit	Public	Private Non-profit	Private For-profit			
1	1	0	1	1	0	0	1	1

Note: Figures cover institutions located within the Santa Rosa-Petaluma, CA Metropolitan Statistical Area and include main campuses only; (1) includes schools accredited by the Liaison Committee on Medical Education and the American Osteopathic Association's Commission on Osteopathic College Accreditation; (2) includes ABA-accredited schools, schools with provisional ABA accreditation, and state accredited schools; (3) includes all schools with programs that are less than 2 years.
Source: National Center for Education Statistics, Integrated Postsecondary Education System (IPEDS), 2021-22; Wikipedia, List of Medical Schools in the United States, accessed April 10, 2023; Wikipedia, List of Law Schools in the United States, accessed April 10, 2023

EMPLOYERS

Major Employers

Company Name	Industry
Amy's Kitchen	Food manufacturing
AT&T	Utility company
Bear Republic Brewing Co.	Brewing company
Empire College	Education
Exchange Bank	Financial services
G&G Supermarket	Grocery stores
Ghilotti Construction Co.	Construction
Graton Resort & Casino	Casino resort
Hansel Auto Group	Auto sales
Hyatt Vineyard Creek Hotel & Spa	Hotels & motels
Jackson Family Wines	Winery
JDSU	Optical communications networks, communications equip
Kaiser Permanente	Healthcare
Keysight Technologies	Test equipment for labratories
Korbel	Korbel
La Tortilla Factory	Grocery stores
Mary's Pizza Shack	Grocery stores
Medtronic	Medical device manufacturer
Redwood Credit Union	Credit union
River Rock Casino	Casino resort
Sonoma Media Investments	Financial services
St. Joseph Health, Sonoma County	Healthcare
Sutter Santa Rosa Regional Hospital	Healthcare

Note: Companies shown are located within the Santa Rosa-Petaluma, CA Metropolitan Statistical Area.
Source: Hoovers.com; Wikipedia

PUBLIC SAFETY

Crime Rate

Area	Total Crime	Violent Crime Rate				Property Crime Rate		
		Murder	Rape[3]	Robbery	Aggrav. Assault	Burglary	Larceny -Theft	Motor Vehicle Theft
City	2,120.0	2.3	62.2	76.3	375.3	306.3	1,059.7	237.9
Suburbs[1]	1,554.3	1.9	41.1	41.8	329.5	232.8	807.9	99.2
Metro[2]	1,758.4	2.0	48.7	54.2	346.0	259.4	898.8	149.2
U.S.	2,356.7	6.5	38.4	73.9	279.7	314.2	1,398.0	246.0

Note: Figures are crimes per 100,000 population; (1) All areas within the metro area that are located outside the city limits; (2) Figures cover the Santa Rosa, CA Metropolitan Statistical Area; (3) All figures shown were reported using the revised Uniform Crime Reporting (UCR) definition of rape; Due to the transition to the National Incident-Based Reporting System (NIBRS), limited city and metro area data was released for 2021.
Source: FBI Uniform Crime Reports, 2020

Hate Crimes

Area	Number of Quarters Reported	Number of Incidents per Bias Motivation					
		Race/Ethnicity/ Ancestry	Religion	Sexual Orientation	Disability	Gender	Gender Identity
City	4	6	4	1	0	0	0
U.S.	4	5,227	1,244	1,110	130	75	266

Note: Due to the transition to the National Incident-Based Reporting System (NIBRS), limited crime data was released for 2021.
Source: Federal Bureau of Investigation, Hate Crime Statistics 2020

Identity Theft Consumer Reports

Area	Reports	Reports per 100,000 Population	Rank[2]
MSA[1]	802	161	226
U.S.	1,108,609	339	-

Note: (1) Figures cover the Santa Rosa-Petaluma, CA Metropolitan Statistical Area; (2) Rank ranges from 1 to 391 where 1 indicates greatest number of identity theft reports per 100,000 population
Source: Federal Trade Commission, Consumer Sentinel Network Data Book 2022

Fraud and Other Consumer Reports

Area	Reports	Reports per 100,000 Population	Rank[2]
MSA[1]	3,931	791	224
U.S.	4,064,520	1,245	-

Note: (1) Figures cover the Santa Rosa-Petaluma, CA Metropolitan Statistical Area; (2) Rank ranges from 1 to 391 where 1 indicates greatest number of fraud and other consumer reports per 100,000 population
Source: Federal Trade Commission, Consumer Sentinel Network Data Book 2022

POLITICS

2020 Presidential Election Results

Area	Biden	Trump	Jorgensen	Hawkins	Other
Sonoma County	74.5	23.0	1.3	0.6	0.6
U.S.	51.3	46.8	1.2	0.3	0.5

Note: Results are percentages and may not add to 100% due to rounding
Source: Dave Leip's Atlas of U.S. Presidential Elections

SPORTS

Professional Sports Teams

Team Name	League	Year Established

No teams are located in the metro area
Source: Wikipedia, Major Professional Sports Teams of the United States and Canada, April 12, 2023

CLIMATE

Average and Extreme Temperatures

Temperature	Jan	Feb	Mar	Apr	May	Jun	Jul	Aug	Sep	Oct	Nov	Dec	Yr.
Extreme High (°F)	69	72	83	89	99	102	103	105	109	94	85	73	109
Average High (°F)	56	61	65	69	74	79	81	84	84	75	65	58	71
Average Temp. (°F)	46	50	51	55	60	63	65	66	65	60	52	47	57
Average Low (°F)	35	38	36	41	45	47	49	47	46	44	39	35	42
Extreme Low (°F)	24	26	25	29	32	36	41	40	36	32	28	23	23

Note: Figures cover the years 1948-1990
Source: National Climatic Data Center, International Station Meteorological Climate Summary, 9/96

Average Precipitation/Snowfall/Humidity

Precip./Humidity	Jan	Feb	Mar	Apr	May	Jun	Jul	Aug	Sep	Oct	Nov	Dec	Yr.
Avg. Precip. (in.)	5.6	6.2	4.5	0.7	0.9	0.1	0.0	0.0	0.0	2.3	4.7	4.0	29.0
Avg. Snowfall (in.)	n/a	n/a	n/a	0	0	0	0	0	0	0	n/a	n/a	n/a
Avg. Rel. Hum. (%)	85	74	70	69	68	63	71	68	66	74	81	82	73

Note: Figures cover the years 1948-1990
Source: National Climatic Data Center, International Station Meteorological Climate Summary, 9/96

Weather Conditions

Temperature			Daytime Sky			Precipitation		
0°F & below	32°F & below	90°F & above	Clear	Partly cloudy	Cloudy	0.01 inch or more precip.	0.1 inch or more snow/ice	Thunder-storms
0	43	30	n/a	n/a	n/a	n/a	n/a	2

Note: Figures are average number of days per year and cover the years 1948-1990
Source: National Climatic Data Center, International Station Meteorological Climate Summary, 9/96

HAZARDOUS WASTE

Superfund Sites

The Santa Rosa-Petaluma, CA metro area has no sites on the EPA's Superfund Final National Priorities List. There are a total of 1,165 Superfund sites with a status of proposed or final on the list in the U.S. *U.S. Environmental Protection Agency, National Priorities List, April 12, 2023*

AIR QUALITY

Air Quality Trends: Ozone

	1990	1995	2000	2005	2010	2015	2018	2019	2020	2021
MSA[1]	0.063	0.071	0.061	0.050	0.053	0.059	0.055	0.052	0.052	0.052
U.S.	0.087	0.089	0.081	0.080	0.072	0.067	0.069	0.065	0.065	0.067

Note: (1) Data covers the Santa Rosa-Petaluma, CA Metropolitan Statistical Area. The values shown are the composite ozone concentration averages among trend sites based on the highest fourth daily maximum 8-hour concentration in parts per million. These trends are based on sites having an adequate record of monitoring data during the trend period. Data from exceptional events are included.
Source: U.S. Environmental Protection Agency, Air Quality Monitoring Information, "Air Quality Trends by City, 1990-2021"

Air Quality Index

Area	Percent of Days when Air Quality was...[2]						AQI Statistics[2]	
	Good	Moderate	Unhealthy for Sensitive Groups	Unhealthy	Very Unhealthy		Maximum	Median
MSA[1]	87.9	12.1	0.0	0.0	0.0		88	33

Note: (1) Data covers the Santa Rosa-Petaluma, CA Metropolitan Statistical Area; (2) Based on 365 days with AQI data in 2021. Air Quality Index (AQI) is an index for reporting daily air quality. EPA calculates the AQI for five major air pollutants regulated by the Clean Air Act: ground-level ozone, particle pollution (aka particulate matter), carbon monoxide, sulfur dioxide, and nitrogen dioxide. The AQI runs from 0 to 500. The higher the AQI value, the greater the level of air pollution and the greater the health concern. There are six AQI categories: "Good" AQI is between 0 and 50. Air quality is considered satisfactory; "Moderate" AQI is between 51 and 100. Air quality is acceptable; "Unhealthy for Sensitive Groups" When AQI values are between 101 and 150, members of sensitive groups may experience health effects; "Unhealthy" When AQI values are between 151 and 200 everyone may begin to experience health effects; "Very Unhealthy" AQI values between 201 and 300 trigger a health alert; "Hazardous" AQI values over 300 trigger warnings of emergency conditions (not shown).
Source: U.S. Environmental Protection Agency, Air Quality Index Report, 2021

Air Quality Index Pollutants

Area	Percent of Days when AQI Pollutant was...[2]					
	Carbon Monoxide	Nitrogen Dioxide	Ozone	Sulfur Dioxide	Particulate Matter 2.5	Particulate Matter 10
MSA[1]	0.0	0.0	59.5	(3)	37.5	3.0

Note: (1) Data covers the Santa Rosa-Petaluma, CA Metropolitan Statistical Area; (2) Based on 365 days with AQI data in 2021. The Air Quality Index (AQI) is an index for reporting daily air quality. EPA calculates the AQI for five major air pollutants regulated by the Clean Air Act: ground-level ozone, particle pollution (also known as particulate matter), carbon monoxide, sulfur dioxide, and nitrogen dioxide. The AQI runs from 0 to 500. The higher the AQI value, the greater the level of air pollution and the greater the health concern; (3) Sulfur dioxide is no longer included in this table (as of December 8, 2021) because SO_2 concentrations tend to be very localized and not necessarily representative of broad geographical areas like counties and CBSAs.
Source: U.S. Environmental Protection Agency, Air Quality Index Report, 2021

Maximum Air Pollutant Concentrations: Particulate Matter, Ozone, CO and Lead

	Particulate Matter 10 (ug/m³)	Particulate Matter 2.5 Wtd AM (ug/m³)	Particulate Matter 2.5 24-Hr (ug/m³)	Ozone (ppm)	Carbon Monoxide (ppm)	Lead (ug/m³)
MSA[1] Level	53	n/a	n/a	0.055	1	n/a
NAAQS[2]	150	15	35	0.075	9	0.15
Met NAAQS[2]	Yes	n/a	n/a	Yes	Yes	n/a

Note: (1) Data covers the Santa Rosa-Petaluma, CA Metropolitan Statistical Area; Data from exceptional events are included; (2) National Ambient Air Quality Standards; ppm = parts per million; ug/m³ = micrograms per cubic meter; n/a not available.
Concentrations: Particulate Matter 10 (coarse particulate)—highest second maximum 24-hour concentration; Particulate Matter 2.5 Wtd AM (fine particulate)—highest weighted annual mean concentration; Particulate Matter 2.5 24-Hour (fine particulate)—highest 98th percentile 24-hour concentration; Ozone—highest fourth daily maximum 8-hour concentration; Carbon Monoxide—highest second maximum non-overlapping 8-hour concentration; Lead—maximum running 3-month average
Source: U.S. Environmental Protection Agency, Air Quality Monitoring Information, "Air Quality Statistics by City, 2021"

Maximum Air Pollutant Concentrations: Nitrogen Dioxide and Sulfur Dioxide

	Nitrogen Dioxide AM (ppb)	Nitrogen Dioxide 1-Hr (ppb)	Sulfur Dioxide AM (ppb)	Sulfur Dioxide 1-Hr (ppb)	Sulfur Dioxide 24-Hr (ppb)
MSA[1] Level	3	20	n/a	n/a	n/a
NAAQS[2]	53	100	30	75	140
Met NAAQS[2]	Yes	Yes	n/a	n/a	n/a

Note: (1) Data covers the Santa Rosa-Petaluma, CA Metropolitan Statistical Area; Data from exceptional events are included; (2) National Ambient Air Quality Standards; ppm = parts per million; ug/m³ = micrograms per cubic meter; n/a not available.
Concentrations: Nitrogen Dioxide AM—highest arithmetic mean concentration; Nitrogen Dioxide 1-Hr—highest 98th percentile 1-hour daily maximum concentration; Sulfur Dioxide AM—highest annual mean concentration; Sulfur Dioxide 1-Hr—highest 99th percentile 1-hour daily maximum concentration; Sulfur Dioxide 24-Hr—highest second maximum 24-hour concentration
Source: U.S. Environmental Protection Agency, Air Quality Monitoring Information, "Air Quality Statistics by City, 2021"

Seattle, Washington

Background

Believe it or not, the virgin hinterlands and wide curving arch of Elliot Bay in present-day Seattle were once named New York. The city was renamed Seattle in 1853, for the Native American Indian Chief Seattle, two years after its first five families from Illinois had settled into the narrow strip of land between Puget Sound and Lake Washington.

The lush, green forests of the "Emerald City," created by frequent rain and its many natural waterways, gave birth to Seattle's first major industry—lumber, which also bred a society of bearded, rabble-rousing bachelors. To alleviate that problem, Asa Mercer, president of the Territorial University, which later became the University of Washington, trekked back east, and recruited marriageable women, aka "Mercer girls."

Today, the city does not rely on lumber as its major industry, but boasts commercial aircraft production and missile research, importing and exporting, and technology. As the closest U.S. mainland port to Asia, Seattle has become a key trade center for goods such as cars, forest products, electronic equipment, bananas, and petroleum products. The city is home to ten Fortune 500 companies including Amazon, Microsoft, Costco, and Starbucks. Other major employers in Seattle are Nordstrom, Avanade, and Alaska Airlines.

Seattle continues to move toward becoming the next Silicon Valley. It is predominantly a software town dominated by Microsoft, in nearby Redmond, announced that expansion of their campus - 17 new buildings and a parking facility for 6,500 cars—opens this year.

The Seattle Seaport Terminal Project, comprised of small-and-large-scale projects designed to improve the port's facilities for businesses, passengers, residents, and tourists, included a major renovation of Terminal 5, construction of a Cruise Ship Terminal improvement, and port facilities improvements. Seattle is the fourth largest container port in North America.

Seattle has undergone a cultural and commercial reemergence of its downtown. Tourists and locals are drawn by luxury hotels, restaurants, a 16-screen movie theater, and other entertainment-oriented businesses, including the first in a nationwide chain of Game Works, computerized playgrounds for adults. Center City Seattle continues to see renovation and development projects, as city planners try to deal with more people living, working, and visiting in the city.

The arts are a vital part of Seattle life. The world-famous Seattle Opera, now performing in a state-of-the-art hall dedicated in 2003, is well known for its summer presentations of Wagner's *Ring* cycle. The Seattle Philharmonic Orchestra celebrated its 50th anniversary in 2004; its annual Bushnell Concerto Competition features promising new area musicians. The city's jazz scene developed the early careers of Ray Charles and Quincy Jones, and is the birthplace of rocker Jimi Hendrix, the bands Nirvana, Pearl Jam, Soundgarden, and Foo Fighters, and the alternative rock movement grunge.

The Seattle Museum constructed in Olympic Sculpture Park turned disused waterfront property into a permanent green space with plantings native to Puget Sound. The Seattle Museum of Flight's remarkable collection—the largest on the West Coast—includes a Concorde and the Boeing 707 used as Air Force One by presidents from Eisenhower to Nixon.

Seattle's professional sports teams are popular and many. Football's Seattle Seahawks are Super Bowl XLVIII champions. Major league rugby team, Seattle Seawolves won back-to-back championships in 2018 and 2019.

Seattle has a distinctly marine climate. The city's location on Puget Sound and between two mountain ranges ensures a mild climate year-round with moderate variations in temperature, and also puts it in a major earthquake zone. Summers are generally sunny and, while winters are rainy, most of the rain falls between October and March.

Rankings

General Rankings

- For its "Best for Vets: Places to Live 2019" rankings, *Military Times* evaluated 599 cities (83 large, 234 medium, 282 small) and compared the locations across three broad categories: veteran and military culture/services; economic indicators; and livability factors such as health, crime, traffic, and school quality. Seattle ranked #7 out of the top 25, in the large city category (population of more than 250,000). Data points more specific to veterans and the military weighed more heavily than others. *rebootcamp.militarytimes.com, "Military Times Best Places to Live 2019," September 10, 2018*

- The Seattle metro area was identified as one of America's fastest-growing areas in terms of population and business growth by *MagnifyMoney*. The area ranked #20 out of 35. The 100 most populous metro areas in the U.S. were evaluated on their change from 2011 to 2016 in the following categories: people and housing; workforce and employment opportunities; growing industry. *www.businessinsider.com, "The 35 Cities in the US with the Biggest Influx of People, the Most Work Opportunities, and the Hottest Business Growth," August 12, 2018*

- The Seattle metro area was identified as one of America's fastest-growing areas in terms of population and economy by *Forbes*. The area ranked #2 out of 25. The 100 most populous metro areas in the U.S. were evaluated on the following criteria: estimated population growth; employment; economic output; wages; home values. *Forbes, "America's Fastest-Growing Cities 2018," February 28, 2018*

- The human resources consulting firm Mercer ranked 231 major cities worldwide in terms of overall quality of life. Seattle ranked #46. Criteria: political, social, economic, and socio-cultural factors; medical and health considerations; schools and education; public services and transportation; recreation; consumer goods; housing; and natural environment. *Mercer, "Mercer 2019 Quality of Living Survey," March 13, 2019*

- For its 35th annual "Readers' Choice Awards" survey, *Condé Nast Traveler* ranked its readers' favorite cities in the U.S. Whether it be a longed-for visit or a first on the list, these are the places that inspired a return to travel. The list was broken into large cities and cities under 250,000. Seattle ranked #10 in the big city category. *Condé Nast Traveler, Readers' Choice Awards 2022, "Best Big Cities in the U.S." October 4, 2022*

Business/Finance Rankings

- According to *Business Insider*, the Seattle metro area is a prime place to run a startup or move an existing business to. The area ranked #5. More than 300 metro areas were analyzed for factors that were of top concern to new business owners. Data was based on the 2019 U.S. Census Bureau American Community Survey, statistics from the CDC, Bureau of Labor Statistics employment report, and University of Chicago analysis. Criteria: business formations; percentage of vaccinated population; percentage of households with internet subscriptions; median household income; and share of work that can be done from home. *www.businessinsider.com, "The 20 Best Cities for Starting a Business in 2022 Include Baltimore, Boulder, and Boston," January 5, 2022*

- Based on metro area social media reviews, the employment opinion group Glassdoor surveyed 50 of the most populous U.S. metro areas and equally weighed cost of living, hiring opportunity, and job satisfaction to compose a list of "25 Best Cities for Jobs." Median pay and home value, and number of active job openings were also factored in. The Seattle metro area was ranked #23 in overall job satisfaction. *www.glassdoor.com, "Best Cities for Jobs," February 25, 2020*

- The Brookings Institution ranked the nation's largest cities based on income inequality. Seattle was ranked #34 (#1 = greatest inequality). Criteria: the "95/20 ratio," a figure representing the income at which a household earns more than 95 percent of all other households, divided by the income at which a household earns more than only 20 percent of all other households. *Brookings Institution, "Household Income Inequality, Largest Cities of 97 Large U.S. Metro Areas, 2014-2016," February 5, 2018*

- The Brookings Institution ranked the 100 largest metro areas in the U.S. based on income inequality. Seattle was ranked #71 (#1 = greatest inequality). Criteria: the "95/20 ratio," a figure representing the income at which a household earns more than 95 percent of all other households, divided by the income at which a household earns more than only 20 percent of all other households. *Brookings Institution, "Household Income Inequality, 100 Largest U.S. Metro Areas, 2014-2016," February 5, 2018*

- Payscale.com ranked the 32 largest metro areas in terms of wage growth. The Seattle metro area ranked #28. Criteria: quarterly changes in private industry employee and education professional wage growth from the previous year. *PayScale, "Wage Trends by Metro Area-1st Quarter," April 20, 2023*

- The Seattle metro area was identified as one of the most debt-ridden places in America by the finance site Credit.com. The metro area was ranked #9. Criteria: residents' average credit card debt as well as median income. *Credit.com, "25 Cities With the Most Credit Card Debt," February 28, 2018*

- For its annual survey of the "Most Expensive U.S. Cities to Live In," Kiplinger applied Cost of Living Index statistics developed by the Council for Community and Economic Research to U.S. Census Bureau population and median household income data for 265 urban areas. Seattle ranked #8 among the most expensive in the country. *Kiplinger.com, "The 11 Most Expensive Cities to Live in the U.S.," April 15, 2023*

- The Seattle metro area appeared on the Milken Institute "2022 Best Performing Cities" list. Rank: #6 out of 200 large metro areas (population over 250,000). Criteria: job growth; wage and salary growth; high-tech output growth; housing affordability; household broadband access. *Milken Institute, "Best-Performing Cities 2022," March 28, 2022*

- *Forbes* ranked the 200 most populous metro areas to determine the nation's "Best Places for Business and Careers." The Seattle metro area was ranked #1. Criteria: costs (business and living); job growth (past and projected); income growth; quality of life; educational attainment (college and high school); projected economic growth; cultural and leisure opportunities; workplace tolerance laws; net migration patterns. *Forbes, "The Best Places for Business and Careers 2019: Seattle Still On Top," October 30, 2019*

- Mercer Human Resources Consulting ranked 227 cities worldwide in terms of cost-of-living. Seattle ranked #45 (the lower the ranking, the higher the cost-of-living). The survey measured the comparative cost of over 200 items (such as housing, food, clothing, domestic supplies, transportation, and recreation/entertainment) in each location. *Mercer, "2022 Cost of Living City Ranking," June 29, 2022*

Dating/Romance Rankings

- Seattle was selected as one of the nation's most romantic cities with 100,000 or more residents by Amazon.com. The city ranked #14 of 20. Criteria: per capita sales of romance novels, relationship books, romantic comedy movies, romantic music, and sexual wellness products. *Amazon.com, "Top 20 Most Romantic Cities in the U.S.," February 1, 2017*

Education Rankings

- Personal finance website *WalletHub* analyzed the 150 largest U.S. metropolitan statistical areas to determine where the most educated Americans are putting their degrees to work. Criteria: education levels; percentage of workers with degrees; education quality and attainment gap; public school quality rankings; quality and enrollment of each metro area's universities. Seattle was ranked #9 (#1 = most educated city). *www.WalletHub.com, "Most & Least Educated Cities in America," July 18, 2022*

- Seattle was selected as one of the best cities for post grads by *Rent.com*. The city ranked among the top 10. Criteria: jobs per capita; unemployment rate; mean annual income; cost of living; rental inventory. *Rent.com, "Best Cities for College Grads," December 11, 2018*

- Seattle was selected as one of America's most literate cities. The city ranked #1 out of the 84 largest U.S. cities. Criteria: number of booksellers; library resources; Internet resources; educational attainment; periodical publishing resources; newspaper circulation. *Central Connecticut State University, "America's Most Literate Cities, 2018," February 2019*

Environmental Rankings

- Sperling's BestPlaces assessed the 50 largest metropolitan areas of the United States for the likelihood of dangerously extreme weather events or earthquakes. In general the Southeast and South-Central regions have the highest risk of weather extremes and earthquakes, while the Pacific Northwest enjoys the lowest risk. Of the least risky metropolitan areas, the Seattle metro area was ranked #5. *www.bestplaces.net, "Avoid Natural Disasters: BestPlaces Reveals The Top 10 Safest Places to Live," October 25, 2017*

- The U.S. Environmental Protection Agency (EPA) released its list of U.S. metropolitan areas with the most ENERGY STAR certified buildings in 2022. The Seattle metro area was ranked #13 out of 25. *U.S. Environmental Protection Agency, "2023 Energy Star Top Cities," April 26, 2023*

Food/Drink Rankings

- The U.S. Chamber of Commerce Foundation conducted an in-depth study on local food truck regulations, surveyed 288 food truck owners, and ranked 20 major American cities based on how friendly they are for operating a food truck. The compiled index assessed the following: procedures for obtaining permits and licenses; complying with restrictions; and financial obligations associated with operating a food truck. Seattle ranked #17 overall (1 being the best). *www.foodtrucknation.us, "Food Truck Nation," March 20, 2018*

- T-Mobile Park was selected as one of PETA's "Top 10 Vegan-Friendly Ballparks" for 2019. The park ranked #8. *People for the Ethical Treatment of Animals, "Top 10 Vegan-Friendly Ballparks," May 23, 2019*

Health/Fitness Rankings

- For each of the 100 largest cities in the United States, the American Fitness Index®, compiled in partnership between the American College of Sports Medicine and the Elevance Health Foundation, evaluated community infrastructure and 34 health behaviors including preventive health, levels of chronic disease conditions, food insecurity, sleep quality, pedestrian safety, air quality, and community/environment resources that support physical activity. Seattle ranked #5 for "community fitness." *americanfitnessindex.org, "2022 ACSM American Fitness Index Summary Report," July 12, 2022*

- Seattle was identified as one of the 10 most walkable cities in the U.S. by Walk Score. The city ranked #8. Walk Score measures walkability by analyzing hundreds of walking routes to nearby amenities, and also measures pedestrian friendliness by analyzing population density and road metrics such as block length and intersection density. *WalkScore.com, April 13, 2021*

- The Seattle metro area was identified as one of the worst cities for bed bugs in America by pest control company Orkin. The area ranked #39 out of 50 based on the number of bed bug treatments Orkin performed from December 2021 to November 2022. *Orkin, "The Windy City Can't Blow Bed Bugs Away: Chicago Ranks #1 For Third Consecutive Year On Orkin's Bed Bug Cities List," January 9, 2023*

- Seattle was identified as a "2022 Spring Allergy Capital." The area ranked #99 out of 100. Three groups of factors were used to identify the most challenging cities for people with allergies during the spring season: annual spring pollen scores; over the counter allergy medicine use; number of board-certified allergy specialists. *Asthma and Allergy Foundation of America, "Spring Allergy Capitals 2022," March 2, 2022*

- Seattle was identified as a "2022 Fall Allergy Capital." The area ranked #100 out of 100. Three groups of factors were used to identify the most challenging cities for people with allergies during the fall season: annual fall pollen scores; over the counter allergy medicine use; number of board-certified allergy specialists. *Asthma and Allergy Foundation of America, "Fall Allergy Capitals 2022," March 2, 2022*

- Seattle was identified as a "2022 Asthma Capital." The area ranked #76 out of the nation's 100 largest metropolitan areas. Criteria: estimated asthma prevalence; asthma-related mortality; and ER visits due to asthma. Risk factors analyzed but not factored in the rankings: annual pollen score; annual air quality; public smoking laws; access to board-certified asthma specialists; rescue and controller medication use; uninsured rate; poverty rate. *Asthma and Allergy Foundation of America, "Asthma Capitals 2022: The Most Challenging Places to Live With Asthma," September 14, 2022*

- The Sharecare Community Well-Being Index evaluates 10 individual and social health factors in order to measure what matters to Americans in the communities in which they live. The Seattle metro area ranked #9 in the top 10 across all 10 domains. Criteria: access to healthcare, food, and community resources; housng and transportation; economic security; feeling of purpose; physical, financial, social, and community well-being. *www.sharecare.com, "Community Well-Being Index: 2020 Metro Area & County Rankings Report," August 30, 2021*

Real Estate Rankings

- *WalletHub* compared the most populated U.S. cities to determine which had the best markets for real estate agents. Seattle ranked #1 where demand was high and pay was the best. Criteria: sales per agent; annual median wage for real-estate agents; monthly average starting salary for real estate agents; real estate job density and competition; unemployment rate; home turnover rate; housing-market health index; and other relevant metrics. *www.WalletHub.com, "2021 Best Places to Be a Real Estate Agent," May 12, 2021*

- The Seattle metro area was identified as one of the 20 least affordable housing markets in the U.S. in 2022. The area ranked #178 out of 186 markets. Criteria: qualification for a mortgage loan with a 10 percent down payment on a typical home. *National Association of Realtors®, Qualifying Income Based on Sales Price of Existing Single-Family Homes for Metropolitan Areas, 2022*

- Seattle was ranked #193 out of 235 metro areas in terms of housing affordability in 2022 by the National Association of Home Builders (#1 = most affordable). Criteria: the share of homes sold in that area affordable to a family earning the local median income, based on standard mortgage underwriting criteria. *National Association of Home Builders®, NAHB-Wells Fargo Housing Opportunity Index, 4th Quarter 2022*

Safety Rankings

- Allstate ranked the 200 largest cities in America in terms of driver safety. Seattle ranked #155. Criteria: internal property damage claims over a two-year period from January 2016 to December 2017. The report helps increase the importance of safety and awareness behind the wheel. *Allstate, "Allstate America's Best Drivers Report, 2019" June 24, 2019*

- The National Insurance Crime Bureau ranked 390 metro areas in the U.S. in terms of per capita rates of vehicle theft. The Seattle metro area ranked #9 (#1 = highest rate). Criteria: number of vehicle theft offenses per 100,000 inhabitants in 2021. *National Insurance Crime Bureau, "Hot Spots 2021," September 1, 2022*

Seniors/Retirement Rankings

- From its Best Cities for Successful Aging indexes, the Milken Institute generated rankings for metropolitan areas, weighing data in nine categories—health care, wellness, living arrangements, transportation and convenience, financial characteristics, education, employment, community engagement, and overall livability. The Seattle metro area was ranked #35 overall in the large metro area category. *Milken Institute, "Best Cities for Successful Aging, 2017" March 14, 2017*

Sports/Recreation Rankings

- Seattle was chosen as one of America's best cities for bicycling. The city ranked #1 out of 50. Criteria: cycling infrastructure that is safe and friendly for all ages; energy and bike culture. The editors evaluated cities with populations of 100,000 or more. *Bicycling, "The 50 Best Bike Cities in America," October 10, 2018*

Transportation Rankings

- Business Insider presented an AllTransit Performance Score ranking of public transportation in major U.S. cities and towns, with populations over 250,000, in which Seattle earned the #16-ranked "Transit Score," awarded for frequency of service, access to jobs, quality and number of stops, and affordability. *www.businessinsider.com, "The 17 Major U.S. Cities with the Best Public Transportation," April 17, 2018*

- Seattle was identified as one of the most congested metro areas in the U.S. The area ranked #6 out of 10. Criteria: yearly delay per auto commuter in hours. *Texas A&M Transportation Institute, "2021 Urban Mobility Report," June 2021*

- According to the INRIX "2022 Global Traffic Scorecard," Seattle was identified as one of the most congested metro areas in the U.S. The area ranked #19 out of 25. Criteria: average annual time spent in traffic and average cost of congestion per motorist. *Inrix.com, "Return to Work, Higher Gas Prices & Inflation Drove Americans to Spend Hundreds More in Time and Money Commuting," January 10, 2023*

Women/Minorities Rankings

- Seattle was selected as one of the queerest cities in America by *The Advocate*. The city ranked #24 out of 25. Criteria, among many: Trans Pride parades/festivals; gay rugby teams; lesbian bars; LGBTQ centers; theater screenings of "Moonlight"; LGBTQ-inclusive nondiscrimination ordinances; and gay bowling teams. *The Advocate, "Queerest Cities in America 2017" January 12, 2017*

- Personal finance website *WalletHub* compared more than 180 U.S. cities across two key dimensions, "Hispanic Business-Friendliness" and "Hispanic Purchasing Power," to arrive at the most favorable conditions for Hispanic entrepreneurs. Seattle was ranked #107 out of 182. Criteria includes: share of Hispanic-Owned Businesses; Hispanic entrepreneurship rate to median annual income of Hispanics; Small Business-Friendliness score; cost of living; and number of Hispanics with at least a bachelor's degree. *WalletHub.com, "2019's Best Cities for Hispanic Entrepreneurs," May 1, 2019*

Miscellaneous Rankings

- *MoveHub* ranked 446 hipster cities across 20 countries, using its new and improved *alternative* Hipster Index and Seattle came out as #4 among the top 50. Criteria: population over 150,000; number of vintage boutiques; density of tattoo parlors; vegan places to eat; coffee shops; and density of vinyl record stores. *www.movehub.com, "The Hipster Index: Brighton Pips Portland to Global Top Spot," July 28, 2021*

- The watchdog site, Charity Navigator, conducted a study of charities in major markets both to analyze statistical differences in their financial, accountability, and transparency practices and to track year-to-year variations in individual philanthropic communities. The Seattle metro area was ranked #25 among the 30 metro markets in the rating category of Overall Score. *www.charitynavigator.org, "2017 Metro Market Study," May 1, 2017*

- *WalletHub* compared the 150 most populated U.S. cities to determine their operating efficiency. A "Quality of Services" score was constructed for each city and then divided by the total budget per capita to reveal which were managed the best. Seattle ranked #118. Criteria: financial stability; economy; education; safety; health; infrastructure and pollution. *www.WalletHub.com, "2022's Best- & Worst-Run Cities in America," June 21, 2022*

- The National Alliance to End Homelessness listed the 25 most populous metro areas with the highest rate of homelessness. The Seattle metro area had a high rate of homelessness. Criteria: number of homeless people per 10,000 population in 2016. *National Alliance to End Homelessness, "Homelessness in the 25 Most Populous U.S. Metro Areas," September 1, 2017*

Business Environment

DEMOGRAPHICS

Population Growth

Area	1990 Census	2000 Census	2010 Census	2020 Census	Population Growth (%)	
					1990-2020	2010-2020
City	516,262	563,374	608,660	737,015	42.8	21.1
MSA[1]	2,559,164	3,043,878	3,439,809	4,018,762	57.0	16.8
U.S.	248,709,873	281,421,906	308,745,538	331,449,281	33.3	7.4

Note: (1) Figures cover the Seattle-Tacoma-Bellevue, WA Metropolitan Statistical Area
Source: U.S. Census Bureau, 1990 Census, 2000 Census, 2010 Census, 2020 Census

Race

Area	White Alone[2] (%)	Black Alone[2] (%)	Asian Alone[2] (%)	AIAN[3] Alone[2] (%)	NHOPI[4] Alone[2] (%)	Other Race Alone[2] (%)	Two or More Races (%)
City	61.3	7.0	17.1	0.7	0.3	3.2	10.5
MSA[1]	60.1	6.1	15.4	1.1	1.1	5.3	11.0
U.S.	61.6	12.4	6.0	1.1	0.2	8.4	10.2

Note: (1) Figures cover the Seattle-Tacoma-Bellevue, WA Metropolitan Statistical Area; (2) Alone is defined as not being in combination with one or more other races; (3) American Indian and Alaska Native; (4) Native Hawaiian and Other Pacific Islander
Source: U.S. Census Bureau, 2020 Census

Hispanic or Latino Origin

Area	Total (%)	Mexican (%)	Puerto Rican (%)	Cuban (%)	Other (%)
City	7.2	4.2	0.4	0.2	2.4
MSA[1]	10.5	7.3	0.6	0.2	2.5
U.S.	18.4	11.2	1.8	0.7	4.7

Note: Persons of Hispanic or Latino origin can be of any race; (1) Figures cover the Seattle-Tacoma-Bellevue, WA Metropolitan Statistical Area
Source: U.S. Census Bureau, 2017-2021 American Community Survey 5-Year Estimates

Age

Area	Percent of Population									Median Age
	Under Age 5	Age 5–19	Age 20–34	Age 35–44	Age 45–54	Age 55–64	Age 65–74	Age 75–84	Age 85+	
City	4.4	12.6	33.1	16.0	11.8	9.7	7.7	3.3	1.5	35.0
MSA[1]	5.7	17.9	22.7	14.9	12.7	12.1	8.5	3.9	1.5	37.2
U.S.	5.6	19.2	20.2	12.7	12.4	13.1	10.0	4.9	1.9	38.8

Note: (1) Figures cover the Seattle-Tacoma-Bellevue, WA Metropolitan Statistical Area
Source: U.S. Census Bureau, 2020 Census

Disability by Age

Area	All Ages	Under 18 Years Old	18 to 64 Years Old	65 Years and Over
City	9.3	2.5	7.2	30.6
MSA[1]	10.8	3.9	8.7	32.8
U.S.	12.6	4.4	10.3	33.4

Note: Figures show percent of the civilian noninstitutionalized population that reported having a disability. Disability status is determined from six types of difficulty: vision, hearing, cognitive, ambulatory, self-care, and independent living. For children under 5 years old, hearing and vision difficulty are used to determine disability status. For children between the ages of 5 and 14, disability status is determined from hearing, vision, cognitive, ambulatory, and self-care difficulties. For people aged 15 years and older, they are considered to have a disability if they have difficulty with any one of the six difficulty types; Note: (1) Figures cover the Seattle-Tacoma-Bellevue, WA Metropolitan Statistical Area
Source: U.S. Census Bureau, 2017-2021 American Community Survey 5-Year Estimates

Ancestry

Area	German	Irish	English	American	Italian	Polish	French[2]	Scottish	Dutch
City	14.4	11.0	11.1	2.3	4.5	2.6	3.0	2.8	1.3
MSA[1]	13.8	9.4	10.1	3.0	3.5	1.8	2.6	2.5	1.3
U.S.	12.8	9.6	8.1	5.7	5.0	2.7	2.2	1.6	1.1

Note: Figures are the percentage of the total population reporting a particular ancestry. The nine most commonly reported ancestries in the U.S. are shown. Figures include multiple ancestries (e.g. if a person reported being Irish and Italian, they were included in both columns); (1) Figures cover the Seattle-Tacoma-Bellevue, WA Metropolitan Statistical Area; (2) Excludes Basque
Source: U.S. Census Bureau, 2017-2021 American Community Survey 5-Year Estimates

Foreign-born Population

Area	Percent of Population Born in								
	Any Foreign Country	Asia	Mexico	Europe	Caribbean	Central America[2]	South America	Africa	Canada
City	19.3	11.0	1.3	2.6	0.1	0.4	0.5	2.0	1.0
MSA[1]	19.5	10.4	2.3	2.8	0.2	0.6	0.6	1.6	0.7
U.S.	13.6	4.2	3.3	1.5	1.4	1.1	1.1	0.8	0.2

Note: (1) Figures cover the Seattle-Tacoma-Bellevue, WA Metropolitan Statistical Area; (2) Excludes Mexico.
Source: U.S. Census Bureau, 2017-2021 American Community Survey 5-Year Estimates

Household Size

Area	Persons in Household (%)							Average Household Size
	One	Two	Three	Four	Five	Six	Seven or More	
City	39.9	35.0	12.1	9.0	2.6	0.8	0.5	2.10
MSA[1]	27.3	34.0	16.0	14.0	5.4	2.0	1.3	2.50
U.S.	28.1	33.8	15.5	12.9	6.0	2.3	1.4	2.60

Note: (1) Figures cover the Seattle-Tacoma-Bellevue, WA Metropolitan Statistical Area
Source: U.S. Census Bureau, 2017-2021 American Community Survey 5-Year Estimates

Household Relationships

Area	House-holder	Opposite-sex Spouse	Same-sex Spouse	Opposite-sex Unmarried Partner	Same-sex Unmarried Partner	Child[2]	Grand-child	Other Relatives	Non-relatives
City	46.9	15.2	0.8	4.3	0.6	17.5	0.7	2.8	7.3
MSA[1]	38.9	18.3	0.3	2.9	0.2	26.7	1.5	4.6	4.7
U.S.	38.3	17.5	0.2	2.5	0.2	28.3	2.4	4.8	3.4

Note: Figures are percent of the total population; (1) Figures cover the Seattle-Tacoma-Bellevue, WA Metropolitan Statistical Area; (2) Includes biological, adopted, and stepchildren of the householder
Source: U.S. Census Bureau, 2020 Census

Gender

Area	Males	Females	Males per 100 Females
City	371,247	365,768	101.5
MSA[1]	2,007,150	2,011,612	99.8
U.S.	162,685,811	168,763,470	96.4

Note: (1) Figures cover the Seattle-Tacoma-Bellevue, WA Metropolitan Statistical Area
Source: U.S. Census Bureau, 2020 Census

Marital Status

Area	Never Married	Now Married[2]	Separated	Widowed	Divorced
City	45.5	40.3	1.2	3.0	10.0
MSA[1]	33.2	50.7	1.3	4.0	10.8
U.S.	33.8	48.0	1.8	5.6	10.8

Note: Figures are percentages and cover the population 15 years of age and older; (1) Figures cover the Seattle-Tacoma-Bellevue, WA Metropolitan Statistical Area; (2) Excludes separated
Source: U.S. Census Bureau, 2017-2021 American Community Survey 5-Year Estimates

Religious Groups by Family

Area	Catholic	Baptist	Methodist	LDS[2]	Pentecostal	Lutheran	Islam	Adventist	Other
MSA[1]	11.0	1.0	0.7	2.6	2.8	1.2	0.6	1.4	19.8
U.S.	18.7	7.3	3.0	2.0	1.8	1.7	1.3	1.3	11.6

Note: Figures are the number of adherents as a percentage of the total population and cover the eight largest religious groups in the U.S.; (1) Figures cover the Seattle-Tacoma-Bellevue, WA Metropolitan Statistical Area; (2) Church of Jesus Christ of Latter-day Saints
Sources: 2020 U.S. Religion Census, Association of Statisticians of American Religious Bodies; The Association of Religion Data Archives (ARDA)

Religious Groups by Tradition

Area	Catholic	Evangelical Protestant	Mainline Protestant	Black Protestant	Islam	Judaism	Hinduism	Orthodox	Buddhism
MSA[1]	11.0	19.5	2.7	0.6	0.6	0.4	0.4	0.6	1.6
U.S.	18.7	16.5	5.2	2.3	1.3	0.6	0.4	0.4	0.3

Note: Figures are the number of adherents as a percentage of the total population; (1) Figures cover the Seattle-Tacoma-Bellevue, WA Metropolitan Statistical Area
Sources: 2020 U.S. Religion Census, Association of Statisticians of American Religious Bodies; The Association of Religion Data Archives (ARDA)

ECONOMY

Gross Metropolitan Product

Area	2020	2021	2022	2023	Rank[2]
MSA[1]	426.9	470.6	509.3	539.7	10

Note: Figures are in billions of dollars; (1) Figures cover the Seattle-Tacoma-Bellevue, WA Metropolitan Statistical Area; (2) Rank is based on 2021 data and ranges from 1 to 381
Source: U.S. Conference of Mayors, U.S. Metro Economies: U.S. Metros Compared to Global and State Economies, June 2022

Economic Growth

Area	2018-20 (%)	2021 (%)	2022 (%)	2023 (%)	Rank[2]
MSA[1]	2.2	7.2	3.3	2.6	26
U.S.	-0.6	5.7	3.1	2.9	–

Note: Figures are real gross metropolitan product (GMP) growth rates and represent average annual percent change; (1) Figures cover the Seattle-Tacoma-Bellevue, WA Metropolitan Statistical Area; (2) Rank is based on 2020 2-year average annual percent change and ranges from 1 to 381
Source: U.S. Conference of Mayors, U.S. Metro Economies: U.S. Metros Compared to Global and State Economies, June 2022

Metropolitan Area Exports

Area	2016	2017	2018	2019	2020	2021	Rank[2]
MSA[1]	61,881.0	59,007.0	59,742.9	41,249.0	23,851.0	28,866.7	14

Note: Figures are in millions of dollars; (1) Figures cover the Seattle-Tacoma-Bellevue, WA Metropolitan Statistical Area; (2) Rank is based on 2021 data and ranges from 1 to 388
Source: U.S. Department of Commerce, International Trade Administration, Office of Trade and Economic Analysis, Industry and Analysis, Exports by Metropolitan Area, data extracted March 16, 2023

Building Permits

Area	Single-Family			Multi-Family			Total		
	2021	2022	Pct. Chg.	2021	2022	Pct. Chg.	2021	2022	Pct. Chg.
City	264	418	58.3	11,716	8,572	-26.8	11,980	8,990	-25.0
MSA[1]	8,828	7,029	-20.4	21,915	19,632	-10.4	30,743	26,661	-13.3
U.S.	1,115,400	975,600	-12.5	621,600	689,500	10.9	1,737,000	1,665,100	-4.1

Note: (1) Figures cover the Seattle-Tacoma-Bellevue, WA Metropolitan Statistical Area; Figures represent new, privately-owned housing units authorized (unadjusted data); All permit data are based on estimates with imputation
Source: U.S. Census Bureau, Manufacturing, Mining, and Construction Statistics, Building Permits, 2021, 2022

Bankruptcy Filings

Area	Business Filings			Nonbusiness Filings		
	2021	2022	% Chg.	2021	2022	% Chg.
King County	56	55	-1.8	1,094	979	-10.5
U.S.	14,347	13,481	-6.0	399,269	374,240	-6.3

Note: Business filings include Chapter 7, Chapter 9, Chapter 11, Chapter 12, Chapter 13, Chapter 15, and Section 304; Nonbusiness filings include Chapter 7, Chapter 11, and Chapter 13
Source: Administrative Office of the U.S. Courts, Business and Nonbusiness Bankruptcy, County Cases Commenced by Chapter of the Bankruptcy Code, During the 12-Month Period Ending December 31, 2021 and Business and Nonbusiness Bankruptcy, County Cases Commenced by Chapter of the Bankruptcy Code, During the 12-Month Period Ending December 31, 2022

Housing Vacancy Rates

Area	Gross Vacancy Rate[2] (%)			Year-Round Vacancy Rate[3] (%)			Rental Vacancy Rate[4] (%)			Homeowner Vacancy Rate[5] (%)		
	2020	2021	2022	2020	2021	2022	2020	2021	2022	2020	2021	2022
MSA[1]	4.7	6.2	5.7	4.5	5.5	5.2	3.6	5.3	4.9	0.6	0.7	0.7
U.S.	10.6	10.8	10.5	8.2	8.4	8.2	6.3	6.1	5.8	1.0	0.9	0.8

Note: (1) Figures cover the Seattle-Tacoma-Bellevue, WA Metropolitan Statistical Area; (2) The percentage of the total housing inventory that is vacant; (3) The percentage of the housing inventory (excluding seasonal units) that is year-round vacant; (4) The percentage of rental inventory that is vacant for rent; (5) The percentage of homeowner inventory that is vacant for sale
Source: U.S. Census Bureau, Housing Vacancies and Homeownership Annual Statistics: 2020, 2021, 2022

INCOME

Income

Area	Per Capita ($)	Median Household ($)	Average Household ($)
City	68,836	105,391	144,955
MSA[1]	51,872	97,675	130,964
U.S.	37,638	69,021	97,196

Note: (1) Figures cover the Seattle-Tacoma-Bellevue, WA Metropolitan Statistical Area
Source: U.S. Census Bureau, 2017-2021 American Community Survey 5-Year Estimates

Household Income Distribution

Area	Percent of Households Earning							
	Under $15,000	$15,000 -$24,999	$25,000 -$34,999	$35,000 -$49,999	$50,000 -$74,999	$75,000 -$99,999	$100,000 -$149,999	$150,000 and up
City	7.8	4.5	4.7	7.5	12.8	10.6	17.9	34.1
MSA[1]	5.9	4.6	5.1	8.2	14.7	12.5	19.8	29.2
U.S.	9.4	7.8	8.2	11.4	16.8	12.8	16.3	17.3

Note: (1) Figures cover the Seattle-Tacoma-Bellevue, WA Metropolitan Statistical Area
Source: U.S. Census Bureau, 2017-2021 American Community Survey 5-Year Estimates

Poverty Rate

Area	All Ages	Under 18 Years Old	18 to 64 Years Old	65 Years and Over
City	10.0	9.5	9.9	11.2
MSA[1]	8.3	9.7	7.9	7.8
U.S.	12.6	17.0	11.8	9.6

Note: Figures are percentage of people whose income during the past 12 months was below the poverty level;
(1) Figures cover the Seattle-Tacoma-Bellevue, WA Metropolitan Statistical Area
Source: U.S. Census Bureau, 2017-2021 American Community Survey 5-Year Estimates

EMPLOYMENT

Labor Force and Employment

Area	Civilian Labor Force			Workers Employed		
	Dec. 2021	Dec. 2022	% Chg.	Dec. 2021	Dec. 2022	% Chg.
City	483,713	490,565	1.4	471,546	477,991	1.4
MD[1]	1,724,262	1,779,111	3.2	1,675,402	1,725,495	3.0
U.S.	161,696,000	164,224,000	1.6	155,732,000	158,872,000	2.0

Note: Data is not seasonally adjusted and covers workers 16 years of age and older; (1) Figures cover the Seattle-Bellevue-Kent, WA Metropolitan Division
Source: Bureau of Labor Statistics, Local Area Unemployment Statistics

Unemployment Rate

Area	2022											
	Jan.	Feb.	Mar.	Apr.	May	Jun.	Jul.	Aug.	Sep.	Oct.	Nov.	Dec.
City	3.0	2.5	2.1	1.6	1.9	2.4	2.6	2.8	2.6	2.6	2.7	2.6
MD[1]	3.3	2.8	2.6	2.3	2.6	3.0	3.3	3.3	3.3	3.4	2.9	3.0
U.S.	4.4	4.1	3.8	3.3	3.4	3.8	3.8	3.8	3.3	3.4	3.4	3.3

Note: Data is not seasonally adjusted and covers workers 16 years of age and older; (1) Figures cover the Seattle-Bellevue-Kent, WA Metropolitan Division
Source: Bureau of Labor Statistics, Local Area Unemployment Statistics

Average Wages

Occupation	$/Hr.	Occupation	$/Hr.
Accountants and Auditors	45.25	Maintenance and Repair Workers	27.19
Automotive Mechanics	28.69	Marketing Managers	82.15
Bookkeepers	26.09	Network and Computer Systems Admin.	53.30
Carpenters	35.16	Nurses, Licensed Practical	35.34
Cashiers	17.95	Nurses, Registered	50.74
Computer Programmers	64.30	Nursing Assistants	21.40
Computer Systems Analysts	62.53	Office Clerks, General	24.29
Computer User Support Specialists	36.00	Physical Therapists	50.43
Construction Laborers	28.67	Physicians	120.27
Cooks, Restaurant	21.69	Plumbers, Pipefitters and Steamfitters	41.46
Customer Service Representatives	24.71	Police and Sheriff's Patrol Officers	48.78
Dentists	84.44	Postal Service Mail Carriers	28.57
Electricians	44.45	Real Estate Sales Agents	34.93
Engineers, Electrical	60.98	Retail Salespersons	19.75
Fast Food and Counter Workers	17.49	Sales Representatives, Technical/Scientific	74.86
Financial Managers	87.94	Secretaries, Exc. Legal/Medical/Executive	26.09
First-Line Supervisors of Office Workers	37.50	Security Guards	20.72
General and Operations Managers	72.41	Surgeons	97.57
Hairdressers/Cosmetologists	23.93	Teacher Assistants, Exc. Postsecondary*	22.89
Home Health and Personal Care Aides	18.81	Teachers, Secondary School, Exc. Sp. Ed.*	44.03
Janitors and Cleaners	20.41	Telemarketers	20.78
Landscaping/Groundskeeping Workers	23.52	Truck Drivers, Heavy/Tractor-Trailer	30.34
Lawyers	83.85	Truck Drivers, Light/Delivery Services	24.18
Maids and Housekeeping Cleaners	18.50	Waiters and Waitresses	23.47

Note: Wage data covers the Seattle-Tacoma-Bellevue, WA Metropolitan Statistical Area; (*) Hourly wages were calculated from annual wage data based on a 40 hour work week; n/a not available.
Source: Bureau of Labor Statistics, Metro Area Occupational Employment & Wage Estimates, May 2022

Employment by Industry

Sector	MD[1]		U.S.
	Number of Employees	Percent of Total	Percent of Total
Construction	108,600	6.0	5.0
Private Education and Health Services	233,600	12.9	16.1
Financial Activities	89,400	5.0	5.9
Government	211,000	11.7	14.5
Information	142,100	7.9	2.0
Leisure and Hospitality	157,200	8.7	10.3
Manufacturing	146,800	8.1	8.4
Mining and Logging	700	<0.1	0.4
Other Services	58,900	3.3	3.7
Professional and Business Services	361,800	20.0	14.7
Retail Trade	145,800	8.1	10.2
Transportation, Warehousing, and Utilities	76,700	4.2	4.9
Wholesale Trade	73,200	4.1	3.9

Note: Figures are non-farm employment as of December 2022. Figures are not seasonally adjusted and include workers 16 years of age and older; (1) Figures cover the Seattle-Bellevue-Kent, WA Metropolitan Division
Source: Bureau of Labor Statistics, Current Employment Statistics, Employment, Hours, and Earnings

Employment by Occupation

Occupation Classification	City (%)	MSA[1] (%)	U.S. (%)
Management, Business, Science, and Arts	63.7	48.5	40.3
Natural Resources, Construction, and Maintenance	3.0	7.4	8.7
Production, Transportation, and Material Moving	5.4	10.8	13.1
Sales and Office	15.4	18.5	20.9
Service	12.4	14.9	17.0

Note: Figures cover employed civilians 16 years of age and older; (1) Figures cover the Seattle-Tacoma-Bellevue, WA Metropolitan Statistical Area
Source: U.S. Census Bureau, 2017-2021 American Community Survey 5-Year Estimates

Occupations with Greatest Projected Employment Growth: 2022 – 2024

Occupation[1]	2022 Employment	2024 Projected Employment	Numeric Employment Change	Percent Employment Change
Software Developers and Software Quality Assurance Analysts and Testers	134,340	146,090	11,750	8.7
Fast Food and Counter Workers	108,420	112,150	3,730	3.4
Business Operations Specialists, All Other	70,170	72,940	2,770	3.9
Web Developers and Digital Interface Designers	23,750	26,230	2,480	10.4
Home Health and Personal Care Aides	67,900	70,330	2,430	3.6
Laborers and Freight, Stock, and Material Movers, Hand	62,650	65,050	2,400	3.8
Office Clerks, General	78,060	80,150	2,090	2.7
Management Analysts	34,780	36,700	1,920	5.5
Farmworkers and Laborers, Crop, Nursery, and Greenhouse	68,790	70,710	1,920	2.8
Waiters and Waitresses	47,700	49,500	1,800	3.8

Note: Projections cover Washington; (1) Sorted by numeric employment change
Source: www.projectionscentral.com, State Occupational Projections, 2022–2024 Short-Term Projections

Fastest-Growing Occupations: 2022 – 2024

Occupation[1]	2022 Employment	2024 Projected Employment	Numeric Employment Change	Percent Employment Change
Computer Hardware Engineers	2,100	2,350	250	11.9
Computer and Information Research Scientists (SOC 2018)	2,880	3,200	320	11.1
Industrial Truck and Tractor Operators	15,690	17,430	1,740	11.1
Web Developers and Digital Interface Designers	23,750	26,230	2,480	10.4
Software Developers and Software Quality Assurance Analysts and Testers	134,340	146,090	11,750	8.7
Computer Programmers (SOC 2018)	6,490	7,010	520	8.0
Soil and Plant Scientists	910	980	70	7.7
First-Line Supervisors of Gaming Workers	660	710	50	7.6
Gaming Change Persons and Booth Cashiers	850	910	60	7.1
Gaming Cage Workers	1,120	1,200	80	7.1

Note: Projections cover Washington; (1) Sorted by percent employment change and excludes occupations with numeric employment change less than 50
Source: www.projectionscentral.com, State Occupational Projections, 2022–2024 Short-Term Projections

CITY FINANCES

City Government Finances

Component	2020 ($000)	2020 ($ per capita)
Total Revenues	4,628,465	6,141
Total Expenditures	4,045,021	5,367
Debt Outstanding	5,522,397	7,327
Cash and Securities[1]	2,822,579	3,745

Note: (1) Cash and security holdings of a government at the close of its fiscal year, including those of its dependent agencies, utilities, and liquor stores.
Source: U.S. Census Bureau, State & Local Government Finances 2020

City Government Revenue by Source

Source	2020 ($000)	2020 ($ per capita)	2020 (%)
General Revenue			
From Federal Government	46,387	62	1.0
From State Government	172,269	229	3.7
From Local Governments	10,309	14	0.2
Taxes			
Property	691,680	918	14.9
Sales and Gross Receipts	784,069	1,040	16.9
Personal Income	0	0	0.0
Corporate Income	0	0	0.0
Motor Vehicle License	71,721	95	1.5
Other Taxes	237,905	316	5.1
Current Charges	1,005,262	1,334	21.7
Liquor Store	0	0	0.0
Utility	1,315,308	1,745	28.4

Source: U.S. Census Bureau, State & Local Government Finances 2020

City Government Expenditures by Function

Function	2020 ($000)	2020 ($ per capita)	2020 (%)
General Direct Expenditures			
Air Transportation	0	0	0.0
Corrections	0	0	0.0
Education	64,915	86	1.6
Employment Security Administration	0	0	0.0
Financial Administration	11,013	14	0.3
Fire Protection	188,900	250	4.7
General Public Buildings	0	0	0.0
Governmental Administration, Other	87,898	116	2.2
Health	13,774	18	0.3
Highways	364,942	484	9.0
Hospitals	0	0	0.0
Housing and Community Development	94,076	124	2.3
Interest on General Debt	94,111	124	2.3
Judicial and Legal	55,482	73	1.4
Libraries	79,006	104	2.0
Parking	9,589	12	0.2
Parks and Recreation	338,336	448	8.4
Police Protection	253,480	336	6.3
Public Welfare	123,612	164	3.1
Sewerage	198,430	263	4.9
Solid Waste Management	162,026	215	4.0
Veterans' Services	0	0	0.0
Liquor Store	0	0	0.0
Utility	1,390,757	1,845	34.4

Source: U.S. Census Bureau, State & Local Government Finances 2020

TAXES

State Corporate Income Tax Rates

State	Tax Rate (%)	Income Brackets ($)	Num. of Brackets	Financial Institution Tax Rate (%)[a]	Federal Income Tax Ded.
Washington	None	–	–	–	–

Note: Tax rates as of January 1, 2023; (a) Rates listed are the corporate income tax rate applied to financial institutions or excise taxes based on income. Some states have other taxes based upon the value of deposits or shares.
Source: Federation of Tax Administrators, State Corporate Income Tax Rates, January 1, 2023

State Individual Income Tax Rates

State	Tax Rate (%)	Income Brackets ($)	Personal Exemptions ($)			Standard Ded. ($)	
			Single	Married	Depend.	Single	Married
Washington			– No state income tax –				

Note: Tax rates as of January 1, 2023; Local- and county-level taxes are not included
Source: Federation of Tax Administrators, State Individual Income Tax Rates, January 1, 2023

Various State Sales and Excise Tax Rates

State	State Sales Tax (%)	Gasoline[1] ($/gal.)	Cigarette[2] ($/pack)	Spirits[3] ($/gal.)	Wine[4] ($/gal.)	Beer[5] ($/gal.)	Recreational Marijuana (%)
Washington	6.5	0.494	3.025	36.55	0.87	0.26	(t)

Note: All tax rates as of January 1, 2023; (1) The American Petroleum Institute has developed a methodology for determining the average tax rate on a gallon of fuel. Rates may include any of the following: excise taxes, environmental fees, storage tank fees, other fees or taxes, general sales tax, and local taxes; (2) The federal excise tax of $1.0066 per pack and local taxes are not included; (3) Rates are those applicable to off-premise sales of 40% alcohol by volume (a.b.v.) distilled spirits in 750ml containers. Local excise taxes are excluded; (4) Rates are those applicable to off-premise sales of 11% a.b.v. non-carbonated wine in 750ml containers; (5) Rates are those applicable to off-premise sales of 4.7% a.b.v. beer in 12 ounce containers; (t) 37% excise tax (retail price)
Source: Tax Foundation, 2023 Facts & Figures: How Does Your State Compare?

State Business Tax Climate Index Rankings

State	Overall Rank	Corporate Tax Rank	Individual Income Tax Rank	Sales Tax Rank	Property Tax Rank	Unemployment Insurance Tax Rank
Washington	28	37	8	49	22	25

Note: The index is a measure of how each state's tax laws affect economic performance. The lower the rank, the more favorable a state's tax system is for business. States without a given tax are given a ranking of 1. The scores/rankings for the District of Columbia do not affect other states. The 2023 index represents the tax climate as of July 1, 2022.
Source: Tax Foundation, State Business Tax Climate Index 2023

TRANSPORTATION

Means of Transportation to Work

Area	Car/Truck/Van		Public Transportation			Bicycle	Walked	Other Means	Worked at Home
	Drove Alone	Car-pooled	Bus	Subway	Railroad				
City	40.5	6.1	15.4	1.0	0.1	2.8	9.7	2.9	21.4
MSA[1]	62.4	9.1	6.7	0.3	0.4	0.9	3.6	1.6	14.9
U.S.	73.2	8.6	2.0	1.6	0.5	0.5	2.5	1.5	9.7

Note: Figures are percentages and cover workers 16 years of age and older; (1) Figures cover the Seattle-Tacoma-Bellevue, WA Metropolitan Statistical Area
Source: U.S. Census Bureau, 2017-2021 American Community Survey 5-Year Estimates

Travel Time to Work

Area	Less Than 10 Minutes	10 to 19 Minutes	20 to 29 Minutes	30 to 44 Minutes	45 to 59 Minutes	60 to 89 Minutes	90 Minutes or More
City	7.3	24.0	24.1	27.6	10.6	5.0	1.5
MSA[1]	8.2	22.3	21.1	25.2	11.2	8.6	3.4
U.S.	12.4	28.5	21.0	20.9	8.2	6.2	2.9

Note: Note: Figures are percentages and include workers 16 years old and over; (1) Figures cover the Seattle-Tacoma-Bellevue, WA Metropolitan Statistical Area
Source: U.S. Census Bureau, 2017-2021 American Community Survey 5-Year Estimates

Key Congestion Measures

Measure	1990	2000	2010	2015	2020
Annual Hours of Delay, Total (000)	53,681	92,925	137,010	162,517	69,016
Annual Hours of Delay, Per Auto Commuter	43	55	64	74	31
Annual Congestion Cost, Per Auto Commuter ($)	946	1,231	1,442	1,580	685

Note: Covers the Seattle WA urban area
Source: Texas A&M Transportation Institute, 2021 Urban Mobility Report

Freeway Travel Time Index

Measure	1985	1990	1995	2000	2005	2010	2015	2020
Urban Area Index[1]	1.22	1.26	1.29	1.33	1.37	1.36	1.37	1.11
Urban Area Rank[1,2]	4	3	3	3	3	4	5	20

Note: Freeway Travel Time Index—the ratio of travel time in the peak period to the travel time at free-flow conditions. For example, a value of 1.30 indicates a 20-minute free-flow trip takes 26 minutes in the peak (20 minutes x 1.30 = 26 minutes); (1) Covers the Seattle WA urban area; (2) Rank is based on 101 larger urban areas (#1 = highest travel time index)
Source: Texas A&M Transportation Institute, 2021 Urban Mobility Report

Public Transportation

Agency Name / Mode of Transportation	Vehicles Operated in Maximum Service[1]	Annual Unlinked Passenger Trips[2] (in thous.)	Annual Passenger Miles[3] (in thous.)
King County Department of Transportation (KC Metro)			
Bus (directly operated)	824	42,112.0	173,679.8
Bus (purchased transportation)	41	424.2	1,631.4
Demand Response (purchased transportation)	230	468.1	4,681.1
Demand Response - Taxi	79	88.9	1,034.5
Ferryboat (directly operated)	2	286.8	984.1
Streetcar Rail (directly operated)	10	830.0	992.8
Trolleybus (directly operated)	126	7,976.2	14,349.3
Vanpool (directly operated)	1,038	512.2	10,548.4
Central Puget Sound Regional Transit Authority (Sound Transit)			
Commuter Bus (directly operated)	170	4,122.1	57,972.9
Commuter Bus (purchased transportation)	36	1,024.3	16,310.6
Commuter Rail (purchased transportation)	77	734.5	18,482.2
Light Rail (directly operated)	72	11,516.1	86,103.5
Streetcar Rail (directly operated)	2	371.9	338.4
Washington State Ferries			
Ferryboat (directly operated)	17	15,326.7	108,124.7
City of Seattle (Seattle Center Monorail)			
Monorail and Automated Guideway (purchased transportation)	8	666.9	600.2

Note: (1) Number of revenue vehicles operated by the given mode and type of service to meet the annual maximum service requirement. This is the revenue vehicle count during the peak season of the year; on the week and day that maximum service is provided. Vehicles operated in maximum service (VOMS) exclude atypical days and one-time special events; (2) Number of passengers who boarded public transportation vehicles. Passengers are counted each time they board a vehicle no matter how many vehicles they use to travel from their origin to their destination. (3) Sum of the distances ridden by all passengers during the entire fiscal year.
Source: Federal Transit Administration, National Transit Database, 2021

Air Transportation

Airport Name and Code / Type of Service	Passenger Airlines[1]	Passenger Enplanements	Freight Carriers[2]	Freight (lbs)
Seattle-Tacoma International (SEA)				
Domestic service (U.S. carriers - 2022)	18	20,045,715	19	318,132,458
International service (U.S. carriers - 2021)	6	418,231	6	20,327,596

Note: (1) Includes all U.S.-based major, minor and commuter airlines that carried at least one passenger during the year; (2) Includes all U.S.-based airlines and freight carriers that transported at least one pound of freight during the year.
Source: Bureau of Transportation Statistics, The Intermodal Transportation Database, Air Carriers: T-100 Domestic Market (U.S. Carriers), 2022; Bureau of Transportation Statistics, The Intermodal Transportation Database, Air Carriers: T-100 International Market (U.S. Carriers), 2021

BUSINESSES

Major Business Headquarters

Company Name	Industry	Rankings Fortune[1]	Forbes[2]
Amazon	Internet services and retailing	2	-
Expedia Group	Travel technology	404	-
Expeditors Intl. of Washington	Transportation and logistics	225	-
Nordstrom	General merchandisers	245	-
Saltchuk	Transportation	-	118
Starbucks	Food services	120	-
Trident Seafoods	Food, drink & tobacco	-	213
Zillow Group	Real estate	424	-

Note: (1) Companies that produce a 10-K are ranked 1 to 500 based on 2021 revenue; (2) All private companies with at least $2 billion in annual revenue through the end of their most current fiscal year are ranked 1 to 246; companies listed are headquartered in the city; dashes indicate no ranking
Source: Fortune, "Fortune 500," 2022; Forbes, "America's Largest Private Companies," 2022

Fastest-Growing Businesses

According to *Inc.*, Seattle is home to four of America's 500 fastest-growing private companies: **Coinme** (#227); **FlavorCloud** (#251); **Anvil Secure** (#303); **Knack** (#333). Criteria: must be an independent, privately-held, for-profit, U.S. corporation, proprietorship or partnership as of December 31, 2021; revenues must be at least $100,000 in 2018 and $2 million in 2021; must have four-year operating/sales history. *Inc., "America's 500 Fastest-Growing Private Companies," 2022*

According to *Initiative for a Competitive Inner City (ICIC)*, Seattle is home to one of America's 100 fastest-growing "inner city" companies: **ABC Towing** (#91). Criteria for inclusion: company must be headquartered in or have 51 percent or more of its physical operations in an economically distressed urban area; must be an independent, for-profit corporation, partnership or proprietorship; must have 10 or more employees and have a five-year sales history that includes sales of at least $200,000 in the base year and at least $1 million in the current year with no decrease in sales over the two most recent years. Companies were ranked overall by revenue growth over the five-year period between 2017 and 2021. *Initiative for a Competitive Inner City (ICIC), "Inner City 100 Companies," 2022*

According to Deloitte, Seattle is home to 13 of North America's 500 fastest-growing high-technology companies: **Vontive** (#10); **Alpine Immune Sciences** (#53); **Coinme** (#73); **Syndio** (#126); **Highspot** (#248); **Zillow Group** (#287); **Outreach** (#288); **Qumulo** (#293); **Skilljar** (#306); **Remitly** (#307); **Flexe** (#338); **Redfin Corp** (#428); **Chinook Therapeutics** (#495). Companies are ranked by percentage growth in revenue over a four-year period. Criteria for inclusion: company must be headquartered within North America; must own proprietary intellectual property or technology that is sold to customers in products that contributes to a significant portion of the company's operating revenue; must have been in business for a minumum of four years with 2018 operating revenues of at least $50,000 USD/CD and 2021 operating revenues of at least $5 million USD/CD. *Deloitte, 2022 Technology Fast 500™*

Living Environment

COST OF LIVING

Cost of Living Index

Composite Index	Groceries	Housing	Utilities	Transportation	Health Care	Misc. Goods/ Services
149.9	125.1	211.2	105.8	123.4	129.9	131.8

Note: The Cost of Living Index measures regional differences in the cost of consumer goods and services, excluding taxes and non-consumer expenditures, for professional and managerial households in the top income quintile. It is based on more than 50,000 prices covering almost 60 different items for which prices are collected three times a year by chambers of commerce, economic development organizations or university applied economic centers in each participating urban area. The numbers shown should be read as a percentage above or below the national average of 100. For example, a value of 115.4 in the groceries column indicates that grocery prices are 15.4% higher than the national average. Small differences in the index numbers should not be interpreted as significant; Figures cover the Seattle WA urban area.
Source: The Council for Community and Economic Research, Cost of Living Index, 2022

Grocery Prices

Area[1]	T-Bone Steak ($/pound)	Frying Chicken ($/pound)	Whole Milk ($/half gal.)	Eggs ($/dozen)	Orange Juice ($/64 oz.)	Coffee ($/11.5 oz.)
City[2]	17.83	2.43	2.97	2.23	4.41	6.55
Avg.	13.81	1.59	2.43	2.25	3.85	4.95
Min.	10.17	0.90	1.51	1.30	2.90	3.46
Max.	19.35	3.30	4.32	4.32	5.31	8.59

*Note: (1) Values for the local area are compared with the average, minimum and maximum values for all 286 areas in the Cost of Living Index; (2) Figures cover the Seattle WA urban area; **T-Bone Steak** (price per pound); **Frying Chicken** (price per pound, whole fryer); **Whole Milk** (half gallon carton); **Eggs** (price per dozen, Grade A, large); **Orange Juice** (64 oz. Tropicana or Florida Natural); **Coffee** (11.5 oz. can, vacuum-packed, Maxwell House, Hills Bros, or Folgers).*
Source: The Council for Community and Economic Research, Cost of Living Index, 2022

Housing and Utility Costs

Area[1]	New Home Price ($)	Apartment Rent ($/month)	All Electric ($/month)	Part Electric ($/month)	Other Energy ($/month)	Telephone ($/month)
City[2]	940,665	3,031	188.83	-	-	198.78
Avg.	450,913	1,371	176.41	99.93	76.96	190.22
Min.	229,283	546	100.84	31.56	27.15	174.27
Max.	2,434,977	4,569	356.86	249.59	272.24	208.31

*Note: (1) Values for the local area are compared with the average, minimum and maximum values for all 286 areas in the Cost of Living Index; (2) Figures cover the Seattle WA urban area; **New Home Price** (2,400 sf living area, 8,000 sf lot, in urban area with full utilities); **Apartment Rent** (950 sf 2 bedroom/1.5 or 2 bath, unfurnished, excluding all utilities except water); **All Electric** (average monthly cost for an all-electric home); **Part Electric** (average monthly cost for a part-electric home); **Other Energy** (average monthly cost for natural gas, fuel oil, coal, wood, and any other forms of energy except electricity); **Telephone** (price includes the base monthly rate plus taxes and fees for three lines of mobile phone service).*
Source: The Council for Community and Economic Research, Cost of Living Index, 2022

Health Care, Transportation, and Other Costs

Area[1]	Doctor ($/visit)	Dentist ($/visit)	Optometrist ($/visit)	Gasoline ($/gallon)	Beauty Salon ($/visit)	Men's Shirt ($)
City[2]	176.92	144.83	170.85	4.95	65.43	43.45
Avg.	124.91	107.77	117.66	3.86	43.31	34.21
Min.	36.61	58.25	51.79	2.90	22.18	13.05
Max.	250.21	162.58	371.96	5.54	85.61	63.54

*Note: (1) Values for the local area are compared with the average, minimum and maximum values for all 286 areas in the Cost of Living Index; (2) Figures cover the Seattle WA urban area; **Doctor** (general practitioners routine exam of an established patient); **Dentist** (adult teeth cleaning and periodic oral examination); **Optometrist** (full vision eye exam for established adult patient); **Gasoline** (one gallon regular unleaded, national brand, including all taxes, cash price at self-service pump if available); **Beauty Salon** (woman's shampoo, trim, and blow-dry); **Men's Shirt** (cotton/polyester dress shirt, pinpoint weave, long sleeves).*
Source: The Council for Community and Economic Research, Cost of Living Index, 2022

HOUSING

Homeownership Rate

Area	2015 (%)	2016 (%)	2017 (%)	2018 (%)	2019 (%)	2020 (%)	2021 (%)	2022 (%)
MSA[1]	59.5	57.7	59.5	62.5	61.5	59.4	58.0	62.7
U.S.	63.7	63.4	63.9	64.4	64.6	66.6	65.5	65.8

Note: (1) Figures cover the Seattle-Tacoma-Bellevue, WA Metropolitan Statistical Area
Source: U.S. Census Bureau, Housing Vacancies and Homeownership Annual Statistics: 2015-2022

House Price Index (HPI)

Area	National Ranking[2]	Quarterly Change (%)	One-Year Change (%)	Five-Year Change (%)	Since 1991Q1 (%)
MD[1]	236	-3.59	6.21	48.84	436.06
U.S.[3]	–	0.34	8.41	58.44	289.08

Note: The HPI is a weighted repeat sales index. It measures average price changes in repeat sales or refinancings on the same properties. This information is obtained by reviewing repeat mortgage transactions on single-family properties whose mortgages have been purchased or securitized by Fannie Mae or Freddie Mac since January 1975; (1) Figures cover the Seattle-Bellevue-Everett, WA Metropolitan Division; (2) Rankings are based on annual percentage change for all metro areas containing at least 15,000 transactions over the last 10 years and ranges from 1 to 257; (3) figures based on a weighted average of Census Division estimates using a seasonally adjusted, purchase-only index; all figures are for the period ending December 31, 2022
Source: Federal Housing Finance Agency, Change in FHFA Metropolitan Area House Price Indexes, 2022Q4

Median Single-Family Home Prices

Area	2020	2021	2022p	Percent Change 2021 to 2022
MSA[1]	596.9	698.6	756.2	8.2
U.S. Average	300.2	357.1	392.6	9.9

Note: Figures are median sales prices of existing single-family homes in thousands of dollars; (p) preliminary; (1) Figures cover the Seattle-Tacoma-Bellevue, WA Metropolitan Statistical Area
Source: National Association of Realtors, Median Sales Price of Existing Single-Family Homes for Metropolitan Areas, 4th Quarter 2022

Qualifying Income Based on Median Sales Price of Existing Single-Family Homes

Area	With 5% Down ($)	With 10% Down ($)	With 20% Down ($)
MSA[1]	212,091	200,929	178,603
U.S. Average	112,234	106,237	94,513

Note: Figures are preliminary; Qualifying income is based on a mortgage rate of 6.77%. Monthly principal and interest payment is limited to 25% of income; (1) Figures cover the Seattle-Tacoma-Bellevue, WA Metropolitan Statistical Area
Source: National Association of Realtors, Qualifying Income Based on Median Sales Price of Existing Single-Family Homes for Metropolitan Areas, 4th Quarter 2022

Home Value

Area	Under $100,000	$100,000 -$199,999	$200,000 -$299,999	$300,000 -$399,999	$400,000 -$499,999	$500,000 -$999,999	$1,000,000 or more	Median ($)
City	1.1	0.6	2.7	6.3	8.6	55.3	25.4	767,500
MSA[1]	3.3	3.2	9.5	16.3	15.8	39.3	12.5	518,000
U.S.	16.2	24.2	20.1	13.6	8.3	13.6	4.1	244,900

Note: Figures are percentages except for median and cover owner-occupied housing units; (1) Figures cover the Seattle-Tacoma-Bellevue, WA Metropolitan Statistical Area
Source: U.S. Census Bureau, 2017-2021 American Community Survey 5-Year Estimates

Year Housing Structure Built

Area	2020 or Later	2010 -2019	2000 -2009	1990 -1999	1980 -1989	1970 -1979	1960 -1969	1950 -1959	1940 -1949	Before 1940	Median Year
City	0.1	14.7	11.9	8.3	7.6	7.7	8.3	9.1	8.0	24.2	1971
MSA[1]	0.2	10.6	14.7	15.2	14.1	13.4	10.8	7.1	4.2	9.7	1983
U.S.	0.2	7.3	13.6	13.6	13.2	14.8	10.3	10.0	4.7	12.2	1979

Note: Figures are percentages except for Median Year; Note: (1) Figures cover the Seattle-Tacoma-Bellevue, WA Metropolitan Statistical Area
Source: U.S. Census Bureau, 2017-2021 American Community Survey 5-Year Estimates

Gross Monthly Rent

Area	Under $500	$500 -$999	$1,000 -$1,499	$1,500 -$1,999	$2,000 -$2,499	$2,500 -$2,999	$3,000 and up	Median ($)
City	5.4	6.3	21.6	27.9	19.6	9.7	9.6	1,801
MSA[1]	4.3	8.4	25.0	30.5	17.7	7.5	6.6	1,701
U.S.	8.1	30.5	30.8	16.8	7.3	3.1	3.5	1,163

Note: Figures are percentages except for median; Gross rent is the contract rent plus the estimated average monthly cost of utilities (electricity, gas, and water and sewer) and fuels (oil, coal, kerosene, wood, etc.) if these are paid by the renter (or paid for the renter by someone else); (1) Figures cover the Seattle-Tacoma-Bellevue, WA Metropolitan Statistical Area
Source: U.S. Census Bureau, 2017-2021 American Community Survey 5-Year Estimates

HEALTH

Health Risk Factors

Category	MD[1] (%)	U.S. (%)
Adults aged 18–64 who have any kind of health care coverage	92.6	90.9
Adults who reported being in good or better health	88.4	85.2
Adults who have been told they have high blood cholesterol	33.1	35.7
Adults who have been told they have high blood pressure	26.3	32.4
Adults who are current smokers	8.3	14.4
Adults who currently use e-cigarettes	5.5	6.7
Adults who currently use chewing tobacco, snuff, or snus	2.1	3.5
Adults who are heavy drinkers[2]	6.8	6.3
Adults who are binge drinkers[3]	15.3	15.4
Adults who are overweight (BMI 25.0 - 29.9)	33.1	34.4
Adults who are obese (BMI 30.0 - 99.8)	25.4	33.9
Adults who participated in any physical activities in the past month	84.6	76.3

Note: (1) Figures cover the Seattle-Bellevue-Everett, WA Metropolitan Division; (2) Heavy drinkers are classified as adult men having more than 14 drinks per week and adult women having more than 7 drinks per week; (3) Binge drinkers are classified as males having five or more drinks on one occasion or females having four or more drinks on one occasion
Source: Centers for Disease Control and Prevention, Behaviorial Risk Factor Surveillance System, SMART: Selected Metropolitan Area Risk Trends, 2021

Acute and Chronic Health Conditions

Category	MD[1] (%)	U.S. (%)
Adults who have ever been told they had a heart attack	2.1	4.0
Adults who have ever been told they have angina or coronary heart disease	2.3	3.8
Adults who have ever been told they had a stroke	2.5	3.0
Adults who have ever been told they have asthma	15.0	14.9
Adults who have ever been told they have arthritis	21.5	25.8
Adults who have ever been told they have diabetes[2]	6.9	10.9
Adults who have ever been told they had skin cancer	6.5	6.6
Adults who have ever been told they had any other types of cancer	6.2	7.5
Adults who have ever been told they have COPD	3.4	6.1
Adults who have ever been told they have kidney disease	2.6	3.0
Adults who have ever been told they have a form of depression	22.4	20.5

Note: (1) Figures cover the Seattle-Bellevue-Everett, WA Metropolitan Division; (2) Figures do not include pregnancy-related, borderline, or pre-diabetes
Source: Centers for Disease Control and Prevention, Behaviorial Risk Factor Surveillance System, SMART: Selected Metropolitan Area Risk Trends, 2021

Health Screening and Vaccination Rates

Category	MD[1] (%)	U.S. (%)
Adults who have ever been tested for HIV	41.1	34.9
Adults who have had their blood cholesterol checked within the last five years	85.1	85.2
Adults aged 65+ who have had flu shot within the past year	75.2	68.6
Adults aged 65+ who have ever had a pneumonia vaccination	77.5	71.0

Note: (1) Figures cover the Seattle-Bellevue-Everett, WA Metropolitan Division.
Source: Centers for Disease Control and Prevention, Behaviorial Risk Factor Surveillance System, SMART: Selected Metropolitan Area Risk Trends, 2021

Disability Status

Category	MD[1] (%)	U.S. (%)
Adults who reported being deaf	4.9	7.2
Are you blind or have serious difficulty seeing, even when wearing glasses?	3.0	4.8
Are you limited in any way in any of your usual activities due to arthritis?	9.0	11.1
Do you have difficulty doing errands alone?	5.3	7.0
Do you have difficulty dressing or bathing?	2.5	3.6
Do you have serious difficulty concentrating/remembering/making decisions?	10.7	12.1
Do you have serious difficulty walking or climbing stairs?	8.1	12.8

Note: (1) Figures cover the Seattle-Bellevue-Everett, WA Metropolitan Division.
Source: Centers for Disease Control and Prevention, Behaviorial Risk Factor Surveillance System, SMART: Selected Metropolitan Area Risk Trends, 2021

Mortality Rates for the Top 10 Causes of Death in the U.S.

ICD-10[a] Sub-Chapter	ICD-10[a] Code	Crude Mortality Rate[1] per 100,000 population	
		County[2]	U.S.
Malignant neoplasms	C00-C97	129.0	182.6
Ischaemic heart diseases	I20-I25	72.5	113.1
Other forms of heart disease	I30-I51	30.2	64.4
Other degenerative diseases of the nervous system	G30-G31	51.9	51.0
Cerebrovascular diseases	I60-I69	29.8	47.8
Other external causes of accidental injury	W00-X59	38.5	46.4
Chronic lower respiratory diseases	J40-J47	19.1	45.7
Organic, including symptomatic, mental disorders	F01-F09	17.6	35.9
Hypertensive diseases	I10-I15	26.6	35.0
Diabetes mellitus	E10-E14	19.5	29.6

Note: (a) ICD-10 = International Classification of Diseases 10th Revision; (1) Crude mortality rates are a three-year average covering 2019-2021; (2) Figures cover King County.
Source: Centers for Disease Control and Prevention, National Center for Health Statistics. National Vital Statistics System, Mortality 2018-2021 on CDC WONDER Online Database

Mortality Rates for Selected Causes of Death

ICD-10[a] Sub-Chapter	ICD-10[a] Code	Crude Mortality Rate[1] per 100,000 population	
		County[2]	U.S.
Assault	X85-Y09	4.1	7.0
Diseases of the liver	K70-K76	15.3	19.8
Human immunodeficiency virus (HIV) disease	B20-B24	1.0	1.5
Influenza and pneumonia	J09-J18	7.2	14.7
Intentional self-harm	X60-X84	12.9	14.3
Malnutrition	E40-E46	2.1	4.3
Obesity and other hyperalimentation	E65-E68	2.2	3.0
Renal failure	N17-N19	3.6	15.7
Transport accidents	V01-V99	6.7	13.6
Viral hepatitis	B15-B19	1.4	1.2

Note: (a) ICD-10 = International Classification of Diseases 10th Revision; (1) Crude mortality rates are a three-year average covering 2019-2021; (2) Figures cover King County; Data are suppressed when the data meet the criteria for confidentiality constraints; Crude mortality rates are flagged as unreliable when the rate would be calculated with a numerator of 20 or less.
Source: Centers for Disease Control and Prevention, National Center for Health Statistics. National Vital Statistics System, Mortality 2018-2021 on CDC WONDER Online Database

Health Insurance Coverage

Area	With Health Insurance	With Private Health Insurance	With Public Health Insurance	Without Health Insurance	Population Under Age 19 Without Health Insurance
City	95.6	80.7	23.5	4.4	1.5
MSA[1]	94.3	75.8	29.2	5.7	2.6
U.S.	91.2	67.8	35.4	8.8	5.3

Note: Figures are percentages that cover the civilian noninstitutionalized population; (1) Figures cover the Seattle-Tacoma-Bellevue, WA Metropolitan Statistical Area
Source: U.S. Census Bureau, 2017-2021 American Community Survey 5-Year Estimates

Number of Medical Professionals

Area	MDs[3]	DOs[3,4]	Dentists	Podiatrists	Chiropractors	Optometrists
County[1] (number)	11,427	378	2,556	141	1,075	513
County[1] (rate[2])	502.8	16.6	113.5	6.3	47.7	22.8
U.S. (rate[2])	289.3	23.5	72.5	6.2	28.7	17.4

Note: Data as of 2021 unless noted; (1) Data covers King County; (2) Rate per 100,000 population; (3) Data as of 2020 and includes all active, non-federal physicians; (4) Doctor of Osteopathic Medicine
Source: U.S. Department of Health and Human Services, Health Resources and Services Administration, Bureau of Health Professions, Area Resource File (ARF) 2021-2022

Best Hospitals

According to *U.S. News,* the Seattle-Bellevue-Kent, WA metro area is home to four of the best hospitals in the U.S.: **Fred Hutchinson Cancer Center/University of Washington Medical Center** (1 adult specialty); **Swedish Medical Center-Cherry Hill** (1 adult specialty); **UW Medicine-Harborview Medical Center** (1 adult specialty); **UW Medicine-University of Washington Medical Center** (7 adult specialties). The hospitals listed were nationally ranked in at least one of 15 adult or 10 pediatric specialties. The number of specialties shown cover the parent hospital. Only 164 U.S. hospitals performed well enough to be nationally ranked in one or more specialties. Twenty hospitals in the U.S. made the Honor Roll. The Best Hospitals Honor Roll takes both the national rankings and the procedure and condition ratings into account. Hospitals received points if they were nationally ranked in one of the 15 adult specialties—the higher they ranked, the more points they got—and how many ratings of "high performing" they earned in the 17 procedures and conditions. *U.S. News Online, "America's Best Hospitals 2022-23"*

According to *U.S. News,* the Seattle-Bellevue-Kent, WA metro area is home to one of the best children's hospitals in the U.S.: **Seattle Children's Hospital** (10 pediatric specialties). The hospital listed was highly ranked in at least one of 10 pediatric specialties. Eighty-six children's hospitals in the U.S. were nationally ranked in at least one specialty. Hospitals received points for being ranked in a specialty, and the 10 hospitals with the most points across the 10 specialties make up the Honor Roll. *U.S. News Online, "America's Best Children's Hospitals 2022-23"*

EDUCATION

Public School District Statistics

District Name	Schls	Pupils	Pupil/ Teacher Ratio	Minority Pupils[1] (%)	LEP/ELL[2] (%)	IEP[3] (%)
Seattle Public Schools	109	51,443	16.5	54.6	11.9	13.9

Note: Table includes school districts with 2,000 or more students; (1) Percentage of students that are not non-Hispanic white; (2) Percentage of students that are Limited English Proficient or English Language Learners (2018-19); (3) Percentage of students that have an Individualized Education Program (2019-20).
Source: U.S. Department of Education, National Center for Education Statistics, Common Core of Data, Local Education Agency (School District) Universe Survey: School Year 2021-2022

Highest Level of Education

Area	Less than H.S.	H.S. Diploma	Some College, No Deg.	Associate Degree	Bachelor's Degree	Master's Degree	Prof. School Degree	Doctorate Degree
City	4.5	9.7	13.9	6.0	37.3	19.4	5.3	3.9
MSA[1]	6.8	19.1	20.3	9.4	27.1	12.5	2.7	2.0
U.S.	11.1	26.5	20.0	8.7	20.6	9.3	2.2	1.5

Note: Figures cover persons age 25 and over; (1) Figures cover the Seattle-Tacoma-Bellevue, WA Metropolitan Statistical Area
Source: U.S. Census Bureau, 2017-2021 American Community Survey 5-Year Estimates

Educational Attainment by Race

Area	High School Graduate or Higher (%)					Bachelor's Degree or Higher (%)				
	Total	White	Black	Asian	Hisp.[2]	Total	White	Black	Asian	Hisp.[2]
City	95.5	98.2	89.8	90.1	85.7	65.9	70.7	32.9	66.9	46.5
MSA[1]	93.2	95.5	90.8	90.0	75.9	44.3	44.9	27.5	58.3	25.0
U.S.	88.9	91.4	87.2	87.6	71.2	33.7	35.5	23.3	55.6	18.4

Note: Figures shown cover persons 25 years old and over; (1) Figures cover the Seattle-Tacoma-Bellevue, WA Metropolitan Statistical Area; (2) People of Hispanic origin can be of any race
Source: U.S. Census Bureau, 2017-2021 American Community Survey 5-Year Estimates

School Enrollment by Grade and Control

Area	Preschool (%)		Kindergarten (%)		Grades 1 - 4 (%)		Grades 5 - 8 (%)		Grades 9 - 12 (%)	
	Public	Private	Public	Private	Public	Private	Public	Private	Public	Private
City	36.3	63.7	79.0	21.0	79.2	20.8	73.5	26.5	77.3	22.7
MSA[1]	42.0	58.0	82.0	18.0	86.4	13.6	86.9	13.1	90.2	9.8
U.S.	58.8	41.2	86.3	13.7	88.3	11.7	88.6	11.4	89.4	10.6

Note: Figures shown cover persons 3 years old and over; (1) Figures cover the Seattle-Tacoma-Bellevue, WA Metropolitan Statistical Area
Source: U.S. Census Bureau, 2017-2021 American Community Survey 5-Year Estimates

Higher Education

Four-Year Colleges			Two-Year Colleges			Medical Schools[1]	Law Schools[2]	Voc/ Tech[3]
Public	Private Non-profit	Private For-profit	Public	Private Non-profit	Private For-profit			
16	13	3	3	1	3	1	2	9

Note: Figures cover institutions located within the Seattle-Tacoma-Bellevue, WA Metropolitan Statistical Area and include main campuses only; (1) includes schools accredited by the Liaison Committee on Medical Education and the American Osteopathic Association's Commission on Osteopathic College Accreditation; (2) includes ABA-accredited schools, schools with provisional ABA accreditation, and state accredited schools; (3) includes all schools with programs that are less than 2 years.
Source: National Center for Education Statistics, Integrated Postsecondary Education System (IPEDS), 2021-22; Wikipedia, List of Medical Schools in the United States, accessed April 10, 2023; Wikipedia, List of Law Schools in the United States, accessed April 10, 2023

According to *U.S. News & World Report,* the Seattle-Bellevue-Kent, WA metro division is home to two of the top 200 national universities in the U.S.: **University of Washington** (#55 tie); **Seattle University** (#137 tie). The indicators used to capture academic quality fall into a number of categories: assessment by administrators at peer institutions; retention of students; faculty resources; student selectivity; financial resources; alumni giving; high school counselor ratings of colleges; and graduation rate. *U.S. News & World Report, "America's Best Colleges 2023"*

According to *U.S. News & World Report*, the Seattle-Bellevue-Kent, WA metro division is home to one of the top 100 law schools in the U.S.: **University of Washington** (#49 tie). The rankings are based on a weighted average of 12 measures of quality: peer assessment score; assessment score by lawyers/judges; median LSAT scores; median undergrad GPA; acceptance rate; employment rates for graduates; placement success; bar passage rate; faculty resources; expenditures per student; student/faculty ratio; and library resources. *U.S. News & World Report, "America's Best Graduate Schools, Law, 2023"*

According to *U.S. News & World Report*, the Seattle-Bellevue-Kent, WA metro division is home to one of the top 75 medical schools for research in the U.S.: **University of Washington** (#9). The rankings are based on a weighted average of 11 measures of quality: quality assessment; peer assessment score; assessment score by residency directors; research activity; total research activity; average research activity per faculty member; student selectivity; median MCAT total score; median undergraduate GPA; acceptance rate; and faculty resources. *U.S. News & World Report, "America's Best Graduate Schools, Medical, 2023"*

According to *U.S. News & World Report*, the Seattle-Bellevue-Kent, WA metro division is home to one of the top 75 business schools in the U.S.: **University of Washington (Foster)** (#22 tie). The rankings are based on a weighted average of the following nine measures: quality assessment; peer assessment; recruiter assessment; placement success; mean starting salary and bonus; student selectivity; mean GMAT and GRE scores; mean undergraduate GPA; and acceptance rate. *U.S. News & World Report, "America's Best Graduate Schools, Business, 2023"*

EMPLOYERS

Major Employers

Company Name	Industry
City of Tacoma	Municipal government
Costco Wholesale Corporation	Miscellaneous general merchandise stores
County of Snohomish	County government
Evergreen Healthcare	General medical & surgical hospitals
Harborview Medical Center	General medical & surgical hospitals
King County Public Hospital Dist No. 2	Hospital & health services consultant
Microsoft	Prepackaged software
Prologix Distribution Services	General merchandise, non-durable
R U Corporation	American restaurant
SNC-Lavalin Constructors	Heavy construction, nec
Swedish Health Services	General medical & surgical hospitals
T-Mobile USA	Radio, telephone communication
The Boeing Company	Airplanes, fixed or rotary wing
Tulalip Resort Casino	Casino hotels
United States Department of the Army	Medical centers
University of Washington	Colleges & universities
Virginia Mason Medical Center	General medical & surgical hospitals
Virginia Mason Seattle Main Clinic	Clinic, operated by physicians
Washington Dept of Social & Health Svcs	General medical & surgical hospitals

Note: Companies shown are located within the Seattle-Tacoma-Bellevue, WA Metropolitan Statistical Area.
Source: Hoovers.com; Wikipedia

Best Companies to Work For

Perkins Coie; Slalom Consulting, headquartered in Seattle, are among "The 100 Best Companies to Work For." To pick the best companies, *Fortune* partnered with the Great Place to Work Institute. Two-thirds of a company's score is based on the results of the Institute's Trust Index survey, which is sent to a random sample of employees from each company. The questions related to attitudes about management's credibility, job satisfaction, and camaraderie. The other third of the scoring is based on the company's responses to the Institute's Culture Audit, which includes detailed questions about pay and benefit programs, and a series of open-ended questions about hiring practices, internal communication, training, recognition programs, and diversity efforts. Any company that is at least five years old with more than 1,000 U.S. employees is eligible. *Fortune, "The 100 Best Companies to Work For," 2023*

Avanade; Perkins Coie; Slalom Consulting; Zillow Group, headquartered in Seattle, are among "Fortune's Best Workplaces for Women." To pick the best companies, *Fortune* partnered with the Great Place to Work Institute. To be considered for the list, companies must be Great Place To Work-Certified. Companies must also employ at least 50 women, at least 20% of their non-executive managers must be female, and at least one executive must be female. To determine the Best Workplaces for Women, Great Place To Work measured the differences in women's survey responses to those of their peers and assesses the impact of demographics and roles on the quality and consistency of women's experiences. Great Place To Work also analyzed the gender balance of each workplace, how it compared to each company's industry, and patterns in representation as women rise from front-line positions to the board of directors. *Fortune, "Best Workplaces for Women," 2022*

Avanade; Outreach; Slalom Consulting; Zillow Group, headquartered in Seattle, are among "Fortune's Best Workplaces for Parents." To pick the best companies, *Fortune* partnered with the Great Place to Work Institute. To be considered for the list, companies must be Great Place To Work-Certified and have at least 50 responses from parents in the US. The survey enables employees to share confidential quantitative and qualitative feedback about their organization's culture by responding to 60 statements on a 5-point scale and answering two open-ended questions. Collectively, these statements describe a great employee experience, defined by high levels of trust, respect, credibility, fairness, pride, and camaraderie. In addition, companies provide organizational data like size, location, industry, demographics, roles, and levels; and provide information about parental leave, adoption, flexible schedule, childcare and dependent health care benefits. *Fortune, "Best Workplaces for Parents," 2022*

Avanade, headquartered in Seattle, is among the "100 Best Places to Work in IT." To qualify, companies had to have a minimum of 100 total employees and five IT employees. The best places to work were selected based on DEI (diversity, equity, and inclusion) practices; IT turnover, promotions, and growth; IT retention and engagement programs; remote/hybrid working; benefits and perks (such as elder care and child care, flextime, and reimbursement for college tuition); and training and career development opportunities. *Computerworld, "Best Places to Work in IT," 2023*

PUBLIC SAFETY

Crime Rate

Area	Total Crime	Violent Crime Rate				Property Crime Rate		
		Murder	Rape[3]	Robbery	Aggrav. Assault	Burglary	Larceny -Theft	Motor Vehicle Theft
City	5,498.9	6.7	39.0	190.7	389.9	1,351.5	2,884.6	636.5
Suburbs[1]	3,022.6	4.0	29.2	70.5	168.3	442.6	1,893.4	414.8
Metro[2]	3,496.7	4.5	31.1	93.5	210.7	616.6	2,083.1	457.2
U.S.	2,356.7	6.5	38.4	73.9	279.7	314.2	1,398.0	246.0

Note: Figures are crimes per 100,000 population; (1) All areas within the metro area that are located outside the city limits; (2) Figures cover the Seattle-Bellevue-Everett, WA Metropolitan Division; (3) All figures shown were reported using the revised Uniform Crime Reporting (UCR) definition of rape; Due to the transition to the National Incident-Based Reporting System (NIBRS), limited city and metro area data was released for 2021.
Source: FBI Uniform Crime Reports, 2020

Hate Crimes

Area	Number of Quarters Reported	Number of Incidents per Bias Motivation					
		Race/Ethnicity/ Ancestry	Religion	Sexual Orientation	Disability	Gender	Gender Identity
City[1]	4	100	6	27	3	4	8
U.S.	4	5,227	1,244	1,110	130	75	266

Note: (1) Figures include one incident reported with more than one bias motivation; Due to the transition to the National Incident-Based Reporting System (NIBRS), limited crime data was released for 2021.
Source: Federal Bureau of Investigation, Hate Crime Statistics 2020

Identity Theft Consumer Reports

Area	Reports	Reports per 100,000 Population	Rank[2]
MSA[1]	6,944	177	198
U.S.	1,108,609	339	-

Note: (1) Figures cover the Seattle-Tacoma-Bellevue, WA Metropolitan Statistical Area; (2) Rank ranges from 1 to 391 where 1 indicates greatest number of identity theft reports per 100,000 population
Source: Federal Trade Commission, Consumer Sentinel Network Data Book 2022

Fraud and Other Consumer Reports

Area	Reports	Reports per 100,000 Population	Rank[2]
MSA[1]	40,415	1,029	84
U.S.	4,064,520	1,245	-

Note: (1) Figures cover the Seattle-Tacoma-Bellevue, WA Metropolitan Statistical Area; (2) Rank ranges from 1 to 391 where 1 indicates greatest number of fraud and other consumer reports per 100,000 population
Source: Federal Trade Commission, Consumer Sentinel Network Data Book 2022

POLITICS

2020 Presidential Election Results

Area	Biden	Trump	Jorgensen	Hawkins	Other
King County	75.0	22.2	1.5	0.5	0.8
U.S.	51.3	46.8	1.2	0.3	0.5

Note: Results are percentages and may not add to 100% due to rounding
Source: Dave Leip's Atlas of U.S. Presidential Elections

SPORTS

Professional Sports Teams

Team Name	League	Year Established
Seattle Kraken	National Hockey League (NHL)	2021
Seattle Mariners	Major League Baseball (MLB)	1977
Seattle Seahawks	National Football League (NFL)	1976
Seattle Sounders FC	Major League Soccer (MLS)	2009

Note: Includes teams located in the Seattle-Tacoma-Bellevue, WA Metropolitan Statistical Area.
Source: Wikipedia, Major Professional Sports Teams of the United States and Canada, April 12, 2023

CLIMATE

Average and Extreme Temperatures

Temperature	Jan	Feb	Mar	Apr	May	Jun	Jul	Aug	Sep	Oct	Nov	Dec	Yr.
Extreme High (°F)	64	70	75	85	93	96	98	99	98	89	74	63	99
Average High (°F)	44	48	52	57	64	69	75	74	69	59	50	45	59
Average Temp. (°F)	39	43	45	49	55	61	65	65	60	52	45	41	52
Average Low (°F)	34	36	38	41	46	51	54	55	51	45	39	36	44
Extreme Low (°F)	0	1	11	29	28	38	43	44	35	28	6	6	0

Note: Figures cover the years 1948-1990
Source: National Climatic Data Center, International Station Meteorological Climate Summary, 9/96

Average Precipitation/Snowfall/Humidity

Precip./Humidity	Jan	Feb	Mar	Apr	May	Jun	Jul	Aug	Sep	Oct	Nov	Dec	Yr.
Avg. Precip. (in.)	5.7	4.2	3.7	2.4	1.7	1.4	0.8	1.1	1.9	3.5	5.9	5.9	38.4
Avg. Snowfall (in.)	5	2	1	Tr	Tr	0	0	0	0	Tr	1	3	13
Avg. Rel. Hum. 7am (%)	83	83	84	83	80	79	79	84	87	88	85	85	83
Avg. Rel. Hum. 4pm (%)	76	69	63	57	54	54	49	51	57	68	76	79	63

Note: Figures cover the years 1948-1990; Tr = Trace amounts (<0.05 in. of rain; <0.5 in. of snow)
Source: National Climatic Data Center, International Station Meteorological Climate Summary, 9/96

Weather Conditions

Temperature			Daytime Sky			Precipitation		
5°F & below	32°F & below	90°F & above	Clear	Partly cloudy	Cloudy	0.01 inch or more precip.	0.1 inch or more snow/ice	Thunder-storms
< 1	38	3	57	120	188	157	8	8

Note: Figures are average number of days per year and cover the years 1948-1990
Source: National Climatic Data Center, International Station Meteorological Climate Summary, 9/96

HAZARDOUS WASTE

Superfund Sites

The Seattle-Bellevue-Kent, WA metro division is home to nine sites on the EPA's Superfund National Priorities List: **Harbor Island (Lead)** (final); **Lockheed West Seattle** (final); **Lower Duwamish Waterway** (final); **Midway Landfill** (final); **Pacific Car & Foundry Co.** (final); **Pacific Sound Resources** (final); **Queen City Farms** (final); **Quendall Terminals** (final); **Seattle Municipal Landfill (Kent Highlands)** (final). There are a total of 1,165 Superfund sites with a status of proposed or final on the list in the U.S. *U.S. Environmental Protection Agency, National Priorities List, April 12, 2023*

AIR QUALITY

Air Quality Trends: Ozone

	1990	1995	2000	2005	2010	2015	2018	2019	2020	2021
MSA[1]	0.082	0.062	0.056	0.053	0.053	0.059	0.067	0.052	0.052	0.052
U.S.	0.087	0.089	0.081	0.080	0.072	0.067	0.069	0.065	0.065	0.067

Note: (1) Data covers the Seattle-Tacoma-Bellevue, WA Metropolitan Statistical Area. The values shown are the composite ozone concentration averages among trend sites based on the highest fourth daily maximum 8-hour concentration in parts per million. These trends are based on sites having an adequate record of monitoring data during the trend period. Data from exceptional events are included.
Source: U.S. Environmental Protection Agency, Air Quality Monitoring Information, "Air Quality Trends by City, 1990-2021"

Air Quality Index

| Area | Percent of Days when Air Quality was...[2] | | | | | AQI Statistics[2] | |
	Good	Moderate	Unhealthy for Sensitive Groups	Unhealthy	Very Unhealthy	Maximum	Median
MSA[1]	72.1	26.0	1.4	0.5	0.0	177	43

Note: (1) Data covers the Seattle-Tacoma-Bellevue, WA Metropolitan Statistical Area; (2) Based on 365 days with AQI data in 2021. Air Quality Index (AQI) is an index for reporting daily air quality. EPA calculates the AQI for five major air pollutants regulated by the Clean Air Act: ground-level ozone, particle pollution (aka particulate matter), carbon monoxide, sulfur dioxide, and nitrogen dioxide. The AQI runs from 0 to 500. The higher the AQI value, the greater the level of air pollution and the greater the health concern. There are six AQI categories: "Good" AQI is between 0 and 50. Air quality is considered satisfactory; "Moderate" AQI is between 51 and 100. Air quality is acceptable; "Unhealthy for Sensitive Groups" When AQI values are between 101 and 150, members of sensitive groups may experience health effects; "Unhealthy" When AQI values are between 151 and 200 everyone may begin to experience health effects; "Very Unhealthy" AQI values between 201 and 300 trigger a health alert; "Hazardous" AQI values over 300 trigger warnings of emergency conditions (not shown).
Source: U.S. Environmental Protection Agency, Air Quality Index Report, 2021

Air Quality Index Pollutants

| Area | Percent of Days when AQI Pollutant was...[2] | | | | | |
	Carbon Monoxide	Nitrogen Dioxide	Ozone	Sulfur Dioxide	Particulate Matter 2.5	Particulate Matter 10
MSA[1]	0.0	2.2	62.2	(3)	35.6	0.0

Note: (1) Data covers the Seattle-Tacoma-Bellevue, WA Metropolitan Statistical Area; (2) Based on 365 days with AQI data in 2021. The Air Quality Index (AQI) is an index for reporting daily air quality. EPA calculates the AQI for five major air pollutants regulated by the Clean Air Act: ground-level ozone, particle pollution (also known as particulate matter), carbon monoxide, sulfur dioxide, and nitrogen dioxide. The AQI runs from 0 to 500. The higher the AQI value, the greater the level of air pollution and the greater the health concern; (3) Sulfur dioxide is no longer included in this table (as of December 8, 2021) because SO_2 concentrations tend to be very localized and not necessarily representative of broad geographical areas like counties and CBSAs.
Source: U.S. Environmental Protection Agency, Air Quality Index Report, 2021

Maximum Air Pollutant Concentrations: Particulate Matter, Ozone, CO and Lead

	Particulate Matter 10 (ug/m^3)	Particulate Matter 2.5 Wtd AM (ug/m^3)	Particulate Matter 2.5 24-Hr (ug/m^3)	Ozone (ppm)	Carbon Monoxide (ppm)	Lead (ug/m^3)
MSA[1] Level	22	7.1	22	0.078	1	n/a
NAAQS[2]	150	15	35	0.075	9	0.15
Met NAAQS[2]	Yes	Yes	Yes	No	Yes	n/a

Note: (1) Data covers the Seattle-Tacoma-Bellevue, WA Metropolitan Statistical Area; Data from exceptional events are included; (2) National Ambient Air Quality Standards; ppm = parts per million; ug/m^3 = micrograms per cubic meter; n/a not available.
Concentrations: Particulate Matter 10 (coarse particulate)—highest second maximum 24-hour concentration; Particulate Matter 2.5 Wtd AM (fine particulate)—highest weighted annual mean concentration; Particulate Matter 2.5 24-Hour (fine particulate)—highest 98th percentile 24-hour concentration; Ozone—highest fourth daily maximum 8-hour concentration; Carbon Monoxide—highest second maximum non-overlapping 8-hour concentration; Lead—maximum running 3-month average
Source: U.S. Environmental Protection Agency, Air Quality Monitoring Information, "Air Quality Statistics by City, 2021"

Maximum Air Pollutant Concentrations: Nitrogen Dioxide and Sulfur Dioxide

	Nitrogen Dioxide AM (ppb)	Nitrogen Dioxide 1-Hr (ppb)	Sulfur Dioxide AM (ppb)	Sulfur Dioxide 1-Hr (ppb)	Sulfur Dioxide 24-Hr (ppb)
MSA[1] Level	16	49	n/a	3	n/a
NAAQS[2]	53	100	30	75	140
Met NAAQS[2]	Yes	Yes	n/a	Yes	n/a

Note: (1) Data covers the Seattle-Tacoma-Bellevue, WA Metropolitan Statistical Area; Data from exceptional events are included; (2) National Ambient Air Quality Standards; ppm = parts per million; ug/m^3 = micrograms per cubic meter; n/a not available.
Concentrations: Nitrogen Dioxide AM—highest arithmetic mean concentration; Nitrogen Dioxide 1-Hr—highest 98th percentile 1-hour daily maximum concentration; Sulfur Dioxide AM—highest annual mean concentration; Sulfur Dioxide 1-Hr—highest 99th percentile 1-hour daily maximum concentration; Sulfur Dioxide 24-Hr—highest second maximum 24-hour concentration
Source: U.S. Environmental Protection Agency, Air Quality Monitoring Information, "Air Quality Statistics by City, 2021"

Tucson, Arizona

Background

Tucson lies in a high desert valley that was once the floor of an ancient inland sea. Its name derives from the Papago tribe's term for the ancient settlement, Stukshon, which in Spanish is Tuquison. It is believed that the Spanish Jesuit Eusebio Francesco Kino, who established the San Xavier Mission, was the first European to visit the area in 1700. Spanish prospectors who came after Father Kino were driven out by the native tribes trying to protect their territory.

Tucson came under Mexican jurisdiction in 1821, when Mexico was no longer ruled by Spain. In 1853 Mexico sold the area to the U.S. and soon, overland stage service from San Antonio was instituted. The Civil War interrupted travel along this route to California. After the war, Tucson continued as a supply and distribution point, first for the army and then for miners. From 1867 to 1877, it was the capital of the territory.

Tucson grew slowly until World War II when it became more industrialized. Today, the city is both an industrial center and a health resort. Aircraft and missile manufacturing, optics, electronics research, tourism, and education are chief industries. The University of Arizona is the city's largest employer while Raytheon Missile Systems, Davis-Monthan Air Force Base, the state of Arizona, and Walmart are other top employers.

Recreation in Tucson revolves around its breathtaking natural beauty. Its attractions include the Arizona-Sonoran Desert Museum—21 acres of wild desert inhabited by over 300 animal species and 1,200 types of plants—and Kitt Peak National Observatory atop a 6,882-foot mountain, where visitors can peek through its many optical telescopes and radio telescopes and enjoy exhibits and tours. Saguaro National Park is a 91,000-acre park featuring one of the world's largest saguaro, or tall cactus. Mount Lemmon, over 9,000 feet high, offers hiking, camping, picnicking, and skiing. Biosphere 2, the world's largest controlled environment dedicated to understanding the impact of climate change is in nearby Oracle. This 3.14-acre laboratory is home to world-class research and education programs under the stewardship of the University of Arizona and a popular tourist attraction.

To deal with its ever-present water scarcity, the city embarked on a water harvesting program which saved 52.1 million gallons of water in 2018-2019. Today, Tucson is offering financial incentives to residents who harvest their rainwater as the city works to become carbon-neutral by 2030.

Arizona State Museum features extensive basketry and fiber arts exhibits, celebrating the Southwest United States' ancient fiber-weaving traditions. The unparalleled collections of basketry and pottery have been named National Treasures by the National Endowment for the Humanities. Other notable museums include the University of Arizona Museum of Art, Arizona-Sonora Desert Museum, and Pima Air & Space Museum. The city is home to numerous annual events, including the Tucson Gem & Mineral Show, the Tucson Festival of Books, the Tucson Folk Festival, and the All-Souls Procession Weekend.

The college scene in Tucson includes the University of Arizona, one of the top research universities in the U.S., with 45,000 national and international students, and Pima Community College, serving 75,000 students on six campuses with occupational and special interest courses. Tucson's sports focuses on the University of Arizona, with competitive men's basketball women's softball teams. A 2018 addition to the city was the Indoor Football League expansion team, the Tucson Sugar Skulls, playing in the renovated Tucson Arena.

Nightlife in Tucson abounds with music of all kinds—blues, jazz, country, folk, Latino, and reggae. The diverse restaurant scene, including Japanese, Southwestern, and Italian, is world-renowned.

The region is known for its nearly perfect climate. Surrounded by four mountain ranges, Tucson has much sunshine, dry air, and rich desert vegetation.

Rankings

Business/Finance Rankings

- The Brookings Institution ranked the nation's largest cities based on income inequality. Tucson was ranked #58 (#1 = greatest inequality). Criteria: the "95/20 ratio," a figure representing the income at which a household earns more than 95 percent of all other households, divided by the income at which a household earns more than only 20 percent of all other households. *Brookings Institution, "Household Income Inequality, Largest Cities of 97 Large U.S. Metro Areas, 2014-2016," February 5, 2018*

- The Brookings Institution ranked the 100 largest metro areas in the U.S. based on income inequality. Tucson was ranked #24 (#1 = greatest inequality). Criteria: the "95/20 ratio," a figure representing the income at which a household earns more than 95 percent of all other households, divided by the income at which a household earns more than only 20 percent of all other households. *Brookings Institution, "Household Income Inequality, 100 Largest U.S. Metro Areas, 2014-2016," February 5, 2018*

- The Tucson metro area appeared on the Milken Institute "2022 Best Performing Cities" list. Rank: #38 out of 200 large metro areas (population over 250,000). Criteria: job growth; wage and salary growth; high-tech output growth; housing affordability; household broadband access. *Milken Institute, "Best-Performing Cities 2022," March 28, 2022*

- *Forbes* ranked the 200 most populous metro areas to determine the nation's "Best Places for Business and Careers." The Tucson metro area was ranked #107. Criteria: costs (business and living); job growth (past and projected); income growth; quality of life; educational attainment (college and high school); projected economic growth; cultural and leisure opportunities; workplace tolerance laws; net migration patterns. *Forbes, "The Best Places for Business and Careers 2019: Seattle Still On Top," October 30, 2019*

Children/Family Rankings

- Tucson was selected as one of the most playful cities in the U.S. by KaBOOM! The organization's Playful City USA initiative honors cities and towns across the nation that have made their communities more playable. Criteria: pledging to integrate play as a solution to challenges in their communities; making it easy for children to get active and balanced play; creating more family-friendly and innovative communities as a result. *KaBOOM! National Campaign for Play, "2017 Playful City USA Communities"*

Education Rankings

- Personal finance website *WalletHub* analyzed the 150 largest U.S. metropolitan statistical areas to determine where the most educated Americans are putting their degrees to work. Criteria: education levels; percentage of workers with degrees; education quality and attainment gap; public school quality rankings; quality and enrollment of each metro area's universities. Tucson was ranked #44 (#1 = most educated city). *www.WalletHub.com, "Most & Least Educated Cities in America," July 18, 2022*

- Tucson was selected as one of America's most literate cities. The city ranked #56 out of the 84 largest U.S. cities. Criteria: number of booksellers; library resources; Internet resources; educational attainment; periodical publishing resources; newspaper circulation. *Central Connecticut State University, "America's Most Literate Cities, 2018," February 2019*

Health/Fitness Rankings

- For each of the 100 largest cities in the United States, the American Fitness Index®, compiled in partnership between the American College of Sports Medicine and the Elevance Health Foundation, evaluated community infrastructure and 34 health behaviors including preventive health, levels of chronic disease conditions, food insecurity, sleep quality, pedestrian safety, air quality, and community/environment resources that support physical activity. Tucson ranked #35 for "community fitness." *americanfitnessindex.org, "2022 ACSM American Fitness Index Summary Report," July 12, 2022*

- Tucson was identified as a "2022 Spring Allergy Capital." The area ranked #49 out of 100. Three groups of factors were used to identify the most challenging cities for people with allergies during the spring season: annual spring pollen scores; over the counter allergy medicine use; number of board-certified allergy specialists. *Asthma and Allergy Foundation of America, "Spring Allergy Capitals 2022," March 2, 2022*

- Tucson was identified as a "2022 Fall Allergy Capital." The area ranked #39 out of 100. Three groups of factors were used to identify the most challenging cities for people with allergies during the fall season: annual fall pollen scores; over the counter allergy medicine use; number of board-certified allergy specialists. *Asthma and Allergy Foundation of America, "Fall Allergy Capitals 2022," March 2, 2022*

- Tucson was identified as a "2022 Asthma Capital." The area ranked #27 out of the nation's 100 largest metropolitan areas. Criteria: estimated asthma prevalence; asthma-related mortality; and ER visits due to asthma. Risk factors analyzed but not factored in the rankings: annual pollen score; annual air quality; public smoking laws; access to board-certified asthma specialists; rescue and controller medication use; uninsured rate; poverty rate. *Asthma and Allergy Foundation of America, "Asthma Capitals 2022: The Most Challenging Places to Live With Asthma," September 14, 2022*

Real Estate Rankings

- *WalletHub* compared the most populated U.S. cities to determine which had the best markets for real estate agents. Tucson ranked #67 where demand was high and pay was the best. Criteria: sales per agent; annual median wage for real-estate agents; monthly average starting salary for real estate agents; real estate job density and competition; unemployment rate; home turnover rate; housing-market health index; and other relevant metrics. *www.WalletHub.com, "2021 Best Places to Be a Real Estate Agent," May 12, 2021*

- Tucson was ranked #139 out of 235 metro areas in terms of housing affordability in 2022 by the National Association of Home Builders (#1 = most affordable). Criteria: the share of homes sold in that area affordable to a family earning the local median income, based on standard mortgage underwriting criteria. *National Association of Home Builders®, NAHB-Wells Fargo Housing Opportunity Index, 4th Quarter 2022*

Safety Rankings

- Allstate ranked the 200 largest cities in America in terms of driver safety. Tucson ranked #40. Criteria: internal property damage claims over a two-year period from January 2016 to December 2017. The report helps increase the importance of safety and awareness behind the wheel. *Allstate, "Allstate America's Best Drivers Report, 2019" June 24, 2019*

- The National Insurance Crime Bureau ranked 390 metro areas in the U.S. in terms of per capita rates of vehicle theft. The Tucson metro area ranked #88 (#1 = highest rate). Criteria: number of vehicle theft offenses per 100,000 inhabitants in 2021. *National Insurance Crime Bureau, "Hot Spots 2021," September 1, 2022*

Seniors/Retirement Rankings

- From its Best Cities for Successful Aging indexes, the Milken Institute generated rankings for metropolitan areas, weighing data in nine categories—health care, wellness, living arrangements, transportation and convenience, financial characteristics, education, employment, community engagement, and overall livability. The Tucson metro area was ranked #60 overall in the large metro area category. *Milken Institute, "Best Cities for Successful Aging, 2017" March 14, 2017*

- Tucson made the 2022 *Forbes* list of "25 Best Places to Retire." Criteria, focused on overall affordability as well as quality of life indicators, include: housing/living costs compared to the national average and state taxes; air quality; crime rates; home price appreciation; risk associated with climate-change/natural hazards; availability of medical care; bikeability; walkability; healthy living. *Forbes.com, "The Best Places to Retire in 2022," May 13, 2022*

- Tucson was identified as #4 of 20 most popular places to retire in the Southwest region by *Topretirements.com*. The site separated its annual "Best Places to Retire" list by major U.S. regions for 2019. The list reflects the 20 cities that visitors to the website are most interested in for retirement, based on the number of times a city's review was viewed on the website. *Topretirements.com, "20 Most Popular Places to Retire in the Southwest for 2019," October 2, 2019*

Sports/Recreation Rankings

- Tucson was chosen as one of America's best cities for bicycling. The city ranked #24 out of 50. Criteria: cycling infrastructure that is safe and friendly for all ages; energy and bike culture. The editors evaluated cities with populations of 100,000 or more. *Bicycling, "The 50 Best Bike Cities in America," October 10, 2018*

Women/Minorities Rankings

- The *Houston Chronicle* listed the Tucson metro area as #10 in top places for young Latinos to live in the U.S. Research was largely based on housing and occupational data from the largest metropolitan areas performed by *Forbes* and NBC Universo. Criteria: percentage of 18-34 year-olds; Latino college grad rates; and diversity. *blog.chron.com, "The 15 Best Big Cities for Latino Millenials," January 26, 2016*

- Personal finance website *WalletHub* compared more than 180 U.S. cities across two key dimensions, "Hispanic Business-Friendliness" and "Hispanic Purchasing Power," to arrive at the most favorable conditions for Hispanic entrepreneurs. Tucson was ranked #92 out of 182. Criteria includes: share of Hispanic-Owned Businesses; Hispanic entrepreneurship rate to median annual income of Hispanics; Small Business-Friendliness score; cost of living; and number of Hispanics with at least a bachelor's degree. *WalletHub.com, "2019's Best Cities for Hispanic Entrepreneurs," May 1, 2019*

Miscellaneous Rankings

- In *Condé Nast Traveler* magazine's 2022 Readers' Choice Survey, Tucson made the top ten list of friendliest American cities. Tucson ranked #6. *www.cntraveler.com, "The 10 Friendliest Cities in the U.S.," December 20, 2022*

- *WalletHub* compared the 150 most populated U.S. cities to determine their operating efficiency. A "Quality of Services" score was constructed for each city and then divided by the total budget per capita to reveal which were managed the best. Tucson ranked #33. Criteria: financial stability; economy; education; safety; health; infrastructure and pollution. *www.WalletHub.com, "2022's Best- & Worst-Run Cities in America," June 21, 2022*

Business Environment

DEMOGRAPHICS

Population Growth

Area	1990 Census	2000 Census	2010 Census	2020 Census	Population Growth (%) 1990-2020	Population Growth (%) 2010-2020
City	417,942	486,699	520,116	542,629	29.8	4.3
MSA[1]	666,880	843,746	980,263	1,043,433	56.5	6.4
U.S.	248,709,873	281,421,906	308,745,538	331,449,281	33.3	7.4

Note: (1) Figures cover the Tucson, AZ Metropolitan Statistical Area
Source: U.S. Census Bureau, 1990 Census, 2000 Census, 2010 Census, 2020 Census

Race

Area	White Alone[2] (%)	Black Alone[2] (%)	Asian Alone[2] (%)	AIAN[3] Alone[2] (%)	NHOPI[4] Alone[2] (%)	Other Race Alone[2] (%)	Two or More Races (%)
City	54.5	5.6	3.2	2.9	0.3	15.2	18.3
MSA[1]	60.7	3.8	3.0	3.3	0.2	12.2	16.7
U.S.	61.6	12.4	6.0	1.1	0.2	8.4	10.2

Note: (1) Figures cover the Tucson, AZ Metropolitan Statistical Area; (2) Alone is defined as not being in combination with one or more other races; (3) American Indian and Alaska Native; (4) Native Hawaiian and Other Pacific Islander
Source: U.S. Census Bureau, 2020 Census

Hispanic or Latino Origin

Area	Total (%)	Mexican (%)	Puerto Rican (%)	Cuban (%)	Other (%)
City	44.6	39.8	0.9	0.2	3.7
MSA[1]	38.0	33.7	0.9	0.2	3.2
U.S.	18.4	11.2	1.8	0.7	4.7

Note: Persons of Hispanic or Latino origin can be of any race; (1) Figures cover the Tucson, AZ Metropolitan Statistical Area
Source: U.S. Census Bureau, 2017-2021 American Community Survey 5-Year Estimates

Age

Area	Under Age 5	Age 5–19	Age 20–34	Age 35–44	Age 45–54	Age 55–64	Age 65–74	Age 75–84	Age 85+	Median Age
City	5.3	18.2	24.8	12.0	10.9	12.1	9.9	4.8	1.9	36.2
MSA[1]	4.9	17.8	19.8	11.5	10.9	13.1	12.7	6.8	2.4	41.2
U.S.	5.6	19.2	20.2	12.7	12.4	13.1	10.0	4.9	1.9	38.8

Note: (1) Figures cover the Tucson, AZ Metropolitan Statistical Area
Source: U.S. Census Bureau, 2020 Census

Disability by Age

Area	All Ages	Under 18 Years Old	18 to 64 Years Old	65 Years and Over
City	15.0	5.8	12.8	37.5
MSA[1]	14.9	5.3	12.1	33.4
U.S.	12.6	4.4	10.3	33.4

Note: Figures show percent of the civilian noninstitutionalized population that reported having a disability. Disability status is determined from six types of difficulty: vision, hearing, cognitive, ambulatory, self-care, and independent living. For children under 5 years old, hearing and vision difficulty are used to determine disability status. For children between the ages of 5 and 14, disability status is determined from hearing, vision, cognitive, ambulatory, and self-care difficulties. For people aged 15 years and older, they are considered to have a disability if they have difficulty with any one of the six difficulty types; Note: (1) Figures cover the Tucson, AZ Metropolitan Statistical Area
Source: U.S. Census Bureau, 2017-2021 American Community Survey 5-Year Estimates

Ancestry

Area	German	Irish	English	American	Italian	Polish	French[2]	Scottish	Dutch
City	11.1	8.1	7.4	2.8	3.5	1.9	1.8	1.5	0.8
MSA[1]	13.1	8.9	9.1	3.3	3.9	2.3	2.1	1.9	1.0
U.S.	12.8	9.6	8.1	5.7	5.0	2.7	2.2	1.6	1.1

Note: Figures are the percentage of the total population reporting a particular ancestry. The nine most commonly reported ancestries in the U.S. are shown. Figures include multiple ancestries (e.g. if a person reported being Irish and Italian, they were included in both columns); (1) Figures cover the Tucson, AZ Metropolitan Statistical Area; (2) Excludes Basque
Source: U.S. Census Bureau, 2017-2021 American Community Survey 5-Year Estimates

Foreign-born Population

Area	Any Foreign Country	Percent of Population Born in							
		Asia	Mexico	Europe	Caribbean	Central America[2]	South America	Africa	Canada
City	14.2	2.3	8.8	1.0	0.1	0.3	0.4	0.9	0.2
MSA[1]	12.2	2.2	7.0	1.2	0.2	0.3	0.3	0.6	0.3
U.S.	13.6	4.2	3.3	1.5	1.4	1.1	1.1	0.8	0.2

Note: (1) Figures cover the Tucson, AZ Metropolitan Statistical Area; (2) Excludes Mexico.
Source: U.S. Census Bureau, 2017-2021 American Community Survey 5-Year Estimates

Household Size

Area	Persons in Household (%)							Average Household Size
	One	Two	Three	Four	Five	Six	Seven or More	
City	35.0	31.0	14.3	11.2	5.3	2.0	1.2	2.40
MSA[1]	30.7	35.5	13.5	11.4	5.3	2.4	1.3	2.40
U.S.	28.1	33.8	15.5	12.9	6.0	2.3	1.4	2.60

Note: (1) Figures cover the Tucson, AZ Metropolitan Statistical Area
Source: U.S. Census Bureau, 2017-2021 American Community Survey 5-Year Estimates

Household Relationships

Area	House-holder	Opposite-sex Spouse	Same-sex Spouse	Opposite-sex Unmarried Partner	Same-sex Unmarried Partner	Child[2]	Grand-child	Other Relatives	Non-relatives
City	41.1	13.3	0.3	3.3	0.3	25.4	2.8	4.8	4.5
MSA[1]	40.9	17.2	0.3	2.9	0.2	25.5	2.6	4.4	3.4
U.S.	38.3	17.5	0.2	2.5	0.2	28.3	2.4	4.8	3.4

Note: Figures are percent of the total population; (1) Figures cover the Tucson, AZ Metropolitan Statistical Area; (2) Includes biological, adopted, and stepchildren of the householder
Source: U.S. Census Bureau, 2020 Census

Gender

Area	Males	Females	Males per 100 Females
City	269,110	273,519	98.4
MSA[1]	512,753	530,680	96.6
U.S.	162,685,811	168,763,470	96.4

Note: (1) Figures cover the Tucson, AZ Metropolitan Statistical Area
Source: U.S. Census Bureau, 2020 Census

Marital Status

Area	Never Married	Now Married[2]	Separated	Widowed	Divorced
City	42.0	36.7	2.2	5.2	13.9
MSA[1]	34.3	45.5	1.7	5.6	12.9
U.S.	33.8	48.0	1.8	5.6	10.8

Note: Figures are percentages and cover the population 15 years of age and older; (1) Figures cover the Tucson, AZ Metropolitan Statistical Area; (2) Excludes separated
Source: U.S. Census Bureau, 2017-2021 American Community Survey 5-Year Estimates

Religious Groups by Family

Area	Catholic	Baptist	Methodist	LDS[2]	Pentecostal	Lutheran	Islam	Adventist	Other
MSA[1]	18.9	1.9	0.6	2.8	1.3	1.1	1.0	1.4	9.7
U.S.	18.7	7.3	3.0	2.0	1.8	1.7	1.3	1.3	11.6

Note: Figures are the number of adherents as a percentage of the total population and cover the eight largest religious groups in the U.S.; (1) Figures cover the Tucson, AZ Metropolitan Statistical Area; (2) Church of Jesus Christ of Latter-day Saints
Sources: 2020 U.S. Religion Census, Association of Statisticians of American Religious Bodies; The Association of Religion Data Archives (ARDA)

Religious Groups by Tradition

Area	Catholic	Evangelical Protestant	Mainline Protestant	Black Protestant	Islam	Judaism	Hinduism	Orthodox	Buddhism
MSA[1]	18.9	10.4	2.4	0.6	1.0	0.4	0.4	0.2	0.3
U.S.	18.7	16.5	5.2	2.3	1.3	0.6	0.4	0.4	0.3

Note: Figures are the number of adherents as a percentage of the total population; (1) Figures cover the Tucson, AZ Metropolitan Statistical Area
Sources: 2020 U.S. Religion Census, Association of Statisticians of American Religious Bodies; The Association of Religion Data Archives (ARDA)

ECONOMY

Gross Metropolitan Product

Area	2020	2021	2022	2023	Rank[2]
MSA[1]	45.2	49.1	53.1	56.2	72

Note: Figures are in billions of dollars; (1) Figures cover the Tucson, AZ Metropolitan Statistical Area; (2) Rank is based on 2021 data and ranges from 1 to 381
Source: U.S. Conference of Mayors, U.S. Metro Economies: U.S. Metros Compared to Global and State Economies, June 2022

Economic Growth

Area	2018-20 (%)	2021 (%)	2022 (%)	2023 (%)	Rank[2]
MSA[1]	-1.3	4.0	2.1	2.5	240
U.S.	-0.6	5.7	3.1	2.9	–

Note: Figures are real gross metropolitan product (GMP) growth rates and represent average annual percent change; (1) Figures cover the Tucson, AZ Metropolitan Statistical Area; (2) Rank is based on 2020 2-year average annual percent change and ranges from 1 to 381
Source: U.S. Conference of Mayors, U.S. Metro Economies: U.S. Metros Compared to Global and State Economies, June 2022

Metropolitan Area Exports

Area	2016	2017	2018	2019	2020	2021	Rank[2]
MSA[1]	2,563.9	2,683.9	2,824.8	2,943.7	2,640.7	2,846.1	87

Note: Figures are in millions of dollars; (1) Figures cover the Tucson, AZ Metropolitan Statistical Area; (2) Rank is based on 2021 data and ranges from 1 to 388
Source: U.S. Department of Commerce, International Trade Administration, Office of Trade and Economic Analysis, Industry and Analysis, Exports by Metropolitan Area, data extracted March 16, 2023

Building Permits

Area	Single-Family			Multi-Family			Total		
	2021	2022	Pct. Chg.	2021	2022	Pct. Chg.	2021	2022	Pct. Chg.
City	1,134	918	-19.0	959	962	0.3	2,093	1,880	-10.2
MSA[1]	5,116	3,735	-27.0	1,168	1,979	69.4	6,284	5,714	-9.1
U.S.	1,115,400	975,600	-12.5	621,600	689,500	10.9	1,737,000	1,665,100	-4.1

Note: (1) Figures cover the Tucson, AZ Metropolitan Statistical Area; Figures represent new, privately-owned housing units authorized (unadjusted data); All permit data are based on estimates with imputation
Source: U.S. Census Bureau, Manufacturing, Mining, and Construction Statistics, Building Permits, 2021, 2022

Bankruptcy Filings

Area	Business Filings			Nonbusiness Filings		
	2021	2022	% Chg.	2021	2022	% Chg.
Pima County	21	22	4.8	1,379	1,310	-5.0
U.S.	14,347	13,481	-6.0	399,269	374,240	-6.3

Note: Business filings include Chapter 7, Chapter 9, Chapter 11, Chapter 12, Chapter 13, Chapter 15, and Section 304; Nonbusiness filings include Chapter 7, Chapter 11, and Chapter 13
Source: Administrative Office of the U.S. Courts, Business and Nonbusiness Bankruptcy, County Cases Commenced by Chapter of the Bankruptcy Code, During the 12-Month Period Ending December 31, 2021 and Business and Nonbusiness Bankruptcy, County Cases Commenced by Chapter of the Bankruptcy Code, During the 12-Month Period Ending December 31, 2022

Housing Vacancy Rates

Area	Gross Vacancy Rate[2] (%)			Year-Round Vacancy Rate[3] (%)			Rental Vacancy Rate[4] (%)			Homeowner Vacancy Rate[5] (%)		
	2020	2021	2022	2020	2021	2022	2020	2021	2022	2020	2021	2022
MSA[1]	12.1	10.0	13.5	7.7	6.9	10.3	8.6	5.0	8.0	0.5	0.6	1.4
U.S.	10.6	10.8	10.5	8.2	8.4	8.2	6.3	6.1	5.8	1.0	0.9	0.8

Note: (1) Figures cover the Tucson, AZ Metropolitan Statistical Area; (2) The percentage of the total housing inventory that is vacant; (3) The percentage of the housing inventory (excluding seasonal units) that is year-round vacant; (4) The percentage of rental inventory that is vacant for rent; (5) The percentage of homeowner inventory that is vacant for sale
Source: U.S. Census Bureau, Housing Vacancies and Homeownership Annual Statistics: 2020, 2021, 2022

INCOME

Income

Area	Per Capita ($)	Median Household ($)	Average Household ($)
City	26,373	48,058	63,665
MSA[1]	33,016	59,215	80,772
U.S.	37,638	69,021	97,196

Note: (1) Figures cover the Tucson, AZ Metropolitan Statistical Area
Source: U.S. Census Bureau, 2017-2021 American Community Survey 5-Year Estimates

Household Income Distribution

Area				Percent of Households Earning				
	Under $15,000	$15,000 -$24,999	$25,000 -$34,999	$35,000 -$49,999	$50,000 -$74,999	$75,000 -$99,999	$100,000 -$149,999	$150,000 and up
City	13.9	11.4	11.3	15.2	18.1	12.0	11.7	6.4
MSA[1]	10.8	9.2	9.6	13.4	17.3	13.1	14.9	11.7
U.S.	9.4	7.8	8.2	11.4	16.8	12.8	16.3	17.3

Note: (1) Figures cover the Tucson, AZ Metropolitan Statistical Area
Source: U.S. Census Bureau, 2017-2021 American Community Survey 5-Year Estimates

Poverty Rate

Area	All Ages	Under 18 Years Old	18 to 64 Years Old	65 Years and Over
City	19.8	25.3	19.7	12.5
MSA[1]	15.1	20.2	15.5	8.6
U.S.	12.6	17.0	11.8	9.6

Note: Figures are percentage of people whose income during the past 12 months was below the poverty level;
(1) Figures cover the Tucson, AZ Metropolitan Statistical Area
Source: U.S. Census Bureau, 2017-2021 American Community Survey 5-Year Estimates

EMPLOYMENT

Labor Force and Employment

Area	Civilian Labor Force			Workers Employed		
	Dec. 2021	Dec. 2022	% Chg.	Dec. 2021	Dec. 2022	% Chg.
City	257,903	262,655	1.8	249,443	254,180	1.9
MSA[1]	482,383	492,280	2.1	468,330	477,224	1.9
U.S.	161,696,000	164,224,000	1.6	155,732,000	158,872,000	2.0

Note: Data is not seasonally adjusted and covers workers 16 years of age and older; (1) Figures cover the
Tucson, AZ Metropolitan Statistical Area
Source: Bureau of Labor Statistics, Local Area Unemployment Statistics

Unemployment Rate

Area	2022											
	Jan.	Feb.	Mar.	Apr.	May	Jun.	Jul.	Aug.	Sep.	Oct.	Nov.	Dec.
City	4.0	3.9	3.1	3.4	3.6	4.2	4.2	4.3	4.3	4.2	3.6	3.2
MSA[1]	3.6	3.6	2.8	3.1	3.3	3.9	3.9	4.0	4.1	4.0	3.4	3.1
U.S.	4.4	4.1	3.8	3.3	3.4	3.8	3.8	3.8	3.3	3.4	3.4	3.3

Note: Data is not seasonally adjusted and covers workers 16 years of age and older; (1) Figures cover the
Tucson, AZ Metropolitan Statistical Area
Source: Bureau of Labor Statistics, Local Area Unemployment Statistics

Average Wages

Occupation	$/Hr.	Occupation	$/Hr.
Accountants and Auditors	34.99	Maintenance and Repair Workers	20.08
Automotive Mechanics	23.11	Marketing Managers	58.86
Bookkeepers	21.61	Network and Computer Systems Admin.	41.53
Carpenters	21.37	Nurses, Licensed Practical	29.01
Cashiers	14.27	Nurses, Registered	40.19
Computer Programmers	39.03	Nursing Assistants	17.25
Computer Systems Analysts	51.23	Office Clerks, General	20.55
Computer User Support Specialists	27.18	Physical Therapists	44.89
Construction Laborers	19.78	Physicians	n/a
Cooks, Restaurant	16.51	Plumbers, Pipefitters and Steamfitters	25.56
Customer Service Representatives	17.76	Police and Sheriff's Patrol Officers	30.75
Dentists	87.60	Postal Service Mail Carriers	27.62
Electricians	24.71	Real Estate Sales Agents	27.03
Engineers, Electrical	56.86	Retail Salespersons	16.59
Fast Food and Counter Workers	14.40	Sales Representatives, Technical/Scientific	48.00
Financial Managers	62.10	Secretaries, Exc. Legal/Medical/Executive	19.49
First-Line Supervisors of Office Workers	27.35	Security Guards	15.65
General and Operations Managers	44.86	Surgeons	n/a
Hairdressers/Cosmetologists	19.75	Teacher Assistants, Exc. Postsecondary*	14.47
Home Health and Personal Care Aides	14.57	Teachers, Secondary School, Exc. Sp. Ed.*	23.84
Janitors and Cleaners	15.53	Telemarketers	n/a
Landscaping/Groundskeeping Workers	16.04	Truck Drivers, Heavy/Tractor-Trailer	23.82
Lawyers	61.60	Truck Drivers, Light/Delivery Services	21.31
Maids and Housekeeping Cleaners	14.58	Waiters and Waitresses	20.77

Note: Wage data covers the Tucson, AZ Metropolitan Statistical Area; (*) Hourly wages were calculated from
annual wage data based on a 40 hour work week; n/a not available.
Source: Bureau of Labor Statistics, Metro Area Occupational Employment & Wage Estimates, May 2022

Employment by Industry

Sector	MSA[1]		U.S.
	Number of Employees	Percent of Total	Percent of Total
Construction	19,700	4.9	5.0
Private Education and Health Services	68,100	16.8	16.1
Financial Activities	19,600	4.8	5.9
Government	78,100	19.3	14.5
Information	5,200	1.3	2.0
Leisure and Hospitality	45,300	11.2	10.3
Manufacturing	29,000	7.2	8.4
Mining and Logging	2,000	0.5	0.4
Other Services	14,100	3.5	3.7
Professional and Business Services	51,600	12.8	14.7
Retail Trade	42,900	10.6	10.2
Transportation, Warehousing, and Utilities	21,100	5.2	4.9
Wholesale Trade	7,900	2.0	3.9

Note: Figures are non-farm employment as of December 2022. Figures are not seasonally adjusted and include workers 16 years of age and older; (1) Figures cover the Tucson, AZ Metropolitan Statistical Area
Source: Bureau of Labor Statistics, Current Employment Statistics, Employment, Hours, and Earnings

Employment by Occupation

Occupation Classification	City (%)	MSA[1] (%)	U.S. (%)
Management, Business, Science, and Arts	35.5	39.4	40.3
Natural Resources, Construction, and Maintenance	8.9	8.4	8.7
Production, Transportation, and Material Moving	10.2	9.4	13.1
Sales and Office	22.7	22.5	20.9
Service	22.7	20.3	17.0

Note: Figures cover employed civilians 16 years of age and older; (1) Figures cover the Tucson, AZ Metropolitan Statistical Area
Source: U.S. Census Bureau, 2017-2021 American Community Survey 5-Year Estimates

Occupations with Greatest Projected Employment Growth: 2022 – 2024

Occupation[1]	2022 Employment	2024 Projected Employment	Numeric Employment Change	Percent Employment Change
Home Health and Personal Care Aides	71,650	75,090	3,440	4.8
Laborers and Freight, Stock, and Material Movers, Hand	63,960	67,090	3,130	4.9
General and Operations Managers	82,890	85,760	2,870	3.5
Stockers and Order Fillers	56,490	59,310	2,820	5.0
Cooks, Restaurant	29,560	32,170	2,610	8.8
Heavy and Tractor-Trailer Truck Drivers	43,800	45,870	2,070	4.7
Fast Food and Counter Workers	57,520	59,510	1,990	3.5
Waiters and Waitresses	50,910	52,850	1,940	3.8
Software Developers	38,570	40,370	1,800	4.7
Industrial Truck and Tractor Operators	18,980	20,500	1,520	8.0

Note: Projections cover Arizona; (1) Sorted by numeric employment change
Source: www.projectionscentral.com, State Occupational Projections, 2022–2024 Short-Term Projections

Fastest-Growing Occupations: 2022 – 2024

Occupation[1]	2022 Employment	2024 Projected Employment	Numeric Employment Change	Percent Employment Change
Ushers, Lobby Attendants, and Ticket Takers	1,080	1,370	290	26.9
Media and Communication Workers, All Other	450	520	70	15.6
Paper Goods Machine Setters, Operators, and Tenders	800	900	100	12.5
Molders, Shapers, and Casters, Except Metal and Plastic	570	640	70	12.3
Nurse Practitioners	5,570	6,220	650	11.7
Chemical Equipment Operators and Tenders	1,380	1,540	160	11.6
Cooks, All Other	800	890	90	11.3
Packaging and Filling Machine Operators and Tenders	3,500	3,880	380	10.9
Logisticians	3,730	4,120	390	10.5
Solar Photovoltaic Installers	1,180	1,300	120	10.2

Note: Projections cover Arizona; (1) Sorted by percent employment change and excludes occupations with numeric employment change less than 50
Source: www.projectionscentral.com, State Occupational Projections, 2022–2024 Short-Term Projections

CITY FINANCES

City Government Finances

Component	2020 ($000)	2020 ($ per capita)
Total Revenues	1,019,687	1,860
Total Expenditures	1,226,824	2,238
Debt Outstanding	438,561	800
Cash and Securities[1]	512,150	934

Note: (1) Cash and security holdings of a government at the close of its fiscal year, including those of its dependent agencies, utilities, and liquor stores.
Source: U.S. Census Bureau, State & Local Government Finances 2020

City Government Revenue by Source

Source	2020 ($000)	2020 ($ per capita)	2020 (%)
General Revenue			
From Federal Government	70,056	128	6.9
From State Government	218,467	399	21.4
From Local Governments	0	0	0.0
Taxes			
Property	59,133	108	5.8
Sales and Gross Receipts	292,579	534	28.7
Personal Income	0	0	0.0
Corporate Income	0	0	0.0
Motor Vehicle License	0	0	0.0
Other Taxes	13,311	24	1.3
Current Charges	118,204	216	11.6
Liquor Store	0	0	0.0
Utility	226,824	414	22.2

Source: U.S. Census Bureau, State & Local Government Finances 2020

City Government Expenditures by Function

Function	2020 ($000)	2020 ($ per capita)	2020 (%)
General Direct Expenditures			
Air Transportation	62,200	113	5.1
Corrections	0	0	0.0
Education	0	0	0.0
Employment Security Administration	0	0	0.0
Financial Administration	26,924	49	2.2
Fire Protection	118,663	216	9.7
General Public Buildings	1,096	2	0.1
Governmental Administration, Other	26,264	47	2.1
Health	0	0	0.0
Highways	134,175	244	10.9
Hospitals	0	0	0.0
Housing and Community Development	80,798	147	6.6
Interest on General Debt	9,585	17	0.8
Judicial and Legal	33,701	61	2.7
Libraries	0	0	0.0
Parking	6,233	11	0.5
Parks and Recreation	47,296	86	3.9
Police Protection	251,510	458	20.5
Public Welfare	0	0	0.0
Sewerage	0	0	0.0
Solid Waste Management	68,023	124	5.5
Veterans' Services	0	0	0.0
Liquor Store	0	0	0.0
Utility	331,406	604	27.0

Source: U.S. Census Bureau, State & Local Government Finances 2020

TAXES

State Corporate Income Tax Rates

State	Tax Rate (%)	Income Brackets ($)	Num. of Brackets	Financial Institution Tax Rate (%)[a]	Federal Income Tax Ded.
Arizona	4.9 (b)	Flat rate	1	4.9 (b)	No

Note: Tax rates as of January 1, 2023; (a) Rates listed are the corporate income tax rate applied to financial institutions or excise taxes based on income. Some states have other taxes based upon the value of deposits or shares; (b) Minimum tax is $800 in California, $250 in District of Columbia, $50 in Arizona and North Dakota (banks), $400 ($100 banks) in Rhode Island, $200 per location in South Dakota (banks), $100 in Utah, $300 in Vermont.
Source: Federation of Tax Administrators, State Corporate Income Tax Rates, January 1, 2023

State Individual Income Tax Rates

State	Tax Rate (%)	Income Brackets ($)	Personal Exemptions ($) Single	Married	Depend.	Standard Ded. ($) Single	Married
Arizona	2.5	27,808 - 166,843 (b)	–		100 (c)	12,950	25,900

Note: Tax rates as of January 1, 2023; Local- and county-level taxes are not included; Federal income tax is not deductible on state income tax returns; (b) For joint returns, taxes are twice the tax on half the couple's income; (c) The personal exemption takes the form of a tax credit instead of a deduction
Source: Federation of Tax Administrators, State Individual Income Tax Rates, January 1, 2023

Various State Sales and Excise Tax Rates

State	State Sales Tax (%)	Gasoline[1] ($/gal.)	Cigarette[2] ($/pack)	Spirits[3] ($/gal.)	Wine[4] ($/gal.)	Beer[5] ($/gal.)	Recreational Marijuana (%)
Arizona	5.6	0.19	2.00	3.00	0.84	0.16	(b)

Note: All tax rates as of January 1, 2023; (1) The American Petroleum Institute has developed a methodology for determining the average tax rate on a gallon of fuel. Rates may include any of the following: excise taxes, environmental fees, storage tank fees, other fees or taxes, general sales tax, and local taxes; (2) The federal excise tax of $1.0066 per pack and local taxes are not included; (3) Rates are those applicable to off-premise sales of 40% alcohol by volume (a.b.v.) distilled spirits in 750ml containers. Local excise taxes are excluded; (4) Rates are those applicable to off-premise sales of 11% a.b.v. non-carbonated wine in 750ml containers; (5) Rates are those applicable to off-premise sales of 4.7% a.b.v. beer in 12 ounce containers; (b) 16% excise tax (retail price)
Source: Tax Foundation, 2023 Facts & Figures: How Does Your State Compare?

State Business Tax Climate Index Rankings

State	Overall Rank	Corporate Tax Rank	Individual Income Tax Rank	Sales Tax Rank	Property Tax Rank	Unemployment Insurance Tax Rank
Arizona	19	23	16	41	11	14

Note: The index is a measure of how each state's tax laws affect economic performance. The lower the rank, the more favorable a state's tax system is for business. States without a given tax are given a ranking of 1. The scores/rankings for the District of Columbia do not affect other states. The 2023 index represents the tax climate as of July 1, 2022.
Source: Tax Foundation, State Business Tax Climate Index 2023

TRANSPORTATION

Means of Transportation to Work

Area	Car/Truck/Van		Public Transportation			Bicycle	Walked	Other Means	Worked at Home
	Drove Alone	Car-pooled	Bus	Subway	Railroad				
City	71.3	10.4	2.6	0.0	0.0	1.9	2.9	1.7	9.2
MSA[1]	73.4	9.7	1.7	0.0	0.0	1.2	2.1	1.7	10.3
U.S.	73.2	8.6	2.0	1.6	0.5	0.5	2.5	1.5	9.7

Note: Figures are percentages and cover workers 16 years of age and older; (1) Figures cover the Tucson, AZ Metropolitan Statistical Area
Source: U.S. Census Bureau, 2017-2021 American Community Survey 5-Year Estimates

Travel Time to Work

Area	Less Than 10 Minutes	10 to 19 Minutes	20 to 29 Minutes	30 to 44 Minutes	45 to 59 Minutes	60 to 89 Minutes	90 Minutes or More
City	11.8	34.9	25.4	19.6	4.7	2.0	1.6
MSA[1]	10.6	29.4	24.7	24.1	7.0	2.4	1.7
U.S.	12.4	28.5	21.0	20.9	8.2	6.2	2.9

Note: Note: Figures are percentages and include workers 16 years old and over; (1) Figures cover the Tucson, AZ Metropolitan Statistical Area
Source: U.S. Census Bureau, 2017-2021 American Community Survey 5-Year Estimates

Key Congestion Measures

Measure	1990	2000	2010	2015	2020
Annual Hours of Delay, Total (000)	9,594	18,225	27,738	30,850	13,189
Annual Hours of Delay, Per Auto Commuter	28	40	43	49	21
Annual Congestion Cost, Per Auto Commuter ($)	470	673	816	836	381

Note: Covers the Tucson AZ urban area
Source: Texas A&M Transportation Institute, 2021 Urban Mobility Report

Freeway Travel Time Index

Measure	1985	1990	1995	2000	2005	2010	2015	2020
Urban Area Index[1]	1.10	1.14	1.16	1.20	1.21	1.20	1.21	1.07
Urban Area Rank[1,2]	27	26	32	29	35	36	36	57

Note: Freeway Travel Time Index—the ratio of travel time in the peak period to the travel time at free-flow conditions. For example, a value of 1.30 indicates a 20-minute free-flow trip takes 26 minutes in the peak (20 minutes x 1.30 = 26 minutes); (1) Covers the Tucson AZ urban area; (2) Rank is based on 101 larger urban areas (#1 = highest travel time index)
Source: Texas A&M Transportation Institute, 2021 Urban Mobility Report

Public Transportation

Agency Name / Mode of Transportation	Vehicles Operated in Maximum Service[1]	Annual Unlinked Passenger Trips[2] (in thous.)	Annual Passenger Miles[3] (in thous.)
City of Tucson (COT)			
Bus (purchased transportation)	174	10,894.8	46,374.5
Demand Response (purchased transportation)	87	291.2	2,199.6
Streetcar Rail (purchased transportation)	6	438.8	491.5

Note: (1) Number of revenue vehicles operated by the given mode and type of service to meet the annual maximum service requirement. This is the revenue vehicle count during the peak season of the year; on the week and day that maximum service is provided. Vehicles operated in maximum service (VOMS) exclude atypical days and one-time special events; (2) Number of passengers who boarded public transportation vehicles. Passengers are counted each time they board a vehicle no matter how many vehicles they use to travel from their origin to their destination. (3) Sum of the distances ridden by all passengers during the entire fiscal year.
Source: Federal Transit Administration, National Transit Database, 2021

Air Transportation

Airport Name and Code / Type of Service	Passenger Airlines[1]	Passenger Enplanements	Freight Carriers[2]	Freight (lbs)
Tucson International (TUS)				
Domestic service (U.S. carriers - 2022)	25	1,698,404	13	31,666,107
International service (U.S. carriers - 2021)	1	4	1	23,806

Note: (1) Includes all U.S.-based major, minor and commuter airlines that carried at least one passenger during the year; (2) Includes all U.S.-based airlines and freight carriers that transported at least one pound of freight during the year.
Source: Bureau of Transportation Statistics, The Intermodal Transportation Database, Air Carriers: T-100 Domestic Market (U.S. Carriers), 2022; Bureau of Transportation Statistics, The Intermodal Transportation Database, Air Carriers: T-100 International Market (U.S. Carriers), 2021

BUSINESSES

Major Business Headquarters

Company Name	Industry	Rankings	
		Fortune[1]	Forbes[2]
No companies listed	-	-	-

Note: (1) Companies that produce a 10-K are ranked 1 to 500 based on 2021 revenue; (2) All private companies with at least $2 billion in annual revenue through the end of their most current fiscal year are ranked 1 to 246; companies listed are headquartered in the city; dashes indicate no ranking
Source: Fortune, "Fortune 500," 2022; Forbes, "America's Largest Private Companies," 2022

Fastest-Growing Businesses

According to *Inc.*, Tucson is home to one of America's 500 fastest-growing private companies: **Paradigm Laboratories** (#432). Criteria: must be an independent, privately-held, for-profit, U.S. corporation, proprietorship or partnership as of December 31, 2021; revenues must be at least $100,000 in 2018 and $2 million in 2021; must have four-year operating/sales history. *Inc., "America's 500 Fastest-Growing Private Companies," 2022*

According to *Initiative for a Competitive Inner City (ICIC)*, Tucson is home to one of America's 100 fastest-growing "inner city" companies: **Cushman & Wakefield | Picor** (#75). Criteria for inclusion: company must be headquartered in or have 51 percent or more of its physical operations in an economically distressed urban area; must be an independent, for-profit corporation, partnership or proprietorship; must have 10 or more employees and have a five-year sales history that includes sales of at least $200,000 in the base year and at least $1 million in the current year with no decrease in sales over the two most recent years. Companies were ranked overall by revenue growth over the five-year period between 2017 and 2021. *Initiative for a Competitive Inner City (ICIC), "Inner City 100 Companies," 2022*

According to Deloitte, Tucson is home to one of North America's 500 fastest-growing high-technology companies: **AudioEye** (#392). Companies are ranked by percentage growth in revenue over a four-year period. Criteria for inclusion: company must be headquartered within North America; must own proprietary intellectual property or technology that is sold to customers in products that contributes to a significant portion of the company's operating revenue; must have been in business for a minumum of four years with 2018 operating revenues of at least $50,000 USD/CD and 2021 operating revenues of at least $5 million USD/CD. *Deloitte, 2022 Technology Fast 500™*

Living Environment

COST OF LIVING

Cost of Living Index

Composite Index	Groceries	Housing	Utilities	Trans-portation	Health Care	Misc. Goods/Services
103.7	103.9	105.5	97.8	106.7	101.3	103.2

Note: The Cost of Living Index measures regional differences in the cost of consumer goods and services, excluding taxes and non-consumer expenditures, for professional and managerial households in the top income quintile. It is based on more than 50,000 prices covering almost 60 different items for which prices are collected three times a year by chambers of commerce, economic development organizations or university applied economic centers in each participating urban area. The numbers shown should be read as a percentage above or below the national average of 100. For example, a value of 115.4 in the groceries column indicates that grocery prices are 15.4% higher than the national average. Small differences in the index numbers should not be interpreted as significant; Figures cover the Tucson AZ urban area.
Source: The Council for Community and Economic Research, Cost of Living Index, 2022

Grocery Prices

Area[1]	T-Bone Steak ($/pound)	Frying Chicken ($/pound)	Whole Milk ($/half gal.)	Eggs ($/dozen)	Orange Juice ($/64 oz.)	Coffee ($/11.5 oz.)
City[2]	12.19	1.47	2.37	2.22	4.03	5.97
Avg.	13.81	1.59	2.43	2.25	3.85	4.95
Min.	10.17	0.90	1.51	1.30	2.90	3.46
Max.	19.35	3.30	4.32	4.32	5.31	8.59

*Note: (1) Values for the local area are compared with the average, minimum and maximum values for all 286 areas in the Cost of Living Index; (2) Figures cover the Tucson AZ urban area; **T-Bone Steak** (price per pound); **Frying Chicken** (price per pound, whole fryer); **Whole Milk** (half gallon carton); **Eggs** (price per dozen, Grade A, large); **Orange Juice** (64 oz. Tropicana or Florida Natural); **Coffee** (11.5 oz. can, vacuum-packed, Maxwell House, Hills Bros, or Folgers).*
Source: The Council for Community and Economic Research, Cost of Living Index, 2022

Housing and Utility Costs

Area[1]	New Home Price ($)	Apartment Rent ($/month)	All Electric ($/month)	Part Electric ($/month)	Other Energy ($/month)	Telephone ($/month)
City[2]	481,931	1,410	-	103.78	69.05	186.26
Avg.	450,913	1,371	176.41	99.93	76.96	190.22
Min.	229,283	546	100.84	31.56	27.15	174.27
Max.	2,434,977	4,569	356.86	249.59	272.24	208.31

*Note: (1) Values for the local area are compared with the average, minimum and maximum values for all 286 areas in the Cost of Living Index; (2) Figures cover the Tucson AZ urban area; **New Home Price** (2,400 sf living area, 8,000 sf lot, in urban area with full utilities); **Apartment Rent** (950 sf 2 bedroom/1.5 or 2 bath, unfurnished, excluding all utilities except water); **All Electric** (average monthly cost for an all-electric home); **Part Electric** (average monthly cost for a part-electric home); **Other Energy** (average monthly cost for natural gas, fuel oil, coal, wood, and any other forms of energy except electricity); **Telephone** (price includes the base monthly rate plus taxes and fees for three lines of mobile phone service).*
Source: The Council for Community and Economic Research, Cost of Living Index, 2022

Health Care, Transportation, and Other Costs

Area[1]	Doctor ($/visit)	Dentist ($/visit)	Optometrist ($/visit)	Gasoline ($/gallon)	Beauty Salon ($/visit)	Men's Shirt ($)
City[2]	140.00	101.33	108.10	4.09	39.50	37.99
Avg.	124.91	107.77	117.66	3.86	43.31	34.21
Min.	36.61	58.25	51.79	2.90	22.18	13.05
Max.	250.21	162.58	371.96	5.54	85.61	63.54

*Note: (1) Values for the local area are compared with the average, minimum and maximum values for all 286 areas in the Cost of Living Index; (2) Figures cover the Tucson AZ urban area; **Doctor** (general practitioners routine exam of an established patient); **Dentist** (adult teeth cleaning and periodic oral examination); **Optometrist** (full vision eye exam for established adult patient); **Gasoline** (one gallon regular unleaded, national brand, including all taxes, cash price at self-service pump if available); **Beauty Salon** (woman's shampoo, trim, and blow-dry); **Men's Shirt** (cotton/polyester dress shirt, pinpoint weave, long sleeves).*
Source: The Council for Community and Economic Research, Cost of Living Index, 2022

HOUSING

Homeownership Rate

Area	2015 (%)	2016 (%)	2017 (%)	2018 (%)	2019 (%)	2020 (%)	2021 (%)	2022 (%)
MSA[1]	61.4	56.0	60.1	63.8	60.1	67.1	63.5	71.6
U.S.	63.7	63.4	63.9	64.4	64.6	66.6	65.5	65.8

Note: (1) Figures cover the Tucson, AZ Metropolitan Statistical Area
Source: U.S. Census Bureau, Housing Vacancies and Homeownership Annual Statistics: 2015-2022

House Price Index (HPI)

Area	National Ranking[2]	Quarterly Change (%)	One-Year Change (%)	Five-Year Change (%)	Since 1991Q1 (%)
MSA[1]	73	-1.74	13.68	74.77	329.80
U.S.[3]	—	0.34	8.41	58.44	289.08

Note: The HPI is a weighted repeat sales index. It measures average price changes in repeat sales or refinancings on the same properties. This information is obtained by reviewing repeat mortgage transactions on single-family properties whose mortgages have been purchased or securitized by Fannie Mae or Freddie Mac since January 1975; (1) Figures cover the Tucson, AZ Metropolitan Statistical Area; (2) Rankings are based on annual percentage change for all metro areas containing at least 15,000 transactions over the last 10 years and ranges from 1 to 257; (3) figures based on a weighted average of Census Division estimates using a seasonally adjusted, purchase-only index; all figures are for the period ending December 31, 2022
Source: Federal Housing Finance Agency, Change in FHFA Metropolitan Area House Price Indexes, 2022Q4

Median Single-Family Home Prices

Area	2020	2021	2022[p]	Percent Change 2021 to 2022
MSA[1]	265.1	331.2	371.9	12.3
U.S. Average	300.2	357.1	392.6	9.9

Note: Figures are median sales prices of existing single-family homes in thousands of dollars; (p) preliminary; (1) Figures cover the Tucson, AZ Metropolitan Statistical Area
Source: National Association of Realtors, Median Sales Price of Existing Single-Family Homes for Metropolitan Areas, 4th Quarter 2022

Qualifying Income Based on Median Sales Price of Existing Single-Family Homes

Area	With 5% Down ($)	With 10% Down ($)	With 20% Down ($)
MSA[1]	110,159	104,362	92,766
U.S. Average	112,234	106,237	94,513

Note: Figures are preliminary; Qualifying income is based on a mortgage rate of 6.77%. Monthly principal and interest payment is limited to 25% of income; (1) Figures cover the Tucson, AZ Metropolitan Statistical Area
Source: National Association of Realtors, Qualifying Income Based on Median Sales Price of Existing Single-Family Homes for Metropolitan Areas, 4th Quarter 2022

Home Value

Area	Under $100,000	$100,000 -$199,999	$200,000 -$299,999	$300,000 -$399,999	$400,000 -$499,999	$500,000 -$999,999	$1,000,000 or more	Median ($)
City	17.8	41.3	26.3	8.4	3.0	2.4	0.7	177,800
MSA[1]	15.0	29.7	26.3	13.5	6.8	7.4	1.3	217,700
U.S.	16.2	24.2	20.1	13.6	8.3	13.6	4.1	244,900

Note: Figures are percentages except for median and cover owner-occupied housing units; (1) Figures cover the Tucson, AZ Metropolitan Statistical Area
Source: U.S. Census Bureau, 2017-2021 American Community Survey 5-Year Estimates

Year Housing Structure Built

Area	2020 or Later	2010 -2019	2000 -2009	1990 -1999	1980 -1989	1970 -1979	1960 -1969	1950 -1959	1940 -1949	Before 1940	Median Year
City	0.1	3.4	12.6	13.3	17.2	20.5	11.0	13.9	4.6	3.4	1978
MSA[1]	0.2	6.2	18.1	17.3	17.7	19.1	8.4	8.2	2.8	2.0	1985
U.S.	0.2	7.3	13.6	13.6	13.2	14.8	10.3	10.0	4.7	12.2	1979

Note: Figures are percentages except for Median Year; Note: (1) Figures cover the Tucson, AZ Metropolitan Statistical Area
Source: U.S. Census Bureau, 2017-2021 American Community Survey 5-Year Estimates

Gross Monthly Rent

Area	Under $500	$500 -$999	$1,000 -$1,499	$1,500 -$1,999	$2,000 -$2,499	$2,500 -$2,999	$3,000 and up	Median ($)
City	6.0	53.6	30.2	8.0	1.2	0.5	0.6	907
MSA[1]	5.5	46.8	33.6	10.3	1.9	0.8	1.1	976
U.S.	8.1	30.5	30.8	16.8	7.3	3.1	3.5	1,163

Note: Figures are percentages except for median; Gross rent is the contract rent plus the estimated average monthly cost of utilities (electricity, gas, and water and sewer) and fuels (oil, coal, kerosene, wood, etc.) if these are paid by the renter (or paid for the renter by someone else); (1) Figures cover the Tucson, AZ Metropolitan Statistical Area
Source: U.S. Census Bureau, 2017-2021 American Community Survey 5-Year Estimates

HEALTH

Health Risk Factors

Category	MSA[1] (%)	U.S. (%)
Adults aged 18–64 who have any kind of health care coverage	n/a	90.9
Adults who reported being in good or better health	n/a	85.2
Adults who have been told they have high blood cholesterol	n/a	35.7
Adults who have been told they have high blood pressure	n/a	32.4
Adults who are current smokers	n/a	14.4
Adults who currently use e-cigarettes	n/a	6.7
Adults who currently use chewing tobacco, snuff, or snus	n/a	3.5
Adults who are heavy drinkers[2]	n/a	6.3
Adults who are binge drinkers[3]	n/a	15.4
Adults who are overweight (BMI 25.0 - 29.9)	n/a	34.4
Adults who are obese (BMI 30.0 - 99.8)	n/a	33.9
Adults who participated in any physical activities in the past month	n/a	76.3

Note: (1) Figures for the Tucson, AZ Metropolitan Statistical Area were not available.
(2) Heavy drinkers are classified as adult men having more than 14 drinks per week and adult women having more than 7 drinks per week; (3) Binge drinkers are classified as males having five or more drinks on one occasion or females having four or more drinks on one occasion
Source: Centers for Disease Control and Prevention, Behaviorial Risk Factor Surveillance System, SMART: Selected Metropolitan Area Risk Trends, 2021

Acute and Chronic Health Conditions

Category	MSA[1] (%)	U.S. (%)
Adults who have ever been told they had a heart attack	n/a	4.0
Adults who have ever been told they have angina or coronary heart disease	n/a	3.8
Adults who have ever been told they had a stroke	n/a	3.0
Adults who have ever been told they have asthma	n/a	14.9
Adults who have ever been told they have arthritis	n/a	25.8
Adults who have ever been told they have diabetes[2]	n/a	10.9
Adults who have ever been told they had skin cancer	n/a	6.6
Adults who have ever been told they had any other types of cancer	n/a	7.5
Adults who have ever been told they have COPD	n/a	6.1
Adults who have ever been told they have kidney disease	n/a	3.0
Adults who have ever been told they have a form of depression	n/a	20.5

Note: (1) Figures for the Tucson, AZ Metropolitan Statistical Area were not available.
(2) Figures do not include pregnancy-related, borderline, or pre-diabetes
Source: Centers for Disease Control and Prevention, Behaviorial Risk Factor Surveillance System, SMART: Selected Metropolitan Area Risk Trends, 2021

Health Screening and Vaccination Rates

Category	MSA[1] (%)	U.S. (%)
Adults who have ever been tested for HIV	n/a	34.9
Adults who have had their blood cholesterol checked within the last five years	n/a	85.2
Adults aged 65+ who have had flu shot within the past year	n/a	68.6
Adults aged 65+ who have ever had a pneumonia vaccination	n/a	71.0

Note: (1) Figures for the Tucson, AZ Metropolitan Statistical Area were not available.
Source: Centers for Disease Control and Prevention, Behaviorial Risk Factor Surveillance System, SMART: Selected Metropolitan Area Risk Trends, 2021

Disability Status

Category	MSA[1] (%)	U.S. (%)
Adults who reported being deaf	n/a	7.2
Are you blind or have serious difficulty seeing, even when wearing glasses?	n/a	4.8
Are you limited in any way in any of your usual activities due to arthritis?	n/a	11.1
Do you have difficulty doing errands alone?	n/a	7.0
Do you have difficulty dressing or bathing?	n/a	3.6
Do you have serious difficulty concentrating/remembering/making decisions?	n/a	12.1
Do you have serious difficulty walking or climbing stairs?	n/a	12.8

Note: (1) Figures for the Tucson, AZ Metropolitan Statistical Area were not available.
Source: Centers for Disease Control and Prevention, Behaviorial Risk Factor Surveillance System, SMART: Selected Metropolitan Area Risk Trends, 2021

Mortality Rates for the Top 10 Causes of Death in the U.S.

ICD-10[a] Sub-Chapter	ICD-10[a] Code	Crude Mortality Rate[1] per 100,000 population	
		County[2]	U.S.
Malignant neoplasms	C00-C97	196.0	182.6
Ischaemic heart diseases	I20-I25	124.0	113.1
Other forms of heart disease	I30-I51	48.2	64.4
Other degenerative diseases of the nervous system	G30-G31	79.5	51.0
Cerebrovascular diseases	I60-I69	52.6	47.8
Other external causes of accidental injury	W00-X59	62.1	46.4
Chronic lower respiratory diseases	J40-J47	51.5	45.7
Organic, including symptomatic, mental disorders	F01-F09	20.1	35.9
Hypertensive diseases	I10-I15	42.7	35.0
Diabetes mellitus	E10-E14	37.7	29.6

Note: (a) ICD-10 = International Classification of Diseases 10th Revision; (1) Crude mortality rates are a three-year average covering 2019-2021; (2) Figures cover Pima County.
Source: Centers for Disease Control and Prevention, National Center for Health Statistics. National Vital Statistics System, Mortality 2018-2021 on CDC WONDER Online Database

Mortality Rates for Selected Causes of Death

ICD-10[a] Sub-Chapter	ICD-10[a] Code	Crude Mortality Rate[1] per 100,000 population	
		County[2]	U.S.
Assault	X85-Y09	7.5	7.0
Diseases of the liver	K70-K76	29.1	19.8
Human immunodeficiency virus (HIV) disease	B20-B24	0.9	1.5
Influenza and pneumonia	J09-J18	16.1	14.7
Intentional self-harm	X60-X84	22.1	14.3
Malnutrition	E40-E46	8.7	4.3
Obesity and other hyperalimentation	E65-E68	3.6	3.0
Renal failure	N17-N19	13.7	15.7
Transport accidents	V01-V99	17.2	13.6
Viral hepatitis	B15-B19	1.9	1.2

Note: (a) ICD-10 = International Classification of Diseases 10th Revision; (1) Crude mortality rates are a three-year average covering 2019-2021; (2) Figures cover Pima County; Data are suppressed when the data meet the criteria for confidentiality constraints; Crude mortality rates are flagged as unreliable when the rate would be calculated with a numerator of 20 or less.
Source: Centers for Disease Control and Prevention, National Center for Health Statistics. National Vital Statistics System, Mortality 2018-2021 on CDC WONDER Online Database

Health Insurance Coverage

Area	With Health Insurance	With Private Health Insurance	With Public Health Insurance	Without Health Insurance	Population Under Age 19 Without Health Insurance
City	88.7	57.2	42.3	11.3	7.6
MSA[1]	91.1	62.9	42.4	8.9	6.9
U.S.	91.2	67.8	35.4	8.8	5.3

Note: Figures are percentages that cover the civilian noninstitutionalized population; (1) Figures cover the Tucson, AZ Metropolitan Statistical Area
Source: U.S. Census Bureau, 2017-2021 American Community Survey 5-Year Estimates

Number of Medical Professionals

Area	MDs[3]	DOs[3,4]	Dentists	Podiatrists	Chiropractors	Optometrists
County[1] (number)	3,893	256	707	62	202	179
County[1] (rate[2])	372.3	24.5	67.2	5.9	19.2	17.0
U.S. (rate[2])	289.3	23.5	72.5	6.2	28.7	17.4

Note: Data as of 2021 unless noted; (1) Data covers Pima County; (2) Rate per 100,000 population; (3) Data as of 2020 and includes all active, non-federal physicians; (4) Doctor of Osteopathic Medicine
Source: U.S. Department of Health and Human Services, Health Resources and Services Administration, Bureau of Health Professions, Area Resource File (ARF) 2021-2022

EDUCATION

Public School District Statistics

District Name	Schls	Pupils	Pupil/ Teacher Ratio	Minority Pupils[1] (%)	LEP/ELL[2] (%)	IEP[3] (%)
Amphitheater Unified District	22	12,396	14.7	57.1	5.8	18.1
Catalina Foothills Unified District	8	5,319	18.7	44.2	1.7	8.9
Flowing Wells Unified District	11	5,450	16.9	76.3	7.6	16.4
Leman Academy of Excellence	7	4,928	n/a	49.2	1.4	7.9
Sunnyside Unified District	22	14,569	18.9	96.7	15.5	12.6
Tanque Verde Unified District	4	2,218	17.3	27.0	0.3	13.1
Tucson Unified District	90	42,002	14.9	81.2	8.5	14.6

Note: Table includes school districts with 2,000 or more students; (1) Percentage of students that are not non-Hispanic white; (2) Percentage of students that are Limited English Proficient or English Language Learners (2018-19); (3) Percentage of students that have an Individualized Education Program (2019-20). Source: U.S. Department of Education, National Center for Education Statistics, Common Core of Data, Local Education Agency (School District) Universe Survey: School Year 2021-2022

Best High Schools

According to *U.S. News,* Tucson is home to two of the top 500 high schools in the U.S.: **University High School (Tucson)** (#28); **BASIS Tucson North** (#54). Nearly 18,000 public, magnet and charter schools were ranked based on their performance on state assessments and how well they prepare students for college. *U.S. News & World Report, "Best High Schools 2022"*

Highest Level of Education

Area	Less than H.S.	H.S. Diploma	Some College, No Deg.	Associate Degree	Bachelor's Degree	Master's Degree	Prof. School Degree	Doctorate Degree
City	13.7	22.8	25.7	8.9	17.5	8.2	1.4	1.8
MSA[1]	10.6	21.4	24.6	9.0	19.7	10.2	2.2	2.2
U.S.	11.1	26.5	20.0	8.7	20.6	9.3	2.2	1.5

Note: Figures cover persons age 25 and over; (1) Figures cover the Tucson, AZ Metropolitan Statistical Area Source: U.S. Census Bureau, 2017-2021 American Community Survey 5-Year Estimates

Educational Attainment by Race

Area	High School Graduate or Higher (%)					Bachelor's Degree or Higher (%)				
	Total	White	Black	Asian	Hisp.[2]	Total	White	Black	Asian	Hisp.[2]
City	86.3	89.9	84.2	87.3	75.0	28.9	32.7	20.8	51.6	15.5
MSA[1]	89.4	92.5	87.6	87.7	77.9	34.4	38.1	27.6	55.7	18.5
U.S.	88.9	91.4	87.2	87.6	71.2	33.7	35.5	23.3	55.6	18.4

Note: Figures shown cover persons 25 years old and over; (1) Figures cover the Tucson, AZ Metropolitan Statistical Area; (2) People of Hispanic origin can be of any race Source: U.S. Census Bureau, 2017-2021 American Community Survey 5-Year Estimates

School Enrollment by Grade and Control

Area	Preschool (%)		Kindergarten (%)		Grades 1 - 4 (%)		Grades 5 - 8 (%)		Grades 9 - 12 (%)	
	Public	Private	Public	Private	Public	Private	Public	Private	Public	Private
City	70.3	29.7	84.3	15.7	86.8	13.2	88.9	11.1	93.6	6.4
MSA[1]	67.5	32.5	85.8	14.2	87.9	12.1	88.9	11.1	91.0	9.0
U.S.	58.8	41.2	86.3	13.7	88.3	11.7	88.6	11.4	89.4	10.6

Note: Figures shown cover persons 3 years old and over; (1) Figures cover the Tucson, AZ Metropolitan Statistical Area Source: U.S. Census Bureau, 2017-2021 American Community Survey 5-Year Estimates

Higher Education

Four-Year Colleges			Two-Year Colleges			Medical Schools[1]	Law Schools[2]	Voc/ Tech[3]
Public	Private Non-profit	Private For-profit	Public	Private Non-profit	Private For-profit			
1	0	3	2	0	2	1	1	7

Note: Figures cover institutions located within the Tucson, AZ Metropolitan Statistical Area and include main campuses only; (1) includes schools accredited by the Liaison Committee on Medical Education and the American Osteopathic Association's Commission on Osteopathic College Accreditation; (2) includes ABA-accredited schools, schools with provisional ABA accreditation, and state accredited schools; (3) includes all schools with programs that are less than 2 years. Source: National Center for Education Statistics, Integrated Postsecondary Education System (IPEDS), 2021-22; Wikipedia, List of Medical Schools in the United States, accessed April 10, 2023; Wikipedia, List of Law Schools in the United States, accessed April 10, 2023

According to *U.S. News & World Report,* the Tucson, AZ metro area is home to one of the top 200 national universities in the U.S.: **University of Arizona** (#105 tie). The indicators used to capture academic quality fall into a number of categories: assessment by administrators at peer institutions; retention of students; faculty resources; student selectivity; financial resources; alumni giving; high school counselor ratings of colleges; and graduation rate. *U.S. News & World Report, "America's Best Colleges 2023"*

According to *U.S. News & World Report,* the Tucson, AZ metro area is home to one of the top 100 law schools in the U.S.: **University of Arizona (Rogers)** (#45). The rankings are based on a weighted average of 12 measures of quality: peer assessment score; assessment score by lawyers/judges; median LSAT scores; median undergrad GPA; acceptance rate; employment rates for graduates; placement success; bar passage rate; faculty resources; expenditures per student; student/faculty ratio; and library resources. *U.S. News & World Report, "America's Best Graduate Schools, Law, 2023"*

According to *U.S. News & World Report,* the Tucson, AZ metro area is home to one of the top 75 medical schools for research in the U.S.: **University of Arizona—Tucson** (#74 tie). The rankings are based on a weighted average of 11 measures of quality: quality assessment; peer assessment score; assessment score by residency directors; research activity; total research activity; average research activity per faculty member; student selectivity; median MCAT total score; median undergraduate GPA; acceptance rate; and faculty resources. *U.S. News & World Report, "America's Best Graduate Schools, Medical, 2023"*

According to *U.S. News & World Report,* the Tucson, AZ metro area is home to one of the top 75 business schools in the U.S.: **University of Arizona (Eller)** (#47 tie). The rankings are based on a weighted average of the following nine measures: quality assessment; peer assessment; recruiter assessment; placement success; mean starting salary and bonus; student selectivity; mean GMAT and GRE scores; mean undergraduate GPA; and acceptance rate. *U.S. News & World Report, "America's Best Graduate Schools, Business, 2023"*

EMPLOYERS

Major Employers

Company Name	Industry
Banner University Medical Center Tucson	General medical & surgical hospitals
Davis-Monthan Air Force Base	U.S. military
Freeport-McMoran Copper & Gold	Mining
Pima County	County government
Raytheon Missile Systems	Missile systems
State of Arizona	State government
Tucson Unified School District	School districts
U.S. Customs and Border Protection	Federal government
University of Arizona	Public research university
Wal-Mart Stores	Retail stores

Note: Companies shown are located within the Tucson, AZ Metropolitan Statistical Area.
Source: Hoovers.com; Wikipedia

PUBLIC SAFETY

Crime Rate

Area	Total Crime	Violent Crime Rate				Property Crime Rate		
		Murder	Rape[3]	Robbery	Aggrav. Assault	Burglary	Larceny -Theft	Motor Vehicle Theft
City	4,319.0	11.1	84.1	177.7	425.3	381.0	2,898.7	341.2
Suburbs[1]	2,196.1	4.9	16.1	37.5	172.4	257.0	1,582.6	125.6
Metro[2]	3,298.3	8.1	51.4	110.3	303.7	321.4	2,265.9	237.5
U.S.	2,356.7	6.5	38.4	73.9	279.7	314.2	1,398.0	246.0

Note: Figures are crimes per 100,000 population; (1) All areas within the metro area that are located outside the city limits; (2) Figures cover the Tucson, AZ Metropolitan Statistical Area; (3) All figures shown were reported using the revised Uniform Crime Reporting (UCR) definition of rape; Due to the transition to the National Incident-Based Reporting System (NIBRS), limited city and metro area data was released for 2021.
Source: FBI Uniform Crime Reports, 2020

Hate Crimes

Area	Number of Quarters Reported	Number of Incidents per Bias Motivation					
		Race/Ethnicity/ Ancestry	Religion	Sexual Orientation	Disability	Gender	Gender Identity
City	n/a	n/a	n/a	n/a	n/a	n/a	n/a
U.S.	4	5,227	1,244	1,110	130	75	266

Note: n/a not available; Due to the transition to the National Incident-Based Reporting System (NIBRS), limited crime data was released for 2021.
Source: Federal Bureau of Investigation, Hate Crime Statistics 2020

Identity Theft Consumer Reports

Area	Reports	Reports per 100,000 Population	Rank[2]
MSA[1]	1,890	182	193
U.S.	1,108,609	339	-

Note: (1) Figures cover the Tucson, AZ Metropolitan Statistical Area; (2) Rank ranges from 1 to 391 where 1 indicates greatest number of identity theft reports per 100,000 population
Source: Federal Trade Commission, Consumer Sentinel Network Data Book 2022

Fraud and Other Consumer Reports

Area	Reports	Reports per 100,000 Population	Rank[2]
MSA[1]	10,093	972	107
U.S.	4,064,520	1,245	-

Note: (1) Figures cover the Tucson, AZ Metropolitan Statistical Area; (2) Rank ranges from 1 to 391 where 1 indicates greatest number of fraud and other consumer reports per 100,000 population
Source: Federal Trade Commission, Consumer Sentinel Network Data Book 2022

POLITICS

2020 Presidential Election Results

Area	Biden	Trump	Jorgensen	Hawkins	Other
Pima County	58.4	39.8	1.5	0.0	0.3
U.S.	51.3	46.8	1.2	0.3	0.5

Note: Results are percentages and may not add to 100% due to rounding
Source: Dave Leip's Atlas of U.S. Presidential Elections

SPORTS

Professional Sports Teams

Team Name	League	Year Established

No teams are located in the metro area
Source: Wikipedia, Major Professional Sports Teams of the United States and Canada, April 12, 2023

CLIMATE

Average and Extreme Temperatures

Temperature	Jan	Feb	Mar	Apr	May	Jun	Jul	Aug	Sep	Oct	Nov	Dec	Yr.
Extreme High (°F)	87	92	99	104	107	117	114	108	107	101	90	84	117
Average High (°F)	64	68	73	81	89	99	99	96	94	84	73	65	82
Average Temp. (°F)	51	54	59	66	74	84	86	84	81	71	59	52	69
Average Low (°F)	38	40	44	51	58	68	74	72	67	57	45	39	55
Extreme Low (°F)	16	20	20	33	38	47	62	61	44	26	24	16	16

Note: Figures cover the years 1946-1990
Source: National Climatic Data Center, International Station Meteorological Climate Summary, 9/96

Average Precipitation/Snowfall/Humidity

Precip./Humidity	Jan	Feb	Mar	Apr	May	Jun	Jul	Aug	Sep	Oct	Nov	Dec	Yr.
Avg. Precip. (in.)	0.9	0.7	0.7	0.3	0.1	0.2	2.5	2.2	1.4	0.9	0.6	0.9	11.6
Avg. Snowfall (in.)	Tr	Tr	Tr	Tr	0	0	0	0	0	0	Tr	Tr	2
Avg. Rel. Hum. 5am (%)	62	58	52	41	34	32	58	65	55	52	54	61	52
Avg. Rel. Hum. 5pm (%)	31	26	22	16	13	13	29	32	26	24	27	33	24

Note: Figures cover the years 1946-1990; Tr = Trace amounts (<0.05 in. of rain; <0.5 in. of snow)
Source: National Climatic Data Center, International Station Meteorological Climate Summary, 9/96

Weather Conditions

Temperature			Daytime Sky			Precipitation		
10°F & below	32°F & below	90°F & above	Clear	Partly cloudy	Cloudy	0.01 inch or more precip.	0.1 inch or more snow/ice	Thunder-storms
0	18	140	177	119	69	54	2	42

Note: Figures are average number of days per year and cover the years 1946-1990
Source: National Climatic Data Center, International Station Meteorological Climate Summary, 9/96

HAZARDOUS WASTE

Superfund Sites

The Tucson, AZ metro area has no sites on the EPA's Superfund Final National Priorities List. There are a total of 1,165 Superfund sites with a status of proposed or final on the list in the U.S. *U.S. Environmental Protection Agency, National Priorities List, April 12, 2023*

AIR QUALITY

Air Quality Trends: Ozone

	1990	1995	2000	2005	2010	2015	2018	2019	2020	2021
MSA[1]	0.073	0.078	0.074	0.075	0.068	0.065	0.069	0.065	0.070	0.068
U.S.	0.087	0.089	0.081	0.080	0.072	0.067	0.069	0.065	0.065	0.067

Note: (1) Data covers the Tucson, AZ Metropolitan Statistical Area. The values shown are the composite ozone concentration averages among trend sites based on the highest fourth daily maximum 8-hour concentration in parts per million. These trends are based on sites having an adequate record of monitoring data during the trend period. Data from exceptional events are included.
Source: U.S. Environmental Protection Agency, Air Quality Monitoring Information, "Air Quality Trends by City, 1990-2021"

Air Quality Index

Area	Percent of Days when Air Quality was...[2]					AQI Statistics[2]	
	Good	Moderate	Unhealthy for Sensitive Groups	Unhealthy	Very Unhealthy	Maximum	Median
MSA[1]	39.2	57.0	3.6	0.0	0.0	315	53

Note: (1) Data covers the Tucson, AZ Metropolitan Statistical Area; (2) Based on 365 days with AQI data in 2021. Air Quality Index (AQI) is an index for reporting daily air quality. EPA calculates the AQI for five major air pollutants regulated by the Clean Air Act: ground-level ozone, particle pollution (aka particulate matter), carbon monoxide, sulfur dioxide, and nitrogen dioxide. The AQI runs from 0 to 500. The higher the AQI value, the greater the level of air pollution and the greater the health concern. There are six AQI categories: "Good" AQI is between 0 and 50. Air quality is considered satisfactory; "Moderate" AQI is between 51 and 100. Air quality is acceptable; "Unhealthy for Sensitive Groups" When AQI values are between 101 and 150, members of sensitive groups may experience health effects; "Unhealthy" When AQI values are between 151 and 200 everyone may begin to experience health effects; "Very Unhealthy" AQI values between 201 and 300 trigger a health alert; "Hazardous" AQI values over 300 trigger warnings of emergency conditions (not shown).
Source: U.S. Environmental Protection Agency, Air Quality Index Report, 2021

Air Quality Index Pollutants

Area	Percent of Days when AQI Pollutant was...[2]					
	Carbon Monoxide	Nitrogen Dioxide	Ozone	Sulfur Dioxide	Particulate Matter 2.5	Particulate Matter 10
MSA[1]	0.0	0.0	54.8	(3)	15.9	29.3

Note: (1) Data covers the Tucson, AZ Metropolitan Statistical Area; (2) Based on 365 days with AQI data in 2021. The Air Quality Index (AQI) is an index for reporting daily air quality. EPA calculates the AQI for five major air pollutants regulated by the Clean Air Act: ground-level ozone, particle pollution (also known as particulate matter), carbon monoxide, sulfur dioxide, and nitrogen dioxide. The AQI runs from 0 to 500. The higher the AQI value, the greater the level of air pollution and the greater the health concern; (3) Sulfur dioxide is no longer included in this table (as of December 8, 2021) because SO_2 concentrations tend to be very localized and not necessarily representative of broad geographical areas like counties and CBSAs.
Source: U.S. Environmental Protection Agency, Air Quality Index Report, 2021

Maximum Air Pollutant Concentrations: Particulate Matter, Ozone, CO and Lead

	Particulate Matter 10 (ug/m³)	Particulate Matter 2.5 Wtd AM (ug/m³)	Particulate Matter 2.5 24-Hr (ug/m³)	Ozone (ppm)	Carbon Monoxide (ppm)	Lead (ug/m³)
MSA[1] Level	249	6.6	14	0.068	1	n/a
NAAQS[2]	150	15	35	0.075	9	0.15
Met NAAQS[2]	No	Yes	Yes	Yes	Yes	n/a

Note: (1) Data covers the Tucson, AZ Metropolitan Statistical Area; Data from exceptional events are included; (2) National Ambient Air Quality Standards; ppm = parts per million; ug/m³ = micrograms per cubic meter; n/a not available.
Concentrations: Particulate Matter 10 (coarse particulate)—highest second maximum 24-hour concentration; Particulate Matter 2.5 Wtd AM (fine particulate)—highest weighted annual mean concentration; Particulate Matter 2.5 24-Hour (fine particulate)—highest 98th percentile 24-hour concentration; Ozone—highest fourth daily maximum 8-hour concentration; Carbon Monoxide—highest second maximum non-overlapping 8-hour concentration; Lead—maximum running 3-month average
Source: U.S. Environmental Protection Agency, Air Quality Monitoring Information, "Air Quality Statistics by City, 2021"

Maximum Air Pollutant Concentrations: Nitrogen Dioxide and Sulfur Dioxide

	Nitrogen Dioxide AM (ppb)	Nitrogen Dioxide 1-Hr (ppb)	Sulfur Dioxide AM (ppb)	Sulfur Dioxide 1-Hr (ppb)	Sulfur Dioxide 24-Hr (ppb)
MSA[1] Level	8	38	n/a	1	n/a
NAAQS[2]	53	100	30	75	140
Met NAAQS[2]	Yes	Yes	n/a	Yes	n/a

Note: (1) Data covers the Tucson, AZ Metropolitan Statistical Area; Data from exceptional events are included; (2) National Ambient Air Quality Standards; ppm = parts per million; ug/m^3 = micrograms per cubic meter; n/a not available.
Concentrations: Nitrogen Dioxide AM—highest arithmetic mean concentration; Nitrogen Dioxide 1-Hr—highest 98th percentile 1-hour daily maximum concentration; Sulfur Dioxide AM—highest annual mean concentration; Sulfur Dioxide 1-Hr—highest 99th percentile 1-hour daily maximum concentration; Sulfur Dioxide 24-Hr—highest second maximum 24-hour concentration
Source: U.S. Environmental Protection Agency, Air Quality Monitoring Information, "Air Quality Statistics by City, 2021"

Appendixes

Appendix A: Comparative Statistics

Table of Contents

Population Growth: City

Area	1990 Census	2000 Census	2010 Census	2020 Census	Population Growth (%) 1990-2020	2010-2020
Albuquerque, NM	388,375	448,607	545,852	564,559	45.4	3.4
Allentown, PA	105,066	106,632	118,032	125,845	19.8	6.6
Anchorage, AK	226,338	260,283	291,826	291,247	28.7	-0.2
Ann Arbor, MI	111,018	114,024	113,934	123,851	11.6	8.7
Athens, GA	86,561	100,266	115,452	127,315	47.1	10.3
Atlanta, GA	394,092	416,474	420,003	498,715	26.5	18.7
Austin, TX	499,053	656,562	790,390	961,855	92.7	21.7
Baltimore, MD	736,014	651,154	620,961	585,708	-20.4	-5.7
Boise City, ID	144,317	185,787	205,671	235,684	63.3	14.6
Boston, MA	574,283	589,141	617,594	675,647	17.7	9.4
Boulder, CO	87,737	94,673	97,385	108,250	23.4	11.2
Brownsville, TX	114,025	139,722	175,023	186,738	63.8	6.7
Cape Coral, FL	75,507	102,286	154,305	194,016	157.0	25.7
Cedar Rapids, IA	110,829	120,758	126,326	137,710	24.3	9.0
Charleston, SC	96,102	96,650	120,083	150,227	56.3	25.1
Charlotte, NC	428,283	540,828	731,424	874,579	104.2	19.6
Chicago, IL	2,783,726	2,896,016	2,695,598	2,746,388	-1.3	1.9
Cincinnati, OH	363,974	331,285	296,943	309,317	-15.0	4.2
Clarksville, TN	78,569	103,455	132,929	166,722	112.2	25.4
Cleveland, OH	505,333	478,403	396,815	372,624	-26.3	-6.1
College Station, TX	53,318	67,890	93,857	120,511	126.0	28.4
Colorado Springs, CO	283,798	360,890	416,427	478,961	68.8	15.0
Columbia, MO	71,069	84,531	108,500	126,254	77.6	16.4
Columbia, SC	115,475	116,278	129,272	136,632	18.3	5.7
Columbus, OH	648,656	711,470	787,033	905,748	39.6	15.1
Dallas, TX	1,006,971	1,188,580	1,197,816	1,304,379	29.5	8.9
Davenport, IA	95,705	98,359	99,685	101,724	6.3	2.0
Denver, CO	467,153	554,636	600,158	715,522	53.2	19.2
Des Moines, IA	193,569	198,682	203,433	214,133	10.6	5.3
Durham, NC	151,737	187,035	228,330	283,506	86.8	24.2
Edison, NJ	88,680	97,687	99,967	107,588	21.3	7.6
El Paso, TX	515,541	563,662	649,121	678,815	31.7	4.6
Fargo, ND	74,372	90,599	105,549	125,990	69.4	19.4
Fort Collins, CO	89,555	118,652	143,986	169,810	89.6	17.9
Fort Wayne, IN	205,671	205,727	253,691	263,886	28.3	4.0
Fort Worth, TX	448,311	534,694	741,206	918,915	105.0	24.0
Grand Rapids, MI	189,145	197,800	188,040	198,917	5.2	5.8
Greeley, CO	60,887	76,930	92,889	108,795	78.7	17.1
Green Bay, WI	96,466	102,313	104,057	107,395	11.3	3.2
Greensboro, NC	193,389	223,891	269,666	299,035	54.6	10.9
Honolulu, HI	376,465	371,657	337,256	350,964	-6.8	4.1
Houston, TX	1,697,610	1,953,631	2,099,451	2,304,580	35.8	9.8
Huntsville, AL	161,842	158,216	180,105	215,006	32.8	19.4
Indianapolis, IN	730,993	781,870	820,445	887,642	21.4	8.2
Jacksonville, FL	635,221	735,617	821,784	949,611	49.5	15.6
Kansas City, MO	434,967	441,545	459,787	508,090	16.8	10.5
Lafayette, LA	104,735	110,257	120,623	121,374	15.9	0.6
Las Cruces, NM	63,267	74,267	97,618	111,385	76.1	14.1
Las Vegas, NV	261,374	478,434	583,756	641,903	145.6	10.0
Lexington, KY	225,366	260,512	295,803	322,570	43.1	9.0
Lincoln, NE	193,629	225,581	258,379	291,082	50.3	12.7
Little Rock, AR	177,519	183,133	193,524	202,591	14.1	4.7
Los Angeles, CA	3,487,671	3,694,820	3,792,621	3,898,747	11.8	2.8
Louisville, KY	269,160	256,231	597,337	386,884	43.7	-35.2
Madison, WI	193,451	208,054	233,209	269,840	39.5	15.7

Table continued on following page.

Area	1990 Census	2000 Census	2010 Census	2020 Census	Population Growth (%) 1990-2020	Population Growth (%) 2010-2020
Manchester, NH	99,567	107,006	109,565	115,644	16.1	5.5
Miami, FL	358,843	362,470	399,457	442,241	23.2	10.7
Midland, TX	89,358	94,996	111,147	132,524	48.3	19.2
Milwaukee, WI	628,095	596,974	594,833	577,222	-8.1	-3.0
Minneapolis, MN	368,383	382,618	382,578	429,954	16.7	12.4
Nashville, TN	488,364	545,524	601,222	689,447	41.2	14.7
New Haven, CT	130,474	123,626	129,779	134,023	2.7	3.3
New Orleans, LA	496,938	484,674	343,829	383,997	-22.7	11.7
New York, NY	7,322,552	8,008,278	8,175,133	8,804,190	20.2	7.7
Oklahoma City, OK	445,065	506,132	579,999	681,054	53.0	17.4
Omaha, NE	371,972	390,007	408,958	486,051	30.7	18.9
Orlando, FL	161,172	185,951	238,300	307,573	90.8	29.1
Philadelphia, PA	1,585,577	1,517,550	1,526,006	1,603,797	1.1	5.1
Phoenix, AZ	989,873	1,321,045	1,445,632	1,608,139	62.5	11.2
Pittsburgh, PA	369,785	334,563	305,704	302,971	-18.1	-0.9
Portland, OR	485,833	529,121	583,776	652,503	34.3	11.8
Providence, RI	160,734	173,618	178,042	190,934	18.8	7.2
Provo, UT	87,148	105,166	112,488	115,162	32.1	2.4
Raleigh, NC	226,841	276,093	403,892	467,665	106.2	15.8
Reno, NV	139,950	180,480	225,221	264,165	88.8	17.3
Richmond, VA	202,783	197,790	204,214	226,610	11.7	11.0
Rochester, MN	74,151	85,806	106,769	121,395	63.7	13.7
Sacramento, CA	368,923	407,018	466,488	524,943	42.3	12.5
St. Louis, MO	396,685	348,189	319,294	301,578	-24.0	-5.5
Salem, OR	112,046	136,924	154,637	175,535	56.7	13.5
Salt Lake City, UT	159,796	181,743	186,440	199,723	25.0	7.1
San Antonio, TX	997,258	1,144,646	1,327,407	1,434,625	43.9	8.1
San Diego, CA	1,111,048	1,223,400	1,307,402	1,386,932	24.8	6.1
San Francisco, CA	723,959	776,733	805,235	873,965	20.7	8.5
San Jose, CA	784,324	894,943	945,942	1,013,240	29.2	7.1
Santa Rosa, CA	123,297	147,595	167,815	178,127	44.5	6.1
Savannah, GA	138,038	131,510	136,286	147,780	7.1	8.4
Seattle, WA	516,262	563,374	608,660	737,015	42.8	21.1
Sioux Falls, SD	102,262	123,975	153,888	192,517	88.3	25.1
Springfield, IL	108,997	111,454	116,250	114,394	5.0	-1.6
Tampa, FL	279,960	303,447	335,709	384,959	37.5	14.7
Tucson, AZ	417,942	486,699	520,116	542,629	29.8	4.3
Tulsa, OK	367,241	393,049	391,906	413,066	12.5	5.4
Tuscaloosa, AL	81,075	77,906	90,468	99,600	22.8	10.1
Virginia Beach, VA	393,069	425,257	437,994	459,470	16.9	4.9
Washington, DC	606,900	572,059	601,723	689,545	13.6	14.6
Wichita, KS	313,693	344,284	382,368	397,532	26.7	4.0
Wilmington, NC	64,609	75,838	106,476	115,451	78.7	8.4
Winston-Salem, NC	168,139	185,776	229,617	249,545	48.4	8.7
Worcester, MA	169,759	172,648	181,045	206,518	21.7	14.1
U.S.	248,709,873	281,421,906	308,745,538	331,449,281	33.3	7.4

Source: U.S. Census Bureau, 1990 Census,, 2000 Census,, 2010 Census,, 2020 Census

Population Growth: Metro Area

Area	1990 Census	2000 Census	2010 Census	2020 Census	Population Growth (%) 1990-2020	Population Growth (%) 2010-2020
Albuquerque, NM	599,416	729,649	887,077	916,528	52.9	3.3
Allentown, PA	686,666	740,395	821,173	861,889	25.5	5.0
Anchorage, AK	266,021	319,605	380,821	398,328	49.7	4.6
Ann Arbor, MI	282,937	322,895	344,791	372,258	31.6	8.0
Athens, GA	136,025	166,079	192,541	215,415	58.4	11.9
Atlanta, GA	3,069,411	4,247,981	5,268,860	6,089,815	98.4	15.6
Austin, TX	846,217	1,249,763	1,716,289	2,283,371	169.8	33.0
Baltimore, MD	2,382,172	2,552,994	2,710,489	2,844,510	19.4	4.9
Boise City, ID	319,596	464,840	616,561	764,718	139.3	24.0
Boston, MA	4,133,895	4,391,344	4,552,402	4,941,632	19.5	8.5
Boulder, CO	208,898	269,758	294,567	330,758	58.3	12.3
Brownsville, TX	260,120	335,227	406,220	421,017	61.9	3.6
Cape Coral, FL	335,113	440,888	618,754	760,822	127.0	23.0
Cedar Rapids, IA	210,640	237,230	257,940	276,520	31.3	7.2
Charleston, SC	506,875	549,033	664,607	799,636	57.8	20.3
Charlotte, NC	1,024,331	1,330,448	1,758,038	2,660,329	159.7	51.3
Chicago, IL	8,182,076	9,098,316	9,461,105	9,618,502	17.6	1.7
Cincinnati, OH	1,844,917	2,009,632	2,130,151	2,256,884	22.3	5.9
Clarksville, TN	189,277	232,000	273,949	320,535	69.3	17.0
Cleveland, OH	2,102,219	2,148,143	2,077,240	2,088,251	-0.7	0.5
College Station, TX	150,998	184,885	228,660	268,248	77.7	17.3
Colorado Springs, CO	409,482	537,484	645,613	755,105	84.4	17.0
Columbia, MO	122,010	145,666	172,786	210,864	72.8	22.0
Columbia, SC	548,325	647,158	767,598	829,470	51.3	8.1
Columbus, OH	1,405,176	1,612,694	1,836,536	2,138,926	52.2	16.5
Dallas, TX	3,989,294	5,161,544	6,371,773	7,637,387	91.4	19.9
Davenport, IA	368,151	376,019	379,690	384,324	4.4	1.2
Denver, CO	1,666,935	2,179,296	2,543,482	2,963,821	77.8	16.5
Des Moines, IA	416,346	481,394	569,633	709,466	70.4	24.5
Durham, NC	344,646	426,493	504,357	649,903	88.6	28.9
Edison, NJ	16,845,992	18,323,002	18,897,109	20,140,470	19.6	6.6
El Paso, TX	591,610	679,622	800,647	868,859	46.9	8.5
Fargo, ND	153,296	174,367	208,777	249,843	63.0	19.7
Fort Collins, CO	186,136	251,494	299,630	359,066	92.9	19.8
Fort Wayne, IN	354,435	390,156	416,257	419,601	18.4	0.8
Fort Worth, TX	3,989,294	5,161,544	6,371,773	7,637,387	91.4	19.9
Grand Rapids, MI	645,914	740,482	774,160	1,087,592	68.4	40.5
Greeley, CO	131,816	180,926	252,825	328,981	149.6	30.1
Green Bay, WI	243,698	282,599	306,241	328,268	34.7	7.2
Greensboro, NC	540,257	643,430	723,801	776,566	43.7	7.3
Honolulu, HI	836,231	876,156	953,207	1,016,508	21.6	6.6
Houston, TX	3,767,335	4,715,407	5,946,800	7,122,240	89.1	19.8
Huntsville, AL	293,047	342,376	417,593	491,723	67.8	17.8
Indianapolis, IN	1,294,217	1,525,104	1,756,241	2,111,040	63.1	20.2
Jacksonville, FL	925,213	1,122,750	1,345,596	1,605,848	73.6	19.3
Kansas City, MO	1,636,528	1,836,038	2,035,334	2,192,035	33.9	7.7
Lafayette, LA	208,740	239,086	273,738	478,384	129.2	74.8
Las Cruces, NM	135,510	174,682	209,233	219,561	62.0	4.9
Las Vegas, NV	741,459	1,375,765	1,951,269	2,265,461	205.5	16.1
Lexington, KY	348,428	408,326	472,099	516,811	48.3	9.5
Lincoln, NE	229,091	266,787	302,157	340,217	48.5	12.6
Little Rock, AR	535,034	610,518	699,757	748,031	39.8	6.9
Los Angeles, CA	11,273,720	12,365,627	12,828,837	13,200,998	17.1	2.9
Louisville, KY	1,055,973	1,161,975	1,283,566	1,285,439	21.7	0.1
Madison, WI	432,323	501,774	568,593	680,796	57.5	19.7

Table continued on following page.

Area	1990 Census	2000 Census	2010 Census	2020 Census	Population Growth (%) 1990-2020	2010-2020
Manchester, NH	336,073	380,841	400,721	422,937	25.8	5.5
Miami, FL	4,056,100	5,007,564	5,564,635	6,138,333	51.3	10.3
Midland, TX	106,611	116,009	136,872	175,220	64.4	28.0
Milwaukee, WI	1,432,149	1,500,741	1,555,908	1,574,731	10.0	1.2
Minneapolis, MN	2,538,834	2,968,806	3,279,833	3,690,261	45.4	12.5
Nashville, TN	1,048,218	1,311,789	1,589,934	1,989,519	89.8	25.1
New Haven, CT	804,219	824,008	862,477	864,835	7.5	0.3
New Orleans, LA	1,264,391	1,316,510	1,167,764	1,271,845	0.6	8.9
New York, NY	16,845,992	18,323,002	18,897,109	20,140,470	19.6	6.6
Oklahoma City, OK	971,042	1,095,421	1,252,987	1,425,695	46.8	13.8
Omaha, NE	685,797	767,041	865,350	967,604	41.1	11.8
Orlando, FL	1,224,852	1,644,561	2,134,411	2,673,376	118.3	25.3
Philadelphia, PA	5,435,470	5,687,147	5,965,343	6,245,051	14.9	4.7
Phoenix, AZ	2,238,480	3,251,876	4,192,887	4,845,832	116.5	15.6
Pittsburgh, PA	2,468,289	2,431,087	2,356,285	2,370,930	-3.9	0.6
Portland, OR	1,523,741	1,927,881	2,226,009	2,512,859	64.9	12.9
Providence, RI	1,509,789	1,582,997	1,600,852	1,676,579	11.0	4.7
Provo, UT	269,407	376,774	526,810	671,185	149.1	27.4
Raleigh, NC	541,081	797,071	1,130,490	1,413,982	161.3	25.1
Reno, NV	257,193	342,885	425,417	490,596	90.8	15.3
Richmond, VA	949,244	1,096,957	1,258,251	1,314,434	38.5	4.5
Rochester, MN	141,945	163,618	186,011	226,329	59.4	21.7
Sacramento, CA	1,481,126	1,796,857	2,149,127	2,397,382	61.9	11.6
St. Louis, MO	2,580,897	2,698,687	2,812,896	2,820,253	9.3	0.3
Salem, OR	278,024	347,214	390,738	433,353	55.9	10.9
Salt Lake City, UT	768,075	968,858	1,124,197	1,257,936	63.8	11.9
San Antonio, TX	1,407,745	1,711,703	2,142,508	2,558,143	81.7	19.4
San Diego, CA	2,498,016	2,813,833	3,095,313	3,298,634	32.1	6.6
San Francisco, CA	3,686,592	4,123,740	4,335,391	4,749,008	28.8	9.5
San Jose, CA	1,534,280	1,735,819	1,836,911	2,000,468	30.4	8.9
Santa Rosa, CA	388,222	458,614	483,878	488,863	25.9	1.0
Savannah, GA	258,060	293,000	347,611	404,798	56.9	16.5
Seattle, WA	2,559,164	3,043,878	3,439,809	4,018,762	57.0	16.8
Sioux Falls, SD	153,500	187,093	228,261	276,730	80.3	21.2
Springfield, IL	189,550	201,437	210,170	208,640	10.1	-0.7
Tampa, FL	2,067,959	2,395,997	2,783,243	3,175,275	53.5	14.1
Tucson, AZ	666,880	843,746	980,263	1,043,433	56.5	6.4
Tulsa, OK	761,019	859,532	937,478	1,015,331	33.4	8.3
Tuscaloosa, AL	176,123	192,034	219,461	268,674	52.5	22.4
Virginia Beach, VA	1,449,389	1,576,370	1,671,683	1,799,674	24.2	7.7
Washington, DC	4,122,914	4,796,183	5,582,170	6,385,162	54.9	14.4
Wichita, KS	511,111	571,166	623,061	647,610	26.7	3.9
Wilmington, NC	200,124	274,532	362,315	285,905	42.9	-21.1
Winston-Salem, NC	361,091	421,961	477,717	675,966	87.2	41.5
Worcester, MA	709,728	750,963	798,552	978,529	37.9	22.5
U.S.	248,709,873	281,421,906	308,745,538	331,449,281	33.3	7.4

Note: Figures cover the Metropolitan Statistical Area (MSA)
Source: U.S. Census Bureau, 1990 Census,, 2000 Census,, 2010 Census,, 2020 Census

Male/Female Ratio: City

City	Males	Females	Males per 100 Females
Albuquerque, NM	274,173	290,386	94.4
Allentown, PA	60,577	65,268	92.8
Anchorage, AK	147,894	143,353	103.2
Ann Arbor, MI	61,263	62,588	97.9
Athens, GA	59,963	67,352	89.0
Atlanta, GA	245,444	253,271	96.9
Austin, TX	485,739	476,116	102.0
Baltimore, MD	274,635	311,073	88.3
Boise City, ID	116,758	118,926	98.2
Boston, MA	319,326	356,321	89.6
Boulder, CO	55,982	52,268	107.1
Brownsville, TX	89,293	97,445	91.6
Cape Coral, FL	95,028	98,988	96.0
Cedar Rapids, IA	67,218	70,492	95.4
Charleston, SC	71,681	78,546	91.3
Charlotte, NC	421,316	453,263	93.0
Chicago, IL	1,332,725	1,413,663	94.3
Cincinnati, OH	149,736	159,581	93.8
Clarksville, TN	81,849	84,873	96.4
Cleveland, OH	180,991	191,633	94.4
College Station, TX	61,203	59,308	103.2
Colorado Springs, CO	236,731	242,230	97.7
Columbia, MO	60,766	65,488	92.8
Columbia, SC	67,155	69,477	96.7
Columbus, OH	441,869	463,879	95.3
Dallas, TX	647,963	656,416	98.7
Davenport, IA	49,751	51,973	95.7
Denver, CO	358,405	357,117	100.4
Des Moines, IA	105,618	108,515	97.3
Durham, NC	133,353	150,153	88.8
Edison, NJ	53,123	54,465	97.5
El Paso, TX	326,540	352,275	92.7
Fargo, ND	63,707	62,283	102.3
Fort Collins, CO	84,217	85,593	98.4
Fort Wayne, IN	128,678	135,208	95.2
Fort Worth, TX	449,923	468,992	95.9
Grand Rapids, MI	97,037	101,880	95.2
Greeley, CO	53,848	54,947	98.0
Green Bay, WI	53,407	53,988	98.9
Greensboro, NC	138,465	160,570	86.2
Honolulu, HI	172,783	178,181	97.0
Houston, TX	1,140,598	1,163,982	98.0
Huntsville, AL	104,200	110,806	94.0
Indianapolis, IN	430,358	457,284	94.1
Jacksonville, FL	459,204	490,407	93.6
Kansas City, MO	247,776	260,314	95.2
Lafayette, LA	58,213	63,161	92.2
Las Cruces, NM	53,571	57,814	92.7
Las Vegas, NV	317,700	324,203	98.0
Lexington, KY	155,876	166,694	93.5
Lincoln, NE	145,790	145,292	100.3
Little Rock, AR	96,018	106,573	90.1
Los Angeles, CA	1,925,675	1,973,072	97.6
Louisville, KY	186,813	200,071	93.4
Madison, WI	133,922	135,918	98.5

Table continued on following page.

City	Males	Females	Males per 100 Females
Manchester, NH	57,668	57,976	99.5
Miami, FL	218,706	223,535	97.8
Midland, TX	66,552	65,972	100.9
Milwaukee, WI	278,386	298,836	93.2
Minneapolis, MN	216,381	213,573	101.3
Nashville, TN	332,568	356,879	93.2
New Haven, CT	64,141	69,882	91.8
New Orleans, LA	181,171	202,826	89.3
New York, NY	4,184,548	4,619,642	90.6
Oklahoma City, OK	335,613	345,441	97.2
Omaha, NE	239,675	246,376	97.3
Orlando, FL	148,481	159,092	93.3
Philadelphia, PA	760,383	843,414	90.2
Phoenix, AZ	799,456	808,683	98.9
Pittsburgh, PA	148,157	154,814	95.7
Portland, OR	322,690	329,813	97.8
Providence, RI	92,861	98,073	94.7
Provo, UT	56,944	58,218	97.8
Raleigh, NC	224,994	242,671	92.7
Reno, NV	134,002	130,163	102.9
Richmond, VA	107,678	118,932	90.5
Rochester, MN	58,643	62,752	93.5
Sacramento, CA	255,987	268,956	95.2
St. Louis, MO	147,340	154,238	95.5
Salem, OR	87,574	87,961	99.6
Salt Lake City, UT	102,530	97,193	105.5
San Antonio, TX	699,905	734,720	95.3
San Diego, CA	694,107	692,825	100.2
San Francisco, CA	446,144	427,821	104.3
San Jose, CA	509,260	503,980	101.0
Santa Rosa, CA	86,767	91,360	95.0
Savannah, GA	69,878	77,902	89.7
Seattle, WA	371,247	365,768	101.5
Sioux Falls, SD	95,676	96,841	98.8
Springfield, IL	54,215	60,179	90.1
Tampa, FL	187,761	197,198	95.2
Tucson, AZ	269,110	273,519	98.4
Tulsa, OK	201,814	211,252	95.5
Tuscaloosa, AL	47,020	52,580	89.4
Virginia Beach, VA	224,059	235,411	95.2
Washington, DC	322,777	366,768	88.0
Wichita, KS	196,575	200,957	97.8
Wilmington, NC	54,189	61,262	88.5
Winston-Salem, NC	116,698	132,847	87.8
Worcester, MA	100,540	105,978	94.9
U.S.	162,685,811	168,763,470	96.4

Source: U.S. Census Bureau, 2020 Census

Male/Female Ratio: Metro Area

Metro Area	Males	Females	Males per 100 Females
Albuquerque, NM	449,092	467,436	96.1
Allentown, PA	419,780	442,109	94.9
Anchorage, AK	203,277	195,051	104.2
Ann Arbor, MI	182,825	189,433	96.5
Athens, GA	103,235	112,180	92.0
Atlanta, GA	2,933,974	3,155,841	93.0
Austin, TX	1,138,942	1,144,429	99.5
Baltimore, MD	1,365,439	1,479,071	92.3
Boise City, ID	380,892	383,826	99.2
Boston, MA	2,390,705	2,550,927	93.7
Boulder, CO	166,794	163,964	101.7
Brownsville, TX	203,223	217,794	93.3
Cape Coral, FL	371,444	389,378	95.4
Cedar Rapids, IA	136,845	139,675	98.0
Charleston, SC	389,850	409,786	95.1
Charlotte, NC	1,289,221	1,371,108	94.0
Chicago, IL	4,694,560	4,923,942	95.3
Cincinnati, OH	1,107,410	1,149,474	96.3
Clarksville, TN	159,552	160,983	99.1
Cleveland, OH	1,008,568	1,079,683	93.4
College Station, TX	134,329	133,919	100.3
Colorado Springs, CO	379,052	376,053	100.8
Columbia, MO	102,929	107,935	95.4
Columbia, SC	398,440	431,030	92.4
Columbus, OH	1,050,767	1,088,159	96.6
Dallas, TX	3,753,384	3,884,003	96.6
Davenport, IA	189,247	195,077	97.0
Denver, CO	1,481,349	1,482,472	99.9
Des Moines, IA	349,805	359,661	97.3
Durham, NC	312,256	337,647	92.5
Edison, NJ	9,693,702	10,446,768	92.8
El Paso, TX	422,688	446,171	94.7
Fargo, ND	125,674	124,169	101.2
Fort Collins, CO	177,804	181,262	98.1
Fort Wayne, IN	205,785	213,816	96.2
Fort Worth, TX	3,753,384	3,884,003	96.6
Grand Rapids, MI	540,561	547,031	98.8
Greeley, CO	164,843	164,138	100.4
Green Bay, WI	163,689	164,579	99.5
Greensboro, NC	370,483	406,083	91.2
Honolulu, HI	509,569	506,939	100.5
Houston, TX	3,505,374	3,616,866	96.9
Huntsville, AL	241,092	250,631	96.2
Indianapolis, IN	1,033,439	1,077,601	95.9
Jacksonville, FL	779,083	826,765	94.2
Kansas City, MO	1,076,104	1,115,931	96.4
Lafayette, LA	231,864	246,520	94.1
Las Cruces, NM	107,150	112,411	95.3
Las Vegas, NV	1,126,444	1,139,017	98.9
Lexington, KY	250,691	266,120	94.2
Lincoln, NE	170,718	169,499	100.7
Little Rock, AR	361,694	386,337	93.6
Los Angeles, CA	6,469,965	6,731,033	96.1
Louisville, KY	628,220	657,219	95.6
Madison, WI	338,757	342,039	99.0

Table continued on following page.

Metro Area	Males	Females	Males per 100 Females
Manchester, NH	209,879	213,058	98.5
Miami, FL	2,954,448	3,183,885	92.8
Midland, TX	88,457	86,763	102.0
Milwaukee, WI	766,278	808,453	94.8
Minneapolis, MN	1,824,100	1,866,161	97.7
Nashville, TN	968,381	1,021,138	94.8
New Haven, CT	415,391	449,444	92.4
New Orleans, LA	610,653	661,192	92.4
New York, NY	9,693,702	10,446,768	92.8
Oklahoma City, OK	702,324	723,371	97.1
Omaha, NE	478,627	488,977	97.9
Orlando, FL	1,296,256	1,377,120	94.1
Philadelphia, PA	3,015,319	3,229,732	93.4
Phoenix, AZ	2,395,320	2,450,512	97.7
Pittsburgh, PA	1,157,964	1,212,966	95.5
Portland, OR	1,240,947	1,271,912	97.6
Providence, RI	812,496	864,083	94.0
Provo, UT	336,952	334,233	100.8
Raleigh, NC	687,440	726,542	94.6
Reno, NV	247,924	242,672	102.2
Richmond, VA	632,849	681,585	92.8
Rochester, MN	111,433	114,896	97.0
Sacramento, CA	1,170,850	1,226,532	95.5
St. Louis, MO	1,369,631	1,450,622	94.4
Salem, OR	214,703	218,650	98.2
Salt Lake City, UT	632,295	625,641	101.1
San Antonio, TX	1,254,014	1,304,129	96.2
San Diego, CA	1,642,796	1,655,838	99.2
San Francisco, CA	2,344,775	2,404,233	97.5
San Jose, CA	1,007,254	993,214	101.4
Santa Rosa, CA	238,535	250,328	95.3
Savannah, GA	194,814	209,984	92.8
Seattle, WA	2,007,150	2,011,612	99.8
Sioux Falls, SD	138,437	138,293	100.1
Springfield, IL	100,412	108,228	92.8
Tampa, FL	1,535,385	1,639,890	93.6
Tucson, AZ	512,753	530,680	96.6
Tulsa, OK	499,555	515,776	96.9
Tuscaloosa, AL	127,913	140,761	90.9
Virginia Beach, VA	879,439	920,235	95.6
Washington, DC	3,091,711	3,293,451	93.9
Wichita, KS	321,349	326,261	98.5
Wilmington, NC	137,791	148,114	93.0
Winston-Salem, NC	324,467	351,499	92.3
Worcester, MA	482,355	496,174	97.2
U.S.	162,685,811	168,763,470	96.4

Note: Figures cover the Metropolitan Statistical Area (MSA)
Source: U.S. Census Bureau, 2020 Census

Race: City

City	White Alone[1] (%)	Black Alone[1] (%)	Asian Alone[1] (%)	AIAN[2] Alone[1] (%)	NHOPI[3] Alone[1] (%)	Other Race Alone[1] (%)	Two or More Races (%)
Albuquerque, NM	52.2	3.5	3.4	5.6	0.1	14.2	21.0
Allentown, PA	38.3	13.2	2.1	0.8	0.1	30.1	15.5
Anchorage, AK	56.5	5.0	9.5	8.1	3.4	3.5	14.0
Ann Arbor, MI	67.6	6.8	15.7	0.2	0.1	1.8	7.9
Athens, GA	58.1	24.7	3.9	0.5	0.1	6.1	6.7
Atlanta, GA	39.8	47.2	4.5	0.3	0.0	2.4	5.8
Austin, TX	54.7	7.3	9.0	1.0	0.1	11.9	16.1
Baltimore, MD	27.8	57.8	3.6	0.4	0.0	4.8	5.5
Boise City, ID	81.2	2.3	3.6	0.7	0.3	3.5	8.5
Boston, MA	47.1	20.6	11.3	0.4	0.1	10.1	10.5
Boulder, CO	78.8	1.3	6.4	0.6	0.1	4.7	8.1
Brownsville, TX	34.9	0.3	0.6	0.7	0.1	20.5	42.9
Cape Coral, FL	72.3	4.3	1.7	0.3	0.1	5.8	15.6
Cedar Rapids, IA	77.8	10.4	2.7	0.3	0.4	1.7	6.8
Charleston, SC	73.5	17.0	2.2	0.3	0.1	1.6	5.3
Charlotte, NC	41.7	33.1	7.1	0.6	0.1	9.6	7.9
Chicago, IL	35.9	29.2	7.0	1.3	0.0	15.8	10.8
Cincinnati, OH	47.7	40.6	2.5	0.3	0.1	3.0	5.8
Clarksville, TN	57.0	24.4	2.5	0.5	0.5	4.2	10.9
Cleveland, OH	34.5	48.4	2.8	0.4	0.0	6.3	7.6
College Station, TX	63.5	8.1	10.2	0.5	0.1	7.4	10.2
Colorado Springs, CO	70.3	5.9	3.4	1.1	0.3	6.2	12.8
Columbia, MO	72.5	11.9	5.6	0.3	0.1	2.2	7.4
Columbia, SC	50.7	38.5	3.1	0.3	0.1	2.3	5.1
Columbus, OH	53.2	28.6	6.2	0.4	0.0	4.3	7.2
Dallas, TX	36.1	23.3	3.7	1.2	0.1	19.5	16.2
Davenport, IA	74.1	12.0	2.2	0.4	0.0	2.6	8.7
Denver, CO	60.6	8.9	3.9	1.5	0.2	11.3	13.5
Des Moines, IA	64.5	11.7	6.8	0.7	0.1	6.6	9.6
Durham, NC	40.2	36.2	5.6	0.7	0.0	9.8	7.4
Edison, NJ	28.1	7.6	53.7	0.4	0.0	4.7	5.5
El Paso, TX	36.8	3.7	1.5	1.1	0.2	20.6	36.0
Fargo, ND	78.9	8.8	4.1	1.6	0.1	1.2	5.3
Fort Collins, CO	80.8	1.5	3.6	0.8	0.1	3.6	9.6
Fort Wayne, IN	65.0	15.3	5.8	0.5	0.0	5.6	7.8
Fort Worth, TX	44.9	19.6	5.2	0.9	0.1	14.2	15.1
Grand Rapids, MI	60.3	18.9	2.3	0.9	0.0	9.0	8.7
Greeley, CO	62.0	2.7	2.0	1.8	0.1	14.8	16.6
Green Bay, WI	66.6	5.5	4.4	4.4	0.1	8.4	10.6
Greensboro, NC	40.0	42.0	5.1	0.6	0.0	5.6	6.6
Honolulu, HI	16.4	1.7	52.9	0.2	9.2	1.3	18.2
Houston, TX	32.1	22.6	7.3	1.2	0.1	20.7	16.1
Huntsville, AL	56.6	29.3	2.5	0.7	0.1	3.4	7.3
Indianapolis, IN	52.0	27.9	4.3	0.5	0.0	7.7	7.5
Jacksonville, FL	50.1	30.6	5.1	0.4	0.1	4.6	9.1
Kansas City, MO	55.3	26.1	3.1	0.6	0.3	5.5	9.0
Lafayette, LA	58.1	30.7	2.6	0.4	0.0	2.3	5.8
Las Cruces, NM	51.9	2.7	1.9	2.3	0.1	16.6	24.5
Las Vegas, NV	46.0	12.9	7.2	1.1	0.7	17.0	15.0
Lexington, KY	68.3	14.9	4.2	0.3	0.0	5.2	7.1
Lincoln, NE	78.7	4.7	4.8	0.9	0.1	3.5	7.5
Little Rock, AR	43.5	40.6	3.5	0.6	0.0	6.0	5.7
Los Angeles, CA	34.9	8.6	11.9	1.7	0.2	29.5	13.3
Louisville, KY	66.3	17.5	3.5	0.3	0.1	4.2	8.0

Table continued on following page.

City	White Alone[1] (%)	Black Alone[1] (%)	Asian Alone[1] (%)	AIAN[2] Alone[1] (%)	NHOPI[3] Alone[1] (%)	Other Race Alone[1] (%)	Two or More Races (%)
Madison, WI	71.0	7.4	9.5	0.5	0.1	3.8	7.8
Manchester, NH	76.7	5.5	4.2	0.3	0.0	5.2	7.9
Miami, FL	30.2	12.9	1.4	0.4	0.0	14.3	40.7
Midland, TX	57.6	7.9	2.6	0.9	0.1	12.5	18.4
Milwaukee, WI	36.1	38.6	5.2	0.9	0.0	9.0	10.1
Minneapolis, MN	59.5	19.1	5.8	1.7	0.0	5.9	8.0
Nashville, TN	55.2	24.6	4.0	0.6	0.0	8.1	7.6
New Haven, CT	32.7	32.2	6.8	1.0	0.1	15.3	12.0
New Orleans, LA	32.9	54.2	2.8	0.3	0.0	3.2	6.4
New York, NY	34.1	22.1	15.7	1.0	0.1	17.0	10.1
Oklahoma City, OK	53.6	14.0	4.6	3.4	0.2	11.1	13.1
Omaha, NE	65.5	12.4	4.6	1.1	0.1	7.2	9.1
Orlando, FL	40.0	23.8	4.3	0.4	0.1	12.3	19.0
Philadelphia, PA	36.3	39.3	8.3	0.4	0.1	8.7	6.9
Phoenix, AZ	49.7	7.8	4.1	2.6	0.2	20.1	15.5
Pittsburgh, PA	62.7	22.8	6.5	0.2	0.0	1.8	5.9
Portland, OR	68.8	5.9	8.1	1.1	0.6	4.8	10.7
Providence, RI	37.7	13.5	6.1	1.5	0.1	26.9	14.2
Provo, UT	74.6	0.9	2.5	1.0	1.5	8.2	11.3
Raleigh, NC	53.3	26.3	5.0	0.6	0.1	7.5	7.4
Reno, NV	62.7	3.1	7.1	1.4	0.8	12.0	13.0
Richmond, VA	43.3	40.4	2.8	0.4	0.1	6.8	6.2
Rochester, MN	73.2	8.9	7.9	0.4	0.1	2.9	6.6
Sacramento, CA	34.8	13.2	19.9	1.4	1.6	15.3	13.8
St. Louis, MO	43.9	43.0	4.1	0.3	0.0	2.6	6.1
Salem, OR	69.1	1.7	3.2	1.7	1.4	10.9	12.1
Salt Lake City, UT	68.4	2.9	5.5	1.4	2.1	9.7	9.9
San Antonio, TX	44.3	7.2	3.3	1.2	0.1	16.7	27.1
San Diego, CA	46.4	5.9	17.9	0.9	0.4	14.1	14.4
San Francisco, CA	41.3	5.3	33.9	0.7	0.4	8.4	9.9
San Jose, CA	27.3	2.9	38.5	1.4	0.4	18.2	11.2
Santa Rosa, CA	55.7	2.3	6.1	2.3	0.6	19.1	13.9
Savannah, GA	37.9	49.1	3.8	0.3	0.2	3.1	5.5
Seattle, WA	61.3	7.0	17.1	0.7	0.3	3.2	10.5
Sioux Falls, SD	79.0	6.3	2.8	2.7	0.0	2.9	6.1
Springfield, IL	68.9	20.4	2.9	0.3	0.0	1.1	6.4
Tampa, FL	49.7	21.9	5.4	0.4	0.1	7.6	14.8
Tucson, AZ	54.5	5.6	3.2	2.9	0.3	15.2	18.3
Tulsa, OK	51.8	14.9	3.5	5.2	0.2	9.8	14.6
Tuscaloosa, AL	48.7	41.2	2.4	0.3	0.1	2.1	5.3
Virginia Beach, VA	60.7	18.6	7.5	0.4	0.2	3.0	9.6
Washington, DC	39.6	41.4	4.9	0.5	0.1	5.4	8.1
Wichita, KS	63.4	11.0	5.1	1.3	0.1	7.4	11.7
Wilmington, NC	70.9	16.5	1.6	0.4	0.1	3.9	6.6
Winston-Salem, NC	45.8	32.5	2.5	0.7	0.1	10.7	7.6
Worcester, MA	53.3	14.8	7.1	0.5	0.0	12.9	11.3
U.S.	61.6	12.4	6.0	1.1	0.2	8.4	10.2

Note: (1) Alone is defined as not being in combination with one or more other races; (2) American Indian and Alaska Native; (3) Native Hawaiian and Other Pacific Islander
Source: U.S. Census Bureau, 2020 Census

Race: Metro Area

Metro Area	White Alone[1] (%)	Black Alone[1] (%)	Asian Alone[1] (%)	AIAN[2] Alone[1] (%)	NHOPI[3] Alone[1] (%)	Other Race Alone[1] (%)	Two or More Races (%)
Albuquerque, NM	52.8	2.8	2.5	6.6	0.1	14.5	20.6
Allentown, PA	72.9	6.3	3.2	0.3	0.0	8.5	8.8
Anchorage, AK	62.1	3.9	7.3	7.7	2.6	3.0	13.3
Ann Arbor, MI	69.2	11.5	9.0	0.3	0.1	2.0	7.9
Athens, GA	67.0	17.9	3.6	0.4	0.0	4.7	6.3
Atlanta, GA	45.5	33.6	6.6	0.5	0.0	6.0	7.7
Austin, TX	57.3	7.0	7.1	0.9	0.1	11.1	16.5
Baltimore, MD	53.9	28.5	6.3	0.4	0.0	4.0	6.8
Boise City, ID	80.0	1.3	2.1	0.9	0.3	5.9	9.6
Boston, MA	68.4	7.4	8.7	0.3	0.0	6.9	8.4
Boulder, CO	77.4	1.0	5.0	0.8	0.1	5.8	10.0
Brownsville, TX	38.6	0.5	0.7	0.7	0.0	19.0	40.4
Cape Coral, FL	69.7	7.7	1.7	0.5	0.0	7.5	12.8
Cedar Rapids, IA	84.7	6.1	2.0	0.2	0.2	1.2	5.6
Charleston, SC	64.0	23.0	2.0	0.5	0.1	3.9	6.5
Charlotte, NC	59.5	21.9	4.3	0.6	0.1	6.4	7.2
Chicago, IL	54.0	16.4	7.1	0.9	0.0	11.3	10.2
Cincinnati, OH	76.7	12.1	3.0	0.3	0.1	2.1	5.7
Clarksville, TN	65.8	19.1	2.0	0.5	0.4	3.2	9.0
Cleveland, OH	68.9	19.6	2.6	0.2	0.0	2.6	6.0
College Station, TX	60.7	11.0	5.6	0.7	0.1	9.8	12.1
Colorado Springs, CO	71.3	5.8	3.0	1.0	0.4	5.8	12.7
Columbia, MO	77.7	9.3	3.8	0.3	0.1	1.8	7.1
Columbia, SC	55.7	32.4	2.3	0.4	0.1	3.1	6.0
Columbus, OH	70.1	15.7	4.9	0.3	0.0	2.7	6.3
Dallas, TX	48.9	16.0	7.9	1.0	0.1	12.2	13.9
Davenport, IA	78.2	8.3	2.4	0.4	0.0	3.2	7.5
Denver, CO	66.7	5.6	4.6	1.2	0.2	8.8	12.8
Des Moines, IA	79.8	5.6	4.3	0.4	0.1	3.2	6.7
Durham, NC	54.3	25.0	4.9	0.7	0.0	7.9	7.2
Edison, NJ	46.5	16.1	12.5	0.8	0.1	14.1	10.0
El Paso, TX	36.3	3.3	1.4	1.2	0.2	21.7	35.8
Fargo, ND	82.8	6.5	2.7	1.5	0.0	1.1	5.3
Fort Collins, CO	82.4	1.1	2.4	0.8	0.1	3.8	9.4
Fort Wayne, IN	73.7	10.6	4.4	0.4	0.0	4.0	6.8
Fort Worth, TX	48.9	16.0	7.9	1.0	0.1	12.2	13.9
Grand Rapids, MI	78.0	6.9	2.8	0.6	0.0	4.7	7.0
Greeley, CO	70.5	1.4	1.8	1.3	0.1	11.2	13.8
Green Bay, WI	81.8	2.6	2.7	2.5	0.0	3.8	6.6
Greensboro, NC	56.7	26.7	4.1	0.6	0.0	5.5	6.4
Honolulu, HI	18.5	2.0	43.0	0.2	10.0	1.7	24.5
Houston, TX	41.4	17.4	8.4	1.0	0.1	16.0	15.7
Huntsville, AL	65.0	21.4	2.5	0.7	0.1	2.9	7.3
Indianapolis, IN	69.6	15.0	3.9	0.4	0.0	4.5	6.6
Jacksonville, FL	61.6	21.2	4.2	0.4	0.1	3.6	8.8
Kansas City, MO	70.9	12.0	3.1	0.6	0.2	4.2	9.0
Lafayette, LA	65.8	24.5	1.9	0.4	0.0	2.3	5.1
Las Cruces, NM	47.5	1.9	1.2	1.9	0.1	20.1	27.4
Las Vegas, NV	44.9	12.7	10.5	1.0	0.9	15.4	14.7
Lexington, KY	74.9	11.1	2.9	0.3	0.0	4.2	6.6
Lincoln, NE	80.8	4.1	4.2	0.8	0.1	3.1	6.9
Little Rock, AR	64.0	23.2	1.8	0.6	0.1	3.7	6.6
Los Angeles, CA	35.2	6.4	16.7	1.5	0.3	25.2	14.7
Louisville, KY	72.7	14.8	2.5	0.3	0.1	2.9	6.8

Table continued on following page.

Metro Area	White Alone[1] (%)	Black Alone[1] (%)	Asian Alone[1] (%)	AIAN[2] Alone[1] (%)	NHOPI[3] Alone[1] (%)	Other Race Alone[1] (%)	Two or More Races (%)
Madison, WI	80.2	4.7	5.4	0.4	0.0	2.9	6.4
Manchester, NH	82.8	2.6	3.9	0.2	0.0	3.5	6.9
Miami, FL	39.6	19.5	2.7	0.4	0.0	9.7	28.1
Midland, TX	58.2	6.4	2.3	0.9	0.1	13.2	18.9
Milwaukee, WI	66.7	16.3	4.2	0.6	0.0	4.6	7.6
Minneapolis, MN	73.0	9.1	7.2	0.8	0.0	3.3	6.6
Nashville, TN	70.0	14.3	3.1	0.5	0.1	5.1	7.0
New Haven, CT	62.9	13.8	4.3	0.5	0.1	9.0	9.5
New Orleans, LA	50.3	33.3	2.9	0.5	0.0	4.8	8.1
New York, NY	46.5	16.1	12.5	0.8	0.1	14.1	10.0
Oklahoma City, OK	62.5	10.3	3.3	4.0	0.1	7.2	12.6
Omaha, NE	74.9	7.7	3.5	0.8	0.1	5.0	8.0
Orlando, FL	50.4	15.4	4.7	0.4	0.1	11.4	17.7
Philadelphia, PA	60.7	20.4	6.6	0.3	0.0	5.1	6.8
Phoenix, AZ	60.2	5.8	4.3	2.5	0.3	13.4	13.5
Pittsburgh, PA	82.7	8.4	2.9	0.1	0.0	0.9	4.9
Portland, OR	71.5	3.0	7.1	1.1	0.6	6.0	10.7
Providence, RI	73.9	5.2	3.1	0.6	0.0	8.0	9.1
Provo, UT	81.8	0.7	1.6	0.7	1.0	5.4	8.9
Raleigh, NC	60.1	18.3	7.0	0.6	0.0	6.4	7.6
Reno, NV	64.2	2.5	5.9	1.8	0.7	11.8	13.0
Richmond, VA	56.5	27.7	4.3	0.5	0.1	4.4	6.4
Rochester, MN	82.3	5.1	4.7	0.3	0.0	2.2	5.4
Sacramento, CA	52.5	7.0	14.9	1.1	0.9	10.4	13.2
St. Louis, MO	71.2	18.0	2.9	0.3	0.0	1.6	6.0
Salem, OR	69.6	1.1	2.1	2.0	1.0	12.2	12.0
Salt Lake City, UT	72.3	1.9	4.1	1.1	1.8	9.1	9.8
San Antonio, TX	50.3	7.1	2.9	1.1	0.2	14.0	24.4
San Diego, CA	49.5	4.7	12.5	1.2	0.5	15.8	15.8
San Francisco, CA	39.3	7.1	27.5	1.0	0.7	12.7	11.7
San Jose, CA	32.5	2.3	38.1	1.2	0.4	14.6	11.0
Santa Rosa, CA	62.7	1.6	4.7	1.8	0.4	15.3	13.5
Savannah, GA	55.6	30.8	3.1	0.4	0.1	3.4	6.6
Seattle, WA	60.1	6.1	15.4	1.1	1.1	5.3	11.0
Sioux Falls, SD	83.4	4.6	2.0	2.2	0.0	2.3	5.5
Springfield, IL	78.4	12.5	2.1	0.2	0.0	0.9	5.8
Tampa, FL	64.4	11.8	3.9	0.4	0.1	6.2	13.1
Tucson, AZ	60.7	3.8	3.0	3.3	0.2	12.2	16.7
Tulsa, OK	61.3	7.9	2.8	8.1	0.1	5.4	14.2
Tuscaloosa, AL	57.5	33.9	1.3	0.4	0.0	2.5	4.3
Virginia Beach, VA	54.0	30.3	4.1	0.4	0.2	2.9	8.1
Washington, DC	44.5	24.5	11.0	0.6	0.1	9.3	10.1
Wichita, KS	71.7	7.5	3.7	1.2	0.1	5.4	10.4
Wilmington, NC	75.6	12.2	1.3	0.5	0.1	3.8	6.4
Winston-Salem, NC	67.0	17.2	1.8	0.6	0.0	6.7	6.5
Worcester, MA	74.5	5.2	4.9	0.4	0.0	6.3	8.6
U.S.	61.6	12.4	6.0	1.1	0.2	8.4	10.2

Note: Figures cover the Metropolitan Statistical Area (MSA); (1) Alone is defined as not being in combination with one or more other races;
(2) American Indian and Alaska Native; (3) Native Hawaiian & Other Pacific Islander
Source: U.S. Census Bureau, 2020 Census

Hispanic Origin: City

City	Hispanic or Latino (%)	Mexican (%)	Puerto Rican (%)	Cuban (%)	Other Hispanic or Latino (%)
Albuquerque, NM	49.8	29.7	0.7	0.4	19.0
Allentown, PA	54.5	2.6	27.6	0.8	23.5
Anchorage, AK	9.5	4.6	1.5	0.4	3.0
Ann Arbor, MI	4.6	2.4	0.3	0.3	1.7
Athens, GA	11.0	5.9	0.4	0.6	4.0
Atlanta, GA	5.0	1.9	0.8	0.3	2.0
Austin, TX	33.1	25.6	1.0	0.7	5.8
Baltimore, MD	5.6	1.1	0.8	0.3	3.3
Boise City, ID	8.8	6.4	0.5	0.1	1.9
Boston, MA	19.8	1.1	5.2	0.4	13.1
Boulder, CO	10.6	6.3	0.4	0.4	3.6
Brownsville, TX	94.7	90.5	0.2	0.1	3.8
Cape Coral, FL	23.2	1.7	4.9	9.7	7.0
Cedar Rapids, IA	4.4	3.2	0.2	0.1	1.0
Charleston, SC	4.2	1.9	0.6	0.1	1.6
Charlotte, NC	14.9	5.3	1.1	0.6	7.9
Chicago, IL	28.7	21.2	3.5	0.3	3.8
Cincinnati, OH	4.4	1.4	0.6	0.2	2.2
Clarksville, TN	11.7	5.6	3.0	0.4	2.8
Cleveland, OH	12.2	1.6	8.6	0.2	1.8
College Station, TX	17.7	12.8	0.7	0.2	4.1
Colorado Springs, CO	18.4	12.1	1.2	0.3	4.9
Columbia, MO	3.7	2.1	0.3	0.0	1.2
Columbia, SC	5.6	2.4	1.1	0.3	1.8
Columbus, OH	6.5	3.1	1.0	0.1	2.3
Dallas, TX	42.0	34.7	0.6	0.3	6.4
Davenport, IA	8.9	8.2	0.3	0.1	0.3
Denver, CO	29.4	22.6	0.7	0.3	5.9
Des Moines, IA	14.6	11.6	0.3	0.2	2.4
Durham, NC	13.2	6.4	0.9	0.3	5.7
Edison, NJ	10.8	1.4	2.8	0.7	6.0
El Paso, TX	81.6	76.9	1.0	0.2	3.5
Fargo, ND	3.2	2.0	0.3	0.0	0.9
Fort Collins, CO	12.6	9.0	0.5	0.1	3.0
Fort Wayne, IN	9.5	7.2	0.6	0.1	1.6
Fort Worth, TX	35.3	29.8	1.2	0.4	3.9
Grand Rapids, MI	15.7	9.6	1.6	0.3	4.1
Greeley, CO	40.3	33.0	0.9	0.1	6.3
Green Bay, WI	16.6	13.0	1.9	0.0	1.8
Greensboro, NC	8.4	4.5	1.1	0.2	2.6
Honolulu, HI	7.2	2.2	2.0	0.1	2.8
Houston, TX	44.5	30.3	0.7	0.8	12.8
Huntsville, AL	6.4	3.6	1.1	0.2	1.6
Indianapolis, IN	10.8	7.3	0.7	0.2	2.6
Jacksonville, FL	10.9	2.0	3.4	1.6	3.9
Kansas City, MO	10.7	7.7	0.4	0.4	2.2
Lafayette, LA	4.6	1.4	0.1	0.2	2.9
Las Cruces, NM	61.8	51.1	0.6	0.2	9.9
Las Vegas, NV	34.1	24.9	1.2	1.4	6.5
Lexington, KY	7.4	4.7	0.6	0.2	1.9
Lincoln, NE	8.1	5.5	0.4	0.2	2.0
Little Rock, AR	7.8	4.7	0.2	0.3	2.5
Los Angeles, CA	48.4	31.5	0.5	0.4	16.1
Louisville, KY	6.5	2.3	0.4	2.3	1.4
Madison, WI	7.8	4.5	0.7	0.2	2.4

Table continued on following page.

City	Hispanic or Latino (%)	Mexican (%)	Puerto Rican (%)	Cuban (%)	Other Hispanic or Latino (%)
Manchester, NH	11.0	1.6	3.9	0.1	5.4
Miami, FL	72.3	1.9	3.5	33.4	33.5
Midland, TX	46.5	42.5	0.5	1.0	2.5
Milwaukee, WI	19.9	13.4	4.9	0.2	1.4
Minneapolis, MN	9.8	5.3	0.5	0.2	3.8
Nashville, TN	10.6	5.9	0.6	0.4	3.8
New Haven, CT	30.3	5.3	16.5	0.4	8.1
New Orleans, LA	5.6	1.2	0.2	0.6	3.5
New York, NY	28.9	3.8	7.7	0.5	16.9
Oklahoma City, OK	19.9	16.1	0.4	0.1	3.3
Omaha, NE	14.5	10.9	0.5	0.2	2.9
Orlando, FL	34.2	1.8	15.8	3.0	13.6
Philadelphia, PA	15.4	1.3	8.7	0.3	5.1
Phoenix, AZ	42.7	37.9	0.7	0.4	3.8
Pittsburgh, PA	3.5	1.2	0.7	0.1	1.6
Portland, OR	10.3	7.0	0.5	0.4	2.3
Providence, RI	42.9	1.3	7.9	0.3	33.4
Provo, UT	17.8	11.3	0.7	0.2	5.6
Raleigh, NC	11.3	5.0	1.4	0.4	4.5
Reno, NV	23.3	17.8	0.7	0.3	4.6
Richmond, VA	7.3	1.3	0.8	0.3	4.9
Rochester, MN	5.8	3.7	0.6	0.1	1.4
Sacramento, CA	28.9	24.1	0.9	0.2	3.7
St. Louis, MO	4.2	2.5	0.2	0.2	1.3
Salem, OR	22.4	19.5	0.6	0.1	2.2
Salt Lake City, UT	19.9	14.2	0.4	0.3	5.0
San Antonio, TX	65.7	56.7	1.4	0.3	7.3
San Diego, CA	30.1	25.6	0.8	0.3	3.4
San Francisco, CA	15.4	7.8	0.7	0.3	6.7
San Jose, CA	31.0	26.0	0.5	0.2	4.3
Santa Rosa, CA	34.0	29.3	0.5	0.1	4.1
Savannah, GA	6.5	2.1	2.0	0.4	2.0
Seattle, WA	7.2	4.2	0.4	0.2	2.4
Sioux Falls, SD	5.5	2.6	0.3	0.1	2.6
Springfield, IL	2.9	1.5	0.6	0.1	0.7
Tampa, FL	26.2	3.1	6.9	8.0	8.3
Tucson, AZ	44.6	39.8	0.9	0.2	3.7
Tulsa, OK	17.1	13.4	0.6	0.1	3.0
Tuscaloosa, AL	4.4	2.5	0.6	0.3	0.9
Virginia Beach, VA	8.6	2.7	2.2	0.3	3.4
Washington, DC	11.3	1.9	0.9	0.5	8.0
Wichita, KS	17.6	15.1	0.5	0.1	1.9
Wilmington, NC	7.1	2.7	1.3	0.4	2.7
Winston-Salem, NC	16.2	9.7	1.5	0.2	4.8
Worcester, MA	23.9	0.8	14.7	0.3	8.1
U.S.	18.4	11.2	1.8	0.7	4.7

Note: Persons of Hispanic or Latino origin can be of any race
Source: U.S. Census Bureau, 2017-2021 American Community Survey 5-Year Estimates

Hispanic Origin: Metro Area

Metro Area	Hispanic or Latino (%)	Mexican (%)	Puerto Rican (%)	Cuban (%)	Other Hispanic or Latino (%)
Albuquerque, NM	49.7	29.0	0.7	0.4	19.7
Allentown, PA	18.4	1.3	9.3	0.4	7.3
Anchorage, AK	8.4	4.1	1.3	0.4	2.6
Ann Arbor, MI	5.0	2.8	0.5	0.2	1.5
Athens, GA	8.9	4.7	0.8	0.4	2.9
Atlanta, GA	11.0	5.5	1.1	0.4	3.9
Austin, TX	32.7	26.3	1.0	0.5	5.0
Baltimore, MD	6.2	1.4	1.0	0.2	3.6
Boise City, ID	14.1	11.5	0.5	0.1	2.0
Boston, MA	11.6	0.7	2.8	0.3	7.8
Boulder, CO	14.0	9.9	0.5	0.3	3.3
Brownsville, TX	90.0	86.0	0.3	0.1	3.6
Cape Coral, FL	22.6	5.4	4.6	5.7	6.8
Cedar Rapids, IA	3.2	2.4	0.1	0.0	0.7
Charleston, SC	5.9	2.7	0.8	0.1	2.3
Charlotte, NC	10.6	4.6	1.1	0.4	4.6
Chicago, IL	22.5	17.5	2.2	0.3	2.6
Cincinnati, OH	3.5	1.6	0.4	0.1	1.4
Clarksville, TN	9.3	4.7	2.4	0.2	2.0
Cleveland, OH	6.2	1.4	3.5	0.1	1.1
College Station, TX	25.7	21.8	0.4	0.3	3.1
Colorado Springs, CO	17.5	10.9	1.4	0.4	4.9
Columbia, MO	3.4	2.1	0.2	0.1	1.0
Columbia, SC	5.8	2.8	1.1	0.2	1.7
Columbus, OH	4.5	2.1	0.8	0.1	1.6
Dallas, TX	29.3	23.6	0.8	0.3	4.5
Davenport, IA	9.1	8.0	0.3	0.1	0.7
Denver, CO	23.4	17.5	0.6	0.2	5.0
Des Moines, IA	7.4	5.5	0.3	0.1	1.5
Durham, NC	11.3	5.9	0.8	0.3	4.3
Edison, NJ	24.8	2.9	5.9	0.8	15.3
El Paso, TX	82.9	78.1	0.9	0.2	3.6
Fargo, ND	3.4	2.4	0.3	0.0	0.7
Fort Collins, CO	12.0	8.8	0.4	0.2	2.6
Fort Wayne, IN	7.4	5.6	0.4	0.1	1.3
Fort Worth, TX	29.3	23.6	0.8	0.3	4.5
Grand Rapids, MI	9.9	6.8	0.9	0.3	1.9
Greeley, CO	30.0	24.5	0.5	0.2	4.8
Green Bay, WI	8.1	6.1	0.9	0.1	1.0
Greensboro, NC	8.8	5.7	1.0	0.2	1.9
Honolulu, HI	10.2	3.2	3.5	0.1	3.5
Houston, TX	37.9	27.3	0.7	0.7	9.2
Huntsville, AL	5.4	3.2	0.8	0.1	1.3
Indianapolis, IN	7.1	4.6	0.6	0.1	1.8
Jacksonville, FL	9.6	1.9	3.0	1.3	3.5
Kansas City, MO	9.4	7.0	0.4	0.2	1.8
Lafayette, LA	4.1	1.8	0.2	0.1	2.0
Las Cruces, NM	68.9	60.8	0.4	0.1	7.6
Las Vegas, NV	31.8	23.3	1.1	1.5	5.9
Lexington, KY	6.3	4.2	0.5	0.1	1.5
Lincoln, NE	7.2	4.9	0.3	0.2	1.7
Little Rock, AR	5.5	3.7	0.2	0.1	1.5
Los Angeles, CA	45.2	34.5	0.5	0.4	9.8
Louisville, KY	5.3	2.4	0.4	1.3	1.1
Madison, WI	6.1	3.7	0.5	0.1	1.7

Table continued on following page.

Metro Area	Hispanic or Latino (%)	Mexican (%)	Puerto Rican (%)	Cuban (%)	Other Hispanic or Latino (%)
Manchester, NH	7.4	1.1	2.5	0.2	3.5
Miami, FL	45.6	2.5	3.8	18.6	20.6
Midland, TX	46.3	42.7	0.4	0.9	2.3
Milwaukee, WI	11.3	7.5	2.6	0.2	1.1
Minneapolis, MN	6.1	3.8	0.4	0.1	1.8
Nashville, TN	7.7	4.3	0.6	0.3	2.5
New Haven, CT	19.2	2.2	10.6	0.4	6.0
New Orleans, LA	9.1	1.7	0.5	0.6	6.3
New York, NY	24.8	2.9	5.9	0.8	15.3
Oklahoma City, OK	13.9	10.9	0.4	0.1	2.5
Omaha, NE	11.0	8.2	0.5	0.1	2.1
Orlando, FL	31.8	2.8	15.0	2.5	11.5
Philadelphia, PA	9.9	1.9	4.6	0.3	3.2
Phoenix, AZ	31.5	27.1	0.7	0.3	3.4
Pittsburgh, PA	1.9	0.6	0.5	0.1	0.7
Portland, OR	12.5	9.4	0.4	0.3	2.4
Providence, RI	13.7	0.9	4.4	0.2	8.3
Provo, UT	12.1	7.5	0.3	0.1	4.1
Raleigh, NC	10.8	5.6	1.4	0.4	3.5
Reno, NV	25.1	19.3	0.7	0.4	4.6
Richmond, VA	6.7	1.6	1.0	0.2	3.8
Rochester, MN	4.7	2.9	0.4	0.1	1.3
Sacramento, CA	22.2	17.8	0.7	0.2	3.5
St. Louis, MO	3.2	2.0	0.3	0.1	0.9
Salem, OR	24.9	22.1	0.4	0.1	2.3
Salt Lake City, UT	18.5	13.1	0.5	0.2	4.7
San Antonio, TX	56.0	48.2	1.4	0.3	6.0
San Diego, CA	34.3	29.9	0.8	0.2	3.4
San Francisco, CA	22.0	14.1	0.7	0.2	7.0
San Jose, CA	26.2	21.5	0.5	0.2	4.1
Santa Rosa, CA	27.5	22.7	0.4	0.2	4.2
Savannah, GA	6.5	2.9	1.6	0.5	1.6
Seattle, WA	10.5	7.3	0.6	0.2	2.5
Sioux Falls, SD	4.6	2.3	0.2	0.1	2.1
Springfield, IL	2.4	1.4	0.4	0.1	0.5
Tampa, FL	20.5	3.7	6.3	4.3	6.3
Tucson, AZ	38.0	33.7	0.9	0.2	3.2
Tulsa, OK	10.5	8.1	0.4	0.1	1.9
Tuscaloosa, AL	3.8	2.4	0.3	0.2	0.9
Virginia Beach, VA	7.2	2.4	1.9	0.3	2.5
Washington, DC	16.2	2.3	1.2	0.3	12.4
Wichita, KS	13.6	11.5	0.4	0.1	1.6
Wilmington, NC	6.2	2.5	1.0	0.3	2.4
Winston-Salem, NC	10.8	6.7	1.1	0.2	2.8
Worcester, MA	12.3	0.9	7.2	0.2	4.0
U.S.	18.4	11.2	1.8	0.7	4.7

Note: Persons of Hispanic or Latino origin can be of any race; Figures cover the Metropolitan Statistical Area (MSA)
Source: U.S. Census Bureau, 2017-2021 American Community Survey 5-Year Estimates

Household Size: City

| City | Persons in Household (%) | | | | | | | Average Household Size |
	One	Two	Three	Four	Five	Six	Seven or More	
Albuquerque, NM	36.4	32.9	13.6	10.1	4.7	1.2	0.7	2.36
Allentown, PA	29.4	29.5	14.0	14.3	7.3	3.0	2.1	2.65
Anchorage, AK	26.8	32.9	15.5	13.5	6.2	2.6	2.1	2.68
Ann Arbor, MI	33.6	37.5	13.0	10.6	2.8	1.6	0.5	2.21
Athens, GA	34.2	34.4	14.9	11.1	3.4	1.1	0.6	2.22
Atlanta, GA	45.8	31.9	10.9	6.7	2.5	1.1	0.7	2.06
Austin, TX	34.7	33.7	14.3	10.4	4.2	1.5	0.8	2.28
Baltimore, MD	41.4	29.8	13.8	8.1	3.7	1.6	1.1	2.32
Boise City, ID	31.6	36.5	14.9	9.9	4.9	1.3	0.5	2.37
Boston, MA	36.2	32.7	15.1	9.4	3.9	1.6	0.9	2.30
Boulder, CO	35.7	35.9	13.9	10.5	2.7	0.4	0.5	2.21
Brownsville, TX	19.2	23.6	17.0	19.2	12.4	4.6	3.5	3.31
Cape Coral, FL	26.0	42.6	13.7	10.6	5.0	1.1	0.7	2.59
Cedar Rapids, IA	33.7	34.3	14.6	10.3	4.4	1.4	0.9	2.31
Charleston, SC	35.0	38.5	13.2	9.6	2.7	0.6	0.1	2.23
Charlotte, NC	34.1	31.7	15.0	11.9	4.6	1.5	0.9	2.47
Chicago, IL	38.2	29.5	13.5	10.0	4.9	2.1	1.4	2.41
Cincinnati, OH	44.5	30.2	11.4	8.4	3.0	1.3	0.8	2.11
Clarksville, TN	24.5	32.7	17.0	15.9	6.0	2.3	1.4	2.69
Cleveland, OH	46.0	27.9	12.0	7.3	3.7	1.7	1.0	2.15
College Station, TX	32.4	31.1	14.8	14.9	3.5	2.4	0.5	2.51
Colorado Springs, CO	27.5	36.0	15.0	12.4	5.5	2.2	1.1	2.48
Columbia, MO	35.6	31.7	13.7	11.1	5.7	1.2	0.7	2.33
Columbia, SC	39.1	32.6	13.4	8.9	4.0	1.4	0.2	2.19
Columbus, OH	35.8	32.6	13.3	10.1	4.8	1.7	1.3	2.32
Dallas, TX	36.3	29.5	13.1	10.3	6.4	2.4	1.6	2.49
Davenport, IA	34.3	35.7	13.1	9.1	5.0	1.7	0.8	2.36
Denver, CO	38.5	33.5	11.7	9.4	3.8	1.5	1.2	2.21
Des Moines, IA	34.8	30.5	14.3	10.8	5.1	2.5	1.6	2.40
Durham, NC	35.5	33.9	14.1	9.6	4.3	1.6	0.7	2.27
Edison, NJ	17.7	28.6	20.6	22.7	6.3	2.2	1.7	2.90
El Paso, TX	25.4	28.5	17.5	15.6	8.2	3.0	1.4	2.83
Fargo, ND	38.0	33.9	13.2	9.0	4.1	1.1	0.4	2.15
Fort Collins, CO	25.2	37.4	17.6	14.0	4.0	1.1	0.4	2.36
Fort Wayne, IN	32.8	32.7	14.1	10.8	5.6	2.6	1.1	2.42
Fort Worth, TX	26.6	29.4	16.5	14.6	7.5	3.1	2.0	2.81
Grand Rapids, MI	33.2	30.9	15.1	10.2	6.0	2.2	2.1	2.47
Greeley, CO	25.4	32.8	16.1	13.5	7.3	3.0	1.6	2.73
Green Bay, WI	34.9	32.2	13.5	10.6	5.5	1.5	1.3	2.36
Greensboro, NC	35.1	31.9	15.5	10.3	4.5	1.4	0.9	2.36
Honolulu, HI	34.9	30.4	14.1	10.5	4.9	2.1	2.8	2.54
Houston, TX	32.7	29.1	15.6	11.9	6.2	2.5	1.5	2.57
Huntsville, AL	36.6	34.9	14.4	8.5	3.9	0.8	0.5	2.21
Indianapolis, IN	36.8	32.2	12.9	9.7	5.1	1.8	1.1	2.46
Jacksonville, FL	32.2	32.8	16.3	10.7	5.1	1.6	0.9	2.50
Kansas City, MO	36.7	32.0	12.7	10.8	4.4	1.9	1.1	2.31
Lafayette, LA	33.6	36.0	14.1	8.6	4.7	1.5	1.1	2.30
Las Cruces, NM	31.9	31.4	15.8	12.6	5.5	1.6	0.7	2.46
Las Vegas, NV	30.2	31.3	15.5	12.1	6.1	2.7	1.7	2.65
Lexington, KY	33.0	34.2	14.3	11.4	4.2	1.7	0.8	2.30
Lincoln, NE	31.6	33.7	13.7	11.8	5.4	2.4	0.9	2.37
Little Rock, AR	37.6	31.8	13.8	9.9	4.4	1.4	0.7	2.33
Los Angeles, CA	30.5	28.5	15.4	13.1	6.7	2.9	2.5	2.75
Louisville, KY	33.8	32.9	15.1	10.7	4.9	1.4	0.9	2.39

Table continued on following page.

City	Persons in Household (%)							Average Household Size
	One	Two	Three	Four	Five	Six	Seven or More	
Madison, WI	37.7	35.2	12.4	9.4	3.4	1.0	0.5	2.16
Manchester, NH	33.9	33.2	15.8	10.3	3.5	1.9	1.0	2.32
Miami, FL	35.9	32.2	16.2	9.2	3.8	1.3	1.0	2.38
Midland, TX	26.8	28.2	17.2	15.2	8.2	2.8	1.3	2.57
Milwaukee, WI	37.7	28.8	13.7	10.0	5.7	2.3	1.5	2.45
Minneapolis, MN	40.4	31.6	11.5	9.5	3.4	1.7	1.5	2.24
Nashville, TN	35.2	33.3	14.5	9.6	4.6	1.4	1.1	2.34
New Haven, CT	36.7	29.1	16.1	9.0	5.3	2.0	1.4	2.48
New Orleans, LA	46.4	28.7	12.5	7.9	2.7	1.1	0.4	2.37
New York, NY	32.4	28.6	16.3	12.1	5.7	2.5	2.0	2.63
Oklahoma City, OK	31.3	31.8	15.1	11.6	6.4	2.5	1.0	2.49
Omaha, NE	33.6	31.6	13.6	10.7	6.1	2.5	1.6	2.44
Orlando, FL	32.8	33.5	16.0	10.8	4.3	1.3	1.0	2.53
Philadelphia, PA	37.1	29.4	14.9	10.2	4.8	1.8	1.3	2.40
Phoenix, AZ	27.9	30.0	15.2	13.0	7.4	3.6	2.7	2.71
Pittsburgh, PA	44.2	32.4	12.4	6.7	2.5	1.0	0.5	2.04
Portland, OR	34.9	35.2	13.7	10.3	3.5	1.2	0.8	2.26
Providence, RI	33.6	29.0	15.5	11.1	7.0	1.9	1.6	2.56
Provo, UT	15.1	34.8	17.3	14.9	7.2	6.9	3.4	3.10
Raleigh, NC	34.6	32.8	14.4	12.0	4.2	1.2	0.5	2.37
Reno, NV	31.9	34.0	14.6	11.2	5.3	1.4	1.2	2.37
Richmond, VA	42.4	33.0	12.0	7.6	2.8	1.3	0.5	2.19
Rochester, MN	31.0	34.7	13.0	12.2	5.5	1.9	1.4	2.40
Sacramento, CA	30.5	30.3	14.6	13.0	6.1	2.8	2.4	2.63
St. Louis, MO	46.2	30.2	10.8	7.3	3.2	0.9	1.0	2.08
Salem, OR	29.6	33.2	14.8	11.0	6.4	2.7	2.0	2.58
Salt Lake City, UT	38.2	32.7	11.9	9.3	4.1	1.9	1.7	2.32
San Antonio, TX	30.6	29.5	15.4	12.7	6.9	2.9	1.7	2.64
San Diego, CA	27.8	34.0	15.7	12.9	5.6	2.1	1.5	2.64
San Francisco, CA	36.5	32.9	13.9	10.1	3.6	1.4	1.3	2.34
San Jose, CA	19.7	28.9	18.8	17.9	8.0	3.2	3.2	3.08
Santa Rosa, CA	28.4	32.4	15.0	13.8	6.6	2.0	1.3	2.60
Savannah, GA	32.8	35.4	15.2	9.6	4.5	1.3	0.9	2.46
Seattle, WA	39.9	35.0	12.1	8.9	2.5	0.8	0.5	2.08
Sioux Falls, SD	32.2	33.4	14.0	11.2	6.1	1.8	1.0	2.37
Springfield, IL	39.3	32.5	12.3	9.5	3.8	1.2	1.0	2.18
Tampa, FL	35.9	31.1	15.6	10.7	4.2	1.5	0.6	2.41
Tucson, AZ	34.9	31.0	14.2	11.2	5.2	2.0	1.2	2.35
Tulsa, OK	35.5	32.2	13.2	10.4	5.0	2.2	1.1	2.41
Tuscaloosa, AL	37.2	32.9	14.0	9.9	3.8	1.3	0.6	2.45
Virginia Beach, VA	24.5	35.5	17.6	13.7	6.0	1.7	0.6	2.53
Washington, DC	45.4	30.6	11.6	7.3	3.1	1.0	0.6	2.08
Wichita, KS	32.8	32.4	13.0	11.2	6.2	2.5	1.7	2.51
Wilmington, NC	39.9	36.9	11.5	7.4	3.0	0.6	0.3	2.10
Winston-Salem, NC	36.0	31.7	14.7	9.3	4.6	2.4	1.0	2.43
Worcester, MA	34.9	28.3	17.0	11.9	4.4	2.1	1.0	2.40
U.S.	28.0	33.8	15.5	12.8	5.9	2.2	1.4	2.60

U.S. Census Bureau, 2017-2021 American Community Survey 5-Year Estimates

Household Size: Metro Area

Metro Area	Persons in Household (%)							Average Household Size
	One	Two	Three	Four	Five	Six	Seven or More	
Albuquerque, NM	32.3	34.7	14.2	10.7	5.1	1.7	1.0	2.49
Allentown, PA	26.5	35.6	15.2	13.6	5.8	1.9	1.1	2.52
Anchorage, AK	25.7	33.3	15.5	13.4	6.7	2.8	2.3	2.70
Ann Arbor, MI	29.9	36.6	14.7	11.7	4.2	1.8	0.8	2.39
Athens, GA	28.7	34.5	16.6	13.2	4.5	1.3	0.9	2.46
Atlanta, GA	26.7	31.7	17.0	14.2	6.2	2.4	1.4	2.69
Austin, TX	27.2	33.7	15.9	13.5	5.9	2.2	1.2	2.54
Baltimore, MD	29.1	32.7	16.1	12.9	5.6	2.0	1.1	2.55
Boise City, ID	24.7	36.0	15.3	12.5	6.5	3.1	1.6	2.67
Boston, MA	27.5	33.0	16.6	14.4	5.5	1.7	0.9	2.50
Boulder, CO	29.4	36.3	14.8	13.1	4.2	1.5	0.4	2.41
Brownsville, TX	20.4	26.8	16.4	17.5	10.4	4.9	3.3	3.21
Cape Coral, FL	28.6	44.2	11.5	8.8	4.6	1.3	0.7	2.49
Cedar Rapids, IA	29.5	36.6	14.1	11.9	5.1	1.6	0.9	2.41
Charleston, SC	28.7	36.1	16.2	11.8	4.9	1.4	0.7	2.50
Charlotte, NC	27.4	34.0	16.1	13.8	5.6	1.8	0.9	2.59
Chicago, IL	29.2	31.1	15.6	13.6	6.5	2.3	1.4	2.61
Cincinnati, OH	29.2	33.9	15.0	12.8	5.5	2.1	1.1	2.49
Clarksville, TN	25.1	33.1	17.6	13.9	6.1	2.5	1.3	2.68
Cleveland, OH	34.8	33.5	13.9	10.5	4.5	1.5	0.8	2.32
College Station, TX	30.8	32.6	14.6	12.7	5.3	2.6	1.1	2.56
Colorado Springs, CO	24.5	35.7	15.9	13.2	6.6	2.3	1.5	2.60
Columbia, MO	31.5	35.1	13.7	11.9	5.3	1.4	0.8	2.41
Columbia, SC	30.4	34.2	15.4	11.8	5.1	1.9	0.9	2.46
Columbus, OH	28.8	33.9	15.2	12.8	5.8	2.0	1.2	2.49
Dallas, TX	25.1	30.7	16.7	14.9	7.7	2.9	1.7	2.77
Davenport, IA	31.2	36.3	13.2	11.4	5.0	1.8	0.8	2.39
Denver, CO	28.4	34.4	15.0	13.1	5.3	2.2	1.3	2.51
Des Moines, IA	28.5	34.1	14.2	13.7	6.2	2.0	1.0	2.48
Durham, NC	30.7	36.0	15.0	11.2	4.8	1.4	0.7	2.40
Edison, NJ	28.0	29.5	17.0	14.4	6.4	2.5	1.9	2.71
El Paso, TX	23.6	27.7	17.7	16.2	9.1	3.6	1.7	2.94
Fargo, ND	33.2	33.8	13.9	11.2	5.4	1.4	0.8	2.33
Fort Collins, CO	24.8	39.8	15.7	12.2	4.9	1.4	0.8	2.38
Fort Wayne, IN	29.0	34.3	14.1	12.1	6.1	2.6	1.4	2.51
Fort Worth, TX	25.1	30.7	16.7	14.9	7.7	2.9	1.7	2.77
Grand Rapids, MI	25.0	34.3	15.2	14.3	7.2	2.4	1.4	2.61
Greeley, CO	20.1	34.4	16.3	15.8	8.1	3.2	1.6	2.84
Green Bay, WI	28.3	37.5	14.0	11.7	5.5	1.7	0.9	2.41
Greensboro, NC	30.0	34.5	16.1	11.5	4.9	1.8	0.9	2.47
Honolulu, HI	24.5	30.4	16.5	13.4	7.1	3.7	4.0	2.96
Houston, TX	24.2	29.6	17.2	15.7	8.0	3.0	1.8	2.83
Huntsville, AL	29.3	36.0	15.3	11.9	5.0	1.5	0.6	2.42
Indianapolis, IN	29.2	34.1	14.7	12.9	5.8	1.8	1.1	2.54
Jacksonville, FL	28.0	34.8	16.4	12.1	5.7	1.8	1.0	2.57
Kansas City, MO	29.1	34.4	14.3	13.0	5.7	2.0	1.2	2.50
Lafayette, LA	27.5	33.6	16.7	13.1	5.7	2.0	1.1	2.56
Las Cruces, NM	27.3	33.2	15.7	13.5	6.4	2.0	1.5	2.66
Las Vegas, NV	28.0	32.7	15.5	12.2	6.7	2.7	1.8	2.71
Lexington, KY	29.8	35.1	15.5	12.1	4.5	1.8	0.8	2.39
Lincoln, NE	29.9	35.2	13.6	12.0	5.6	2.4	1.0	2.41
Little Rock, AR	30.3	34.4	15.8	11.7	5.1	1.7	0.7	2.47
Los Angeles, CA	24.6	28.6	17.0	15.4	7.9	3.3	2.8	2.95
Louisville, KY	30.3	34.4	15.5	11.7	5.2	1.7	0.9	2.47

Table continued on following page.

Metro Area	Persons in Household (%)							Average Household Size
	One	Two	Three	Four	Five	Six	Seven or More	
Madison, WI	31.5	36.8	13.6	11.4	4.3	1.4	0.7	2.31
Manchester, NH	27.1	35.7	16.3	13.0	4.8	2.1	0.7	2.50
Miami, FL	28.0	32.4	17.0	13.3	5.9	2.0	1.1	2.68
Midland, TX	25.7	28.1	17.0	15.7	8.6	2.6	2.0	2.61
Milwaukee, WI	32.2	34.3	13.7	11.5	5.2	1.7	0.9	2.40
Minneapolis, MN	28.1	34.1	14.7	13.5	5.8	2.1	1.4	2.53
Nashville, TN	26.9	34.8	16.2	13.1	5.7	1.8	1.1	2.57
New Haven, CT	30.6	33.1	16.4	12.2	4.7	1.6	0.9	2.49
New Orleans, LA	34.1	32.0	15.3	11.2	4.6	1.6	0.9	2.52
New York, NY	28.0	29.5	17.0	14.4	6.4	2.5	1.9	2.71
Oklahoma City, OK	28.5	33.4	15.7	12.2	6.3	2.5	1.1	2.53
Omaha, NE	28.9	33.5	14.5	12.2	6.6	2.4	1.4	2.53
Orlando, FL	24.1	34.6	17.0	13.9	6.6	2.2	1.2	2.83
Philadelphia, PA	29.2	32.1	16.1	13.4	5.7	1.9	1.1	2.53
Phoenix, AZ	25.9	34.5	14.6	12.7	6.8	3.0	2.2	2.65
Pittsburgh, PA	33.7	35.3	14.1	10.7	4.1	1.2	0.5	2.27
Portland, OR	26.9	35.5	15.4	13.3	5.3	2.0	1.3	2.53
Providence, RI	29.6	33.1	16.7	12.7	5.1	1.6	0.8	2.46
Provo, UT	12.4	28.6	15.5	15.9	12.5	8.9	5.9	3.52
Raleigh, NC	25.4	34.1	16.6	14.8	5.9	1.9	0.9	2.61
Reno, NV	27.4	34.9	15.5	12.5	5.8	2.0	1.5	2.51
Richmond, VA	29.4	34.5	15.7	12.3	5.3	1.7	0.8	2.51
Rochester, MN	27.4	36.9	13.3	13.0	6.1	1.9	1.1	2.46
Sacramento, CA	24.6	32.9	15.9	14.7	6.9	2.7	1.9	2.73
St. Louis, MO	30.5	34.5	15.0	12.2	5.1	1.5	0.8	2.43
Salem, OR	25.3	34.1	15.2	12.4	7.4	3.3	2.0	2.74
Salt Lake City, UT	23.1	30.9	15.7	13.8	8.5	4.6	3.1	2.92
San Antonio, TX	26.2	30.9	16.2	14.0	7.5	3.0	1.8	2.74
San Diego, CA	24.0	32.8	16.8	14.6	6.8	2.7	1.9	2.81
San Francisco, CA	26.4	31.8	16.8	14.8	6.1	2.2	1.6	2.71
San Jose, CA	20.4	30.4	19.1	17.7	7.2	2.7	2.2	2.94
Santa Rosa, CA	26.9	35.1	14.8	13.7	6.1	1.9	1.1	2.56
Savannah, GA	27.9	36.7	15.8	12.1	4.8	1.5	0.9	2.56
Seattle, WA	27.2	33.9	16.0	13.9	5.4	1.9	1.3	2.53
Sioux Falls, SD	28.7	34.4	14.5	12.2	6.8	2.0	1.1	2.45
Springfield, IL	33.7	35.4	13.4	10.4	4.6	1.3	0.9	2.28
Tampa, FL	30.7	36.3	14.9	10.8	4.6	1.5	0.8	2.46
Tucson, AZ	30.7	35.4	13.4	11.3	5.2	2.3	1.3	2.41
Tulsa, OK	28.8	33.7	15.2	12.2	6.0	2.5	1.3	2.57
Tuscaloosa, AL	30.1	34.6	15.5	11.7	5.4	1.5	0.8	2.62
Virginia Beach, VA	27.8	34.4	16.9	12.5	5.5	1.8	0.8	2.49
Washington, DC	27.8	30.7	16.1	14.5	6.5	2.6	1.6	2.67
Wichita, KS	29.7	33.4	13.9	11.8	6.6	2.5	1.8	2.56
Wilmington, NC	33.6	36.4	14.4	10.1	3.6	1.2	0.4	2.30
Winston-Salem, NC	30.1	35.7	15.6	10.7	4.7	2.0	0.9	2.47
Worcester, MA	27.0	33.0	17.4	14.5	5.3	1.6	0.8	2.52
U.S.	28.0	33.8	15.5	12.8	5.9	2.2	1.4	2.60

Note: Figures cover the Metropolitan Statistical Area (MSA)
Source: U.S. Census Bureau, 2017-2021 American Community Survey 5-Year Estimates

Household Relationships: City

City	House-holder	Opposite-sex Spouse	Same-sex Spouse	Opposite-sex Unmarried Partner	Same-sex Unmarried Partner	Child[1]	Grand-child	Other Relatives	Non-relatives
Albuquerque, NM	42.1	15.1	0.3	3.4	0.3	27.0	2.5	4.6	3.2
Allentown, PA	36.3	11.6	0.2	3.7	0.2	30.6	3.2	6.8	4.1
Anchorage, AK	37.5	17.0	0.2	3.0	0.2	28.3	1.9	4.6	4.2
Ann Arbor, MI	40.3	13.3	0.3	2.4	0.2	17.1	0.5	1.6	11.5
Athens, GA	40.1	11.6	0.2	2.7	0.2	20.8	2.0	3.7	10.7
Atlanta, GA	45.7	10.4	0.5	3.1	0.6	20.7	2.1	3.9	5.9
Austin, TX	42.7	14.5	0.4	3.6	0.4	23.2	1.5	4.1	6.4
Baltimore, MD	42.9	9.6	0.3	3.3	0.3	24.9	3.7	5.8	6.1
Boise City, ID	41.4	17.8	0.2	3.2	0.2	24.7	1.3	2.9	5.4
Boston, MA	41.4	10.4	0.5	3.1	0.4	20.6	1.7	5.3	9.7
Boulder, CO	40.2	13.0	0.3	3.1	0.2	16.4	0.3	1.6	12.3
Brownsville, TX	30.8	15.0	0.1	1.4	0.1	36.7	4.7	8.3	1.6
Cape Coral, FL	39.5	21.2	0.3	3.2	0.1	25.5	2.1	4.8	2.8
Cedar Rapids, IA	42.2	16.7	0.2	3.5	0.2	26.8	1.3	2.9	3.4
Charleston, SC	45.0	17.0	0.3	3.1	0.2	21.8	1.4	2.7	5.3
Charlotte, NC	40.6	15.2	0.2	2.8	0.2	28.0	2.1	4.9	4.2
Chicago, IL	41.6	12.2	0.3	3.0	0.3	26.6	3.0	6.4	4.8
Cincinnati, OH	45.1	10.2	0.3	3.4	0.3	24.6	2.2	3.4	5.3
Clarksville, TN	36.6	16.9	0.2	2.5	0.1	31.2	2.4	3.9	3.5
Cleveland, OH	45.0	8.5	0.2	3.5	0.3	27.0	3.3	5.0	3.8
College Station, TX	35.2	11.2	0.2	1.8	0.1	19.7	0.7	2.7	13.7
Colorado Springs, CO	39.7	18.3	0.3	2.6	0.2	27.5	1.9	3.6	4.3
Columbia, MO	40.5	14.1	0.2	2.8	0.2	22.4	1.0	2.5	7.8
Columbia, SC	39.2	10.5	0.2	2.1	0.2	19.5	1.6	2.8	5.8
Columbus, OH	42.2	12.9	0.3	3.6	0.3	26.2	2.1	4.4	5.2
Dallas, TX	40.1	13.4	0.4	2.6	0.3	28.6	3.2	6.2	4.0
Davenport, IA	41.9	15.9	0.2	3.7	0.2	27.0	2.0	3.0	3.2
Denver, CO	44.4	14.0	0.5	4.1	0.4	22.3	1.9	4.4	5.9
Des Moines, IA	41.1	14.2	0.3	3.5	0.2	27.9	2.0	4.4	3.9
Durham, NC	42.0	14.8	0.4	2.9	0.3	24.6	1.8	4.4	4.6
Edison, NJ	34.3	21.2	0.1	1.1	0.1	32.2	1.4	6.8	1.9
El Paso, TX	35.9	15.8	0.2	1.8	0.1	32.7	3.9	6.4	2.0
Fargo, ND	44.5	15.5	0.1	3.6	0.2	23.5	0.7	2.5	5.0
Fort Collins, CO	39.9	16.0	0.2	3.3	0.2	22.1	0.9	2.4	9.0
Fort Wayne, IN	40.7	15.6	0.2	3.1	0.2	29.7	2.0	3.4	3.0
Fort Worth, TX	35.2	15.8	0.2	2.1	0.1	33.0	3.1	5.6	3.0
Grand Rapids, MI	40.2	13.1	0.3	3.6	0.3	26.1	2.1	4.0	6.6
Greeley, CO	34.9	15.8	0.2	2.5	0.1	29.4	2.6	5.0	5.1
Green Bay, WI	40.7	15.2	0.2	4.0	0.2	28.6	1.6	3.4	3.0
Greensboro, NC	40.9	13.6	0.2	2.6	0.2	26.4	2.0	4.1	3.6
Honolulu, HI	39.1	15.0	0.3	2.4	0.2	22.2	3.1	9.1	5.6
Houston, TX	38.9	14.0	0.3	2.4	0.2	29.5	2.9	6.5	3.6
Huntsville, AL	42.8	16.5	0.2	2.2	0.2	25.1	2.1	3.5	3.1
Indianapolis, IN	40.7	14.0	0.3	3.4	0.3	28.6	2.5	4.5	3.9
Jacksonville, FL	39.9	15.6	0.2	2.8	0.2	27.7	2.8	4.9	3.6
Kansas City, MO	42.6	14.5	0.3	3.3	0.3	27.2	2.3	4.0	3.8
Lafayette, LA	43.0	15.3	0.2	2.8	0.2	27.0	2.3	3.5	3.8
Las Cruces, NM	41.1	14.9	0.2	3.4	0.3	28.5	2.5	4.5	3.6
Las Vegas, NV	37.5	15.2	0.3	2.9	0.2	29.3	2.7	6.7	4.3
Lexington, KY	41.7	16.0	0.3	2.9	0.3	25.3	1.6	3.4	4.4
Lincoln, NE	40.1	16.9	0.2	2.8	0.1	26.6	1.1	2.7	4.6
Little Rock, AR	43.5	14.5	0.3	2.4	0.3	27.1	2.3	3.9	3.1
Los Angeles, CA	36.2	13.1	0.3	2.8	0.3	26.5	2.8	9.0	6.3
Louisville, KY	40.0	18.0	0.2	2.9	0.2	28.8	2.6	4.2	2.7
Madison, WI	44.8	14.5	0.4	3.8	0.3	19.7	0.7	2.4	8.2

Table continued on following page.

City	House-holder	Opposite-sex Spouse	Same-sex Spouse	Opposite-sex Unmarried Partner	Same-sex Unmarried Partner	Child[1]	Grand-child	Other Relatives	Non-relatives
Manchester, NH	42.5	14.9	0.3	4.3	0.2	24.3	1.6	4.3	4.7
Miami, FL	42.4	12.6	0.5	3.3	0.3	22.5	2.4	8.7	5.8
Midland, TX	36.4	18.5	0.1	2.1	0.1	31.9	3.0	4.2	2.5
Milwaukee, WI	40.8	10.2	0.2	3.6	0.2	30.2	2.7	4.9	4.4
Minneapolis, MN	43.7	12.0	0.6	3.9	0.5	22.1	1.1	3.5	8.0
Nashville, TN	42.1	14.3	0.3	3.0	0.3	24.0	1.9	4.7	5.7
New Haven, CT	39.0	9.4	0.3	2.9	0.2	27.0	2.5	5.0	5.7
New Orleans, LA	43.0	11.0	0.3	3.1	0.4	26.1	3.2	4.6	4.3
New York, NY	38.3	12.7	0.3	2.2	0.2	27.6	2.5	8.3	5.3
Oklahoma City, OK	39.4	16.6	0.2	2.6	0.2	29.4	2.3	4.3	3.1
Omaha, NE	39.8	16.0	0.2	2.8	0.2	29.6	1.8	3.7	3.6
Orlando, FL	41.7	13.7	0.5	3.5	0.4	26.1	2.0	5.9	5.0
Philadelphia, PA	41.0	10.9	0.3	3.1	0.3	26.8	3.6	5.9	5.2
Phoenix, AZ	36.3	14.4	0.3	3.1	0.3	30.2	2.9	6.6	4.2
Pittsburgh, PA	46.1	11.5	0.3	3.6	0.4	19.3	1.7	3.1	6.7
Portland, OR	43.2	14.9	0.7	4.4	0.6	21.2	1.1	3.7	7.2
Providence, RI	36.5	10.5	0.3	2.9	0.3	27.3	1.9	5.7	6.1
Provo, UT	29.6	15.9	0.1	0.6	0.0	25.7	1.6	4.0	12.7
Raleigh, NC	41.8	15.1	0.2	2.9	0.2	25.5	1.4	3.9	5.0
Reno, NV	41.1	15.2	0.3	3.8	0.2	24.8	1.7	4.7	5.7
Richmond, VA	45.2	10.4	0.4	4.0	0.4	20.8	2.1	4.3	7.4
Rochester, MN	41.1	18.5	0.2	2.8	0.1	27.8	0.9	2.8	3.3
Sacramento, CA	36.7	13.5	0.4	3.0	0.3	28.0	2.6	7.5	4.7
St. Louis, MO	48.0	10.3	0.4	3.7	0.4	22.5	2.6	4.0	4.3
Salem, OR	36.6	16.0	0.2	3.1	0.2	28.1	1.9	4.6	4.2
Salt Lake City, UT	42.3	13.9	0.5	3.4	0.4	22.1	1.7	4.2	7.6
San Antonio, TX	37.5	14.7	0.3	2.7	0.2	30.3	3.8	5.5	3.2
San Diego, CA	37.2	15.7	0.4	2.6	0.3	25.0	2.0	6.2	6.1
San Francisco, CA	42.6	13.6	0.8	3.3	0.6	17.6	1.3	6.8	10.3
San Jose, CA	32.4	17.1	0.2	1.9	0.1	28.6	2.3	9.8	6.1
Santa Rosa, CA	37.6	16.2	0.4	3.0	0.2	27.3	1.8	6.2	5.5
Savannah, GA	39.9	11.2	0.3	2.7	0.3	24.9	3.2	4.4	5.0
Seattle, WA	46.9	15.2	0.8	4.3	0.6	17.5	0.7	2.8	7.3
Sioux Falls, SD	40.7	18.0	0.1	3.2	0.1	28.4	1.1	2.7	3.1
Springfield, IL	44.8	15.5	0.2	3.2	0.2	25.7	1.9	2.8	2.8
Tampa, FL	40.9	13.8	0.3	3.2	0.3	25.8	2.3	4.9	4.5
Tucson, AZ	41.1	13.3	0.3	3.3	0.3	25.4	2.8	4.8	4.5
Tulsa, OK	41.6	14.8	0.2	2.9	0.2	27.8	2.3	4.3	3.4
Tuscaloosa, AL	41.0	10.6	0.1	2.1	0.1	21.3	2.4	3.5	8.7
Virginia Beach, VA	38.8	18.6	0.2	2.4	0.1	28.7	2.2	4.0	3.5
Washington, DC	45.3	10.3	0.6	3.1	0.5	20.4	2.4	4.2	7.1
Wichita, KS	40.0	16.4	0.2	2.7	0.2	29.1	2.2	3.7	3.1
Wilmington, NC	45.7	14.9	0.3	3.4	0.3	21.2	1.5	3.0	5.9
Winston-Salem, NC	40.9	14.6	0.2	2.5	0.2	28.1	2.4	4.3	2.7
Worcester, MA	38.3	12.2	0.3	2.8	0.2	26.3	1.7	5.7	5.3
U.S.	38.3	17.5	0.2	2.5	0.2	28.3	2.4	4.8	3.4

Note: Figures are percent of the total population; (1) Includes biological, adopted, and stepchildren of the householder
Source: U.S. Census Bureau, 2020 Census

Household Relationships: Metro Area

Metro Area	House-holder	Opposite-sex Spouse	Same-sex Spouse	Opposite-sex Unmarried Partner	Same-sex Unmarried Partner	Child[1]	Grand-child	Other Relatives	Non-relatives
Albuquerque, NM	40.1	16.3	0.3	3.1	0.3	27.7	3.1	4.6	2.9
Allentown, PA	38.8	18.7	0.2	2.9	0.1	28.2	2.0	4.1	2.5
Anchorage, AK	37.1	17.6	0.2	2.9	0.1	29.1	1.9	4.2	4.0
Ann Arbor, MI	39.7	17.0	0.3	2.4	0.2	24.3	1.3	2.5	5.8
Athens, GA	38.6	15.6	0.2	2.3	0.2	25.1	2.3	3.7	7.3
Atlanta, GA	37.1	16.7	0.2	2.1	0.2	30.4	2.7	5.7	3.5
Austin, TX	38.6	17.3	0.3	2.7	0.3	27.8	1.9	4.4	4.6
Baltimore, MD	38.7	16.8	0.2	2.4	0.2	28.7	2.5	4.8	3.5
Boise City, ID	36.6	19.5	0.2	2.5	0.1	29.7	1.9	3.5	3.8
Boston, MA	38.7	17.4	0.3	2.5	0.2	27.1	1.6	4.5	4.4
Boulder, CO	40.1	18.0	0.3	2.8	0.2	23.8	1.0	2.6	6.8
Brownsville, TX	31.5	15.3	0.1	1.7	0.1	36.1	5.2	7.4	1.7
Cape Coral, FL	41.8	20.9	0.3	3.0	0.2	22.4	1.8	4.4	3.3
Cedar Rapids, IA	40.9	19.3	0.1	3.0	0.1	27.9	1.2	2.3	2.5
Charleston, SC	39.9	18.1	0.2	2.4	0.1	27.3	2.6	3.8	3.5
Charlotte, NC	38.9	18.3	0.2	2.4	0.2	29.2	2.4	4.2	2.8
Chicago, IL	38.2	17.1	0.2	2.3	0.1	30.3	2.4	5.1	2.8
Cincinnati, OH	39.5	18.1	0.2	2.7	0.1	28.9	2.3	3.2	2.9
Clarksville, TN	36.7	18.2	0.2	2.2	0.1	30.5	2.5	3.6	3.0
Cleveland, OH	42.5	17.1	0.1	2.7	0.1	27.7	2.1	3.3	2.3
College Station, TX	36.9	14.6	0.1	2.0	0.1	24.7	1.9	3.5	8.3
Colorado Springs, CO	37.5	19.3	0.2	2.2	0.1	28.5	2.0	3.6	3.8
Columbia, MO	39.8	16.5	0.2	2.8	0.2	24.9	1.4	2.5	5.7
Columbia, SC	39.9	17.0	0.2	2.1	0.2	27.5	2.7	3.8	3.0
Columbus, OH	39.4	17.4	0.2	2.9	0.2	28.5	2.0	3.5	3.3
Dallas, TX	36.2	17.6	0.2	2.0	0.2	31.7	2.7	5.5	2.9
Davenport, IA	41.4	18.8	0.2	2.9	0.1	27.9	1.8	2.5	2.2
Denver, CO	39.4	17.9	0.3	2.9	0.2	27.4	1.9	4.4	4.3
Des Moines, IA	39.6	19.2	0.2	2.7	0.1	29.6	1.3	2.8	2.6
Durham, NC	40.3	17.2	0.3	2.5	0.2	25.1	1.9	3.8	3.9
Edison, NJ	36.8	15.8	0.2	2.0	0.2	29.7	2.1	7.1	4.1
El Paso, TX	34.2	15.8	0.2	1.7	0.1	33.5	4.2	6.5	1.8
Fargo, ND	41.5	17.7	0.1	3.2	0.1	27.0	0.7	2.2	3.9
Fort Collins, CO	40.2	19.4	0.2	2.8	0.2	24.0	1.2	2.7	6.0
Fort Wayne, IN	39.5	18.0	0.2	2.7	0.1	30.5	1.9	2.9	2.5
Fort Worth, TX	36.2	17.6	0.2	2.0	0.2	31.7	2.7	5.5	2.9
Grand Rapids, MI	37.3	19.0	0.1	2.5	0.1	29.6	1.7	2.9	3.5
Greeley, CO	34.6	19.3	0.1	2.2	0.1	31.5	2.4	4.6	3.6
Green Bay, WI	40.5	19.8	0.1	3.3	0.1	28.1	1.2	2.2	2.2
Greensboro, NC	40.2	17.1	0.2	2.4	0.2	27.4	2.3	3.9	2.6
Honolulu, HI	33.1	16.3	0.2	1.9	0.1	26.2	4.5	9.2	4.9
Houston, TX	35.2	17.1	0.2	2.0	0.1	32.7	2.8	6.1	2.6
Huntsville, AL	40.1	19.3	0.1	1.9	0.1	27.8	2.3	3.4	2.3
Indianapolis, IN	39.2	17.9	0.2	2.8	0.2	29.6	2.1	3.5	2.8
Jacksonville, FL	39.1	17.9	0.2	2.6	0.2	28.0	2.6	4.3	3.2
Kansas City, MO	39.6	18.4	0.2	2.6	0.2	29.4	2.0	3.3	2.7
Lafayette, LA	39.5	17.1	0.2	2.7	0.2	30.4	2.9	3.5	2.5
Las Cruces, NM	37.5	15.9	0.2	2.7	0.2	30.0	3.6	5.1	2.7
Las Vegas, NV	37.3	15.5	0.3	3.0	0.2	28.7	2.6	7.0	4.4
Lexington, KY	40.5	17.4	0.2	2.8	0.2	26.5	2.0	3.4	3.7
Lincoln, NE	39.5	17.9	0.2	2.6	0.1	27.2	1.1	2.6	4.1
Little Rock, AR	40.8	17.7	0.2	2.3	0.2	27.9	2.6	3.6	2.7
Los Angeles, CA	34.0	15.2	0.2	2.3	0.2	29.0	3.0	9.1	5.1
Louisville, KY	40.5	17.7	0.2	2.8	0.2	27.6	2.5	3.6	2.9
Madison, WI	42.2	18.6	0.3	3.3	0.2	25.0	0.8	2.1	4.5

Table continued on following page.

Metro Area	House-holder	Opposite-sex Spouse	Same-sex Spouse	Opposite-sex Unmarried Partner	Same-sex Unmarried Partner	Child[1]	Grand-child	Other Relatives	Non-relatives
Manchester, NH	39.7	19.2	0.3	3.2	0.1	27.2	1.6	3.5	3.2
Miami, FL	38.0	16.0	0.3	2.6	0.2	27.6	2.5	7.8	3.7
Midland, TX	35.8	18.6	0.1	2.0	0.1	32.3	3.2	4.4	2.6
Milwaukee, WI	41.3	17.5	0.2	2.9	0.2	28.7	1.6	3.1	2.7
Minneapolis, MN	38.9	18.7	0.2	2.8	0.2	29.4	1.2	3.3	3.3
Nashville, TN	38.8	18.2	0.2	2.4	0.2	28.1	2.2	4.1	3.8
New Haven, CT	39.7	16.5	0.2	2.6	0.2	28.1	2.0	4.4	2.9
New Orleans, LA	40.3	15.3	0.2	2.7	0.2	28.8	3.1	4.6	2.9
New York, NY	36.8	15.8	0.2	2.0	0.2	29.7	2.1	7.1	4.1
Oklahoma City, OK	38.8	17.7	0.2	2.4	0.2	29.0	2.3	3.8	3.1
Omaha, NE	38.8	18.4	0.2	2.6	0.1	30.6	1.6	3.1	2.8
Orlando, FL	37.0	17.0	0.3	2.7	0.2	28.4	2.4	6.0	4.2
Philadelphia, PA	38.7	16.9	0.2	2.5	0.2	29.2	2.5	4.4	3.0
Phoenix, AZ	36.9	17.2	0.2	2.8	0.2	29.0	2.5	5.4	3.7
Pittsburgh, PA	43.2	19.0	0.2	2.8	0.2	25.6	1.6	2.6	2.4
Portland, OR	39.0	18.1	0.4	3.2	0.3	26.7	1.6	4.2	4.9
Providence, RI	40.0	16.9	0.2	3.0	0.2	27.2	1.9	4.1	3.0
Provo, UT	28.0	18.8	0.1	0.7	0.0	39.0	2.1	4.0	4.8
Raleigh, NC	38.4	19.2	0.2	2.2	0.2	30.0	1.5	3.7	3.0
Reno, NV	39.5	17.2	0.2	3.4	0.2	26.1	2.1	5.0	4.9
Richmond, VA	39.5	17.3	0.2	2.5	0.2	27.7	2.4	4.0	3.3
Rochester, MN	40.1	20.5	0.1	2.7	0.1	28.9	1.0	2.2	2.5
Sacramento, CA	36.2	17.1	0.3	2.4	0.2	29.4	2.2	6.0	4.2
St. Louis, MO	40.8	18.2	0.2	2.6	0.2	28.5	2.2	3.0	2.4
Salem, OR	35.7	17.6	0.2	2.7	0.1	29.3	2.3	5.0	4.1
Salt Lake City, UT	34.0	17.4	0.3	2.1	0.2	32.4	2.5	5.3	4.4
San Antonio, TX	36.2	16.9	0.2	2.3	0.2	31.0	3.5	5.1	2.8
San Diego, CA	35.1	16.9	0.3	2.3	0.2	27.8	2.3	6.6	5.1
San Francisco, CA	36.7	17.0	0.4	2.3	0.3	26.3	1.8	6.9	5.9
San Jose, CA	33.8	18.4	0.2	1.8	0.1	28.3	1.9	7.9	5.6
Santa Rosa, CA	38.4	17.6	0.4	2.9	0.2	26.1	1.9	5.2	5.5
Savannah, GA	38.7	16.6	0.2	2.4	0.2	28.0	2.8	4.1	3.4
Seattle, WA	38.9	18.3	0.3	2.9	0.2	26.7	1.5	4.6	4.7
Sioux Falls, SD	39.5	19.4	0.1	2.9	0.1	29.8	1.1	2.3	2.6
Springfield, IL	42.9	18.2	0.2	3.0	0.2	27.2	1.8	2.4	2.4
Tampa, FL	41.2	17.6	0.3	3.1	0.2	25.5	2.2	4.6	3.4
Tucson, AZ	40.9	17.2	0.3	2.9	0.2	25.5	2.6	4.4	3.4
Tulsa, OK	39.1	18.2	0.2	2.4	0.1	29.0	2.6	3.9	2.7
Tuscaloosa, AL	39.8	15.2	0.1	1.9	0.1	26.5	3.2	3.9	4.5
Virginia Beach, VA	39.0	17.4	0.2	2.3	0.1	27.7	2.5	4.0	3.3
Washington, DC	37.0	17.3	0.3	2.0	0.2	29.3	2.0	5.9	4.4
Wichita, KS	39.0	18.2	0.1	2.4	0.1	29.8	2.1	3.2	2.6
Wilmington, NC	42.3	18.7	0.2	2.9	0.2	24.4	1.9	3.1	3.9
Winston-Salem, NC	40.9	18.6	0.2	2.3	0.1	27.5	2.4	3.7	2.2
Worcester, MA	38.6	17.9	0.2	2.9	0.1	28.1	1.7	4.0	3.1
U.S.	38.3	17.5	0.2	2.5	0.2	28.3	2.4	4.8	3.4

Note: Figures are percent of the total population; Figures cover the Metropolitan Statistical Area; (1) Includes biological, adopted, and stepchildren of the householder
Source: U.S. Census Bureau, 2020 Census

Age: City

City	Percent of Population									Median Age
	Under Age 5	Age 5–19	Age 20–34	Age 35–44	Age 45–54	Age 55–64	Age 65–74	Age 75–84	Age 85+	
Albuquerque, NM	5.1	18.6	21.8	13.2	11.7	12.7	10.2	4.9	1.9	38.2
Allentown, PA	6.8	21.0	23.3	12.4	11.4	11.6	7.8	3.9	1.7	34.2
Anchorage, AK	6.4	19.6	23.4	13.7	11.7	12.6	8.3	3.1	0.9	35.2
Ann Arbor, MI	3.9	15.5	42.4	9.6	7.8	8.1	7.3	3.6	1.7	27.9
Athens, GA	5.1	16.6	38.4	10.7	8.8	8.5	7.3	3.5	1.2	28.2
Atlanta, GA	4.9	15.5	33.3	14.3	11.2	9.5	6.8	3.3	1.3	33.1
Austin, TX	5.5	16.7	31.8	16.1	11.4	9.0	6.1	2.5	1.0	33.0
Baltimore, MD	5.5	16.6	27.0	13.1	10.7	12.6	8.9	4.0	1.6	35.5
Boise City, ID	5.1	18.4	23.4	13.6	11.7	12.0	9.5	4.5	1.8	37.1
Boston, MA	4.5	14.1	37.6	12.0	9.6	9.8	7.2	3.7	1.5	31.7
Boulder, CO	3.0	19.4	34.9	10.4	10.3	9.1	7.7	3.6	1.6	30.0
Brownsville, TX	6.6	25.8	20.0	12.3	12.0	10.1	7.9	3.8	1.5	32.9
Cape Coral, FL	4.5	16.6	14.9	11.3	13.4	16.0	14.5	6.8	2.1	47.2
Cedar Rapids, IA	6.3	19.1	22.5	13.0	11.2	12.0	8.9	4.6	2.4	36.4
Charleston, SC	5.6	14.6	28.5	13.9	10.3	11.2	9.7	4.4	1.8	35.7
Charlotte, NC	6.1	19.3	25.8	14.6	12.6	10.5	6.9	3.0	1.1	34.2
Chicago, IL	5.5	16.9	27.5	14.4	11.9	11.1	7.7	3.7	1.4	35.1
Cincinnati, OH	6.1	18.3	29.2	11.9	10.0	11.5	8.0	3.3	1.7	32.7
Clarksville, TN	8.3	21.9	28.4	13.0	9.9	9.2	5.8	2.5	0.8	29.9
Cleveland, OH	6.0	18.2	24.2	11.8	11.5	13.9	9.0	3.9	1.7	36.1
College Station, TX	5.4	24.3	43.8	8.4	6.3	5.2	3.8	2.1	0.6	22.5
Colorado Springs, CO	5.9	19.0	23.7	13.2	11.3	12.2	8.9	4.1	1.6	35.9
Columbia, MO	5.5	20.5	32.8	11.4	9.1	8.9	7.0	3.3	1.5	29.2
Columbia, SC	4.6	22.1	30.7	11.1	9.5	9.8	7.7	3.2	1.3	29.9
Columbus, OH	6.6	18.1	30.0	13.4	10.7	10.3	6.9	2.9	1.2	32.3
Dallas, TX	6.5	19.3	26.6	14.2	11.7	10.6	6.8	3.1	1.3	33.6
Davenport, IA	6.1	18.8	21.8	12.5	11.5	12.8	9.7	4.6	2.1	37.5
Denver, CO	5.4	15.5	31.0	15.8	11.1	9.4	7.4	3.2	1.3	34.1
Des Moines, IA	6.6	19.7	24.0	13.1	11.3	11.8	8.2	3.6	1.7	34.8
Durham, NC	6.0	17.6	28.2	13.9	11.1	10.4	8.1	3.4	1.3	33.9
Edison, NJ	5.3	19.7	18.1	16.5	13.3	12.2	8.9	4.2	1.9	39.0
El Paso, TX	5.9	21.7	21.9	11.9	11.9	11.9	8.6	4.3	1.9	35.4
Fargo, ND	6.2	17.8	30.1	13.0	9.7	10.3	7.7	3.5	1.8	32.5
Fort Collins, CO	4.4	19.4	31.1	12.7	10.2	9.5	7.7	3.4	1.6	31.7
Fort Wayne, IN	6.9	20.8	21.9	12.4	11.2	11.9	9.1	4.1	1.9	35.3
Fort Worth, TX	7.0	22.7	23.1	14.3	12.1	10.3	6.6	2.9	1.1	33.2
Grand Rapids, MI	6.4	18.1	31.1	12.2	9.3	10.1	7.3	3.4	2.1	31.7
Greeley, CO	6.9	22.5	25.0	12.3	10.2	9.8	7.9	3.9	1.6	31.9
Green Bay, WI	6.5	20.6	22.5	12.9	11.1	12.4	8.6	3.7	1.5	35.2
Greensboro, NC	5.5	20.0	24.9	12.1	11.5	11.3	8.7	4.2	1.8	34.7
Honolulu, HI	4.5	14.3	20.5	13.0	12.7	13.7	11.5	6.0	3.6	42.9
Houston, TX	6.6	19.7	25.1	14.3	11.6	10.7	7.3	3.4	1.3	34.2
Huntsville, AL	5.6	17.7	24.2	12.0	11.2	13.1	9.0	5.2	2.2	36.9
Indianapolis, IN	6.6	20.2	24.0	13.4	11.3	11.8	7.9	3.5	1.3	34.5
Jacksonville, FL	6.0	18.2	22.3	12.9	12.2	13.1	9.3	4.2	1.6	37.4
Kansas City, MO	6.2	18.5	25.0	13.6	11.4	11.9	8.2	3.7	1.5	35.1
Lafayette, LA	5.6	17.9	23.5	12.4	10.9	13.0	10.2	4.6	2.0	37.3
Las Cruces, NM	5.8	20.1	23.5	11.9	10.0	11.2	10.0	5.4	2.1	35.5
Las Vegas, NV	5.7	20.0	20.0	13.5	13.1	12.1	9.4	4.7	1.5	38.0
Lexington, KY	5.7	19.2	24.7	13.3	11.4	11.2	8.6	4.0	1.6	35.2
Lincoln, NE	6.0	20.5	24.9	12.9	10.4	10.8	8.8	3.9	1.7	34.0
Little Rock, AR	6.0	18.7	22.1	13.5	11.8	12.2	9.7	4.3	1.8	37.2
Los Angeles, CA	4.9	17.0	25.6	14.6	12.9	11.5	8.0	3.9	1.7	36.5
Louisville, KY	5.9	19.2	18.9	12.8	12.8	13.4	10.0	4.8	1.9	39.5

Table continued on following page.

| City | Percent of Population | | | | | | | | | Median Age |
	Under Age 5	Age 5–19	Age 20–34	Age 35–44	Age 45–54	Age 55–64	Age 65–74	Age 75–84	Age 85+	
Madison, WI	5.0	16.4	33.7	12.6	9.4	9.6	8.1	3.5	1.6	32.0
Manchester, NH	5.3	15.7	26.0	12.6	12.1	13.4	9.0	3.9	2.0	37.0
Miami, FL	4.8	13.6	24.0	15.0	13.5	12.4	8.8	5.5	2.5	39.7
Midland, TX	7.9	21.7	23.5	14.4	10.3	11.0	6.7	3.0	1.5	33.3
Milwaukee, WI	6.8	21.9	25.6	12.6	10.8	10.8	7.3	2.9	1.3	32.1
Minneapolis, MN	5.6	16.1	32.8	14.7	10.3	9.7	7.1	2.6	1.0	32.6
Nashville, TN	6.1	16.6	29.5	14.1	10.7	10.8	7.5	3.3	1.3	33.8
New Haven, CT	5.6	20.8	30.4	12.8	10.0	9.4	6.6	3.1	1.2	31.0
New Orleans, LA	5.5	17.5	24.9	14.0	11.1	12.3	9.4	3.9	1.5	36.2
New York, NY	5.4	16.7	24.8	13.9	12.2	12.0	8.7	4.4	1.9	36.8
Oklahoma City, OK	6.7	20.7	22.7	13.9	11.2	11.4	8.3	3.8	1.5	34.9
Omaha, NE	6.6	20.7	23.1	13.0	11.0	11.7	8.4	3.8	1.6	34.7
Orlando, FL	5.7	17.6	27.2	15.6	12.4	10.1	6.8	3.2	1.3	34.7
Philadelphia, PA	5.5	17.6	27.2	12.9	10.9	11.6	8.5	4.0	1.7	34.8
Phoenix, AZ	6.3	21.6	22.9	13.7	12.4	11.3	7.5	3.2	1.1	34.5
Pittsburgh, PA	4.4	14.5	34.3	11.5	8.8	11.1	9.1	4.2	2.0	33.0
Portland, OR	4.5	14.6	25.8	17.2	13.1	10.8	8.9	3.7	1.4	37.6
Providence, RI	5.6	21.3	29.4	12.4	10.4	9.8	6.6	3.0	1.4	30.9
Provo, UT	7.1	21.4	44.5	8.3	6.1	5.4	3.8	2.2	1.1	23.8
Raleigh, NC	5.5	18.5	28.0	14.0	12.1	10.1	7.0	3.3	1.4	33.7
Reno, NV	5.5	18.0	24.5	12.7	11.3	11.9	9.9	4.6	1.5	36.3
Richmond, VA	5.5	15.8	33.4	12.0	9.3	10.8	8.2	3.4	1.5	32.4
Rochester, MN	6.5	18.6	23.3	13.4	10.5	11.9	8.5	5.0	2.3	36.0
Sacramento, CA	5.9	18.8	24.6	14.1	11.5	11.2	8.5	3.7	1.6	35.4
St. Louis, MO	5.3	15.1	28.8	13.6	10.9	12.8	8.7	3.4	1.4	35.4
Salem, OR	5.9	20.3	21.7	13.6	11.5	11.2	9.6	4.5	1.8	36.3
Salt Lake City, UT	5.1	16.7	33.3	14.1	10.3	9.2	7.0	2.9	1.3	32.1
San Antonio, TX	6.1	20.6	23.4	13.0	11.8	11.4	8.2	3.9	1.6	34.9
San Diego, CA	5.0	16.8	26.7	14.2	11.9	11.3	8.3	4.0	1.7	35.8
San Francisco, CA	4.0	10.5	29.3	15.8	12.5	11.4	9.2	4.6	2.4	38.2
San Jose, CA	5.3	18.5	22.2	14.7	13.9	12.2	7.7	4.0	1.6	37.6
Santa Rosa, CA	5.1	18.5	19.4	13.7	12.1	12.5	10.9	5.4	2.5	39.9
Savannah, GA	5.8	18.4	28.0	12.2	10.2	11.2	8.6	4.0	1.6	33.5
Seattle, WA	4.4	12.6	33.1	16.0	11.8	9.7	7.7	3.3	1.5	35.0
Sioux Falls, SD	7.0	19.8	22.7	13.8	10.7	11.4	8.7	4.0	1.8	35.3
Springfield, IL	5.8	17.6	19.4	12.2	11.6	14.1	11.5	5.5	2.4	40.7
Tampa, FL	5.4	18.7	24.6	13.6	12.4	11.9	8.0	3.8	1.5	35.8
Tucson, AZ	5.3	18.2	24.8	12.0	10.9	12.1	9.9	4.8	1.9	36.2
Tulsa, OK	6.5	19.8	22.5	12.9	11.1	11.8	9.0	4.3	2.0	35.8
Tuscaloosa, AL	5.1	20.8	34.3	10.0	8.8	9.0	7.2	3.3	1.5	27.1
Virginia Beach, VA	5.8	18.6	22.4	13.3	11.8	12.9	9.1	4.4	1.7	37.1
Washington, DC	5.4	13.9	32.9	15.2	10.0	9.9	7.4	3.6	1.5	33.9
Wichita, KS	6.3	21.0	21.7	12.4	11.1	12.4	9.1	4.1	1.8	35.7
Wilmington, NC	4.3	15.1	27.2	11.8	11.0	12.1	10.8	5.7	2.3	37.8
Winston-Salem, NC	5.8	20.5	22.0	12.2	11.6	12.1	9.1	4.5	2.0	36.2
Worcester, MA	5.4	18.9	26.8	12.1	11.5	11.9	7.9	3.7	1.9	34.3
U.S.	5.6	19.2	20.2	12.7	12.4	13.1	10.0	4.9	1.9	38.8

Source: U.S. Census Bureau, 2020 Census

Age: Metro Area

Metro Area	Percent of Population									Median Age
	Under Age 5	Age 5–19	Age 20–34	Age 35–44	Age 45–54	Age 55–64	Age 65–74	Age 75–84	Age 85+	
Albuquerque, NM	5.1	19.2	19.8	12.6	11.7	13.4	11.0	5.2	1.8	39.4
Allentown, PA	5.0	18.5	18.2	11.8	12.9	14.6	11.0	5.6	2.5	41.9
Anchorage, AK	6.5	20.4	22.2	13.7	11.8	12.7	8.6	3.1	0.9	35.5
Ann Arbor, MI	4.7	17.5	28.4	11.6	11.3	11.6	9.1	4.1	1.6	34.5
Athens, GA	5.3	18.8	28.8	11.6	10.9	10.5	8.6	4.2	1.3	32.5
Atlanta, GA	5.7	20.6	20.9	13.7	13.8	12.1	8.3	3.7	1.2	36.9
Austin, TX	5.9	20.0	24.8	15.3	12.4	10.3	7.3	3.1	1.1	34.7
Baltimore, MD	5.6	18.8	20.5	13.0	12.4	13.6	9.6	4.7	1.9	38.6
Boise City, ID	5.9	21.8	19.7	13.4	11.9	11.7	9.5	4.6	1.6	36.9
Boston, MA	4.9	17.2	22.6	12.5	12.6	13.5	9.8	4.8	2.1	39.0
Boulder, CO	4.2	19.0	23.5	12.7	12.7	12.5	9.7	4.2	1.6	37.6
Brownsville, TX	6.5	25.3	19.3	12.0	11.9	10.6	8.6	4.3	1.6	34.0
Cape Coral, FL	4.3	15.4	15.4	10.1	11.0	14.7	16.4	9.7	3.0	49.7
Cedar Rapids, IA	5.9	19.9	19.1	12.8	11.9	13.2	9.7	5.1	2.2	38.8
Charleston, SC	5.8	18.6	21.4	13.5	11.8	12.6	10.0	4.6	1.5	37.8
Charlotte, NC	5.8	20.2	20.0	13.6	13.7	12.3	8.8	4.2	1.4	37.8
Chicago, IL	5.5	19.3	20.8	13.4	12.9	12.9	9.0	4.3	1.8	38.2
Cincinnati, OH	5.9	20.1	19.8	12.4	12.3	13.4	9.7	4.5	1.8	38.2
Clarksville, TN	7.9	21.3	25.4	12.4	10.7	10.6	7.3	3.3	1.1	31.8
Cleveland, OH	5.2	17.7	18.8	11.7	12.4	14.6	11.3	5.6	2.5	41.7
College Station, TX	5.9	22.0	32.3	10.5	8.8	9.1	6.8	3.3	1.3	27.5
Colorado Springs, CO	6.0	20.0	23.1	12.9	11.4	12.4	8.8	3.9	1.4	35.6
Columbia, MO	5.7	20.6	26.7	12.0	10.2	10.9	8.4	3.9	1.5	32.8
Columbia, SC	5.4	20.2	20.1	12.4	12.4	13.2	10.2	4.6	1.6	38.4
Columbus, OH	6.2	19.8	22.2	13.4	12.3	12.0	8.6	3.9	1.5	36.2
Dallas, TX	6.2	21.8	21.4	14.1	13.0	11.4	7.4	3.4	1.1	35.3
Davenport, IA	5.7	19.5	17.9	12.4	11.8	13.6	11.0	5.6	2.3	40.3
Denver, CO	5.5	18.8	23.0	14.7	12.6	11.7	8.5	3.7	1.4	36.6
Des Moines, IA	6.5	20.8	20.2	13.8	12.0	11.9	8.7	4.1	1.7	36.6
Durham, NC	5.2	18.4	23.1	12.7	12.1	12.3	9.9	4.6	1.6	37.4
Edison, NJ	5.4	18.0	21.5	13.3	12.8	13.0	9.2	4.7	2.1	38.7
El Paso, TX	6.1	22.6	22.4	12.1	11.8	11.5	8.0	3.9	1.7	34.2
Fargo, ND	6.7	19.9	25.7	13.7	10.4	10.7	7.7	3.5	1.7	33.5
Fort Collins, CO	4.6	18.5	23.6	12.9	11.0	12.4	10.5	4.8	1.8	37.4
Fort Wayne, IN	6.7	21.3	19.9	12.4	11.7	12.4	9.4	4.4	1.8	36.6
Fort Worth, TX	6.2	21.8	21.4	14.1	13.0	11.4	7.4	3.4	1.1	35.3
Grand Rapids, MI	6.1	20.6	21.8	12.5	11.5	12.5	8.9	4.3	1.8	36.2
Greeley, CO	6.9	22.6	21.3	13.9	11.6	11.1	8.0	3.4	1.2	34.5
Green Bay, WI	5.8	19.8	18.8	12.6	12.2	14.0	10.1	4.8	1.8	39.3
Greensboro, NC	5.3	19.6	19.9	11.7	12.9	13.2	10.2	5.1	1.9	39.4
Honolulu, HI	5.4	17.3	21.1	12.6	12.2	12.9	10.4	5.4	2.8	39.8
Houston, TX	6.5	22.1	21.0	14.3	12.7	11.4	7.7	3.3	1.1	35.3
Huntsville, AL	5.6	19.2	20.4	12.6	12.8	13.9	9.1	4.7	1.7	38.7
Indianapolis, IN	6.2	20.7	20.2	13.5	12.5	12.5	8.8	4.1	1.5	37.0
Jacksonville, FL	5.6	18.9	19.5	12.8	12.6	13.6	10.4	4.8	1.7	39.6
Kansas City, MO	6.1	20.2	19.9	13.4	12.1	12.8	9.3	4.4	1.7	37.7
Lafayette, LA	6.3	20.5	19.3	12.9	11.7	13.5	9.6	4.5	1.6	37.8
Las Cruces, NM	5.8	21.3	21.6	11.4	10.6	12.2	10.2	5.2	1.9	36.0
Las Vegas, NV	5.7	19.4	20.6	13.9	13.1	12.1	9.5	4.6	1.3	38.0
Lexington, KY	5.9	19.7	22.2	13.2	12.1	12.1	9.2	4.2	1.6	36.5
Lincoln, NE	6.0	20.9	23.4	12.9	10.6	11.4	9.1	4.1	1.7	34.8
Little Rock, AR	5.9	19.9	20.2	13.1	12.0	12.7	10.0	4.7	1.6	38.0
Los Angeles, CA	5.0	18.3	22.5	13.7	13.3	12.4	8.6	4.4	1.9	37.9
Louisville, KY	5.8	18.9	19.5	12.9	12.6	13.6	10.2	4.7	1.8	39.3

Table continued on following page.

Metro Area	Percent of Population									Median Age
	Under Age 5	Age 5–19	Age 20–34	Age 35–44	Age 45–54	Age 55–64	Age 65–74	Age 75–84	Age 85+	
Madison, WI	5.3	18.3	23.6	13.3	11.5	12.3	9.6	4.2	1.8	36.9
Manchester, NH	5.0	17.5	20.0	12.3	13.5	15.2	10.0	4.7	1.9	40.9
Miami, FL	4.8	17.1	18.7	13.0	13.8	13.7	10.2	6.0	2.6	42.1
Midland, TX	7.8	22.3	22.9	14.3	10.7	11.2	6.7	2.9	1.3	33.3
Milwaukee, WI	5.8	19.6	19.9	12.6	12.0	13.5	9.7	4.6	2.1	38.5
Minneapolis, MN	6.1	19.8	20.5	13.7	12.3	13.0	8.9	4.1	1.7	37.5
Nashville, TN	6.0	19.6	22.1	13.9	12.5	12.1	8.6	3.9	1.3	36.4
New Haven, CT	4.9	18.1	20.3	11.9	12.6	14.1	10.4	5.3	2.5	40.4
New Orleans, LA	5.7	18.9	20.3	13.3	11.9	13.4	10.3	4.6	1.7	38.6
New York, NY	5.4	18.0	21.5	13.3	12.8	13.0	9.2	4.7	2.1	38.7
Oklahoma City, OK	6.2	21.0	21.6	13.4	11.3	12.0	8.9	4.2	1.6	35.8
Omaha, NE	6.6	21.5	20.4	13.4	11.5	12.2	8.8	4.0	1.6	36.0
Orlando, FL	5.2	19.5	21.2	13.5	12.9	12.2	9.2	4.6	1.7	37.9
Philadelphia, PA	5.3	18.7	20.7	12.6	12.4	13.7	9.8	4.8	2.1	39.1
Phoenix, AZ	5.7	20.5	20.5	12.8	12.1	11.9	9.8	5.1	1.7	37.5
Pittsburgh, PA	4.9	16.3	19.3	11.8	12.1	14.9	12.0	5.9	2.8	42.9
Portland, OR	5.2	18.3	21.0	14.8	12.8	12.0	9.8	4.4	1.6	38.6
Providence, RI	4.8	17.9	20.0	12.1	12.8	14.5	10.6	5.2	2.4	40.8
Provo, UT	8.9	27.9	26.5	12.8	8.9	6.9	4.9	2.5	0.9	25.9
Raleigh, NC	5.8	21.0	20.5	14.3	13.8	11.7	8.0	3.6	1.2	36.8
Reno, NV	5.4	18.5	21.4	12.3	11.8	13.1	10.9	5.0	1.5	38.5
Richmond, VA	5.5	18.9	20.8	12.7	12.3	13.3	10.1	4.6	1.8	38.6
Rochester, MN	6.2	19.8	19.3	13.2	11.2	13.4	9.4	5.3	2.3	38.4
Sacramento, CA	5.6	19.8	20.3	13.2	12.1	12.7	9.8	4.8	2.0	38.2
St. Louis, MO	5.6	18.9	19.4	12.6	12.1	14.1	10.3	5.0	2.1	39.7
Salem, OR	5.9	20.8	20.0	12.7	11.3	11.9	10.4	5.1	1.9	37.4
Salt Lake City, UT	6.7	22.8	23.7	14.7	11.1	9.7	7.0	3.1	1.1	32.8
San Antonio, TX	6.1	21.4	21.0	13.2	12.2	11.8	8.7	4.1	1.5	36.0
San Diego, CA	5.3	18.5	23.2	13.4	12.2	12.2	9.0	4.3	1.9	37.1
San Francisco, CA	5.0	16.8	21.7	14.7	13.3	12.4	9.3	4.7	2.0	39.1
San Jose, CA	5.3	18.4	22.4	14.6	13.6	12.0	7.7	4.2	1.9	37.5
Santa Rosa, CA	4.6	17.3	18.2	12.9	12.2	14.2	12.7	5.8	2.3	42.6
Savannah, GA	5.9	19.7	22.5	13.0	11.7	12.2	9.3	4.3	1.5	36.3
Seattle, WA	5.7	17.9	22.7	14.9	12.7	12.1	8.5	3.9	1.5	37.2
Sioux Falls, SD	7.0	20.9	20.5	13.8	11.1	11.9	8.8	4.0	1.7	36.0
Springfield, IL	5.6	18.9	17.6	12.5	12.1	14.5	11.4	5.3	2.1	41.2
Tampa, FL	4.8	17.1	18.3	12.3	12.8	14.2	11.8	6.2	2.3	42.7
Tucson, AZ	4.9	17.8	19.8	11.5	10.9	13.1	12.7	6.8	2.4	41.2
Tulsa, OK	6.2	20.6	19.6	12.8	11.8	12.7	9.7	4.9	1.8	37.6
Tuscaloosa, AL	5.8	20.1	24.7	11.9	11.1	11.8	9.0	4.1	1.5	34.5
Virginia Beach, VA	5.8	18.8	22.2	12.5	11.5	13.4	9.5	4.6	1.7	37.3
Washington, DC	5.8	19.4	21.5	14.3	13.2	12.3	8.2	3.9	1.4	37.2
Wichita, KS	6.2	21.6	19.9	12.5	11.2	12.9	9.5	4.4	1.9	36.7
Wilmington, NC	4.8	16.9	20.5	12.7	12.6	13.3	11.7	5.7	2.0	41.1
Winston-Salem, NC	5.3	19.2	18.2	11.6	13.2	14.0	10.8	5.6	2.1	41.1
Worcester, MA	5.0	18.5	19.8	12.3	13.4	14.6	9.9	4.6	2.0	40.3
U.S.	5.6	19.2	20.2	12.7	12.4	13.1	10.0	4.9	1.9	38.8

Note: Figures cover the Metropolitan Statistical Area (MSA)
Source: U.S. Census Bureau, 2020 Census

Ancestry: City

City	German	Irish	English	American	Italian	Polish	French[1]	Scottish	Dutch
Albuquerque, NM	9.2	7.6	7.8	3.3	3.2	1.4	1.8	1.4	0.9
Allentown, PA	9.8	4.7	2.0	2.7	4.2	1.8	0.7	0.4	0.8
Anchorage, AK	13.8	9.4	8.5	3.6	3.2	2.0	2.3	1.9	1.3
Ann Arbor, MI	17.0	10.4	10.1	2.7	4.9	6.0	2.7	2.6	2.4
Athens, GA	8.4	8.2	9.8	3.5	3.4	1.5	2.0	2.8	0.8
Atlanta, GA	6.8	5.9	8.1	4.8	2.9	1.4	1.8	1.5	0.5
Austin, TX	10.9	8.3	8.7	2.9	3.0	1.8	2.4	2.1	0.7
Baltimore, MD	6.1	5.7	3.3	2.8	3.1	2.3	0.9	0.7	0.3
Boise City, ID	16.9	12.1	18.1	4.4	4.2	1.9	2.2	3.2	1.7
Boston, MA	4.8	13.1	4.9	2.2	7.2	2.1	1.8	1.1	0.4
Boulder, CO	16.2	11.5	11.4	2.4	6.0	3.6	2.4	3.3	1.3
Brownsville, TX	0.9	0.5	0.6	1.7	0.4	0.1	0.4	0.1	0.2
Cape Coral, FL	14.2	11.5	7.8	12.3	9.6	3.4	2.0	1.5	0.9
Cedar Rapids, IA	29.0	13.5	9.0	3.6	1.7	1.3	1.9	1.7	1.6
Charleston, SC	10.8	10.5	11.4	21.1	4.2	2.2	2.5	2.3	0.7
Charlotte, NC	8.0	6.9	7.0	4.8	3.4	1.5	1.3	1.7	0.5
Chicago, IL	7.3	7.3	2.8	2.1	3.9	5.2	0.9	0.7	0.5
Cincinnati, OH	17.3	9.4	6.2	3.5	3.8	1.6	1.4	1.1	0.9
Clarksville, TN	12.2	8.6	7.1	6.1	4.2	1.0	1.4	1.6	1.1
Cleveland, OH	9.5	8.5	3.2	2.2	4.6	3.9	0.9	0.6	0.5
College Station, TX	15.9	8.4	8.8	3.3	3.5	1.8	2.9	1.7	0.8
Colorado Springs, CO	17.7	10.6	11.4	4.2	4.7	2.2	2.7	2.7	1.4
Columbia, MO	24.6	12.0	11.0	4.4	3.6	2.2	1.9	2.3	1.2
Columbia, SC	9.6	6.9	7.7	5.5	3.3	1.1	1.9	1.9	0.6
Columbus, OH	15.2	10.2	6.9	4.0	4.9	2.1	1.3	1.6	0.8
Dallas, TX	5.1	4.2	5.1	4.2	1.7	0.8	1.2	1.1	0.4
Davenport, IA	27.7	15.3	7.5	3.4	2.2	2.0	1.5	1.6	1.6
Denver, CO	13.9	10.1	9.0	2.6	5.0	2.7	2.1	2.1	1.1
Des Moines, IA	19.1	11.9	8.2	3.1	3.6	1.2	1.5	1.2	2.3
Durham, NC	8.1	6.5	9.4	3.7	3.3	1.7	1.6	1.6	0.6
Edison, NJ	4.4	5.8	1.6	1.7	7.8	3.3	1.0	0.5	0.2
El Paso, TX	3.8	2.5	1.9	2.2	1.3	0.5	0.7	0.4	0.2
Fargo, ND	35.0	8.2	5.0	2.5	1.0	2.1	3.5	1.2	1.0
Fort Collins, CO	23.4	12.9	13.0	3.6	5.8	3.0	3.2	3.3	1.8
Fort Wayne, IN	23.1	9.4	7.8	5.5	2.3	2.2	2.7	1.6	1.1
Fort Worth, TX	7.2	6.1	6.5	4.2	1.8	1.0	1.3	1.5	0.7
Grand Rapids, MI	14.1	8.0	6.4	2.5	3.0	6.3	1.9	1.6	13.0
Greeley, CO	16.6	8.4	7.5	3.1	2.7	1.6	1.6	1.9	1.0
Green Bay, WI	28.7	8.5	4.3	4.1	2.1	8.0	3.6	1.0	2.6
Greensboro, NC	6.5	5.5	8.6	4.4	2.4	1.0	1.2	1.6	0.5
Honolulu, HI	4.4	3.1	3.2	1.4	1.7	0.8	0.8	0.6	0.2
Houston, TX	4.8	3.5	4.3	3.4	1.6	0.9	1.4	0.9	0.4
Huntsville, AL	9.4	8.9	10.6	10.2	2.3	1.2	1.8	1.9	0.9
Indianapolis, IN	12.8	8.2	7.0	4.9	2.0	1.5	1.6	1.5	0.9
Jacksonville, FL	7.5	7.6	6.5	5.7	3.7	1.4	1.3	1.5	0.6
Kansas City, MO	15.2	10.1	8.1	4.1	3.6	1.7	1.7	1.4	0.8
Lafayette, LA	8.0	5.4	5.9	5.9	3.6	0.3	16.2	1.0	0.4
Las Cruces, NM	7.0	5.8	6.4	2.6	1.9	1.0	1.2	1.1	0.8
Las Vegas, NV	8.5	7.3	6.2	3.2	5.2	1.8	1.6	1.3	0.7
Lexington, KY	13.1	11.0	12.1	8.2	3.1	1.6	1.6	2.6	1.1
Lincoln, NE	31.5	11.5	8.9	3.3	2.0	2.4	1.8	1.4	1.6
Little Rock, AR	7.3	6.2	8.8	5.2	1.4	0.9	1.5	1.6	0.4
Los Angeles, CA	3.8	3.6	3.1	3.9	2.7	1.4	1.1	0.7	0.4
Louisville, KY	15.2	11.5	9.3	6.5	2.6	1.1	1.7	1.6	0.9
Madison, WI	29.4	12.0	8.8	2.0	4.0	5.5	2.4	1.8	1.8
Manchester, NH	6.2	19.3	9.5	2.9	8.8	3.8	11.4	2.7	0.3

Table continued on following page.

City	German	Irish	English	American	Italian	Polish	French[1]	Scottish	Dutch
Miami, FL	1.8	1.3	1.0	2.7	2.5	0.7	0.9	0.2	0.2
Midland, TX	5.8	5.2	6.0	4.7	1.0	0.5	1.5	1.4	0.3
Milwaukee, WI	15.1	5.6	2.1	1.3	2.5	5.9	1.2	0.4	0.6
Minneapolis, MN	20.9	10.5	6.5	1.9	2.6	3.9	2.7	1.4	1.3
Nashville, TN	8.4	7.8	8.7	6.8	2.6	1.4	1.6	1.9	0.7
New Haven, CT	3.9	6.2	3.2	2.0	8.2	2.0	1.2	0.5	0.5
New Orleans, LA	6.1	5.7	4.9	2.2	3.7	0.9	5.2	1.0	0.4
New York, NY	2.9	4.4	1.9	3.8	6.1	2.3	0.8	0.5	0.3
Oklahoma City, OK	10.0	7.8	7.7	5.7	1.8	0.7	1.3	1.6	0.9
Omaha, NE	24.7	13.0	7.8	3.0	4.0	3.5	1.9	1.6	1.4
Orlando, FL	6.2	5.7	5.7	5.6	4.7	1.6	1.5	1.0	0.6
Philadelphia, PA	6.7	9.9	2.8	2.5	6.9	3.1	0.8	0.6	0.3
Phoenix, AZ	9.8	7.4	6.3	2.8	3.8	1.8	1.6	1.2	0.8
Pittsburgh, PA	17.9	13.8	5.4	3.0	12.1	6.7	1.4	1.3	0.5
Portland, OR	15.3	11.2	11.9	4.5	4.5	2.3	2.8	2.9	1.7
Providence, RI	3.7	8.0	3.9	2.1	6.9	1.4	2.9	0.8	0.3
Provo, UT	9.9	5.2	25.3	2.6	1.8	0.7	1.4	4.1	1.7
Raleigh, NC	9.0	8.1	10.4	8.4	3.9	2.0	1.7	2.3	0.9
Reno, NV	12.0	10.6	10.5	4.2	5.7	1.9	2.4	2.0	1.2
Richmond, VA	7.3	7.0	8.9	4.5	3.5	1.4	1.5	1.9	0.5
Rochester, MN	28.7	10.2	6.7	3.1	1.5	2.9	1.8	1.3	1.6
Sacramento, CA	6.6	5.9	5.5	1.8	3.5	1.0	1.5	1.1	0.6
St. Louis, MO	15.7	9.7	5.4	4.4	4.0	1.7	2.3	1.2	0.8
Salem, OR	16.9	9.3	11.1	3.6	2.9	1.4	2.7	2.5	1.8
Salt Lake City, UT	10.9	6.9	17.7	3.2	4.1	1.4	2.1	3.5	1.8
San Antonio, TX	7.0	4.3	4.0	3.2	1.8	1.0	1.4	0.8	0.3
San Diego, CA	8.3	7.1	6.2	2.3	4.2	1.8	1.7	1.4	0.7
San Francisco, CA	6.9	7.6	5.5	2.5	4.6	1.8	2.1	1.3	0.7
San Jose, CA	4.6	4.0	3.8	1.8	3.3	0.8	1.1	0.8	0.5
Santa Rosa, CA	11.1	9.8	9.6	2.5	6.6	1.6	2.8	1.7	1.1
Savannah, GA	6.5	7.6	5.4	4.0	3.1	1.5	1.6	1.3	0.6
Seattle, WA	14.4	11.0	11.1	2.3	4.5	2.6	3.0	2.8	1.3
Sioux Falls, SD	33.6	10.9	6.5	4.2	1.6	1.5	1.8	0.9	6.1
Springfield, IL	18.9	11.4	9.6	4.1	4.5	2.0	1.9	1.8	1.1
Tampa, FL	8.7	7.5	6.7	6.5	6.2	2.0	1.8	1.4	0.7
Tucson, AZ	11.1	8.1	7.4	2.8	3.5	1.9	1.8	1.5	0.8
Tulsa, OK	10.8	8.7	9.3	5.4	2.0	0.9	1.9	2.0	0.8
Tuscaloosa, AL	5.2	6.1	6.4	5.7	1.9	0.7	1.3	2.1	0.5
Virginia Beach, VA	11.3	10.7	10.1	7.8	5.6	2.1	2.2	2.2	0.8
Washington, DC	7.5	7.3	6.1	2.8	4.3	2.2	1.6	1.4	0.7
Wichita, KS	19.0	9.6	9.7	4.8	1.6	0.9	2.0	1.6	1.2
Wilmington, NC	10.2	9.4	11.7	4.7	5.3	2.0	1.8	2.7	0.8
Winston-Salem, NC	8.7	6.4	8.5	4.8	2.4	0.9	1.2	1.9	0.7
Worcester, MA	3.0	14.0	4.6	3.7	8.9	4.2	5.7	1.0	0.3
U.S.	12.8	9.6	8.1	5.7	5.0	2.7	2.2	1.6	1.1

Note: Figures are the percentage of the total population reporting a particular ancestry. The nine most commonly reported ancestries in the U.S. are shown. Figures include multiple ancestries (e.g. if a person reported being Irish and Italian, they were included in both columns); (1) Excludes Basque
Source: U.S. Census Bureau, 2017-2021 American Community Survey 5-Year Estimates

Ancestry: Metro Area

Metro Area	German	Irish	English	American	Italian	Polish	French[1]	Scottish	Dutch
Albuquerque, NM	9.2	7.2	7.7	3.9	3.1	1.3	1.7	1.5	0.7
Allentown, PA	22.8	12.8	6.1	4.9	11.8	4.9	1.4	1.0	1.8
Anchorage, AK	14.7	9.9	8.8	4.0	3.0	2.0	2.4	2.0	1.4
Ann Arbor, MI	18.3	10.6	10.8	5.9	4.6	6.3	2.9	2.7	2.0
Athens, GA	8.4	10.1	11.7	6.7	2.9	1.1	1.8	2.6	1.0
Atlanta, GA	6.5	6.4	8.0	8.0	2.6	1.2	1.3	1.6	0.6
Austin, TX	12.3	8.1	9.1	3.7	2.8	1.6	2.3	2.1	0.8
Baltimore, MD	14.3	11.3	8.0	4.6	5.9	3.8	1.4	1.5	0.6
Boise City, ID	16.4	10.2	17.6	4.9	3.5	1.4	2.4	2.9	1.9
Boston, MA	5.8	20.3	9.7	3.3	12.4	3.1	4.2	2.1	0.5
Boulder, CO	18.4	11.9	13.4	3.0	5.4	3.2	2.7	3.0	1.7
Brownsville, TX	1.9	1.1	1.8	1.9	0.5	0.2	0.5	0.3	0.1
Cape Coral, FL	13.5	10.7	8.4	12.5	7.8	3.1	2.1	1.7	1.1
Cedar Rapids, IA	32.6	14.2	9.1	4.1	1.7	1.1	2.2	1.9	2.0
Charleston, SC	10.1	9.5	10.6	11.8	3.9	1.8	2.1	2.3	0.6
Charlotte, NC	10.7	8.5	8.9	8.8	3.9	1.8	1.5	2.1	0.8
Chicago, IL	13.7	10.5	4.5	2.5	6.4	8.3	1.3	0.9	1.1
Cincinnati, OH	26.1	13.2	10.0	6.2	4.0	1.6	1.8	1.8	1.0
Clarksville, TN	11.8	8.8	8.3	7.4	3.2	1.1	1.4	1.7	1.0
Cleveland, OH	18.7	13.4	7.7	4.2	9.4	7.4	1.5	1.4	0.8
College Station, TX	13.5	7.6	7.6	3.8	2.8	1.8	2.4	1.6	0.7
Colorado Springs, CO	17.8	10.6	10.9	4.4	4.5	2.3	2.6	2.6	1.4
Columbia, MO	25.0	11.7	11.6	6.2	2.9	1.7	2.1	2.1	1.3
Columbia, SC	9.5	7.1	8.3	7.5	2.3	1.3	1.4	1.8	0.6
Columbus, OH	20.7	12.7	9.6	5.7	5.2	2.3	1.7	2.1	1.1
Dallas, TX	8.2	6.5	7.6	5.9	2.1	1.0	1.5	1.5	0.6
Davenport, IA	25.9	13.5	8.2	4.0	2.3	2.1	1.7	1.4	1.8
Denver, CO	17.1	10.7	10.5	3.3	5.0	2.4	2.4	2.2	1.4
Des Moines, IA	26.2	13.0	10.1	4.0	3.1	1.4	1.7	1.5	3.6
Durham, NC	9.3	8.0	11.1	5.4	3.5	1.8	1.7	2.1	0.7
Edison, NJ	6.0	8.9	2.9	4.0	11.6	3.7	0.9	0.6	0.5
El Paso, TX	3.5	2.3	1.8	2.2	1.2	0.5	0.6	0.4	0.2
Fargo, ND	35.4	7.8	4.8	2.5	1.1	2.2	3.1	1.1	1.1
Fort Collins, CO	25.2	13.1	14.1	4.1	5.2	2.8	3.2	3.4	2.1
Fort Wayne, IN	26.4	9.5	8.3	6.4	2.5	2.1	3.1	1.6	1.1
Fort Worth, TX	8.2	6.5	7.6	5.9	2.1	1.0	1.5	1.5	0.6
Grand Rapids, MI	18.8	9.5	8.9	3.4	3.0	6.3	2.5	1.7	18.0
Greeley, CO	20.5	10.1	9.7	4.1	3.7	1.9	1.9	1.8	1.4
Green Bay, WI	35.4	9.6	4.8	3.8	2.1	9.5	3.9	0.8	4.1
Greensboro, NC	8.5	7.0	9.4	7.3	2.4	1.1	1.3	2.1	0.8
Honolulu, HI	5.2	3.9	3.7	1.3	1.9	0.8	1.1	0.8	0.4
Houston, TX	7.3	5.0	5.8	3.8	2.0	1.1	1.9	1.1	0.6
Huntsville, AL	8.9	9.5	11.1	11.7	2.2	1.3	1.6	1.9	0.8
Indianapolis, IN	16.6	9.6	9.5	8.1	2.5	1.7	1.7	1.7	1.2
Jacksonville, FL	9.3	9.4	8.9	7.9	4.3	1.8	1.7	2.0	0.7
Kansas City, MO	19.9	12.3	11.1	4.9	3.2	1.6	2.1	1.9	1.2
Lafayette, LA	6.3	4.3	4.2	6.4	2.6	0.4	16.5	0.6	0.3
Las Cruces, NM	6.5	4.7	5.3	2.5	1.6	0.7	1.1	1.1	0.7
Las Vegas, NV	8.2	6.9	6.3	3.0	4.9	1.8	1.5	1.2	0.6
Lexington, KY	12.7	11.3	12.6	11.4	2.8	1.4	1.6	2.5	1.1
Lincoln, NE	32.9	11.3	8.7	3.6	1.9	2.3	1.8	1.3	1.8
Little Rock, AR	8.9	8.8	9.6	7.1	1.5	0.8	1.5	1.8	0.7
Los Angeles, CA	5.1	4.3	4.1	3.5	2.9	1.2	1.2	0.8	0.5
Louisville, KY	17.3	12.5	10.8	8.1	2.5	1.2	1.9	1.9	1.0
Madison, WI	35.2	12.9	9.1	2.7	3.6	5.1	2.5	1.6	1.7
Manchester, NH	8.0	20.7	13.9	3.3	9.8	4.0	11.2	3.3	0.7

Table continued on following page.

Metro Area	German	Irish	English	American	Italian	Polish	French[1]	Scottish	Dutch
Miami, FL	4.3	4.2	2.9	5.9	4.9	1.8	1.2	0.6	0.4
Midland, TX	6.0	5.0	5.7	5.0	1.2	0.5	1.4	1.2	0.2
Milwaukee, WI	31.9	9.5	4.6	2.1	4.2	10.3	2.2	0.9	1.2
Minneapolis, MN	28.1	10.9	6.3	3.0	2.6	4.1	3.2	1.2	1.4
Nashville, TN	9.9	9.3	11.1	10.2	2.7	1.3	1.7	2.1	0.8
New Haven, CT	7.5	14.2	7.1	2.9	19.9	5.4	3.0	1.0	0.5
New Orleans, LA	9.6	7.9	5.5	4.8	7.3	0.7	11.0	1.0	0.4
New York, NY	6.0	8.9	2.9	4.0	11.6	3.7	0.9	0.6	0.5
Oklahoma City, OK	11.6	8.9	9.1	7.0	1.8	0.8	1.5	1.8	1.0
Omaha, NE	28.3	13.1	9.1	3.5	3.9	3.7	1.9	1.5	1.6
Orlando, FL	8.1	7.2	6.5	8.2	5.1	1.8	1.7	1.2	0.7
Philadelphia, PA	14.1	17.4	7.4	3.2	12.4	4.7	1.2	1.2	0.7
Phoenix, AZ	12.5	8.6	8.6	3.8	4.4	2.3	1.9	1.6	1.0
Pittsburgh, PA	25.1	17.0	8.6	3.3	15.2	8.1	1.6	1.9	1.0
Portland, OR	16.4	10.5	11.7	4.6	3.7	1.8	2.7	2.7	1.7
Providence, RI	4.5	17.2	10.7	3.2	13.1	3.4	8.6	1.5	0.4
Provo, UT	10.0	4.9	29.5	4.2	2.2	0.5	1.6	4.3	1.5
Raleigh, NC	9.9	9.1	11.6	8.2	4.6	2.1	1.8	2.4	0.8
Reno, NV	12.5	10.6	10.9	3.8	6.2	1.8	2.6	2.0	1.2
Richmond, VA	9.0	7.9	11.7	6.7	3.8	1.5	1.5	1.9	0.7
Rochester, MN	34.2	11.0	6.8	3.4	1.3	2.8	1.9	1.2	1.9
Sacramento, CA	10.1	7.9	8.7	2.6	4.7	1.2	1.9	1.6	0.9
St. Louis, MO	26.1	12.9	8.6	5.4	4.6	2.3	3.0	1.5	1.0
Salem, OR	16.9	9.0	10.6	3.7	2.8	1.2	2.6	2.3	1.8
Salt Lake City, UT	9.7	5.7	21.7	4.0	2.9	0.9	1.9	3.6	1.7
San Antonio, TX	10.0	5.7	5.8	3.6	2.1	1.4	1.7	1.2	0.4
San Diego, CA	8.9	7.4	6.7	2.7	4.1	1.7	1.8	1.4	0.8
San Francisco, CA	7.3	7.0	6.2	2.3	4.4	1.4	1.8	1.4	0.7
San Jose, CA	5.8	4.7	4.7	2.0	3.7	1.1	1.3	0.9	0.6
Santa Rosa, CA	12.8	12.2	10.9	2.5	8.3	1.7	3.1	2.5	1.2
Savannah, GA	9.1	9.9	8.7	7.4	3.5	1.4	1.7	1.7	0.6
Seattle, WA	13.8	9.4	10.1	3.0	3.5	1.8	2.6	2.5	1.3
Sioux Falls, SD	35.2	10.4	6.1	5.2	1.4	1.4	1.8	0.9	6.4
Springfield, IL	21.5	12.5	10.9	5.1	4.8	1.9	2.2	1.9	1.3
Tampa, FL	11.6	10.3	8.5	8.6	7.3	2.9	2.4	1.7	0.9
Tucson, AZ	13.1	8.9	9.1	3.3	3.9	2.3	2.1	1.9	1.0
Tulsa, OK	12.6	10.2	9.9	5.6	1.9	0.9	2.0	2.0	1.1
Tuscaloosa, AL	5.0	6.5	6.9	10.9	1.5	0.4	0.9	1.9	0.5
Virginia Beach, VA	9.5	8.8	9.8	8.5	4.0	1.7	1.8	1.7	0.7
Washington, DC	9.0	8.4	7.5	4.0	4.2	2.1	1.5	1.5	0.7
Wichita, KS	21.4	9.9	10.0	5.7	1.7	0.9	2.0	1.8	1.3
Wilmington, NC	11.3	10.8	12.1	5.8	5.6	2.3	1.8	3.0	0.8
Winston-Salem, NC	11.3	8.1	11.0	8.5	2.3	1.1	1.2	2.2	0.8
Worcester, MA	5.5	17.6	9.3	5.5	11.8	5.6	9.5	2.0	0.5
U.S.	12.8	9.6	8.1	5.7	5.0	2.7	2.2	1.6	1.1

Note: Figures are the percentage of the total population reporting a particular ancestry. The nine most commonly reported ancestries in the U.S. are shown. Figures include multiple ancestries (e.g. if a person reported being Irish and Italian, they were included in both columns); Figures cover the Metropolitan Statistical Area; (1) Excludes Basque
Source: U.S. Census Bureau, 2017-2021 American Community Survey 5-Year Estimates

Foreign-born Population: City

City	Any Foreign Country	Percent of Population Born in							
		Asia	Mexico	Europe	Caribbean	Central America[1]	South America	Africa	Canada
Albuquerque, NM	10.2	2.5	5.1	0.9	0.4	0.1	0.4	0.5	0.1
Allentown, PA	20.4	3.1	1.0	0.8	11.5	0.8	2.0	1.3	0.1
Anchorage, AK	11.0	6.1	0.7	1.0	0.6	0.2	0.5	0.6	0.4
Ann Arbor, MI	18.6	12.3	0.5	2.9	0.1	0.1	0.7	1.2	0.8
Athens, GA	9.5	2.9	2.4	0.9	0.3	1.0	1.0	1.0	0.2
Atlanta, GA	8.3	3.4	0.7	1.4	0.8	0.2	0.8	0.8	0.3
Austin, TX	18.5	6.3	6.3	1.5	0.6	1.7	0.8	0.9	0.3
Baltimore, MD	8.1	2.2	0.3	0.9	1.3	1.0	0.4	1.9	0.1
Boise City, ID	6.5	2.8	1.1	1.2	0.1	0.0	0.3	0.5	0.5
Boston, MA	28.1	7.6	0.4	3.1	8.6	2.5	2.3	3.0	0.4
Boulder, CO	10.6	4.4	0.9	3.0	0.2	0.5	0.7	0.3	0.5
Brownsville, TX	27.1	0.5	25.5	0.2	0.0	0.7	0.1	0.0	0.1
Cape Coral, FL	17.4	1.5	0.6	2.4	8.3	0.9	3.2	0.1	0.5
Cedar Rapids, IA	6.8	2.6	0.7	0.5	0.1	0.2	0.2	2.3	0.1
Charleston, SC	5.0	1.5	0.6	1.3	0.4	0.1	0.6	0.3	0.1
Charlotte, NC	17.3	5.3	2.5	1.3	1.2	3.1	1.5	2.1	0.2
Chicago, IL	20.2	5.1	8.1	3.4	0.3	0.9	1.1	1.0	0.2
Cincinnati, OH	6.6	1.9	0.4	0.9	0.2	0.8	0.3	2.0	0.1
Clarksville, TN	6.3	2.0	1.3	0.8	0.5	0.7	0.4	0.4	0.2
Cleveland, OH	6.0	2.4	0.4	1.1	0.6	0.4	0.3	0.7	0.1
College Station, TX	12.3	7.3	1.5	0.9	0.2	0.3	1.1	0.8	0.2
Colorado Springs, CO	7.5	2.2	2.0	1.5	0.3	0.4	0.4	0.4	0.4
Columbia, MO	8.4	5.1	0.6	0.9	0.1	0.2	0.3	1.0	0.1
Columbia, SC	4.8	2.1	0.3	0.6	0.6	0.2	0.4	0.5	0.1
Columbus, OH	13.3	5.0	1.1	0.9	0.5	0.8	0.4	4.7	0.1
Dallas, TX	23.8	2.8	13.9	0.8	0.4	2.9	0.7	2.1	0.2
Davenport, IA	4.5	1.6	1.8	0.4	0.2	0.1	0.0	0.2	0.1
Denver, CO	14.2	2.8	6.6	1.4	0.3	0.6	0.7	1.4	0.3
Des Moines, IA	13.8	5.2	3.6	0.8	0.1	1.1	0.1	2.8	0.1
Durham, NC	14.6	4.4	2.8	1.4	0.6	2.7	0.7	1.5	0.3
Edison, NJ	46.1	37.1	0.5	2.2	1.8	0.6	1.8	1.8	0.3
El Paso, TX	22.8	1.0	20.2	0.5	0.2	0.3	0.2	0.3	0.0
Fargo, ND	9.9	3.7	0.1	0.5	0.1	0.1	0.2	4.8	0.5
Fort Collins, CO	7.3	2.9	1.4	1.4	0.1	0.3	0.6	0.3	0.2
Fort Wayne, IN	8.6	4.3	2.0	0.6	0.1	0.6	0.2	0.6	0.1
Fort Worth, TX	16.7	3.7	9.2	0.6	0.3	0.8	0.6	1.3	0.2
Grand Rapids, MI	10.8	2.4	3.2	1.0	0.7	1.4	0.2	1.7	0.2
Greeley, CO	12.2	0.8	8.3	0.5	0.1	1.1	0.2	1.2	0.1
Green Bay, WI	9.2	2.0	5.2	0.4	0.2	0.4	0.3	0.6	0.1
Greensboro, NC	12.1	4.1	1.8	1.2	0.7	0.5	0.7	2.9	0.2
Honolulu, HI	27.5	22.9	0.2	0.9	0.2	0.1	0.2	0.2	0.2
Houston, TX	28.9	5.9	10.6	1.1	1.0	6.5	1.6	2.0	0.2
Huntsville, AL	6.4	1.9	1.5	0.8	0.3	0.5	0.3	0.7	0.1
Indianapolis, IN	10.0	3.0	2.8	0.5	0.5	0.9	0.4	1.9	0.1
Jacksonville, FL	12.0	4.2	0.6	1.9	2.2	0.8	1.4	0.6	0.2
Kansas City, MO	8.0	2.3	2.2	0.5	0.6	0.6	0.3	1.3	0.1
Lafayette, LA	5.5	2.3	0.4	0.7	0.2	1.1	0.6	0.1	0.1
Las Cruces, NM	11.0	2.3	7.0	0.8	0.1	0.1	0.2	0.4	0.1
Las Vegas, NV	20.8	5.3	8.8	1.6	1.1	2.4	0.8	0.4	0.4
Lexington, KY	10.1	3.8	2.0	1.1	0.3	0.7	0.5	1.5	0.2
Lincoln, NE	9.1	4.9	1.3	1.0	0.4	0.5	0.3	0.8	0.1
Little Rock, AR	7.1	2.6	1.7	0.5	0.1	1.1	0.4	0.4	0.1
Los Angeles, CA	36.2	10.9	12.0	2.4	0.3	8.4	1.1	0.7	0.4
Louisville, KY	8.6	2.6	0.8	0.9	2.0	0.5	0.3	1.4	0.2

Table continued on following page.

City	Percent of Population Born in								
	Any Foreign Country	Asia	Mexico	Europe	Caribbean	Central America[1]	South America	Africa	Canada
Madison, WI	12.0	6.2	1.4	1.6	0.2	0.3	1.0	1.0	0.3
Manchester, NH	14.6	4.3	0.5	2.7	1.7	1.4	1.0	2.1	1.0
Miami, FL	58.1	1.4	1.1	1.9	31.0	11.9	10.3	0.3	0.2
Midland, TX	15.1	2.1	9.0	0.2	1.0	0.5	0.5	1.3	0.5
Milwaukee, WI	10.1	2.8	4.9	0.7	0.4	0.3	0.2	0.8	0.1
Minneapolis, MN	14.8	3.7	1.8	1.2	0.3	0.4	1.5	5.8	0.3
Nashville, TN	13.7	4.0	2.8	0.9	0.3	2.0	0.3	3.0	0.3
New Haven, CT	17.4	4.2	2.7	2.4	2.6	1.3	2.3	1.5	0.3
New Orleans, LA	5.4	1.9	0.3	0.7	0.4	1.3	0.4	0.2	0.2
New York, NY	36.3	10.8	1.8	5.2	9.9	1.4	4.9	1.7	0.3
Oklahoma City, OK	11.6	3.2	5.3	0.5	0.2	1.2	0.4	0.6	0.2
Omaha, NE	10.8	3.3	3.4	0.7	0.1	1.2	0.4	1.5	0.2
Orlando, FL	22.8	2.8	0.6	2.0	6.7	1.1	8.8	0.5	0.3
Philadelphia, PA	14.3	5.5	0.5	2.1	2.9	0.7	0.9	1.6	0.1
Phoenix, AZ	19.2	3.2	11.7	1.4	0.4	0.9	0.4	0.8	0.4
Pittsburgh, PA	9.0	4.5	0.3	1.8	0.4	0.1	0.5	1.0	0.3
Portland, OR	13.1	6.0	1.9	2.5	0.2	0.4	0.3	0.9	0.5
Providence, RI	30.7	3.8	0.3	2.5	13.9	5.4	1.2	3.1	0.4
Provo, UT	11.3	1.9	4.3	0.4	0.4	0.9	2.4	0.4	0.4
Raleigh, NC	13.0	3.9	2.4	1.2	0.9	1.2	0.8	2.3	0.2
Reno, NV	15.6	5.4	5.1	1.4	0.2	1.7	0.4	0.6	0.4
Richmond, VA	7.5	1.6	0.6	0.8	0.6	2.7	0.4	0.7	0.1
Rochester, MN	13.6	5.4	1.0	1.7	0.1	0.2	0.5	4.5	0.2
Sacramento, CA	20.9	10.3	5.8	1.4	0.1	0.7	0.4	0.5	0.2
St. Louis, MO	6.8	2.8	0.7	1.2	0.2	0.3	0.2	1.3	0.1
Salem, OR	11.3	2.4	5.8	1.1	0.1	0.4	0.2	0.2	0.2
Salt Lake City, UT	15.3	4.1	4.9	1.9	0.2	0.7	1.3	1.0	0.4
San Antonio, TX	14.2	2.5	8.9	0.5	0.3	0.9	0.5	0.4	0.1
San Diego, CA	25.1	11.8	8.2	2.2	0.2	0.5	0.9	0.9	0.4
San Francisco, CA	34.1	22.0	2.4	4.5	0.2	2.4	1.1	0.5	0.6
San Jose, CA	40.7	26.4	8.6	2.3	0.1	1.2	0.7	0.8	0.3
Santa Rosa, CA	21.1	4.6	11.9	1.9	0.0	1.1	0.3	0.6	0.4
Savannah, GA	6.1	2.5	0.8	0.8	0.5	0.5	0.5	0.3	0.2
Seattle, WA	19.3	11.0	1.3	2.6	0.1	0.4	0.5	2.0	1.0
Sioux Falls, SD	8.7	2.1	0.5	1.1	0.1	1.1	0.1	3.4	0.1
Springfield, IL	4.4	2.3	0.5	0.5	0.1	0.1	0.2	0.6	0.0
Tampa, FL	18.1	3.8	1.1	1.8	7.1	1.2	2.3	0.5	0.3
Tucson, AZ	14.2	2.3	8.8	1.0	0.1	0.3	0.4	0.9	0.2
Tulsa, OK	11.0	2.6	5.2	0.6	0.2	1.0	0.5	0.6	0.1
Tuscaloosa, AL	4.5	2.3	1.0	0.4	0.1	0.3	0.1	0.2	0.1
Virginia Beach, VA	9.3	4.9	0.4	1.4	0.5	0.6	0.8	0.4	0.2
Washington, DC	13.5	3.0	0.6	2.4	1.2	2.4	1.5	2.1	0.3
Wichita, KS	9.9	3.7	4.2	0.5	0.1	0.5	0.3	0.5	0.1
Wilmington, NC	4.7	1.2	1.1	1.0	0.2	0.4	0.4	0.1	0.2
Winston-Salem, NC	10.2	2.2	4.1	0.6	0.5	1.5	0.7	0.7	0.1
Worcester, MA	21.9	6.1	0.3	3.6	3.0	1.3	2.5	4.9	0.1
U.S.	13.6	4.2	3.3	1.5	1.4	1.1	1.1	0.8	0.2

Note: (1) Excludes Mexico
Source: U.S. Census Bureau, 2017-2021 American Community Survey 5-Year Estimates

Foreign-born Population: Metro Area

| Metro Area | Any Foreign Country | Percent of Population Born in | | | | | | | |
		Asia	Mexico	Europe	Caribbean	Central America[1]	South America	Africa	Canada
Albuquerque, NM	8.9	1.9	4.9	0.8	0.3	0.2	0.3	0.4	0.1
Allentown, PA	9.7	2.7	0.4	1.4	2.8	0.5	1.1	0.6	0.1
Anchorage, AK	9.0	4.8	0.6	1.1	0.4	0.2	0.4	0.4	0.4
Ann Arbor, MI	12.5	7.3	0.6	2.3	0.1	0.2	0.5	0.9	0.6
Athens, GA	7.4	2.5	1.7	0.7	0.2	0.8	0.7	0.6	0.2
Atlanta, GA	14.1	4.7	2.3	1.1	1.6	1.2	1.2	1.7	0.2
Austin, TX	15.2	4.8	5.8	1.2	0.4	1.2	0.7	0.7	0.3
Baltimore, MD	10.5	4.3	0.4	1.3	0.8	1.1	0.5	1.9	0.1
Boise City, ID	6.5	1.5	2.7	1.0	0.0	0.2	0.4	0.3	0.3
Boston, MA	19.3	6.3	0.2	3.2	3.6	1.6	2.2	1.7	0.4
Boulder, CO	9.9	3.4	2.3	2.3	0.1	0.3	0.6	0.3	0.5
Brownsville, TX	22.8	0.6	20.8	0.2	0.1	0.7	0.1	0.0	0.1
Cape Coral, FL	17.1	1.3	2.3	2.0	6.3	1.9	2.2	0.1	0.9
Cedar Rapids, IA	4.3	1.8	0.4	0.3	0.1	0.1	0.1	1.2	0.1
Charleston, SC	5.8	1.5	1.0	1.1	0.3	0.6	0.7	0.2	0.2
Charlotte, NC	10.5	3.1	2.0	1.1	0.7	1.5	1.0	1.0	0.2
Chicago, IL	17.7	5.3	6.3	3.7	0.2	0.5	0.7	0.7	0.2
Cincinnati, OH	5.1	2.2	0.5	0.7	0.1	0.4	0.2	0.8	0.1
Clarksville, TN	4.9	1.5	0.9	0.6	0.3	0.4	0.3	0.6	0.2
Cleveland, OH	6.0	2.2	0.4	2.2	0.2	0.2	0.2	0.4	0.2
College Station, TX	11.5	3.8	5.0	0.7	0.2	0.5	0.7	0.5	0.1
Colorado Springs, CO	6.7	1.9	1.6	1.5	0.4	0.3	0.4	0.3	0.3
Columbia, MO	5.7	3.3	0.5	0.7	0.1	0.2	0.2	0.7	0.1
Columbia, SC	5.3	1.8	1.0	0.7	0.4	0.6	0.3	0.3	0.1
Columbus, OH	8.8	3.7	0.7	0.8	0.3	0.4	0.3	2.4	0.1
Dallas, TX	18.7	5.7	7.8	0.8	0.3	1.6	0.7	1.6	0.2
Davenport, IA	5.3	1.7	1.7	0.5	0.1	0.1	0.1	0.9	0.1
Denver, CO	12.0	3.3	4.6	1.4	0.2	0.5	0.6	1.1	0.3
Des Moines, IA	8.1	3.2	1.5	1.0	0.1	0.5	0.2	1.5	0.1
Durham, NC	11.8	3.6	2.7	1.4	0.4	1.8	0.6	1.0	0.3
Edison, NJ	29.4	8.7	1.4	4.3	6.9	1.9	4.5	1.4	0.2
El Paso, TX	23.7	0.9	21.3	0.4	0.2	0.3	0.2	0.2	0.0
Fargo, ND	7.0	2.8	0.1	0.5	0.1	0.0	0.1	3.0	0.4
Fort Collins, CO	5.8	1.8	1.4	1.2	0.1	0.2	0.5	0.3	0.2
Fort Wayne, IN	6.7	3.3	1.5	0.6	0.1	0.4	0.2	0.4	0.1
Fort Worth, TX	18.7	5.7	7.8	0.8	0.3	1.6	0.7	1.6	0.2
Grand Rapids, MI	6.6	2.1	1.6	0.9	0.4	0.5	0.2	0.7	0.2
Greeley, CO	8.9	0.8	6.0	0.5	0.1	0.7	0.2	0.5	0.1
Green Bay, WI	4.9	1.6	2.1	0.4	0.1	0.3	0.1	0.2	0.1
Greensboro, NC	9.1	3.0	2.4	0.8	0.4	0.5	0.5	1.4	0.1
Honolulu, HI	19.5	15.7	0.2	0.7	0.2	0.1	0.2	0.2	0.2
Houston, TX	23.5	6.0	8.4	1.1	0.8	3.8	1.6	1.5	0.3
Huntsville, AL	5.2	1.9	1.0	0.7	0.2	0.4	0.3	0.4	0.1
Indianapolis, IN	7.3	2.7	1.6	0.6	0.2	0.5	0.4	1.2	0.1
Jacksonville, FL	9.8	3.3	0.5	1.8	1.6	0.7	1.2	0.4	0.2
Kansas City, MO	6.8	2.3	2.0	0.5	0.2	0.6	0.2	0.8	0.1
Lafayette, LA	3.3	1.3	0.5	0.3	0.2	0.7	0.2	0.1	0.1
Las Cruces, NM	16.0	1.4	13.3	0.6	0.1	0.1	0.1	0.2	0.1
Las Vegas, NV	22.0	7.3	7.8	1.5	1.2	2.0	0.9	0.8	0.4
Lexington, KY	7.6	2.6	1.7	1.0	0.2	0.5	0.3	1.1	0.2
Lincoln, NE	8.0	4.2	1.1	0.9	0.3	0.4	0.2	0.7	0.1
Little Rock, AR	4.2	1.4	1.2	0.4	0.1	0.6	0.2	0.2	0.1
Los Angeles, CA	32.5	12.7	11.5	1.7	0.3	4.3	1.0	0.6	0.3
Louisville, KY	6.4	2.0	0.9	0.7	1.1	0.4	0.2	0.9	0.1

Table continued on following page.

Metro Area	Percent of Population Born in								
	Any Foreign Country	Asia	Mexico	Europe	Caribbean	Central America[1]	South America	Africa	Canada
Madison, WI	7.6	3.5	1.2	1.0	0.1	0.2	0.6	0.6	0.2
Manchester, NH	10.0	3.4	0.3	1.9	1.3	0.5	0.8	0.8	0.9
Miami, FL	41.2	2.2	1.2	2.3	20.9	4.2	9.5	0.4	0.6
Midland, TX	13.7	1.9	8.5	0.3	0.8	0.4	0.4	1.0	0.4
Milwaukee, WI	7.5	2.8	2.3	1.2	0.2	0.2	0.3	0.4	0.1
Minneapolis, MN	10.7	4.1	1.1	1.0	0.1	0.4	0.6	3.0	0.2
Nashville, TN	8.5	2.6	1.9	0.7	0.3	1.1	0.4	1.3	0.2
New Haven, CT	13.4	3.2	1.1	2.9	2.1	0.6	2.1	1.0	0.3
New Orleans, LA	7.6	2.1	0.5	0.5	0.9	2.7	0.4	0.3	0.1
New York, NY	29.4	8.7	1.4	4.3	6.9	1.9	4.5	1.4	0.2
Oklahoma City, OK	7.9	2.3	3.3	0.4	0.1	0.8	0.3	0.5	0.2
Omaha, NE	7.6	2.5	2.4	0.6	0.1	0.7	0.3	1.0	0.1
Orlando, FL	19.3	3.0	1.0	1.7	5.6	1.1	6.0	0.6	0.3
Philadelphia, PA	11.2	4.6	0.8	1.9	1.4	0.5	0.7	1.2	0.2
Phoenix, AZ	14.0	3.2	7.0	1.3	0.3	0.6	0.4	0.6	0.6
Pittsburgh, PA	4.1	2.0	0.1	0.9	0.2	0.1	0.2	0.3	0.1
Portland, OR	12.7	5.1	2.9	2.4	0.2	0.5	0.3	0.6	0.4
Providence, RI	13.9	2.3	0.3	4.1	2.6	1.6	1.2	1.6	0.2
Provo, UT	7.2	1.0	2.5	0.5	0.2	0.6	1.6	0.2	0.3
Raleigh, NC	12.2	4.7	2.4	1.3	0.6	0.9	0.6	1.2	0.3
Reno, NV	14.0	4.0	5.7	1.2	0.2	1.4	0.4	0.4	0.4
Richmond, VA	8.1	3.1	0.6	1.0	0.4	1.6	0.5	0.7	0.1
Rochester, MN	8.5	3.2	0.7	1.1	0.1	0.2	0.4	2.4	0.2
Sacramento, CA	18.6	9.1	4.3	2.7	0.1	0.7	0.4	0.4	0.3
St. Louis, MO	4.8	2.2	0.5	1.1	0.1	0.2	0.2	0.5	0.1
Salem, OR	11.5	1.5	7.2	1.1	0.1	0.5	0.3	0.1	0.2
Salt Lake City, UT	12.4	3.1	4.3	1.3	0.1	0.6	1.5	0.6	0.3
San Antonio, TX	11.7	2.1	7.1	0.6	0.3	0.7	0.4	0.3	0.1
San Diego, CA	22.7	8.8	9.6	1.8	0.2	0.6	0.7	0.6	0.4
San Francisco, CA	30.7	17.8	4.7	2.8	0.2	2.5	1.1	0.9	0.5
San Jose, CA	39.3	26.2	6.7	3.1	0.1	1.0	0.8	0.7	0.5
Santa Rosa, CA	16.3	3.1	8.9	1.9	0.1	0.9	0.4	0.3	0.4
Savannah, GA	6.0	1.9	1.2	1.0	0.6	0.3	0.4	0.3	0.2
Seattle, WA	19.5	10.4	2.3	2.8	0.2	0.6	0.6	1.6	0.7
Sioux Falls, SD	6.5	1.5	0.5	0.9	0.1	0.8	0.1	2.4	0.1
Springfield, IL	2.9	1.5	0.3	0.4	0.1	0.0	0.2	0.3	0.0
Tampa, FL	14.4	2.8	1.3	2.2	4.0	0.8	2.2	0.5	0.6
Tucson, AZ	12.2	2.2	7.0	1.2	0.2	0.3	0.3	0.6	0.3
Tulsa, OK	6.7	1.9	2.8	0.5	0.1	0.5	0.3	0.3	0.1
Tuscaloosa, AL	3.3	1.2	1.1	0.3	0.1	0.4	0.1	0.1	0.1
Virginia Beach, VA	6.6	2.8	0.4	1.1	0.6	0.7	0.4	0.4	0.1
Washington, DC	22.9	8.2	0.8	1.8	1.1	4.8	2.3	3.6	0.2
Wichita, KS	7.3	2.7	2.9	0.5	0.1	0.4	0.2	0.4	0.1
Wilmington, NC	4.6	1.0	1.0	0.9	0.1	0.6	0.4	0.2	0.2
Winston-Salem, NC	7.0	1.4	2.7	0.6	0.3	0.9	0.5	0.3	0.1
Worcester, MA	12.0	3.7	0.3	2.3	1.1	0.6	2.0	1.6	0.4
U.S.	13.6	4.2	3.3	1.5	1.4	1.1	1.1	0.8	0.2

Note: Figures cover the Metropolitan Statistical Area—see Appendix B for areas included; (1) Excludes Mexico
Source: U.S. Census Bureau, 2017-2021 American Community Survey 5-Year Estimates

Marital Status: City

City	Never Married	Now Married[1]	Separated	Widowed	Divorced
Albuquerque, NM	38.2	40.1	1.4	5.5	14.8
Allentown, PA	46.7	34.6	3.9	5.0	9.8
Anchorage, AK	33.6	48.9	1.9	3.6	12.0
Ann Arbor, MI	56.5	34.4	0.4	2.4	6.3
Athens, GA	53.8	31.8	1.7	3.7	9.0
Atlanta, GA	55.1	29.0	1.8	4.0	10.1
Austin, TX	43.0	41.9	1.4	3.0	10.6
Baltimore, MD	52.3	27.2	3.1	6.0	11.4
Boise City, ID	34.8	47.0	1.0	4.4	12.9
Boston, MA	55.7	30.9	2.5	3.6	7.3
Boulder, CO	56.1	31.2	0.7	2.5	9.5
Brownsville, TX	34.2	47.6	4.3	6.2	7.8
Cape Coral, FL	24.4	53.3	1.2	7.3	13.8
Cedar Rapids, IA	35.5	45.7	1.0	5.6	12.2
Charleston, SC	40.3	43.3	1.6	5.1	9.8
Charlotte, NC	41.4	42.0	2.4	3.9	10.3
Chicago, IL	48.9	35.5	2.3	5.0	8.3
Cincinnati, OH	52.6	29.1	2.2	4.5	11.7
Clarksville, TN	30.2	50.3	2.1	3.9	13.6
Cleveland, OH	53.1	24.0	2.9	5.9	14.1
College Station, TX	59.4	31.9	0.8	2.4	5.5
Colorado Springs, CO	30.9	50.2	1.6	4.5	12.9
Columbia, MO	47.8	39.2	1.3	3.1	8.7
Columbia, SC	55.7	29.6	2.3	4.0	8.4
Columbus, OH	45.4	36.7	2.1	4.2	11.6
Dallas, TX	42.3	40.2	2.9	4.3	10.3
Davenport, IA	36.9	43.5	1.3	5.6	12.7
Denver, CO	43.4	39.6	1.6	3.5	11.8
Des Moines, IA	39.5	39.8	2.1	5.5	13.0
Durham, NC	43.1	40.7	2.2	4.1	9.9
Edison, NJ	26.3	61.4	0.8	5.3	6.1
El Paso, TX	34.9	44.8	3.6	5.7	11.1
Fargo, ND	43.0	43.4	1.0	3.9	8.6
Fort Collins, CO	46.6	40.9	0.7	3.3	8.5
Fort Wayne, IN	36.1	44.2	1.5	5.9	12.3
Fort Worth, TX	35.5	46.7	2.2	4.4	11.1
Grand Rapids, MI	45.3	38.1	1.2	4.9	10.5
Greeley, CO	35.4	46.5	1.9	4.8	11.4
Green Bay, WI	37.4	42.2	1.2	5.2	14.0
Greensboro, NC	43.8	36.8	2.6	5.9	11.0
Honolulu, HI	37.5	44.7	1.1	6.7	10.0
Houston, TX	41.1	41.2	3.0	4.5	10.2
Huntsville, AL	36.1	43.6	2.1	5.9	12.4
Indianapolis, IN	41.8	39.4	1.7	4.8	12.3
Jacksonville, FL	36.0	42.4	2.1	5.5	14.0
Kansas City, MO	39.3	40.6	2.0	4.8	13.3
Lafayette, LA	40.6	41.4	2.1	6.0	9.9
Las Cruces, NM	41.9	39.4	1.7	4.7	12.4
Las Vegas, NV	35.6	43.7	2.0	5.2	13.5
Lexington, KY	38.6	43.4	1.5	4.6	11.8
Lincoln, NE	39.7	45.3	0.9	4.0	10.1
Little Rock, AR	38.2	40.4	1.8	5.6	14.1
Los Angeles, CA	46.1	38.9	2.5	4.4	8.1
Louisville, KY	36.9	42.0	2.1	6.3	12.7
Madison, WI	50.3	37.2	0.7	3.3	8.5
Manchester, NH	39.2	39.2	1.8	5.4	14.3

Table continued on following page.

City	Never Married	Now Married[1]	Separated	Widowed	Divorced
Miami, FL	39.7	37.3	3.5	6.0	13.6
Midland, TX	28.6	55.1	1.9	4.5	9.9
Milwaukee, WI	54.4	29.4	1.9	4.4	9.9
Minneapolis, MN	51.2	34.3	1.4	3.0	10.1
Nashville, TN	41.5	40.4	1.9	4.6	11.6
New Haven, CT	59.1	25.5	2.4	3.9	9.1
New Orleans, LA	49.7	29.4	2.6	5.5	12.8
New York, NY	43.8	39.9	2.9	5.3	8.1
Oklahoma City, OK	33.3	46.6	2.1	5.3	12.7
Omaha, NE	37.2	45.6	1.4	4.8	11.1
Orlando, FL	43.2	37.8	2.4	3.9	12.7
Philadelphia, PA	50.5	31.5	3.0	5.7	9.2
Phoenix, AZ	39.1	42.5	2.1	4.0	12.2
Pittsburgh, PA	53.1	30.4	1.9	5.4	9.2
Portland, OR	41.6	41.1	1.3	3.6	12.4
Providence, RI	53.6	31.9	2.0	4.2	8.4
Provo, UT	48.8	43.8	0.9	2.2	4.3
Raleigh, NC	43.2	40.0	2.1	3.8	11.0
Reno, NV	36.5	42.1	1.9	4.9	14.8
Richmond, VA	51.2	29.4	2.8	5.2	11.4
Rochester, MN	33.3	51.7	1.2	4.7	9.2
Sacramento, CA	40.5	41.1	2.6	4.8	11.2
St. Louis, MO	48.8	30.7	2.9	5.2	12.3
Salem, OR	34.6	45.1	1.6	5.2	13.4
Salt Lake City, UT	44.4	40.3	1.3	3.1	10.8
San Antonio, TX	38.3	41.7	2.8	5.1	12.0
San Diego, CA	40.1	44.8	1.6	4.0	9.5
San Francisco, CA	46.0	40.1	1.4	4.5	8.0
San Jose, CA	36.2	50.3	1.5	4.2	7.8
Santa Rosa, CA	33.8	46.4	2.0	5.4	12.3
Savannah, GA	47.5	32.1	2.6	5.6	12.2
Seattle, WA	45.5	40.3	1.2	3.0	10.0
Sioux Falls, SD	34.5	48.6	1.2	4.3	11.4
Springfield, IL	37.6	39.5	1.6	6.2	15.1
Tampa, FL	40.3	39.1	2.5	5.0	13.1
Tucson, AZ	42.0	36.7	2.2	5.2	13.9
Tulsa, OK	35.0	42.4	2.4	5.7	14.4
Tuscaloosa, AL	52.3	32.6	1.8	4.0	9.4
Virginia Beach, VA	30.9	50.8	2.1	5.1	11.2
Washington, DC	55.8	30.9	1.7	3.5	8.2
Wichita, KS	33.7	45.6	1.9	5.0	13.8
Wilmington, NC	41.6	39.1	2.2	5.3	11.7
Winston-Salem, NC	41.9	39.1	2.6	5.4	11.0
Worcester, MA	47.8	34.0	2.0	4.9	11.3
U.S.	33.8	48.0	1.8	5.6	10.8

Note: Figures are percentages and cover the population 15 years of age and older; (1) Excludes separated
Source: U.S. Census Bureau, 2017-2021 American Community Survey 5-Year Estimates

Marital Status: Metro Area

Metro Area	Never Married	Now Married[1]	Separated	Widowed	Divorced
Albuquerque, NM	35.6	43.5	1.4	5.5	14.1
Allentown, PA	32.7	49.3	1.9	6.2	9.9
Anchorage, AK	32.2	50.5	1.8	3.8	11.8
Ann Arbor, MI	43.1	44.4	0.7	3.6	8.1
Athens, GA	43.0	41.5	1.6	4.4	9.5
Atlanta, GA	35.7	47.6	1.8	4.4	10.6
Austin, TX	35.5	49.4	1.4	3.5	10.3
Baltimore, MD	36.0	46.3	1.9	5.7	10.0
Boise City, ID	29.1	53.3	1.1	4.3	12.2
Boston, MA	37.3	47.6	1.6	4.9	8.7
Boulder, CO	38.5	45.5	0.9	3.7	11.4
Brownsville, TX	33.6	48.2	3.5	6.3	8.4
Cape Coral, FL	25.9	51.9	1.5	7.9	12.8
Cedar Rapids, IA	30.6	51.3	1.1	5.5	11.5
Charleston, SC	33.8	48.5	2.1	5.3	10.3
Charlotte, NC	33.1	49.3	2.3	5.0	10.3
Chicago, IL	37.2	47.0	1.6	5.2	8.9
Cincinnati, OH	32.8	48.7	1.5	5.6	11.4
Clarksville, TN	29.6	51.1	1.9	4.9	12.5
Cleveland, OH	35.8	44.4	1.5	6.3	11.9
College Station, TX	45.5	40.1	1.8	4.1	8.5
Colorado Springs, CO	29.5	53.3	1.4	4.0	11.7
Columbia, MO	40.0	44.8	1.3	4.0	9.8
Columbia, SC	36.3	45.0	2.6	5.6	10.6
Columbus, OH	34.8	47.6	1.7	4.8	11.1
Dallas, TX	32.8	50.8	1.9	4.2	10.3
Davenport, IA	30.5	49.9	1.4	6.2	12.0
Denver, CO	33.6	49.8	1.4	3.8	11.5
Des Moines, IA	30.9	51.7	1.2	4.9	11.2
Durham, NC	37.3	46.1	2.0	4.8	9.8
Edison, NJ	38.1	46.1	2.2	5.5	8.1
El Paso, TX	34.9	45.8	3.5	5.4	10.4
Fargo, ND	37.5	49.1	0.9	4.0	8.5
Fort Collins, CO	34.5	51.3	0.8	4.0	9.4
Fort Wayne, IN	31.5	50.0	1.3	5.6	11.6
Fort Worth, TX	32.8	50.8	1.9	4.2	10.3
Grand Rapids, MI	32.2	52.1	0.9	4.5	10.3
Greeley, CO	28.7	55.2	1.4	4.0	10.7
Green Bay, WI	30.6	52.2	0.7	5.1	11.4
Greensboro, NC	34.1	45.5	2.8	6.2	11.4
Honolulu, HI	34.4	49.7	1.2	6.0	8.7
Houston, TX	33.8	50.2	2.3	4.3	9.4
Huntsville, AL	29.9	51.5	1.6	5.5	11.4
Indianapolis, IN	33.0	49.2	1.3	4.9	11.5
Jacksonville, FL	31.7	47.7	1.8	5.6	13.2
Kansas City, MO	30.8	50.5	1.5	5.0	12.1
Lafayette, LA	33.8	47.9	2.1	5.6	10.6
Las Cruces, NM	38.8	43.7	2.0	4.9	10.7
Las Vegas, NV	35.2	44.3	2.1	5.0	13.4
Lexington, KY	34.1	47.0	1.5	5.1	12.3
Lincoln, NE	37.3	48.1	0.8	4.1	9.7
Little Rock, AR	30.6	48.1	1.9	5.8	13.6
Los Angeles, CA	40.3	44.5	2.0	4.7	8.4
Louisville, KY	31.9	47.5	1.8	6.0	12.9
Madison, WI	37.1	48.2	0.8	4.1	9.9
Manchester, NH	31.3	50.2	1.2	5.1	12.1

Table continued on following page.

Metro Area	Never Married	Now Married[1]	Separated	Widowed	Divorced
Miami, FL	34.1	44.4	2.5	6.2	12.9
Midland, TX	27.9	55.4	1.7	4.5	10.5
Milwaukee, WI	37.4	46.2	1.1	5.1	10.1
Minneapolis, MN	33.7	51.0	1.0	4.1	10.1
Nashville, TN	32.6	50.0	1.5	4.9	11.0
New Haven, CT	38.2	43.7	1.6	5.7	10.8
New Orleans, LA	37.8	41.7	2.3	6.0	12.1
New York, NY	38.1	46.1	2.2	5.5	8.1
Oklahoma City, OK	31.4	49.2	1.8	5.4	12.3
Omaha, NE	32.2	51.3	1.2	4.7	10.7
Orlando, FL	35.2	46.2	2.0	5.0	11.6
Philadelphia, PA	37.3	45.8	2.0	5.7	9.2
Phoenix, AZ	33.7	48.2	1.6	4.8	11.7
Pittsburgh, PA	32.6	48.7	1.7	6.9	10.1
Portland, OR	32.8	49.6	1.3	4.3	12.0
Providence, RI	36.5	45.0	1.5	5.9	11.1
Provo, UT	33.0	58.1	0.8	2.5	5.5
Raleigh, NC	32.2	51.9	2.0	4.2	9.7
Reno, NV	32.4	47.4	1.7	4.9	13.7
Richmond, VA	34.7	46.7	2.3	5.6	10.7
Rochester, MN	29.0	56.0	0.9	4.7	9.3
Sacramento, CA	33.9	48.6	2.0	4.9	10.6
St. Louis, MO	32.2	48.7	1.7	5.9	11.4
Salem, OR	31.8	48.7	1.7	5.3	12.6
Salt Lake City, UT	32.7	52.3	1.4	3.6	10.1
San Antonio, TX	34.0	47.6	2.4	4.9	11.1
San Diego, CA	36.2	47.9	1.6	4.4	9.8
San Francisco, CA	36.6	48.6	1.4	4.6	8.7
San Jose, CA	34.4	52.7	1.4	4.1	7.4
Santa Rosa, CA	32.3	48.7	1.5	5.1	12.5
Savannah, GA	35.7	45.2	2.3	5.3	11.7
Seattle, WA	33.2	50.7	1.3	4.0	10.8
Sioux Falls, SD	30.6	53.2	1.0	4.4	10.8
Springfield, IL	32.4	46.6	1.3	6.1	13.6
Tampa, FL	31.3	46.5	1.9	6.8	13.5
Tucson, AZ	34.3	45.5	1.7	5.6	12.9
Tulsa, OK	29.1	49.8	1.9	6.1	13.0
Tuscaloosa, AL	39.5	43.1	1.7	5.4	10.3
Virginia Beach, VA	33.6	47.7	2.4	5.5	10.8
Washington, DC	36.2	49.2	1.7	4.2	8.7
Wichita, KS	30.3	50.2	1.4	5.4	12.7
Wilmington, NC	33.0	48.2	2.2	5.7	11.0
Winston-Salem, NC	31.0	48.9	2.4	6.4	11.3
Worcester, MA	34.4	47.7	1.5	5.4	11.0
U.S.	33.8	48.0	1.8	5.6	10.8

Note: Figures are percentages and cover the population 15 years of age and older; Figures cover the Metropolitan Statistical Area;
(1) Excludes separated
Source: U.S. Census Bureau, 2017-2021 American Community Survey 5-Year Estimates

Disability by Age: City

City	All Ages	Under 18 Years Old	18 to 64 Years Old	65 Years and Over
Albuquerque, NM	14.2	4.3	12.3	35.3
Allentown, PA	16.0	9.9	15.3	33.5
Anchorage, AK	11.1	3.8	10.0	33.3
Ann Arbor, MI	7.1	4.2	4.9	24.0
Athens, GA	11.8	6.1	9.6	35.6
Atlanta, GA	11.4	4.7	9.3	35.0
Austin, TX	8.7	4.1	7.4	28.5
Baltimore, MD	15.9	6.0	14.1	39.0
Boise City, ID	11.3	4.2	9.4	29.7
Boston, MA	11.8	6.3	8.7	38.3
Boulder, CO	6.6	2.9	4.7	23.1
Brownsville, TX	10.6	4.2	7.8	40.6
Cape Coral, FL	13.4	3.8	9.7	29.3
Cedar Rapids, IA	10.0	3.1	8.1	27.2
Charleston, SC	9.3	2.9	6.2	30.5
Charlotte, NC	7.8	2.6	6.5	27.9
Chicago, IL	10.9	3.3	8.8	34.8
Cincinnati, OH	12.8	5.2	11.8	32.0
Clarksville, TN	15.7	6.1	16.4	43.8
Cleveland, OH	19.5	8.4	18.5	41.9
College Station, TX	6.8	5.1	5.3	27.8
Colorado Springs, CO	13.1	5.2	12.1	30.9
Columbia, MO	11.4	4.6	9.8	33.9
Columbia, SC	12.8	5.1	10.7	38.5
Columbus, OH	11.6	5.2	10.3	34.5
Dallas, TX	10.5	4.5	9.0	34.3
Davenport, IA	13.1	5.2	11.3	31.6
Denver, CO	9.7	3.5	7.6	32.3
Des Moines, IA	13.7	5.3	12.8	35.6
Durham, NC	9.6	3.0	7.6	31.7
Edison, NJ	7.6	4.2	4.5	26.9
El Paso, TX	13.6	5.2	11.1	42.1
Fargo, ND	10.2	5.1	7.7	32.0
Fort Collins, CO	8.4	2.7	6.8	28.0
Fort Wayne, IN	13.9	5.5	12.8	34.2
Fort Worth, TX	9.7	3.4	8.6	34.4
Grand Rapids, MI	11.7	3.9	11.0	30.4
Greeley, CO	11.9	3.4	11.1	33.5
Green Bay, WI	13.8	6.7	12.2	34.9
Greensboro, NC	11.1	4.9	8.9	32.1
Honolulu, HI	11.5	3.1	6.9	32.4
Houston, TX	9.9	3.9	8.0	34.7
Huntsville, AL	13.5	4.4	11.3	33.7
Indianapolis, IN	13.5	5.3	12.4	35.5
Jacksonville, FL	13.1	4.8	11.3	35.3
Kansas City, MO	12.5	3.9	11.1	34.2
Lafayette, LA	12.1	2.8	9.7	34.5
Las Cruces, NM	15.9	7.9	13.6	38.0
Las Vegas, NV	12.5	4.0	10.4	34.8
Lexington, KY	12.5	4.9	10.8	33.2
Lincoln, NE	10.7	4.4	8.9	30.0
Little Rock, AR	13.2	4.7	11.6	34.5
Los Angeles, CA	10.3	3.1	7.5	36.6
Louisville, KY	14.3	4.5	12.8	35.6
Madison, WI	8.3	4.4	6.4	25.0

Table continued on following page.

City	All Ages	Under 18 Years Old	18 to 64 Years Old	65 Years and Over
Manchester, NH	13.9	6.6	11.8	34.7
Miami, FL	11.9	4.5	7.6	37.2
Midland, TX	9.8	2.7	8.1	41.1
Milwaukee, WI	12.5	5.0	11.6	36.6
Minneapolis, MN	11.0	4.9	9.8	32.2
Nashville, TN	11.2	4.6	9.1	34.5
New Haven, CT	10.3	4.2	8.8	33.4
New Orleans, LA	13.7	4.7	11.8	34.0
New York, NY	10.9	3.6	8.0	33.9
Oklahoma City, OK	13.1	4.3	11.9	36.6
Omaha, NE	10.9	3.6	9.6	30.9
Orlando, FL	9.6	4.9	7.7	32.0
Philadelphia, PA	16.9	7.0	15.0	42.0
Phoenix, AZ	10.8	4.2	9.7	32.9
Pittsburgh, PA	14.3	7.7	11.3	35.4
Portland, OR	12.1	4.8	9.9	33.4
Providence, RI	13.6	5.9	12.4	36.4
Provo, UT	9.6	4.9	8.1	41.8
Raleigh, NC	9.0	4.2	7.2	30.1
Reno, NV	11.2	3.2	9.0	31.1
Richmond, VA	14.2	6.5	12.1	35.7
Rochester, MN	10.3	4.2	7.9	30.7
Sacramento, CA	11.8	3.3	9.6	36.7
St. Louis, MO	15.4	6.2	13.3	38.5
Salem, OR	15.2	6.3	13.9	35.5
Salt Lake City, UT	11.0	4.0	9.4	32.6
San Antonio, TX	15.0	6.3	13.2	41.6
San Diego, CA	9.2	3.3	6.5	31.3
San Francisco, CA	10.1	2.6	6.3	33.5
San Jose, CA	8.9	3.1	6.0	33.1
Santa Rosa, CA	11.7	3.2	9.5	29.7
Savannah, GA	15.7	6.4	13.1	42.3
Seattle, WA	9.3	2.5	7.2	30.6
Sioux Falls, SD	10.1	3.4	9.0	28.9
Springfield, IL	14.7	6.2	13.0	31.2
Tampa, FL	12.1	3.7	9.6	38.9
Tucson, AZ	15.0	5.8	12.8	37.5
Tulsa, OK	14.2	4.7	13.1	34.6
Tuscaloosa, AL	9.9	2.9	8.3	28.0
Virginia Beach, VA	11.5	4.3	9.4	31.3
Washington, DC	11.2	4.4	9.2	33.7
Wichita, KS	14.8	5.7	13.7	35.4
Wilmington, NC	13.0	5.1	10.0	32.0
Winston-Salem, NC	11.3	3.5	9.9	30.6
Worcester, MA	14.3	4.7	12.9	37.3
U.S.	12.6	4.4	10.3	33.4

Note: Figures show percent of the civilian noninstitutionalized population that reported having a disability. Disability status is determined from from six types of difficulty: vision, hearing, cognitive, ambulatory, self-care, and independent living. For children under 5 years old, hearing and vision difficulty are used to determine disability status. For children between the ages of 5 and 14, disability status is determined from hearing, vision, cognitive, ambulatory, and self-care difficulties. For people aged 15 years and older, they are considered to have a disability if they have difficulty with any one of the six difficulty types.
Source: U.S. Census Bureau, 2017-2021 American Community Survey 5-Year Estimates

Disability by Age: Metro Area

Metro Area	All Ages	Under 18 Years Old	18 to 64 Years Old	65 Years and Over
Albuquerque, NM	15.1	4.2	13.2	36.3
Allentown, PA	12.7	5.5	10.2	30.3
Anchorage, AK	11.7	3.8	10.7	33.9
Ann Arbor, MI	9.7	3.8	7.7	27.2
Athens, GA	12.5	5.6	10.2	34.4
Atlanta, GA	10.3	4.0	8.6	31.5
Austin, TX	9.3	3.8	7.8	29.4
Baltimore, MD	11.8	4.6	9.7	30.8
Boise City, ID	12.1	4.4	10.6	31.6
Boston, MA	10.5	4.2	7.8	30.2
Boulder, CO	8.4	3.3	6.1	25.5
Brownsville, TX	12.2	5.6	9.5	39.0
Cape Coral, FL	13.6	3.9	9.8	26.9
Cedar Rapids, IA	10.3	4.1	8.1	27.2
Charleston, SC	11.6	3.9	9.2	32.1
Charlotte, NC	10.4	3.5	8.5	31.5
Chicago, IL	10.1	3.3	7.9	30.3
Cincinnati, OH	12.4	5.0	10.6	31.8
Clarksville, TN	16.7	7.1	16.3	42.9
Cleveland, OH	14.0	5.0	11.6	32.6
College Station, TX	9.9	5.5	7.6	33.3
Colorado Springs, CO	12.5	5.1	11.5	30.8
Columbia, MO	12.8	4.9	11.1	33.8
Columbia, SC	14.2	4.7	12.3	36.3
Columbus, OH	11.9	5.0	10.1	32.7
Dallas, TX	9.5	3.8	8.0	32.1
Davenport, IA	12.7	5.2	10.4	30.1
Denver, CO	9.7	3.5	7.8	29.8
Des Moines, IA	10.5	3.7	9.0	30.4
Durham, NC	11.0	3.4	8.6	30.7
Edison, NJ	10.1	3.3	7.3	30.5
El Paso, TX	13.3	5.4	10.9	43.0
Fargo, ND	9.8	4.0	7.8	31.7
Fort Collins, CO	10.0	2.7	7.7	28.8
Fort Wayne, IN	12.4	4.7	11.0	32.0
Fort Worth, TX	9.5	3.8	8.0	32.1
Grand Rapids, MI	10.9	3.8	9.4	29.8
Greeley, CO	10.7	3.6	9.1	34.7
Green Bay, WI	11.3	4.5	9.7	27.7
Greensboro, NC	13.1	4.9	10.9	32.7
Honolulu, HI	11.2	3.0	7.5	33.0
Houston, TX	9.6	3.8	7.9	32.6
Huntsville, AL	13.1	4.0	11.1	35.4
Indianapolis, IN	12.3	4.8	10.8	32.9
Jacksonville, FL	13.0	4.6	10.9	33.2
Kansas City, MO	11.7	4.0	9.9	32.2
Lafayette, LA	14.1	4.9	12.4	37.8
Las Cruces, NM	15.2	6.6	13.4	35.7
Las Vegas, NV	12.1	4.0	9.9	33.9
Lexington, KY	13.5	5.2	11.8	34.2
Lincoln, NE	10.7	4.1	8.8	30.4
Little Rock, AR	15.6	5.8	13.8	38.4
Los Angeles, CA	9.8	3.2	7.0	33.0
Louisville, KY	13.9	4.4	12.1	35.1
Madison, WI	8.9	4.2	6.9	24.6

Table continued on following page.

Metro Area	All Ages	Under 18 Years Old	18 to 64 Years Old	65 Years and Over
Manchester, NH	11.6	4.7	9.5	29.8
Miami, FL	10.8	3.7	7.2	31.1
Midland, TX	9.9	2.6	8.2	41.3
Milwaukee, WI	11.0	3.9	8.9	29.8
Minneapolis, MN	10.0	3.9	8.2	28.5
Nashville, TN	11.6	4.0	9.7	33.6
New Haven, CT	11.6	3.7	9.2	29.9
New Orleans, LA	14.9	5.4	12.7	36.4
New York, NY	10.1	3.3	7.3	30.5
Oklahoma City, OK	14.0	4.5	12.4	38.4
Omaha, NE	11.0	3.6	9.5	31.4
Orlando, FL	12.3	5.7	9.6	33.8
Philadelphia, PA	12.7	5.1	10.5	32.2
Phoenix, AZ	11.8	4.3	9.7	31.4
Pittsburgh, PA	14.4	5.7	11.3	32.5
Portland, OR	12.1	4.1	10.0	32.3
Providence, RI	13.7	5.4	11.5	31.9
Provo, UT	8.3	3.6	8.0	31.9
Raleigh, NC	9.7	3.9	7.9	30.4
Reno, NV	11.7	4.0	9.2	30.9
Richmond, VA	12.8	5.3	10.5	32.1
Rochester, MN	10.0	3.8	7.6	28.6
Sacramento, CA	11.5	3.4	9.0	33.7
St. Louis, MO	13.0	4.7	10.8	32.4
Salem, OR	14.9	5.3	13.0	36.5
Salt Lake City, UT	9.5	3.9	8.4	30.0
San Antonio, TX	14.1	5.9	12.3	38.7
San Diego, CA	10.0	3.3	7.4	31.7
San Francisco, CA	9.6	3.1	6.7	30.0
San Jose, CA	8.3	2.7	5.5	30.7
Santa Rosa, CA	11.6	3.4	8.8	28.4
Savannah, GA	14.2	4.9	12.5	36.6
Seattle, WA	10.8	3.9	8.7	32.8
Sioux Falls, SD	9.9	3.2	8.7	28.5
Springfield, IL	13.7	6.2	11.6	30.4
Tampa, FL	14.1	5.0	10.8	33.6
Tucson, AZ	14.9	5.3	12.1	33.4
Tulsa, OK	14.7	4.8	13.1	37.4
Tuscaloosa, AL	14.3	4.5	12.5	37.4
Virginia Beach, VA	13.3	5.3	11.3	33.7
Washington, DC	8.8	3.3	6.8	28.2
Wichita, KS	14.5	5.8	12.9	35.7
Wilmington, NC	12.9	4.5	10.6	30.3
Winston-Salem, NC	13.5	4.2	11.2	33.6
Worcester, MA	12.4	4.3	10.5	31.6
U.S.	12.6	4.4	10.3	33.4

Note: Figures show percent of the civilian noninstitutionalized population that reported having a disability. Disability status is determined from from six types of difficulty: vision, hearing, cognitive, ambulatory, self-care, and independent living. For children under 5 years old, hearing and vision difficulty are used to determine disability status. For children between the ages of 5 and 14, disability status is determined from hearing, vision, cognitive, ambulatory, and self-care difficulties. For people aged 15 years and older, they are considered to have a disability if they have difficulty with any one of the six difficulty types; Figures cover the Metropolitan Statistical Area
Source: U.S. Census Bureau, 2017-2021 American Community Survey 5-Year Estimates

Religious Groups by Family

Area[1]	Catholic	Baptist	Methodist	LDS[2]	Pentecostal	Lutheran	Islam	Adventist	Other
Albuquerque, NM	32.6	3.2	0.9	2.7	1.7	0.4	0.7	1.5	10.8
Allentown, PA	18.6	0.4	2.3	0.4	0.6	5.4	0.7	1.2	11.0
Anchorage, AK	4.9	3.4	1.0	5.1	1.7	1.5	0.1	1.7	16.3
Ann Arbor, MI	9.7	2.0	2.4	0.8	1.5	2.3	2.2	0.9	10.0
Athens, GA	6.4	12.8	5.7	1.0	2.4	0.3	0.2	1.3	7.9
Atlanta, GA	10.7	14.7	6.7	0.8	2.0	0.4	1.9	1.9	12.4
Austin, TX	18.8	6.5	2.2	1.3	0.7	1.1	1.0	1.0	9.9
Baltimore, MD	12.4	3.2	4.4	0.6	1.2	1.4	3.3	1.2	11.7
Boise City, ID	13.0	0.8	2.5	15.0	1.6	0.8	0.3	1.7	10.0
Boston, MA	37.0	1.0	0.7	0.5	0.7	0.2	2.2	0.9	7.1
Boulder, CO	16.0	0.3	0.7	0.7	0.5	1.7	0.4	0.9	15.2
Brownsville, TX	36.8	2.8	0.7	1.2	1.0	0.2	0.1	2.5	9.4
Cape Coral, FL	18.8	2.5	1.7	0.6	3.0	0.7	0.2	2.0	12.2
Cedar Rapids, IA	16.8	1.0	5.3	1.0	1.3	8.1	1.3	0.6	9.6
Charleston, SC	11.5	7.7	8.0	0.8	1.9	0.7	0.2	1.0	12.8
Charlotte, NC	12.1	13.9	7.0	0.7	2.2	1.1	1.7	1.4	15.9
Chicago, IL	28.6	3.4	1.4	0.3	1.5	2.1	4.7	1.1	9.2
Cincinnati, OH	17.0	5.7	2.3	0.6	1.5	0.8	1.1	0.7	21.8
Clarksville, TN	4.6	23.2	4.4	1.4	3.2	0.5	0.1	0.8	12.4
Cleveland, OH	26.1	4.3	2.3	0.4	1.5	1.8	1.1	1.3	16.8
College Station, TX	17.2	10.6	4.3	1.7	0.5	1.1	0.6	0.5	6.8
Colorado Springs, CO	16.4	2.6	1.3	3.0	1.0	1.2	0.1	1.0	16.2
Columbia, MO	7.1	9.0	3.5	1.7	1.1	1.6	1.4	1.2	12.4
Columbia, SC	6.6	15.1	8.5	1.2	3.8	2.3	0.3	1.3	15.4
Columbus, OH	11.7	3.4	3.0	0.8	1.9	1.7	2.1	0.9	17.5
Dallas, TX	14.2	14.3	4.7	1.4	2.2	0.5	1.8	1.3	13.8
Davenport, IA	13.2	3.2	3.6	0.8	1.5	6.6	0.7	0.8	6.7
Denver, CO	16.1	1.5	1.0	2.1	0.6	1.4	0.3	1.1	10.4
Des Moines, IA	12.1	1.8	4.0	0.9	2.5	6.6	1.6	0.8	8.7
Durham, NC	8.5	12.3	6.5	0.9	1.3	0.3	1.5	1.1	13.7
Edison, NJ	32.5	1.7	1.2	0.3	0.9	0.5	4.5	1.4	10.6
El Paso, TX	47.9	2.5	0.4	1.2	1.1	0.2	0.1	2.1	6.9
Fargo, ND	14.2	0.2	1.0	0.6	1.3	24.0	<0.1	0.6	8.1
Fort Collins, CO	9.9	1.2	1.3	4.0	2.7	2.5	<0.1	1.2	12.1
Fort Wayne, IN	13.1	8.1	3.9	0.4	1.1	7.1	1.0	0.9	17.6
Fort Worth, TX	14.2	14.3	4.7	1.4	2.2	0.5	1.8	1.3	13.8
Grand Rapids, MI	13.1	1.3	1.8	0.4	1.3	1.8	0.8	1.2	19.9
Greeley, CO	14.1	0.5	0.9	2.9	1.1	1.2	<0.1	1.1	6.1
Green Bay, WI	31.8	0.3	1.4	0.5	1.1	10.8	0.4	0.9	7.0
Greensboro, NC	7.9	10.0	8.0	0.7	2.8	0.4	1.5	1.4	17.8
Honolulu, HI	18.0	1.4	0.5	4.1	2.6	0.2	<0.1	1.9	9.8
Houston, TX	18.3	13.1	3.7	1.2	1.6	0.7	1.7	1.5	13.1
Huntsville, AL	7.5	23.6	6.6	1.4	1.2	0.4	0.8	2.7	17.5
Indianapolis, IN	11.5	6.2	3.3	0.7	1.3	1.1	1.1	1.0	17.4
Jacksonville, FL	13.0	14.5	3.0	1.0	1.4	0.4	0.6	1.3	20.5
Kansas City, MO	11.3	9.1	5.0	1.6	2.7	1.7	1.0	1.0	12.1
Lafayette, LA	44.3	9.3	2.0	0.4	1.8	0.1	0.1	0.8	7.0
Las Cruces, NM	19.3	4.1	1.6	2.5	2.5	0.4	0.6	2.2	4.2
Las Vegas, NV	26.2	1.9	0.3	5.8	1.5	0.6	0.3	1.3	5.5
Lexington, KY	5.8	14.9	5.5	1.2	1.6	0.3	0.5	1.2	16.6
Lincoln, NE	13.2	1.0	5.7	1.2	3.1	9.1	0.1	1.8	10.0
Little Rock, AR	4.9	23.5	6.2	0.8	3.7	0.4	0.4	1.0	13.6
Los Angeles, CA	31.1	2.6	0.8	1.5	2.4	0.4	1.4	1.5	9.1
Louisville, KY	11.9	14.5	3.2	0.8	0.9	0.5	1.0	1.0	12.4
Madison, WI	14.4	0.5	2.0	0.7	0.2	9.2	1.2	0.7	8.4
Manchester, NH	16.3	0.6	0.6	0.6	0.3	0.3	0.1	0.8	8.1

Table continued on following page.

Area[1]	Catholic	Baptist	Methodist	LDS[2]	Pentecostal	Lutheran	Islam	Adventist	Other
Miami, FL	23.8	5.1	0.9	0.5	1.3	0.3	0.8	2.4	11.1
Midland, TX	15.4	25.5	2.5	2.0	1.2	0.3	0.4	1.3	16.5
Milwaukee, WI	24.5	3.0	1.0	0.4	2.8	9.1	2.8	0.9	10.7
Minneapolis, MN	19.8	0.8	1.4	0.5	2.5	10.7	2.9	0.7	7.4
Nashville, TN	6.2	16.4	4.8	0.9	1.6	0.4	0.8	1.3	19.4
New Haven, CT	29.9	1.4	1.2	0.4	1.2	0.4	0.9	1.2	9.9
New Orleans, LA	42.1	9.3	2.5	0.5	2.1	0.5	1.4	1.0	8.0
New York, NY	32.5	1.7	1.2	0.3	0.9	0.5	4.5	1.4	10.6
Oklahoma City, OK	10.0	16.6	6.2	1.3	3.9	0.6	0.6	0.9	21.4
Omaha, NE	19.9	2.8	2.8	1.6	1.0	6.1	0.2	1.0	9.0
Orlando, FL	17.6	5.7	2.1	0.9	2.7	0.6	1.3	2.8	14.6
Philadelphia, PA	26.8	3.3	2.4	0.3	1.0	1.2	2.6	1.0	10.5
Phoenix, AZ	22.9	1.7	0.6	6.2	1.5	1.0	1.9	1.5	9.3
Pittsburgh, PA	30.6	1.9	4.3	0.4	1.3	2.5	0.6	0.6	12.5
Portland, OR	11.8	0.8	0.6	3.3	1.4	1.1	0.2	2.0	14.4
Providence, RI	37.9	0.9	0.6	0.3	0.6	0.3	0.5	0.9	6.1
Provo, UT	4.9	0.1	<0.1	82.6	0.1	<0.1	0.3	0.3	0.4
Raleigh, NC	12.4	9.8	5.4	1.2	1.9	0.7	3.2	1.5	12.8
Reno, NV	24.4	1.4	0.5	4.0	0.9	0.5	0.3	1.4	5.3
Richmond, VA	12.3	14.2	4.8	0.9	3.2	0.5	2.1	1.2	14.8
Rochester, MN	15.6	0.4	2.8	1.5	1.9	19.3	1.0	0.7	10.1
Sacramento, CA	17.1	1.9	1.1	3.1	2.2	0.6	1.9	1.9	8.2
St. Louis, MO	21.2	8.6	2.9	0.7	1.4	3.2	1.3	0.8	11.1
Salem, OR	19.5	0.5	0.6	3.8	2.9	1.2	n/a	2.5	10.7
Salt Lake City, UT	9.0	0.6	0.2	52.0	0.7	0.2	1.6	0.7	2.6
San Antonio, TX	27.3	6.4	2.1	1.4	1.6	1.1	0.5	1.5	11.0
San Diego, CA	22.9	1.5	0.6	2.1	1.0	0.6	1.5	1.9	9.4
San Francisco, CA	21.5	2.2	0.9	1.5	1.4	0.4	2.0	1.0	7.7
San Jose, CA	27.2	1.2	0.6	1.4	0.9	0.4	2.0	1.3	11.4
Santa Rosa, CA	23.5	1.1	0.5	1.4	0.5	0.5	0.2	1.8	6.9
Savannah, GA	5.5	11.9	4.8	0.8	1.5	1.1	0.2	1.4	12.3
Seattle, WA	11.0	1.0	0.7	2.6	2.8	1.2	0.6	1.4	19.8
Sioux Falls, SD	13.1	0.7	2.9	0.7	1.7	16.4	0.1	0.6	20.3
Springfield, IL	15.2	4.7	4.3	0.5	1.5	4.7	0.5	0.8	14.6
Tampa, FL	23.1	6.3	2.9	0.5	1.9	0.6	0.7	1.8	12.1
Tucson, AZ	18.9	1.9	0.6	2.8	1.3	1.1	1.0	1.4	9.7
Tulsa, OK	5.6	15.5	7.7	1.2	2.5	0.5	0.5	1.2	22.2
Tuscaloosa, AL	2.6	25.1	6.2	0.6	1.5	0.1	0.3	0.7	13.3
Virginia Beach, VA	8.3	9.5	4.8	0.7	2.0	0.5	1.0	0.9	16.1
Washington, DC	16.1	6.0	4.1	1.1	1.3	0.8	3.3	1.5	12.6
Wichita, KS	12.7	23.5	4.5	1.5	1.4	1.3	0.1	1.1	15.0
Wilmington, NC	13.2	9.9	8.1	1.0	1.0	0.7	0.7	1.4	12.6
Winston-Salem, NC	9.3	12.8	11.4	0.5	1.0	0.6	0.8	1.4	22.5
Worcester, MA	30.1	0.8	0.8	0.3	1.0	0.4	0.6	1.4	7.1
U.S.	18.7	7.3	3.0	2.0	1.8	1.7	1.3	1.3	11.6

Note: Figures are the number of adherents as a percentage of the total population; (1) Figures cover the Metropolitan Statistical Area; (2) Church of Jesus Christ of Latter-day Saints
Source: 2020 U.S. Religion Census, Association of Statisticians of American Religious Bodies; The Association of Religion Data Archives (ARDA)

Religious Groups by Tradition

Area	Catholic	Evangelical Protestant	Mainline Protestant	Black Protestant	Islam	Judaism	Hinduism	Orthodox	Buddhism
Albuquerque, NM	32.6	13.4	2.2	0.5	0.7	0.2	0.2	0.1	0.6
Allentown, PA	18.6	6.2	11.9	0.2	0.7	0.5	0.6	0.4	0.1
Anchorage, AK	4.9	19.2	2.4	0.9	0.1	0.1	0.1	0.5	1.3
Ann Arbor, MI	9.7	8.1	5.6	2.5	2.2	0.8	0.5	0.4	0.3
Athens, GA	6.4	19.1	7.2	2.6	0.2	0.2	0.2	0.1	<0.1
Atlanta, GA	10.7	22.3	7.4	5.3	1.9	0.5	0.7	0.3	0.2
Austin, TX	18.8	13.5	4.0	1.7	1.0	0.2	0.6	0.2	0.3
Baltimore, MD	12.4	10.6	5.9	3.3	3.3	1.7	0.1	0.5	0.1
Boise City, ID	13.0	11.9	3.9	<0.1	0.3	0.1	0.2	0.1	0.1
Boston, MA	37.0	3.4	3.2	0.3	2.2	1.1	0.3	0.9	0.4
Boulder, CO	16.0	12.7	3.4	n/a	0.4	0.7	0.5	0.2	1.0
Brownsville, TX	36.8	13.1	1.2	0.1	0.1	n/a	n/a	n/a	n/a
Cape Coral, FL	18.8	16.4	3.0	0.6	0.2	0.2	0.2	0.1	0.1
Cedar Rapids, IA	16.8	11.9	12.2	0.4	1.3	0.1	0.7	0.1	<0.1
Charleston, SC	11.5	17.1	6.8	6.6	0.2	0.4	<0.1	0.2	n/a
Charlotte, NC	12.1	26.4	9.5	3.4	1.7	0.2	0.2	0.4	0.1
Chicago, IL	28.6	8.2	3.7	3.6	4.7	0.7	0.4	0.7	0.4
Cincinnati, OH	17.0	24.9	4.1	2.0	1.1	0.4	0.3	0.3	0.1
Clarksville, TN	4.6	35.7	4.8	3.4	0.1	n/a	n/a	0.1	n/a
Cleveland, OH	26.1	15.1	5.6	3.5	1.1	1.3	0.3	0.8	0.2
College Station, TX	17.2	16.1	5.3	1.8	0.6	n/a	0.1	0.1	n/a
Colorado Springs, CO	16.4	18.3	2.9	0.9	0.1	<0.1	<0.1	0.1	0.3
Columbia, MO	7.1	19.4	6.3	1.9	1.4	0.2	0.1	0.1	<0.1
Columbia, SC	6.6	27.9	10.7	5.6	0.3	0.2	0.4	0.1	0.3
Columbus, OH	11.7	18.1	6.8	1.5	2.1	0.4	0.4	0.5	0.2
Dallas, TX	14.2	25.4	5.9	3.3	1.8	0.3	0.5	0.3	0.2
Davenport, IA	13.2	8.5	10.6	1.9	0.7	0.1	0.2	0.1	n/a
Denver, CO	16.1	9.6	2.8	0.6	0.3	0.4	0.5	0.4	0.5
Des Moines, IA	12.1	10.3	12.2	1.0	1.6	<0.1	0.2	0.1	0.1
Durham, NC	8.5	20.0	8.8	4.3	1.5	0.5	0.1	0.3	0.1
Edison, NJ	32.5	4.4	3.0	1.5	4.5	4.4	1.0	0.8	0.3
El Paso, TX	47.9	9.9	0.6	0.4	0.1	0.2	<0.1	<0.1	0.2
Fargo, ND	14.2	11.1	23.4	n/a	<0.1	<0.1	n/a	0.1	n/a
Fort Collins, CO	9.9	15.6	3.3	0.4	<0.1	n/a	0.1	0.1	0.1
Fort Wayne, IN	13.1	24.7	6.1	6.5	1.0	0.1	0.1	0.2	0.4
Fort Worth, TX	14.2	25.4	5.9	3.3	1.8	0.3	0.5	0.3	0.2
Grand Rapids, MI	13.1	17.6	7.4	1.0	0.8	0.1	0.2	0.2	<0.1
Greeley, CO	14.1	7.8	2.1	<0.1	<0.1	n/a	n/a	<0.1	0.2
Green Bay, WI	31.8	14.6	6.2	<0.1	0.4	n/a	n/a	<0.1	<0.1
Greensboro, NC	7.9	24.9	10.1	3.5	1.5	0.3	0.3	0.1	0.1
Honolulu, HI	18.0	8.1	2.3	0.2	<0.1	0.1	0.2	<0.1	4.0
Houston, TX	18.3	23.8	4.7	2.3	1.7	0.3	0.7	0.3	0.3
Huntsville, AL	7.5	34.8	8.2	7.2	0.8	0.1	0.9	0.1	0.1
Indianapolis, IN	11.5	16.8	7.6	4.2	1.1	0.4	0.2	0.3	0.1
Jacksonville, FL	13.0	29.8	3.5	5.6	0.6	0.3	0.3	0.3	0.2
Kansas City, MO	11.3	19.1	7.1	3.6	1.0	0.3	0.4	0.1	0.2
Lafayette, LA	44.3	12.6	2.4	5.0	0.1	n/a	<0.1	<0.1	0.1
Las Cruces, NM	19.3	9.8	2.4	0.2	0.6	0.1	0.2	<0.1	n/a
Las Vegas, NV	26.2	6.6	1.0	0.5	0.3	0.3	0.2	0.6	0.7
Lexington, KY	5.8	26.9	8.1	3.5	0.5	0.3	0.1	0.2	<0.1
Lincoln, NE	13.2	16.6	12.9	0.3	0.1	0.1	0.1	0.1	0.1
Little Rock, AR	4.9	32.1	6.6	8.5	0.4	0.1	<0.1	0.1	0.1
Los Angeles, CA	31.1	9.3	1.5	1.7	1.4	0.8	0.4	0.9	0.9
Louisville, KY	11.9	21.1	5.0	4.6	1.0	0.2	0.4	0.2	0.2
Madison, WI	14.4	8.0	10.6	0.2	1.2	0.4	0.1	0.1	0.9

Table continued on following page.

Area	Catholic	Evangelical Protestant	Mainline Protestant	Black Protestant	Islam	Judaism	Hinduism	Orthodox	Buddhism
Manchester, NH	16.3	5.8	2.7	n/a	0.1	0.3	<0.1	0.9	n/a
Miami, FL	23.8	13.7	1.6	2.2	0.8	1.2	0.3	0.2	0.3
Midland, TX	15.4	35.5	3.0	7.6	0.4	n/a	0.2	n/a	n/a
Milwaukee, WI	24.5	16.3	5.4	3.3	2.8	0.4	0.4	0.5	0.4
Minneapolis, MN	19.8	10.6	10.3	0.5	2.9	0.6	0.2	0.3	0.3
Nashville, TN	6.2	30.1	6.0	5.2	0.8	0.2	0.4	1.1	0.2
New Haven, CT	29.9	6.4	4.4	1.4	0.9	1.0	0.3	0.5	0.4
New Orleans, LA	42.1	13.5	3.0	4.9	1.4	0.4	0.3	0.1	0.3
New York, NY	32.5	4.4	3.0	1.5	4.5	4.4	1.0	0.8	0.3
Oklahoma City, OK	10.0	38.7	7.1	2.2	0.6	0.1	0.4	0.1	0.4
Omaha, NE	19.9	10.8	7.9	1.5	0.2	0.3	1.0	0.2	0.2
Orlando, FL	17.6	20.6	2.5	2.7	1.3	0.2	0.5	0.3	0.3
Philadelphia, PA	26.8	7.3	6.6	2.2	2.6	1.1	0.6	0.4	0.4
Phoenix, AZ	22.9	11.0	1.6	0.3	1.9	0.3	0.5	0.4	0.2
Pittsburgh, PA	30.6	8.8	10.1	1.3	0.6	0.6	1.2	0.6	0.1
Portland, OR	11.8	14.6	2.3	0.4	0.2	0.3	0.7	0.3	0.4
Providence, RI	37.9	4.0	3.2	0.1	0.5	0.6	0.1	0.5	0.2
Provo, UT	4.9	0.4	<0.1	n/a	0.3	n/a	0.1	n/a	n/a
Raleigh, NC	12.4	19.3	7.4	2.8	3.2	0.2	0.4	0.3	0.4
Reno, NV	24.4	6.8	1.3	0.2	0.3	0.1	0.1	0.1	0.2
Richmond, VA	12.3	23.1	9.3	3.1	2.1	0.3	1.3	0.4	0.2
Rochester, MN	15.6	15.0	19.1	n/a	1.0	0.1	0.1	0.2	0.2
Sacramento, CA	17.1	10.4	1.4	1.1	1.9	0.2	0.4	0.3	0.5
St. Louis, MO	21.2	16.1	5.7	3.9	1.3	0.6	0.2	0.2	0.3
Salem, OR	19.5	14.4	2.0	0.2	n/a	0.1	<0.1	<0.1	<0.1
Salt Lake City, UT	9.0	2.4	0.7	0.1	1.6	0.1	0.3	0.4	0.3
San Antonio, TX	27.3	17.7	3.1	0.8	0.5	0.2	0.1	0.1	0.3
San Diego, CA	22.9	9.5	1.5	0.6	1.5	0.4	0.3	0.4	0.7
San Francisco, CA	21.5	5.2	2.2	1.8	2.0	0.7	1.1	0.7	1.1
San Jose, CA	27.2	8.4	1.4	0.3	2.0	0.6	2.4	0.6	1.2
Santa Rosa, CA	23.5	5.3	1.5	<0.1	0.2	0.4	0.3	0.4	1.7
Savannah, GA	5.5	19.0	5.7	5.9	0.2	0.7	0.5	0.1	n/a
Seattle, WA	11.0	19.5	2.7	0.6	0.6	0.4	0.4	0.6	1.6
Sioux Falls, SD	13.1	21.0	20.2	0.1	0.1	n/a	n/a	0.8	<0.1
Springfield, IL	15.2	19.0	7.7	2.4	0.5	0.2	0.3	0.1	<0.1
Tampa, FL	23.1	16.9	3.8	1.7	0.7	0.4	0.3	0.8	0.4
Tucson, AZ	18.9	10.4	2.4	0.6	1.0	0.4	0.4	0.2	0.3
Tulsa, OK	5.6	37.8	8.6	1.7	0.5	0.2	0.1	0.1	<0.1
Tuscaloosa, AL	2.6	34.3	4.6	7.3	0.3	0.1	n/a	n/a	n/a
Virginia Beach, VA	8.3	21.3	6.9	3.7	1.0	0.3	0.2	0.3	0.3
Washington, DC	16.1	12.3	6.5	3.3	3.3	1.0	0.9	0.9	0.5
Wichita, KS	12.7	19.4	23.2	2.6	0.1	<0.1	0.1	0.2	0.5
Wilmington, NC	13.2	17.9	9.3	4.6	0.7	0.3	0.1	0.3	n/a
Winston-Salem, NC	9.3	31.4	13.6	3.4	0.8	n/a	<0.1	0.3	0.1
Worcester, MA	30.1	4.9	3.6	0.2	0.6	0.4	0.3	1.0	0.4
U.S.	18.7	16.5	5.2	2.3	1.3	0.6	0.4	0.4	0.3

Note: Figures are the number of adherents as a percentage of the total population; (1) Figures cover the Metropolitan Statistical Area
Source: 2020 U.S. Religion Census, Association of Statisticians of American Religious Bodies; The Association of Religion Data Archives (ARDA)

Gross Metropolitan Product

MSA[1]	2020	2021	2022	2023	Rank[2]
Albuquerque, NM	45.1	50.3	56.1	58.2	70
Allentown, PA	46.7	51.6	56.6	59.9	67
Anchorage, AK	25.8	28.3	31.3	32.6	112
Ann Arbor, MI	25.8	28.1	30.4	32.1	113
Athens, GA	10.5	11.5	12.8	13.4	213
Atlanta, GA	425.4	465.1	507.9	540.7	11
Austin, TX	168.4	192.3	215.9	231.0	22
Baltimore, MD	205.8	219.9	238.6	255.0	19
Boise City, ID	37.9	42.9	46.9	50.4	80
Boston, MA	480.3	526.5	569.8	601.7	8
Boulder, CO	29.7	32.7	35.9	38.1	101
Brownsville, TX	11.9	13.1	14.8	15.6	195
Cape Coral, FL	34.5	38.8	42.7	45.6	85
Cedar Rapids, IA	18.5	20.7	21.9	23.3	147
Charleston, SC	45.6	50.4	55.3	59.2	69
Charlotte, NC	184.0	204.1	222.9	238.2	21
Chicago, IL	693.0	757.2	819.9	861.2	3
Cincinnati, OH	152.1	165.2	178.8	190.5	27
Clarksville, TN	12.3	13.7	14.8	15.6	191
Cleveland, OH	133.6	144.9	157.7	167.2	35
College Station, TX	13.6	14.9	16.6	17.4	185
Colorado Springs, CO	39.5	43.7	47.3	49.9	78
Columbia, MO	10.4	11.6	12.5	13.3	211
Columbia, SC	44.4	48.2	51.8	55.2	74
Columbus, OH	137.3	151.0	164.2	175.3	33
Dallas, TX	538.4	608.8	686.1	722.1	5
Davenport, IA	22.1	24.6	26.3	27.6	126
Denver, CO	223.1	246.9	271.0	286.2	18
Des Moines, IA	55.0	63.3	67.6	71.4	57
Durham, NC	51.6	57.3	61.8	65.6	60
Edison, NJ	1,844.7	1,993.2	2,157.6	2,278.7	1
El Paso, TX	34.1	37.5	40.5	42.6	89
Fargo, ND	15.7	18.0	19.9	20.6	160
Fort Collins, CO	21.6	23.7	25.7	27.3	130
Fort Wayne, IN	24.3	27.3	29.8	31.6	114
Fort Worth, TX	538.4	608.8	686.1	722.1	5
Grand Rapids, MI	61.4	67.8	73.0	78.0	55
Greeley, CO	16.7	17.9	20.0	22.3	162
Green Bay, WI	20.5	22.2	24.3	26.0	139
Greensboro, NC	42.0	46.1	49.5	51.7	75
Honolulu, HI	62.1	66.8	74.3	80.2	56
Houston, TX	488.1	543.0	619.8	654.0	7
Huntsville, AL	30.9	33.5	36.5	39.2	98
Indianapolis, IN	146.9	163.9	178.6	190.0	28
Jacksonville, FL	91.0	100.3	109.1	115.5	42
Kansas City, MO	142.5	154.3	165.9	176.9	32
Lafayette, LA	20.6	22.6	24.8	26.2	135
Las Cruces, NM	7.6	8.5	9.6	10.0	258
Las Vegas, NV	119.4	134.8	151.1	164.0	36
Lexington, KY	29.8	32.5	35.1	36.8	103
Lincoln, NE	21.2	23.8	25.4	26.9	129
Little Rock, AR	38.6	42.3	45.8	48.0	81
Los Angeles, CA	1,007.0	1,129.4	1,226.9	1,295.5	2
Louisville, KY	75.6	83.6	90.5	94.4	47
Madison, WI	51.5	56.1	60.8	64.9	63
Manchester, NH	28.8	32.2	34.1	35.6	104

Table continued on following page.

MSA[1]	2020	2021	2022	2023	Rank[2]
Miami, FL	365.0	402.9	442.8	471.0	12
Midland, TX	21.8	25.3	30.1	33.9	121
Milwaukee, WI	102.4	110.1	119.2	126.3	38
Minneapolis, MN	270.7	298.9	324.7	344.9	15
Nashville, TN	136.6	157.4	173.7	184.5	31
New Haven, CT	53.0	57.1	61.7	64.7	61
New Orleans, LA	76.4	82.6	91.2	96.5	48
New York, NY	1,844.7	1,993.2	2,157.6	2,278.7	1
Oklahoma City, OK	74.4	81.6	92.9	98.2	49
Omaha, NE	69.1	77.9	83.2	88.2	50
Orlando, FL	144.1	160.5	180.2	194.2	30
Philadelphia, PA	439.1	478.2	521.7	553.7	9
Phoenix, AZ	281.0	310.1	336.3	358.7	14
Pittsburgh, PA	153.4	165.5	178.3	189.7	26
Portland, OR	168.4	184.1	201.8	214.4	25
Providence, RI	87.9	95.6	104.0	109.3	45
Provo, UT	31.9	36.5	40.2	43.1	91
Raleigh, NC	95.3	106.6	117.3	125.7	39
Reno, NV	31.8	35.9	39.3	41.9	92
Richmond, VA	91.2	97.3	104.5	110.5	44
Rochester, MN	14.2	15.8	17.1	18.1	178
Sacramento, CA	145.4	161.7	176.8	188.8	29
St. Louis, MO	171.5	187.7	201.8	212.8	23
Salem, OR	19.2	21.0	22.9	24.2	144
Salt Lake City, UT	103.9	114.9	124.5	132.3	37
San Antonio, TX	132.1	146.4	161.1	169.2	34
San Diego, CA	240.4	269.0	294.4	313.2	17
San Francisco, CA	588.3	652.7	713.1	748.9	4
San Jose, CA	360.5	400.1	431.2	450.9	13
Santa Rosa, CA	31.2	35.6	39.1	41.5	93
Savannah, GA	22.0	25.3	27.7	28.7	122
Seattle, WA	426.9	470.6	509.3	539.7	10
Sioux Falls, SD	23.4	26.6	28.7	30.6	118
Springfield, IL	11.7	13.1	13.8	14.6	196
Tampa, FL	169.3	187.4	205.4	217.8	24
Tucson, AZ	45.2	49.1	53.1	56.2	72
Tulsa, OK	53.7	58.3	65.1	68.5	59
Tuscaloosa, AL	11.4	12.2	13.2	13.9	205
Virginia Beach, VA	95.3	102.4	109.4	116.0	41
Washington, DC	560.7	600.8	647.6	688.6	6
Wichita, KS	36.7	40.2	44.0	47.1	83
Wilmington, NC	16.0	18.0	19.3	20.3	161
Winston-Salem, NC	34.0	37.6	40.9	43.7	88
Worcester, MA	50.9	55.1	59.3	62.5	64

Note: Figures are in billions of dollars; (1) Metropolitan Statistical Area; (2) Rank is based on 2021 data and ranges from 1 to 381.
Source: The U.S. Conference of Mayors, U.S. Metro Economies: U.S. Metros Compared to Global and State Economies,, June 2022

Economic Growth

MSA[1]	2018-20 (%)	2021 (%)	2022 (%)	2023	Rank[2]
Albuquerque, NM	-0.4	5.6	4.6	3.6	167
Allentown, PA	-0.3	5.9	3.6	2.6	159
Anchorage, AK	-2.4	0.4	2.3	2.9	323
Ann Arbor, MI	-0.4	5.0	2.9	2.6	164
Athens, GA	-2.1	5.6	6.1	1.6	288
Atlanta, GA	-0.1	5.9	3.3	3.1	151
Austin, TX	3.2	10.1	5.9	3.8	13
Baltimore, MD	-2.0	3.2	2.7	3.5	284
Boise City, ID	2.0	7.4	3.2	4.2	35
Boston, MA	-0.1	6.7	3.2	2.4	146
Boulder, CO	1.5	5.6	3.5	3.8	49
Brownsville, TX	1.3	6.2	4.4	2.9	56
Cape Coral, FL	-0.4	8.7	5.0	2.9	165
Cedar Rapids, IA	-2.3	4.9	-0.2	3.5	310
Charleston, SC	0.4	6.3	3.8	3.8	106
Charlotte, NC	0.5	6.6	3.2	3.6	103
Chicago, IL	-2.4	5.5	2.6	1.8	324
Cincinnati, OH	0.0	4.2	2.4	3.3	145
Clarksville, TN	0.7	7.1	3.0	1.6	91
Cleveland, OH	-1.3	4.3	3.1	2.7	238
College Station, TX	1.1	5.1	4.2	2.8	61
Colorado Springs, CO	1.6	6.0	2.1	3.0	47
Columbia, MO	2.1	5.6	2.9	3.3	29
Columbia, SC	0.1	4.4	1.7	3.2	137
Columbus, OH	0.1	5.8	3.1	3.5	136
Dallas, TX	0.8	8.3	5.3	3.2	84
Davenport, IA	-0.6	5.6	1.2	1.8	184
Denver, CO	0.8	6.2	3.5	3.1	82
Des Moines, IA	1.7	8.2	0.9	2.7	46
Durham, NC	2.7	6.7	2.5	2.9	19
Edison, NJ	-1.5	5.6	3.3	2.4	250
El Paso, TX	2.0	5.5	2.3	1.9	36
Fargo, ND	-0.4	6.0	-0.2	1.2	170
Fort Collins, CO	2.2	5.3	2.6	4.0	27
Fort Wayne, IN	-2.0	8.3	3.1	2.7	285
Fort Worth, TX	0.8	8.3	5.3	3.2	84
Grand Rapids, MI	-2.1	6.3	1.8	3.7	294
Greeley, CO	-4.3	3.2	5.5	9.1	366
Green Bay, WI	-2.5	3.7	3.7	3.9	326
Greensboro, NC	-2.2	5.4	1.5	1.4	302
Honolulu, HI	-5.4	3.6	5.2	4.6	376
Houston, TX	-1.6	4.9	4.4	4.7	254
Huntsville, AL	1.8	4.9	3.4	3.9	42
Indianapolis, IN	-0.2	7.3	3.2	3.1	155
Jacksonville, FL	2.1	6.1	3.1	2.6	30
Kansas City, MO	0.0	4.0	1.7	3.5	140
Lafayette, LA	-3.7	4.2	2.6	3.3	356
Las Cruces, NM	-1.8	6.3	7.3	3.2	273
Las Vegas, NV	-3.4	7.7	5.7	5.1	349
Lexington, KY	-1.6	4.1	1.8	1.6	261
Lincoln, NE	0.1	5.0	0.9	2.8	131
Little Rock, AR	-0.6	5.2	2.2	1.9	182
Los Angeles, CA	-1.6	8.8	3.3	2.6	256
Louisville, KY	-0.4	5.8	2.2	1.2	169
Madison, WI	0.1	4.4	2.7	3.7	132
Manchester, NH	0.9	8.3	1.2	1.0	78

Table continued on following page.

MSA[1]	2018-20 (%)	2021 (%)	2022 (%)	2023	Rank[2]
Miami, FL	-1.4	6.4	4.2	3.1	245
Midland, TX	3.5	15.8	10.1	12.3	12
Milwaukee, WI	-1.8	3.1	2.5	2.8	271
Minneapolis, MN	-1.9	5.9	2.8	3.0	276
Nashville, TN	-1.2	10.6	4.4	3.0	228
New Haven, CT	-0.9	4.6	2.8	1.7	206
New Orleans, LA	-2.2	2.6	1.8	3.3	304
New York, NY	-1.5	5.6	3.3	2.4	250
Oklahoma City, OK	-2.2	2.3	4.2	4.8	307
Omaha, NE	0.2	5.3	0.8	3.0	127
Orlando, FL	-1.2	7.5	6.4	4.4	229
Philadelphia, PA	-1.2	4.9	3.3	2.8	235
Phoenix, AZ	1.9	5.8	2.7	3.4	39
Pittsburgh, PA	-1.6	3.8	1.9	3.1	257
Portland, OR	-0.6	5.8	4.2	2.9	179
Providence, RI	-1.1	5.6	3.4	1.9	224
Provo, UT	5.1	10.9	6.1	4.3	3
Raleigh, NC	-0.1	7.7	4.4	4.0	148
Reno, NV	2.1	7.5	2.8	3.2	31
Richmond, VA	-0.3	3.0	1.7	2.3	160
Rochester, MN	-0.9	6.6	2.9	2.5	209
Sacramento, CA	0.0	7.4	3.6	3.6	142
St. Louis, MO	-1.2	5.3	1.6	2.0	232
Salem, OR	0.3	5.6	4.2	2.6	119
Salt Lake City, UT	1.9	6.1	2.7	3.1	38
San Antonio, TX	0.8	6.2	3.7	2.4	88
San Diego, CA	-0.5	8.2	3.9	3.3	174
San Francisco, CA	1.2	7.1	4.0	1.9	60
San Jose, CA	5.2	8.6	3.3	1.6	2
Santa Rosa, CA	-1.8	9.7	5.0	3.1	269
Savannah, GA	-1.6	10.3	4.8	0.1	262
Seattle, WA	2.2	7.2	3.3	2.6	26
Sioux Falls, SD	0.4	7.1	1.9	3.7	111
Springfield, IL	-3.3	9.4	0.6	2.6	346
Tampa, FL	1.0	7.2	4.1	2.8	72
Tucson, AZ	-1.3	4.0	2.1	2.5	240
Tulsa, OK	-1.7	1.1	3.1	3.5	266
Tuscaloosa, AL	0.9	3.1	3.9	2.4	80
Virginia Beach, VA	-1.4	3.5	1.1	2.5	247
Washington, DC	-0.7	4.0	2.5	3.0	192
Wichita, KS	-2.0	4.3	2.9	4.1	286
Wilmington, NC	1.5	8.5	1.8	1.3	52
Winston-Salem, NC	-4.0	6.0	2.8	3.6	358
Worcester, MA	-0.9	5.3	2.5	2.4	204
U.S.	-0.6	5.7	3.1	2.9	–

Note: Figures are real gross metropolitan product (GMP) growth rates and represent annual average percent change;
(1) Metropolitan Statistical Area; (2) Rank is based on 2020 2-year average annual percent change and ranges from 1 to 381
Source: The U.S. Conference of Mayors, U.S. Metro Economies: U.S. Metros Compared to Global and State Economies,, June 2022

Metropolitan Area Exports

MSA[1]	2016	2017	2018	2019	2020	2021	Rank[2]
Albuquerque, NM	999.7	624.2	771.5	1,629.7	1,265.3	2,215.0	101
Allentown, PA	3,657.2	3,639.4	3,423.2	3,796.3	3,207.4	4,088.7	68
Anchorage, AK	1,215.4	1,675.9	1,510.8	1,348.0	990.9	n/a	n/a
Ann Arbor, MI	1,207.9	1,447.4	1,538.7	1,432.7	1,183.1	1,230.7	141
Athens, GA	332.1	297.7	378.1	442.1	338.7	448.1	223
Atlanta, GA	20,480.1	21,748.0	24,091.6	25,800.8	25,791.0	28,116.4	16
Austin, TX	10,682.7	12,451.5	12,929.9	12,509.0	13,041.5	15,621.9	25
Baltimore, MD	5,288.6	4,674.3	6,039.2	7,081.8	6,084.6	8,200.6	43
Boise City, ID	3,021.7	2,483.3	2,771.7	2,062.8	1,632.9	1,937.1	110
Boston, MA	21,168.0	23,116.2	24,450.1	23,505.8	23,233.8	32,084.2	12
Boulder, CO	956.3	1,012.0	1,044.1	1,014.9	1,110.4	1,078.0	152
Brownsville, TX	5,016.7	n/a	6,293.0	4,741.8	n/a	6,953.0	47
Cape Coral, FL	540.3	592.3	668.0	694.9	654.8	797.5	183
Cedar Rapids, IA	945.0	1,071.6	1,025.0	1,028.4	832.0	980.0	160
Charleston, SC	9,508.1	8,845.2	10,943.2	16,337.9	6,110.5	3,381.6	77
Charlotte, NC	11,944.1	13,122.5	14,083.2	13,892.4	8,225.6	10,554.3	33
Chicago, IL	43,932.7	46,140.2	47,287.8	42,438.8	41,279.4	54,498.1	4
Cincinnati, OH	26,326.2	28,581.8	27,396.3	28,778.3	21,002.2	23,198.7	19
Clarksville, TN	376.1	360.2	435.5	341.8	246.8	288.7	268
Cleveland, OH	8,752.9	8,944.9	9,382.9	8,829.9	7,415.8	8,560.4	41
College Station, TX	113.2	145.4	153.0	160.5	114.9	110.3	346
Colorado Springs, CO	786.9	819.7	850.6	864.2	979.2	866.9	175
Columbia, MO	213.7	224.0	238.6	291.4	256.2	335.4	255
Columbia, SC	2,007.7	2,123.9	2,083.8	2,184.6	2,058.8	2,100.2	104
Columbus, OH	5,675.4	5,962.2	7,529.5	7,296.6	6,304.8	6,557.9	51
Dallas, TX	27,187.8	30,269.1	36,260.9	39,474.0	35,642.0	43,189.0	6
Davenport, IA	4,497.6	5,442.7	6,761.9	6,066.3	5,097.5	6,341.0	52
Denver, CO	3,649.3	3,954.7	4,544.3	4,555.6	4,604.4	4,670.8	62
Des Moines, IA	1,052.2	1,141.2	1,293.7	1,437.8	1,414.0	1,706.6	118
Durham, NC	2,937.4	3,128.4	3,945.8	4,452.9	3,359.3	3,326.4	78
Edison, NJ	89,649.5	93,693.7	97,692.4	87,365.7	75,745.4	103,930.9	2
El Paso, TX	26,452.8	25,814.1	30,052.0	32,749.6	27,154.4	32,397.9	11
Fargo, ND	474.5	519.5	553.5	515.0	438.3	539.4	210
Fort Collins, CO	993.8	1,034.1	1,021.8	1,060.0	1,092.5	1,132.5	146
Fort Wayne, IN	1,322.2	1,422.8	1,593.3	1,438.5	1,144.6	1,592.7	123
Fort Worth, TX	27,187.8	30,269.1	36,260.9	39,474.0	35,642.0	43,189.0	6
Grand Rapids, MI	5,168.5	5,385.8	5,420.9	5,214.1	4,488.3	5,171.7	57
Greeley, CO	1,539.6	1,492.8	1,366.5	1,439.2	1,480.4	2,022.6	109
Green Bay, WI	1,044.0	1,054.8	1,044.3	928.2	736.4	765.6	185
Greensboro, NC	3,730.4	3,537.9	3,053.5	2,561.8	2,007.3	2,356.2	97
Honolulu, HI	330.3	393.6	438.9	308.6	169.0	164.3	319
Houston, TX	84,105.5	95,760.3	120,714.3	129,656.0	104,538.2	140,750.4	1
Huntsville, AL	1,827.3	1,889.2	1,608.7	1,534.2	1,263.0	1,579.5	124
Indianapolis, IN	9,655.4	10,544.2	11,069.9	11,148.7	11,100.4	12,740.4	30
Jacksonville, FL	2,159.0	2,141.7	2,406.7	2,975.5	2,473.3	2,683.7	90
Kansas City, MO	6,709.8	7,015.0	7,316.9	7,652.6	7,862.7	9,177.6	38
Lafayette, LA	1,335.2	954.8	1,001.7	1,086.2	946.2	895.7	167
Las Cruces, NM	1,568.6	1,390.2	1,467.5	n/a	2,149.5	2,408.2	95
Las Vegas, NV	2,312.3	2,710.6	2,240.6	2,430.8	1,705.9	1,866.2	115
Lexington, KY	2,069.6	2,119.8	2,148.0	2,093.8	1,586.3	1,880.0	113
Lincoln, NE	796.9	860.9	885.6	807.0	726.3	872.6	171
Little Rock, AR	1,871.0	2,146.1	1,607.4	1,642.5	n/a	1,370.6	132
Los Angeles, CA	61,245.7	63,752.9	64,814.6	61,041.1	50,185.4	58,588.4	3
Louisville, KY	7,793.3	8,925.9	8,987.0	9,105.5	8,360.3	10,262.8	35
Madison, WI	2,204.8	2,187.7	2,460.2	2,337.6	2,450.5	2,756.3	89
Manchester, NH	1,465.2	1,714.7	1,651.4	1,587.1	1,704.9	2,077.6	106

Table continued on following page.

MSA[1]	2016	2017	2018	2019	2020	2021	Rank[2]
Miami, FL	32,734.5	34,780.5	35,650.2	35,498.9	29,112.1	36,011.3	7
Midland, TX	69.6	69.4	63.6	63.7	57.7	49.9	372
Milwaukee, WI	7,256.2	7,279.1	7,337.6	6,896.3	6,624.0	7,282.8	46
Minneapolis, MN	18,329.2	19,070.9	20,016.2	18,633.0	17,109.5	21,098.8	21
Nashville, TN	9,460.1	10,164.3	8,723.7	7,940.7	6,569.9	8,256.1	42
New Haven, CT	1,819.8	1,876.3	2,082.3	2,133.8	2,330.5	2,667.5	91
New Orleans, LA	29,518.8	31,648.5	36,570.4	34,109.6	31,088.4	35,773.5	8
New York, NY	89,649.5	93,693.7	97,692.4	87,365.7	75,745.4	103,930.9	2
Oklahoma City, OK	1,260.0	1,278.8	1,489.4	1,434.5	1,326.6	1,773.2	116
Omaha, NE	3,509.7	3,756.2	4,371.6	3,725.7	3,852.5	4,595.1	64
Orlando, FL	3,363.9	3,196.7	3,131.7	3,363.9	2,849.8	3,313.6	79
Philadelphia, PA	21,359.9	21,689.7	23,663.2	24,721.3	23,022.1	28,724.4	15
Phoenix, AZ	12,838.2	13,223.1	13,614.9	15,136.6	11,073.9	14,165.1	27
Pittsburgh, PA	7,971.0	9,322.7	9,824.2	9,672.9	7,545.1	9,469.6	36
Portland, OR	20,256.8	20,788.8	21,442.9	23,761.9	27,824.7	33,787.5	10
Providence, RI	6,595.7	7,125.4	6,236.6	7,424.8	6,685.2	6,708.2	49
Provo, UT	1,894.8	2,065.3	1,788.1	1,783.7	1,888.5	2,053.8	108
Raleigh, NC	2,620.4	2,865.8	3,193.2	3,546.8	3,372.0	3,962.7	71
Reno, NV	2,382.1	2,517.3	2,631.7	2,598.3	4,553.3	4,503.0	66
Richmond, VA	3,525.7	3,663.7	3,535.0	3,203.2	2,719.1	3,010.7	84
Rochester, MN	398.0	495.3	537.6	390.1	194.0	224.9	292
Sacramento, CA	7,032.1	6,552.6	6,222.8	5,449.2	4,980.9	5,682.3	54
St. Louis, MO	8,346.5	9,662.9	10,866.8	10,711.1	9,089.4	10,486.1	34
Salem, OR	358.2	339.0	410.2	405.7	350.5	372.0	244
Salt Lake City, UT	8,653.7	7,916.9	9,748.6	13,273.9	13,565.5	13,469.1	28
San Antonio, TX	5,621.2	9,184.1	11,678.1	11,668.0	10,987.9	13,086.4	29
San Diego, CA	18,086.6	18,637.1	20,156.8	19,774.1	18,999.7	23,687.8	18
San Francisco, CA	24,506.3	29,103.8	27,417.0	28,003.8	23,864.5	29,972.0	13
San Jose, CA	21,716.8	21,464.7	22,224.2	20,909.4	19,534.5	22,293.6	20
Santa Rosa, CA	1,194.3	1,168.2	1,231.7	1,234.5	1,131.4	1,301.8	137
Savannah, GA	4,263.4	4,472.0	5,407.8	4,925.5	4,557.0	5,520.5	55
Seattle, WA	61,881.0	59,007.0	59,742.9	41,249.0	23,851.0	28,866.7	14
Sioux Falls, SD	334.3	386.8	400.0	431.5	524.9	547.3	207
Springfield, IL	88.3	107.5	91.2	99.8	90.5	98.9	351
Tampa, FL	5,702.9	6,256.0	4,966.7	6,219.7	5,082.2	5,754.7	53
Tucson, AZ	2,563.9	2,683.9	2,824.8	2,943.7	2,640.7	2,846.1	87
Tulsa, OK	2,363.0	2,564.7	3,351.7	3,399.2	2,567.8	3,064.8	81
Tuscaloosa, AL	n/a	n/a	n/a	n/a	5,175.0	6,675.5	50
Virginia Beach, VA	3,291.1	3,307.2	3,950.6	3,642.4	4,284.3	4,566.3	65
Washington, DC	13,582.4	12,736.1	13,602.7	14,563.8	13,537.3	12,210.8	31
Wichita, KS	3,054.9	3,299.2	3,817.0	3,494.7	2,882.1	3,615.3	74
Wilmington, NC	598.7	759.8	634.4	526.4	553.6	497.8	218
Winston-Salem, NC	1,234.6	1,131.7	1,107.5	1,209.1	913.1	918.2	164
Worcester, MA	3,093.5	2,929.6	2,573.6	2,221.5	2,026.4	2,624.6	92

Note: Figures are in millions of dollars; (1) Metropolitan Statistical Area; (2) Rank is based on 2021 data and ranges from 1 to 388
Source: U.S. Department of Commerce, International Trade Administration, Office of Trade and Economic Analysis, Industry and Analysis, Exports by Metropolitan Area, extracted March 16, 2023

Building Permits: City

City	Single-Family			Multi-Family			Total		
	2021	2022	Pct. Chg.	2021	2022	Pct. Chg.	2021	2022	Pct. Chg.
Albuquerque, NM	773	707	-8.5	894	902	0.9	1,667	1,609	-3.5
Allentown, PA	0	27	–	0	0	0.0	0	27	–
Anchorage, AK	840	124	-85.2	293	31	-89.4	1,133	155	-86.3
Ann Arbor, MI	175	135	-22.9	52	4	-92.3	227	139	-38.8
Athens, GA	180	227	26.1	986	1,548	57.0	1,166	1,775	52.2
Atlanta, GA	855	1,775	107.6	1,558	10,078	546.9	2,413	11,853	391.2
Austin, TX	4,180	3,344	-20.0	14,542	15,102	3.9	18,722	18,446	-1.5
Baltimore, MD	191	118	-38.2	1,366	1,539	12.7	1,557	1,657	6.4
Boise City, ID	856	392	-54.2	1,165	1,210	3.9	2,021	1,602	-20.7
Boston, MA	53	53	0.0	3,459	3,882	12.2	3,512	3,935	12.0
Boulder, CO	41	35	-14.6	253	269	6.3	294	304	3.4
Brownsville, TX	883	817	-7.5	246	353	43.5	1,129	1,170	3.6
Cape Coral, FL	4,279	3,813	-10.9	1,133	922	-18.6	5,412	4,735	-12.5
Cedar Rapids, IA	158	129	-18.4	280	225	-19.6	438	354	-19.2
Charleston, SC	1,091	942	-13.7	378	459	21.4	1,469	1,401	-4.6
Charlotte, NC	n/a	n/a	n/a	n/a	n/a	n/a	n/a	n/a	n/a
Chicago, IL	414	412	-0.5	4,927	6,712	36.2	5,341	7,124	33.4
Cincinnati, OH	206	104	-49.5	932	689	-26.1	1,138	793	-30.3
Clarksville, TN	1,452	973	-33.0	1,813	2,160	19.1	3,265	3,133	-4.0
Cleveland, OH	104	158	51.9	27	363	1,244.4	131	521	297.7
College Station, TX	674	592	-12.2	318	97	-69.5	992	689	-30.5
Colorado Springs, CO	n/a	n/a	n/a	n/a	n/a	n/a	n/a	n/a	n/a
Columbia, MO	487	303	-37.8	189	135	-28.6	676	438	-35.2
Columbia, SC	804	772	-4.0	896	1,359	51.7	1,700	2,131	25.4
Columbus, OH	913	642	-29.7	3,555	5,535	55.7	4,468	6,177	38.2
Dallas, TX	2,245	2,349	4.6	7,769	7,880	1.4	10,014	10,229	2.1
Davenport, IA	84	160	90.5	0	0	0.0	84	160	90.5
Denver, CO	1,550	1,323	-14.6	8,450	6,973	-17.5	10,000	8,296	-17.0
Des Moines, IA	248	256	3.2	380	284	-25.3	628	540	-14.0
Durham, NC	1,960	1,595	-18.6	1,361	2,771	103.6	3,321	4,366	31.5
Edison, NJ	105	104	-1.0	250	17	-93.2	355	121	-65.9
El Paso, TX	1,961	1,649	-15.9	272	319	17.3	2,233	1,968	-11.9
Fargo, ND	410	413	0.7	736	820	11.4	1,146	1,233	7.6
Fort Collins, CO	381	287	-24.7	458	515	12.4	839	802	-4.4
Fort Wayne, IN	n/a	n/a	n/a	n/a	n/a	n/a	n/a	n/a	n/a
Fort Worth, TX	7,236	7,421	2.6	4,338	4,557	5.0	11,574	11,978	3.5
Grand Rapids, MI	43	23	-46.5	243	211	-13.2	286	234	-18.2
Greeley, CO	315	345	9.5	600	1,725	187.5	915	2,070	126.2
Green Bay, WI	58	37	-36.2	2	0	-100.0	60	37	-38.3
Greensboro, NC	529	467	-11.7	1,363	676	-50.4	1,892	1,143	-39.6
Honolulu, HI	n/a	n/a	n/a	n/a	n/a	n/a	n/a	n/a	n/a
Houston, TX	7,146	6,800	-4.8	8,103	8,945	10.4	15,249	15,745	3.3
Huntsville, AL	1,483	1,083	-27.0	1,328	47	-96.5	2,811	1,130	-59.8
Indianapolis, IN	1,221	1,099	-10.0	968	1,011	4.4	2,189	2,110	-3.6
Jacksonville, FL	6,191	5,484	-11.4	3,778	5,862	55.2	9,969	11,346	13.8
Kansas City, MO	890	746	-16.2	1,448	1,241	-14.3	2,338	1,987	-15.0
Lafayette, LA	n/a	n/a	n/a	n/a	n/a	n/a	n/a	n/a	n/a
Las Cruces, NM	763	685	-10.2	99	26	-73.7	862	711	-17.5
Las Vegas, NV	2,700	3,001	11.1	1,048	1,024	-2.3	3,748	4,025	7.4
Lexington, KY	792	686	-13.4	863	1,045	21.1	1,655	1,731	4.6
Lincoln, NE	1,093	943	-13.7	1,227	2,179	77.6	2,320	3,122	34.6
Little Rock, AR	666	377	-43.4	460	644	40.0	1,126	1,021	-9.3
Los Angeles, CA	2,475	3,182	28.6	11,613	13,525	16.5	14,088	16,707	18.6
Louisville, KY	1,382	1,151	-16.7	466	1,637	251.3	1,848	2,788	50.9

Table continued on following page.

City	Single-Family			Multi-Family			Total		
	2021	2022	Pct. Chg.	2021	2022	Pct. Chg.	2021	2022	Pct. Chg.
Madison, WI	327	314	-4.0	3,299	2,046	-38.0	3,626	2,360	-34.9
Manchester, NH	126	132	4.8	8	6	-25.0	134	138	3.0
Miami, FL	102	127	24.5	6,153	4,231	-31.2	6,255	4,358	-30.3
Midland, TX	858	593	-30.9	0	0	0.0	858	593	-30.9
Milwaukee, WI	28	42	50.0	176	134	-23.9	204	176	-13.7
Minneapolis, MN	63	55	-12.7	3,119	3,626	16.3	3,182	3,681	15.7
Nashville, TN	3,932	3,977	1.1	12,205	10,818	-11.4	16,137	14,795	-8.3
New Haven, CT	13	10	-23.1	286	491	71.7	299	501	67.6
New Orleans, LA	716	615	-14.1	860	1,007	17.1	1,576	1,622	2.9
New York, NY	151	61	-59.6	19,772	21,429	8.4	19,923	21,490	7.9
Oklahoma City, OK	4,127	3,298	-20.1	140	260	85.7	4,267	3,558	-16.6
Omaha, NE	1,620	1,217	-24.9	1,547	2,552	65.0	3,167	3,769	19.0
Orlando, FL	990	1,286	29.9	2,734	2,229	-18.5	3,724	3,515	-5.6
Philadelphia, PA	1,553	478	-69.2	23,704	2,745	-88.4	25,257	3,223	-87.2
Phoenix, AZ	4,922	3,982	-19.1	6,570	10,616	61.6	11,492	14,598	27.0
Pittsburgh, PA	198	115	-41.9	617	1,913	210.0	815	2,028	148.8
Portland, OR	474	489	3.2	2,554	1,708	-33.1	3,028	2,197	-27.4
Providence, RI	1	28	2,700.0	53	271	411.3	54	299	453.7
Provo, UT	98	134	36.7	617	327	-47.0	715	461	-35.5
Raleigh, NC	1,354	1,875	38.5	5,133	6,760	31.7	6,487	8,635	33.1
Reno, NV	1,414	1,158	-18.1	2,539	2,535	-0.2	3,953	3,693	-6.6
Richmond, VA	502	457	-9.0	565	2,192	288.0	1,067	2,649	148.3
Rochester, MN	251	234	-6.8	374	847	126.5	625	1,081	73.0
Sacramento, CA	1,004	905	-9.9	2,079	1,149	-44.7	3,083	2,054	-33.4
St. Louis, MO	146	122	-16.4	809	1,054	30.3	955	1,176	23.1
Salem, OR	447	318	-28.9	399	851	113.3	846	1,169	38.2
Salt Lake City, UT	172	144	-16.3	3,519	3,489	-0.9	3,691	3,633	-1.6
San Antonio, TX	6,567	4,686	-28.6	4,591	9,496	106.8	11,158	14,182	27.1
San Diego, CA	539	506	-6.1	4,249	3,916	-7.8	4,788	4,422	-7.6
San Francisco, CA	33	38	15.2	2,486	2,006	-19.3	2,519	2,044	-18.9
San Jose, CA	299	553	84.9	359	1,450	303.9	658	2,003	204.4
Santa Rosa, CA	420	286	-31.9	1,031	911	-11.6	1,451	1,197	-17.5
Savannah, GA	487	408	-16.2	5	24	380.0	492	432	-12.2
Seattle, WA	264	418	58.3	11,716	8,572	-26.8	11,980	8,990	-25.0
Sioux Falls, SD	1,313	1,036	-21.1	1,819	3,429	88.5	3,132	4,465	42.6
Springfield, IL	137	55	-59.9	87	10	-88.5	224	65	-71.0
Tampa, FL	1,312	1,058	-19.4	1,093	3,753	243.4	2,405	4,811	100.0
Tucson, AZ	1,134	918	-19.0	959	962	0.3	2,093	1,880	-10.2
Tulsa, OK	652	452	-30.7	165	369	123.6	817	821	0.5
Tuscaloosa, AL	401	299	-25.4	725	329	-54.6	1,126	628	-44.2
Virginia Beach, VA	335	231	-31.0	128	966	654.7	463	1,197	158.5
Washington, DC	376	409	8.8	4,364	7,296	67.2	4,740	7,705	62.6
Wichita, KS	760	787	3.6	368	276	-25.0	1,128	1,063	-5.8
Wilmington, NC	n/a	n/a	n/a	n/a	n/a	n/a	n/a	n/a	n/a
Winston-Salem, NC	1,087	1,291	18.8	0	0	0.0	1,087	1,291	18.8
Worcester, MA	66	94	42.4	112	718	541.1	178	812	356.2
U.S.	1,115,400	975,600	-12.5	621,600	689,500	10.9	1,737,000	1,665,100	-4.1

Note: Figures represent new, privately-owned housing units authorized (unadjusted data); All permit data are based on estimates with imputation
Source: U.S. Census Bureau, Manufacturing, Mining, and Construction Statistics, Building Permits, 2021, 2022

Building Permits: Metro Area

Metro Area	Single-Family			Multi-Family			Total		
	2021	2022	Pct. Chg.	2021	2022	Pct. Chg.	2021	2022	Pct. Chg.
Albuquerque, NM	2,535	2,002	-21.0	1,486	1,055	-29.0	4,021	3,057	-24.0
Allentown, PA	1,716	1,586	-7.6	890	723	-18.8	2,606	2,309	-11.4
Anchorage, AK	877	166	-81.1	306	47	-84.6	1,183	213	-82.0
Ann Arbor, MI	795	580	-27.0	121	49	-59.5	916	629	-31.3
Athens, GA	856	771	-9.9	992	1,574	58.7	1,848	2,345	26.9
Atlanta, GA	31,560	26,623	-15.6	7,906	21,484	171.7	39,466	48,107	21.9
Austin, TX	24,486	19,717	-19.5	26,421	22,647	-14.3	50,907	42,364	-16.8
Baltimore, MD	4,783	2,832	-40.8	3,051	3,756	23.1	7,834	6,588	-15.9
Boise City, ID	8,342	5,925	-29.0	3,854	4,550	18.1	12,196	10,475	-14.1
Boston, MA	4,820	3,985	-17.3	11,782	10,469	-11.1	16,602	14,454	-12.9
Boulder, CO	343	661	92.7	894	981	9.7	1,237	1,642	32.7
Brownsville, TX	1,573	1,940	23.3	479	569	18.8	2,052	2,509	22.3
Cape Coral, FL	11,020	9,145	-17.0	2,374	4,476	88.5	13,394	13,621	1.7
Cedar Rapids, IA	546	453	-17.0	352	494	40.3	898	947	5.5
Charleston, SC	5,913	6,329	7.0	2,369	2,994	26.4	8,282	9,323	12.6
Charlotte, NC	20,830	19,029	-8.6	9,296	8,183	-12.0	30,126	27,212	-9.7
Chicago, IL	10,071	8,563	-15.0	8,440	9,073	7.5	18,511	17,636	-4.7
Cincinnati, OH	5,358	4,126	-23.0	3,071	2,084	-32.1	8,429	6,210	-26.3
Clarksville, TN	2,217	1,501	-32.3	1,895	2,592	36.8	4,112	4,093	-0.5
Cleveland, OH	2,949	2,915	-1.2	391	820	109.7	3,340	3,735	11.8
College Station, TX	1,765	1,545	-12.5	535	230	-57.0	2,300	1,775	-22.8
Colorado Springs, CO	5,074	3,646	-28.1	4,261	5,198	22.0	9,335	8,844	-5.3
Columbia, MO	838	628	-25.1	191	151	-20.9	1,029	779	-24.3
Columbia, SC	5,853	4,101	-29.9	1,028	1,703	65.7	6,881	5,804	-15.7
Columbus, OH	6,844	5,623	-17.8	5,218	6,472	24.0	12,062	12,095	0.3
Dallas, TX	51,996	43,645	-16.1	26,709	34,249	28.2	78,705	77,894	-1.0
Davenport, IA	436	416	-4.6	193	181	-6.2	629	597	-5.1
Denver, CO	13,113	10,108	-22.9	16,893	13,368	-20.9	30,006	23,476	-21.8
Des Moines, IA	4,888	3,646	-25.4	2,081	2,476	19.0	6,969	6,122	-12.2
Durham, NC	3,735	3,170	-15.1	2,165	3,222	48.8	5,900	6,392	8.3
Edison, NJ	12,947	12,089	-6.6	43,714	46,323	6.0	56,661	58,412	3.1
El Paso, TX	2,655	2,147	-19.1	334	319	-4.5	2,989	2,466	-17.5
Fargo, ND	1,229	1,123	-8.6	1,060	1,191	12.4	2,289	2,314	1.1
Fort Collins, CO	2,149	1,385	-35.6	1,072	1,187	10.7	3,221	2,572	-20.1
Fort Wayne, IN	1,799	1,453	-19.2	179	882	392.7	1,978	2,335	18.0
Fort Worth, TX	51,996	43,645	-16.1	26,709	34,249	28.2	78,705	77,894	-1.0
Grand Rapids, MI	2,811	2,488	-11.5	894	1,710	91.3	3,705	4,198	13.3
Greeley, CO	3,814	3,203	-16.0	1,454	2,940	102.2	5,268	6,143	16.6
Green Bay, WI	830	627	-24.5	578	622	7.6	1,408	1,249	-11.3
Greensboro, NC	2,593	2,161	-16.7	1,371	832	-39.3	3,964	2,993	-24.5
Honolulu, HI	938	652	-30.5	500	1,901	280.2	1,438	2,553	77.5
Houston, TX	52,719	47,701	-9.5	16,544	28,027	69.4	69,263	75,728	9.3
Huntsville, AL	4,230	3,617	-14.5	1,942	418	-78.5	6,172	4,035	-34.6
Indianapolis, IN	10,159	8,578	-15.6	3,292	4,915	49.3	13,451	13,493	0.3
Jacksonville, FL	16,536	14,410	-12.9	6,202	8,759	41.2	22,738	23,169	1.9
Kansas City, MO	7,051	5,204	-26.2	4,203	6,015	43.1	11,254	11,219	-0.3
Lafayette, LA	3,040	2,051	-32.5	4	20	400.0	3,044	2,071	-32.0
Las Cruces, NM	1,239	1,079	-12.9	99	26	-73.7	1,338	1,105	-17.4
Las Vegas, NV	12,156	9,199	-24.3	4,151	3,867	-6.8	16,307	13,066	-19.9
Lexington, KY	1,760	1,460	-17.0	1,183	1,249	5.6	2,943	2,709	-8.0
Lincoln, NE	1,378	1,132	-17.9	1,229	2,217	80.4	2,607	3,349	28.5
Little Rock, AR	2,505	1,863	-25.6	1,130	1,475	30.5	3,635	3,338	-8.2
Los Angeles, CA	11,090	11,184	0.8	20,061	21,326	6.3	31,151	32,510	4.4
Louisville, KY	4,136	3,345	-19.1	1,372	2,111	53.9	5,508	5,456	-0.9

Table continued on following page.

Metro Area	Single-Family			Multi-Family			Total		
	2021	2022	Pct. Chg.	2021	2022	Pct. Chg.	2021	2022	Pct. Chg.
Madison, WI	1,737	1,530	-11.9	5,457	4,049	-25.8	7,194	5,579	-22.4
Manchester, NH	683	623	-8.8	659	224	-66.0	1,342	847	-36.9
Miami, FL	8,316	6,970	-16.2	16,997	13,051	-23.2	25,313	20,021	-20.9
Midland, TX	872	594	-31.9	0	0	0.0	872	594	-31.9
Milwaukee, WI	1,779	1,557	-12.5	1,150	1,609	39.9	2,929	3,166	8.1
Minneapolis, MN	11,734	9,114	-22.3	14,343	14,611	1.9	26,077	23,725	-9.0
Nashville, TN	17,422	15,388	-11.7	14,769	12,804	-13.3	32,191	28,192	-12.4
New Haven, CT	497	493	-0.8	486	770	58.4	983	1,263	28.5
New Orleans, LA	4,018	3,101	-22.8	1,264	1,065	-15.7	5,282	4,166	-21.1
New York, NY	12,947	12,089	-6.6	43,714	46,323	6.0	56,661	58,412	3.1
Oklahoma City, OK	7,637	5,971	-21.8	443	940	112.2	8,080	6,911	-14.5
Omaha, NE	3,677	2,651	-27.9	2,705	3,469	28.2	6,382	6,120	-4.1
Orlando, FL	17,795	16,213	-8.9	12,823	12,470	-2.8	30,618	28,683	-6.3
Philadelphia, PA	8,868	8,532	-3.8	27,439	5,881	-78.6	36,307	14,413	-60.3
Phoenix, AZ	34,347	26,857	-21.8	16,234	20,410	25.7	50,581	47,267	-6.6
Pittsburgh, PA	3,891	3,184	-18.2	1,332	2,481	86.3	5,223	5,665	8.5
Portland, OR	8,008	6,029	-24.7	7,015	6,949	-0.9	15,023	12,978	-13.6
Providence, RI	1,788	1,559	-12.8	470	563	19.8	2,258	2,122	-6.0
Provo, UT	7,562	5,153	-31.9	3,613	3,134	-13.3	11,175	8,287	-25.8
Raleigh, NC	14,227	12,488	-12.2	7,422	9,080	22.3	21,649	21,568	-0.4
Reno, NV	2,717	2,184	-19.6	2,620	3,628	38.5	5,337	5,812	8.9
Richmond, VA	5,946	4,503	-24.3	3,601	5,911	64.1	9,547	10,414	9.1
Rochester, MN	721	641	-11.1	414	1,080	160.9	1,135	1,721	51.6
Sacramento, CA	9,390	8,170	-13.0	3,044	2,630	-13.6	12,434	10,800	-13.1
St. Louis, MO	5,716	4,743	-17.0	2,610	4,388	68.1	8,326	9,131	9.7
Salem, OR	1,368	874	-36.1	786	1,943	147.2	2,154	2,817	30.8
Salt Lake City, UT	5,338	3,992	-25.2	6,304	6,110	-3.1	11,642	10,102	-13.2
San Antonio, TX	13,945	10,226	-26.7	8,319	14,113	69.6	22,264	24,339	9.3
San Diego, CA	3,227	3,517	9.0	6,821	5,829	-14.5	10,048	9,346	-7.0
San Francisco, CA	4,301	3,370	-21.6	9,305	7,834	-15.8	13,606	11,204	-17.7
San Jose, CA	2,400	3,899	62.5	2,129	4,308	102.3	4,529	8,207	81.2
Santa Rosa, CA	1,227	954	-22.2	1,391	1,310	-5.8	2,618	2,264	-13.5
Savannah, GA	2,752	2,228	-19.0	475	966	103.4	3,227	3,194	-1.0
Seattle, WA	8,828	7,029	-20.4	21,915	19,632	-10.4	30,743	26,661	-13.3
Sioux Falls, SD	1,893	1,626	-14.1	2,093	3,928	87.7	3,986	5,554	39.3
Springfield, IL	239	146	-38.9	93	64	-31.2	332	210	-36.7
Tampa, FL	19,305	15,678	-18.8	5,526	14,291	158.6	24,831	29,969	20.7
Tucson, AZ	5,116	3,735	-27.0	1,168	1,979	69.4	6,284	5,714	-9.1
Tulsa, OK	4,354	3,843	-11.7	566	1,280	126.1	4,920	5,123	4.1
Tuscaloosa, AL	771	714	-7.4	725	329	-54.6	1,496	1,043	-30.3
Virginia Beach, VA	4,712	3,680	-21.9	2,665	2,633	-1.2	7,377	6,313	-14.4
Washington, DC	13,729	11,657	-15.1	13,685	20,736	51.5	27,414	32,393	18.2
Wichita, KS	1,618	1,586	-2.0	766	1,264	65.0	2,384	2,850	19.5
Wilmington, NC	2,671	2,489	-6.8	1,747	1,932	10.6	4,418	4,421	0.1
Winston-Salem, NC	3,887	3,983	2.5	319	67	-79.0	4,206	4,050	-3.7
Worcester, MA	1,177	1,172	-0.4	876	1,080	23.3	2,053	2,252	9.7
U.S.	1,115,400	975,600	-12.5	621,600	689,500	10.9	1,737,000	1,665,100	-4.1

Note: Figures cover the Metropolitan Statistical Area; Figures represent new, privately-owned housing units authorized (unadjusted data); All permit data are based on estimates with imputation
Source: U.S. Census Bureau, Manufacturing, Mining, and Construction Statistics, Building Permits, 2021, 2022

Housing Vacancy Rates

MSA[1]	Gross Vacancy Rate[2] (%)			Year-Round Vacancy Rate[3] (%)			Rental Vacancy Rate[4] (%)			Homeowner Vacancy Rate[5] (%)		
	2020	2021	2022	2020	2021	2022	2020	2021	2022	2020	2021	2022
Albuquerque, NM	5.1	5.3	5.3	4.9	5.1	5.1	5.4	6.4	5.5	1.4	0.5	1.0
Allentown, PA	4.9	5.2	8.7	4.8	4.3	8.0	3.9	4.0	6.1	0.7	0.1	1.2
Anchorage, AK	n/a	n/a	n/a	n/a	n/a	n/a	n/a	n/a	n/a	n/a	n/a	n/a
Ann Arbor, MI	n/a	n/a	n/a	n/a	n/a	n/a	n/a	n/a	n/a	n/a	n/a	n/a
Athens, GA	n/a	n/a	n/a	n/a	n/a	n/a	n/a	n/a	n/a	n/a	n/a	n/a
Atlanta, GA	5.8	6.1	5.9	5.4	5.7	5.7	6.4	5.2	6.7	0.8	1.0	0.8
Austin, TX	7.0	6.5	5.5	6.8	6.2	4.9	6.6	8.5	5.6	2.0	1.3	0.6
Baltimore, MD	7.2	6.8	5.9	7.0	6.6	5.7	7.0	6.1	5.3	1.0	1.0	0.5
Boise City, ID	n/a	n/a	n/a	n/a	n/a	n/a	n/a	n/a	n/a	n/a	n/a	n/a
Boston, MA	6.8	7.4	6.2	5.6	6.2	5.4	4.7	4.5	2.5	0.4	0.5	0.7
Boulder, CO	n/a	n/a	n/a	n/a	n/a	n/a	n/a	n/a	n/a	n/a	n/a	n/a
Brownsville, TX	n/a	n/a	n/a	n/a	n/a	n/a	n/a	n/a	n/a	n/a	n/a	n/a
Cape Coral, FL	35.1	36.4	38.2	15.8	13.0	16.9	15.5	10.7	11.6	1.9	2.4	3.9
Cedar Rapids, IA	n/a	n/a	n/a	n/a	n/a	n/a	n/a	n/a	n/a	n/a	n/a	n/a
Charleston, SC	18.1	12.9	10.6	16.5	10.5	7.5	27.7	15.4	8.8	2.3	1.3	0.4
Charlotte, NC	6.6	7.7	7.4	6.3	7.4	7.0	5.6	6.8	5.9	1.0	1.3	0.7
Chicago, IL	7.4	8.7	7.3	7.2	8.6	7.1	7.4	8.0	6.1	1.2	1.3	1.1
Cincinnati, OH	6.6	7.9	6.8	6.2	7.3	6.3	7.9	7.2	6.3	0.7	0.5	0.3
Clarksville, TN	n/a	n/a	n/a	n/a	n/a	n/a	n/a	n/a	n/a	n/a	n/a	n/a
Cleveland, OH	9.3	7.7	7.0	8.8	7.5	6.8	5.5	3.6	3.2	0.7	0.4	1.0
College Station, TX	n/a	n/a	n/a	n/a	n/a	n/a	n/a	n/a	n/a	n/a	n/a	n/a
Colorado Springs, CO	n/a	n/a	n/a	n/a	n/a	n/a	n/a	n/a	n/a	n/a	n/a	n/a
Columbia, MO	n/a	n/a	n/a	n/a	n/a	n/a	n/a	n/a	n/a	n/a	n/a	n/a
Columbia, SC	7.2	7.6	12.0	7.1	7.6	12.0	4.5	4.7	6.1	0.7	1.1	0.6
Columbus, OH	4.7	6.8	5.6	4.5	6.6	5.4	5.9	6.5	3.8	0.3	0.8	0.8
Dallas, TX	6.4	6.6	6.6	6.4	6.5	6.3	7.2	7.0	6.8	0.7	0.7	0.7
Davenport, IA	n/a	n/a	n/a	n/a	n/a	n/a	n/a	n/a	n/a	n/a	n/a	n/a
Denver, CO	5.8	6.5	5.8	5.1	5.3	5.2	4.8	4.6	5.1	0.5	1.0	0.3
Des Moines, IA	n/a	n/a	n/a	n/a	n/a	n/a	n/a	n/a	n/a	n/a	n/a	n/a
Durham, NC	n/a	n/a	n/a	n/a	n/a	n/a	n/a	n/a	n/a	n/a	n/a	n/a
Edison, NJ	9.1	9.8	8.2	7.8	8.7	7.0	4.5	5.2	3.5	1.3	1.2	1.0
El Paso, TX	n/a	n/a	n/a	n/a	n/a	n/a	n/a	n/a	n/a	n/a	n/a	n/a
Fargo, ND	n/a	n/a	n/a	n/a	n/a	n/a	n/a	n/a	n/a	n/a	n/a	n/a
Fort Collins, CO	n/a	n/a	n/a	n/a	n/a	n/a	n/a	n/a	n/a	n/a	n/a	n/a
Fort Wayne, IN	n/a	n/a	n/a	n/a	n/a	n/a	n/a	n/a	n/a	n/a	n/a	n/a
Fort Worth, TX	6.4	6.6	6.6	6.4	6.5	6.3	7.2	7.0	6.8	0.7	0.7	0.7
Grand Rapids, MI	7.1	7.0	4.9	4.7	4.2	3.0	4.6	3.4	2.4	1.1	0.7	0.1
Greeley, CO	n/a	n/a	n/a	n/a	n/a	n/a	n/a	n/a	n/a	n/a	n/a	n/a
Green Bay, WI	n/a	n/a	n/a	n/a	n/a	n/a	n/a	n/a	n/a	n/a	n/a	n/a
Greensboro, NC	8.3	5.9	8.7	8.2	5.9	8.7	7.2	2.7	10.2	0.7	0.5	0.7
Honolulu, HI	10.0	10.6	10.6	9.6	10.1	10.0	5.5	5.1	5.7	1.0	0.6	0.6
Houston, TX	6.8	7.2	6.9	6.3	6.6	6.3	9.7	8.8	8.9	1.1	0.8	0.6
Huntsville, AL	n/a	n/a	n/a	n/a	n/a	n/a	n/a	n/a	n/a	n/a	n/a	n/a
Indianapolis, IN	7.3	6.2	7.7	7.0	6.1	7.2	10.4	8.2	11.0	0.8	0.7	1.0
Jacksonville, FL	9.5	8.3	8.9	9.3	7.6	7.7	7.5	5.6	6.2	1.5	0.4	1.7
Kansas City, MO	9.1	8.3	7.1	9.1	8.2	7.1	9.4	8.9	7.8	0.7	1.2	0.6
Lafayette, LA	n/a	n/a	n/a	n/a	n/a	n/a	n/a	n/a	n/a	n/a	n/a	n/a
Las Cruces, NM	n/a	n/a	n/a	n/a	n/a	n/a	n/a	n/a	n/a	n/a	n/a	n/a
Las Vegas, NV	7.8	7.7	9.2	7.1	7.1	8.3	5.0	3.7	5.7	1.1	0.9	0.9
Lexington, KY	n/a	n/a	n/a	n/a	n/a	n/a	n/a	n/a	n/a	n/a	n/a	n/a
Lincoln, NE	n/a	n/a	n/a	n/a	n/a	n/a	n/a	n/a	n/a	n/a	n/a	n/a
Little Rock, AR	9.4	11.4	9.4	9.1	11.2	9.2	9.1	10.0	11.4	1.3	1.2	0.7
Los Angeles, CA	5.5	6.4	5.9	4.8	5.9	5.5	3.6	4.6	4.1	0.6	0.7	0.5
Louisville, KY	6.9	8.3	5.7	6.9	8.3	5.7	6.4	8.5	5.3	1.4	0.7	0.5

Table continued on following page.

MSA[1]	Gross Vacancy Rate[2] (%)			Year-Round Vacancy Rate[3] (%)			Rental Vacancy Rate[4] (%)			Homeowner Vacancy Rate[5] (%)		
	2020	2021	2022	2020	2021	2022	2020	2021	2022	2020	2021	2022
Madison, WI	n/a	n/a	n/a	n/a	n/a	n/a	n/a	n/a	n/a	n/a	n/a	n/a
Manchester, NH	n/a	n/a	n/a	n/a	n/a	n/a	n/a	n/a	n/a	n/a	n/a	n/a
Miami, FL	12.6	12.2	12.6	6.8	6.8	7.5	5.4	5.5	6.3	1.4	1.0	1.1
Midland, TX	n/a	n/a	n/a	n/a	n/a	n/a	n/a	n/a	n/a	n/a	n/a	n/a
Milwaukee, WI	6.6	5.2	5.2	6.3	5.1	5.1	4.6	2.2	5.9	0.6	0.5	0.1
Minneapolis, MN	4.7	5.3	4.8	3.7	4.6	4.5	4.0	4.9	6.7	0.5	0.6	0.8
Nashville, TN	6.5	7.1	7.6	6.1	6.8	7.1	7.3	7.9	6.4	0.7	1.0	0.9
New Haven, CT	9.4	7.9	6.8	8.4	7.2	6.4	7.8	5.4	2.6	0.2	0.5	1.1
New Orleans, LA	10.7	12.6	13.4	9.8	11.1	11.5	6.1	7.2	6.6	1.3	1.0	1.6
New York, NY	9.1	9.8	8.2	7.8	8.7	7.0	4.5	5.2	3.5	1.3	1.2	1.0
Oklahoma City, OK	7.5	6.1	8.6	7.3	6.0	8.5	6.4	5.7	10.6	0.9	0.8	0.9
Omaha, NE	5.6	6.0	5.4	5.3	5.7	5.0	6.5	5.1	4.2	0.5	0.7	0.8
Orlando, FL	12.9	9.5	9.6	9.8	7.5	7.4	8.6	7.5	6.5	1.2	0.5	1.4
Philadelphia, PA	6.0	6.1	5.5	5.8	5.9	5.4	5.4	4.8	4.2	0.7	0.5	1.0
Phoenix, AZ	8.9	9.0	10.9	5.3	5.6	6.7	4.9	4.9	6.4	0.7	0.6	0.9
Pittsburgh, PA	11.5	11.4	11.5	11.3	10.8	11.0	9.3	9.4	8.3	1.0	0.4	0.7
Portland, OR	5.5	6.0	5.4	4.9	5.6	5.1	4.3	5.2	4.0	0.8	0.9	1.2
Providence, RI	8.7	7.9	9.5	6.6	5.8	7.6	3.5	2.7	4.5	0.8	0.7	0.4
Provo, UT	n/a	n/a	n/a	n/a	n/a	n/a	n/a	n/a	n/a	n/a	n/a	n/a
Raleigh, NC	4.6	6.3	7.4	4.5	6.3	7.3	2.3	2.9	7.1	0.4	1.1	0.5
Reno, NV	n/a	n/a	n/a	n/a	n/a	n/a	n/a	n/a	n/a	n/a	n/a	n/a
Richmond, VA	6.0	5.8	6.1	6.0	5.8	6.1	2.7	1.8	3.0	0.9	1.0	0.7
Rochester, MN	n/a	n/a	n/a	n/a	n/a	n/a	n/a	n/a	n/a	n/a	n/a	n/a
Sacramento, CA	6.1	6.7	6.3	5.8	6.5	6.1	4.2	3.6	2.3	1.0	0.7	0.6
St. Louis, MO	6.4	7.0	7.2	6.3	7.0	7.1	5.3	6.5	6.8	0.7	0.5	1.4
Salem, OR	n/a	n/a	n/a	n/a	n/a	n/a	n/a	n/a	n/a	n/a	n/a	n/a
Salt Lake City, UT	5.7	4.1	5.1	5.6	3.9	4.5	6.2	4.1	4.6	0.3	0.8	0.6
San Antonio, TX	7.4	7.6	7.5	6.7	6.9	7.1	7.2	8.4	8.1	1.0	1.1	0.9
San Diego, CA	6.0	6.9	6.9	5.6	6.7	6.6	3.9	3.1	3.6	0.8	0.7	0.6
San Francisco, CA	6.4	7.6	7.9	6.2	7.3	7.7	5.3	6.5	5.4	0.5	1.1	1.3
San Jose, CA	4.7	5.9	5.8	4.7	5.6	5.8	4.4	6.6	4.7	n/a	0.4	0.4
Santa Rosa, CA	n/a	n/a	n/a	n/a	n/a	n/a	n/a	n/a	n/a	n/a	n/a	n/a
Savannah, GA	n/a	n/a	n/a	n/a	n/a	n/a	n/a	n/a	n/a	n/a	n/a	n/a
Seattle, WA	4.7	6.2	5.7	4.5	5.5	5.2	3.6	5.3	4.9	0.6	0.7	0.7
Sioux Falls, SD	n/a	n/a	n/a	n/a	n/a	n/a	n/a	n/a	n/a	n/a	n/a	n/a
Springfield, IL	n/a	n/a	n/a	n/a	n/a	n/a	n/a	n/a	n/a	n/a	n/a	n/a
Tampa, FL	13.0	14.2	13.3	10.1	10.5	9.9	8.9	7.3	8.1	1.5	1.0	1.2
Tucson, AZ	12.1	10.0	13.5	7.7	6.9	10.3	8.6	5.0	8.0	0.5	0.6	1.4
Tulsa, OK	9.4	11.0	8.9	8.8	10.0	8.5	8.6	5.3	5.6	0.8	1.5	0.7
Tuscaloosa, AL	n/a	n/a	n/a	n/a	n/a	n/a	n/a	n/a	n/a	n/a	n/a	n/a
Virginia Beach, VA	7.9	7.7	8.1	7.0	6.9	7.3	5.5	5.5	6.3	0.6	0.6	1.0
Washington, DC	6.5	5.5	5.2	6.2	5.3	5.0	5.5	5.9	5.3	0.7	0.5	0.6
Wichita, KS	n/a	n/a	n/a	n/a	n/a	n/a	n/a	n/a	n/a	n/a	n/a	n/a
Wilmington, NC	n/a	n/a	n/a	n/a	n/a	n/a	n/a	n/a	n/a	n/a	n/a	n/a
Winston-Salem, NC	n/a	n/a	n/a	n/a	n/a	n/a	n/a	n/a	n/a	n/a	n/a	n/a
Worcester, MA	4.8	5.5	4.5	4.6	4.9	4.0	1.3	2.2	1.6	0.4	0.7	0.4
U.S.	10.6	10.8	10.5	8.2	8.4	8.2	6.3	6.1	5.8	1.0	0.9	0.8

Note: (1) Metropolitan Statistical Area; (2) The percentage of the total housing inventory that is vacant; (3) The percentage of the housing inventory (excluding seasonal units) that is year-round vacant; (4) The percentage of rental inventory that is vacant for rent; (5) The percentage of homeowner inventory that is vacant for sale; n/a not available
Source: U.S. Census Bureau, Housing Vacancies and Homeownership Annual Statistics: 2020, 2021, 2022

Bankruptcy Filings

City	Area Covered	Business Filings			Nonbusiness Filings		
		2021	2022	% Chg.	2021	2022	% Chg.
Albuquerque, NM	Bernalillo County	21	15	-28.6	560	383	-31.6
Allentown, PA	Lehigh County	5	7	40.0	346	283	-18.2
Anchorage, AK	Anchorage Borough	12	4	-66.7	116	77	-33.6
Ann Arbor, MI	Washtenaw County	8	24	200.0	352	350	-0.6
Athens, GA	Clarke County	10	4	-60.0	162	212	30.9
Atlanta, GA	Fulton County	87	124	42.5	2,072	2,323	12.1
Austin, TX	Travis County	113	76	-32.7	443	372	-16.0
Baltimore, MD	Baltimore City	18	17	-5.6	1,323	1,167	-11.8
Boise City, ID	Ada County	13	16	23.1	393	326	-17.0
Boston, MA	Suffolk County	23	42	82.6	224	221	-1.3
Boulder, CO	Boulder County	13	27	107.7	216	160	-25.9
Brownsville, TX	Cameron County	0	4	n/a	171	195	14.0
Cape Coral, FL	Lee County	39	31	-20.5	928	711	-23.4
Cedar Rapids, IA	Linn County	6	10	66.7	193	166	-14.0
Charleston, SC	Charleston County	8	5	-37.5	176	228	29.5
Charlotte, NC	Mecklenburg County	56	21	-62.5	460	459	-0.2
Chicago, IL	Cook County	270	237	-12.2	10,430	10,849	4.0
Cincinnati, OH	Hamilton County	28	25	-10.7	1,500	1,164	-22.4
Clarksville, TN	Montgomery County	11	6	-45.5	333	352	5.7
Cleveland, OH	Cuyahoga County	48	53	10.4	3,240	2,994	-7.6
College Station, TX	Brazos County	8	4	-50.0	66	47	-28.8
Colorado Springs, CO	El Paso County	22	19	-13.6	728	609	-16.3
Columbia, MO	Boone County	1	5	400.0	193	171	-11.4
Columbia, SC	Richland County	8	13	62.5	348	424	21.8
Columbus, OH	Franklin County	128	38	-70.3	2,223	2,029	-8.7
Dallas, TX	Dallas County	186	237	27.4	1,797	1,984	10.4
Davenport, IA	Scott County	5	9	80.0	163	140	-14.1
Denver, CO	Denver County	72	37	-48.6	764	590	-22.8
Des Moines, IA	Polk County	22	17	-22.7	550	474	-13.8
Durham, NC	Durham County	10	5	-50.0	175	143	-18.3
Edison, NJ	Middlesex County	45	30	-33.3	843	746	-11.5
El Paso, TX	El Paso County	46	41	-10.9	961	1,092	13.6
Fargo, ND	Cass County	4	2	-50.0	131	100	-23.7
Fort Collins, CO	Larimer County	14	14	0.0	306	283	-7.5
Fort Wayne, IN	Allen County	6	13	116.7	872	767	-12.0
Fort Worth, TX	Tarrant County	151	200	32.5	2,277	2,447	7.5
Grand Rapids, MI	Kent County	8	10	25.0	469	439	-6.4
Greeley, CO	Weld County	9	16	77.8	447	400	-10.5
Green Bay, WI	Brown County	2	7	250.0	388	290	-25.3
Greensboro, NC	Guilford County	23	8	-65.2	369	336	-8.9
Honolulu, HI	Honolulu County	28	35	25.0	830	671	-19.2
Houston, TX	Harris County	269	213	-20.8	2,310	2,541	10.0
Huntsville, AL	Madison County	18	12	-33.3	894	806	-9.8
Indianapolis, IN	Marion County	45	37	-17.8	2,705	2,399	-11.3
Jacksonville, FL	Duval County	58	38	-34.5	1,336	1,226	-8.2
Kansas City, MO	Jackson County	22	16	-27.3	1,027	1,037	1.0
Lafayette, LA	Lafayette Parish	17	29	70.6	263	296	12.5
Las Cruces, NM	Dona Ana County	8	4	-50.0	187	178	-4.8
Las Vegas, NV	Clark County	181	163	-9.9	5,825	4,525	-22.3
Lexington, KY	Fayette County	8	7	-12.5	450	410	-8.9
Lincoln, NE	Lancaster County	6	14	133.3	430	304	-29.3
Little Rock, AR	Pulaski County	23	19	-17.4	1,157	1,352	16.9
Los Angeles, CA	Los Angeles County	672	626	-6.8	11,316	8,314	-26.5
Louisville, KY	Jefferson County	19	20	5.3	1,918	1,883	-1.8
Madison, WI	Dane County	26	10	-61.5	436	383	-12.2

Table continued on following page.

City	Area Covered	Business Filings			Nonbusiness Filings		
		2021	2022	% Chg.	2021	2022	% Chg.
Manchester, NH	Hillsborough County	19	11	-42.1	253	204	-19.4
Miami, FL	Miami-Dade County	201	224	11.4	6,432	5,081	-21.0
Midland, TX	Midland County	18	7	-61.1	64	73	14.1
Milwaukee, WI	Milwaukee County	20	20	0.0	3,237	2,957	-8.6
Minneapolis, MN	Hennepin County	52	55	5.8	1,240	1,200	-3.2
Nashville, TN	Davidson County	37	32	-13.5	959	989	3.1
New Haven, CT	New Haven County	14	12	-14.3	864	719	-16.8
New Orleans, LA	Orleans Parish	31	11	-64.5	263	287	9.1
New York, NY	Bronx County	23	27	17.4	1,219	862	-29.3
New York, NY	Kings County	108	212	96.3	1,238	1,062	-14.2
New York, NY	New York County	398	240	-39.7	721	595	-17.5
New York, NY	Queens County	82	126	53.7	1,447	1,478	2.1
New York, NY	Richmond County	24	25	4.2	310	352	13.5
Oklahoma City, OK	Oklahoma County	52	50	-3.8	1,424	1,199	-15.8
Omaha, NE	Douglas County	20	21	5.0	807	628	-22.2
Orlando, FL	Orange County	100	127	27.0	1,909	1,588	-16.8
Philadelphia, PA	Philadelphia County	31	28	-9.7	741	952	28.5
Phoenix, AZ	Maricopa County	223	172	-22.9	6,402	5,811	-9.2
Pittsburgh, PA	Allegheny County	79	72	-8.9	1,266	1,135	-10.3
Portland, OR	Multnomah County	33	17	-48.5	802	749	-6.6
Providence, RI	Providence County	16	21	31.3	638	507	-20.5
Provo, UT	Utah County	22	19	-13.6	814	790	-2.9
Raleigh, NC	Wake County	53	50	-5.7	614	536	-12.7
Reno, NV	Washoe County	25	26	4.0	592	467	-21.1
Richmond, VA	Richmond city	21	6	-71.4	590	511	-13.4
Rochester, MN	Olmsted County	0	1	n/a	90	119	32.2
Sacramento, CA	Sacramento County	80	61	-23.8	1,731	1,275	-26.3
St. Louis, MO	Saint Louis City	12	15	25.0	1,395	1,247	-10.6
Salem, OR	Marion County	7	4	-42.9	489	439	-10.2
Salt Lake City, UT	Salt Lake County	27	23	-14.8	2,389	2,147	-10.1
San Antonio, TX	Bexar County	143	84	-41.3	1,102	1,028	-6.7
San Diego, CA	San Diego County	194	158	-18.6	4,533	3,136	-30.8
San Francisco, CA	San Francisco County	65	55	-15.4	334	342	2.4
San Jose, CA	Santa Clara County	80	77	-3.8	868	655	-24.5
Santa Rosa, CA	Sonoma County	23	29	26.1	329	278	-15.5
Savannah, GA	Chatham County	9	7	-22.2	546	591	8.2
Seattle, WA	King County	56	55	-1.8	1,094	979	-10.5
Sioux Falls, SD	Minnehaha County	7	6	-14.3	221	201	-9.0
Springfield, IL	Sangamon County	6	5	-16.7	221	186	-15.8
Tampa, FL	Hillsborough County	87	94	8.0	2,061	1,686	-18.2
Tucson, AZ	Pima County	21	22	4.8	1,379	1,310	-5.0
Tulsa, OK	Tulsa County	30	51	70.0	874	758	-13.3
Tuscaloosa, AL	Tuscaloosa County	4	9	125.0	679	821	20.9
Virginia Beach, VA	Virginia Beach City	11	15	36.4	788	711	-9.8
Washington, DC	District of Columbia	36	36	0.0	264	200	-24.2
Wichita, KS	Sedgwick County	20	14	-30.0	760	658	-13.4
Wilmington, NC	New Hanover County	12	6	-50.0	144	138	-4.2
Winston-Salem, NC	Forsyth County	10	6	-40.0	240	240	0.0
Worcester, MA	Worcester County	24	26	8.3	569	550	-3.3
U.S.	U.S.	14,347	13,481	-6.0	399,269	374,240	-6.3

Note: Business filings include Chapter 7, Chapter 9, Chapter 11, Chapter 12, Chapter 13, Chapter 15, and Section 304; Nonbusiness filings include Chapter 7, Chapter 11, and Chapter 13
Source: Administrative Office of the U.S. Courts, Business and Nonbusiness Bankruptcy, County Cases Commenced by Chapter of the Bankruptcy Code, During the 12-Month Period Ending December 31, 2021 and Business and Nonbusiness Bankruptcy, County Cases Commenced by Chapter of the Bankruptcy Code, During the 12-Month Period Ending December 31, 2022

Income: City

City	Per Capita ($)	Median Household ($)	Average Household ($)
Albuquerque, NM	33,494	56,366	76,833
Allentown, PA	22,976	47,703	61,780
Anchorage, AK	43,125	88,871	113,873
Ann Arbor, MI	47,883	73,276	107,368
Athens, GA	27,194	43,466	65,960
Atlanta, GA	54,466	69,164	118,074
Austin, TX	48,550	78,965	111,233
Baltimore, MD	34,378	54,124	79,399
Boise City, ID	40,056	68,373	93,693
Boston, MA	50,344	81,744	120,939
Boulder, CO	52,057	74,902	123,606
Brownsville, TX	18,207	43,174	58,147
Cape Coral, FL	34,586	65,282	84,169
Cedar Rapids, IA	35,566	63,170	82,815
Charleston, SC	50,240	76,556	111,903
Charlotte, NC	43,080	68,367	104,228
Chicago, IL	41,821	65,781	100,347
Cincinnati, OH	34,060	45,235	73,412
Clarksville, TN	27,437	58,838	71,824
Cleveland, OH	23,415	33,678	49,942
College Station, TX	28,705	50,089	76,307
Colorado Springs, CO	37,979	71,957	93,740
Columbia, MO	32,784	57,463	80,898
Columbia, SC	32,954	48,791	79,637
Columbus, OH	32,481	58,575	75,482
Dallas, TX	37,719	58,231	92,785
Davenport, IA	32,431	56,315	76,281
Denver, CO	50,642	78,177	111,981
Des Moines, IA	31,276	58,444	74,131
Durham, NC	39,496	66,623	91,960
Edison, NJ	47,410	110,896	136,606
El Paso, TX	25,165	51,325	69,692
Fargo, ND	37,522	60,243	82,974
Fort Collins, CO	38,949	72,932	96,301
Fort Wayne, IN	29,268	53,978	70,654
Fort Worth, TX	32,569	67,927	90,141
Grand Rapids, MI	29,060	55,385	72,017
Greeley, CO	28,480	60,601	78,033
Green Bay, WI	29,822	55,221	70,879
Greensboro, NC	31,812	51,667	76,282
Honolulu, HI	41,571	76,495	105,724
Houston, TX	35,578	56,019	90,511
Huntsville, AL	38,838	60,959	87,475
Indianapolis, IN	31,538	54,321	75,792
Jacksonville, FL	32,654	58,263	79,817
Kansas City, MO	35,352	60,042	81,577
Lafayette, LA	35,348	55,329	82,752
Las Cruces, NM	26,290	47,722	64,425
Las Vegas, NV	33,363	61,356	86,008
Lexington, KY	37,475	61,526	88,901
Lincoln, NE	33,955	62,566	83,225
Little Rock, AR	39,141	56,928	89,748
Los Angeles, CA	39,378	69,778	106,931
Louisville, KY	34,195	58,357	81,393
Madison, WI	42,693	70,466	94,746
Manchester, NH	36,440	66,929	83,913

Table continued on following page.

City	Per Capita ($)	Median Household ($)	Average Household ($)
Miami, FL	34,295	47,860	79,886
Midland, TX	44,218	87,900	115,425
Milwaukee, WI	25,564	45,318	61,529
Minneapolis, MN	43,925	70,099	99,741
Nashville, TN	39,509	65,565	92,866
New Haven, CT	29,348	48,973	73,450
New Orleans, LA	34,036	45,594	76,715
New York, NY	43,952	70,663	113,315
Oklahoma City, OK	33,162	59,679	81,931
Omaha, NE	36,749	65,359	90,389
Orlando, FL	36,596	58,968	88,128
Philadelphia, PA	32,344	52,649	77,454
Phoenix, AZ	33,718	64,927	90,481
Pittsburgh, PA	37,655	54,306	80,248
Portland, OR	47,289	78,476	106,948
Providence, RI	31,757	55,787	83,046
Provo, UT	23,440	53,572	76,163
Raleigh, NC	42,632	72,996	102,100
Reno, NV	39,104	67,557	93,306
Richmond, VA	38,132	54,795	82,939
Rochester, MN	43,827	79,159	106,381
Sacramento, CA	35,793	71,074	93,320
St. Louis, MO	33,326	48,751	68,681
Salem, OR	31,610	62,185	82,450
Salt Lake City, UT	42,081	65,880	97,628
San Antonio, TX	28,579	55,084	74,154
San Diego, CA	46,460	89,457	121,230
San Francisco, CA	77,267	126,187	178,742
San Jose, CA	53,574	125,075	162,521
Santa Rosa, CA	41,880	84,823	108,164
Savannah, GA	27,952	49,832	69,653
Seattle, WA	68,836	105,391	144,955
Sioux Falls, SD	36,430	66,761	87,676
Springfield, IL	35,851	57,596	79,460
Tampa, FL	40,962	59,893	97,942
Tucson, AZ	26,373	48,058	63,665
Tulsa, OK	33,492	52,438	79,727
Tuscaloosa, AL	27,789	44,880	69,736
Virginia Beach, VA	41,803	81,810	105,521
Washington, DC	63,793	93,547	138,421
Wichita, KS	31,558	56,374	77,762
Wilmington, NC	38,890	54,066	83,853
Winston-Salem, NC	30,859	50,204	75,459
Worcester, MA	30,855	56,746	76,859
U.S.	37,638	69,021	97,196

Source: U.S. Census Bureau, 2017-2021 American Community Survey 5-Year Estimates

Income: Metro Area

Metro Area	Per Capita ($)	Median Household ($)	Average Household ($)
Albuquerque, NM	32,622	58,335	78,771
Allentown, PA	37,945	73,091	96,205
Anchorage, AK	41,201	86,252	109,817
Ann Arbor, MI	45,500	79,198	110,102
Athens, GA	31,392	52,958	80,272
Atlanta, GA	39,267	75,267	104,478
Austin, TX	44,830	85,398	114,103
Baltimore, MD	45,226	87,513	115,291
Boise City, ID	35,114	69,801	92,742
Boston, MA	53,033	99,039	135,411
Boulder, CO	52,401	92,466	128,190
Brownsville, TX	19,371	43,057	60,107
Cape Coral, FL	37,550	63,235	89,228
Cedar Rapids, IA	37,291	70,210	90,560
Charleston, SC	39,923	70,275	98,682
Charlotte, NC	38,783	69,559	98,559
Chicago, IL	42,097	78,790	109,339
Cincinnati, OH	37,846	70,308	94,687
Clarksville, TN	28,243	57,963	74,308
Cleveland, OH	36,907	61,320	85,864
College Station, TX	30,182	53,541	78,104
Colorado Springs, CO	37,650	75,641	97,647
Columbia, MO	33,131	61,901	82,741
Columbia, SC	32,508	58,992	79,903
Columbus, OH	38,167	71,020	95,315
Dallas, TX	38,609	76,916	105,647
Davenport, IA	34,859	63,282	83,352
Denver, CO	47,026	88,512	117,250
Des Moines, IA	39,333	75,134	97,364
Durham, NC	40,502	68,913	99,164
Edison, NJ	47,591	86,445	127,555
El Paso, TX	23,934	50,849	68,522
Fargo, ND	38,367	68,560	91,642
Fort Collins, CO	42,596	80,664	104,442
Fort Wayne, IN	32,207	62,031	80,675
Fort Worth, TX	38,609	76,916	105,647
Grand Rapids, MI	34,581	70,347	91,126
Greeley, CO	35,707	80,843	99,568
Green Bay, WI	35,678	68,952	87,144
Greensboro, NC	31,655	55,544	77,839
Honolulu, HI	40,339	92,600	118,470
Houston, TX	36,821	72,551	103,497
Huntsville, AL	38,800	71,057	94,763
Indianapolis, IN	36,867	67,330	92,858
Jacksonville, FL	36,316	66,664	91,361
Kansas City, MO	39,175	73,299	96,817
Lafayette, LA	30,758	55,539	77,448
Las Cruces, NM	24,645	47,151	65,405
Las Vegas, NV	33,461	64,210	87,879
Lexington, KY	36,123	63,360	88,439
Lincoln, NE	35,055	65,508	87,123
Little Rock, AR	33,523	58,441	81,542
Los Angeles, CA	39,895	81,652	115,584
Louisville, KY	35,613	64,533	87,361
Madison, WI	43,359	77,519	100,891
Manchester, NH	45,238	86,930	111,733

Table continued on following page.

Metro Area	Per Capita ($)	Median Household ($)	Average Household ($)
Miami, FL	36,174	62,870	94,059
Midland, TX	43,287	87,812	114,916
Milwaukee, WI	38,930	67,448	92,423
Minneapolis, MN	45,301	87,397	114,491
Nashville, TN	39,269	72,537	99,987
New Haven, CT	41,192	75,043	102,367
New Orleans, LA	33,792	57,656	83,052
New York, NY	47,591	86,445	127,555
Oklahoma City, OK	34,136	63,351	85,884
Omaha, NE	38,289	73,757	97,122
Orlando, FL	32,999	65,086	89,689
Philadelphia, PA	43,195	79,070	109,757
Phoenix, AZ	36,842	72,211	97,412
Pittsburgh, PA	39,416	65,894	90,001
Portland, OR	42,946	82,901	108,110
Providence, RI	39,267	74,422	97,540
Provo, UT	29,817	82,742	105,296
Raleigh, NC	42,554	83,581	110,195
Reno, NV	40,299	74,216	100,824
Richmond, VA	40,254	74,592	100,389
Rochester, MN	42,841	80,865	106,479
Sacramento, CA	39,510	81,264	107,069
St. Louis, MO	39,168	69,635	94,953
Salem, OR	31,447	65,881	85,642
Salt Lake City, UT	36,688	82,506	105,669
San Antonio, TX	32,580	65,355	88,127
San Diego, CA	42,696	88,240	118,474
San Francisco, CA	62,070	118,547	165,749
San Jose, CA	64,169	138,370	187,324
Santa Rosa, CA	47,580	91,607	121,206
Savannah, GA	34,908	64,703	89,172
Seattle, WA	51,872	97,675	130,964
Sioux Falls, SD	37,200	72,547	92,236
Springfield, IL	37,961	66,999	87,390
Tampa, FL	35,879	61,121	86,382
Tucson, AZ	33,016	59,215	80,772
Tulsa, OK	33,647	60,866	84,069
Tuscaloosa, AL	28,204	54,449	72,452
Virginia Beach, VA	37,548	71,612	93,415
Washington, DC	54,663	111,252	145,303
Wichita, KS	32,124	61,445	81,209
Wilmington, NC	38,607	63,036	89,355
Winston-Salem, NC	31,238	55,454	76,451
Worcester, MA	40,750	80,333	104,366
U.S.	37,638	69,021	97,196

Note: Figures cover the Metropolitan Statistical Area (MSA)
Source: U.S. Census Bureau, 2017-2021 American Community Survey 5-Year Estimates

Household Income Distribution: City

City	Percent of Households Earning							
	Under $15,000	$15,000 -$24,999	$25,000 -$34,999	$35,000 -$49,999	$50,000 -$74,999	$75,000 -$99,999	$100,000 -$149,999	$150,000 and up
Albuquerque, NM	13.1	8.9	9.8	12.9	18.0	11.6	14.8	10.9
Allentown, PA	13.0	12.4	10.9	16.1	19.7	11.2	10.9	5.7
Anchorage, AK	5.5	5.1	5.5	9.0	17.1	14.1	20.2	23.6
Ann Arbor, MI	14.5	6.2	6.2	8.9	15.2	11.2	15.7	22.2
Athens, GA	17.8	12.2	12.4	12.8	15.4	9.2	11.3	8.8
Atlanta, GA	14.2	8.1	7.3	9.4	14.5	11.0	13.5	22.0
Austin, TX	8.3	5.5	6.7	10.4	16.8	12.6	17.7	22.1
Baltimore, MD	16.6	9.1	8.9	12.2	17.1	10.8	12.7	12.8
Boise City, ID	7.6	7.6	8.6	12.4	18.5	13.9	15.7	15.7
Boston, MA	14.9	7.2	5.5	7.7	11.9	10.5	16.1	26.2
Boulder, CO	13.1	7.8	6.7	8.9	13.6	9.5	13.8	26.6
Brownsville, TX	18.6	13.1	10.0	13.0	18.2	10.7	10.6	5.9
Cape Coral, FL	7.6	6.2	8.7	13.7	20.5	15.4	17.2	10.6
Cedar Rapids, IA	7.1	8.5	9.5	13.6	19.9	14.8	14.9	11.7
Charleston, SC	9.1	6.5	6.2	11.3	15.8	12.3	18.6	20.3
Charlotte, NC	7.8	6.7	8.5	12.7	18.3	12.5	15.8	17.7
Chicago, IL	13.1	8.7	8.2	10.2	14.9	11.7	14.7	18.6
Cincinnati, OH	18.0	11.9	10.5	12.6	15.3	10.1	10.6	11.0
Clarksville, TN	9.6	6.8	9.9	15.2	20.6	15.3	15.5	7.2
Cleveland, OH	25.4	13.8	12.4	13.8	14.7	8.7	7.0	4.4
College Station, TX	19.7	10.2	8.8	11.2	15.3	10.0	12.3	12.4
Colorado Springs, CO	7.8	6.6	7.6	12.0	18.0	14.2	17.3	16.4
Columbia, MO	12.8	9.6	9.8	12.6	17.3	11.5	13.2	13.2
Columbia, SC	18.9	10.2	9.7	12.6	14.8	10.5	11.2	12.1
Columbus, OH	10.8	8.4	9.5	13.6	19.5	13.5	15.3	9.5
Dallas, TX	11.3	8.6	9.6	13.7	18.4	11.3	12.1	14.8
Davenport, IA	10.9	9.1	9.0	13.6	20.8	12.8	14.6	9.2
Denver, CO	8.6	6.1	6.4	10.3	16.9	12.4	17.0	22.2
Des Moines, IA	10.0	8.9	9.4	14.7	20.2	14.3	13.6	8.9
Durham, NC	8.9	6.8	9.7	12.2	17.2	13.1	15.7	16.4
Edison, NJ	4.6	3.4	3.5	7.2	13.3	12.4	21.8	34.0
El Paso, TX	13.8	11.4	10.6	13.3	18.8	10.7	12.7	8.8
Fargo, ND	9.8	9.1	9.7	12.9	18.4	13.0	15.5	11.7
Fort Collins, CO	9.6	6.7	7.5	11.0	16.5	13.0	17.2	18.5
Fort Wayne, IN	10.4	10.4	10.8	14.8	19.8	13.2	13.1	7.5
Fort Worth, TX	8.7	7.0	8.7	11.6	18.6	13.5	17.2	14.6
Grand Rapids, MI	12.5	9.8	8.1	14.1	19.0	14.1	14.3	8.0
Greeley, CO	10.3	8.2	9.7	13.9	16.1	13.7	17.9	10.3
Green Bay, WI	10.1	9.4	10.0	15.0	21.7	13.0	13.6	7.3
Greensboro, NC	12.2	9.7	10.9	15.7	17.5	11.3	12.7	9.9
Honolulu, HI	9.1	6.3	6.1	11.0	16.5	13.2	17.1	20.6
Houston, TX	11.9	9.5	10.6	13.1	17.1	10.7	12.1	14.9
Huntsville, AL	11.5	9.2	10.1	12.3	15.2	11.4	14.4	15.9
Indianapolis, IN	12.1	9.6	9.9	14.5	18.8	11.9	12.9	10.4
Jacksonville, FL	10.9	8.4	9.6	13.8	18.9	13.2	14.3	10.9
Kansas City, MO	11.4	8.8	9.6	12.7	17.2	12.7	15.2	12.3
Lafayette, LA	16.0	8.5	9.7	11.5	15.4	11.4	13.3	14.2
Las Cruces, NM	17.5	12.3	10.4	12.2	17.4	9.8	13.1	7.4
Las Vegas, NV	11.6	8.1	8.7	12.9	17.3	13.1	15.2	13.0
Lexington, KY	10.6	8.9	9.5	12.1	17.6	12.3	14.9	14.1
Lincoln, NE	8.4	7.9	9.8	13.0	20.2	12.4	16.1	12.0
Little Rock, AR	11.5	10.1	10.4	13.4	16.2	11.5	12.3	14.4
Los Angeles, CA	11.6	7.8	7.8	10.4	15.1	11.7	15.4	20.1
Louisville, KY	11.2	8.8	9.5	13.3	18.5	12.3	14.3	11.9

Table continued on following page.

City	Percent of Households Earning							
	Under $15,000	$15,000 -$24,999	$25,000 -$34,999	$35,000 -$49,999	$50,000 -$74,999	$75,000 -$99,999	$100,000 -$149,999	$150,000 and up
Madison, WI	10.0	6.8	7.5	11.0	17.5	14.1	16.9	16.0
Manchester, NH	8.0	7.7	7.3	13.7	19.8	14.0	17.0	12.5
Miami, FL	17.7	11.8	10.1	11.8	16.1	9.4	11.1	12.0
Midland, TX	8.0	5.8	6.5	8.5	14.7	12.5	19.6	24.4
Milwaukee, WI	16.5	11.5	11.7	14.6	17.8	11.6	10.5	5.8
Minneapolis, MN	11.3	7.1	7.5	11.0	16.1	12.6	15.9	18.5
Nashville, TN	9.1	7.1	8.2	12.9	19.1	13.2	15.6	14.8
New Haven, CT	18.5	11.0	9.8	11.2	17.2	10.3	11.4	10.6
New Orleans, LA	21.3	11.3	9.5	10.4	15.0	9.4	10.8	12.3
New York, NY	13.2	8.0	7.3	9.6	14.0	11.0	15.0	21.9
Oklahoma City, OK	10.7	7.7	9.6	13.9	18.7	12.8	14.6	12.1
Omaha, NE	9.5	7.3	8.4	12.5	18.9	13.7	15.5	14.1
Orlando, FL	11.2	9.3	8.7	13.6	17.9	11.7	13.0	14.5
Philadelphia, PA	17.1	9.8	9.2	12.0	16.4	11.3	12.4	11.7
Phoenix, AZ	8.4	7.6	8.8	13.5	18.2	13.5	15.3	14.8
Pittsburgh, PA	16.3	9.8	9.6	11.2	16.1	11.7	12.6	12.8
Portland, OR	9.8	6.3	6.7	9.7	15.7	12.6	17.5	21.8
Providence, RI	15.7	10.6	8.8	11.3	17.4	11.9	12.0	12.4
Provo, UT	11.4	10.2	11.3	14.1	19.1	12.7	10.7	10.5
Raleigh, NC	7.5	6.5	8.7	12.1	16.7	12.9	17.0	18.8
Reno, NV	8.6	7.7	8.6	11.5	18.1	13.4	16.7	15.3
Richmond, VA	14.1	9.6	9.4	13.7	17.4	11.3	11.7	12.7
Rochester, MN	6.9	6.3	5.8	10.4	18.0	13.9	18.8	19.9
Sacramento, CA	10.5	6.9	7.2	10.4	17.3	13.8	17.2	16.7
St. Louis, MO	17.0	10.3	10.7	12.9	17.5	10.5	12.1	8.9
Salem, OR	9.9	8.3	8.7	12.8	19.4	13.0	16.6	11.3
Salt Lake City, UT	11.2	6.9	8.6	10.9	18.1	13.1	15.0	16.2
San Antonio, TX	12.2	9.5	10.3	13.6	19.1	12.0	13.3	10.0
San Diego, CA	7.3	5.4	5.9	8.6	15.2	12.6	19.0	26.0
San Francisco, CA	9.2	4.9	4.5	6.0	9.1	8.3	14.9	43.2
San Jose, CA	5.2	4.2	4.2	6.3	10.9	9.9	17.7	41.6
Santa Rosa, CA	7.3	4.9	6.0	10.1	15.6	13.8	20.2	22.1
Savannah, GA	14.7	11.5	10.4	13.6	18.3	11.2	11.7	8.6
Seattle, WA	7.8	4.5	4.7	7.5	12.8	10.6	17.9	34.1
Sioux Falls, SD	7.3	7.4	9.7	12.4	19.1	15.0	17.1	11.9
Springfield, IL	13.8	9.1	9.7	11.9	16.0	13.3	15.0	11.2
Tampa, FL	12.9	8.5	9.4	12.0	15.8	10.8	13.3	17.3
Tucson, AZ	13.9	11.4	11.3	15.2	18.1	12.0	11.7	6.4
Tulsa, OK	12.7	9.8	11.0	14.2	17.7	11.5	11.7	11.5
Tuscaloosa, AL	19.5	10.8	10.9	11.9	15.4	8.7	12.8	10.0
Virginia Beach, VA	5.6	4.5	6.3	10.5	18.8	14.6	20.9	18.8
Washington, DC	11.9	5.1	5.5	6.8	12.2	11.3	15.9	31.3
Wichita, KS	10.8	9.3	10.3	14.0	18.9	12.8	13.6	10.3
Wilmington, NC	14.8	9.7	8.2	13.5	18.5	10.4	12.5	12.5
Winston-Salem, NC	13.8	10.6	11.2	14.2	16.4	12.3	11.7	9.8
Worcester, MA	15.5	9.8	8.5	12.0	15.8	11.7	14.8	11.8
U.S.	9.4	7.8	8.2	11.4	16.8	12.8	16.3	17.3

Source: U.S. Census Bureau, 2017-2021 American Community Survey 5-Year Estimates

Household Income Distribution: Metro Area

Metro Area	Percent of Households Earning							
	Under $15,000	$15,000 -$24,999	$25,000 -$34,999	$35,000 -$49,999	$50,000 -$74,999	$75,000 -$99,999	$100,000 -$149,999	$150,000 and up
Albuquerque, NM	12.0	8.9	9.3	13.0	18.0	12.3	15.0	11.5
Allentown, PA	7.3	7.6	7.6	11.8	17.0	13.7	17.9	17.2
Anchorage, AK	6.1	5.5	5.7	9.0	17.1	14.1	20.1	22.4
Ann Arbor, MI	9.7	6.0	6.9	9.7	15.5	12.5	17.4	22.3
Athens, GA	14.0	10.2	11.1	12.3	15.9	10.2	13.7	12.5
Atlanta, GA	7.6	6.5	7.5	11.1	17.2	13.3	17.3	19.5
Austin, TX	6.8	5.1	6.3	9.7	16.1	13.6	19.1	23.4
Baltimore, MD	8.0	5.5	5.9	9.3	14.8	12.5	18.8	25.1
Boise City, ID	7.0	7.1	7.6	12.0	20.4	14.6	17.3	14.2
Boston, MA	8.1	5.6	5.2	7.6	12.5	11.4	18.2	31.3
Boulder, CO	7.9	5.7	5.5	8.3	13.7	12.1	18.2	28.5
Brownsville, TX	16.8	13.4	11.5	12.9	17.9	10.7	10.6	6.3
Cape Coral, FL	9.1	7.9	9.2	13.2	19.0	13.8	14.9	12.8
Cedar Rapids, IA	6.6	7.4	8.5	12.1	19.2	14.9	17.0	14.4
Charleston, SC	8.4	7.7	7.8	11.6	17.3	13.4	17.1	16.7
Charlotte, NC	7.9	7.3	8.3	12.1	17.7	13.1	16.4	17.2
Chicago, IL	8.7	6.6	7.1	9.9	15.6	12.8	17.9	21.5
Cincinnati, OH	9.2	7.6	8.0	11.1	17.0	13.3	17.5	16.3
Clarksville, TN	10.8	7.6	10.3	14.0	19.6	14.5	14.8	8.5
Cleveland, OH	11.6	8.6	9.0	12.5	17.2	12.7	15.0	13.5
College Station, TX	16.0	9.6	8.9	12.5	17.0	11.2	13.1	11.7
Colorado Springs, CO	6.9	6.2	6.9	11.5	18.1	14.1	18.4	17.9
Columbia, MO	10.8	8.5	9.5	12.3	18.3	13.3	14.8	12.5
Columbia, SC	12.0	8.3	9.4	12.8	18.2	13.1	14.4	11.8
Columbus, OH	8.1	7.0	7.9	11.6	17.9	13.3	17.6	16.6
Dallas, TX	7.1	6.0	7.4	11.1	17.3	13.3	17.9	20.0
Davenport, IA	9.6	8.2	8.7	12.4	18.8	13.7	16.5	12.0
Denver, CO	6.2	4.8	5.7	9.5	16.3	13.2	19.9	24.5
Des Moines, IA	6.4	6.3	7.4	11.8	18.1	14.1	19.0	16.9
Durham, NC	9.2	7.1	9.1	11.5	16.4	12.4	15.6	18.8
Edison, NJ	9.7	6.6	6.3	8.6	13.3	11.2	16.7	27.5
El Paso, TX	13.8	11.2	10.7	13.5	19.0	10.9	12.5	8.3
Fargo, ND	8.7	7.9	7.9	11.8	17.3	13.8	17.9	14.7
Fort Collins, CO	7.9	6.2	6.6	10.0	16.0	14.2	18.8	20.3
Fort Wayne, IN	8.2	8.9	9.5	13.5	19.5	14.9	15.3	10.3
Fort Worth, TX	7.1	6.0	7.4	11.1	17.3	13.3	17.9	20.0
Grand Rapids, MI	7.1	7.4	7.5	12.3	19.2	14.8	17.9	13.9
Greeley, CO	6.6	5.7	7.3	10.2	16.7	14.3	22.2	16.9
Green Bay, WI	7.0	7.1	8.7	12.3	19.2	15.2	18.3	12.1
Greensboro, NC	11.3	9.5	10.3	14.5	17.9	12.1	13.8	10.5
Honolulu, HI	6.5	4.5	5.4	9.0	14.7	13.5	20.0	26.3
Houston, TX	8.4	7.1	8.2	11.0	16.6	12.3	16.5	19.8
Huntsville, AL	8.8	8.0	8.2	11.7	15.4	12.8	16.9	18.2
Indianapolis, IN	8.6	7.4	8.3	12.1	18.4	13.4	16.2	15.6
Jacksonville, FL	9.0	7.1	8.6	12.5	18.3	13.7	15.8	15.0
Kansas City, MO	7.5	6.9	8.1	11.4	17.1	13.9	18.1	17.0
Lafayette, LA	13.7	10.4	10.0	11.9	15.8	12.9	14.4	11.1
Las Cruces, NM	16.8	12.7	10.8	12.2	17.7	9.5	12.9	7.3
Las Vegas, NV	9.7	7.7	8.8	12.8	18.2	13.4	15.7	13.6
Lexington, KY	10.0	8.2	9.3	12.4	17.6	12.9	16.1	13.4
Lincoln, NE	7.8	7.5	9.4	12.6	19.7	12.8	17.1	13.1
Little Rock, AR	11.0	9.2	10.1	13.3	17.5	12.4	14.9	11.6
Los Angeles, CA	9.0	6.4	6.8	9.5	14.8	12.3	17.4	23.8
Louisville, KY	9.2	7.9	8.9	12.9	18.3	13.2	16.0	13.6

Table continued on following page.

Metro Area	Percent of Households Earning							
	Under $15,000	$15,000 -$24,999	$25,000 -$34,999	$35,000 -$49,999	$50,000 -$74,999	$75,000 -$99,999	$100,000 -$149,999	$150,000 and up
Madison, WI	6.9	6.0	6.7	11.1	17.7	14.3	18.9	18.3
Manchester, NH	5.4	5.5	6.2	10.2	15.7	13.2	20.1	23.7
Miami, FL	10.8	8.5	9.0	12.2	17.2	12.2	14.6	15.5
Midland, TX	7.6	5.8	7.1	8.8	14.1	12.8	19.2	24.6
Milwaukee, WI	9.4	7.8	8.5	11.8	17.1	13.2	16.7	15.5
Minneapolis, MN	6.1	5.2	6.1	9.7	16.0	13.7	20.2	23.2
Nashville, TN	7.4	6.5	7.4	12.1	18.2	13.9	17.5	16.9
New Haven, CT	9.4	7.6	6.9	10.1	15.8	12.5	17.1	20.4
New Orleans, LA	14.1	9.6	9.1	11.5	16.5	11.7	14.0	13.5
New York, NY	9.7	6.6	6.3	8.6	13.3	11.2	16.7	27.5
Oklahoma City, OK	9.4	7.9	9.1	13.0	18.6	13.4	15.6	12.8
Omaha, NE	7.6	6.5	7.7	11.3	17.7	14.2	18.5	16.4
Orlando, FL	8.3	7.9	9.0	12.9	18.5	13.6	15.8	14.0
Philadelphia, PA	9.3	6.7	7.1	9.7	15.1	12.5	17.3	22.5
Phoenix, AZ	7.4	6.6	7.7	12.0	18.1	13.9	17.7	16.7
Pittsburgh, PA	9.7	8.4	8.7	11.8	17.0	12.9	16.5	14.9
Portland, OR	7.2	5.7	6.3	10.0	16.3	13.6	19.5	21.5
Providence, RI	9.7	7.9	7.3	10.1	15.2	13.2	18.2	18.3
Provo, UT	5.1	5.0	6.4	10.4	17.9	15.7	20.8	18.6
Raleigh, NC	6.3	6.0	7.0	10.4	15.8	12.8	19.5	22.3
Reno, NV	7.2	6.7	7.8	10.8	18.0	14.0	18.3	17.2
Richmond, VA	7.9	6.7	7.2	11.2	17.2	13.1	18.3	18.3
Rochester, MN	6.2	6.0	6.4	10.1	17.8	14.0	20.1	19.5
Sacramento, CA	8.3	6.1	6.7	9.5	15.9	13.2	18.3	22.1
St. Louis, MO	8.6	7.4	8.1	11.8	17.5	13.5	16.9	16.3
Salem, OR	8.5	7.8	8.7	12.3	18.9	13.8	17.5	12.3
Salt Lake City, UT	6.0	4.8	6.3	10.2	17.9	14.8	20.6	19.3
San Antonio, TX	9.6	7.9	8.9	12.0	18.2	13.0	16.1	14.4
San Diego, CA	6.9	5.7	6.3	9.1	15.0	12.6	18.9	25.5
San Francisco, CA	6.7	4.3	4.5	6.4	10.8	10.0	17.1	40.0
San Jose, CA	4.9	3.6	3.7	5.5	9.9	9.2	16.8	46.6
Santa Rosa, CA	6.5	5.0	5.9	9.0	14.3	13.4	19.6	26.3
Savannah, GA	9.4	7.9	8.6	12.0	18.6	14.1	15.9	13.5
Seattle, WA	5.9	4.6	5.1	8.2	14.7	12.5	19.8	29.2
Sioux Falls, SD	6.2	6.7	8.7	11.8	18.7	15.7	18.9	13.3
Springfield, IL	10.4	7.9	8.4	11.5	16.2	14.1	18.0	13.7
Tampa, FL	9.9	8.6	9.5	13.2	18.0	12.7	14.6	13.7
Tucson, AZ	10.8	9.2	9.6	13.4	17.3	13.1	14.9	11.7
Tulsa, OK	9.6	8.5	9.9	13.1	18.6	12.8	15.3	12.2
Tuscaloosa, AL	14.3	9.9	10.2	12.1	17.3	12.0	14.5	9.6
Virginia Beach, VA	8.0	7.0	7.6	11.3	18.3	13.9	18.4	15.5
Washington, DC	5.7	3.7	4.4	6.8	12.6	12.0	19.6	35.4
Wichita, KS	9.2	8.6	9.1	13.4	19.6	13.4	15.5	11.0
Wilmington, NC	11.0	8.7	7.8	12.4	18.0	12.0	16.0	14.0
Winston-Salem, NC	11.0	10.0	10.7	13.7	18.1	13.1	13.3	10.1
Worcester, MA	8.6	6.8	7.0	9.6	15.3	12.5	18.5	21.8
U.S.	9.4	7.8	8.2	11.4	16.8	12.8	16.3	17.3

Note: Figures cover the Metropolitan Statistical Area (MSA)
Source: Source: U.S. Census Bureau, 2017-2021 American Community Survey 5-Year Estimates

Poverty Rate: City

City	All Ages	Under 18 Years Old	18 to 64 Years Old	65 Years and Over
Albuquerque, NM	16.2	21.0	15.7	11.7
Allentown, PA	23.3	34.9	19.6	16.6
Anchorage, AK	9.1	11.1	8.8	6.8
Ann Arbor, MI	22.5	10.8	27.7	6.3
Athens, GA	26.6	25.8	29.5	11.1
Atlanta, GA	18.5	27.1	16.5	16.9
Austin, TX	12.5	15.9	11.7	11.3
Baltimore, MD	20.3	27.9	18.2	18.6
Boise City, ID	11.6	13.8	11.6	8.6
Boston, MA	17.6	23.7	15.6	21.0
Boulder, CO	20.9	8.6	25.6	6.4
Brownsville, TX	26.5	36.4	21.2	28.2
Cape Coral, FL	9.9	15.4	8.7	8.8
Cedar Rapids, IA	11.2	15.5	10.9	6.4
Charleston, SC	12.0	14.6	12.6	6.4
Charlotte, NC	11.6	17.3	10.1	8.7
Chicago, IL	17.1	24.2	15.1	15.9
Cincinnati, OH	24.7	37.4	22.3	14.7
Clarksville, TN	13.2	16.9	12.4	7.2
Cleveland, OH	31.4	45.7	28.3	22.8
College Station, TX	28.2	13.2	34.3	5.9
Colorado Springs, CO	10.9	13.7	10.7	7.5
Columbia, MO	19.9	14.9	23.7	6.1
Columbia, SC	24.3	31.3	23.5	16.7
Columbus, OH	18.4	27.1	16.5	11.6
Dallas, TX	17.7	26.9	14.7	14.7
Davenport, IA	15.8	24.7	14.1	9.8
Denver, CO	11.6	16.0	10.4	11.3
Des Moines, IA	15.3	22.6	13.6	9.8
Durham, NC	13.5	19.6	12.5	8.9
Edison, NJ	5.8	7.1	5.1	6.6
El Paso, TX	18.3	25.3	15.1	19.1
Fargo, ND	12.9	14.1	14.1	4.8
Fort Collins, CO	15.7	8.9	18.7	7.3
Fort Wayne, IN	15.5	23.9	13.7	8.3
Fort Worth, TX	13.4	19.1	11.3	10.7
Grand Rapids, MI	18.6	25.6	17.1	13.9
Greeley, CO	15.3	20.5	14.5	9.1
Green Bay, WI	15.4	21.5	14.2	10.3
Greensboro, NC	17.4	24.3	15.9	13.0
Honolulu, HI	11.0	13.3	10.4	10.8
Houston, TX	19.5	29.7	16.3	15.1
Huntsville, AL	14.6	21.8	13.9	8.3
Indianapolis, IN	16.4	23.3	14.9	10.5
Jacksonville, FL	14.9	21.1	13.0	12.7
Kansas City, MO	15.0	22.2	13.4	10.1
Lafayette, LA	19.5	29.0	17.8	12.9
Las Cruces, NM	21.8	26.9	22.4	11.5
Las Vegas, NV	14.9	20.8	13.6	11.3
Lexington, KY	15.7	18.6	16.5	7.6
Lincoln, NE	13.0	13.5	14.4	6.1
Little Rock, AR	15.6	22.9	14.2	9.2
Los Angeles, CA	16.6	22.9	14.7	16.3
Louisville, KY	15.2	22.6	14.0	9.4
Madison, WI	16.6	13.0	19.2	7.1

Table continued on following page.

City	All Ages	Under 18 Years Old	18 to 64 Years Old	65 Years and Over
Manchester, NH	12.5	22.1	10.7	8.6
Miami, FL	20.9	27.8	16.6	30.9
Midland, TX	10.6	13.5	9.1	11.8
Milwaukee, WI	24.1	33.4	21.6	15.9
Minneapolis, MN	17.0	21.2	16.3	13.6
Nashville, TN	14.5	22.7	12.7	10.4
New Haven, CT	24.6	31.4	23.3	17.4
New Orleans, LA	23.8	33.8	21.5	20.6
New York, NY	17.0	23.2	14.7	17.8
Oklahoma City, OK	14.9	21.5	13.6	8.4
Omaha, NE	12.1	15.7	11.4	8.4
Orlando, FL	15.5	21.5	13.7	14.5
Philadelphia, PA	22.8	31.9	20.6	18.9
Phoenix, AZ	15.4	22.7	13.3	10.5
Pittsburgh, PA	19.7	28.8	19.0	14.0
Portland, OR	12.6	13.5	12.7	10.6
Providence, RI	21.5	30.3	18.8	19.5
Provo, UT	24.6	17.7	28.2	10.0
Raleigh, NC	12.1	15.8	11.8	7.2
Reno, NV	12.6	13.6	12.4	11.8
Richmond, VA	19.8	30.2	18.3	13.5
Rochester, MN	8.7	9.6	8.9	6.4
Sacramento, CA	14.8	18.5	14.1	12.1
St. Louis, MO	19.6	27.3	18.3	15.4
Salem, OR	14.7	18.0	14.5	10.2
Salt Lake City, UT	14.7	15.4	15.2	10.3
San Antonio, TX	17.6	25.8	15.3	13.6
San Diego, CA	11.6	13.9	11.3	9.4
San Francisco, CA	10.3	10.1	9.4	14.4
San Jose, CA	7.7	8.2	7.1	9.5
Santa Rosa, CA	9.8	12.9	9.0	9.0
Savannah, GA	19.8	29.7	18.1	12.1
Seattle, WA	10.0	9.5	9.9	11.2
Sioux Falls, SD	9.5	10.6	9.6	6.8
Springfield, IL	18.5	28.2	17.6	9.2
Tampa, FL	17.2	23.7	14.6	19.3
Tucson, AZ	19.8	25.3	19.7	12.5
Tulsa, OK	18.0	26.8	16.7	8.8
Tuscaloosa, AL	22.6	21.7	24.5	14.8
Virginia Beach, VA	7.8	10.5	7.6	4.8
Washington, DC	15.4	22.8	13.7	13.9
Wichita, KS	15.2	20.8	14.5	8.5
Wilmington, NC	18.8	25.3	19.8	8.7
Winston-Salem, NC	19.0	30.1	16.9	9.5
Worcester, MA	19.3	24.8	18.1	16.6
U.S.	12.6	17.0	11.8	9.6

Note: Figures are percentage of people whose income during the past 12 months was below the poverty level;
Source: U.S. Census Bureau, 2017-2021 American Community Survey 5-Year Estimates

Poverty Rate: Metro Area

Metro Area	All Ages	Under 18 Years Old	18 to 64 Years Old	65 Years and Over
Albuquerque, NM	15.3	19.5	14.9	11.3
Allentown, PA	10.4	15.9	9.4	7.3
Anchorage, AK	9.6	11.5	9.2	7.4
Ann Arbor, MI	13.4	11.1	15.8	5.8
Athens, GA	20.1	20.5	22.3	9.5
Atlanta, GA	11.1	15.5	9.9	8.5
Austin, TX	10.2	12.0	9.9	8.3
Baltimore, MD	9.8	12.7	9.0	8.8
Boise City, ID	9.9	11.2	9.9	7.6
Boston, MA	9.0	10.3	8.4	9.5
Boulder, CO	11.0	7.1	13.2	6.4
Brownsville, TX	26.3	37.9	21.2	21.8
Cape Coral, FL	12.0	18.7	11.5	9.0
Cedar Rapids, IA	9.5	12.0	9.4	6.5
Charleston, SC	12.1	18.2	10.9	8.1
Charlotte, NC	10.7	14.9	9.7	8.4
Chicago, IL	11.1	15.1	10.1	9.4
Cincinnati, OH	11.6	15.5	10.9	8.1
Clarksville, TN	13.5	17.0	12.6	9.2
Cleveland, OH	13.7	19.6	12.8	9.7
College Station, TX	22.3	20.5	25.3	8.6
Colorado Springs, CO	9.5	12.0	9.2	6.6
Columbia, MO	16.2	14.6	18.7	6.8
Columbia, SC	14.9	19.9	14.2	10.6
Columbus, OH	12.3	17.0	11.5	7.7
Dallas, TX	10.9	15.4	9.4	8.9
Davenport, IA	12.6	18.5	11.8	7.6
Denver, CO	8.1	10.2	7.6	7.1
Des Moines, IA	9.0	11.5	8.6	6.6
Durham, NC	13.2	17.8	12.9	8.2
Edison, NJ	12.3	16.6	10.8	12.1
El Paso, TX	19.3	26.5	15.9	20.0
Fargo, ND	11.3	12.1	12.2	5.5
Fort Collins, CO	11.1	8.8	13.0	6.6
Fort Wayne, IN	12.1	17.9	10.9	6.9
Fort Worth, TX	10.9	15.4	9.4	8.9
Grand Rapids, MI	9.8	11.7	9.5	7.8
Greeley, CO	9.7	12.1	9.0	7.7
Green Bay, WI	9.4	12.0	9.0	7.1
Greensboro, NC	15.1	21.5	14.0	10.3
Honolulu, HI	8.6	11.0	7.9	8.0
Houston, TX	13.3	18.9	11.5	10.5
Huntsville, AL	11.0	15.0	10.1	8.9
Indianapolis, IN	11.1	15.0	10.2	7.7
Jacksonville, FL	12.3	17.2	11.3	9.3
Kansas City, MO	9.8	13.5	9.0	7.0
Lafayette, LA	18.5	26.6	16.6	12.9
Las Cruces, NM	23.2	30.9	22.2	14.7
Las Vegas, NV	13.6	19.0	12.5	9.8
Lexington, KY	14.1	17.2	14.4	8.3
Lincoln, NE	11.8	11.9	13.1	5.9
Little Rock, AR	14.0	18.8	13.4	9.1
Los Angeles, CA	12.9	17.2	11.6	12.4
Louisville, KY	12.0	17.0	11.1	8.2
Madison, WI	10.1	9.0	11.5	5.8

Table continued on following page.

Metro Area	All Ages	Under 18 Years Old	18 to 64 Years Old	65 Years and Over
Manchester, NH	7.2	9.8	6.5	6.2
Miami, FL	13.6	18.0	11.6	15.6
Midland, TX	11.2	15.9	8.9	11.2
Milwaukee, WI	12.6	17.7	11.6	9.0
Minneapolis, MN	8.1	10.1	7.7	6.8
Nashville, TN	10.9	14.6	10.2	8.3
New Haven, CT	11.5	15.8	11.1	7.9
New Orleans, LA	17.3	24.6	15.7	13.3
New York, NY	12.3	16.6	10.8	12.1
Oklahoma City, OK	13.6	18.6	12.9	7.8
Omaha, NE	9.3	11.2	9.0	7.1
Orlando, FL	12.6	17.1	11.7	9.9
Philadelphia, PA	11.7	16.0	10.9	9.2
Phoenix, AZ	12.0	16.9	11.0	8.3
Pittsburgh, PA	10.7	14.2	10.3	8.3
Portland, OR	9.9	11.3	9.8	8.2
Providence, RI	11.2	15.2	10.3	9.6
Provo, UT	9.3	7.9	10.7	5.2
Raleigh, NC	9.3	12.1	8.7	6.9
Reno, NV	11.0	12.8	10.6	9.9
Richmond, VA	10.2	14.1	9.4	7.7
Rochester, MN	7.4	8.6	7.4	6.0
Sacramento, CA	12.2	14.9	12.0	8.8
St. Louis, MO	10.5	14.4	9.9	7.7
Salem, OR	13.1	16.8	12.8	8.8
Salt Lake City, UT	8.2	9.2	8.0	6.5
San Antonio, TX	13.8	19.4	12.1	10.7
San Diego, CA	10.7	13.2	10.3	8.9
San Francisco, CA	8.4	9.1	8.1	9.1
San Jose, CA	6.7	6.8	6.3	8.2
Santa Rosa, CA	8.7	10.3	8.6	7.4
Savannah, GA	12.5	17.5	11.5	8.6
Seattle, WA	8.3	9.7	7.9	7.8
Sioux Falls, SD	7.9	8.5	8.0	6.3
Springfield, IL	13.6	20.0	13.2	7.3
Tampa, FL	12.9	17.4	12.1	10.9
Tucson, AZ	15.1	20.2	15.5	8.6
Tulsa, OK	13.4	19.0	12.6	7.6
Tuscaloosa, AL	17.5	22.8	17.0	11.8
Virginia Beach, VA	10.9	16.1	9.8	7.6
Washington, DC	7.7	9.9	7.0	7.1
Wichita, KS	12.6	16.7	12.0	7.6
Wilmington, NC	13.4	16.6	14.2	7.0
Winston-Salem, NC	15.1	23.7	13.6	9.0
Worcester, MA	10.0	12.0	9.6	8.8
U.S.	12.6	17.0	11.8	9.6

Note: Figures are percentage of people whose income during the past 12 months was below the poverty level; Figures cover the Metropolitan Statistical Area
Source: U.S. Census Bureau, 2017-2021 American Community Survey 5-Year Estimates

Employment by Industry

Metro Area[1]	(A)	(B)	(C)	(D)	(E)	(F)	(G)	(H)	(I)	(J)	(K)	(L)	(M)	(N)
Albuquerque, NM	6.2	n/a	16.6	5.0	19.4	1.4	10.6	4.2	n/a	2.9	16.6	10.5	3.7	2.8
Allentown, PA	3.4	n/a	20.9	3.3	10.0	1.3	8.6	10.5	n/a	3.7	13.2	10.4	11.0	3.7
Anchorage, AK	6.2	5.1	18.4	4.5	19.2	1.9	10.8	1.3	1.1	3.6	11.3	11.5	8.5	2.8
Ann Arbor, MI	2.0	n/a	13.1	3.1	38.2	2.6	7.0	5.5	n/a	2.6	13.6	7.2	2.2	3.0
Athens, GA	n/a	n/a	n/a	n/a	27.8	n/a	11.5	n/a	n/a	n/a	9.0	11.1	n/a	n/a
Atlanta, GA	4.7	4.6	13.1	6.7	11.3	3.8	9.8	5.9	0.1	3.5	19.4	10.1	6.5	5.3
Austin, TX	5.9	n/a	11.2	6.0	14.3	4.1	11.2	5.5	n/a	3.8	21.6	9.2	2.8	4.5
Baltimore, MD	6.0	n/a	19.1	5.5	16.0	1.1	8.6	4.2	n/a	3.4	17.7	9.0	5.8	3.7
Boise City, ID	8.4	n/a	14.8	5.8	13.2	1.2	10.1	7.6	n/a	3.4	15.4	10.6	4.4	5.0
Boston, MA[4]	3.9	n/a	22.9	8.3	10.3	3.6	9.0	4.0	n/a	3.4	21.9	7.2	2.5	3.0
Boulder, CO	2.9	n/a	12.7	3.5	19.4	4.0	9.5	10.8	n/a	4.0	20.6	8.0	1.1	3.6
Brownsville, TX	2.3	n/a	30.2	3.2	18.6	0.4	11.0	4.6	n/a	2.2	10.7	11.5	3.4	2.0
Cape Coral, FL	12.5	n/a	11.7	5.0	14.6	1.1	14.9	2.6	n/a	3.7	14.5	14.3	2.4	2.8
Cedar Rapids, IA	6.0	n/a	15.3	7.4	11.5	2.1	8.2	13.9	n/a	3.5	10.8	10.3	6.9	4.1
Charleston, SC	5.4	n/a	11.7	4.9	16.7	2.2	12.5	7.6	n/a	3.9	16.2	10.9	5.1	3.0
Charlotte, NC	5.6	n/a	10.4	9.1	12.2	2.0	10.6	8.3	n/a	3.7	16.9	10.5	6.0	4.8
Chicago, IL[2]	3.5	3.4	16.2	7.2	10.5	1.9	9.5	7.3	<0.1	4.1	19.2	8.9	6.6	5.0
Cincinnati, OH	4.5	n/a	14.7	6.8	11.2	1.2	10.4	10.4	n/a	3.5	16.2	9.4	6.4	5.1
Clarksville, TN	4.3	n/a	13.2	3.4	19.4	1.2	12.1	12.0	n/a	3.4	10.2	14.2	3.4	n/a
Cleveland, OH	3.7	n/a	19.4	7.0	12.3	1.5	9.0	11.4	n/a	3.6	14.4	9.1	3.6	5.0
College Station, TX	5.7	n/a	11.3	3.2	34.3	1.1	13.9	4.4	n/a	2.6	9.5	10.0	1.9	2.1
Colorado Springs, CO	5.9	n/a	13.8	5.8	17.7	1.6	12.1	3.7	n/a	6.8	17.0	10.3	3.3	2.0
Columbia, MO	n/a	n/a	n/a	n/a	28.2	n/a	n/a	n/a	n/a	n/a	n/a	10.5	n/a	n/a
Columbia, SC	4.0	n/a	12.8	8.6	19.9	1.2	9.2	7.6	n/a	4.1	13.7	10.8	4.2	3.8
Columbus, OH	4.2	n/a	14.1	7.3	16.0	1.6	9.1	6.4	n/a	3.8	16.5	9.0	8.5	3.6
Dallas, TX[2]	5.3	n/a	11.4	9.7	10.9	2.8	9.2	6.5	n/a	3.0	20.6	8.9	5.9	5.9
Davenport, IA	n/a	n/a	n/a	n/a	n/a	n/a	n/a	n/a	n/a	n/a	n/a	n/a	n/a	n/a
Denver, CO	6.9	n/a	12.2	7.3	12.7	3.3	10.6	4.5	n/a	4.1	19.6	8.9	5.0	4.9
Des Moines, IA	5.9	n/a	14.3	14.3	12.3	1.6	8.7	5.9	n/a	3.3	13.5	10.6	4.5	5.0
Durham, NC	2.9	n/a	21.9	4.8	18.9	1.8	7.7	8.5	n/a	3.4	17.5	7.1	2.5	2.8
Edison, NJ[2]	3.6	n/a	22.7	9.0	12.4	3.9	8.9	2.6	n/a	4.0	16.5	8.3	4.3	3.7
El Paso, TX	5.1	n/a	14.5	3.9	20.7	1.8	11.7	5.5	n/a	2.7	12.2	12.1	6.4	3.6
Fargo, ND	6.0	n/a	19.2	7.5	13.5	1.8	9.6	7.9	n/a	3.3	10.0	10.0	5.0	6.1
Fort Collins, CO	6.8	n/a	10.9	4.0	24.0	1.5	11.9	8.3	n/a	3.6	11.9	11.4	2.4	3.2
Fort Wayne, IN	5.2	n/a	18.4	5.5	9.4	0.8	9.0	16.4	n/a	5.0	9.7	10.7	5.1	4.8
Fort Worth, TX[2]	6.6	n/a	12.8	6.4	11.9	0.9	10.5	9.3	n/a	3.4	13.4	10.7	9.0	4.9
Grand Rapids, MI	4.7	n/a	16.5	4.8	8.6	1.2	8.2	20.0	n/a	3.9	13.8	8.7	3.5	6.0
Greeley, CO	15.1	n/a	9.9	4.1	16.5	0.5	9.3	12.3	n/a	3.2	10.5	10.6	4.2	4.0
Green Bay, WI	4.7	n/a	15.3	6.2	11.5	0.8	8.9	17.7	n/a	4.5	10.6	9.9	5.1	5.0
Greensboro, NC	4.8	n/a	14.6	4.6	11.9	1.1	9.9	13.8	n/a	3.4	12.6	11.2	6.3	5.8
Honolulu, HI	6.2	n/a	14.5	4.7	21.0	1.6	15.3	2.1	n/a	4.4	12.2	9.7	5.4	3.0
Houston, TX	8.8	6.7	13.2	5.5	13.4	1.0	10.3	6.9	2.0	3.5	16.6	9.8	5.9	5.2
Huntsville, AL	3.9	n/a	8.5	3.1	20.4	1.0	8.2	12.0	n/a	3.3	25.5	10.1	1.7	2.4
Indianapolis, IN	5.3	5.2	14.9	6.6	12.1	1.1	9.0	8.3	0.1	3.9	16.6	9.0	8.3	4.8
Jacksonville, FL	6.4	6.3	15.2	9.4	10.0	1.7	11.2	4.5	0.1	3.4	16.3	10.9	7.4	3.7
Kansas City, MO	5.1	n/a	14.5	7.0	12.9	1.5	9.7	7.6	n/a	4.0	17.1	9.8	6.3	4.6
Lafayette, LA	10.5	5.4	17.2	5.5	12.8	0.9	10.6	8.1	5.2	3.5	10.4	12.9	3.2	4.4
Las Cruces, NM	4.7	n/a	22.7	3.1	26.7	0.8	11.4	4.4	n/a	2.1	9.1	9.9	3.2	1.9
Las Vegas, NV	7.3	7.3	10.8	5.4	10.0	1.2	25.9	2.6	<0.1	2.9	14.8	10.4	6.4	2.4
Lexington, KY	4.8	n/a	13.0	4.0	19.0	1.0	11.1	10.8	n/a	4.4	13.2	10.2	4.5	3.8
Lincoln, NE	5.5	n/a	15.7	5.6	22.1	1.9	9.4	7.7	n/a	3.9	10.3	9.8	5.8	2.2
Little Rock, AR	4.9	n/a	16.2	6.4	17.9	1.5	8.6	5.1	n/a	6.6	12.3	10.2	5.8	4.6
Los Angeles, CA[2]	3.2	3.2	19.4	4.7	12.3	5.0	11.4	6.9	<0.1	3.4	14.9	9.2	5.1	4.4
Louisville, KY	4.3	n/a	14.7	6.8	10.5	1.3	9.3	12.4	n/a	3.7	12.9	9.4	10.2	4.6
Madison, WI	4.8	n/a	12.3	5.8	21.7	4.6	7.9	9.3	n/a	5.0	12.6	9.5	2.8	3.7
Manchester, NH[3]	5.0	n/a	22.7	6.5	10.3	2.2	8.4	6.9	n/a	4.1	16.2	10.8	3.0	3.9

Table continued on following page.

Metro Area[1]	(A)	(B)	(C)	(D)	(E)	(F)	(G)	(H)	(I)	(J)	(K)	(L)	(M)	(N)
Miami, FL[2]	4.0	4.0	16.4	7.1	10.9	1.9	11.1	3.4	<0.1	3.7	16.4	11.6	7.5	6.0
Midland, TX	33.3	n/a	6.6	4.5	8.4	1.0	9.8	4.2	n/a	3.5	9.8	8.3	4.9	5.7
Milwaukee, WI	4.0	3.9	20.3	6.0	9.6	1.4	8.4	13.5	0.1	5.2	13.9	8.9	4.2	4.6
Minneapolis, MN	4.1	n/a	18.0	7.6	12.5	1.5	8.9	10.5	n/a	3.6	15.4	9.3	4.3	4.3
Nashville, TN	5.2	n/a	14.6	6.7	10.9	2.8	11.0	7.5	n/a	4.1	17.3	9.2	6.6	4.2
New Haven, CT[3]	3.7	n/a	29.2	3.9	11.9	1.3	8.7	7.8	n/a	3.5	10.4	9.0	6.7	3.9
New Orleans, LA	5.6	5.1	19.0	5.1	12.1	1.6	14.0	5.3	0.6	4.0	13.5	10.6	5.3	3.9
New York, NY[2]	3.6	n/a	22.7	9.0	12.4	3.9	8.9	2.6	n/a	4.0	16.5	8.3	4.3	3.7
Oklahoma City, OK	6.6	4.9	15.4	5.4	18.8	0.9	11.2	5.2	1.6	4.2	13.3	10.4	5.2	3.4
Omaha, NE	6.3	n/a	16.3	8.3	13.3	2.0	9.7	6.9	n/a	3.8	14.2	10.5	5.3	3.3
Orlando, FL	6.0	6.0	12.6	6.3	8.9	1.9	19.4	3.7	<0.1	3.1	19.3	10.8	4.5	3.6
Philadelphia, PA[2]	2.5	n/a	31.6	6.5	12.7	2.0	9.1	3.3	n/a	4.0	14.5	7.4	4.2	2.4
Phoenix, AZ	6.6	6.4	15.9	9.3	10.2	1.8	10.1	6.4	0.1	3.1	17.0	10.5	5.1	4.0
Pittsburgh, PA	5.4	4.7	21.2	6.5	9.7	1.9	9.6	7.2	0.7	4.0	16.6	10.1	4.4	3.6
Portland, OR	6.7	6.6	15.0	6.2	12.2	2.3	9.4	10.2	0.1	3.4	16.2	9.7	4.3	4.6
Providence, RI[3]	4.8	4.8	20.8	6.4	12.8	1.2	10.6	8.6	<0.1	4.4	12.7	10.9	3.4	3.4
Provo, UT	10.0	n/a	19.8	4.2	11.7	4.7	8.6	7.7	n/a	2.3	15.0	11.7	1.8	2.5
Raleigh, NC	6.6	n/a	13.0	5.7	13.8	3.6	10.4	4.7	n/a	4.0	20.4	10.2	3.5	4.1
Reno, NV	8.4	8.3	11.1	4.4	12.1	1.4	14.4	10.8	0.1	2.4	12.7	9.3	9.4	3.9
Richmond, VA	5.8	n/a	14.1	8.0	16.2	0.9	9.2	4.6	n/a	4.5	17.7	9.6	5.4	4.0
Rochester, MN	4.0	n/a	43.3	2.4	10.5	0.9	8.5	7.9	n/a	3.0	5.4	9.9	2.1	2.1
Sacramento, CA	6.8	6.8	16.9	4.9	22.7	1.0	10.3	3.7	<0.1	3.5	14.0	9.6	4.0	2.6
Salem, OR	7.6	7.3	17.8	3.8	24.5	0.9	8.8	6.7	0.3	3.0	9.5	11.0	4.1	2.3
Salt Lake City, UT	7.0	n/a	11.5	7.6	13.6	3.2	8.3	7.8	n/a	2.8	17.8	9.9	5.8	4.5
San Antonio, TX	5.9	5.3	14.9	8.9	15.6	1.7	12.2	5.1	0.6	3.5	14.0	10.9	4.1	3.3
San Diego, CA	5.7	5.6	15.0	4.8	15.9	1.4	12.8	7.6	<0.1	3.6	18.6	9.1	2.7	2.8
San Francisco, CA[2]	3.4	3.4	13.1	7.4	10.9	10.6	10.2	3.3	<0.1	3.2	26.3	5.7	4.1	1.9
San Jose, CA	4.8	4.7	16.3	3.3	8.3	9.1	8.5	15.4	<0.1	2.1	21.7	6.4	1.8	2.4
Santa Rosa, CA	7.9	7.8	17.3	4.0	12.7	1.3	12.4	11.5	0.1	3.6	12.2	11.4	2.3	3.5
Savannah, GA	4.7	n/a	14.1	3.5	11.8	0.8	13.7	9.8	n/a	4.0	12.6	12.0	9.5	3.5
Seattle, WA[2]	6.1	6.0	12.9	5.0	11.7	7.9	8.7	8.1	<0.1	3.3	20.0	8.1	4.2	4.1
Sioux Falls, SD	5.8	n/a	21.6	9.1	9.1	1.5	9.5	8.7	n/a	3.9	9.8	11.8	3.8	5.5
Springfield, IL	3.4	n/a	19.2	5.6	24.1	2.0	9.6	3.3	n/a	5.5	11.4	10.9	2.3	2.9
St. Louis, MO	5.0	n/a	18.6	6.9	10.9	2.0	10.0	8.3	n/a	3.8	15.5	9.6	4.7	4.8
Tampa, FL	6.2	6.2	15.2	9.1	10.2	1.9	10.8	4.9	<0.1	3.3	19.3	11.3	3.6	4.1
Tucson, AZ	5.4	4.9	16.8	4.8	19.3	1.3	11.2	7.2	0.5	3.5	12.8	10.6	5.2	2.0
Tulsa, OK	6.1	5.3	16.0	5.2	12.7	1.2	10.1	10.7	0.8	4.5	13.8	11.0	5.2	3.7
Tuscaloosa, AL	5.7	n/a	8.5	3.5	25.7	0.7	10.3	16.8	n/a	4.1	9.3	10.4	3.1	1.9
Virginia Beach, VA	5.2	n/a	14.8	5.0	19.7	1.2	11.1	7.4	n/a	4.2	14.7	10.4	4.0	2.4
Washington, DC[2]	4.8	n/a	12.9	4.4	22.2	2.5	9.2	1.4	n/a	6.2	24.3	7.6	2.7	1.9
Wichita, KS	5.7	n/a	14.9	3.9	14.3	1.2	10.8	16.8	n/a	3.7	11.3	10.3	4.0	3.1
Wilmington, NC	7.4	n/a	17.0	5.1	12.6	2.0	14.8	4.2	n/a	4.2	13.1	12.7	3.3	3.5
Winston-Salem, NC	4.3	n/a	20.1	5.0	11.3	0.7	10.5	12.6	n/a	3.5	12.9	11.6	4.5	3.1
Worcester, MA[3]	4.1	n/a	23.5	4.8	15.7	0.9	8.3	9.2	n/a	3.6	11.1	10.2	5.3	3.2
U.S.	5.4	5.0	16.1	5.9	14.5	2.0	10.3	8.4	0.4	3.7	14.7	10.2	4.9	3.9

Note: All figures are percentages covering non-farm employment as of December 2022 and are not seasonally adjusted;
(1) Figures cover the Metropolitan Statistical Area (MSA) except where noted. See Appendix B for areas included; (2) Metropolitan Division; (3) New England City and Town Area; (4) New England City and Town Area Division; (A) Construction, Mining, and Logging (some areas report Construction separate from Mining and Logging); (B) Construction; (C) Private Education and Health Services; (D) Financial Activities; (E) Government; (F) Information; (G) Leisure and Hospitality; (H) Manufacturing; (I) Mining and Logging; (J) Other Services; (K) Professional and Business Services; (L) Retail Trade; (M) Transportation and Utilities; (N) Wholesale Trade; n/a not available
Source: Bureau of Labor Statistics, Current Employment Statistics, Employment, Hours, and Earnings, December 2022

Labor Force, Employment and Job Growth: City

City	Civilian Labor Force			Workers Employed		
	Dec. 2021	Dec. 2022	% Chg.	Dec. 2021	Dec. 2022	% Chg.
Albuquerque, NM	286,208	278,969	-2.5	272,867	270,719	-0.7
Allentown, PA	55,657	56,449	1.4	52,269	54,138	3.5
Anchorage, AK	154,601	155,471	0.5	148,017	150,605	1.7
Ann Arbor, MI	63,522	64,736	1.9	62,006	63,139	1.8
Athens, GA	60,379	61,240	1.4	58,643	59,627	1.6
Atlanta, GA	271,164	274,219	1.1	261,888	265,951	1.5
Austin, TX	626,475	642,058	2.4	609,403	625,541	2.6
Baltimore, MD	280,450	278,592	-0.6	262,676	266,256	1.3
Boise City, ID	135,152	140,433	3.9	132,075	137,857	4.3
Boston, MA	394,417	392,029	-0.6	379,015	380,790	0.4
Boulder, CO	66,246	67,538	1.9	64,727	66,197	2.2
Brownsville, TX	78,951	79,589	0.8	73,562	74,739	1.6
Cape Coral, FL	96,606	100,709	4.2	93,922	97,833	4.1
Cedar Rapids, IA	69,935	70,822	1.2	66,849	68,200	2.0
Charleston, SC	75,129	76,762	2.1	73,011	74,897	2.5
Charlotte, NC	498,644	513,354	2.9	481,757	496,911	3.1
Chicago, IL	1,370,152	1,365,082	-0.3	1,301,665	1,299,230	-0.1
Cincinnati, OH	147,147	145,962	-0.8	141,899	140,924	-0.6
Clarksville, TN	64,581	62,625	-3.0	62,259	60,449	-2.9
Cleveland, OH	154,230	153,656	-0.3	144,455	146,635	1.5
College Station, TX	63,443	64,403	1.5	61,598	62,625	1.6
Colorado Springs, CO	243,995	246,112	0.8	234,766	238,820	1.7
Columbia, MO	68,593	68,729	0.2	67,043	67,523	0.7
Columbia, SC	56,736	55,816	-1.6	54,797	54,043	-1.3
Columbus, OH	484,399	482,990	-0.2	469,341	467,547	-0.3
Dallas, TX	707,758	735,922	3.9	679,409	711,095	4.6
Davenport, IA	50,142	51,938	3.5	47,788	49,912	4.4
Denver, CO	428,646	439,359	2.5	411,447	426,400	3.6
Des Moines, IA	109,744	111,230	1.3	104,975	107,148	2.0
Durham, NC	155,641	159,589	2.5	151,405	155,264	2.5
Edison, NJ	55,370	56,778	2.5	53,727	55,594	3.4
El Paso, TX	302,469	303,815	0.4	288,907	292,314	1.1
Fargo, ND	72,514	72,188	-0.4	70,902	70,818	-0.1
Fort Collins, CO	100,891	102,741	1.8	98,235	100,394	2.2
Fort Wayne, IN	126,450	130,964	3.5	124,397	127,828	2.7
Fort Worth, TX	462,444	475,802	2.8	444,256	459,728	3.4
Grand Rapids, MI	101,134	105,118	3.9	96,771	100,836	4.2
Greeley, CO	51,681	51,829	0.2	49,366	50,105	1.5
Green Bay, WI	53,463	52,666	-1.4	52,235	51,500	-1.4
Greensboro, NC	143,008	144,251	0.8	137,220	138,826	1.1
Honolulu, HI	459,370	457,096	-0.5	440,467	441,407	0.2
Houston, TX	1,138,573	1,173,802	3.0	1,085,474	1,128,659	3.9
Huntsville, AL	102,295	104,297	1.9	100,086	102,254	2.1
Indianapolis, IN	450,127	464,032	3.0	441,617	452,513	2.4
Jacksonville, FL	470,543	493,413	4.8	456,509	481,988	5.5
Kansas City, MO	257,158	258,850	0.6	247,609	252,172	1.8
Lafayette, LA	59,534	60,606	1.8	57,818	58,830	1.7
Las Cruces, NM	48,477	48,211	-0.5	46,260	46,735	1.0
Las Vegas, NV	301,290	316,801	5.1	286,123	299,424	4.6
Lexington, KY	175,989	174,916	-0.6	170,668	170,430	-0.1
Lincoln, NE	161,763	164,641	1.7	159,144	161,093	1.2
Little Rock, AR	95,576	95,929	0.3	92,287	93,043	0.8
Los Angeles, CA	2,047,789	2,027,026	-1.0	1,931,445	1,935,875	0.2
Louisville, KY	400,329	398,800	-0.3	384,379	387,119	0.7
Madison, WI	162,642	161,298	-0.8	160,375	158,871	-0.9

Table continued on following page.

City	Civilian Labor Force			Workers Employed		
	Dec. 2021	Dec. 2022	% Chg.	Dec. 2021	Dec. 2022	% Chg.
Manchester, NH	63,249	66,044	4.4	61,619	64,357	4.4
Miami, FL	227,422	231,754	1.9	220,939	228,420	3.3
Midland, TX	83,370	84,916	1.8	80,102	82,715	3.2
Milwaukee, WI	272,797	266,036	-2.4	262,401	257,421	-1.9
Minneapolis, MN	241,913	246,063	1.7	235,948	240,094	1.7
Nashville, TN	413,734	407,521	-1.5	402,245	397,879	-1.0
New Haven, CT	65,615	66,515	1.3	62,503	64,310	2.8
New Orleans, LA	175,708	180,265	2.5	166,032	172,381	3.8
New York, NY	4,085,159	4,113,259	0.6	3,782,405	3,907,975	3.3
Oklahoma City, OK	327,538	333,291	1.7	320,689	324,655	1.2
Omaha, NE	250,414	253,695	1.3	244,895	246,725	0.7
Orlando, FL	168,524	173,274	2.8	162,788	169,122	3.8
Philadelphia, PA	712,569	723,233	1.5	667,785	690,464	3.4
Phoenix, AZ	865,943	889,029	2.6	842,267	864,868	2.6
Pittsburgh, PA	148,500	152,028	2.3	142,551	147,423	3.4
Portland, OR	387,410	393,179	1.4	373,537	376,724	0.8
Providence, RI	88,878	88,200	-0.7	85,136	85,603	0.5
Provo, UT	70,289	73,861	5.0	69,267	72,590	4.8
Raleigh, NC	255,398	264,381	3.5	247,896	256,967	3.6
Reno, NV	134,416	141,155	5.0	131,188	136,416	3.9
Richmond, VA	115,165	116,068	0.7	110,750	112,086	1.2
Rochester, MN	67,368	68,064	1.0	65,967	66,601	0.9
Sacramento, CA	237,842	239,915	0.8	226,017	231,146	2.2
Salem, OR	84,706	83,973	-0.8	81,711	80,171	-1.8
Salt Lake City, UT	121,702	125,773	3.3	119,545	123,299	3.1
San Antonio, TX	735,449	751,540	2.1	707,860	727,368	2.7
San Diego, CA	711,954	721,000	1.2	684,180	701,197	2.4
San Francisco, CA	560,450	578,421	3.2	543,659	566,695	4.2
San Jose, CA	546,462	558,687	2.2	529,424	546,728	3.2
Santa Rosa, CA	85,496	86,918	1.6	82,307	84,605	2.7
Savannah, GA	69,179	68,684	-0.7	66,698	66,661	0.0
Seattle, WA	483,713	490,565	1.4	471,546	477,991	1.3
Sioux Falls, SD	109,388	111,832	2.2	106,662	109,520	2.6
Springfield, IL	55,434	55,938	0.9	53,040	53,888	1.6
St. Louis, MO	150,418	149,690	-0.4	143,212	145,026	1.2
Tampa, FL	211,042	219,467	3.9	205,058	214,586	4.6
Tucson, AZ	257,903	262,655	1.8	249,443	254,180	1.9
Tulsa, OK	194,312	199,027	2.4	189,673	193,469	2.0
Tuscaloosa, AL	46,912	47,393	1.0	45,459	46,256	1.7
Virginia Beach, VA	222,270	227,788	2.4	216,500	221,941	2.5
Washington, DC	378,144	386,520	2.2	358,132	370,787	3.5
Wichita, KS	190,708	192,293	0.8	184,998	186,223	0.6
Wilmington, NC	65,317	66,641	2.0	63,471	64,589	1.7
Winston-Salem, NC	116,216	117,459	1.0	112,011	113,308	1.1
Worcester, MA	93,362	90,627	-2.9	88,807	87,239	-1.7
U.S.	161,696,000	164,224,000	1.6	155,732,000	158,872,000	2.0

Note: Data is not seasonally adjusted and covers workers 16 years of age and older
Source: Bureau of Labor Statistics, Local Area Unemployment Statistics

Labor Force, Employment and Job Growth: Metro Area

Metro Area[1]	Civilian Labor Force			Workers Employed		
	Dec. 2021	Dec. 2022	% Chg.	Dec. 2021	Dec. 2022	% Chg.
Albuquerque, NM	445,726	434,352	-2.5	424,396	421,074	-0.7
Allentown, PA	447,351	458,516	2.5	428,287	443,287	3.5
Anchorage, AK	205,827	206,845	0.4	196,305	199,569	1.6
Ann Arbor, MI	192,598	196,315	1.9	187,000	190,417	1.8
Athens, GA	102,226	103,727	1.4	99,578	101,194	1.6
Atlanta, GA	3,175,581	3,216,104	1.2	3,085,734	3,133,430	1.5
Austin, TX	1,339,834	1,372,624	2.4	1,301,083	1,335,791	2.6
Baltimore, MD	1,501,247	1,502,740	0.1	1,434,164	1,455,751	1.5
Boise City, ID	400,832	416,686	3.9	390,861	407,819	4.3
Boston, MA[4]	1,673,210	1,666,434	-0.4	1,614,446	1,622,005	0.4
Boulder, CO	198,590	201,887	1.6	193,073	197,458	2.2
Brownsville, TX	175,175	176,374	0.6	163,657	166,276	1.6
Cape Coral, FL	362,039	377,849	4.3	352,239	366,908	4.1
Cedar Rapids, IA	140,768	142,727	1.3	135,170	137,743	1.9
Charleston, SC	400,171	408,735	2.1	388,529	398,569	2.5
Charlotte, NC	1,377,149	1,414,791	2.7	1,332,923	1,371,461	2.8
Chicago, IL[2]	3,826,621	3,838,545	0.3	3,671,983	3,676,358	0.1
Cincinnati, OH	1,123,242	1,116,215	-0.6	1,088,875	1,082,108	-0.6
Clarksville, TN	120,311	117,511	-2.3	115,795	113,311	-2.1
Cleveland, OH	1,006,515	1,010,141	0.3	963,990	975,650	1.2
College Station, TX	138,941	140,832	1.3	134,636	136,870	1.6
Colorado Springs, CO	364,630	367,853	0.8	350,819	356,889	1.7
Columbia, MO	100,630	100,708	0.0	98,278	98,981	0.7
Columbia, SC	399,511	392,721	-1.7	387,182	381,702	-1.4
Columbus, OH	1,121,138	1,118,600	-0.2	1,088,089	1,084,246	-0.3
Dallas, TX[2]	2,825,024	2,943,498	4.1	2,723,620	2,851,201	4.6
Davenport, IA	185,485	190,708	2.8	177,815	183,615	3.2
Denver, CO	1,691,446	1,735,541	2.6	1,629,015	1,687,640	3.6
Des Moines, IA	362,322	367,598	1.4	350,192	357,259	2.0
Durham, NC	311,304	319,367	2.5	303,354	310,936	2.5
Edison, NJ[2]	6,978,612	7,057,593	1.1	6,599,840	6,759,099	2.4
El Paso, TX	365,233	366,661	0.3	347,953	352,057	1.1
Fargo, ND	143,613	142,810	-0.5	140,498	140,046	-0.3
Fort Collins, CO	208,863	212,087	1.5	202,604	207,057	2.2
Fort Wayne, IN	213,153	220,727	3.5	210,157	215,921	2.7
Fort Worth, TX[2]	1,345,295	1,384,350	2.9	1,295,323	1,340,078	3.4
Grand Rapids, MI	563,869	586,790	4.0	545,813	568,603	4.1
Greeley, CO	167,574	168,716	0.6	161,228	163,640	1.5
Green Bay, WI	173,797	170,959	-1.6	170,171	167,408	-1.6
Greensboro, NC	360,317	364,357	1.1	347,114	351,304	1.2
Honolulu, HI	459,370	457,096	-0.5	440,467	441,407	0.2
Houston, TX	3,460,832	3,565,905	3.0	3,294,015	3,425,418	3.9
Huntsville, AL	239,285	244,014	1.9	234,543	239,596	2.1
Indianapolis, IN	1,076,300	1,110,642	3.1	1,060,871	1,086,712	2.4
Jacksonville, FL	806,862	847,564	5.0	785,663	829,550	5.5
Kansas City, MO	1,138,286	1,149,586	0.9	1,105,453	1,121,442	1.4
Lafayette, LA	211,602	215,089	1.6	204,894	208,467	1.7
Las Cruces, NM	99,600	99,107	-0.5	94,429	95,399	1.0
Las Vegas, NV	1,093,227	1,149,504	5.1	1,039,029	1,087,331	4.6
Lexington, KY	275,622	274,006	-0.5	267,238	266,822	-0.1
Lincoln, NE	188,166	191,439	1.7	185,143	187,374	1.2
Little Rock, AR	350,674	353,640	0.8	341,122	343,843	0.8
Los Angeles, CA[2]	5,001,852	4,965,511	-0.7	4,701,620	4,747,043	0.9
Louisville, KY	672,926	678,057	0.7	650,589	659,926	1.4
Madison, WI	400,355	395,887	-1.1	393,718	389,430	-1.0

Table continued on following page.

Metro Area[1]	Civilian Labor Force			Workers Employed		
	Dec. 2021	Dec. 2022	% Chg.	Dec. 2021	Dec. 2022	% Chg.
Manchester, NH[3]	118,844	124,173	4.4	116,140	121,300	4.4
Miami, FL[2]	1,345,385	1,397,307	3.8	1,304,718	1,369,536	4.9
Midland, TX	103,649	105,497	1.7	99,519	102,761	3.2
Milwaukee, WI	817,582	799,375	-2.2	796,196	780,437	-1.9
Minneapolis, MN	1,991,752	2,028,489	1.8	1,943,478	1,975,295	1.6
Nashville, TN	1,124,910	1,111,047	-1.2	1,096,732	1,085,200	-1.0
New Haven, CT[3]	327,755	334,058	1.9	315,344	324,400	2.8
New Orleans, LA	582,640	600,820	3.1	558,375	579,744	3.8
New York, NY[2]	6,978,612	7,057,593	1.1	6,599,840	6,759,099	2.4
Oklahoma City, OK	699,178	711,592	1.7	685,472	694,168	1.2
Omaha, NE	502,000	508,654	1.3	490,956	495,693	0.9
Orlando, FL	1,366,646	1,407,116	2.9	1,323,163	1,374,399	3.8
Philadelphia, PA[2]	1,004,235	1,021,788	1.7	946,859	979,293	3.4
Phoenix, AZ	2,518,007	2,590,356	2.8	2,453,226	2,520,303	2.7
Pittsburgh, PA	1,147,805	1,177,164	2.5	1,096,709	1,134,155	3.4
Portland, OR	1,369,607	1,391,563	1.6	1,322,133	1,334,787	0.9
Providence, RI[3]	706,157	698,803	-1.0	679,845	680,282	0.0
Provo, UT	345,721	363,397	5.1	340,264	356,597	4.8
Raleigh, NC	737,649	764,883	3.6	718,092	744,560	3.6
Reno, NV	249,159	261,626	5.0	243,158	252,847	3.9
Richmond, VA	664,206	670,336	0.9	643,038	650,950	1.2
Rochester, MN	126,103	127,371	1.0	123,345	124,243	0.7
Sacramento, CA	1,102,380	1,115,511	1.1	1,055,002	1,078,900	2.2
Salem, OR	210,043	208,341	-0.8	202,733	198,916	-1.8
Salt Lake City, UT	699,196	722,471	3.3	686,309	707,898	3.1
San Antonio, TX	1,217,217	1,244,094	2.2	1,171,224	1,203,295	2.7
San Diego, CA	1,570,184	1,588,968	1.2	1,505,925	1,543,381	2.4
San Francisco, CA[2]	1,003,772	1,035,986	3.2	974,872	1,015,702	4.1
San Jose, CA	1,067,389	1,093,480	2.4	1,036,363	1,070,252	3.2
Santa Rosa, CA	243,938	248,408	1.8	235,525	242,101	2.7
Savannah, GA	199,752	198,853	-0.4	194,065	193,933	0.0
Seattle, WA[2]	1,724,262	1,779,111	3.1	1,675,402	1,725,495	2.9
Sioux Falls, SD	159,168	162,847	2.3	155,392	159,650	2.7
Springfield, IL	103,907	105,050	1.1	99,703	101,310	1.6
St. Louis, MO	1,460,514	1,459,027	-0.1	1,407,703	1,422,207	1.0
Tampa, FL	1,596,468	1,661,495	4.0	1,552,983	1,625,105	4.6
Tucson, AZ	482,383	492,280	2.0	468,330	477,224	1.9
Tulsa, OK	479,679	491,520	2.4	468,777	478,458	2.0
Tuscaloosa, AL	114,876	116,118	1.0	111,656	113,579	1.7
Virginia Beach, VA	821,309	840,432	2.3	795,009	815,342	2.5
Washington, DC[2]	2,676,340	2,681,074	0.1	2,582,644	2,604,564	0.8
Wichita, KS	317,498	320,744	1.0	309,104	311,289	0.7
Wilmington, NC	154,267	157,407	2.0	150,051	152,775	1.8
Winston-Salem, NC	322,524	326,477	1.2	312,552	316,261	1.1
Worcester, MA[3]	358,980	351,150	-2.1	344,046	339,514	-1.3
U.S.	161,696,000	164,224,000	1.6	155,732,000	158,872,000	2.0

Note: Data is not seasonally adjusted and covers workers 16 years of age and older; (1) Figures cover the Metropolitan Statistical Area (MSA) except where noted. See Appendix B for areas included; (2) Metropolitan Division; (3) New England City and Town Area; (4) New England City and Town Area Division
Source: Bureau of Labor Statistics, Local Area Unemployment Statistics

Unemployment Rate: City

City	2022											
	Jan.	Feb.	Mar.	Apr.	May	Jun.	Jul.	Aug.	Sep.	Oct.	Nov.	Dec.
Albuquerque, NM	4.9	4.3	4.0	3.9	3.7	4.4	4.1	4.0	4.0	3.6	3.2	3.0
Allentown, PA	7.3	6.5	6.1	6.0	5.8	6.2	6.2	6.5	5.0	4.6	4.6	4.1
Anchorage, AK	4.8	4.4	4.0	3.9	3.7	3.8	3.6	2.9	2.9	3.1	3.3	3.1
Ann Arbor, MI	2.7	3.1	2.5	2.5	3.0	3.4	3.3	2.9	2.7	2.7	2.5	2.5
Athens, GA	3.2	3.2	3.2	2.3	2.7	3.5	2.9	3.2	2.5	3.1	2.7	2.6
Atlanta, GA	4.0	3.8	3.9	2.9	3.1	3.7	3.4	3.5	3.1	3.4	3.2	3.0
Austin, TX	3.2	3.2	2.6	2.4	2.6	2.9	2.9	2.9	2.7	2.7	2.6	2.6
Baltimore, MD	6.3	6.1	5.8	4.9	5.1	6.1	5.6	5.9	5.1	5.6	5.0	4.4
Boise City, ID	2.8	2.7	2.5	2.0	2.0	2.4	2.2	2.3	2.3	2.4	2.3	1.8
Boston, MA	4.4	3.5	3.2	3.0	3.2	3.5	3.6	3.5	3.0	2.9	2.7	2.9
Boulder, CO	2.6	2.7	2.3	2.1	2.2	2.8	3.0	2.4	2.3	2.6	2.7	2.0
Brownsville, TX	7.9	7.4	6.1	6.0	6.1	7.1	6.9	6.4	5.9	5.5	5.7	6.1
Cape Coral, FL	3.4	2.9	2.6	2.3	2.4	2.8	2.7	2.6	2.5	4.2	3.6	2.9
Cedar Rapids, IA	4.9	3.9	3.6	2.7	2.9	3.4	3.7	3.8	3.3	3.4	3.7	3.7
Charleston, SC	3.1	3.5	2.9	2.1	2.5	2.8	2.6	2.6	2.4	2.8	2.2	2.4
Charlotte, NC	4.0	3.8	3.7	3.5	3.5	3.9	3.6	3.9	3.3	3.8	3.7	3.2
Chicago, IL	5.8	5.5	5.0	4.7	4.9	5.7	5.8	5.9	5.6	5.2	5.3	4.8
Cincinnati, OH	4.6	4.2	3.8	3.5	3.5	4.6	4.8	4.8	3.9	4.2	3.3	3.5
Clarksville, TN	4.0	3.6	3.4	3.5	3.9	4.8	4.6	4.1	3.6	4.1	3.9	3.5
Cleveland, OH	7.7	8.0	8.2	7.5	7.2	7.7	6.5	6.0	5.9	6.4	5.8	4.6
College Station, TX	3.5	3.4	2.7	2.6	2.8	3.6	3.3	3.3	3.0	3.0	3.2	2.8
Colorado Springs, CO	4.1	4.2	3.6	3.2	3.1	3.4	3.8	3.6	3.5	3.7	3.5	3.0
Columbia, MO	3.0	2.2	2.4	1.7	2.4	1.9	2.4	2.5	1.5	1.9	1.9	1.8
Columbia, SC	3.7	4.3	3.5	2.9	3.9	4.0	3.9	3.7	3.4	4.2	3.3	3.2
Columbus, OH	3.9	3.8	3.4	3.1	3.1	3.9	3.8	4.0	3.4	3.7	2.9	3.2
Dallas, TX	4.5	4.4	3.6	3.4	3.5	4.0	4.0	3.9	3.6	3.6	3.5	3.4
Davenport, IA	5.5	4.4	4.1	3.1	3.2	4.0	4.0	3.9	3.3	3.4	3.8	3.9
Denver, CO	4.3	4.3	3.9	3.4	3.3	3.4	3.6	3.6	3.5	3.7	3.4	2.9
Des Moines, IA	5.7	4.7	4.3	3.0	2.8	3.0	3.2	3.3	2.8	2.9	3.2	3.7
Durham, NC	3.2	3.0	3.0	2.9	3.1	3.5	3.1	3.3	2.7	3.4	3.2	2.7
Edison, NJ	3.3	3.0	2.9	2.5	2.5	2.8	2.7	2.6	2.0	2.1	2.1	2.1
El Paso, TX	5.1	5.0	4.1	4.0	4.2	4.7	4.5	4.4	4.1	4.1	4.1	3.8
Fargo, ND	2.7	2.5	2.7	2.1	1.8	2.2	1.7	1.8	1.4	1.5	1.6	1.9
Fort Collins, CO	3.0	3.2	2.7	2.4	2.4	2.8	2.9	2.7	2.6	2.8	2.8	2.3
Fort Wayne, IN	2.5	2.7	2.8	2.5	2.6	3.3	3.6	3.1	2.3	2.9	2.9	2.4
Fort Worth, TX	4.5	4.4	3.6	3.4	3.6	4.2	4.2	4.0	3.7	3.6	3.5	3.4
Grand Rapids, MI	5.0	5.0	4.3	4.2	4.6	5.2	5.0	4.6	4.3	4.2	4.0	4.1
Greeley, CO	4.9	5.0	4.4	3.7	3.5	3.9	4.5	3.9	3.8	3.9	3.7	3.3
Green Bay, WI	3.1	3.1	3.1	2.9	2.8	3.4	3.2	3.4	3.3	2.9	2.5	2.2
Greensboro, NC	4.6	4.5	4.4	4.3	4.3	4.8	4.6	4.8	4.0	4.5	4.4	3.8
Honolulu, HI	3.7	3.5	3.2	3.3	3.4	3.9	3.5	3.4	3.3	3.4	3.8	3.4
Houston, TX	5.3	5.2	4.3	4.1	4.2	4.7	4.8	4.6	4.2	4.1	4.0	3.8
Huntsville, AL	2.8	2.6	2.1	1.7	2.1	3.0	2.8	2.6	2.3	2.3	2.1	2.0
Indianapolis, IN	2.7	3.0	3.0	2.5	2.8	3.5	3.8	3.4	2.4	2.9	3.0	2.5
Jacksonville, FL	3.6	3.2	2.7	2.5	2.6	3.3	3.2	3.1	2.7	2.8	2.7	2.3
Kansas City, MO	4.3	4.3	4.1	3.1	3.2	2.6	3.4	3.4	2.2	2.7	2.7	2.6
Lafayette, LA	3.6	3.1	3.1	2.9	3.1	3.9	3.8	3.2	3.0	2.7	2.6	2.9
Las Cruces, NM	4.8	3.9	3.6	3.5	3.4	4.9	4.7	4.6	4.5	3.8	3.4	3.1
Las Vegas, NV	5.9	5.4	5.2	5.2	5.4	5.8	5.7	5.8	5.4	5.8	5.7	5.5
Lexington, KY	3.3	3.0	3.1	2.8	2.9	3.5	3.3	3.0	2.8	3.3	3.1	2.6
Lincoln, NE	2.3	2.1	2.2	1.8	1.9	2.4	2.3	2.1	1.9	2.1	2.1	2.2
Little Rock, AR	4.3	4.2	3.7	3.8	3.6	4.1	4.6	3.9	3.9	3.3	3.2	3.0
Los Angeles, CA	6.3	5.5	5.0	4.9	4.6	5.3	5.2	5.1	4.6	4.6	4.6	4.5
Louisville, KY	4.7	3.9	4.7	3.1	4.1	3.8	4.1	3.4	3.0	3.5	3.3	2.9
Madison, WI	1.9	2.0	2.0	1.9	2.2	2.8	2.5	2.4	2.6	2.2	2.0	1.5

Table continued on following page.

City	2022											
	Jan.	Feb.	Mar.	Apr.	May	Jun.	Jul.	Aug.	Sep.	Oct.	Nov.	Dec.
Manchester, NH	3.6	2.6	2.5	2.3	1.9	2.0	2.0	2.4	2.4	2.7	2.7	2.6
Miami, FL	3.0	2.6	2.8	2.4	2.2	2.0	2.2	2.2	1.9	1.7	1.5	1.4
Midland, TX	4.3	4.3	3.4	3.2	3.2	3.6	3.5	3.3	3.0	3.0	2.8	2.6
Milwaukee, WI	4.8	5.1	5.0	5.0	4.9	5.4	5.5	5.5	4.8	4.6	4.1	3.2
Minneapolis, MN	3.0	2.2	2.4	1.5	1.7	2.4	2.2	2.3	2.0	1.9	2.0	2.4
Nashville, TN	3.3	2.9	2.7	2.7	2.9	3.5	3.2	2.9	2.5	2.8	2.7	2.4
New Haven, CT	5.5	5.4	4.4	4.1	4.8	5.0	5.6	5.4	4.7	4.7	4.0	3.3
New Orleans, LA	6.5	6.0	5.9	5.5	5.5	6.5	6.6	5.5	4.8	4.1	4.0	4.4
New York, NY	7.8	7.2	6.3	5.7	5.4	5.5	5.4	5.2	4.5	5.0	5.0	5.0
Oklahoma City, OK	2.9	3.0	2.9	2.7	2.8	3.4	3.0	3.3	3.2	3.4	2.9	2.6
Omaha, NE	2.9	2.8	2.7	2.3	2.3	2.9	3.1	2.7	2.4	2.6	2.5	2.7
Orlando, FL	3.9	3.6	3.1	2.9	2.9	3.3	3.1	3.1	2.7	2.8	2.7	2.4
Philadelphia, PA	7.7	6.8	6.3	6.0	5.7	6.2	6.2	6.4	4.9	4.7	4.8	4.5
Phoenix, AZ	3.4	3.3	2.5	2.8	3.0	3.4	3.4	3.5	3.6	3.5	3.0	2.7
Pittsburgh, PA	4.9	4.1	4.0	3.8	3.9	4.3	4.4	4.4	3.2	3.1	3.0	3.0
Portland, OR	4.5	3.9	3.9	3.4	3.0	3.5	3.7	4.1	3.8	3.8	4.1	4.2
Providence, RI	5.5	5.3	3.7	3.3	3.5	3.5	4.0	5.0	4.3	4.1	4.3	2.9
Provo, UT	1.8	1.5	1.6	1.7	2.0	2.4	1.8	1.8	1.6	1.8	1.8	1.7
Raleigh, NC	3.3	3.3	3.2	3.1	3.3	3.6	3.4	3.5	3.0	3.5	3.4	2.8
Reno, NV	3.1	2.8	2.5	2.7	2.9	3.3	3.2	3.5	3.1	3.6	3.5	3.4
Richmond, VA	4.6	4.1	3.7	3.5	3.9	3.8	3.7	4.1	3.4	3.5	3.9	3.4
Rochester, MN	2.6	2.0	2.1	1.2	1.3	1.9	1.7	1.8	1.6	1.5	1.6	2.1
Sacramento, CA	5.7	4.9	4.3	3.7	3.3	3.8	3.8	4.1	3.8	3.9	4.2	3.7
Salem, OR	4.4	4.0	4.0	3.7	3.1	3.8	4.2	4.5	4.1	4.2	4.3	4.5
Salt Lake City, UT	2.4	2.1	2.0	2.1	2.1	2.3	2.1	2.1	1.9	2.1	2.0	2.0
San Antonio, TX	4.3	4.2	3.5	3.3	3.5	4.0	3.9	3.8	3.5	3.5	3.4	3.2
San Diego, CA	4.5	3.9	3.3	2.9	2.6	3.0	2.9	3.2	2.9	3.0	3.2	2.7
San Francisco, CA	3.5	3.0	2.5	2.2	1.9	2.2	2.1	2.3	2.1	2.2	2.3	2.0
San Jose, CA	3.5	3.1	2.6	2.3	2.0	2.4	2.3	2.5	2.2	2.3	2.5	2.1
Santa Rosa, CA	4.3	3.8	3.3	2.7	2.4	2.8	2.7	2.9	2.7	2.8	3.1	2.7
Savannah, GA	4.2	4.0	4.1	3.1	3.2	3.8	3.3	3.5	3.0	3.4	3.1	2.9
Seattle, WA	3.0	2.5	2.1	1.6	1.9	2.4	2.6	2.8	2.6	2.6	2.7	2.6
Sioux Falls, SD	2.6	2.8	2.4	2.0	1.9	2.1	1.7	2.0	1.6	1.9	1.8	2.1
Springfield, IL	5.3	5.0	4.6	4.9	5.2	4.6	4.8	4.9	4.3	4.5	4.3	3.7
St. Louis, MO	5.4	5.0	4.9	3.6	3.8	3.3	4.1	4.1	2.5	3.0	3.2	3.1
Tampa, FL	3.5	3.0	2.6	2.3	2.4	2.9	2.8	2.8	2.6	2.7	2.6	2.2
Tucson, AZ	4.0	3.9	3.1	3.4	3.6	4.2	4.2	4.3	4.3	4.2	3.6	3.2
Tulsa, OK	3.2	3.3	3.2	3.0	3.1	3.7	3.4	3.7	3.6	3.7	3.2	2.8
Tuscaloosa, AL	3.6	3.4	2.6	2.4	2.9	4.1	4.0	3.4	2.9	3.1	2.7	2.4
Virginia Beach, VA	3.2	2.7	2.6	2.4	2.9	2.9	2.8	3.0	2.5	2.7	2.9	2.6
Washington, DC	6.3	5.6	5.1	4.2	4.3	4.9	4.7	4.6	4.1	4.3	4.1	4.1
Wichita, KS	3.7	3.6	3.6	2.8	3.2	3.5	4.1	3.8	3.1	3.2	3.1	3.2
Wilmington, NC	3.4	3.4	3.2	3.3	3.5	3.9	3.5	3.7	3.1	3.6	3.6	3.1
Winston-Salem, NC	4.1	4.0	3.9	3.8	4.0	4.5	4.3	4.4	3.8	4.3	4.1	3.5
Worcester, MA	5.5	4.6	4.1	3.9	4.2	4.6	4.6	4.6	4.0	3.7	3.5	3.7
U.S.	4.4	4.1	3.8	3.3	3.4	3.8	3.8	3.8	3.3	3.4	3.4	3.3

Note: Data is not seasonally adjusted and covers workers 16 years of age and older; All figures are percentages
Source: Bureau of Labor Statistics, Local Area Unemployment Statistics

Unemployment Rate: Metro Area

Metro Area[1]	2022											
	Jan.	Feb.	Mar.	Apr.	May	Jun.	Jul.	Aug.	Sep.	Oct.	Nov.	Dec.
Albuquerque, NM	5.1	4.4	4.1	4.0	3.8	4.6	4.3	4.1	4.2	3.7	3.3	3.1
Allentown, PA	5.5	4.8	4.5	4.1	3.9	4.4	4.5	4.5	3.3	3.2	3.3	3.3
Anchorage, AK	5.3	4.9	4.5	4.3	4.0	4.2	3.9	3.2	3.2	3.3	3.6	3.5
Ann Arbor, MI	3.3	3.7	3.1	3.0	3.6	4.1	4.0	3.5	3.3	3.3	3.1	3.0
Athens, GA	2.9	2.9	2.9	2.1	2.5	3.1	2.6	2.9	2.3	2.9	2.5	2.4
Atlanta, GA	3.3	3.2	3.2	2.4	2.6	3.2	2.8	3.0	2.5	2.9	2.7	2.6
Austin, TX	3.3	3.3	2.7	2.5	2.7	3.1	3.1	3.0	2.8	2.8	2.8	2.7
Baltimore, MD	4.2	4.3	4.2	3.3	3.6	4.6	4.1	4.3	3.7	4.0	3.5	3.1
Boise City, ID	3.1	3.0	2.8	2.4	2.2	2.7	2.6	2.7	2.5	2.6	2.5	2.1
Boston, MA[4]	4.2	3.4	3.1	2.8	2.9	3.1	3.0	3.0	2.7	2.7	2.5	2.7
Boulder, CO	3.1	3.2	2.8	2.4	2.4	2.8	2.9	2.6	2.5	2.8	2.6	2.2
Brownsville, TX	7.6	7.3	6.1	5.9	6.0	6.9	6.8	6.4	5.8	5.6	5.7	5.7
Cape Coral, FL	3.4	2.9	2.5	2.2	2.4	2.9	2.8	2.7	2.6	4.0	3.6	2.9
Cedar Rapids, IA	4.9	4.0	3.7	2.6	2.6	3.0	3.2	3.4	2.9	3.0	3.3	3.5
Charleston, SC	3.2	3.6	2.9	2.3	2.8	3.0	2.7	2.8	2.7	3.1	2.2	2.5
Charlotte, NC	3.7	3.7	3.5	3.2	3.4	3.8	3.4	3.6	3.1	3.7	3.5	3.1
Chicago, IL[2]	5.2	5.0	4.4	4.3	4.5	5.3	5.1	5.2	4.6	4.5	4.4	4.2
Cincinnati, OH	3.9	3.8	3.5	3.0	3.0	3.9	3.9	3.8	3.3	3.6	3.0	3.1
Clarksville, TN	4.1	3.7	3.6	3.6	4.0	4.7	4.5	4.1	3.6	4.0	3.9	3.6
Cleveland, OH	5.6	6.0	5.6	4.8	4.9	5.3	4.9	4.5	4.1	3.9	3.6	3.4
College Station, TX	3.7	3.5	2.9	2.7	2.9	3.6	3.5	3.5	3.1	3.1	3.1	2.8
Colorado Springs, CO	4.1	4.2	3.8	3.3	3.3	3.5	3.9	3.6	3.5	3.8	3.6	3.0
Columbia, MO	3.0	2.3	2.6	1.7	2.3	1.8	2.3	2.4	1.4	1.9	1.8	1.7
Columbia, SC	3.5	3.8	3.1	2.5	3.0	3.3	3.1	3.1	2.9	3.4	2.6	2.8
Columbus, OH	3.8	3.7	3.3	2.9	2.9	3.8	3.7	3.8	3.3	3.5	2.7	3.1
Dallas, TX[2]	4.1	4.0	3.3	3.1	3.3	3.8	3.7	3.6	3.4	3.3	3.2	3.1
Davenport, IA	5.3	4.6	4.4	3.7	3.8	3.7	3.8	3.8	3.4	3.5	3.7	3.7
Denver, CO	4.0	4.0	3.6	3.2	3.1	3.3	3.5	3.3	3.2	3.5	3.3	2.8
Des Moines, IA	4.2	3.4	3.2	2.1	2.2	2.5	2.6	2.7	2.3	2.5	2.8	2.8
Durham, NC	3.0	2.9	2.8	2.8	3.0	3.4	3.1	3.2	2.7	3.3	3.2	2.6
Edison, NJ[2]	6.1	5.6	5.1	4.7	4.6	4.9	5.3	5.4	4.1	4.1	4.2	4.2
El Paso, TX	5.4	5.3	4.3	4.2	4.3	4.9	4.8	4.6	4.4	4.3	4.2	4.0
Fargo, ND	2.8	2.4	2.7	1.9	1.6	2.1	1.7	1.7	1.4	1.4	1.5	1.9
Fort Collins, CO	3.4	3.5	3.1	2.7	2.6	2.9	3.0	2.8	2.7	2.9	2.8	2.4
Fort Wayne, IN	2.2	2.4	2.6	2.2	2.3	3.0	3.2	2.8	2.0	2.7	2.6	2.2
Fort Worth, TX[2]	4.2	4.2	3.4	3.2	3.4	3.9	3.9	3.8	3.5	3.4	3.4	3.2
Grand Rapids, MI	3.7	3.8	3.3	3.1	3.4	3.9	3.8	3.4	3.2	3.1	3.0	3.1
Greeley, CO	4.2	4.3	3.9	3.4	3.3	3.6	3.8	3.6	3.4	3.7	3.5	3.0
Green Bay, WI	2.8	3.0	3.0	2.7	2.6	3.2	3.0	3.0	2.9	2.6	2.4	2.1
Greensboro, NC	4.2	4.1	4.0	3.8	4.0	4.5	4.2	4.4	3.7	4.3	4.1	3.6
Honolulu, HI	3.7	3.5	3.2	3.3	3.4	3.9	3.5	3.4	3.3	3.4	3.8	3.4
Houston, TX	5.5	5.3	4.4	4.1	4.3	4.8	4.8	4.6	4.2	4.1	4.0	3.9
Huntsville, AL	2.6	2.4	1.9	1.6	1.9	2.7	2.6	2.3	2.1	2.2	2.0	1.8
Indianapolis, IN	2.2	2.5	2.5	2.0	2.4	3.0	3.3	2.8	2.1	2.6	2.6	2.2
Jacksonville, FL	3.2	2.9	2.5	2.2	2.3	2.9	2.8	2.8	2.5	2.5	2.5	2.1
Kansas City, MO	3.4	3.7	3.3	2.4	2.7	2.6	3.2	3.1	2.2	2.6	2.5	2.4
Lafayette, LA	3.8	3.4	3.4	3.1	3.2	4.1	4.0	3.3	3.2	2.8	2.7	3.1
Las Cruces, NM	5.7	5.1	4.8	4.8	4.4	5.3	5.0	4.6	4.8	4.2	4.0	3.7
Las Vegas, NV	5.8	5.3	5.0	5.0	5.2	5.7	5.6	5.7	5.3	5.6	5.6	5.4
Lexington, KY	3.4	3.1	3.1	2.8	2.9	3.5	3.3	3.0	2.8	3.3	3.1	2.6
Lincoln, NE	2.3	2.1	2.1	1.8	1.9	2.4	2.3	2.1	1.9	2.0	2.1	2.1
Little Rock, AR	3.8	3.8	3.3	3.2	3.2	3.7	4.0	3.5	3.5	2.8	2.9	2.8
Los Angeles, CA[2]	6.5	5.8	5.2	4.8	4.5	4.9	4.9	4.7	4.3	4.5	4.5	4.4
Louisville, KY	4.1	3.5	4.3	2.8	3.7	3.5	3.8	3.1	2.7	3.3	3.1	2.7
Madison, WI	2.3	2.5	2.4	2.1	2.2	2.8	2.5	2.5	2.6	2.2	2.0	1.6

Table continued on following page.

Metro Area[1]	2022											
	Jan.	Feb.	Mar.	Apr.	May	Jun.	Jul.	Aug.	Sep.	Oct.	Nov.	Dec.
Manchester, NH[3]	3.3	2.3	2.3	2.1	1.8	1.9	1.9	2.2	2.3	2.5	2.4	2.3
Miami, FL[2]	3.2	2.9	3.0	2.6	2.5	2.6	2.8	2.9	2.6	2.4	2.1	2.0
Midland, TX	4.4	4.3	3.5	3.2	3.3	3.6	3.5	3.3	3.0	2.9	2.8	2.6
Milwaukee, WI	3.4	3.7	3.6	3.5	3.4	4.0	4.0	3.9	3.6	3.3	3.0	2.4
Minneapolis, MN	3.0	2.4	2.6	1.5	1.6	2.2	2.0	2.2	1.9	1.7	1.9	2.6
Nashville, TN	2.9	2.7	2.4	2.5	2.8	3.4	3.1	2.7	2.4	2.7	2.6	2.3
New Haven, CT[3]	4.6	4.6	3.9	3.5	3.8	3.9	4.2	4.1	3.7	3.7	3.3	2.9
New Orleans, LA	4.9	4.5	4.4	4.1	4.1	5.1	5.0	4.1	3.8	3.3	3.1	3.5
New York, NY[2]	6.1	5.6	5.1	4.7	4.6	4.9	5.3	5.4	4.1	4.1	4.2	4.2
Oklahoma City, OK	2.8	2.9	2.7	2.6	2.7	3.2	2.9	3.1	3.1	3.3	2.8	2.4
Omaha, NE	2.9	2.7	2.6	2.1	2.1	2.7	2.7	2.5	2.2	2.4	2.4	2.5
Orlando, FL	3.8	3.4	2.9	2.6	2.7	3.2	3.0	2.9	2.7	2.8	2.7	2.3
Philadelphia, PA[2]	7.0	6.2	5.7	5.5	5.2	5.7	5.7	5.9	4.5	4.3	4.4	4.2
Phoenix, AZ	3.2	3.1	2.4	2.7	2.9	3.4	3.3	3.4	3.5	3.5	3.0	2.7
Pittsburgh, PA	5.8	5.1	4.6	4.2	4.0	4.6	4.7	4.8	3.4	3.3	3.5	3.7
Portland, OR	4.4	3.9	3.9	3.4	3.1	3.5	3.6	4.0	3.7	3.7	3.9	4.1
Providence, RI[3]	4.9	4.7	3.4	3.0	2.9	3.0	3.3	4.0	3.4	3.3	3.4	2.7
Provo, UT	2.0	1.8	1.8	1.8	2.0	2.3	1.8	1.9	1.7	1.9	1.9	1.9
Raleigh, NC	3.1	3.0	2.9	2.9	3.1	3.4	3.1	3.3	2.8	3.3	3.2	2.7
Reno, NV	3.2	2.8	2.6	2.7	2.9	3.3	3.2	3.5	3.1	3.5	3.5	3.4
Richmond, VA	3.7	3.2	2.9	2.8	3.2	3.2	3.1	3.4	2.8	3.0	3.2	2.9
Rochester, MN	3.0	2.3	2.4	1.3	1.3	1.9	1.7	1.8	1.5	1.4	1.6	2.5
Sacramento, CA	5.0	4.4	3.7	3.3	2.9	3.4	3.3	3.6	3.3	3.4	3.7	3.3
Salem, OR	4.5	3.9	3.9	3.6	3.1	3.7	4.0	4.4	4.0	4.2	4.3	4.5
Salt Lake City, UT	2.4	2.2	2.1	2.1	2.2	2.4	2.1	2.1	1.9	2.1	2.0	2.0
San Antonio, TX	4.3	4.2	3.5	3.3	3.5	4.0	4.0	3.8	3.5	3.5	3.4	3.3
San Diego, CA	4.7	4.0	3.4	3.0	2.7	3.2	3.1	3.4	3.1	3.2	3.3	2.9
San Francisco, CA[2]	3.3	2.9	2.4	2.1	1.8	2.1	2.1	2.3	2.1	2.1	2.3	2.0
San Jose, CA	3.4	3.0	2.5	2.2	1.9	2.3	2.2	2.4	2.2	2.2	2.4	2.1
Santa Rosa, CA	4.0	3.5	3.0	2.6	2.3	2.7	2.6	2.8	2.6	2.6	2.9	2.5
Savannah, GA	3.3	3.2	3.2	2.4	2.6	3.1	2.7	2.9	2.5	2.9	2.6	2.5
Seattle, WA[2]	3.3	2.8	2.6	2.3	2.6	3.0	3.3	3.3	3.3	3.4	2.9	3.0
Sioux Falls, SD	2.5	2.7	2.3	1.9	1.9	2.1	1.7	2.0	1.5	1.8	1.7	2.0
Springfield, IL	5.1	4.8	4.5	4.6	4.7	4.2	4.3	4.3	3.8	3.9	3.9	3.6
St. Louis, MO	4.3	3.7	3.7	2.9	3.2	2.8	3.2	3.3	2.3	2.7	2.7	2.5
Tampa, FL	3.3	2.9	2.5	2.3	2.4	2.9	2.7	2.7	2.5	2.6	2.6	2.2
Tucson, AZ	3.6	3.6	2.8	3.1	3.3	3.9	3.9	4.0	4.1	4.0	3.4	3.1
Tulsa, OK	3.1	3.3	3.1	2.9	3.0	3.6	3.3	3.4	3.4	3.5	3.0	2.7
Tuscaloosa, AL	3.5	3.2	2.5	2.1	2.5	3.6	3.4	3.0	2.6	2.7	2.4	2.2
Virginia Beach, VA	3.9	3.4	3.1	3.0	3.4	3.4	3.3	3.6	3.0	3.2	3.4	3.0
Washington, DC[2]	4.0	3.6	3.5	3.0	3.3	3.6	3.4	3.6	3.0	3.2	3.1	2.9
Wichita, KS	3.4	3.3	3.3	2.6	3.0	3.2	3.8	3.5	2.9	3.0	2.9	2.9
Wilmington, NC	3.3	3.2	3.1	3.0	3.3	3.7	3.3	3.5	3.0	3.6	3.4	2.9
Winston-Salem, NC	3.6	3.5	3.4	3.3	3.6	4.0	3.6	3.8	3.3	3.8	3.7	3.1
Worcester, MA[3]	5.0	4.4	3.9	3.4	3.5	3.7	3.7	3.8	3.3	3.3	3.4	3.3
U.S.	4.4	4.1	3.8	3.3	3.4	3.8	3.8	3.8	3.3	3.4	3.4	3.3

Note: Data is not seasonally adjusted and covers workers 16 years of age and older; All figures are percentages; (1) Figures cover the Metropolitan Statistical Area (MSA) except where noted. See Appendix B for areas included; (2) Metropolitan Division; (3) New England City and Town Area; (4) New England City and Town Area Division
Source: Bureau of Labor Statistics, Local Area Unemployment Statistics

Average Hourly Wages: Occupations A – C

Metro Area[1]	Accountants/ Auditors	Automotive Mechanics	Book-keepers	Carpenters	Cashiers	Computer Program-mers	Computer Systems Analysts
Albuquerque, NM	35.62	21.48	20.91	23.25	13.53	39.45	44.30
Allentown, PA	38.74	23.90	21.73	26.50	12.78	48.46	45.52
Anchorage, AK	38.08	28.88	25.34	35.06	16.27	47.28	47.93
Ann Arbor, MI	41.17	24.91	22.53	27.04	13.30	46.31	50.46
Athens, GA	35.00	22.03	20.51	23.47	11.77	29.81	35.56
Atlanta, GA	42.89	23.34	23.13	24.77	12.29	47.05	50.28
Austin, TX	41.33	25.45	22.37	24.23	13.85	46.80	48.67
Baltimore, MD	42.20	24.80	24.11	26.91	14.41	50.01	51.61
Boise City, ID	34.92	22.86	21.24	21.41	13.64	37.89	44.85
Boston, MA[2]	46.85	25.85	27.28	34.31	16.21	55.26	57.55
Boulder, CO	46.88	27.50	24.94	27.55	16.30	71.67	61.71
Brownsville, TX	31.30	20.87	17.66	18.88	11.54	n/a	40.71
Cape Coral, FL	37.19	23.44	21.35	21.78	12.98	43.01	46.18
Cedar Rapids, IA	36.04	23.48	22.67	24.39	13.19	42.82	43.29
Charleston, SC	38.80	22.64	20.63	23.50	12.44	n/a	51.58
Charlotte, NC	45.21	24.42	22.12	22.36	12.80	54.86	52.23
Chicago, IL	42.15	25.15	25.13	35.45	14.91	43.54	49.11
Cincinnati, OH	38.18	21.73	22.50	26.23	12.78	44.15	50.79
Clarksville, TN	32.20	21.35	19.54	21.38	11.96	n/a	39.23
Cleveland, OH	39.26	22.70	22.17	27.47	12.94	40.92	48.16
College Station, TX	36.77	21.75	19.34	20.12	12.47	36.69	39.40
Colorado Springs, CO	36.34	25.04	21.56	25.51	14.94	56.28	53.00
Columbia, MO	32.30	21.77	20.39	25.95	12.91	37.12	38.74
Columbia, SC	31.51	22.42	19.63	22.23	11.56	46.56	41.41
Columbus, OH	38.54	23.63	22.84	26.80	12.98	44.12	48.82
Dallas, TX	43.06	24.09	22.81	23.70	13.14	46.27	54.07
Davenport, IA	34.44	23.03	21.58	25.54	13.39	41.58	42.03
Denver, CO	43.21	26.75	24.91	26.47	16.03	59.06	58.10
Des Moines, IA	36.71	23.68	23.50	25.01	13.40	44.45	45.98
Durham, NC	42.03	24.33	23.51	22.09	12.86	51.67	48.44
Edison, NJ	54.94	26.81	26.44	37.06	16.55	57.97	60.54
El Paso, TX	33.19	19.58	18.00	18.84	11.04	32.89	38.82
Fargo, ND	33.62	23.74	21.80	24.78	14.30	43.53	46.07
Fort Collins, CO	40.07	25.91	23.02	25.81	15.48	47.61	50.60
Fort Wayne, IN	35.91	21.07	20.51	24.46	12.43	41.88	40.51
Fort Worth, TX	43.06	24.09	22.81	23.70	13.14	46.27	54.07
Grand Rapids, MI	36.05	23.88	21.43	25.03	13.24	43.23	45.05
Greeley, CO	40.39	26.16	22.81	25.71	14.89	42.19	47.48
Green Bay, WI	35.84	24.15	21.27	27.33	13.29	48.63	44.13
Greensboro, NC	39.53	23.26	20.74	21.12	11.95	47.79	44.56
Honolulu, HI	35.01	25.53	23.01	40.03	15.19	40.35	44.09
Houston, TX	45.35	24.26	22.16	23.53	12.84	44.09	53.59
Huntsville, AL	38.65	23.32	19.18	21.60	12.06	48.90	59.97
Indianapolis, IN	38.48	24.17	21.02	26.70	12.72	55.30	46.41
Jacksonville, FL	37.78	21.66	22.39	21.96	12.81	45.61	47.46
Kansas City, MO	37.26	22.90	22.32	28.49	13.42	32.32	43.98
Lafayette, LA	33.20	21.50	19.60	21.95	10.71	46.32	40.06
Las Cruces, NM	31.08	19.52	19.12	19.82	12.79	32.88	40.51
Las Vegas, NV	32.32	23.93	22.52	31.29	12.95	46.77	45.39
Lexington, KY	34.78	19.88	21.74	24.79	12.65	41.29	41.63
Lincoln, NE	33.19	25.66	21.09	22.21	12.89	42.91	38.01
Little Rock, AR	34.54	21.76	20.43	20.73	12.61	39.86	36.35
Los Angeles, CA	44.41	27.03	25.38	32.48	16.40	52.39	56.78
Louisville, KY	37.30	20.62	21.86	24.50	12.91	39.53	43.77
Madison, WI	37.27	24.24	22.60	27.63	14.13	56.02	44.74

Table continued on following page.

Metro Area[1]	Accountants/ Auditors	Automotive Mechanics	Book- keepers	Carpenters	Cashiers	Computer Program- mers	Computer Systems Analysts
Manchester, NH[2]	38.41	25.34	23.03	25.30	13.47	37.37	55.74
Miami, FL	40.21	23.98	22.09	23.23	13.04	57.52	49.49
Midland, TX	45.27	22.73	23.16	24.74	13.53	46.24	60.82
Milwaukee, WI	38.84	25.28	22.52	27.42	13.47	48.26	47.82
Minneapolis, MN	41.61	26.35	24.93	31.05	14.83	56.92	51.73
Nashville, TN	37.26	23.62	22.19	23.17	13.16	55.27	45.76
New Haven, CT[2]	40.18	25.11	25.93	29.63	14.82	46.28	50.48
New Orleans, LA	35.71	22.89	21.05	23.83	11.45	n/a	42.24
New York, NY	54.94	26.81	26.44	37.06	16.55	57.97	60.54
Oklahoma City, OK	37.21	22.78	20.87	21.48	12.66	43.42	43.52
Omaha, NE	36.79	24.01	22.22	22.88	13.40	45.89	44.58
Orlando, FL	39.04	22.82	21.76	22.25	13.41	44.68	49.23
Philadelphia, PA	41.83	25.23	23.94	30.34	13.39	48.86	51.32
Phoenix, AZ	40.79	24.61	23.11	24.95	14.93	42.27	50.03
Pittsburgh, PA	36.77	22.54	21.77	27.30	12.18	44.53	44.54
Portland, OR	40.08	26.62	24.24	30.98	16.34	54.65	56.22
Providence, RI[2]	44.90	22.35	24.22	29.76	14.61	43.32	51.67
Provo, UT	36.53	24.47	21.59	22.45	13.70	50.42	42.69
Raleigh, NC	40.68	23.79	21.92	22.09	12.55	51.36	48.99
Reno, NV	36.36	26.22	23.68	30.24	13.43	47.35	51.99
Richmond, VA	39.80	24.06	22.01	22.95	13.04	46.05	49.01
Rochester, MN	39.00	23.13	22.86	28.86	14.39	43.06	50.23
Sacramento, CA	41.27	28.35	25.70	32.41	16.67	54.48	52.53
Salem, OR	37.81	26.17	23.29	27.37	15.07	43.99	48.05
Salt Lake City, UT	38.26	24.06	23.32	24.89	13.79	48.36	47.68
San Antonio, TX	40.79	22.70	21.14	21.56	13.19	42.04	48.72
San Diego, CA	43.86	27.06	25.51	32.52	16.54	61.76	55.08
San Francisco, CA	54.83	31.95	30.30	38.33	18.96	64.89	70.44
San Jose, CA	55.92	37.42	29.94	37.76	19.15	70.63	79.75
Santa Rosa, CA	44.48	28.50	27.43	37.66	17.71	51.79	53.46
Savannah, GA	37.20	21.80	21.94	22.17	12.01	40.03	51.98
Seattle, WA	45.25	28.69	26.09	35.16	17.95	64.30	62.53
Sioux Falls, SD	36.65	24.92	19.54	20.96	13.46	31.23	41.70
Springfield, IL	37.41	23.85	22.33	28.27	13.91	43.32	48.50
St. Louis, MO	37.46	23.04	23.29	29.99	13.92	39.08	49.69
Tampa, FL	39.60	22.77	21.91	22.26	12.70	42.78	47.41
Tucson, AZ	34.99	23.11	21.61	21.37	14.27	39.03	51.23
Tulsa, OK	39.68	22.38	20.66	21.83	12.73	44.62	44.82
Tuscaloosa, AL	35.59	21.58	19.16	21.27	11.34	40.66	45.86
Virginia Beach, VA	36.48	23.14	20.67	23.04	12.50	45.16	49.26
Washington, DC	48.98	27.98	26.17	28.25	15.21	59.90	58.64
Wichita, KS	36.01	21.40	19.47	23.61	12.22	33.61	40.07
Wilmington, NC	37.58	21.31	19.94	21.32	11.98	51.25	42.16
Winston-Salem, NC	38.18	21.78	20.62	20.32	11.93	48.29	46.37
Worcester, MA[2]	42.78	26.08	24.24	29.55	15.32	49.03	50.87

Notes: (1) Figures cover the Metropolitan Statistical Area (MSA) except where noted. See Appendix B for areas included;
(2) New England City and Town Area; n/a not available
Source: Bureau of Labor Statistics, May 2022 Metro Area Occupational Employment and Wage Estimates

Average Hourly Wages: Occupations C – E

Metro Area	Comp. User Support Specialists	Construction Laborers	Cooks, Restaurant	Customer Service Reps.	Dentists	Electricians	Engineers, Electrical
Albuquerque, NM	25.04	17.98	15.25	17.46	92.90	27.76	63.45
Allentown, PA	29.17	23.73	15.53	19.08	76.30	35.65	52.01
Anchorage, AK	31.03	26.21	18.32	20.61	86.58	38.38	51.77
Ann Arbor, MI	26.14	23.76	16.10	19.39	76.15	34.45	48.28
Athens, GA	23.39	17.59	14.12	16.00	83.95	25.40	51.99
Atlanta, GA	30.05	19.06	14.12	19.35	n/a	27.76	56.29
Austin, TX	28.69	19.04	15.59	19.39	85.63	27.12	62.22
Baltimore, MD	28.42	20.10	16.72	20.48	78.23	31.44	56.06
Boise City, ID	26.11	19.73	15.37	18.74	71.88	26.06	55.65
Boston, MA[2]	35.38	31.95	19.78	24.00	89.08	39.81	61.23
Boulder, CO	37.04	20.81	18.99	21.92	77.69	28.91	61.37
Brownsville, TX	21.36	14.98	12.36	16.29	n/a	21.42	44.90
Cape Coral, FL	27.26	18.06	16.07	18.46	77.81	23.54	48.44
Cedar Rapids, IA	27.05	22.70	14.19	20.25	95.40	28.53	47.69
Charleston, SC	26.98	18.51	15.93	18.41	87.52	25.86	46.55
Charlotte, NC	30.39	18.19	15.26	19.72	98.68	25.03	49.35
Chicago, IL	29.52	32.85	17.06	21.26	67.54	42.79	50.03
Cincinnati, OH	25.81	24.39	15.01	19.74	86.77	28.47	48.44
Clarksville, TN	22.21	17.54	13.67	17.08	n/a	25.15	45.92
Cleveland, OH	26.60	26.17	15.16	20.42	78.04	29.88	46.94
College Station, TX	22.57	17.19	13.51	16.40	n/a	25.15	44.21
Colorado Springs, CO	31.65	20.22	17.67	19.52	88.61	27.65	54.86
Columbia, MO	26.05	25.63	14.43	17.49	80.29	27.19	40.87
Columbia, SC	26.44	18.07	14.25	17.29	76.98	25.73	41.58
Columbus, OH	26.03	26.04	15.34	20.25	69.07	29.48	53.22
Dallas, TX	28.45	18.68	15.57	19.64	76.46	26.46	50.66
Davenport, IA	27.11	23.89	14.54	19.17	75.24	30.25	46.40
Denver, CO	33.31	20.88	18.61	21.35	73.17	29.06	53.05
Des Moines, IA	27.24	22.43	14.73	21.45	80.98	30.12	48.91
Durham, NC	31.57	18.55	15.87	19.93	106.19	27.22	56.69
Edison, NJ	35.55	30.93	19.55	23.75	89.01	41.22	53.37
El Paso, TX	20.96	15.44	12.46	15.69	78.62	21.95	40.61
Fargo, ND	27.94	22.00	15.80	19.82	80.70	29.07	47.71
Fort Collins, CO	30.99	20.70	17.57	19.06	n/a	28.15	54.42
Fort Wayne, IN	25.05	22.43	14.31	19.63	81.34	29.66	48.26
Fort Worth, TX	28.45	18.68	15.57	19.64	76.46	26.46	50.66
Grand Rapids, MI	27.43	21.17	15.94	19.17	88.95	27.51	43.36
Greeley, CO	33.01	20.70	17.40	18.44	65.47	27.92	50.58
Green Bay, WI	29.31	22.68	15.04	20.32	81.73	30.20	43.80
Greensboro, NC	25.86	17.39	14.20	18.33	85.11	24.46	46.74
Honolulu, HI	29.83	32.93	19.44	20.16	n/a	43.15	50.24
Houston, TX	27.70	18.56	14.67	18.59	74.27	27.69	55.91
Huntsville, AL	24.38	16.49	14.48	17.51	87.97	25.26	53.71
Indianapolis, IN	25.93	23.51	14.76	20.25	98.07	31.79	46.72
Jacksonville, FL	27.33	18.20	15.75	19.12	82.64	24.62	48.04
Kansas City, MO	28.08	22.55	15.09	19.33	85.61	32.19	49.54
Lafayette, LA	26.07	17.53	12.87	16.84	63.45	25.23	43.20
Las Cruces, NM	22.91	17.03	14.13	15.26	76.28	25.44	44.62
Las Vegas, NV	25.53	21.97	17.17	18.68	n/a	33.87	42.86
Lexington, KY	25.84	20.07	14.54	17.87	n/a	25.25	44.15
Lincoln, NE	25.23	19.61	15.58	17.91	73.53	25.71	47.33
Little Rock, AR	22.91	17.13	14.00	18.06	85.98	21.91	46.55
Los Angeles, CA	33.66	25.96	18.92	22.21	n/a	37.09	65.13
Louisville, KY	26.08	21.24	14.55	19.09	87.22	28.92	45.08
Madison, WI	29.94	23.76	16.05	20.72	83.83	34.25	46.88

Table continued on following page.

Metro Area	Comp. User Support Specialists	Construction Laborers	Cooks, Restaurant	Customer Service Reps.	Dentists	Electricians	Engineers, Electrical
Manchester, NH[2]	30.81	20.40	17.24	20.95	139.57	28.40	53.87
Miami, FL	27.62	18.58	16.91	19.16	80.27	25.35	47.59
Midland, TX	29.09	19.01	15.29	19.91	n/a	29.47	42.56
Milwaukee, WI	27.77	24.14	15.78	21.30	86.72	36.15	46.03
Minneapolis, MN	30.92	27.61	17.93	22.61	93.89	37.09	50.35
Nashville, TN	25.45	19.33	15.20	18.93	89.30	28.19	47.79
New Haven, CT[2]	31.79	25.19	17.29	21.99	95.87	33.24	50.00
New Orleans, LA	25.14	18.62	13.82	17.57	88.12	27.99	51.29
New York, NY	35.55	30.93	19.55	23.75	89.01	41.22	53.37
Oklahoma City, OK	26.61	19.08	14.94	18.11	84.37	27.58	47.89
Omaha, NE	26.48	20.49	15.05	18.92	78.54	27.41	47.76
Orlando, FL	26.77	17.79	17.07	18.69	91.27	24.05	50.65
Philadelphia, PA	31.04	26.48	16.51	21.24	93.37	38.35	53.63
Phoenix, AZ	29.29	21.22	18.08	19.49	87.37	25.61	49.97
Pittsburgh, PA	29.16	24.33	14.67	19.68	68.86	34.15	49.62
Portland, OR	30.08	25.00	18.56	21.22	91.21	41.15	51.53
Providence, RI[2]	29.79	26.46	17.00	21.03	97.31	30.94	54.51
Provo, UT	28.02	21.54	15.72	18.34	65.12	26.76	56.26
Raleigh, NC	31.64	18.40	15.45	19.52	107.63	24.71	52.39
Reno, NV	26.75	25.44	17.06	19.43	56.35	32.25	48.35
Richmond, VA	28.49	17.43	15.43	18.72	79.72	27.27	50.41
Rochester, MN	31.25	25.20	16.86	20.61	83.58	33.41	51.22
Sacramento, CA	44.86	26.69	18.68	22.15	81.12	35.93	59.48
Salem, OR	29.88	23.00	17.44	19.55	94.78	37.27	52.49
Salt Lake City, UT	30.53	20.17	16.82	20.02	64.38	28.08	58.74
San Antonio, TX	26.07	18.15	14.44	18.47	90.08	25.79	50.10
San Diego, CA	31.80	26.98	18.75	22.23	70.37	33.63	61.94
San Francisco, CA	40.10	31.48	20.39	25.95	98.09	46.31	77.67
San Jose, CA	39.13	30.35	21.53	26.29	103.12	47.71	n/a
Santa Rosa, CA	34.14	28.67	19.90	23.15	79.52	36.36	60.81
Savannah, GA	26.01	17.96	15.06	16.30	n/a	25.68	56.50
Seattle, WA	36.00	28.67	21.69	24.71	84.44	44.45	60.98
Sioux Falls, SD	21.59	18.01	15.46	18.54	69.39	26.54	46.30
Springfield, IL	26.48	30.22	16.03	19.00	72.48	35.32	47.34
St. Louis, MO	30.84	27.50	15.55	20.00	n/a	33.40	50.08
Tampa, FL	29.20	18.14	15.73	18.73	77.98	24.40	49.32
Tucson, AZ	27.18	19.78	16.51	17.76	87.60	24.71	56.86
Tulsa, OK	26.87	19.26	14.72	18.17	83.90	27.67	48.62
Tuscaloosa, AL	29.58	15.23	14.27	17.16	93.58	25.75	55.16
Virginia Beach, VA	26.21	17.52	14.70	17.30	78.65	27.29	47.22
Washington, DC	33.96	21.29	18.00	22.02	85.40	34.04	59.45
Wichita, KS	27.25	18.13	13.72	17.53	76.11	28.57	43.15
Wilmington, NC	25.96	18.29	14.56	18.04	76.66	23.28	48.09
Winston-Salem, NC	26.98	17.33	14.50	18.08	91.37	23.79	49.50
Worcester, MA[2]	31.83	28.53	18.32	21.98	n/a	37.55	57.13

Notes: (1) Figures cover the Metropolitan Statistical Area (MSA) except where noted. See Appendix B for areas included;
(2) New England City and Town Area; n/a not available
Source: Bureau of Labor Statistics, May 2022 Metro Area Occupational Employment and Wage Estimates

Average Hourly Wages: Occupations F – J

Metro Area	Fast Food and Counter Workers	Financial Managers	First-Line Supervisors/ of Office Workers	General and Operations Managers	Hair-dressers/ Cosme-tologists	Home Health and Personal Care Aides	Janitors/ Cleaners
Albuquerque, NM	12.75	59.44	27.81	58.98	13.60	13.30	14.36
Allentown, PA	12.66	74.84	31.48	58.15	16.54	13.96	16.71
Anchorage, AK	14.73	72.72	32.44	54.98	15.13	17.28	16.95
Ann Arbor, MI	13.66	71.39	31.10	62.22	19.87	14.08	17.50
Athens, GA	11.00	67.23	27.18	47.82	17.24	12.56	14.99
Atlanta, GA	11.65	83.96	31.25	59.75	18.59	12.95	15.06
Austin, TX	12.48	81.29	32.79	56.28	16.04	12.07	14.63
Baltimore, MD	14.31	76.62	32.11	55.22	19.90	15.32	16.24
Boise City, ID	11.97	56.23	27.15	38.95	15.45	13.80	14.80
Boston, MA[2]	16.22	88.25	36.88	74.45	23.51	17.13	19.76
Boulder, CO	16.24	90.26	34.38	77.36	23.64	17.40	18.80
Brownsville, TX	10.12	59.69	25.20	41.63	12.81	10.33	12.36
Cape Coral, FL	12.56	69.72	30.29	51.54	18.15	15.99	14.30
Cedar Rapids, IA	12.59	60.69	29.72	45.54	15.24	16.20	15.98
Charleston, SC	11.69	65.85	29.33	52.71	16.62	13.41	13.93
Charlotte, NC	12.43	84.45	30.59	64.62	18.90	12.92	14.10
Chicago, IL	14.28	78.05	33.78	63.64	21.49	15.66	17.40
Cincinnati, OH	12.33	74.98	31.83	54.62	19.64	13.84	15.79
Clarksville, TN	11.02	59.25	27.42	46.82	16.59	12.82	13.88
Cleveland, OH	12.12	74.24	31.50	57.05	17.94	13.45	16.17
College Station, TX	10.89	65.41	26.24	47.87	13.68	11.46	13.57
Colorado Springs, CO	14.73	83.92	31.26	65.50	23.17	16.66	16.75
Columbia, MO	12.77	n/a	27.71	47.42	18.61	13.29	15.66
Columbia, SC	10.98	59.98	30.75	48.46	15.32	12.35	13.42
Columbus, OH	12.65	71.54	32.35	57.91	20.68	13.75	16.00
Dallas, TX	12.14	79.36	31.46	56.66	16.24	11.66	14.42
Davenport, IA	12.80	60.84	29.38	47.04	16.42	14.44	16.52
Denver, CO	15.81	94.94	34.80	75.18	21.59	16.85	17.70
Des Moines, IA	13.07	72.01	31.64	49.19	16.70	15.41	15.75
Durham, NC	13.08	84.49	31.92	70.01	22.31	13.24	16.43
Edison, NJ	16.08	110.67	38.32	83.82	20.85	17.10	20.14
El Paso, TX	10.10	62.87	24.90	40.58	13.11	9.83	12.05
Fargo, ND	13.47	68.39	30.87	48.98	16.61	16.62	16.77
Fort Collins, CO	14.91	86.90	31.88	63.72	26.75	16.84	17.15
Fort Wayne, IN	11.84	56.74	29.78	57.29	15.67	13.51	15.11
Fort Worth, TX	12.14	79.36	31.46	56.66	16.24	11.66	14.42
Grand Rapids, MI	13.09	65.10	29.78	55.04	18.45	14.38	15.34
Greeley, CO	14.57	83.73	32.68	64.82	19.24	16.62	17.37
Green Bay, WI	11.72	67.97	32.04	64.87	16.41	14.33	15.45
Greensboro, NC	11.81	73.43	28.58	57.79	18.33	12.20	13.36
Honolulu, HI	13.92	65.00	29.47	57.59	15.94	15.75	16.29
Houston, TX	11.74	84.66	31.01	56.99	13.81	11.18	13.63
Huntsville, AL	11.05	69.15	28.19	67.02	18.45	12.03	13.17
Indianapolis, IN	12.43	70.85	32.23	62.85	15.39	14.07	15.71
Jacksonville, FL	12.07	73.04	31.15	55.91	16.72	13.54	14.39
Kansas City, MO	13.01	74.13	31.26	52.71	19.13	13.99	16.10
Lafayette, LA	10.23	58.26	26.05	58.46	12.89	9.92	12.05
Las Cruces, NM	12.21	46.68	25.64	50.87	13.04	12.29	13.56
Las Vegas, NV	12.19	58.11	29.10	60.12	13.20	15.34	15.69
Lexington, KY	11.82	65.06	29.85	45.50	13.22	14.88	14.75
Lincoln, NE	12.48	61.87	26.83	47.07	17.83	14.17	14.69
Little Rock, AR	12.41	56.25	26.41	41.68	13.73	12.92	13.43
Los Angeles, CA	16.43	87.66	34.56	67.77	22.18	15.68	18.46
Louisville, KY	11.98	70.09	32.22	48.89	14.19	15.29	14.97

Table continued on following page.

Metro Area	Fast Food and Counter Workers	Financial Managers	First-Line Supervisors/ of Office Workers	General and Operations Managers	Hair-dressers/ Cosme-tologists	Home Health and Personal Care Aides	Janitors/ Cleaners
Madison, WI	12.42	72.88	33.73	65.92	17.32	14.89	16.04
Manchester, NH[2]	13.09	72.83	33.58	67.22	16.38	15.63	17.06
Miami, FL	12.93	81.34	31.90	56.01	15.37	13.24	14.03
Midland, TX	12.27	94.45	32.60	59.45	14.46	12.12	14.35
Milwaukee, WI	12.08	74.52	33.87	68.48	18.97	13.83	15.71
Minneapolis, MN	14.79	76.74	34.96	56.37	20.87	15.64	17.94
Nashville, TN	12.17	72.46	32.48	67.20	19.75	13.96	15.14
New Haven, CT[2]	14.76	71.48	34.08	70.00	18.17	16.48	18.12
New Orleans, LA	12.70	67.00	26.71	61.48	14.26	11.09	12.91
New York, NY	16.08	110.67	38.32	83.82	20.85	17.10	20.14
Oklahoma City, OK	11.19	64.38	30.11	48.66	17.09	12.14	13.56
Omaha, NE	12.76	65.55	28.58	47.42	21.04	14.54	15.19
Orlando, FL	12.49	77.76	30.12	55.62	17.02	13.54	13.87
Philadelphia, PA	13.26	78.78	33.31	68.82	17.70	14.31	17.24
Phoenix, AZ	15.53	76.99	30.64	54.46	20.15	15.17	15.82
Pittsburgh, PA	11.65	73.72	29.71	55.74	16.69	13.88	16.22
Portland, OR	15.88	75.43	32.27	56.83	18.86	17.48	18.11
Providence, RI[2]	14.82	81.58	34.07	65.29	15.61	17.07	17.99
Provo, UT	12.33	68.82	29.37	47.51	18.44	15.63	13.80
Raleigh, NC	12.10	74.45	29.75	64.48	21.68	13.39	14.13
Reno, NV	12.62	59.63	29.96	61.79	16.20	17.81	15.57
Richmond, VA	12.47	80.46	31.31	59.05	18.60	13.05	14.79
Rochester, MN	14.09	65.15	31.71	51.56	19.51	15.54	18.28
Sacramento, CA	16.46	79.36	35.50	67.53	21.69	15.29	18.34
Salem, OR	14.60	64.50	30.14	46.82	18.25	17.28	17.05
Salt Lake City, UT	13.19	69.34	30.21	53.16	19.62	16.45	14.30
San Antonio, TX	11.50	73.39	30.02	50.98	14.16	10.89	14.02
San Diego, CA	16.37	83.73	33.77	n/a	21.87	16.23	18.06
San Francisco, CA	18.38	107.34	40.24	80.86	23.34	16.61	21.39
San Jose, CA	18.80	103.92	41.82	90.32	20.99	17.24	20.64
Santa Rosa, CA	17.13	81.95	34.88	64.13	21.59	16.52	22.75
Savannah, GA	11.64	71.42	27.26	51.37	16.53	12.70	14.18
Seattle, WA	17.49	87.94	37.50	72.41	23.93	18.81	20.41
Sioux Falls, SD	13.18	76.40	28.08	71.87	19.15	15.27	15.35
Springfield, IL	13.61	64.09	30.02	52.04	18.76	14.39	16.63
St. Louis, MO	13.40	72.89	31.51	54.93	18.85	13.32	16.09
Tampa, FL	12.44	76.40	30.65	53.47	17.46	13.80	13,88
Tucson, AZ	14.40	62.10	27.35	44.86	19.75	14.57	15.53
Tulsa, OK	11.21	72.14	29.35	51.65	16.50	12.65	14.02
Tuscaloosa, AL	11.34	62.63	28.60	55.95	17.32	11.32	14.40
Virginia Beach, VA	12.47	72.27	28.99	54.70	17.34	12.57	14.20
Washington, DC	15.12	87.75	35.74	72.97	22.54	15.70	17.34
Wichita, KS	11.16	70.00	28.52	46.78	16.45	12.10	14.45
Wilmington, NC	11.32	74.45	26.02	53.42	19.04	12.45	13.87
Winston-Salem, NC	12.15	74.71	27.78	58.23	18.87	12.67	13.23
Worcester, MA[2]	15.52	71.84	32.65	61.97	21.83	16.77	18.83

Notes: (1) Figures cover the Metropolitan Statistical Area (MSA) except where noted. See Appendix B for areas included;
(2) New England City and Town Area; n/a not available
Source: Bureau of Labor Statistics, May 2022 Metro Area Occupational Employment and Wage Estimates

Average Hourly Wages: Occupations L – N

Metro Area	Landscapers	Lawyers	Maids/ House- keepers	Main- tenance/ Repairers	Marketing Managers	Network Admin.	Nurses, Licensed Practical
Albuquerque, NM	16.24	54.41	13.69	20.91	61.49	44.73	28.50
Allentown, PA	17.57	64.68	14.89	24.13	66.34	41.40	26.64
Anchorage, AK	21.00	58.26	15.86	24.49	52.64	42.70	31.62
Ann Arbor, MI	17.82	60.75	15.15	22.11	66.72	43.40	28.93
Athens, GA	15.97	n/a	12.50	19.81	54.36	36.48	24.20
Atlanta, GA	17.07	84.73	13.58	21.53	73.79	50.54	26.03
Austin, TX	16.91	72.31	13.88	20.40	70.73	46.20	27.17
Baltimore, MD	18.68	77.46	14.74	23.34	69.41	52.41	28.83
Boise City, ID	17.90	48.56	15.14	20.73	51.10	39.68	27.38
Boston, MA[2]	21.78	97.55	19.01	27.11	80.96	52.37	33.67
Boulder, CO	21.69	n/a	17.31	27.19	85.56	48.32	29.85
Brownsville, TX	12.90	56.07	10.80	15.45	56.84	36.42	22.93
Cape Coral, FL	16.34	58.21	14.40	20.21	65.93	42.44	25.89
Cedar Rapids, IA	16.78	57.59	13.71	22.16	61.42	41.95	25.54
Charleston, SC	16.99	53.48	13.47	21.41	52.80	46.31	25.74
Charlotte, NC	17.24	78.03	13.43	22.36	71.03	44.85	26.52
Chicago, IL	18.93	78.47	17.07	26.11	70.74	44.98	30.01
Cincinnati, OH	16.69	64.18	13.58	23.48	69.92	46.45	25.99
Clarksville, TN	16.66	51.48	11.75	22.30	50.21	34.09	22.40
Cleveland, OH	17.23	64.28	14.02	23.06	69.27	45.69	26.09
College Station, TX	15.78	75.98	12.68	18.38	57.23	37.16	23.08
Colorado Springs, CO	n/a	53.62	16.06	22.51	79.04	47.29	27.54
Columbia, MO	15.24	58.60	13.42	20.64	52.19	38.68	23.50
Columbia, SC	15.84	53.72	12.62	20.68	59.00	43.75	25.20
Columbus, OH	17.46	65.26	13.91	23.16	69.18	47.97	26.41
Dallas, TX	16.86	87.42	13.78	21.23	67.66	45.36	26.59
Davenport, IA	16.43	56.57	13.68	22.09	60.27	40.41	25.09
Denver, CO	20.25	84.07	16.80	25.27	86.32	50.59	30.30
Des Moines, IA	17.60	59.08	14.22	22.01	64.50	44.01	25.09
Durham, NC	17.41	73.85	14.21	23.68	75.77	48.52	26.52
Edison, NJ	20.81	92.92	21.40	26.67	93.41	55.75	30.31
El Paso, TX	13.79	65.20	11.07	16.87	49.29	37.25	22.95
Fargo, ND	19.28	61.05	14.33	22.10	61.40	39.32	25.14
Fort Collins, CO	19.43	88.05	16.17	22.69	87.40	43.41	28.74
Fort Wayne, IN	16.18	62.54	13.34	23.13	56.84	37.68	25.80
Fort Worth, TX	16.86	87.42	13.78	21.23	67.66	45.36	26.59
Grand Rapids, MI	17.18	64.19	14.27	21.10	64.10	41.89	27.34
Greeley, CO	20.33	67.70	16.09	25.25	80.70	41.55	29.06
Green Bay, WI	17.41	72.57	14.43	22.47	75.00	42.60	23.59
Greensboro, NC	15.69	66.92	13.04	21.27	64.13	41.11	25.19
Honolulu, HI	19.21	50.95	23.06	25.25	59.72	44.72	27.07
Houston, TX	16.29	84.79	14.27	20.87	71.45	47.28	26.65
Huntsville, AL	15.92	69.72	11.97	20.71	68.35	45.60	22.75
Indianapolis, IN	17.19	74.02	14.20	23.30	65.78	42.49	27.80
Jacksonville, FL	16.00	62.74	13.79	20.57	72.46	43.58	24.97
Kansas City, MO	17.47	70.16	14.27	22.59	68.75	42.01	26.30
Lafayette, LA	14.42	53.24	10.93	18.12	47.53	41.24	21.48
Las Cruces, NM	15.38	53.03	12.60	18.02	n/a	41.48	27.19
Las Vegas, NV	17.85	82.94	17.87	23.05	51.14	49.43	30.50
Lexington, KY	15.64	51.22	12.88	22.07	55.36	38.28	24.21
Lincoln, NE	16.86	56.01	13.97	21.04	49.76	40.83	24.46
Little Rock, AR	15.21	50.96	12.84	18.37	51.80	38.74	23.12
Los Angeles, CA	19.81	93.69	18.69	24.86	81.73	49.56	32.95
Louisville, KY	16.00	52.07	13.67	23.69	68.37	40.49	25.32
Madison, WI	18.73	66.28	14.97	22.80	70.25	43.19	25.83

Table continued on following page.

Metro Area	Landscapers	Lawyers	Maids/ House- keepers	Main- tenance/ Repairers	Marketing Managers	Network Admin.	Nurses, Licensed Practical
Manchester, NH[2]	19.05	69.50	15.17	23.02	70.51	42.70	31.39
Miami, FL	16.61	69.69	14.17	20.30	73.31	45.42	26.47
Midland, TX	16.75	87.92	13.55	20.19	76.35	46.75	26.25
Milwaukee, WI	17.75	80.34	14.73	22.70	68.47	46.07	26.39
Minneapolis, MN	19.96	83.25	17.58	25.64	78.99	46.85	27.70
Nashville, TN	17.05	73.05	13.44	21.40	76.32	44.89	23.71
New Haven, CT[2]	20.86	73.87	15.86	24.69	71.85	45.08	30.20
New Orleans, LA	14.72	68.27	12.41	20.69	61.89	39.84	24.25
New York, NY	20.81	92.92	21.40	26.67	93.41	55.75	30.31
Oklahoma City, OK	16.15	53.26	12.31	18.75	64.04	41.84	23.45
Omaha, NE	17.69	59.74	14.69	22.11	58.09	44.11	25.44
Orlando, FL	16.23	70.07	14.29	20.33	76.95	43.75	26.40
Philadelphia, PA	18.71	76.88	15.47	23.49	71.68	47.15	28.52
Phoenix, AZ	17.31	72.30	16.08	22.41	68.83	45.37	30.07
Pittsburgh, PA	16.84	66.28	14.29	22.49	60.70	45.38	25.74
Portland, OR	20.88	73.57	17.60	24.55	66.94	48.17	33.26
Providence, RI[2]	20.58	74.38	16.14	24.78	79.73	51.47	31.28
Provo, UT	18.30	72.07	14.71	21.46	62.12	43.16	25.28
Raleigh, NC	17.40	67.47	14.15	22.67	71.21	45.26	26.69
Reno, NV	18.37	72.00	16.74	23.76	64.64	55.57	32.19
Richmond, VA	16.43	80.05	13.35	22.55	72.33	48.67	25.75
Rochester, MN	18.74	57.71	15.90	23.54	62.16	48.04	25.78
Sacramento, CA	20.30	79.67	20.36	24.95	77.80	43.18	34.27
Salem, OR	19.59	67.46	16.44	22.28	52.32	46.22	30.83
Salt Lake City, UT	18.82	65.12	16.12	23.79	65.16	45.48	29.02
San Antonio, TX	15.69	68.81	13.15	19.50	60.00	41.81	25.93
San Diego, CA	19.61	89.63	18.37	24.59	84.68	49.31	32.57
San Francisco, CA	23.72	115.06	22.92	29.95	100.73	61.21	38.69
San Jose, CA	24.14	128.77	22.48	30.88	113.98	72.84	38.75
Santa Rosa, CA	21.42	88.92	20.35	26.12	75.37	46.00	36.88
Savannah, GA	15.94	n/a	11.85	20.32	68.95	44.17	24.10
Seattle, WA	23.52	83.85	18.50	27.19	82.15	53.30	35.34
Sioux Falls, SD	16.41	60.68	13.76	20.54	66.13	35.57	22.26
Springfield, IL	18.70	61.68	16.39	23.40	62.68	36.92	25.11
St. Louis, MO	17.58	68.34	14.77	24.01	64.07	45.06	26.06
Tampa, FL	15.63	66.40	13.55	19.72	72.41	44.44	25.31
Tucson, AZ	16.04	61.60	14.58	20.08	58.86	41.53	29.01
Tulsa, OK	15.90	60.61	12.45	19.66	69.45	41.63	24.26
Tuscaloosa, AL	15.89	55.63	11.48	18.71	54.09	37.32	21.53
Virginia Beach, VA	16.35	61.10	13.16	21.28	70.40	44.66	24.37
Washington, DC	19.67	101.85	17.03	25.65	84.53	55.96	29.10
Wichita, KS	15.78	54.07	12.87	19.99	63.35	40.60	23.92
Wilmington, NC	16.23	61.99	12.83	19.80	67.91	39.92	25.28
Winston-Salem, NC	16.17	81.73	13.42	21.32	72.60	42.13	25.36
Worcester, MA[2]	20.03	69.75	17.11	24.75	73.90	47.65	30.85

Notes: (1) Figures cover the Metropolitan Statistical Area (MSA) except where noted. See Appendix B for areas included;
(2) New England City and Town Area; n/a not available
Source: Bureau of Labor Statistics, May 2022 Metro Area Occupational Employment and Wage Estimates

Average Hourly Wages: Occupations N – P

Metro Area	Nurses, Registered	Nursing Assistants	Office Clerks	Physical Therapists	Physicians	Plumbers	Police Officers
Albuquerque, NM	41.94	16.74	16.26	44.66	129.51	25.36	27.99
Allentown, PA	39.14	17.79	20.19	48.05	n/a	32.16	36.38
Anchorage, AK	49.59	20.50	22.26	49.64	112.03	43.11	47.16
Ann Arbor, MI	41.54	18.36	19.11	46.21	120.10	33.25	34.05
Athens, GA	38.59	14.53	19.23	49.24	106.67	26.88	24.49
Atlanta, GA	43.40	17.12	19.42	46.86	123.80	28.56	26.02
Austin, TX	41.69	16.17	19.06	47.33	136.94	28.42	35.58
Baltimore, MD	43.03	17.71	19.28	45.91	120.21	28.83	34.65
Boise City, ID	39.06	17.88	17.66	43.44	148.73	28.88	30.67
Boston, MA[2]	51.44	20.42	23.38	46.36	106.88	39.70	36.32
Boulder, CO	44.57	19.72	25.81	48.20	142.09	32.34	40.88
Brownsville, TX	35.07	13.19	14.88	45.71	116.21	20.29	26.68
Cape Coral, FL	38.04	16.24	19.43	43.77	177.87	24.29	31.19
Cedar Rapids, IA	33.68	17.02	19.34	40.86	125.70	32.41	31.90
Charleston, SC	36.96	17.18	17.46	41.79	141.24	24.76	25.12
Charlotte, NC	38.24	15.93	18.96	46.12	133.48	25.11	28.24
Chicago, IL	40.99	18.37	21.22	48.81	100.40	43.17	41.59
Cincinnati, OH	38.82	16.53	19.80	45.46	108.34	31.67	33.83
Clarksville, TN	34.52	14.53	16.20	42.52	143.21	24.18	23.65
Cleveland, OH	38.95	17.21	20.05	47.43	79.22	31.97	34.02
College Station, TX	37.59	14.34	15.70	46.21	n/a	24.11	31.36
Colorado Springs, CO	39.78	18.31	23.24	45.18	n/a	28.01	37.67
Columbia, MO	34.00	15.71	18.99	41.76	132.62	28.50	24.89
Columbia, SC	35.37	15.81	16.30	41.97	142.61	22.81	24.96
Columbus, OH	38.80	16.67	20.13	48.56	102.84	31.99	37.43
Dallas, TX	42.24	16.34	18.59	50.76	118.86	26.94	35.82
Davenport, IA	32.77	16.26	18.58	41.53	n/a	32.66	32.09
Denver, CO	42.21	19.35	24.74	47.13	156.83	31.18	41.85
Des Moines, IA	34.16	17.50	19.96	41.72	105.11	31.79	34.32
Durham, NC	n/a	16.82	19.49	40.71	n/a	26.00	25.40
Edison, NJ	50.41	21.50	21.90	53.25	128.42	42.38	42.43
El Paso, TX	36.36	13.69	15.17	45.54	105.87	22.73	30.10
Fargo, ND	36.60	17.94	22.07	40.35	105.75	29.18	34.03
Fort Collins, CO	40.85	18.30	23.55	42.61	n/a	29.30	43.64
Fort Wayne, IN	35.21	15.77	18.98	44.25	n/a	33.18	31.73
Fort Worth, TX	42.24	16.34	18.59	50.76	118.86	26.94	35.82
Grand Rapids, MI	36.98	17.03	20.33	42.66	126.06	30.06	31.96
Greeley, CO	41.14	17.60	23.36	47.67	n/a	26.96	36.95
Green Bay, WI	37.41	17.41	19.40	44.40	177.48	33.56	34.37
Greensboro, NC	38.59	14.93	17.77	45.22	n/a	23.39	24.52
Honolulu, HI	55.38	19.29	20.72	49.00	132.28	37.07	43.41
Houston, TX	42.73	16.18	18.74	52.20	138.31	28.24	32.31
Huntsville, AL	31.99	14.59	13.92	46.53	139.48	24.93	25.54
Indianapolis, IN	38.68	16.97	20.15	45.55	161.40	33.28	32.70
Jacksonville, FL	37.74	15.99	19.42	44.49	132.91	23.81	27.88
Kansas City, MO	36.82	17.33	20.48	44.96	104.46	31.93	29.20
Lafayette, LA	35.91	12.92	13.92	44.44	140.81	25.47	22.67
Las Cruces, NM	37.30	14.84	15.58	40.75	135.79	22.92	27.37
Las Vegas, NV	46.96	19.90	19.84	51.20	126.98	31.07	36.94
Lexington, KY	37.36	16.43	17.56	40.93	146.74	29.90	24.95
Lincoln, NE	35.52	16.53	16.75	44.49	131.40	25.79	33.34
Little Rock, AR	34.48	15.09	17.64	44.50	90.44	22.44	23.08
Los Angeles, CA	60.26	20.49	21.66	52.02	113.43	34.45	50.13
Louisville, KY	39.08	16.62	18.11	43.91	144.45	29.23	25.96
Madison, WI	41.46	18.71	20.66	43.49	152.61	35.91	35.34

Table continued on following page.

Metro Area	Nurses, Registered	Nursing Assistants	Office Clerks	Physical Therapists	Physicians	Plumbers	Police Officers
Manchester, NH[2]	39.38	18.40	22.10	43.45	n/a	28.32	30.78
Miami, FL	39.33	16.17	19.87	42.11	102.65	24.64	43.87
Midland, TX	39.34	16.60	20.43	50.09	124.58	26.81	34.27
Milwaukee, WI	39.44	17.93	19.83	45.40	104.93	35.62	35.72
Minneapolis, MN	44.32	22.36	22.34	43.60	145.35	39.07	39.69
Nashville, TN	37.13	16.08	17.70	44.33	131.73	26.77	26.07
New Haven, CT[2]	46.18	18.43	21.09	48.79	130.80	34.63	36.86
New Orleans, LA	38.18	14.49	14.52	46.62	151.73	27.73	23.68
New York, NY	50.41	21.50	21.90	53.25	128.42	42.38	42.43
Oklahoma City, OK	37.19	14.90	16.78	44.06	126.14	24.68	33.22
Omaha, NE	36.18	17.53	18.19	43.62	142.86	32.29	34.43
Orlando, FL	38.04	16.41	18.94	45.58	133.16	23.14	29.83
Philadelphia, PA	42.23	18.17	21.08	48.69	n/a	34.76	37.93
Phoenix, AZ	42.03	18.44	21.73	48.80	98.99	28.48	35.65
Pittsburgh, PA	36.65	17.51	19.95	45.42	59.50	34.72	36.66
Portland, OR	53.66	21.15	21.40	46.36	111.11	40.51	40.50
Providence, RI[2]	42.39	18.87	21.07	45.70	100.09	32.22	34.35
Provo, UT	34.96	15.59	18.82	43.16	82.30	25.73	28.90
Raleigh, NC	37.82	16.03	19.56	42.43	140.14	24.57	26.56
Reno, NV	44.85	19.69	21.19	49.42	142.69	32.67	35.21
Richmond, VA	39.75	15.79	18.79	46.28	79.68	25.66	29.03
Rochester, MN	43.30	19.09	21.24	41.61	143.61	37.05	34.21
Sacramento, CA	69.82	21.17	21.97	58.89	145.43	33.87	48.52
Salem, OR	46.17	21.59	20.38	45.54	158.13	34.34	37.37
Salt Lake City, UT	38.16	16.66	19.23	45.74	120.76	30.62	32.06
San Antonio, TX	39.92	15.47	18.02	45.42	145.35	24.88	31.55
San Diego, CA	56.65	20.39	21.38	52.92	125.61	34.09	47.51
San Francisco, CA	79.21	25.13	26.29	60.61	114.31	44.23	57.43
San Jose, CA	76.94	24.81	25.56	64.33	124.09	46.57	62.36
Santa Rosa, CA	72.67	20.99	22.86	60.31	112.97	36.74	49.57
Savannah, GA	40.41	14.89	18.02	45.44	100.61	28.19	25.28
Seattle, WA	50.74	21.40	24.29	50.43	120.27	41.46	48.78
Sioux Falls, SD	30.18	15.47	15.70	41.62	n/a	25.38	31.52
Springfield, IL	37.80	17.22	20.11	46.06	146.21	38.31	34.84
St. Louis, MO	36.14	16.41	20.76	44.14	142.81	35.55	29.89
Tampa, FL	38.42	16.72	19.64	46.29	132.49	23.00	33.26
Tucson, AZ	40.19	17.25	20.55	44.89	n/a	25.56	30.75
Tulsa, OK	38.32	15.05	17.16	43.95	78.82	26.43	26.48
Tuscaloosa, AL	30.81	14.13	13.87	48.68	105.13	23.92	27.48
Virginia Beach, VA	38.20	15.13	18.11	45.34	n/a	26.56	27.70
Washington, DC	44.61	18.33	22.52	49.52	101.91	30.71	37.25
Wichita, KS	33.08	15.61	14.16	43.47	100.53	27.23	25.83
Wilmington, NC	36.27	14.86	17.25	41.09	112.33	22.57	23.49
Winston-Salem, NC	38.57	15.34	17.36	47.28	n/a	22.79	24.14
Worcester, MA[2]	47.38	18.71	21.03	44.80	108.84	40.47	30.41

Notes: (1) Figures cover the Metropolitan Statistical Area (MSA) except where noted. See Appendix B for areas included;
(2) New England City and Town Area; n/a not available
Source: Bureau of Labor Statistics, May 2022 Metro Area Occupational Employment and Wage Estimates

Average Hourly Wages: Occupations P – S

Metro Area	Postal Mail Carriers	R.E. Sales Agents	Retail Sales-persons	Sales Reps., Technical/ Scientific	Secretaries, Exc. Leg./ Med./Exec.	Security Guards	Surgeons
Albuquerque, NM	26.30	22.73	15.08	37.39	20.16	15.37	n/a
Allentown, PA	27.45	27.37	16.75	51.14	20.39	17.28	n/a
Anchorage, AK	25.73	34.80	18.27	36.27	20.62	20.74	n/a
Ann Arbor, MI	27.10	33.57	16.77	128.93	22.52	18.34	n/a
Athens, GA	25.97	21.38	14.84	41.34	17.79	19.33	n/a
Atlanta, GA	26.65	28.00	15.55	52.79	19.44	16.02	212.04
Austin, TX	27.22	39.51	16.52	44.57	21.45	17.41	n/a
Baltimore, MD	27.22	32.50	15.99	50.13	21.48	20.09	162.71
Boise City, ID	27.00	21.80	16.72	41.57	18.67	16.67	n/a
Boston, MA[2]	28.27	38.33	18.39	54.97	25.44	19.80	148.22
Boulder, CO	28.10	49.41	18.86	n/a	22.19	21.46	n/a
Brownsville, TX	26.80	24.87	14.27	n/a	16.45	15.55	n/a
Cape Coral, FL	26.49	24.97	15.73	53.67	18.53	14.53	n/a
Cedar Rapids, IA	27.18	30.06	15.63	51.91	20.40	17.15	n/a
Charleston, SC	26.88	29.27	15.26	37.04	19.15	14.67	n/a
Charlotte, NC	27.50	27.29	15.72	54.96	20.17	14.89	276.15
Chicago, IL	27.84	21.56	17.49	56.01	23.34	17.98	136.81
Cincinnati, OH	28.15	27.69	16.23	51.86	20.51	17.09	184.17
Clarksville, TN	25.40	28.07	15.47	32.81	18.04	18.30	n/a
Cleveland, OH	27.79	20.71	16.56	52.20	20.38	17.47	n/a
College Station, TX	26.30	31.28	14.39	39.76	18.70	14.38	n/a
Colorado Springs, CO	26.35	34.84	17.44	46.25	19.90	17.50	n/a
Columbia, MO	26.18	20.94	14.99	n/a	18.33	16.33	n/a
Columbia, SC	25.68	28.52	14.63	40.39	18.64	13.48	n/a
Columbus, OH	27.37	21.29	16.00	58.13	20.96	17.83	n/a
Dallas, TX	27.30	38.08	16.19	43.31	20.33	16.99	142.82
Davenport, IA	26.31	33.24	15.72	50.09	19.78	18.10	n/a
Denver, CO	28.16	40.40	19.03	54.91	22.11	19.02	146.05
Des Moines, IA	27.78	34.49	15.88	54.80	21.22	17.63	n/a
Durham, NC	27.82	26.02	15.72	58.46	21.42	18.04	n/a
Edison, NJ	27.72	47.01	19.51	63.64	23.24	19.89	149.60
El Paso, TX	26.59	27.97	14.09	n/a	16.30	15.14	n/a
Fargo, ND	27.52	29.08	17.14	54.63	20.53	16.86	n/a
Fort Collins, CO	27.22	33.68	17.51	46.18	21.02	16.93	n/a
Fort Wayne, IN	26.91	27.25	14.91	51.06	18.31	17.67	n/a
Fort Worth, TX	27.30	38.08	16.19	43.31	20.33	16.99	142.82
Grand Rapids, MI	27.01	27.56	16.20	52.99	20.23	14.75	121.07
Greeley, CO	26.49	52.77	18.12	47.78	20.32	16.95	n/a
Green Bay, WI	27.20	29.62	16.28	34.34	20.34	16.22	n/a
Greensboro, NC	27.21	26.84	15.24	42.34	19.33	14.54	n/a
Honolulu, HI	26.72	26.75	17.85	54.70	23.30	17.09	205.79
Houston, TX	26.87	38.86	16.04	46.77	20.43	15.78	162.09
Huntsville, AL	26.36	41.38	14.54	38.34	20.21	15.35	n/a
Indianapolis, IN	27.71	32.61	15.60	52.85	20.15	16.75	185.56
Jacksonville, FL	27.22	29.37	15.49	46.55	19.30	15.13	n/a
Kansas City, MO	27.63	26.48	16.44	53.53	19.21	18.98	119.29
Lafayette, LA	26.29	17.52	13.84	40.17	17.91	13.48	n/a
Las Cruces, NM	25.66	22.91	13.98	n/a	18.37	15.27	n/a
Las Vegas, NV	26.97	38.35	16.82	41.45	21.22	15.06	n/a
Lexington, KY	27.17	27.67	15.76	45.14	20.09	14.57	n/a
Lincoln, NE	27.48	19.09	15.39	43.72	19.78	14.91	n/a
Little Rock, AR	26.80	n/a	14.90	44.97	18.48	15.34	n/a
Los Angeles, CA	28.35	35.65	18.93	52.61	24.22	18.19	n/a
Louisville, KY	27.28	22.31	15.89	49.19	19.91	16.60	194.02
Madison, WI	27.00	33.85	16.03	36.52	21.15	17.01	n/a

Table continued on following page.

Metro Area	Postal Mail Carriers	R.E. Sales Agents	Retail Sales-persons	Sales Reps., Technical/ Scientific	Secretaries, Exc. Leg./ Med./Exec.	Security Guards	Surgeons
Manchester, NH[2]	27.77	30.34	16.93	41.73	20.73	18.41	n/a
Miami, FL	27.09	26.19	16.30	50.86	20.66	16.16	92.08
Midland, TX	25.08	48.44	16.59	48.08	20.58	17.08	n/a
Milwaukee, WI	27.42	24.00	16.36	39.18	20.72	16.44	n/a
Minneapolis, MN	27.77	n/a	17.68	47.57	23.29	18.79	176.40
Nashville, TN	27.31	19.02	16.18	40.84	20.51	15.94	135.32
New Haven, CT[2]	26.76	29.22	18.46	45.89	26.88	18.52	n/a
New Orleans, LA	26.86	24.99	14.66	40.90	18.95	15.17	n/a
New York, NY	27.72	47.01	19.51	63.64	23.24	19.89	149.60
Oklahoma City, OK	27.22	n/a	15.14	39.45	18.26	15.95	n/a
Omaha, NE	27.42	29.75	16.07	41.32	19.89	17.42	158.30
Orlando, FL	26.72	26.11	15.51	46.62	18.93	15.30	n/a
Philadelphia, PA	27.23	27.12	16.66	57.64	21.81	18.05	196.21
Phoenix, AZ	27.93	29.19	17.07	46.98	21.31	17.03	n/a
Pittsburgh, PA	26.80	30.60	15.60	50.53	19.68	16.59	n/a
Portland, OR	27.17	28.64	19.03	56.64	24.16	18.14	n/a
Providence, RI[2]	27.29	35.48	17.17	39.71	22.88	17.75	n/a
Provo, UT	27.30	27.88	16.90	43.62	19.25	15.75	n/a
Raleigh, NC	27.38	27.61	16.28	55.59	20.25	15.48	n/a
Reno, NV	27.69	24.89	17.26	42.94	22.47	16.07	n/a
Richmond, VA	26.92	35.50	15.56	47.20	19.90	17.63	n/a
Rochester, MN	27.15	n/a	16.90	35.30	21.71	17.79	156.35
Sacramento, CA	28.15	32.19	19.11	58.98	23.74	18.43	n/a
Salem, OR	26.44	29.11	17.64	53.51	22.97	18.21	n/a
Salt Lake City, UT	28.08	26.96	18.75	57.43	20.26	17.09	219.11
San Antonio, TX	26.74	32.87	15.92	41.27	19.44	15.80	n/a
San Diego, CA	27.48	41.65	18.69	57.24	23.50	18.37	n/a
San Francisco, CA	29.20	39.87	21.47	60.73	28.82	21.09	75.20
San Jose, CA	29.08	36.25	21.34	78.03	28.34	21.24	n/a
Santa Rosa, CA	27.31	39.25	19.94	53.84	25.29	19.11	n/a
Savannah, GA	26.97	23.15	14.40	40.36	18.89	15.54	n/a
Seattle, WA	28.57	34.93	19.75	74.86	26.09	20.72	97.57
Sioux Falls, SD	27.07	n/a	18.12	57.97	17.76	16.09	n/a
Springfield, IL	26.37	26.10	16.08	39.68	20.55	17.77	n/a
St. Louis, MO	27.22	23.21	17.00	48.57	19.80	17.68	n/a
Tampa, FL	26.91	27.94	16.01	45.68	18.84	15.00	191.11
Tucson, AZ	27.62	27.03	16.59	48.00	19.49	15.65	n/a
Tulsa, OK	27.22	40.04	15.59	38.20	18.07	15.18	n/a
Tuscaloosa, AL	27.01	29.05	14.09	n/a	19.12	15.31	n/a
Virginia Beach, VA	26.24	33.80	15.11	45.63	20.00	16.42	n/a
Washington, DC	27.72	36.03	17.61	62.98	24.44	23.65	186.07
Wichita, KS	26.65	27.02	15.34	51.87	17.74	15.50	n/a
Wilmington, NC	26.03	28.16	15.41	60.83	19.24	15.17	n/a
Winston-Salem, NC	27.50	33.61	14.59	44.22	19.35	16.60	n/a
Worcester, MA[2]	27.11	n/a	17.84	55.25	23.77	18.53	n/a

Notes: (1) Figures cover the Metropolitan Statistical Area (MSA) except where noted. See Appendix B for areas included;
(2) New England City and Town Area; n/a not available
Source: Bureau of Labor Statistics, May 2022 Metro Area Occupational Employment and Wage Estimates

Average Hourly Wages: Occupations T – W

Metro Area	Teacher Assistants[3]	Teachers, Secondary School[3]	Telemarketers	Truck Drivers, Heavy	Truck Drivers, Light	Waiters/ Waitresses
Albuquerque, NM	14.88	28.99	20.16	22.67	20.43	16.14
Allentown, PA	16.36	35.24	14.10	27.04	22.74	15.35
Anchorage, AK	17.44	36.14	n/a	27.93	26.04	13.47
Ann Arbor, MI	15.21	35.99	n/a	24.45	23.48	17.37
Athens, GA	11.12	31.25	n/a	26.85	22.03	13.09
Atlanta, GA	14.07	34.25	15.50	26.24	21.28	14.52
Austin, TX	15.16	30.16	16.31	23.73	22.03	13.42
Baltimore, MD	19.37	34.31	18.80	26.63	22.04	17.63
Boise City, ID	14.04	27.88	17.64	25.05	24.37	14.76
Boston, MA[2]	20.14	40.58	19.82	27.78	23.55	19.76
Boulder, CO	18.12	35.67	17.68	26.67	24.66	20.98
Brownsville, TX	13.50	26.50	n/a	22.21	18.91	10.94
Cape Coral, FL	14.90	33.25	16.95	22.84	20.22	15.70
Cedar Rapids, IA	14.26	28.59	n/a	25.17	19.97	13.27
Charleston, SC	12.32	27.85	n/a	25.58	19.54	11.64
Charlotte, NC	13.20	26.35	16.09	25.66	19.89	13.70
Chicago, IL	16.89	37.13	15.52	27.99	24.27	15.53
Cincinnati, OH	16.00	33.81	14.72	26.16	21.77	14.51
Clarksville, TN	14.59	26.06	n/a	22.96	19.13	11.97
Cleveland, OH	16.13	35.16	14.85	25.57	20.45	14.38
College Station, TX	13.43	25.97	n/a	22.43	22.97	12.47
Colorado Springs, CO	15.06	26.75	19.45	24.71	22.21	19.75
Columbia, MO	14.65	n/a	n/a	24.11	22.20	15.51
Columbia, SC	12.00	26.34	10.78	23.99	19.35	10.82
Columbus, OH	16.49	34.42	15.65	26.61	22.93	15.07
Dallas, TX	14.09	30.46	18.24	24.73	22.27	13.17
Davenport, IA	15.10	31.35	14.97	26.12	20.97	13.22
Denver, CO	17.40	32.50	20.16	27.32	23.68	18.48
Des Moines, IA	14.28	32.05	15.86	26.85	21.17	13.46
Durham, NC	13.63	26.62	15.07	24.94	19.89	14.16
Edison, NJ	18.07	45.24	20.35	29.43	23.63	23.01
El Paso, TX	12.23	27.72	14.74	20.95	18.70	11.05
Fargo, ND	16.83	28.97	n/a	27.94	23.00	14.71
Fort Collins, CO	16.36	28.98	18.28	25.19	22.91	19.93
Fort Wayne, IN	13.32	27.57	15.78	25.45	20.20	13.17
Fort Worth, TX	14.09	30.46	18.24	24.73	22.27	13.17
Grand Rapids, MI	15.09	31.35	15.93	24.69	20.89	17.53
Greeley, CO	16.03	27.26	n/a	26.14	23.11	18.76
Green Bay, WI	15.77	29.64	n/a	25.81	21.30	15.02
Greensboro, NC	12.50	24.32	18.68	24.84	18.97	12.88
Honolulu, HI	16.06	29.35	16.92	26.64	21.01	16.89
Houston, TX	13.73	30.64	17.46	24.72	22.19	13.02
Huntsville, AL	10.75	28.00	n/a	23.90	20.20	11.55
Indianapolis, IN	14.25	30.46	17.62	26.92	23.09	13.35
Jacksonville, FL	14.72	31.72	15.08	24.87	21.39	15.33
Kansas City, MO	15.24	28.68	20.21	26.24	22.59	15.86
Lafayette, LA	11.25	24.62	n/a	21.71	17.50	11.88
Las Cruces, NM	14.06	33.00	n/a	21.52	17.37	15.04
Las Vegas, NV	16.36	30.96	15.02	24.98	20.79	13.18
Lexington, KY	16.94	29.65	n/a	26.48	21.58	14.02
Lincoln, NE	12.27	28.33	13.08	35.10	21.50	14.17
Little Rock, AR	14.46	25.70	n/a	26.45	22.85	13.89
Los Angeles, CA	20.58	43.33	18.39	26.10	22.77	18.08
Louisville, KY	15.01	30.29	15.36	27.04	23.90	13.48
Madison, WI	16.63	29.79	n/a	25.52	20.60	15.98

Table continued on following page.

Metro Area	Teacher Assistants[3]	Teachers, Secondary School[3]	Telemarketers	Truck Drivers, Heavy	Truck Drivers, Light	Waiters/ Waitresses
Manchester, NH[2]	16.19	33.56	15.33	25.70	20.52	16.61
Miami, FL	14.59	31.87	16.79	24.62	21.37	16.13
Midland, TX	13.37	30.50	n/a	25.69	20.91	12.89
Milwaukee, WI	16.86	33.03	16.38	26.40	21.54	15.68
Minneapolis, MN	18.50	31.91	22.98	28.77	23.50	13.34
Nashville, TN	13.61	26.44	n/a	26.23	21.56	11.99
New Haven, CT[2]	18.30	36.32	23.10	26.23	21.59	19.08
New Orleans, LA	14.50	27.00	n/a	24.66	19.53	12.15
New York, NY	18.07	45.24	20.35	29.43	23.63	23.01
Oklahoma City, OK	11.92	27.00	18.98	24.66	20.54	12.33
Omaha, NE	13.94	28.50	13.51	32.23	21.83	15.36
Orlando, FL	13.42	26.07	14.29	24.63	21.37	16.41
Philadelphia, PA	16.04	35.76	16.16	27.40	22.39	15.81
Phoenix, AZ	15.19	30.07	17.98	25.42	22.85	22.24
Pittsburgh, PA	15.05	39.73	16.91	25.67	20.10	14.85
Portland, OR	19.64	41.94	19.08	28.25	22.77	18.37
Providence, RI[2]	17.68	36.31	16.60	27.14	22.45	16.64
Provo, UT	13.34	31.61	17.82	25.28	20.06	17.18
Raleigh, NC	12.44	25.67	15.51	24.80	19.06	14.41
Reno, NV	18.08	36.23	n/a	26.51	21.26	13.12
Richmond, VA	14.32	37.47	n/a	24.27	20.61	16.35
Rochester, MN	17.00	31.98	n/a	26.90	21.79	12.51
Sacramento, CA	19.35	41.56	18.78	26.24	23.03	17.51
Salem, OR	19.13	39.59	16.13	26.69	21.33	16.15
Salt Lake City, UT	14.52	33.46	15.85	26.89	21.89	17.80
San Antonio, TX	14.17	29.61	17.04	22.61	20.69	13.14
San Diego, CA	19.50	47.51	17.68	25.83	22.99	17.49
San Francisco, CA	22.38	44.23	22.03	30.83	25.29	18.52
San Jose, CA	22.29	46.64	20.56	29.99	24.72	19.37
Santa Rosa, CA	20.52	43.10	n/a	27.66	24.22	18.13
Savannah, GA	15.18	29.79	n/a	24.85	20.20	13.87
Seattle, WA	22.89	44.03	20.78	30.34	24.18	23.47
Sioux Falls, SD	12.99	24.57	n/a	26.46	21.01	13.23
Springfield, IL	15.04	30.36	n/a	24.23	23.13	14.77
St. Louis, MO	15.52	29.12	18.25	26.27	22.92	16.19
Tampa, FL	14.33	32.73	14.35	23.41	20.06	15.84
Tucson, AZ	14.47	23.84	n/a	23.82	21.31	20.77
Tulsa, OK	12.67	28.15	18.01	24.99	19.91	11.71
Tuscaloosa, AL	10.07	26.64	n/a	24.19	20.50	10.78
Virginia Beach, VA	16.04	31.98	17.71	23.13	19.47	15.39
Washington, DC	19.39	40.33	20.08	27.54	23.67	19.91
Wichita, KS	14.41	28.44	n/a	23.66	20.17	14.48
Wilmington, NC	12.82	25.18	15.79	22.70	20.42	13.33
Winston-Salem, NC	11.63	25.01	n/a	24.69	18.96	12.01
Worcester, MA[2]	19.32	38.25	19.51	26.93	22.55	18.31

Notes: (1) Figures cover the Metropolitan Statistical Area (MSA) except where noted. See Appendix B for areas included; (2) New England City and Town Area; (3) Hourly wages were calculated from annual wage data assuming a 40 hour work week; n/a not available

Source: Bureau of Labor Statistics, May 2022 Metro Area Occupational Employment and Wage Estimates

Means of Transportation to Work: City

City	Car/Truck/Van		Public Transportation			Bicycle	Walked	Other Means	Worked at Home
	Drove Alone	Car-pooled	Bus	Subway	Railroad				
Albuquerque, NM	76.6	8.9	1.3	0.0	0.1	0.8	1.9	1.1	9.4
Allentown, PA	67.4	15.5	3.7	0.0	0.0	0.1	4.4	1.9	6.9
Anchorage, AK	73.7	12.1	1.4	0.0	0.0	0.9	2.6	2.1	7.1
Ann Arbor, MI	48.5	4.9	7.9	0.2	0.0	3.1	15.5	0.6	19.1
Athens, GA	72.0	8.0	2.7	0.0	0.0	1.4	4.8	1.0	10.2
Atlanta, GA	59.8	4.8	4.8	3.6	0.2	1.0	4.4	2.8	18.6
Austin, TX	66.2	7.7	2.5	0.1	0.1	1.0	2.6	1.4	18.4
Baltimore, MD	58.2	7.8	11.8	1.2	1.1	0.8	5.9	2.7	10.8
Boise City, ID	73.8	6.9	0.5	0.0	0.0	2.5	2.9	1.6	11.7
Boston, MA	36.1	5.5	10.6	15.5	1.1	2.0	14.4	2.6	12.3
Boulder, CO	45.8	4.3	6.5	0.0	0.0	8.8	9.1	1.3	24.3
Brownsville, TX	80.7	10.2	0.7	0.0	0.0	0.1	1.3	1.2	5.7
Cape Coral, FL	79.3	7.8	0.1	0.0	0.0	0.2	0.9	1.9	9.8
Cedar Rapids, IA	80.2	7.6	0.4	0.0	0.0	0.5	2.0	1.0	8.5
Charleston, SC	74.5	6.2	0.8	0.0	0.0	1.8	3.8	1.3	11.6
Charlotte, NC	68.8	8.6	1.9	0.3	0.1	0.1	1.8	1.8	16.7
Chicago, IL	47.4	7.5	11.1	10.7	1.4	1.5	5.8	2.2	12.3
Cincinnati, OH	69.0	8.5	6.1	0.0	0.0	0.3	5.5	1.4	9.2
Clarksville, TN	84.5	7.7	0.7	0.0	0.0	0.0	1.2	1.4	4.5
Cleveland, OH	68.6	9.9	7.3	0.4	0.1	0.5	4.7	1.7	6.9
College Station, TX	74.7	8.8	2.1	0.0	0.0	1.8	2.6	0.9	9.0
Colorado Springs, CO	74.7	9.8	0.7	0.0	0.0	0.5	1.7	1.1	11.4
Columbia, MO	75.0	9.0	0.9	0.0	0.0	1.2	6.4	0.7	6.8
Columbia, SC	63.8	5.7	1.5	0.0	0.0	0.4	20.3	1.6	6.7
Columbus, OH	75.0	7.2	2.5	0.0	0.0	0.4	2.7	1.1	11.0
Dallas, TX	72.3	11.2	2.3	0.3	0.2	0.2	2.2	1.6	9.7
Davenport, IA	83.4	6.5	0.6	0.0	0.0	0.2	2.3	0.7	6.3
Denver, CO	62.7	6.8	3.5	0.6	0.4	2.0	4.4	2.3	17.2
Des Moines, IA	75.4	10.6	1.4	0.1	0.0	0.5	2.4	1.4	8.2
Durham, NC	70.7	8.0	2.6	0.0	0.0	0.5	2.2	1.3	14.6
Edison, NJ	64.0	8.1	0.7	0.5	9.9	0.1	1.1	1.3	14.1
El Paso, TX	79.1	10.2	1.4	0.0	0.0	0.1	1.1	2.4	5.7
Fargo, ND	79.5	7.8	1.2	0.0	0.0	0.5	3.5	1.9	5.5
Fort Collins, CO	66.7	6.3	1.8	0.0	0.0	4.4	4.3	1.1	15.5
Fort Wayne, IN	80.9	9.6	1.0	0.0	0.0	0.5	1.5	0.8	5.8
Fort Worth, TX	77.3	11.0	0.5	0.0	0.1	0.2	1.3	1.0	8.6
Grand Rapids, MI	71.5	10.0	3.3	0.0	0.0	0.9	4.4	1.0	8.8
Greeley, CO	76.0	12.4	0.5	0.0	0.0	0.5	3.1	0.7	6.8
Green Bay, WI	77.7	10.7	1.1	0.0	0.0	0.2	2.3	1.1	6.9
Greensboro, NC	78.2	7.7	2.3	0.0	0.0	0.2	2.3	1.0	8.3
Honolulu, HI	57.7	13.1	9.4	0.0	0.0	1.6	8.2	3.6	6.4
Houston, TX	73.7	9.8	3.4	0.1	0.0	0.4	1.9	2.4	8.3
Huntsville, AL	81.8	6.2	0.4	0.0	0.0	0.2	1.2	0.8	9.4
Indianapolis, IN	77.6	9.3	1.6	0.0	0.0	0.4	1.9	0.9	8.4
Jacksonville, FL	77.3	8.7	1.4	0.0	0.0	0.3	1.4	2.0	8.8
Kansas City, MO	77.2	7.4	2.2	0.0	0.0	0.2	1.7	1.5	9.8
Lafayette, LA	83.4	4.8	0.8	0.0	0.0	0.5	2.4	1.0	7.0
Las Cruces, NM	74.3	13.2	0.5	0.0	0.0	1.6	1.7	1.4	7.4
Las Vegas, NV	75.5	9.8	2.8	0.0	0.0	0.2	1.3	2.9	7.4
Lexington, KY	77.0	8.1	1.7	0.0	0.0	0.6	3.5	1.1	8.2
Lincoln, NE	78.2	9.1	1.0	0.0	0.0	0.8	3.3	0.7	7.0
Little Rock, AR	78.5	9.7	0.7	0.0	0.0	0.2	1.8	1.5	7.7
Los Angeles, CA	65.2	8.9	6.6	0.8	0.1	0.7	3.2	2.1	12.4
Louisville, KY	76.6	8.4	2.6	0.0	0.0	0.3	1.9	1.6	8.5

Table continued on following page.

| City | Car/Truck/Van | | Public Transportation | | | Bicycle | Walked | Other Means | Worked at Home |
	Drove Alone	Car-pooled	Bus	Subway	Railroad				
Madison, WI	60.5	6.6	7.0	0.0	0.1	3.6	8.9	1.3	12.1
Manchester, NH	77.8	8.9	0.5	0.0	0.0	0.2	2.6	1.2	8.8
Miami, FL	65.9	7.7	6.1	1.1	0.1	0.8	4.8	3.5	10.1
Midland, TX	82.4	10.4	0.2	0.0	0.0	0.3	0.6	0.7	5.5
Milwaukee, WI	71.2	9.5	5.8	0.0	0.0	0.6	4.1	1.0	7.7
Minneapolis, MN	56.4	6.3	8.6	0.6	0.2	2.9	6.6	2.6	15.8
Nashville, TN	72.8	9.1	1.6	0.0	0.1	0.2	2.2	1.3	12.7
New Haven, CT	58.6	8.0	7.5	0.1	1.1	2.1	11.6	1.9	9.1
New Orleans, LA	65.6	8.9	4.6	0.1	0.0	2.6	5.4	2.9	9.9
New York, NY	22.4	4.4	9.7	38.4	1.2	1.4	9.5	2.5	10.7
Oklahoma City, OK	80.0	9.7	0.4	0.0	0.0	0.2	1.6	1.4	6.8
Omaha, NE	77.2	8.9	1.3	0.0	0.0	0.2	2.1	1.0	9.3
Orlando, FL	75.2	8.1	2.3	0.0	0.0	0.6	1.4	2.7	9.7
Philadelphia, PA	48.3	7.8	13.5	5.2	2.2	2.0	7.6	2.7	10.8
Phoenix, AZ	70.8	11.5	2.1	0.0	0.0	0.5	1.5	1.9	11.5
Pittsburgh, PA	52.1	6.6	14.5	0.3	0.0	1.2	9.7	1.8	13.9
Portland, OR	53.8	7.4	7.2	0.5	0.2	4.7	5.1	3.2	18.0
Providence, RI	64.0	11.3	3.3	0.1	1.0	0.9	7.3	1.7	10.4
Provo, UT	59.2	11.2	3.2	0.1	0.9	2.0	11.8	1.0	10.5
Raleigh, NC	70.9	7.1	1.7	0.0	0.0	0.2	1.4	1.4	17.2
Reno, NV	71.1	12.0	2.7	0.0	0.0	0.7	2.8	2.5	8.3
Richmond, VA	67.8	8.5	4.2	0.1	0.0	1.8	4.5	1.6	11.5
Rochester, MN	67.8	11.9	5.4	0.0	0.0	0.8	4.2	1.2	8.8
Sacramento, CA	68.9	9.6	1.7	0.2	0.3	1.6	2.9	2.2	12.6
St. Louis, MO	69.9	6.6	5.8	0.4	0.1	0.9	4.4	1.4	10.5
Salem, OR	71.7	9.5	2.2	0.0	0.0	1.4	3.4	1.2	10.5
Salt Lake City, UT	63.1	8.8	3.8	0.3	0.6	2.1	4.8	3.2	13.2
San Antonio, TX	74.6	11.8	2.1	0.0	0.0	0.2	1.8	1.6	8.0
San Diego, CA	68.9	8.2	2.8	0.1	0.1	0.7	3.2	2.0	14.0
San Francisco, CA	29.4	6.5	17.8	7.0	1.3	3.3	11.0	5.6	18.0
San Jose, CA	69.2	10.5	2.0	0.3	0.9	0.6	1.9	1.8	13.0
Santa Rosa, CA	76.1	10.3	1.4	0.1	0.1	0.8	1.8	1.4	7.9
Savannah, GA	71.7	10.7	3.1	0.0	0.0	1.2	4.2	1.8	7.3
Seattle, WA	40.5	6.1	15.4	1.0	0.1	2.8	9.7	2.9	21.4
Sioux Falls, SD	81.7	7.8	0.6	0.0	0.0	0.3	2.1	0.7	6.8
Springfield, IL	79.6	6.4	1.6	0.1	0.0	0.5	1.6	1.7	8.7
Tampa, FL	71.9	8.2	1.9	0.0	0.0	0.8	2.1	1.9	13.2
Tucson, AZ	71.3	10.4	2.6	0.0	0.0	1.9	2.9	1.7	9.2
Tulsa, OK	78.4	9.9	0.6	0.0	0.0	0.2	1.8	1.9	7.2
Tuscaloosa, AL	80.0	9.7	1.4	0.0	0.0	0.5	1.8	1.0	5.6
Virginia Beach, VA	79.1	7.6	0.7	0.0	0.0	0.4	2.1	1.6	8.4
Washington, DC	30.7	4.7	10.0	16.7	0.2	3.7	11.3	2.7	19.8
Wichita, KS	81.4	9.8	0.6	0.0	0.0	0.4	1.2	1.4	5.1
Wilmington, NC	75.4	7.5	0.7	0.0	0.0	0.6	2.5	0.8	12.6
Winston-Salem, NC	77.7	8.9	1.3	0.0	0.0	0.3	2.1	1.2	8.5
Worcester, MA	68.3	11.4	1.9	0.2	0.6	0.2	6.2	2.9	8.3
U.S.	73.2	8.6	2.0	1.6	0.5	0.5	2.5	1.5	9.7

Note: Figures are percentages and cover workers 16 years of age and older
Source: U.S. Census Bureau, 2017-2021 American Community Survey 5-Year Estimates

Means of Transportation to Work: Metro Area

Metro Area	Car/Truck/Van		Public Transportation			Bicycle	Walked	Other Means	Worked at Home
	Drove Alone	Car-pooled	Bus	Subway	Railroad				
Albuquerque, NM	76.8	9.4	1.0	0.0	0.1	0.6	1.7	1.1	9.4
Allentown, PA	78.4	7.9	1.2	0.1	0.1	0.1	2.3	1.2	8.7
Anchorage, AK	73.7	11.5	1.2	0.0	0.0	0.8	2.4	3.0	7.4
Ann Arbor, MI	66.1	6.5	4.1	0.1	0.0	1.3	6.9	0.8	14.2
Athens, GA	75.1	8.0	1.6	0.0	0.0	0.8	3.4	1.2	9.9
Atlanta, GA	72.7	8.7	1.5	0.7	0.1	0.2	1.2	1.7	13.2
Austin, TX	69.7	8.4	1.3	0.0	0.1	0.6	1.8	1.3	16.8
Baltimore, MD	72.5	7.4	3.4	0.7	0.7	0.2	2.3	1.5	11.2
Boise City, ID	76.4	7.9	0.2	0.0	0.0	1.1	1.9	1.3	11.0
Boston, MA	62.2	6.6	3.2	5.5	1.8	0.9	5.0	1.7	13.0
Boulder, CO	60.1	6.6	3.9	0.0	0.0	3.6	4.0	1.1	20.8
Brownsville, TX	81.3	9.1	0.4	0.0	0.0	0.1	1.6	1.2	6.3
Cape Coral, FL	76.3	9.6	0.5	0.0	0.0	0.7	1.0	2.3	9.6
Cedar Rapids, IA	80.3	7.0	0.3	0.0	0.0	0.3	1.8	0.8	9.4
Charleston, SC	79.1	7.6	0.6	0.0	0.0	0.6	1.8	1.2	9.1
Charlotte, NC	74.7	8.4	0.9	0.1	0.0	0.1	1.3	1.3	13.1
Chicago, IL	66.7	7.6	3.7	3.6	2.6	0.6	2.8	1.5	10.9
Cincinnati, OH	78.8	7.7	1.4	0.0	0.0	0.2	1.9	0.9	9.1
Clarksville, TN	82.2	8.6	0.5	0.0	0.0	0.2	2.9	1.3	4.3
Cleveland, OH	77.9	7.4	2.1	0.1	0.0	0.3	2.1	1.2	8.8
College Station, TX	78.2	9.5	1.1	0.0	0.0	1.1	1.7	1.2	7.2
Colorado Springs, CO	73.8	9.6	0.5	0.0	0.0	0.3	3.2	1.0	11.4
Columbia, MO	77.1	9.6	0.6	0.0	0.0	0.8	4.4	0.8	6.7
Columbia, SC	78.7	8.1	0.6	0.0	0.0	0.1	4.2	1.6	6.7
Columbus, OH	77.1	6.7	1.3	0.0	0.0	0.3	2.0	1.0	11.6
Dallas, TX	75.8	9.5	0.6	0.1	0.2	0.1	1.2	1.3	11.1
Davenport, IA	83.9	6.8	0.7	0.0	0.0	0.2	2.2	0.7	5.6
Denver, CO	69.8	7.5	2.2	0.3	0.2	0.8	2.1	1.7	15.4
Des Moines, IA	78.3	7.6	0.6	0.0	0.0	0.2	1.7	1.1	10.5
Durham, NC	70.8	7.7	2.6	0.0	0.0	0.6	2.3	1.3	14.5
Edison, NJ	47.4	6.1	6.7	17.4	3.1	0.7	5.5	2.3	10.6
El Paso, TX	78.6	10.6	1.1	0.0	0.0	0.1	1.4	2.3	5.8
Fargo, ND	79.8	8.0	0.9	0.0	0.0	0.4	2.6	1.4	6.9
Fort Collins, CO	70.7	6.4	1.1	0.1	0.0	2.4	2.8	1.1	15.4
Fort Wayne, IN	82.1	8.7	0.7	0.0	0.0	0.4	1.3	0.7	6.2
Fort Worth, TX	75.8	9.5	0.6	0.1	0.2	0.1	1.2	1.3	11.1
Grand Rapids, MI	79.0	8.5	1.2	0.0	0.0	0.4	2.2	0.7	7.9
Greeley, CO	76.7	10.4	0.4	0.0	0.0	0.2	1.9	0.8	9.5
Green Bay, WI	81.4	7.6	0.5	0.0	0.0	0.1	1.8	0.8	7.8
Greensboro, NC	79.8	8.8	1.1	0.0	0.0	0.2	1.5	1.1	7.5
Honolulu, HI	65.4	13.2	6.3	0.0	0.0	0.9	5.2	2.5	6.4
Houston, TX	77.1	9.3	1.7	0.0	0.0	0.3	1.2	1.6	8.7
Huntsville, AL	83.6	5.8	0.2	0.0	0.0	0.1	0.7	1.0	8.6
Indianapolis, IN	78.7	8.2	0.7	0.0	0.0	0.2	1.4	0.9	9.8
Jacksonville, FL	76.8	8.2	0.9	0.0	0.0	0.4	1.3	1.9	10.5
Kansas City, MO	79.0	7.3	0.7	0.0	0.0	0.1	1.1	1.0	10.6
Lafayette, LA	83.9	6.7	0.3	0.0	0.0	0.2	1.9	1.2	5.8
Las Cruces, NM	76.4	12.3	0.4	0.0	0.0	0.9	1.7	1.3	7.1
Las Vegas, NV	75.8	10.1	2.6	0.0	0.0	0.2	1.3	2.5	7.4
Lexington, KY	78.2	8.4	1.1	0.0	0.0	0.4	2.9	1.0	8.0
Lincoln, NE	78.5	8.9	0.8	0.0	0.0	0.8	3.2	0.7	7.2
Little Rock, AR	81.6	9.4	0.4	0.0	0.0	0.1	1.1	1.1	6.3
Los Angeles, CA	70.9	9.3	3.4	0.4	0.2	0.6	2.3	1.8	11.2
Louisville, KY	78.9	8.2	1.5	0.0	0.0	0.2	1.4	1.1	8.7

Table continued on following page.

Metro Area	Car/Truck/Van		Public Transportation			Bicycle	Walked	Other Means	Worked at Home
	Drove Alone	Car-pooled	Bus	Subway	Railroad				
Madison, WI	71.0	6.5	3.3	0.0	0.0	1.8	4.9	1.0	11.5
Manchester, NH	77.6	7.2	0.6	0.1	0.1	0.2	1.8	0.9	11.5
Miami, FL	75.1	9.1	2.1	0.3	0.1	0.5	1.5	2.1	9.2
Midland, TX	82.7	9.9	0.1	0.0	0.0	0.2	1.2	0.7	5.1
Milwaukee, WI	77.4	7.1	2.4	0.0	0.0	0.4	2.3	0.8	9.5
Minneapolis, MN	72.1	7.4	3.2	0.1	0.1	0.6	2.1	1.3	13.1
Nashville, TN	76.7	8.6	0.7	0.0	0.1	0.1	1.2	1.1	11.6
New Haven, CT	74.9	8.1	2.3	0.1	0.7	0.4	3.4	1.3	8.7
New Orleans, LA	76.2	9.6	1.7	0.0	0.0	0.9	2.4	1.7	7.4
New York, NY	47.4	6.1	6.7	17.4	3.1	0.7	5.5	2.3	10.6
Oklahoma City, OK	80.6	9.1	0.3	0.0	0.0	0.3	1.6	1.2	7.0
Omaha, NE	79.5	8.0	0.7	0.0	0.0	0.1	1.7	1.0	9.0
Orlando, FL	75.8	9.4	1.1	0.0	0.1	0.4	1.1	1.9	10.2
Philadelphia, PA	68.2	7.1	4.2	1.7	1.7	0.6	3.2	1.5	11.7
Phoenix, AZ	71.6	10.3	1.3	0.0	0.0	0.6	1.4	1.8	13.0
Pittsburgh, PA	73.0	7.4	4.2	0.2	0.0	0.2	3.0	1.3	10.8
Portland, OR	66.2	8.4	3.6	0.4	0.2	1.7	3.1	2.0	14.4
Providence, RI	77.8	8.3	1.2	0.1	0.7	0.2	2.7	1.0	7.8
Provo, UT	70.1	10.3	1.0	0.1	0.7	0.7	3.3	1.0	12.8
Raleigh, NC	72.9	7.4	0.7	0.0	0.0	0.1	1.1	1.0	16.8
Reno, NV	73.1	12.0	2.0	0.0	0.0	0.5	2.0	2.0	8.3
Richmond, VA	76.2	7.7	1.2	0.0	0.1	0.4	1.4	1.1	11.9
Rochester, MN	71.2	11.0	3.4	0.0	0.0	0.5	3.5	1.0	9.4
Sacramento, CA	72.1	8.8	1.3	0.1	0.2	1.1	1.6	1.7	13.1
St. Louis, MO	79.2	6.7	1.4	0.2	0.1	0.2	1.6	1.0	9.8
Salem, OR	74.3	10.1	1.3	0.0	0.0	0.8	2.6	1.1	9.8
Salt Lake City, UT	71.0	10.3	1.5	0.2	0.4	0.6	1.9	1.7	12.5
San Antonio, TX	75.6	10.7	1.3	0.0	0.0	0.2	1.6	1.4	9.1
San Diego, CA	71.6	8.4	2.0	0.1	0.1	0.5	2.9	2.0	12.5
San Francisco, CA	53.4	8.6	6.1	5.7	1.2	1.6	4.3	2.8	16.3
San Jose, CA	67.1	9.4	1.8	0.3	1.0	1.4	2.1	1.6	15.3
Santa Rosa, CA	72.8	10.0	1.2	0.1	0.2	0.6	2.3	1.5	11.3
Savannah, GA	79.8	8.6	1.3	0.0	0.0	0.6	1.9	1.7	6.2
Seattle, WA	62.4	9.1	6.7	0.3	0.4	0.9	3.6	1.6	14.9
Sioux Falls, SD	81.7	7.6	0.5	0.0	0.0	0.3	1.9	0.6	7.4
Springfield, IL	81.6	6.4	0.9	0.1	0.0	0.4	1.4	1.3	8.0
Tampa, FL	74.8	8.2	1.0	0.0	0.0	0.5	1.3	1.6	12.4
Tucson, AZ	73.4	9.7	1.7	0.0	0.0	1.2	2.1	1.7	10.3
Tulsa, OK	80.7	9.1	0.3	0.0	0.0	0.1	1.3	1.3	7.1
Tuscaloosa, AL	82.3	10.3	0.8	0.0	0.0	0.2	0.9	0.6	5.0
Virginia Beach, VA	78.3	7.9	1.3	0.0	0.0	0.3	3.1	1.6	7.5
Washington, DC	60.7	8.5	3.6	5.8	0.6	0.7	2.9	1.7	15.4
Wichita, KS	82.2	8.7	0.4	0.0	0.0	0.3	1.5	1.3	5.6
Wilmington, NC	77.5	8.0	0.3	0.0	0.0	0.4	1.4	0.6	11.8
Winston-Salem, NC	80.7	8.8	0.6	0.0	0.0	0.1	1.3	0.9	7.6
Worcester, MA	76.2	7.6	0.7	0.2	0.7	0.2	2.6	1.7	10.2
U.S.	73.2	8.6	2.0	1.6	0.5	0.5	2.5	1.5	9.7

Note: Figures are percentages and cover workers 16 years of age and older; (1) Figures cover the Metropolitan Statistical Area
Source: U.S. Census Bureau, 2017-2021 American Community Survey 5-Year Estimates

Travel Time to Work: City

City	Less Than 10 Minutes	10 to 19 Minutes	20 to 29 Minutes	30 to 44 Minutes	45 to 59 Minutes	60 to 89 Minutes	90 Minutes or More
Albuquerque, NM	11.0	35.9	27.8	18.1	3.1	2.5	1.6
Allentown, PA	10.6	33.2	30.0	15.2	4.3	4.6	2.1
Anchorage, AK	16.1	44.4	23.4	11.2	2.1	1.2	1.6
Ann Arbor, MI	13.9	45.7	18.6	14.0	5.0	2.4	0.5
Athens, GA	18.0	45.8	16.6	9.8	3.5	3.5	2.8
Atlanta, GA	6.9	29.5	25.6	21.8	7.3	5.4	3.5
Austin, TX	9.7	32.0	24.5	21.7	6.9	3.7	1.5
Baltimore, MD	6.7	23.6	23.3	25.6	8.7	7.4	4.7
Boise City, ID	13.6	44.5	26.2	11.4	1.6	1.5	1.2
Boston, MA	6.9	20.4	19.6	29.8	12.1	9.1	2.1
Boulder, CO	19.7	44.5	16.1	9.5	5.8	3.2	1.2
Brownsville, TX	8.7	42.9	28.9	14.3	2.5	1.7	1.0
Cape Coral, FL	8.0	25.3	22.2	27.4	9.4	5.4	2.3
Cedar Rapids, IA	20.0	48.9	17.0	9.2	1.9	1.5	1.5
Charleston, SC	11.4	30.7	26.6	20.6	7.6	1.6	1.4
Charlotte, NC	8.6	29.6	26.7	23.2	6.5	3.3	2.1
Chicago, IL	4.7	16.4	18.4	30.5	15.1	11.9	3.1
Cincinnati, OH	11.4	33.0	26.8	19.1	4.3	3.2	2.1
Clarksville, TN	10.3	33.0	25.3	14.1	6.8	8.5	2.2
Cleveland, OH	10.2	34.0	27.0	20.0	3.9	3.0	2.1
College Station, TX	17.6	55.5	17.1	6.2	0.5	2.0	1.1
Colorado Springs, CO	11.5	35.9	28.0	15.9	3.3	2.9	2.5
Columbia, MO	20.0	54.4	13.7	7.3	2.5	1.0	1.1
Columbia, SC	29.8	36.0	19.0	10.0	2.1	1.8	1.4
Columbus, OH	10.3	34.2	30.4	18.7	3.2	1.9	1.3
Dallas, TX	8.2	26.9	23.3	25.8	8.0	5.9	1.9
Davenport, IA	16.5	47.5	22.0	8.2	3.1	1.8	1.0
Denver, CO	7.9	29.0	24.7	26.0	7.2	3.7	1.4
Des Moines, IA	13.5	43.1	26.6	12.3	2.2	1.3	1.1
Durham, NC	9.2	38.4	25.5	17.9	4.8	2.7	1.4
Edison, NJ	7.6	22.0	18.1	17.8	12.2	12.6	9.6
El Paso, TX	9.5	33.5	28.5	19.7	4.7	2.2	1.8
Fargo, ND	20.6	56.3	15.2	3.6	1.4	1.9	0.9
Fort Collins, CO	15.4	43.8	20.6	10.0	5.4	3.3	1.5
Fort Wayne, IN	12.8	38.2	28.0	13.5	3.0	2.6	1.8
Fort Worth, TX	7.7	29.0	22.9	23.9	8.7	5.8	2.0
Grand Rapids, MI	14.5	44.0	23.5	11.6	3.7	2.0	0.8
Greeley, CO	15.9	37.3	15.3	14.4	5.9	9.2	1.9
Green Bay, WI	18.2	48.6	19.5	8.5	2.8	1.3	1.1
Greensboro, NC	12.5	40.0	23.6	15.9	3.2	3.0	2.0
Honolulu, HI	8.7	38.2	22.6	20.6	5.0	3.6	1.2
Houston, TX	7.2	25.5	23.0	27.7	8.9	5.9	1.8
Huntsville, AL	13.1	41.0	26.2	15.5	2.5	1.0	0.8
Indianapolis, IN	9.5	30.4	28.8	22.7	4.3	2.4	1.8
Jacksonville, FL	8.7	28.5	27.2	25.4	6.0	2.8	1.4
Kansas City, MO	11.6	33.4	27.9	20.3	4.0	1.7	1.2
Lafayette, LA	15.8	44.0	19.3	11.9	2.8	3.6	2.6
Las Cruces, NM	16.2	49.2	16.2	9.5	3.5	4.8	0.7
Las Vegas, NV	7.3	24.0	30.6	27.4	6.2	2.7	1.9
Lexington, KY	13.2	39.5	26.2	13.9	2.9	2.4	1.8
Lincoln, NE	16.7	44.7	22.8	9.9	2.6	2.1	1.2
Little Rock, AR	15.4	45.3	23.6	11.0	2.3	1.5	0.9
Los Angeles, CA	5.9	22.2	19.3	28.5	10.5	10.1	3.6
Louisville, KY	9.6	32.6	31.4	19.1	3.9	2.0	1.4
Madison, WI	14.9	39.6	24.8	15.1	3.0	1.8	0.8

Table continued on following page.

City	Less Than 10 Minutes	10 to 19 Minutes	20 to 29 Minutes	30 to 44 Minutes	45 to 59 Minutes	60 to 89 Minutes	90 Minutes or More
Manchester, NH	12.6	35.5	23.4	14.6	6.4	5.1	2.4
Miami, FL	6.0	21.8	24.7	30.5	9.1	6.6	1.4
Midland, TX	14.2	47.3	18.9	12.0	2.9	2.4	2.4
Milwaukee, WI	10.4	36.6	26.1	19.1	3.5	2.7	1.7
Minneapolis, MN	7.9	32.6	30.2	20.9	4.5	2.7	1.1
Nashville, TN	9.1	29.0	26.6	23.2	7.0	3.6	1.5
New Haven, CT	13.2	40.4	21.6	13.6	4.5	4.2	2.5
New Orleans, LA	11.0	34.8	24.2	19.5	5.0	3.5	2.0
New York, NY	4.0	12.3	13.5	27.1	16.3	19.2	7.6
Oklahoma City, OK	10.5	36.0	29.0	18.2	3.5	1.4	1.4
Omaha, NE	14.5	41.2	26.7	12.4	2.5	1.9	0.9
Orlando, FL	7.2	25.4	27.6	26.6	7.2	3.9	2.2
Philadelphia, PA	6.1	19.2	20.2	28.1	12.9	9.5	4.0
Phoenix, AZ	8.6	26.6	26.6	24.5	7.4	4.5	1.8
Pittsburgh, PA	9.4	32.3	26.6	21.8	4.6	3.6	1.7
Portland, OR	8.3	28.2	26.8	24.0	7.1	4.1	1.5
Providence, RI	10.3	40.4	19.4	15.3	6.2	5.5	2.8
Provo, UT	21.4	44.2	16.8	9.8	3.5	3.1	1.2
Raleigh, NC	9.3	32.4	27.0	20.8	5.7	3.0	1.8
Reno, NV	15.6	40.3	22.8	12.5	4.7	2.7	1.4
Richmond, VA	11.4	37.4	27.3	16.8	2.9	2.7	1.5
Rochester, MN	17.7	55.5	14.1	6.5	2.8	2.2	1.2
Sacramento, CA	8.4	31.3	24.9	22.4	5.6	4.2	3.1
St. Louis, MO	9.2	35.2	26.5	19.7	4.3	2.9	2.1
Salem, OR	13.0	41.0	19.7	12.7	6.0	6.0	1.6
Salt Lake City, UT	14.1	45.1	21.4	12.6	3.5	2.2	1.2
San Antonio, TX	9.4	31.4	26.3	21.8	6.0	3.4	1.7
San Diego, CA	7.7	32.9	27.5	20.9	5.7	3.6	1.7
San Francisco, CA	4.5	19.3	21.4	29.5	11.6	10.1	3.7
San Jose, CA	5.6	24.6	23.2	26.1	10.1	7.5	3.0
Santa Rosa, CA	12.6	40.1	21.3	14.4	4.3	4.0	3.3
Savannah, GA	15.7	39.1	22.8	13.3	4.8	2.8	1.5
Seattle, WA	7.3	24.0	24.1	27.6	10.6	5.0	1.5
Sioux Falls, SD	16.7	51.6	22.0	5.8	1.7	1.2	1.0
Springfield, IL	17.4	53.1	17.9	6.3	1.8	2.3	1.3
Tampa, FL	11.1	30.2	22.5	23.4	6.8	4.3	1.8
Tucson, AZ	11.8	34.9	25.4	19.6	4.7	2.0	1.6
Tulsa, OK	14.2	44.9	26.3	10.1	1.9	1.4	1.2
Tuscaloosa, AL	16.8	46.6	21.7	7.6	3.1	3.1	1.1
Virginia Beach, VA	10.1	30.9	27.9	22.0	5.3	2.5	1.4
Washington, DC	5.3	19.0	22.3	33.1	11.6	6.6	2.1
Wichita, KS	14.3	44.9	26.7	9.9	1.6	1.4	1.2
Wilmington, NC	16.1	47.0	21.7	9.5	2.5	1.7	1.5
Winston-Salem, NC	14.0	40.3	22.6	14.3	4.6	2.6	1.7
Worcester, MA	13.4	34.6	19.5	17.8	5.9	6.3	2.5
U.S.	12.4	28.5	21.0	20.9	8.2	6.2	2.9

Note: Figures are percentages and include workers 16 years old and over
Source: U.S. Census Bureau, 2017-2021 American Community Survey 5-Year Estimates

Travel Time to Work: Metro Area

Metro Area	Less Than 10 Minutes	10 to 19 Minutes	20 to 29 Minutes	30 to 44 Minutes	45 to 59 Minutes	60 to 89 Minutes	90 Minutes or More
Albuquerque, NM	10.7	31.5	26.0	20.7	5.7	3.5	1.8
Allentown, PA	12.6	27.7	23.5	18.5	7.3	6.6	3.8
Anchorage, AK	15.0	40.4	21.8	11.4	4.5	4.1	2.7
Ann Arbor, MI	11.5	32.6	24.5	19.1	7.3	3.8	1.1
Athens, GA	14.2	38.2	21.9	13.5	5.2	4.0	3.0
Atlanta, GA	6.9	22.5	19.9	25.2	12.2	9.6	3.5
Austin, TX	9.3	26.6	22.1	23.8	10.1	6.3	1.9
Baltimore, MD	8.0	23.3	21.0	24.7	11.0	8.3	3.7
Boise City, ID	12.8	33.4	25.0	19.7	5.5	2.2	1.4
Boston, MA	9.1	22.7	18.6	24.4	11.7	10.1	3.3
Boulder, CO	14.5	33.4	20.5	17.6	7.6	4.8	1.6
Brownsville, TX	12.8	40.5	25.7	15.0	3.4	1.6	1.0
Cape Coral, FL	8.6	25.3	22.8	26.0	9.8	5.2	2.3
Cedar Rapids, IA	18.8	40.1	20.6	12.8	4.3	2.0	1.5
Charleston, SC	8.8	26.0	24.1	25.1	9.5	4.8	1.7
Charlotte, NC	9.8	27.8	22.6	23.3	9.3	5.1	2.1
Chicago, IL	8.5	21.9	19.0	25.3	12.2	10.0	3.1
Cincinnati, OH	10.9	28.2	25.2	23.1	7.5	3.5	1.6
Clarksville, TN	14.8	31.0	22.4	16.1	6.5	6.5	2.7
Cleveland, OH	11.6	28.2	25.9	23.2	6.7	2.9	1.6
College Station, TX	16.1	49.4	18.4	10.4	2.3	2.1	1.4
Colorado Springs, CO	11.5	32.8	26.9	18.0	4.7	3.6	2.5
Columbia, MO	17.3	44.2	19.4	11.9	3.8	1.7	1.7
Columbia, SC	12.6	28.8	24.1	22.2	6.9	3.3	2.2
Columbus, OH	11.4	29.5	26.7	21.7	6.1	3.1	1.5
Dallas, TX	8.6	25.2	21.7	25.6	10.3	6.7	2.0
Davenport, IA	18.3	36.1	24.9	13.1	3.9	2.4	1.3
Denver, CO	8.4	25.1	23.0	26.5	9.6	5.5	1.9
Des Moines, IA	15.0	35.0	27.5	16.1	3.7	1.5	1.1
Durham, NC	9.8	31.4	24.8	21.0	7.3	4.2	1.5
Edison, NJ	7.0	18.5	16.3	24.0	12.7	14.7	6.8
El Paso, TX	10.3	31.9	27.4	21.0	5.2	2.3	1.9
Fargo, ND	17.8	52.1	18.3	6.0	2.4	1.9	1.4
Fort Collins, CO	13.5	35.4	21.8	15.9	6.3	4.9	2.2
Fort Wayne, IN	13.0	35.3	28.4	15.7	3.4	2.4	1.8
Fort Worth, TX	8.6	25.2	21.7	25.6	10.3	6.7	2.0
Grand Rapids, MI	14.8	35.3	24.7	16.1	5.0	2.6	1.5
Greeley, CO	11.6	26.7	18.8	22.8	9.8	8.1	2.3
Green Bay, WI	17.9	40.4	21.9	13.0	3.6	1.7	1.4
Greensboro, NC	12.8	34.6	24.4	18.6	4.8	3.0	1.9
Honolulu, HI	9.8	26.1	19.9	24.9	9.4	7.3	2.6
Houston, TX	7.6	23.2	20.4	26.7	11.6	8.2	2.3
Huntsville, AL	10.1	31.7	27.7	22.1	5.2	1.9	1.2
Indianapolis, IN	11.4	27.7	23.9	24.5	7.4	3.4	1.7
Jacksonville, FL	9.1	26.1	24.3	26.1	8.6	4.2	1.6
Kansas City, MO	12.3	30.6	25.5	21.6	6.3	2.5	1.3
Lafayette, LA	13.3	33.5	20.9	18.5	5.9	3.8	4.0
Las Cruces, NM	13.9	40.3	20.0	14.2	5.2	4.8	1.7
Las Vegas, NV	7.8	27.5	29.4	25.4	5.4	2.6	1.9
Lexington, KY	14.5	35.6	24.5	16.8	4.3	2.6	1.7
Lincoln, NE	16.9	41.6	23.5	11.6	3.0	2.2	1.3
Little Rock, AR	13.0	32.7	22.6	20.4	7.0	2.9	1.4
Los Angeles, CA	7.1	24.8	19.9	25.4	9.9	9.3	3.5
Louisville, KY	9.7	30.1	28.8	22.0	5.7	2.4	1.5
Madison, WI	15.9	32.2	24.8	18.2	5.3	2.5	1.1

Table continued on following page.

Metro Area	Less Than 10 Minutes	10 to 19 Minutes	20 to 29 Minutes	30 to 44 Minutes	45 to 59 Minutes	60 to 89 Minutes	90 Minutes or More
Manchester, NH	10.9	29.7	21.2	19.5	8.7	6.7	3.4
Miami, FL	6.6	22.6	22.7	27.7	10.2	7.6	2.6
Midland, TX	14.7	42.7	21.0	13.5	3.3	2.5	2.2
Milwaukee, WI	12.1	32.1	25.7	21.2	5.0	2.5	1.4
Minneapolis, MN	10.6	28.0	25.2	23.2	7.7	4.0	1.4
Nashville, TN	9.4	26.2	21.5	23.5	10.9	6.5	2.0
New Haven, CT	11.7	31.6	23.1	19.7	6.3	4.6	3.0
New Orleans, LA	10.9	30.8	21.8	20.7	8.0	5.5	2.4
New York, NY	7.0	18.5	16.3	24.0	12.7	14.7	6.8
Oklahoma City, OK	11.9	32.3	25.4	20.6	5.7	2.5	1.6
Omaha, NE	14.1	36.1	27.3	16.0	3.6	1.9	1.1
Orlando, FL	7.2	22.9	22.3	28.1	11.2	6.0	2.4
Philadelphia, PA	9.6	23.9	20.6	24.0	11.1	7.8	3.1
Phoenix, AZ	9.9	26.1	24.0	23.6	8.9	5.6	1.9
Pittsburgh, PA	11.8	27.0	21.3	22.9	9.1	5.8	2.1
Portland, OR	10.8	27.5	23.0	22.7	8.9	5.1	2.0
Providence, RI	11.7	30.4	21.3	19.8	7.8	6.2	2.8
Provo, UT	17.1	34.7	20.2	16.5	6.2	3.9	1.5
Raleigh, NC	8.6	26.7	24.4	24.4	9.1	4.9	1.9
Reno, NV	13.0	35.6	24.5	17.2	5.2	2.9	1.6
Richmond, VA	9.3	28.8	26.7	23.5	6.6	3.1	2.1
Rochester, MN	18.1	41.7	18.6	12.6	4.3	2.9	1.9
Sacramento, CA	9.9	28.3	22.4	23.1	7.9	4.7	3.7
St. Louis, MO	11.0	27.3	24.4	24.0	7.9	3.8	1.7
Salem, OR	13.7	32.6	20.9	16.9	7.6	6.3	2.0
Salt Lake City, UT	10.8	33.5	26.9	19.2	5.5	3.0	1.2
San Antonio, TX	9.2	27.8	24.1	23.2	8.7	4.8	2.2
San Diego, CA	8.1	29.4	24.5	23.5	7.5	5.0	2.1
San Francisco, CA	7.0	22.9	17.8	23.6	11.9	12.0	4.9
San Jose, CA	7.0	26.5	23.0	24.3	9.1	7.0	3.1
Santa Rosa, CA	14.0	32.4	20.4	17.1	6.4	6.0	3.8
Savannah, GA	11.0	29.3	24.8	21.8	8.2	3.6	1.5
Seattle, WA	8.2	22.3	21.1	25.2	11.2	8.6	3.4
Sioux Falls, SD	16.8	43.8	24.1	10.0	2.6	1.4	1.2
Springfield, IL	15.0	43.3	23.5	11.8	2.5	2.1	1.8
Tampa, FL	9.6	26.9	21.0	23.7	10.2	6.3	2.3
Tucson, AZ	10.6	29.4	24.7	24.1	7.0	2.4	1.7
Tulsa, OK	13.3	33.7	26.9	18.0	4.6	2.1	1.4
Tuscaloosa, AL	11.1	33.8	23.3	17.4	6.7	5.7	2.0
Virginia Beach, VA	11.1	31.1	23.5	21.4	7.1	4.0	1.7
Washington, DC	6.1	19.3	18.2	26.2	13.7	12.1	4.3
Wichita, KS	16.1	37.2	26.2	15.1	2.7	1.5	1.3
Wilmington, NC	12.7	38.0	22.6	16.0	5.7	2.8	2.1
Winston-Salem, NC	12.5	32.5	24.3	19.3	6.1	3.2	2.2
Worcester, MA	12.3	26.0	18.5	20.6	10.4	8.5	3.8
U.S.	12.4	28.5	21.0	20.9	8.2	6.2	2.9

Note: Figures are percentages and include workers 16 years old and over; Figures cover the Metropolitan Statistical Area
Source: U.S. Census Bureau, 2017-2021 American Community Survey 5-Year Estimates

2020 Presidential Election Results

City	Area Covered	Biden	Trump	Jorgensen	Hawkins	Other
Albuquerque, NM	Bernalillo County	61.0	36.6	1.5	0.5	0.4
Allentown, PA	Lehigh County	53.1	45.5	1.2	0.1	0.2
Anchorage, AK	State of Alaska	42.8	52.8	2.5	0.0	1.9
Ann Arbor, MI	Washtenaw County	72.4	25.9	0.9	0.3	0.4
Athens, GA	Clarke County	70.1	28.1	1.6	0.1	0.1
Atlanta, GA	Fulton County	72.6	26.2	1.2	0.0	0.0
Austin, TX	Travis County	71.4	26.4	1.5	0.3	0.4
Baltimore, MD	Baltimore City	87.3	10.7	0.7	0.6	0.7
Boise City, ID	Ada County	46.1	50.0	2.0	0.1	1.8
Boston, MA	Suffolk County	80.6	17.5	0.9	0.5	0.5
Boulder, CO	Boulder County	77.2	20.6	1.2	0.3	0.6
Brownsville, TX	Cameron County	56.0	42.9	0.6	0.3	0.1
Cape Coral, FL	Lee County	39.9	59.1	0.5	0.1	0.3
Cedar Rapids, IA	Linn County	55.6	41.9	1.6	0.3	0.7
Charleston, SC	Charleston County	55.5	42.6	1.5	0.3	0.1
Charlotte, NC	Mecklenburg County	66.7	31.6	1.0	0.3	0.5
Chicago, IL	Cook County	74.2	24.0	0.8	0.5	0.5
Cincinnati, OH	Hamilton County	57.1	41.3	1.2	0.3	0.0
Clarksville, TN	Montgomery County	42.3	55.0	1.9	0.2	0.7
Cleveland, OH	Cuyahoga County	66.4	32.3	0.7	0.3	0.3
College Station, TX	Brazos County	41.4	55.7	2.1	0.3	0.4
Colorado Springs, CO	El Paso County	42.7	53.5	2.4	0.3	1.0
Columbia, MO	Boone County	54.8	42.3	2.2	0.3	0.4
Columbia, SC	Richland County	68.4	30.1	1.0	0.4	0.1
Columbus, OH	Franklin County	64.7	33.4	1.2	0.3	0.4
Dallas, TX	Dallas County	64.9	33.3	1.0	0.4	0.4
Davenport, IA	Scott County	50.7	47.2	1.2	0.2	0.7
Denver, CO	Denver County	79.6	18.2	1.2	0.3	0.7
Des Moines, IA	Polk County	56.5	41.3	1.3	0.2	0.7
Durham, NC	Durham County	80.4	18.0	0.8	0.3	0.4
Edison, NJ	Middlesex County	60.2	38.2	0.7	0.3	0.6
El Paso, TX	El Paso County	66.7	31.6	1.0	0.5	0.2
Fargo, ND	Cass County	46.8	49.5	2.9	0.0	0.7
Fort Collins, CO	Larimer County	56.2	40.8	1.8	0.3	0.9
Fort Wayne, IN	Allen County	43.2	54.3	2.2	0.0	0.3
Fort Worth, TX	Tarrant County	49.3	49.1	1.2	0.3	0.0
Grand Rapids, MI	Kent County	51.9	45.8	1.5	0.3	0.5
Greeley, CO	Weld County	39.6	57.6	1.7	0.2	0.9
Green Bay, WI	Brown County	45.5	52.7	1.3	0.0	0.5
Greensboro, NC	Guilford County	60.8	37.7	0.8	0.2	0.4
Honolulu, HI	Honolulu County	62.5	35.7	0.9	0.6	0.4
Houston, TX	Harris County	55.9	42.7	1.0	0.3	0.0
Huntsville, AL	Madison County	44.8	52.8	1.9	0.0	0.5
Indianapolis, IN	Marion County	63.3	34.3	1.8	0.1	0.4
Jacksonville, FL	Duval County	51.1	47.3	1.0	0.2	0.5
Kansas City, MO	Jackson County	59.8	37.9	1.4	0.4	0.5
Lafayette, LA	Lafayette Parish	34.7	63.3	1.3	0.0	0.7
Las Cruces, NM	Dona Ana County	58.0	39.7	1.4	0.5	0.4
Las Vegas, NV	Clark County	53.7	44.3	0.9	0.0	1.1
Lexington, KY	Fayette County	59.2	38.5	1.6	0.1	0.6
Lincoln, NE	Lancaster County	52.3	44.6	2.4	0.0	0.7
Little Rock, AR	Pulaski County	60.0	37.5	1.0	0.3	1.3
Los Angeles, CA	Los Angeles County	71.0	26.9	0.8	0.5	0.8
Louisville, KY	Jefferson County	58.9	38.8	1.2	0.1	1.0
Madison, WI	Dane County	75.5	22.9	1.1	0.1	0.6
Manchester, NH	Hillsborough County	52.8	45.2	1.7	0.0	0.3

Table continued on following page.

City	Area Covered	Biden	Trump	Jorgensen	Hawkins	Other
Miami, FL	Miami-Dade County	53.3	46.0	0.3	0.1	0.3
Midland, TX	Midland County	20.9	77.3	1.3	0.2	0.2
Milwaukee, WI	Milwaukee County	69.1	29.3	0.9	0.0	0.7
Minneapolis, MN	Hennepin County	70.5	27.2	1.0	0.3	1.0
Nashville, TN	Davidson County	64.5	32.4	1.1	0.2	1.8
New Haven, CT	New Haven County	58.0	40.6	0.9	0.4	0.0
New Orleans, LA	Orleans Parish	83.1	15.0	0.9	0.0	1.0
New York, NY	Bronx County	83.3	15.9	0.2	0.3	0.3
New York, NY	Kings County	76.8	22.1	0.3	0.4	0.4
New York, NY	New York County	86.4	12.2	0.5	0.4	0.5
New York, NY	Queens County	72.0	26.9	0.3	0.4	0.4
New York, NY	Richmond County	42.0	56.9	0.4	0.3	0.4
Oklahoma City, OK	Oklahoma County	48.1	49.2	1.8	0.0	0.9
Omaha, NE	Douglas County	54.4	43.1	2.0	0.0	0.6
Orlando, FL	Orange County	60.9	37.8	0.7	0.2	0.4
Philadelphia, PA	Philadelphia County	81.2	17.9	0.7	0.1	0.2
Phoenix, AZ	Maricopa County	50.1	48.0	1.5	0.0	0.3
Pittsburgh, PA	Allegheny County	59.4	39.0	1.2	0.0	0.4
Portland, OR	Multnomah County	79.2	17.9	1.2	0.6	1.0
Providence, RI	Providence County	60.5	37.6	0.8	0.0	1.0
Provo, UT	Utah County	26.3	66.7	3.6	0.3	3.1
Raleigh, NC	Wake County	62.3	35.8	1.2	0.3	0.5
Reno, NV	Washoe County	50.8	46.3	1.4	0.0	1.5
Richmond, VA	Richmond City	82.9	14.9	1.5	0.0	0.6
Rochester, MN	Olmsted County	54.2	43.4	1.2	0.3	0.9
Sacramento, CA	Sacramento County	61.4	36.1	1.4	0.5	0.7
St. Louis, MO	St. Louis City	81.9	16.0	1.1	0.4	0.5
Salem, OR	Marion County	48.9	47.7	2.0	0.5	0.9
Salt Lake City, UT	Salt Lake County	53.0	42.1	2.2	0.4	2.2
San Antonio, TX	Bexar County	58.2	40.1	1.1	0.4	0.2
San Diego, CA	San Diego County	60.2	37.5	1.3	0.5	0.5
San Francisco, CA	San Francisco County	85.3	12.7	0.7	0.6	0.7
San Jose, CA	Santa Clara County	72.6	25.2	1.1	0.5	0.6
Santa Rosa, CA	Sonoma County	74.5	23.0	1.3	0.6	0.6
Savannah, GA	Chatham County	58.6	39.9	1.4	0.0	0.0
Seattle, WA	King County	75.0	22.2	1.5	0.5	0.8
Sioux Falls, SD	Minnehaha County	43.8	53.3	2.8	0.0	0.0
Springfield, IL	Sangamon County	46.5	50.9	1.4	0.6	0.6
Tampa, FL	Hillsborough County	52.7	45.8	0.8	0.2	0.5
Tucson, AZ	Pima County	58.4	39.8	1.5	0.0	0.3
Tulsa, OK	Tulsa County	40.9	56.5	1.8	0.0	0.8
Tuscaloosa, AL	Tuscaloosa County	41.9	56.7	1.0	0.0	0.4
Virginia Beach, VA	Virginia Beach City	51.6	46.2	1.8	0.0	0.4
Washington, DC	District of Columbia	92.1	5.4	0.6	0.5	1.4
Wichita, KS	Sedgwick County	42.6	54.4	2.4	0.0	0.5
Wilmington, NC	New Hanover County	50.2	48.0	1.2	0.3	0.4
Winston-Salem, NC	Forsyth County	56.2	42.3	0.9	0.2	0.4
Worcester, MA	Worcester County	57.6	39.7	1.7	0.6	0.4
U.S.	U.S.	51.3	46.8	1.2	0.3	0.5

Note: Results are percentages and may not add to 100% due to rounding
Source: Dave Leip's Atlas of U.S. Presidential Elections

House Price Index (HPI)

Metro Area[1]	National Ranking[3]	Quarterly Change (%)	One-Year Change (%)	Five-Year Change (%)	Since 1991Q1 (%)
Albuquerque, NM	67	0.95	14.03	58.76	256.02
Allentown, PA	104	-0.97	12.09	52.30	165.53
Anchorage, AK	215	-0.36	8.00	27.30	235.38
Ann Arbor, MI	210	-4.46	8.26	40.08	220.18
Athens, GA	33	0.64	16.98	76.16	301.70
Atlanta, GA	40	-0.35	16.14	73.42	274.52
Austin, TX	222	-5.35	7.56	75.92	618.91
Baltimore, MD	199	0.91	8.63	34.77	214.03
Boise City, ID	256	-6.44	1.06	96.45	501.63
Boston, MA[2]	195	-1.14	8.90	44.63	310.81
Boulder, CO	150	-1.96	10.66	47.80	588.29
Brownsville, TX	n/a	n/a	n/a	n/a	n/a
Cape Coral, FL	6	-0.47	20.91	83.64	358.39
Cedar Rapids, IA	243	-4.60	5.29	30.92	170.24
Charleston, SC	29	-0.34	17.51	66.55	441.52
Charlotte, NC	19	0.48	18.66	78.79	310.41
Chicago, IL[2]	205	-1.86	8.51	31.58	168.46
Cincinnati, OH	96	-0.52	12.38	55.37	199.65
Clarksville, TN	n/a	n/a	n/a	n/a	n/a
Cleveland, OH	189	-1.76	9.23	49.32	153.83
College Station, TX	n/a	n/a	n/a	n/a	n/a
Colorado Springs, CO	231	-3.83	6.63	67.59	425.90
Columbia, MO	148	1.10	10.69	48.19	225.68
Columbia, SC	23	1.44	18.32	59.58	209.37
Columbus, OH	94	-1.27	12.41	59.08	243.03
Dallas, TX[2]	43	-1.44	15.77	61.60	325.13
Davenport, IA	220	0.26	7.72	30.21	202.26
Denver, CO	216	-2.41	7.96	52.15	548.72
Des Moines, IA	108	0.29	12.00	40.34	223.17
Durham, NC	45	-3.85	15.68	66.89	294.13
Edison, NJ[2]	212	-0.09	8.22	34.61	258.57
El Paso, TX	21	2.05	18.42	54.29	201.64
Fargo, ND	133	0.78	11.14	32.39	270.20
Fort Collins, CO	141	-2.34	10.88	51.04	508.13
Fort Wayne, IN	68	1.56	14.01	67.52	186.04
Fort Worth, TX[2]	53	-1.47	15.09	66.00	306.95
Grand Rapids, MI	116	n/a	11.72	62.74	262.62
Greeley, CO	207	-3.14	8.35	53.74	462.73
Green Bay, WI	25	3.83	17.89	59.68	250.27
Greensboro, NC	26	0.70	17.71	64.64	188.62
Honolulu, HI	122	-5.39	11.51	33.52	222.93
Houston, TX	81	0.53	13.01	46.44	300.24
Huntsville, AL	109	-1.12	11.99	73.58	211.74
Indianapolis, IN	99	-1.53	12.29	62.22	209.62
Jacksonville, FL	35	-1.80	16.79	76.35	371.41
Kansas City, MO	102	-0.14	12.17	58.36	257.00
Lafayette, LA	179	-0.60	9.73	25.29	232.27
Las Cruces, NM	n/a	n/a	n/a	n/a	n/a
Las Vegas, NV	157	-3.37	10.38	70.87	260.78
Lexington, KY	72	0.70	13.70	53.19	235.38
Lincoln, NE	107	0.03	12.01	49.08	257.46
Little Rock, AR	119	0.21	11.59	41.21	196.34
Los Angeles, CA[2]	200	-1.90	8.62	46.01	298.97
Louisville, KY	147	1.02	10.70	47.57	251.74
Madison, WI	121	-1.67	11.52	45.50	303.94

Table continued on following page.

Metro Area[1]	National Ranking[3]	Quarterly Change (%)	One-Year Change (%)	Five-Year Change (%)	Since 1991Q1 (%)
Manchester, NH	126	-0.32	11.34	59.79	253.04
Miami, FL[2]	4	2.23	21.62	75.85	539.14
Midland, TX	n/a	n/a	n/a	n/a	n/a
Milwaukee, WI	134	-1.54	11.11	45.94	239.44
Minneapolis, MN	239	-1.83	6.08	41.05	273.41
Nashville, TN	34	-1.19	16.94	75.36	429.41
New Haven, CT	113	0.91	11.80	48.13	135.81
New Orleans, LA	202	0.06	8.58	36.52	291.68
New York, NY[2]	212	-0.09	8.22	34.61	258.57
Oklahoma City, OK	97	0.36	12.37	49.27	260.86
Omaha, NE	161	-0.79	10.26	51.61	252.12
Orlando, FL	13	0.53	19.76	74.99	330.12
Philadelphia, PA[2]	187	1.72	9.32	47.35	257.72
Phoenix, AZ	144	-4.25	10.82	83.46	453.06
Pittsburgh, PA	224	-1.54	7.43	42.48	223.87
Portland, OR	247	-2.87	4.63	43.13	493.76
Providence, RI	153	-0.93	10.48	54.47	232.15
Provo, UT	206	-3.27	8.39	75.92	514.28
Raleigh, NC	57	-2.71	14.97	69.49	298.33
Reno, NV	244	-1.71	5.01	60.21	333.43
Richmond, VA	79	-0.25	13.11	53.64	254.70
Rochester, MN	234	-3.55	6.25	42.75	234.69
Sacramento, CA	253	-3.63	3.17	45.83	234.41
St. Louis, MO	190	-0.80	9.10	40.60	193.95
Salem, OR	204	-1.19	8.51	62.82	461.52
Salt Lake City, UT	197	-2.92	8.70	74.37	596.70
San Antonio, TX	50	0.79	15.27	62.24	345.76
San Diego, CA	181	-2.11	9.62	51.34	344.82
San Francisco, CA[2]	177	3.28	9.77	19.08	360.06
San Jose, CA	101	1.47	12.23	31.21	389.33
Santa Rosa, CA	250	-4.80	3.50	26.56	276.48
Savannah, GA	12	1.20	19.86	70.81	361.13
Seattle, WA[2]	236	-3.59	6.21	48.84	436.06
Sioux Falls, SD	92	-1.20	12.49	55.67	315.04
Springfield, IL	158	-0.16	10.38	29.11	125.30
Tampa, FL	10	-0.71	19.98	91.22	438.13
Tucson, AZ	73	-1.74	13.68	74.77	329.80
Tulsa, OK	58	0.72	14.67	52.24	236.95
Tuscaloosa, AL	n/a	n/a	n/a	n/a	n/a
Virginia Beach, VA	131	0.74	11.17	43.79	243.78
Washington, DC[2]	238	-1.35	6.16	35.79	253.98
Wichita, KS	151	-1.84	10.63	47.99	197.78
Wilmington, NC	18	-1.23	18.70	72.00	356.80
Winston-Salem, NC	37	0.94	16.66	66.13	201.85
Worcester, MA	184	-1.36	9.48	52.36	218.67
U.S.[4]	—	0.34	8.41	58.44	289.08

Note: The HPI is a weighted repeat sales index. It measures average price changes in repeat sales or refinancings on the same properties. This information is obtained by reviewing repeat mortgage transactions on single-family properties whose mortgages have been purchased or securitized by Fannie Mae or Freddie Mac since January 1975; all figures are for the period ended December 31, 2022; (1) figures cover the Metropolitan Statistical Area (MSA) unless noted otherwise; (2) Metropolitan Division; (3) Rankings are based on annual percentage change, for all MSAs containing at least 15,000 transactions over the last 10 years and ranges from 1 to 257; (4) figures based on a weighted division average; (a) Not ranked because of increased index variability due to smaller sample size; n/a not available
Source: Federal Housing Finance Agency, Change in FHFA Metropolitan Area House Price Indexes, 2022Q4

Home Value: City

City	Under $100,000	$100,000 -$199,999	$200,000 -$299,999	$300,000 -$399,999	$400,000 -$499,999	$500,000 -$999,999	$1,000,000 or more	Median ($)
Albuquerque, NM	8.2	36.2	31.9	13.0	5.9	4.2	0.6	214,600
Allentown, PA	19.9	58.7	14.0	3.6	1.8	1.4	0.5	145,700
Anchorage, AK	6.7	10.2	25.3	28.2	13.9	14.3	1.4	327,500
Ann Arbor, MI	2.4	10.8	20.5	24.6	18.8	19.9	3.0	366,600
Athens, GA	16.0	34.3	25.3	10.4	5.8	6.9	1.2	199,300
Atlanta, GA	8.9	17.3	17.4	13.6	10.3	23.2	9.3	346,600
Austin, TX	3.6	8.4	20.6	21.5	15.3	24.7	6.0	381,400
Baltimore, MD	21.5	35.5	21.4	10.3	4.3	5.9	1.0	175,300
Boise City, ID	5.2	12.8	27.2	22.0	13.5	17.2	2.3	322,300
Boston, MA	2.6	1.0	5.5	11.1	15.0	48.4	16.5	610,400
Boulder, CO	5.2	3.5	3.6	5.3	6.9	44.1	31.4	790,100
Brownsville, TX	53.5	34.4	9.1	1.4	0.6	0.8	0.1	95,700
Cape Coral, FL	3.4	25.6	35.3	19.8	6.7	8.1	1.2	255,700
Cedar Rapids, IA	18.6	53.5	19.0	5.4	1.7	1.5	0.3	149,000
Charleston, SC	3.1	7.6	23.0	23.5	11.5	23.2	8.1	369,500
Charlotte, NC	7.8	27.5	23.8	14.8	8.8	13.3	4.0	258,000
Chicago, IL	8.5	22.4	24.5	16.5	9.6	14.2	4.3	277,600
Cincinnati, OH	24.5	35.2	17.3	9.2	4.7	7.2	1.8	162,300
Clarksville, TN	13.0	51.0	25.3	6.3	1.6	2.6	0.3	172,700
Cleveland, OH	67.7	23.2	4.6	2.2	0.7	1.3	0.2	74,700
College Station, TX	2.2	18.2	39.2	25.7	7.6	6.3	0.7	269,100
Colorado Springs, CO	4.6	11.0	28.1	26.0	14.7	14.1	1.4	324,100
Columbia, MO	8.9	35.8	29.2	14.1	6.5	5.1	0.5	215,300
Columbia, SC	17.9	34.1	18.9	9.7	5.5	11.7	2.2	193,100
Columbus, OH	19.2	40.1	25.2	9.3	2.9	2.8	0.5	174,400
Dallas, TX	17.6	27.3	15.3	11.0	8.6	14.8	5.5	230,000
Davenport, IA	28.0	44.6	17.1	7.5	1.1	1.4	0.3	138,000
Denver, CO	2.3	4.6	12.8	20.0	17.5	34.9	7.9	459,100
Des Moines, IA	20.9	53.8	17.0	4.6	1.5	1.9	0.3	149,700
Durham, NC	5.0	24.8	31.4	20.4	8.2	9.0	1.1	264,100
Edison, NJ	3.9	3.9	14.5	26.0	20.3	29.1	2.3	408,100
El Paso, TX	25.7	52.3	14.1	4.5	1.7	1.4	0.3	137,600
Fargo, ND	7.4	30.1	36.2	16.5	4.6	4.4	0.7	232,900
Fort Collins, CO	4.0	2.8	10.0	24.0	29.5	27.3	2.4	431,300
Fort Wayne, IN	32.7	46.5	14.2	4.0	1.2	1.1	0.2	130,700
Fort Worth, TX	15.9	29.7	31.6	12.1	4.7	4.8	1.2	212,300
Grand Rapids, MI	16.4	49.8	24.0	6.0	2.0	1.4	0.3	168,700
Greeley, CO	9.3	8.9	33.0	31.0	10.6	6.8	0.3	296,300
Green Bay, WI	17.2	57.2	16.1	5.1	2.4	1.8	0.2	151,000
Greensboro, NC	19.7	40.5	20.3	9.3	4.4	4.8	1.0	169,100
Honolulu, HI	1.6	1.6	5.5	11.7	10.7	41.2	27.6	726,000
Houston, TX	19.1	30.8	17.1	11.0	6.7	11.3	4.0	200,700
Huntsville, AL	21.0	30.5	21.8	12.5	6.6	6.4	1.1	194,500
Indianapolis, IN	23.7	43.7	17.7	7.2	3.1	3.9	0.7	156,300
Jacksonville, FL	17.0	32.0	28.0	12.0	4.8	4.9	1.4	203,400
Kansas City, MO	23.0	34.6	21.2	11.4	4.1	4.8	0.8	175,400
Lafayette, LA	13.7	33.6	25.7	11.7	7.0	6.7	1.6	209,100
Las Cruces, NM	17.4	49.1	21.5	7.7	1.5	2.5	0.3	167,800
Las Vegas, NV	4.3	14.0	31.2	23.5	11.7	13.1	2.2	302,100
Lexington, KY	9.0	36.1	25.2	14.5	6.4	7.6	1.2	216,800
Lincoln, NE	9.6	42.9	27.9	11.1	4.5	3.2	0.7	193,800
Little Rock, AR	22.0	33.4	17.9	11.1	5.5	8.4	1.6	179,500
Los Angeles, CA	2.2	1.3	2.4	6.2	11.3	50.1	26.6	705,900
Louisville, KY	17.5	40.5	20.3	10.8	5.0	5.1	0.9	174,400
Madison, WI	3.4	18.6	35.0	22.5	10.9	8.3	1.3	277,800

Table continued on following page.

City	Under $100,000	$100,000 -$199,999	$200,000 -$299,999	$300,000 -$399,999	$400,000 -$499,999	$500,000 -$999,999	$1,000,000 or more	Median ($)
Manchester, NH	4.7	21.9	39.9	23.6	6.6	3.1	0.1	258,100
Miami, FL	4.5	9.8	20.4	22.1	14.7	20.0	8.4	369,100
Midland, TX	11.2	22.4	32.5	17.2	6.3	8.8	1.5	250,300
Milwaukee, WI	30.6	48.6	14.1	3.3	1.2	1.8	0.5	135,600
Minneapolis, MN	4.2	19.5	31.1	20.3	9.7	12.6	2.5	284,400
Nashville, TN	4.4	18.9	29.1	21.3	9.6	13.3	3.3	291,400
New Haven, CT	11.0	36.4	29.4	10.5	5.4	5.7	1.6	207,600
New Orleans, LA	9.7	28.7	20.4	13.4	8.3	15.2	4.2	255,500
New York, NY	4.3	3.6	5.5	8.2	10.8	44.7	22.9	660,700
Oklahoma City, OK	23.1	38.5	21.4	8.2	3.8	3.8	1.2	168,900
Omaha, NE	15.7	42.7	23.3	9.7	4.0	3.9	0.7	177,700
Orlando, FL	7.5	23.3	22.9	20.6	10.8	12.3	2.6	283,700
Philadelphia, PA	21.6	33.0	22.8	10.0	4.6	6.6	1.4	184,100
Phoenix, AZ	7.3	19.8	28.5	18.6	9.6	13.8	2.4	277,700
Pittsburgh, PA	33.7	31.4	13.9	7.9	4.8	7.2	1.1	147,600
Portland, OR	2.6	2.8	9.9	21.8	20.5	38.3	4.1	462,800
Providence, RI	4.9	27.5	34.7	14.0	4.1	11.6	3.2	248,900
Provo, UT	5.3	9.2	27.9	26.4	12.3	16.1	2.7	328,500
Raleigh, NC	4.0	21.6	28.3	18.3	11.0	14.2	2.7	285,400
Reno, NV	5.9	5.9	14.6	25.8	20.2	24.1	3.5	391,500
Richmond, VA	9.5	26.4	21.0	16.5	8.6	14.2	3.8	263,000
Rochester, MN	5.8	30.7	30.8	16.9	8.6	6.8	0.5	236,400
Sacramento, CA	4.0	5.0	19.4	25.1	19.3	24.0	3.0	385,500
St. Louis, MO	29.9	36.3	17.8	8.4	3.4	3.4	0.9	153,200
Salem, OR	7.5	13.6	32.7	26.7	11.1	7.9	0.5	289,500
Salt Lake City, UT	3.8	10.8	19.8	19.3	14.6	26.2	5.3	380,200
San Antonio, TX	24.0	38.4	21.9	8.7	3.3	3.1	0.6	167,700
San Diego, CA	2.6	1.4	3.1	8.1	13.7	51.4	19.8	664,000
San Francisco, CA	1.5	0.8	1.0	1.9	1.6	26.1	67.1	1,194,500
San Jose, CA	2.3	2.5	2.0	1.6	2.6	40.3	48.6	986,700
Santa Rosa, CA	4.1	2.6	4.0	7.3	13.6	60.0	8.4	598,700
Savannah, GA	19.1	41.2	21.4	6.7	4.4	5.9	1.3	170,500
Seattle, WA	1.1	0.6	2.7	6.3	8.6	55.3	25.4	767,500
Sioux Falls, SD	10.1	32.4	31.9	12.6	6.1	5.6	1.3	218,600
Springfield, IL	34.4	38.8	15.9	6.3	2.4	1.9	0.4	132,900
Tampa, FL	9.0	22.7	22.8	14.6	9.9	14.9	6.1	277,700
Tucson, AZ	17.8	41.3	26.3	8.4	3.0	2.4	0.7	177,800
Tulsa, OK	28.0	36.9	15.4	8.2	4.4	5.5	1.5	151,500
Tuscaloosa, AL	14.2	37.7	19.5	11.1	6.0	10.0	1.6	194,500
Virginia Beach, VA	3.8	15.6	32.0	21.6	11.7	12.8	2.6	295,900
Washington, DC	1.8	2.2	7.5	12.3	12.7	42.1	21.4	635,900
Wichita, KS	31.2	39.6	17.3	6.7	2.2	2.7	0.3	145,300
Wilmington, NC	5.9	23.6	25.8	19.2	8.2	13.7	3.7	279,900
Winston-Salem, NC	22.4	44.2	16.7	7.0	3.5	5.6	0.6	158,600
Worcester, MA	4.7	20.1	40.8	22.2	6.8	4.6	0.9	259,800
U.S.	16.2	24.2	20.1	13.6	8.3	13.6	4.1	244,900

Note: Figures are percentages except for median and cover owner-occupied housing units.
Source: U.S. Census Bureau, 2017-2021 American Community Survey 5-Year Estimates

Home Value: Metro Area

MSA[1]	Under $100,000	$100,000 -$199,999	$200,000 -$299,999	$300,000 -$399,999	$400,000 -$499,999	$500,000 -$999,999	$1,000,000 or more	Median ($)
Albuquerque, NM	11.7	34.6	28.4	12.3	5.9	5.9	1.1	210,700
Allentown, PA	9.9	31.5	28.8	17.1	7.2	5.1	0.6	227,900
Anchorage, AK	6.7	12.7	28.8	26.2	12.5	12.0	1.1	306,700
Ann Arbor, MI	9.2	18.2	24.0	19.4	12.7	14.5	1.9	293,800
Athens, GA	16.8	30.0	23.5	12.5	7.6	8.0	1.7	211,500
Atlanta, GA	8.9	26.9	25.0	16.1	9.3	11.7	2.0	252,100
Austin, TX	6.2	12.5	25.9	20.6	12.6	18.1	4.1	326,400
Baltimore, MD	6.7	15.8	23.5	20.6	12.8	18.2	2.4	319,500
Boise City, ID	6.9	15.9	25.8	21.3	13.1	14.9	2.1	306,300
Boston, MA	2.5	3.6	10.6	18.0	17.3	38.5	9.4	487,600
Boulder, CO	4.1	2.1	5.7	13.1	16.3	44.3	14.5	575,700
Brownsville, TX	53.6	31.8	8.9	2.9	1.1	1.4	0.2	94,200
Cape Coral, FL	12.0	23.6	27.5	16.4	7.3	10.5	2.8	248,300
Cedar Rapids, IA	17.2	44.7	22.6	8.4	3.7	3.0	0.5	165,500
Charleston, SC	10.8	21.0	24.9	16.5	8.1	14.0	4.6	270,700
Charlotte, NC	13.0	27.8	23.7	15.3	8.0	10.0	2.3	237,300
Chicago, IL	8.6	25.3	26.7	17.5	8.5	10.9	2.5	258,500
Cincinnati, OH	16.4	37.7	23.2	11.6	4.9	5.4	0.9	187,000
Clarksville, TN	19.0	41.2	23.4	9.2	2.9	3.7	0.7	174,300
Cleveland, OH	23.8	37.8	20.5	9.2	4.1	3.9	0.6	164,400
College Station, TX	20.3	25.9	24.8	14.8	5.2	7.7	1.3	213,600
Colorado Springs, CO	4.6	10.9	26.6	25.1	14.8	16.3	1.6	331,300
Columbia, MO	14.6	36.8	24.4	12.8	5.2	5.2	1.0	195,600
Columbia, SC	22.5	38.6	19.7	9.2	4.2	4.9	1.0	167,800
Columbus, OH	14.2	32.0	25.3	14.2	6.8	6.6	0.9	213,600
Dallas, TX	10.9	24.1	26.2	17.0	9.3	10.2	2.4	255,600
Davenport, IA	27.9	41.0	17.1	8.3	2.8	2.6	0.4	145,200
Denver, CO	3.2	3.4	11.5	22.5	21.7	32.8	4.9	443,400
Des Moines, IA	12.8	35.7	26.8	13.6	5.6	5.0	0.6	205,200
Durham, NC	10.6	23.8	24.0	17.7	9.2	12.7	1.9	264,400
Edison, NJ	3.5	5.2	11.1	16.7	16.1	36.2	11.2	483,500
El Paso, TX	29.8	49.6	13.5	4.1	1.4	1.2	0.3	131,200
Fargo, ND	8.0	29.3	32.7	16.9	6.0	6.3	0.8	235,600
Fort Collins, CO	4.9	3.0	11.4	25.9	23.2	28.1	3.4	420,200
Fort Wayne, IN	26.2	42.9	18.0	6.8	2.7	2.8	0.5	150,600
Fort Worth, TX	10.9	24.1	26.2	17.0	9.3	10.2	2.4	255,600
Grand Rapids, MI	14.0	34.9	27.4	12.2	5.7	4.7	1.1	203,500
Greeley, CO	7.1	7.0	21.1	28.5	17.5	17.3	1.5	352,000
Green Bay, WI	12.8	41.4	26.0	10.9	4.6	3.6	0.7	188,800
Greensboro, NC	22.8	39.9	19.0	9.0	4.4	4.2	0.7	162,700
Honolulu, HI	1.6	1.6	3.6	8.3	9.7	53.8	21.5	726,800
Houston, TX	13.5	30.4	25.4	13.7	6.5	8.0	2.5	221,400
Huntsville, AL	17.1	33.2	24.5	12.5	6.2	5.8	0.7	199,000
Indianapolis, IN	17.1	37.2	22.1	11.7	5.5	5.6	0.9	186,700
Jacksonville, FL	13.2	26.5	26.7	15.0	7.8	8.5	2.2	235,300
Kansas City, MO	15.2	31.5	24.6	14.0	6.8	6.8	1.1	211,900
Lafayette, LA	28.0	34.1	21.1	9.0	3.7	3.3	0.7	167,400
Las Cruces, NM	26.6	38.7	19.7	7.3	3.9	3.4	0.4	162,200
Las Vegas, NV	5.6	12.8	29.4	25.2	12.4	12.3	2.3	308,800
Lexington, KY	10.9	37.5	24.2	13.2	6.0	7.1	1.2	206,000
Lincoln, NE	9.4	39.9	27.0	12.5	5.5	4.7	0.9	202,300
Little Rock, AR	23.2	39.9	20.4	8.5	3.2	4.0	0.8	164,200
Los Angeles, CA	3.2	1.7	3.2	7.0	11.9	52.3	20.7	671,700
Louisville, KY	15.4	37.8	23.3	12.0	5.0	5.4	0.9	189,900
Madison, WI	5.1	20.5	30.8	21.7	10.9	9.4	1.6	277,400

Table continued on following page.

MSA[1]	Under $100,000	$100,000 -$199,999	$200,000 -$299,999	$300,000 -$399,999	$400,000 -$499,999	$500,000 -$999,999	$1,000,000 or more	Median ($)
Manchester, NH	4.2	13.5	30.7	27.5	12.9	10.7	0.5	306,000
Miami, FL	8.7	15.9	21.8	20.7	12.8	15.2	4.9	317,800
Midland, TX	16.5	20.8	29.5	16.1	6.9	8.7	1.4	243,400
Milwaukee, WI	10.6	29.0	27.8	16.4	7.5	7.4	1.2	235,100
Minneapolis, MN	4.6	17.1	32.2	21.8	11.2	11.4	1.7	287,600
Nashville, TN	6.6	19.5	27.4	19.2	9.9	14.1	3.2	286,800
New Haven, CT	6.4	25.9	29.4	18.7	10.0	8.3	1.2	259,400
New Orleans, LA	11.5	34.6	25.7	13.3	5.8	7.5	1.7	214,300
New York, NY	3.5	5.2	11.1	16.7	16.1	36.2	11.2	483,500
Oklahoma City, OK	21.7	39.2	20.6	9.0	4.1	4.1	1.2	169,300
Omaha, NE	13.4	38.4	24.8	12.5	5.4	4.7	0.8	195,000
Orlando, FL	10.4	20.5	30.9	19.9	8.1	8.3	1.9	260,800
Philadelphia, PA	9.6	21.9	25.7	18.4	10.4	12.1	1.8	270,400
Phoenix, AZ	8.3	15.9	27.3	20.3	11.4	13.9	2.9	294,700
Pittsburgh, PA	25.5	34.6	19.9	9.9	4.5	4.9	0.7	167,500
Portland, OR	4.2	3.7	12.4	25.2	21.3	29.7	3.5	421,300
Providence, RI	3.5	12.7	31.4	24.1	12.7	13.5	2.1	309,600
Provo, UT	3.1	6.2	22.3	28.1	17.5	20.2	2.6	365,500
Raleigh, NC	7.0	20.0	25.5	20.2	12.4	13.2	1.7	289,700
Reno, NV	5.5	6.4	16.4	25.0	18.1	22.9	5.9	387,400
Richmond, VA	6.4	24.3	29.8	18.4	9.3	10.4	1.5	262,900
Rochester, MN	9.2	29.8	26.8	16.1	8.6	8.3	1.2	234,700
Sacramento, CA	4.1	3.6	11.7	22.0	20.6	33.7	4.4	441,800
St. Louis, MO	20.0	33.1	22.7	12.1	5.2	5.7	1.2	189,600
Salem, OR	8.1	12.8	29.6	24.3	12.1	12.1	1.0	298,400
Salt Lake City, UT	3.8	8.2	22.9	24.5	16.6	21.1	2.9	361,600
San Antonio, TX	18.7	31.5	24.5	12.0	5.8	6.2	1.3	199,200
San Diego, CA	4.2	2.2	3.5	7.9	14.3	52.3	15.7	627,200
San Francisco, CA	2.0	1.4	1.7	3.8	5.9	40.7	44.4	933,300
San Jose, CA	2.1	2.0	1.7	1.6	2.3	32.2	58.0	1,113,700
Santa Rosa, CA	3.9	2.9	2.9	5.1	9.9	58.1	17.2	665,800
Savannah, GA	14.2	32.9	25.4	11.2	5.1	9.1	2.1	210,400
Seattle, WA	3.3	3.2	9.5	16.3	15.8	39.3	12.5	518,000
Sioux Falls, SD	11.0	31.1	29.9	14.0	6.4	6.5	1.2	221,500
Springfield, IL	29.8	38.6	19.5	7.3	2.4	2.0	0.4	148,000
Tampa, FL	16.4	25.3	26.4	14.8	6.9	8.1	2.0	229,400
Tucson, AZ	15.0	29.7	26.3	13.5	6.8	7.4	1.3	217,700
Tulsa, OK	24.2	39.1	19.5	8.6	3.5	4.1	0.9	163,100
Tuscaloosa, AL	24.9	35.9	20.8	9.4	3.6	4.6	0.8	171,100
Virginia Beach, VA	6.5	23.8	31.1	18.5	9.8	9.0	1.3	261,800
Washington, DC	2.4	4.9	14.2	19.7	16.6	34.4	7.8	453,100
Wichita, KS	28.6	40.0	18.4	7.4	2.6	2.6	0.4	151,900
Wilmington, NC	9.2	24.0	25.8	18.0	8.9	11.6	2.4	262,500
Winston-Salem, NC	20.7	42.5	19.5	8.7	3.7	4.4	0.5	165,000
Worcester, MA	3.6	16.4	30.3	22.9	12.3	13.1	1.3	298,900
U.S.	16.2	24.2	20.1	13.6	8.3	13.6	4.1	244,900

Note: (1) Figures cover the Metropolitan Statistical Area (MSA); Figures are percentages except for median and cover owner-occupied housing units.
Source: U.S. Census Bureau, 2017-2021 American Community Survey 5-Year Estimates

Homeownership Rate

Metro Area	2015	2016	2017	2018	2019	2020	2021	2022
Albuquerque, NM	64.3	66.9	67.0	67.9	70.0	69.5	66.5	67.3
Allentown, PA	69.2	68.9	73.1	72.1	67.8	68.8	70.4	73.1
Anchorage, AK	n/a	n/a	n/a	n/a	n/a	n/a	n/a	n/a
Ann Arbor, MI	n/a	n/a	n/a	n/a	n/a	n/a	n/a	n/a
Athens, GA	n/a	n/a	n/a	n/a	n/a	n/a	n/a	n/a
Atlanta, GA	61.7	61.5	62.4	64.0	64.2	66.4	64.2	64.4
Austin, TX	57.5	56.5	55.6	56.1	59.0	65.4	62.2	62.4
Baltimore, MD	65.3	68.5	67.5	63.5	66.5	70.7	67.5	70.4
Boise City, ID	n/a	n/a	n/a	n/a	n/a	n/a	n/a	n/a
Boston, MA	59.3	58.9	58.8	61.0	60.9	61.2	60.7	59.4
Boulder, CO	n/a	n/a	n/a	n/a	n/a	n/a	n/a	n/a
Brownsville, TX	n/a	n/a	n/a	n/a	n/a	n/a	n/a	n/a
Cape Coral, FL	62.9	66.5	65.5	75.1	72.0	77.4	76.1	70.8
Cedar Rapids, IA	n/a	n/a	n/a	n/a	n/a	n/a	n/a	n/a
Charleston, SC	65.8	62.1	67.7	68.8	70.7	75.5	73.2	71.9
Charlotte, NC	62.3	66.2	64.6	67.9	72.3	73.3	70.0	68.7
Chicago, IL	64.3	64.5	64.1	64.6	63.4	66.0	67.5	66.8
Cincinnati, OH	65.9	64.9	65.7	67.3	67.4	71.1	72.1	67.1
Clarksville, TN	n/a	n/a	n/a	n/a	n/a	n/a	n/a	n/a
Cleveland, OH	68.4	64.8	66.6	66.7	64.4	66.3	64.7	63.0
College Station, TX	n/a	n/a	n/a	n/a	n/a	n/a	n/a	n/a
Colorado Springs, CO	n/a	n/a	n/a	n/a	n/a	n/a	n/a	n/a
Columbia, MO	n/a	n/a	n/a	n/a	n/a	n/a	n/a	n/a
Columbia, SC	66.1	63.9	70.7	69.3	65.9	69.7	69.4	70.9
Columbus, OH	59.0	57.5	57.9	64.8	65.7	65.6	64.6	61.5
Dallas, TX	57.8	59.7	61.8	62.0	60.6	64.7	61.8	60.4
Davenport, IA	n/a	n/a	n/a	n/a	n/a	n/a	n/a	n/a
Denver, CO	61.6	61.6	59.3	60.1	63.5	62.9	62.8	64.6
Des Moines, IA	n/a	n/a	n/a	n/a	n/a	n/a	n/a	n/a
Durham, NC	n/a	n/a	n/a	n/a	n/a	n/a	n/a	n/a
Edison, NJ	49.9	50.4	49.9	49.7	50.4	50.9	50.7	50.5
El Paso, TX	n/a	n/a	n/a	n/a	n/a	n/a	n/a	n/a
Fargo, ND	n/a	n/a	n/a	n/a	n/a	n/a	n/a	n/a
Fort Collins, CO	n/a	n/a	n/a	n/a	n/a	n/a	n/a	n/a
Fort Wayne, IN	n/a	n/a	n/a	n/a	n/a	n/a	n/a	n/a
Fort Worth, TX	57.8	59.7	61.8	62.0	60.6	64.7	61.8	60.4
Grand Rapids, MI	75.8	76.2	71.7	73.0	75.2	71.8	65.0	68.1
Greeley, CO	n/a	n/a	n/a	n/a	n/a	n/a	n/a	n/a
Green Bay, WI	n/a	n/a	n/a	n/a	n/a	n/a	n/a	n/a
Greensboro, NC	65.4	62.9	61.9	63.2	61.7	65.8	61.9	70.0
Honolulu, HI	59.6	57.9	53.8	57.7	59.0	56.9	55.9	57.7
Houston, TX	60.3	59.0	58.9	60.1	61.3	65.3	64.1	63.7
Huntsville, AL	n/a	n/a	n/a	n/a	n/a	n/a	n/a	n/a
Indianapolis, IN	64.6	63.9	63.9	64.3	66.2	70.0	70.1	68.8
Jacksonville, FL	62.5	61.8	65.2	61.4	63.1	64.8	68.1	70.6
Kansas City, MO	65.0	62.4	62.4	64.3	65.0	66.7	63.8	63.8
Lafayette, LA	n/a	n/a	n/a	n/a	n/a	n/a	n/a	n/a
Las Cruces, NM	n/a	n/a	n/a	n/a	n/a	n/a	n/a	n/a
Las Vegas, NV	52.1	51.3	54.4	58.1	56.0	57.3	57.7	58.7
Lexington, KY	n/a	n/a	n/a	n/a	n/a	n/a	n/a	n/a
Lincoln, NE	n/a	n/a	n/a	n/a	n/a	n/a	n/a	n/a
Little Rock, AR	65.8	64.9	61.0	62.2	65.0	67.7	64.6	64.4
Los Angeles, CA	49.1	47.1	49.1	49.5	48.2	48.5	47.9	48.3
Louisville, KY	67.7	67.6	71.7	67.9	64.9	69.3	71.4	71.7
Madison, WI	n/a	n/a	n/a	n/a	n/a	n/a	n/a	n/a
Manchester, NH	n/a	n/a	n/a	n/a	n/a	n/a	n/a	n/a

Table continued on following page.

Metro Area	2015	2016	2017	2018	2019	2020	2021	2022
Miami, FL	58.6	58.4	57.9	59.9	60.4	60.6	59.4	58.3
Midland, TX	n/a	n/a	n/a	n/a	n/a	n/a	n/a	n/a
Milwaukee, WI	57.0	60.4	63.9	62.3	56.9	58.5	56.8	57.3
Minneapolis, MN	67.9	69.1	70.1	67.8	70.2	73.0	75.0	73.0
Nashville, TN	67.4	65.0	69.4	68.3	69.8	69.8	65.7	70.4
New Haven, CT	64.6	59.4	58.7	65.0	65.1	63.4	61.0	63.3
New Orleans, LA	62.8	59.3	61.7	62.6	61.1	66.3	66.2	66.3
New York, NY	49.9	50.4	49.9	49.7	50.4	50.9	50.7	50.5
Oklahoma City, OK	61.4	63.1	64.7	64.6	64.3	68.3	61.9	64.8
Omaha, NE	69.6	69.2	65.5	67.8	66.9	68.6	68.6	67.9
Orlando, FL	58.4	58.5	59.5	58.5	56.1	64.2	63.0	62.1
Philadelphia, PA	67.0	64.7	65.6	67.4	67.4	69.2	69.8	68.2
Phoenix, AZ	61.0	62.6	64.0	65.3	65.9	67.9	65.2	68.0
Pittsburgh, PA	71.0	72.2	72.7	71.7	71.5	69.8	69.1	72.7
Portland, OR	58.9	61.8	61.1	59.2	60.0	62.5	64.1	65.2
Providence, RI	60.0	57.5	58.6	61.3	63.5	64.8	64.1	66.3
Provo, UT	n/a	n/a	n/a	n/a	n/a	n/a	n/a	n/a
Raleigh, NC	67.4	65.9	68.2	64.9	63.0	68.2	62.7	65.1
Reno, NV	n/a	n/a	n/a	n/a	n/a	n/a	n/a	n/a
Richmond, VA	67.4	61.7	63.1	62.9	66.4	66.5	64.9	66.3
Rochester, MN	n/a	n/a	n/a	n/a	n/a	n/a	n/a	n/a
Sacramento, CA	60.8	60.5	60.1	64.1	61.6	63.4	63.2	63.5
St. Louis, MO	68.7	66.4	65.6	65.8	68.1	71.1	73.8	69.9
Salem, OR	n/a	n/a	n/a	n/a	n/a	n/a	n/a	n/a
Salt Lake City, UT	69.1	69.2	68.1	69.5	69.2	68.0	64.1	66.6
San Antonio, TX	66.0	61.6	62.5	64.4	62.6	64.2	62.7	62.9
San Diego, CA	51.8	53.3	56.0	56.1	56.7	57.8	52.6	51.6
San Francisco, CA	56.3	55.8	55.7	55.6	52.8	53.0	54.7	56.4
San Jose, CA	50.7	49.9	50.4	50.4	52.4	52.6	48.4	53.1
Santa Rosa, CA	n/a	n/a	n/a	n/a	n/a	n/a	n/a	n/a
Savannah, GA	n/a	n/a	n/a	n/a	n/a	n/a	n/a	n/a
Seattle, WA	59.5	57.7	59.5	62.5	61.5	59.4	58.0	62.7
Sioux Falls, SD	n/a	n/a	n/a	n/a	n/a	n/a	n/a	n/a
Springfield, IL	n/a	n/a	n/a	n/a	n/a	n/a	n/a	n/a
Tampa, FL	64.9	62.9	60.4	64.9	68.0	72.2	68.3	68.4
Tucson, AZ	61.4	56.0	60.1	63.8	60.1	67.1	63.5	71.6
Tulsa, OK	65.2	65.4	66.8	68.3	70.5	70.1	63.8	63.7
Tuscaloosa, AL	n/a	n/a	n/a	n/a	n/a	n/a	n/a	n/a
Virginia Beach, VA	59.4	59.6	65.3	62.8	63.0	65.8	64.4	61.4
Washington, DC	64.6	63.1	63.3	62.9	64.7	67.9	65.8	66.2
Wichita, KS	n/a	n/a	n/a	n/a	n/a	n/a	n/a	n/a
Wilmington, NC	n/a	n/a	n/a	n/a	n/a	n/a	n/a	n/a
Winston-Salem, NC	n/a	n/a	n/a	n/a	n/a	n/a	n/a	n/a
Worcester, MA	64.2	65.5	64.9	63.4	62.7	65.9	68.7	64.8
U.S.	63.7	63.4	63.9	64.4	64.6	66.6	65.5	65.8

Note: Figures are percentages and cover the Metropolitan Statistical Area; n/a not available
Source: U.S. Census Bureau, Housing Vacancies and Homeownership Annual Statistics: 2015-2022

Year Housing Structure Built: City

City	2020 or Later	2010 -2019	2000 -2009	1990 -1999	1980 -1989	1970 -1979	1960 -1969	1950 -1959	1940 -1949	Before 1940	Median Year
Albuquerque, NM	0.2	5.7	16.1	14.9	15.1	19.1	9.8	11.8	4.3	3.1	1981
Allentown, PA	0.1	2.3	4.6	3.4	5.3	10.8	11.5	15.0	7.2	39.7	1952
Anchorage, AK	<0.1	4.7	11.9	11.9	25.8	28.0	10.2	5.8	1.2	0.5	1982
Ann Arbor, MI	0.2	5.0	5.8	11.7	11.3	16.9	18.0	11.1	5.0	15.0	1971
Athens, GA	0.1	5.7	17.6	18.6	15.8	15.8	12.5	6.6	2.2	5.1	1985
Atlanta, GA	0.4	12.7	22.0	10.2	7.6	7.7	11.0	10.6	5.7	12.1	1984
Austin, TX	0.2	17.5	17.1	14.7	18.6	15.0	7.7	4.5	2.1	2.6	1990
Baltimore, MD	<0.1	3.4	3.6	3.9	4.3	5.7	8.6	15.8	11.9	42.8	1946
Boise City, ID	0.1	9.0	11.0	22.5	15.8	17.1	7.8	6.8	3.9	6.2	1985
Boston, MA	0.2	7.2	6.6	4.4	5.6	7.5	7.6	7.3	5.4	48.2	1943
Boulder, CO	0.1	7.9	7.7	12.0	16.7	19.6	17.7	9.0	1.7	7.7	1977
Brownsville, TX	0.2	12.9	22.9	18.0	14.8	15.5	6.2	4.4	2.8	2.3	1992
Cape Coral, FL	0.1	8.4	34.8	17.6	21.6	11.7	4.6	0.8	0.2	0.1	1996
Cedar Rapids, IA	0.1	7.7	11.5	10.5	7.1	14.6	14.8	12.8	4.1	16.8	1971
Charleston, SC	0.3	18.9	20.0	10.6	12.0	8.8	8.5	5.5	3.4	11.9	1990
Charlotte, NC	0.2	13.2	21.5	19.3	14.4	11.2	8.7	6.3	2.5	2.7	1992
Chicago, IL	<0.1	3.8	8.0	5.1	4.8	7.7	9.6	11.8	8.8	40.3	1951
Cincinnati, OH	0.1	3.3	3.7	4.2	6.0	9.4	12.2	11.5	8.4	41.4	1950
Clarksville, TN	0.2	15.6	22.2	20.2	12.9	12.0	7.2	4.8	2.8	2.1	1994
Cleveland, OH	0.1	2.9	3.5	3.4	2.8	5.5	7.8	12.7	11.2	50.0	<1940
College Station, TX	0.6	20.8	20.7	20.0	16.6	14.8	3.5	2.0	0.4	0.6	1996
Colorado Springs, CO	0.3	9.5	14.7	15.4	18.9	17.2	9.4	7.0	2.0	5.5	1985
Columbia, MO	0.1	15.5	20.0	18.1	11.8	12.1	10.5	4.4	2.3	5.3	1992
Columbia, SC	0.2	9.3	15.2	11.3	10.2	10.2	10.2	13.9	10.1	9.5	1976
Columbus, OH	0.1	8.0	11.7	15.1	12.9	14.3	11.5	10.4	4.3	11.8	1978
Dallas, TX	0.2	9.8	10.5	10.8	16.4	16.5	12.5	13.2	4.9	5.2	1979
Davenport, IA	<0.1	3.9	8.5	8.7	6.8	15.2	12.5	10.9	5.6	27.8	1965
Denver, CO	0.3	12.8	11.1	6.7	7.6	12.7	10.6	14.2	5.8	18.2	1971
Des Moines, IA	0.1	5.5	6.7	7.0	6.4	13.6	10.0	14.9	7.8	28.0	1960
Durham, NC	0.4	17.0	17.9	16.6	14.6	10.4	8.1	5.7	3.3	5.9	1991
Edison, NJ	0.1	2.5	5.7	9.8	24.2	11.6	18.6	17.8	4.0	5.5	1973
El Paso, TX	0.1	12.1	14.1	12.9	14.4	16.3	10.5	11.1	3.7	4.8	1982
Fargo, ND	0.3	18.3	14.2	15.1	13.1	14.2	6.1	8.0	2.3	8.3	1988
Fort Collins, CO	0.3	13.1	18.0	21.0	15.0	16.8	6.7	3.0	1.5	4.6	1991
Fort Wayne, IN	0.1	2.2	6.7	13.6	11.5	17.5	14.9	12.8	6.5	14.2	1971
Fort Worth, TX	0.3	14.8	21.3	12.3	13.5	9.4	7.7	10.2	4.9	5.7	1989
Grand Rapids, MI	<0.1	3.8	4.9	6.3	6.6	8.5	9.0	14.9	8.9	37.1	1953
Greeley, CO	0.1	9.4	17.2	16.7	10.2	21.2	9.4	6.4	2.2	7.2	1984
Green Bay, WI	0.1	2.3	7.0	10.4	12.0	18.6	12.9	15.6	6.5	14.7	1970
Greensboro, NC	0.1	8.0	15.0	16.8	16.5	13.3	11.3	10.2	3.7	5.1	1984
Honolulu, HI	0.1	6.0	6.8	8.2	9.8	26.1	21.0	11.9	5.2	5.0	1973
Houston, TX	0.2	11.8	12.7	9.8	14.6	19.6	13.0	10.0	4.2	4.2	1980
Huntsville, AL	0.2	13.6	12.4	11.0	15.8	12.8	20.6	8.6	2.4	2.6	1982
Indianapolis, IN	0.1	5.0	9.2	12.5	11.5	12.9	13.6	12.8	6.2	16.3	1971
Jacksonville, FL	0.6	8.4	18.1	14.7	15.6	12.4	9.9	10.8	4.5	5.0	1985
Kansas City, MO	0.2	6.9	9.8	9.2	8.9	11.8	12.5	13.4	5.9	21.3	1968
Lafayette, LA	<0.1	10.1	10.7	10.1	19.5	22.0	12.8	9.0	3.2	2.5	1980
Las Cruces, NM	0.3	10.7	19.9	15.0	16.9	15.5	8.1	8.9	2.1	2.6	1988
Las Vegas, NV	0.2	7.1	21.8	31.0	16.3	10.1	7.6	4.2	1.1	0.5	1993
Lexington, KY	0.2	8.4	14.2	16.5	13.2	15.2	13.5	8.9	2.9	7.1	1982
Lincoln, NE	0.1	10.3	13.1	14.2	10.4	15.4	9.4	10.7	3.4	13.0	1979
Little Rock, AR	0.0	8.0	11.4	12.3	13.7	18.5	13.8	9.4	5.1	7.8	1978
Los Angeles, CA	0.1	4.8	5.5	6.0	10.6	13.4	13.6	16.8	9.3	19.7	1963
Louisville, KY	0.2	6.6	11.0	11.1	6.9	12.4	13.6	14.6	7.2	16.5	1969
Madison, WI	0.1	10.1	13.5	12.8	9.8	13.7	11.8	9.4	4.5	14.2	1977

Table continued on following page.

City	2020 or Later	2010 -2019	2000 -2009	1990 -1999	1980 -1989	1970 -1979	1960 -1969	1950 -1959	1940 -1949	Before 1940	Median Year
Manchester, NH	0.3	2.5	6.2	8.3	16.3	11.9	8.1	10.1	7.2	29.1	1965
Miami, FL	0.2	11.5	18.0	6.6	7.5	12.8	10.0	14.4	9.9	9.1	1975
Midland, TX	0.2	18.2	8.1	13.4	18.0	11.7	8.9	17.8	2.6	1.2	1984
Milwaukee, WI	0.1	2.6	3.5	3.3	4.1	8.7	11.4	19.5	10.4	36.5	1952
Minneapolis, MN	<0.1	7.3	6.3	4.0	6.8	8.2	7.5	9.0	6.9	43.9	1949
Nashville, TN	0.8	13.4	13.8	12.3	14.5	13.5	11.6	9.7	4.0	6.4	1983
New Haven, CT	0.0	3.8	4.6	3.1	6.8	9.5	11.2	10.3	7.4	43.2	1949
New Orleans, LA	0.1	4.4	6.9	3.3	7.6	13.9	10.9	12.1	7.3	33.4	1958
New York, NY	<0.1	4.1	5.4	3.8	4.9	7.0	12.5	12.9	9.5	39.9	1950
Oklahoma City, OK	0.3	12.0	13.4	9.9	14.2	15.9	11.5	10.0	5.0	7.9	1980
Omaha, NE	0.1	5.1	8.3	12.4	10.9	15.1	14.4	10.9	4.6	18.3	1971
Orlando, FL	0.2	13.7	20.3	14.7	15.6	14.5	7.2	8.3	2.8	2.8	1989
Philadelphia, PA	0.1	3.6	3.0	3.2	4.0	7.4	11.1	15.7	11.2	40.7	1948
Phoenix, AZ	0.2	6.4	16.3	15.4	17.5	19.4	11.0	9.6	2.4	1.9	1983
Pittsburgh, PA	0.1	3.9	3.0	3.6	4.4	6.6	8.3	13.2	8.3	48.8	1941
Portland, OR	0.2	8.9	9.9	7.9	6.8	10.8	8.6	11.4	7.8	27.7	1964
Providence, RI	0.1	1.2	4.6	4.6	5.7	7.9	5.4	7.1	5.7	57.7	<1940
Provo, UT	0.4	6.9	10.7	18.8	14.4	18.5	9.9	7.8	5.0	7.6	1981
Raleigh, NC	0.3	14.6	23.4	18.5	16.8	9.9	7.6	4.2	1.6	3.1	1994
Reno, NV	1.0	9.8	19.0	17.3	13.8	18.0	8.8	6.1	3.1	3.1	1988
Richmond, VA	0.1	6.5	5.3	5.8	7.1	9.9	11.8	14.7	9.1	29.6	1958
Rochester, MN	0.4	12.3	18.0	14.4	12.0	12.5	10.0	8.8	3.4	8.1	1986
Sacramento, CA	0.1	4.6	14.5	8.7	15.6	14.2	11.4	12.3	7.3	11.3	1975
St. Louis, MO	<0.1	2.4	4.0	3.0	3.2	4.4	6.5	10.2	8.1	58.2	<1940
Salem, OR	0.2	6.9	12.5	16.8	9.7	19.9	9.5	10.6	4.9	9.0	1978
Salt Lake City, UT	0.2	8.1	6.8	6.4	7.6	11.3	9.8	12.8	9.2	27.8	1960
San Antonio, TX	0.2	10.2	14.9	12.9	16.2	14.4	10.3	9.9	5.5	5.4	1983
San Diego, CA	0.2	5.7	10.2	11.0	17.5	20.7	12.5	11.5	4.1	6.7	1977
San Francisco, CA	0.1	5.4	6.3	4.2	5.4	7.2	7.9	8.6	8.8	46.2	1944
San Jose, CA	0.2	6.4	9.2	10.1	12.5	24.3	18.0	11.1	2.8	5.3	1975
Santa Rosa, CA	0.5	4.6	12.5	13.2	17.9	21.1	12.0	8.1	4.7	5.5	1979
Savannah, GA	0.1	9.6	9.7	6.5	10.9	11.5	12.2	14.5	8.0	17.0	1969
Seattle, WA	0.1	14.7	11.9	8.3	7.6	7.7	8.3	9.1	8.0	24.2	1971
Sioux Falls, SD	0.3	17.8	17.9	14.7	9.7	12.1	7.0	8.3	3.1	9.1	1990
Springfield, IL	<0.1	3.0	8.6	13.0	8.8	17.4	12.6	10.8	6.0	19.7	1971
Tampa, FL	0.3	10.8	17.3	12.5	11.9	11.3	9.3	13.0	5.1	8.6	1982
Tucson, AZ	0.1	3.4	12.6	13.3	17.2	20.5	11.0	13.9	4.6	3.4	1978
Tulsa, OK	0.1	4.6	6.2	9.2	13.4	20.6	14.4	16.5	6.4	8.7	1972
Tuscaloosa, AL	0.1	16.7	16.7	14.4	11.6	14.9	9.8	8.3	3.9	3.6	1988
Virginia Beach, VA	0.1	6.4	11.1	14.1	27.1	20.4	12.4	6.1	1.2	1.1	1983
Washington, DC	0.2	10.3	7.9	3.1	4.7	6.8	11.1	12.1	10.8	32.9	1955
Wichita, KS	0.1	5.9	9.9	12.2	12.3	13.1	9.8	18.6	8.0	10.2	1973
Wilmington, NC	0.1	10.8	15.0	17.3	15.3	12.9	6.7	6.8	5.5	9.6	1986
Winston-Salem, NC	0.1	6.4	13.2	13.0	14.3	16.4	11.8	12.2	4.9	7.7	1978
Worcester, MA	0.0	2.1	4.6	5.2	10.1	7.9	7.8	11.6	7.5	43.3	1949
U.S.	0.2	7.3	13.6	13.6	13.2	14.8	10.3	10.0	4.7	12.2	1979

Note: Figures are percentages except for median year
Source: U.S. Census Bureau, 2017-2021 American Community Survey 5-Year Estimates

Year Housing Structure Built: Metro Area

Metro Area	2020 or Later	2010 -2019	2000 -2009	1990 -1999	1980 -1989	1970 -1979	1960 -1969	1950 -1959	1940 -1949	Before 1940	Median Year
Albuquerque, NM	0.2	5.9	17.2	17.3	16.8	17.8	8.7	9.3	3.6	3.2	1984
Allentown, PA	0.1	4.0	11.4	10.3	11.0	12.0	9.5	10.9	5.2	25.7	1969
Anchorage, AK	0.1	6.4	17.2	13.3	25.0	23.5	8.3	4.7	1.0	0.5	1985
Ann Arbor, MI	0.2	4.8	12.8	17.0	11.2	16.0	12.4	9.7	4.5	11.5	1977
Athens, GA	0.2	7.5	17.8	20.4	16.4	15.2	10.0	5.3	1.9	5.2	1988
Atlanta, GA	0.3	9.4	23.6	20.8	17.1	12.4	7.3	4.5	1.7	2.8	1992
Austin, TX	0.6	22.4	22.8	16.7	15.5	10.6	4.9	3.0	1.5	2.1	1997
Baltimore, MD	0.1	6.0	9.4	13.4	13.4	12.9	10.4	12.8	6.2	15.4	1974
Boise City, ID	0.5	14.3	23.2	20.7	9.8	14.1	5.2	4.3	2.8	5.2	1994
Boston, MA	0.1	5.8	7.5	7.4	10.4	10.8	10.1	10.7	5.0	32.2	1962
Boulder, CO	0.2	9.4	11.7	19.4	16.4	19.7	10.6	4.8	1.3	6.3	1984
Brownsville, TX	0.2	11.0	22.2	17.0	17.9	16.0	5.7	5.3	2.6	2.1	1990
Cape Coral, FL	0.2	8.9	29.7	17.4	21.0	14.4	5.2	2.2	0.4	0.6	1994
Cedar Rapids, IA	0.1	8.3	13.7	12.7	7.2	13.8	12.3	10.4	3.5	18.0	1974
Charleston, SC	0.3	16.4	20.8	15.5	15.4	13.0	7.7	4.8	2.4	3.7	1992
Charlotte, NC	0.2	13.6	22.6	18.9	12.9	10.8	7.7	6.3	2.9	4.1	1993
Chicago, IL	0.1	3.6	11.4	11.2	9.1	14.1	11.5	12.7	5.9	20.5	1969
Cincinnati, OH	0.1	5.3	12.0	13.8	10.7	13.8	10.5	11.6	4.8	17.3	1974
Clarksville, TN	0.4	13.8	19.7	20.2	12.2	13.9	7.9	6.0	2.9	3.0	1992
Cleveland, OH	0.1	3.4	6.8	8.9	6.9	12.4	13.6	17.7	7.6	22.5	1962
College Station, TX	0.6	17.0	18.8	18.0	16.6	14.4	6.0	4.3	2.1	2.3	1992
Colorado Springs, CO	0.3	10.7	17.8	16.4	17.6	16.2	8.1	6.2	1.6	5.1	1987
Columbia, MO	<0.1	12.1	18.1	17.6	13.2	14.8	9.6	4.7	2.6	7.2	1988
Columbia, SC	0.3	11.3	18.6	18.3	13.7	14.9	9.2	6.7	3.2	3.7	1989
Columbus, OH	0.2	8.0	14.2	15.9	11.6	13.8	10.7	9.8	3.7	12.2	1980
Dallas, TX	0.4	14.0	19.1	15.6	17.3	13.3	8.3	7.1	2.4	2.6	1989
Davenport, IA	0.1	4.6	7.9	8.5	6.8	15.9	12.8	12.1	7.2	24.2	1965
Denver, CO	0.3	10.7	16.0	14.8	13.8	17.2	9.0	9.0	2.6	6.5	1984
Des Moines, IA	0.3	14.1	15.7	12.5	8.0	13.3	7.9	8.8	3.9	15.4	1981
Durham, NC	0.5	13.4	17.9	18.2	15.3	12.0	8.4	6.1	2.9	5.3	1990
Edison, NJ	0.1	4.1	6.5	6.2	7.8	9.7	13.5	15.6	8.5	28.1	1959
El Paso, TX	0.2	14.0	15.8	14.1	14.5	15.2	9.2	9.4	3.3	4.3	1986
Fargo, ND	0.4	17.5	17.3	13.6	10.2	15.0	6.8	7.8	2.5	8.9	1989
Fort Collins, CO	0.4	14.9	18.1	19.1	12.4	17.9	6.6	3.3	1.8	5.6	1991
Fort Wayne, IN	0.2	5.9	11.5	14.3	10.4	15.3	12.4	11.0	5.4	13.7	1975
Fort Worth, TX	0.4	14.0	19.1	15.6	17.3	13.3	8.3	7.1	2.4	2.6	1989
Grand Rapids, MI	0.2	6.9	12.6	15.8	11.3	13.6	9.3	10.0	5.1	15.2	1978
Greeley, CO	0.7	16.2	26.7	15.4	7.2	14.6	5.6	3.9	1.9	7.7	1996
Green Bay, WI	<0.1	7.5	13.4	16.3	11.6	15.4	9.8	9.5	4.3	12.3	1979
Greensboro, NC	0.1	7.3	15.8	17.9	14.5	14.4	10.4	9.5	4.1	6.0	1984
Honolulu, HI	0.1	6.7	9.7	11.8	12.4	24.3	17.9	10.1	3.8	3.1	1976
Houston, TX	0.4	15.6	20.3	13.9	15.3	15.8	8.1	5.9	2.4	2.4	1990
Huntsville, AL	0.2	14.6	18.9	16.7	16.1	10.6	13.0	5.9	1.9	2.1	1990
Indianapolis, IN	0.2	8.8	14.9	16.3	10.3	12.1	10.6	10.1	4.5	12.3	1980
Jacksonville, FL	0.7	11.2	21.2	15.9	16.4	12.0	7.7	7.7	3.2	4.0	1989
Kansas City, MO	0.2	7.1	13.3	14.1	12.0	14.7	11.7	11.0	4.3	11.7	1978
Lafayette, LA	0.2	12.8	14.8	12.9	15.8	15.9	10.3	9.0	3.7	4.5	1984
Las Cruces, NM	0.2	11.0	17.9	19.3	18.3	15.3	7.0	6.3	1.9	2.7	1989
Las Vegas, NV	0.3	10.0	29.1	27.6	14.2	10.6	4.9	2.1	0.7	0.4	1996
Lexington, KY	0.2	8.7	16.1	17.4	13.4	14.8	11.1	7.7	3.0	7.6	1984
Lincoln, NE	0.1	10.1	13.5	14.2	10.1	15.6	9.6	9.8	3.3	13.7	1979
Little Rock, AR	0.3	12.0	17.4	16.6	14.0	15.9	10.0	6.8	3.2	3.8	1987
Los Angeles, CA	0.1	4.2	6.1	7.7	12.4	16.1	15.5	18.2	8.0	11.7	1968
Louisville, KY	0.2	6.7	12.8	13.8	9.2	14.8	12.1	12.2	5.9	12.3	1975
Madison, WI	0.2	9.4	15.4	15.5	10.7	14.3	9.5	7.6	3.5	13.9	1981

Table continued on following page.

Metro Area	2020 or Later	2010 -2019	2000 -2009	1990 -1999	1980 -1989	1970 -1979	1960 -1969	1950 -1959	1940 -1949	Before 1940	Median Year
Manchester, NH	0.1	4.2	9.7	10.9	20.4	15.6	9.5	7.0	3.8	18.8	1977
Miami, FL	0.2	6.0	12.7	14.6	19.2	21.0	11.9	9.8	2.7	2.1	1981
Midland, TX	0.2	19.5	11.0	14.2	17.8	10.9	7.8	14.6	2.6	1.4	1987
Milwaukee, WI	0.1	4.2	8.2	10.9	7.8	12.9	11.5	15.7	6.9	21.8	1965
Minneapolis, MN	0.2	7.0	13.5	13.9	14.2	14.3	9.8	9.5	3.7	13.8	1979
Nashville, TN	0.6	15.4	18.5	16.8	13.5	12.5	8.8	6.4	2.8	4.5	1991
New Haven, CT	<0.1	2.5	5.8	7.4	12.6	13.6	12.2	14.8	7.1	23.9	1963
New Orleans, LA	0.2	5.1	12.1	10.0	13.3	19.0	12.9	9.7	4.6	13.0	1975
New York, NY	0.1	4.1	6.5	6.2	7.8	9.7	13.5	15.6	8.5	28.1	1959
Oklahoma City, OK	0.3	11.8	14.7	11.0	14.3	16.8	11.4	9.2	4.6	5.9	1981
Omaha, NE	0.3	9.0	14.4	12.5	9.8	14.1	11.7	8.4	3.5	16.3	1977
Orlando, FL	0.3	12.7	22.2	19.4	19.4	12.6	5.8	5.1	1.2	1.5	1992
Philadelphia, PA	0.1	4.3	7.9	9.4	9.8	12.0	12.0	15.3	7.2	22.0	1965
Phoenix, AZ	0.3	9.8	24.5	19.4	16.8	15.4	6.9	4.8	1.2	0.9	1992
Pittsburgh, PA	0.1	4.0	6.2	7.6	7.7	12.0	11.4	16.5	8.6	25.9	1959
Portland, OR	0.3	9.2	14.0	17.3	11.3	16.7	8.2	6.9	4.5	11.7	1982
Providence, RI	0.1	2.7	6.1	8.1	11.2	12.1	10.7	11.5	6.0	31.4	1961
Provo, UT	0.4	19.6	24.2	17.6	8.9	12.7	4.7	5.0	2.7	4.2	1997
Raleigh, NC	0.5	17.9	23.9	21.6	14.6	8.6	5.4	3.4	1.4	2.7	1996
Reno, NV	0.7	8.8	20.1	18.8	14.8	18.9	8.6	4.7	2.3	2.3	1989
Richmond, VA	0.2	8.7	14.2	15.0	15.6	14.5	9.6	8.8	4.3	9.0	1982
Rochester, MN	0.3	9.6	17.9	14.4	10.8	13.2	9.0	7.6	3.4	13.8	1983
Sacramento, CA	0.2	5.3	16.9	14.9	16.7	18.0	10.6	9.7	3.4	4.2	1982
St. Louis, MO	0.2	5.3	11.4	12.1	11.1	13.0	12.6	12.6	5.5	16.2	1972
Salem, OR	0.2	6.5	13.4	17.3	9.7	22.3	10.3	8.0	4.0	8.4	1979
Salt Lake City, UT	0.2	12.6	14.8	15.1	11.9	17.4	8.6	8.3	3.5	7.5	1984
San Antonio, TX	0.5	16.2	19.2	13.9	14.5	12.4	8.0	7.2	3.8	4.3	1990
San Diego, CA	0.2	5.1	11.8	12.2	18.6	22.2	11.9	10.5	3.4	4.2	1979
San Francisco, CA	0.1	4.6	7.6	8.1	10.9	14.7	13.1	13.6	7.7	19.7	1967
San Jose, CA	0.2	7.5	8.9	10.0	12.1	21.3	17.6	13.9	3.5	5.0	1975
Santa Rosa, CA	0.3	4.0	10.3	13.7	18.2	20.6	11.6	8.9	4.4	8.0	1978
Savannah, GA	0.3	13.3	19.8	14.7	13.2	11.2	7.6	7.8	4.2	8.0	1989
Seattle, WA	0.2	10.6	14.7	15.2	14.1	13.4	10.8	7.1	4.2	9.7	1983
Sioux Falls, SD	0.2	16.0	18.0	14.9	8.7	12.7	6.7	7.4	3.2	12.2	1989
Springfield, IL	<0.1	4.3	10.0	13.2	8.7	17.3	11.7	11.0	6.0	17.8	1972
Tampa, FL	0.3	8.2	15.8	14.0	19.9	19.9	9.1	8.3	2.0	2.6	1984
Tucson, AZ	0.2	6.2	18.1	17.3	17.7	19.1	8.4	8.2	2.8	2.0	1985
Tulsa, OK	0.3	9.1	13.7	12.1	14.1	18.8	10.5	10.5	4.3	6.7	1980
Tuscaloosa, AL	0.1	12.4	18.5	18.3	13.5	14.7	9.0	6.6	3.2	3.6	1989
Virginia Beach, VA	0.2	8.0	12.6	14.8	18.4	15.2	11.6	9.3	4.2	5.7	1982
Washington, DC	0.2	9.0	14.0	14.0	15.4	13.5	11.8	8.9	4.9	8.3	1982
Wichita, KS	0.1	6.7	11.8	13.5	12.4	13.1	8.8	16.4	6.5	10.7	1976
Wilmington, NC	0.3	12.4	20.4	20.9	15.1	12.0	5.6	4.6	3.4	5.3	1992
Winston-Salem, NC	0.1	6.8	15.2	16.6	14.8	16.6	10.2	9.2	4.1	6.2	1982
Worcester, MA	0.1	3.8	8.7	9.5	12.4	11.3	8.9	11.0	5.6	28.9	1965
U.S.	0.2	7.3	13.6	13.6	13.2	14.8	10.3	10.0	4.7	12.2	1979

Note: Figures are percentages except for median year; Figures cover the Metropolitan Statistical Area
Source: U.S. Census Bureau, 2017-2021 American Community Survey 5-Year Estimates

Gross Monthly Rent: City

City	Under $500	$500 -$999	$1,000 -$1,499	$1,500 -$1,999	$2,000 -$2,499	$2,500 -$2,999	$3,000 and up	Median ($)
Albuquerque, NM	7.3	49.4	31.5	9.8	1.1	0.5	0.5	932
Allentown, PA	7.6	31.1	44.6	14.9	1.3	0.3	0.3	1,100
Anchorage, AK	4.8	20.1	34.7	23.1	11.6	4.0	1.8	1,350
Ann Arbor, MI	3.9	17.0	37.0	24.4	9.7	3.5	4.4	1,382
Athens, GA	5.4	52.2	29.1	9.4	2.2	0.8	0.8	939
Atlanta, GA	11.0	18.0	31.3	25.2	9.2	2.9	2.4	1,342
Austin, TX	2.8	10.6	43.9	26.9	10.3	3.0	2.6	1,415
Baltimore, MD	14.9	22.2	37.2	17.6	5.5	1.5	1.1	1,146
Boise City, ID	4.2	34.8	42.3	15.3	1.9	0.7	0.8	1,103
Boston, MA	14.1	10.7	13.3	20.9	17.7	9.6	13.6	1,783
Boulder, CO	3.1	6.2	29.1	27.4	16.5	6.4	11.3	1,711
Brownsville, TX	20.5	54.9	19.9	3.9	0.7	0.2	0.0	794
Cape Coral, FL	1.2	11.9	40.8	37.8	5.8	0.9	1.5	1,456
Cedar Rapids, IA	12.8	56.9	24.8	3.1	0.6	0.2	1.7	836
Charleston, SC	5.1	13.9	39.7	27.1	8.4	2.8	3.0	1,400
Charlotte, NC	3.4	19.6	48.2	21.7	4.5	1.5	1.2	1,260
Chicago, IL	8.6	25.4	32.7	17.7	8.6	3.9	3.2	1,209
Cincinnati, OH	15.9	52.7	21.5	6.4	2.1	0.7	0.7	814
Clarksville, TN	4.2	44.4	38.0	10.4	2.6	0.3	0.1	1,016
Cleveland, OH	20.3	53.7	19.1	4.7	1.3	0.6	0.4	774
College Station, TX	2.2	44.2	33.0	14.9	3.9	1.4	0.5	1,042
Colorado Springs, CO	3.3	21.7	39.4	25.1	6.5	2.8	1.2	1,300
Columbia, MO	5.7	52.3	30.3	6.6	4.2	0.8	0.1	935
Columbia, SC	10.3	38.9	37.0	11.2	2.0	0.3	0.3	1,007
Columbus, OH	5.2	37.8	43.6	10.1	2.3	0.4	0.6	1,061
Dallas, TX	3.5	28.7	42.6	16.5	5.2	1.7	1.8	1,178
Davenport, IA	9.4	61.7	21.9	4.3	0.7	0.5	1.5	815
Denver, CO	7.1	10.5	32.7	27.6	14.0	5.1	3.0	1,495
Des Moines, IA	7.8	52.1	31.7	6.4	1.7	0.2	0.2	916
Durham, NC	6.7	26.5	44.8	17.4	3.1	0.4	1.1	1,157
Edison, NJ	3.2	3.3	26.6	39.0	22.8	4.0	1.1	1,716
El Paso, TX	12.3	48.4	31.0	6.7	1.2	0.3	0.2	910
Fargo, ND	5.7	65.4	21.2	5.3	1.9	0.3	0.2	841
Fort Collins, CO	2.0	17.4	34.7	28.6	13.4	2.2	1.7	1,443
Fort Wayne, IN	9.5	63.9	22.8	3.0	0.4	0.2	0.2	823
Fort Worth, TX	3.7	28.4	40.5	19.2	5.9	1.4	0.9	1,187
Grand Rapids, MI	10.7	38.1	37.4	9.2	3.4	0.8	0.4	1,013
Greeley, CO	9.1	29.7	37.4	16.2	6.0	1.1	0.5	1,134
Green Bay, WI	9.1	66.5	22.1	1.8	0.2	0.0	0.2	805
Greensboro, NC	5.7	53.2	33.2	5.9	1.2	0.3	0.6	944
Honolulu, HI	6.7	10.1	27.5	24.0	13.2	7.9	10.7	1,620
Houston, TX	3.4	34.1	38.9	15.8	4.4	1.5	1.8	1,136
Huntsville, AL	7.5	52.1	31.9	6.8	0.7	0.5	0.5	912
Indianapolis, IN	6.0	49.3	34.3	7.9	1.7	0.4	0.4	962
Jacksonville, FL	5.4	29.0	43.7	17.5	3.6	0.5	0.4	1,146
Kansas City, MO	7.2	39.0	38.6	11.6	2.4	0.7	0.5	1,040
Lafayette, LA	6.9	50.5	32.1	8.7	1.0	0.2	0.6	948
Las Cruces, NM	13.0	56.6	25.0	4.0	1.0	0.1	0.4	824
Las Vegas, NV	4.0	25.7	42.9	20.6	4.9	1.0	0.9	1,219
Lexington, KY	6.4	47.7	34.5	8.1	2.3	0.5	0.4	967
Lincoln, NE	6.2	53.4	30.1	7.6	1.4	0.3	1.1	920
Little Rock, AR	7.8	49.3	33.3	6.7	1.4	0.7	0.8	940
Los Angeles, CA	4.9	11.1	27.1	24.6	15.1	8.1	9.2	1,641
Louisville, KY	11.4	47.2	32.6	6.8	1.2	0.2	0.6	931
Madison, WI	4.2	25.0	44.1	17.9	5.5	1.6	1.7	1,212

Table continued on following page.

City	Under $500	$500 -$999	$1,000 -$1,499	$1,500 -$1,999	$2,000 -$2,499	$2,500 -$2,999	$3,000 and up	Median ($)
Manchester, NH	7.0	21.3	43.4	20.8	5.4	1.4	0.8	1,220
Miami, FL	9.1	17.6	31.5	20.1	11.7	5.0	4.9	1,361
Midland, TX	2.8	19.5	44.3	19.5	9.2	3.6	1.1	1,273
Milwaukee, WI	7.7	55.0	28.4	6.3	1.6	0.6	0.4	910
Minneapolis, MN	10.9	27.0	33.1	17.8	7.4	2.0	1.9	1,159
Nashville, TN	7.4	20.6	41.1	20.6	6.9	1.9	1.5	1,250
New Haven, CT	13.5	14.2	40.8	20.6	7.4	2.4	1.1	1,267
New Orleans, LA	10.9	31.7	36.8	13.8	4.6	1.2	0.8	1,079
New York, NY	9.5	12.4	24.4	23.3	13.3	6.6	10.5	1,579
Oklahoma City, OK	6.5	51.2	32.1	7.8	1.6	0.4	0.4	933
Omaha, NE	5.4	44.7	36.8	10.2	1.6	0.4	0.9	999
Orlando, FL	3.4	15.1	45.7	26.9	6.3	1.6	1.1	1,346
Philadelphia, PA	9.3	27.7	38.4	15.3	5.5	2.0	1.8	1,149
Phoenix, AZ	3.8	28.5	43.3	18.5	4.2	0.9	0.8	1,175
Pittsburgh, PA	13.0	33.7	31.0	13.9	5.5	2.0	0.9	1,043
Portland, OR	5.6	14.2	37.6	25.6	10.8	3.9	2.3	1,406
Providence, RI	19.3	21.5	38.2	14.8	3.7	1.3	1.2	1,098
Provo, UT	9.1	44.7	29.6	11.4	4.1	0.5	0.6	973
Raleigh, NC	3.2	19.5	52.4	19.0	4.3	0.9	0.9	1,237
Reno, NV	5.7	27.4	37.5	21.1	6.4	1.0	1.0	1,213
Richmond, VA	11.2	26.1	41.7	16.2	3.6	0.6	0.7	1,132
Rochester, MN	7.8	34.8	32.6	17.7	3.4	1.3	2.4	1,120
Sacramento, CA	5.5	16.1	33.0	30.1	11.3	2.5	1.6	1,434
St. Louis, MO	10.6	54.3	26.8	6.1	1.7	0.3	0.2	873
Salem, OR	6.3	30.7	43.7	15.2	2.8	0.6	0.7	1,125
Salt Lake City, UT	8.0	30.3	36.6	17.7	5.4	1.2	0.8	1,141
San Antonio, TX	6.2	34.8	41.6	13.5	2.6	0.7	0.6	1,090
San Diego, CA	2.7	6.1	19.8	27.8	21.3	11.6	10.7	1,885
San Francisco, CA	8.6	10.0	13.7	14.1	13.3	11.6	28.5	2,130
San Jose, CA	3.7	5.6	9.3	17.0	19.6	18.0	26.7	2,366
Santa Rosa, CA	4.9	5.3	21.2	27.5	21.2	11.7	8.1	1,837
Savannah, GA	8.6	29.0	45.1	13.3	2.8	0.5	0.7	1,116
Seattle, WA	5.4	6.3	21.6	27.9	19.6	9.7	9.6	1,801
Sioux Falls, SD	6.2	58.7	27.7	5.7	0.6	0.4	0.8	892
Springfield, IL	10.6	58.7	23.8	4.8	0.9	0.8	0.4	852
Tampa, FL	7.4	21.2	39.2	19.4	8.2	2.4	2.1	1,249
Tucson, AZ	6.0	53.6	30.2	8.0	1.2	0.5	0.6	907
Tulsa, OK	8.9	54.8	28.8	4.8	1.3	0.5	0.9	882
Tuscaloosa, AL	11.0	51.3	28.3	5.9	2.0	0.6	0.9	907
Virginia Beach, VA	2.3	9.1	45.2	30.5	8.6	2.5	1.8	1,433
Washington, DC	9.2	10.4	22.3	22.4	15.2	9.2	11.3	1,681
Wichita, KS	8.1	60.2	26.3	3.9	0.8	0.2	0.5	856
Wilmington, NC	10.1	31.3	40.1	15.0	2.5	0.5	0.6	1,093
Winston-Salem, NC	8.8	57.2	26.5	5.3	1.3	0.3	0.6	871
Worcester, MA	13.8	21.1	41.4	18.7	3.6	0.7	0.7	1,179
U.S.	8.1	30.5	30.8	16.8	7.3	3.1	3.5	1,163

Note: Figures are percentages except for Median; Gross rent is the contract rent plus the estimated average monthly cost of utilities (electricity, gas, and water and sewer) and fuels (oil, coal, kerosene, wood, etc.) if these are paid by the renter (or paid for the renter by someone else).

Source: U.S. Census Bureau, 2017-2021 American Community Survey 5-Year Estimates

Gross Monthly Rent: Metro Area

MSA[1]	Under $500	$500 -$999	$1,000 -$1,499	$1,500 -$1,999	$2,000 -$2,499	$2,500 -2,999	$3,000 and up	Median ($)
Albuquerque, NM	7.2	47.4	32.9	10.2	1.3	0.4	0.5	952
Allentown, PA	8.9	28.4	39.4	17.7	3.9	0.9	0.9	1,141
Anchorage, AK	5.1	21.7	34.9	22.4	10.8	3.5	1.5	1,314
Ann Arbor, MI	5.1	24.0	40.6	18.9	6.1	2.2	3.1	1,218
Athens, GA	5.6	51.9	28.9	9.1	2.7	0.9	0.8	939
Atlanta, GA	4.3	19.1	43.9	23.8	6.2	1.5	1.2	1,294
Austin, TX	2.6	12.4	43.5	26.5	9.9	2.7	2.4	1,398
Baltimore, MD	8.2	14.4	35.1	26.4	11.0	3.0	2.0	1,387
Boise City, ID	6.5	32.7	40.5	16.2	2.6	0.8	0.7	1,107
Boston, MA	10.9	10.8	20.5	24.5	16.4	8.4	8.6	1,659
Boulder, CO	3.5	7.0	27.3	31.3	15.9	6.9	8.0	1,694
Brownsville, TX	18.4	59.0	18.3	3.2	0.7	0.2	0.2	785
Cape Coral, FL	3.6	19.1	45.6	21.7	5.9	1.8	2.4	1,307
Cedar Rapids, IA	13.4	57.1	23.0	4.2	0.8	0.1	1.4	806
Charleston, SC	4.6	20.9	43.3	20.1	6.9	2.0	2.1	1,274
Charlotte, NC	4.8	31.3	41.3	16.7	3.6	1.2	1.0	1,147
Chicago, IL	6.9	25.3	36.0	18.6	7.6	2.9	2.5	1,209
Cincinnati, OH	10.6	49.6	28.4	7.8	2.1	0.7	0.8	906
Clarksville, TN	7.7	45.9	35.8	8.3	1.9	0.2	0.1	967
Cleveland, OH	11.5	52.2	27.1	6.5	1.4	0.5	0.8	880
College Station, TX	5.0	44.7	32.9	12.3	3.1	1.2	0.7	1,003
Colorado Springs, CO	3.3	20.8	36.2	28.6	7.6	2.6	1.1	1,349
Columbia, MO	7.4	52.9	29.9	5.6	3.5	0.6	0.2	917
Columbia, SC	7.1	43.7	35.6	9.8	2.7	0.5	0.5	993
Columbus, OH	6.0	38.6	41.3	10.3	2.4	0.7	0.6	1,049
Dallas, TX	2.6	22.1	43.0	21.2	7.7	1.9	1.5	1,264
Davenport, IA	12.9	58.7	21.1	4.7	1.2	0.4	1.1	808
Denver, CO	4.5	9.6	32.5	31.5	14.2	5.0	2.7	1,554
Des Moines, IA	6.8	46.8	34.7	8.9	2.0	0.3	0.6	972
Durham, NC	6.6	30.7	41.7	15.5	3.6	0.7	1.3	1,127
Edison, NJ	8.4	11.4	26.5	24.9	13.4	6.3	9.1	1,573
El Paso, TX	12.0	48.6	30.8	7.0	1.2	0.2	0.2	908
Fargo, ND	6.6	60.9	22.5	7.6	1.6	0.4	0.3	855
Fort Collins, CO	2.8	17.7	34.1	28.7	12.2	2.9	1.7	1,433
Fort Wayne, IN	8.9	62.4	23.7	4.1	0.6	0.2	0.2	839
Fort Worth, TX	2.6	22.1	43.0	21.2	7.7	1.9	1.5	1,264
Grand Rapids, MI	8.4	45.1	34.9	7.7	2.5	0.9	0.6	973
Greeley, CO	7.1	26.4	33.6	21.2	7.5	2.6	1.6	1,234
Green Bay, WI	6.8	64.8	24.4	2.9	0.3	0.3	0.4	851
Greensboro, NC	9.0	55.6	28.9	4.6	1.1	0.3	0.6	900
Honolulu, HI	5.4	8.4	20.9	20.8	15.0	12.0	17.6	1,870
Houston, TX	3.3	29.1	39.7	19.2	5.7	1.5	1.6	1,189
Huntsville, AL	8.0	51.8	30.9	7.1	1.1	0.6	0.5	912
Indianapolis, IN	5.7	46.0	35.5	9.7	2.0	0.5	0.6	987
Jacksonville, FL	4.9	27.9	41.7	18.9	4.6	1.0	1.0	1,175
Kansas City, MO	6.5	38.5	38.5	11.8	3.0	0.8	0.9	1,052
Lafayette, LA	13.8	54.5	25.3	4.8	1.1	0.1	0.4	853
Las Cruces, NM	16.4	55.8	22.5	3.8	1.2	0.1	0.3	785
Las Vegas, NV	2.3	24.0	42.7	23.4	5.6	1.2	0.8	1,257
Lexington, KY	7.5	50.4	32.5	7.0	1.8	0.4	0.3	934
Lincoln, NE	6.5	53.2	30.0	7.4	1.5	0.3	1.1	918
Little Rock, AR	8.1	55.9	29.1	5.3	0.9	0.4	0.4	893
Los Angeles, CA	3.8	8.7	24.8	26.8	17.5	8.9	9.5	1,737
Louisville, KY	11.0	47.2	33.5	6.2	1.3	0.2	0.6	934
Madison, WI	4.5	31.5	41.8	15.7	4.3	1.1	1.2	1,143

Table continued on following page.

MSA[1]	Under $500	$500 -$999	$1,000 -$1,499	$1,500 -$1,999	$2,000 -$2,499	$2,500 -2,999	$3,000 and up	Median ($)
Manchester, NH	6.7	18.6	40.2	24.7	6.8	1.9	1.1	1,305
Miami, FL	4.5	11.5	34.6	28.5	12.9	4.5	3.6	1,492
Midland, TX	4.2	19.9	43.6	19.0	9.0	3.3	1.0	1,271
Milwaukee, WI	6.9	48.0	32.3	9.1	2.4	0.7	0.5	963
Minneapolis, MN	8.1	24.0	37.9	20.4	6.3	1.7	1.6	1,207
Nashville, TN	6.7	25.1	39.7	20.0	5.7	1.6	1.2	1,211
New Haven, CT	10.6	19.5	41.4	19.9	5.6	1.6	1.4	1,223
New Orleans, LA	8.0	35.7	39.3	12.2	3.5	0.7	0.6	1,064
New York, NY	8.4	11.4	26.5	24.9	13.4	6.3	9.1	1,573
Oklahoma City, OK	6.8	50.2	32.3	8.0	1.6	0.5	0.6	937
Omaha, NE	6.4	43.7	36.5	10.2	1.7	0.5	1.2	1,000
Orlando, FL	2.7	16.2	43.2	27.2	7.5	1.9	1.2	1,363
Philadelphia, PA	7.2	22.3	40.2	19.2	6.7	2.3	2.0	1,230
Phoenix, AZ	3.0	23.1	41.3	22.9	6.3	1.7	1.7	1,268
Pittsburgh, PA	14.0	47.0	26.4	7.9	2.9	0.9	0.9	892
Portland, OR	4.1	12.6	38.8	28.4	10.8	3.2	2.0	1,434
Providence, RI	14.9	29.3	35.5	14.2	4.1	1.0	0.9	1,066
Provo, UT	4.6	31.0	36.2	20.0	6.2	1.0	1.1	1,193
Raleigh, NC	4.4	22.5	46.4	19.1	5.2	1.2	1.2	1,230
Reno, NV	4.8	26.6	36.7	22.2	6.7	1.5	1.5	1,250
Richmond, VA	6.6	23.4	45.3	18.7	3.9	0.9	1.2	1,202
Rochester, MN	10.2	39.0	30.7	14.7	2.8	1.0	1.8	1,013
Sacramento, CA	4.3	14.1	34.2	27.8	13.3	3.9	2.5	1,465
St. Louis, MO	7.9	47.8	33.0	7.6	2.1	0.6	1.1	952
Salem, OR	5.9	30.4	45.3	14.0	2.9	1.0	0.5	1,128
Salt Lake City, UT	4.6	21.7	43.4	22.2	6.0	1.1	0.9	1,253
San Antonio, TX	5.6	32.5	41.5	15.3	3.5	0.9	0.7	1,122
San Diego, CA	2.9	5.9	21.1	29.4	19.7	10.6	10.4	1,842
San Francisco, CA	5.6	7.0	13.2	18.3	19.2	14.0	22.8	2,155
San Jose, CA	3.0	4.7	7.8	14.7	19.4	18.5	31.9	2,511
Santa Rosa, CA	4.8	7.8	19.2	25.6	21.0	11.3	10.3	1,856
Savannah, GA	5.5	26.3	47.1	16.1	3.7	0.6	0.6	1,161
Seattle, WA	4.3	8.4	25.0	30.5	17.7	7.5	6.6	1,701
Sioux Falls, SD	7.0	57.8	27.5	5.8	0.8	0.3	0.7	889
Springfield, IL	10.4	57.4	25.5	4.8	0.8	0.6	0.5	857
Tampa, FL	4.1	24.2	42.4	19.8	6.2	1.8	1.5	1,230
Tucson, AZ	5.5	46.8	33.6	10.3	1.9	0.8	1.1	976
Tulsa, OK	8.7	51.9	30.3	6.3	1.6	0.4	0.8	909
Tuscaloosa, AL	14.9	50.5	27.1	4.8	1.5	0.6	0.5	879
Virginia Beach, VA	6.1	22.2	42.3	21.1	5.5	1.5	1.3	1,227
Washington, DC	4.3	6.4	20.9	32.5	19.2	8.6	8.1	1,783
Wichita, KS	8.8	57.8	26.3	5.4	0.9	0.4	0.5	868
Wilmington, NC	8.0	29.7	41.7	15.1	3.2	1.5	0.8	1,118
Winston-Salem, NC	11.0	59.4	23.7	4.3	1.0	0.2	0.4	834
Worcester, MA	13.2	26.4	37.7	15.9	4.7	1.2	1.0	1,126
U.S.	8.1	30.5	30.8	16.8	7.3	3.1	3.5	1,163

Note: (1) Figures cover the Metropolitan Statistical Area (MSA); Figures are percentages except for Median; Gross rent is the contract rent plus the estimated average monthly cost of utilities (electricity, gas, and water and sewer) and fuels (oil, coal, kerosene, wood, etc.) if these are paid by the renter (or paid for the renter by someone else).
Source: U.S. Census Bureau, 2017-2021 American Community Survey 5-Year Estimates

Highest Level of Education: City

City	Less than H.S.	H.S. Diploma	Some College, No Deg.	Associate Degree	Bachelors Degree	Masters Degree	Profess. School Degree	Doctorate Degree
Albuquerque, NM	9.1	21.8	22.7	9.1	20.4	11.5	2.9	2.6
Allentown, PA	19.4	36.5	19.3	7.5	11.5	3.8	1.1	0.8
Anchorage, AK	5.8	23.7	25.0	8.6	22.8	9.8	2.8	1.3
Ann Arbor, MI	2.2	7.6	8.9	4.0	30.5	26.8	8.3	11.6
Athens, GA	10.3	19.2	17.0	6.4	23.4	14.8	2.7	6.1
Atlanta, GA	7.9	17.5	13.6	5.4	31.6	15.8	5.6	2.7
Austin, TX	9.4	14.4	15.7	5.4	34.2	14.9	3.5	2.6
Baltimore, MD	13.7	28.1	18.8	5.2	17.2	11.3	3.2	2.5
Boise City, ID	4.8	20.4	22.8	8.3	28.0	10.8	2.8	2.0
Boston, MA	11.8	18.5	12.9	4.7	27.8	15.7	5.1	3.6
Boulder, CO	3.1	5.9	10.6	3.6	37.1	25.0	5.7	9.0
Brownsville, TX	32.0	24.2	16.0	7.3	14.6	4.7	0.9	0.3
Cape Coral, FL	7.1	37.1	23.0	9.2	15.6	5.3	1.5	1.3
Cedar Rapids, IA	6.2	25.7	22.8	12.5	22.7	7.2	2.0	0.8
Charleston, SC	4.2	16.8	16.1	7.3	34.5	13.6	4.8	2.9
Charlotte, NC	10.3	16.9	19.2	7.9	29.5	12.2	2.9	1.2
Chicago, IL	13.7	21.9	17.0	5.7	24.1	12.2	3.6	1.8
Cincinnati, OH	11.4	24.0	17.6	7.4	23.0	11.0	3.4	2.2
Clarksville, TN	6.4	26.9	26.3	11.6	18.7	8.2	0.8	1.1
Cleveland, OH	17.4	33.3	22.8	7.4	11.4	5.2	1.7	0.8
College Station, TX	5.2	13.1	17.0	6.7	30.3	15.4	2.1	10.3
Colorado Springs, CO	6.1	19.1	24.0	10.7	24.3	12.0	2.3	1.7
Columbia, MO	4.5	17.5	17.6	6.6	28.4	15.5	4.6	5.3
Columbia, SC	9.5	19.3	18.8	7.7	25.1	11.7	4.5	3.3
Columbus, OH	9.7	24.8	20.3	7.4	24.3	10.0	2.1	1.6
Dallas, TX	20.4	21.8	17.4	4.8	22.1	9.0	3.2	1.3
Davenport, IA	7.9	31.4	22.0	11.7	17.9	6.6	1.6	0.9
Denver, CO	10.0	16.0	16.0	5.6	32.0	13.9	4.5	2.1
Des Moines, IA	12.9	29.6	20.2	9.2	19.3	6.2	1.8	0.8
Durham, NC	9.4	16.2	14.7	6.9	27.7	15.8	4.3	5.0
Edison, NJ	7.9	18.1	11.9	5.8	30.1	21.4	2.6	2.3
El Paso, TX	18.6	23.1	22.7	8.8	17.7	6.6	1.4	1.0
Fargo, ND	5.2	19.3	20.3	13.6	28.1	9.9	1.8	2.0
Fort Collins, CO	3.0	14.4	17.3	8.6	32.8	17.5	2.5	3.8
Fort Wayne, IN	11.1	28.9	21.9	10.1	19.0	7.1	1.1	0.8
Fort Worth, TX	16.5	24.5	20.8	7.2	20.6	7.8	1.6	1.1
Grand Rapids, MI	11.3	22.2	20.1	7.6	25.6	9.7	2.2	1.4
Greeley, CO	16.4	26.0	22.8	8.8	15.9	7.7	1.4	1.2
Green Bay, WI	12.2	31.3	19.7	11.7	18.3	5.0	0.9	0.8
Greensboro, NC	9.8	21.3	20.4	9.0	24.5	10.7	2.4	1.9
Honolulu, HI	9.6	23.1	18.1	10.8	24.0	9.1	3.1	2.1
Houston, TX	20.5	21.6	17.2	6.0	20.9	9.1	3.0	1.8
Huntsville, AL	8.9	17.6	20.9	7.9	26.7	13.7	1.9	2.5
Indianapolis, IN	13.3	27.3	18.8	7.6	21.1	8.2	2.3	1.2
Jacksonville, FL	9.7	28.7	21.5	9.9	20.3	7.2	1.6	1.0
Kansas City, MO	9.0	24.9	22.2	7.4	23.0	9.8	2.6	1.2
Lafayette, LA	9.7	26.2	19.5	5.2	24.9	8.7	3.9	1.9
Las Cruces, NM	12.5	19.8	22.0	9.3	20.5	11.7	2.2	2.0
Las Vegas, NV	14.6	27.4	24.0	8.0	16.7	6.4	1.9	0.9
Lexington, KY	7.6	18.9	20.0	7.9	25.9	12.2	4.2	3.4
Lincoln, NE	7.1	20.7	20.9	11.2	25.3	9.8	2.2	2.8
Little Rock, AR	8.1	21.7	19.8	6.4	25.3	11.8	4.3	2.8
Los Angeles, CA	21.6	18.8	17.2	6.3	23.7	8.1	3.0	1.5
Louisville, KY	9.8	28.2	22.1	8.3	18.9	9.0	2.1	1.5
Madison, WI	4.4	14.2	15.4	7.5	32.5	15.9	4.2	5.9

Table continued on following page.

City	Less than H.S.	H.S. Diploma	Some College, No Deg.	Associate Degree	Bachelors Degree	Masters Degree	Profess. School Degree	Doctorate Degree
Manchester, NH	11.4	28.8	18.8	9.1	21.5	8.0	1.5	1.0
Miami, FL	20.8	25.8	12.6	7.8	19.8	8.2	3.9	1.1
Midland, TX	15.5	23.4	22.1	8.1	22.5	6.4	1.4	0.6
Milwaukee, WI	15.1	30.9	21.1	7.4	16.3	6.7	1.4	1.0
Minneapolis, MN	9.3	14.2	16.4	7.4	31.7	14.5	3.9	2.5
Nashville, TN	10.0	21.5	18.4	6.2	27.5	10.7	3.2	2.6
New Haven, CT	14.6	30.2	14.2	4.6	16.3	11.9	4.0	4.3
New Orleans, LA	11.8	22.4	21.6	5.0	21.9	10.4	4.5	2.2
New York, NY	16.8	23.6	13.5	6.5	22.9	11.8	3.3	1.6
Oklahoma City, OK	12.5	24.6	22.5	8.1	20.5	8.0	2.6	1.2
Omaha, NE	9.7	21.7	22.0	7.8	24.9	9.1	3.1	1.6
Orlando, FL	8.4	23.2	16.8	11.5	25.0	10.3	3.1	1.7
Philadelphia, PA	13.4	31.4	16.7	6.0	18.4	9.3	3.0	1.8
Phoenix, AZ	16.5	22.9	22.1	8.0	19.1	8.2	2.1	1.2
Pittsburgh, PA	6.5	24.7	14.9	8.2	23.5	13.7	4.6	3.9
Portland, OR	6.7	15.1	19.4	6.9	31.2	13.9	4.3	2.4
Providence, RI	16.5	30.6	14.6	5.1	17.4	9.5	3.5	2.9
Provo, UT	7.3	14.4	25.3	8.6	31.6	8.7	1.6	2.4
Raleigh, NC	7.7	15.7	16.9	7.3	32.7	13.7	3.5	2.5
Reno, NV	10.2	22.7	23.3	8.3	21.6	9.2	2.5	2.3
Richmond, VA	12.3	20.4	19.2	5.0	25.1	12.1	3.7	2.2
Rochester, MN	5.6	18.6	15.8	11.3	26.6	13.1	5.2	3.6
Sacramento, CA	13.6	20.3	22.6	8.4	22.2	8.4	3.2	1.4
St. Louis, MO	10.8	24.4	20.3	6.5	21.3	11.3	3.2	2.2
Salem, OR	11.6	23.2	25.8	9.4	18.4	8.4	1.8	1.4
Salt Lake City, UT	8.9	16.6	17.9	6.7	28.3	13.4	4.6	3.5
San Antonio, TX	16.7	25.5	22.5	8.0	16.9	7.2	2.0	1.2
San Diego, CA	10.7	15.4	18.6	7.7	27.9	12.8	3.6	3.4
San Francisco, CA	11.2	11.4	12.7	5.2	35.4	16.0	5.1	3.0
San Jose, CA	14.5	16.3	16.2	7.6	26.0	14.5	2.2	2.8
Santa Rosa, CA	14.5	18.0	23.2	10.0	21.3	8.7	3.0	1.3
Savannah, GA	11.2	26.9	24.6	6.8	19.3	7.9	2.1	1.2
Seattle, WA	4.5	9.7	13.9	6.0	37.3	19.4	5.3	3.9
Sioux Falls, SD	6.7	24.6	20.5	12.2	24.3	8.3	2.4	1.0
Springfield, IL	8.7	26.6	22.1	8.2	20.2	9.6	3.5	1.2
Tampa, FL	11.6	23.4	15.3	7.9	24.8	10.6	4.4	2.0
Tucson, AZ	13.7	22.8	25.7	8.9	17.5	8.2	1.4	1.8
Tulsa, OK	12.1	25.3	22.1	8.0	20.7	7.7	2.7	1.3
Tuscaloosa, AL	9.9	27.1	18.6	6.8	20.5	11.0	2.1	4.0
Virginia Beach, VA	5.5	20.8	24.1	11.0	24.3	10.7	2.3	1.4
Washington, DC	7.8	15.5	12.4	3.0	25.5	21.9	9.7	4.3
Wichita, KS	11.8	26.2	23.4	8.1	19.3	8.4	1.7	1.1
Wilmington, NC	6.5	19.7	20.0	10.3	28.3	10.2	3.2	1.8
Winston-Salem, NC	12.0	24.9	20.7	7.7	20.3	9.2	2.8	2.2
Worcester, MA	14.2	28.3	17.1	8.2	19.2	8.8	2.0	2.3
U.S.	11.1	26.5	20.0	8.7	20.6	9.3	2.2	1.5

Note: Figures cover persons age 25 and over
Source: U.S. Census Bureau, 2017-2021 American Community Survey 5-Year Estimates

Highest Level of Education: Metro Area

Metro Area	Less than H.S.	H.S. Diploma	Some College, No Deg.	Associate Degree	Bachelors Degree	Masters Degree	Profess. School Degree	Doctorate Degree
Albuquerque, NM	10.0	23.8	23.2	9.2	18.6	10.5	2.4	2.2
Allentown, PA	9.1	33.6	16.6	9.4	19.5	8.7	1.6	1.4
Anchorage, AK	6.0	26.2	25.5	9.1	20.9	8.8	2.4	1.2
Ann Arbor, MI	4.3	14.6	17.0	6.9	26.9	19.0	5.0	6.2
Athens, GA	10.6	22.7	17.6	7.4	20.8	13.0	3.2	4.7
Atlanta, GA	9.5	23.3	18.9	7.8	24.9	11.1	2.6	1.6
Austin, TX	9.0	18.2	18.9	6.5	30.1	12.7	2.6	2.0
Baltimore, MD	8.4	24.1	18.9	6.9	22.7	13.7	3.0	2.3
Boise City, ID	7.9	24.1	24.9	9.2	22.6	8.1	1.9	1.3
Boston, MA	7.9	21.2	14.1	7.1	26.9	15.8	3.6	3.5
Boulder, CO	4.5	11.1	15.0	6.6	34.5	19.1	3.9	5.3
Brownsville, TX	30.5	26.1	17.1	7.4	13.2	4.4	0.9	0.5
Cape Coral, FL	10.2	30.8	20.5	9.4	17.8	7.5	2.3	1.4
Cedar Rapids, IA	5.2	28.0	21.3	13.4	22.1	7.4	1.7	0.9
Charleston, SC	8.5	24.3	19.7	9.5	24.0	10.0	2.6	1.4
Charlotte, NC	10.1	22.9	20.5	9.4	24.5	9.7	2.0	0.9
Chicago, IL	10.5	23.4	19.0	7.3	23.8	11.6	2.8	1.5
Cincinnati, OH	8.2	29.3	18.7	8.4	21.9	9.8	2.1	1.5
Clarksville, TN	8.6	28.9	25.1	11.0	17.0	7.4	1.2	0.9
Cleveland, OH	8.6	28.5	21.3	8.8	19.8	9.2	2.5	1.3
College Station, TX	12.1	23.4	19.3	6.7	21.6	9.8	2.0	5.1
Colorado Springs, CO	5.4	19.8	24.4	10.9	23.9	12.0	1.9	1.6
Columbia, MO	5.9	23.1	18.3	7.5	25.4	12.6	3.3	3.8
Columbia, SC	9.4	26.0	21.5	9.5	20.5	9.2	2.1	1.8
Columbus, OH	7.9	26.7	19.4	7.6	24.0	10.4	2.5	1.5
Dallas, TX	13.4	22.0	20.6	7.3	23.8	9.8	1.9	1.2
Davenport, IA	8.2	29.9	22.9	11.1	17.8	7.7	1.5	0.9
Denver, CO	8.1	19.2	18.9	7.6	29.1	12.5	2.8	1.8
Des Moines, IA	6.6	25.6	19.5	10.7	25.8	8.4	2.1	1.3
Durham, NC	9.9	19.0	15.8	7.9	24.4	14.1	4.1	4.8
Edison, NJ	12.7	24.0	14.4	6.8	24.2	12.7	3.4	1.7
El Paso, TX	20.4	23.8	22.3	9.0	16.5	6.0	1.3	0.8
Fargo, ND	4.8	19.7	21.1	14.1	27.8	8.9	1.8	1.7
Fort Collins, CO	3.7	17.4	20.4	9.1	29.5	14.4	2.4	3.1
Fort Wayne, IN	9.8	29.0	21.0	11.0	19.8	7.1	1.5	1.0
Fort Worth, TX	13.4	22.0	20.6	7.3	23.8	9.8	1.9	1.2
Grand Rapids, MI	7.7	26.7	21.6	9.5	22.5	9.1	1.8	1.2
Greeley, CO	11.9	25.4	23.8	9.5	19.3	7.8	1.3	1.1
Green Bay, WI	7.5	31.5	19.1	12.8	20.5	6.3	1.4	0.8
Greensboro, NC	11.8	26.7	21.4	9.7	19.8	7.9	1.5	1.3
Honolulu, HI	7.3	25.6	19.8	11.1	23.2	8.9	2.5	1.6
Houston, TX	15.6	22.7	20.2	7.4	21.6	8.8	2.2	1.5
Huntsville, AL	9.2	20.9	21.0	8.0	25.2	12.4	1.5	1.8
Indianapolis, IN	9.4	27.3	18.9	8.0	23.2	9.4	2.3	1.3
Jacksonville, FL	8.6	27.5	21.0	9.9	21.6	8.4	2.0	1.1
Kansas City, MO	7.3	25.1	21.6	8.0	23.8	10.6	2.4	1.3
Lafayette, LA	14.0	36.5	18.4	6.5	17.0	5.1	1.7	0.8
Las Cruces, NM	19.3	21.5	20.9	8.3	17.5	9.2	1.7	1.7
Las Vegas, NV	13.6	28.0	24.3	8.3	17.1	6.2	1.7	0.9
Lexington, KY	8.3	23.8	20.5	8.3	22.4	10.8	3.4	2.5
Lincoln, NE	6.6	21.4	20.7	11.7	25.1	9.8	2.1	2.6
Little Rock, AR	8.4	29.1	22.2	8.3	19.9	8.6	2.2	1.4
Los Angeles, CA	18.4	19.6	18.8	7.2	23.2	8.6	2.7	1.5
Louisville, KY	9.1	29.3	21.7	8.7	18.9	8.8	2.1	1.4
Madison, WI	4.3	20.6	17.5	9.8	28.8	12.3	3.1	3.5

Table continued on following page.

Metro Area	Less than H.S.	H.S. Diploma	Some College, No Deg.	Associate Degree	Bachelors Degree	Masters Degree	Profess. School Degree	Doctorate Degree
Manchester, NH	7.1	25.6	17.7	9.9	25.0	11.4	1.7	1.6
Miami, FL	13.5	25.8	16.9	9.6	21.1	8.6	3.2	1.3
Midland, TX	15.6	24.5	23.1	8.2	20.0	6.8	1.2	0.5
Milwaukee, WI	7.9	26.1	19.7	8.9	24.3	9.4	2.3	1.5
Minneapolis, MN	6.0	20.5	19.4	10.6	28.3	10.9	2.6	1.7
Nashville, TN	9.0	25.7	19.6	7.3	24.9	9.4	2.3	1.8
New Haven, CT	9.7	29.6	16.7	7.3	19.4	11.9	3.2	2.2
New Orleans, LA	11.9	26.9	22.4	6.5	20.0	8.0	2.9	1.3
New York, NY	12.7	24.0	14.4	6.8	24.2	12.7	3.4	1.7
Oklahoma City, OK	10.2	26.4	22.9	8.1	20.7	8.1	2.2	1.4
Omaha, NE	7.7	23.1	22.0	9.4	24.3	9.6	2.4	1.4
Orlando, FL	9.9	25.4	19.4	11.6	21.9	8.6	2.0	1.1
Philadelphia, PA	8.4	27.9	16.5	7.3	23.3	11.5	2.9	2.0
Phoenix, AZ	11.3	22.8	23.8	9.0	20.9	9.0	2.0	1.3
Pittsburgh, PA	5.5	31.4	16.0	10.5	22.2	10.3	2.3	1.7
Portland, OR	7.2	20.1	22.9	8.9	25.5	10.8	2.7	2.0
Providence, RI	12.0	28.7	17.5	8.6	20.2	9.4	2.0	1.6
Provo, UT	4.9	17.2	25.6	10.4	29.0	9.4	1.7	1.7
Raleigh, NC	7.4	17.3	17.7	9.0	30.1	13.6	2.6	2.3
Reno, NV	11.4	23.8	23.9	8.6	19.8	8.5	2.2	1.8
Richmond, VA	8.9	24.6	19.9	7.6	23.7	11.0	2.5	1.7
Rochester, MN	5.3	23.2	17.8	12.6	23.9	10.6	4.1	2.4
Sacramento, CA	10.2	20.8	24.1	9.9	22.3	8.3	2.8	1.5
St. Louis, MO	7.2	25.7	21.7	9.2	21.5	10.9	2.2	1.6
Salem, OR	13.2	25.1	26.3	9.7	16.7	6.8	1.3	1.0
Salt Lake City, UT	8.2	22.8	23.5	9.2	23.4	9.3	2.2	1.5
San Antonio, TX	13.6	25.2	22.7	8.2	19.0	8.2	1.9	1.2
San Diego, CA	11.7	18.2	21.5	8.4	24.5	10.5	2.9	2.3
San Francisco, CA	10.3	15.1	16.5	6.7	29.9	14.5	3.9	3.1
San Jose, CA	11.0	14.1	14.7	6.9	27.5	18.7	2.8	4.4
Santa Rosa, CA	10.8	18.3	24.2	9.5	23.2	9.2	3.3	1.5
Savannah, GA	9.3	26.5	22.9	7.8	20.7	9.0	2.4	1.5
Seattle, WA	6.8	19.1	20.3	9.4	27.1	12.5	2.7	2.0
Sioux Falls, SD	6.3	25.7	20.2	13.0	24.1	7.8	2.0	1.0
Springfield, IL	7.1	28.0	22.7	8.8	20.3	9.4	2.6	1.1
Tampa, FL	9.6	28.1	20.0	9.8	20.8	8.2	2.2	1.2
Tucson, AZ	10.6	21.4	24.6	9.0	19.7	10.2	2.2	2.2
Tulsa, OK	10.0	28.8	23.3	9.2	19.2	6.7	1.8	1.0
Tuscaloosa, AL	11.5	31.7	20.2	8.8	16.6	7.6	1.2	2.4
Virginia Beach, VA	7.6	24.7	23.8	10.1	20.6	9.8	1.9	1.4
Washington, DC	8.5	17.7	15.5	6.0	26.4	18.2	4.6	3.3
Wichita, KS	9.8	26.5	23.8	8.8	20.1	8.5	1.5	1.0
Wilmington, NC	7.2	20.8	21.3	10.9	26.2	9.4	2.8	1.5
Winston-Salem, NC	12.0	29.1	21.8	9.6	17.7	6.7	1.7	1.3
Worcester, MA	8.7	27.8	17.9	9.2	21.5	11.4	1.8	1.8
U.S.	11.1	26.5	20.0	8.7	20.6	9.3	2.2	1.5

Note: Figures cover persons age 25 and over; Figures cover the Metropolitan Statistical Area
Source: U.S. Census Bureau, 2017-2021 American Community Survey 5-Year Estimates

School Enrollment by Grade and Control: City

City	Preschool (%)		Kindergarten (%)		Grades 1 - 4 (%)		Grades 5 - 8 (%)		Grades 9 - 12 (%)	
	Public	Private	Public	Private	Public	Private	Public	Private	Public	Private
Albuquerque, NM	57.2	42.8	86.7	13.3	86.7	13.3	90.7	9.3	91.7	8.3
Allentown, PA	80.2	19.8	86.2	13.8	87.7	12.3	90.5	9.5	89.0	11.0
Anchorage, AK	50.1	49.9	91.5	8.5	87.5	12.5	89.0	11.0	92.0	8.0
Ann Arbor, MI	34.0	66.0	86.6	13.4	88.7	11.3	87.6	12.4	94.0	6.0
Athens, GA	61.1	38.9	96.2	3.8	91.8	8.2	88.7	11.3	91.8	8.2
Atlanta, GA	50.7	49.3	75.7	24.3	85.9	14.1	78.5	21.5	79.9	20.1
Austin, TX	52.0	48.0	87.1	12.9	88.8	11.2	87.9	12.1	90.9	9.1
Baltimore, MD	69.2	30.8	83.5	16.5	84.0	16.0	85.0	15.0	85.3	14.7
Boise City, ID	32.0	68.0	77.1	22.9	89.8	10.2	91.7	8.3	88.4	11.6
Boston, MA	51.0	49.0	87.0	13.0	84.7	15.3	86.1	13.9	88.8	11.2
Boulder, CO	50.4	49.6	88.4	11.6	88.7	11.3	90.1	9.9	89.7	10.3
Brownsville, TX	95.8	4.2	92.3	7.7	95.6	4.4	94.7	5.3	97.5	2.5
Cape Coral, FL	73.5	26.5	96.9	3.1	88.6	11.4	94.2	5.8	90.2	9.8
Cedar Rapids, IA	69.1	30.9	85.6	14.4	88.0	12.0	91.4	8.6	87.2	12.8
Charleston, SC	42.4	57.6	81.0	19.0	83.5	16.5	83.8	16.2	76.6	23.4
Charlotte, NC	48.9	51.1	86.9	13.1	89.2	10.8	85.8	14.2	89.3	10.7
Chicago, IL	54.2	45.8	80.2	19.8	82.7	17.3	84.1	15.9	86.0	14.0
Cincinnati, OH	64.4	35.6	70.7	29.3	76.8	23.2	78.9	21.1	80.3	19.7
Clarksville, TN	61.1	38.9	85.7	14.3	93.4	6.6	92.1	7.9	87.1	12.9
Cleveland, OH	71.3	28.7	80.0	20.0	81.4	18.6	78.8	21.2	78.0	22.0
College Station, TX	51.4	48.6	86.9	13.1	91.0	9.0	93.9	6.1	88.3	11.7
Colorado Springs, CO	56.0	44.0	89.3	10.7	88.6	11.4	89.0	11.0	91.0	9.0
Columbia, MO	42.1	57.9	84.4	15.6	86.5	13.5	85.4	14.6	91.4	8.6
Columbia, SC	50.6	49.4	75.0	25.0	88.4	11.6	86.6	13.4	91.7	8.3
Columbus, OH	63.4	36.6	78.5	21.5	84.4	15.6	84.8	15.2	86.2	13.8
Dallas, TX	71.3	28.7	91.0	9.0	91.3	8.7	91.4	8.6	90.6	9.4
Davenport, IA	59.7	40.3	83.7	16.3	85.5	14.5	86.6	13.4	94.0	6.0
Denver, CO	57.4	42.6	85.2	14.8	90.6	9.4	89.6	10.4	91.8	8.2
Des Moines, IA	73.4	26.6	90.8	9.2	89.8	10.2	89.4	10.6	92.0	8.0
Durham, NC	53.6	46.4	84.7	15.3	89.3	10.7	84.4	15.6	88.5	11.5
Edison, NJ	18.4	81.6	71.4	28.6	88.2	11.8	89.7	10.3	91.9	8.1
El Paso, TX	88.6	11.4	92.5	7.5	94.3	5.7	94.0	6.0	95.8	4.2
Fargo, ND	43.0	57.0	92.4	7.6	92.6	7.4	90.6	9.4	94.5	5.5
Fort Collins, CO	44.8	55.2	89.3	10.7	93.6	6.4	93.0	7.0	93.8	6.2
Fort Wayne, IN	50.8	49.2	76.9	23.1	79.4	20.6	82.2	17.8	79.9	20.1
Fort Worth, TX	62.1	37.9	83.6	16.4	90.6	9.4	90.1	9.9	92.2	7.8
Grand Rapids, MI	66.8	33.2	74.2	25.8	78.3	21.7	82.3	17.7	82.3	17.7
Greeley, CO	72.4	27.6	92.8	7.2	94.1	5.9	92.8	7.2	94.4	5.6
Green Bay, WI	70.8	29.2	87.5	12.5	87.8	12.2	84.9	15.1	91.3	8.7
Greensboro, NC	55.5	44.5	90.0	10.0	93.3	6.7	91.0	9.0	89.1	10.9
Honolulu, HI	40.2	59.8	73.5	26.5	79.4	20.6	75.4	24.6	71.9	28.1
Houston, TX	64.5	35.5	89.1	10.9	93.1	6.9	92.0	8.0	92.5	7.5
Huntsville, AL	58.2	41.8	85.2	14.8	81.8	18.2	78.4	21.6	82.1	17.9
Indianapolis, IN	58.5	41.5	86.4	13.6	83.9	16.1	84.2	15.8	87.5	12.5
Jacksonville, FL	54.4	45.6	85.0	15.0	83.7	16.3	80.4	19.6	84.8	15.2
Kansas City, MO	55.9	44.1	86.9	13.1	87.6	12.4	88.5	11.5	83.8	16.2
Lafayette, LA	63.6	36.4	67.4	32.6	70.2	29.8	72.4	27.6	79.5	20.5
Las Cruces, NM	84.8	15.2	91.5	8.5	92.9	7.1	96.6	3.4	96.2	3.8
Las Vegas, NV	63.4	36.6	88.2	11.8	90.3	9.7	91.1	8.9	92.5	7.5
Lexington, KY	37.3	62.7	84.6	15.4	83.2	16.8	83.9	16.1	85.4	14.6
Lincoln, NE	50.3	49.7	73.0	27.0	83.5	16.5	83.1	16.9	87.0	13.0
Little Rock, AR	67.9	32.1	88.9	11.1	78.3	21.7	79.1	20.9	76.2	23.8
Los Angeles, CA	57.1	42.9	85.7	14.3	88.0	12.0	87.6	12.4	89.1	10.9
Louisville, KY	51.6	48.4	80.2	19.8	82.9	17.1	82.3	17.7	78.3	21.7
Madison, WI	51.2	48.8	87.9	12.1	88.7	11.3	88.1	11.9	90.6	9.4

Table continued on following page.

City	Preschool (%)		Kindergarten (%)		Grades 1 - 4 (%)		Grades 5 - 8 (%)		Grades 9 - 12 (%)	
	Public	Private	Public	Private	Public	Private	Public	Private	Public	Private
Manchester, NH	58.7	41.3	86.5	13.5	89.0	11.0	93.0	7.0	92.0	8.0
Miami, FL	58.9	41.1	85.5	14.5	85.8	14.2	84.2	15.8	90.8	9.2
Midland, TX	70.6	29.4	83.7	16.3	83.1	16.9	77.6	22.4	83.9	16.1
Milwaukee, WI	74.3	25.7	77.9	22.1	75.8	24.2	74.5	25.5	81.4	18.6
Minneapolis, MN	55.0	45.0	85.0	15.0	87.3	12.7	88.9	11.1	90.7	9.3
Nashville, TN	48.4	51.6	84.0	16.0	84.6	15.4	80.0	20.0	81.9	18.1
New Haven, CT	80.4	19.6	89.7	10.3	95.2	4.8	93.4	6.6	92.5	7.5
New Orleans, LA	49.2	50.8	78.4	21.6	81.5	18.5	81.9	18.1	80.2	19.8
New York, NY	63.8	36.2	79.0	21.0	81.8	18.2	80.9	19.1	80.3	19.7
Oklahoma City, OK	70.9	29.1	87.6	12.4	89.5	10.5	88.2	11.8	88.1	11.9
Omaha, NE	52.7	47.3	81.2	18.8	82.9	17.1	83.3	16.7	83.2	16.8
Orlando, FL	62.9	37.1	84.3	15.7	88.0	12.0	87.0	13.0	86.7	13.3
Philadelphia, PA	54.6	45.4	78.1	21.9	79.2	20.8	80.8	19.2	79.4	20.6
Phoenix, AZ	61.2	38.8	86.5	13.5	90.6	9.4	91.6	8.4	93.1	6.9
Pittsburgh, PA	50.4	49.6	76.4	23.6	76.9	23.1	76.5	23.5	79.5	20.5
Portland, OR	37.9	62.1	84.9	15.1	87.2	12.8	88.2	11.8	87.1	12.9
Providence, RI	56.9	43.1	80.9	19.1	88.4	11.6	84.5	15.5	89.6	10.4
Provo, UT	63.9	36.1	91.4	8.6	92.1	7.9	95.5	4.5	90.2	9.8
Raleigh, NC	37.3	62.7	87.2	12.8	85.6	14.4	87.7	12.3	87.7	12.3
Reno, NV	59.8	40.2	92.4	7.6	94.3	5.7	92.0	8.0	93.1	6.9
Richmond, VA	50.9	49.1	89.3	10.7	85.0	15.0	84.6	15.4	83.6	16.4
Rochester, MN	52.1	47.9	90.2	9.8	90.8	9.2	88.0	12.0	89.3	10.7
Sacramento, CA	65.0	35.0	91.0	9.0	93.1	6.9	91.5	8.5	90.9	9.1
St. Louis, MO	56.8	43.2	73.9	26.1	82.9	17.1	78.8	21.2	80.6	19.4
Salem, OR	61.3	38.7	87.8	12.2	90.0	10.0	93.3	6.7	96.5	3.5
Salt Lake City, UT	42.5	57.5	86.4	13.6	88.6	11.4	91.0	9.0	94.8	5.2
San Antonio, TX	74.0	26.0	89.7	10.3	92.1	7.9	92.3	7.7	91.5	8.5
San Diego, CA	46.8	53.2	89.4	10.6	90.4	9.6	91.7	8.3	91.2	8.8
San Francisco, CA	34.0	66.0	67.4	32.6	71.0	29.0	66.6	33.4	75.5	24.5
San Jose, CA	43.4	56.6	81.8	18.2	87.0	13.0	87.6	12.4	85.9	14.1
Santa Rosa, CA	53.7	46.3	86.2	13.8	92.9	7.1	89.1	10.9	93.8	6.2
Savannah, GA	77.0	23.0	89.0	11.0	91.9	8.1	91.5	8.5	88.5	11.5
Seattle, WA	36.3	63.7	79.0	21.0	79.2	20.8	73.5	26.5	77.3	22.7
Sioux Falls, SD	53.8	46.2	92.3	7.7	86.4	13.6	88.8	11.2	84.6	15.4
Springfield, IL	53.6	46.4	80.8	19.2	80.5	19.5	86.1	13.9	86.8	13.2
Tampa, FL	51.4	48.6	81.9	18.1	87.9	12.1	83.5	16.5	82.2	17.8
Tucson, AZ	70.3	29.7	84.3	15.7	86.8	13.2	88.9	11.1	93.6	6.4
Tulsa, OK	63.6	36.4	82.4	17.6	85.0	15.0	83.0	17.0	81.8	18.2
Tuscaloosa, AL	78.7	21.3	94.7	5.3	84.3	15.7	96.4	3.6	94.9	5.1
Virginia Beach, VA	35.4	64.6	75.9	24.1	90.1	9.9	90.1	9.9	92.2	7.8
Washington, DC	74.2	25.8	90.9	9.1	88.6	11.4	82.4	17.6	80.7	19.3
Wichita, KS	62.8	37.2	84.4	15.6	86.4	13.6	83.7	16.3	84.5	15.5
Wilmington, NC	62.4	37.6	84.8	15.2	75.5	24.5	74.3	25.7	88.8	11.2
Winston-Salem, NC	56.5	43.5	90.6	9.4	91.7	8.3	91.4	8.6	91.9	8.1
Worcester, MA	54.7	45.3	96.0	4.0	93.5	6.5	92.0	8.0	88.1	11.9
U.S.	58.8	41.2	86.3	13.7	88.3	11.7	88.6	11.4	89.4	10.6

Note: Figures shown cover persons 3 years old and over
Source: U.S. Census Bureau, 2017-2021 American Community Survey 5-Year Estimates

School Enrollment by Grade and Control: Metro Area

Metro Area	Preschool (%)		Kindergarten (%)		Grades 1 - 4 (%)		Grades 5 - 8 (%)		Grades 9 - 12 (%)	
	Public	Private	Public	Private	Public	Private	Public	Private	Public	Private
Albuquerque, NM	57.8	42.2	84.8	15.2	86.4	13.6	89.8	10.2	90.8	9.2
Allentown, PA	52.6	47.4	86.9	13.1	89.7	10.3	91.2	8.8	91.3	8.7
Anchorage, AK	51.6	48.4	90.9	9.1	87.2	12.8	88.1	11.9	90.9	9.1
Ann Arbor, MI	49.9	50.1	89.4	10.6	87.1	12.9	88.1	11.9	93.0	7.0
Athens, GA	64.9	35.1	93.2	6.8	89.6	10.4	87.0	13.0	88.4	11.6
Atlanta, GA	54.8	45.2	85.7	14.3	89.8	10.2	88.2	11.8	89.0	11.0
Austin, TX	49.5	50.5	89.5	10.5	90.6	9.4	89.8	10.2	91.7	8.3
Baltimore, MD	47.8	52.2	82.9	17.1	85.3	14.7	84.6	15.4	83.2	16.8
Boise City, ID	35.5	64.5	84.5	15.5	87.8	12.2	90.3	9.7	89.0	11.0
Boston, MA	45.1	54.9	88.5	11.5	91.0	9.0	89.6	10.4	86.5	13.5
Boulder, CO	50.1	49.9	84.8	15.2	90.1	9.9	90.4	9.6	94.6	5.4
Brownsville, TX	95.5	4.5	95.8	4.2	97.0	3.0	96.5	3.5	96.7	3.3
Cape Coral, FL	60.7	39.3	89.9	10.1	90.4	9.6	90.7	9.3	90.5	9.5
Cedar Rapids, IA	69.0	31.0	86.7	13.3	89.3	10.7	90.5	9.5	91.0	9.0
Charleston, SC	46.6	53.4	83.0	17.0	86.2	13.8	88.5	11.5	88.5	11.5
Charlotte, NC	50.3	49.7	87.4	12.6	89.5	10.5	87.5	12.5	89.9	10.1
Chicago, IL	56.6	43.4	84.4	15.6	88.3	11.7	88.6	11.4	90.3	9.7
Cincinnati, OH	53.2	46.8	79.7	20.3	82.8	17.2	83.5	16.5	82.3	17.7
Clarksville, TN	62.6	37.4	88.2	11.8	86.8	13.2	88.6	11.4	87.0	13.0
Cleveland, OH	52.8	47.2	79.0	21.0	81.1	18.9	82.0	18.0	82.4	17.6
College Station, TX	59.9	40.1	86.3	13.7	91.4	8.6	92.1	7.9	92.3	7.7
Colorado Springs, CO	58.9	41.1	87.2	12.8	88.7	11.3	90.1	9.9	90.8	9.2
Columbia, MO	52.3	47.7	87.6	12.4	85.9	14.1	87.6	12.4	91.3	8.7
Columbia, SC	58.5	41.5	90.7	9.3	92.0	8.0	92.7	7.3	92.9	7.1
Columbus, OH	57.3	42.7	82.1	17.9	87.4	12.6	87.9	12.1	88.7	11.3
Dallas, TX	59.0	41.0	88.8	11.2	91.3	8.7	91.6	8.4	91.9	8.1
Davenport, IA	68.6	31.4	88.3	11.7	91.0	9.0	92.0	8.0	92.1	7.9
Denver, CO	58.0	42.0	88.1	11.9	90.8	9.2	90.9	9.1	91.5	8.5
Des Moines, IA	67.2	32.8	90.4	9.6	91.9	8.1	90.5	9.5	92.2	7.8
Durham, NC	47.9	52.1	81.8	18.2	88.9	11.1	86.0	14.0	90.4	9.6
Edison, NJ	56.6	43.4	81.6	18.4	84.6	15.4	84.8	15.2	84.1	15.9
El Paso, TX	88.3	11.7	93.1	6.9	94.3	5.7	94.7	5.3	96.3	3.7
Fargo, ND	59.7	40.3	91.9	8.1	91.0	9.0	91.1	8.9	91.6	8.4
Fort Collins, CO	45.2	54.8	88.9	11.1	88.9	11.1	86.8	13.2	88.3	11.7
Fort Wayne, IN	46.6	53.4	75.5	24.5	76.6	23.4	77.4	22.6	80.7	19.3
Fort Worth, TX	59.0	41.0	88.8	11.2	91.3	8.7	91.6	8.4	91.9	8.1
Grand Rapids, MI	61.5	38.5	81.4	18.6	82.3	17.7	85.8	14.2	85.3	14.7
Greeley, CO	71.5	28.5	91.2	8.8	92.1	7.9	91.7	8.3	94.2	5.8
Green Bay, WI	67.1	32.9	86.7	13.3	88.4	11.6	86.7	13.3	91.8	8.2
Greensboro, NC	55.7	44.3	86.7	13.3	88.5	11.5	88.1	11.9	88.2	11.8
Honolulu, HI	38.4	61.6	78.3	21.7	82.6	17.4	79.3	20.7	75.9	24.1
Houston, TX	56.6	43.4	88.9	11.1	92.0	8.0	92.4	7.6	92.5	7.5
Huntsville, AL	57.2	42.8	80.7	19.3	82.7	17.3	81.5	18.5	81.8	18.2
Indianapolis, IN	52.2	47.8	87.2	12.8	86.8	13.2	87.0	13.0	88.4	11.6
Jacksonville, FL	54.8	45.2	86.3	13.7	84.9	15.1	83.2	16.8	87.2	12.8
Kansas City, MO	59.2	40.8	88.2	11.8	88.3	11.7	89.5	10.5	88.8	11.2
Lafayette, LA	66.3	33.7	78.7	21.3	80.8	19.2	78.8	21.2	78.7	21.3
Las Cruces, NM	83.3	16.7	92.7	7.3	90.3	9.7	96.5	3.5	94.7	5.3
Las Vegas, NV	60.9	39.1	88.6	11.4	91.5	8.5	92.4	7.6	92.7	7.3
Lexington, KY	44.3	55.7	82.5	17.5	85.0	15.0	84.0	16.0	86.6	13.4
Lincoln, NE	49.5	50.5	74.6	25.4	81.6	18.4	83.9	16.1	87.2	12.8
Little Rock, AR	70.5	29.5	90.1	9.9	87.0	13.0	86.6	13.4	86.4	13.6
Los Angeles, CA	55.8	44.2	86.9	13.1	90.0	10.0	90.1	9.9	91.1	8.9
Louisville, KY	52.4	47.6	81.8	18.2	82.3	17.7	82.4	17.6	80.7	19.3
Madison, WI	67.4	32.6	88.0	12.0	89.6	10.4	90.2	9.8	94.3	5.7

Table continued on following page.

Metro Area	Preschool (%)		Kindergarten (%)		Grades 1 - 4 (%)		Grades 5 - 8 (%)		Grades 9 - 12 (%)	
	Public	Private	Public	Private	Public	Private	Public	Private	Public	Private
Manchester, NH	49.7	50.3	81.7	18.3	87.4	12.6	87.8	12.2	88.9	11.1
Miami, FL	51.1	48.9	82.4	17.6	85.2	14.8	85.6	14.4	86.1	13.9
Midland, TX	75.7	24.3	79.8	20.2	83.8	16.2	82.0	18.0	85.2	14.8
Milwaukee, WI	58.0	42.0	78.8	21.2	79.9	20.1	79.6	20.4	85.4	14.6
Minneapolis, MN	61.4	38.6	87.3	12.7	89.0	11.0	89.6	10.4	91.6	8.4
Nashville, TN	50.2	49.8	85.0	15.0	85.7	14.3	84.7	15.3	83.3	16.7
New Haven, CT	65.6	34.4	93.4	6.6	92.1	7.9	90.4	9.6	88.9	11.1
New Orleans, LA	54.1	45.9	76.7	23.3	77.8	22.2	77.5	22.5	74.9	25.1
New York, NY	56.6	43.4	81.6	18.4	84.6	15.4	84.8	15.2	84.1	15.9
Oklahoma City, OK	71.5	28.5	87.9	12.1	89.2	10.8	88.8	11.2	89.1	10.9
Omaha, NE	57.9	42.1	83.0	17.0	85.1	14.9	85.4	14.6	85.4	14.6
Orlando, FL	50.4	49.6	81.5	18.5	84.1	15.9	85.5	14.5	87.5	12.5
Philadelphia, PA	46.2	53.8	81.2	18.8	84.8	15.2	84.6	15.4	83.3	16.7
Phoenix, AZ	61.7	38.3	86.0	14.0	89.6	10.4	91.1	8.9	92.7	7.3
Pittsburgh, PA	50.8	49.2	82.7	17.3	88.7	11.3	89.0	11.0	89.6	10.4
Portland, OR	41.3	58.7	85.1	14.9	87.5	12.5	89.1	10.9	90.2	9.8
Providence, RI	56.5	43.5	88.3	11.7	90.4	9.6	89.4	10.6	88.4	11.6
Provo, UT	54.2	45.8	89.1	10.9	91.5	8.5	93.7	6.3	94.4	5.6
Raleigh, NC	33.6	66.4	84.1	15.9	86.7	13.3	86.5	13.5	88.1	11.9
Reno, NV	54.1	45.9	89.2	10.8	93.0	7.0	92.3	7.7	92.1	7.9
Richmond, VA	44.8	55.2	87.7	12.3	88.8	11.2	89.4	10.6	90.2	9.8
Rochester, MN	63.8	36.2	91.4	8.6	90.6	9.4	89.8	10.2	91.2	8.8
Sacramento, CA	59.9	40.1	90.0	10.0	91.7	8.3	91.9	8.1	91.7	8.3
St. Louis, MO	53.6	46.4	80.8	19.2	83.8	16.2	82.7	17.3	85.1	14.9
Salem, OR	59.7	40.3	86.9	13.1	89.6	10.4	91.7	8.3	93.9	6.1
Salt Lake City, UT	55.1	44.9	86.9	13.1	90.6	9.4	93.7	6.3	93.7	6.3
San Antonio, TX	67.2	32.8	89.3	10.7	91.6	8.4	91.2	8.8	91.1	8.9
San Diego, CA	49.0	51.0	89.7	10.3	90.8	9.2	91.8	8.2	92.3	7.7
San Francisco, CA	40.5	59.5	83.1	16.9	85.1	14.9	84.7	15.3	86.2	13.8
San Jose, CA	36.0	64.0	78.9	21.1	85.4	14.6	86.0	14.0	85.9	14.1
Santa Rosa, CA	48.2	51.8	87.3	12.7	92.4	7.6	89.8	10.2	92.0	8.0
Savannah, GA	53.9	46.1	81.7	18.3	85.0	15.0	88.0	12.0	85.4	14.6
Seattle, WA	42.0	58.0	82.0	18.0	86.4	13.6	86.9	13.1	90.2	9.8
Sioux Falls, SD	56.2	43.8	91.6	8.4	87.3	12.7	90.0	10.0	87.1	12.9
Springfield, IL	58.6	41.4	85.1	14.9	85.1	14.9	89.7	10.3	90.4	9.6
Tampa, FL	54.7	45.3	82.3	17.7	84.8	15.2	85.9	14.1	87.4	12.6
Tucson, AZ	67.5	32.5	85.8	14.2	87.9	12.1	88.9	11.1	91.0	9.0
Tulsa, OK	66.3	33.7	85.2	14.8	86.1	13.9	86.5	13.5	85.9	14.1
Tuscaloosa, AL	71.4	28.6	87.3	12.7	86.8	13.2	89.9	10.1	88.1	11.9
Virginia Beach, VA	50.5	49.5	79.9	20.1	88.8	11.2	90.0	10.0	90.1	9.9
Washington, DC	45.8	54.2	84.0	16.0	87.7	12.3	87.4	12.6	88.2	11.8
Wichita, KS	64.9	35.1	83.7	16.3	86.6	13.4	86.2	13.8	87.4	12.6
Wilmington, NC	48.0	52.0	81.2	18.8	83.4	16.6	82.0	18.0	88.8	11.2
Winston-Salem, NC	52.2	47.8	88.5	11.5	90.0	10.0	89.8	10.2	88.4	11.6
Worcester, MA	59.0	41.0	91.1	8.9	92.2	7.8	90.6	9.4	90.5	9.5
U.S.	58.8	41.2	86.3	13.7	88.3	11.7	88.6	11.4	89.4	10.6

Note: Figures shown cover persons 3 years old and over; Figures cover the Metropolitan Statistical Area
Source: U.S. Census Bureau, 2017-2021 American Community Survey 5-Year Estimates

Educational Attainment by Race: City

City	High School Graduate or Higher (%)					Bachelor's Degree or Higher (%)				
	Total	White	Black	Asian	Hisp.[1]	Total	White	Black	Asian	Hisp.[1]
Albuquerque, NM	90.9	93.0	94.3	87.7	84.8	37.4	41.1	36.2	54.1	24.3
Allentown, PA	80.6	84.7	83.6	80.4	70.5	17.3	21.5	11.2	42.3	7.7
Anchorage, AK	94.2	96.4	93.2	88.4	85.6	36.8	44.0	21.6	26.4	24.5
Ann Arbor, MI	97.8	98.5	93.2	98.0	92.7	77.2	79.5	36.4	85.6	69.9
Athens, GA	89.7	94.3	83.2	92.5	67.4	47.1	59.0	23.3	72.4	27.0
Atlanta, GA	92.1	98.3	86.3	96.7	84.0	55.6	79.9	29.9	86.1	48.0
Austin, TX	90.6	93.2	89.5	92.7	76.2	55.1	59.5	31.6	76.5	30.9
Baltimore, MD	86.3	91.5	84.1	90.2	72.2	34.2	59.7	18.7	71.6	32.9
Boise City, ID	95.2	96.2	78.5	90.0	82.7	43.7	43.9	31.0	57.7	26.7
Boston, MA	88.2	94.7	85.2	80.6	72.7	52.1	68.7	25.0	57.1	25.7
Boulder, CO	96.9	98.2	89.2	95.5	81.4	76.8	78.0	34.2	84.3	51.2
Brownsville, TX	68.0	67.8	78.7	92.7	66.5	20.5	20.4	37.3	61.2	19.3
Cape Coral, FL	92.9	94.0	84.8	87.3	88.5	23.6	23.9	22.7	44.4	16.4
Cedar Rapids, IA	93.8	95.3	83.0	86.2	82.8	32.8	33.6	17.8	51.5	22.4
Charleston, SC	95.8	97.8	89.2	98.6	86.5	55.7	63.7	24.3	66.2	41.3
Charlotte, NC	89.7	94.7	91.2	84.3	60.8	45.7	59.2	30.8	61.5	19.1
Chicago, IL	86.3	90.8	86.4	87.6	70.9	41.7	55.5	23.5	64.1	18.5
Cincinnati, OH	88.6	92.9	83.1	94.7	76.9	39.6	54.9	16.8	80.3	33.3
Clarksville, TN	93.6	94.2	94.0	87.4	87.1	28.7	30.6	25.3	37.3	17.2
Cleveland, OH	82.6	85.7	81.1	75.3	71.4	19.2	27.6	11.2	46.9	9.2
College Station, TX	94.8	95.9	91.0	94.2	87.1	58.0	58.7	31.9	78.7	41.2
Colorado Springs, CO	93.9	95.5	93.8	85.8	82.6	40.2	43.4	28.1	42.7	20.4
Columbia, MO	95.5	96.6	92.6	94.7	89.1	53.8	56.5	29.4	68.9	47.1
Columbia, SC	90.5	96.2	83.5	95.7	87.6	44.7	63.4	21.6	76.0	35.4
Columbus, OH	90.3	93.0	87.0	86.5	73.5	37.9	44.5	20.1	60.7	24.1
Dallas, TX	79.6	80.5	88.4	87.4	55.4	35.6	44.3	22.3	66.0	13.5
Davenport, IA	92.1	93.9	87.7	71.8	78.3	27.1	29.1	13.6	35.3	15.4
Denver, CO	90.0	93.6	89.8	85.6	69.6	52.5	60.7	27.7	56.5	19.4
Des Moines, IA	87.1	91.9	82.1	58.6	60.2	28.1	31.1	16.4	21.8	10.1
Durham, NC	90.6	93.8	90.0	93.0	54.7	52.8	65.7	35.4	77.8	19.8
Edison, NJ	92.1	94.0	95.0	92.0	86.3	56.4	38.6	43.0	76.2	25.0
El Paso, TX	81.4	84.1	96.1	88.5	77.8	26.7	28.7	32.3	56.8	22.7
Fargo, ND	94.8	96.7	79.3	82.7	91.6	41.8	43.5	19.0	57.2	16.4
Fort Collins, CO	97.0	97.6	91.7	93.4	87.4	56.6	58.0	36.7	73.4	33.1
Fort Wayne, IN	88.9	93.5	85.4	47.6	63.7	28.0	31.6	15.3	21.6	11.6
Fort Worth, TX	83.5	88.1	89.1	80.9	63.5	31.0	37.5	22.7	44.5	14.4
Grand Rapids, MI	88.7	92.6	86.4	80.6	57.7	38.8	46.0	20.4	44.7	13.3
Greeley, CO	83.6	86.1	69.8	81.6	64.7	26.1	28.3	21.9	50.3	9.1
Green Bay, WI	87.8	90.7	76.5	75.1	57.7	25.1	27.0	16.9	26.0	9.3
Greensboro, NC	90.2	93.9	89.3	77.0	68.0	39.5	50.5	26.7	47.0	19.3
Honolulu, HI	90.4	97.9	94.5	87.4	93.9	38.4	54.2	31.3	37.9	31.6
Houston, TX	79.5	82.2	89.1	87.1	59.6	34.7	42.7	25.0	62.3	15.5
Huntsville, AL	91.1	93.8	86.8	88.8	72.3	44.8	51.8	29.4	56.2	29.2
Indianapolis, IN	86.7	89.7	85.3	70.5	60.6	32.9	38.4	20.9	44.3	15.8
Jacksonville, FL	90.3	92.0	88.2	87.8	83.9	30.2	33.0	21.3	49.4	27.0
Kansas City, MO	91.0	93.9	88.6	86.1	71.3	36.5	45.2	16.9	48.4	19.0
Lafayette, LA	90.3	95.1	80.3	92.2	72.5	39.4	49.1	15.2	63.9	33.0
Las Cruces, NM	87.5	90.4	83.9	85.3	83.2	36.4	38.7	47.4	63.0	24.8
Las Vegas, NV	85.4	89.5	88.3	91.9	66.0	25.9	29.4	18.8	43.3	11.6
Lexington, KY	92.4	94.8	88.9	89.4	64.1	45.6	49.7	23.7	69.0	25.3
Lincoln, NE	92.9	95.0	87.1	79.8	69.0	40.1	41.7	26.6	43.7	19.9
Little Rock, AR	91.9	94.1	90.0	87.5	67.6	44.1	57.8	25.7	61.9	13.0
Los Angeles, CA	78.4	84.6	89.3	90.9	58.3	36.2	44.9	29.3	56.8	14.0
Louisville, KY	90.2	91.8	88.2	80.0	77.1	31.6	35.2	18.8	50.7	24.4
Madison, WI	95.6	97.2	88.8	92.4	79.2	58.5	60.9	24.7	70.9	40.0

Table continued on following page.

City	High School Graduate or Higher (%)					Bachelor's Degree or Higher (%)				
	Total	White	Black	Asian	Hisp.[1]	Total	White	Black	Asian	Hisp.[1]
Manchester, NH	88.6	90.4	78.2	81.0	67.1	31.9	32.9	17.6	40.8	13.0
Miami, FL	79.2	80.7	75.7	96.5	76.5	33.1	37.3	15.6	68.9	29.6
Midland, TX	84.5	88.0	88.2	72.1	71.2	30.9	35.0	16.2	45.8	15.5
Milwaukee, WI	84.9	90.5	84.9	74.8	64.4	25.5	37.6	13.5	32.7	10.8
Minneapolis, MN	90.7	96.7	74.7	84.7	66.1	52.6	63.7	17.2	57.3	25.6
Nashville, TN	90.0	92.2	89.3	80.3	59.3	43.9	50.7	28.8	52.3	17.2
New Haven, CT	85.4	87.2	87.3	94.8	71.6	36.5	49.2	22.5	78.5	14.5
New Orleans, LA	88.2	96.4	83.7	76.7	80.9	39.1	65.3	21.0	47.9	40.4
New York, NY	83.2	90.5	84.7	76.8	70.8	39.6	54.6	25.3	44.0	20.1
Oklahoma City, OK	87.5	89.5	91.2	80.6	57.6	32.3	35.4	24.3	42.3	10.4
Omaha, NE	90.3	93.1	87.9	72.2	60.3	38.7	42.8	17.7	49.8	13.8
Orlando, FL	91.6	94.7	84.5	92.5	90.2	40.1	48.5	20.6	54.5	32.2
Philadelphia, PA	86.6	91.8	86.9	73.2	71.9	32.5	46.4	19.3	41.4	18.1
Phoenix, AZ	83.5	87.0	89.8	86.8	65.5	30.6	33.8	25.9	60.2	12.0
Pittsburgh, PA	93.5	95.0	89.1	92.5	87.3	45.7	51.2	19.8	77.7	49.3
Portland, OR	93.3	95.7	89.2	79.9	79.1	51.9	56.1	26.6	43.6	34.5
Providence, RI	83.5	88.8	85.7	84.1	73.3	33.3	41.9	27.0	50.4	12.3
Provo, UT	92.7	94.5	95.3	84.4	73.5	44.3	46.4	17.0	47.4	19.3
Raleigh, NC	92.3	96.3	91.6	89.4	62.6	52.4	64.4	32.6	61.7	23.0
Reno, NV	89.8	93.9	90.8	92.4	66.3	35.5	38.3	31.1	49.5	13.5
Richmond, VA	87.7	94.7	81.5	88.6	58.3	43.1	68.0	14.8	70.7	22.5
Rochester, MN	94.4	96.8	70.6	88.5	76.7	48.7	49.9	19.9	61.8	33.6
Sacramento, CA	86.4	91.5	91.3	81.6	75.4	35.1	42.6	24.8	39.3	21.6
St. Louis, MO	89.2	94.4	83.1	87.1	79.1	38.0	53.9	16.6	57.9	36.7
Salem, OR	88.4	92.3	95.0	84.5	61.8	30.0	32.6	27.1	44.4	11.1
Salt Lake City, UT	91.1	95.3	84.5	83.1	69.3	49.8	54.8	32.1	57.8	21.2
San Antonio, TX	83.3	84.8	91.5	86.1	76.7	27.3	28.9	25.7	55.7	18.0
San Diego, CA	89.3	91.8	91.2	89.2	73.4	47.6	52.0	28.3	55.1	22.6
San Francisco, CA	88.8	97.3	87.3	80.4	79.2	59.5	75.4	31.5	48.9	38.1
San Jose, CA	85.5	90.9	91.4	87.6	69.6	45.4	48.2	38.3	57.5	16.6
Santa Rosa, CA	85.5	92.6	83.5	86.8	62.4	34.3	40.0	27.4	48.4	14.4
Savannah, GA	88.8	94.8	84.1	78.6	84.0	30.5	45.4	16.3	50.7	31.9
Seattle, WA	95.5	98.2	89.8	90.1	85.7	65.9	70.7	32.9	66.9	46.5
Sioux Falls, SD	93.3	95.3	83.9	74.3	73.5	36.0	37.9	20.0	44.2	17.9
Springfield, IL	91.3	93.6	80.0	94.0	86.8	34.4	37.2	14.3	69.9	43.3
Tampa, FL	88.4	91.9	84.1	87.7	78.2	41.8	49.8	18.7	65.4	26.7
Tucson, AZ	86.3	89.9	84.2	87.3	75.0	28.9	32.7	20.8	51.6	15.5
Tulsa, OK	87.9	90.8	89.6	74.0	59.8	32.4	37.6	17.8	37.0	11.5
Tuscaloosa, AL	90.1	95.5	85.9	91.4	66.5	37.6	57.4	15.7	67.5	20.2
Virginia Beach, VA	94.5	96.0	92.5	89.5	87.4	38.6	41.7	29.3	40.9	30.1
Washington, DC	92.2	98.6	88.0	94.4	78.6	61.4	90.8	31.1	82.4	52.8
Wichita, KS	88.2	91.6	87.8	73.7	63.9	30.5	33.6	17.7	35.1	13.3
Wilmington, NC	93.5	95.6	87.4	84.0	78.0	43.6	49.0	20.9	60.7	32.3
Winston-Salem, NC	88.0	90.7	88.1	89.9	58.9	34.6	43.0	20.9	70.4	15.1
Worcester, MA	85.8	88.9	89.5	74.9	69.5	32.2	33.9	31.7	41.7	13.9
U.S.	88.9	91.4	87.2	87.6	71.2	33.7	35.5	23.3	55.6	18.4

Note: Figures shown cover persons 25 years old and over; (1) People of Hispanic origin can be of any race
Source: U.S. Census Bureau, 2017-2021 American Community Survey 5-Year Estimates

Educational Attainment by Race: Metro Area

Metro Area	High School Graduate or Higher (%)					Bachelor's Degree or Higher (%)				
	Total	White	Black	Asian	Hisp.[1]	Total	White	Black	Asian	Hisp.[1]
Albuquerque, NM	90.0	92.1	92.0	89.6	83.8	33.7	37.5	34.4	54.4	21.7
Allentown, PA	90.9	92.5	87.6	89.0	77.5	31.2	32.2	21.7	61.7	15.7
Anchorage, AK	94.0	95.8	92.9	88.2	86.4	33.3	38.1	21.8	26.1	24.3
Ann Arbor, MI	95.7	96.8	90.8	95.7	87.2	57.2	58.9	29.1	82.1	46.1
Athens, GA	89.4	92.3	82.2	89.7	69.1	41.7	46.6	21.7	67.5	30.6
Atlanta, GA	90.5	92.5	91.5	87.7	67.2	40.4	44.6	32.6	59.7	22.9
Austin, TX	91.0	93.4	92.3	92.8	77.1	47.4	50.3	33.1	73.7	26.1
Baltimore, MD	91.6	93.9	89.0	89.1	76.2	41.8	46.4	28.4	63.1	32.4
Boise City, ID	92.1	94.1	80.8	88.2	70.7	33.9	35.1	25.3	52.0	16.6
Boston, MA	92.1	95.1	86.2	86.6	73.7	49.7	52.5	29.6	64.1	24.9
Boulder, CO	95.5	97.0	86.9	92.5	75.8	62.9	64.6	30.4	70.8	31.3
Brownsville, TX	69.5	70.7	82.1	89.3	66.1	19.0	18.7	26.6	59.8	16.2
Cape Coral, FL	89.8	92.0	81.0	91.5	74.4	29.0	30.9	16.7	50.0	14.7
Cedar Rapids, IA	94.8	95.7	83.9	87.6	79.9	32.1	32.5	18.5	49.3	23.6
Charleston, SC	91.5	94.6	85.7	89.7	70.2	38.0	45.2	18.5	50.8	23.0
Charlotte, NC	89.9	92.2	89.9	86.7	65.7	37.1	40.0	28.1	60.8	20.5
Chicago, IL	89.5	92.9	88.7	91.1	70.5	39.7	44.4	24.5	66.5	16.8
Cincinnati, OH	91.8	92.7	87.3	89.4	77.4	35.4	36.4	21.6	65.9	29.4
Clarksville, TN	91.4	91.9	90.6	87.5	85.7	26.5	27.3	23.3	42.7	18.7
Cleveland, OH	91.4	93.3	86.1	86.8	77.9	32.7	36.2	16.8	63.5	17.6
College Station, TX	87.9	89.3	87.7	94.5	67.8	38.6	40.7	18.3	76.8	17.3
Colorado Springs, CO	94.6	95.8	95.1	87.2	84.7	39.4	41.9	29.6	42.2	21.4
Columbia, MO	94.1	94.7	91.6	94.2	88.0	45.1	46.2	25.5	67.1	38.5
Columbia, SC	90.6	92.8	88.1	92.3	70.0	33.6	37.9	24.7	62.2	23.1
Columbus, OH	92.1	93.6	87.6	88.4	76.8	38.4	40.3	22.7	64.1	27.4
Dallas, TX	86.6	88.9	91.8	88.8	63.9	36.8	38.9	30.0	62.8	16.2
Davenport, IA	91.8	93.9	80.3	78.7	75.3	27.9	29.0	11.8	51.7	16.9
Denver, CO	91.9	94.5	90.4	84.9	74.1	46.2	50.1	29.2	53.1	19.6
Des Moines, IA	93.4	95.6	84.8	71.0	68.2	37.6	39.0	20.7	37.1	15.8
Durham, NC	90.1	93.0	87.9	92.8	56.5	47.4	54.2	30.3	77.1	21.3
Edison, NJ	87.3	92.2	86.3	84.1	73.1	42.0	49.1	26.8	56.0	21.3
El Paso, TX	79.6	82.4	96.1	89.2	76.0	24.6	26.5	32.2	54.0	20.8
Fargo, ND	95.2	96.5	78.9	85.9	86.7	40.3	41.5	20.4	55.6	21.7
Fort Collins, CO	96.3	96.9	94.2	93.2	84.3	49.4	50.0	33.0	66.7	28.5
Fort Wayne, IN	90.2	93.3	86.0	55.8	66.3	29.3	31.4	16.4	30.4	12.5
Fort Worth, TX	86.6	88.9	91.8	88.8	63.9	36.8	38.9	30.0	62.8	16.2
Grand Rapids, MI	92.3	94.3	87.7	75.5	69.4	34.5	36.4	20.6	40.5	16.2
Greeley, CO	88.1	90.1	79.6	89.1	67.8	29.5	31.3	31.0	41.1	10.1
Green Bay, WI	92.5	94.3	76.4	83.4	61.7	29.1	29.8	19.0	47.3	13.4
Greensboro, NC	88.2	90.3	87.8	78.5	61.1	30.5	32.9	24.1	47.0	14.3
Honolulu, HI	92.7	97.6	97.1	90.3	95.1	36.2	50.0	33.8	37.4	28.7
Houston, TX	84.4	86.6	91.8	87.3	66.4	34.2	36.5	30.0	56.9	16.7
Huntsville, AL	90.8	92.5	87.5	89.5	74.7	40.9	43.4	32.1	60.6	27.7
Indianapolis, IN	90.6	92.5	86.5	81.0	67.3	36.3	38.5	22.9	55.5	21.3
Jacksonville, FL	91.4	92.8	88.4	89.4	85.5	33.1	35.6	22.0	49.9	27.9
Kansas City, MO	92.7	94.3	89.8	88.2	72.4	38.0	40.9	20.4	56.2	19.1
Lafayette, LA	86.0	88.8	79.2	76.0	70.7	24.6	27.7	13.2	38.0	19.1
Las Cruces, NM	80.7	83.8	84.8	88.6	73.5	30.0	32.5	44.9	60.3	19.8
Las Vegas, NV	86.4	90.0	89.9	90.6	68.4	25.8	28.3	19.8	41.0	11.9
Lexington, KY	91.7	93.3	89.0	89.2	63.6	39.0	40.9	22.8	65.5	22.1
Lincoln, NE	93.4	95.2	87.1	79.5	69.3	39.6	40.9	26.6	43.4	20.1
Little Rock, AR	91.6	92.8	90.2	87.1	70.1	32.1	34.4	24.8	51.1	15.5
Los Angeles, CA	81.6	86.5	90.5	88.8	64.5	36.0	40.8	29.5	54.5	15.1
Louisville, KY	90.9	91.9	88.1	85.5	73.8	31.1	32.7	19.7	57.5	21.6
Madison, WI	95.7	96.8	90.1	90.5	77.2	47.7	48.1	25.2	68.5	30.6

Table continued on following page.

Metro Area	High School Graduate or Higher (%)					Bachelor's Degree or Higher (%)				
	Total	White	Black	Asian	Hisp.[1]	Total	White	Black	Asian	Hisp.[1]
Manchester, NH	92.9	93.8	82.8	89.8	73.6	39.6	39.8	20.5	62.1	19.0
Miami, FL	86.5	88.7	83.6	87.9	81.2	34.1	38.5	21.2	54.3	29.8
Midland, TX	84.4	87.4	89.1	75.0	71.5	28.5	31.3	16.7	51.6	14.1
Milwaukee, WI	92.1	95.2	85.9	86.1	71.0	37.4	42.3	15.1	53.3	16.6
Minneapolis, MN	94.0	96.6	82.8	82.7	73.9	43.5	46.1	23.6	46.0	24.1
Nashville, TN	91.0	92.2	90.0	86.0	64.9	38.4	39.9	30.0	55.3	19.4
New Haven, CT	90.3	92.7	88.2	89.7	74.5	36.6	39.8	23.0	64.1	15.6
New Orleans, LA	88.1	91.7	84.1	80.3	74.7	32.2	39.2	19.9	43.4	22.4
New York, NY	87.3	92.2	86.3	84.1	73.1	42.0	49.1	26.8	56.0	21.3
Oklahoma City, OK	89.8	91.3	91.6	83.3	62.2	32.4	34.4	24.0	47.2	13.2
Omaha, NE	92.3	94.2	88.8	75.9	66.1	37.7	39.7	20.5	49.0	17.3
Orlando, FL	90.1	92.1	85.6	89.2	85.5	33.7	36.3	23.3	52.0	25.7
Philadelphia, PA	91.6	94.4	89.0	84.5	73.0	39.8	44.5	23.0	58.3	20.7
Phoenix, AZ	88.7	91.3	91.7	89.3	71.8	33.1	35.2	28.2	59.7	14.9
Pittsburgh, PA	94.5	95.1	90.8	87.5	88.5	36.6	37.0	21.6	69.2	37.5
Portland, OR	92.8	94.6	90.8	87.6	73.2	41.0	41.6	31.3	54.0	22.1
Providence, RI	88.0	89.8	84.7	86.4	73.3	33.2	34.9	25.8	53.2	15.5
Provo, UT	95.1	95.8	95.1	93.1	79.7	41.9	42.6	34.1	54.0	24.9
Raleigh, NC	92.6	95.1	91.1	92.7	65.6	48.6	52.8	32.3	75.7	21.1
Reno, NV	88.6	92.8	90.7	92.0	64.2	32.3	34.9	28.0	47.1	13.2
Richmond, VA	91.1	94.0	87.4	89.9	68.9	38.9	45.5	22.8	65.6	22.8
Rochester, MN	94.7	96.1	71.8	88.1	77.4	41.0	41.1	19.5	59.6	31.3
Sacramento, CA	89.8	93.2	91.2	84.7	76.7	35.0	36.8	25.5	44.8	20.1
St. Louis, MO	92.8	94.2	87.5	90.8	82.3	36.2	38.6	20.4	68.0	31.3
Salem, OR	86.8	90.9	92.8	81.5	60.7	25.7	28.0	25.2	37.3	10.0
Salt Lake City, UT	91.8	94.9	84.6	86.6	73.5	36.4	38.9	25.4	49.1	17.1
San Antonio, TX	86.4	88.1	92.7	87.8	78.4	30.3	32.0	31.4	53.9	19.4
San Diego, CA	88.3	90.8	91.6	90.0	73.1	40.3	43.2	27.4	53.0	19.6
San Francisco, CA	89.7	95.0	91.3	88.1	73.1	51.4	58.7	31.6	57.6	23.9
San Jose, CA	89.0	92.7	92.4	91.4	71.9	53.4	53.4	41.7	67.5	19.0
Santa Rosa, CA	89.2	94.2	87.2	88.3	66.1	37.1	41.5	32.1	48.5	15.9
Savannah, GA	90.7	93.4	87.0	83.3	84.4	33.6	39.7	21.0	51.4	25.1
Seattle, WA	93.2	95.5	90.8	90.0	75.9	44.3	44.9	27.5	58.3	25.0
Sioux Falls, SD	93.7	95.1	84.5	75.7	73.0	34.8	36.1	19.6	44.4	18.6
Springfield, IL	92.9	94.4	80.8	90.9	89.3	33.4	34.8	15.5	68.2	42.6
Tampa, FL	90.4	91.9	88.7	85.1	81.4	32.4	33.1	25.0	51.8	24.6
Tucson, AZ	89.4	92.5	87.6	87.7	77.9	34.4	38.1	27.6	55.7	18.5
Tulsa, OK	90.0	91.7	90.1	76.7	65.8	28.7	31.1	19.6	34.9	14.0
Tuscaloosa, AL	88.5	91.2	84.9	86.9	64.6	27.8	34.2	15.3	61.0	17.4
Virginia Beach, VA	92.4	94.9	88.7	88.4	84.8	33.8	38.2	23.8	44.2	28.3
Washington, DC	91.5	95.1	92.4	91.3	70.4	52.4	61.3	37.2	66.0	28.0
Wichita, KS	90.2	92.8	87.6	74.2	66.9	31.1	33.0	19.0	35.5	16.4
Wilmington, NC	92.8	94.4	87.9	82.0	78.9	39.9	43.0	22.5	63.9	27.1
Winston-Salem, NC	88.0	89.3	87.7	88.3	60.1	27.4	28.9	21.0	54.6	13.5
Worcester, MA	91.3	92.9	89.3	85.0	73.7	36.4	36.4	34.4	59.8	16.6
U.S.	88.9	91.4	87.2	87.6	71.2	33.7	35.5	23.3	55.6	18.4

Note: Figures shown cover persons 25 years old and over; Figures cover the Metropolitan Statistical Area; (1) People of Hispanic origin can be of any race
Source: U.S. Census Bureau, 2017-2021 American Community Survey 5-Year Estimates

Cost of Living Index

Urban Area	Composite	Groceries	Housing	Utilities	Transp.	Health	Misc.
Albuquerque, NM	93.8	104.8	84.5	87.7	97.2	99.8	96.6
Allentown, PA	104.4	98.4	114.0	103.4	104.8	94.6	100.6
Anchorage, AK	124.5	132.6	140.0	124.0	114.8	144.2	109.7
Ann Arbor, MI	n/a	n/a	n/a	n/a	n/a	n/a	n/a
Athens, GA	n/a	n/a	n/a	n/a	n/a	n/a	n/a
Atlanta, GA	102.8	103.4	103.5	85.1	103.6	107.1	106.0
Austin, TX	99.7	91.2	105.5	95.2	90.7	105.8	101.4
Baltimore, MD	n/a	n/a	n/a	n/a	n/a	n/a	n/a
Boise City, ID	98.7	94.5	97.5	81.9	108.5	103.0	102.8
Boston, MA	151.0	109.3	228.6	120.5	112.0	118.3	129.3
Boulder, CO	n/a	n/a	n/a	n/a	n/a	n/a	n/a
Brownsville, TX	76.6	80.2	58.0	108.2	88.1	80.3	79.6
Cape Coral, FL	100.6	107.8	89.6	98.8	98.7	108.5	106.3
Cedar Rapids, IA	96.2	94.8	83.0	102.1	96.6	107.0	103.9
Charleston, SC	97.2	99.7	93.2	120.4	86.6	97.5	95.9
Charlotte, NC	98.2	101.7	88.8	95.6	90.7	105.1	106.0
Chicago, IL	120.6	101.9	155.7	92.4	125.9	100.0	109.4
Cincinnati, OH	99.7	91.2	105.5	95.2	90.7	105.8	101.4
Clarksville, TN	n/a	n/a	n/a	n/a	n/a	n/a	n/a
Cleveland, OH	96.9	106.0	83.3	96.1	99.4	104.4	102.6
College Station, TX	n/a	n/a	n/a	n/a	n/a	n/a	n/a
Colorado Springs, CO	101.1	95.9	101.3	97.2	97.7	108.6	104.1
Columbia, MO	91.8	95.5	75.0	100.0	92.0	102.6	99.8
Columbia, SC	93.5	103.1	72.7	126.2	87.1	79.9	100.5
Columbus, OH	92.6	98.6	81.2	89.1	95.5	88.5	99.7
Dallas, TX	108.2	100.2	118.8	106.8	96.7	105.4	106.7
Davenport, IA	92.0	99.7	76.9	98.9	105.8	105.3	93.7
Denver, CO	111.3	98.3	139.3	80.5	100.9	103.6	106.6
Des Moines, IA	89.9	95.2	80.2	90.1	99.1	95.4	92.3
Durham, NC[1]	n/a	n/a	n/a	n/a	n/a	n/a	n/a
Edison, NJ[2]	120.6	108.7	149.3	105.8	107.8	102.5	112.4
El Paso, TX	87.7	102.3	73.7	85.7	99.0	99.3	89.0
Fargo, ND	98.6	111.5	77.6	90.5	100.4	120.1	108.9
Fort Collins, CO	n/a	n/a	n/a	n/a	n/a	n/a	n/a
Fort Wayne, IN	86.9	86.7	62.3	95.7	99.5	101.5	98.6
Fort Worth, TX	94.9	92.4	88.4	107.2	96.9	101.5	96.2
Grand Rapids, MI	94.1	92.8	87.4	98.5	104.1	92.3	96.3
Greeley, CO	n/a	n/a	n/a	n/a	n/a	n/a	n/a
Green Bay, WI	91.1	91.0	77.9	97.4	97.7	101.8	96.6
Greensboro, NC	n/a	n/a	n/a	n/a	n/a	n/a	n/a
Honolulu, HI	192.9	165.0	332.6	172.3	138.2	118.8	124.2
Houston, TX	95.8	88.4	91.2	105.8	95.2	92.0	100.3
Huntsville, AL	91.3	95.1	66.6	99.0	97.3	96.4	104.7
Indianapolis, IN	92.4	94.1	78.4	105.4	97.9	90.6	98.0
Jacksonville, FL	91.7	98.4	88.0	97.7	86.0	83.7	92.7
Kansas City, MO	95.8	102.4	82.6	100.6	92.6	105.9	101.7
Lafayette, LA	88.9	101.8	72.0	88.0	104.7	88.0	93.3
Las Cruces, NM	n/a	n/a	n/a	n/a	n/a	n/a	n/a
Las Vegas, NV	103.6	95.8	118.3	98.6	114.0	100.2	94.2
Lexington, KY	92.7	89.9	83.7	95.6	96.7	78.9	100.7
Lincoln, NE	93.0	95.6	78.7	90.2	93.4	105.8	102.2
Little Rock, AR	96.0	95.1	88.1	97.4	94.7	89.6	103.2
Los Angeles, CA	146.7	116.3	230.6	106.2	134.8	110.8	112.0
Louisville, KY	94.1	91.8	79.8	94.6	98.1	105.2	103.7
Madison, WI	107.0	107.6	108.6	99.8	104.4	124.0	106.0
Manchester, NH	108.9	102.2	109.6	117.9	104.1	116.0	108.9

Table continued on following page.

Urban Area	Composite	Groceries	Housing	Utilities	Transp.	Health	Misc.
Miami, FL	115.0	110.5	144.3	102.0	101.5	100.6	102.7
Midland, TX	102.1	93.6	91.5	106.6	104.1	96.5	112.6
Milwaukee, WI	96.7	93.4	100.5	94.8	99.8	115.9	92.4
Minneapolis, MN	106.6	103.6	102.9	97.5	104.4	105.6	113.9
Nashville, TN	98.9	99.5	98.5	97.0	97.9	92.4	100.4
New Haven, CT	122.3	111.0	128.5	136.7	110.6	115.8	121.9
New Orleans, LA	105.0	102.6	125.5	81.5	101.3	115.1	96.1
New York, NY[3]	181.6	128.4	339.0	121.4	113.7	107.1	123.1
Oklahoma City, OK	86.0	93.3	69.6	95.3	86.2	95.0	92.1
Omaha, NE	92.3	96.8	83.6	99.4	98.3	96.4	93.3
Orlando, FL	92.1	100.7	85.1	97.2	89.3	88.3	94.1
Philadelphia, PA	110.9	118.7	116.5	105.6	116.1	101.8	104.8
Phoenix, AZ	99.3	99.7	103.8	109.5	107.2	90.1	91.9
Pittsburgh, PA	103.1	111.9	105.7	116.1	114.0	93.1	92.6
Portland, OR	134.7	112.4	186.4	87.1	131.0	115.6	119.4
Providence, RI	119.2	106.7	132.8	126.4	112.1	109.3	114.6
Provo, UT	98.2	93.0	96.1	84.7	100.7	94.5	105.4
Raleigh, NC	95.4	92.7	89.0	98.3	90.9	103.8	100.9
Reno, NV	114.1	118.7	125.8	85.9	126.3	113.9	107.6
Richmond, VA	94.2	89.0	86.0	97.6	86.9	106.7	102.1
Rochester, MN	n/a	n/a	n/a	n/a	n/a	n/a	n/a
Sacramento, CA	118.4	120.2	134.2	102.9	139.0	113.6	104.8
Saint Louis, MO	n/a	n/a	n/a	n/a	n/a	n/a	n/a
Salem, OR	n/a	n/a	n/a	n/a	n/a	n/a	n/a
Salt Lake City, UT	103.6	108.0	106.7	87.8	103.6	105.7	103.6
San Antonio, TX	89.5	88.0	82.2	87.6	89.1	87.2	96.5
San Diego, CA	142.1	116.1	216.3	123.2	129.2	107.3	107.3
San Francisco, CA	197.9	131.3	368.9	123.0	145.3	129.6	133.4
San Jose, CA	n/a	n/a	n/a	n/a	n/a	n/a	n/a
Santa Rosa, CA	n/a	n/a	n/a	n/a	n/a	n/a	n/a
Savannah, GA	89.5	95.7	66.2	96.0	94.9	106.1	100.0
Seattle, WA	157.5	129.1	227.6	108.0	137.8	128.6	136.2
Sioux Falls, SD	92.5	96.3	86.3	84.7	91.9	107.7	96.3
Springfield, IL	n/a	n/a	n/a	n/a	n/a	n/a	n/a
Tampa, FL	91.2	104.8	79.2	85.9	99.4	98.3	93.7
Tucson, AZ	97.5	100.5	87.9	99.9	101.1	98.7	102.0
Tulsa, OK	86.0	96.2	62.7	99.5	84.4	91.6	96.1
Tuscaloosa, AL	n/a	n/a	n/a	n/a	n/a	n/a	n/a
Virginia Beach, VA[4]	94.1	92.7	89.1	97.4	92.2	90.4	98.7
Washington, DC	159.9	116.0	277.1	117.9	110.6	95.8	118.1
Wichita, KS	91.1	94.3	69.6	99.3	95.3	96.1	102.5
Wilmington, NC	n/a	n/a	n/a	n/a	n/a	n/a	n/a
Winston-Salem, NC	90.8	101.4	66.7	94.6	92.0	119.5	100.5
Worcester, MA	n/a	n/a	n/a	n/a	n/a	n/a	n/a
U.S.	100.0	100.0	100.0	100.0	100.0	100.0	100.0

Note: The Cost of Living Index measures regional differences in the cost of consumer goods and services, excluding taxes and non-consumer expenditures, for professional and managerial households in the top income quintile. It is based on more than 50,000 prices covering almost 60 different items for which prices are collected three times a year by chambers of commerce, economic development organizations or university applied economic centers in each participating urban area. The numbers shown should be read as a percentage above or below the national average of 100. For example, a value of 115.4 in the groceries column indicates that grocery prices are 15.4% higher than the national average. Small differences in the index numbers should not be interpreted as significant. In cases where data is not available for the city, data for the metro area or for a neighboring city has been provided and noted as follows: (1) Chapel Hill NC; (2) Middlesex-Monmouth NJ; (3) Brooklyn, NY; (4) Hampton Roads-SE Virginia
Source: The Council for Community and Economic Research, Cost of Living Index, 2022

Grocery Prices

Urban Area	T-Bone Steak ($/pound)	Frying Chicken ($/pound)	Whole Milk ($/half gal.)	Eggs ($/dozen)	Orange Juice ($/64 oz.)	Coffee ($/11.5 oz.)
Albuquerque, NM	11.88	1.01	2.29	2.30	3.89	5.52
Allentown, PA	15.80	1.61	2.56	2.11	3.74	3.90
Anchorage, AK	16.43	2.25	2.85	2.16	4.61	6.29
Ann Arbor, MI	n/a	n/a	n/a	n/a	n/a	n/a
Athens, GA	n/a	n/a	n/a	n/a	n/a	n/a
Atlanta, GA	12.23	1.21	1.94	1.87	3.63	4.51
Austin, TX	11.44	1.08	2.14	2.18	3.36	4.26
Baltimore, MD	15.04	1.96	2.45	2.54	4.38	5.31
Boise City, ID	13.59	1.60	2.21	1.69	3.58	5.27
Boston, MA	n/a	n/a	n/a	n/a	n/a	n/a
Boulder, CO	n/a	n/a	n/a	n/a	n/a	n/a
Brownsville, TX	10.74	1.02	2.10	2.06	3.34	3.77
Cape Coral, FL	14.43	2.34	2.55	1.83	4.28	4.04
Cedar Rapids, IA	14.03	1.66	2.19	2.32	3.68	5.08
Charleston, SC	12.23	1.63	2.11	2.00	4.07	4.90
Charlotte, NC	13.63	1.23	2.11	2.12	3.68	5.31
Chicago, IL	n/a	n/a	n/a	n/a	n/a	n/a
Cincinnati, OH	13.66	2.66	2.15	1.68	3.92	6.05
Clarksville, TN	n/a	n/a	n/a	n/a	n/a	n/a
Cleveland, OH	16.00	2.16	1.86	2.08	3.91	4.91
College Station, TX	n/a	n/a	n/a	n/a	n/a	n/a
Colorado Springs, CO	14.09	1.35	2.17	2.04	3.53	5.14
Columbia, MO	12.00	1.39	3.08	2.51	3.99	5.68
Columbia, SC	12.03	1.56	2.36	2.02	3.66	4.95
Columbus, OH	14.20	1.44	1.93	1.99	4.00	5.76
Dallas, TX	12.76	1.26	2.34	2.12	3.60	4.62
Davenport, IA	13.66	2.17	2.57	2.18	3.81	5.91
Denver, CO	13.30	1.65	2.07	2.07	3.66	4.97
Des Moines, IA	11.66	2.33	2.79	2.40	3.41	5.05
Durham, NC[1]	13.15	1.77	1.97	2.14	4.23	5.04
Edison, NJ[2]	n/a	n/a	n/a	n/a	n/a	n/a
El Paso, TX	14.35	2.08	2.19	2.14	3.96	5.58
Fargo, ND	n/a	n/a	n/a	n/a	n/a	n/a
Fort Collins, CO	n/a	n/a	n/a	n/a	n/a	n/a
Fort Wayne, IN	12.91	1.22	2.46	1.84	3.53	4.98
Fort Worth, TX	13.46	1.51	2.16	2.25	3.40	4.73
Grand Rapids, MI	15.24	1.48	1.92	2.07	3.33	3.68
Greeley, CO	n/a	n/a	n/a	n/a	n/a	n/a
Green Bay, WI	15.09	1.55	2.25	1.74	3.86	4.01
Greensboro, NC	n/a	n/a	n/a	n/a	n/a	n/a
Honolulu, HI	18.12	2.74	4.32	4.32	5.31	8.59
Houston, TX	11.65	1.42	2.10	2.00	3.76	4.58
Huntsville, AL	14.42	1.54	2.22	2.04	3.86	5.03
Indianapolis, IN	14.69	1.70	2.12	1.99	3.50	4.75
Jacksonville, FL	13.82	1.79	2.26	2.53	3.59	4.86
Kansas City, MO	13.21	1.90	2.42	2.03	3.44	4.53
Lafayette, LA	12.53	1.49	2.57	3.19	3.66	5.04
Las Cruces, NM	13.28	1.47	2.51	2.47	3.97	5.37
Las Vegas, NV	14.35	1.87	2.51	2.43	4.05	5.47
Lexington, KY	13.65	1.26	2.02	1.80	3.65	4.54
Lincoln, NE	13.05	1.58	2.23	1.79	3.20	4.97
Little Rock, AR	12.30	1.41	2.12	2.08	3.74	3.90
Los Angeles, CA	14.79	1.77	2.76	3.66	4.20	6.21
Louisville, KY	14.49	1.35	1.51	1.48	3.61	4.28
Madison, WI	16.50	1.80	2.27	1.88	3.60	5.26

Table continued on following page.

Urban Area	T-Bone Steak ($/pound)	Frying Chicken ($/pound)	Whole Milk ($/half gal.)	Eggs ($/dozen)	Orange Juice ($/64 oz.)	Coffee ($/11.5 oz.)
Manchester, NH	16.69	1.85	2.66	2.57	4.36	5.25
Miami, FL	11.37	1.69	3.62	2.72	4.62	5.14
Midland, TX	12.66	1.09	2.11	2.23	3.77	4.78
Milwaukee, WI	15.29	1.57	2.52	2.18	3.77	4.12
Minneapolis, MN	14.32	1.95	2.28	1.83	3.78	4.69
Nashville, TN	14.63	1.68	2.33	1.83	3.95	4.92
New Haven, CT	13.03	1.44	2.84	2.53	3.81	4.79
New Orleans, LA	15.23	1.37	2.57	2.32	3.68	4.26
New York, NY[3]	16.18	1.70	2.88	2.77	4.42	4.89
Oklahoma City, OK	12.72	1.51	2.34	2.04	3.32	4.72
Omaha, NE	15.11	1.71	2.00	1.72	3.59	5.20
Orlando, FL	13.49	1.37	2.67	2.44	3.89	3.89
Philadelphia, PA	16.43	1.91	2.57	2.47	4.19	5.67
Phoenix, AZ	14.66	1.65	2.06	2.51	4.00	5.82
Pittsburgh, PA	16.67	2.16	2.50	1.93	3.90	5.33
Portland, OR	12.15	1.28	2.88	2.75	4.10	6.48
Providence, RI	15.73	1.68	2.42	2.52	3.90	3.94
Provo, UT	14.23	1.44	2.04	2.18	4.02	5.39
Raleigh, NC	11.98	1.14	1.99	1.71	4.00	3.54
Reno, NV	13.35	1.68	2.82	2.46	3.75	5.69
Richmond, VA	12.49	1.38	2.09	1.44	3.87	4.49
Rochester, MN	n/a	n/a	n/a	n/a	n/a	n/a
Sacramento, CA	12.12	1.51	3.08	3.34	4.02	5.25
Saint Louis, MO	17.61	1.85	1.97	2.17	3.66	4.65
Salem, OR	n/a	n/a	n/a	n/a	n/a	n/a
Salt Lake City, UT	13.19	1.85	2.28	2.25	4.46	5.46
San Antonio, TX	11.06	1.05	2.20	1.86	3.41	4.07
San Diego, CA	14.80	1.85	2.70	3.71	4.32	5.91
San Francisco, CA	18.36	1.95	3.38	3.83	4.48	7.00
San Jose, CA	n/a	n/a	n/a	n/a	n/a	n/a
Santa Rosa, CA	n/a	n/a	n/a	n/a	n/a	n/a
Savannah, GA	13.73	1.29	2.24	1.99	3.42	4.55
Seattle, WA	17.83	2.43	2.97	2.23	4.41	6.55
Sioux Falls, SD	12.85	1.47	2.61	2.26	3.63	5.53
Springfield, IL	14.11	2.05	1.85	1.54	3.88	4.88
Tampa, FL	12.92	1.93	2.78	2.83	4.18	4.31
Tucson, AZ	12.19	1.47	2.37	2.22	4.03	5.97
Tulsa, OK	13.52	1.46	2.57	1.97	3.57	4.66
Tuscaloosa, AL	n/a	n/a	n/a	n/a	n/a	n/a
Virginia Beach, VA[4]	12.02	1.45	2.24	1.64	3.95	3.93
Washington, DC	13.41	1.21	2.91	2.62	4.08	5.36
Wichita, KS	13.71	1.63	2.05	1.95	4.15	4.95
Wilmington, NC	n/a	n/a	n/a	n/a	n/a	n/a
Winston-Salem, NC	13.05	1.11	2.31	2.28	3.98	4.30
Worcester, MA	n/a	n/a	n/a	n/a	n/a	n/a
Average*	13.81	1.59	2.43	2.25	3.85	4.95
Minimum*	10.17	0.90	1.51	1.30	2.90	3.46
Maximum*	19.35	3.30	4.32	4.32	5.31	8.59

*Note: **T-Bone Steak** (price per pound); **Frying Chicken** (price per pound, whole fryer); **Whole Milk** (half gallon carton); **Eggs** (price per dozen, Grade A, large); **Orange Juice** (64 oz. Tropicana or Florida Natural); **Coffee** (11.5 oz. can, vacuum-packed, Maxwell House, Hills Bros, or Folgers); (*) Average, minimum, and maximum values for all 286 areas in the Cost of Living Index report; n/a not available; In cases where data is not available for the city, data for the metro area or for a neighboring city has been provided and noted as follows: (1) Chapel Hill NC; (2) Middlesex-Monmouth NJ; (3) Brooklyn, NY; (4) Hampton Roads-SE Virginia*
Source: The Council for Community and Economic Research, Cost of Living Index, 2022

Housing and Utility Costs

Urban Area	New Home Price ($)	Apartment Rent ($/month)	All Electric ($/month)	Part Electric ($/month)	Other Energy ($/month)	Telephone ($/month)
Albuquerque, NM	383,227	1,215	-	107.21	43.71	191.37
Allentown, PA	485,339	1,679	-	99.25	82.35	193.11
Anchorage, AK	656,122	1,516	-	102.07	130.31	188.62
Ann Arbor, MI	n/a	n/a	n/a	n/a	n/a	n/a
Athens, GA	n/a	n/a	n/a	n/a	n/a	n/a
Atlanta, GA	489,573	1,551	-	90.61	44.15	188.95
Austin, TX	484,044	1,807	-	101.22	51.85	196.79
Baltimore, MD	440,295	1,868	-	92.51	93.60	196.85
Boise City, ID	576,971	1,640	-	63.81	63.35	174.27
Boston, MA	n/a	n/a	n/a	n/a	n/a	n/a
Boulder, CO	n/a	n/a	n/a	n/a	n/a	n/a
Brownsville, TX	274,631	757	-	139.72	54.99	196.56
Cape Coral, FL	495,794	1,824	182.94	-	-	195.37
Cedar Rapids, IA	339,825	846	-	106.96	45.22	189.46
Charleston, SC	423,780	1,572	224.48	-	-	195.28
Charlotte, NC	377,295	1,498	155.34	-	-	184.19
Chicago, IL	n/a	n/a	n/a	n/a	n/a	n/a
Cincinnati, OH	368,833	1,083	-	76.34	81.75	184.60
Clarksville, TN	n/a	n/a	n/a	n/a	n/a	n/a
Cleveland, OH	347,809	1,302	-	89.55	82.10	188.12
College Station, TX	n/a	n/a	n/a	n/a	n/a	n/a
Colorado Springs, CO	497,622	1,512	-	104.56	85.71	186.39
Columbia, MO	442,644	861	-	96.49	65.29	194.74
Columbia, SC	322,903	1,107	-	112.85	167.25	190.68
Columbus, OH	366,506	1,200	-	88.37	72.63	184.15
Dallas, TX	439,403	1,563	-	136.69	79.10	196.79
Davenport, IA	285,682	1,014	-	88.01	57.06	198.79
Denver, CO	639,886	1,841	-	58.60	78.48	190.08
Des Moines, IA	337,128	741	-	79.63	53.25	188.32
Durham, NC[1]	582,565	1,411	-	85.31	62.68	176.30
Edison, NJ[2]	n/a	n/a	n/a	n/a	n/a	n/a
El Paso, TX	292,519	1,130	-	93.81	47.74	200.02
Fargo, ND	n/a	n/a	n/a	n/a	n/a	n/a
Fort Collins, CO	n/a	n/a	n/a	n/a	n/a	n/a
Fort Wayne, IN	296,241	1,083	-	105.04	65.35	191.60
Fort Worth, TX	372,205	1,327	-	137.89	75.49	199.27
Grand Rapids, MI	384,672	1,273	-	105.38	79.74	190.37
Greeley, CO	n/a	n/a	n/a	n/a	n/a	n/a
Green Bay, WI	382,340	881	-	83.06	80.95	186.93
Greensboro, NC	n/a	n/a	n/a	n/a	n/a	n/a
Honolulu, HI	1,605,915	3,589	309.47	-	-	182.54
Houston, TX	378,106	1,292	-	123.18	45.33	195.79
Huntsville, AL	350,811	1,023	173.74	-	-	186.08
Indianapolis, IN	340,588	1,325	-	111.24	89.87	188.71
Jacksonville, FL	385,800	1,507	187.84	-	-	196.12
Kansas City, MO	439,207	1,471	-	98.92	78.39	198.58
Lafayette, LA	284,856	1,063	-	89.62	58.12	186.23
Las Cruces, NM	364,513	926	-	95.18	40.12	192.31
Las Vegas, NV	491,447	1,600	-	121.78	57.89	196.21
Lexington, KY	351,975	982	-	90.87	109.72	189.80
Lincoln, NE	359,724	1,066	-	63.75	64.03	199.14
Little Rock, AR	395,450	946	-	81.77	91.69	204.44
Los Angeles, CA	1,098,874	3,182	-	123.99	84.34	192.21
Louisville, KY	338,400	1,315	-	90.92	105.78	184.63
Madison, WI	475,954	1,205	-	114.02	94.46	183.66

Table continued on following page.

Urban Area	New Home Price ($)	Apartment Rent ($/month)	All Electric ($/month)	Part Electric ($/month)	Other Energy ($/month)	Telephone ($/month)
Manchester, NH	441,922	2,064	-	107.51	118.35	184.25
Miami, FL	584,754	2,690	192.68	-	-	195.67
Midland, TX	366,614	927	-	121.06	40.30	195.66
Milwaukee, WI	432,791	1,481	-	104.40	98.25	186.18
Minneapolis, MN	404,076	1,318	-	102.55	74.40	188.30
Nashville, TN	483,320	1,465	-	90.92	51.95	190.02
New Haven, CT	434,014	2,127	-	166.18	115.11	186.44
New Orleans, LA	654,349	1,851	-	71.40	46.62	187.68
New York, NY[3]	1,349,755	3,727	-	106.15	87.34	195.04
Oklahoma City, OK	333,325	860	-	90.04	66.60	195.02
Omaha, NE	350,853	1,290	-	92.74	60.25	198.80
Orlando, FL	448,493	1,766	154.33	-	-	192.14
Philadelphia, PA	430,067	1,542	-	105.62	103.27	196.34
Phoenix, AZ	497,561	2,083	187.70	-	-	185.99
Pittsburgh, PA	418,872	1,281	-	118.68	149.99	194.84
Portland, OR	661,664	2,636	-	80.74	76.64	181.33
Providence, RI	462,061	2,085	-	132.22	119.10	193.25
Provo, UT	532,268	1,449	-	67.96	72.66	194.35
Raleigh, NC	400,445	1,614	-	112.40	74.47	184.19
Reno, NV	576,610	1,515	-	97.93	44.46	185.65
Richmond, VA	383,637	1,334	-	95.49	99.23	182.67
Rochester, MN	n/a	n/a	n/a	n/a	n/a	n/a
Sacramento, CA	582,334	2,402	-	152.89	43.30	189.21
Saint Louis, MO	339,758	981	-	80.89	68.47	201.40
Salem, OR	n/a	n/a	n/a	n/a	n/a	n/a
Salt Lake City, UT	575,689	1,609	-	77.74	74.42	194.94
San Antonio, TX	327,632	1,388	-	99.94	37.03	198.89
San Diego, CA	1,001,748	3,057	-	145.75	74.47	183.97
San Francisco, CA	1,502,557	3,585	-	172.31	95.33	201.38
San Jose, CA	n/a	n/a	n/a	n/a	n/a	n/a
Santa Rosa, CA	n/a	n/a	n/a	n/a	n/a	n/a
Savannah, GA	297,041	1,176	158.44	-	-	186.50
Seattle, WA	940,665	3,031	188.83	-	-	198.78
Sioux Falls, SD	450,933	1,111	-	84.19	47.87	182.72
Springfield, IL	408,667	1,152	-	91.51	94.77	185.67
Tampa, FL	414,223	1,528	167.09	-	-	192.89
Tucson, AZ	481,931	1,410	-	103.78	69.05	186.26
Tulsa, OK	313,413	852	-	90.90	68.43	190.79
Tuscaloosa, AL	n/a	n/a	n/a	n/a	n/a	n/a
Virginia Beach, VA[4]	395,804	1,258	-	98.78	95.60	184.73
Washington, DC	1,156,418	3,220	-	117.06	100.23	188.98
Wichita, KS	314,516	978	-	93.16	71.97	198.70
Wilmington, NC	n/a	n/a	n/a	n/a	n/a	n/a
Winston-Salem, NC	319,961	1,290	157.68	-	-	180.76
Worcester, MA	n/a	n/a	n/a	n/a	n/a	n/a
Average*	450,913	1,371	176.41	99.93	76.96	190.22
Minimum*	229,283	546	100.84	31.56	27.15	174.27
Maximum*	2,434,977	4,569	356.86	249.59	272.24	208.31

Note: **New Home Price** (2,400 sf living area, 8,000 sf lot, in urban area with full utilities); **Apartment Rent** (950 sf 2 bedroom/1.5 or 2 bath, unfurnished, excluding all utilities except water); **All Electric** (average monthly cost for an all-electric home); **Part Electric** (average monthly cost for a part-electric home); **Other Energy** (average monthly cost for natural gas, fuel oil, coal, wood, and any other forms of energy except electricity); **Telephone** (price includes the base monthly rate plus taxes and fees for three lines of mobile phone service); (*) Average, minimum, and maximum values for all 286 areas in the Cost of Living Index report; n/a not available; In cases where data is not available for the city, data for the metro area or for a neighboring city has been provided and noted as follows: (1) Chapel Hill NC; (2) Middlesex-Monmouth NJ; (3) Brooklyn, NY; (4) Hampton Roads-SE Virginia
Source: The Council for Community and Economic Research, Cost of Living Index, 2022

Health Care, Transportation, and Other Costs

Urban Area	Doctor ($/visit)	Dentist ($/visit)	Optometrist ($/visit)	Gasoline ($/gallon)	Beauty Salon ($/visit)	Men's Shirt ($)
Albuquerque, NM	114.36	105.38	123.65	3.81	45.00	29.72
Allentown, PA	107.20	115.92	108.43	4.12	53.07	35.54
Anchorage, AK	228.37	152.08	252.89	4.49	55.00	34.08
Ann Arbor, MI	n/a	n/a	n/a	n/a	n/a	n/a
Athens, GA	n/a	n/a	n/a	n/a	n/a	n/a
Atlanta, GA	115.86	132.58	128.60	3.87	51.09	40.24
Austin, TX	122.17	119.14	118.78	3.47	52.91	34.72
Baltimore, MD	80.00	115.58	87.78	3.67	56.91	27.22
Boise City, ID	140.88	86.46	138.00	4.43	39.00	43.44
Boston, MA	n/a	n/a	n/a	n/a	n/a	n/a
Boulder, CO	n/a	n/a	n/a	n/a	n/a	n/a
Brownsville, TX	90.00	91.61	73.32	3.46	23.67	13.19
Cape Coral, FL	127.67	112.88	96.64	3.86	50.60	29.74
Cedar Rapids, IA	139.68	101.88	94.68	3.84	34.39	26.11
Charleston, SC	146.94	92.17	71.32	3.61	59.17	37.27
Charlotte, NC	140.33	135.13	125.78	3.68	31.70	49.35
Chicago, IL	n/a	n/a	n/a	n/a	n/a	n/a
Cincinnati, OH	142.44	100.47	107.60	4.01	43.10	45.33
Clarksville, TN	n/a	n/a	n/a	n/a	n/a	n/a
Cleveland, OH	113.00	109.47	94.21	3.86	35.71	41.99
College Station, TX	n/a	n/a	n/a	n/a	n/a	n/a
Colorado Springs, CO	134.96	108.29	123.36	3.96	47.60	44.38
Columbia, MO	125.84	92.11	110.19	3.84	43.33	29.87
Columbia, SC	124.17	82.50	53.00	3.26	42.36	37.12
Columbus, OH	118.38	87.19	61.70	3.77	42.53	38.24
Dallas, TX	141.13	129.77	139.62	3.39	64.32	38.33
Davenport, IA	136.67	84.83	102.07	3.46	34.89	37.75
Denver, CO	106.00	118.21	115.00	3.72	47.09	35.52
Des Moines, IA	131.59	90.21	119.28	3.34	39.44	39.61
Durham, NC[1]	143.27	113.91	132.86	3.70	53.11	22.22
Edison, NJ[2]	n/a	n/a	n/a	n/a	n/a	n/a
El Paso, TX	146.74	84.59	98.23	3.61	28.33	30.52
Fargo, ND	n/a	n/a	n/a	n/a	n/a	n/a
Fort Collins, CO	n/a	n/a	n/a	n/a	n/a	n/a
Fort Wayne, IN	140.00	105.42	88.55	3.70	34.67	39.66
Fort Worth, TX	92.61	96.41	111.17	3.58	55.08	32.87
Grand Rapids, MI	104.35	109.29	109.72	4.13	36.00	26.03
Greeley, CO	n/a	n/a	n/a	n/a	n/a	n/a
Green Bay, WI	152.75	98.67	75.78	3.45	27.46	26.90
Greensboro, NC	n/a	n/a	n/a	n/a	n/a	n/a
Honolulu, HI	168.32	97.93	209.95	5.03	75.67	53.63
Houston, TX	99.00	115.42	103.21	3.53	64.48	26.78
Huntsville, AL	124.50	99.17	88.78	3.55	49.33	33.22
Indianapolis, IN	97.22	99.33	68.63	3.65	39.23	42.46
Jacksonville, FL	90.43	93.90	72.66	3.68	63.00	25.84
Kansas City, MO	90.64	101.00	89.60	3.40	33.07	36.41
Lafayette, LA	109.56	100.77	100.99	3.43	43.28	30.76
Las Cruces, NM	114.46	118.68	146.98	3.89	41.11	36.87
Las Vegas, NV	108.58	98.81	101.71	4.55	46.52	20.35
Lexington, KY	97.28	98.17	80.03	3.78	58.71	52.93
Lincoln, NE	157.42	104.71	103.26	3.64	38.48	50.37
Little Rock, AR	116.78	58.25	94.06	3.52	52.55	37.55
Los Angeles, CA	130.00	128.20	132.27	5.54	82.67	36.49
Louisville, KY	82.50	87.22	61.89	4.13	84.44	45.50
Madison, WI	207.78	115.45	65.67	3.59	54.45	43.08

Table continued on following page.

Urban Area	Doctor ($/visit)	Dentist ($/visit)	Optometrist ($/visit)	Gasoline ($/gallon)	Beauty Salon ($/visit)	Men's Shirt ($)
Manchester, NH	175.70	152.18	115.00	4.03	59.17	41.12
Miami, FL	109.83	94.65	100.82	3.81	80.15	24.94
Midland, TX	118.20	107.50	108.50	3.51	45.00	25.17
Milwaukee, WI	181.86	123.58	75.00	3.66	37.70	33.64
Minneapolis, MN	161.06	88.15	100.90	3.94	37.88	35.74
Nashville, TN	106.23	100.08	86.77	3.57	41.35	27.39
New Haven, CT	146.79	125.96	131.33	4.04	46.14	28.74
New Orleans, LA	168.89	125.56	105.55	3.92	42.78	39.00
New York, NY[3]	124.61	125.08	113.20	4.34	68.52	42.89
Oklahoma City, OK	111.16	120.92	115.53	3.36	43.00	21.10
Omaha, NE	140.67	89.91	120.78	3.75	30.74	28.27
Orlando, FL	98.00	108.72	79.50	3.83	60.44	45.42
Philadelphia, PA	136.17	96.17	118.67	4.19	63.11	34.67
Phoenix, AZ	99.00	99.00	117.08	4.30	50.83	19.04
Pittsburgh, PA	98.25	112.80	96.58	3.99	37.03	20.62
Portland, OR	142.04	113.83	122.48	4.72	56.61	32.88
Providence, RI	143.54	117.33	120.06	3.98	51.00	34.08
Provo, UT	105.44	95.74	116.76	4.24	40.94	46.89
Raleigh, NC	121.09	115.41	113.39	3.86	50.42	26.62
Reno, NV	124.83	110.67	109.50	4.63	36.67	21.59
Richmond, VA	145.32	104.74	115.73	3.61	49.08	29.41
Rochester, MN	n/a	n/a	n/a	n/a	n/a	n/a
Sacramento, CA	176.26	109.67	149.00	5.48	57.08	33.30
Saint Louis, MO	86.89	101.96	85.05	3.81	39.83	21.57
Salem, OR	n/a	n/a	n/a	n/a	n/a	n/a
Salt Lake City, UT	114.47	93.33	109.59	4.14	39.28	46.00
San Antonio, TX	123.35	111.47	125.52	3.43	58.84	35.83
San Diego, CA	116.25	118.33	126.18	5.50	66.33	36.49
San Francisco, CA	174.07	148.07	154.96	5.42	85.61	50.77
San Jose, CA	n/a	n/a	n/a	n/a	n/a	n/a
Santa Rosa, CA	n/a	n/a	n/a	n/a	n/a	n/a
Savannah, GA	119.64	141.34	89.22	3.40	37.92	35.96
Seattle, WA	176.92	144.83	170.85	4.95	65.43	43.45
Sioux Falls, SD	164.33	103.08	126.50	3.57	33.33	24.13
Springfield, IL	120.00	103.33	123.00	3.95	28.33	17.09
Tampa, FL	100.17	104.90	106.73	3.80	31.35	28.97
Tucson, AZ	140.00	101.33	108.10	4.09	39.50	37.99
Tulsa, OK	126.65	101.50	105.72	3.23	43.68	29.27
Tuscaloosa, AL	n/a	n/a	n/a	n/a	n/a	n/a
Virginia Beach, VA[4]	88.07	115.80	111.36	3.72	40.74	32.74
Washington, DC	129.71	105.20	75.00	3.98	81.00	37.83
Wichita, KS	106.36	92.39	162.06	3.75	41.30	51.01
Wilmington, NC	n/a	n/a	n/a	n/a	n/a	n/a
Winston-Salem, NC	142.38	133.67	132.58	3.71	45.00	35.83
Worcester, MA	n/a	n/a	n/a	n/a	n/a	n/a
Average*	124.91	107.77	117.66	3.86	43.31	34.21
Minimum*	36.61	58.25	51.79	2.90	22.18	13.05
Maximum*	250.21	162.58	371.96	5.54	85.61	63.54

*Note: **Doctor** (general practitioners routine exam of an established patient); **Dentist** (adult teeth cleaning and periodic oral examination); **Optometrist** (full vision eye exam for established adult patient); **Gasoline** (one gallon regular unleaded, national brand, including all taxes, cash price at self-service pump if available); **Beauty Salon** (woman's shampoo, trim, and blow-dry); **Men's Shirt** (cotton/polyester dress shirt, pinpoint weave, long sleeves); (*) Average, minimum, and maximum values for all 286 areas in the Cost of Living Index report; n/a not available; In cases where data is not available for the city, data for the metro area or for a neighboring city has been provided and noted as follows: (1) Chapel Hill NC; (2) Middlesex-Monmouth NJ; (3) Brooklyn, NY; (4) Hampton Roads-SE Virginia*
Source: The Council for Community and Economic Research, Cost of Living Index, 2022

Number of Medical Professionals

City	Area Covered	MDs[1]	DOs[1,2]	Dentists	Podiatrists	Chiropractors	Optometrists
Albuquerque, NM	Bernalillo County	472.2	22.0	87.6	8.9	25.1	16.3
Allentown, PA	Lehigh County	359.4	84.6	88.1	12.5	28.8	20.8
Anchorage, AK	Anchorage Borough	383.0	45.1	130.5	5.6	64.2	31.2
Ann Arbor, MI	Washtenaw County	1,319.8	42.2	198.4	7.9	26.8	18.4
Athens, GA	Clarke County	326.1	16.3	52.1	4.7	22.5	15.5
Atlanta, GA	Fulton County	536.7	14.7	74.5	5.3	58.4	19.8
Austin, TX	Travis County	327.2	18.8	74.5	4.5	35.0	17.9
Baltimore, MD	Baltimore City	1,113.1	23.8	82.9	8.3	14.9	16.0
Boise City, ID	Ada County	283.7	33.7	81.1	3.9	53.3	20.7
Boston, MA	Suffolk County	1,576.4	17.2	235.9	9.9	15.7	36.8
Boulder, CO	Boulder County	361.2	31.7	107.7	6.1	82.8	27.9
Brownsville, TX	Cameron County	140.1	7.1	31.4	3.1	7.8	6.6
Cape Coral, FL	Lee County	203.1	31.1	53.7	8.1	27.9	13.2
Cedar Rapids, IA	Linn County	182.0	23.5	74.3	7.9	58.5	17.5
Charleston, SC	Charleston County	831.9	31.3	113.3	5.8	52.1	24.5
Charlotte, NC	Mecklenburg County	343.0	16.9	72.0	3.7	35.2	14.5
Chicago, IL	Cook County	434.1	22.5	95.4	12.6	29.2	21.1
Cincinnati, OH	Hamilton County	614.9	25.9	76.1	10.2	20.5	22.8
Clarksville, TN	Montgomery County	97.7	16.3	43.0	2.2	12.3	11.8
Cleveland, OH	Cuyahoga County	715.5	51.1	110.1	18.9	19.1	17.3
College Station, TX	Brazos County	270.8	16.2	55.3	3.4	17.7	16.5
Colorado Springs, CO	El Paso County	207.1	31.6	104.2	5.3	45.4	25.1
Columbia, MO	Boone County	808.6	57.6	71.6	5.4	38.2	28.5
Columbia, SC	Richland County	357.2	15.4	93.7	7.2	22.5	19.8
Columbus, OH	Franklin County	442.5	62.5	93.6	7.6	25.4	28.6
Dallas, TX	Dallas County	357.1	21.3	93.4	4.3	37.6	14.7
Davenport, IA	Scott County	240.7	53.3	81.0	4.6	184.3	17.2
Denver, CO	Denver County	611.2	31.8	81.0	6.5	39.4	16.9
Des Moines, IA	Polk County	215.9	99.2	77.3	11.3	59.4	21.7
Durham, NC	Durham County	1,130.5	16.3	75.4	4.3	19.9	14.1
Edison, NJ	Middlesex County	377.3	20.2	88.4	9.9	24.9	20.0
El Paso, TX	El Paso County	204.1	13.3	47.4	3.9	9.1	10.4
Fargo, ND	Cass County	404.1	21.1	82.5	4.3	75.6	32.7
Fort Collins, CO	Larimer County	251.3	31.4	83.6	6.1	56.8	21.2
Fort Wayne, IN	Allen County	263.0	29.3	66.9	5.9	23.4	26.0
Fort Worth, TX	Tarrant County	190.1	33.9	62.9	4.5	29.2	16.6
Grand Rapids, MI	Kent County	358.3	69.8	76.9	5.0	39.2	25.4
Greeley, CO	Weld County	126.4	18.1	46.2	2.1	23.2	12.9
Green Bay, WI	Brown County	253.8	27.9	80.9	3.0	49.7	18.5
Greensboro, NC	Guilford County	257.0	14.8	60.5	4.8	14.4	10.3
Honolulu, HI	Honolulu County	351.4	16.2	97.1	3.6	20.4	24.8
Houston, TX	Harris County	348.8	12.3	73.7	4.9	23.1	21.2
Huntsville, AL	Madison County	274.6	13.3	51.6	3.3	23.5	19.0
Indianapolis, IN	Marion County	451.2	21.7	92.0	6.4	16.8	20.9
Jacksonville, FL	Duval County	341.1	22.8	79.5	7.1	25.9	15.9
Kansas City, MO	Jackson County	314.4	59.1	91.9	6.4	47.6	20.2
Lafayette, LA	Lafayette Parish	377.7	11.6	71.7	3.7	32.8	14.3
Las Cruces, NM	Dona Ana County	166.0	13.6	59.1	6.3	18.5	8.6
Las Vegas, NV	Clark County	182.9	36.0	65.4	4.5	20.5	14.1
Lexington, KY	Fayette County	764.3	38.2	146.7	7.8	24.5	26.4
Lincoln, NE	Lancaster County	223.6	13.0	102.6	5.5	47.1	21.3
Little Rock, AR	Pulaski County	743.0	15.3	77.7	4.8	22.1	21.9
Los Angeles, CA	Los Angeles County	315.0	14.6	94.2	6.5	30.7	19.7
Louisville, KY	Jefferson County	480.0	18.7	104.9	8.1	27.8	16.6
Madison, WI	Dane County	615.0	20.6	73.4	4.8	45.0	20.9
Manchester, NH	Hillsborough County	240.8	24.4	82.8	5.7	26.2	21.9

Table continued on following page.

City	Area Covered	MDs[1]	DOs[1,2]	Dentists	Podiatrists	Chiropractors	Optometrists
Miami, FL	Miami-Dade County	375.0	18.6	75.2	10.2	19.4	15.6
Midland, TX	Midland County	157.4	7.6	63.7	2.4	13.1	12.5
Milwaukee, WI	Milwaukee County	388.3	22.2	88.0	7.1	21.1	11.5
Minneapolis, MN	Hennepin County	532.0	24.0	103.5	5.2	77.1	21.6
Nashville, TN	Davidson County	647.1	14.1	81.0	5.3	26.8	17.5
New Haven, CT	New Haven County	577.3	10.3	77.7	9.6	27.2	16.6
New Orleans, LA	Orleans Parish	887.3	24.0	81.2	4.2	10.1	8.2
New York, NY	New York City	471.8	16.8	87.4	13.4	16.3	18.2
Oklahoma City, OK	Oklahoma County	423.1	43.0	109.1	5.3	28.9	20.5
Omaha, NE	Douglas County	547.3	26.0	101.4	5.0	42.2	21.7
Orlando, FL	Orange County	323.9	23.6	51.7	3.8	28.7	13.2
Philadelphia, PA	Philadelphia County	587.8	43.6	81.6	16.8	15.4	19.0
Phoenix, AZ	Maricopa County	255.3	33.2	71.1	7.0	33.9	16.7
Pittsburgh, PA	Allegheny County	640.1	44.3	97.1	9.2	44.0	20.7
Portland, OR	Multnomah County	646.7	32.2	101.6	5.1	76.3	24.8
Providence, RI	Providence County	489.8	17.1	58.3	9.7	21.1	21.6
Provo, UT	Utah County	119.4	20.8	59.3	4.7	26.4	11.7
Raleigh, NC	Wake County	289.4	12.4	72.7	3.7	28.3	16.8
Reno, NV	Washoe County	298.1	20.5	69.5	3.9	29.0	23.9
Richmond, VA	Richmond City	777.8	27.8	150.5	11.9	7.5	16.8
Rochester, MN	Olmsted County	2,470.7	46.0	125.4	6.7	44.1	22.6
Sacramento, CA	Sacramento County	329.3	16.6	80.7	4.6	21.8	18.4
St. Louis, MO	St. Louis City	1,222.5	35.3	63.1	4.8	21.1	19.4
Salem, OR	Marion County	182.0	15.0	84.4	5.8	34.0	16.4
Salt Lake City, UT	Salt Lake County	387.4	18.7	79.5	6.4	.28.2	14.1
San Antonio, TX	Bexar County	329.0	18.9	94.2	5.4	17.2	18.9
San Diego, CA	San Diego County	346.3	19.7	96.3	4.7	35.5	20.4
San Francisco, CA	San Francisco County	834.7	13.1	171.0	11.8	43.1	31.8
San Jose, CA	Santa Clara County	445.9	12.0	124.2	6.9	45.0	28.8
Santa Rosa, CA	Sonoma County	284.4	19.0	96.7	7.4	43.0	18.3
Savannah, GA	Chatham County	352.3	19.0	68.5	6.7	20.2	13.8
Seattle, WA	King County	502.8	16.6	113.5	6.3	47.7	22.8
Sioux Falls, SD	Minnehaha County	369.1	23.8	56.1	5.5	58.1	19.0
Springfield, IL	Sangamon County	644.3	24.0	86.3	5.6	39.0	21.6
Tampa, FL	Hillsborough County	366.3	31.8	61.6	6.0	27.7	15.0
Tucson, AZ	Pima County	372.3	24.5	67.2	5.9	19.2	17.0
Tulsa, OK	Tulsa County	264.3	111.5	70.3	4.3	38.8	23.6
Tuscaloosa, AL	Tuscaloosa County	223.2	9.2	44.9	4.0	18.9	15.9
Virginia Beach, VA	Virginia Beach City	259.3	14.6	80.6	6.6	26.2	17.3
Washington, DC	District of Columbia	817.4	19.0	128.8	9.6	10.4	14.0
Wichita, KS	Sedgwick County	252.9	34.0	69.1	1.9	43.3	29.0
Wilmington, NC	New Hanover County	359.2	30.5	82.1	8.7	36.7	24.9
Winston-Salem, NC	Forsyth County	680.1	29.8	65.6	6.0	17.6	18.4
Worcester, MA	Worcester County	360.6	19.0	75.4	6.6	19.8	18.9
U.S.	U.S.	289.3	23.5	72.5	6.2	28.7	17.4

Note: All figures are rates per 100,000 population; Data as of 2021 unless noted; (1) Data as of 2020 and includes all active, non-federal physicians; (2) Doctor of Osteopathic Medicine
Source: U.S. Department of Health and Human Services, Health Resources and Services Administration, Bureau of Health Professions, Area Resource File (ARF) 2021-2022

Health Insurance Coverage: City

City	With Health Insurance	With Private Health Insurance	With Public Health Insurance	Without Health Insurance	Population Under Age 19 Without Health Insurance
Albuquerque, NM	92.1	60.6	44.2	7.9	4.3
Allentown, PA	88.6	46.4	50.2	11.4	4.7
Anchorage, AK	89.5	69.7	32.7	10.5	7.6
Ann Arbor, MI	97.4	87.5	20.3	2.6	1.3
Athens, GA	87.5	70.8	25.1	12.5	9.1
Atlanta, GA	89.4	70.1	27.0	10.6	6.2
Austin, TX	87.2	74.3	20.3	12.8	7.9
Baltimore, MD	94.1	59.3	45.9	5.9	3.4
Boise City, ID	92.1	75.5	28.2	7.9	4.2
Boston, MA	96.6	68.6	35.9	3.4	1.7
Boulder, CO	96.0	83.6	21.0	4.0	1.1
Brownsville, TX	69.2	37.3	35.7	30.8	18.5
Cape Coral, FL	87.2	64.4	38.6	12.8	10.1
Cedar Rapids, IA	95.2	73.2	34.4	4.8	2.2
Charleston, SC	93.2	79.8	25.0	6.8	2.4
Charlotte, NC	87.2	68.2	26.4	12.8	7.7
Chicago, IL	90.2	61.6	35.5	9.8	3.6
Cincinnati, OH	92.7	60.4	40.5	7.3	5.2
Clarksville, TN	91.5	71.6	34.9	8.5	3.5
Cleveland, OH	92.5	44.5	56.6	7.5	3.3
College Station, TX	91.3	84.1	14.3	8.7	5.6
Colorado Springs, CO	92.1	69.2	36.4	7.9	4.6
Columbia, MO	92.5	80.0	22.1	7.5	3.8
Columbia, SC	91.4	70.7	30.7	8.6	3.4
Columbus, OH	90.7	63.4	34.7	9.3	5.6
Dallas, TX	76.5	53.3	29.3	23.5	16.0
Davenport, IA	93.3	66.2	39.9	6.7	4.9
Denver, CO	90.4	66.9	31.3	9.6	5.5
Des Moines, IA	93.7	63.7	42.0	6.3	2.2
Durham, NC	88.1	69.6	27.9	11.9	7.7
Edison, NJ	95.2	80.5	23.8	4.8	1.9
El Paso, TX	80.0	54.6	33.9	20.0	10.2
Fargo, ND	93.8	79.9	25.1	6.2	3.8
Fort Collins, CO	93.9	78.5	23.9	6.1	5.1
Fort Wayne, IN	90.8	64.6	37.0	9.2	6.2
Fort Worth, TX	81.2	61.1	26.9	18.8	12.5
Grand Rapids, MI	91.6	63.6	37.7	8.4	4.9
Greeley, CO	90.2	60.8	40.2	9.8	5.1
Green Bay, WI	91.7	64.2	36.7	8.3	5.5
Greensboro, NC	90.3	66.3	34.1	9.7	4.1
Honolulu, HI	96.0	76.9	36.2	4.0	1.9
Houston, TX	76.2	51.7	30.5	23.8	14.5
Huntsville, AL	90.1	72.6	33.3	9.9	3.9
Indianapolis, IN	90.2	62.4	37.4	9.8	6.3
Jacksonville, FL	87.9	64.4	34.2	12.1	6.9
Kansas City, MO	88.2	68.9	28.9	11.8	6.9
Lafayette, LA	91.5	64.4	38.6	8.5	4.0
Las Cruces, NM	92.0	54.9	50.8	8.0	2.2
Las Vegas, NV	87.1	60.7	36.0	12.9	8.6
Lexington, KY	93.2	70.9	33.1	6.8	3.1
Lincoln, NE	92.6	77.1	26.4	7.4	4.9
Little Rock, AR	91.3	63.9	38.7	8.7	4.4
Los Angeles, CA	89.3	55.1	40.8	10.7	3.8
Louisville, KY	94.4	66.2	41.2	5.6	3.4
Madison, WI	96.0	82.9	23.3	4.0	2.4

Table continued on following page.

City	With Health Insurance	With Private Health Insurance	With Public Health Insurance	Without Health Insurance	Population Under Age 19 Without Health Insurance
Manchester, NH	90.9	65.9	35.1	9.1	3.8
Miami, FL	81.0	49.9	34.5	19.0	8.1
Midland, TX	83.5	69.9	20.7	16.5	14.2
Milwaukee, WI	90.6	54.1	44.8	9.4	3.5
Minneapolis, MN	93.9	68.8	33.0	6.1	3.1
Nashville, TN	87.6	68.7	29.3	12.4	8.2
New Haven, CT	92.2	51.9	46.3	7.8	3.1
New Orleans, LA	91.2	54.1	45.3	8.8	5.0
New York, NY	93.1	58.8	43.6	6.9	2.4
Oklahoma City, OK	85.6	64.7	32.3	14.4	7.5
Omaha, NE	89.7	70.8	28.7	10.3	7.0
Orlando, FL	84.9	64.3	27.5	15.1	8.9
Philadelphia, PA	92.6	57.7	45.8	7.4	4.1
Phoenix, AZ	85.5	57.9	35.0	14.5	10.0
Pittsburgh, PA	94.5	73.0	33.7	5.5	3.9
Portland, OR	93.9	72.1	31.8	6.1	2.3
Providence, RI	93.2	55.8	45.4	6.8	3.9
Provo, UT	89.3	78.1	17.5	10.7	10.8
Raleigh, NC	89.6	74.3	24.5	10.4	6.1
Reno, NV	90.0	69.1	30.5	10.0	8.4
Richmond, VA	89.3	63.7	35.5	10.7	6.9
Rochester, MN	96.2	79.1	30.9	3.8	2.0
Sacramento, CA	94.3	64.2	40.8	5.7	2.4
St. Louis, MO	89.5	62.6	35.2	10.5	4.3
Salem, OR	92.9	64.7	41.5	7.1	2.1
Salt Lake City, UT	88.9	74.0	22.7	11.1	9.9
San Antonio, TX	82.8	58.9	33.4	17.2	9.2
San Diego, CA	92.8	71.1	31.1	7.2	3.7
San Francisco, CA	96.4	76.2	29.5	3.6	1.9
San Jose, CA	94.9	72.9	29.9	5.1	2.1
Santa Rosa, CA	92.4	68.5	36.9	7.6	5.5
Savannah, GA	84.3	58.4	35.4	15.7	7.7
Seattle, WA	95.6	80.7	23.5	4.4	1.5
Sioux Falls, SD	92.0	77.5	26.1	8.0	5.2
Springfield, IL	95.7	69.7	41.8	4.3	1.4
Tampa, FL	88.9	63.5	33.0	11.1	5.1
Tucson, AZ	88.7	57.2	42.3	11.3	7.6
Tulsa, OK	83.3	58.7	35.8	16.7	8.7
Tuscaloosa, AL	92.1	70.9	32.9	7.9	2.3
Virginia Beach, VA	92.9	79.8	27.6	7.1	4.3
Washington, DC	96.6	71.9	34.7	3.4	2.2
Wichita, KS	87.8	65.8	33.6	12.2	5.8
Wilmington, NC	88.9	70.3	32.6	11.1	6.5
Winston-Salem, NC	87.7	62.3	36.6	12.3	4.5
Worcester, MA	97.0	61.1	46.4	3.0	1.5
U.S.	91.2	67.8	35.4	8.8	5.3

Note: Figures are percentages that cover the civilian noninstitutionalized population
Source: U.S. Census Bureau, 2017-2021 American Community Survey 5-Year Estimates

Health Insurance Coverage: Metro Area

Metro Area	With Health Insurance	With Private Health Insurance	With Public Health Insurance	Without Health Insurance	Population Under Age 19 Without Health Insurance
Albuquerque, NM	92.0	60.1	45.5	8.0	4.7
Allentown, PA	94.6	72.8	35.7	5.4	2.9
Anchorage, AK	88.6	68.1	33.5	11.4	9.0
Ann Arbor, MI	96.6	82.5	27.2	3.4	1.8
Athens, GA	88.1	70.2	27.8	11.9	7.0
Atlanta, GA	87.4	69.4	27.2	12.6	7.9
Austin, TX	87.7	75.1	21.7	12.3	8.1
Baltimore, MD	95.2	75.1	33.7	4.8	3.2
Boise City, ID	90.5	72.3	30.7	9.5	5.4
Boston, MA	97.0	76.8	32.6	3.0	1.6
Boulder, CO	95.4	79.9	26.0	4.6	2.3
Brownsville, TX	71.5	38.4	38.3	28.5	17.1
Cape Coral, FL	86.9	61.9	43.5	13.1	9.8
Cedar Rapids, IA	96.2	75.9	33.5	3.8	1.8
Charleston, SC	89.7	71.5	31.4	10.3	6.7
Charlotte, NC	89.7	70.1	29.6	10.3	5.5
Chicago, IL	92.4	70.5	31.6	7.6	3.3
Cincinnati, OH	94.6	72.7	33.0	5.4	3.5
Clarksville, TN	91.6	69.8	36.8	8.4	5.6
Cleveland, OH	94.6	68.7	38.7	5.4	3.4
College Station, TX	87.5	73.3	23.8	12.5	8.4
Colorado Springs, CO	92.7	71.3	35.4	7.3	4.7
Columbia, MO	92.4	78.6	25.0	7.6	4.7
Columbia, SC	90.4	69.8	34.4	9.6	4.5
Columbus, OH	93.0	71.1	31.8	7.0	4.5
Dallas, TX	83.4	66.4	24.5	16.6	11.7
Davenport, IA	94.5	71.5	37.8	5.5	3.5
Denver, CO	92.2	72.6	29.1	7.8	4.7
Des Moines, IA	95.7	76.3	31.8	4.3	2.2
Durham, NC	90.0	71.8	30.0	10.0	5.7
Edison, NJ	93.2	67.3	36.5	6.8	3.0
El Paso, TX	78.7	52.8	33.7	21.3	10.9
Fargo, ND	94.5	80.8	25.2	5.5	4.4
Fort Collins, CO	94.0	76.6	28.9	6.0	4.4
Fort Wayne, IN	91.9	69.8	33.3	8.1	6.1
Fort Worth, TX	83.4	66.4	24.5	16.6	11.7
Grand Rapids, MI	95.0	76.1	31.3	5.0	3.0
Greeley, CO	91.2	68.7	32.3	8.8	4.7
Green Bay, WI	94.9	74.8	31.6	5.1	3.7
Greensboro, NC	89.9	64.9	36.0	10.1	4.5
Honolulu, HI	96.5	79.2	34.3	3.5	2.3
Houston, TX	81.3	61.6	26.6	18.7	12.3
Huntsville, AL	91.9	77.2	29.5	8.1	3.1
Indianapolis, IN	92.4	71.4	31.8	7.6	5.2
Jacksonville, FL	89.3	68.7	33.1	10.7	6.7
Kansas City, MO	90.9	74.8	27.2	9.1	5.6
Lafayette, LA	91.9	61.3	41.3	8.1	3.5
Las Cruces, NM	89.4	48.3	52.6	10.6	4.8
Las Vegas, NV	88.1	63.3	34.7	11.9	8.0
Lexington, KY	93.9	71.2	34.6	6.1	3.4
Lincoln, NE	93.1	78.1	26.2	6.9	4.7
Little Rock, AR	92.3	66.2	39.1	7.7	4.3
Los Angeles, CA	91.4	61.2	37.6	8.6	3.6
Louisville, KY	94.6	70.7	37.3	5.4	3.5
Madison, WI	96.1	83.0	25.6	3.9	2.4

Table continued on following page.

Metro Area	With Health Insurance	With Private Health Insurance	With Public Health Insurance	Without Health Insurance	Population Under Age 19 Without Health Insurance
Manchester, NH	93.8	77.2	28.7	6.2	3.4
Miami, FL	85.3	59.9	33.0	14.7	8.3
Midland, TX	84.0	69.8	21.3	16.0	13.0
Milwaukee, WI	94.3	71.8	34.1	5.7	2.8
Minneapolis, MN	95.7	77.9	29.9	4.3	2.8
Nashville, TN	90.5	72.7	28.4	9.5	5.7
New Haven, CT	94.9	66.9	39.6	5.1	2.5
New Orleans, LA	91.2	58.8	42.8	8.8	4.5
New York, NY	93.2	67.3	36.5	6.8	3.0
Oklahoma City, OK	87.4	68.4	31.5	12.6	6.9
Omaha, NE	92.3	75.4	27.6	7.7	5.0
Orlando, FL	87.8	65.8	31.3	12.2	6.8
Philadelphia, PA	94.7	73.0	34.8	5.3	3.2
Phoenix, AZ	89.2	65.8	34.2	10.8	8.6
Pittsburgh, PA	96.3	76.2	36.5	3.7	1.9
Portland, OR	93.9	73.0	32.9	6.1	3.1
Providence, RI	96.0	70.2	39.4	4.0	2.2
Provo, UT	92.2	82.4	17.0	7.8	6.2
Raleigh, NC	90.9	75.9	25.2	9.1	5.2
Reno, NV	90.2	69.8	31.2	9.8	7.8
Richmond, VA	92.5	74.5	31.1	7.5	4.7
Rochester, MN	95.7	79.6	30.8	4.3	3.3
Sacramento, CA	95.1	70.1	38.0	4.9	2.6
St. Louis, MO	93.7	74.5	30.5	6.3	3.4
Salem, OR	92.2	63.8	41.9	7.8	3.1
Salt Lake City, UT	90.2	77.7	20.2	9.8	8.2
San Antonio, TX	85.0	64.7	31.2	15.0	8.9
San Diego, CA	92.5	69.4	33.6	7.5	3.9
San Francisco, CA	95.9	76.0	30.5	4.1	2.3
San Jose, CA	95.8	77.5	26.7	4.2	1.9
Santa Rosa, CA	94.1	72.5	36.2	5.9	3.5
Savannah, GA	87.2	68.1	30.9	12.8	6.3
Seattle, WA	94.3	75.8	29.2	5.7	2.6
Sioux Falls, SD	92.8	79.1	25.2	7.2	4.7
Springfield, IL	96.2	74.4	37.3	3.8	1.4
Tampa, FL	88.3	63.7	36.4	11.7	6.2
Tucson, AZ	91.1	62.9	42.4	8.9	6.9
Tulsa, OK	86.3	65.3	33.3	13.7	7.7
Tuscaloosa, AL	92.6	70.5	34.5	7.4	2.6
Virginia Beach, VA	92.3	74.5	32.6	7.7	4.4
Washington, DC	92.7	77.8	26.4	7.3	4.5
Wichita, KS	89.8	70.6	31.6	10.2	5.2
Wilmington, NC	89.7	72.8	32.3	10.3	7.2
Winston-Salem, NC	89.0	65.0	36.4	11.0	4.8
Worcester, MA	97.4	73.0	37.5	2.6	1.3
U.S.	91.2	67.8	35.4	8.8	5.3

Note: Figures are percentages that cover the civilian noninstitutionalized population; Figures cover the Metropolitan Statistical Area (MSA)—see Appendix B for areas included
Source: U.S. Census Bureau, 2017-2021 American Community Survey 5-Year Estimates

Crime Rate: City

City	Total Crime	Violent Crime Rate				Property Crime Rate		
		Murder	Rape	Robbery	Aggrav. Assault	Burglary	Larceny -Theft	Motor Vehicle Theft
Albuquerque, NM	6,355.7	14.2	78.5	256.0	994.9	902.9	3,225.8	883.3
Allentown, PA[1]	2,669.6	5.7	52.5	139.5	188.7	427.6	1,656.1	199.4
Anchorage, AK	4,659.4	6.3	194.8	194.8	816.4	504.2	2,541.7	401.2
Ann Arbor, MI	1,563.2	0.8	40.6	31.5	170.7	126.8	1,125.6	67.1
Athens, GA	3,463.9	3.1	81.9	79.6	345.7	465.9	2,213.8	273.9
Atlanta, GA[2]	5,423.2	17.7	49.4	221.5	480.1	621.2	3,366.4	666.8
Austin, TX	4,098.2	4.4	47.8	110.1	304.7	477.3	2,747.3	406.6
Baltimore, MD[1]	6,169.9	58.3	54.2	813.1	933.1	906.5	2,745.1	659.5
Boise City, ID	1,933.2	1.7	73.5	23.8	193.8	207.2	1,312.6	120.7
Boston, MA	2,490.8	8.3	26.4	131.8	457.9	243.5	1,439.4	183.6
Boulder, CO	4,092.0	1.9	29.1	67.5	223.3	613.5	2,808.7	348.0
Brownsville, TX	2,250.2	3.8	45.2	83.3	269.6	219.5	1,563.0	65.9
Cape Coral, FL	1,195.5	0.5	9.0	10.0	108.3	152.9	848.1	66.7
Cedar Rapids, IA	3,488.4	8.2	11.9	75.9	225.6	619.4	2,132.8	414.7
Charleston, SC	2,771.1	12.2	38.7	71.6	343.2	233.6	1,747.4	324.5
Charlotte, NC	4,076.6	12.4	25.6	184.0	614.4	449.9	2,478.9	311.4
Chicago, IL	n/a	28.6	50.0	292.1	616.2	320.9	n/a	373.2
Cincinnati, OH	4,576.3	30.2	70.6	246.1	546.1	762.0	2,427.1	494.2
Clarksville, TN	2,852.9	9.3	52.1	48.4	500.1	273.6	1,715.6	253.8
Cleveland, OH	5,727.5	42.2	103.7	420.2	1,090.7	973.8	2,321.2	775.7
College Station, TX	2,082.2	1.7	45.5	22.3	110.1	265.7	1,463.2	173.8
Colorado Springs, CO	3,976.6	7.4	82.5	77.5	429.6	533.5	2,344.8	501.4
Columbia, MO	3,106.6	10.4	71.3	46.5	314.0	323.6	1,985.1	355.7
Columbia, SC	5,227.8	14.4	65.3	156.3	516.0	552.4	3,442.2	481.1
Columbus, OH	3,686.0	19.1	89.5	197.1	249.9	609.1	2,180.6	340.7
Dallas, TX	4,291.0	17.3	41.7	241.5	544.2	727.6	1,955.6	763.1
Davenport, IA	4,661.8	9.8	65.8	133.6	527.5	895.8	2,568.6	460.7
Denver, CO	5,506.6	13.1	90.8	165.1	588.9	708.0	2,800.8	1,139.9
Des Moines, IA	4,606.3	15.3	55.3	114.3	519.8	894.1	2,347.1	660.5
Durham, NC	4,596.6	12.6	43.9	219.7	582.6	668.9	2,730.2	338.7
Edison, NJ	1,242.2	1.0	9.0	31.1	62.3	131.5	889.7	117.5
El Paso, TX	1,557.6	4.1	38.1	42.2	231.9	123.6	1,057.2	60.6
Fargo, ND	3,929.0	5.5	84.3	48.1	322.2	800.5	2,302.1	366.4
Fort Collins, CO[1]	2,389.9	0.6	24.0	21.1	171.5	204.8	1,834.5	133.4
Fort Wayne, IN	2,659.5	14.3	35.6	90.0	272.9	240.6	1,818.8	187.3
Fort Worth, TX	3,274.2	11.8	48.0	93.3	387.9	366.9	1,988.9	377.4
Grand Rapids, MI	2,666.0	13.8	59.7	94.8	544.2	228.6	1,437.9	286.9
Greeley, CO	2,888.6	8.1	48.0	70.6	298.6	333.9	1,774.6	354.7
Green Bay, WI	2,056.4	5.7	67.8	43.0	410.9	196.8	1,222.2	109.9
Greensboro, NC	4,513.0	19.7	31.7	193.7	656.6	737.6	2,501.9	371.8
Honolulu, HI	n/a	n/a	n/a	n/a	n/a	n/a	n/a	n/a
Houston, TX	5,435.1	17.0	48.5	373.2	817.5	672.9	2,875.9	630.0
Huntsville, AL	n/a	n/a	n/a	n/a	n/a	n/a	n/a	n/a
Indianapolis, IN	4,440.6	24.3	64.3	243.2	538.9	580.6	2,376.9	612.5
Jacksonville, FL	3,569.3	15.2	49.5	100.8	532.3	419.3	2,129.5	322.6
Kansas City, MO	5,705.4	35.2	76.5	257.3	1,216.8	615.2	2,595.1	909.2
Lafayette, LA	5,081.3	11.1	13.4	116.0	421.5	843.9	3,352.6	322.9
Las Cruces, NM[1]	4,077.5	9.7	61.8	55.1	370.0	631.8	2,652.6	296.6
Las Vegas, NV	2,738.2	5.7	63.1	100.8	358.1	416.8	1,390.7	403.0
Lexington, KY	3,191.6	8.6	54.6	102.8	154.1	445.0	2,108.3	318.2
Lincoln, NE[1]	3,133.7	1.7	110.9	57.0	213.3	339.4	2,255.4	155.9
Little Rock, AR	6,707.0	24.8	99.1	190.2	1,535.8	772.4	3,572.3	512.4
Los Angeles, CA	2,869.9	8.8	49.6	200.3	463.3	344.3	1,274.6	529.1
Louisville, KY[1]	4,578.4	13.9	29.8	149.2	494.0	638.9	2,670.2	582.4

Table continued on following page.

City	Total Crime	Violent Crime Rate				Property Crime Rate		
		Murder	Rape	Robbery	Aggrav. Assault	Burglary	Larceny -Theft	Motor Vehicle Theft
Madison, WI	3,099.3	3.8	28.2	62.8	225.7	497.5	2,034.7	246.6
Manchester, NH	2,858.0	4.4	64.6	97.3	426.5	253.9	1,854.6	156.6
Miami, FL	3,305.4	12.8	19.7	128.1	394.9	305.2	2,104.0	340.7
Midland, TX	2,436.7	6.6	53.8	33.2	271.0	268.4	1,494.1	309.6
Milwaukee, WI	4,325.4	32.4	73.2	326.8	1,164.5	578.5	1,388.2	761.8
Minneapolis, MN	5,713.0	18.2	83.0	409.5	644.2	899.8	2,747.1	911.3
Nashville, TN	5,228.7	16.4	56.0	253.2	830.1	544.3	3,086.9	441.9
New Haven, CT	4,218.8	16.1	22.3	257.9	411.4	419.8	2,507.3	584.0
New Orleans, LA	5,863.9	51.0	180.8	280.9	811.6	506.4	3,138.3	894.9
New York, NY	2,136.3	5.6	27.1	158.8	386.2	167.5	1,279.4	111.5
Oklahoma City, OK	4,621.5	9.5	84.2	123.1	509.1	881.3	2,444.3	569.9
Omaha, NE	3,805.8	7.7	73.1	96.6	453.9	316.7	2,227.2	630.7
Orlando, FL	4,663.8	10.6	57.6	172.8	619.4	408.4	3,003.8	391.3
Philadelphia, PA[2]	4,005.6	22.1	69.0	331.6	486.0	409.4	2,329.5	357.9
Phoenix, AZ	3,788.0	10.9	62.5	191.8	533.2	433.4	2,121.4	434.7
Pittsburgh, PA[2]	3,594.8	18.8	40.0	230.0	289.9	443.2	2,331.9	241.0
Portland, OR	5,261.6	8.0	39.5	121.7	353.4	567.0	3,211.0	960.9
Providence, RI	2,900.8	9.5	36.7	101.9	338.0	335.2	1,776.7	302.9
Provo, UT[1]	1,623.0	0.9	37.5	11.1	65.7	139.1	1,259.5	109.2
Raleigh, NC	2,412.8	4.4	34.2	97.0	256.5	270.0	1,468.3	282.4
Reno, NV	2,710.2	6.6	108.4	110.4	338.0	426.4	1,345.1	375.4
Richmond, VA	3,269.8	28.3	8.6	117.4	194.6	330.4	2,328.7	261.8
Rochester, MN	2,172.3	4.2	61.5	36.6	147.1	275.9	1,519.1	128.0
Sacramento, CA	3,428.4	8.1	24.1	169.3	481.8	546.0	1,715.2	483.8
Saint Louis, MO	7,846.6	88.1	78.4	416.2	1,433.5	855.2	3,895.8	1,079.3
Salem, OR	4,187.2	1.1	15.9	83.8	294.4	383.8	2,780.4	627.9
Salt Lake City, UT	8,274.5	8.4	137.0	240.9	536.1	764.1	5,503.8	1,084.1
San Antonio, TX	4,362.2	8.3	75.5	137.5	514.2	503.4	2,679.8	443.7
San Diego, CA	2,060.6	3.9	33.7	84.0	247.3	231.2	1,116.0	344.5
San Francisco, CA	4,938.4	5.4	22.5	270.9	245.3	845.4	2,872.2	676.8
San Jose, CA	2,741.2	3.9	55.0	115.1	251.0	392.9	1,237.2	686.2
Santa Rosa, CA	2,120.0	2.3	62.2	76.3	375.3	306.3	1,059.7	237.9
Savannah, GA[2]	2,865.5	11.6	35.1	110.2	248.5	364.9	1,824.4	270.8
Seattle, WA	5,498.9	6.7	39.0	190.7	389.9	1,351.5	2,884.6	636.5
Sioux Falls, SD	3,729.0	6.9	51.8	54.4	484.6	365.1	2,273.0	493.1
Springfield, IL	n/a	9.7	88.7	171.2	676.8	822.6	n/a	223.0
Tampa, FL	1,885.4	10.1	24.8	79.8	405.5	227.1	980.2	157.8
Tucson, AZ	4,319.0	11.1	84.1	177.7	425.3	381.0	2,898.7	341.2
Tulsa, OK	6,244.2	17.9	94.0	184.3	836.5	1,095.8	3,045.0	970.7
Tuscaloosa, AL[2]	4,843.6	4.9	46.2	137.6	316.4	739.9	3,289.0	309.5
Virginia Beach, VA	1,610.5	3.8	13.3	27.5	54.1	110.7	1,262.7	138.4
Washington, DC	4,389.2	27.8	43.1	309.8	577.3	275.4	2,683.2	472.8
Wichita, KS[1]	6,462.8	9.0	94.1	118.2	919.8	686.3	4,044.6	590.9
Wilmington, NC	3,175.8	17.5	52.5	113.7	445.2	473.0	1,915.8	158.2
Winston-Salem, NC	n/a	n/a	n/a	n/a	n/a	n/a	n/a	n/a
Worcester, MA	2,631.3	5.4	21.6	113.6	491.8	360.8	1,396.3	241.8
U.S.	2,356.7	6.5	38.4	73.9	279.7	314.2	1,398.0	246.0

Note: Figures are crimes per 100,000 population in 2020 except where noted; n/a not available; (1) 2019 data; (2) 2018 data; Due to the transition to the National Incident-Based Reporting System (NIBRS), limited city and metro area data was released for 2021
Source: FBI Uniform Crime Reports, 2018, 2019, 2020

Crime Rate: Suburbs

Suburbs[1]	Total Crime	Violent Crime Rate				Property Crime Rate		
		Murder	Rape	Robbery	Aggrav. Assault	Burglary	Larceny -Theft	Motor Vehicle Theft
Albuquerque, NM	2,025.9	1.9	34.6	40.4	405.3	354.2	870.1	319.4
Allentown, PA	n/a	n/a	n/a	n/a	n/a	n/a	n/a	n/a
Anchorage, AK	3,312.3	0.0	63.6	42.4	445.2	233.2	2,247.1	280.9
Ann Arbor, MI	1,734.3	3.2	74.1	38.7	378.3	167.6	942.7	129.7
Athens, GA	1,270.6	2.3	20.5	11.4	171.1	219.0	735.7	110.6
Atlanta, GA[3]	2,666.3	4.6	24.0	82.5	168.8	373.2	1,770.4	242.7
Austin, TX	1,578.6	2.3	40.3	25.2	129.8	227.0	1,028.7	125.3
Baltimore, MD[2]	2,213.3	3.9	31.8	88.1	260.3	217.8	1,485.2	126.1
Boise City, ID	1,206.5	1.9	52.0	6.9	189.1	178.4	674.0	104.3
Boston, MA	1,043.0	1.2	21.0	22.6	147.3	96.5	677.6	76.8
Boulder, CO	2,552.6	0.9	66.0	30.7	181.8	304.8	1,686.2	282.2
Brownsville, TX	2,358.5	2.5	38.8	39.2	248.9	317.7	1,598.9	112.6
Cape Coral, FL	1,333.2	5.3	37.6	48.3	222.8	148.9	761.7	108.6
Cedar Rapids, IA	1,291.6	0.7	39.3	10.0	135.0	318.6	660.1	127.9
Charleston, SC	2,958.7	11.2	35.6	81.5	313.9	324.5	1,914.7	277.3
Charlotte, NC	n/a	n/a	n/a	n/a	n/a	n/a	n/a	n/a
Chicago, IL	n/a	n/a	n/a	n/a	n/a	n/a	n/a	n/a
Cincinnati, OH	1,469.5	1.9	27.0	24.3	78.3	177.6	1,049.2	111.1
Clarksville, TN	1,659.2	4.0	32.5	25.9	161.9	300.0	988.2	146.7
Cleveland, OH	1,328.9	3.0	20.9	35.0	104.7	154.4	907.3	103.7
College Station, TX	2,209.2	5.4	86.2	41.4	262.1	349.1	1,310.7	154.2
Colorado Springs, CO	1,620.4	4.1	66.6	24.3	191.2	193.8	966.8	173.6
Columbia, MO	1,789.7	2.3	52.8	19.9	179.4	218.1	1,128.2	188.8
Columbia, SC	3,572.6	8.2	37.6	61.2	415.2	504.0	2,183.1	363.3
Columbus, OH	1,664.0	1.5	28.2	27.2	77.2	205.1	1,223.7	101.1
Dallas, TX	n/a	n/a	n/a	n/a	n/a	n/a	n/a	n/a
Davenport, IA	n/a	5.8	57.2	48.2	268.5	345.6	n/a	174.3
Denver, CO	3,233.8	3.8	57.7	70.7	238.2	357.6	1,904.0	601.8
Des Moines, IA	1,384.2	2.2	25.9	9.9	141.1	218.8	859.4	126.9
Durham, NC	1,768.6	4.6	17.6	32.3	169.1	319.6	1,113.7	111.7
Edison, NJ	n/a	n/a	n/a	n/a	n/a	n/a	n/a	n/a
El Paso, TX	1,026.7	3.1	36.2	20.0	217.8	121.7	554.9	73.0
Fargo, ND	2,397.0	5.8	53.5	17.3	159.7	489.9	1,455.9	214.9
Fort Collins, CO[2]	1,855.9	1.1	44.9	14.6	189.3	184.4	1,296.7	124.9
Fort Wayne, IN	988.4	1.4	22.3	16.7	146.5	136.7	579.0	85.8
Fort Worth, TX	n/a	n/a	n/a	n/a	n/a	n/a	n/a	n/a
Grand Rapids, MI	1,390.3	2.5	70.8	21.3	172.1	149.8	837.9	135.8
Greeley, CO	2,286.0	3.2	56.2	25.4	188.9	212.4	1,410.9	389.1
Green Bay, WI	816.1	0.9	22.7	3.2	54.1	122.4	580.0	32.8
Greensboro, NC	2,458.1	7.5	28.3	53.6	282.3	415.1	1,477.5	193.7
Honolulu, HI	n/a	n/a	n/a	n/a	n/a	n/a	n/a	n/a
Houston, TX	2,188.3	5.4	42.8	68.3	212.3	270.6	1,338.7	250.2
Huntsville, AL	n/a	n/a	n/a	n/a	n/a	n/a	n/a	n/a
Indianapolis, IN	n/a	n/a	n/a	n/a	n/a	n/a	n/a	n/a
Jacksonville, FL	1,375.4	2.4	28.0	23.8	169.5	172.0	880.2	99.5
Kansas City, MO	n/a	n/a	n/a	n/a	n/a	n/a	n/a	n/a
Lafayette, LA	2,189.8	7.4	23.9	35.5	344.1	400.2	1,210.2	168.4
Las Cruces, NM[2]	1,781.8	1.7	52.3	10.5	546.8	362.8	699.5	108.1
Las Vegas, NV	1,944.4	5.0	31.6	99.0	209.5	261.9	1,057.0	280.4
Lexington, KY	2,178.6	1.5	29.6	28.6	75.6	317.7	1,508.9	216.6
Lincoln, NE[2]	1,017.1	0.0	77.9	0.0	41.1	119.0	705.4	73.6
Little Rock, AR	3,185.5	8.9	56.1	52.4	493.6	457.2	1,830.0	287.2
Los Angeles, CA	2,435.2	4.2	28.0	102.7	228.4	355.9	1,303.4	412.7
Louisville, KY[2]	1,847.8	1.9	21.7	30.8	98.0	230.7	1,263.0	201.7

Table continued on following page.

Suburbs[1]	Total Crime	Violent Crime Rate				Property Crime Rate		
		Murder	Rape	Robbery	Aggrav. Assault	Burglary	Larceny -Theft	Motor Vehicle Theft
Madison, WI	1,304.6	1.7	21.3	17.4	85.0	157.7	930.9	90.6
Manchester, NH	801.4	0.0	34.0	8.8	36.6	64.3	609.1	48.6
Miami, FL	2,551.6	7.0	31.8	85.7	280.9	220.2	1,689.2	236.7
Midland, TX	2,973.5	8.2	30.0	13.6	360.1	349.2	1,606.8	605.6
Milwaukee, WI	1,624.3	1.5	20.3	29.8	78.2	114.7	1,274.1	105.6
Minneapolis, MN	n/a	n/a	n/a	n/a	n/a	n/a	n/a	n/a
Nashville, TN	1,755.3	3.0	29.0	27.7	266.9	199.9	1,090.1	138.6
New Haven, CT	2,076.3	4.2	20.2	61.1	82.9	193.7	1,413.6	300.7
New Orleans, LA	2,268.4	8.6	24.1	45.2	233.6	244.1	1,581.0	131.9
New York, NY	n/a	n/a	n/a	n/a	n/a	n/a	n/a	n/a
Oklahoma City, OK	2,313.8	6.3	37.1	28.2	177.5	392.7	1,432.3	239.8
Omaha, NE	1,602.2	1.5	37.1	23.2	163.9	191.7	977.7	207.1
Orlando, FL	1,994.4	5.4	40.1	59.7	267.8	251.1	1,217.2	153.1
Philadelphia, PA[3]	1,935.5	7.6	16.3	96.8	235.8	202.8	1,235.3	140.9
Phoenix, AZ	2,118.2	3.8	35.2	43.8	211.2	276.5	1,380.4	167.3
Pittsburgh, PA[3]	1,402.7	3.5	23.7	33.2	168.7	159.1	958.5	55.9
Portland, OR	n/a	n/a	41.7	37.9	150.0	262.3	1,381.0	296.2
Providence, RI	1,264.5	1.7	40.2	29.7	189.1	149.7	749.5	104.7
Provo, UT[2]	1,312.0	1.1	30.2	7.2	46.1	131.5	1,018.1	77.8
Raleigh, NC	1,376.5	2.8	12.2	21.8	100.3	201.3	956.0	82.2
Reno, NV	1,808.3	4.5	59.7	39.2	243.4	304.1	959.0	198.4
Richmond, VA	1,784.2	5.9	23.2	30.9	126.7	136.3	1,342.0	119.3
Rochester, MN	824.5	1.0	36.1	2.9	75.1	191.3	456.7	61.5
Sacramento, CA	2,102.6	3.8	27.9	64.5	196.3	323.1	1,274.4	212.6
Saint Louis, MO	n/a	5.6	29.6	39.0	241.8	262.7	n/a	283.8
Salem, OR	2,400.4	1.9	29.2	29.6	123.4	258.0	1,578.0	380.3
Salt Lake City, UT	3,411.8	4.1	53.4	45.4	176.7	364.6	2,327.6	439.9
San Antonio, TX	1,759.0	3.9	36.2	22.5	151.5	297.8	1,074.4	172.6
San Diego, CA	1,655.8	3.1	25.4	69.7	229.9	210.0	887.9	229.9
San Francisco, CA	3,106.9	5.3	33.9	157.3	219.7	345.9	1,757.2	587.6
San Jose, CA	2,331.9	1.7	27.1	56.1	116.6	343.6	1,474.4	312.3
Santa Rosa, CA	1,554.3	1.9	41.1	41.8	329.5	232.8	807.9	99.2
Savannah, GA[3]	3,497.3	5.3	37.2	67.1	245.2	497.1	2,366.1	279.1
Seattle, WA	3,022.6	4.0	29.2	70.5	168.3	442.6	1,893.4	414.8
Sioux Falls, SD	1,410.7	2.3	31.5	8.2	172.8	462.4	597.9	135.5
Springfield, IL	n/a	1.1	36.1	21.9	259.1	349.8	n/a	122.4
Tampa, FL	1,648.1	3.1	34.5	42.4	204.3	176.5	1,068.6	118.6
Tucson, AZ	2,196.1	4.9	16.1	37.5	172.4	257.0	1,582.6	125.6
Tulsa, OK	2,005.9	3.6	31.0	21.9	174.2	380.7	1,150.1	244.3
Tuscaloosa, AL[3]	2,503.0	3.3	28.5	41.7	249.6	518.3	1,449.1	212.5
Virginia Beach, VA	2,536.3	12.5	30.6	67.3	327.6	197.9	1,701.5	198.8
Washington, DC	n/a	n/a	n/a	n/a	n/a	n/a	n/a	n/a
Wichita, KS[2]	n/a	1.6	42.3	14.5	156.8	271.8	n/a	129.8
Wilmington, NC	1,803.5	2.3	27.7	24.3	135.2	300.9	1,220.4	92.7
Winston-Salem, NC	n/a	n/a	n/a	n/a	n/a	n/a	n/a	n/a
Worcester, MA	922.7	0.4	32.3	16.3	166.2	115.4	522.3	69.7
U.S.	2,356.7	6.5	38.4	73.9	279.7	314.2	1,398.0	246.0

Note: Figures are crimes per 100,000 population in 2020 except where noted; n/a not available; (1) All areas within the metro area that are located outside the city limits; (2) 2019 data; (3) 2018 data; Due to the transition to the National Incident-Based Reporting System (NIBRS), limited city and metro area data was released for 2021
Source: FBI Uniform Crime Reports, 2018, 2019, 2020

Crime Rate: Metro Area

Metro Area[1]	Total Crime	Violent Crime Rate				Property Crime Rate		
		Murder	Rape	Robbery	Aggrav. Assault	Burglary	Larceny -Theft	Motor Vehicle Theft
Albuquerque, NM	4,660.5	9.4	61.3	171.6	764.1	688.1	2,303.5	662.5
Allentown, PA[3]	n/a	n/a	n/a	n/a	n/a	n/a	n/a	n/a
Anchorage, AK	4,576.1	5.9	186.7	185.4	793.4	487.5	2,523.4	393.8
Ann Arbor, MI	1,678.4	2.4	63.2	36.3	310.4	154.3	1,002.5	109.3
Athens, GA	2,572.9	2.8	57.0	51.9	274.8	365.6	1,613.3	207.6
Atlanta, GA[4]	2,895.7	5.7	26.1	94.1	194.7	393.9	1,903.2	278.0
Austin, TX	2,682.2	3.2	43.6	62.4	206.4	336.6	1,781.5	248.5
Baltimore, MD[3]	3,057.2	15.5	36.6	242.7	403.8	364.7	1,753.9	239.9
Boise City, ID	1,424.4	1.8	58.5	11.9	190.5	187.0	865.5	109.2
Boston, MA[2]	1,249.7	2.2	21.8	38.2	191.6	117.5	786.3	92.1
Boulder, CO	3,053.3	1.2	54.0	42.7	195.3	405.2	2,051.3	303.6
Brownsville, TX	2,311.6	3.1	41.6	58.3	257.9	275.1	1,583.3	92.3
Cape Coral, FL	1,298.3	4.1	30.4	38.6	193.8	149.9	783.6	98.0
Cedar Rapids, IA	2,367.4	4.4	25.9	42.3	179.4	465.9	1,381.3	268.3
Charleston, SC	2,926.8	11.3	36.1	79.8	318.9	309.0	1,886.2	285.4
Charlotte, NC	n/a	n/a	n/a	n/a	n/a	n/a	n/a	n/a
Chicago, IL[2]	n/a	n/a	n/a	n/a	n/a	n/a	n/a	n/a
Cincinnati, OH	1,894.4	5.7	33.0	54.6	142.3	257.5	1,237.7	163.5
Clarksville, TN	2,276.1	6.7	42.6	37.5	336.7	286.4	1,364.1	202.0
Cleveland, OH	2,145.2	10.3	36.2	106.5	287.7	306.5	1,169.7	228.4
College Station, TX	2,152.0	3.7	67.9	32.8	193.6	311.5	1,379.4	163.0
Colorado Springs, CO	3,139.6	6.2	76.8	58.6	344.9	412.8	1,855.2	384.9
Columbia, MO	2,572.2	7.1	63.8	35.7	259.4	280.8	1,637.3	288.0
Columbia, SC	3,830.0	9.2	41.9	76.0	430.9	511.5	2,378.9	381.6
Columbus, OH	2,523.0	9.0	54.3	99.3	150.6	376.7	1,630.2	202.9
Dallas, TX[2]	n/a	n/a	n/a	n/a	n/a	n/a	n/a	n/a
Davenport, IA	n/a	6.9	59.6	71.2	338.3	493.9	n/a	251.4
Denver, CO	3,793.1	6.1	65.8	93.9	324.5	443.9	2,124.7	734.2
Des Moines, IA	2,362.1	6.2	34.8	41.6	256.0	423.8	1,310.9	288.8
Durham, NC	3,000.9	8.1	29.1	113.9	349.3	471.8	1,818.1	210.6
Edison, NJ[2]	n/a	n/a	n/a	n/a	n/a	n/a	n/a	n/a
El Paso, TX	1,457.0	3.9	37.7	38.0	229.2	123.2	962.0	62.9
Fargo, ND	3,180.0	5.6	69.3	33.0	242.8	648.6	1,888.3	292.3
Fort Collins, CO[3]	2,112.3	0.8	34.8	17.7	180.7	194.2	1,555.0	129.0
Fort Wayne, IN	2,083.1	9.9	31.0	64.7	229.3	204.7	1,391.1	152.3
Fort Worth, TX[2]	n/a	n/a	n/a	n/a	n/a	n/a	n/a	n/a
Grand Rapids, MI	1,628.8	4.6	68.8	35.1	241.6	164.6	950.1	164.0
Greeley, CO	2,487.0	4.8	53.4	40.4	225.5	253.0	1,532.2	377.6
Green Bay, WI	1,216.1	2.5	37.3	16.0	169.2	146.4	787.1	57.6
Greensboro, NC	3,250.8	12.2	29.6	107.7	426.7	539.5	1,872.7	262.4
Honolulu, HI[3]	n/a	n/a	n/a	n/a	n/a	n/a	n/a	n/a
Houston, TX	3,249.2	9.2	44.7	167.9	410.0	402.1	1,841.0	374.3
Huntsville, AL	n/a	n/a	n/a	n/a	n/a	n/a	n/a	n/a
Indianapolis, IN	n/a	n/a	n/a	n/a	n/a	n/a	n/a	n/a
Jacksonville, FL	2,653.0	9.9	40.5	68.6	380.8	316.0	1,607.7	229.4
Kansas City, MO	n/a	n/a	n/a	n/a	n/a	n/a	n/a	n/a
Lafayette, LA	2,937.4	8.4	21.2	56.3	364.1	514.9	1,764.1	208.4
Las Cruces, NM[3]	2,871.0	5.5	56.8	31.6	462.9	490.4	1,626.2	197.5
Las Vegas, NV	2,525.2	5.5	54.6	100.3	318.2	375.2	1,301.2	370.1
Lexington, KY	2,811.4	5.9	45.2	75.0	124.6	397.2	1,883.4	280.1
Lincoln, NE[3]	2,843.7	1.5	106.4	49.2	189.7	309.2	2,043.0	144.7
Little Rock, AR	4,117.3	13.1	67.5	88.9	769.4	540.6	2,291.0	346.8
Los Angeles, CA[2]	2,567.7	5.6	34.6	132.5	300.0	352.3	1,294.6	448.2
Louisville, KY[3]	3,300.8	8.3	26.0	93.8	308.7	447.9	2,011.8	404.3

Table continued on following page.

Metro Area[1]	Total Crime	Violent Crime Rate				Property Crime Rate		
		Murder	Rape	Robbery	Aggrav. Assault	Burglary	Larceny -Theft	Motor Vehicle Theft
Madison, WI	2,007.2	2.5	24.0	35.2	140.1	290.7	1,363.0	151.7
Manchester, NH	1,355.7	1.2	42.2	32.7	141.6	115.4	944.8	77.7
Miami, FL[2]	2,609.4	7.5	30.9	88.9	289.6	226.7	1,721.0	244.7
Midland, TX	2,541.9	6.9	49.1	29.4	288.5	284.2	1,516.1	367.5
Milwaukee, WI	2,634.0	13.1	40.0	140.8	484.3	288.1	1,316.8	350.9
Minneapolis, MN	n/a	n/a	n/a	n/a	n/a	n/a	n/a	n/a
Nashville, TN	2,968.8	7.7	38.4	106.5	463.7	320.3	1,787.7	244.5
New Haven, CT	2,425.5	6.1	20.5	93.2	136.5	230.5	1,591.8	346.9
New Orleans, LA	3,378.9	21.7	72.5	118.0	412.2	325.1	2,061.9	367.5
New York, NY[2]	n/a	n/a	n/a	n/a	n/a	n/a	n/a	n/a
Oklahoma City, OK	3,387.0	7.8	59.0	72.3	331.7	619.9	1,902.9	393.3
Omaha, NE	2,710.6	4.6	55.2	60.1	309.8	254.6	1,606.2	420.2
Orlando, FL	2,288.9	5.9	42.0	72.2	306.6	268.4	1,414.3	179.4
Philadelphia, PA[2,4]	3,462.1	18.3	55.2	270.0	420.3	355.2	2,042.3	300.9
Phoenix, AZ	2,681.7	6.2	44.4	93.8	319.9	329.5	1,630.4	257.5
Pittsburgh, PA[4]	1,687.7	5.5	25.8	58.8	184.5	196.1	1,137.0	80.0
Portland, OR	n/a	n/a	41.1	60.0	203.7	342.7	1,864.0	471.6
Providence, RI	1,445.8	2.5	39.8	37.7	205.6	170.2	863.3	126.6
Provo, UT[3]	1,368.4	1.1	31.6	7.9	49.6	132.9	1,061.8	83.5
Raleigh, NC	1,727.9	3.3	19.7	47.3	153.3	224.6	1,129.7	150.1
Reno, NV	2,291.8	5.6	85.8	77.4	294.1	369.6	1,165.9	293.3
Richmond, VA	2,050.3	9.9	20.6	46.4	138.8	171.1	1,518.7	144.8
Rochester, MN	1,552.4	2.7	49.8	21.1	114.0	237.0	1,030.4	97.4
Sacramento, CA	2,393.6	4.8	27.0	87.5	259.0	372.0	1,371.2	272.1
Saint Louis, MO	n/a	14.3	34.8	79.2	368.7	325.8	n/a	368.6
Salem, OR	3,123.1	1.6	23.8	51.5	192.6	308.9	2,064.3	480.4
Salt Lake City, UT	4,200.7	4.8	67.0	77.1	235.0	429.5	2,842.9	544.4
San Antonio, TX	3,339.5	6.6	60.1	92.3	371.7	422.6	2,049.1	337.2
San Diego, CA	1,830.5	3.4	29.0	75.8	237.4	219.1	986.3	279.3
San Francisco, CA[2]	3,448.3	5.3	31.8	178.5	224.5	439.0	1,965.0	604.2
San Jose, CA	2,543.9	2.8	41.6	86.7	186.2	369.1	1,351.5	506.0
Santa Rosa, CA	1,758.4	2.0	48.7	54.2	346.0	259.4	898.8	149.2
Savannah, GA[4]	3,107.5	9.2	35.9	93.7	247.2	415.6	2,032.0	274.0
Seattle, WA[2]	3,496.7	4.5	31.1	93.5	210.7	616.6	2,083.1	457.2
Sioux Falls, SD	3,001.8	5.5	45.4	39.9	386.8	395.6	1,747.6	381.0
Springfield, IL	n/a	5.8	65.2	104.7	490.8	612.0	n/a	178.2
Tampa, FL	1,678.0	4.0	33.3	47.1	229.7	182.8	1,057.5	123.6
Tucson, AZ	3,298.3	8.1	51.4	110.3	303.7	321.4	2,265.9	237.5
Tulsa, OK	3,701.1	9.3	56.2	86.8	439.1	666.7	1,908.0	534.9
Tuscaloosa, AL[4]	3,445.1	4.0	35.6	80.3	276.5	607.5	2,189.7	251.6
Virginia Beach, VA	2,301.0	10.3	26.2	57.2	258.1	175.7	1,590.0	183.5
Washington, DC[2]	n/a	n/a	n/a	n/a	n/a	n/a	n/a	n/a
Wichita, KS[3]	n/a	6.1	74.0	77.9	623.3	525.2	n/a	411.7
Wilmington, NC	2,373.9	8.6	38.0	61.5	264.0	372.4	1,509.5	120.0
Winston-Salem, NC	n/a	n/a	n/a	n/a	n/a	n/a	n/a	n/a
Worcester, MA	1,285.0	1.5	30.1	36.9	235.2	167.5	707.6	106.2
U.S.	2,356.7	6.5	38.4	73.9	279.7	314.2	1,398.0	246.0

Note: Figures are crimes per 100,000 population in 2020 except where noted; n/a not available; (1) Figures cover the Metropolitan Statistical Area except where noted; (2) Metropolitan Division (MD); (3) 2019 data; (4) 2018 data; Due to the transition to the National Incident-Based Reporting System (NIBRS), limited city and metro area data was released for 2021
Source: FBI Uniform Crime Reports, 2018, 2019, 2020

Temperature & Precipitation: Yearly Averages and Extremes

City	Extreme Low (°F)	Average Low (°F)	Average Temp. (°F)	Average High (°F)	Extreme High (°F)	Average Precip. (in.)	Average Snow (in.)
Albuquerque, NM	-17	43	57	70	105	8.5	11
Allentown, PA	-12	42	52	61	105	44.2	32
Anchorage, AK	-34	29	36	43	85	15.7	71
Ann Arbor, MI	-21	39	49	58	104	32.4	41
Athens, GA	-8	52	62	72	105	49.8	2
Atlanta, GA	-8	52	62	72	105	49.8	2
Austin, TX	-2	58	69	79	109	31.1	1
Baltimore, MD	-7	45	56	65	105	41.2	21
Boise City, ID	-25	39	51	63	111	11.8	22
Boston, MA	-12	44	52	59	102	42.9	41
Boulder, CO	-25	37	51	64	103	15.5	63
Brownsville, TX	16	65	74	83	106	25.8	Trace
Cape Coral, FL	26	65	75	84	103	53.9	0
Cedar Rapids, IA	-34	36	47	57	105	34.4	33
Charleston, SC	6	55	66	76	104	52.1	1
Charlotte, NC	-5	50	61	71	104	42.8	6
Chicago, IL	-27	40	49	59	104	35.4	39
Cincinnati, OH	-25	44	54	64	103	40.9	23
Clarksville, TN	-17	49	60	70	107	47.4	11
Cleveland, OH	-19	41	50	59	104	37.1	55
College Station, TX	-2	58	69	79	109	31.1	1
Colorado Springs, CO	-24	36	49	62	99	17.0	48
Columbia, MO	-20	44	54	64	111	40.6	25
Columbia, SC	-1	51	64	75	107	48.3	2
Columbus, OH	-19	42	52	62	104	37.9	28
Dallas, TX	-2	56	67	77	112	33.9	3
Davenport, IA	-24	40	50	60	108	31.8	33
Denver, CO	-25	37	51	64	103	15.5	63
Des Moines, IA	-24	40	50	60	108	31.8	33
Durham, NC	-9	48	60	71	105	42.0	8
Edison, NJ	-8	46	55	63	105	43.5	27
El Paso, TX	-8	50	64	78	114	8.6	6
Fargo, ND	-36	31	41	52	106	19.6	40
Fort Collins, CO	-25	37	51	64	103	15.5	63
Fort Wayne, IN	-22	40	50	60	106	35.9	33
Fort Worth, TX	-1	55	66	76	113	32.3	3
Grand Rapids, MI	-22	38	48	57	102	34.7	73
Greeley, CO	-25	37	51	64	103	15.5	63
Green Bay, WI	-31	34	44	54	99	28.3	46
Greensboro, NC	-8	47	58	69	103	42.5	10
Honolulu, HI	52	70	77	84	94	22.4	0
Houston, TX	7	58	69	79	107	46.9	Trace
Huntsville, AL	-11	50	61	71	104	56.8	4
Indianapolis, IN	-23	42	53	62	104	40.2	25
Jacksonville, FL	7	58	69	79	103	52.0	0
Kansas City, MO	-23	44	54	64	109	38.1	21
Lafayette, LA	8	57	68	78	103	58.5	Trace
Las Cruces, NM	-8	50	64	78	114	8.6	6
Las Vegas, NV	8	53	67	80	116	4.0	1
Lexington, KY	-21	45	55	65	103	45.1	17
Lincoln, NE	-33	39	51	62	108	29.1	27
Little Rock, AR	-5	51	62	73	112	50.7	5
Los Angeles, CA	27	55	63	70	110	11.3	Trace
Louisville, KY	-20	46	57	67	105	43.9	17
Madison, WI	-37	35	46	57	104	31.1	42

Table continued on following page.

City	Extreme Low (°F)	Average Low (°F)	Average Temp. (°F)	Average High (°F)	Extreme High (°F)	Average Precip. (in.)	Average Snow (in.)
Manchester, NH	-33	34	46	57	102	36.9	63
Miami, FL	30	69	76	83	98	57.1	0
Midland, TX	-11	50	64	77	116	14.6	4
Milwaukee, WI	-26	38	47	55	103	32.0	49
Minneapolis, MN	-34	35	45	54	105	27.1	52
Nashville, TN	-17	49	60	70	107	47.4	11
New Haven, CT	-7	44	52	60	103	41.4	25
New Orleans, LA	11	59	69	78	102	60.6	Trace
New York, NY	-2	47	55	62	104	47.0	23
Oklahoma City, OK	-8	49	60	71	110	32.8	10
Omaha, NE	-23	40	51	62	110	30.1	29
Orlando, FL	19	62	72	82	100	47.7	Trace
Philadelphia, PA	-7	45	55	64	104	41.4	22
Phoenix, AZ	17	59	72	86	122	7.3	Trace
Pittsburgh, PA	-18	41	51	60	103	37.1	43
Portland, OR	-3	45	54	62	107	37.5	7
Providence, RI	-13	42	51	60	104	45.3	35
Provo, UT	-22	40	52	64	107	15.6	63
Raleigh, NC	-9	48	60	71	105	42.0	8
Reno, NV	-16	33	50	67	105	7.2	24
Richmond, VA	-8	48	58	69	105	43.0	13
Rochester, MN	-40	34	44	54	102	29.4	47
Sacramento, CA	18	48	61	73	115	17.3	Trace
Saint Louis, MO	-18	46	56	66	115	36.8	20
Salem, OR	-12	41	52	63	108	40.2	7
Salt Lake City, UT	-22	40	52	64	107	15.6	63
San Antonio, TX	0	58	69	80	108	29.6	1
San Diego, CA	29	57	64	71	111	9.5	Trace
San Francisco, CA	24	49	57	65	106	19.3	Trace
San Jose, CA	21	50	59	68	105	13.5	Trace
Santa Rosa, CA	23	42	57	71	109	29.0	n/a
Savannah, GA	3	56	67	77	105	50.3	Trace
Seattle, WA	0	44	52	59	99	38.4	13
Sioux Falls, SD	-36	35	46	57	110	24.6	38
Springfield, IL	-24	44	54	63	112	34.9	21
Tampa, FL	18	63	73	82	99	46.7	Trace
Tucson, AZ	16	55	69	82	117	11.6	2
Tulsa, OK	-8	50	61	71	112	38.9	10
Tuscaloosa, AL	-6	51	63	74	106	53.5	2
Virginia Beach, VA	-3	51	60	69	104	44.8	8
Washington, DC	-5	49	58	67	104	39.5	18
Wichita, KS	-21	45	57	68	113	29.3	17
Wilmington, NC	0	53	64	74	104	55.0	2
Winston-Salem, NC	-8	47	58	69	103	42.5	10
Worcester, MA	-13	38	47	56	99	47.6	62

Source: National Climatic Data Center, International Station Meteorological Climate Summary, 9/96; NOAA

Weather Conditions

City	Temperature			Daytime Sky			Precipitation		
	10°F & below	32°F & below	90°F & above	Clear	Partly cloudy	Cloudy	0.01 inch or more precip.	1.0 inch or more snow/ice	Thunder-storms
Albuquerque, NM	4	114	65	140	161	64	60	9	38
Allentown, PA	n/a	123	15	77	148	140	123	20	31
Anchorage, AK	n/a	194	n/a	50	115	200	113	49	2
Ann Arbor, MI	n/a	136	12	74	134	157	135	38	32
Athens, GA	1	49	38	98	147	120	116	3	48
Atlanta, GA	1	49	38	98	147	120	116	3	48
Austin, TX	< 1	20	111	105	148	112	83	1	41
Baltimore, MD	6	97	31	91	143	131	113	13	27
Boise City, ID	n/a	124	45	106	133	126	91	22	14
Boston, MA	n/a	97	12	88	127	150	253	48	18
Boulder, CO	24	155	33	99	177	89	90	38	39
Brownsville, TX	n/a	n/a	116	86	180	99	72	0	27
Cape Coral, FL	n/a	n/a	115	93	220	52	110	0	92
Cedar Rapids, IA	n/a	156	16	89	132	144	109	28	42
Charleston, SC	< 1	33	53	89	162	114	114	1	59
Charlotte, NC	1	65	44	98	142	125	113	3	41
Chicago, IL	n/a	132	17	83	136	146	125	31	38
Cincinnati, OH	14	107	23	80	126	159	127	25	39
Clarksville, TN	5	76	51	98	135	132	119	8	54
Cleveland, OH	n/a	123	12	63	127	175	157	48	34
College Station, TX	< 1	20	111	105	148	112	83	1	41
Colorado Springs, CO	21	161	18	108	157	100	98	33	49
Columbia, MO	17	108	36	99	127	139	110	17	52
Columbia, SC	< 1	58	77	97	149	119	110	1	53
Columbus, OH	n/a	118	19	72	137	156	136	29	40
Dallas, TX	1	34	102	108	160	97	78	2	49
Davenport, IA	n/a	137	26	99	129	137	106	25	46
Denver, CO	24	155	33	99	177	89	90	38	39
Des Moines, IA	n/a	137	26	99	129	137	106	25	46
Durham, NC	n/a	n/a	39	98	143	124	110	3	42
Edison, NJ	n/a	90	24	80	146	139	122	16	46
El Paso, TX	1	59	106	147	164	54	49	3	35
Fargo, ND	n/a	180	15	81	145	139	100	38	31
Fort Collins, CO	24	155	33	99	177	89	90	38	39
Fort Wayne, IN	n/a	131	16	75	140	150	131	31	39
Fort Worth, TX	1	40	100	123	136	106	79	3	47
Grand Rapids, MI	n/a	146	11	67	119	179	142	57	34
Greeley, CO	24	155	33	99	177	89	90	38	39
Green Bay, WI	n/a	163	7	86	125	154	120	40	33
Greensboro, NC	3	85	32	94	143	128	113	5	43
Honolulu, HI	n/a	n/a	23	25	286	54	98	0	7
Houston, TX	n/a	n/a	96	83	168	114	101	1	62
Huntsville, AL	2	66	49	70	118	177	116	2	54
Indianapolis, IN	19	119	19	83	128	154	127	24	43
Jacksonville, FL	< 1	16	83	86	181	98	114	1	65
Kansas City, MO	22	110	39	112	134	119	103	17	51
Lafayette, LA	< 1	21	86	99	150	116	113	< 1	73
Las Cruces, NM	1	59	106	147	164	54	49	3	35
Las Vegas, NV	< 1	37	134	185	132	48	27	2	13
Lexington, KY	11	96	22	86	136	143	129	17	44
Lincoln, NE	n/a	145	40	108	135	122	94	19	46
Little Rock, AR	1	57	73	110	142	113	104	4	57
Los Angeles, CA	0	< 1	5	131	125	109	34	0	1
Louisville, KY	8	90	35	82	143	140	125	15	45

Table continued on following page.

City	Temperature			Daytime Sky			Precipitation		
	10°F & below	32°F & below	90°F & above	Clear	Partly cloudy	Cloudy	0.01 inch or more precip.	1.0 inch or more snow/ice	Thunder-storms
Madison, WI	n/a	161	14	88	119	158	118	38	40
Manchester, NH	n/a	171	12	87	131	147	125	32	19
Miami, FL	n/a	n/a	55	48	263	54	128	0	74
Midland, TX	1	62	102	144	138	83	52	3	38
Milwaukee, WI	n/a	141	10	90	118	157	126	38	35
Minneapolis, MN	n/a	156	16	93	125	147	113	41	37
Nashville, TN	5	76	51	98	135	132	119	8	54
New Haven, CT	n/a	n/a	7	80	146	139	118	17	22
New Orleans, LA	0	13	70	90	169	106	114	1	69
New York, NY	n/a	n/a	18	85	166	114	120	11	20
Oklahoma City, OK	5	79	70	124	131	110	80	8	50
Omaha, NE	n/a	139	35	100	142	123	97	20	46
Orlando, FL	n/a	n/a	90	76	208	81	115	0	80
Philadelphia, PA	5	94	23	81	146	138	117	14	27
Phoenix, AZ	0	10	167	186	125	54	37	< 1	23
Pittsburgh, PA	n/a	121	8	62	137	166	154	42	35
Portland, OR	n/a	37	11	67	116	182	152	4	7
Providence, RI	n/a	117	9	85	134	146	123	21	21
Provo, UT	n/a	128	56	94	152	119	92	38	38
Raleigh, NC	n/a	n/a	39	98	143	124	110	3	42
Reno, NV	14	178	50	143	139	83	50	17	14
Richmond, VA	3	79	41	90	147	128	115	7	43
Rochester, MN	n/a	165	9	87	126	152	114	40	41
Sacramento, CA	0	21	73	175	111	79	58	< 1	2
Saint Louis, MO	13	100	43	97	138	130	109	14	46
Salem, OR	n/a	66	16	78	118	169	146	6	5
Salt Lake City, UT	n/a	128	56	94	152	119	92	38	38
San Antonio, TX	n/a	n/a	112	97	153	115	81	1	36
San Diego, CA	0	< 1	4	115	126	124	40	0	5
San Francisco, CA	0	6	4	136	130	99	63	< 1	5
San Jose, CA	0	5	5	106	180	79	57	< 1	6
Santa Rosa, CA	n/a	43	30	n/a	365	n/a	n/a	n/a	2
Savannah, GA	< 1	29	70	97	155	113	111	< 1	63
Seattle, WA	n/a	38	3	57	121	187	157	8	8
Sioux Falls, SD	n/a	n/a	n/a	95	136	134	n/a	n/a	n/a
Springfield, IL	19	111	34	96	126	143	111	18	49
Tampa, FL	n/a	n/a	85	81	204	80	107	< 1	87
Tucson, AZ	0	18	140	177	119	69	54	2	42
Tulsa, OK	6	78	74	117	141	107	88	8	50
Tuscaloosa, AL	1	57	59	91	161	113	119	1	57
Virginia Beach, VA	< 1	53	33	89	149	127	115	5	38
Washington, DC	2	71	34	84	144	137	112	9	30
Wichita, KS	13	110	63	117	132	116	87	13	54
Wilmington, NC	< 1	42	46	96	150	119	115	1	47
Winston-Salem, NC	3	85	32	94	143	128	113	5	43
Worcester, MA	n/a	141	4	81	144	140	131	32	23

Note: Figures are average number of days per year
Source: National Climatic Data Center, International Station Meteorological Climate Summary, 9/96; NOAA

Air Quality Index

MSA[1] (Days[2])	Percent of Days when Air Quality was...					AQI Statistics	
	Good	Moderate	Unhealthy for Sensitive Groups	Unhealthy	Very Unhealthy	Maximum	Median
Albuquerque, NM (365)	23.6	70.7	5.2	0.5	0.0	166	62
Allentown, PA (365)	69.9	29.0	0.8	0.3	0.0	153	43
Anchorage, AK (365)	80.3	18.6	0.8	0.3	0.0	160	25
Ann Arbor, MI (365)	76.2	23.8	0.0	0.0	0.0	100	40
Athens, GA (365)	71.8	27.9	0.3	0.0	0.0	107	41
Atlanta, GA (365)	57.3	40.5	2.2	0.0	0.0	150	47
Austin, TX (365)	68.2	31.5	0.3	0.0	0.0	101	43
Baltimore, MD (365)	68.8	27.1	4.1	0.0	0.0	140	45
Boise City, ID (365)	55.1	39.5	4.4	1.1	0.0	168	49
Boston, MA (365)	77.0	21.6	1.1	0.3	0.0	153	40
Boulder, CO (365)	55.9	34.5	8.8	0.8	0.0	159	48
Brownsville, TX (365)	64.4	35.6	0.0	0.0	0.0	99	43
Cape Coral, FL (365)	91.0	9.0	0.0	0.0	0.0	97	36
Cedar Rapids, IA (365)	64.4	34.5	1.1	0.0	0.0	123	44
Charleston, SC (365)	79.5	20.5	0.0	0.0	0.0	93	40
Charlotte, NC (365)	64.4	34.8	0.8	0.0	0.0	128	46
Chicago, IL (365)	34.2	58.1	7.1	0.5	0.0	169	58
Cincinnati, OH (365)	45.8	52.1	2.2	0.0	0.0	140	52
Clarksville, TN (365)	70.4	29.3	0.3	0.0	0.0	138	43
Cleveland, OH (365)	47.4	50.4	2.2	0.0	0.0	122	52
College Station, TX (356)	87.6	12.4	0.0	0.0	0.0	84	30
Colorado Springs, CO (365)	64.7	27.7	7.7	0.0	0.0	140	47
Columbia, MO (245)	95.1	4.9	0.0	0.0	0.0	77	37
Columbia, SC (365)	74.0	25.5	0.5	0.0	0.0	102	41
Columbus, OH (365)	71.2	28.8	0.0	0.0	0.0	100	43
Dallas, TX (365)	54.0	37.5	7.4	0.8	0.3	209	49
Davenport, IA (365)	56.2	43.0	0.8	0.0	0.0	112	49
Denver, CO (365)	30.1	51.5	13.7	4.7	0.0	177	61
Des Moines, IA (365)	77.8	21.9	0.3	0.0	0.0	110	40
Durham, NC (365)	81.6	18.4	0.0	0.0	0.0	90	40
Edison, NJ (365)	54.8	39.5	4.9	0.8	0.0	154	49
El Paso, TX (365)	38.6	56.2	5.2	0.0	0.0	150	54
Fargo, ND (363)	76.6	18.7	2.2	2.5	0.0	192	37
Fort Collins, CO (365)	54.0	36.4	8.8	0.8	0.0	156	50
Fort Wayne, IN (365)	70.7	29.3	0.0	0.0	0.0	100	41
Fort Worth, TX (365)	54.0	37.5	7.4	0.8	0.3	209	49
Grand Rapids, MI (365)	62.2	36.4	1.4	0.0	0.0	143	44
Greeley, CO (365)	54.5	36.2	9.0	0.3	0.0	154	49
Green Bay, WI (365)	73.4	25.2	1.4	0.0	0.0	125	40
Greensboro, NC (365)	75.9	24.1	0.0	0.0	0.0	100	42
Honolulu, HI (365)	99.7	0.3	0.0	0.0	0.0	52	26
Houston, TX (365)	38.6	53.2	5.8	2.5	0.0	179	54
Huntsville, AL (357)	75.4	24.1	0.6	0.0	0.0	105	41
Indianapolis, IN (365)	42.2	55.9	1.9	0.0	0.0	114	53
Jacksonville, FL (365)	73.4	26.6	0.0	0.0	0.0	93	43
Kansas City, MO (365)	52.9	43.6	3.6	0.0	0.0	147	50
Lafayette, LA (365)	81.6	18.4	0.0	0.0	0.0	87	38
Las Cruces, NM (365)	38.4	53.2	5.5	2.2	0.3	665	55
Las Vegas, NV (365)	32.6	58.1	8.5	0.8	0.0	174	59
Lexington, KY (363)	77.4	22.0	0.6	0.0	0.0	108	40
Lincoln, NE (276)	93.1	6.9	0.0	0.0	0.0	84	35
Little Rock, AR (365)	58.4	41.1	0.5	0.0	0.0	112	47
Los Angeles, CA (365)	10.7	62.5	19.5	7.1	0.3	281	77
Louisville, KY (365)	60.8	37.3	1.9	0.0	0.0	143	46

Table continued on following page.

MSA[1] (Days[2])	Percent of Days when Air Quality was...					AQI Statistics	
	Good	Moderate	Unhealthy for Sensitive Groups	Unhealthy	Very Unhealthy	Maximum	Median
Madison, WI (365)	67.1	32.6	0.3	0.0	0.0	101	42
Manchester, NH (365)	91.8	7.7	0.5	0.0	0.0	144	36
Miami, FL (365)	70.4	28.8	0.8	0.0	0.0	135	44
Midland, TX (n/a)	n/a	n/a	n/a	n/a	n/a	n/a	n/a
Milwaukee, WI (365)	57.3	39.5	3.3	0.0	0.0	129	47
Minneapolis, MN (365)	63.0	34.8	1.4	0.8	0.0	182	44
Nashville, TN (365)	60.5	38.1	1.4	0.0	0.0	133	46
New Haven, CT (365)	77.0	19.2	3.3	0.5	0.0	159	40
New Orleans, LA (365)	76.4	22.7	0.8	0.0	0.0	108	42
New York, NY (365)	54.8	39.5	4.9	0.8	0.0	154	49
Oklahoma City, OK (365)	48.2	49.0	2.7	0.0	0.0	140	51
Omaha, NE (365)	72.9	25.8	1.4	0.0	0.0	150	42
Orlando, FL (365)	82.7	17.3	0.0	0.0	0.0	97	39
Philadelphia, PA (365)	49.9	46.0	3.6	0.5	0.0	152	51
Phoenix, AZ (365)	3.0	32.1	28.2	16.7	20.0	272	123
Pittsburgh, PA (365)	44.9	52.6	2.2	0.3	0.0	153	53
Portland, OR (365)	79.7	20.0	0.0	0.3	0.0	161	37
Providence, RI (365)	76.2	22.7	1.1	0.0	0.0	147	41
Provo, UT (365)	60.0	35.3	4.7	0.0	0.0	144	46
Raleigh, NC (365)	71.0	29.0	0.0	0.0	0.0	97	43
Reno, NV (365)	54.2	36.2	4.4	4.4	0.8	291	49
Richmond, VA (365)	76.4	22.7	0.8	0.0	0.0	112	42
Rochester, MN (361)	83.4	16.1	0.6	0.0	0.0	125	36
Sacramento, CA (365)	37.8	46.3	10.4	3.3	1.4	448	62
St. Louis, MO (365)	38.1	57.8	3.6	0.5	0.0	187	55
Salem, OR (363)	87.1	12.9	0.0	0.0	0.0	93	33
Salt Lake City, UT (365)	47.4	39.5	10.7	2.5	0.0	177	52
San Antonio, TX (365)	54.5	42.2	3.3	0.0	0.0	147	48
San Diego, CA (365)	26.8	68.8	4.4	0.0	0.0	133	64
San Francisco, CA (365)	58.1	39.2	2.5	0.3	0.0	151	46
San Jose, CA (365)	60.5	37.5	1.9	0.0	0.0	147	46
Santa Rosa, CA (365)	87.9	12.1	0.0	0.0	0.0	88	33
Savannah, GA (363)	75.8	24.0	0.3	0.0	0.0	103	41
Seattle, WA (365)	72.1	26.0	1.4	0.5	0.0	182	43
Sioux Falls, SD (349)	81.7	16.9	0.9	0.6	0.0	182	36
Springfield, IL (362)	80.7	19.3	0.0	0.0	0.0	97	38
Tampa, FL (365)	72.9	26.8	0.3	0.0	0.0	129	44
Tucson, AZ (365)	39.2	57.0	3.6	0.0	0.0	315	53
Tulsa, OK (365)	60.3	37.0	2.2	0.5	0.0	163	47
Tuscaloosa, AL (281)	94.3	5.7	0.0	0.0	0.0	90	31
Virginia Beach, VA (365)	85.8	14.2	0.0	0.0	0.0	94	38
Washington, DC (365)	61.6	35.6	2.5	0.3	0.0	153	46
Wichita, KS (365)	59.7	38.9	1.4	0.0	0.0	147	47
Wilmington, NC (360)	89.4	10.6	0.0	0.0	0.0	93	34
Winston-Salem, NC (365)	67.4	31.8	0.8	0.0	0.0	124	44
Worcester, MA (365)	81.6	17.5	0.8	0.0	0.0	140	39

Note: The Air Quality Index (AQI) is an index for reporting daily air quality. EPA calculates the AQI for five major air pollutants regulated by the Clean Air Act: ground-level ozone, particle pollution (also known as particulate matter), carbon monoxide, sulfur dioxide, and nitrogen dioxide. The AQI runs from 0 to 500. The higher the AQI value, the greater the level of air pollution and the greater the health concern. There are six AQI categories: "Good" The AQI is between 0 and 50. Air quality is considered satisfactory; "Moderate" The AQI is between 51 and 100. Air quality is acceptable; "Unhealthy for Sensitive Groups" When AQI values are between 101 and 150, members of sensitive groups may experience health effects; "Unhealthy" When AQI values are between 151 and 200 everyone may begin to experience health effects; "Very Unhealthy" AQI values between 201 and 300 trigger a health alert; "Hazardous" AQI values over 300 trigger health warnings of emergency conditions; (1) Data covers the Metropolitan Statistical Area; (2) Number of days with AQI data in 2021
Source: U.S. Environmental Protection Agency, Air Quality Index Report, 2021

Air Quality Index Pollutants

MSA[1] (Days[2])	Carbon Monoxide	Nitrogen Dioxide	Ozone	Sulfur Dioxide	Particulate Matter 2.5	Particulate Matter 10
	Carbon Monoxide	Nitrogen Dioxide	Ozone	Sulfur Dioxide	Particulate Matter 2.5	Particulate Matter 10
Albuquerque, NM (365)	0.0	0.0	49.6	(3)	16.7	33.7
Allentown, PA (365)	0.0	1.6	48.8	(3)	49.6	0.0
Anchorage, AK (365)	0.0	0.0	0.0	(3)	68.5	31.5
Ann Arbor, MI (365)	0.0	0.0	62.5	(3)	37.5	0.0
Athens, GA (365)	0.0	0.0	32.9	(3)	67.1	0.0
Atlanta, GA (365)	0.0	3.6	40.8	(3)	55.6	0.0
Austin, TX (365)	0.0	1.6	50.7	(3)	46.6	1.1
Baltimore, MD (365)	0.0	7.4	60.5	(3)	32.1	0.0
Boise City, ID (365)	0.0	0.8	44.9	(3)	51.2	3.0
Boston, MA (365)	0.0	3.3	53.4	(3)	43.0	0.3
Boulder, CO (365)	0.0	0.0	74.8	(3)	24.7	0.5
Brownsville, TX (365)	0.0	0.0	31.2	(3)	68.8	0.0
Cape Coral, FL (365)	0.0	0.0	66.0	(3)	32.9	1.1
Cedar Rapids, IA (365)	0.0	0.0	35.1	(3)	64.7	0.3
Charleston, SC (365)	0.0	0.0	41.4	(3)	58.6	0.0
Charlotte, NC (365)	0.0	0.3	59.2	(3)	40.5	0.0
Chicago, IL (365)	0.0	4.9	34.2	(3)	51.0	9.9
Cincinnati, OH (365)	0.0	3.0	28.8	(3)	64.1	4.1
Clarksville, TN (365)	0.0	0.0	47.4	(3)	52.6	0.0
Cleveland, OH (365)	0.0	1.4	35.9	(3)	60.8	1.9
College Station, TX (356)	0.0	0.0	0.0	(3)	100.0	0.0
Colorado Springs, CO (365)	0.0	0.0	95.1	(3)	4.9	0.0
Columbia, MO (245)	0.0	0.0	100.0	(3)	0.0	0.0
Columbia, SC (365)	0.0	0.0	51.8	(3)	48.2	0.0
Columbus, OH (365)	0.0	2.7	44.7	(3)	52.6	0.0
Dallas, TX (365)	0.0	3.3	61.4	(3)	35.3	0.0
Davenport, IA (365)	0.0	0.0	33.4	(3)	46.8	19.7
Denver, CO (365)	0.0	18.6	63.6	(3)	11.2	6.6
Des Moines, IA (365)	0.0	3.6	43.3	(3)	51.8	1.4
Durham, NC (365)	0.0	0.0	51.8	(3)	48.2	0.0
Edison, NJ (365)	0.0	12.3	41.4	(3)	46.3	0.0
El Paso, TX (365)	0.0	5.8	53.2	(3)	35.9	5.2
Fargo, ND (363)	0.0	1.4	54.5	(3)	44.1	0.0
Fort Collins, CO (365)	0.0	0.0	91.0	(3)	9.0	0.0
Fort Wayne, IN (365)	0.0	0.0	51.0	(3)	49.0	0.0
Fort Worth, TX (365)	0.0	3.3	61.4	(3)	35.3	0.0
Grand Rapids, MI (365)	0.0	1.9	50.1	(3)	47.9	0.0
Greeley, CO (365)	0.0	0.3	78.6	(3)	21.1	0.0
Green Bay, WI (365)	0.0	0.0	48.8	(3)	51.2	0.0
Greensboro, NC (365)	0.0	0.0	52.9	(3)	46.3	0.8
Honolulu, HI (365)	0.3	0.8	83.8	(3)	11.5	3.6
Houston, TX (365)	0.0	0.8	38.9	(3)	55.3	4.9
Huntsville, AL (357)	0.0	0.0	33.3	(3)	63.0	3.6
Indianapolis, IN (365)	0.0	2.2	25.5	(3)	72.3	0.0
Jacksonville, FL (365)	0.0	0.0	36.4	(3)	63.6	0.0
Kansas City, MO (365)	0.0	0.3	38.6	(3)	50.1	11.0
Lafayette, LA (365)	0.0	0.0	61.9	(3)	38.1	0.0
Las Cruces, NM (365)	0.0	2.5	58.1	(3)	6.3	33.2
Las Vegas, NV (365)	0.0	1.6	66.6	(3)	24.9	6.8
Lexington, KY (363)	0.0	5.5	38.3	(3)	55.9	0.3
Lincoln, NE (276)	0.0	0.0	78.6	(3)	21.4	0.0
Little Rock, AR (365)	0.0	1.6	27.9	(3)	70.4	0.0
Los Angeles, CA (365)	0.0	6.6	46.0	(3)	45.2	2.2
Louisville, KY (365)	0.0	2.2	39.5	(3)	58.4	0.0

Table continued on following page.

MSA[1] (Days[2])	Percent of Days when AQI Pollutant was...					
	Carbon Monoxide	Nitrogen Dioxide	Ozone	Sulfur Dioxide	Particulate Matter 2.5	Particulate Matter 10
Madison, WI (365)	0.0	0.0	39.2	(3)	60.8	0.0
Manchester, NH (365)	0.0	0.0	92.1	(3)	7.9	0.0
Miami, FL (365)	0.0	6.8	33.7	(3)	59.5	0.0
Midland, TX (n/a)	n/a	n/a	n/a	(3)	n/a	n/a
Milwaukee, WI (365)	0.0	1.4	52.3	(3)	43.6	2.7
Minneapolis, MN (365)	0.0	3.3	47.7	(3)	41.1	7.9
Nashville, TN (365)	0.0	5.2	33.4	(3)	61.4	0.0
New Haven, CT (365)	0.0	5.2	55.9	(3)	37.5	1.4
New Orleans, LA (365)	0.0	0.0	48.2	(3)	51.5	0.3
New York, NY (365)	0.0	12.3	41.4	(3)	46.3	0.0
Oklahoma City, OK (365)	0.0	3.0	41.6	(3)	54.8	0.5
Omaha, NE (365)	0.0	0.0	53.4	(3)	38.4	8.2
Orlando, FL (365)	0.0	0.0	66.0	(3)	33.2	0.8
Philadelphia, PA (365)	0.0	6.0	39.7	(3)	54.0	0.3
Phoenix, AZ (365)	0.0	0.0	75.3	(3)	6.3	18.4
Pittsburgh, PA (365)	0.0	0.3	32.6	(3)	67.1	0.0
Portland, OR (365)	0.0	0.5	61.1	(3)	38.4	0.0
Providence, RI (365)	0.0	2.2	63.0	(3)	34.8	0.0
Provo, UT (365)	0.0	3.3	78.9	(3)	16.4	1.4
Raleigh, NC (365)	0.0	0.5	53.7	(3)	45.8	0.0
Reno, NV (365)	0.0	1.4	72.6	(3)	24.9	1.1
Richmond, VA (365)	0.0	6.3	51.8	(3)	41.9	0.0
Rochester, MN (361)	0.0	0.0	61.5	(3)	38.5	0.0
Sacramento, CA (365)	0.0	0.0	66.0	(3)	33.4	0.5
St. Louis, MO (365)	0.0	0.5	25.8	(3)	70.1	3.6
Salem, OR (363)	0.0	0.0	39.7	(3)	60.3	0.0
Salt Lake City, UT (365)	0.0	7.9	64.4	(3)	24.1	3.6
San Antonio, TX (365)	0.0	0.3	44.9	(3)	54.2	0.5
San Diego, CA (365)	0.0	1.1	59.5	(3)	38.6	0.8
San Francisco, CA (365)	0.0	1.1	47.9	(3)	51.0	0.0
San Jose, CA (365)	0.0	0.0	54.8	(3)	44.1	1.1
Santa Rosa, CA (365)	0.0	0.0	59.5	(3)	37.5	3.0
Savannah, GA (363)	0.0	0.0	24.5	(3)	75.5	0.0
Seattle, WA (365)	0.0	2.2	62.2	(3)	35.6	0.0
Sioux Falls, SD (349)	0.0	4.6	65.9	(3)	22.3	7.2
Springfield, IL (362)	0.0	0.0	43.1	(3)	56.9	0.0
Tampa, FL (365)	0.0	0.0	51.2	(3)	48.2	0.5
Tucson, AZ (365)	0.0	0.0	54.8	(3)	15.9	29.3
Tulsa, OK (365)	0.0	0.0	52.9	(3)	46.3	0.8
Tuscaloosa, AL (281)	0.0	0.0	72.6	(3)	27.4	0.0
Virginia Beach, VA (365)	0.0	6.8	49.6	(3)	43.6	0.0
Washington, DC (365)	0.0	8.5	52.1	(3)	39.5	0.0
Wichita, KS (365)	0.0	0.5	42.7	(3)	48.8	7.9
Wilmington, NC (360)	0.0	0.0	46.7	(3)	53.3	0.0
Winston-Salem, NC (365)	0.0	1.6	46.6	(3)	51.8	0.0
Worcester, MA (365)	0.0	2.5	58.1	(3)	39.2	0.3

Note: The Air Quality Index (AQI) is an index for reporting daily air quality. EPA calculates the AQI for five major air pollutants regulated by the Clean Air Act: ground-level ozone, particle pollution (also known as particulate matter), carbon monoxide, sulfur dioxide, and nitrogen dioxide. The AQI runs from 0 to 500. The higher the AQI value, the greater the level of air pollution and the greater the health concern; (1) Data covers the Metropolitan Statistical Area—see Appendix B for areas included; (2) Number of days with AQI data in 2021; (3) Sulfur dioxide is no longer included in this table (as of December 8, 2021) because SO_2 concentrations tend to be very localized and not necessarily representative of broad geographical areas like counties and CBSAs.
Source: U.S. Environmental Protection Agency, Air Quality Index Report, 2021

Air Quality Trends: Ozone

MSA[1]	1990	1995	2000	2005	2010	2015	2018	2019	2020	2021
Albuquerque, NM	0.072	0.070	0.072	0.073	0.066	0.066	0.074	0.067	0.071	0.071
Allentown, PA	0.093	0.091	0.091	0.086	0.080	0.070	0.067	0.064	0.063	0.063
Anchorage, AK	n/a	n/a	n/a	n/a	n/a	n/a	n/a	n/a	n/a	n/a
Ann Arbor, MI	0.025	0.034	0.035	0.023	0.034	0.064	0.072	0.058	0.067	0.063
Athens, GA	n/a	n/a	n/a	n/a	n/a	n/a	n/a	n/a	n/a	n/a
Atlanta, GA	0.088	0.089	0.089	0.077	0.067	0.069	0.068	0.070	0.059	0.064
Austin, TX	0.088	0.089	0.088	0.082	0.074	0.073	0.072	0.065	0.066	0.066
Baltimore, MD	0.100	0.103	0.088	0.089	0.084	0.073	0.071	0.070	0.064	0.071
Boise City, ID	n/a	n/a	n/a	n/a	n/a	n/a	n/a	n/a	n/a	n/a
Boston, MA	0.078	0.085	0.067	0.075	0.066	0.065	0.061	0.052	0.053	0.059
Boulder, CO	n/a	n/a	n/a	n/a	n/a	n/a	n/a	n/a	n/a	n/a
Brownsville, TX	n/a	n/a	n/a	n/a	n/a	n/a	n/a	n/a	n/a	n/a
Cape Coral, FL	0.069	0.066	0.073	0.071	0.065	0.058	0.065	0.062	0.061	0.055
Cedar Rapids, IA	n/a	n/a	n/a	n/a	n/a	n/a	n/a	n/a	n/a	n/a
Charleston, SC	0.068	0.071	0.078	0.073	0.067	0.054	0.058	0.064	0.059	0.062
Charlotte, NC	0.094	0.091	0.099	0.089	0.082	0.071	0.070	0.073	0.060	0.067
Chicago, IL	0.074	0.094	0.073	0.084	0.070	0.066	0.073	0.069	0.076	0.071
Cincinnati, OH	0.083	0.082	0.074	0.075	0.069	0.069	0.073	0.067	0.067	0.065
Clarksville, TN	n/a	n/a	n/a	n/a	n/a	n/a	n/a	n/a	n/a	n/a
Cleveland, OH	0.084	0.090	0.079	0.084	0.074	0.069	0.072	0.067	0.069	0.066
College Station, TX	n/a	n/a	n/a	n/a	n/a	n/a	n/a	n/a	n/a	n/a
Colorado Springs, CO	n/a	n/a	n/a	n/a	n/a	n/a	n/a	n/a	n/a	n/a
Columbia, MO	n/a	n/a	n/a	n/a	n/a	n/a	n/a	n/a	n/a	n/a
Columbia, SC	0.091	0.079	0.089	0.082	0.069	0.058	0.059	0.063	0.053	0.061
Columbus, OH	0.090	0.091	0.085	0.084	0.073	0.066	0.062	0.060	0.062	0.061
Dallas, TX	0.094	0.103	0.096	0.096	0.079	0.078	0.079	0.070	0.070	0.076
Davenport, IA	0.065	0.072	0.064	0.065	0.057	0.060	0.067	0.066	0.063	0.066
Denver, CO	0.077	0.070	0.069	0.072	0.070	0.073	0.071	0.068	0.079	0.080
Des Moines, IA	n/a	n/a	n/a	n/a	n/a	n/a	n/a	n/a	n/a	n/a
Durham, NC	0.078	0.080	0.082	0.079	0.074	0.061	0.063	0.063	0.051	0.063
Edison, NJ	0.101	0.105	0.089	0.090	0.080	0.074	0.073	0.067	0.064	0.069
El Paso, TX	0.080	0.078	0.082	0.074	0.072	0.071	0.077	0.074	0.076	0.071
Fargo, ND	n/a	n/a	n/a	n/a	n/a	n/a	n/a	n/a	n/a	n/a
Fort Collins, CO	0.066	0.072	0.074	0.075	0.072	0.070	0.073	0.065	0.070	0.077
Fort Wayne, IN	0.086	0.094	0.086	0.081	0.067	0.061	0.071	0.063	0.064	0.062
Fort Worth, TX	0.094	0.103	0.096	0.096	0.079	0.078	0.079	0.070	0.070	0.076
Grand Rapids, MI	0.098	0.092	0.073	0.084	0.069	0.066	0.070	0.063	0.074	0.067
Greeley, CO	0.076	0.072	0.069	0.078	0.073	0.073	0.073	0.065	0.072	0.076
Green Bay, WI	n/a	n/a	n/a	n/a	n/a	n/a	n/a	n/a	n/a	n/a
Greensboro, NC	0.097	0.089	0.089	0.082	0.076	0.064	0.067	0.064	0.057	0.066
Honolulu, HI	0.034	0.049	0.044	0.042	0.046	0.048	0.046	0.053	0.044	0.045
Houston, TX	0.119	0.114	0.102	0.087	0.079	0.083	0.073	0.074	0.067	0.072
Huntsville, AL	0.079	0.080	0.088	0.075	0.071	0.063	0.065	0.063	0.057	0.061
Indianapolis, IN	0.085	0.095	0.081	0.081	0.070	0.065	0.076	0.066	0.065	0.067
Jacksonville, FL	0.080	0.068	0.072	0.076	0.068	0.060	0.060	0.062	0.057	0.061
Kansas City, MO	0.075	0.095	0.087	0.082	0.067	0.063	0.072	0.061	0.064	0.067
Lafayette, LA	n/a	n/a	n/a	n/a	n/a	n/a	n/a	n/a	n/a	n/a
Las Cruces, NM	0.073	0.075	0.075	0.070	0.060	0.070	0.072	0.068	0.071	0.079
Las Vegas, NV	n/a	n/a	n/a	n/a	n/a	n/a	n/a	n/a	n/a	n/a
Lexington, KY	0.078	0.088	0.077	0.078	0.070	0.069	0.063	0.059	0.060	0.064
Lincoln, NE	0.057	0.060	0.057	0.056	0.050	0.061	0.062	0.056	0.054	0.059
Little Rock, AR	0.080	0.086	0.090	0.083	0.072	0.063	0.066	0.059	0.062	0.066
Los Angeles, CA	0.128	0.109	0.090	0.086	0.074	0.082	0.082	0.080	0.096	0.076
Louisville, KY	0.082	0.091	0.087	0.083	0.076	0.071	0.069	0.064	0.063	0.064
Madison, WI	0.077	0.084	0.072	0.079	0.062	0.064	0.066	0.059	0.070	0.066
Manchester, NH	0.085	0.088	0.070	0.082	0.067	0.061	0.066	0.054	0.055	0.061

Table continued on following page.

MSA[1]	1990	1995	2000	2005	2010	2015	2018	2019	2020	2021
Miami, FL	0.068	0.072	0.075	0.065	0.064	0.061	0.064	0.058	0.058	0.057
Midland, TX	n/a	n/a	n/a	n/a	n/a	n/a	n/a	n/a	n/a	n/a
Milwaukee, WI	0.095	0.106	0.082	0.092	0.079	0.069	0.073	0.066	0.074	0.072
Minneapolis, MN	0.068	0.084	0.065	0.074	0.066	0.061	0.065	0.059	0.060	0.067
Nashville, TN	0.089	0.092	0.084	0.078	0.073	0.065	0.068	0.064	0.061	0.064
New Haven, CT	0.121	0.117	0.087	0.092	0.079	0.081	0.077	0.084	0.080	0.083
New Orleans, LA	0.082	0.088	0.091	0.079	0.074	0.067	0.065	0.062	0.061	0.060
New York, NY	0.101	0.105	0.089	0.090	0.080	0.074	0.073	0.067	0.064	0.069
Oklahoma City, OK	0.080	0.087	0.083	0.077	0.071	0.067	0.072	0.065	0.066	0.068
Omaha, NE	0.054	0.075	0.063	0.069	0.058	0.055	0.063	0.050	0.055	0.055
Orlando, FL	0.081	0.075	0.080	0.083	0.069	0.060	0.062	0.062	0.059	0.061
Philadelphia, PA	0.102	0.109	0.099	0.091	0.083	0.074	0.075	0.067	0.065	0.068
Phoenix, AZ	0.080	0.086	0.082	0.077	0.075	0.072	0.073	0.071	0.079	0.079
Pittsburgh, PA	0.080	0.100	0.084	0.083	0.077	0.070	0.070	0.062	0.066	0.066
Portland, OR	0.081	0.065	0.059	0.059	0.056	0.064	0.062	0.058	0.058	0.058
Providence, RI	0.106	0.107	0.087	0.090	0.072	0.070	0.074	0.064	0.065	0.067
Provo, UT	n/a	n/a	n/a	n/a	n/a	n/a	n/a	n/a	n/a	n/a
Raleigh, NC	0.093	0.081	0.087	0.082	0.071	0.065	0.063	0.064	0.054	0.062
Reno, NV	0.074	0.069	0.067	0.069	0.068	0.071	0.077	0.063	0.073	0.078
Richmond, VA	0.083	0.089	0.080	0.082	0.079	0.062	0.062	0.061	0.054	0.061
Rochester, MN	n/a	n/a	n/a	n/a	n/a	n/a	n/a	n/a	n/a	n/a
Sacramento, CA	0.087	0.092	0.085	0.084	0.072	0.073	0.074	0.067	0.072	0.073
St. Louis, MO	0.077	0.084	0.074	0.078	0.069	0.067	0.072	0.066	0.066	0.067
Salem, OR	n/a	n/a	n/a	n/a	n/a	n/a	n/a	n/a	n/a	n/a
Salt Lake City, UT	n/a	n/a	n/a	n/a	n/a	n/a	n/a	n/a	n/a	n/a
San Antonio, TX	0.090	0.095	0.078	0.084	0.072	0.079	0.072	0.075	0.069	0.070
San Diego, CA	0.110	0.085	0.079	0.074	0.073	0.068	0.069	0.069	0.078	0.068
San Francisco, CA	0.062	0.077	0.060	0.060	0.063	0.064	0.056	0.062	0.062	0.064
San Jose, CA	0.078	0.084	0.065	0.063	0.072	0.067	0.059	0.061	0.066	0.067
Santa Rosa, CA	0.063	0.071	0.061	0.050	0.053	0.059	0.055	0.052	0.052	0.052
Savannah, GA	n/a	n/a	n/a	n/a	n/a	n/a	n/a	n/a	n/a	n/a
Seattle, WA	0.082	0.062	0.056	0.053	0.053	0.059	0.067	0.052	0.052	0.052
Sioux Falls, SD	n/a	n/a	n/a	n/a	n/a	n/a	n/a	n/a	n/a	n/a
Springfield, IL	n/a	n/a	n/a	n/a	n/a	n/a	n/a	n/a	n/a	n/a
Tampa, FL	0.080	0.075	0.081	0.075	0.067	0.062	0.065	0.065	0.063	0.060
Tucson, AZ	0.073	0.078	0.074	0.075	0.068	0.065	0.069	0.065	0.070	0.068
Tulsa, OK	0.086	0.091	0.081	0.072	0.069	0.061	0.067	0.062	0.061	0.063
Tuscaloosa, AL	n/a	n/a	n/a	n/a	n/a	n/a	n/a	n/a	n/a	n/a
Virginia Beach, VA	0.085	0.084	0.083	0.078	0.074	0.061	0.061	0.059	0.053	0.057
Washington, DC	0.075	0.083	0.073	0.069	0.069	0.067	0.068	0.064	0.057	0.066
Wichita, KS	0.077	0.069	0.080	0.074	0.075	0.064	0.064	0.062	0.059	0.061
Wilmington, NC	0.082	0.079	0.080	0.075	0.062	0.057	0.062	0.059	0.054	0.062
Winston-Salem, NC	0.084	0.086	0.089	0.080	0.078	0.065	0.064	0.062	0.058	0.062
Worcester, MA	0.097	0.096	0.076	0.085	0.070	0.063	0.065	0.060	0.063	0.063
U.S.	0.087	0.089	0.081	0.080	0.072	0.067	0.069	0.065	0.065	0.067

Note: (1) Data covers the Metropolitan Statistical Area; n/a not available. The values shown are the composite ozone concentration averages among trend sites based on the highest fourth daily maximum 8-hour concentration in parts per million. These trends are based on sites having an adequate record of monitoring data during the trend period. Data from exceptional events are included.
Source: U.S. Environmental Protection Agency, Air Quality Monitoring Information, "Air Quality Trends by City, 1990-2021"

Maximum Air Pollutant Concentrations: Particulate Matter, Ozone, CO and Lead

Metro Aea	PM 10 (ug/m³)	PM 2.5 Wtd AM (ug/m³)	PM 2.5 24-Hr (ug/m³)	Ozone (ppm)	Carbon Monoxide (ppm)	Lead (ug/m³)
Albuquerque, NM	221	11.3	28	0.076	1	n/a
Allentown, PA	44	9.9	27	0.069	n/a	0.06
Anchorage, AK	97	6	21	n/a	2	n/a
Ann Arbor, MI	n/a	8.8	18	0.066	n/a	n/a
Athens, GA	n/a	10.1	25	0.06	n/a	n/a
Atlanta, GA	44	9.7	22	0.07	2	n/a
Austin, TX	91	9.4	21	0.066	1	n/a
Baltimore, MD	27	8.9	21	0.075	1	n/a
Boise City, ID	113	9.2	37	0.075	1	n/a
Boston, MA	50	8.3	18	0.067	1	n/a
Boulder, CO	51	10	54	0.082	n/a	n/a
Brownsville, TX	n/a	9.2	24	0.056	n/a	n/a
Cape Coral, FL	54	7.3	17	0.055	n/a	n/a
Cedar Rapids, IA	57	8.8	24	0.064	n/a	n/a
Charleston, SC	40	9.5	20	0.059	n/a	n/a
Charlotte, NC	39	9.3	21	0.067	1	n/a
Chicago, IL	166	10.8	27	0.079	1	0.03
Cincinnati, OH	178	12.1	27	0.07	2	n/a
Clarksville, TN	n/a	10.4	27	0.06	n/a	n/a
Cleveland, OH	89	12.6	29	0.072	2	0.01
College Station, TX	n/a	8	21	n/a	n/a	n/a
Colorado Springs, CO	39	6	21	0.078	1	n/a
Columbia, MO	n/a	n/a	n/a	0.058	n/a	n/a
Columbia, SC	42	9	22	0.064	1	n/a
Columbus, OH	32	9.9	24	0.064	1	n/a
Dallas, TX	56	9.6	23	0.085	1	0.02
Davenport, IA	137	9.4	26	0.066	1	n/a
Denver, CO	96	10.3	41	0.089	2	n/a
Des Moines, IA	54	8.3	23	0.061	n/a	n/a
Durham, NC	40	8	18	0.063	n/a	n/a
Edison, NJ	40	9.8	26	0.079	2	n/a
El Paso, TX	153	9.2	37	0.073	3	n/a
Fargo, ND	n/a	11	60	0.063	n/a	n/a
Fort Collins, CO	n/a	8.5	29	0.085	1	n/a
Fort Wayne, IN	n/a	9	21	0.065	n/a	n/a
Fort Worth, TX	56	9.6	23	0.085	1	0.02
Grand Rapids, MI	42	10.1	26	0.069	1	Lead
Greeley, CO	n/a	9.8	31	0.083	1	n/a
Green Bay, WI	n/a	8.7	26	0.068	n/a	n/a
Greensboro, NC	35	7.7	18	0.066	n/a	n/a
Honolulu, HI	34	3.3	6	0.047	2	n/a
Houston, TX	103	11.4	24	0.083	2	n/a
Huntsville, AL	36	7.5	17	0.061	n/a	n/a
Indianapolis, IN	55	12.6	32	0.067	2	n/a
Jacksonville, FL	54	8.8	18	0.061	1	n/a
Kansas City, MO	103	11.2	31	0.071	1	n/a
Lafayette, LA	56	7.6	16	0.063	n/a	n/a
Las Cruces, NM	439	9.3	26	0.086	n/a	n/a
Las Vegas, NV	176	9.9	33	0.076	2	n/a
Lexington, KY	27	9.6	23	0.064	n/a	n/a
Lincoln, NE	n/a	7.1	21	0.059	n/a	n/a
Little Rock, AR	32	9.7	25	0.067	1	n/a
Los Angeles, CA	113	13.4	48	0.097	3	0.06
Louisville, KY	46	11.2	28	0.073	1	n/a
Madison, WI	49	9.5	27	0.066	n/a	n/a

Table continued on following page.

Metro Aea	PM 10 (ug/m³)	PM 2.5 Wtd AM (ug/m³)	PM 2.5 24-Hr (ug/m³)	Ozone (ppm)	Carbon Monoxide (ppm)	Lead (ug/m³)
Manchester, NH	n/a	4.5	13	0.062	1	n/a
Miami, FL	73	9.5	26	0.058	1	n/a
Midland, TX	n/a	n/a	n/a	n/a	n/a	n/a
Milwaukee, WI	70	10.2	27	0.073	1	n/a
Minneapolis, MN	115	8.8	30	0.07	2	0.08
Nashville, TN	50	9.4	24	0.066	2	n/a
New Haven, CT	68	8.8	22	0.083	1	n/a
New Orleans, LA	45	7.6	17	0.063	1	0.05
New York, NY	40	9.8	26	0.079	2	n/a
Oklahoma City, OK	64	11.2	28	0.07	1	n/a
Omaha, NE	70	8.9	26	0.066	1	0.09
Orlando, FL	51	7.6	15	0.062	1	n/a
Philadelphia, PA	60	10.1	25	0.077	1	0
Phoenix, AZ	225	12.7	36	0.083	3	n/a
Pittsburgh, PA	81	11.8	30	0.068	4	0
Portland, OR	29	6.4	16	0.062	1	n/a
Providence, RI	29	9.3	21	0.069	1	n/a
Provo, UT	100	7.7	31	0.077	1	n/a
Raleigh, NC	56	9.2	22	0.066	1	n/a
Reno, NV	284	12.4	105	0.08	2	n/a
Richmond, VA	40	8.3	19	0.066	1	n/a
Rochester, MN	n/a	n/a	n/a	0.067	n/a	n/a
Sacramento, CA	406	11.3	57	0.085	1	n/a
St. Louis, MO	161	10	23	0.073	1	0.06
Salem, OR	n/a	n/a	n/a	0.063	n/a	n/a
Salt Lake City, UT	103	10.3	43	0.087	1	n/a
San Antonio, TX	87	8.9	22	0.078	1	n/a
San Diego, CA	119	11.2	24	0.078	1	0.02
San Francisco, CA	35	9.1	23	0.074	2	n/a
San Jose, CA	76	10.9	25	0.074	1	n/a
Santa Rosa, CA	53	n/a	n/a	0.055	1	n/a
Savannah, GA	n/a	10.1	22	0.058	n/a	n/a
Seattle, WA	22	7.1	22	0.078	1	n/a
Sioux Falls, SD	110	n/a	n/a	0.065	1	n/a
Springfield, IL	n/a	8.7	22	0.057	n/a	n/a
Tampa, FL	61	8.5	18	0.063	1	0.08
Tucson, AZ	249	6.6	14	0.068	1	n/a
Tulsa, OK	99	10.1	29	0.068	1	n/a
Tuscaloosa, AL	n/a	7.8	20	0.053	n/a	n/a
Virginia Beach, VA	44	7.2	16	0.061	1	n/a
Washington, DC	47	9.6	21	0.072	2	n/a
Wichita, KS	89	11.3	31	0.067	n/a	n/a
Wilmington, NC	41	4.8	13	0.062	n/a	n/a
Winston-Salem, NC	41	9.2	41	0.066	n/a	n/a
Worcester, MA	31	9.1	19	0.068	1	n/a
NAAQS[1]	150	15.0	35	0.075	9	0.15

Note: Data from exceptional events are included; Data covers the Metropolitan Statistical Area; (1) National Ambient Air Quality Standards; ppm = parts per million; ug/m³ = micrograms per cubic meter; n/a not available

Concentrations: Particulate Matter 10 (coarse particulate)—highest second maximum 24-hour concentration; Particulate Matter 2.5 Wtd AM (fine particulate)—highest weighted annual mean concentration; Particulate Matter 2.5 24-Hour (fine particulate)—highest 98th percentile 24-hour concentration; Ozone—highest fourth daily maximum 8-hour concentration; Carbon Monoxide—highest second maximum non-overlapping 8-hour concentration; Lead—maximum running 3-month average

Source: U.S. Environmental Protection Agency, Air Quality Monitoring Information, "Air Quality Statistics by City, 2021"

Maximum Air Pollutant Concentrations: Nitrogen Dioxide and Sulfur Dioxide

Metro Area	Nitrogen Dioxide AM (ppb)	Nitrogen Dioxide 1-Hr (ppb)	Sulfur Dioxide AM (ppb)	Sulfur Dioxide 1-Hr (ppb)	Sulfur Dioxide 24-Hr (ppb)
Albuquerque, NM	8	44	n/a	3	n/a
Allentown, PA	10	42	n/a	6	n/a
Anchorage, AK	n/a	n/a	n/a	n/a	n/a
Ann Arbor, MI	n/a	n/a	n/a	n/a	n/a
Athens, GA	n/a	n/a	n/a	n/a	n/a
Atlanta, GA	17	50	n/a	4	n/a
Austin, TX	13	44	n/a	3	n/a
Baltimore, MD	16	51	n/a	16	n/a
Boise City, ID	10	45	n/a	2	n/a
Boston, MA	12	45	n/a	9	n/a
Boulder, CO	n/a	n/a	n/a	n/a	n/a
Brownsville, TX	n/a	n/a	n/a	n/a	n/a
Cape Coral, FL	n/a	n/a	n/a	n/a	n/a
Cedar Rapids, IA	n/a	n/a	n/a	40	n/a
Charleston, SC	n/a	n/a	n/a	9	n/a
Charlotte, NC	7	37	n/a	2	n/a
Chicago, IL	17	54	n/a	73	n/a
Cincinnati, OH	16	49	n/a	28	n/a
Clarksville, TN	n/a	n/a	n/a	n/a	n/a
Cleveland, OH	9	38	n/a	39	n/a
College Station, TX	n/a	n/a	n/a	11	n/a
Colorado Springs, CO	n/a	n/a	n/a	10	n/a
Columbia, MO	n/a	n/a	n/a	n/a	n/a
Columbia, SC	n/a	n/a	n/a	1	n/a
Columbus, OH	10	47	n/a	2	n/a
Dallas, TX	13	48	n/a	8	n/a
Davenport, IA	n/a	n/a	n/a	4	n/a
Denver, CO	26	71	n/a	7	n/a
Des Moines, IA	6	34	n/a	n/a	n/a
Durham, NC	n/a	n/a	n/a	1	n/a
Edison, NJ	19	65	n/a	17	n/a
El Paso, TX	14	57	n/a	n/a	n/a
Fargo, ND	4	31	n/a	n/a	n/a
Fort Collins, CO	n/a	n/a	n/a	n/a	n/a
Fort Wayne, IN	n/a	n/a	n/a	n/a	n/a
Fort Worth, TX	13	48	n/a	8	n/a
Grand Rapids, MI	8	39	n/a	4	n/a
Greeley, CO	6	42	n/a	n/a	n/a
Green Bay, WI	n/a	n/a	n/a	5	n/a
Greensboro, NC	n/a	n/a	n/a	n/a	n/a
Honolulu, HI	3	22	n/a	44	n/a
Houston, TX	12	49	n/a	16	n/a
Huntsville, AL	n/a	n/a	n/a	n/a	n/a
Indianapolis, IN	12	40	n/a	3	n/a
Jacksonville, FL	11	41	n/a	39	n/a
Kansas City, MO	10	44	n/a	9	n/a
Lafayette, LA	n/a	n/a	n/a	n/a	n/a
Las Cruces, NM	8	48	n/a	n/a	n/a
Las Vegas, NV	22	53	n/a	3	n/a
Lexington, KY	6	n/a	n/a	5	n/a
Lincoln, NE	n/a	n/a	n/a	n/a	n/a
Little Rock, AR	7	38	n/a	6	n/a
Los Angeles, CA	25	76	n/a	4	n/a
Louisville, KY	15	50	n/a	13	n/a
Madison, WI	n/a	n/a	n/a	2	n/a

Table continued on following page.

Metro Area	Nitrogen Dioxide AM (ppb)	Nitrogen Dioxide 1-Hr (ppb)	Sulfur Dioxide AM (ppb)	Sulfur Dioxide 1-Hr (ppb)	Sulfur Dioxide 24-Hr (ppb)
Manchester, NH	n/a	n/a	n/a	1	n/a
Miami, FL	13	49	n/a	2	n/a
Midland, TX	n/a	n/a	n/a	n/a	n/a
Milwaukee, WI	13	42	n/a	n/a	n/a
Minneapolis, MN	8	38	n/a	14	n/a
Nashville, TN	13	52	n/a	4	n/a
New Haven, CT	12	48	n/a	3	n/a
New Orleans, LA	9	37	n/a	56	n/a
New York, NY	19	65	n/a	17	n/a
Oklahoma City, OK	13	47	n/a	1	n/a
Omaha, NE	n/a	n/a	n/a	48	n/a
Orlando, FL	n/a	n/a	n/a	n/a	n/a
Philadelphia, PA	14	54	n/a	6	n/a
Phoenix, AZ	26	59	n/a	7	n/a
Pittsburgh, PA	10	36	n/a	54	n/a
Portland, OR	9	31	n/a	3	n/a
Providence, RI	16	36	n/a	3	n/a
Provo, UT	9	42	n/a	n/a	n/a
Raleigh, NC	8	31	n/a	2	n/a
Reno, NV	12	47	n/a	3	n/a
Richmond, VA	13	48	n/a	3	n/a
Rochester, MN	n/a	n/a	n/a	n/a	n/a
Sacramento, CA	7	41	n/a	n/a	n/a
St. Louis, MO	10	46	n/a	34	n/a
Salem, OR	n/a	n/a	n/a	n/a	n/a
Salt Lake City, UT	16	51	n/a	7	n/a
San Antonio, TX	7	32	n/a	3	n/a
San Diego, CA	13	54	n/a	1	n/a
San Francisco, CA	12	40	n/a	11	n/a
San Jose, CA	12	39	n/a	2	n/a
Santa Rosa, CA	3	20	n/a	n/a	n/a
Savannah, GA	n/a	n/a	n/a	50	n/a
Seattle, WA	16	49	n/a	3	n/a
Sioux Falls, SD	n/a	n/a	n/a	n/a	n/a
Springfield, IL	n/a	n/a	n/a	n/a	n/a
Tampa, FL	9	37	n/a	29	n/a
Tucson, AZ	8	38	n/a	1	n/a
Tulsa, OK	7	38	n/a	5	n/a
Tuscaloosa, AL	n/a	n/a	n/a	n/a	n/a
Virginia Beach, VA	7	40	n/a	3	n/a
Washington, DC	15	50	n/a	3	n/a
Wichita, KS	7	39	n/a	4	n/a
Wilmington, NC	n/a	n/a	n/a	n/a	n/a
Winston-Salem, NC	6	32	n/a	4	n/a
Worcester, MA	9	44	n/a	2	n/a
NAAQS[1]	53	100	30	75	140

Note: Data from exceptional events are included; Data covers the Metropolitan Statistical Area; (1) National Ambient Air Quality Standards; ppb = parts per billion; n/a not available
Concentrations: Nitrogen Dioxide AM—highest arithmetic mean concentration; Nitrogen Dioxide 1-Hr—highest 98th percentile 1-hour daily maximum concentration; Sulfur Dioxide AM—highest annual mean concentration; Sulfur Dioxide 1-Hr—highest 99th percentile 1-hour daily maximum concentration; Sulfur Dioxide 24-Hr—highest second maximum 24-hour concentration
Source: U.S. Environmental Protection Agency, Air Quality Monitoring Information, "Air Quality Statistics by City, 2021"

Appendix B: Metropolitan Area Definitions

Metropolitan Statistical Areas (MSA), Metropolitan Divisions (MD), New England City and Town Areas (NECTA), and New England City and Town Area Divisions (NECTAD)

Note: In March 2020, the Office of Management and Budget (OMB) announced changes to metropolitan and micropolitan statistical area definitions. Both current and historical definitions (December 2009) are shown below. If the change only affected the name of the metro area, the counties included were not repeated.

Albuquerque, NM MSA
Bernalillo, Sandoval, Torrance, and Valencia Counties

Allentown-Bethlehem-Easton, PA-NJ MSA
Carbon, Lehigh, and Northampton Counties, PA; Warren County, NJ

Anchorage, AK MSA
Anchorage Municipality and Matanuska-Susitna Borough

Ann Arbor, MI MSA
Washtenaw County

Athens-Clarke County, GA MSA
Clarke, Madison, Oconee, and Oglethorpe Counties

Atlanta-Sandy Springs-Roswell, GA MSA
Barrow, Bartow, Butts, Carroll, Cherokee, Clayton, Cobb, Coweta, Dawson, DeKalb, Douglas, Fayette, Forsyth, Fulton, Gwinnett, Haralson, Heard, Henry, Jasper, Lamar, Meriwether, Morgan, Newton, Paulding, Pickens, Pike, Rockdale, Spalding, and Walton Counties
Previously Atlanta-Sandy Springs-Marietta, GA MSA
Barrow, Bartow, Butts, Carroll, Cherokee, Clayton, Cobb, Coweta, Dawson, DeKalb, Douglas, Fayette, Forsyth, Fulton, Gwinnett, Haralson, Heard, Henry, Jasper, Lamar, Meriwether, Newton, Paulding, Pickens, Pike, Rockdale, Spalding, and Walton Counties

Austin-Round Rock, TX MSA
Previously Austin-Round Rock-San Marcos, TX MSA
Bastrop, Caldwell, Hays, Travis, and Williamson Counties

Baltimore-Columbia-Towson, MD MSA
Previously Baltimore-Towson, MD MSA
Baltimore city; Anne Arundel, Baltimore, Carroll, Harford, Howard, and Queen Anne's Counties

Boise City, ID MSA
Previously Boise City-Nampa, ID MSA
Ada, Boise, Canyon, Gem, and Owyhee Counties

Boston, MA

Boston-Cambridge-Newton, MA-NH MSA
Previously Boston-Cambridge-Quincy, MA-NH MSA
Essex, Middlesex, Norfolk, Plymouth, and Suffolk Counties, MA; Rockingham and Strafford Counties, NH

Boston, MA MD
Previously Boston-Quincy, MA MD
Norfolk, Plymouth, and Suffolk Counties

Boston-Cambridge-Nashua, MA-NH NECTA
Includes 157 cities and towns in Massachusetts and 34 cities and towns in New Hampshire
Previously Boston-Cambridge-Quincy, MA-NH NECTA
Includes 155 cities and towns in Massachusetts and 38 cities and towns in New Hampshire

Boston-Cambridge-Newton, MA NECTA Division
Includes 92 cities and towns in Massachusetts
Previously Boston-Cambridge-Quincy, MA NECTA Division
Includes 97 cities and towns in Massachusetts

Boulder, CO MSA
Boulder County

Brownsville-Harlingen, TX MSA
Cameron County

Cape Coral-Fort Myers, FL MSA
Lee County

Cedar Rapids, IA, MSA
Benton, Jones, and Linn Counties

Charleston-North Charleston, SC MSA
Previously Charleston-North Charleston-Summerville, SC MSA
Berkeley, Charleston, and Dorchester Counties

Charlotte-Concord-Gastonia, NC-SC MSA
Cabarrus, Gaston, Iredell, Lincoln, Mecklenburg, Rowan, and Union Counties, NC; Chester, Lancaster, and York Counties, SC
Previously Charlotte-Gastonia-Rock Hill, NC-SC MSA
Anson, Cabarrus, Gaston, Mecklenburg, and Union Counties, NC; York County, SC

Chicago, IL

Chicago-Naperville-Elgin, IL-IN-WI MSA
Previous name: Chicago-Joliet-Naperville, IL-IN-WI MSA
Cook, DeKalb, DuPage, Grundy, Kane, Kendall, Lake, McHenry, and Will Counties, IL; Jasper, Lake, Newton, and Porter Counties, IN; Kenosha County, WI

Chicago-Naperville-Arlington Heights, IL MD
Cook, DuPage, Grundy, Kendall, McHenry, and Will Counties
Previous name: Chicago-Joliet-Naperville, IL MD
Cook, DeKalb, DuPage, Grundy, Kane, Kendall, McHenry, and Will Counties

Elgin, IL MD
DeKalb and Kane Counties
Previously part of the Chicago-Joliet-Naperville, IL MD

Gary, IN MD
Jasper, Lake, Newton, and Porter Counties

Lake County-Kenosha County, IL-WI MD
Lake County, IL; Kenosha County, WI

Cincinnati, OH-KY-IN MSA
Brown, Butler, Clermont, Hamilton, and Warren Counties, OH; Boone, Bracken, Campbell, Gallatin, Grant, Kenton, and Pendleton County, KY; Dearborn, Franklin, Ohio, and Union Counties, IN
Previously Cincinnati-Middletown, OH-KY-IN MSA
Brown, Butler, Clermont, Hamilton, and Warren Counties, OH; Boone, Bracken, Campbell, Gallatin, Grant, Kenton, and Pendleton County, KY; Dearborn, Franklin, and Ohio Counties, IN

Clarksville, TN-KY MSA
Montgomery and Stewart Counties, TN; Christian and Trigg Counties, KY

Cleveland-Elyria-Mentor, OH MSA
Cuyahoga, Geauga, Lake, Lorain, and Medina Counties

College Station-Bryan, TX MSA
Brazos, Burleson and Robertson Counties

Colorado Springs, CO MSA
El Paso and Teller Counties

Columbia, MO MSA
Boone and Howard Counties

Columbia, SC MSA
Calhoun, Fairfield, Kershaw, Lexington, Richland and Saluda Counties

Columbus, OH MSA
Delaware, Fairfield, Franklin, Licking, Madison, Morrow, Pickaway, and Union Counties

Dallas, TX

Dallas-Fort Worth-Arlington, TX MSA
Collin, Dallas, Denton, Ellis, Hunt, Johnson, Kaufman, Parker, Rockwall, Tarrant, and Wise Counties

Dallas-Plano-Irving, TX MD
Collin, Dallas, Denton, Ellis, Hunt, Kaufman, and Rockwall Counties

Davenport-Moline-Rock Island, IA-IL MSA
Henry, Mercer, and Rock Island Counties, IA; Scott County

Denver-Aurora-Lakewood, CO MSA
Previously Denver-Aurora-Broomfield, CO MSA
Adams, Arapahoe, Broomfield, Clear Creek, Denver, Douglas, Elbert, Gilpin, Jefferson, and Park Counties

Des Moines-West Des Moines, IA MSA
Dallas, Guthrie, Madison, Polk, and Warren Counties

Durham-Chapel Hill, NC MSA
Chatham, Durham, Orange, and Person Counties

Edison, NJ
See New York, NY (New York-Jersey City-White Plains, NY-NJ MD)

El Paso, TX MSA
El Paso County

Fargo, ND-MN MSA
Cass County, ND; Clay County, MN

Fort Collins, CO MSA
Previously Fort Collins-Loveland, CO MSA
Larimer County

Fort Wayne, IN MSA
Allen, Wells, and Whitley Counties

Fort Worth, TX

Dallas-Fort Worth-Arlington, TX MSA
Collin, Dallas, Denton, Ellis, Hunt, Johnson, Kaufman, Parker, Rockwall, Tarrant, and Wise Counties

Fort Worth-Arlington, TX MD
Hood, Johnson, Parker, Somervell, Tarrant, and Wise Counties

Grand Rapids-Wyoming, MI MSA
Barry, Kent, Montcalm, and Ottawa Counties
Previously Grand Rapids-Wyoming, MI MSA
Barry, Ionia, Kent, and Newaygo Counties

Greeley, CO MSA
Weld County

Green Bay, WI MSA
Brown, Kewaunee, and Oconto Counties

Greensboro-High Point, NC MSA
Guilford, Randolph, and Rockingham Counties

Honolulu, HI MSA
Honolulu County

Houston-The Woodlands-Sugar Land-Baytown, TX MSA
Austin, Brazoria, Chambers, Fort Bend, Galveston, Harris, Liberty, Montgomery, and Waller Counties
Previously Houston-Sugar Land-Baytown, TX MSA
Austin, Brazoria, Chambers, Fort Bend, Galveston, Harris, Liberty, Montgomery, San Jacinto, and Waller Counties

Huntsville, AL MSA
Limestone and Madison Counties

Indianapolis-Carmel, IN MSA
Boone, Brown, Hamilton, Hancock, Hendricks, Johnson, Marion, Morgan, Putnam, and Shelby Counties

Jacksonville, FL MSA
Baker, Clay, Duval, Nassau, and St. Johns Counties

Kansas City, MO-KS MSA
Franklin, Johnson, Leavenworth, Linn, Miami, and Wyandotte Counties, KS; Bates, Caldwell, Cass, Clay, Clinton, Jackson, Lafayette, Platte, and Ray Counties, MO

Lafayette, LA MSA
Acadia, Iberia, Lafayette, St. Martin, and Vermilion Parishes

Las Cruces, NM MSA
Doña Ana County
Previously Las Cruces, NM MSA
Doña Ana and San Miguel Counties

Las Vegas-Henderson-Paradise, NV MSA
Previously Las Vegas-Paradise, NV MSA
Clark County

Lexington-Fayette, KY MSA
Bourbon, Clark, Fayette, Jessamine, Scott, and Woodford Counties

Lincoln, NE MSA
Lancaster and Seward Counties

Little Rock-North Little Rock-Conway, AR MSA
Faulkner, Grant, Lonoke, Perry, Pulaski, and Saline Counties

Los Angeles, CA

Los Angeles-Long Beach-Anaheim, CA MSA
Previously Los Angeles-Long Beach-Santa Ana, CA MSA
Los Angeles and Orange Counties

Los Angeles-Long Beach-Glendale, CA MD
Los Angeles County

Anaheim-Santa Ana-Irvine, CA MD
Previously Santa Ana-Anaheim-Irvine, CA MD
Orange County

Louisville/Jefferson, KY-IN MSA
Clark, Floyd, Harrison, Scott, and Washington Counties, IN; Bullitt, Henry, Jefferson, Oldham, Shelby, Spencer, and Trimble Counties, KY

Madison, WI MSA
Columbia, Dane, and Iowa Counties

Manchester, NH

Manchester-Nashua, NH MSA
Hillsborough County

Manchester, NH NECTA
Includes 11 cities and towns in New Hampshire
Previously Manchester, NH NECTA
Includes 9 cities and towns in New Hampshire

Miami, FL

Miami-Fort Lauderdale-West Palm Beach, FL MSA
Previously Miami-Fort Lauderdale-Pompano Beach, FL MSA
Broward, Miami-Dade, and Palm Beach Counties

Miami-Miami Beach-Kendall, FL MD
Miami-Dade County

Midland, TX MSA
Martin, and Midland Counties

Milwaukee-Waukesha-West Allis, WI MSA
Milwaukee, Ozaukee, Washington, and Waukesha Counties

Minneapolis-St. Paul-Bloomington, MN-WI MSA
Anoka, Carver, Chisago, Dakota, Hennepin, Isanti, Le Sueur, Mille
Lacs, Ramsey, Scott, Sherburne, Sibley, Washington, and Wright
Counties, MN; Pierce and St. Croix Counties, WI

Nashville-Davidson-Murfreesboro-Franklin, TN MSA
Cannon, Cheatham, Davidson, Dickson, Hickman, Macon, Robertson,
Rutherford, Smith, Sumner, Trousdale, Williamson, and Wilson Counties

New Haven-Milford, CT MSA
New Haven County

New Orleans-Metarie-Kenner, LA MSA
Jefferson, Orleans, Plaquemines, St. Bernard, St. Charles, St. James,
St. John the Baptist, and St. Tammany Parish
Previously New Orleans-Metarie-Kenner, LA MSA
Jefferson, Orleans, Plaquemines, St. Bernard, St. Charles, St. John the
Baptist, and St. Tammany Parish

New York, NY

New York-Newark-Jersey City, NY-NJ-PA MSA
Bergen, Essex, Hudson, Hunterdon, Middlesex, Monmouth, Morris,
Ocean, Passaic, Somerset, Sussex, and Union Counties, NJ; Bronx,
Dutchess, Kings, Nassau, New York, Orange, Putnam, Queens,
Richmond, Rockland, Suffolk, and Westchester Counties, NY; Pike
County, PA
Previous name: New York-Northern New Jersey-Long Island,
NY-NJ-PA MSA
Bergen, Essex, Hudson, Hunterdon, Middlesex, Monmouth, Morris,
Ocean, Passaic, Somerset, Sussex, and Union Counties, NJ; Bronx,
Kings, Nassau, New York, Putnam, Queens, Richmond, Rockland,
Suffolk, and Westchester Counties, NY; Pike County, PA

Dutchess County-Putnam County, NY MD
Dutchess and Putnam Counties
Dutchess County was previously part of the
Poughkeepsie-Newburgh-Middletown, NY MSA. Putnam County was
previously part of the New York-Wayne-White Plains, NY-NJ MD

Nassau-Suffolk, NY MD
Nassau and Suffolk Counties

New York-Jersey City-White Plains, NY-NJ MD
Bergen, Hudson, Middlesex, Monmouth, Ocean, and Passaic
Counties, NJ; Bronx, Kings, New York, Orange, Queens, Richmond,
Rockland, and Westchester Counties, NY
Previous name: New York-Wayne-White Plains, NY-NJ MD
Bergen, Hudson, and Passaic Counties, NJ; Bronx, Kings, New York,
Putnam, Queens, Richmond, Rockland, and Westchester Counties, NY

Newark, NJ-PA MD
Essex, Hunterdon, Morris, Somerset, Sussex, and Union Counties, NJ;
Pike County, PA
Previous name: Newark-Union, NJ-PA MD
Essex, Hunterdon, Morris, Sussex, and Union Counties, NJ; Pike
County, PA

Oklahoma City, OK MSA
Canadian, Cleveland, Grady, Lincoln, Logan, McClain, and Oklahoma
Counties

Omaha-Council Bluffs, NE-IA MSA
Harrison, Mills, and Pottawattamie Counties, IA; Cass, Douglas,
Sarpy, Saunders, and Washington Counties, NE

Orlando-Kissimmee-Sanford, FL MSA
Lake, Orange, Osceola, and Seminole Counties

Philadelphia, PA

Philadelphia-Camden-Wilmington, PA-NJ-DE-MD MSA
New Castle County, DE; Cecil County, MD; Burlington, Camden,
Gloucester, and Salem Counties, NJ; Bucks, Chester, Delaware,
Montgomery, and Philadelphia Counties, PA

Camden, NJ MD
Burlington, Camden, and Gloucester Counties

Montgomery County-Bucks County-Chester County, PA MD
Bucks, Chester, and Montgomery Counties
Previously part of the Philadelphia, PA MD

Philadelphia, PA MD
Delaware and Philadelphia Counties
Previous name: Philadelphia, PA MD
Bucks, Chester, Delaware, Montgomery, and Philadelphia Counties

Wilmington, DE-MD-NJ MD
New Castle County, DE; Cecil County, MD; Salem County, NJ

Phoenix-Mesa-Scottsdale, AZ MSA
Previously Phoenix-Mesa-Glendale, AZ MSA
Maricopa and Pinal Counties

Pittsburgh, PA MSA
Allegheny, Armstrong, Beaver, Butler, Fayette, Washington, and
Westmoreland Counties

Portland-Vancouver-Hillsboro, OR-WA MSA
Clackamas, Columbia, Multnomah, Washington, and Yamhill
Counties, OR; Clark and Skamania Counties, WA

Providence, RI

Providence-New Bedford-Fall River, RI-MA MSA
Previously Providence-New Bedford-Fall River, RI-MA MSA
Bristol County, MA; Bristol, Kent, Newport, Providence, and
Washington Counties, RI

Providence-Warwick, RI-MA NECTA
Includes 12 cities and towns in Massachusetts and 36 cities and towns
in Rhode Island
Previously Providence-Fall River-Warwick, RI-MA NECTA
Includes 12 cities and towns in Massachusetts and 37 cities and towns
in Rhode Island

Provo-Orem, UT MSA
Juab and Utah Counties

Raleigh, NC MSA
Previously Raleigh-Cary, NC MSA
Franklin, Johnston, and Wake Counties

Reno, NV MSA
Previously Reno-Sparks, NV MSA
Storey and Washoe Counties

Richmond, VA MSA
Amelia, Caroline, Charles City, Chesterfield, Dinwiddie, Goochland, Hanover, Henrico, King William, New Kent, Powhatan, Prince George, and Sussex Counties; Colonial Heights, Hopewell, Petersburg, and Richmond Cities

Rochester, MN MSA
Dodge, Fillmore, Olmsted, and Wabasha Counties

Sacramento—Roseville—Arden-Arcade, CA MSA
El Dorado, Placer, Sacramento, and Yolo Counties

Saint Louis, MO-IL MSA
Bond, Calhoun, Clinton, Jersey, Macoupin, Madison, Monroe, and St. Clair Counties, IL; St. Louis city; Franklin, Jefferson, Lincoln, St. Charles, St. Louis, and Warren Counties, MO
Previously Saint Louis, MO-IL MSA
Bond, Calhoun, Clinton, Jersey, Macoupin, Madison, Monroe, and St. Clair Counties, IL; St. Louis city; Crawford (part), Franklin, Jefferson, Lincoln, St. Charles, St. Louis, Warren, and Washington Counties, MO

Salem, OR MSA
Marion and Polk Counties

Salt Lake City, UT MSA
Salt Lake and Tooele Counties

San Antonio-New Braunfels, TX MSA
Atascosa, Bandera, Bexar, Comal, Guadalupe, Kendall, Medina, and Wilson Counties

San Diego-Carlsbad, CA MSA
Previously San Diego-Carlsbad-San Marcos, CA MSA
San Diego County

San Francisco, CA

San Francisco-Oakland-Hayward, CA MSA
Previously San Francisco-Oakland- Fremont, CA MSA
Alameda, Contra Costa, Marin, San Francisco, and San Mateo Counties

San Francisco-Redwood City-South San Francisco, CA MD
San Francisco and San Mateo Counties

Previously San Francisco-San Mateo-Redwood City, CA MD
Marin, San Francisco, and San Mateo Counties

San Jose-Sunnyvale-Santa Clara, CA MSA
San Benito and Santa Clara Counties

Santa Rosa, CA MSA
Previously Santa Rosa-Petaluma, CA MSA
Sonoma County

Savannah, GA MSA
Bryan, Chatham, and Effingham Counties

Seattle, WA

Seattle-Tacoma-Bellevue, WA MSA
King, Pierce, and Snohomish Counties

Seattle-Bellevue-Everett, WA MD
King and Snohomish Counties

Sioux Falls, SD MSA
Lincoln, McCook, Minnehaha, and Turner Counties

Springfield, IL MSA
Menard and Sangamon Counties

Tampa-St. Petersburg-Clearwater, FL MSA
Hernando, Hillsborough, Pasco, and Pinellas Counties

Tucson, AZ MSA
Pima County

Tulsa, OK MSA
Creek, Okmulgee, Osage, Pawnee, Rogers, Tulsa, and Wagoner Counties

Tuscaloosa, AL MSA
Hale, Pickens, and Tuscaloosa Counties

Virginia Beach-Norfolk-Newport News, VA-NC MSA
Currituck County, NC; Chesapeake, Hampton, Newport News, Norfolk, Poquoson, Portsmouth, Suffolk, Virginia Beach and Williamsburg cities, VA; Gloucester, Isle of Wight, James City, Mathews, Surry, and York Counties, VA

Washington, DC

Washington-Arlington-Alexandria, DC-VA-MD-WV MSA
District of Columbia; Calvert, Charles, Frederick, Montgomery, and Prince George's Counties, MD; Alexandria, Fairfax, Falls Church, Fredericksburg, Manassas Park, and Manassas cities, VA; Arlington, Clarke, Culpepper, Fairfax, Fauquier, Loudoun, Prince William, Rappahannock, Spotsylvania, Stafford, and Warren Counties, VA; Jefferson County, WV
Previously Washington-Arlington-Alexandria, DC-VA-MD-WV MSA
District of Columbia; Calvert, Charles, Frederick, Montgomery, and Prince George's Counties, MD; Alexandria, Fairfax, Falls Church, Fredericksburg, Manassas Park, and Manassas cities, VA; Arlington, Clarke, Fairfax, Fauquier, Loudoun, Prince William, Spotsylvania, Stafford, and Warren Counties, VA; Jefferson County, WV

Washington-Arlington-Alexandria, DC-VA-MD-WV MD
District of Columbia; Calvert, Charles, and Prince George's Counties, MD; Alexandria, Fairfax, Falls Church, Fredericksburg, Manassas Park, and Manassas cities, VA; Arlington, Clarke, Culpepper, Fairfax, Fauquier, Loudoun, Prince William, Rappahannock, Spotsylvania, Stafford, and Warren Counties, VA; Jefferson County, WV
Previously Washington-Arlington-Alexandria, DC-VA-MD-WV MD
District of Columbia; Calvert, Charles, and Prince George's Counties, MD; Alexandria, Fairfax, Falls Church, Fredericksburg, Manassas Park, and Manassas cities, VA; Arlington, Clarke, Fairfax, Fauquier, Loudoun, Prince William, Spotsylvania, Stafford, and Warren Counties, VA; Jefferson County, WV

Wichita, KS MSA
Butler, Harvey, Kingman, Sedgwick, and Sumner Counties

Wilmington, NC MSA
New Hanover and Pender Counties
Previously Wilmington, NC MSA
Brunswick, New Hanover and Pender Counties

Winston-Salem, NC MSA
Davidson, Davie, Forsyth, Stokes, and Yadkin Counties

Worcester, MA

Worcester, MA-CT MSA
Windham County, CT; Worcester County, MA
Previously Worcester, MA MSA
Worcester County

Worcester, MA-CT NECTA
Includes 40 cities and towns in Massachusetts and 8 cities and towns in Connecticut
Previously Worcester, MA-CT NECTA
Includes 37 cities and towns in Massachusetts and 3 cities and towns in Connecticut

Appendix C: Government Type and Primary County

This appendix includes the government structure of each place included in this book. It also includes the county or county equivalent in which each place is located. If a place spans more than one county, the county in which the majority of the population resides is shown.

Albuquerque, NM
Government Type: City
County: Bernalillo

Allentown, PA
Government Type: City
County: Lehigh

Anchorage, AK
Government Type: Municipality
Borough: Anchorage

Ann Arbor, MI
Government Type: City
County: Washtenaw

Athens, GA
Government Type: Consolidated
   city-county
County: Clarke

Atlanta, GA
Government Type: City
County: Fulton

Austin, TX
Government Type: City
County: Travis

Baltimore, MD
Government Type: Independent city

Baton Rouge, LA
Government Type: Consolidated city-parish
Parish: East Baton Rouge

Boise City, ID
Government Type: City
County: Ada

Boston, MA
Government Type: City
County: Suffolk

Boulder, CO
Government Type: City
County: Boulder

Brownsville, TX
Government Type: City
County: Cameron

Cape Coral, FL
Government Type: City
County: Lee

Cedar Rapids, IA
Government Type: City
County: Linn

Charleston, SC
Government Type: City
County: Charleston

Charlotte, NC
Government Type: City
County: Mecklenburg

Chicago, IL
Government Type: City
County: Cook

Cincinnati, OH
Government Type: City
County: Hamilton

Clarksville, TN
Government Type: City
County: Montgomery

Cleveland, OH
Government Type: City
County: Cuyahoga

College Station, TX
Government Type: City
County: Brazos

Colorado Springs, CO
Government Type: City
County: El Paso

Columbia, MO
Government Type: City
County: Boone

Columbia, SC
Government Type: City
County: Richland

Columbus, OH
Government Type: City
County: Franklin

Dallas, TX
Government Type: City
County: Dallas

Davenport, IA
Government Type: City
County: Scott

Denver, CO
Government Type: City
County: Denver

Des Moines, IA
Government Type: City
County: Polk

Durham, NC
Government Type: City
County: Durham

Edison, NJ
Government Type: Township
County: Middlesex

El Paso, TX
Government Type: City
County: El Paso

Fargo, ND
Government Type: City
County: Cass

Fort Collins, CO
Government Type: City
County: Larimer

Fort Wayne, IN
Government Type: City
County: Allen

Fort Worth, TX
Government Type: City
County: Tarrant

Grand Rapids, MI
Government Type: City
County: Kent

Greeley, CO
Government Type: City
County: Weld

Green Bay, WI
Government Type: City
County: Brown

Greensboro, NC
Government Type: City
County: Guilford

Honolulu, HI
Government Type: Census Designated Place (CDP)
County: Honolulu

Houston, TX
Government Type: City
County: Harris

Huntsville, AL
Government Type: City
County: Madison

Indianapolis, IN
Government Type: City
County: Marion

Jacksonville, FL
Government Type: City
County: Duval

Kansas City, MO
Government Type: City
County: Jackson

Lafayette, LA
Government Type: City
Parish: Lafayette

Las Cruces, NM
Government Type: City
County: Doña Ana

Las Vegas, NV
Government Type: City
County: Clark

Lexington, KY
Government Type: Consolidated city-county
County: Fayette

Lincoln, NE
Government Type: City
County: Lancaster

Little Rock, AR
Government Type: City
County: Pulaski

Los Angeles, CA
Government Type: City
County: Los Angeles

Louisville, KY
Government Type: Consolidated city-county
County: Jefferson

Madison, WI
Government Type: City
County: Dane

Manchester, NH
Government Type: City
County: Hillsborough

Memphis, TN
Government Type: City
County: Shelby

Miami, FL
Government Type: City
County: Miami-Dade

Midland, TX
Government Type: City
County: Midland

Milwaukee, WI
Government Type: City
County: Milwaukee

Minneapolis, MN
Government Type: City
County: Hennepin

Nashville, TN
Government Type: Consolidated city-county
County: Davidson

New Haven, CT
Government Type: City
County: New Haven

New Orleans, LA
Government Type: City
Parish: Orleans

New York, NY
Government Type: City
Counties: Bronx; Kings; New York; Queens;
    Staten Island

Oklahoma City, OK
Government Type: City
County: Oklahoma

Omaha, NE
Government Type: City
County: Douglas

Orlando, FL
Government Type: City
County: Orange

Philadelphia, PA
Government Type: City
County: Philadelphia

Phoenix, AZ
Government Type: City
County: Maricopa

Pittsburgh, PA
Government Type: City
County: Allegheny

Portland, OR
Government Type: City
County: Multnomah

Providence, RI
Government Type: City
County: Providence

Provo, UT
Government Type: City
County: Utah

Raleigh, NC
Government Type: City
County: Wake

Reno, NV
Government Type: City
County: Washoe

Richmond, VA
Government Type: Independent city

Riverside, CA
Government Type: City
County: Riverside

Rochester, MN
Government Type: City
County: Olmsted

Rochester, NY
Government Type: City
County: Monroe

Sacramento, CA
Government Type: City
County: Sacramento

Saint Louis, MO
Government Type: Independent city

Salem, OR
Government Type: City
County: Marion

Salt Lake City, UT
Government Type: City
County: Salt Lake

San Antonio, TX
Government Type: City
County: Bexar

San Diego, CA
Government Type: City
County: San Diego

San Francisco, CA
Government Type: City
County: San Francisco

San Jose, CA
Government Type: City
County: Santa Clara

Santa Rosa, CA
Government Type: City
County: Sonoma

Savannah, GA
Government Type: City
County: Chatham

Seattle, WA
Government Type: City
County: King

Sioux Falls, SD
Government Type: City
County: Minnehaha

Springfield, IL
Government Type: City
County: Sangamon

Tampa, FL
Government Type: City
County: Hillsborough

Tucson, AZ
Government Type: City
County: Pima

Tulsa, OK
Government Type: City
County: Tulsa

Tuscaloosa, AL
Government Type: City
County: Tuscaloosa

Virginia Beach, VA
Government Type: Independent city

Washington, DC
Government Type: City
County: District of Columbia

Wichita, KS
Government Type: City
County: Sedgwick

Wilmington, NC
Government Type: City
County: New Hanover

Winston-Salem, NC
Government Type: City
County: Forsyth

Worcester, MA
Government Type: City
County: Worcester

Appendix D: Chambers of Commerce

Albuquerque, NM
Albuquerque Chamber of Commerce
P.O. Box 25100
Albuquerque, NM 87125
Phone: (505) 764-3700
Fax: (505) 764-3714
www.abqchamber.com

Albuquerque Economic Development Dept
851 University Blvd SE, Suite 203
Albuquerque, NM 87106
Phone: (505) 246-6200
Fax: (505) 246-6219
www.cabq.gov/econdev

Allentown, PA
Greater Lehigh Valley Chamber of
Commerce
Allentown Office
840 Hamilton Street, Suite 205
Allentown, PA 18101
Phone: (610) 751-4929
Fax: (610) 437-4907
www.lehighvalleychamber.org

Anchorage, AK
Anchorage Chamber of Commerce
1016 W Sixth Avenue
Suite 303
Anchorage, AK 99501
Phone: (907) 272-2401
Fax: (907) 272-4117
www.anchoragechamber.org

Anchorage Economic Development
Department
900 W 5th Avenue
Suite 300
Anchorage, AK 99501
Phone: (907) 258-3700
Fax: (907) 258-6646
aedcweb.com

Ann Arbor, MI
Ann Arbor Area Chamber of Commerce
115 West Huron
3rd Floor
Ann Arbor, MI 48104
Phone: (734) 665-4433
Fax: (734) 665-4191
www.annarborchamber.org

Ann Arbor Economic Development
Department
201 S Division
Suite 430
Ann Arbor, MI 48104
Phone: (734) 761-9317
www.annarborspark.org

Athens, GA
Athens Area Chamber of Commerce
246 W Hancock Avenue
Athens, GA 30601
Phone: (706) 549-6800
Fax: (706) 549-5636
www.aacoc.org

Athens-Clarke County Economic
Development Department
246 W. Hancock Avenue
Athens, GA 30601
Phone: (706) 613-3233
Fax: (706) 613-3812
www.athensbusiness.org

Atlanta, GA
Metro Atlanta Chamber of Commerce
235 Andrew Young International Blvd NW
Atlanta, GA 30303
Phone: (404) 880-9000
Fax: (404) 586-8464
www.metroatlantachamber.com

Austin, TX
Greater Austin Chamber of Commerce
210 Barton Springs Road
Suite 400
Austin, TX 78704
Phone: (512) 478-9383
Fax: (512) 478-6389
www.austin-chamber.org

Baltimore, MD
Baltimore City Chamber of Commerce
P.O. Box 43121
Baltimore, MD 21236
443-860-2020
baltimorecitychamber.org

Baltimore County Chamber of Commerce
102 W. Pennsylvania Avenue
Suite 305
Towson, MD, 21204
Phone: (410) 825-6200
Fax: (410) 821-9901
www.baltcountychamber.com

Boise City, ID
Boise Metro Chamber of Commerce
250 S 5th Street
Suite 800
Boise City, ID 83701
Phone: (208) 472-5200
Fax: (208) 472-5201
www.boisechamber.org

Boston, MA
Greater Boston Chamber of Commerce
265 Franklin Street
12th Floor
Boston, MA 02110
Phone: (617) 227-4500
Fax: (617) 227-7505
www.bostonchamber.com

Boulder, CO
Boulder Chamber of Commerce
2440 Pearl Street
Boulder, CO 80302
Phone: (303) 442-1044
Fax: (303) 938-8837
www.boulderchamber.com

City of Boulder Economic Vitality Program
P.O. Box 791
Boulder, CO 80306
Phone: (303) 441-3090
www.bouldercolorado.gov

Brownsville, TX
Brownsville Chamber of Commerce
1600 University Blvd.
Brownsville, TX 78520
Phone: (956) 542-4341
brownsvillechamber.com

Cape Coral, FL
Chamber of Commerce of Cape Coral
2051 Cape Coral Parkway East
Cape Coral, FL 33904
Phone: (239) 549-6900
Fax: (239) 549-9609
www.capecoralchamber.com

Cedar Rapids, IA
Cedar Rapids Chamber of Commerce
424 First Avenue NE
Cedar Rapids, IA 52401
Phone: (319) 398-5317
Fax: (319) 398-5228
www.cedarrapids.org

Cedar Rapids Economic Development
50 Second Avenue Bridge, Sixth Floor
Cedar Rapids, IA 52401-1256
Phone: (319) 286-5041
Fax: (319) 286-5141
www.cedar-rapids.org

Charleston, SC
Charleston Metro Chamber of Commerce
P.O. Box 975
Charleston, SC 29402
Phone: (843) 577-2510
www.charlestonchamber.net

Charlotte, NC
Charlotte Chamber of Commerce
330 S Tryon Street
P.O. Box 32785
Charlotte, NC 28232
Phone: (704) 378-1300
Fax: (704) 374-1903
www.charlottechamber.com

Charlotte Regional Partnership
1001 Morehead Square Drive, Suite 200
Charlotte, NC 28203
Phone: (704) 347-8942
Fax: (704) 347-8981
www.charlotteusa.com

Chicago, IL
Chicagoland Chamber of Commerce
200 E Randolph Street
Suite 2200
Chicago, IL 60601-6436
Phone: (312) 494-6700
Fax: (312) 861-0660
www.chicagolandchamber.org

City of Chicago Department of Planning
and Development
City Hall, Room 1000
121 North La Salle Street
Chicago, IL 60602
Phone: (312) 744-4190
Fax: (312) 744-2271
www.cityofchicago.org/city/en/depts/dcd.html

Cincinnati, OH
Cincinnati USA Regional Chamber
3 East 4th Street, Suite 200
Cincinnati, Ohio 45202
Phone: (513) 579-3111
www.cincinnatichamber.com

Clarksville, TN
Clarksville Area Chamber of Commerce
25 Jefferson Street, Suite 300
Clarksville, TN 37040
Phone: (931) 647-2331
www.clarksvillechamber.com

Cleveland, OH
Greater Cleveland Partnership
1240 Huron Rd. E, Suite 300
Cleveland, OH 44115
Phone: (216) 621-3300
www.gcpartnership.com

College Station, TX
Bryan-College Station Chamber of
Commerce
4001 East 29th St, Suite 175
Bryan, TX 77802
Phone: (979) 260-5200
www.bcschamber.org

Colorado Springs, CO
Colorado Springs Chamber and EDC
102 South Tejon Street
Suite 430
Colorado Springs, CO 80903
Phone: (719) 471-8183
coloradospringschamberedc.com

Columbia, MO
Columbia Chamber of Commerce
300 South Providence Rd.
P.O. Box 1016
Columbia, MO 65205-1016
Phone: (573) 874-1132
Fax: (573) 443-3986
www.columbiamochamber.com

Columbia, SC
The Columbia Chamber
930 Richland Street
Columbia, SC 29201
Phone: (803) 733-1110
Fax: (803) 733-1113
www.columbiachamber.com

Columbus, OH
Greater Columbus Chamber
37 North High Street
Columbus, OH 43215
Phone: (614) 221-1321
Fax: (614) 221-1408
www.columbus.org

Dallas, TX
City of Dallas Economic Development
Department
1500 Marilla Street
5C South
Dallas, TX 75201
Phone: (214) 670-1685
Fax: (214) 670-0158
www.dallas-edd.org

Greater Dallas Chamber of Commerce
700 North Pearl Street
Suite1200
Dallas, TX 75201
Phone: (214) 746-6600
Fax: (214) 746-6799
www.dallaschamber.org

Davenport, IA
Quad Cities Chamber
331 W. 3rd Street
Suite 100
Davenport, IA 52801
Phone: (563) 322-1706
quadcitieschamber.com

Denver, CO
Denver Metro Chamber of Commerce
1445 Market Street
Denver, CO 80202
Phone: (303) 534-8500
Fax: (303) 534-3200
www.denverchamber.org

Downtown Denver Partnership
511 16th Street
Suite 200
Denver, CO 80202
Phone: (303) 534-6161
Fax: (303) 534-2803
www.downtowndenver.com

Des Moines, IA
Des Moines Downtown Chamber
301 Grand Ave
Des Moines, IA 50309
Phone: (515) 309-3229
desmoinesdowntownchamber.com

Greater Des Moines Partnership
700 Locust Street
Suite 100
Des Moines, IA 50309
Phone: (515) 286-4950
Fax: (515) 286-4974
www.desmoinesmetro.com

Durham, NC
Durham Chamber of Commerce
P.O. Box 3829
Durham, NC 27702
Phone: (919) 682-2133
Fax: (919) 688-8351
www.durhamchamber.org

North Carolina Institute of Minority
Economic Development
114 W Parish Street
Durham, NC 27701
Phone: (919) 956-8889
Fax: (919) 688-7668
www.ncimed.com

Edison, NJ
Edison Chamber of Commerce
939 Amboy Avenue
Edison, NJ 08837
Phone: (732) 738-9482
www.edisonchamber.com

El Paso, TX
City of El Paso Department of Economic
Development
2 Civic Center Plaza
El Paso, TX 79901
Phone: (915) 541-4000
Fax: (915) 541-1316
www.elpasotexas.gov

Greater El Paso Chamber of Commerce
10 Civic Center Plaza
El Paso, TX 79901
Phone: (915) 534-0500
Fax: (915) 534-0510
www.elpaso.org

Fargo, ND
Chamber of Commerce of Fargo Moorhead
202 First Avenue North
Fargo, ND 56560
Phone: (218) 233-1100
Fax: (218) 233-1200
www.fmchamber.com

Greater Fargo-Moorhead Economic
Development Corporation
51 Broadway, Suite 500
Fargo, ND 58102
Phone: (701) 364-1900
Fax: (701) 293-7819
www.gfmedc.com

Fort Collins, CO
Fort Collins Chamber of Commerce
225 South Meldrum
Fort Collins, CO 80521
Phone: (970) 482-3746
Fax: (970) 482-3774
fortcollinschamber.com

Fort Wayne, IN
City of Fort Wayne Economic Development
1 Main St
1 Main Street
Fort Wayne, IN 46802
Phone: (260) 427-1111
Fax: (260) 427-1375
www.cityoffortwayne.org

Greater Fort Wayne Chamber of Commerce
826 Ewing Street
Fort Wayne, IN 46802
Phone: (260) 424-1435
Fax: (260) 426-7232
www.fwchamber.org

Fort Worth, TX
City of Fort Worth Economic Development
City Hall
900 Monroe Street
Suite 301
Fort Worth, TX 76102
Phone: (817) 392-6103
Fax: (817) 392-2431
www.fortworthgov.org

Fort Worth Chamber of Commerce
777 Taylor Street, Suite 900
Fort Worth, TX 76102-4997
Phone: (817) 336-2491
Fax: (817) 877-4034
www.fortworthchamber.com

Grand Rapids, MI
Grands Rapids Area Chamber of Commerce
111 Pearl Street N.W.
Grand Rapids, MI 49503
Phone: (616) 771-0300
Fax: (616) 771-0318
www.grandrapids.org

Greeley, CO
Greeley Area Chamber of Commerce
902 7th Avenue
Greeley, CO 80631
Phone: (970) 352-3566
www.greeleychamber.com

Green Bay, WI
Economic Development
100 N Jefferson Street
Room 202
Green Bay, WI 54301
Phone: (920) 448-3397
Fax: (920) 448-3063
www.ci.green-bay.wi.us

Green Bay Area Chamber of Commerce
300 N. Broadway
Suite 3A
Green Bay, WI 54305-1660
Phone: (920) 437-8704
Fax: (920) 593-3468
www.titletown.org

Greensboro, NC
Greensboro Chamber of Commerce
111 W. February One Place
Greensboro, NC 27401
Phone: (336) 387-8301
greensboro.org

Honolulu, HI
The Chamber of Commerce of Hawaii
1132 Bishop Street
Suite 402
Honolulu, HI 96813
Phone: (808) 545-4300
Fax: (808) 545-4369
www.cochawaii.com

Houston, TX
Greater Houston Partnership
1200 Smith Street, Suite 700
Houston, TX 77002-4400
Phone: (713) 844-3600
Fax: (713) 844-0200
www.houston.org

Huntsville, AL
Chamber of Commerce of
Huntsville/Madison County
225 Church Street
Huntsville, AL 35801
Phone: (256) 535-2000
Fax: (256) 535-2015
www.huntsvillealabamausa.com

Indianapolis, IN
Greater Indianapolis Chamber of Commerce
111 Monument Circle, Suite 1950
Indianapolis, IN 46204
Phone: (317) 464-2222
Fax: (317) 464-2217
www.indychamber.com

The Indy Partnership
111 Monument Circle, Suite 1800
Indianapolis, IN 46204
Phone: (317) 236-6262
Fax: (317) 236-6275
indypartnership.com

Jacksonville, FL
Jacksonville Chamber of Commerce
3 Independent Drive
Jacksonville, FL 32202
Phone: (904) 366-6600
Fax: (904) 632-0617
www.myjaxchamber.com

Kansas City, MO
Greater Kansas City Chamber of Commerce
2600 Commerce Tower
911 Main Street
Kansas City, MO 64105
Phone: (816) 221-2424
Fax: (816) 221-7440
www.kcchamber.com

Kansas City Area Development Council
2600 Commerce Tower
911 Main Street
Kansas City, MO 64105
Phone: (816) 221-2121
Fax: (816) 842-2865
www.thinkkc.com

Lafayette, LA
Greater Lafayette Chamber of Commerce
804 East Saint Mary Blvd.
Lafayette, LA 70503
Phone: (337) 233-2705
Fax: (337) 234-8671
www.lafchamber.org

Las Cruces, NM
Greater Las Cruces Chamber of Commerce
505 S Main Street, Suite 134
Las Cruces, NM 88001
Phone: (575) 524-1968
Fax: (575) 527-5546
www.lascruces.org

Las Vegas, NV
Las Vegas Chamber of Commerce
6671 Las Vegas Blvd South
Suite 300
Las Vegas, NV 89119
Phone: (702) 735-1616
Fax: (702) 735-0406
www.lvchamber.org

Las Vegas Office of Business Development
400 Stewart Avenue
City Hall
Las Vegas, NV 89101
Phone: (702) 229-6011
Fax: (702) 385-3128
www.lasvegasnevada.gov

Lexington, KY
Greater Lexington Chamber of Commerce
330 East Main Street
Suite 100
Lexington, KY 40507
Phone: (859) 254-4447
Fax: (859) 233-3304
www.commercelexington.com

Lexington Downtown Development
Authority
101 East Vine Street
Suite 500
Lexington, KY 40507
Phone: (859) 425-2296
Fax: (859) 425-2292
www.lexingtondda.com

Lincoln, NE
Lincoln Chamber of Commerce
1135 M Street
Suite 200
Lincoln, NE 68508
Phone: (402) 436-2350
Fax: (402) 436-2360
www.lcoc.com

Little Rock, AR
Little Rock Regional Chamber
One Chamber Plaza
Little Rock, AR 72201
Phone: (501) 374-2001
Fax: (501) 374-6018
www.littlerockchamber.com

Los Angeles, CA
Los Angeles Area Chamber of Commerce
350 South Bixel Street
Los Angeles, CA 90017
Phone: (213) 580-7500
Fax: (213) 580-7511
www.lachamber.org

Los Angeles County Economic
Development Corporation
444 South Flower Street
34th Floor
Los Angeles, CA 90071
Phone: (213) 622-4300
Fax: (213) 622-7100
www.laedc.org

Louisville, KY
The Greater Louisville Chamber of
Commerce
614 West Main Street
Suite 6000
Louisville, KY 40202
Phone: (502) 625-0000
Fax: (502) 625-0010
www.greaterlouisville.com

Madison, WI
Greater Madison Chamber of Commerce
615 East Washington Avenue
P.O. Box 71
Madison, WI 53701-0071
Phone: (608) 256-8348
Fax: (608) 256-0333
www.greatermadisonchamber.com

Manchester, NH

Greater Manchester Chamber of Commerce
889 Elm Street
Manchester, NH 03101
Phone: (603) 666-6600
Fax: (603) 626-0910
www.manchester-chamber.org

Manchester Economic Development Office
One City Hall Plaza
Manchester, NH 03101
Phone: (603) 624-6505
Fax: (603) 624-6308
www.yourmanchesternh.com

Miami, FL

Greater Miami Chamber of Commerce
1601 Biscayne Boulevard
Miami, FL 33132-1260
Phone: (305) 350-7700
Fax: (305) 374-6902
www.miamichamber.com

The Beacon Council
80 Southwest 8th Street, Suite 2400
Miami, FL 33130
Phone: (305) 579-1300
Fax: (305) 375-0271
www.beaconcouncil.com

Midland, TX

Midland Chamber of Commerce
109 N. Main
Midland, TX 79701
Phone: (432) 683-3381
Fax: (432) 686-3556
www.midlandtxchamber.com

Milwaukee, WI

Greater Milwaukee Chamber of Commerce
6815 W. Capitol Drive
Suite 300
Milwaukee, WI 53216
Phone: (414) 465-2422
www.gmcofc.org

Metropolitan Milwaukee Association of
Commerce
756 N. Milwaukee Street
Suite 400
Milwaukee, WI 53202
Phone: (414) 287-4100
Fax: (414) 271-7753
www.mmac.org

Minneapolis, MN

Minneapolis Regional Chamber
81 South Ninth Street, Suite 200
Minneapolis, MN 55402
Phone: (612) 370-9100
Fax: (612) 370-9195
www.minneapolischamber.org

Minneapolis Community Development
Agency
Crown Roller Mill
105 5th Avenue South
Suite 200
Minneapolis, MN 55401
Phone: (612) 673-5095
Fax: (612) 673-5100
www.ci.minneapolis.mn.us

Nashville, TN

Nashville Area Chamber of Commerce
211 Commerce Street, Suite 100
Nashville, TN 37201
Phone: (615) 743-3000
Fax: (615) 256-3074
www.nashvillechamber.com

Tennessee Valley Authority Economic
Development
400 West Summit Hill Drive
Knoxville TN 37902
Phone: (865) 632-2101
www.tvaed.com

New Haven, CT

Greater New Haven Chamber of Commerce
900 Chapel Street, 10th Floor
New Haven, CT 06510
Phone: (203) 787-6735
www.gnhcc.com

New Orleans, LA

New Orleans Chamber of Commerce
1515 Poydras Street
Suite 1010
New Orleans, LA 70112
Phone: (504) 799-4260
Fax: (504) 799-4259
www.neworleanschamber.org

New York, NY

New York City Economic Development
Corporation
110 William Street
New York, NY 10038
Phone: (212) 619-5000
www.nycedc.com

The Partnership for New York City
One Battery Park Plaza
5th Floor
New York, NY 10004
Phone: (212) 493-7400
Fax: (212) 344-3344
www.pfnyc.org

Oklahoma City, OK

Greater Oklahoma City Chamber of
Commerce
123 Park Avenue
Oklahoma City, OK 73102
Phone: (405) 297-8900
Fax: (405) 297-8916
www.okcchamber.com

Omaha, NE

Omaha Chamber of Commerce
1301 Harney Street
Omaha, NE 68102
Phone: (402) 346-5000
Fax: (402) 346-7050
www.omahachamber.org

Orlando, FL

Metro Orlando Economic Development
Commission of Mid-Florida
301 East Pine Street, Suite 900
Orlando, FL 32801
Phone: (407) 422-7159
Fax: (407) 425.6428
www.orlandoedc.com

Orlando Regional Chamber of Commerce
75 South Ivanhoe Boulevard
P.O. Box 1234
Orlando, FL 32802
Phone: (407) 425-1234
Fax: (407) 839-5020
www.orlando.org

Philadelphia, PA

Greater Philadelphia Chamber of
Commerce
200 South Broad Street
Suite 700
Philadelphia, PA 19102
Phone: (215) 545-1234
Fax: (215) 790-3600
www.greaterphilachamber.com

Phoenix, AZ

Greater Phoenix Chamber of Commerce
201 North Central Avenue
27th Floor
Phoenix, AZ 85073
Phone: (602) 495-2195
Fax: (602) 495-8913
www.phoenixchamber.com

Greater Phoenix Economic Council
2 North Central Avenue
Suite 2500
Phoenix, AZ 85004
Phone: (602) 256-7700
Fax: (602) 256-7744
www.gpec.org

Pittsburgh, PA

Allegheny County Industrial Development
Authority
425 6th Avenue
Suite 800
Pittsburgh, PA 15219
Phone: (412) 350-1067
Fax: (412) 642-2217
www.alleghenycounty.us

Greater Pittsburgh Chamber of Commerce
425 6th Avenue
12th Floor
Pittsburgh, PA 15219
Phone: (412) 392-4500
Fax: (412) 392-4520
www.alleghenyconference.org

Portland, OR

Portland Business Alliance
200 SW Market Street
Suite 1770
Portland, OR 97201
Phone: (503) 224-8684
Fax: (503) 323-9186
www.portlandalliance.com

Providence, RI

Greater Providence Chamber of Commerce
30 Exchange Terrace
Fourth Floor
Providence, RI 02903
Phone: (401) 521-5000
Fax: (401) 351-2090
www.provchamber.com

Rhode Island Economic Development
Corporation
Providence City Hall
25 Dorrance Street
Providence, RI 02903
Phone: (401) 421-7740
Fax: (401) 751-0203
www.providenceri.com

Provo, UT
Provo-Orem Chamber of Commerce
51 South University Avenue, Suite 215
Provo, UT 84601
Phone: (801) 851-2555
Fax: (801) 851-2557
www.thechamber.org

Raleigh, NC
Greater Raleigh Chamber of Commerce
800 South Salisbury Street
Raleigh, NC 27601-2978
Phone: (919) 664-7000
Fax: (919) 664-7099
www.raleighchamber.org

Reno, NV
Greater Reno-Sparks Chamber of Commerce
1 East First Street, 16th Floor
Reno, NV 89505
Phone: (775) 337-3030
Fax: (775) 337-3038
www.reno-sparkschamber.org

The Chamber Reno-Sparks-Northern Nevada
449 S. Virginia Street, 2nd Floor
Reno, NV 89501
Phone: (775) 636-9550
www.thechambernv.org

Richmond, VA
Greater Richmond Chamber
600 East Main Street
Suite 700
Richmond, VA 23219
Phone: (804) 648-1234
www.grcc.com

Greater Richmond Partnership
901 East Byrd Street
Suite 801
Richmond, VA 23219-4070
Phone: (804) 643-3227
Fax: (804) 343-7167
www.grpva.com

Rochester, MN
Rochester Area Chamber of Commerce
220 South Broadway
Suite 100
Rochester, MN 55904
Phone: (507) 288-1122
Fax: (507) 282-8960
www.rochestermnchamber.com

Sacramento, CA
Sacramento Metro Chamber
One Capitol Mall
Suite 700
Sacramento, CA 95814
Phone: (916) 552-6800
metrochamber.org

Saint Louis, MO
St. Louis Regional Chamber
One Metropolitan Square, Suite 1300
St. Louis, MO 63102
Phone: (314) 231-5555
www.stlregionalchamber.com

Salem, OR
Salem Chamber
1110 Commercial Street NE
Salem, OR 97301
Phone: (503) 581-1466
salemchamber.org

Salt Lake City, UT
Salt Lake Chamber
175 E. University Blvd. (400 S), Suite 600
Salt Lake City, UT 84111
Phone: (801) 364-3631
www.slchamber.com

San Antonio, TX
The Greater San Antonio Chamber of
Commerce
602 E. Commerce Street
San Antonio, TX 78205
Phone: (210) 229-2100
Fax: (210) 229-1600
www.sachamber.org

San Antonio Economic Development
Department
P.O. Box 839966
San Antonio, TX 78283-3966
Phone: (210) 207-8080
Fax: (210) 207-8151
www.sanantonio.gov/edd

San Diego, CA
San Diego Economic Development Corp.
401 B Street
Suite 1100
San Diego, CA 92101
Phone: (619) 234-8484
Fax: (619) 234-1935
www.sandiegobusiness.org

San Diego Regional Chamber of Commerce
402 West Broadway
Suite 1000
San Diego, CA 92101-3585
Phone: (619) 544-1300
Fax: (619) 744-7481
www.sdchamber.org

San Francisco, CA
San Francisco Chamber of Commerce
235 Montgomery Street
12th Floor
San Francisco, CA 94104
Phone: (415) 392-4520
Fax: (415) 392-0485
www.sfchamber.com

San Jose, CA
Office of Economic Development
60 South Market Street
Suite 470
San Jose, CA 95113
Phone: (408) 277-5880
Fax: (408) 277-3615
www.sba.gov

The Silicon Valley Organization
101 W Santa Clara Street
San Jose, CA 95113
Phone: (408) 291-5250
www.thesvo.com

Santa Rosa, CA
Santa Rosa Chamber of Commerce
1260 North Dutton Avenue
Suite 272
Santa Rosa, CA 95401
Phone: (707) 545-1414
www.santarosachamber.com

Savannah, GA
Economic Development Authority
131 Hutchinson Island Road
4th Floor
Savannah, GA 31421
Phone: (912) 447-8450
Fax: (912) 447-8455
www.seda.org

Savannah Chamber of Commerce
101 E. Bay Street
Savannah, GA 31402
Phone: (912) 644-6400
Fax: (912) 644-6499
www.savannahchamber.com

Seattle, WA
Greater Seattle Chamber of Commerce
1301 Fifth Avenue
Suite 2500
Seattle, WA 98101
Phone: (206) 389-7200
Fax: (206) 389-7288
www.seattlechamber.com

Sioux Falls, SD
Sioux Falls Area Chamber of Commerce
200 N. Phillips Avenue
Suite 102
Sioux Falls, SD 57104
Phone: (605) 336-1620
Fax: (605) 336-6499
www.siouxfallschamber.com

Springfield, IL
The Greater Springfield Chamber of
Commerce
1011 S. Second Street
Springfield, IL 62704
Phone: (217) 525-1173
Fax: (217) 525-8768
www.gscc.org

Tampa, FL
Greater Tampa Chamber of Commerce
P.O. Box 420
Tampa, FL 33601-0420
Phone: (813) 276-9401
Fax: (813) 229-7855
www.tampachamber.com

Tucson, AZ
Tucson Metro Chamber
212 E. Broadway Blvd
Tucson, AZ 85701
Phone: (520) 792-1212
tucsonchamber.org

Tulsa, OK
Tulsa Regional Chamber
One West Third Street
Suite 100
Tulsa, OK 74103
Phone: (918) 585-1201
www.tulsachamber.com

Tuscaloosa, AL
The Chamber of Commerce of West
Alabama
2201 Jack Warner Parkway
Building C
Tuscaloosa, AL 35401
Phone: (205) 758-7588
tuscaloosachamber.com

Virginia Beach, VA
Hampton Roads Chamber of Commerce
500 East Main Street, Suite 700
Virginia Beach, VA 23510
Phone: (757) 664-2531
www.hamptonroadschamber.com

Washington, DC
District of Columbia Chamber of Commerce
1213 K Street NW
Washington, DC 20005
Phone: (202) 347-7201
Fax: (202) 638-6762
www.dcchamber.org

District of Columbia Office of Planning and
Economic Development
J.A. Wilson Building
1350 Pennsylvania Ave NW, Suite 317
Washington, DC 20004
Phone: (202) 727-6365
Fax: (202) 727-6703
www.dcbiz.dc.gov

Wichita, KS
Wichita Regional Chamber of Commerce
350 W Douglas Avennue
Wichita, KS 67202
Phone: (316) 265-7771
www.wichitachamber.org

Wilmington, NC
Wilmington Chamber of Commerce
One Estell Lee Place
Wilmington, NC 28401
Phone: (910) 762-2611
www.wilmingtonchamber.org

Winston-Salem, NC
Winston-Salem Chamber of Commerce
411 West Fourth Street
Suite 211
Winston-Salem, NC 27101
Phone: (336) 728-9200
www.winstonsalem.com

Worcester, MA
Worcester Regional Chamber of Commerce
311 Main Street, Suite 200
Worcester, MA 01608
Phone: (508) 753-2924
worcesterchamber.org

Appendix E: State Departments of Labor

Alabama
Alabama Department of Labor
P.O. Box 303500
Montgomery, AL 36130-3500
Phone: (334) 242-3072
www.labor.alabama.gov

Alaska
Dept of Labor and Workforce Devel.
P.O. Box 11149
Juneau, AK 99822-2249
Phone: (907) 465-2700
www.labor.state.ak.us

Arizona
Industrial Commission or Arizona
800 West Washington Street
Phoenix, AZ 85007
Phone: (602) 542-4411
www.azica.gov

Arkansas
Department of Labor
10421 West Markham
Little Rock, AR 72205
Phone: (501) 682-4500
www.labor.ar.gov

California
Labor and Workforce Development
445 Golden Gate Ave., 10th Floor
San Francisco, CA 94102
Phone: (916) 263-1811
www.labor.ca.gov

Colorado
Dept of Labor and Employment
633 17th St., 2nd Floor
Denver, CO 80202-3660
Phone: (888) 390-7936
cdle.colorado.gov

Connecticut
Department of Labor
200 Folly Brook Blvd.
Wethersfield, CT 06109-1114
Phone: (860) 263-6000
www.ctdol.state.ct.us

Delaware
Department of Labor
4425 N. Market St., 4th Floor
Wilmington, DE 19802
Phone: (302) 451-3423
dol.delaware.gov

District of Columbia
Department of Employment Services
614 New York Ave., NE, Suite 300
Washington, DC 20002
Phone: (202) 671-1900
does.dc.gov

Florida
Florida Department of Economic Opportunity
The Caldwell Building
107 East Madison St. Suite 100
Tallahassee, FL 32399-4120
Phone: (800) 342-3450
www.floridajobs.org

Georgia
Department of Labor
Sussex Place, Room 600
148 Andrew Young Intl Blvd., NE
Atlanta, GA 30303
Phone: (404) 656-3011
dol.georgia.gov

Hawaii
Dept of Labor & Industrial Relations
830 Punchbowl Street
Honolulu, HI 96813
Phone: (808) 586-8842
labor.hawaii.gov

Idaho
Department of Labor
317 W. Main St.
Boise, ID 83735-0001
Phone: (208) 332-3579
www.labor.idaho.gov

Illinois
Department of Labor
160 N. LaSalle Street, 13th Floor
Suite C-1300
Chicago, IL 60601
Phone: (312) 793-2800
www.illinois.gov/idol

Indiana
Indiana Department of Labor
402 West Washington Street, Room W195
Indianapolis, IN 46204
Phone: (317) 232-2655
www.in.gov/dol

Iowa
Iowa Workforce Development
1000 East Grand Avenue
Des Moines, IA 50319-0209
Phone: (515) 242-5870
www.iowadivisionoflabor.gov

Kansas
Department of Labor
401 S.W. Topeka Blvd.
Topeka, KS 66603-3182
Phone: (785) 296-5000
www.dol.ks.gov

Kentucky
Department of Labor
1047 U.S. Hwy 127 South, Suite 4
Frankfort, KY 40601-4381
Phone: (502) 564-3070
www.labor.ky.gov

Louisiana
Louisiana Workforce Commission
1001 N. 23rd Street
Baton Rouge, LA 70804-9094
Phone: (225) 342-3111
www.laworks.net

Maine
Department of Labor
45 Commerce Street
Augusta, ME 04330
Phone: (207) 623-7900
www.state.me.us/labor

Maryland
Department of Labor, Licensing & Regulation
500 N. Calvert Street
Suite 401
Baltimore, MD 21202
Phone: (410) 767-2357
www.dllr.state.md.us

Massachusetts
Dept of Labor & Workforce Development
One Ashburton Place
Room 2112
Boston, MA 02108
Phone: (617) 626-7100
www.mass.gov/lwd

Michigan
Department of Licensing and Regulatory
Affairs
611 W. Ottawa
P.O. Box 30004
Lansing, MI 48909
Phone: (517) 373-1820
www.michigan.gov/lara

Minnesota
Dept of Labor and Industry
443 Lafayette Road North
Saint Paul, MN 55155
Phone: (651) 284-5070
www.doli.state.mn.us

Mississippi
Dept of Employment Security
P.O. Box 1699
Jackson, MS 39215-1699
Phone: (601) 321-6000
www.mdes.ms.gov

Missouri
Labor and Industrial Relations
P.O. Box 599
3315 W. Truman Boulevard
Jefferson City, MO 65102-0599
Phone: (573) 751-7500
labor.mo.gov

Montana
Dept of Labor and Industry
P.O. Box 1728
Helena, MT 59624-1728
Phone: (406) 444-9091
www.dli.mt.gov

Nebraska
Department of Labor
550 S 16th Street
Lincoln, NE 68508
Phone: (402) 471-9000
dol.nebraska.gov

Nevada
Dept of Business and Industry
3300 W. Sahara Ave, Suite 425
Las Vegas, NV 89102
Phone: (702) 486-2750
business.nv.gov

New Hampshire
Department of Labor
State Office Park South
95 Pleasant Street
Concord, NH 03301
Phone: (603) 271-3176
www.nh.gov/labor

New Jersey
Department of Labor & Workforce Devel.
John Fitch Plaza, 13th Floor, Suite D
Trenton, NJ 08625-0110
Phone: (609) 777-3200
lwd.dol.state.nj.us/labor

New Mexico
Department of Workforce Solutions
401 Broadway, NE
Albuquerque, NM 87103-1928
Phone: (505) 841-8450
www.dws.state.nm.us

New York
Department of Labor
State Office Bldg. # 12
W.A. Harriman Campus
Albany, NY 12240
Phone: (518) 457-9000
www.labor.ny.gov

North Carolina
Department of Labor
4 West Edenton Street
Raleigh, NC 27601-1092
Phone: (919) 733-7166
www.labor.nc.gov

North Dakota
North Dakota Department of Labor and
Human Rights
State Capitol Building
600 East Boulevard, Dept 406
Bismark, ND 58505-0340
Phone: (701) 328-2660
www.nd.gov/labor

Ohio
Department of Commerce
77 South High Street, 22nd Floor
Columbus, OH 43215
Phone: (614) 644-2239
www.com.state.oh.us

Oklahoma
Department of Labor
4001 N. Lincoln Blvd.
Oklahoma City, OK 73105-5212
Phone: (405) 528-1500
www.ok.gov/odol

Oregon
Bureau of Labor and Industries
800 NE Oregon St., #32
Portland, OR 97232
Phone: (971) 673-0761
www.oregon.gov/boli

Pennsylvania
Dept of Labor and Industry
1700 Labor and Industry Bldg
7th and Forster Streets
Harrisburg, PA 17120
Phone: (717) 787-5279
www.dli.pa.gov

Rhode Island
Department of Labor and Training
1511 Pontiac Avenue
Cranston, RI 02920
Phone: (401) 462-8000
www.dlt.state.ri.us

South Carolina
Dept of Labor, Licensing & Regulations
P.O. Box 11329
Columbia, SC 29211-1329
Phone: (803) 896-4300
www.llr.state.sc.us

South Dakota
Department of Labor & Regulation
700 Governors Drive
Pierre, SD 57501-2291
Phone: (605) 773-3682
dlr.sd.gov

Tennessee
Dept of Labor & Workforce Development
Andrew Johnson Tower
710 James Robertson Pkwy
Nashville, TN 37243-0655
Phone: (615) 741-6642
www.tn.gov/workforce

Texas
Texas Workforce Commission
101 East 15th St.
Austin, TX 78778
Phone: (512) 475-2670
www.twc.state.tx.us

Utah
Utah Labor Commission
160 East 300 South, 3rd Floor
Salt Lake City, UT 84114-6600
Phone: (801) 530-6800
laborcommission.utah.gov

Vermont
Department of Labor
5 Green Mountain Drive
P.O. Box 488
Montpelier, VT 05601-0488
Phone: (802) 828-4000
labor.vermont.gov

Virginia
Dept of Labor and Industry
Powers-Taylor Building
13 S. 13th Street
Richmond, VA 23219
Phone: (804) 371-2327
www.doli.virginia.gov

Washington
Dept of Labor and Industries
P.O. Box 44001
Olympia, WA 98504-4001
Phone: (360) 902-4200
www.lni.wa.gov

West Virginia
Division of Labor
749 B Building 6
Capitol Complex
Charleston, WV 25305
Phone: (304) 558-7890
labor.wv.gov

Wisconsin
Dept of Workforce Development
201 E. Washington Ave., #A400
P.O. Box 7946
Madison, WI 53707-7946
Phone: (608) 266-6861
dwd.wisconsin.gov

Wyoming
Department of Workforce Services
1510 East Pershing Blvd.
Cheyenne, WY 82002
Phone: (307) 777-7261
www.wyomingworkforce.org

Titles from Grey House

Visit www.GreyHouse.com for Product Information, Table of Contents, and Sample Pages.

Opinions Throughout History

Opinions Throughout History: Church & State
Opinions Throughout History: Conspiracy Theories
Opinions Throughout History: The Death Penalty
Opinions Throughout History: Diseases & Epidemics
Opinions Throughout History: Drug Use & Abuse
Opinions Throughout History: The Environment
Opinions Throughout History: Free Speech & Censorship
Opinions Throughout History: Gender: Roles & Rights
Opinions Throughout History: Globalization
Opinions Throughout History: Guns in America
Opinions Throughout History: Immigration
Opinions Throughout History: Law Enforcement in America
Opinions Throughout History: Mental Health
Opinions Throughout History: Nat'l Security vs. Civil & Privacy Rights
Opinions Throughout History: Presidential Authority
Opinions Throughout History: Robotics & Artificial Intelligence
Opinions Throughout History: Social Media Issues
Opinions Throughout History: The Supreme Court
Opinions Throughout History: Voters' Rights
Opinions Throughout History: War & the Military
Opinions Throughout History: Workers Rights & Wages

This is Who We Were

This is Who We Were: Colonial America (1492-1775)
This is Who We Were: 1880-1899
This is Who We Were: In the 1900s
This is Who We Were: In the 1910s
This is Who We Were: In the 1920s
This is Who We Were: A Companion to the 1940 Census
This is Who We Were: In the 1940s (1940-1949)
This is Who We Were: In the 1950s
This is Who We Were: In the 1960s
This is Who We Were: In the 1970s
This is Who We Were: In the 1980s
This is Who We Were: In the 1990s
This is Who We Were: In the 2000s
This is Who We Were: In the 2010s

Working Americans

Working Americans—Vol. 1: The Working Class
Working Americans—Vol. 2: The Middle Class
Working Americans—Vol. 3: The Upper Class
Working Americans—Vol. 4: Children
Working Americans—Vol. 5: At War
Working Americans—Vol. 6: Working Women
Working Americans—Vol. 7: Social Movements
Working Americans—Vol. 8: Immigrants
Working Americans—Vol. 9: Revolutionary War to the Civil War
Working Americans—Vol. 10: Sports & Recreation
Working Americans—Vol. 11: Inventors & Entrepreneurs
Working Americans—Vol. 12: Our History through Music
Working Americans—Vol. 13: Education & Educators
Working Americans—Vol. 14: African Americans
Working Americans—Vol. 15: Politics & Politicians
Working Americans—Vol. 16: Farming & Ranching
Working Americans—Vol. 17: Teens in America
Working Americans—Vol. 18: Health Care Workers
Working Americans—Vol. 19: The Performing Arts

Grey House Health & Wellness Guides

Addiction Handbook & Resource Guide
The Autism Spectrum Handbook & Resource Guide
Autoimmune Disorders Handbook & Resource Guide
Cardiovascular Disease Handbook & Resource Guide
Dementia Handbook & Resource Guide
Depression Handbook & Resource Guide
Diabetes Handbook & Resource Guide
Nutrition, Obesity & Eating Disorders Handbook & Resource Guide

Consumer Health

Complete Mental Health Resource Guide
Complete Resource Guide for Pediatric Disorders
Complete Resource Guide for People with Chronic Illness
Complete Resource Guide for People with Disabilities
Older Americans Information Resource
Parenting: Styles & Strategies
Teens: Growing Up, Skills & Strategies

General Reference

American Environmental Leaders
Constitutional Amendments
Encyclopedia of African-American Writing
Encyclopedia of Invasions & Conquests
Encyclopedia of Prisoners of War & Internment
Encyclopedia of the Continental Congresses
Encyclopedia of the United States Cabinet
Encyclopedia of War Journalism
The Environmental Debate
Financial Literacy Starter Kit
From Suffrage to the Senate
The Gun Debate: Gun Rights & Gun Control in the U.S.
Historical Warrior Peoples & Modern Fighting Groups
Human Rights and the United States
Political Corruption in America
Privacy Rights in the Digital Age
The Religious Right and American Politics
Speakers of the House of Representatives, 1789-2021
US Land & Natural Resources Policy
The Value of a Dollar 1600-1865 Colonial to Civil War
The Value of a Dollar 1860-2019

Business Information

Business Information Resources
Complete Broadcasting Industry Guide: TV, Radio, Cable & Streaming
Directory of Mail Order Catalogs
Environmental Resource Handbook
Food & Beverage Market Place
The Grey House Guide to Homeland Security Resources
The Grey House Performing Arts Industry Guide
Guide to Healthcare Group Purchasing Organizations
Guide to U.S. HMOs and PPOs
Guide to Venture Capital & Private Equity Firms
Hudson's Washington News Media Contacts Guide
New York State Directory
Sports Market Place

Grey House Publishing | Salem Press | H.W. Wilson | 4919 Route 22, PO Box 56, Amenia, NY 12501-0056

Grey House Imprints

Visit www.GreyHouse.com for Product Information, Table of Contents, and Sample Pages.

Grey House Titles, continued

Education

Complete Learning Disabilities Resource Guide
Digital Literacy: Skills & Strategies
Educators Resource Guide
The Comparative Guide to Elem. & Secondary Schools
Special Education: Policy & Curriculum Development

Statistics & Demographics

America's Top-Rated Cities
America's Top-Rated Smaller Cities
The Comparative Guide to American Suburbs
Profiles of America
Profiles of California
Profiles of Florida
Profiles of Illinois
Profiles of Indiana
Profiles of Massachusetts
Profiles of Michigan
Profiles of New Jersey
Profiles of New York
Profiles of North Carolina & South Carolina
Profiles of Ohio
Profiles of Pennsylvania
Profiles of Texas
Profiles of Virginia
Profiles of Wisconsin

Canadian Resources

Associations Canada
Canadian Almanac & Directory
Canadian Environmental Resource Guide
Canadian Parliamentary Guide
Canadian Venture Capital & Private Equity Firms
Canadian Who's Who
Cannabis Canada
Careers & Employment Canada
Financial Post: Directory of Directors
Financial Services Canada
FP Bonds: Corporate
FP Bonds: Government
FP Equities: Preferreds & Derivatives
FP Survey: Industrials
FP Survey: Mines & Energy
FP Survey: Predecessor & Defunct
Health Guide Canada
Libraries Canada

Weiss Financial Ratings

Financial Literacy Basics
Financial Literacy: How to Become an Investor
Financial Literacy: Planning for the Future
Weiss Ratings Consumer Guides
Weiss Ratings Guide to Banks
Weiss Ratings Guide to Credit Unions
Weiss Ratings Guide to Health Insurers
Weiss Ratings Guide to Life & Annuity Insurers
Weiss Ratings Guide to Property & Casualty Insurers
Weiss Ratings Investment Research Guide to Bond & Money Market
    Mutual Funds
Weiss Ratings Investment Research Guide to Exchange-Traded Funds
Weiss Ratings Investment Research Guide to Stock Mutual Funds
Weiss Ratings Investment Research Guide to Stocks

Books in Print Series

American Book Publishing Record® Annual
American Book Publishing Record® Monthly
Books In Print®
Books In Print® Supplement
Books Out Loud™
Bowker's Complete Video Directory™
Children's Books In Print®
El-Hi Textbooks & Serials In Print®
Forthcoming Books®
Law Books & Serials In Print™
Medical & Health Care Books In Print™
Publishers, Distributors & Wholesalers of the US™
Subject Guide to Books In Print®
Subject Guide to Children's Books In Print®

Grey House Publishing | Salem Press | H.W. Wilson | 4919 Route, 22 PO Box 56, Amenia NY 12501-0056

SALEM PRESS

Titles from Salem Press

SALEM PRESS

Visit www.SalemPress.com for Product Information, Table of Contents, and Sample Pages.

LITERATURE

Critical Insights: Authors

Louisa May Alcott
Sherman Alexie
Isabel Allende
Maya Angelou
Isaac Asimov
Margaret Atwood
Jane Austen
James Baldwin
Saul Bellow
Roberto Bolano
Ray Bradbury
The Brontë Sisters
Gwendolyn Brooks
Albert Camus
Raymond Carver
Willa Cather
Geoffrey Chaucer
John Cheever
Joseph Conrad
Charles Dickens
Emily Dickinson
Frederick Douglass
T. S. Eliot
George Eliot
Harlan Ellison
Ralph Waldo Emerson
Louise Erdrich
William Faulkner
F. Scott Fitzgerald
Gustave Flaubert
Horton Foote
Benjamin Franklin
Robert Frost
Neil Gaiman
Gabriel Garcia Marquez
Thomas Hardy
Nathaniel Hawthorne
Robert A. Heinlein
Lillian Hellman
Ernest Hemingway
Langston Hughes
Zora Neale Hurston
Henry James
Thomas Jefferson
James Joyce
Jamaica Kincaid
Stephen King
Martin Luther King, Jr.
Barbara Kingsolver
Abraham Lincoln
C.S. Lewis
Mario Vargas Llosa
Jack London
James McBride
Cormac McCarthy
Herman Melville
Arthur Miller
Toni Morrison
Alice Munro
Tim O'Brien
Flannery O'Connor
Eugene O'Neill
George Orwell

Sylvia Plath
Edgar Allan Poe
Philip Roth
Salman Rushdie
J.D. Salinger
Mary Shelley
John Steinbeck
Amy Tan
Leo Tolstoy
Mark Twain
John Updike
Kurt Vonnegut
Alice Walker
David Foster Wallace
Edith Wharton
Walt Whitman
Oscar Wilde
Tennessee Williams
Virginia Woolf
Richard Wright
Malcolm X

Critical Insights: Works

Absalom, Absalom!
Adventures of Huckleberry Finn
The Adventures of Tom Sawyer
Aeneid
All Quiet on the Western Front
All the Pretty Horses
Animal Farm
Anna Karenina
The Awakening
The Bell Jar
Beloved
Billy Budd, Sailor
The Book Thief
Brave New World
The Canterbury Tales
Catch-22
The Catcher in the Rye
The Color Purple
The Crucible
Death of a Salesman
The Diary of a Young Girl
Dracula
Fahrenheit 451
The Grapes of Wrath
Great Expectations
The Great Gatsby
Hamlet
The Handmaid's Tale
Harry Potter Series
Heart of Darkness
The Hobbit
The House on Mango Street
How the Garcia Girls Lost Their Accents
The Hunger Games Trilogy
I Know Why the Caged Bird Sings
In Cold Blood
The Inferno
Invisible Man
Jane Eyre
The Joy Luck Club
Julius Caesar
King Lear

The Kite Runner
Life of Pi
Little Women
Lolita
Lord of the Flies
The Lord of the Rings
Macbeth
The Merchant of Venice
The Metamorphosis
Midnight's Children
A Midsummer Night's Dream
Moby-Dick
Mrs. Dalloway
Nineteen Eighty-Four
The Odyssey
Of Mice and Men
The Old Man and the Sea
On the Road
One Flew Over the Cuckoo's Nest
One Hundred Years of Solitude
Othello
The Outsiders
Paradise Lost
The Pearl
The Plague
The Poetry of Baudelaire
The Poetry of Edgar Allan Poe
A Portrait of the Artist as a Young Man
Pride and Prejudice
A Raisin in the Sun
The Red Badge of Courage
Romeo and Juliet
The Scarlet Letter
Sense and Sensibility
Short Fiction of Flannery O'Connor
Slaughterhouse-Five
The Sound and the Fury
A Streetcar Named Desire
The Sun Also Rises
A Tale of Two Cities
The Tales of Edgar Allan Poe
Their Eyes Were Watching God
Things Fall Apart
To Kill a Mockingbird
War and Peace
The Woman Warrior

Critical Insights: Themes

The American Comic Book
American Creative Non-Fiction
The American Dream
American Multicultural Identity
American Road Literature
American Short Story
American Sports Fiction
The American Thriller
American Writers in Exile
Censored & Banned Literature
Civil Rights Literature, Past & Present
Coming of Age
Conspiracies
Contemporary Canadian Fiction
Contemporary Immigrant Short Fiction
Contemporary Latin American Fiction
Contemporary Speculative Fiction

Grey House Publishing | Salem Press | H.W. Wilson | 4919 Route, 22 PO Box 56, Amenia NY 12501-0056

SALEM PRESS

Titles from Salem Press

Visit www.SalemPress.com for Product Information, Table of Contents, and Sample Pages.

SALEM PRESS

HISTORY
The Decades
The 1910s in America
The Twenties in America
The Thirties in America
The Forties in America
The Fifties in America
The Sixties in America
The Seventies in America
The Eighties in America
The Nineties in America
The 2000s in America
The 2010s in America

Defining Documents in American History
Defining Documents: The 1900s
Defining Documents: The 1910s
Defining Documents: The 1920s
Defining Documents: The 1930s
Defining Documents: The 1950s
Defining Documents: The 1960s
Defining Documents: The 1970s
Defining Documents: The 1980s
Defining Documents: American Citizenship
Defining Documents: The American Economy
Defining Documents: The American Revolution
Defining Documents: The American West
Defining Documents: Business Ethics
Defining Documents: Capital Punishment
Defining Documents: Civil Rights
Defining Documents: Civil War
Defining Documents: The Constitution
Defining Documents: The Cold War
Defining Documents: Dissent & Protest
Defining Documents: Domestic Terrorism & Extremism
Defining Documents: Drug Policy
Defining Documents: The Emergence of Modern America
Defining Documents: Environment & Conservation
Defining Documents: Espionage & Intrigue
Defining Documents: Exploration and Colonial America
Defining Documents: The First Amendment
Defining Documents: The Free Press
Defining Documents: The Great Depression
Defining Documents: The Great Migration
Defining Documents: The Gun Debate
Defining Documents: Immigration & Immigrant Communities
Defining Documents: The Legacy of 9/11
Defining Documents: LGBTQ+
Defining Documents: Manifest Destiny and the New Nation
Defining Documents: Native Americans
Defining Documents: Political Campaigns, Candidates & Discourse
Defining Documents: Postwar 1940s
Defining Documents: Prison Reform
Defining Documents: Secrets, Leaks & Scandals
Defining Documents: Slavery
Defining Documents: Supreme Court Decisions
Defining Documents: Reconstruction Era
Defining Documents: The Vietnam War
Defining Documents: U.S. Involvement in the Middle East
Defining Documents: Workers' Rights
Defining Documents: World War I
Defining Documents: World War II

Defining Documents in World History
Defining Documents: The 17th Century
Defining Documents: The 18th Century
Defining Documents: The 19th Century
Defining Documents: The 20th Century (1900-1950)
Defining Documents: The Ancient World
Defining Documents: Asia
Defining Documents: Genocide & the Holocaust
Defining Documents: Human Rights
Defining Documents: The Middle Ages
Defining Documents: The Middle East
Defining Documents: Nationalism & Populism
Defining Documents: The Nuclear Age
Defining Documents: Pandemics, Plagues & Public Health
Defining Documents: Renaissance & Early Modern Era
Defining Documents: Revolutions
Defining Documents: Women's Rights

Great Events from History
Great Events from History: American History, Exploration to the
 Colonial Era, 1492-1775
Great Events from History: The Ancient World
Great Events from History: The Middle Ages
Great Events from History: The Renaissance & Early Modern Era
Great Events from History: The 17th Century
Great Events from History: The 18th Century
Great Events from History: The 19th Century
Great Events from History: The 20th Century, 1901-1940
Great Events from History: The 20th Century, 1941-1970
Great Events from History: The 20th Century, 1971-2000
Great Events from History: Modern Scandals
Great Events from History: African American History
Great Events from History: The 21st Century, 2000-2016
Great Events from History: LGBTQ Events
Great Events from History: Human Rights
Great Events from History: Women's History

Great Lives from History
Great Athletes
Great Athletes of the Twenty-First Century
Great Lives from History: The 17th Century
Great Lives from History: The 18th Century
Great Lives from History: The 19th Century
Great Lives from History: The 20th Century
Great Lives from History: The 21st Century, 2000-2017
Great Lives from History: African Americans
Great Lives from History: The Ancient World
Great Lives from History: American Heroes
Great Lives from History: American Women
Great Lives from History: Asian and Pacific Islander Americans
Great Lives from History: Autocrats & Dictators
Great Lives from History: The Incredibly Wealthy
Great Lives from History: Inventors & Inventions
Great Lives from History: Jewish Americans
Great Lives from History: Latinos
Great Lives from History: The Middle Ages
Great Lives from History: The Renaissance & Early Modern Era
Great Lives from History: Scientists and Science

Grey House Publishing | Salem Press | H.W. Wilson | 4919 Route, 22 PO Box 56, Amenia NY 12501-0056

Titles from Salem Press

Visit www.SalemPress.com for Product Information, Table of Contents, and Sample Pages.

History & Government

American First Ladies
American Presidents
The 50 States
The Ancient World: Extraordinary People in Extraordinary Societies
The Bill of Rights
The Criminal Justice System
The U.S. Supreme Court

Innovators

Computer Technology Innovators
Fashion Innovators
Human Rights Innovators
Internet Innovators
Music Innovators
Musicians and Composers of the 20th Century
World Political Innovators

SOCIAL SCIENCES

Civil Rights Movements: Past & Present
Countries, Peoples and Cultures
Countries: Their Wars & Conflicts: A World Survey
Education Today: Issues, Policies & Practices
Encyclopedia of American Immigration
Ethics: Questions & Morality of Human Actions
Issues in U.S. Immigration
Principles of Sociology: Group Relationships & Behavior
Principles of Sociology: Personal Relationships & Behavior
Principles of Sociology: Societal Issues & Behavior
Racial & Ethnic Relations in America
Weapons, Warfare & Military Technology
World Geography

HEALTH

Addictions, Substance Abuse & Alcoholism
Adolescent Health & Wellness
Aging
Cancer
Community & Family Health Issues
Integrative, Alternative & Complementary Medicine
Genetics and Inherited Conditions
Infectious Diseases and Conditions
Magill's Medical Guide
Nutrition
Parenting: Styles & Strategies
Psychology & Behavioral Health
Teens: Growing Up, Skills & Strategies
Women's Health

Principles of Health

Principles of Health: Allergies & Immune Disorders
Principles of Health: Anxiety & Stress
Principles of Health: Depression
Principles of Health: Diabetes
Principles of Health: Nursing
Principles of Health: Obesity
Principles of Health: Occupational Therapy & Physical Therapy
Principles of Health: Pain Management
Principles of Health: Prescription Drug Abuse

SCIENCE

Ancient Creatures
Applied Science
Applied Science: Engineering & Mathematics
Applied Science: Science & Medicine
Applied Science: Technology
Biomes and Ecosystems
Digital Literacy: Skills & Strategies
Earth Science: Earth Materials and Resources
Earth Science: Earth's Surface and History
Earth Science: Earth's Weather, Water and Atmosphere
Earth Science: Physics and Chemistry of the Earth
Encyclopedia of Climate Change
Encyclopedia of Energy
Encyclopedia of Environmental Issues
Encyclopedia of Global Resources
Encyclopedia of Mathematics and Society
Forensic Science
Notable Natural Disasters
The Solar System
USA in Space

Principles of Science

Principles of Aeronautics
Principles of Anatomy
Principles of Astronomy
Principles of Behavioral Science
Principles of Biology
Principles of Biotechnology
Principles of Botany
Principles of Chemistry
Principles of Climatology
Principles of Computer-aided Design
Principles of Computer Science
Principles of Digital Arts & Multimedia
Principles of Ecology
Principles of Energy
Principles of Fire Science
Principles of Forestry & Conservation
Principles of Geology
Principles of Information Technology
Principles of Marine Science
Principles of Mathematics
Principles of Mechanics
Principles of Microbiology
Principles of Modern Agriculture
Principles of Pharmacology
Principles of Physical Science
Principles of Physics
Principles of Programming & Coding
Principles of Robotics & Artificial Intelligence
Principles of Scientific Research
Principles of Sports Medicine & Exercise Science
Principles of Sustainability
Principles of Zoology

Grey House Publishing | Salem Press | H.W. Wilson | 4919 Route, 22 PO Box 56, Amenia NY 12501-0056

SALEM PRESS

Titles from Salem Press

Visit www.SalemPress.com for Product Information, Table of Contents, and Sample Pages.

SALEM PRESS

CAREERS

Careers: Paths to Entrepreneurship
Careers in Archaeology & Museum Services
Careers in Artificial Intelligence
Careers in the Arts: Fine, Performing & Visual
Careers in the Automotive Industry
Careers in Biology
Careers in Biotechnology
Careers in Building Construction
Careers in Business
Careers in Chemistry
Careers in Communications & Media
Careers in Cybersecurity
Careers in Education & Training
Careers in Engineering
Careers in Environment & Conservation
Careers in Financial Services
Careers in Fish & Wildlife
Careers in Forensic Science
Careers in Gaming
Careers in Green Energy
Careers in Healthcare
Careers in Hospitality & Tourism
Careers in Human Services
Careers in Information Technology
Careers in Law, Criminal Justice & Emergency Services
Careers in the Music Industry
Careers in Manufacturing & Production
Careers in Nursing
Careers in Physics
Careers in Protective Services
Careers in Psychology & Behavioral Health
Careers in Public Administration
Careers in Sales, Insurance & Real Estate
Careers in Science & Engineering
Careers in Social Media
Careers in Sports & Fitness
Careers in Sports Medicine & Training
Careers in Technical Services & Equipment Repair
Careers in Transportation
Careers in Writing & Editing
Careers Outdoors
Careers Overseas
Careers Working with Infants & Children
Careers Working with Animals

BUSINESS

Principles of Business: Accounting
Principles of Business: Economics
Principles of Business: Entrepreneurship
Principles of Business: Finance
Principles of Business: Globalization
Principles of Business: Leadership
Principles of Business: Management
Principles of Business: Marketing

Grey House Publishing | Salem Press | H.W. Wilson | 4919 Route, 22 PO Box 56, Amenia NY 12501-0056

Titles from H.W. Wilson

Visit www.HWWilsonInPrint.com for Product Information, Table of Contents, and Sample Pages.

The Reference Shelf

Affordable Housing
Aging in America
Alternative Facts, Post-Truth and the Information War
The American Dream
Artificial Intelligence
The Business of Food
Campaign Trends & Election Law
College Sports
Democracy Evolving
The Digital Age
Embracing New Paradigms in Education
Food Insecurity & Hunger in the United States
Future of U.S. Economic Relations: Mexico, Cuba, & Venezuela
Gene Editing & Genetic Engineering
Global Climate Change
Guns in America
Hacktivism
Hate Crimes
Immigration
Income Inequality
Internet Abuses & Privacy Rights
Internet Law
LGBTQ in the 21st Century
Marijuana Reform
Mental Health Awareness
Money in Politics
National Debate Topic 2014/2015: The Ocean
National Debate Topic 2015/2016: Surveillance
National Debate Topic 2016/2017: US/China Relations
National Debate Topic 2017/2018: Education Reform
National Debate Topic 2018/2019: Immigration
National Debate Topic 2019/2021: Arms Sales
National Debate Topic 2020/2021: Criminal Justice Reform
National Debate Topic 2021/2022: Water Resources
National Debate Topic 2022/2023: Emerging Technologies & International Security
National Debate Topic 2023/2024: Economic Inequality
New Frontiers in Space
Policing in 2020
Pollution
Prescription Drug Abuse
Propaganda and Misinformation
Racial Tension in a Postracial Age
Reality Television
Renewable Energy
Representative American Speeches, Annual Editions
Rethinking Work
Revisiting Gender
The South China Sea Conflict
Sports in America
The Supreme Court
The Transformation of American Cities
The Two Koreas
UFOs
Vaccinations
Voting Rights
Whistleblowers

Core Collections

Children's Core Collection
Fiction Core Collection
Graphic Novels Core Collection
Middle & Junior High School Core
Public Library Core Collection: Nonfiction
Senior High Core Collection
Young Adult Fiction Core Collection

Current Biography

Current Biography Cumulative Index 1946-2021
Current Biography Monthly Magazine
Current Biography Yearbook

Readers' Guide to Periodical Literature

Abridged Readers' Guide to Periodical Literature
Readers' Guide to Periodical Literature

Indexes

Index to Legal Periodicals & Books
Short Story Index
Book Review Digest

Sears List

Sears List of Subject Headings
Sears List of Subject Headings, Online Database
Sears: Lista de Encabezamientos de Materia

History

American Game Changers: Invention, Innovation & Transformation
American Reformers
Speeches of the American Presidents

Facts About Series

Facts About the 20th Century
Facts About American Immigration
Facts About China
Facts About the Presidents
Facts About the World's Languages

Nobel Prize Winners

Nobel Prize Winners: 1901-1986
Nobel Prize Winners: 1987-1991
Nobel Prize Winners: 1992-1996
Nobel Prize Winners: 1997-2001
Nobel Prize Winners: 2002-2018

Famous First Facts

Famous First Facts
Famous First Facts About American Politics
Famous First Facts About Sports
Famous First Facts About the Environment
Famous First Facts: International Edition

American Book of Days

The American Book of Days
The International Book of Days

Grey House Publishing | Salem Press | H.W. Wilson | 4919 Route, 22 PO Box 56, Amenia NY 12501-0056